Direct Social Work Practice

Direct Social Work Practice
Theory and Skills

Eighth Edition

DEAN H. HEPWORTH

Professor Emeritus, University of Utah and Arizona State University

RONALD H. ROONEY

University of Minnesota

GLENDA DEWBERRY ROONEY

Augsburg College

KIMBERLY STROM-GOTTFRIED

University of North Carolina at Chapel Hill

JO ANN LARSEN

Private Practice, Salt Lake City

BROOKS/COLE
CENGAGE Learning

Australia • Brazil • Japan • Korea • Mexico • Singapore • Spain • United Kingdom • United States

BROOKS/COLE
CENGAGE Learning

Direct Social Work Practice: Theory and Skills, Eighth Edition
Dean H. Hepworth, Ronald H. Rooney, Glenda Dewberry Rooney, Kimberly Strom-Gottfried, and Jo Ann Larsen

Acquisitions Editor: Seth Dobrin

Assistant Editor: Allison Bowie

Editorial Assistant: Rachel McDonald

Media Editor: Andrew Keay

Senior Marketing Manager: Trent Whatcott

Marketing Assistant: Darlene Macanan

Senior Marketing Communications Manager: Tami Strang

Project Manager, Editorial Production: Christy Krueger

Creative Director: Rob Hugel

Senior Art Director: Caryl Gorska

Print Buyer: Judy Inouye

Permissions Editor, Text: Mardell Glinski Schultz

Production Service: Pre-PressPMG

Copy Editor: Kelly Birch

Cover Designer: Gia Giasullo

Cover Image: Vincenzo Lombardo/ Getty Images

Compositor: Pre-PressPMG

For product information and technology assistance, contact us at **Cengage Learning Customer & Sales Support, 1-800-354-9706**

For permission to use material from this text or product, submit all requests online at **www.cengage.com/permissions**. Further permissions questions can be emailed to **permissionrequest@cengage.com**.

Library of Congress Control Number: 2008943641

ISBN-13: 978-0-495-60167-8

ISBN-10: 0-495-60167-5

Brooks/Cole
10 Davis Drive
Belmont, CA 94002-3098
USA

Cengage Learning is a leading provider of customized learning solutions with office locations around the globe, including Singapore, the United Kingdom, Australia, Mexico, Brazil, and Japan. Locate your local office at: **www.cengage.com/international**

Cengage Learning products are represented in Canada by Nelson Education, Ltd.

To learn more about Brooks/Cole, visit **www.cengage.com/brookscole**

Printed in the United States of America
3 4 5 6 7 13 12 11

Brief Contents

Preface xv
About the Authors xvii

PART 1
INTRODUCTION 1

1 The Challenges of Social Work 3
2 Direct Practice: Domain, Philosophy, and Roles 23
3 Overview of the Helping Process 33
4 Operationalizing the Cardinal Social Work Values 53

PART 2
EXPLORING, ASSESSING, AND PLANNING 81

5 Building Blocks of Communication: Communicating with
   Empathy and Authenticity 83
6 Verbal Following, Exploring, and Focusing Skills 129
7 Eliminating Counterproductive Communication Patterns 155
8 Assessment: Exploring and Understanding Problems and Strengths 171
9 Assessment: Intrapersonal, Interpersonal, and Environmental Factors 199
10 Assessing Family Functioning in Diverse Family and Cultural Contexts 227
11 Forming and Assessing Social Work Groups 273
12 Developing Goals and Formulating a Contract 303

PART 3
THE CHANGE-ORIENTED PHASE 353

13 Planning and Implementing Change-Oriented Strategies 355
14 Developing Resources, Organizing, Planning, and Advocacy
    as Intervention Strategies 411
15 Enhancing Family Relationships 455
16 Intervening in Social Work Groups 491

17 **Additive Empathy, Interpretation, and Confrontation**   519

18 **Managing Barriers to Change**   539

PART 4
THE TERMINATION PHASE 567

19 **The Final Phase: Evaluation and Termination**   569

Bibliography   585
Author Index   629
Subject Index   637

Contents

Preface xv

About the Authors xvii

PART 1
INTRODUCTION 1

CHAPTER 1
The Challenges of Social Work 3

The Mission of Social Work   4

Purposes of Social Work   5

Social Work Values   6
  Values and Ethics   8
  Social Work's Code of Ethics   9
  Orienting Frameworks to Achieve Competencies   15

Deciding on and Carrying out Interventions   18
  Guidelines Influencing Intervention Selection   20

Summary   21

CHAPTER 2
Direct Practice: Domain, Philosophy,
  and Roles 23

Domain   23
  Generalist Practice   23
  Direct Practice   25

A Philosophy of Direct Practice   26

Roles of Direct Practitioners   26
  Direct Provision of Services   26
  System Linkage Roles   27
  System Maintenance and Enhancement   29
  Researcher/Research Consumer   30
  System Development   30

Summary   31

CHAPTER 3
Overview of the Helping Process 33

Common Elements among Diverse Theorists and Social
  Workers   33

The Helping Process   34
  Phase I: Exploration, Engagement, Assessment,
    and Planning   34
  Phase II: Implementation and Goal Attainment   39
  Phase III: Termination   41

The Interviewing Process: Structure and Skills   42
  Physical Conditions   43
  Structure of Interviews   43
  Establishing Rapport   44
  The Exploration Process   47
  Focusing in Depth   48
  Employing Outlines   49
  Assessing Emotional Functioning   49
  Exploring Cognitive Functioning   49
  Exploring Substance Abuse, Violence,
    and Sexual Abuse   49
  Negotiating Goals and a Contract   49
  Ending Interviews   50
  Goal Attainment   50

Summary   51

Notes   51

CHAPTER 4
Operationalizing the Cardinal Social Work
  Values 53

The Interaction between Personal and Professional
  Values   53

The Cardinal Values of Social Work   53

Challenges in Embracing the Profession's Values   61

Ethics   61

The Intersection of Laws and Ethics   62
Key Ethical Principles   63
What Are the Limits on Confidentiality?   68
Understanding and Resolving Ethical Dilemmas   73

Summary   76

Related Online Content   76

Skill Development Exercises in Managing Ethical Dilemmas   76

Skill Development Exercises in Operationalizing Cardinal Values   77

Client Statements   78

Modeled Responses   78

Notes   79

PART 2
EXPLORING, ASSESSING, AND PLANNING . . . 81

CHAPTER 5
Building Blocks of Communication: Communicating with Empathy and Authenticity 83

Roles of the Participants   83

Communicating about Informed Consent, Confidentiality, and Agency Policies   87

Facilitative Conditions   87

Empathic Communication   88

Developing Perceptiveness to Feelings   89

Affective Words and Phrases   90
Use of the Lists of Affective Words and Phrases   92
Exercises in Identifying Surface and Underlying Feelings   94

Accurately Conveying Empathy   95
Empathic Communication Scale   95
Exercises in Discriminating Levels of Empathic Responding   99

Client Statements   99

Responding with Reciprocal Empathy   100
Constructing Reciprocal Responses   100
Leads for Empathic Responses   101
Employing Empathic Responding   102
Multiple Uses of Empathic Communication   102
Teaching Clients to Respond Empathically   105

Authenticity   106
Types of Self-Disclosure   107
Timing and Intensity of Self-Disclosure   108
A Paradigm for Responding Authentically   108
Guidelines for Responding Authentically   109
Cues for Authentic Responding   112
Positive Feedback: A Form of Authentic Responding   116

Relating Assertively to Clients   118
Making Requests and Giving Directives   118
Maintaining Focus and Managing Interruptions   119
Interrupting Dysfunctional Processes   119
"Leaning Into" Clients' Anger   120
Saying No and Setting Limits   120

Summary   122

Related Online Content   122

Notes   127

CHAPTER 6
Verbal Following, Exploring, and Focusing Skills 129

Maintaining Psychological Contact with Clients and Exploring Their Problems   129

Verbal Following Skills   130

Furthering Responses   130
Minimal Prompts   130
Accent Responses   130

Paraphrasing Responses   130
Exercises in Paraphrasing   131

Closed- and Open-Ended Responses   132
Exercises in Identifying Closed- and Open-Ended Responses   133
Discriminant Use of Closed- and Open-Ended Responses   133

Seeking Concreteness   135
Types of Responses That Facilitate Specificity of Expression by Clients   136
Specificity of Expression by Social Workers   141
Exercises in Seeking Concreteness   142

Focusing: A Complex Skill   143
Selecting Topics for Exploration   143
Exploring Topics in Depth   144
Blending Open-Ended, Empathic, and Concrete Responses to Maintain Focus   146
Managing Obstacles to Focusing   148

Summarizing Responses   150
Highlighting Key Aspects of Problems   150
Summarizing Lengthy Messages   151
Reviewing Focal Points of a Session   152
Providing Focus and Continuity   152
Analyzing Your Verbal Following Skills   152

Summary   154

Modeled Responses to Exercise in Paraphrasing   154

Answers to Exercise in Identifying Closed- and Open-Ended Responses   154

Modeled Open-Ended Responses   154

Notes   154

CHAPTER 7
Eliminating Counterproductive Communication Patterns 155

Impacts of Counterproductive Communication Patterns 155

Eliminating Nonverbal Barriers to Effective Communication 155
  Physical Attending 155
  Cultural Nuances of Nonverbal Cues 156
  Other Nonverbal Behaviors 156
  Taking Inventory of Nonverbal Patterns of Responding 157

Eliminating Verbal Barriers to Communication 158
  Reassuring, Sympathizing, Consoling, or Excusing 159
  Advising and Giving Suggestions or Solutions Prematurely 159
  Using Sarcasm or Employing Humor Inappropriately 160
  Judging, Criticizing, or Placing Blame 161
  Trying to Convince Clients about the Right Point of View through Logic, Lecturing, Instructing, or Arguing 161
  Analyzing, Diagnosing, or Making Glib or Dramatic Interpretations 162
  Threatening, Warning, or Counterattacking 163
  Stacking Questions 163
  Asking Leading Questions 164
  Interrupting Inappropriately or Excessively 164
  Dominating the Interaction 164
  Fostering Safe Social Interaction 165
  Responding Infrequently 165
  Parroting or Overusing Certain Phrases or Clichés 166
  Dwelling on the Remote Past 166
  Going on Fishing Expeditions 166

Gauging the Effectiveness of Your Responses 167

The Challenge of Learning New Skills 168

Summary 170

Notes 170

CHAPTER 8
Assessment: Exploring and Understanding Problems and Strengths 171

The Multidimensionality of Assessment 171

Defining Assessment: Process and Product 172

Assessment and Diagnosis 174
  The Diagnostic and Statistical Manual (DSM-IV-TR) 174

Culturally Competent Assessment 175

Emphasizing Strengths in Assessments 177

The Role of Knowledge and Theory in Assessments 179

Sources of Information 181

Questions to Answer in Problem Assessment 184
  Getting Started 185
  Identifying the Problem, Its Expressions, and Other Critical Concerns 186
  The Interaction of Other People or Systems 187
  Assessing Developmental Needs and Wants 187
  Typical Wants Involved in Presenting Problems 188
  Stresses Associated with Life Transitions 189
  Severity of the Problem 189
  Meanings That Clients Ascribe to Problems 189
  Sites of Problematic Behaviors 190
  Temporal Context of Problematic Behaviors 190
  Frequency of Problematic Behaviors 191
  Duration of the Problem 191
  Other Issues Affecting Client Functioning 191
  Clients' Emotional Reactions to Problems 192
  Coping Efforts and Needed Skills 192
  Cultural, Societal, and Social Class Factors 193
  External Resources Needed 194

Assessing Children and Older Adults 194
  Maltreatment 195

Summary 196

Skill Development Exercises in Exploring Strengths and Problems 196

Related Online Content 197

Notes 197

CHAPTER 9
Assessment: Intrapersonal, Interpersonal, and Environmental Factors 199

The Interaction of Multiple Systems in Human Problems 199

Intrapersonal Systems 199

Biophysical Functioning 200
  Physical Characteristics and Presentation 200
  Physical Health 201

Assessing Use and Abuse of Medications, Alcohol, and Drugs 202
  Alcohol Use and Abuse 202
  Use and Abuse of Other Substances 203
  Dual Diagnosis: Addictive and Mental Disorders 205
  Using Interviewing Skills to Assess Substance Use 206

Assessing Cognitive/Perceptual Functioning 206
  Intellectual Functioning 206
  Judgment 207
  Reality Testing 207
  Coherence 208
  Cognitive Flexibility 208
  Values 208
  Misconceptions 209
  Self-Concept 209

Assessing Emotional Functioning   209
Emotional Control   210
Range of Emotions   211
Appropriateness of Affect   211
Affective Disorders   212
Suicidal Risk   213
Depression and Suicidal Risk with Children and
Adolescents   214
Depression and Suicidal Risk with
Older Adults   215

Assessing Behavioral Functioning   215

Assessing Motivation   217

Assessing Environmental Systems   217
Physical Environment   218
Social Support Systems   220
Spirituality and Affiliation with a
Faith Community   221

Written Assessments   222
Case Notes   225

Summary   225

Skill Development Exercises in Assessment   226

Related Online Content   226

Notes   226

CHAPTER 10
**Assessing Family Functioning in Diverse
Family and Cultural Contexts** 227

Social Work Practice with Families   227

Defining Family   227

Family Functions   228

Family Stressors   230
Public Policy   230
Poverty   231
Who are the Poor and Why?   232
Impact on Children   232
Life Transitions and Separations   233
Extraordinary Family Transitions   233
Work and Family   234
Resilience in Families   235

**A Systems Framework for Assessing Family
Functioning**   235
Family Assessment Instruments   236
Strengths-Based and Risk Assessments   237

Systems Concepts   237
Application of Systems Concepts   238
Family Homeostasis   238

Family Rules   239
Functional and Rigid Rules   240
Violation of Rules   241
Flexibility of Rules   241

Content and Process Levels of Family Interactions   242
Sequences of Interaction   243
Employing "Circular" Explanations of Behavior   245

**Assessing Problems Using the Systems
Framework**   246

Dimensions of Family Assessment   247
Family Context   248
Family Strengths   251
Boundaries and Boundary Maintenance of Family
Systems   252
Family Power Structure   256
Family Decision-Making Processes   259
Family Goals   261
Family Myths and Cognitive Patterns   263
Family Roles   264
Communication Styles of Family Members   265
Family Life Cycle   269

Summary   270

Related Online Content   270

Skill Development Exercises   270

Notes   271

CHAPTER 11
**Forming and Assessing Social
Work Groups** 273

Classification of Groups   273

Formation of Treatment Groups   275
Determining the Need for the Group   275
Establishing the Group Purpose   275
Deciding on Leadership · 277
Establishing Specific Individual and
Group Goals   278
Conducting a Preliminary Interview   278
Deciding on Group Composition   280
Open versus Closed Groups   281
Determining Group Size and Location   281
Setting the Frequency and Duration
of Meetings   282
Formulating Group Guidelines   282

Assessing Group Processes   286
A Systems Framework for Assessing Groups   286
Assessing Individuals' Patterned Behaviors   287
Assessing Individuals' Cognitive Patterns   290
Assessing Groups' Patterned Behaviors   291
Assessing Group Alliances   292
Assessing Power and Decision-Making Styles   294
Assessing Group Norms, Values, and Cohesion   295

Formation of Task Groups   297
Planning for Task Groups   297
Beginning the Task Group   298

Ethics in Practice with Groups   298
First Session   299

Summary 301

Related Online Content 301

Skills Development Exercises in Planning Groups 301

Notes 302

CHAPTER 12
Developing Goals and Formulating a Contract ... 303

Goals 303
The Purpose and Function of Goals 303
Linking Goals to Target Concerns 303
Program Objectives and Goals 305
Factors That Influence the Development of Goals 306
Types of Goals 309
Guidelines for Selecting and Defining Goals 310
Motivational Congruence 311
Agreeable Mandate 312
Let's Make a Deal 312
Getting Rid of the Mandate 313
Partializing Goals 315
Involuntary Clients' Mandated Case Plans 317

Applying Goal Development Guidelines with Minors 321
School-based Group Example 322
Process of Negotiating Goals 325

Measurement and Evaluation 331
Methods of Evaluation and Measuring Progress 332
Evaluation Resources 332
Cautions and Strengths 333
Quantitative Measurements 333
Qualitative Measurement 338

Contracts 341
The Rationale for Contracts 342
Formal and Informal Contracts 342
Developing Contracts 343
Sample Contracts 346

Summary 346

Skill Development Exercises 349

Notes 351

PART 3
THE CHANGE-ORIENTED PHASE 353

CHAPTER 13
Planning and Implementing Change-Oriented Strategies 355

Change-Oriented Approaches 355

Planning Goal Attainment Strategies 356
What is the Problem and What are the Goals? 356
Is the Approach Appropriate to the Person, Family, or Group? 356

Child Development and Family Lifecycle 357
Stressful Transitions 357
Minority Groups 358
What Empirical or Conceptual Evidence Supports the Effectiveness of the Approach? 360
Is the Approach Compatible with Basic Values and Ethics of Social Work? 360
Am I Sufficiently Knowledgeable and Skilled Enough in this Approach? 363

Models & Techniques of Practice 363
The Task-Centered System 363
Tenets of the Task-Centered Approach 363
Theoretical Framework 363
Empirical Evidence and Uses of the Task-Centered Model 363
Application with Diverse Groups 364

Procedures of the Task-Centered Model 364
Developing General Tasks 364
Partializing Group or Family Goals 365
General Tasks for the Social Worker 366
Developing Specific Tasks 366
Brainstorming Task Alternatives 367
Task Implementation Sequence 368
Maintaining Focus and Continuity 375
Failure to Complete Tasks 375
Monitoring Progress 378

Crisis Intervention 379
Tenets of the Crisis Intervention Equilibrium Model 379
Definition and Stages of Crisis 380
Duration of Contact 381
Considerations for Minors 381
Theoretical Framework 383
Application with Diverse Groups 384
Process and Procedures of Crisis Intervention 385
Strengths and Limitations 389

Cognitive Restructuring 390
Theoretical Framework 390
Tenets of Cognitive Behavioral Therapy-Cognitive Restructuring 391
What are Cognitive Distortions? 391
Empirical Evidence and Uses of Cognitive Restructuring 393
Application of Cognitive Restructuring with Diverse Groups 394
Procedure of Cognitive Restructuring 395
Strengths, Limitations, and Cautions 402

Solution-focused Brief Treatment 403
Tenets of Solution-Focused 403
Theoretical Framework 403
Empirical Evidence and Uses of Solution-Focused Strategies 403
Application with Diverse Groups 404
Solution-Focused Procedures and Techniques 404
Strengths and Limitations 406

Summary   408

Trends and Challenges in Problem-Solving Intervention Approaches   409

Skill Development Exercises   410

Related Online Content   410

Notes   410

CHAPTER 14
Developing Resources, Organizing, Planning, and Advocacy as Intervention Strategies 411

Social Work's Commitment   411
   Defining Macro Practice   412

Linking Micro and Macro Practice   412

Macro Practice Activities   413

Intervention Strategies   414
   Empowerment and Strengths   414
   Analyzing Social Problems and Conditions   415

Developing and Supplementing Resources   418
   Supplementing Existing Resources   420
   Mobilizing Community Resources   422
   Developing Resources with Diverse Groups   424

Utilizing and Enhancing Support Systems   424
   Community Support Systems and Networks   425
   Organizations as Support Systems   426
   Immigrant and Refugee Groups   427
   Cautions and Advice   428

Advocacy and Social Action   428
   Policies and Legislation   429
   Cause Advocacy and Social Action   430
   Indications for Advocacy or Social Action   430
   Competence and Skills   431
   Techniques and Steps of Advocacy and
      Social Action   432

Community Organization   433

Models and Strategies of Community Intervention   433

Steps and Skills of Community Intervention   434
   Organizing Skills   435
   Organizing and Planning with Diverse Groups   435

Ethical Issues in Community Organizing   436

Improving Institutional Environments   437
   Change within Organizations   437

Organizational Environments   439
   Staff   439
   Policies and Practices   441
   Institutional Programs   448

Service Coordination and Interorganizational Collaboration   449
   Organizational Relationships   450
   Case Management   450
   Collaboration: A Case Example   452

Macro Practice Evaluation   453

Summary   454

Related Online Content   454

Skill Development Exercises   454

Notes   454

CHAPTER 15
Enhancing Family Relationships 455

Approaches to Work with Families   455

Initial Contacts   456
   Managing Initial Contact with Couples and
      Families   457
   Managing Initial Contacts with Parents   459

Orchestrating the Initial Family or Couple Session   460
   The Dynamics of Minority Status and Culture in
      Exploring Reservations   462

Intervening with Families: Cultural and Ecological Perspectives   467
   Differences in Communication Styles   467
   Hierarchical Considerations   468
   Authority of the Social Worker   468
   Engaging the Family   469
   Understanding Families Using an Ecological
      Perspective   470
   Twanna, the Adolescent Mother   470
   Anna and Jackie, a Lesbian Couple   471

Intervening with Families: Focusing on the Future   472

Communication Patterns and Styles   473

Giving and Receiving Feedback   473
   Engaging Clients in Assessing How Well They Give and
      Receive Positive Feedback   473
   Educating Clients about the Vital Role of Positive
      Feedback   473
   Cultivating Positive Cognitive Sets   474
   Enabling Clients to Give and Receive Positive
      Feedback   475

Intervening with Families: Strategies to Modify Interactions   477
   Metacommunication   477
   Modifying Family Rules   478
   On-the-Spot Interventions   480
   Assisting Clients to Disengage from Conflict   482
   Modifying Complementary Interactions   483
   Negotiating Agreements for Reciprocal Changes   483

Intervening with Families: Modifying Misconceptions and Distorted Perceptions   485

Intervening with Families: Modifying Family Alignments   486

Summary   488

Skill Development Exercises   489

Related Online Content   489

CHAPTER 16
Intervening in Social Work Groups 491

Stages of Group Development 491

Stage 1. Preaffiliation: Approach and Avoidance Behavior 492

Stage 2. Power and Control: A Time of Transition 493

Stage 3. Intimacy: Developing a Familial Frame of Reference 494

Stage 4. Differentiation: Developing Group Identity and an Internal Frame of Reference 495

Stage 5. Separation: Breaking Away 496

The Leader's Role in the Stages of Group Development 497

Intervention into Structural Elements of a Group 497

Fostering Cohesion 499

Addressing Group Norms 500

Intervening with Members' Roles 501

Addressing Subgroups 502

Purposeful Use of the Leadership Role 502

Interventions Across Stages of Group Development 503

Common Mistakes: Overemphasizing Content and Lecturing in the HEART Group 504

Interventions in the Preaffiliation Stage 504

Seeking Concreteness 505

Interventions in the Power and Control Stage 506

Interventions in the Intimacy and Differentiation Stages 510

Unhelpful Thoughts from the HEART Group Selectively Focusing 511

Interventions in the Termination Stage 512

New Developments in Social Work with Groups 513

Work with Task Groups 515

Problem Identification 515

Getting Members Involved 515

Enhancing Awareness of Stages of Development 516

Summary 516

Related Online Content 516

Skills Development Exercises in Group Interventions 516

Client Statements 517

Modeled Responses 517

Notes 517

CHAPTER 17
Additive Empathy, Interpretation, and Confrontation 519

The Meaning and Significance of Client Self-Awareness 519

Additive Empathy and Interpretation 519

Deeper Feelings 521

Underlying Meanings of Feelings, Thoughts, and Behavior 522

Wants and Goals 523

Hidden Purposes of Behavior 523

Unrealized Strengths and Potentialities 524

Guidelines for Employing Interpretation and Additive Empathy 525

Confrontation 526

Guidelines for Employing Confrontation 530

Indications for Assertive Confrontation 531

Summary 533

Skill Development Exercises in Additive Empathy and Interpretation 533

Client Statements 533

Modeled Responses for Interpretation and Additive Empathy 534

Skill Development Exercises in Confrontation 534

Situations and Dialogue 535

Modeled Responses for Confrontation 536

Notes 537

CHAPTER 18
Managing Barriers to Change 539

Barriers to Change 539

Relational Reactions 539

Under- and Over-Involvement of Social Workers with Clients 541

Burnout, Compassion Fatigue and Vicarious Trauma 544

Pathological or Inept Social Workers 546

Cross-Racial and Cross-Cultural Barriers 547

Difficulties in Establishing Trust 550

Transference Reactions 551

Countertransference Reactions 555

Realistic Practitioner Reactions 557

Sexual Attraction toward Clients 557

Managing Opposition to Change 558

Preventing Opposition to Change 559

Transference Resistance 560

Manifestations of Opposition to Change 560

Exploring and Managing Opposition 561

Positive Connotation 562

Redefining Problems as Opportunities for Growth 562

Relabeling 562

Reframing 563

Confronting Patterns of Opposition 563

Summary 564

Related Online Content 564

Skill Development Exercises 564

Skill Development Exercises in Managing Relational Reactions and Opposition 564

Client Statements 565

Modeled Responses 565

Notes 566

PART 4
THE TERMINATION PHASE 567

CHAPTER 19
The Final Phase: Evaluation and Termination . . 569

Evaluation 569
   Outcomes 569
   Process 571
   Satisfaction 571
   Types of Termination 572

Understanding and Responding to Clients' Termination
   Reactions 577
   Social Workers' Reactions to Termination 579

**Consolidating Gains and Planning Maintenance
Strategies** 580
   Follow-Up Sessions 580
   Ending Rituals 581

Summary 582

Related Online Content 582

**Skills Development Exercises in Evaluation and
Termination** 582

Notes 583

Bibliography 585
Author Index 629
Subject Index 637

Preface

Welcome to the eighth edition of *Direct Social Work Practice!* We are eager to provide readers with this tool for effective and ethical beginning social work practice.

Goals for the Eighth Edition

The eighth edition of *Direct Social Work Practice* presents a variety of models, theories, and techniques chosen based on the particular mission and values of social work. The approaches selected are both evidence-based and consistent with strength and empowerment perspectives. The book is strongly influenced by the task-centered, crisis, cognitive–behavioral, solution-focused, and motivational interviewing approaches. We also include interventions for modifying environments, as we take a multidimensional view toward assessment and intervention. Several new and enhanced features are reflected in the eighth edition:

- Application of content to practice with minors and elderly clients
- Identification of societal challenges to contemporary practice such as immigration policies, finite resources, and economic challenges
- Attention to competencies drawn from the Council on Social Work Education's Educational Policy and Accreditation Standards (EPAS)
- Skill-building exercises associated with each chapter
- Videotaped interviews depicting an array of clientele and settings. These accompany the text in DVD format and excerpts are referenced in the text. The videos and the examples drawn from them will help faculty and students to apply

practice concepts; identify, model, and learn skills; and stimulate classroom discussions and exercises.

The Structure of the Text

The book has four parts. Part 1 introduces the reader to the social work profession and direct practice and provides an overview of the helping process. Chapter 1 describes the ways that the EPAS standards are addressed in the text and examines the status of evidence-based practice in social work. Chapter 2 presents roles and the domain of the social work field. Chapter 3 provides an overview of the helping process. Part 1 concludes with Chapter 4, which presents the cardinal values of social work, core ethical standards for the profession, and strategies for ethical decision making.

Part 2 presents the beginning phase of the helping process, and each chapter includes examples from the videotapes developed for the text. It opens with Chapter 5, which focuses on relationship-building skills. Chapter 6 presents theories and skills related to eliciting concerns, exploring problems in depth, and providing direction and focus to sessions. Chapter 7 addresses barriers to communication. Chapter 8 covers the process of assessment and problem and strengths exploration. It includes material on culturally competent and solution-focused assessments, as well as assessments with children. Chapter 9 covers the assessment of intrapersonal and environmental systems. It includes information on conducting mental status exams, using the *DSM-IV-TR,* and writing biopsychosocial assessments.

Chapter 10 focuses on family assessment. It includes content on family stressors and resilience as well as an array of instruments to assist in assessing family strengths and stressors. Chapter 11 considers the role of group work in a variety of settings and concepts for forming different types of groups. Chapter 12 presents information on goal setting and recording in ways that are both efficient and client-focused.

Part 3 presents the middle, or goal attainment, phase of the helping process. It begins with Chapter 13, which describes change-oriented strategies, including updated material on task-centered, crisis intervention, cognitive restructuring, and solution-focused approaches to practice.

In Chapter 14, the focus shifts to modifying environments, assessing needs and developing or supplementing resources, and empowerment. This chapter also highlights potential ethical issues in advocacy, social action, and community organizing. Chapter 15 presents methods for enhancing family relationships and illustrates them with novel case examples. Chapter 16 describes theories and skills that are applicable to work with groups, including ethical challenges in group work and innovations such as culturally specific groups and single-session groups. Chapter 17 offers coverage of additive empathy, interpretation, and confrontation with new examples and references. Chapter 18 focuses on dealing with obstacles and barriers to change and likewise includes new content on compassion fatigue and burnout, as well as client and social worker' reactions and case examples.

Part 4 deals with the terminal phase of the helping process. Chapter 19 incorporates material on evaluation and elaborates on termination to address an array of planned and unplanned endings to the social work relationship.

Alternative Chapter Order

The eighth edition of this book has been structured around phases of practice at systems levels ranging from individual, to family, to group, to macro practice. Some instructors prefer to teach all content about a particular mode of practice in one block. In particular, those instructors whose courses emphasize individual contacts may choose to present chapters in a different order than we have organized them (see Table 1). They may teach content in Chapters 5–9, skip ahead to Chapters 12 and 13, and then delve into chapters 17 and 18. Similarly, family content can be organized by using Chapters 10 and 15 together, and groups by using 11 and 16 together. We have presented the chapters in the

TABLE 1 ORGANIZATION OF CHAPTERS BY MODE OF PRACTICE

MODE OF PRACTICE	
Across levels	Chapters 1–4 and 19
Individual	Chapters 5–8, 12, 13, 17, and 18
Family	Chapters 10 and 15
Group	Chapters 11 and 16
Macro	Chapter 14

book in the current order because we think that presentation of intervention by phases fits a systems perspective better than beginning with a choice of intervention mode.

Acknowledgments

We would like to thank the following colleagues for their help in providing useful comments and suggestions. We have been supported by members of our writers' groups, including Mike Chovanec, Annete Gerten, Elena Izaksonas, Rachel Roiblatt, and Nancy Rodenborg. We also want to thank research assistants David DeVito and Tonya VanDeinse for their research, reviews, construction of cases, and management of the bibliography. We owe a special debt of gratitude to our video and simulation participants: Sarah Gottfried, Shannon Van Osdel, Emily Williams, Heather Parnell, Kristen Lukasiewicz, Erika Johnson, Angela Brandt, Irwin Thompson, Ali Vogel, Mrs. Janic Mays, Dorothy Flaherty, Val Velazquez, Kathy Ringham, Mary Pattridge, and Cali Carpenter. Also, for the countless hours of video development and editing, we are grateful for the expertise of Keith Brown and Pete McCauley, University of Minnesota. Finally, we wish to thank our students—the users of this text—and social workers in the field for their suggestions, case examples, and encouragement.

This edition could not have been completed without the support, inspiration, and challenge of our colleagues, friends, and families, including George Gottfried, Lola Dewberry, and Chris Rooney. And finally we want to express special appreciation to Seth Dobrin and his team from Cengage for their enthusiasm, expertise, and patience.

About the Authors

Dean H. Hepworth is Professor Emeritus at the School of Social Work, Arizona State University, Tempe Arizona, and the University of Utah. Dean has extensive practice experience in individual psychotherapy, and marriage and family therapy. Dean was the lead author and active in the production of the first four editions, and he is the co-author of *Improving Therapeutic Communication*. He is now retired and lives in Phoenix, Arizona.

Ronald H. Rooney is Professor, School of Social Work, University of Minnesota, Twin Cities. Ron's practice background is primarily in public and private child welfare, including work with involuntary clients, about which he does training and consultation. Ron is the editor of the second edition of *Strategies for Work with Involuntary Clients*.

Glenda Dewberry Rooney is a Professor at Augsburg College, Department of Social Work, Minneapolis, Minnesota. She teaches undergraduate and graduate micro and macro practice courses, HBSE, ethics, child welfare and research. In addition to her practice experience, she has been involved with agencies concerned with children, youth, and families as a trainer, clinical and management consultant and in community-based research projects. She continues to be an advocate regarding the disparate impact of child welfare policies on families of color. Dr. Rooney is a contributing author to *Strategies for Work with Involuntary Clients (2nd ed)*.

Kim Strom-Gottfried is the Smith B. Theimann Distinguished Professor of Ethics and Professional Practice at the UNC-Chapel Hill School of Social Work. She teaches in the areas of direct practice, communities and organizations, and human resource management and her scholarly interests involve ethics, moral courage, and professional education. Kim's practice experience has been in the nonprofit and public sectors, focusing on mental health and suicide prevention, intervention, and bereavement. She has written numerous articles, monographs and chapters on the ethics of practice and is the author of *Straight Talk about Professional Ethics* and *The Ethics of Practice with*

Minors: High Stakes and Hard Choices. Dr. Strom-Gottfried is also the co-author of *Teaching Social Work Values and Ethics: A Curriculum Resource.*

 **Jo Ann Larsen** is in private practice in Salt Lake City, Utah, and was formerly a faculty member at the School of Social Work, University of Utah. Jo Ann was active in the preparation of the first four editions of the book. Jo Ann has extensive experience in psychotherapy with individuals, families, and groups. Jo Ann is the author of four books on women's issues.

PART 1

Introduction

1   The Challenges of Social Work
2   Direct Practice: Domain, Philosophy, and Roles
3   Overview of the Helping Process
4   Operationalizing the Cardinal Social Work Values

Part 1 of this book provides you with a background of concepts, values, historical perspectives, and information about systems. This information will, in turn, prepare you to learn the specific direct practice skills described in Part 2.

Chapter 1 introduces you to the social work profession; explains its mission, purposes, and values; and describes how systems perspectives can guide you in conceptualizing your work.

Chapter 2 elaborates on the roles played by social workers, including the distinctions made between clinical and direct social work practice, and presents a philosophy of direct practice.

Chapter 3 offers an overview of the helping process, including exploration, implementation, and termination.

Finally, Chapter 4 introduces the cardinal values and ethical concerns underlying social work.

CHAPTER 1

The Challenges of Social Work

- introduces the mission of social work and the purposes of social work services

- illustrates the roles played by social workers within the organizational context for such services

- identifies the value perspectives that guide social workers

- introduces systems and ecological concepts for understanding the interaction of individuals and families with their environment

Case Example

Marta Ramirez was referred to child welfare services because her two elementary school-aged children had more than seven days of unexcused absences from school during the semester, the standard for educational neglect in her state. When Tobias, a child welfare social worker, met with Mrs. Ramirez, he found that the children had missed similar amounts of time when they had previously lived in another state, as well as earlier, before they had immigrated without documents from Mexico. There had not been earlier investigations, however, as legal standards for educational neglect were different in the previous state. Mrs. Ramirez noted that her children had been frequently ill with 'flu and asthma. She said that the children did not feel comfortable at the school. They felt that the teachers were mean to them because they are Hispanic. In addition, Mrs. Ramirez had sustained a back injury on her job that limited her ability to get out of bed some mornings. As an immigrant without documents, Mrs. Ramirez was ineligible for the surgery she needed. Finally, she acknowledged experiencing depression and anxiety.

Tobias shared with Mrs. Ramirez the reason for the referral under statute and asked for her perspective on school attendance. He explained

that child welfare workers are called on to assist families in having their children educated. He also asked about how things were going for Mrs. Ramirez and her family in their community. In so doing, Tobias explained his dual roles of responding to the law violation by statute and helping families address issues of concern to them.

Many social workers practice in settings, such as schools, in which they perform dual roles, protecting both the community at large and vulnerable individuals, in addition to playing other supportive roles (Trotter, 2006). No matter where they are employed, social workers are influenced by the social work value of self-determination for their clients. For this reason, in addition to exploring school attendance issues with Mrs. Ramirez and her children, Tobias addressed Mrs. Ramirez's other concerns.

Mrs. Ramirez acknowledged that her children's school attendance had been sporadic. She attributed this to their illnesses, their feeling uncomfortable and unwelcome in the school, and her own health difficulties that inhibited her in getting the children ready for school.

Tobias asked Mrs. Ramirez if she would like to receive assistance in problem solving, both about how to get the children to school and how to help them to have a better educational experience there. In addition, while health issues were not served directly by his child welfare agency, Tobias offered to explore linkages with the medical field to address Mrs. Ramirez's health and depression concerns.

This case example highlights several aspects of social work practice. As a profession, we are committed to the pursuit of social justice for poor, disadvantaged, disenfranchised, and oppressed people (Marsh, 2005; Finn & Jacobson, 2003; Pelton, 2003; Van Wormer, 2002; Carniol, 1992). In this case, in addition to seeing

Mrs. Ramirez as a parent struggling with school attendance issues, Tobias also saw her as a client experiencing challenges possibly related to the ambivalence and unresolved issues in the United States surrounding immigrants without documentation (Padilla et al., 2008). A law passed by the U.S. House of Representatives in 2005, but not in the Senate, would have made it a crime for service providers to assist undocumented immigrants. However, according to the National Association of Social Workers' (NASW) Immigration Toolkit (NASW, 2006, p. 4), "the plight of refugees and immigrants must be considered on the basis of human values and needs rather than on the basis of an ideological struggle related to foreign policy." The contrast between these two positions suggests that social workers grapple with issues of social justice in their everyday practice. As a social worker, Tobias could not personally resolve the uncertain situation of undocumented immigrants. However, he could work with Mrs. Ramirez and local health institutions to problem-solve around what was possible. Social workers are not the only helping professionals who provide direct services to clients in need. We have a special interest, however, in helping empower members of oppressed groups (Parsons, 2002).

Social workers work in quite diverse settings—governmental agencies, schools, health care centers, family and child welfare agencies, mental health centers, business and industry, correctional settings, and private practice. Social workers work with people of all ages, races, ethnic groups, socioeconomic levels, religions, sexual orientations, and abilities. Social workers themselves variously describe their work as rewarding, frustrating, satisfying, discouraging, stressful, and, most of all, challenging.

In the case example, Mrs. Ramirez did not seek assistance. Instead, she was *referred* by school staff because of her children's poor class attendance, although she acknowledged problems in getting the children to school, as well as her health and depression concerns. Those who *apply* for services are most clearly *voluntary clients*. Many potential clients, including Mrs. Ramirez become more voluntary if their own concerns are explicitly addressed. Social workers practice with clients whose level of voluntarism ranges from *applicants* who seek a service to *legally mandated clients* who receive services under the threat of a court order. Many potential clients fall between these two extremes, as they are neither legally coerced nor seeking a service (Trotter, 2006). These potential clients who experience non-legal pressures

from family members, teachers, and referral sources are known as *nonvoluntary clients* (Rooney, 2009).

With each type of client (voluntary, legally mandated, and non-voluntary), social work assessments include three facets:

1. Exploration of multiple concerns expressed by potential clients
2. Circumstances that might involve legally mandated intervention or concerns about health or safety
3. Other potential problems that emerge from the assessment

Such assessments also include strengths and potential resources. For example, Mrs. Ramirez's potential strengths and resources include her determination that her children have a better life than their parents, and other community and spiritual support systems, both locally and in Mexico. Those potential resources must be assessed in the context of challenges, both internal and external, such as the lack of a safety net for health concerns of undocumented immigrants and Mrs. Ramirez's own medical and psychological concerns.

The Mission of Social Work

The perspectives taken by social workers in their professional roles will influence how Mrs. Ramirez's concerns are conceptualized and addressed. According to the National Association of Social Workers (NASW), "the primary mission of the social work profession is to enhance human well-being and help meet the basic human needs of all people with particular attention to the needs and empowerment of people who are vulnerable, oppressed, and living in poverty" (NASW, 1999, p. 1). The International Federation of Social Workers defines the purpose of social work as including the promotion of social change and the empowerment and liberation of people to enhance well-being (IFSW, 2000, p. 1). Reviews of the definition of the mission of social work maintain the focus on marginalized peoples and empowerment, but add an emphasis on global and cultural sensitivity (Bidgood, Holosko, & Taylor, 2003).

In this book, we will delineate the core elements that lie at the heart of social work wherever it is practiced. These core elements can be classified into two dimensions: purposes of the profession and core competencies. Core competencies include characteristic knowledge, values, and practice behaviors (CSWE, 2008, p. 1). Chapter 1 presents the purposes of social work and the first nine core competencies. The tenth competency, which is to "engage, assess, intervene, and evaluate with individuals, families, groups, organizations, and communities" (EPAS, 2008, p. 7) will be reviewed in Chapter 3 and will become the foundation of the remaining chapters.

Purposes of Social Work

Social work practitioners help clients move toward specific objectives. The means of accomplishing those objectives, however, varies based on the unique circumstances of each client. Even so, all social workers share common goals that constitute the purpose and objectives of the profession. These goals unify the profession and help members avoid developing too-narrow perspectives that are limited to particular practice settings. To best serve their clients, social workers must be willing to assume responsibilities and engage in actions that expand upon the functions of specific social agencies and their designated individual roles as staff members. For example, the child welfare social worker who met with Mrs. Ramirez assessed issues and concerns with her that went beyond the child protection mission of the child welfare setting.

According to CSWE, the purpose of the social work profession is to "promote human and community well-being" (EPAS, 2008, p. 1). Furthermore, that purpose "is actualized through its quest for social and economic justice, the prevention of conditions that limit human rights, the elimination of poverty, and the enhancement of the quality of life for all persons" (EPAS, 2008, p. 1). Hence, the pursuit of social and economic justice is central to social work's purpose. Social justice refers to the creation of social institutions that support the welfare of individuals and groups (Center for Economic and Social Justice, www.cesj.org/thirdway/economicjustice-defined.htm). Economic justice, then, refers to those aspects of social justice that relate to economic well-being, such as a livable wage, pay equity, job discrimination, and social security.

In 2007, the columnist George Will and a group of conservative scholars charged that the social work Code of Ethics, as well as the authors of the previous edition of this book, prescribed political orthodoxy in violation of freedom of speech and in opposition to critical thinking (Will, 2007; NAS, 2007). While support for social and economic justice as national priorities ebbs and flows in the political landscape of the United States, the social work profession supports those goals at all times as part of our core mission. It is not relevant to the profession whether the political majority in such times label themselves as liberal, conservative, green, independent, or any other political affiliation. Social workers ally with those political groups that benefit the oppressed groups who form their core constituencies. Following this purpose, social workers seek to promote social and economic justice for both Americans and immigrants with or without documents. The prevention of conditions that limit human rights and quality of life principle guides Tobias to take seriously the allegation that Mrs. Ramirez and her family have not been made to feel welcome at the school. Indeed, with national priorities of raising testing scores for reading and writing, attention to the needs of those who speak English as a second language may be in conflict with the goal of increasing test scores.

The purposes outlined above also suggest that Tobias might assist Mrs. Ramirez and her family in a variety of ways to meet their needs. Those ways include the creation of policies to find solutions to the health needs of immigrants without documents. Social workers perform preventive, restorative, and remedial functions in pursuit of this purpose.

- Prevention *involves the timely provision of services to vulnerable persons, promoting social functioning before problems develop. It includes programs and activities such as family planning, well-baby clinics, parent education, premarital and pre-retirement counseling, and marital enrichment programs.*
- Restoration *seeks to restore functioning that has been impaired by physical or mental difficulties. Included in this group of clients are persons with varying degrees of paralysis caused by severe spinal injury, individuals afflicted with chronic mental illness, persons with developmental disabilities, persons with deficient educational backgrounds, and individuals with many other types of disability.*
- Remediation *entails the elimination or amelioration of existing social problems. Many potential clients in this category are similar to Mrs. Ramirez in that they are referred by others such as the school system, family members, neighbors, and doctors who have perceived a need.*

The purpose of promoting human and community well-being is "guided by a person and environment construct, a global perspective, respect for human diversity, and knowledge based on scientific inquiry (EPAS, 2008, p. 1). "Guided by a person and environment construct" suggests that social workers always examine individual behavior in its context, reflecting on how that behavior is both a response to and, in turn, influences the individual's environment. Adopting a global perspective suggests that the profession look beyond national borders in assessing needs. A "global perspective" also suggests that Tobias and his agency be aware of the significance of Mrs. Ramirez's migration from Mexico as part of the context of her current circumstances related to school attendance and health care.

The Educational Policy and Accreditation Standards (EPAS) affirms the commitment of social programs to the core values of the profession: service, social justice, dignity and worth of the person, importance of human relationships, integrity, competence, human rights, and scientific inquiry (NASW, 1999, EPAS, 2008).

Social Work Values

All professions have value preferences that give purpose and direction to their practitioners. Indeed, the purpose and objectives of social work and other professions come from their respective value systems. Professional values, however, are not separate from societal values. Rather, professions espouse selected societal values. Society, in turn, sanctions the activities of professions through supportive legislation, funding, delegation of responsibility for certain societal functions, and mechanisms for ensuring that those functions are adequately discharged. Because a profession is linked to certain societal values, it tends to serve as society's conscience with respect to those particular values.

Values represent strongly held beliefs about how the world should be, about how people should normally behave, and about what the preferred conditions of life are. Broad societal values in the United States are reflected in the Declaration of Independence, the Constitution, and the laws of the land, which declare and ensure certain rights of the people. In addition, societal values are reflected in governmental entities and programs designed to safeguard the rights of people and to promote the common good. Interpretations of values and rights, however, are not always uniform. Consider, for example, the heated national debates over the right of women to have abortions; the controversy over the rights of gays, lesbians, and bisexuals to enjoy the benefits of marriage; and conflicts between advocates of gun control and those espousing individual rights.

The values of the social work profession also reflect strongly held beliefs about the rights of people to free choice and opportunity. They recognize the preferred conditions of life that enhance people's welfare, ways that members of the profession should view and treat people, preferred goals for people, and ways in which those goals should be reached. We next consider five values and purposes that guide social work education. Chapter 4 will examine these values and describe others that are contained in the NASW Code of Ethics. These five values are italicized, and the content that follows each is our commentary.

1. *Social workers' professional relationships are built on regard for individual worth and dignity, and are advanced by mutual participation, acceptance, confidentiality, honesty, and responsible handling of conflict* (EPAS, 2008). This value is also reflected in several parts of the Code of Ethics. The first value of the code is simple: "Social workers' primary goal is to serve" (NASW, 1999, p. 5). That is, service to others is elevated above self-interest and social workers should use their knowledge, values, and skills to help people in need and to address social problems. The second value states that they serve others in a fashion such that "social workers respect the inherent dignity and worth of the person." Every person is unique and has inherent worth; therefore, social workers' interactions with people as they pursue and utilize resources should enhance their dignity and individuality, enlarge their competence, and increase their problem-solving and coping abilities.

   People who receive social work services are often overwhelmed by their difficult circumstances and have exhausted their coping resources. Many feel stressed by a multitude of problems. In addition to helping clients reduce their stress level, practitioners aid clients in many other ways: They help them view their difficulties from a fresh perspective, consider various remedial alternatives, foster awareness of strengths, mobilize both active and latent coping resources, enhance self-awareness, and teach problem-solving strategies and interpersonal skills.

   Social workers perform these functions while recognizing "the central importance of human relationships" (NASW, 1999, p. 5). This principle suggests that social workers engage clients as partners in purposeful efforts to promote, restore, maintain, and enhance the clients' well-being. This value is reflected in yet another Code of Ethics principle: "Social workers behave in a trustworthy manner" (p. 6). This principle suggests that social workers practice consistently with the profession's mission, values, and ethical standards, and that they promote ethical practices in the organizations with which they are affiliated (p. 6).

2. *Social workers respect the individual's right to make independent decisions and to participate actively in the helping process.* People have a right to freedom as long as they do not infringe on the rights of others. Therefore, transactions with people who are seeking and utilizing resources should enhance their independence and self-determination. Too often in the past, social workers and other helping professionals have focused on "deficit, disease and dysfunction" (Cowger, 1992). The attention currently devoted to empowerment and strengths behooves social workers to assist clients in increasing their personal potential and political power such that clients can improve their life situation (Finn & Jacobson, 2003; Parsons, 2002; Saleebey, 1997). Consistent with this value, this book incorporates an empowerment and strength-oriented perspective for working with clients. Chapter 13 focuses on skills designed to enhance clients' empowerment and capacity for independent action.

3. *Social workers are committed to assisting client systems to obtain needed resources.* People should have access to the resources they need to meet life's challenges and difficulties as well as access to opportunities to realize their potentialities throughout their lives. Our commitment to client self-determination and empowerment is hollow if clients lack access to the resources necessary to achieve their goals (Hartman, 1993). Because people such as Mrs. Ramirez from the case example often know little about available resources, practitioners must act as brokers by referring people to resource systems such as public legal services, health care agencies, child welfare divisions, mental health centers, centers for elderly persons, and family counseling agencies. Some individual clients or families may require goods and services from many different providers and may lack the language facility, physical or mental capacity, experience, or skills needed to avail themselves of essential goods and services. Practitioners then may assume the role of case manager; that is, they may not only provide direct services

but also assume responsibility for linking the client to diverse resources and ensuring that the client receives needed services in a timely fashion. The broker and case manager roles are discussed in Chapters 2 and 14.

Clients sometimes need resource systems that are not available. In these cases, practitioners must act as program developers by creating and organizing new resource systems. Examples of such efforts include the following: working with citizens and public officials to arrange transportation to health care agencies for the elderly, persons with disabilities, and indigent people; developing neighborhood organizations to campaign for better educational and recreational programs; organizing tenants to assert their rights to landlords and housing authorities for improved housing and sanitation; and organizing support groups, skill development groups, and self-help groups to assist people in coping with difficult problems of living.

Social workers also frequently pursue this goal by facilitating access to resources. They perform the role of facilitator or enabler in carrying out the following functions: enhancing communication among family members; coordinating efforts of teachers, school counselors, and social workers in assisting troubled students; helping groups provide maximal support to their members; opening channels of communication between coworkers; including patients or inmates in the governance of institutions; facilitating teamwork among members of different disciplines in hospitals and mental health centers; and providing for consumer input into agency policy-making boards. Later chapters in this book deal specifically with this objective.

4. *Social workers strive to make social institutions more humane and responsive to human needs.* Although direct practitioners work primarily in providing direct service, they also have a responsibility to work toward improving clients' quality of life by promoting policies and legislation that enhance physical and social environments. The problems of individuals, families, groups, and neighborhoods can often be prevented or at least ameliorated by implementing laws and policies that prohibit contamination of the physical environment and enrich both physical and social environments. Therefore, direct social workers should not limit themselves to remedial activities but rather should seek out environmental causes of problems and sponsor or support efforts aimed at improving their clients' environments.

Chapters 14 and 18 discuss this topic at greater length.

Social workers also demonstrate this value when they assume the role of expediter or troubleshooter by scrutinizing the policies and procedures of their own and other organizations to determine whether their clients have ready access to resources and whether services are delivered in ways that enhance their clients' dignity. Complex application procedures, needless delays in providing resources and services, discriminatory policies, inaccessible agency sites, inconvenient service delivery hours, dehumanizing procedures or staff behaviors—these and other factors may deter clients from utilizing resources or subject them to demeaning experiences.

Systematically obtaining input from consumers is one method of monitoring an organization's responsiveness to clients. Advocacy actions in conjunction with and on behalf of clients are sometimes required to secure the services and resources to which clients are entitled (as discussed in more detail in Chapters 14 and 18). Social workers may support this value by performing the roles of coordinator, mediator, or disseminator of information. For example, as a case manager, a social worker may coordinate the medical, educational, mental health, and rehabilitative services provided to a given family by multiple resource systems. A mediator may be required to resolve conflicts between agencies, minority and majority groups, and neighborhood groups. The social worker may disseminate information regarding legislation or new funding sources that could potentially affect the relationships between public and private agencies by strengthening interactions between these resource systems.

Social workers must also collaborate with key organizations to facilitate mutual awareness of changes in policies and procedures that affect ongoing relationships and the availability of resources.

5. *Social workers demonstrate respect for and acceptance of the unique characteristics of diverse populations.* Social workers perform their services with populations that are characterized by great diversity, including the intersection of dimensions such as "age, class, culture, disability, ethnicity, gender, gender identity and expression, immigration status, political ideology, race, religion, sex and sexual orientation, religion, physical or mental ability, age, and national origin" (EPAS, 2008, p. 5). Similarly, NASW's Code of Ethics requires social workers to understand cultures, recognize strengths in cultures, have a knowledge base of their clients' cultures, and deliver services that are sensitive to those cultures (NASW, 1999, 1.05). This value suggests that social workers must be informed about and respectful of differences. They must educate themselves over time as a part of lifelong learning—unfortunately, there is no "how-to" manual that will guide the practitioner in understanding all aspects of diversity. To demonstrate this value, the practitioner must continually update his or her knowledge about the strengths and resources associated with individuals from such groups to increase the sensitivity and effectiveness of the services provided to those clients.

An increasing number of social workers are themselves members of these diverse populations. They face the challenge of working effectively with both clients and agency staff from the majority culture as well as persons from their own group.

Values and Ethics

Turning the five values described above into reality should be the mutual responsibility of individual citizens and of society. Society should foster conditions and provide opportunities for citizens to participate in policy-making processes. Citizens, in turn, should fulfill their responsibilities to society by actively participating in those processes.

Considered individually, these five values and the profession's mission are not unique to social work. Their unique combination, however, differentiates social work from other professions. Considered in their entirety, these ingredients make it clear that social work's identity derives from its connection with the institution of social welfare. According to Gilbert (1977), social welfare represents a special helping mechanism devised to aid those who suffer from the variety of ills found in industrial society: "Whenever other major institutions, be they familial, religious, economic, or educational in nature, fall short in their helping and resource providing functions, social welfare spans the gap" (p. 402).

These five values represent the prized ideals of the profession and, as such, are stated at high levels of abstraction. As Siporin (1975) and Levy (1973) have noted, however, different levels of professional values exist. At an intermediate level, values pertain to various segments of society—for example, characteristics of a strong community. At a third level, values are more operational, referring to preferred behaviors.

For example, the ideal social work practitioner is a warm, caring, open, and responsible person who safeguards the confidentiality of information disclosed by clients. Because you, the reader, have chosen to enter the field of social work, most of your personal values probably coincide with the cardinal values espoused by the majority of social work practitioners. By contrast, at the intermediate and third levels of values, your views may not always be in harmony with the specific value positions taken by the majority of social workers.

Self-determination refers to the right of people to exercise freedom of choice when making decisions. Issues such as those described above may pose value dilemmas for individual practitioners because of conflicts between personal and professional values. In addition, conflicts between two professional values or principles are common. Public positions taken by the profession that emanate from its values also sometimes stand in opposition to the attitudes of a large segment of society. For example, professional support for universal health coverage has not been supported by a majority of the U.S. Congress.

We suggest that social workers should be sufficiently flexible to listen to many differing value positions on most moral and political issues. Different value positions do not necessarily reflect divergence among social workers on the five core values of the social work profession. Rather, they reflect the existence of many means of achieving given ends. Indeed, rigid assumptions about preferred means to an end often crumble when put to the test of hard experience. Consistent with our preference for flexibility, we reaffirm our commitment to the value that social workers, whatever their beliefs, should assert them in a forum of professional organizations such as NASW. We maintain further that social workers should accord colleagues who differ on certain value positions the same respect, dignity, and right to self-determination that would be accorded clients. Differences on issues may be frankly expressed. Those issues can be clarified and cohesiveness among professionals can be fostered by debate conducted in a climate of openness and mutual respect.

Conflicts between personal and/or professional values and the personal values of a client or group sometimes arise. Not infrequently, students (and even seasoned practitioners) experience conflicts over value-laden, problematic situations such as incest, infidelity, rape, child neglect or abuse, spousal abuse, and criminal behavior. Because direct practitioners encounter these and other problems typically viewed by the public as appalling, and because personal values inevitably shape the social worker's attitudes, perceptions, feelings, and responses to clients, it is vital that you remain flexible and nonjudgmental in your work. It is equally vital that you be aware of your own values, recognize how they fit with the profession's values, and assess how they may affect clients whose values differ from your own or whose behavior offends you.

Because values are critical determinants of behavior in interactions with clients and other professional persons, we have devoted Chapter 4 to practice situations involving potential value dilemmas, including exercises to assist you in expanding your awareness of your personal values. Chapter 4 also deals at length with the relationship-enhancing dimension of respect and contains exercises to assist you in responding respectfully to value-laden situations that may potentially be painful for both you and your clients.

Social Work's Code of Ethics

An essential attribute of legitimate professions is a code of ethics consisting of principles that define expectations of each profession's members. A code of ethics specifies rules of conduct to which members must adhere so as to remain in good standing within a professional organization. It thus defines expected responsibilities and behaviors as well as prescribed behaviors. Central to the purposes of a code of ethics is its function as a formalized expression of accountability of (1) the profession to the society that gives it sanction, (2) constituent practitioners to consumers who utilize their services, and (3) practitioners to their profession. By promoting accountability, a code of ethics serves additional vital purposes, including the following:

1. It safeguards the reputation of a professional by providing explicit criteria that can be employed to regulate the behavior of members.
2. It furthers competent and responsible practice by its members.
3. It protects the public from exploitation by unscrupulous or incompetent practitioners.

Most states now have licensing boards that certify social workers for practice and review allegations of unethical conduct (Land, 1988; DeAngelis, 2000). Similarly, local and state chapters of the NASW establish committees of inquiry to investigate alleged violations of the profession's Code of Ethics, and national committees provide consultation to local committees and consider appeals of decisions made by local chapters. We have blended the values in the code of ethics above in our presentation of the five values stated by CSWE.

These values are prescribed to underlie the social work curriculum and support the profession's commitment to respect for all people and quest for social and economic justice (EPAS, 2008, p. 2).

The Education Policy and Accreditation standards of CSWE are based on a competency-based education format that prescribes attention to outcome performance (EPAS, 2008, p. 2). Those competencies are based on knowledge, values, and skills with emphasis on integrating those competencies into practice with individuals, families, groups, and communities. We will state these competencies in terms of what a competent social work graduate should be able to do when they have completed their courses. We hope that you do not feel apprehensive about whether you are capable of performing these competencies now. It will be your task and that of your educational program to prepare you to reach those competencies by the time that you graduate. (see box 1-1)

Box 1-1 EPAS Competencies

EPAS Competency 2.1

specifies that students identify themselves as professional social workers and conduct themselves accordingly. In order to meet this competency, social workers should be knowledgeable about the profession's history and commit to the enhancement of the profession and their own professional conduct and growth. A social worker meeting this competency will ensure client access to services; engage in self-reflection, self-monitoring, and correction; attend to professional roles and boundaries; demonstrate professional demeanor in behavior, appearance, and communication; engage in career-long learning; and use supervision and consultation (EPAS, 2008, p. 3). In this text, we will assist you in demonstrating these competencies through materials provided in Chapter 4.

EPAS Competency 2.1.2

requires you to apply social work ethical principles to guide your professional practice. You should be knowledgeable about the profession's value base, ethical standards, and relevant laws. In meeting this competency, social workers recognize and manage their personal values such that professional values guide practice. For example, if Tobias had any personal values that might impede his work with Mrs. Ramirez and her children, he would take care that his professional values supersede those personal values. Social workers also make ethical decisions in applying standards such as the NASW Code of Ethics, tolerate ambiguity in resolving ethical conflicts, and apply strategies of ethical reasoning to arrive at principled decisions (EPAS, 2008, p. 4). Chapter 4 of this text contains content to assist you in meeting this competency.

EPAS Competency 2.1.3

requires you to apply critical thinking to inform and communicate professional judgments. Despite George Will and the National Association of Scholars' (2007) allegation that the social work profession emphasizes political orthodoxy over critical thinking, in fact this competency specifically requires us to use critical thinking in the professional setting. In carrying out this competency, you demonstrate that you are knowledgeable about the principles of logic, scientific inquiry, and discernment. Critical thinking requires the synthesis of relevant information augmented by creativity and curiosity. Applying this competency, social workers distinguish, appraise, and integrate multiple sources of information, including the use of research-based knowledge and empirical wisdom, analysis of assessment models, and creativity to synthesize meanings (EPAS, 2008, p. 4). Following this competency, Tobias would consult research-based knowledge and integrate it with empirical wisdom to guide his practice. Pursuit of this competency requires the social worker to consult multiple sources of information in making decisions. We apply critical thinking as part of each chapter in this book.

EPAS Competency 2.1.4

requires you to be aware of diversity and cultural differences in practice. The dimensions of diversity are understood as "... the intersectionality of multiple factors such as age, class, color, culture, disability, ethnicity, gender, gender identity and expression, immigration status, political ideology, race, religion, sex and sexual orientation" (EPAS, 2008, p. 5). Social workers demonstrate this competency when they appreciate the role of oppression, poverty, marginalization and alienation on the life experiences of many clients as well as the impact of privilege, power, and acclaim for many others who work with them, including social workers (p. 5). This competency links social work's commitment to respecting differences to our commitment to serving oppressed groups. In pursuit of this competency, social workers recognize ways in which structures and values may oppress, marginalize, alienate, or, conversely enhance privilege. Further, they view themselves as learners as they engage with those for whom they work as informants (p. 5). They should also have self-awareness, to "eliminate the influence of personal biases and values in working with diverse groups." (p. 5). While we admire the goal of eliminating personal biases, we suggest that it is a more reasonable, feasible goal to become aware of those biases and manage them appropriately. For example, early on in working with Mrs. Ramirez, Tobias wrote in his case notes that he suspected that, in part, her children were not attending school because she and other undocumented immigrants did not value education as much as their fellow students and families in their new community in the United States. In fact, there is evidence to suggest that Mexican immigrants value education highly (Valencia and Black, 2002). This statement by Tobias might be seen as a belief, a hypothesis, or a possible bias that could have profound implications for his work with Mrs. Ramirez. If he acted on his belief that her children were not attending primarily because she and other Mexican immigrants were not motivated about education, he might not explore other community or school based barriers to their attendance, such as their perception that the children were not welcome. Holding members of oppressed groups personally responsible for all aspects of their condition is an unfortunate value predicated on the Horatio Alger myth that all successful people lifted themselves up by their own bootstraps. This competency requires sensitivity to structures that may act to oppress (p. 5). We include attention to diversity and cultural differences in each chapter.

EPAS Competency 2.1.5

requires you to advance human rights and social justice. This competency asserts that each person in society has basic human rights such as freedom, safety, privacy, an adequate standard of living, health care, and education (EPAS, 2008, p. 5). This competency is also reflected in the second value in the social work Code of Ethics: "Social workers challenge social injustice" (NASW, 1999). This value encourages social workers to pursue social change on behalf of vulnerable or oppressed people who are subject to poverty, discrimination, and other forms of injustice. The focus of efforts geared toward populations at risk should increase the power of these individuals to influence their own lives. While the profession supports critical thinking about the means to achieve these goals, social work education is fully committed to human rights and social justice. If resources and opportunities are to be available to all members of society, then laws, governmental policies, and social programs must assure equal access of citizens to those resources and opportunities. Social workers promote social justice by advocating for clients who have been denied services, resources, or goods to which they are entitled. They also work to develop new resources to meet emerging needs.

To meet this competency, you should be aware of the global implications of oppression; be knowledgeable about theories of justice and strategies to promote human and civil rights; and strive to incorporate social justice practices into organizations, institutions, and society. You should also understand the mechanisms of oppression and discrimination in society and advocate for and engage in practices that advance human rights and social and economic justice. George Will and the National Association of Scholars reported that there were instances in which social work students were required by instructors to advocate for groups in conflict with their own religious beliefs (Will, 2007; NAS, 2007). For example, some students were required to advocate for gay and lesbian people to be able to adopt children. In many states, competency to adopt is not based on sexual orientation. There is room for debate whether it is ethical to require students to advocate for specific oppressed groups; however, this competency clearly specifies that advocating for human rights and social and economic justice is a professional expectation.

Following this competency, Tobias would attempt to understand the issue of children's school attendance in a broader framework of understanding why Mrs. Ramirez and her children had moved to his locality. Awareness of the economic incentive of seeking a better income as an influence on immigration would be appropriate. Chapter 15 of this book is focused on the competencies related to advocacy for social justice. For example, in addition to working with Mrs. Ramirez alone, Tobias or other social workers might approach the circumstance of undocumented immigrants in their community from the standpoint of community organization and advocacy, working on the interests of the group rather than solely on those of the individual. While this book focuses primarily on direct social work intervention, other courses in your program and other texts will provide additional sources of information for pursuit of this goal.

EPAS Competency 2.1.6

requires you to engage in research-informed practice and practice-informed research (EPAS, 2008, p. 5). To fulfill this competency, you use your practice experience to inform research, employ evidence-based interventions, evaluate your own practice, and use research findings to improve practice, policy, and social service delivery (p. 5). You will be knowledgeable about quantitative and qualitative research and understand scientific and ethical approaches to building knowledge. As a social worker, you will use your practice experience to inform scientific inquiry and use research evidence to inform practice (p. 5).

Some proponents suggest that employing evidence-based intervention entails being able to explain an evidence-based approach to clients, creating a useful, realistic evaluation format, refining such intervention and evaluation formats based on knowledge of the client, understanding the relevant elements of evidence-based techniques, incorporating evidence from use of the intervention, and being critical consumers of evidence in practice situations (Pollio, 2006, p. 224). Others suggest that knowledge of the context must also be employed in formulating such interventions, as well as considering the theoretical base in selecting interventions (Walsh, 2006; Payne, 2005; Adams, Matto & Le Croy, in press). Given the range of evidence available in different fields of practice, we agree that evidence-based practice should be a highly valued source of information in the context of planning an intervention. Following this principle, Tobias and his agency would be advised to be mindful of evidence-based interventions that assist families with the problem of low school attendance. He and his agency would become familiar with programs such as Check and Connect that promote personal relationships between school personnel and families around attendance issues (Anderson et al, 2004). They would also need to integrate that knowledge with information about the environmental context and relevant interventions. For example, assisting Mrs. Ramirez in getting the children ready for transportation to school might be one part of the intervention, as well as working with the school to construct a more welcoming environment for the children. Part of this context is Mrs. Ramirez's physical and emotional health. She may be more likely to have her children ready for school if she is linked to health care providers who can assist her with her need for surgery and her depression. This book will provide content pertinent to this competency in each chapter.

EPAS Competency 2.1.7

requires that you apply knowledge of human behavior and the social environment. To meet this competency, you should be knowledgeable about human behavior across the life span. You should also be knowledgeable about the social systems in which people live and how those systems promote or hinder people in maintaining or achieving health and well-being. You will apply theories and knowledge from the liberal arts to understand biological, social, cultural, psychological, and spiritual development (EPAS, 2008, p. 6). You will use those conceptual frameworks to guide the processes of assessment intervention and you will critique and apply that knowledge to understand the person and their environment (p. 6). In

your academic program, you are likely to encounter other course work related to human behavior and the social environment to augment the knowledge available from this book. However, this competency will be specifically addressed in Chapters 8–10 of this book. As social systems theory is one such theory to guide assessment intervention, it will be introduced later in this chapter.

EPAS Competency 2.1.8

requires that you engage in policy practice to advance social and economic well-being and to deliver effective social work services (EPAS, 2008, p. 6). One of the distinguishing features of social work as a helping profession is the understanding that all direct practice occurs in a policy context. Hence, social workers need to know about the history of and current structures for policies and services. In pursuit of this competency, social workers analyze, formulate, and advocate for policies that advance the social well-being of clients (p. 6). They also collaborate with colleagues and clients for effective policy action. While some social workers provide direct services to clients, others act indirectly to influence the environments supporting clients, thereby developing and maintaining the social infrastructure that assists clients in meeting their needs. Many social work programs will contain one or more required courses in policy and practice as well as an advanced practice curriculum in this area. Chapter 15 of this book addresses this competency. Tobias' interaction with Mrs. Ramirez must be considered in the context of policies related to school attendance and policies related to health care access.

EPAS Competency 2.1.9

requires that you respond to and shape an ever-changing professional context. As described above, social work as a helping profession is characterized by its sensitivity not only to the policy context of practice but also a broader professional context related to organizations, communities, and society. In pursuit of this competency, you should be informed, resourceful, and proactive in responding to the evolving organizations, community, and societal context at all levels of practice. You will discover, appraise, and attend to changing locales, populations, scientific and technological developments, and emerging societal trends in order to provide relevant services. Social workers also participate in providing leadership to promote sustainable changes in service delivery and practice to improve the quality of social services (EPAS, 2008, p. 6). Tobias would be acting in fulfillment of this competency if he had or gained knowledge of the circumstances of Hispanic speaking children in the elementary school that Mrs. Ramirez's children attended. As noted above, pressures to increase reading scores for children may indirectly create pressure on children for whom English is a second language. This competency is part of each chapter in this book, with special emphasis in Chapter 15.

EPAS 2.1.10, 2.1.11, 2.1.12, 2.1.13 and 2.1.14

require competency in engaging with, assessing, intervening with, and evaluating individuals, families, groups, organizations, and communities (EPAS, 2008, p. 7). These competencies get at the heart of social work intervention and reflect the knowledge and skills that this book is designed to address.

EPAS Competency 2.1.10.1

refers to engagement. In order to meet this competency, social workers prepare for action with individuals, families, groups, organizations and communities both substantively and emotionally (EPAS, 2008, p. 7). They do this by using empathy and other interpersonal skills and developing a mutually agreed-upon focus of work and identifying desired outcomes (p. 7). We consider this competency so essential that we devote most of Chapters 5, 6, and 7 as well as parts of Chapters 10 and 12 to this area of knowledge and skills. Utilizing these skills, Tobias would attempt to personally engage Mrs. Ramirez and her family. We recognize that the success of such engagement efforts depends in part on sensitivity to cultural norms and hence also includes attention to Competency 2.1.3 on diversity.

EPAS Competency 2.1.10.2

on assessment refers to knowledge and skills required to collect, organize, and interpret client data. In this context, social workers must have skills in assessing both a client system's strengths and limitations. They must be able to develop mutually agreed-upon intervention goals and objectives and be able to select appropriate intervention strategies (EPAS, 2008, p. 7). Chapters 8, 9, and 10 of this book address this competency.

EPAS Competency 2.1.10.3

refers to knowledge and skills associated with intervention. Included here are knowledge and skills associated with prevention strategies designed to enhance client capacities; assist clients in resolving problems; negotiate, mediate, and advocate for client systems; and facilitate transitions and endings. Given this book's focus on direct social work intervention, we devote Chapters 10–19 to this area of competency.

EPAS Competency 2.1.10.4

requires knowledge and skills in evaluation. To meet this competency, social workers must be able to critically analyze, monitor, and evaluate interventions (EPAS, 2008,

p. 7). Following this competency, Tobias would establish goals with Mrs. Ramirez and regularly assess progress with her. This competency is built into several chapters of this book but is addressed most specifically in Chapter 12.

EPAS Competency 2.2

refers to knowledge and skills related to generalist practice. A generalist practitioner is grounded in the liberal arts and the personal and environmental constructs required to promote human and social well-being (EPAS, 2008, p. 8). The generalist practitioner uses a range of prevention and intervention methods to work with individuals, families, groups, organizations, and communities. This competency refers to the fact that many social work practitioners operate in agencies that provide varied services at many levels. Generalist practitioners identify with the social work profession and apply ethical principles and critical thinking in practice (p. 8). They incorporate diversity into their practice and are expected to advocate for human rights and social justice. They do so while building upon the strengths and resiliency of human beings. Finally, they engage in research-informed practice and are proactive in responding to an ever-changing professional context. Social work educations incorporate two practice degrees, BSW and MSW. This competency refers to what is expected of BSW practitioners and incorporates the first year of an MSW curriculum. As Tobias was a BSW practitioner, he was expected to use the range of skills and knowledge required of generalist practice. This competency is most emphasized in Chapters 2 and 3.

EPAS Competency 2.2

refers to knowledge and skills required for advanced practice. Advanced practitioners are expected to be able to assess, intervene, and evaluate in order to promote human and social well-being in ways that are differentiated, discriminating, and self-critical (EPAS, 2008, p. 8). Advanced practitioners are expected to synthesize and apply a broad range of interdisciplinary and multidisciplinary knowledge and skills. Such practitioners are expected to refine and advance the quality of social work practice and the larger social work profession. They incorporate the core competencies augmented by knowledge and skills specific to a specialized concentration. (EPAS, 2008, p. 8). Advanced practice in social work means completion of a concentration as defined by their program. Such concentrations are often divided into those that specialize in some forms of micro, mezzo, and macro practice.

Effective practice requires knowledge related to all three levels of practice. Nevertheless, schools of social work commonly offer "concentrations" in either micro or macro practice and require less preparation in the other methods. Curricula vary, of course. Some schools have generalist practice curricula, which require students to achieve balanced preparation in all three levels of practice. Undergraduate programs and the first year of graduate programs typically feature generalist practice curricula, which aim to prepare students for working with all levels of client systems.

The practice methods that correspond to the three levels of practice are as follows:

- *Micro-level practice*. At this level, the population served by practitioners includes a variety of client systems, including individuals, couples, and families. Practice at the micro-level is designated as direct (or clinical) practice because practitioners deliver services directly to clients in face-to-face contact. Direct practice, however, is by no means limited to such face-to-face contact, as we discuss in Chapter 2.

- *Mezzo-level practice*. The second level is defined as "interpersonal relations that are less intimate than those associated with family life; more meaningful than among organizational and institutional representatives; [including] relationships between individuals in a self-help or therapy group, among peers at school or work or among neighbors" (Sheafor, Horejsi, & Horejsi, 1994, pp. 9–10). Mezzo events are "the interface where the individual and those most immediate and important to him/her meet" (Zastrow & Kirst-Ashman, 1990, p. 11). Mezzo intervention is hence designed to change the systems that directly affect clients, such as the family, peer group, or classroom.

- *Macro-level practice*. Still further removed from face-to-face delivery of services, macro practice involves the processes of social planning and community organization. On this level, social workers serve as professional change agents who assist community action systems composed of individuals, groups, or organizations in dealing with social problems. For example, social workers may work with citizen groups or with private, public, or governmental organizations. Activities of practitioners at this level include the following: (1) development of and work with community groups and organizations; (2) program planning and development; and (3) implementation, administration, and evaluation of programs (Meenaghan, 1987).

Micro practice concentrations are often designated around an area of direct, or micro, practice in particular populations or settings such as child welfare, family practice, group work, school social work, aging, and work with children and adolescents. Macro concentrations often refer to practice in community organization, planning, management, and advocacy.

Administration entails playing a leadership role in human service organizations that seek to effectively deliver services in accordance with the values and laws of society. It includes the processes involved in policy formulation and subsequent translation of that policy into operational goals, program design and implementation, funding and resource allocation, management of internal and interorganizational operation, personnel direction and supervision, organizational representation and public relations, community education, monitoring, evaluation, and innovation to improve organizational productivity (Sarri, 1987, pp. 29–30). Direct practitioners are necessarily involved to some degree in administrative activities, as we discuss in Chapter 2. In addition, many direct practitioners who hold master's degrees become supervisors or administrators later in their professional careers. Knowledge of administration, therefore, is vital to direct practitioners at the master's degree level, and courses in administration are frequently part of the required master's degree curriculum in social work. Although many direct practitioners engage in little or no macro-level practice, those who work in rural areas where practitioners are few and specialists in social planning are not available may work in concert with concerned citizens and community leaders in planning and developing resources to prevent or combat social problems. This text includes advanced practice content in many chapters, but the focus of the book is on an introduction to practice.

EPAS Competency 2.3

refers to the signature pedagogy: field education. Signature pedagogy refers to the forms of instruction and learning by which the social work profession socializes students to perform the role of practitioner. Different professions have varied ways by which they train professionals to connect and integrate theory and practice. That is done in social work through field education. Field education is designed to connect the theoretical and conceptual contributions of classrooms with the practice setting (EPAS, 2008, p. 8). In social work, classroom and field are considered equally important in developing competent social work practice. It is designed, supervised, coordinated and evaluated in such as way that students can demonstrate achievement of program competencies. This text includes many exercises in chapters that are designed to be completed in field placements.

Orienting Frameworks to Achieve Competencies

Practitioners and beginning students need orienting frameworks to ground their work in achieving the competencies described above. There is ever-increasing information from the social sciences, social work, and allied disciplines that point to specific interventions for specific problem situations. Successful use of such interventions represents formidable challenges because available knowledge is often fragmented. Further, since social work often takes place in agency settings with clients whose concerns cut across psychological and environmental needs, an orienting perspective is needed to address these levels of concerns and activities. The ecological systems model is useful in providing an orienting perspective (Germain, 1979, 1981; Meyer, 1983; Pincus & Minahan, 1973; Siporin, 1980).

Ecological Systems Model

Adaptations of this model, originating in biology, make a close conceptual fit with the "person-in-environment" perspective that dominated social work until the mid-1970s. Although that perspective recognized the influence of environmental factors on human functioning, internal factors had received an inordinate emphasis in assessing human problems. In addition, a perception of the environment as constraining the individual did not sufficiently acknowledge the individual's ability to affect the environment.

This heavy emphasis, which resulted from the prominence and wide acceptance of Freud's theories in the 1920s and 1930s, reached its zenith in the 1940s and 1950s. With the emergence of ego psychology, systems theory, theories of family therapy, expanded awareness of the importance of ethnocultural factors, and emphasis on ecological factors in the 1960s and 1970s, increasing importance was accorded to environmental factors and to understanding the ways in which people interact with their environments.

Systems models were first created in the natural sciences. Meanwhile, ecological theory developed from the environmental movement in biology. Ecological systems theory in social work adapted concepts from both systems and ecological theories.

Two concepts of ecological theory that are especially relevant to social workers are habitat and niche. *Habitat* refers to the places where organisms live and, in the case of humans, consists of the physical and social settings within particular cultural contexts. When habitats are rich in the resources required for growth and development, people tend to thrive. When habitats are deficient

in vital resources, physical, social, and emotional development and ongoing functioning may be adversely affected. For example, a substantial body of research indicates that supportive social networks of friends, relatives, neighbors, work and church associates, and pets mitigate the damaging effects of painful life stresses. By contrast, people with deficient social networks may respond to life stresses by becoming severely depressed, resorting to abuse of drugs or alcohol, engaging in violent behavior, or coping in other dysfunctional ways.

Niche refers to the statuses or roles occupied by members of the community. One of the tasks in the course of human maturation is to find one's niche in society, which is essential to achieving self-respect and a stable sense of identity. Being able to locate one's niche, however, presumes that opportunities congruent with human needs exist in society. That presumption may not be valid for members of society who lack equal opportunities because of race, ethnicity, gender, poverty, age, disability, sexual identity, or other factors.

An objective of social work, as noted earlier, is to promote social justice so as to expand opportunities for people to create appropriate niches for themselves. Ecological systems theory posits that individuals constantly engage in transactions with other humans and with other systems in the environment, and that these individuals and systems reciprocally influence each other.

Each system is unique, varying in its characteristics and ways of interacting (e.g., no two individuals, families, groups, or neighborhoods are the same). As a consequence, people do not merely react to environmental forces. Rather, they act on their environments, thereby shaping the responses of other people, groups, institutions, and even the physical environment. For example, people make choices about where to live, whether to upgrade or to neglect their living arrangements, and whether to initiate or support policies that combat urban decay, safeguard the quality of air and water, and provide adequate housing for the elderly poor.

Adequate assessments of human problems and plans of interventions, therefore, must consider how people and environmental systems influence one another. The importance of considering this reciprocal interaction when formulating assessments has been reflected in changing views of certain human problems over the past decade. Disability, for example, is now defined in psychosocial terms rather than in medical or economic terms. As Roth (1987) has clarified, "What is significant can be revealed only by the ecological framework in which the disabled person exists, by the interactions through which society engages a disability, by the attitudes others hold, and by the architecture, means of transportation, and social organization constructed by the able bodied" (p. 434). Disability is thus minimized by maximizing the goodness of fit between the needs of people with physical or mental limitations and the environmental resources that correspond to their special needs (e.g., rehabilitation programs, special physical accommodations, education, and social support systems).

It is clear from the ecological systems perspective that the satisfaction of human needs and mastery of developmental tasks require adequate resources in the environment and positive transactions between people and their environments. For example, effective learning by a student requires adequate schools, competent teachers, parental support, adequate perception and intellectual ability, motivation to learn, and positive relationships between teachers and students. Any gaps in the environmental resources, limitations of individuals who need or utilize these resources, or dysfunctional transactions between individuals and environmental systems threaten to block the fulfillment of human needs and lead to stress or impaired functioning. To reduce or remove this stress requires coping efforts aimed at gratifying the needs—that is, achieving adaptive fit between person and environment. People, however, often do not have access to adequate resources or may lack effective coping methods. Social work involves helping such people meet their needs by linking them with or developing essential resources. It could also include enhancing clients' capacities to utilize resources or cope with environmental forces.

Assessment from an ecological systems perspective obviously requires knowledge of the diverse systems involved in interactions between people and their environments:

- *Subsystems of the individual (biophysical, cognitive, emotional, behavioral, motivational).*
- *Interpersonal systems (parent–child, marital, family, kin, friends, neighbors, cultural reference groups, spiritual belief systems, and other members of social networks).*
- *Organizations, institutions, and communities.*
- *The physical environment (housing, neighborhood environment, buildings, other artificial creations, water, and weather and climate).*

These systems and their interactions are considered in Chapters 8–11.

A major advantage of the ecological systems model is its broad scope. Typical human problems involving

health care, family relations, inadequate income, mental health difficulties, conflicts with law enforcement agencies, unemployment, educational difficulties, and so on can all be subsumed under this model, enabling the practitioner to analyze the complex variables involved in such problems.

Assessing the sources of problems and determining the focuses of interventions are the first steps in applying the ecological systems model.

Pincus and Minahan have adapted systems models to social work practice, suggesting that a *client system* includes those persons who are requesting a change, sanction it, are expected to benefit from it, and contract to receive it (Pincus & Minahan, 1973; Compton & Galaway, 2005). Potential clients who request a change are described as *applicants*. Many clients reach social workers not through their own choice but rather through referral from others. *Referrals* are persons who do not seek services on their own, but do so at the behest of other professionals and family members. Meanwhile, *contacted persons* are approached through an outreach effort (Compton & Galaway, 2005). Some referred and contacted individuals may not experience pressure from that contact. As noted earlier, some individuals do experience pressure and social workers should consider them to be "potential clients" and to be aware of the route that brought them to the social worker and their response to that contact. For example, Mrs. Ramirez could be considered a potential client as she was approached by child welfare services as part of a possible educational neglect assessment.

The next step is to determine what should be done vis-à-vis the pertinent systems involved in the problem situation. In this step, the practitioner surveys the broad spectrum of available practice theories and interventions. To be maximally effective, interventions must be directed to all systems that are critical in a given problem system.

The *target system* refers to the focus of change efforts. With a voluntary client, it will typically encompass the concerns that brought the individual to seek services. With nonvoluntary clients, it may include illegal or dangerous behaviors that the person does not acknowledge (see Figure 1-1). The *client system* consists of those persons who request or are expected to benefit from services. Note that this definition includes both applicants, or voluntary clients, and nonvoluntary clients (see Figure 1-2).

When a client desires assistance on a personal problem, the target and client systems overlap. Frequently, however, clients request assistance with a problem

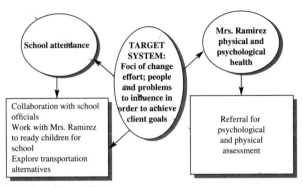

FIG-1-1 Target System

outside themselves. In such instances, that problem could become the center of a target system. For example, Mrs. Ramirez acknowledges psychological and physical health concerns as well as concerns about how welcome her children feel in school. Meanwhile, Tobias must carry out a legally defined educational neglect assessment. These problem areas may merge as a contract is developed to address several concerns. It is important that target problems focus on a target concern rather than on the entire person as the target. Focusing on a person as the target system objectifies that individual and diminishes the respect for individuality to which each person is entitled. Hence, concerns with school attendance can be the target system rather than Mrs. Ramirez and her children.

The *action system* refers to those formal and informal resources and persons that the social worker needs to cooperate with to accomplish a purpose. It often includes family, friends, and other resources as well as more formal resources. For example, an action system for school attendance might include school attendance officers, teachers, relatives, neighbors, spiritual resources or transportation providers, according to the plan agreed upon by Mrs. Ramirez and Tobias (see Figure 1-3).

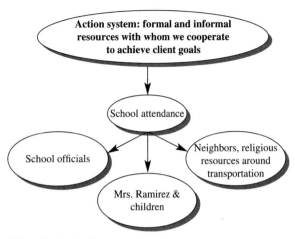

FIG-1-3 Action System

The *agency system* is a special subset of an action system that includes the practitioners and formal service systems involved in work on the target problems (Compton & Galaway, 2005). In this case, the agency system primarily includes the elementary school and the child welfare agency (see Figure 1-4).

Social systems also vary in the degree to which they are open and closed to new information or feedback. Closed systems have relatively rigid *boundaries* that prevent the input or export of information. Open systems have relatively permeable boundaries permitting a more free exchange. Families may vary from being predominantly closed to new information to being excessively open. In fact, all families and human systems exhibit a tension between trying to maintain stability and boundaries in some areas while seeking and responding to change in others. Systems theorists also suggest that change in one part of a system often affects

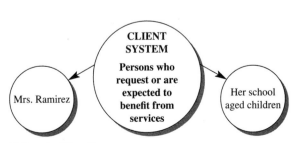

FIG-1-2 Client System

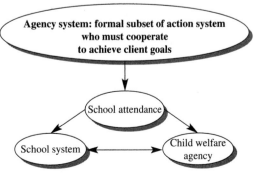

FIG-1-4 Agency System

other parts of the system. For example, Mrs. Ramirez's emotional and physical health may greatly influence her capacity to prepare her children for school. Hence, facilitating a referral for her may have a significant impact on the school attendance issue.

The principle of *equifinality* suggests that the same outcome can be achieved even with different starting points. For example, your classmates have come from different places both geographically and in terms of life experience. Despite their different origins, they have all ended up in the same program of study. The principle of *multifinality* suggests that beginning from the same starting points may end in different outcomes. Just as you and your classmates are engaged in the same course of study, you are likely to end in diverse settings and locales for your own practice experience.

Nonlinear Applications of Systems Theory

Traditional systems theory suggests that systems or organizations are characterized by order, rationality, and stability (Warren, Franklin, & Streeter, 1998). Hence, the emphasis in such stable systems is on concepts such as boundaries, homeostasis, and equilibrium. In addition to ordered circumstances, systems theory can be useful for consideration of nonlinear systems. Systems in the process of change can be very sensitive to initial events and feedback to those events. For example, a nonlinear change would be the circumstance in which an adolescent's voice changes by 1 decibel of loudness resulting in a change of 10 decibels in an adult (Warren et al., 1998). Minor incidents in the past can reverberate throughout a system. Some have suggested that this proliferation supports the notion that family systems can make significant changes as a result of a key intervention that reverberates and is reinforced in a system.

Such nonlinear circumstances emphasize the concept of multifinality—that is, the same initial conditions can lead to quite varied outcomes. Among the implications of multifinality are the possibility of considering chaos not as a lack of order but rather as an opportunity for flexibility and change.

Limitations of Systems Theories

While systems models often provide useful concepts for describing person–situation interactions, they may have limitations in suggesting specific intervention prescriptions (Whittaker & Tracy, 1989). Similarly, Wakefield (1996a, 1996b) has argued that systems concepts do not add much to domain-specific knowledge. Others claim that, however faulty or inadequate, systems

theory provides useful metaphors for conceptualizing the relations between complex organizations.

Perhaps we should not place such high expectations on the theory (Gitterman, 1996). We take the view that systems theory provides useful metaphors for conceptualizing the varied levels of phenomena social workers must recognize. By themselves, those metaphors are insufficient to guide practice. Concepts such as equifinality and multifinality cannot be rigidly applied in all human and social systems.

Deciding on and Carrying out Interventions

How do social workers decide on what interventions they will carry out to assist client systems in reaching their goals? Throughout our professional history, social workers have drawn selectively on theories to help understand circumstances and guide intervention. Psychodynamic theory was an important early source of explanations to guide social work interventions through adaptations such as the functional approach, the psychosocial approach, and the problem-solving approach (Hollis and Woods, 1981; Perlman, 1957; Taft, 1937). In each of these approaches, ego psychology was a particularly valuable source in explaining how individuals coped with their environment. While psychodynamic theory provided a broad-ranging explanatory framework, it was less useful as a source for specific interventions, and the level of abstraction required in the approach did not lend itself well to the evaluation of its effectiveness.

Concerns about the effectiveness of social work services led to an emphasis on employing methods that could be expected to be successful based on proven effectiveness (Fischer, 1973). Rather than seeking single approaches to direct practice in all circumstances, social workers were guided to find the approach that made the best fit for the particular client circumstance and problem (Fischer, 1978). Eclectic practice is designed to meet this goal, but carries its own concerns. For example, selecting techniques employed in particular approaches is best done based on knowledge of the approach the techniques come from and an assessment of the strengths and weaknesses of that approach (Coady and Lehmann, 2008; Marsh, 2004).

Berlin and Marsh suggest that there are legitimate roles for many influences on practice decision making. Those include clear conceptual frameworks to guide the social worker in what to look for, commitments and

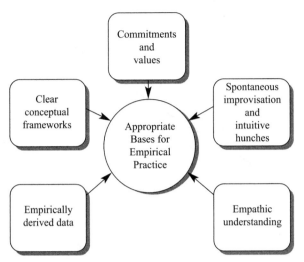

FIG-1-5 **Appropriate Bases for Empirical Practice**
Source: Adapted from Berlin and Marsh, 1993, p. 230.

values, intuitive hunches, spontaneous improvisation, empathic understanding, and empirically derived data (Berlin and Marsh, 1993, p. 230) (see Figure 1-5).

Empirically derived data as a source has a prominent role in determining, together with clients, how to proceed. Empirically based practice refers to promoting models of practice based on scientific evidence (Barker, 2003). In such an approach, problems and outcomes are conceived in measurable terms, and data is gathered to monitor interventions and evaluate effectiveness. Interventions are selected based on their scientific support and effectiveness as systematically measured and evaluated (Cournoyer, 2004; Petr & Walter, 2005). The term "evidence-based practice" has been suggested as broader than "empirically based practice," since external research findings are considered in the context of fit to particular situations, which in turn are considered within the context of informed consent and client values and expectations (Gambrill, 2004; Petr & Walter, 2005, p. 252).

Evidence-based practice began in medicine as an attempt to make conscientious efforts toward identifying best practices for client care, assessing the quality of evidence available, and presenting that evidence to clients and patients so that they could share in decision making (Adams & Drake, 2006; Scheyett, 2006). More recently, two forms of evidence-based practice have become prominent.

The first form, the *process model*, is consistent with the medical definition of evidence-based practice cited above and focuses on the practices of the individual practitioner. Specifically, the individual practitioner learns how to formulate a question that is answerable

with data about his or her work with a client (Rubin, 2007). Based on that question, the practitioner gains access to appropriate empirical literature. The practitioner must have access to appropriate literature through computerized access to online journals and studies. The practitioner does not need to review all the relevant literature from all of the available studies but may seek secondary reviews and meta-analyses of an intervention that summarize the state of knowledge about that intervention. For example, the state of evidence about stages of change in a child welfare context has been summarized by Littell and Girvin (2004). In assessing studies of interventions, a hierarchy of levels has been developed to assess the reliability of an intervention measure. For example, multiple randomized studies are considered to provide potentially strong support for an intervention. With some social problems and settings such as child welfare, such studies are rare; however, studies with other adequate controls may be available (Thomlison, 2005; Whiting Blome, & Steib, 2004; Gira, Kessler, & Poertner, 2001). Whatever the range of studies available, the practitioner needs to have the skills to assess the level of support for the intervention. Based on this assessment of data, the social work practitioner can share that evidence with his or her client in order to better make an informed decision together about what to do. After making this joint decision, the practitioner and client can implement the intervention with fidelity and assess how well it works. This has been characterized as a bottom-up model because the questions raised and interventions selected are assumed to be defined by the people closest to the intervention: the practitioner and client (Rubin, 2007).

There are several assumptions about the process model as presented in this form that must be assessed. It assumes that the practitioner is free to select an intervention and the client is free to accept or reject it. In fact, agency-level practice has many influences that determine which interventions can be utilized (Payne, 2005). Some interventions are supported by the agency and supervisor based on policies, laws, prior training, and accepted practices. Practitioners utilizing the process model hope that such interventions are supported by a review of the research evidence. Recognizing this issue and that the choice of intervention may not be fully in the control of the practitioner, some proponents have suggested that one solution is for teams to study evidence about particular problems and interventions and make recommendations about practices to be used by the team (Proctor, 2007). In partnership with schools of social work, agency teams can identify problems and secure administrative support while the schools provide training in evidence-based practices. Secondly, when clients are not entirely voluntary, practitioners and agencies may and should make evidence-based decisions; but involuntary clients may not feel empowered to reject them (Scheyett, 2006; Kessler et al, 2005). In such cases, however, clients are entitled through informed consent to know the rationale for the intervention and its evidence of effectiveness. This model also assumes that the practitioner has sufficient time to access the appropriate literature and appropriate resources. Finally, it assumes that the practitioner has the skill, training, and supervision to carry out the evidence-based intervention effectively (Rubin, 2007).

Partly in response to the difficulties, described above, associated with the process model, another version of evidence-based practice refers to training in these practices. In this approach, the emphasis is on identifying models of practice that have demonstrated efficacy for particular problems and populations, learning about them, and learning how to implement them. An advantage of this approach, according to proponents, is the fact that it focuses on not just knowing about the intervention but acquiring the skills necessary to carry it out effectively (Rubin, 2007). Critics suggest that this approach carries its own dangers. For one, students often experience anxiety in learning how to become effective practitioners and, having learned one evidence-based practice, might be inclined to generalize it beyond its original effectiveness, thus replicating in part the problem mentioned earlier, of students trained in a theory or model and carrying it out without evidence of effectiveness and without having an alternative: If your only tool is a hammer, all problems may appear to be nails (Scheyette, 2006). Secondly, evidence-based practices have their own limited shelf life, with new studies supporting some methods and qualifying the support for others. Hence, the fact that you learn one evidence-based approach does not preclude and should not preclude learning others. In fact, we believe that becoming effective practitioners is a career-long proposition, not limited by the completion of your academic program. Finally, behavioral and cognitive-behavioral approaches are well-represented among evidence-based practices. Some have suggested that such approaches have some advantage because practice of the approach fits research protocols, and therefore that other approaches have been under-represented (Coady & Lehmann, 2008; Walsh, 2006). It becomes a challenge to other approaches to enhance their effectiveness base rather than question the value of research protocols or representativeness

of the model. There is growing evidence that some emerging approaches, such as the solution-focused approach are in fact increasing their effectiveness base (Kim, 2008).

Advocates suggest that there is room for both such approaches in social work education; that all students should learn how to carry out the process model of evidence-based practice and that all students should become proficient in at least one evidence-based practice modality (Rubin, 2007). These proponents also suggest that this kind of practice may require specialization in certain methods and may not be consistent with those programs that include an advanced generalist curriculum (Howard, Allen-Meares, & Ruffolo, 2007). We do not take sides on this issue, recognizing that programs that have developed advanced generalist curricula have done so mindful of the context and expectations for practitioners in their area, and that generalist practice remains the standard for BSW programs and the first year of MSW programs.

Guidelines Influencing Intervention Selection

We recommend the following guidelines to assist you in deciding when and how to intervene with clients in social work practice.

1. *Social workers value maximum feasible self-determination, empowerment, and enhancing strengths to increase the client's voice in decision making.* Thus, manualized approaches that imply that all major decisions are in the hands of and controlled by the social work practitioner are alien to these values. Following these values, we seek to include clients to the extent possible in access to information that would assist them in making decisions (Coady & Lehmann, 2008).

2. *Social workers assess circumstances from a systems perspective, mindful of the person in the situation, the setting, the community, and the organization.* We assess for the level of the problem and the appropriate level of interventions (Allen-Meares & Garvin, 2000). We recognize that resources are often needed at multiple levels and attempt to avoid a narrow clinical focus on the practitioner and client. Hence our use of data and perspectives to guide us must be governed in part by the multiple roles we play, including systems linkage as well as direct practice or clinical interventions (Richey & Roffman, 1999).

3. *Social workers are sensitive to diversity in considering interventions.* We avoid assumptions that

interventions tested with one population will necessarily generalize to another. In so doing, we are particularly sensitive to the clients' own perspectives about what is appropriate for them (Allen-Meares & Garvin, 2000).

4. *Social workers draw on evidence-based practices at both process and intervention levels as sources in determining, together with the client, how to proceed.* We expect social work practitioners to have access to evidence about efficacious interventions for the problem at hand. Such evidence may occur through individual study, through organizational priorities, or through collaboration with university teams to construct guidelines for practice in critical areas. Because our code of ethics requires us to act within our level of competence and supervision, knowledge of what interventions are efficacious does not mean that we can carry out those interventions. It may be a useful goal to learn how to carry out two or more evidence-based approaches as part of your education program. The goal of this book is, however, to equip you with the basic skills to carry out practice at the beginning level. We are influenced by the process model of evidence-based practice, and we seek to give you useful tools by modeling ways that questions can be asked and that data can be consulted in making decisions with clients. Further, in our chapters on intervention models we will be influenced by evidence-based practice models. It is not realistic at this level to attempt to teach evidence-based practice approaches such that you would be able to implement them right away. We can introduce you to them, but further training and supervision are required.

5. *Social workers think critically about practice, checking out assumptions and examining alternatives.* We try to avoid early social work patterns of applying theories more widely than data suggests by being open to examining alternatives (Briggs & Rzepnicki, 2004; Gambrill, 2004). One danger of following a single approach is that data that does not fit the preferences of the approach is discounted (Maguire, 2002). Conversely, this danger can also apply to selecting an approach based on its label as evidence-based, for example, without assessing fit with client and circumstances (Scheyett, 2006).

Summary

This chapter introduced social work as a profession marked by a specific mission and well-established values. As social workers and their clients operate in many different kinds and levels of environments, ecological and systems concepts are useful metaphors for conceptualizing what social workers and clients must deal with. Chapter 2 will delve deeper into specifying direct practice and the roles that social workers play.

CHAPTER 2

Direct Practice: Domain, Philosophy, and Roles

CHAPTER OVERVIEW

This chapter presents a context and philosophy for direct practice, including definitions of direct and clinical practice, and descriptions of the varied roles played by direct social work practitioners.

Domain

Prior to 1970, social work practice was defined by methodologies or by fields of practice. Social workers were thus variously identified as caseworkers, group workers, community organizers, child welfare workers, psychiatric social workers, school social workers, medical social workers, and so on. The terms *direct practice* and *clinical practice* are relatively new in social work nomenclature.

The profession was unified in 1955 by the creation of the National Association of Social Workers (NASW) and, with the inauguration of the journal *Social Work*, the gradual transformation from more narrow views of practice to the current broader view was under way. This transformation accelerated during the 1960s and 1970s, when social unrest in the United States prompted challenges and criticisms of all institutions, including social work. Persons of color, organized groups of poor people, and other oppressed groups accused the profession of being irrelevant given their pressing needs. These accusations were often justified, because many social workers were engaged in narrowly focused and therapeutically oriented activities that did not address the social problems of concern to oppressed groups (Specht & Courtney, 1994).[1]

Casework had been the predominant social work method during this period. Casework comprised activities in widely varying settings, aimed at assisting individuals, couples, or families to cope more effectively with problems that impaired social functioning. At the same time group work had evolved as a practice method,

and group workers were practicing in settlement houses and neighborhoods, on the streets with youth gangs, in hospitals and correctional institutions, and in other settings. Although the units targeted by group workers were larger, their objectives still did not address broad social problems. It was clear that urgent needs for broadly defined social services could not be met through the narrowly defined remedial (therapeutic) efforts of the casework and group work methods.

The efforts of Gordon (1965) and Bartlett (1970) to formulate a framework (i.e., common base) for social work practice composed of purpose, values, sanction, knowledge, and common skills resulted in a broadened perspective of social work. Because this new perspective was not oriented to methods of practice, a new generic term was created to describe it: *social work practice*.

Generalist Practice

The Council on Social Work Education (CSWE) responded to the evolution of the social work practice framework by adopting a curriculum policy statement stipulating that to meet accreditation standards, social work educational programs must have a curriculum containing foundation courses that embody the common knowledge base of social work practice. Both undergraduate (BSW) and graduate (MSW) programs embody such foundation courses and thus prepare students for generalist practice. BSW curricula, however, are designed primarily to prepare generalist social workers and avoid specialization in practice methods. The rationale for generalist programs, as discussed in Chapter 1, is that practitioners should view problems holistically and be prepared to plan interventions aimed at multiple levels of systems related to client concerns. Similarly, client goals and needs should suggest appropriate interventions, rather than interventions inspiring the selection of compatible goals. Client systems range from micro systems (individuals, couples, families, and groups) to mezzo to macro systems (organizations, institutions, communities, regions, and nations).

Connecting client systems to resource systems that can provide needed goods and services is a paramount function of BSW social workers. Many BSW programs, in fact, prepare students to assume the role of case manager, a role that focuses on linking clients to resource systems. We alluded to this role in Chapter 1 and discuss it briefly later in this chapter and more extensively in Chapter 14.

The first year (foundation year) of MSW programs also prepares graduate students for generalist practice. Although a few MSW programs prepare students for "advanced generalist practice," the vast majority of second-year curricula in the MSW programs permit students to select specializations or "concentrations" within methods of practice or within fields of practice (e.g., substance abuse, aging, child welfare, work with families, health care, or mental health) (Raymond, Teare, & Atherton, 1996). Methods of practice typically are denoted as *micro* or *macro*, the former referring to direct practice and the latter denoting social policy, community organization, and planning to bring about social and economic justice. MSW students thus are prepared for both generalist and specialized practice.

Both similarities in orientation and differences in function between BSW and MSW social workers and the importance of having practitioners at both levels are highlighted in the following case example. Note that similarities and differences exist on a continuum such that some MSW social workers perform some of the tasks otherwise ascribed to the BSW practitioner, and vice versa. Similarly, differences in their tasks may arise based on geographic region, field of practice, and availability of MSW-trained practitioners.

Case Example

Arthur Harrison and Marlene Fisher are unmarried adults, each of whom has developmental disabilities. They have two sons. Mr. Harrison and Ms Fisher came to the attention of child protection services because Roger, the older of their sons who also has a developmental disability, told his teacher that his younger brother, Roy, 13, who does not have a developmental disability, and Roy's friends had sexually molested Roger. Roy admitted to the offense when interviewed, as did his friends. Roy stated that he learned the behavior from a neighbor who had been sexually abusing him since age 7.

The family participated in an assessment conducted by Christine Summers, a BSW social worker employed by the county's child protection agency. Roger was placed in residential care, and Roy was charged with sexual assault. Meanwhile, the neighbor boy was charged with three counts of first-degree sexual assault and was incarcerated pending a hearing. Christine then met with the parents to conduct a strengths-based and risk assessment. This assessment revealed that Mr. Harrison and Ms Fisher had coped well with parenting on many fronts, including maintaining their children in good school performance, and supporting their hobbies and avocations. Some concern was raised about their capacities to protect their children from danger in this instance. As a result of the collaborative assessment conducted by Ms Summers, a plan was developed with the goal of Mr. Harrison and Ms Fisher's resumption of care for their children.

Christine acted as the case manager, coordinating the efforts of several persons who were assisting Mr. Harrison and Ms Fisher and their children in pursuit of their goal of restoration of custody. Christine played dual roles (Trotter, 2006) in this case: (1) ensuring social control designed to protect the public and vulnerable persons and (2) providing assistance to the family (i.e., a helping role). Sometimes those roles can be played simultaneously, sometimes they can be played in sequence, and sometimes only one of the two roles can be filled by the caseworker. In this instance, Ms Summers initially carried out her assessment with her actions largely being guided by her role of protecting the public and vulnerable persons. After she came to agreement with the parents about the plan for regaining custody of their sons, Ms Summers became more able to play a helping role. This plan included a referral to Debra Sontag, an MSW practitioner with special expertise in work with children with sexual behavior difficulties. Ms. Sontag was able to work with Roy, Roger, and their parents and make a recommendation to the child welfare agency and court about when and under what conditions living together as a family would again be safe.

As this example indicates, frequently MSW direct practitioners provide more in-depth individual and family services than fits the caseloads, responsibilities, and training of BSW practitioners. They can coordinate their services to better serve families.

Direct Practice

Direct practice includes work with individuals, couples, families, and groups. Direct social work practitioners perform many roles besides delivering face-to-face service; they work in collaboration with other professionals, organizations, and institutions, and they act as advocates with landlords, agency administrators, policy-making boards, and legislatures, among others. Direct social work practice is conducted in a variety of settings and problem areas. For example, direct practice includes services to clients organized by life-cycle stage (children, adolescents and young adults, aging), problem area (child welfare, domestic violence, health and mental health, substance abuse, anti-poverty issues such as homelessness and housing programs, work programs), mode of intervention (work with families, work with groups), and agency setting (school social work, disability services) (see Figure 2-1).

The term *clinical practice* is used by some as synonymous with *direct practice*. Clinical social work practice has been defined as "the provision of mental health services for the diagnosis, treatment and prevention of mental, behavioral and emotional disorders in individuals, families and groups" (Clinical Social Work Federation, 1997). The focus of clinical work is said to be "to provide mental health treatment in agencies, clinics, hospitals and as private practitioners" (Clinical Social Work Association, 2008). Others suggest a broader definition of practice activities, with psychotherapy at one end of a continuum and advocacy and prevention efforts at the other end (Swenson, 2002). However, pressures exist to emphasize the intensive individual end of the continuum through presenting billable hours

(Frey & Dupper, 2005). Clinical social work practice might be considered to include the function of providing mental health services among its other roles. While mental health treatment may be provided to clients in many settings, such treatment is not the primary function in those settings. For example, while mental health services may be of use to some clients in a homeless shelter, environmental interventions to assist with housing are the primary function.

The *clinical social worker* title has special significance in some states, because an advanced license is labeled as clinical. Licensing provisions are such that diagnosis and treatment of mental health difficulties requires that the provider have a clinical license or be under the supervision of a person with such a license. Achievement of such a license is based on completion of specified hours in training and supervision as well as completion of an exam. Holding such a license then becomes a required credential for social workers to be eligible for third-party reimbursement for delivering psychotherapy or counseling.

While recognizing the significance of these licensing and reimbursement issues, as well as the attached status and prestige of the term "clinical social worker," we do not think it necessary to subsume all direct social work practice under the term clinical practice. Crucial interventions are performed to assist children and families in child welfare, for example, whether or not they are related to mental health services. Some seem to use the term clinical practice to connote "quality social work practice." We prefer to describe clinical services as a particular form of direct service that can be delivered in many fields of practice but which include the

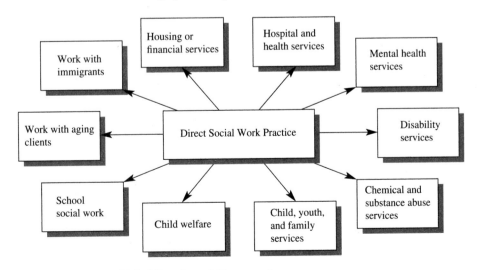

FIG-2-1 **Direct Social Work Practice and Components**

assessment and treatment of mental health issues as one function. In this book, we will use both of the terms *direct practice* and *clinical practice*, guided by the primary functions of the settings in which micro-level services are delivered.

Direct practice encompasses a full range of roles, including acting as a case worker or counselor. Central to assisting people with difficulties is knowledge of and skill in assisting people in deciding how best to work on their concerns. That assistance requires knowledge and skills in assessing human problems and in locating, developing, or utilizing appropriate resource systems. Skills in engaging clients, mutually planning relevant goals, and defining the roles of the participants are also integral parts of the helping process. Likewise, the practitioner must possess knowledge of interventions and skills in implementing them. A more extensive review of the helping process is contained in Chapter 3, and this entire book is devoted to explicating the theory and skills related to direct practice with clients.

Direct practitioners of social work must be knowledgeable and skilled in interviewing and in assessing and intervening in problematic interactions involving individuals, couples, families, and groups. Knowledge of group processes and skills in leading groups are also essential, as are skills in forming natural helping networks, functioning as a member of an interdisciplinary team, and negotiating within and between systems. The negotiating function requires skills in mediating conflicts, advocating for services, and obtaining resources, all of which embody high levels of interpersonal skills.

Some have questioned whether engaging in psychotherapy is appropriate for a profession whose mission focuses on social justice (Specht & Courtney, 1994). Others have countered that a social justice mission is not necessarily inconsistent with use of psychotherapy as one tool in pursuit of this goal (Wakefield, 1996a, 1996b). According to Swenson (1998), clinical work that draws on client strengths, that is mindful of social positions and power relationships, and that attempts to counter oppression is consistent with a social justice perspective. In our opinion, these debates are moot. Many of today's practitioners in social work and other helping professions practice psychotherapy that draws on additional theory bases such as behavioral and family systems models. Clinical practice in a managed care environment focuses on specific problems, strengths, and resources; is highly structured and goal oriented; and develops tangible objectives for each session intended to achieve the overall treatment goals (Franklin, 2002).

A Philosophy of Direct Practice

As a profession evolves, its knowledge base expands and practitioners gain experience in applying abstract values and knowledge to specific practice situations. Instrumental values gradually evolve as part of this transformation; as they are adopted, they become principles or guidelines to practice. Such principles express preferred beliefs about the nature and causes of human problems. They also describe perspectives about people's capacity to deal with problems, desirable goals, and valued qualities in helping relationships. Finally, those principles include beliefs about vital elements of the helping process, the roles of the practitioner and the client, characteristics of effective group leaders, and the nature of the human growth process.

Over many years, we have evolved a philosophy of practice from a synthesis of principles gained from sources too diverse to acknowledge, including our own value preferences. We thus offer as our philosophy of direct practice the principles outlined in Figure 2-2.

Roles of Direct Practitioners

During recent years, increasing attention has been devoted to the various roles that direct practitioners perform in discharging their responsibilities. In Chapter 1, we referred to a number of these roles. In this section, we summarize these and other roles and refer to sections of the book where we discuss certain roles at greater length. We have categorized the roles based in part on a schema presented by Lister (1987) (see Figure 2-3).

Direct Provision of Services

Roles subsumed under this category include those in which social workers meet face to face with clients or consumer groups in providing services:

- *Individual casework or counseling.*
- *Marital and family therapy* (may include sessions with individuals, conjoint sessions, and group sessions).
- *Group work services* (may include support groups, therapy groups, self-help groups, task groups, and skill development groups).
- *Educator/disseminator of information.* The social worker may provide essential information in individual, conjoint, or group sessions or may make educational presentations to consumer groups or to the public. For example, practitioners may conduct educational sessions dealing with parenting skills,

PHILOSOPHY OF DIRECT PRACTICE

1. The problems experienced by social work clients stem from lack of resources, knowledge, and skills (societal, systemic, and personal sources), either alone or in combination.

2. Because social work clients are often subject to poverty, racism, sexism, heterosexism, discrimination, and lack of resources, social workers negotiate systems and advocate for change to ensure that their clients obtain access to their rights, resources, and treatment with dignity. They also attempt to modify or develop resource systems to make them more responsive to client needs.

3. People are capable of making their own choices and decisions. Although controlled to some extent by their environment, they are able to direct their environment more than they realize. Social workers aim to assist in the empowerment of their clients by helping them gain (1) the ability to make decisions and (2) access to critical resources that affect their lives and increase their ability to change those environmental influences that adversely affect them individually and as members of groups.

4. Because social service systems are often funded on the basis of individual dysfunctions, social workers play an educational function in sensitizing service delivery systems to more systemic problem-solving approaches that emphasize health, strengths, and natural support systems.

5. Frequently, social workers deal with persons who are reluctant to receive services through referrals pressured by others or under the threat of legal sanctions. While people have a right to their own values and beliefs, sometimes their behaviors violate the rights of others, and the social worker assists these clients in facing these aspects of their difficulties. Because reluctant or involuntary clients are often not seeking a helping relationship but rather wishing to escape one, negotiation is frequently required.

6. Some clients apply for services because they wish to experience change through a social worker's assistance. Such clients are often helped by having an accepting relationship, with appropriate self-disclosure, which will allow them to seek greater self-awareness and to live more fully in the reality of the moment.

7. All clients, whether voluntary or involuntary, are entitled to be treated with respect and dignity, and to have their choices facilitated.

8. Client behavior is goal directed, although these goals are often not readily discernible. Clients are, however, capable of learning new skills, knowledge, and approaches to resolving their difficulties. Social workers are responsible for helping clients discover their strengths and affirming their capacity for growth and change.

9. While clients' current problems are often influenced by past relationships and concerns, and although limited focus on the past is sometimes beneficial, most difficulties can be alleviated by focusing on present choices and by mobilizing strengths and coping patterns.

FIG-2-2 Principles of a Philosophy of Direct Practice

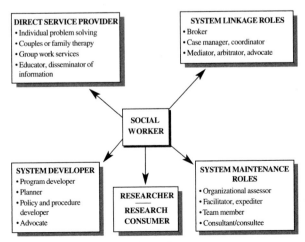

FIG-2-3 Roles Social Workers Play

marital enrichment, stress management, or various aspects of mental health or health care (Dore, 1993).

These roles are primary in the work of most direct service social workers. Because this book is aimed at preparing social workers to provide such direct services, we will not elaborate further on these roles in this section.

System Linkage Roles

Because clients may need resources not provided by a given social agency and lack knowledge of or the ability to utilize other available resources, social workers often perform roles in linking people to other resources.

Broker

To perform the role of broker (i.e., an intermediary who assists in connecting people with resources), social workers must have a thorough knowledge of community resources so that they can make appropriate referrals. Familiarity with the policies of resource systems and working relationships with key contact persons are essential to making successful referrals. In the earlier case example, Christine Summers, the BSW-trained social worker, brokered services for Mr. Harrison, Ms Fisher, and their children, including the referral to Debra Sontag, the MSW-trained sexual behaviors counselor. Before some people are able to avail themselves of resources, they may require the practitioner's assistance in overcoming fears and misconceptions about those services.

Social workers also have responsibilities in developing simple and effective referral mechanisms and ways of monitoring whether clients actually follow through on referrals. Chapter 3 presents guidelines to assist you in gaining skills in referring clients to needed resources.

Case Manager/Coordinator

Some clients lack the ability, skills, knowledge, or resources to follow through on referrals to other systems. In such instances, the social worker may serve as case manager, a person who assumes primary responsibility for assessing the needs of a client and arranging and coordinating the delivery of essential goods and services provided by other resources. Case managers also work directly with clients to ensure that the needed goods and services are provided in a timely manner.

Case managers must maintain close contact with clients (sometimes even providing direct casework services) and with other service providers to ensure that plans for service delivery are in place and are delivered as planned. It is noteworthy that in the case manager role, practitioners function at the interface between the client and the environment more so than in any other role. Because of recent dramatic increases in the numbers of people needing case management services (e.g., homeless individuals, elderly clients, and persons with serious and persistent mental illness), numerous articles have appeared in the literature focusing on the clients who need such services, issues related to case management, and various functions of case managers. Because we discuss these topics at some length in Chapter 14, we defer discussion of them to that chapter.

Mediator/Arbitrator

Occasionally breakdowns occur between clients and service providers so that clients do not receive the needed services to which they are entitled. For example, clients may be seeking a resource to which they believe they are entitled by their health insurance. In other cases, participants in workfare programs may find themselves sanctioned for failure to meet program expectations (Hage, 2004).

Service may be denied for several reasons. Perhaps clients did not adequately represent their eligibility for services, or strains that sometimes develop between clients and service providers may precipitate withdrawals of requests for services by clients or withholding of services by providers.

In such instances, practitioners may serve as mediators with the goal of eliminating obstacles to service delivery. *Mediation* is a process that "provides a neutral forum in which disputants are encouraged to find a mutually satisfactory resolution to their problems" (Chandler, 1985, p. 346). When serving as a mediator, you must carefully listen to and draw out facts and feelings from both parties to determine the cause of the breakdown. It is important not to take sides with either party until you are confident that you have accurate and complete information. When you have determined the nature of the breakdown, you can plan appropriate remedial action aimed at removing barriers, clarifying possible misunderstandings, and working through negative feelings that have impeded service delivery. The communication skills used in this process are delineated in subsequent chapters of this book.

In recent years, knowledge of mediation skills has evolved to a high level of sophistication. Today, a growing number of practitioners are working independently or in tandem with attorneys to mediate conflicts between divorcing partners regarding child custody, visitation rights, and property settlements. These same skills can be used to mediate personnel disputes, labor management conflicts, and victim–offender situations (Nugent et al., 2001).

Client Advocate

Social workers have assumed the role of advocate for a client or group of clients since the inception of the profession. The obligation to assume this role has been reaffirmed most recently in the NASW Code of Ethics, which includes advocacy among the activities performed by social workers in pursuit of the professional mission (NASW, 1996, p. 2).

With respect to linking clients with resources, advocacy is the process of working with and/or on behalf of clients to obtain services and resources that would not otherwise be provided. We discuss circumstances under which this might occur and appropriate remedial measures at length in Chapter 19. We also discuss skills involved in advocacy (including social action for groups of clients) in Chapter 14.

System Maintenance and Enhancement

As staff members of social agencies, social workers bear responsibility for evaluating structures, policies, and functional relationships within agencies that impair effectiveness in service delivery.

Organizational Analyst

Discharging the role of organizational analyst entails pinpointing factors in agency structure, policy, and procedures that have a negative impact on service delivery. Knowledge of organizational and administrative theory is essential to performing this role effectively. We focus on this role in Chapter 14 in more depth. You will also learn more about organizational dynamics in courses concerned with organizational theory.

Facilitator/Expediter

After pinpointing factors that impede service delivery, social workers have a responsibility to plan and implement ways of enhancing service delivery. This may involve providing relevant input to agency boards and administrators, recommending staff meetings to address problems, working collaboratively with other staff members to bring pressure to bear on resistant administrators, encouraging and participating in essential in-service training sessions, and other similar activities.

Team Member

In many agency and institutional settings (e.g., mental health, health care, rehabilitation, and education settings), practitioners function as members of clinical teams that collaborate in assessing clients' problems and delivering services (Sands, 1989; Sands, Stafford, & McClelland, 1990). Such teams commonly consist of a psychiatrist or physician, psychologist, a social worker, a nurse, and perhaps a rehabilitation counselor, occupational therapist, educator, or recreational therapist, depending on the setting. Members of the team have varying types of expertise that are tapped in formulating assessments and planning and implementing therapeutic interventions. As team members, social work practitioners often contribute knowledge related to family dynamics and engage in therapeutic work with family members.

Sometimes such teams are dominated by members from more powerful professions (Bell, 2001). Dane

and Simon (1991) note that social workers in such host settings, in which the mission and decision making may be dominated by non-social workers, often experience a discrepancy between their professional mission and the values of the employing institution. They can act, however, to sensitize team members to strengths and advocate for a more holistic approach while exercising their knowledge of resources and expertise in linking clients with resources. Social workers also are expected to apply their knowledge of community resources in planning for the discharge of patients and facilitating their reentry into the community following periods of hospitalization. In so doing, social workers bring their systems and strengths perspectives to teams that are sometimes more deficit-focused.

Social workers are also involved in interdisciplinary work across systems such as schools and child welfare, which require the ability to work within several systems simultaneously (Bailey-Dempsey & Reid, 1995). As team members, social workers also often serve as case managers in coordinating discharge planning for patients (Dane & Simon, 1991; Kadushin & Kulys, 1993).

Consultant/Consultee

Consultation is a process whereby an expert enables a consultee to deliver services more effectively to a client by increasing, developing, modifying, or freeing the consultee's knowledge, skills, attitudes, or behavior with respect to the problem at hand (Kadushin, 1977). Although social workers both provide and receive consultation, there has been a trend for MSW social workers to serve less as consumers of consultation and more as providers. BSW social workers may provide consultation regarding the availability of specific community resources. More often, however, they are consumers of consultation when they need information about how to work effectively in problem solving that encompasses complex situations and behaviors. Social workers assume the consultee role when they need expert knowledge from doctors and nurses, psychiatrists, psychologists, and other social workers who possess high levels of expertise related to certain types of problems (e.g., substance abuse, child maltreatment, sexual problems).

Social workers serve as consultants to members of other professions and to other social workers in need of their special expertise, including when they fill the role of supervisor. For example, they may provide consultation to school personnel who need assistance in understanding and coping with problem students; to health care providers who seek assistance in understanding a patient's family or ethnic and cultural factors; to court staff regarding matters that bear on child custody decisions and decisions about parole and probation; and in many other similar situations.

Supervisor

Relations between consultants and consultees in social work frequently occur within the supervisory relationship. Supervisors play a critical role in the support of quality direct practice work performed by social work practitioners. Supervisors are responsible for orienting staff to how they can learn through supervision, lines of authority, requirements, and policies of the setting (Munson, 2002, p. 38). Social work supervisors frequently utilize case presentations made by staff social workers as a key mechanism in learning. Such presentations should be organized around questions to be answered. Supervisors assist staff in linking assessment with intervention plans and evaluation. Special responsibilities include helping supervisees identify when client advocacy is needed, identifying and resolving ethical conflicts, and monitoring issues of race, ethnicity, lifestyle, and vulnerability as they affect the client–social worker interaction. In addition, supervisors often take the lead in securing resources for staff and facilitating linkages with other organizations.

Researcher/Research Consumer

Practitioners face responsibilities in both public and private settings to select interventions that can be evaluated, to evaluate the effectiveness of their interventions, and to systematically monitor the progress of their clients. Implementing these processes requires practitioners to conduct and make use of research.

As described in chapter 1, social workers are expected to incorporate research skills into their practice. Such incorporation occurs at several levels. For example, being able to define questions in ways that help in consulting the research literature about effectiveness is one such competency. Conducting ongoing evaluation of the effectiveness of practice is another such competency. Some practitioners utilize single-subject (i.e., single-system) designs. This type of research design enables practitioners to obtain measures of the extent (frequency and severity) of problem behaviors before they implement interventions aimed at eliminating or reducing the problem behaviors or increasing the frequency of currently insufficient behaviors (e.g., doing homework, engaging in prosocial behaviors, setting realistic and consistent limits with children, sending positive messages, abstaining from

drinking). These measures provide a baseline against which the results of the interventions can be assessed by applying the same measures periodically during the course of the interventions, at termination, and at follow-up (Reid, 1994). Perhaps more frequently, practitioners use some form of Goal Attainment Scaling that calls for rating goal achievement on a scale with points designated in advance (Corcoran & Vandiver, 1996).

System Development

Direct practitioners sometimes have opportunities to improve or to expand agency services based on assessment of unmet client needs, gaps in service, needs for preventive services, or research indicating that more promising results might be achieved by interventions other than those currently employed.

Program Developer

As noted earlier, practitioners often have opportunities to develop services in response to emerging needs of clients. Such services may include educational programs (e.g., for immigrants or unwed pregnant teenagers), support groups (e.g., for rape victims, adult children of alcoholics, and victims of incest), and skill development programs (e.g., stress management, parenting, and assertiveness training groups).

Planner

In small communities and rural areas that lack access to community planners, direct practitioners may need to assume a planning role, usually in concert with community leaders. In this role, the practitioner works both formally and informally with influential people to plan programs that respond to unmet and emerging needs. Such needs could include child care programs, transportation for elderly and disabled persons, and recreational and health care programs, to name just a few.

Policy and Procedure Developer

Participation of direct practitioners in formulating policies and procedures typically is limited to the agencies in which they provide direct services to clients. Their degree of participation in such activities is largely determined by the style of administration with a given agency. Able administrators generally solicit and invite input from professional staff about how the agency can more effectively respond to the consumers of its services. Because practitioners serve on the "front lines," they are strategically positioned to evaluate clients' needs and to assess how policies and procedures serve—or fail to serve—the best interests of clients. For these reasons, social workers should become actively involved in decision-making processes related to policies and procedure.

In rural areas and small communities, direct practitioners often participate in policy development concerned with the needs of a broad community rather than the needs of a circumscribed target group. In such instances, social workers must draw from knowledge and skills gained in courses in social welfare policy and services and community planning.

Advocate

Just as social workers may advocate for an individual client, so they may also join client groups, other social workers, and allied professionals in advocating for legislation and social policies aimed at providing needed resources and enhancing social justice. We discuss skills in advocacy and social action in Chapter 14.

Summary

Direct social work practice is characterized by performance of multiple roles. Those roles are carried out at several system levels, depending on the level of the concerns addressed. Knowledge and skills related to some of these roles are taught in segments of the curriculum that lie outside direct practice courses. To do justice in one volume to the knowledge and skills entailed in all these roles is impossible; consequently, we have limited our focus primarily to the roles involved in providing direct service.

CHAPTER 3

Overview of the Helping Process

CHAPTER OVERVIEW

This chapter provides an overview of the three phases of the helping process: exploration, implementation, and termination. The helping process focuses on problem solving with social work clients in a variety of settings, including those found along a continuum of voluntarism. Hence, the process is presented with the larger systems context in mind. In addition, we present the structure and ingredients of interviews that will be examined in more detail in Chapters 5 and 6.

Common Elements among Diverse Theorists and Social Workers

Direct social workers working with individuals, couples, families, groups, and other systems draw on contrasting theories of human behavior, use different models of practice, implement diverse interventions, and serve widely varying clients. Despite these varied factors, such social workers share a common goal: to assist clients in coping more effectively with problems of living and improving the quality of their lives. People are impelled by either internal or external sources to secure social work services because current solutions are not working in their lives. Helping approaches differ in the extent to which they are problem versus goal focused. We take the position that it is important for direct social workers to take seriously the problems compelling clients to seek services as well as to work creatively with them toward achieving solutions that improve upon the initial problematic situation (McMillen et al., 2004).

Whether a potential client perceives a need or seeks help is a critical issue in planning how services may be offered. Their reaction to those internal or external sources plays a part in their motivation for and reaction to the prospects for contact with a social worker. As described in Chapter 1, some potential clients are *applicants* who request services of a social worker to deal with these internal or external problems (Alcabes & Jones, 1985). Often a need for help has been identified by external sources such as teachers, doctors, employers, or family members. Such persons might be best considered *referrals* because they did not apply for service (Compton & Galaway, 2005). Persons who are referred vary in the extent to which they perceive that referral as a source of pressure or simply as a source of potential assistance. As introduced in Chapter 1, others are at least initially *involuntary clients* who respond to perceived requirements to seek help as a result of pressure from other persons or legal sources (Reid, 1978). Individuals who initiate their contact as applicants, referrals, or involuntary clients are all potential clients if they can negotiate a contract addressed to some of their concerns. Children are a special case of potential client as they are rarely applicants and usually referred by teachers or family members for concerns those others have about their behavior.

However potential clients begin their contact, they face a situation of disequilibrium in which they can potentially enhance their problem-solving ability by developing new resources or employing untapped resources in ways that reduce tension and achieve mastery over problems. Whatever their approach to assisting clients, most direct social workers employ a process aimed at reducing client concerns. That is, social workers try to assist clients in assessing the concerns that they perceive or that their environment presses upon them, making decisions about fruitful ways to identify and prioritize those concerns. Next, the social worker and client jointly identify potential approaches to reduce those concerns and make decisions about which courses of action to pursue. Those approaches are selected in part by available evidence about effectiveness reducing the concerns they bring. Involuntary clients face situations in which some of these concerns are not of their choice and some of the approaches to reducing those concerns may be mandated by other parties.

Even in these circumstances, clients have the power to make at least constrained choices regarding how they address these concerns or additional concerns beyond those that they have been mandated to address. After these strategic approaches have been identified and selected, they are implemented. Working together, the client and the social worker then assess the success of their efforts and revise their plans as necessary. Social workers use a variety of communication skills to implement the problem-solving process given the many different systems involved in clients' concerns.

The first portion of this chapter gives an overview of the helping process and its three distinct phases; subsequent parts of the book are organized to correspond to these phases. The latter part of this chapter focuses on the structure and processes involved in interviewing—a critical aspect of dealing with clients. Later chapters deal with the structure, processes, and skills involved in modifying the processes of families and groups.

The Helping Process

The helping process consists of three major phases:

Phase I: Exploration, engagement, assessment, and planning
Phase II: Implementation and goal attainment
Phase III: Termination

Each of these phases has distinct objectives, and the helping process generally proceeds successively through them. The three phases, however, are not sharply demarcated by the activities and skills employed. Indeed, the activities and skills employed in the three phases differ more in terms of their frequency and intensity than in the kind used. The processes of exploration and assessment, for example, are central during Phase I, but these processes continue in somewhat diminished significance during subsequent phases of the helping process.

Phase I: Exploration, Engagement, Assessment, and Planning

The first phase lays the groundwork for subsequent implementation of interventions and strategies aimed at resolving clients' problems and promoting problem-solving skills. It represents a key step in helping relationships of any duration and setting—from crisis intervention and discharge planning to long-term and institutional care. Processes involved and tasks to be accomplished during Phase I include the following:

1. Exploring clients' problems by eliciting comprehensive data about the person(s), the problem, and environmental factors, including forces influencing the referral for contact
2. Establishing rapport and enhancing motivation
3. Formulating a multidimensional assessment of the problem, identifying systems that play a significant role in the difficulties, and identifying relevant resources that can be tapped or must be developed
4. Mutually negotiating goals to be accomplished in remedying or alleviating problems and formulating a contract
5. Making referrals

We briefly discuss each of these five processes in the following sections and refer to portions of the book that include extensive discussions of these processes.

Exploring clients' problems by eliciting comprehensive data about the person(s), the problem, and environmental factors, including forces influencing the referral for contact. Contact begins with an initial exploration of the circumstances that have led the potential client to meet with the social worker. Social workers should not assume that potential clients are applicants at this point, because self-referred persons are the minority of clients served in many settings; even those who self-refer often do so at the suggestion or pressure of others (Cingolani, 1984).

Potential clients may be anxious about the prospect of seeking help and lack knowledge about what to expect. For many, the social worker will have information from an intake form or referral source about the circumstances that have brought them into contact. These many possibilities can be explored by asking questions such as the following:

* *"I have read your intake form. Can you tell me what brings you here, in your own words?"*
* *"How can we help you?"*

These questions should elicit a beginning elaboration of the concern or pressures that the potential client sees as relating to his or her contact. The social worker can begin to determine to what extent the motivation for contact was initiated by the potential client and to what extent the motivation represents a response to external forces. For example, school children are often referred by teachers who are concerned about their classroom behavior or ability to learn in the classroom.

The social worker should begin in such circumstances with a matter-of-fact, non-threatening description of the circumstances that led to the referral, such as:

- *"Your teacher referred you because she was concerned that you're sometimes arriving late to school and appearing tired. How are you feeling about school?"*

The social worker should also give a clear, brief description of his or her own view of the purpose of this first contact and encourage an exploration of how the social worker can be helpful:

- *"We are meeting to both explore the teacher's concerns and also to hear from you about how things are going at school as you see it. My job is to find out what things you would like to see go better and to figure out with you ways that we might work together so that you get more out of school."*

Establishing rapport and enhancing motivation. Effective communication in the helping relationship is crucial. Unless the social worker succeeds in engaging the client, the client may be reluctant to reveal vital information and feelings and, even worse, may not return after the initial session.

Engaging clients successfully means establishing rapport, which reduces the level of threat and gains the trust of clients, who recognize that the social worker intends to be helpful. One condition of rapport is that clients perceive a social worker as understanding and genuinely interested in their well-being. To create such a positive perception among clients who may differ in significant ways from the social worker (including race or ethnicity, gender, sexual orientation, age, for example), the social worker must attend to relevant cultural factors and vary interviewing techniques accordingly (interviewing is discussed later in this chapter and throughout the book). Potential clients may draw conclusions about the openness of the agency to their concerns through the intake forms that they must complete. For example, forms asking for marital status that do not allow for enduring relationships that cannot include legal marriage may communicate insensitivity to gay, lesbian, bisexual, and transgendered people (Charnley & Langley, 2008). Further, when potential clients have been referred by others, these individuals will need to be reassured that their wishes are important and that they do not have to necessarily work on the concerns seen by the referral source.

Potential clients who are not applicants or genuinely self-referred frequently have misgivings about the helping process. They do not perceive themselves as having a problem and often attribute the source of difficulties to another person or to untoward circumstances.

Such clients confront social workers with several challenging tasks:

- *Neutralizing negative feelings*
- *Attempting to help potential clients understand problems identified by others and assessing the advantages and disadvantages of dealing with those concerns*
- *Creating an incentive to work on acknowledged problems*

Skillful social workers often succeed in tapping into the motivation of such involuntary clients, thus affirming the principle from systems theory that motivation is substantially influenced by the interaction between clients and social workers.

In other instances, clients may freely acknowledge problems and do not lack incentive for change but assume a passive role, expecting social workers to magically work out their difficulties for them. Social workers must avoid taking on the impossible role that some clients would ascribe to them. Instead, they should voice a belief in clients' abilities to work as partners in searching for remedial courses of action and mobilize clients' energies in implementing the tasks essential to successful problem resolution. In addition to concerns, it is helpful to identify what things are going well in the client's life and identify ways the client is now coping with difficult situations.

One very useful strategy is to acknowledge the client's problem and explicitly recognize the client's motivation to actively work toward its solution. Potential clients do not lack motivation; rather, they sometimes lack motivation to work on the problems and goals perceived by others. In addition, motivation relates to a person's past experience, which leads him or her to expect that behaviors will be successful or will fail in attempting to reach goals. Hence, individuals with limited expectations for success often appear to lack motivation. As a consequence, social workers must often attempt to increase motivation by assisting clients to discover that their actions can be effective in reaching their goals (Gold, 1990). Motivation can also be seen in terms of stages of change. In some cases, clients can be said to be in *pre-contemplation* and have not yet considered a problem that has been perceived by others (Di Clemente & Prochaska, 1998). For example, the child referred for lateness and perceived tiredness may not have thought about this as an issue of personal responsibility, perhaps feeling powerless over whether adults and siblings help him or her to get to school or to bed on time. Frequently, a client can be in the *contemplation* stage, in that they are aware of the issue but are not fully aware of the options, benefits for changing, and consequences for not changing (Di Clemente & Prochaska, 1998). Such clients can be helped to explore those possibilities. For example, the social worker can gather information from the child about sleeping patterns and rituals involved in getting ready for school. They can explore together what might happen if the child continues to arrive late and be tired in school and how things might be different if behavior patterns were modified to arrive at school on time and rested.

Social workers, therefore, must be able to tap into client motivation and assist those individuals who readily acknowledge a problem but are reluctant to expend the required effort or bear the discomfort involved in effecting essential change. A major task in this process is to provide information to the potential client about what to expect from the helping process. This socialization effort includes identifying the kinds of concerns with which the social worker and agency can help, client rights including confidentiality and circumstances in which it might be abridged, and information about what behavior to expect from the social worker and client (Videka-Sherman, 1988).

The task for clients in groups is twofold: They must develop trust in the social worker, and they must develop trust in the other group members. If group members vary in race, ethnicity, or social class, the group leader must be sensitive to such cultural determinants of behaviors. He or she must assume a facilitative role in breaking down related barriers to rapport not only between the social worker and individual group members, but also among group members.

Developing group norms and mutual expectations together assists in the creation of a group cohesiveness that helps groups become successful. Establishing rapport requires that social workers demonstrate a nonjudgmental attitude, acceptance, respect for clients' right of self-determination, and respect for clients' worth and dignity, uniqueness and individuality, and problem-solving capacities (discussed at length in Chapter 4). Finally, social workers foster rapport when they relate to clients with empathy and authenticity. Both skills are considered in later chapters of this book.

Formulating a multidimensional assessment of the problem, identifying systems that play a significant role in the difficulties, and identifying relevant resources that can be tapped or must be developed. Social

workers must simultaneously establish rapport with their clients and explore their problems. These activities reinforce each other, as astute exploration yields both information and a sense of trust and confidence in the social worker.

A social worker who demonstrates empathy is able to foster rapport and show the client that the social worker understands what he or she is expressing. This, in turn, encourages more openness on the client's part and expands his or her expression of feelings. The greater willingness to share deepens the social worker's understanding of the client's situation and the role that emotions play in both their difficulties and their capabilities. Thus the social worker's communication skills serve multiple functions: They facilitate relationship building, they encourage information sharing, and they establish rapport.

Problem exploration is a critical process, because comprehensive information must be gathered before all of the dimensions of a problem and their interaction can be understood. Exploration begins by attending to the emotional states and immediate concerns manifested by the client. Gradually, the social worker broadens the exploration to encompass relevant systems (individual, interpersonal, and environmental) and explores the most critical aspects of the problem in depth. During this discovery process, the social worker is also alert to and highlights client strengths, realizing that these strengths represent a vital resource to be tapped later during the goal attainment phase. Social workers can assist clients in identifying ways in which they are currently coping and exceptions when problems do not occur (Greene et al., 2005). For example, the social worker working with the child client can help the child identify days on which he or she is on time for school and rested and to trace back the environmental conditions at home that facilitated such an outcome.

Skills that are employed in the exploratory process with individuals, couples, families, and groups are delineated later in this chapter and at length in subsequent chapters. To explore problematic situations thoroughly, social workers must also be knowledgeable about the various systems commonly involved in human difficulties, topics considered at length in Chapters 8–11.

Problem exploration skills are used during the assessment process that begins with the first contact with clients and continues throughout the helping relationship. During interviews, social workers weigh the significance of clients' behavior, thoughts, beliefs, emotions, and, of course, information revealed. These moment-by-moment assessments guide social workers in deciding which aspects of problems to explore in depth, when to explore emotions more deeply, and so on. In addition to this ongoing process of assessment, social workers must formulate a working assessment from which flow the goals and contract upon which Phase II of the problem-solving process is based. An adequate assessment includes analysis of the problem, the person(s), and the ecological context.

Because there are many possible areas that can be explored but limited time available to explore them, focus in assessment is critical. Retaining such a focus is promoted by conducting the assessment in layers. At the first layer, you must focus your attention on issues of client safety, legal mandates, and the client's wishes for service. The rationale for this threefold set of priorities is that client wishes should take precedence in circumstances in which legal mandates do not impinge on choices or in which no dangers to self or others exist.

When you analyze the problem, you can identify which factors are contributing to difficulties—for example, inadequate resources; decisions about a crucial aspect of one's life; difficulties in individual, interpersonal, or societal systems; or interactions between any of the preceding factors. Analysis of the problem also involves making judgments about the duration and severity of a problem as well as the extent to which the problem is susceptible to change, given the client's potential coping capacity. In considering the nature and severity of problems, social workers must weigh these factors against their own competencies and the types of services provided by the agency. If the problems call for services that are beyond the agency's function, such as prescribing medication or rendering speech therapy, referral to another professional or agency may be indicated.

Analysis of the individual system includes assessment of the client's wants and needs, coping capacity, strengths and limitations, and motivation to work on the problem(s). In evaluating the first two dimensions, the social worker must assess such factors as flexibility, judgment, emotional characteristics, degree of responsibility, capacity to tolerate stress, ability to reason critically, and interpersonal skills. These factors, which are critical in selecting appropriate and attainable goals, are discussed at length in Chapter 9.

Assessment of ecological factors entails consideration of the adequacy or deficiency, success or failure, and strengths or weaknesses of salient systems in the environment that bear on the client's problem. Ecological assessment aims to identify systems that must be strengthened, mobilized, or developed to satisfy the client's unmet needs. Systems that often affect clients' needs include couple, family, and social support systems (e.g., kin, friends, neighbors, coworkers, peer groups, and ethnic reference groups); spiritual belief systems; child care, health care, and employment systems; various institutions; and the physical environment. For example, working with the child in our example to identify those persons and conditions in terms of availability of transportation, responsibilities for child care, and availability of others in the evening and in the morning to help the child get ready for school can identify pertinent support systems.

Cultural factors are also vital in ecological assessment, because personal and social needs and the means of satisfying them vary widely from culture to culture. Moreover, the resources that can be tapped to meet clients' needs vary according to cultural contexts. Some cultures include indigenous helping persons, such as folk healers, religious leaders, and relatives from extended family units who have been invested with authority to assist members of that culture in times of crisis. These persons can often provide valuable assistance to social workers and their clients.

Assessment of the client's situational context also requires analyzing the circumstances as well as the actions and reactions of participants in the problematic interaction. Knowledge of the circumstances and specific behaviors of participants before, during, and after troubling events is crucial to understanding the forces that shape and maintain problematic behavior. Assessment, therefore, requires that social workers elicit detailed information about actual transactions between people.

Whether making assessments of individuals per se or assessments of individuals as subsets of couples, families, or groups, it is important to assess the functioning of these larger systems. These systems have unique properties, including power distribution, role definitions, rules, norms, channels of communication, and repetitive interactional patterns. Such systems also boast both strengths and problems that strongly shape the behavior of constituent members. It follows that individual difficulties tend to be related to systemic difficulties, so interventions must therefore be directed to both the system and the individual.

Assessments of systems are based on a variety of data-gathering procedures. With couples and families, social workers may or may not conduct individual interviews, depending on the evidence available about the effectiveness of family intervention with particular concerns, agency practices, and impressions gained during preliminary contacts with family members. If exploration and assessment are implemented exclusively in conjoint sessions, these processes are similar to those employed in individual interviews except that the interaction between the participants assumes major significance. Whereas information gleaned through individual interviews is limited to reports and descriptions by clients, requiring the social worker to make inferences about the actual interaction within the relevant systems, social workers can view interactions directly in conjoint interviews and group sessions. In such cases, the social worker should be alert to strengths and difficulties in communication and interaction and to the properties of the system (see Chapters 10 and 11). As a consequence, assessment focuses heavily on the styles of communication employed by individual participants, interactional patterns among members, and the impact of individual members on processes that occur in the system. These factors are weighed when selecting interventions intended to enhance functioning at these different levels of the larger systems.

Finally, a working assessment involves synthesizing all relevant information gathered as part of the exploration process. To enhance the validity of such assessments, social workers should involve clients in the process by soliciting their perceptions and assisting them in gathering data about their perceived difficulties and hopes. Social workers can share their impressions with their clients, for example, and then invite affirmation or disconfirmation of those impressions. It is also beneficial to highlight their strengths and to identify other relevant resource systems that can be tapped or need to be developed to resolve the difficulties. When social workers and their clients reach agreement about the nature of the problems involved, they are ready to enter the process of negotiating goals, assuming that clients are adequately motivated to advance to Phase II of the helping process.

Mutually negotiating goals to be accomplished in remedying or alleviating the problem and formulating a contract. If the social worker and the individual client, couple, family, or group have reached agreement concerning the nature of the difficulties and the systems that are involved, the participants are ready to negotiate individual and/or group goals. This mutual process aims to identify what needs to be changed and what related actions need to be taken to resolve or ameliorate the problematic situation. We briefly discuss the process of goal selection in this chapter and at length in Chapter 13. If agreement is not reached about the appropriateness of services or clients choose not to continue,

then services may be terminated. In some situations, then, services are finished when the assessment is completed.

In the case of involuntary clients, some may continue the social work contact under pressure even if agreement is not reached about the appropriateness of services or if problems are not acknowledged. After goals have been negotiated, participants undertake the final task of Phase I: formulating a contract. The contract (see Chapter 12), which is also mutually negotiated, consists of a formal agreement or understanding between the social worker and the client that specifies the goals to be accomplished, relevant strategies to be implemented, roles and responsibilities of participants, practical arrangements, and other factors. When the client system is a couple, family, or group, the contract also specifies group goals that tend to accelerate group movement and to facilitate accomplishment of group goals.

Mutually formulating a contract is a vital process because it demystifies the helping process and clarifies for clients what they may realistically expect from the social worker and what is expected of them; what they will mutually be seeking to accomplish and in what ways; and what the problem-solving process entails. Contracting with voluntary clients is relatively straightforward; it specifies what the client desires to accomplish through social work contact. Contracting with involuntary clients contains another layer of legally mandated problems or concerns in addition to the clients' expressed wishes.

The solution-focused approach takes the position that goals are central when working with clients (De Jong & Berg, 2002). Those goals, however, may not be directly related to rectifying or eliminating the concern that initially prompted the contact. Utilizing a solution-focused approach, clients and practitioners can sometimes create or co-construct a solution that will meet the concerns of clients as well as legal requirements (De Jong & Berg, 2001). The solution may be reached without working from a problem viewpoint. For example, a child referred for setting fires might work toward a goal of becoming safe, trustworthy, and reliable in striking matches under adult supervision. By focusing on goals as perceived by clients, an empowering momentum may be created that draws out hidden strengths and resources. We also take the position that empowering clients to discover and make best use of available resources is desirable. Sometimes, focusing on problems can be counterproductive. However, in funding and agency environments that are problem focused both in terms of philosophy and funding streams, ignoring problem conceptions carries risk (McMillen et al., 2004).

In summary, we are influenced by solution-focused methods to support client ownership of goals and methods for seeking them (De Jong, 2001). We differ from the solution-focused method, however, in that we do not assume that all clients have within them the solutions to all of their concerns. Expert information about solutions that have worked for clients in similar situations can often prove valuable (Reid, 2000). Rather than assuming that "the client always knows" or "the social worker always knows," we take the position that the social worker's task is to facilitate a situation in which both client and worker share their information while constructing plans for problem resolution (Reid, 2000). We explore the solution-focused approach more in Chapter 13.

Making referrals. Exploration of clients' problems often reveals that resources or services beyond those provided by the agency are needed to remedy or ameliorate presenting difficulties. This is especially true of clients who have multiple unmet needs. In such instances, referrals to other resources and service providers may be necessary. Unfortunately, clients may lack the knowledge or skills needed to avail themselves of these badly needed resources. Social workers may assume the role of case manager in such instances (e.g., for persons with severe and persistent mental illness, individuals with developmental and physical disabilities, foster children, and infirm elderly clients). Linking clients to other resource systems requires careful handling if clients are to follow through in seeking and obtaining essential resources.

Phase II: Implementation and Goal Attainment

After mutually formulating a contract, the social worker and client(s) enter the heart of the problem-solving process—the implementation and goal attainment phase, also known as the action-oriented or change-oriented phase. Phase II involves translating the plans formulated jointly by the social worker and individual clients, couples, families, or groups into actions. In short, the participants combine their efforts in working toward the goal assigned the highest priority. This process begins by dissecting the goal into general tasks that identify general strategies to be employed in pursuit of the goal. These general tasks are then subdivided into specific tasks that designate what the client and social worker plan to do between one session and the next

(Epstein & Brown, 2002; Reid, 1992; Robinson, 1930; Taft, 1937).[1] Tasks may relate to the individual's personal functioning or to his or her interaction with others present in the client's environment, or they may involve interaction with other resource systems, such as schools, hospitals, or law enforcement agencies. The processes of negotiating goals and tasks are discussed in detail in Chapter 12.

After formulating goals with clients, social workers select and implement interventions designed to assist clients in accomplishing those goals and subsidiary tasks. Interventions should directly relate to the problems that were identified and the goals that were mutually negotiated with clients and derived from accurate assessment. Helping efforts often fail when social workers employ global interventions without considering clients' views of their problems and ignore the uniqueness of each client's problems.

Enhancing Self-Efficacy

Research findings (Dolan et al., 2008, Bandura & Locke, 2003; Washington & Moxley, 2003; Lane, Daugherty, & Nyman, 1998) have strongly indicated that the helping process is greatly enhanced when clients experience an increased sense of self-efficacy as part of this process. *Self-efficacy* refers to an expectation or belief that one can successfully accomplish tasks or perform behaviors associated with specified goals. Note that the concept overlaps with notions of individual empowerment.

The most powerful means for enhancing self-efficacy is to assist clients in actually performing certain behaviors prerequisite to accomplishing their goals. Another potent technique is to make clients aware of their strengths and to recognize incremental progress of clients toward goal attainment.

Family and group members also represent potent resources for enhancing self-efficacy. Social workers can develop and tap these resources by assisting families and groups to accomplish tasks that involve perceiving and accrediting the strengths and progress of group and family members. We consider other sources of self-efficacy and relevant techniques in Chapter 13.

Monitoring Progress

As work toward goal attainment proceeds, it is important to monitor progress on a regular basis.

The reasons for this are fourfold:

1. *To evaluate the effectiveness of change strategies and interventions.* Social workers are increasingly required to document the efficacy of services to satisfy third-party payers with a managed care system.

In addition, social workers owe it to their clients to select interventions based on the best available evidence (Thyer, 2002). If an approach or intervention is not producing desired effects, social workers should determine the reasons for this failure or consider negotiating a different approach.

2. *To guide clients' efforts toward goal attainment.* Evaluating progress toward goals enhances continuity of focus and efforts and promotes efficient use of time (Corcoran & Vandiver, 1996).

3. *To keep abreast of clients' reactions to progress or lack of progress.* When they believe they are not progressing, clients tend to become discouraged and may lose confidence in the helping process. By evaluating progress periodically, social workers will be alerted to negative client reactions that might otherwise undermine the helping process.

4. *To concentrate on goal attainment and evaluate progress.* These efforts will tend to sustain clients' motivation to work on their problems.

Methods of evaluating progress range from eliciting subjective opinions to using various types of measurement instruments. Single-subject research is convenient, involves little or no expense, appeals to most clients, and can be employed with minimal research expertise. In addition, social workers can now access a variety of standardized outcome measurement instruments that are often useful. Chapter 12 includes more extensive discussion of single-subject research and outcome measurement.

Barriers to Goal Accomplishment

As clients strive to accomplish goals and related tasks, their progress is rarely smooth and uneventful. Instead, clients typically encounter obstacles and experience anxiety, uncertainties, fears, and other undesirable reactions as they struggle to solve problems. Furthermore, family or group members or other significant persons may undermine the client's efforts to change by opposing such changes, by ridiculing the client for seeing a social worker, by making derisive comments about the social worker, or by otherwise making change even more difficult for the client. (For this reason, it is vital to involve significant others in the problem-solving process whenever feasible.) Because of the challenges posed by these barriers to change, social workers must be mindful of their clients' struggles and skillful in assisting them to surmount these obstacles.

Barriers to goal accomplishment are frequently encountered in work with families and groups. Such barriers include personality factors that limit participation of certain group members, problematic behaviors of group members, or processes within the group that impede progress. They also encompass impediments in the family's environment.

Still other barriers may involve organizational opposition to change within systems whose resources are essential to goal accomplishment. Denial of resources or services (e.g., health care, rehabilitation services, and public assistance) by organizations, or policies and procedures that unduly restrict clients' access to resources, may require the social worker to assume the role of mediator or advocate. Chapter 14 highlights ways of overcoming this type of organizational opposition.

Relational Reactions

As social workers and clients work together in solving problems, emotional reactions on the part of either party toward the other party may impair the effectiveness of the working partnership and pose an obstacle to goal accomplishment. Clients, for example, may have unrealistic expectations or may misperceive the intent of the social worker. Consequently, clients may experience disappointment, discouragement, hurt, anger, rejection, longing for closeness, or many other emotional reactions that may seriously impede progress toward goals.

Couple partners, parents, and group members may also experience relational reactions to other members of these larger client systems, resulting in problematic interactional patterns within these systems. Not uncommonly, these reactions reflect maladaptive attitudes and beliefs learned from relationships with parents or significant others. In many other instances, however, the social worker or members of clients' systems may unknowingly behave in ways that trigger unfavorable relational reactions by individuals or family or group members. In either event, it is critical to explore and resolve these harmful relational reactions. Otherwise, clients' efforts may be diverted from working toward goal accomplishment or—even worse—clients may prematurely withdraw from the helping process.

Social workers are susceptible to relational reactions as well. Social workers who relate in an authentic manner provide clients with experience that is transferable to the real world of the client's social environment. They communicate that they are human beings who are not immune to making blunders and experiencing emotions and desires as part of their relationships with clients. It is vital that social workers be aware of their unfavorable reactions to clients and understand how to manage them. Otherwise, they may be working on their own problems rather than the client's issues, placing the helping process in severe jeopardy. For example, a student practitioner became aware that she was relating to a client who had difficulty in making and carrying out plans as if the client were a family member, with whom the student had similar difficulties. Becoming aware of those associations through supervision made it possible to separate out the client before her from the family member. Chapter 17 offers advice to assist social workers in coping with potential relational reactions residing with the client(s), the social worker, or both.

Enhancing Clients' Self-Awareness

As clients interact in a novel relationship with a social worker and risk trying out new interpersonal behaviors in their couple, family, or group contacts, they commonly experience emotions that may be pleasing, frightening, confusing, and even overwhelming. Although managing such emotional reactions may require a temporary detour from goal attainment activities, these efforts frequently represent rich opportunities for growth in self-awareness. Self-awareness is the first step to self-realization. Many voluntary clients wish to understand themselves more fully, and they can benefit from becoming more aware of feelings that have previously been buried or denied expression.

Social workers can facilitate the process of self–discovery by employing additive empathic responses during the goal attainment phase. Additive empathic responses focus on deeper feelings than do reciprocal empathic responses (referred to earlier in the discussion of Phase I). This technique can be appropriately applied in both individual and conjoint interviews as well as in group sessions. Additive empathy (discussed at length in Chapter 17) is particularly beneficial in assisting clients to get in touch with their emotions and express those feelings clearly to their significant others.

Another technique used to foster self-awareness is confrontation (a major topic of Chapter 17). This technique helps clients become aware of growth-defeating discrepancies in perceptions, feelings, communications, behavior, values, and attitudes, and then examine these discrepancies in relation to stated goals. Confrontation is also used in circumstances when clients act to violate laws or threaten their own safety or the safety of others. Confrontation must be offered in the context of goodwill, and it requires high skill.

Use of Self

As helping relationships grow stronger during the implementation and goal attainment phase, social workers increasingly use themselves as tools to facilitate growth and accomplishment. Relating spontaneously and appropriately disclosing one's feelings, views, and experiences ensure that clients have an encounter with an open and authentic human being. Modeling authentic behavior encourages clients to reciprocate by risking authentic behavior themselves, thereby achieving significant growth in self-realization and in interpersonal relations.

Indeed, when *group leaders* model authentic behavior in groups, members may follow suit by exhibiting similar behavior. Social workers who relate in an authentic manner provide their clients with experience that is transferable to the clients' real-world social relationships. A contrived, detached, and sterile "professional" relationship, by contrast, lacks transferability to other relationships. Obviously, these issues should be covered in the training process for social workers.

Assertiveness involves dealing tactfully but firmly with problematic behaviors that impinge on the helping relationship or impede progress toward goal attainment. For example, when clients' actions conflict with their goals or are potentially harmful to themselves or others, the social worker must deal with these situations. Further, social workers must sometimes relate assertively to larger client systems—for example, to focus on behavior of group members that hinders the accomplishment of goals. Using oneself to relate authentically and assertively is a major focus of Chapter 5.

Phase III: Termination

The terminal phase of the helping process involves three major aspects:

1. Assessing when client goals have been satisfactorily attained
2. Helping the client develop strategies that maintain change and continue growth following the termination
3. Successfully terminating the helping relationship

Deciding when to terminate is relatively straightforward when time limits are specified in advance as part of the initial contact, as is done with the task-centered approach and other brief treatment strategies. Decisions about when to terminate are also simple when individual or group goals are clear-cut (e.g., to get a job, obtain a prosthetic device, arrange for nursing care, secure tutoring for a child, implement a specific group activity, or hold a public meeting).

In other instances, goals involve growth or changes that have no limits; thus judgments must be made by the social worker and client in tandem about when a satisfactory degree of change has been achieved. Examples of such goals include increasing self-esteem, communicating more effectively, becoming more outgoing in social situations, and resolving conflicts more effectively. In these cases, the ambiguity of termination can be reduced by developing specific, operational indicators of goal achievement, as discussed in Chapter 12. Today, however, many decisions about termination and extension involve third parties, as contracts for service and payers such as managed care may regulate the length and conditions of service (Corcoran & Vandiver, 1996).

Successfully Terminating Helping Relationships

Social workers and clients often respond positively to termination, reflecting pride and accomplishment on the part of both parties (Fortune, Pearlingi, & Rochelle, 1992). Clients who were required or otherwise pressured to see the social worker may experience a sense of relief at getting rid of the pressure or freeing themselves from the strictures of outside scrutiny. In contrast, because voluntary clients share personal problems and are accompanied through rough emotional terrain by a caring social worker, they often feel close to the social worker. Consequently, termination tends to produce mixed feelings for these types of clients. They are likely to feel strong gratitude to the social worker, but are also likely to experience a sense of relief over no longer having to go through the discomfort associated with exploring problems and making changes (not to mention the relief from paying fees).

Although clients are usually optimistic about the prospects of confronting future challenges independently, they sometimes experience a sense of loss over terminating the working relationship. Moreover, uncertainty about their ability to cope independently may be mixed with their optimism.

When they have been engaged in the helping process for a lengthy period of time, clients may develop a strong attachment to a social worker, especially if the social worker has fostered dependency in their relationship. For such individuals, termination involves a painful process of letting go of a relationship that has satisfied significant emotional needs. Moreover, these clients often experience apprehension about facing the future without the reassuring strength represented by the social worker. Group members may experience similar painful reactions as they face the loss of supportive relationships with the social worker and group members as well as a valued resource that has assisted them to cope with their problems.

To effect termination with individuals or groups and minimize psychological stress requires both perceptiveness to emotional reactions and skills in helping clients to work through such reactions. This subject is discussed in detail in Chapter 19.

Planning Change Maintenance Strategies

Social workers have voiced concern over the need to develop strategies that maintain clients' changes and continue their growth after formal social work service is terminated (Rzepnicki, 1991). These concerns have been prompted by findings that after termination many clients relapse or regress to their previous level of functioning. Consequently, more attention is now being paid to strategies for maintaining change. Planning for follow-up sessions not only makes it possible to evaluate the durability of results, but also facilitates the termination process by indicating the social worker's continuing interest in clients, a matter we discuss in Chapter 19.

The Interviewing Process: Structure and Skills

Direct social workers employ interviewing as the primary vehicle of influence, although administrators and social planners also rely heavily on interviewing skills to accomplish their objectives. With the increasing emphasis on evidence-based practice, it becomes yet more important to develop core skills in interviewing that can be applied and revised according to varied situations. Skills in interviewing, active listening, discerning and confronting discrepancies, reframing, and reciprocal empathy skills are key ingredients in the generalist practice model (Adams, Matto, & Le Croy, 2008). These non-specific factors have a considerable impact on outcomes (Drisko, 2004). That is, the relationship or therapeutic alliance has been shown to have considerable influence across studies (Norcross & Lambert, 2006). In fact, such relationship factors have been shown to account for up to 30% of variation in social work outcomes, while particular model and technique factors have accounted for only about 15% (Duncan & Miller, 2000; Hubble, Duncan & Miller, 1999).

Interviews vary according to purpose, types of setting, client characteristics, and number of participants. For example, they may involve interaction between a social worker and individuals, couples, and family units. Interviews are conducted in offices, homes, hospitals, prisons, automobiles, and other diverse settings. Interviews conducted with children are different than interviews with adults or seniors. Despite the numerous variables that affect interviews, certain factors are common to all effective interviews. This section identifies and discusses these essential factors and highlights relevant skills.

Physical Conditions

Interviews sometimes occur in office or interview settings over which the social worker has some control. Interviews that take place in a client's home, of course, are more subject to the client's preferences. The physical climate in which an interview is conducted partly determines the attitudes, feelings, and degree of cooperation and responsiveness of people during interviews. The following conditions are conducive to productive interviews:

1. Adequate ventilation and light
2. Comfortable room temperature
3. Ample space (to avoid a sense of being confined or crowded)
4. Attractive furnishings and décor
5. Chairs that adequately support the back
6. Privacy appropriate to the cultural beliefs of the client
7. Freedom from distraction
8. Open space between participants

The first five items obviously are concerned with providing a pleasant and comfortable environment and need no elaboration.

Privacy is vital, of course, because people are likely to be guarded in revealing personal information and expressing feelings if other people can see or hear them. Likewise, interviewers sometimes have difficulty in concentrating or expressing themselves when others can hear them. Settings vary in the extent to which social workers can control these conditions. For example, in some circumstances families may prefer to have trusted family members, friends, or spiritual leaders present to consider resolution of some issues (Burford & Pennell, 1996). In some settings, it may be impossible to ensure complete privacy. Even when interviewing a patient in a hospital bed, however, privacy can be maximized by closing doors, drawing curtains that separate beds, and requesting that nursing staff avoid nonessential interruptions. Privacy during home interviews may be even more difficult to arrange, but people will often take measures to reduce unnecessary intrusions or distractions if interviewers stress that privacy enhances the productivity of sessions. Social workers in public social service settings often work in cubicle offices. To ensure privacy, they can conduct client interviews in special interview rooms.

Because interviews sometimes involve intense emotional involvement by participants, freedom from distraction is a critical requirement. Telephone calls, knocks on the door, and external noises can impair concentration and disrupt important dialogue. Moreover, clients are unlikely to feel important and valued if social workers permit avoidable intrusions. Other sources of distraction include crying, attention seeking, and restless behavior of clients' infants or children. Small children, of course, cannot be expected to sit quietly for more than short periods of time. For this reason, the social worker should encourage parents to make arrangements for the care of children during interviews (except when it is important to observe interaction between parents and their children). Because requiring such arrangements can create a barrier to service utilization, many social workers and agencies maintain a supply of toys for such occasions.

Having a desk between an interviewer and interviewee(s) emphasizes the authority of the social worker. For some Asian clients, emphasizing the authority or position of the social worker may be a useful way to indicate that he or she occupies a formal, appropriate position. With many other clients, a desk between social worker and client creates a barrier that is not conducive to open communication. If safety of the social worker is an issue, then a desk barrier can be useful. In some instances, an interviewer may believe that maximizing the social worker's authority through a desk barrier will promote his or her service objectives.

In most circumstances, however, social workers strive to foster a sense of equality. Hence, they arrange their desks so that they can rotate their chairs to a position where there is open space between them and their clients. Others prefer to leave their desks entirely and use other chairs in the room when interviewing.

Practitioners who interview children often find it useful to have available a small number of toys or items that the child can manipulate with their hands as well as materials for drawing pictures. Such practitioners have found that such tools or devices seem to reduce tension for children in communicating with unfamiliar adults and assist them in telling their story (Krähenbühl & Blades, 2006; Lamb & Brown, 2006; Lukas, 1993).

Structure of Interviews

Interviews in social work have a purpose, structure, direction, and focus. The purpose is to exchange information systematically with a view toward illuminating and solving problems, promoting growth, or planning strategies or actions aimed at improving the quality of life for people. The structure of interviews varies somewhat from setting to setting, from client to client, and from one phase of the helping process to another. Indeed, skillful interviewers adapt flexibly both to different contexts and to the ebb and flow of each individual session.

Each interview is unique. Nevertheless, effective interviews conform to a general structure, share certain properties, and reflect use of certain basic skills by interviewers. In considering these basic factors, we begin by focusing on the structure and processes involved in initial interviews.

Establishing Rapport

Before starting to explore clients' difficulties, it is important to establish rapport. Rapport with clients fosters open and free communication, which is the hallmark of effective interviews. Achieving rapport enables clients to gain trust in the helpful intent and goodwill of the social worker, such that they will be willing to risk revealing personal and sometimes painful feelings and information. Some clients readily achieve trust and confidence in a social worker, particularly when they have the capacity to form relationships easily. Voluntary clients often ask, "Who am I and why am I in this situation?"; involuntary clients have less reason to be initially trusting and ask, "Who are you and when will you leave?" (Rooney, 2009).

Establishing rapport begins by greeting the client(s) warmly and introducing yourself. If the client system is a family, you should introduce yourself to each family member. In making introductions and addressing clients, it is important to extend the courtesy of asking clients how they prefer to be addressed; doing so conveys your respect and desire to use the title they prefer. Although some clients prefer the informality involved in using first names, social workers should be discreet in using first-name introductions with all clients because of their diverse ethnic and social backgrounds. For example, some adult African Americans and members of other groups may interpret being addressed by their first names as indicative of a lack of respect (Edwards, 1982; McNeely & Badami, 1984).

With many clients, social workers must surmount formidable barriers before establishing rapport. Bear in mind that the majority of clients have had little or no experience with social work agencies and enter initial interviews or group sessions with uncertainty and apprehension. Many did not seek help initially; they may view having to seek assistance with their problems

as evidence of failure, weakness, or inadequacy. Moreover, revealing personal problems is embarrassing and even humiliating for some people, especially those who have difficulty confiding in others.

Cultural factors and language differences compound potential barriers to rapport even further. For example, some Asian Americans who retain strong ties to cultural traditions have been conditioned not to discuss personal or family problems with outsiders. Revealing problems to others may be perceived as a reflection of personal inadequacy and as a stigma upon the entire family. The resultant fear of shame may impede the development of rapport with clients from this ethnic group (Kumabe, Nishida, & Hepworth, 1985; Lum, 1996; Tsui & Schultz, 1985). Some African Americans, Native Americans, and Latinos may also experience difficulty in developing rapport because of distrust that derives from a history of being exploited or discriminated against by other ethnic groups (Longres, 1991; Proctor & Davis, 1994).

Children may be unfamiliar with having conversational exchanges with unfamiliar adults (Lamb & Brown, 2006). For example, their exchanges with teachers may be primarily directive or a test of their knowledge. Asking them to describe events or family situations may be a new experience for them, and they may look for cues from the accompanying adult about how to proceed. Open-ended questions are advised to avoid providing leading questions.

Clients' difficulties in communicating openly tend to be exacerbated when their problems involve allegations of socially unacceptable behavior, such as child abuse, moral infractions, or criminal behavior. In groups, the pain is further compounded by having to expose one's difficulties to other group members, especially in early sessions when the reactions of other members represent the threat of the unknown.

One means of fostering rapport with clients is to employ a "warm-up" period. This is particularly important with some ethnic minority clients for whom such openings are the cultural norm, including Native Americans, persons with strong roots in the cultures of Asia and the Pacific Basin, and Latinos. Aguilar (1972), for example, has stressed the importance of warm-up periods in work with Mexican Americans. Many Native Hawaiians and Samoans also expect to begin new contacts with outside persons by engaging in "talk story," which involves warm, informal, and light personal conversation similar to that described by Aguilar. To plunge into discussion of serious problems without a period of talk story would be regarded by members of these cultural groups as rude and intrusive. Social workers who neglect to engage in a warm-up period are likely to encounter passive-resistant behavior from members of these cultural groups. A warm-up period and a generally slower tempo are also critically important with Native Americans (Hull, 1982). Palmer and Pablo (1978) suggest that social workers who are most successful with Native Americans are low-key, nondirective individuals. Similarly, increased self-disclosure is reported by Hispanic practitioners as a useful part of developing rapport with Hispanic clients (Rosenthal-Gelman, 2004).

Warm-up periods are also important in establishing rapport with adolescents, many of whom are in a stage of emancipating themselves from adults. Consequently, they may be wary of social workers. This is especially true of individuals who are delinquent or are otherwise openly rebelling against authority. Moreover, adolescents who have had little or no experience with social workers have an extremely limited grasp of their roles. Many adolescents, at least initially, are involuntary clients and perceive social workers as adversaries, fearing that their role is to punish or to exercise power over them.

With the majority of clients, a brief warm-up period is usually sufficient. When the preceding barriers do not apply, introductions and a brief discussion of a timely topic (unusual weather, a widely discussed local or national event, or a topic of known interest to the client) will adequately foster a climate conducive to exploring clients' concerns.

Most clients, in fact, expect to immediately plunge into discussion of their problems, and their anxiety level may grow if social workers delay getting to the business at hand (Ivanoff, Blythe, & Tripodi, 1994). This is particularly true with involuntary clients who did not seek the contact. With these clients, rapport often develops rapidly if social workers respond sensitively to their feelings and skillfully give direction to the process of exploration by sharing the circumstances of the referral, thereby defusing the threat sensed by such clients.

Respect for clients is critical to establishing rapport. In both this chapter and Chapter 1, we stressed the importance of respecting clients' dignity and worth, uniqueness, capacities to solve problems, and other factors. An additional aspect of showing respect is demonstrating common courtesy. Being punctual, attending to the client's comfort, listening attentively, remembering the client's name, and assisting a client who has limited mobility convey the message that the social worker values the client and esteems his or her dignity and worth. Courtesy should never be taken lightly.

Verbal and nonverbal messages from social workers that convey understanding and acceptance of clients' feelings and views also facilitate the development of rapport. This does not mean agreeing with or condoning clients' views or problems, but rather apprehending and affirming clients' rights to have their own views, attitudes, and feelings.

Attentiveness to feelings that clients manifest both verbally and nonverbally and empathic responses to these feelings convey understanding in a form that clients can readily discern. Empathic responses clearly convey the message, "I am with you. I understand what you are saying and experiencing." The "workhorse" of successful helping persons, empathic responding, is important not only in Phase I of the helping process but in subsequent phases as well. Mastery of this vital skill (discussed extensively in Chapter 5) requires consistent and sustained practice.

Authenticity, or genuineness, is yet another social worker quality that facilitates rapport. Being authentic during Phase I of the helping process means relating as a genuine person rather than assuming a contrived and sterile professional role. Authentic behavior by social workers also models openness, which encourages clients to reciprocate by lowering their defenses and relating more openly (Doster & Nesbitt, 1979).

Encounters with authentic social workers also provide clients with a relationship experience that more closely approximates relationships in the real world than do relationships with people who conceal their real selves behind a professional facade. A moderate level of authenticity or genuineness during early interviews fosters openness most effectively (Giannandrea & Murphy, 1973; Mann & Murphy, 1975; Simonson, 1976). At this level, the social worker is spontaneous and relates openly by being nondefensive and congruent. In other words, the social worker's behavior and responses match her or his inner experiencing.

Being authentic also permits the constructive use of humor. Relating with a moderate level of authenticity, however, precludes a high level of self-disclosure. Rather, the focus is on the client, and the social worker reveals personal information or shares personal experiences judiciously. During the change-oriented phase of the helping process, however, social workers sometimes engage in self-disclosure when they believe that doing so may facilitate the growth of clients. Self-disclosure is discussed at length in Chapter 5.

Rapport is also enhanced by not employing certain types of responses that block communication. To avoid hindering communication, social workers must be knowledgeable about such types of responses and must eliminate them from their communication repertoires. Toward this end, Chapter 7 identifies various types of responses and interviewing patterns that inhibit communication and describes strategies for eliminating them. Video segments are also presented in the CD accompanying that chapter that will allow you to consider alternative responses to challenging situations.

Beginning social workers often fear that they will forget something, fail to observe something crucial in the interview that will lead to dire consequences, freeze up or become tongue-tied, or talk endlessly to reduce their anxiety (Epstein and Brown, 2002). Practice interviews such as those presented in subsequent chapters will assist in reducing this fear. It also helps to be aware that referred clients need to know the circumstances of the referral and clarify choices, rights, and expectations before they are likely to establish rapport with the social worker.

Starting Where the Client Is

Social work researchers have suggested that *motivational congruence*—that is, the fit between client motivation and what the social worker attempts to provide—is a major factor in explaining more successful findings in studies of social work effectiveness (Reid & Hanrahan, 1982). Starting with client motivation aids social workers in establishing and sustaining rapport and in maintaining psychological contact with clients.

If, for example, a client appears to be in emotional distress at the beginning of the initial interview, the social worker might focus attention on the client's distress before proceeding to explore the client's problematic situation. An example of an appropriate focusing response would be, "I can sense that you are going through a difficult time. Could you tell me what this is like for you right now?" Discussion of the client's emotions and related factors tends to reduce the distress, which might otherwise impede the process of exploration. Moreover, responding sensitively to clients' emotions fosters rapport—clients begin to regard social workers as concerned, perceptive, and understanding persons.

Novice social workers sometimes have difficulty in starting where the client is because they worry that they will not present quickly and clearly the services of the agency, thus neglecting or delaying exploration of client concerns. Practice will allow them to relax and recognize that they can meet the expectations of their supervisors and others by focusing on client concerns while sharing content about the circumstances of referrals and their agency's services.

Starting where the client is has critical significance when you are working with involuntary clients. Because these clients are often compelled by external sources to see social workers, they frequently enter initial interviews with negative, hostile feelings. Social workers, therefore, should begin by eliciting these feelings and focusing on them until they have subsided. By responding empathically to negative feelings and conveying understanding and acceptance of them, skillful social workers often succeed in neutralizing these feelings, which enhances clients' receptivity to exploring their problem situations. For example, social workers can often reduce negative feelings by clarifying the choices available to the involuntary client. If social workers fail to deal with their clients' negativism, they are likely to encounter persistent oppositional responses. These responses are frequently labeled as resistance, opposition to change, and lack of motivation. It is useful to reframe these responses by choosing not to interpret them with deficit labels, but rather replacing them with expectations that these attitudes and behaviors are normal when something an individual values is threatened (Rooney, 2009). As children and adolescents are often referred because adults are concerned about their behavior, and they may therefore be particularly resistant, the practitioner can clarify that he or she wants to hear how things are going from the child's or adolescent's viewpoint.

Language also poses a barrier with many ethnic minority and immigrant clients who may have a limited grasp of the English language, which could cause difficulty in understanding even commonplace expressions. With ethnic minority clients and clients with limited educational levels, social workers must slow down the pace of communication and be especially sensitive to nonverbal indications that clients are confused. To avoid embarrassment, ethnic minority clients sometimes indicate that they understand messages when, in fact, they are perplexed.

Using Interpreters

When ethnic minority and immigrant clients have virtually no command of the English language, effective communication requires the use of an interpreter of the same ethnicity as the client, so that the social worker and client bridge both cultural value differences and language differences. To work effectively together, however, both the social worker and the interpreter must possess special skills. For their part, interpreters must be carefully selected and trained to understand the importance of the interview and their role in the process, as well as to interpret cultural nuances to the social worker. In this way, skilled interpreters assist social workers by translating far more than verbal content—they also convey nonverbal communication, cultural attitudes and beliefs, subtle expressions, emotional reactions, and expectations of clients.

To achieve rapport, of course, the social worker must also convey empathy and establish an emotional connection with the ethnic minority client. The interpreter thus "must have the capacity to act exactly as the interviewer acts—express the same feelings, use the same intonations to the extent possible in another language, and through verbal and nonverbal means convey what the interviewer expresses on several levels" (Freed, 1988, p. 316).

The social worker should explain the interpreter's role to the client and ensure the client of neutrality and confidentiality on the part of both the social worker and the interpreter. Obviously, these factors should also be covered in the training process for interpreters. In addition, successful transcultural work through an interpreter requires that the social worker be acquainted with the history and culture of the client's and the interpreter's country of origin.

Social workers must also adapt to the slower pace of interviews when an interpreter is involved. When social workers and interpreters are skilled in collaborating in interviews, effective working relationships can evolve, and many clients experience the process as beneficial and therapeutic. As implied in this brief discussion, interviewing through an interpreter is a complex process requiring careful preparation of interviewers and interpreters.

The Exploration Process

When clients indicate that they are ready to discuss their problematic situations, it is appropriate to begin the process of exploring their concerns. Messages like the following are typically employed to initiate the exploration process:

- *"Could you tell me about your situation?"*
- *"I'm interested in hearing about what brought you here."*
- *"Tell me about what has been going on with you, and we can think together about what you can do about your difficulties."*
- *"How are things going with school? What subjects to you like? Which ones do you not like so much?"*

The client will generally respond by beginning to relate his or her concerns. The social worker's role at this point is to draw out the client, to respond in ways

that convey understanding, and to seek elaboration of information needed to gain a clear picture of factors involved in the client's difficulties.

Some clients spontaneously provide rich information with little prompting. Others—especially referred and involuntary clients—may hesitate, struggle with their emotions, or have difficulty finding the right words to express themselves. Because referred clients may perceive that they were forced into the interview as the result of others' concerns, they may respond by recounting those external pressures. The social worker can assist in this process by sharing his or her information about the circumstances of the referral.

To facilitate the process of exploration, social workers employ a multitude of skills, often blending two or more in a single response. One such skill, *furthering responses*, encourages clients to continue verbalizing their concerns. Furthering responses, which include minimal prompts (both verbal and nonverbal) and accent responses, convey attention, interest, and an expectation that the client will continue verbalizing. They are discussed in depth in Chapter 6.

Other responses facilitate communication (and rapport) by providing immediate feedback that assures clients that social workers have not only heard but also understood their messages. *Paraphrasing* provides feedback indicating that the social worker has grasped the content of the client's message. In using paraphrasing, the interviewer rephrases (with different words) what the client has expressed. *Empathic responding*, by contrast, shows that the social worker is aware of the emotions the client has experienced or is currently experiencing. Both paraphrasing and empathic responding, which are discussed in Chapters 5 and 6, are especially crucial with clients who have limited language facility, including ethnic minority, immigrant, and developmentally disabled clients. When language barriers exist, social workers should be careful not to assume that they correctly understand the client or that the client understands the social worker. Video examples of paraphrasing and empathic responding and included with Chapters 5 and 6.

With ethnic clients who have been culturally conditioned not to discuss personal or family problems with outsiders, social workers need to make special efforts to grasp their intended meanings. Many of these clients are not accustomed to participating in interviews and tend not to state their concerns openly. Rather, they may send covert (hidden) messages and expect social workers to discern their problems by reading between the lines. Social workers need to use feedback extensively to determine whether their perceptions of the clients' intended meanings are on target.

Using feedback to ascertain that the social worker has understood the client's intended meaning, and vice versa, can avoid unnecessary misunderstandings. In addition, clients generally appreciate a social worker's efforts to reach shared understanding, and they interpret patience and persistence in seeking to understand as evidence that the social worker respects and values them. It is not the ethnic minority client's responsibility, however, to educate the social worker.[2] Conversely, what the social worker thinks he or she knows about the minority client's culture may actually be an inappropriate stereotype, because individuals and families vary on a continuum of assimilation and acculturation with majority culture norms (Congress, 1994). Based on a common Latino value, for example, the social worker might say, "Can you call on other family members for assistance?" Video examples of tuning in to a client's Native American culture are included in Chapter 6.

Exploring Expectations

Before exploring problems, it is important to determine clients' expectations, which vary considerably and are influenced by socioeconomic level, cultural background, level of sophistication, and previous experience with helping professionals. In fact, socialization that includes clarifying expectations about the roles of clients and social workers has been found to be associated with more successful outcomes, especially with involuntary clients (Rooney, 2009; Videka-Sherman, 1988). Video examples of clarifying to a client what information will be shared with a referral source and what information remains confidential are shared in Chapter 5.

In some instances, clients' expectations diverge markedly from what social workers can realistically provide. Unless social workers are aware of and deal successfully with such unrealistic expectations, clients may be keenly disappointed and disinclined to continue beyond the initial interview. In other instances, referred clients may have mistaken impressions about whether they can choose to work on concerns as they see them as opposed to the views of referral sources such as family members. By exploring these expectations, social workers create an opportunity to clarify the nature of the helping process and to work through clients' feelings of disappointment. Being aware of clients' expectations also helps social workers select their approaches and interventions based on their clients' needs and expectations, a matter discussed at greater length in Chapter 5.

Eliciting Essential Information

During the exploration process, the social worker assesses the significance of information revealed as the client discusses problems and interacts with the social worker, group members, or significant others. Indeed, judgments about the meaning and significance of fragments of information guide social workers in deciding issues such as which aspects of a problem are salient and warrant further exploration, how ready a client is to explore certain facets of a problem more deeply, which patterned behaviors of the client or system interfere with effective functioning, and when and when not to draw out intense emotions.

The direction of problem exploration proceeds from general to specific. Clients' initial accounts of their problems are typically general in nature ("We fight over everything," "I don't seem to be able to make friends," "We just don't know how to cope with Scott. He won't do anything we ask," or "Child protection says I don't care for my children"). Clients' concerns typically have many facets, however, and accurate understanding requires careful assessment of each one. Whereas open-ended responses may be effective in launching problem explorations, other types of responses are used to probe for the detailed information needed to identify and unravel the various factors and systems that contribute to and maintain the problem. Responses that seek concreteness are employed to elicit such detailed information. Many types of such responses exist, each of which is considered at length in Chapter 6. Another type of response needed to elicit detailed factual information is the closed-ended question (also discussed in Chapter 6). Video examples of open- and closed-ended questions are included in Chapter 6.

Focusing in Depth

In addition to possessing discrete skills needed to elicit detailed information, social workers must be able to maintain the focus on problems until they have elicited comprehensive information. Adequate assessment of problems is not possible until a social worker possesses sufficient information concerning the various forces (involving individual, interpersonal, and environmental systems) that interact to produce the problems. Focusing skills (discussed at length in Chapter 6, with video examples) blend the various skills identified thus far with summarizing responses.

During the course of exploration, social workers should elicit information relevant to numerous questions, the answers to which are crucial in understanding those factors that bear on the clients' problems, including ecological factors. These questions (discussed in Chapter 8, with video examples) serve as guideposts to social workers and provide direction to interviews.

Employing Outlines

In addition to answering questions that are relevant to virtually all interviews, social workers may need to collect information that answers questions pertinent to specific practice settings. Outlines that list essential questions to be answered for a given situation or problem can prove extremely helpful to beginning social workers. It is important, however, to maintain flexibility in the interview and to focus on the client, not the outline. Chapter 6 provides examples of outlines and suggestions for using them.

Assessing Emotional Functioning

During the process of exploration, social workers must be keenly sensitive to clients' moment-to-moment emotional reactions and to the part that emotional patterns (e.g., inadequate anger control, depression, and widely fluctuating moods) play in their difficulties. Emotional reactions during the interview (e.g., crying, intense anxiety, anger, and hurt feelings) often impede problem exploration and require detours aimed at assisting clients to regain their equanimity. Note that the anxiety and anger exhibited by involuntary clients may be influenced by the circumstances of the involuntary contact as much as by more enduring emotional patterns.

Emotional patterns that powerfully influence behavior in other contexts may also be problems in and of themselves that warrant careful exploration. Depression, for example, is a prevalent problem in our society but generally responds well to proper treatment. When clients exhibit symptoms of depression, the depth of the depression and risk of suicide should be carefully explored. Empathic communication is a major skill employed to explore these types of emotional patterns. Factors to be considered, instruments that assess depression and suicidal risk, and relevant skills are discussed in Chapter 9.

Exploring Cognitive Functioning

Because thought patterns, beliefs, and attitudes are powerful determinants of behavior, it is important to explore clients' opinions and interpretations of those circumstances and events deemed salient to their difficulties. Often, careful exploration reveals that misinformation, distorted meaning attributions, mistaken beliefs, and dysfunctional patterns of thought (such as

rigid, dogmatic thinking) play major roles in clients' difficulties.

Messages commonly employed to explore clients' thinking include the following:

- *"How did you come to that conclusion?"*
- *"What meaning do you make of …?"*
- *"How do you explain what happened?"*
- *"What are your views (or beliefs) about that?"*

Assessment of cognitive functioning and other relevant assessment skills are discussed further in Chapter 9.

Exploring Substance Abuse, Violence, and Sexual Abuse

Because of the prevalence and magnitude of problems associated with substance abuse (including alcohol), violence, and sexual abuse in our society, the possibility that these problems contribute to or represent the primary source of clients' difficulties should be routinely explored. Because of the significance of these problematic behaviors, we devote a major portion of Chapter 9 to their assessment.

Negotiating Goals and a Contract

When social workers and clients believe that they have adequately explored the problems prompting the initial contact, they are ready to enter the process of planning. By this point (if not sooner), it should be apparent whether other resources or services are needed. If other resources are needed or are more appropriate, then the social worker may initiate the process of referring the client elsewhere. If the client's problems match the function of the agency and the client expresses a willingness to continue with the helping process, then it is appropriate to begin negotiating a contract. When involuntary clients are unwilling to participate further in the helping process, their options should be clarified at this point. For example, they can choose to return to court, choose not to comply and risk the legal consequences of this tactic, choose to comply minimally, or choose to work with the social worker on problems as they see them in addition to legal mandates (Rooney, 2009).

In a problem-solving approach, goals specify the end results that will be attained if the problem-solving efforts succeed. Generally, after collaborating in the exploration process, social workers and clients share common views about which results or changes are desirable or essential. In some instances, however, social workers may recognize the importance of accomplishing certain goals that clients have overlooked, and vice versa. Social workers introduce the process of goal negotiation by explaining the rationale for formulating those goals. If stated in explicit terms, goals will give direction to the problem-solving process and serve as progress guideposts and as outcome criteria for the helping efforts. To employ goals effectively, social workers need skills in persuading clients to participate in selecting attainable goals, in formulating general task plans for reaching these goals, and in developing specific task plans to guide the social worker's and client's efforts between sessions.

When resolving the problematic situation requires satisfying more than one goal (the usual case), social workers should assist clients in assigning priorities to those goals so that the first efforts can be directed to the most burdensome aspects of the problem. Stimulating clients to elaborate goals enhances their commitment to actively participate in the problem-solving process by ensuring that goals are of maximal relevance to them. Techniques such as the "miracle question" from the solution-focused approach can be employed to engage clients in elaborating their vision of goals (De Jong & Berg, 2002). Even involuntary clients can often choose the order in which goals are addressed or participate in the process of making that choice. Essential elements of the goal selection process and the contracting process are discussed in depth in Chapter 12.

Ending Interviews

Both initial interviews and the contracting process conclude with a discussion of "housekeeping" arrangements and an agreement about the next steps to be taken. During this final portion of the interview process, social workers should describe the length and frequency of sessions, who will participate in them, the means of accomplishing goals, the duration of the helping period, fees, the date and time of the next appointment, pertinent agency policies and procedures, and other relevant matters. When you have completed these interview processes, or when the time allocated for the interview has elapsed, it is appropriate to conclude the interview. Messages appropriate for ending interviews include the following:

- *"I see our time for today is nearly at an end. Let's stop here, and we'll begin next time by reviewing our experience in carrying out the tasks we discussed."*
- *"Our time is running out, and there are still some areas we need to explore. Let's arrange another*

session when we can finish our exploration and think about where you'd like to go from there."
- *"We have just a few minutes left. Let's summarize what we accomplished today and what you and I are going to work on before our next session."*

Goal Attainment

During Phase II of the helping process, interviewing skills are used to help clients accomplish their goals. Much of the focus during this phase is on identifying and carrying out actions or tasks that clients must implement to accomplish their goals. Not surprisingly, preparing clients to carry out these actions is crucial to successful implementation. Fortunately, effective strategies of preparation are available (see Chapter 13).

As clients undertake the challenging process of making changes in their lives, it is important that they maintain focus on a few high-priority goals until they have made sufficient progress to warrant shifting to other goals. Otherwise, they may jump from one concern to another, dissipating their energies without achieving significant progress. The burden, therefore, falls on the social worker to provide structure for and direction to the client. Toward this end, skills in maintaining focus during single sessions and continuity between sessions are critical (see Chapter 6).

As noted earlier, obstacles to goal attainment commonly arise during the helping process. Individual barriers typically include fears associated with change as well as behavior and thought patterns that are highly resistant to change efforts because they serve a protective function (usually at great psychological cost to the individual). With couples and families, barriers may include entrenched interactional patterns that resist change because they perpetuate power or dependence, maintain safe psychological distance, or foster independence (at the cost of intimacy). In groups, barriers may involve dysfunctional processes that persist despite repeated efforts by leaders to replace these patterns with others that are conducive to group goals and to group maturation.

Additive empathy is used with individuals, couples, and groups as a means to recognize and to resolve emotional barriers that block growth and progress. Confrontation is a high-risk skill used to assist clients in recognizing and resolving resistant patterns of thought and behavior. Because of the sophistication required to use these techniques effectively, we have devoted Chapter 17 to them and have provided relevant skill development exercises. Additional techniques for managing barriers to change (including relational reactions) are discussed in Chapter 18.

Summary

This chapter examined the three phases of the helping process from a global perspective and briefly considered the structure and processes involved in interviewing. The inside cover of the book summarizes the constituent parts of the helping process and demonstrates their interrelationships with various interviewing processes. The remaining parts of the book focus in detail on the three phases of the helping process and on the interviewing skills and interventions employed during each phase.

Notes

1. The idea of specific phases and their accompanying tasks in structuring casework was originally developed by Jessie Taft and Virginia Robinson and the Functional School. This concept was later extended by Reid (2000) and Epstein and Brown (2002) in the task-centered approach.
2. Lila George, Research Director, Leech Lake Tribe (personal communication, 1993).

CHAPTER 4

Operationalizing the Cardinal Social Work Values

CHAPTER OVERVIEW

As we noted in Chapter 1, social work practice is guided by knowledge, skills, and values. Chapter 4 addresses the last of those three areas. It introduces the cardinal values of the profession and the ethical obligations that arise from those values. Because, in practice, values can clash and ethical principles may conflict with each other, the chapter also describes some of these dilemmas and offers guidance about resolving them. As you read this chapter, you will have opportunities to place yourself in complex situations that challenge you to analyze your personal values and to assess their compatibility with social work values. As a result of reading this chapter you will:

- Understand the core social work values and how they play out in practice

- Develop self-awareness and professional competence by examining the tensions that can occur when personal values intersect with professional values

- Learn the role that the NASW Code of Ethics plays in guiding professional practice

- Be familiar with four core ethical issues: self-determination, informed consent, professional boundaries, and confidentiality

- Know the steps for resolving ethical dilemmas and the ways in which these apply to a case

- Understand the complexities in applying ethical standards to minor clients

The Interaction between Personal and Professional Values

Values are "preferred conceptions," or beliefs about how things ought to be. All of us have values: our beliefs about what things are important or proper that then guide our actions and decisions. The profession of social work has values, too. They indicate what is important to social workers and guide the practice of the profession.

Social workers must be attuned to their personal values and be aware of when those values mesh or clash with those espoused by the profession as a whole. Beyond this, social workers must recognize that their clients also have personal values that shape their beliefs and behaviors, and these may conflict with the social worker's own values or with those of the profession. Further, the larger society has values that are articulated through cultural norms, policies, laws, and public opinion. These can also conflict with social workers' own beliefs, their clients' values, or the profession's values.

Self-awareness is the first step in sorting out these potential areas of conflict. The following sections describe the core values of the profession, provide opportunities to become aware of personal values, and describe the difficulties that can occur when social workers impose their own beliefs on clients.

The Cardinal Values of Social Work

The Code of Ethics developed by the National Association of Social Workers (NASW, 1999) and the professional literature articulate the core values of the profession and the ethical principles that represent those values. They can be summarized as follows:

- *All human beings deserve access to the resources they need to deal with life's problems and to develop their full potential. The value of service is embodied in this principle, in that social workers are expected to elevate service to others above their own self-interest. In particular, the profession's values place a premium on working for social justice. Social workers' "change efforts are focused primarily on issues of poverty, unemployment, discrimination, and other forms of social injustice. These activities seek to promote sensitivity to and knowledge about oppression and cultural and ethnic diversity. Social workers strive to ensure access to needed information, services, and resources; equality of opportunity; and meaningful participation in decision making for all people"* (NASW, 1999, p. 5).

- *The value that social workers place on the dignity and worth of the person is demonstrated through respect for the inherent dignity of the persons with whom they work and in efforts to examine prejudicial attitudes that may diminish their ability to embrace each client's individuality.*

- *Social workers view interpersonal relationships as essential for well-being and as "an important vehicle for change"* (NASW, 1999, p. 5). *The value placed on human relationships affects the way social workers relate to their clients and the efforts that social workers make to improve the quality of the relationships in their clients' lives.*

- *The value of integrity means that professional social workers behave in a trustworthy manner. They treat their clients and colleagues in a fair and respectful fashion; they are honest and promote responsible and ethical practices in others.*

- *The value of competence requires that social workers practice only within their areas of ability and continually develop and enhance their professional expertise. As professionals, social workers must take responsibility for assuring that their competence is not diminished by personal problems, by substance abuse, or by other difficulties. Similarly, they should take action to address incompetent, unethical, or impaired practice by other professionals.*

What do these values mean? What difficulties can arise in putting them into practice? How can they conflict with social workers', clients', and society's values? The following sections describe these values and situations in which challenges can occur. Skill-building exercises at the end of the chapter will assist you in identifying and working through value conflicts.

1. *All human beings deserve access to the resources they need to deal with life's problems and to develop to their fullest potential.* A historic and defining feature of social work is the profession's focus on individual well-being in a social context. Attending to the environmental forces that "create, contribute to, and address problems in living" is a fundamental part of social work theory and practice (NASW, 1999, p. 1).

Implementing this value means believing that people have the right to resources. It also means that as a social worker you are committed to helping secure those resources for your clients and to developing policies and implementing programs to fill unmet needs. While this value seems an easy choice to embrace, sometimes specific cases can bring out conflicting beliefs and personal biases that challenge the social worker in upholding it. To enhance your awareness of situations in which you might experience such difficulties, imagine yourself in interviews with the clients in each of the following scenarios. Take note of your feelings and of possible discomfort or conflict. Next, contemplate whether your response is consistent with the social work value in question. If the client has not requested a resource but the need for one is apparent, consider what resource might be developed and how you might go about developing it.

Situation 1 You are a practitioner in a public assistance agency that has limited, special funds available to assist clients to purchase essential devices such as eyeglasses, dentures, hearing aids, and other prosthetic items. Your client, Mr. Y, lives in a large apartment complex for single persons and is disabled by a chronic psychiatric disorder. He requests special aid in purchasing new glasses. He says he accidentally dropped his old glasses and they were stepped on by a passerby. However, you know from talking to his landlord and his previous worker that, due to his confusion, Mr. Y regularly loses his glasses and has received emergency funds for glasses several times in the last year alone.

Situation 2 During a home visit to a large, impoverished family in the central city, you observe Eddy, a teenage boy, drawing pictures of animals. The quality of the drawings reveals an exceptional talent. When you compliment him, Eddy appears shy, but his faint smile expresses his delight over your approval. Eddy's mother then complains that he spends most of his free hours drawing, which she thinks is a waste of time. At her remarks, Eddy's smile dissolves in hurt and discouragement.

Situation 3 During a routine visit to an elderly couple who are recipients of public assistance, you discover that the roof on their home leaks. Your clients have had small repairs on several occasions, but the roof is old and worn out. They have gathered bids for re-roofing, and the lowest bid was more than $3,500. They ask whether your agency can assist them with funding. State policies permit expenditures for such repairs under exceptional circumstances, but much red tape is involved, including securing special approval from the county director of social services, the county advisory board, and the state director of social services.

Situation 4 Mr. M sustained a severe heart attack 3 months ago and took a medical leave from his job as a furniture mover. His medical report indicates that he must limit his future physical activities to light work. Mr. M has given up and is asking you to pursue worker's compensation and other resources that would help support his family. You are concerned that while Mr. M might be entitled to these supports, they may reduce his motivation to pursue rehabilitation and work that he can reasonably do given his physical condition.

The preceding vignettes depict situations in which people need resources or opportunities to develop their skills or potential or to ensure their safety and quality of life. Possible obstacles to responding positively to these needs, according to the sequence of the vignettes, are as follows:

1. A judgmental attitude by the worker
2. Failure to recognize an ability that might be developed, or reluctance to pursue it because it is not related to a goal for work
3. Failure to offer options because of the work involved or the pressure of other responsibilities
4. Skepticism that services will be effective in helping the client and apprehension that they may have unintended effects

As you read the vignettes, you may have experienced some of these reactions or additional ones. This discomfort is not uncommon, but such reactions indicate a need for expanded self-examination and additional experience to embrace the social work value in challenging situations. The next section describes some strategies for addressing these types of conflicting reactions.

2. Social workers respect the inherent dignity and worth of the person. Social workers recognize the central importance of human relationships (NASW, 1999, p. 5). These values mean that social workers believe that all people have intrinsic importance, whatever their past or present behaviors, beliefs, way of life, or social status, and that understanding these qualities is essential in involving clients as partners in change. These values embody several related concepts, sometimes referred to as "unconditional positive regard," "nonpossessive warmth," "acceptance," and "affirmation."

These values also recognize that respect is an essential element of the helping relationship. Before people will risk sharing personal problems and expressing deep emotions, they must first feel fully accepted and experience the goodwill and helpful intent of their service providers. This may be especially difficult when individuals who present for services feel ashamed or inadequate in requesting assistance. When clients are seeking services involuntarily, or when they have violated social norms by engaging in interpersonal violence, criminal behavior, or other infractions, they will be especially alert to perceived judgments or condemnation on the part of the social worker. Your role is not to judge whether clients are to blame for their problems or to determine whether they are good or bad, evil or worthy, guilty or innocent. Rather, your role is to seek to understand them, with all of their difficulties and assets and to assist them in searching for solutions to their problems.

Intertwined with acceptance and nonjudgmental attitude is the equally important value stating that every person is unique and that social workers should affirm the individuality of all people they serve. People are, of course, endowed with widely differing physical and mental characteristics; moreover, their life experiences are infinitely diverse. People differ in terms of their appearance, beliefs, physiological functioning, interests, talents, motivation, goals, values, emotional and behavioral patterns, and many other factors. To affirm the uniqueness of another person, you must be committed to entering that individual's world, endeavoring to understand how that person experiences life. Only by attempting to walk in his or her shoes can you gain a full appreciation of the rich and complex individuality of another person. These recommendations are exemplified in the insights gained by social work students serving as volunteers in a camp for burn-injured children (Williams & Reeves, 2004). Not only did the students overcome feelings of fear, self-consciousness, pity, and horror at the campers' conditions, but they overcame stereotypes and animosity regarding their fellow volunteers (firefighters) who held different values and approaches than the social workers. Through respect, communication, attention to the other (versus oneself), appreciation for individuality over stereotypes, and a focus on shared purpose, all of the volunteers were able to create a successful community in which the campers could experience joy and healing.

Affirming each person's individuality, of course, goes far beyond gaining an appreciation of that person's perspectives on life. You must be able to convey awareness of what your client is experiencing moment by moment and affirm the validity of that experience. This affirmation does not mean agreeing with or condoning all of that person's views and feelings. Part of your role as a social worker entails helping people disentangle their confusing, conflicting thoughts and feelings; align their distorted perceptions with reality; mobilize their particular strengths, and differentiate their irrational reactions from reality. To fulfill this role, you must retain your own separateness and individuality. Otherwise, you may over-identify with clients, thereby losing your ability to provide fresh input. Affirming the experiences of another person, then, means validating those experiences, thus fostering that person's sense of personal identity and self-esteem.

Opportunities for affirming individuality and sense of self-worth are lost when unexamined prejudices and stereotypes (either positive or negative) blind social workers to the uniqueness of each individual client. Labels—such as "gang banger," "sorority girl," "old people," or "mental patient"—perpetuate damaging stereotypes because they obscure the individual characteristics of the people assigned to those labels. Working from these preconceptions, professionals may fail to effectively engage with clients; they may overlook needs or capacities and, as a result, their assessments, goals, and interventions will be distorted.

The consequences of such practice are troubling. Imagine an elderly client whose reversible health problems (associated with inadequate nutrition or need for medication) are dismissed as merely symptomatic of advanced age. Also consider the client with developmental disabilities who is interested in learning about sexuality and contraceptives, but whose social worker fails to address those issues, considering them irrelevant for members of this population. Perhaps the sorority member will fail to disclose symptoms of an eating disorder or suicidal ideation to the social worker who presumes she "has everything going for her." What about the terminally ill patient who is more concerned about allowing her lesbian partner to make her end-of-life decisions than she is about her illness and impending death? Clearly, avoiding assumptions and prejudices is central to effective social work practice.

Sometimes, the ability to embrace these first two sets of values comes with increased experience and exposure to a range of clients. Veteran practitioners have learned that acceptance comes through understanding the life experience of others, not by criticizing or judging their actions. As you work with clients, then, you should try to view them as persons in distress and avoid perceiving them based on labels, such as "lazy," "irresponsible," "delinquent," "dysfunctional," or "promiscuous." As you learn more about your clients, you will find that many of them have suffered various forms of deprivation and have themselves been victims of abusive,

rejecting, or exploitative behavior. Remember also that your clients have abilities and assets that may not be apparent to you. Consistent respect and acceptance on your part are vital in helping them gain the self-esteem and mobilize capacities that are essential to change and to well-being.

However, withholding judgments does not mean condoning or approving of illegal, immoral, abusive, exploitative, or irresponsible behavior. It is often our responsibility to help people live, not according to our particular values and moral codes, but according to the norms and laws of society. In doing so, social workers, without blaming, must assist clients in taking responsibility for the part they play in their difficulties. Indeed, change is possible in many instances only when individuals gain awareness of the effects of their decisions and seek to modify their behavior accordingly. The difference between "blaming" and "defining ownership of responsibilities" lies in the fact that the former tends to be punitive, whereas the latter flows from the social worker's positive intentions to be helpful and to assist clients in change. As a practitioner, you will inevitably confront the challenge of maintaining your own values without imposing them on your clients (Doherty, 1995). A first step toward resolving this issue is addressing your own judgmental tendencies. Yet another challenge is to develop composure, so that you don't reveal embarrassment or dismay when people discuss problems associated with socially unacceptable behavior.

The value clarification exercises that follow will help you to identify your own particular areas of vulnerability. In each situation, imagine yourself in an interview or group session with the client(s). If appropriate, you can role-play the situation with a fellow student, changing roles so that you can benefit by playing the client's role as well. As you imagine or role-play the situation, be aware of your feelings, attitudes, and behavior. After each situation, contemplate or discuss the following questions:

1. What feelings and attitudes did you experience? Were they based on what actually occurred or did they emanate from preconceived beliefs about such situations or individuals?
2. Were you comfortable or uneasy with the client? How did your classmate perceive your attitudes toward the "client"? What cues alerted him or her to your values and reactions?
3. Did any of the situations disturb you more than others? What values were reflected in your feelings, attitudes, and behavior?

4. What assumptions did you make about the needs of the client(s) in each vignette?

5. What actions would you take (or what information would you seek) to move beyond stereotypes in understanding your client(s)?

Situation 5 Your client is a 35-year-old married male who was sentenced by the court to a secure mental health facility following his arrest for peering in the windows of a women's dormitory at your college. He appears uncomfortable and blushes as you introduce yourself.

Situation 6 You are assigned to do a home study for a family interested in adoption. When you arrive at the home for the first interview, you realize that the couple interested in the adoption consists of two gay males.

Situation 7 You are a child protective worker and your client is a 36-year-old stepfather whose 13-year-old stepdaughter ran away from home after he had sexual intercourse with her on several occasions during the past 2 months. In your first meeting, he states that he "doesn't know what the big deal is … it's not like we're related or anything."

Situation 8 Your 68-year-old client has been receiving chemotherapy for terminal cancer at your hospital for the past month. Appearing drawn and dramatically more emaciated than she was last month, the client reports that she has been increasingly suffering with pain and believes her best course of action is to take an overdose of sleeping pills.

Situation 9 You are a probation officer. The judge has ordered you to complete a pre-sentencing investigation of a woman who was arrested for befriending elderly individuals and persons with mental retardation, and then stealing their monthly disability checks.

Situation 10 You have been working for 8 weeks with a 10-year-old boy who has experienced behavioral difficulties at school. During play therapy he demonstrates with toys how he has set fire to or cut up several cats and dogs in his neighborhood.

Situation 11 Your client, Mrs. O, was admitted to a domestic violence shelter following an attack by her husband, in which she sustained a broken collarbone and arm injuries. This occasion is the eighth time she has contacted the shelter. Each previous time she has returned home or allowed her husband to move back into the home with her.

Situation 12 A low-income family with whom you have been working recently received a substantial check as part of a settlement with their former landlord. During a visit in which you plan to help the family budget the funds to pay their past due bills, you find the settlement money is gone—spent on a large television and lost in gambling at a local casino.

Situation 13 You are a Latino outreach worker. One Caucasian client has expressed appreciation for the help you have provided, yet tells you repeatedly that she is angry at her difficulty finding a job, blaming it "on all these illegals."

Situation 14 You are working with a high school senior, the eldest girl in a large family from a strict religious background. Your client wants desperately to attend college but has been told by her parents that she is needed to care for her younger siblings and assist in her family's ministry.

If you experienced uneasy or negative feelings as you read or role-played any of the preceding situations, your reactions were not unusual. While social workers take many situations in stride, each of us may be tripped up by a scenario that is new to us, challenges our imbedded beliefs or triggers value conflicts. It can be challenging to look beyond differences, our comfort zones, or distressing behaviors to see clients as individuals in need. However, by focusing selectively on the person rather than on the behavior, you can gradually overcome the inclination to label people negatively and learn to see them in full perspective.

How does this acceptance play out in practice? Acceptance is conveyed by listening attentively; by responding sensitively to the client's feelings; by using facial expressions, voice intonations, and gestures that convey interest and concern; and by extending courtesies and attending to the client's comfort. These skills are discussed and demonstrated in Chapter 6 and in exercises at the end of this chapter.

If you are unable to be open and accepting of people whose behavior runs counter to your values, your effectiveness in helping them will be diminished, because it is difficult—if not impossible—to conceal negative feelings toward others. Even if you can mask your negative feelings toward certain clients, you are likely to be unsuccessful in helping them, as people quickly detect insincerity. To expand your capacity for openness and acceptance, it may be helpful to view association with others whose beliefs, backgrounds, and behaviors differ strikingly from your own as an opportunity to enrich yourself as you experience their uniqueness. Truly open people relish such opportunities, viewing differences as refreshing and stimulating and seeing these interactions as a chance to better understand the forces that motivate people. By prizing the opportunity to relate to all types of people and by seeking to understand them, you will gain a deeper appreciation of the diversity and complexity of human beings. In so doing, you will be less likely to pass judgment and will achieve personal growth in the process. You might also find it helpful to talk with other social workers who have been in the field for some time. How do they manage value conflicts? How do they develop cultural competence? Are they able to treat others with respect, even if they disdain their actions?

3. *The value of integrity means that social work professionals behave in a trustworthy manner.* As an ethical principle, integrity means that social workers act honestly, encourage ethical practices in their agencies, and take responsibility for their own ethical conduct (Reamer, 1998a). In practice, it means that social workers present themselves and their credentials accurately, avoid other forms of misrepresentation (e.g., in billing practices or in presentation of research findings), and do not participate in fraud and deception. Integrity also refers to the ways that social workers treat their colleagues. Professionals are expected to treat one another with respect, avoid involving clients or others in professional disputes, and be forthright in their dealings with fellow professionals. These expectations are important not only for our individual trustworthiness, but also because each of us serves as a representative of the larger profession and we should act in ways that do not dishonor it.

This may seem to be a relatively straightforward expectation. However, challenges can arise when pressures from other colleagues or employing organizations create ethical dilemmas. In those cases, the challenge is not what is right, but rather how to do it. Following are two examples of such dilemmas involving the principle of integrity. What strategies might you pursue to resolve these dilemmas and act with honesty and professionalism?

Situation 15 Your agency recently received a large federal grant to implement a "Return to Work" program as part of welfare reform. Although the evaluation protocol is very clear about what constitutes "work," the agency is pressuring you and your coworkers (none of whom are social workers) to count clients' volunteer efforts and other nonpaying jobs as "work" in an effort to ensure that this valuable program will continue. The agency maintains that paying jobs are difficult to find, so clients

who are actively working—even in noncompensated jobs—"fit the spirit, if not the letter of the law."

Situation 16 Your supervisor wants to assess your effectiveness in conducting family sessions. Because he fears that if clients know they are being taped, their behaviors will change and his findings will be distorted, he has told you to tape these sessions without their knowledge. The supervisor feels that because he discusses your cases with you anyway, the taping without explicit client permission should be acceptable.

4. *The value of competence requires that social workers practice only within their scope of knowledge and ability and that they enhance and develop their professional expertise.* As with the value of integrity, this principle places the burden for self-awareness and self-regulation on the social worker. An expectation of practice as a professional is that the individual will take responsibility for knowing his or her own limits and seek out the knowledge and experience needed to develop further expertise throughout the span of his or her career. This principle means that social workers will decline cases where they lack sufficient expertise, and that they will seek out supervision for continuous self-examination and professional development. The commitment to utilizing evidence-based practices means that professionals must be lifelong learners, staying abreast of practice-related research findings, discarding ineffective or harmful practices, and tailoring interventions to the client's unique circumstances (Gambrill, 2007). Each of these elements speaks to developing and maintaining professional competence. The NASW Code of Ethics also includes cultural competence among its expectations for social workers, requiring an understanding of various groups, their strengths, the effects of oppression, and the provision of culturally sensitive services (NASW, 1999).

Self-regulation also requires the social worker to be alert to events or problems that affect his or her professional competence. For example, is a health or mental health problem hindering the social worker's service to clients? Are personal reactions to the client (such as anger, partiality, or sexual attraction) impairing the social worker's judgment in a particular case? Are family problems or other stressors detracting from their capacity to respond to clients' needs? *Countertransference* refers broadly to the ways that a worker's experiences and emotional reactions influence his or her perceptions of and interactions with a client. Later in this book you will learn more about the ways that countertransference can be a constructive or destructive factor in the helping process. It is important to be alert to such reactions and use supervisory sessions to examine and address their impact.

Supervision is an essential element in professional development and ongoing competence. In the helping professions, a supervisor is not someone looking over the worker's shoulder to catch and correct mistakes. More typically, supervisors can be thought of as mentors, teachers, coaches, and counselors all wrapped up into one role (Haynes, Corey, & Moulton, 2003). Successful use of supervision requires you to be honest and self-aware in seeking guidance, raising issues for discussion, sharing your challenges and successes, and being open to feedback, praise, critiques, and change. Effective supervisors will help you develop skills to look clearly at yourself, so that you understand your strengths and weaknesses, preferences and prejudices, and become able to manage these for the benefit of your clients.

Developing and maintaining competence is a career-long responsibility, yet it can be challenging to uphold. Consider the following scenarios:

Situation 17 You are a new employee at a small, financially strapped counseling center. The director of your agency just received a contract to do outreach, assessments, and case management for frail elders. Although you took a human behavior course as a social work student, you have never studied or worked with older adults, especially those at risk. The director has asked you to lead this new program and has emphasized how important the new funding is for the agency's survival.

Situation 18 For the past few weeks, you've found yourself attracted to one of your clients, thinking about him or her often and wondering what the client is doing at different times of the day. You wonder if this attraction could affect your objectivity on the case, but are reluctant to discuss the situation with your supervisor because it might affect his or her evaluation of you later this year.

What is competence? Do social workers ever feel totally competent? What is impairment? And how can we tell when it applies to us and our practice? Self-evaluation requires self-knowledge and introspection. Measuring one's competence requires honest self-examination and the pursuit of input from colleagues and supervisors. Professional development requires actively seeking out opportunities to hone existing skills and develop new ones, whether through reading, continuing education, course work, or case conferences. It means knowing what we do not know and being willing to acknowledge our shortcomings. It means being aware of the learning curve in developing new skills or testing new interventions and using staff development and supervision to assure that clients are receiving high quality services (NASW, 1999). It also means that when we lack the skills, abilities, or capacity demanded by a client's situation that we make proper referrals, thereby elevating the clients' needs above our own.

Ideas in Action

One way that social workers can assess and enhance competence is through the review of case recordings. These may be pen-and-paper process recordings of the dialogue in a client session or audio or video tapes of individual, family, or group meetings (Murphy & Dillon, 2008). Many social workers resist taping sessions on the premise that it makes clients uncomfortable, though the greater likelihood is that the client will forget the tape is there; it may be the worker him or herself that is distressed at its presence and at having to look at his or her performance at a later point. Ethical practice, however, requires facing this discomfort for the greater good of evaluating strengths and weaknesses and, ultimately, assuring competent practice. Allie, the worker interviewing Irwin and Angela Corning in the videos that accompany this chapter, received an array of

insights as a result of reviewing the tapes of her sessions. Among her findings are the following:

At the outset of the first session, Irwin clearly stated his frustration with attending the meeting. His comment set the tone for our working relationship, which was strained at first. I remember thinking that exploring his frustration at that time would be a difficult conversation, and I did not want to get off to a bad start. The alternative was hardly any easier to work with. By ignoring his comment, though it was really his tone that got my attention, I communicated to both clients that I was not willing or ready to meet them where they were emotionally. The space between us was muddled for the remainder of the session. I could sense that Irwin was getting tense. I am thankful that rather than explode or walk out, he interjected himself into the conversation to explain his brusque demeanor and negative emotions.

Because I did not address Irwin's frustration, he remained distant, and the business of the meeting was conducted with Angela. For a majority of the first session, my legs are crossed in front of me and I am turned toward Angela. At times, I crossed my arms in front of me over the notepad. You can see by my posture that I am uncomfortable with the tension in the room.

I noticed that my nerves were showing in other ways as well. Occasionally during the interview I explored the details of personal situations with the couple. As I asked these sensitive questions, my voice trailed off, so much so that it is hard to hear the entire question on the recording. In contrast, a calm and even tone would normalize these difficult inquiries and the information they elicit.

It is amazing to hear how many times I said, "You know," and, "So." I never realized it before, but I use these phrases as a pause in my sentences. I have been trying to pay attention to it lately and make sure that when I am working with clients all of my words help to convey a point or information. I also say "you guys" a lot, which seems too casual and potentially disrespectful.

I talked a lot because I was not well prepared for the meeting. Much of the time in the first session was spent sorting through what exactly I could provide the couple. Looking at it on tape, I can see why Angela and Irwin were so frustrated and uncomfortable. I eventually gave them a plan, to provide them with contact information for affordable apartment complexes and employment placement services, but conveyed the information haphazardly. It just got more confusing when I sought the couple's corroboration in a partnership that they knew little about. This is a point in the interview where I could have checked in with the clients to be sure that we were all on the same page.

In the second session, my hesitancy to engage Irwin persisted. At that appointment, Irwin discovered for the first time that he and Angela were carrying a $2,000 balance on their credit card account. The couple exchanged words back and forth, which I remember was a poignant moment in my work with them. As I watch the tape, I am struck by this opportunity to explore the couple's money management methods. Instead of having that discussion, I got into the activity of listing all of the other barriers that the couple would face in attaining a new apartment. My personal goal was to be prepared in the second session. I wanted to be sure to get all of the items on my list, one of which was a discussion of the barriers to attaining the couple's stated goals.

Processing the disclosure of the credit card in the moment with the couple not only would have yielded information and helped the couple to share household financial tasks more effectively but would have also engaged the clients and may have fostered rapport between Irwin and me. Because I did not address the issue, and it was a surprise and disappointment to Irwin, he was unable to follow the thread about barriers. When I checked in with him to see if he wanted to add anything, he revealed that he was consumed with thoughts of the debt discovery over the past several minutes rather than following the discussion.

I did a good job of seeking out which areas the clients wanted to address in their goals. The clients reported that they were happy with the outcomes of our work together and that they became more comfortable with the process as the relationship grew. At the same time, we could have been more detailed in making the task lists. While I was speaking with Irwin about his objectives for employment and career advancement he indicated that in the future he would like to see himself admitted to, or already enrolled in, a masonry apprentice program. This should have been thoughtfully broken down into task steps that Irwin would have control over. Should Irwin meet his objectives, but not attain the goal because of factors out of his control, he would see documentation of his accomplishments and the efficacy of setting objectives and goals. (Unfortunately, we only had enough time to give this goal cursory treatment at the end of the interview.)

Near the end of our time together, Irwin and Angela had made considerable gains in the realms of housing, employment, and communicating with the school. I was glad to have the opportunity to go over the Eco-Map with them to illustrate how much they had done to change their lives. Watching the tape, I realize that I did not emphasize their success and efforts enough. I sense that this was a missed opportunity for offering congratulations and praise.

In the final session, I evaluated the work with Irwin and Angela. I am disclosing too much when I ask, "I didn't seem too nosy, did I?" Watching it, I realize that the wording of the question suggests a need for validation rather than feedback. Actually, one of my focal points for career development is to learn to encourage and foster self-determination as opposed to *doing for* the client. It is important to me that the clients I work with see the relationship as collaborative, with us all on equal ground. I really wanted to know if I seemed too pushy or bossy. I can see how rephrasing my question could allow Irwin and Angela to give more honest feedback. I could have asked, "Did you feel respected in our work together? Did I respond to your needs and concerns?"

Challenges in Embracing the Profession's Values

In this section's presentation of the social work profession's cardinal values, numerous situations and cases have highlighted the potential for value conflicts. Self-awareness, openness to new persons and events, and increasing practice experience are all crucial elements in overcoming value conflicts. But what if you have made these efforts and your values continue to conflict with others' values? Social workers occasionally encounter situations in which they cannot conform to the profession's values or in which a client's behaviors or goals evoke such negative reactions that a positive helping relationship cannot be established. For example, practitioners who have personal experience with child abuse or who are intensely opposed to abortions may find it difficult to accept a pedophile as a client or to offer help to a woman experiencing an unintended pregnancy. In such instances, it is important to acknowledge these feelings and to explore them through supervision or therapy. It may be feasible to help the worker overcome these difficulties in order to be more fully available as a helping person. If this is not possible, however, or if the situation is exceptional, the social worker and his or her supervisor should explore the possibility of transferring the case to another practitioner who can accept both the client and the goals. In such circumstances, it is vital to clarify for clients that the reason for the transfer is not personal rejection of them but rather a recognition that they deserve the best service possible and that the particular social worker cannot provide that service. It is not usually necessary to go into detail about the social worker's challenges. A general explanation conveys goodwill and safeguards clients' well-being. When a transfer is not possible, the social worker is responsible for seeking intensive assistance to ensure that services are provided properly and that ethical and professional responsibilities are upheld. Practitioners who are consistently unable to accept clients or carry out their roles in a professional manner owe it to themselves and to future clients to reflect seriously on their suitability for the social work field.

Cross-cultural and cross-national social work offer further challenges in the application of professional values (Healy, 2007). Are values such as justice, service, and acceptance universally recognized guidelines for behavior, or should their application become tempered by cultural norms? Some have suggested that NASW and other social work codes of ethics place too great a value on individual rights over the collective good and independence over interdependence (Jessop, 1998; Silvawe, 1995). As such, they may reflect a Western bias and give insufficient attention to the values of other cultures. This is not merely a philosophical dispute. It creates significant challenges for practitioners working with individuals or groups with vastly different values. How can workers reconcile their responsibility to advocate for justice and equality while simultaneously demonstrating respect for cultural practices such as female circumcision, corporal punishment of children, arranged marriages, or differential rights based on social class, gender, or sexual orientation? Cultural values shift and evolve over time, and social workers' systems change efforts may appropriately target stances that harm or disenfranchise certain groups. But how can social workers ensure that their efforts are proper and congruent with the desires of the particular cultural group and not a misguided effort borne of paternalism and ethnocentrism?

Healy (2007) recommends a stance of "moderate universalism" (p. 24), where the human rights of equality and protection are promoted along with the importance of cultural diversity and community ties. Ultimately, striking this balance means that social workers, individually and collectively, must be aware of their values and those of their colleagues and clients and engage in ongoing education and conversation in reconciling these value tensions.

Ethics

Codes of ethics are the embodiment of a profession's values. They set forth principles and standards for behavior of members of that profession. In social work, the primary Code of Ethics is promulgated by the NASW. It addresses a range of responsibilities that social workers have as professionals, to their clients, to their colleagues, to their employers, to their profession, and to society as a whole. This section addresses four primary areas of ethical responsibility for social workers: self-determination, informed consent, maintenance of client–social worker boundaries, and confidentiality. First, however, it discusses how ethics are related to legal responsibilities and malpractice risks. The section concludes by summarizing the resources and processes available for resolving ethical dilemmas.

The Intersection of Laws and Ethics

The practice of social work is governed by a vast array of policies, laws, and regulations. Whether established by court cases, the U. S. Congress, state legislatures, licensure boards, or regulatory agencies, these rules affect social workers' decisions and actions. For example, state mandatory reporting laws require social workers to report cases where child abuse is suspected. The Health Insurance Portability and Accountability Act (HIPAA) regulates the storage and sharing of patient records (U. S. Department of Health and Human Services, 2003). Some states' health department rules may require social workers to divulge the names of HIV-positive clients to public health authorities; in other states, rules may forbid the sharing of patient's names or HIV status. Licensure board regulations may forbid social work practice by persons with felony convictions. Federal court cases may extend evidential privilege to communications with social workers (Reamer, 1999). Federal laws may prohibit the provision of certain benefits to undocumented immigrants.

Good social work practice requires workers to be aware of the laws and regulations that govern the profession and apply to their area of practice and the populations they serve. But knowing the laws is not enough. Consider the following case.

Case Example

Alice is a 38-year-old woman who has presented for treatment, filled with guilt as the result of a brief extramarital affair. In her third session, she discloses that she is HIV-positive, but is unwilling to tell her husband of her status because then the affair would be revealed and she fears losing him and her two young daughters. You are concerned about the danger to her husband's health, and press her to tell him or to allow you to do so. Alice responds that if you do, you will be breaking your promise of confidentiality and violating her privacy. She implies that she would sue you or report you to your licensing board and to your profession's ethics committee.

This case neatly captures the clash of ethics, laws, and regulations and illustrates the stakes for workers who make the "wrong" decision. In a scenario such as this one, the social worker just wants a clear answer from a lawyer or supervisor who will tell him or her exactly what to do. Unfortunately, matters are not that simple. Good practice requires knowledge of both the applicable ethical principles and the relevant laws. Even

with this knowledge, dilemmas may persist. In this case example, the ethical principles of self-determination and confidentiality are pitted against the principle to protect others from harm, which itself is derived from a court case (Cohen & Cohen, 1999; Reamer, 1995). The particular state or setting where the case takes place may have laws or regulations that govern the social worker's actions. Finally, the threat of civil litigation for malpractice looms large, even when the social worker's actions are thoughtful, careful, ethical, and legal.

When you think about the intersection of laws and ethics, it may be helpful to think of a Venn diagram, in which two ovals overlap (see Figure 4-1). In the center are areas common to both ethics and laws; within each oval are items that are exclusive to laws and ethics, respectively. Some standards contained in the NASW Code of Ethics are not addressed by laws and regulations (such as the prohibition of sexual relationships with supervisees or standards on treating colleagues with respect). Similarly, some areas of the law are not covered by the Code of Ethics. For example, it is illegal to drive while intoxicated, but the Code of Ethics lacks a standard related to that act. Where the two realms intersect, there can be areas of agreement as well as areas of discord. As the Code of Ethics notes:

> *Social workers' primary responsibility is to promote the well-being of clients. In general, clients' interests are primary. However, social workers' responsibility to the larger society or specific legal obligations may on limited occasions supersede the loyalty owed clients and clients should be so advised. (NASW, 1999, p. 7)*

Also:

> *Instances may arise when social workers' ethical obligations conflict with agency policies or relevant laws or regulations. When such conflicts occur, social workers must make a responsible effort to resolve the conflict in a manner that is consistent with the values, principles, and standards expressed in this*

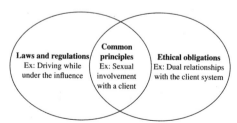

FIG-4-1 The Relationship of Law and Ethics

Code. If a reasonable resolution of the conflict does not appear possible, social workers should seek proper consultation before making a decision. (NASW, 1999, pp. 3–4)

The processes for ethical decision making are addressed later in this chapter. For now, though, it is important to acknowledge that social workers must know both the law and ethical principles to practice effectively. Workers must also recognize that sometimes conflicts will occur between and among ethical and legal imperatives. For example, state laws may prohibit the provision of services or resources to undocumented immigrants, but ethics would expect social workers to fill basic human needs. Thoughtful examination, consultation, and skillful application of the principles will serve as guides when laws and ethics collide.

Key Ethical Principles

The NASW Code of Ethics contains 155 standards, addressing a variety of ethical issues (such as conflicts of interest, competence, or confidentiality) for social workers in a range of roles (such as supervisor, teacher, direct practitioner or administrator). In this section, we examine four key areas of immediate relevance to direct practitioners: self-determination, informed consent, professional boundaries and confidentiality.

Self-Determination

Biestek (1957) has defined self-determination as "the practical recognition of the right and need of clients to freedom in making their own choices and decisions" (p. 103). Self-determination is central to the social worker's ethical responsibility to clients:

Social workers respect and promote the right of clients to self-determination and assist clients in their efforts to identify and clarify their goals. Social workers may limit clients' right to self-determination when, in their professional judgment, clients' actions or potential actions pose a serious, foreseeable, and imminent risk to themselves or others. (NASW, 1999, p. 7)

This value also embodies the beliefs that clients have the capacity to grow and change and to develop solutions to their difficulties, as well as the right and capacity to exercise free choice responsibly. These values are magnified when practitioners adopt a strengths-oriented perspective, looking for positive qualities and undeveloped potential rather than pointing out limitations and past mistakes (Cowger, 1994; Saleeby, 1997). Such a positive perspective engenders hope and courage on the client's part and nurtures self-efficacy. These factors, in turn, enhance the client's motivation, which is indispensable to achieving a successful outcome.

The extent to which you affirm an individual's right to self-determination rests in large measure on your perceptions of the helping role and of the helping process. If you consider your major role to be that of providing solutions or dispensing advice freely, you may foster dependency, demean clients by failing to recognize and affirm their strengths, and relegate them to a position of passive cooperation (or passive resistance, a frequent response under such circumstances).[1] Such domineering behavior is counterproductive. Not only does it discourage open communication, but, equally important, it denies people the opportunity to gain strength and self-respect as they actively wrestle with their difficulties. Fostering dependency generally leaves people weaker rather than stronger and is a disservice to them.

The type of relationship that affirms self-determination and supports growth is a partnership wherein the practitioner and the client (whether an individual, a couple, or a group) are joined in a mutual effort to search for solutions to problems or to promote growth. As enablers of change, social workers facilitate clients in their quest to view their problems realistically, to consider various solutions and their consequences, to implement change-oriented strategies, to understand themselves and others more fully, to gain awareness of previously unrecognized strengths and opportunities for growth, and to tackle obstacles to change and growth. As helpful as these steps are, however, ultimately the responsibility for pursuing these options rests with the client.

Just as fostering self-determination enhances client autonomy, exhibiting paternalism (i.e., preventing self-determination based on a judgment of the client's own good) infringes on autonomy. Linzer (1999) refers to paternalism as "the overriding of a person's wishes or actions through coercion, deception or nondisclosure of information, or for the welfare of others" (p. 137). A similar concept is paternalistic beneficence, wherein the social worker implements protective interventions to enhance the client's quality of life, sometimes despite the client's objections (Abramson, 1985; Murdach, 1996).

Under what conditions might it be acceptable for a social worker to override a client's autonomy? Paternalism may be acceptable when a client is young or judged to be incompetent, when an irreversible act such as suicide can be prevented, or when the interference with the client's decisions or actions ensures other freedoms or liberties, such as preventing a serious crime (Abramson, 1985; Reamer, 1989). Murdach suggests three gradations of beneficent actions, which vary in their level of intrusiveness depending on the degree of risk and the client's decision-making capacity. Yet, even under these circumstances, social workers must weigh the basis for their decisions against the potential outcomes of their actions. For example, if a psychiatric patient refuses medication, some would argue that the client lacks competence to make such a decision, and that forcing him or her to take the medication would be "for the client's own good." Yet diagnosis or placement is not a sufficient basis for overriding a person's autonomy. For this reason, states have developed elaborate administrative and judicial processes that must be traversed before an individual can be involuntarily hospitalized or medicated.

Even when clients have reduced capacity for exercising self-determination, social workers should act to ensure that they exercise their capacities to the fullest feasible extent. For example, self-determination can be extended to individuals who are terminally ill by educating them about their options and encouraging them to articulate their desires through advance directives, which provide instructions to health care personnel regarding which medical interventions are acceptable. These directives become operative when the patient's condition precludes decision-making capacity. Advance directives can take the form of living wills or authorizing an individual to act with durable power of attorney. The latter procedure is broader in scope and more powerful than a living will. The person designated to have durable power of attorney or medical power of attorney is authorized to make decisions as if he or she were the patient when grave illness or accident has obliterated the patient's autonomy.

Operationalizing clients' rights to self-determination sometimes can pose perplexing challenges. Adding to the complexity is the reality that in certain instances, higher-order principles such as safety supersede the right to self-determination. To challenge your thinking about how you might affirm the value of self-determination in practical situations, we have provided exercises that consist of problematic situations actually encountered by the authors or colleagues. As you read each scenario, analyze the alternative courses of action that are available and think of the laws, policies, and resources that you might consult as part of your decision making. Consider how you would work with the client to maximize self-determination, taking care also to promote his or her best interests.

Situation 1 In your work for the state welfare department, you oversee the care of numerous group home residents whose services are paid for by the state. Two of your clients, both in their twenties, reside in the same home and have told you that they are eager to get married. The administrator of the home strenuously protests that "the two are retarded" and, if they marry, might produce a child they could not properly care for. Further, she has stressed that she has no private room for a couple and that if the two marry, they will have to leave the group home.

Situation 2 A 15-year-old runaway, who is 4 months pregnant, has contacted you several times in regard to planning for her child. During her last visit, she confided that she is habituated to heroin. You have expressed your concern that the drug may damage her unborn child, but she does not seem worried, nor does she want to give up use of the drug. You also know that she obtains money for heroin through prostitution and is living on the street.

Situation 3 While making a visit to Mr. and Mrs. F, an elderly couple living in their home on their own savings, you discover that they have hired several home health aides who have stolen from them and provided such poor care that their health and nutrition are endangered. When you discuss with them your concern about the adequacy of their care, they firmly state that they can handle their own problems and "do not want to be put in a nursing home!"

Situation 4 As a rehabilitation worker, you have arranged for a young woman to receive training as a beautician in a local technical college, a vocation in which she expressed intense interest. Although initially enthusiastic, she now tells you that she wants to discontinue the program and go into nursing. According to your client, her supervisor at the college is highly critical of her work and the other trainees tease her and talk about her behind her back. You are torn about what to do, because you know that your client tends to antagonize other people with her quick and barbed remarks. You wonder if, rather than change programs, your client needs to learn more appropriate ways of communicating and relating to her supervisor and coworkers.

Situation 5 A middle-aged woman with cancer was so debilitated by her latest round of chemotherapy that she has decided to refuse further treatment. Her physician states that her age, general health, and stage of her cancer all argue for continuing her treatments, given the likelihood of a successful outcome. Her family is upset at seeing the woman in pain and supports her decision.

Providing Informed Consent

Six principles in the NASW Code of Ethics address facets of informed consent. At its essence, informed consent requires that social workers "use clear and understandable language to inform clients of the purpose of the services, risks related to the services, limits to services because of the requirements of a third-party payer, relevant costs, reasonable alternatives, clients' right to refuse or withdraw consent, and the time frame covered by the consent. Social workers should provide clients with an opportunity to ask questions" (NASW, 1999, pp. 7–8). The Code of Ethics also indicates that clients should be informed when their services are being provided by a student. Timely and understandable informed consent sets the stage for social work services by acquainting the client with expectations for the process. For example, a common element of informed consent involves the limits on client privacy. Social workers explicitly state that in situations involving concerns about the client's danger to him or herself or others, the worker reserves the right to break confidentiality to seek appropriate help. Mandatory reporting requirements (for child and elder abuse and other circumstances such as communicable diseases) are typically also covered at this time. In addition to respectfully educating the client about his or her rights and responsibilities, informed consent lays the groundwork for future actions the worker might need to take. In the earlier case about the woman who refused to let her husband know about her HIV-positive status, informed consent would have alerted the client at the outset to the worker's responsibility to protect others from harm and

her duty to notify public health or other authorities about the risk created by the client's unprotected sexual activity.

Some workers view informed consent as a formality to be disposed of at the first interview or as a legalistic form to have clients sign and then file away. In fact, informed consent should be an active and ongoing part of the helping process. Given the tension and uncertainty that can accompany a first session, clients may not realize the significance of the information you are providing. In addition, new issues may emerge that require discussion of the client's risks, benefits, and options (Strom-Gottfried, 1998b). Therefore, it makes sense to revisit the parameters of service and invite questions throughout the helping process. Having a "fact sheet" that describes relevant policies and answers commonly asked questions can also help clients by giving them something to refer to between meetings, should questions arise (Houston-Vega, Nuehring, & Daguio, 1997).

To facilitate informed consent for persons with hearing, literacy, or language difficulties, social workers should utilize interpreters, translators, and multiple communication methods as appropriate. When clients are temporarily or permanently incapable of providing informed consent, "social workers should protect clients' interests by seeking permission from an appropriate third party, informing clients consistent with the client's level of understanding" and "seek to ensure that the third party acts in a manner consistent with the client's wishes and interests" (NASW, 1999, p. 8). Even clients who are receiving services involuntarily are entitled to know the nature of the services they will be receiving and to understand their right to refuse service.

Ideas in Action

What elements of informed consent were covered in the initial moments of the videotaped interview with Anna and Jackie in "Home for the Holidays?"

- The expectation of confidentiality, by the worker, and by the two clients, in regard to what each other shared in session.
- The limits of confidentiality: risk to self or others.
- Should either partner see the worker in an individual session, the information discussed or revealed there will not be held in confidence during conjoint sessions.

- The amount of time that the worker has set aside for the session (40 minutes).
- The purpose of the first session. The worker tells the clients that this is the time for them to tell her about themselves both as individuals and as a couple and to share their concerns and struggles with her.
- The nature of couples' work. The worker informs the couple that she will not take sides or take the role of a referee. She explains to the couple that her clinical focus is on their interactions, and that

she considers her client to be their relationship rather than either person individually.

- Although the relationship will be the therapeutic focus of the work, at times the worker will push and challenge one of the partners in particular. She explains that this is sometimes necessary to learn more about how the partners interact and to gain clarity about how the relationship works.

What else could have been covered as part of informed consent?

- The worker's experience with couples, specifically her previous work with same-sex partners.
- The worker's preferred theoretical framework for couple's therapy.
- Alternatives to pursuing couple's therapy with the worker (e.g., couple's education groups, group therapy, bibliotherapy).
- Fee schedule and terms of insurance coverage.
- The clients' right to withdraw consent and to cease therapy with the worker.

Preserving Professional Boundaries

Boundaries refer to clear lines of difference that are maintained between the social worker and the client in an effort to preserve the working relationship. They are intended to help prevent conflicts of interest, making the client's interests the primary focus and avoiding situations in which the worker's professional practice is compromised. In part, boundaries help clarify that the client–social worker relationship is not a social one. Also, even though it may involve a high degree of trust and client self-disclosure, the relationship is not an intimate one, such as might be experienced with a friend, partner, or family member. When clients can trust that boundaries exist and will be maintained by the social worker, they are more able to focus on the issues for which they are seeking help. They can freely share of themselves and trust that the social worker's reactions and statements—whether of support, confrontation, or empathy—are artifacts of the working relationship, not social or sexual overtures or personal reactions such as might arise when friends agree or disagree.

Sometimes social workers and other helping professionals have a difficult time with the notion of boundaries, perceiving that they establish a hierarchical relationship in which the client is deemed "less worthy" than the social worker. Some professionals may also feel that establishing such boundaries is a cold and clinical move, treating the client as an object instead of a fellow human deserving of warmth and compassion (Lazarus, 1994). Our viewpoint is that the two positions are not mutually exclusive. Social workers can have relationships with clients that are characterized by collaborative problem solving and mutuality, and they can react to clients authentically and kindly without blurring the boundaries of their relationship or obscuring the purpose of their work.

The NASW Code of Ethics addresses boundaries through six provisions:

1. "Social workers should not take unfair advantage of any professional relationship or exploit others to further their personal, religious, political, or business interests" (NASW, 1999, p. 9).
2. "Social workers should not engage in dual or multiple relationships with clients or former clients in which there is a risk of exploitation or potential harm to the client. In instances when dual or multiple relationships are unavoidable, social workers should take steps to protect clients and are responsible for setting clear, appropriate, and culturally sensitive boundaries. (Dual or multiple relationships occur when social workers relate to clients in more than one relationship, whether professional, social, or business. Dual or multiple relationships can occur simultaneously or consecutively.)" (NASW, 1999, pp. 9–10).
3. "Social workers should not engage in physical contact with clients when there is a possibility of psychological harm to the client as a result of the contact (such as cradling or caressing clients) ..." (NASW, 1999, p. 13).
4. "Social workers should under no circumstances engage in sexual activities or sexual contact with current clients, whether such contact is consensual or forced" (NASW, 1999, p. 13).
5. "Social workers should not engage in sexual activities or sexual contact with clients' relatives or other individuals with whom clients maintain a close personal relationship when there is a risk of exploitation or potential harm to the client. Sexual activity or sexual contact with clients' relatives or other individuals with whom clients maintain a personal relationship has the potential to be harmful to the client and may make it difficult for the

social worker and client to maintain appropriate professional boundaries. Social workers—not their clients, their clients' relatives, or other individuals with whom the client maintains a personal relationship—assume the full burden for setting clear, appropriate, and culturally sensitive boundaries" (NASW, 1999, p. 13).

6. "Social workers should not engage in sexual activities or sexual contact with former clients because of the potential for harm to the client" (NASW, 1999, p. 13).

Although these standards of practice may seem self-evident, they represent an area fraught with difficulty within the profession. Research on ethics complaints indicates that in NASW-adjudicated cases, boundary violations accounted for more than half of all cases in which violations occurred (Strom-Gottfried, 1999a). Similarly, in research on the frequency of malpractice claims against social workers for the period 1961–1990, Reamer (1995) found that sexual violations were the second most common area of claim, and the most expensive in terms of money paid out. Most social workers cannot imagine developing sexual relationships with their clients; yet, this outcome is often the culmination of a "slippery slope" of boundary problems that may include excessive self-disclosure on the part of the worker, the exchange of personal gifts, socializing or meeting for meals outside the office, and arranging for the client to perform office and household chores or other favors (Borys & Pope, 1989; Epstein, Simon, & Kay, 1992; Gabbard, 1996; Gartrell, 1992).

It is not uncommon to experience feelings of sexual attraction for clients. When such feelings arise, however, it is crucial to raise them with faculty or supervisors so they can be acknowledged and examined. Such discussion normalizes and neutralizes these feelings and decreases the likelihood that the worker will act on the attraction (Pope, Keith-Spiegel, & Tabachnick, 1986). These issues will be explored further in Chapter 18 as we discuss relational reactions and their effects on the helping process.

Other boundary issues can be both subtle and complex. For example, you may meet a neighbor in the agency waiting room or run into a client while doing your grocery shopping. You may decide to buy a car and find that the salesperson is a former client. You may visit a relative in the hospital and discover that her roommate is a current or former client. Friends in need of social work services may ask to be assigned to your caseload, because you already know them so well.

A client may ask you to attend a "family" event, such as a graduation or wedding. You may resonate with a particular client and think what a great friend he or she could be. You may sympathize with a particular client's job search plight and consider referring him to a friend who is currently hiring new workers. The possibilities are endless, and addressing them involves other ethical principles, such as maintaining confidentiality and avoiding conflicts of interest. The key is to be alert to dual relationships, to discuss troubling situations with colleagues and a supervisor, and to take care that the primacy of the helping relationship is preserved in questionable boundary situations (Brownlee, 1996; Erickson, 2001; Reamer, 2001). Consultation helps social workers determine whether dual relationships are avoidable or not and whether they are problematic or not. It is incumbent on the social worker to ensure that clients are not taken advantage of and that their services are not obscured or affected detrimentally when boundaries must be crossed.

Safeguarding Confidentiality

From a practical standpoint, confidentiality is a sine qua non of the helping process. Without the assurance of confidentiality, it is unlikely that clients would risk disclosing private aspects of their lives that, if revealed, could cause shame or damage to their reputations. This is especially true when clients' problems involve infidelity, deviant sexual practices, illicit activities, child abuse, and the like. Implied in confidentiality is an assurance that the practitioner will never reveal such personal matters to others.

Social workers are bound by the NASW Code of Ethics to safeguard their clients' confidentiality. Numerous standards operationalize this principle, but in essence, social workers are expected to respect clients' privacy, to gather information only for the purpose of providing effective services, and to disclose information only with clients' consent. Disclosure of information without clients' permission should be done only for compelling reasons, and even under these circumstances, there are limits on what information can be shared and with whom. These exceptions to confidentially will be addressed later in this section.

An unjustified breach of confidentiality is a violation of justice and is tantamount to theft of a secret with which one has been entrusted (Biestek, 1957). Maintaining strict confidentiality requires a strong commitment and constant vigilance, because clients sometimes reveal information that is shocking, humorous, bizarre, or titillating. To fulfill your responsibility in maintaining confidentiality, you must guard against disclosing information in inappropriate situations. Examples include discussing details of your work with family and friends, having gossip sessions with colleagues, dictating within the listening range of others, discussing client situations within earshot of other staff, and making remarks about clients in elevators or other public places.

The emergence of technology that permits the electronic collection, transfer, and storage of information raises new complexities for maintaining client privacy (Gelman, Pollack, & Weiner, 1999). When you leave a voice mail for a client, are you certain that only the client will receive the message? When a colleague sends you a fax on a case, can you be sure that others will not see that information before you retrieve the document? As authors such as Davidson and Davidson (1996) have noted, these technological advances have emerged at the same time that insurance companies and others who fund services are demanding increasingly more detailed information about cases before they will approve reimbursement for services. As a result, clients should be well-informed about the limits of confidentiality and the potential risks of information shared for insurance claims (Corcoran & Winslade, 1994).

Beyond ethical standards, the Health Insurance Portability and Accountability Act of 1996 (HIPAA) established federal standards to protect the privacy of personal health information. HIPAA regulations affect pharmacies, health care settings, and insurance plans as well as individual health and mental health providers. The rules affect identifiable client information in all forms, including paper records, electronic data and communications, and verbal communications. There are several important provisions for social workers in HIPAA (HIPAA Medical Privacy Rule, 2003; Protecting the Privacy of Patients' Health Information, 2003).

- *Psychotherapy notes have a particular protection under HIPAA. The release of those notes requires special, separate authorization. Psychotherapy notes must be kept separately in client files and must meet other criteria in order to be considered protected.*
- *Clients should be provided access to their records, and have the opportunity to seek corrections if they identify errors or mistakes. However, under HIPAA, client access to psychotherapy notes is restricted.*
- *Clients must be given information on the organization's privacy policies and they must sign a form or otherwise indicate that they have received the information.*

- *Client records or data should be protected from non-medical uses, such as marketing, unless the client gives specific permission otherwise.*
- *Clients should understand their rights to request other reasonable efforts to protect confidentiality, such as requesting to be contacted only at certain times or numbers.*
- *Organizations and the individuals who work in them (in clinical, clerical, administrative and other roles) must take care to ensure that security standards are in place and that they are reinforced though staff development and agency policies.*
- *When state laws are more stringent than the provisions in HIPAA (when they offer greater protections for clients) those laws take precedence over HIPAA.*
- *HIPAA recognizes the validity of professional standards, such as those contained in the NASW Code of Ethics, and in some cases, those provisions may be more stringent than HIPAA's.*

What Are the Limits on Confidentiality?

While social workers are expected to safeguard the information they collect in the course of their professional duties, there are several situations in which helping professionals are allowed or compelled to share case information. These include: when seeking supervision or consultation, when the client waives confidentiality, when the client presents a danger to self or others, for reporting suspicions of child or elder maltreatment, and when presented with a subpoena or court order.

Supervision and Consultation

The right to confidentiality is not absolute, because case situations are frequently discussed with supervisors and consultants and may be presented at staff conferences. Disclosing information in these instances, however, is for the purpose of enhancing service to clients, who will generally consent to these uses when their purposes are clarified. The client has a right to be informed that such disclosures may occur, and practitioners seeking supervision have a responsibility to conceal the identity of the client to the fullest extent possible and to reveal no more personal information than is absolutely necessary.

Other personnel such as administrators, volunteers, clerical staff, consultants, board members, researchers, legal counsel, and outside persons who may review records for purposes of quality assurance, peer review, or accreditation may have access to files or case information. This access to information should be for the purposes of better serving the client, and these individuals should sign binding agreements not to misuse confidential information. Further, it is essential that social workers promote policies and norms that protect confidentiality and assure that case information is treated carefully and respectfully.

Client Waivers of Confidentiality

Social workers are often asked by other professionals or agencies to provide confidential information about the nature of their client's difficulties or the services provided. Sometimes, these requests can be made with such authority that the recipient is caught off guard, inadvertently acknowledging a particular person as a client or providing the information requested about the case. In these instances, it is important that such data be provided only with the written, informed consent of clients, which releases the practitioner and agency from liability in disclosing the requested information. Even when informed consent is obtained, however, it is important to reveal information selectively based on the essential needs of the other party.

In some exceptional circumstances, information can be revealed without informed consent, such as a bona fide emergency in which a client's life appears to be at stake or when the social worker is legally compelled, as in the reporting of child abuse. In other instances, it is prudent to obtain supervisory and legal input before disclosing confidential information without the client's written consent for release of information.

A final example of the client's waiver of confidentiality occurs if the client files a malpractice claim against the social worker. Such an action would "terminate the patient or client privilege" (Dickson, 1998, p. 48), freeing the practitioner to share publicly such information as is necessary to mount a defense against the lawsuit.

Danger to Self or Others

In certain instances, the client's right to confidentiality may be less compelling than the rights of other people who could be severely harmed or damaged by actions planned by the client and confided to the practitioner. For example, if the client plans to commit kidnapping, injury, or murder, the practitioner is obligated to disclose these intentions to the intended victim and to law enforcement officials so that timely preventive action can be taken. Indeed, if practitioners fail to make appropriate disclosures under these circumstances, they may be liable to civil prosecution for negligence. The fundamental case in this area is the Tarasoff case (Reamer, 1994). In it, a young man seeing a psychologist at a

university health service threatened his girlfriend, Tatiana Tarasoff. The therapist notified university police; after interviewing the young man, they determined that he did not pose a danger to his girlfriend. Some weeks later the young man murdered Tarasoff, and her family filed a lawsuit alleging that she should have been warned. Ultimately, the court ruled that mental health professionals have an obligation to protect their clients' intended victims.

This court decision has led to varying interpretations in subsequent cases and in resulting state laws, but two principles have consistently resulted from it (Dickson, 1998; Houston-Vega, Nuehring, & Daguio, 1997): If the worker perceives a serious, foreseeable and imminent threat to an identifiable potential victim, the social worker should (1) act to warn that victim or (2) take other precautions (such as notifying police or placing the client in a secure facility) to protect others from harm.

Another application of the duty to protect personal safety involves intervening to prevent a client's suicide. Typically, lawsuits that cite a breach of confidentiality undertaken to protect suicidal clients have not been successful (VandeCreek, Knapp, & Herzog, 1988). Conversely, "liability for wrongful death can be established if appropriate and sufficient action to prevent suicide is not taken" (Houston-Vega, Nuehring, & Daguio, 1997, p. 105). Knowing when the risk is sufficient to warrant breaking a client's confidence is both a clinical decision and an ethical matter. Chapter 8 offers guidelines to use for determining the risk of lethality in suicidal threats or in client aggression.

Suspicion of Child or Elder Abuse

The rights of others also take precedence over the client's right to confidentiality in instances of child abuse or neglect. In fact, all 50 states now have statutes making it mandatory for professionals to report suspected or known child abuse. Moreover, statutes governing the mandatory reporting of child abuse may contain criminal clauses related to the failure to report. Note that practitioners are protected from both civil and criminal liability for a breach of confidentiality resulting from the legal mandate to report (Butz, 1985). Some states have established similar provisions for reporting the suspected abuse of the elderly or other vulnerable adults (Corey, Corey, & Callanan, 2007; Dickson, 1998). The mandate to report suspicions of abuse does not empower the worker to breach confidentiality in other ways. That is, even though the worker is a mandated reporter, he or she should still use caution in the amount of unrelated case information he or she shares with child welfare authorities. Furthermore, the requirement is to report suspicions to specific protective agencies, not to disclose information to the client's family members, teachers, or other parties.

Although afforded immunity from prosecution for reporting, practitioners must still confront the difficult challenge of preserving the helping relationship after having breached the client's confidentiality (Butz, 1985). One way of managing this tension is through informed consent. As noted earlier, clients should know at the outset of service what the "ground rules" for service are and what limits exist on what the social worker can hold as confidential. When clients understand that the social worker must report suspected child abuse, such a report may not be as damaging to the social worker–client relationship. Similarly, the Code of Ethics states, "Social workers should inform clients, to the extent possible, about the disclosure of confidential information and the potential consequences, when feasible before the disclosure is made" (NASW, 1999, p. 10). With informed consent, and careful processing of the decision to file a child abuse report, feelings of betrayal can be diminished and the helping relationship preserved.

The decision to comply with mandated reporting requirements may not always be straightforward, however. As Long (1986) reports, "On Indian reservations and in small rural towns it is often impossible to prevent community awareness of abuse victims, abuse perpetrators, and abuse informants. Despite the best efforts of health care professionals involved, abuse perpetrators may learn of an informant through informal channels or through tribal court procedures" (p. 133). Further, the sense of loyalty to one's clan members may take precedence over the commitment to protect an informant and the need to protect an abused child. Consequently, tribal sanctions may be more severe in relation to the informant than to the abuser. Definitions of abuse also differ from culture to culture, and within certain subcultures even severe abuse (according to common standards) may not be considered a problem by the victim or other family members.

Subcultural differences are by no means limited to members of ethnic minority groups. Long (1986) provides additional documentation indicating how closely knit Anglo health care practitioners discounted reports of child abuse perpetrated by a colleague and hindered effective intervention. Clearly, professional and social class loyalties have shielded abusers and hampered efforts to protect abused children. In part, mandated

reporting measures have emerged in response to professionals' reluctance to break confidentiality in such cases. Loyalty to a subgroup or a particular client should not take precedence over the need to protect vulnerable others from harm. Similarly, skepticism about the merit of an abuse claim or about the capacity of child welfare authorities to respond are insufficient reasons to avoid reporting. Law and ethics clearly articulate professionals' responsibilities to promote child safety and place the responsibility for investigations with child protective services.

Subpoenas and Privileged Communication

Yet another constraint on the client's right to confidentiality is the fact that this right does not necessarily extend into courts of law. Unless social workers are practicing in a state that recognizes the concept of privileged communication, they may be compelled by courts to reveal confidential information and to produce confidential records. "Privileged communication" refers to communications made within a "legally protected relationship," which "cannot be introduced into court without the consent of the person making the communication," typically the patient or client (Dickson, 1998, p. 32).

Determining the presence and applicability of privilege can be complicated, however. As Dickson notes, "Privilege laws can vary with the profession of the individual receiving the communication, the material communicated, the purpose of the communication, whether the proceeding is criminal or civil, and whether the professional is employed by the state or is in private practice, among other factors" (1998, p. 33). At the federal level, the U. S. Supreme Court in *Jaffee v. Redmond* upheld client communications as privileged and specifically extended "that privilege to licensed social workers" (Social Workers and Psychotherapist-Patient Privilege: *Jaffee v. Redmond* Revisited, 2005).

Despite the apparent clarity that this ruling brings to the federal courts, the ambiguity and variability on the state level mean that social workers must understand their state laws and regulations and ensure that clients are fully informed about the limits to confidentiality should records be subpoenaed or testimony required. Bernstein (1977) suggests that practitioners explain to clients that they may be "subpoenaed in court, records in hand, and forced under penalty of contempt to testify under oath, as to what was said between the parties and what was recorded concerning such exchanges" (p. 264).[2] Bernstein further recommends that clients sign a document verifying their understanding of this possibility and that the document be kept in the client's case file.

Laws recognizing privileged communication are created for the protection of the client; thus the privilege belongs to the client and not to the professional (Schwartz, 1989). In other words, if the practitioner were called to take the witness stand, the attorney for the client could invoke the privilege to prohibit the practitioner's testimony (Bernstein, 1977). Conversely, the client's attorney could waive this privilege, in which case the practitioner would be obligated to disclose information as requested by the court.

Another important factor regarding privileged communication is that the client's right is not absolute (Levick, 1981). If, in a court's judgment, disclosure of confidential information would produce benefits that outweigh the injury that might be incurred by revealing that information, the presiding judge may waive the privilege. Occasionally, the privilege is waived in instances of legitimate criminal investigations, because the need for information is deemed more compelling than the need to safeguard confidentiality (Schwartz, 1989). In the final analysis, then, courts make decisions on privilege-related issues on a case-by-case basis.

Because subpoenas, whether for records or testimony, are orders of the court, social workers cannot ignore them. Of course, subpoenas may sometimes be issued for irrelevant or immaterial information. Therefore, social workers should be wary about submitting privileged materials. Careful review of the subpoena, consultation with the client, and consultation with a supervisor and agency attorney can help you determine how to respond. The following sources provide helpful information for social workers contending with subpoenas: Austin, Moline, and Williams (1990); Dickson (1998); Houston-Vega, Nuehring, & Daguio (1997); Polowy and Gilbertson (1997); Barsky and Gould (2004); and the Law Note Series (2008) of the NASW.

Confidentiality in Various Types of Recording

Accreditation standards, funding sources, state and federal laws—all may dictate how agencies maintain record-keeping systems. Because case records can be subpoenaed and because clients and other personnel have access to them, it is essential that practitioners develop and implement policies and practices that provide maximal confidentiality. To this end, social workers should adhere to the following guidelines:

1. Record no more than is essential to the functions of the agency. Identify observed facts and distinguish them from opinions. Use descriptive terms rather than professional jargon, and avoid using psychiatric and medical diagnoses that have not been verified.

2. Omit details of clients' intimate lives from case records; describe intimate problems in general terms. Do not include verbatim or process recordings in case files.

3. Maintain and update records to assure their accuracy, relevancy, timeliness, and completeness.

4. Employ private and soundproof dictation facilities.

5. Keep case records in locked files, and issue keys only to those personnel who require frequent access to the files. Take similar privacy precautions to protect electronically stored data.

6. Do not remove case files from the agency except under extraordinary circumstances and with special authorization.

7. Do not leave case files on desks where others might gain access to them or keep case information on computer screens where it may be observed by others.

8. Take precautions, whenever possible, to ensure that information transmitted through the use of computers, electronic mail, facsimile machines, voice mail, answering machines, and other technology is secure; that it is sent to the correct party; and that identifying information is not conveyed.

9. Use in-service training sessions to stress confidentiality and to monitor adherence to agency policies and practices instituted to safeguard clients' confidentiality.

10. Inform clients of the agency's authority to gather information, the conditions under which that information may be disclosed, the principal uses of the information, and the effects, if any, of limiting what is shared with the agency.

11. Establish procedures to inform clients of the existence of their records, including special measures (if necessary) for disclosure of medical and psychological records and a review of requests to amend or correct the records (Schrier, 1980).

The NASW Code of Ethics reflects most of these provisions, stating that "social workers should provide clients with reasonable access to records concerning the clients" (NASW, 1999, p. 12). It further notes that the social worker should provide "assistance in interpreting the records and consultation with the client" (p. 12) in situations where the worker is concerned about misunderstandings or harm arising from seeing the records. Access to records should be limited "only in exceptional circumstances when there is compelling evidence that such access would cause serious harm to the client" (p. 12). In our opinion, the trend toward greater client access to records has enhanced the rights of clients by avoiding misuse of records and has compelled practitioners to be more prudent, rigorous, and scientific in keeping case records.

Social workers sometimes tape record live interviews or group sessions so that they can analyze interactional patterns or group process at a later time, or scrutinize their own performance with a view toward improving their skills and techniques. Recording is also used extensively for instructional sessions between students and practicum instructors. Yet another use of recordings is to provide firsthand feedback to clients by having them listen to or view their actual behavior in live sessions.

Before tape recording sessions for any of the preceding purposes, social workers should obtain written consent from clients on a form that explicitly specifies how the recording will be used, who will listen to or view the recording, and when it will be erased. A recording should never be made without the client's knowledge and consent. Clients vary widely in their receptivity to having sessions recorded; if they indicate reluctance, their wishes should be respected. The chances of gaining their consent are enhanced by discussing the matter openly and honestly, taking care to explain the client's right to decline. If approached properly, the majority of clients will consent to taping. Indeed, it has been our experience that clients are more comfortable with taping than are students.

Social workers who tape sessions assume a heavy burden of responsibility in safeguarding confidentiality, because live sessions can prove extremely revealing. Such recordings should be guarded to ensure that copies cannot be made and that unauthorized persons do not have access to them. When they have served their designated purpose, tapes should be promptly erased. Failure to heed these guidelines may constitute a breach of professional ethics.

The Ethics of Practice with Minors

A particular challenge in social work practice is interpreting ethical standards as they apply to clients under the age of 18 (Strom-Gottfried, 2008). While minor clients have the right to confidentiality, informed consent, self-determination, and the protection of other ethical principles, their rights are limited by laws and policies, differences in maturity and decision-making capacity, and by their very dependence on adults as their caretakers. As such, parents may retain the right to review a child's treatment record and to be kept informed of issues the child raises in therapy. A 15-year-old teen parent has the right to make decisions about her baby's health care that she cannot legally make about her own. Child welfare experts and other authorities are empowered to decide where to place children and when to move them based on their appraisal of the best interests of the child. A 10-year-old may resist medication or treatments but lacks the ability to withhold consent in light of his age and cognitive capacities. As such, his parents or guardians can compel him to comply, even against his expressed wishes.

Minors' rights are also affected by the particular service setting and by their presenting problems. For example, a youth seeking substance-abuse services would have privacy protections under federal regulations that assure confidentiality (42-CFR) even if his parents insisted on service information (Strom-Gottfried, 2008).

Similarly, a minor in need of prenatal care or treatment for sexually transmitted diseases could offer her own consent for services and be assured of confidentiality. Emergency services may be provided for a minor if delaying for parental consent could jeopardize the minor's well-being. School districts that accept "abstinence only" funding for health care will limit the information that social workers and nurses can share with students about contraception and HIV prevention.

As you can see, practice with minors is a complex tangle of legal, developmental, ethical, and social issues. Unsnarling this web requires a thorough understanding of child development and the physical, emotional, and cognitive capacities that emerge over the first two decades of the life span. It also requires an understanding of ethical standards, so that the worker appreciates the areas in which tensions might arise between legal and developmental limits to a minor's rights and the expectations of the profession for honoring clients' prerogatives, irrespective of age. Professionals in child-serving settings should be familiar with the policies and practices that govern services for their clientele. Through supervision, staff consultation, and careful decision making, social workers must consider various factors on a case-by-case basis in order to ensure that minors' rights are maximized, even amid constraints on those rights.

Understanding and Resolving Ethical Dilemmas

Social workers sometimes experience quandaries in deciding which of two values or ethical principles should take precedence when a conflict exists. In the foregoing discussions of self-determination and confidentiality, for example, we cited examples of how these rights of clients and ethical obligations of social workers are sometimes superseded by higher-order values (e.g., the right to life, safety, and well-being). Thus, clients' right to confidentiality takes second place when they confide that they have physically or sexually abused a child or when they reveal imminent and serious plans for harmful acts that would jeopardize the health or safety of other people. Dilemmas can also arise if you find that certain policies or practices of your employing agency seem detrimental to clients. You may be conflicted about your ethical obligations to advocate for changes, because doing so may jeopardize your employment or pose a threat to your relationships with certain staff members.

Situations such as these present social workers with agonizingly difficult choices. Reamer (1989) has developed general guidelines that can assist you in making these decisions. Here we present our versions of some of these guidelines and illustrate instances of their application.

1. *The right to life, health, well-being, and necessities of life takes precedence over rights to confidentiality and opportunities for additive "goods" such as wealth, education, and recreation.* We have previously alluded to the application of this principle in instances of child abuse or threats of harm to another person. In such circumstances, the rights of both children and adults to health and well-being take precedence over clients' rights to confidentiality.

2. *An individual's basic right to well-being takes precedence over another person's right to privacy, freedom, or self-determination.* As stated in the language of the courts (which have consistently upheld this principle), "The protective privilege ends where the public peril begins" (Reamer, 1994, p. 31). For example, the rights and needs of infants and children to receive medical treatments supersede parents' rights to withhold medical treatment because of their religious beliefs.

3. *A person's right to self-determination takes precedence over his or her right to basic well-being.* This principle maintains that people are entitled to act in ways that may appear contrary to their best interests, provided they are competent to make an informed and voluntary decision with consideration of relevant knowledge, and as long as the consequences of their decisions do not threaten the well-being of others. For example, if an adult chooses to live under a highway overpass, we may find that lifestyle unwise or unhealthy, but we have no power to constrain that choice. This principle affirms the cherished value of freedom to choose and protects the rights of people to make mistakes and to fail. As noted earlier, this principle must yield when an individual's decision might result in either his or her death or in severe and impeding damage to his or her physical or mental health.

4. *A person's rights to well-being may override laws, policies, and arrangements of organizations.* Ordinarily, social workers are obligated to comply with the laws, policies, and procedures of social work agencies, other organizations, and voluntary associations. When a policy is unjust or otherwise harms the well-being of clients or social workers, however, violation of the laws, policies, or procedures may be justified. Examples of this principle include policies or practices that discriminate against or exploit certain persons or groups. An agency, for example, cannot screen clients to select only those who are most healthy or well-to-do (a practice known as "creaming" or "cherry-picking") and then refuse services to those individuals in dire conditions. In situations such as these, the well-being of affected groups takes precedence over compliance with the laws, policies, and arrangements at issue.

Ethical social work includes advocacy for changes in laws and policies that are discriminatory, unfair, or unethical. For example, in regard to the ethical challenges posed by managed care, Sunley (1997) suggests engaging in both "case advocacy" and "cause advocacy" to help both individual clients and groups of clients who may be disadvantaged by particular policies or practices. Resources such as Brager and Holloway (1983), Corey, Corey, and Callanan (2007), and Frey (1990) provide helpful guidance for acting as an effective agent of change within troubled systems.

Although Reamer's guidelines serve as a valuable resource in resolving value dilemmas, applying them to the myriad situations that social workers encounter inevitably involves uncertainties and ambiguities, a reality that practitioners must accept. What should you do when you find yourself confronted with an ethical dilemma? Ethical decision-making models are as yet untested for their capacity to yield high-quality outcomes. Nevertheless, a list of recommended steps can be used to ensure thoughtful and thorough examination of options (Corey, Corey, & Callanan, 2007; Reamer, 1989; Strom-Gottfried, 2007, 2008):

1. Identify the problem or dilemma, gathering as much information about the situation from as many perspectives as possible, including that of the client, if possible.
2. Determine the core principles and the competing issues.
3. Review the relevant codes of ethics.
4. Review the applicable laws and regulations.
5. Consult with colleagues, supervisors, or legal experts.
6. Consider the possible and probable courses of action and examine the consequences of various options.
7. Decide on a particular course of action, weighing the information you have and the impact of your other choices.
8. Develop a strategy for effectively implementing your decision.
9. Evaluate the process and results to determine whether the intended outcome was achieved and consider modifications for future decisions.

These procedures need not be followed in the order listed. For example, consultation can prove useful in revealing options, identifying pros and cons, and rehearsing strategies for implementing the decision. Laws, ethical standards, and values can be examined after options are developed. Even decisions that must be made on the spot with little planning or consultation can be evaluated using this model, so that critical thinking is brought to bear for future dilemmas and actions. The key is to go beyond mere intuition or reactionary decision making to mindful, informed, critically examined choices.

Beyond these steps, you should be sure to document carefully the input and considerations taken into account at each phase of the decision-making process. This documentation may be in the client's formal record, your informal notes, or in the notes from supervisory sessions.

To apply this model, let's use the case of Alice from earlier in the chapter. As you may recall, she is a 38-year-old woman who refuses to notify her husband of her HIV-positive (HIV+) status due to fears that it will lead to the revelation of her extramarital affair.

The dilemma for the social worker in the case arises from Alice's revelation about her HIV+ status and her refusal to tell her husband, which places him at risk for infection. The worker has a loyalty to Alice's needs and wishes but also to preventing her from harming another person, namely, her husband. If the worker reveals the truth, he or she may save the husband's health (and ultimately his life), but in so doing is violating Alice's trust and right to privacy and potentially putting the marriage at risk by exposing the affair. On the other hand, maintaining the secret, although protecting Alice's privacy, could put the unwitting husband at significant risk for contracting a life-limiting or life-ending disease. The worker may also worry about legal liability for actions or inaction in the case. In fact, either party who is disgruntled or damaged in the case could seek to hold the worker accountable: Alice for the breach of privacy, or the husband for negligence in failing to protect him from harm.

Several provisions in the NASW code of ethics (1999) speak to this dilemma:

Social workers should protect the confidentiality of all information obtained in the course of professional service, except for compelling professional reasons. The general expectation that social workers will keep information confidential does not apply when disclosure is necessary to prevent serious, foreseeable, and imminent harm to a client or other identifiable person or when laws or regulations require disclosure without a client's consent. In all instances, social workers should disclose the least amount of confidential information necessary to achieve the desired purpose; only information that is directly relevant to the purpose for which the disclosure is made should be revealed (1.07c).

Social workers should inform clients, to the extent possible, about the disclosure of confidential information and the potential consequences, when feasible before the disclosure is made. This applies whether social workers disclose confidential information on the basis of a legal requirement or client consent (1.07d).

Social workers should discuss with clients and other interested parties the nature of confidentiality and limitations of clients' right to confidentiality. Social workers should review with clients circumstances where confidential information may be requested and where disclosure of confidential information may be legally required. This discussion should occur as soon as possible in the social worker-client relationship and as needed throughout the course of the relationship (1.07e).

Imbedded in these provisions are important ethical concepts—the respect for client self-determination, the importance of informed consent, and the significance of discretion around private information. It would be helpful to know how the social worker handled informed consent with Alice at the outset of services. Did Alice understand the worker's responsibilities should she prove to be a danger to herself or someone else? If so, the question of notifying her husband should not come as a surprise or betrayal, but rather a natural consequence based on the conditions of service and the established limits of confidentiality.

Beyond ethical standards, social workers must be familiar with the laws, regulations, and policies that apply in their jurisdictions and practice settings. The disclosure of HIV+ status is one example where laws and policies vary widely across states. Some states explicitly shield health professionals from liability for making disclosures to protect the health of another, as long as they do so following established procedures. Other states view partner notification as a public health responsibility and require professionals to alert health departments in cases such as Alice's, so that health authorities can undertake necessary disclosures. Preferably, the agency where Alice sought services was already apprised of the laws and incorporated them into policies, and if necessary, informed consent procedures for all clients prior to the outset of service.

Supervisory guidance is essential in this case. Alice's social worker needs help thinking through the implications (for Alice, her husband, the worker, the helping relationship, and the agency). The worker should use supervision to help identify her alternatives of action and the various pros and cons involved, anticipate reactions and prepare to address them, and think through ways to improve her practices in the future. Beyond talking with her supervisor, the worker may get specific consultation from legal and medical experts to address particular questions about her choices, her legal liability, or best practices in working with clients with infectious diseases. In these conversations, the worker should protect the identity of her client, focusing on the issues that gave rise to her dilemma rather than details of the client's case.

As a result of these discussions, the social worker may identify at least five options that can be employed singly or in combination:

- *Honor Alice's wishes and keep the secret.*
- *Work with Alice to institute safe sex practices to limit her husband's exposure to her disease.*
- *Encourage Alice to tell her husband about her HIV+ status by educating her about the implications of her silence.*
- *Offer Alice the chance to tell her husband and let her know that if she does not, the social worker will.*
- *Make an anonymous report to the public health authorities about the risk to Alice's husband.*

Regardless of what option the worker pursues, she should make sure that Alice understands the nature of her disease, is getting proper care, and is taking precautionary steps to protect others from contracting HIV. This is congruent with the ethics of putting the client's needs first, and has the pragmatic effect of mitigating damage resulting from Alice's secrecy about her illness.

The question, however, remains: to tell or not to tell? The options that ultimately involve alerting Alice's husband will protect his health and well-being, clearly an advantage of these choices. These options comply with ethical standards, principles, and policies that require social workers to protect others from significant, foreseeable harm. Alerting the husband will probably make the worker feel more comfortable if she is worried about her complicity and her liability should she keep Alice's secret and he contracts AIDS as a result.

The downsides of telling include violating Alice's expressed desire for privacy, rupturing the trust that is central to the helping relationship, and possibly putting Alice's marriage at risk if the secret of her affair is revealed. Alice may make good on a threat to file a regulatory board complaint or lawsuit against the worker or agency for breach of confidentiality. The options in which the worker encourages Alice to tell may take time to employ, but they have the advantage of empowering her to take control of the situation and face her dilemma head on. Her ability to rely on the worker is essential in this process. The worker can help her look at the long-term effects of deception, in contrast to the short-term effects of revealing her condition and how she contracted HIV. The worker can help Alice anticipate and plan for that very difficult conversation with her husband and family and can be a support to her after the fact, whatever the husband's reactions are. All of the advantages of working *with* the client on this challenging problem are lost if the worker decides to abruptly override Alice's wishes and notify the husband.

Honoring Alice's demands for secrecy without considering the husband's needs and interests fits with the principle of client self-determination, but may be at odds with laws and policies about protecting the safety of others and Alice's own best interests. Social workers must often navigate between clients' wishes and the steps needed to adequately address their problems. Alice's desire to avoid telling her husband in the short run will not spare anyone pain or harm in the long run. In fact, her insistence on silence now may keep her stuck while her health and family relationships suffer. The worker who can empathize with her and help her forthrightly address her fears and problems will be carrying out both ethical responsibilities and professional responsibilities. Should this process fail, the worker may resort to notification against Alice's will. Given the greater expertise and experience of public health authorities in the area of notifications, the worker should probably refer the case to them for assistance.

Self-awareness and self-evaluation are important elements of competent, ethical professional practice. Throughout this process, Alice's social worker should examine her own motivations, decisions, and actions. Supervision is also an important element in self-evaluation. An adept and involved supervisor can help the worker identify strengths and weaknesses in the decision-making process, positive and problematic outcomes, and areas for improvement and skill development. Did the decision adequately resolve the dilemma? If it created unplanned or problematic results, what can be done to remedy them? For example, if the worker's efforts to get Alice to inform her husband of her illness results in Alice's withdrawal from treatment, evaluation will help the worker to determine next steps as well as assess her past actions.

Summary

This chapter introduced the ethics and values that support the social work profession. It provided guidelines for supporting self-determination, respecting confidentiality, obtaining informed consent, maintaining boundaries, and resolving ethical dilemmas. The chapter suggested steps to aid in resolving ethical dilemmas and it applied these steps to a case in which self-determination and client confidentiality conflicted with another's safety. In Chapter 5, we will move toward putting these professional values into action as you learn beginning skills for effective communication with and on behalf of clients.

Related Online Content

Visit the *Direct Social Work Practice* companion Web site at *www.cengage.com/social_work/hepworth* for additional learning tools such as glossary terms, chapter outlines, relevant Web links, and chapter practice quizzes.

Skill Development Exercises in Managing Ethical Dilemmas

The following exercises will give you practice in applying ethics concepts and ethical decision making to specific practice situations. These situations include some of the most difficult ones that we and our colleagues have encountered in practice. Note that the appropriate response or course of action is rarely cut and dried. After reading each situation, consider the following questions:

1. What conflicting principles and feelings are in play in the case?
2. What are the pros and cons of the various courses of action?
3. What guidelines are applicable in resolving this dilemma?
4. What resources could you consult to help you decide on an ethical course of action?

Situation 1 A male client confided in an individual marital therapy session several weeks ago that he is gay, although his wife does not know it. The client's wife, whom you have also seen conjointly with him, calls you today troubled over the lack of progress in solving marital problems and asks you point-blank whether you think her husband could be gay.

Situation 2 You are forming a youth group in a state correctional facility. From past experience, you know that youths sometimes make references in the group to previous offenses that they have committed without being apprehended. You also know that they may talk about plans to escape from the institution or about indiscretions or misdemeanors they (or others) may have committed or plan to commit within the institution, such as smoking marijuana or stealing institutional supplies or property from peers or staff. Are you required to share all of the information you learn in the group? How can you encourage trust and sharing if there are limits to confidentiality?

Situation 3 In conducting an intake interview with a client in a family agency, you observe that both of her young children are withdrawn. One of the children is also badly bruised; the other, an infant, appears malnourished. Throughout the interview, the client seems defensive and suspicious and appears ambivalent about having come for the interview. At one point, she states that she feels overwhelmed with her parenting responsibilities and is having difficulty in coping with her children. She also alludes to her fear that she may hurt them but then abruptly changes the subject. As you encourage her to return to the discussion of her problems with the children, your client says that she has changed her mind about wanting help, takes her children in hand, and hastily leaves the office.

Situation 4 You have seen a husband and wife and their adolescent daughter twice regarding relationship problems between the parents and the girl. The parents are both extremely negative and blaming in their attitudes toward their daughter, stating that their troubles would disappear if she would just "shape up." Today, during an individual interview with the girl, she breaks into tears and tells you that she is pregnant and plans to "go somewhere" with her boyfriend this weekend to get an abortion. She pleads with you not to tell her parents; she feels they would be extremely angry if they knew.

Situation 5 In a mental health agency, you have been working with a male client who has a history, when angered, of becoming violent and physically abusive. He has been under extreme psychological pressure lately because of problems relating to a recent separation from his wife. In an interview today, he is extremely angry, clenching his fists as he tells you that he has heard that his wife has initiated divorce proceedings and plans to move to another state. "If this is true," he loudly protests, "she is doing it to take the kids away from me, and I'll kill her rather than let her do that."

Situation 6 Some of your clients in your private practice rely on their health insurance to pay for their counseling. One client is addressing sensitive issues and is very concerned about anyone else knowing about his situation, especially his employer. Recent experiences have increased the severity of his condition, and you must share this development with the care manager at the insurance company to get further treatment sessions approved. You have concerns about sharing the information with his insurer, especially via its voice mail system. The insurance company representative replies that this practice is organizational policy and, if you cannot abide by it, you are unlikely to get approval for continuing treatment and unlikely to receive further referrals from the insurer.

Situation 7 You and your spouse are advertising for a housekeeper to clean your home once a week. One of the applicants is a former client. In her letter she states that she needs the work very badly and hopes you won't discriminate against her just because she saw you for service in the past.

Situation 8 You are a social work student beginning your first field placement. At orientation, your supervisor informs you that you should not tell clients that you are a student. She acknowledges that the school wants you to inform clients of your status as a social worker in training, but states that it is her opinion and agency policy that the clients not be told. She believes it undermines their confidence in the services they are getting and creates problems when the agency tries to collect fees for its services.

Situation 9 You are a social worker in a high school that has strict rules about student health and safety. Specifically, the rules state that you cannot tell students about contraceptives or safe sex practices, even if asked. Nor can you refer them to someone who is likely to tell them of such options. You are instructed to refer students with such problems or questions only to their parents or their family physician.

Skill Development Exercises in Operationalizing Cardinal Values

To assist you in developing skill in operationalizing the cardinal values in specific practice situations, we have provided a number of exercises with modeled responses. As you read each one, note which values are germane to the situation. To refresh your memory, the values are as follows:

1. Social workers value service to others and a commitment to social justice in helping clients get deserved and needed resources.
2. Social workers value the inherent dignity and worth of others.
3. Social workers value the primacy of human relationships.
4. Social workers behave with integrity.
5. Social workers are responsible for practicing with competence.

Next, assume you are the client's service provider and formulate a response that implements the relevant social work value. After completing each exercise, compare your response with the modeled response that follows the exercises. Bearing in mind that the modeled response is only one of many possible acceptable responses, analyze it and compare it with your own. Also, remember that tone is an essential component of effective, congruent communications. Imagine the modeled responses that follow spoken with different verbal and emotional tones: sensitivity, tentativeness, anger, impatience, pity, kindness, conceit. Which feel genuine to you? Which will help achieve your objectives with the client? Which are congruent with professional values of respect and support for client dignity? By carefully completing these exercises, you will improve your competence in putting values into action in the varied and challenging situations encountered in direct social work practice.

Client Statements

1. *Group member* [*in first group session*]: Before I really open up and talk about myself, I need to be sure what I say isn't blabbed around to other people. [*Turning to social worker.*] How can I be sure that won't happen?

2. *Adolescent in correctional institution* [*after social worker introduces self*]: So you want to help me, huh? I'll tell you how you can help. You can get me out of this damn place—that's how!

3. *Female client, age 21* [*to mental health practitioner*]: Yeah, I know that kicking the habit was a victory of sorts. But I look at my life and I wonder what's there to live for. I've turned my family against me. I've sold my body to more rotten guys than I can count—just to get a fix. I've had three STDs. What do I have to offer anyone? I feel like my life has been one big cesspool.

4. *Teenage male* [*in a group session in a correctional setting*]: [*Takes off shoes and sprawls in his chair. His feet give off a foul odor; other members hold noses and make derisive comments. He responds defensively.*] Hey, get off my back, you creeps. What's the big deal about taking off my shoes?

5. *Female* [*initial interview in family counseling center*]: Before I talk about my marital problems, I need to let you know I'm a Seventh Day Adventist. Do you know anything about my church? I'm asking because a lot of our marital problems involve my religion.

6. *Female client* [*sixth interview*]: Maybe it sounds crazy, but I've been thinking this last week that

you're not really interested in me as a person. I have the feeling I'm just someone for you to analyze or to write about.

7. *Teenage female* [*caught with contraband in her possession by a supervisor-counselor in a residential treatment center*]: Please don't report this, Mrs. Wilson. I've been doing better lately, and I've learned my lesson. You won't need to worry about me. I won't mess with drugs anymore.

8. *Client* [*observing social worker taking notes during initial interview*]: I'm dying to know what you're writing down about me. Maybe you think I'm a nut. Can I take a copy of your notes with me when we're done?

9. *Male parolee, age 27, who has a reputation as a con artist* [*in a mandatory weekly visit to his parole officer*]: Man, you've really got it made. Your office is really fine. But then you deserve what you've got. You've probably got a terrific wife and kids, too. Is that their picture over there?

10. *Female client, age 34* [*in third interview*]: I'm really uptight right now. I've got this tight feeling I get in my chest when I'm nervous. [*Pause.*] Well, I guess I'll have to tell you if I expect to get anything out of this. [*Hesitant.*] You know the marital problems we've talked about? Well, Jack doesn't know this, but I'm attracted to other women. [*Blushes.*] I've tried—I've really tried, but Jack doesn't turn me on. I can't even tolerate sex unless I'm thinking about other women. Jack thinks something's wrong with him, but it's not his fault. [*Chin quivers.*]

11. *Black male probationer* [*to white therapist*]: You're so damn smug. You say you want to help me, but I don't buy that crap. You don't know the first thing about black people. Man, I grew up where it's an accomplishment just to survive. What do you know about life in my world?

Modeled Responses

1. "Ginny raises a good point that concerns all of you. So that you can feel more comfortable about sharing personal feelings and experiences with the group, we need an understanding that each of you will keep what is shared in the strictest confidence. I can assure you that I'll keep information confidential myself, but I am interested in hearing from the rest of you regarding the question that Ginny is asking."

2. "I guess that's what I'd want if I were in your situation. As a matter of fact, that's what I want for you,

too. But we both know the review board won't release you until they feel you're prepared to make it on the outside. I can't get you out, but with your cooperation I can help you to make changes that will get you ready for release."

3. "I can hear that you're down on yourself. Even though you've done a lot that you feel bad about, I'm impressed at what it's taken to get and stay clean. That's a giant step in the right direction. How can we keep your misgivings about the past from sabotaging the path you're on now?"

4. "I think we need to look as a group at how we can give Jim some helpful feedback rather than making fun of him. Let's talk about what just happened. Maybe you could begin, Jim, by sharing with the group what you're feeling just now."

5. "I have to confess I know only a little bit about your religion, which may make you wonder if I can appreciate your problems. I can assure you I'll do my best to understand if you're willing to help me with that. The most important thing, though, is your comfort about it. How do you feel about sharing your problems with me under these circumstances?"

6. "That sounds like a painful feeling—that I'm not personally concerned with you as an individual. I'd like to explore that with you further because that's not at all how I feel about you. Let's talk a bit about how I've come across to you and how you've reached that conclusion?"

7. "I'm sorry you're still involved with drugs, Joy, because of the difficulties it's caused you. I don't like to see you get into trouble but I have no choice. I have to report this. If I didn't, I'd be breaking a rule myself by not reporting you. That wouldn't help you in the long run. Frankly, I'm going to keep worrying about you until I'm satisfied you're really sticking to the rules."

8. [*Chuckling.*] "It's not nutty at all to wonder what I'm thinking and writing. I'm writing down what we talk about. What you tell me is important, and notes help to refresh my memory. You're welcome to look at them if you like. Actually, I would be interested in hearing a little more about your concerns regarding what I might think of you."

9. "As a matter of fact it is, and I think they're pretty terrific. But we're here to talk about you, Rex. I'd like to hear how your job interview went."

10. "Keeping this secret has been very painful for you. I gather you've been afraid I'd condemn you, but I'm pleased you brought it up so that we can work on it together. It took some real courage on your part, and I respect you for that."

11. "I'd be phony if I said I understood all about being black and living in your neighborhood… and I'm sorry if it seems I'm being smug. I am interested in you, and I'd like to understand more about your life."

Notes

1. After goals have been mutually identified and roles in helping the relationship clarified, practitioners need not hesitate to offer advice, because their expertise and input will give impetus and direction to the change efforts. Our point is that giving advice should not be the primary means of assisting clients.

2. Privileged communication is a legal right that protectsclients from having a confidence revealed publicly from the witness stand during legal proceedings. Statutes that recognize privileged communication exempt certain professions from being legally compelled to reveal content disclosed in the context of a confidential relationship.

PART 2
Exploring, Assessing, and Planning

5 Building Blocks of Communication: Communicating with Empathy and Authenticity

6 Verbal Following, Exploring, and Focusing Skills

7 Eliminating Counterproductive Communication Patterns

8 Assessment: Exploring and Understanding Problems and Strengths

9 Assessment: Intrapersonal and Environmental Factors

10 Assessing Family Functioning in Diverse Family and Cultural Contexts

11 Forming and Assessing Social Work Groups

12 Negotiating Goals and Formulating a Contract

Part 2 of this book deals with processes and skills involved in the first phase of the helping process. These processes and skills are also demonstrated in video clips on the CD-ROM accompanying this book. Chapter 5 begins this exploration by setting the context and developing skills for building effective working relationships with clients, one of the two major objectives of initial interviews. Chapter 6 shifts the focus to skills required to accomplish the second major objective: to thoroughly explore clients' difficulties.

Chapter 7 identifies verbal and nonverbal patterns of communication that impede the development of effective working relationships.

Chapters 8 and 9 focus specifically on the process of assessment. Chapter 8 deals with explaining the process, sources of information, delineation of clients' problems, and questions to be addressed during the process. Chapter 9 highlights the many dimensions of ecological assessment, delineating the intrapersonal, interpersonal, cultural, and environmental systems and noting how they reciprocally interact to produce and maintain problems.

Chapter 10 narrows the focus to family systems. It discusses various types of family structures and considers the dimensions of family systems that must be addressed in assessing family functioning, including the cultural context of families.

In Chapter 11, the focus changes to groups. Here the discussion hones in on purposes of groups, selection of group members, arrangements to be made, and ways to begin group process. It then points out various factors to be considered in assessing the functioning of groups.

Part 2 concludes with Chapter 12, which deals with negotiating goals and contracts with both voluntary and involuntary clients. Included in this chapter are theory, skills, and guidelines that address these processes, which lay the foundation for the process of goal attainment.

CHAPTER 5

Building Blocks of Communication: Communicating with Empathy and Authenticity

CHAPTER OVERVIEW

Common factors associated with the worker–client relationship and the therapeutic alliance account for a substantial amount of the improvement, perhaps 70%, of the success of interventions from varied theoretical perspectives (Wampold, 2001, p. 207; Lambert & Ogles, 2004; Drisko, 2004; Norcross & Lambert, 2006). Research on treatment outcomes describes four factors as accounting for much of the improvement in clients: client or extra-therapeutic factors (40%); relationship factors (30%); placebo, hope, and expectancy factors (15%); and model/technique factors (15%) (Duncan & Miller, 2000; Hubble, Duncan, & Miller, 1999; Adams et al., 2008). Consequently, nearly half of the outcome relies on fundamental skills and abilities that social workers need to learn, apart from the type of treatment offered.

The development of social work relationships occurs in a context. Chapter 5 explores how you can develop micro direct practice skills and apply them in a context to help your clients. Interviews follow a structure that reflects predictable elements of contact between a potential client, a social worker, and the setting that the social worker represents. In other words, interviews have beginnings that focus on settling into roles, reviewing legal and ethical limits and boundaries, and attempting to establish rapport. From this point, the social worker engages the client in assessing what has brought the client into contact with the setting or agency. Based on this joint exploration, the social worker and the client then discuss creating a contract or agreement about what they will attempt to do together to address the client's concerns and developing goals to guide the social worker's practice in the case. If contact will last beyond one session, the session ends with the development of tasks or concrete plans about what the social worker and the client will do prior to the next session to advance their common work. This interview structure is held together with practice skills that are designed to help the social worker connect with clients by communicating empathically, assertively, and authentically.

Roles of the Participants

Clients often have little understanding of the helping process and may have expectations that differ from those of the social worker. Unfortunately, these discrepant expectations may impair the helping process. The findings of two classic research studies (Aronson & Overall, 1966; Mayer & Timms, 1969) revealed that unacknowledged discrepancies in expectations produced dissatisfactions and higher rates of discontinuance from therapy of lower-class clients as compared with middle-class clients. The potency of using a "role induction interview" to increase the likelihood that clients will continue contact with the social worker beyond the initial interview was demonstrated by Hoehn-Saric and colleagues (1964). In their study, clients prepared by role induction continued contact at a higher rate and fared better in treatment than control clients who received no special preparation. Kooden (1994) has described how a gay male therapist can serve as a model for socialization of gay adolescents through self-disclosure. Finally, texts on work with involuntary clients emphasize the importance of clarifying the practitioner's and client's roles in developing a working relationship (Rooney, 2009; Trotter, 2006).

The following guidelines will assist you to achieve similar positive results in role clarification.

1. *Determine your clients' expectations.* The varied expectations that clients bring to initial sessions include lectures, magical solutions, advice giving, changing other family members, and so on. With clients who are members of ethnic minority groups and inexperienced with professional helping relationships, sensitively exploring expectations and modifying the social worker's role when necessary are critical.

Clients sometimes explicitly state their expectations without prompting from a social worker. For example, after reciting the difficulties created by her son, a mother declared, "We were hoping you could talk with him and help him understand how much he is hurting us." Notice that the mother's "hope" involved a request for specific action by the social worker. When clients express their expectations spontaneously in this way, you have the opportunity to deal with unrealistic goals. Frequently, however, clients do not openly express their expectations, and you will need to elicit them. It is important not to probe too far into expectations until you have established rapport, however, because the client's request often turns out to be a most intimate revelation.

For this reason, seeking disclosure too soon may put a client on the defensive. The social worker should therefore try to weave exploration of the client's expectations into the natural flow of the session sometime after the client has had ample opportunity to report his or her difficulties and to discern the sensitive understanding and goodwill of the social worker.

If voluntary clients have not spontaneously revealed their requests and the timing appears right, you can elicit their requests by asking a question similar to one of the following:

- *"How do you hope (or wish) I (or the agency) can assist (or help) you?"*
- *"When you thought about coming here, what were your ideas about the kind of help you wanted?"*

For potential clients who were referred or mandated to receive service, practitioners often find it necessary to describe the parameters of what accepting an offer of service might entail since potential clients did not seek the service.

For example, in the video "Getting Back to Shakopee" connected to this chapter, Dorothy, a practitioner in a private child and family service agency, finds that Valerie, a Native American client referred by her employer for job performance issues, has many concerns about confidentiality that need to be addressed before she will consider whether she will accept an offer of service. In many cases it can be useful in such circumstances to elicit client concerns in the following way:

- *"We have explored the reasons why you were referred/required to seek our service. But I would like to know what you hope to gain from this process."*

2. *Briefly explain the nature of the helping process, and define the client–social worker relationship as partners seeking a solution to the client's difficulties.* Clients often hope that social workers will give them advice that they can implement immediately, thereby quickly remedying their problems. They will give up these unrealistic expectations with less disappointment in favor of a more realistic understanding if you clarify how you can actually be of help and why it would be less useful to approach their problems with this kind of "magic potion" strategy. It is very important to convey your intention to help clients find the best possible solution and to clarify that offering advice prematurely would likely be a disservice to them. In the absence of such an explanation, clients may erroneously conclude that you are unwilling to meet their expectations because you are not concerned about them. Indeed, Mayer and Timms (1969) found that clients who were dissatisfied with the service they received for interpersonal problems reasoned that the counselor's failure to give concrete advice stemmed from a lack of interest and desire to help. Taking the time to explore expectations and to clarify how you can help thus prevents clients from drawing unwarranted negative conclusions that may result in premature discontinuance of the contact.

Note that we are not arguing against the value of giving advice to clients. Rather, our point is that to be effective, advice must be based on adequate knowledge of the dynamics of a problem and of the participants in it. This level of understanding is unlikely to be achieved in an initial session.

You can assist many clients to modify their unrealistic expectations and clarify your respective roles by delivering a message similar to the following:

- *"I can sense the urgency you feel in wanting to solve your problems. I wish I could give advice that would lead to an easy solution. You've probably already had plenty of advice, because most people offer advice freely. It has been my experience, though, that what works for one person (couple or family) may not work at all for another."*
- *"As I see it, our task is to work together in considering a number of options so that you can decide which solution best fits you and your situation. In the long run, that's what will work best for you. But finding the right solution takes some time and a lot of thought."*

The preceding role clarification embodies the following essential elements mentioned earlier: (1) acknowledging and empathizing with the client's unrealistic expectation and sense of urgency; (2) expressing the social worker's helpful intent; (3) explaining why the client's unrealistic expectation cannot be fulfilled; and (4) as part of the social worker's expertise, clarifying the helping process and defining a working partnership that places responsibility on the client for actively participating and ultimately making choices as to the courses of action to be taken.

When couples seek help for relationship problems, they commonly view the partner as the source of difficulties and have the unrealistic expectation that the couples counselor will influence the partner to shape up. Because this expectation is so pervasive, we often elicit partners' expectations early in the initial session (individual or conjoint) and clarify the social worker's helping role, thereby setting the stage for more productive use of the exploration to follow. Clarifying the helping process early in the session tends to diminish the partners' tendency toward mutual blaming and competition. Moreover, partners are less likely to respond defensively when the social worker refuses to be drawn into the "blame game" and focuses instead on assisting each person to become aware of his or her part in the difficulties.

> The following excerpt of the session labeled "Home for the Holidays" on your CD-ROM demonstrates how the practitioner can establish ground rules.
>
> *Social worker*: Let me suggest some ground rules for how couples sessions may be useful to you. I want this to be a safe place, so anything said here will be private unless something is shared that would seriously harm someone else, such as possible suicide or transmission of AIDS. I won't take sides in your concerns but will act more like a referee to help you express your concerns.

Implied in the preceding excerpt is another aspect of the client's role—to be open in sharing feelings, thoughts, and events. By explaining the rationale for openness and by expressing your intent to communicate openly, you enhance clients' receptiveness to this factor. To focus on this aspect of the client's role, consider making the following points:

Social worker: For you to receive the greatest benefit, you need to be as open as possible with me. That means not holding back troubling feelings, thoughts, or events that are important. I can understand you and your difficulties only if you're open and honest with me. Only you know what you think and feel; I can know only as much as you share with me.

Sometimes it's painful to share certain thoughts and feelings, but often those are the very feelings that trouble us the most. If you do hold back, remind yourself that you may be letting yourself down. If you're finding it difficult to share certain things, let me know. Discussing what's happening inside you—why it's difficult—may make it easier to discuss those painful things.

I'll be open and honest with you, too. If you have any questions or would like to know more about me, please ask. I'll be frank with you. I may not answer every question, but I'll explain why if I don't.

To enhance clients' participation in the helping process, it is also important to emphasize that they can accelerate their progress by working on their difficulties between appointments. Some clients mistakenly believe that change will result largely from what occurs in sessions. In actuality, the content of sessions is far less significant than how clients apply the information gained from them. The following message clarifies this aspect of a client's responsibility:

Social worker: We'll want to make progress toward your goals as rapidly as possible. One way you can accelerate your progress is by working hard between our sessions. That means carrying out tasks you've agreed to, applying what we talk about in your daily life, and making mental notes or actually writing down thoughts, feelings, and events that relate to your problems so we can consider them in your next session. Actually, what you do between sessions is more important in accomplishing your goals than the session itself. We'll be together only a brief time each week. The rest of the week you have opportunities to apply what we talk about and plan together.

Yet another aspect of the client's role involves keeping appointments. This factor is obvious, but discussing it emphasizes clients' responsibilities and prepares them to cope constructively with obstacles that may cause them to fail or to cancel appointments. The following message clarifies this aspect of the client's role:

Social worker: As we work together, it will be critical for you to keep your appointments. Unforeseen things such as illness happen occasionally, of course, and we can change appointments if such problems arise. At other times, however, you may find yourself feeling discouraged or doubting whether coming here really helps. You may also feel upset over something I've said or done and find yourself not wanting to see me. I won't knowingly say or do anything to offend you, but you may have some troubling feelings toward me anyway. The important thing is that you not miss your appointment, because when you're discouraged or upset we need to talk about it. I know that may not be easy, but it will help you to work out your problematic feelings. If you miss your appointment, you may find it even harder to return.

For example, conversely, when clients are referred, practitioners should not assume that potential clients plan to return for another session. For example, the practitioner, Dorothy, in the "Getting Back to Shakopee" video, suggests near the end of the session:

"If you decide to come back for another session, next time we would break down all of the concerns you are facing and try to address them one at a time, starting with the ones you consider most important."

A final task for the social worker is to emphasize that difficulties are inherent in the process of making changes. Clarifying this reality further prepares clients for the mixed feelings that they will inevitably experience. When these difficulties are highlighted early in the helping process, clients can conceive of such feelings and experiences as natural obstacles that must be surmounted, rather than yield to them or feel defeated. An explanation about these predictable difficulties similar to the following clarifies the vicissitudes of the change process:

Social worker: We've talked about goals you want to achieve. Accomplishing them won't be easy. Making changes is seldom possible without a difficult and sometimes painful struggle. People usually have ups and downs as they seek to make changes. If you understand this, you won't become so discouraged and feel like throwing in the towel. I don't mean to paint a grim picture. In fact, I feel very upbeat about the prospects of your attaining your goals. At the same time, it won't be easy, and I don't want to mislead you. The important thing is that you share your feelings so that we can keep on top of them.

Over the years, numerous clients have reported retrospectively that they appreciated receiving these kinds of explanations during the initial session. When the going became rough and they began to waver in pursuing their goals, they recalled that such discouragement was natural and, rather than discontinuing the contact, mustered up the determination to persevere.

In addition to clarifying the client's role, it is vital to clarify your own role. Stress that you will be a partner in helping clients to understand their difficulties more fully. Because you have an outside vantage point, you may be able to help them see their difficulties from a new perspective and to consider solutions that they may have overlooked. We recommend that you clarify further that, although you will be an active partner in considering possible remedial actions, the final decisions rest with the clients themselves. You will help them to weigh alternatives, but your desire is to see clients develop their strengths and exercise their capacities for independent action to the fullest extent possible. In addition, emphasize that you plan to assist clients in focusing on their strengths and any incremental growth they achieve. Stress that although you will actively perform this function in the initial stage of the helping process, at the same time you will be encouraging your clients to learn to recognize their own strengths and grow independently.

In the "Serving the Squeaky Wheel" video linked to this chapter, the social worker, Ron Rooney, is replacing another social worker who has been abruptly transferred. The client, Molly, has a serious and persistent mental illness. Much of the session is devoted to beginning to develop trust that has been jeopardized by the loss of the previous worker. Such circumstances are not preferable, but occur frequently enough that it is important to have models for dealing with it. The social worker describes his role as helping Molly make a plan in which she will be supported to live safely in a community of her choosing.

Another aspect of the helping role that you should clarify for clients is your intention to assist them in anticipating obstacles they will encounter in striving to attain their goals and your willingness to help them formulate strategies to surmount these obstacles. Clarifying this facet of your role further reinforces the reality that change is difficult but you will be with and behind your clients at all times, offering support and direction. You might share that each family faces its own unique situation and has its own set of values, noting that it will be your job to get to know these values and situations from the clients' point of view. Only then will you attempt to help the clients plan what makes sense for them to do.

Some special hurdles must be overcome to develop productive working relationships between social workers and potential clients in mandated settings, because the mandated client did not seek the contact and often perceives it as being contrary to his or her interests. In the following dialogue, notice how the social worker begins to develop expectations about a collaborative relationship.

Client: I didn't like the earlier workers because they came into my house telling me what I can and can't do. One thing I don't like is someone telling me what I can do with my kids and what I can't.

Social worker: It sounds like you had a negative experience with earlier workers.

Client: Yeah, I did. I did not like it at all because they were telling me what I should do.

Social worker: I'm going to take a different approach with you because I don't feel that I know it all; you know best about the situation occurring in your own family and in your own life. I will want you to tell me about the problems you are concerned about and how we can best resolve those together.

Client: Okay.

Social worker: My job will be to develop a case plan with you. I won't be the one to say, "This is what you need to do." I want you to have input in that decision and to say, "Well, I feel I can do this." I will be willing to share ideas with you as we decide what to work on and how to do it. I will need to include any court-mandated requirements, such as our need to be meeting together, in the agreement. However, I want you to have a lot of say in determining what we work on and how.

The social worker interprets the client's comment about previous workers as pertinent to exploring what their own working relationship might be like. She describes her own role and clarifies what the client can do in a clear and tangible way to work on goals important to her.

Communicating about Informed Consent, Confidentiality, and Agency Policies

The encounter between the social worker and the client exists within a context of limits and possibilities and rights. In this regard, the social worker must share the rights and limits to communication discussed in Chapter 4: discuss confidentiality and its limits, obtain informed consent, and share agency policies and legal

limits. Consider how the social worker in the preceding example might approach this task:

Social worker: What you say to me is private in most circumstances. I will share what we have discussed with my supervisor. In certain circumstances, however, I might have to share what we have discussed with others. For example, if you threatened to seriously harm another person, I would have a duty to warn that would mean that I could not keep that information private. For example, if your children were in danger, I am a mandated reporter and I would have to share that information. Similarly, if you were to seriously consider harming yourself, I would have to share that information. If a judge were to subpoena my records, he or she could gain access to a general summary of what we have done together. Do you have any questions about this?

It is important that this section of the initial interview be presented in language that the client readily understands so that the discussion embodies the spirit of informed consent. The exact content of this discussion will vary with the setting in which you work. It is important that you carry out this duty in a genuine fashion, rather than presenting it as a ritualistic sharing of written forms that has the appearance of obtaining informed consent but ignores its intent. In hurried agency practice, sometimes this principle is violated. Discuss with your supervisor what information needs to be shared with clients and how that is done in ways that are useful to those clients.

> In the video "Getting Back to Shakopee" linked to this chapter, the practitioner, Dorothy, and her Native American client, Valerie, discuss limits to confidentiality for the first several minutes of the video. Valerie is concerned about what material from the session will get back to the supervisor who referred her for service. In addition, she has concerns about Dorothy's mandated reporter responsibilities related to child welfare because her teen-aged daughter supervises younger children in the summer. This video demonstrates how issues are not pro forma with clients who are referred by others in less than voluntary circumstances.

Facilitative Conditions

The social worker uses communication skills as building blocks to help develop a productive working relationship with clients. This chapter focuses on two of the three skills embodied in what have been called the *facilitative conditions* or *core conditions* in helping relationships. These conditions or skills were originally denoted by Carl Rogers (1957) as *empathy, unconditional positive regard*, and *congruence*. Other terms have since evolved, and we shall refer to the conditions as *empathy, respect* or *nonpossessive warmth*, and *authenticity* or *genuineness*. Because we addressed nonpossessive warmth or respect at length in Chapter 4, we limit our focus here to empathy and authenticity.

Research (primarily in psychology) has documented that these three facilitative conditions are associated with positive outcomes. One study by a social worker (Nugent, 1992) further found that these conditions were effective in facilitating positive helping relationships. For these reasons, it is vital that social workers master these skills. While they are particularly useful in treatment situations with voluntary clients, we will also describe ways that the facilitative conditions can serve as building blocks in both involuntary relationships and other situations such as discharge planning that do not have therapy as the primary focus (Bennett, Legon, & Zilberfein, 1989).

Empathic Communication

Empathic communication involves the ability of the social worker to perceive accurately and sensitively the inner feelings of the client and to communicate his or her understanding of these feelings in language attuned to the client's experiencing of the moment. The first dimension of empathy, empathic recognition, is a precondition of the second dimension, demonstrating through accurate reflection of feelings that the social worker comprehends the client's inner experiencing.

Empathic communication plays a vital role in nurturing and sustaining the helping relationship and in providing the vehicle through which the social worker becomes emotionally significant and influential in the client's life. In mandated circumstances in which involuntary clients are not seeking a helping relationship, conveying empathic understanding reduces the level of threat perceived by the client and mitigates his or her defensiveness, conveys interest and helpful intent, and creates an atmosphere conducive to behavior change. In addition, many clients live in environments that constrict resources and opportunities. Social worker empathy with the social and economic context of problems is an important adjunct to empathy with personal experiencing (Keefe, 1978).

In responding to clients' feelings, social workers must avoid being misled by the conventional facades used to conceal emotions. As a consequence, the empathic communicator responds to the feelings that underlie such flippant messages as "Oh, no, it doesn't really matter" or "I don't care what he does!" These messages often mask disappointment or hurt, as do messages such as "I don't need anyone" when the client is experiencing painful loneliness, or "I don't let anyone hurt me" when the client is finding rejection hard to bear. To enter the client's private world of practical experience, the social worker must also avoid making personal interpretations and judgments of the client's private logic and feelings that, in superficial contacts, might appear weak, foolish, or undesirable.

Being empathically attuned involves not only grasping the client's immediately evident feelings, but also, in a mutually shared, exploratory process, identifying the client's underlying emotions and discovering the meaning and personal significance of the client's feelings and behavior. In getting in touch with these camouflaged feelings and meanings, the social worker must tune in not only to verbal messages but also to more subtle cues, including facial expressions, tone of voice, tempo of speech, and postural cues and gestures that amplify and sometimes contradict verbal meanings. Such nonverbal cues as blushing, crying, pausing, stammering, changing voice intonation, clenching jaws or fists, pursing the lips, lowering the head, or shifting the posture often reveal the presence of distressing feelings and thoughts.

Empathic communication involves "stepping into the shoes of another," in the sense that the social worker attempts to perceive the client's world and experiences. When the client feels pressure from an involuntary referral, the empathic social worker understands and is aware of that pressure and how it feels. At the same time, the social worker must remain outside of the client's world and avoid being overwhelmed by his or her fears, anger, joys, and hurts, even as the social worker deeply senses the meaning and significance of these feelings for the client. "Being with" the client means that the social worker focuses intensely on the client's affective state without losing perspective or taking on the emotions experienced by the client.

A person who experiences feelings in common with another person and is similarly affected by whatever the other person is experiencing usually responds sympathetically rather than empathically. Sympathetic responding, which depends on achieving emotional and intellectual accord, involves supporting and condoning the other person's feelings (e.g., "I'd feel the same way if I were in your position" or "I think you're right"). In contrast, empathic responding involves understanding the other person's feelings and circumstances without taking that person's side (e.g., "I sense you're feeling ..." or "You seem to be saying ...").

When social workers support their clients' feelings, the clients may feel no need to examine their behavior or circumstances and may not engage in the process of self-exploration that is so vital to growth and change. Instead, clients tend to look to the social worker to change the behavior of other persons who play significant roles in their problems. Retaining separateness and objectivity thus is a critical dimension in the helping process. Clearly, when social workers assume their clients' feelings and positions, they lose not only the vital perspective that comes from being an outsider but also the ability to be helpful.

Of course, being empathic entails more than just recognizing clients' feelings. Social workers must also respond verbally and nonverbally in ways that affirm their understanding of clients' inner experiencing. It is not unusual for a person to experience empathic feelings for another individual without conveying those feelings in any way to the second party. Exhibiting high-level empathy requires skill in verbally and nonverbally demonstrating understanding. A common mistake made by social workers is to tell clients, "I understand how you feel." Rather than producing a sense of being understood, such a response often creates doubts in the client's mind about the social worker's perceptiveness, because any specific demonstration of understanding is lacking. Indeed, use of this response may mean that the social worker has not explored the client's feelings sufficiently to fully grasp the significance of the problematic situation.

To convey unmistakably the message, "I am with you; I understand," the social worker must respond empathically. Use of this skill creates an atmosphere of acceptance and understanding in which the client is more likely to risk sharing deeper and more personal feelings. Later in this chapter, we present theory and exercises for developing skill in empathic responding. Initially, we provide a list of affective words and phrases intended to expand your vocabulary so that you can meet the challenge of responding to the wide range of emotions experienced by clients. We also provide exercises to help you to refine your ability to perceive the feelings of others—a prerequisite to the mastery of empathic communication. To assist you to discern levels of empathy, we include a rating scale for empathic

responding, accompanied by examples of social worker responses and exercises. These exercises will help you to gain mastery of empathic communication at an effective working level.

Developing Perceptiveness to Feelings

Feelings or emotions exert a powerful influence on behavior and often play a central role in the problems of clients. Applicants or voluntary clients often enter into the helping relationship with openness and hope that they will explore both their concerns and their related feelings. Conversely, involuntary clients experience strong feelings but have not actively sought out a helping relationship for dealing with them (Cingolani, 1984). Hence, use of the skills sometimes takes a slightly different course with these clients, as one of the social worker's goals is to express empathy with the *situation* the involuntary client experiences and the feelings related to them.

To respond to the broad spectrum of emotions and feeling states presented by clients, the social worker must be fully aware of the diversity of human emotion. Further, the social worker needs a rich vocabulary of words and expressions that not only reflect clients' feelings accurately but also capture the intensity of those feelings. For example, dozens of descriptive feeling words may be used to express anger, including *furious, aggravated, vexed, provoked, put out, irritated*, and *impatient*—all of which express different shades and intensities of this feeling.

When used judiciously, such words serve to give sharp and exact focus to clients' feelings. Possessing and utilizing a rich vocabulary of affective words and phrases that accurately reflect these feelings is a skill that often is not developed by even experienced social workers. It is important to realize that high-level empathic responding takes place in two phases: (1) a thinking process and (2) a responding process. A deficient vocabulary for describing feelings limits social workers' ability to conceptualize and hence to reflect the full intensity and range of feelings experienced by clients.

It has been our experience that beginning social workers typically have a limited range of feeling words from which to draw in conveying empathy. Although literally hundreds of words may be used to capture feelings, learners often limit themselves to, and use to excess, a few terms, such as *upset* or *frustrated*, losing much of the richness of client messages in the process.

The accompanying lists illustrate the wide range of expressions available for social workers' use in responding to clients' feelings. Note, however, that using feeling words in a discriminating fashion is not merely important in empathic responding but is indispensable in relating authentically as well. Becoming a competent professional requires passing through a maturing process whereby social workers develop not only the capacity to deeply share the inner experiencing of others, but also a way to express their own personal feelings constructively.

Affective Words and Phrases

Competence/Strength

convinced you can	confident
sense of mastery	powerful
potent	courageous
resolute	determined
strong	influential
brave	impressive
forceful	inspired
successful	secure
in charge	in control
well equipped	committed
sense of accomplishment	daring
feeling one's oats	effective
sure	sense of conviction
trust in yourself	self-reliant
sharp	able
adequate	firm
capable	on top of it
can cope	important
up to it	ready
equal to it	skillful

Happiness/Satisfaction

elated	superb
ecstatic	on cloud nine
on top of the world	organized
fantastic	splendid
exhilarated	jubilant
terrific	euphoric
delighted	marvelous
excited	enthusiastic
thrilled	great
super	in high spirits
joyful	cheerful

Happiness/Satisfaction (continued)

elevated	happy
light-hearted	wonderful
glowing	jolly
neat	glad
fine	pleased
good	contented
hopeful	mellow
satisfied	gratified
fulfilled	tranquil
serene	calm
at ease	awesome

Caring/Love

adore	loving
infatuated	enamored
cherish	idolize
worship	attached to
devoted to	tenderness toward
affection for	hold dear
prize	caring
fond of	regard
respect	admire
concern for	taken with
turned on	trust
close	esteem
hit it off	value
warm toward	friendly
like	positive toward
accept	

Depression/Discouragement

anguished	in despair
dreadful	miserable
dejected	disheartened
rotten	awful
horrible	terrible
hopeless	gloomy
dismal	bleak
depressed	despondent
grieved	grim
brokenhearted	forlorn
distressed	downcast
sorrowful	demoralized
pessimistic	tearful
weepy	down in the dumps
deflated	blue

Depression/Discouragement (continued)

lost	melancholy
in the doldrums	lousy
kaput	unhappy
down	low
bad	blah
disappointed	sad
below par	

Inadequacy/Helplessness

utterly	worthless
good for nothing	washed up
powerless	helpless
impotent	crippled
inferior	emasculated
useless	finished
like a failure	impaired
inadequate	whipped
defeated	stupid
incompetent	puny
inept	clumsy
overwhelmed	ineffective
like a klutz	lacking
awkward	deficient
unable	incapable
small	insignificant
like a wimp	unimportant
over the hill	incomplete
immobilized	like a puppet
at the mercy of	inhibited
insecure	lacking confidence
unsure of self	uncertain
weak	inefficient
unfit	

Anxiety/Tension

terrified	frightened
intimidated	horrified
desperate	panicky
terror-stricken	paralyzed
frantic	stunned
shocked	threatened
afraid	scared
stage fright	dread
vulnerable	fearful
apprehensive	jumpy

Anxiety/Tension (continued)

shaky	distrustful
butterflies	awkward
defensive	uptight
tied in knots	rattled
tense	fidgety
jittery	on edge
nervous	anxious
unsure	hesitant
timid	shy
worried	uneasy
bashful	embarrassed
ill at ease	doubtful
uncomfortable	self-conscious
insecure	alarmed
restless	

Confusion/Troubledness

bewildered	puzzled
tormented by	baffled
perplexed	overwhelmed
trapped	confounded
in a dilemma	befuddled
in a quandary	at loose ends
going around in circles	mixed-up
disorganized	in a fog
troubled	adrift
lost	disconcerted
frustrated	floored
flustered	in a bind
torn	ambivalent
disturbed	conflicted
stumped	feeling pulled apart
mixed feelings about	uncertain
unsure	uncomfortable
bothered	uneasy
undecided	

Rejection/Offensive

crushed	destroyed
ruined	pained
wounded	devastated
tortured	cast off
betrayed	discarded
knifed in the back	hurt
belittled	abused
depreciated	criticized
censured	discredited

Rejection/Offensive (continued)

disparaged	laughed at
maligned	mistreated
ridiculed	devalued
scorned	mocked
scoffed at	used
exploited	debased
slammed	slandered
impugned	cheapened
mistreated	put down
slighted	neglected
overlooked	minimized
let down	disappointed
unappreciated	taken for granted
taken lightly	underestimated
degraded	discounted
shot down	

Anger/Resentment

furious	enraged
livid	seething
could chew nails	fighting mad
burned up	hateful
bitter	galled
vengeful	resentful
indignant	irritated
hostile	pissed off
have hackles up	had it with
upset with	bent out of shape
agitated	annoyed
got dander up	bristle
dismayed	uptight
disgusted	bugged
turned off	put out
miffed	ruffled
irked	perturbed
ticked off	teed off
chagrined	griped
cross	impatient
infuriated	violent

Loneliness

all alone in the universe	isolated
abandoned	totally alone
forsaken	forlorn
lonely	alienated
estranged	rejected

Loneliness (continued)

remote	alone
apart from others	shut out
left out	excluded
lonesome	distant
aloof	cut off

Guilt/Embarrassment

sick at heart	unforgivable
humiliated	disgraced
degraded	horrible
mortified	exposed
branded	could crawl in a hole
like two cents	ashamed
guilty	remorseful
crummy	really rotten
lost face	demeaned
foolish	ridiculous
silly	stupid
egg on face	regretful
wrong	embarrassed
at fault	in error
responsible for	goofed
lament	blew it

Use of the Lists of Affective Words and Phrases

The lists of affective words and phrases may be used with the exercises at the end of the chapter to formulate responses that capture the nature of feelings expressed by clients. Note that potential clients referred by others and involuntary clients may be more likely to initially experience the emotions of anger, resentment, guilt, embarrassment, rejection, confusion, tension, inadequacy, helplessness, depression, and discouragement. In Chapter 7, we will explore barriers to effective communication. One of those barriers can be the social worker's inability to achieve empathy with such involuntary clients, as the social worker may believe that they have brought on these negative feelings as a result of their own irresponsible actions. That is, some social workers feel that perhaps involuntary clients deserve these feelings because they have not fully accepted responsibility for their part in the difficulties they have experienced. As noted in Chapter 4, the social work value of acceptance of worth suggests that we can empathize with feelings of despair and powerlessness *even if* clients have not yet taken responsibility for the consequences of their actions.

In fact, involuntary and referred clients often express anger and frustration about even being in an introductory session with a social worker. You may note how this occurs in the video "Serving the Squeaky Wheel." Notice how the social worker attempts to reflect this anger and frustration and reframe it more constructively.

After you have initially responded to "feeling messages," check the lists to determine whether some other words and phrases might more accurately capture the client's feelings. Also, scan the lists to see whether the client's message involves feelings in addition to those you identified. The lists may similarly assist you in checking out the accuracy of your reflective responses as you review taped sessions.

The lists of affective words and phrases are offered here for the purpose of helping you communicate more empathically with your clients. However, words can have different connotations within the same language based on age, region, ethnic group, and social class. We suggest that you sit down with your coworkers and fellow students to compile your own more specialized list of feeling words for specific groups that you routinely encounter. For example, formulating a list of terms commonly used by adolescents in various socioeconomic and ethnic groupings could be useful. Issues may also arise when you try to use an unfamiliar slang vernacular, thus defeating the purpose of empathizing. However, making the effort to clarify words that accurately describe what the client is feeling often conveys your genuine interest.

Acquisition of a broader emotional vocabulary is a step toward expressing greater empathy for clients. It allows you to more effectively convey your understanding and compassion for what they are experiencing. Because many clients want to change their situations as well as their feelings about it, conveying empathy is the first step toward helping them work on those concerns.

Although the lists of affective words and phrases presented in this chapter are not exhaustive, they encompass many of the feelings and emotions frequently encountered in the helping process. Feeling words are subsumed under 11 categories, running the gamut of emotions from intense anguish and pain (e.g., *grieved, terrified, bewildered, enraged,* and *powerless*) to positive feeling states (e.g., *joy, elation, ecstasy, bliss,* and *pride in accomplishment*). Given our emphasis on clients' strengths, we have taken care to include a grouping of terms to assist social workers in capturing clients' feelings related to growth, strengths, and competence.

Feeling words in each category are roughly graduated by intensity, with words conveying strong intensity grouped toward the beginning of each category and words of moderate to mild intensity appearing toward the end. In responding to client messages, the social worker should choose feeling words that accurately match the intensity of the feelings the client is experiencing.

To illustrate, consider that you are working with an African American client in a drug aftercare program who has returned to work as a meter reader. He reports that when he knocked on the door in a largely white suburb intending to read the meter, the elderly white woman would not let him in, despite his wearing his picture identification name tag on his uniform: "I was so low down and depressed. What can you do? I am doing my thing to keep straight, and I can't even do my job because I'm black." Such a response appropriately calls for an intense response by the social worker: "Sounds like you felt demeaned and humiliated that you couldn't do your job because of this woman's fear of black people. You felt discriminated against, disrespected, yet you did not let these humiliating feelings carry you back to drug use—you kept your head on course, keeping straight, and not being stopped by other people's perceptions."

In addition to using words that accurately reflect the intensity of the client's feelings, it is important to respond with a tone of voice and nonverbal gestures and expressions that similarly reflect the intensity of feelings conveyed by the verbal response. The proper intensity of affect may also be conveyed by using appropriate qualifying words—for example, "You feel (somewhat) (quite) (very) (extremely) discouraged by your low performance on the entrance test."

Clients' messages may also contain multiple feelings. Consider the following client message: "I don't know what to do about my teenage daughter. I know that she's on drugs, but she shuts me out and won't talk to me. All she wants is to be out with her friends, to be left alone. There are times when I think she really dislikes me." Feeling words that would capture the various facets of this message include *confused, bewildered, alarmed, troubled, overwhelmed, lost, desperate, worried, frightened, alienated, rejected,* and *hurt.* A response that included all of these feeling words would be extremely lengthy and overwhelming to the client. However, a well-rounded empathic response should embody at least several of the surface feelings, such as *worried* and *confused*, and be delivered with appropriate timing. The social worker might also bring deeper-level feelings into focus, as explained in the following paragraphs.

Notice in the preceding client message that many feelings were implied but not explicitly stated. Some of these emotions would likely be just beyond the client's level of awareness but could easily be recognized if they were drawn to the client's attention. For example, the client might emphatically confirm a social worker response that sensitively identifies the hurt, rejection, and even anger inherent in the client's message. Without the social worker's assistance, the client might not develop full awareness of those deeper-level feelings.

In responding to client messages, you must be able to distinguish between readily apparent feelings and probable deeper feelings. In the early phase of the helping process, the social worker's objectives of developing a working relationship and creating a climate of understanding are best accomplished by using a reciprocal level of empathy—that is, by focusing on the client's immediately evident feelings. As the client perceives your genuine effort and commitment to understand his or her situation, that experience of being "empathically received" gradually yields a low-threat environment that obviates the need for self-protection.

Note that clients from oppressed groups, such as the African American client in the earlier example, may rightly feel better understood by the social worker yet continue to feel disillusioned by an alien environment. It is important to acknowledge those feelings about the environment. Cingolani (1984) writes of the "negotiated relationship" with such clients as a substitute for the "helping relationship." Even in negotiated relationships, however, increased trust is essential. That trust may be gained by actions taken outside the session that indicate that the social worker is trustworthy and has the client's best interest at heart, as well as by verbal conveyance of empathy during the session. Similarly, Ivanoff, Blythe, and Tripodi suggest that too much emphasis on empathy can feel manipulative to involuntary clients (1994, p. 21). With voluntary clients, the resultant climate of trust sets the stage for self-exploration, a prerequisite to self-understanding, which in turn facilitates behavior change. This positive ambience prepares the way for the use of "additive" or "expanded" levels of empathy to reach for underlying feelings as well as to uncover hidden meanings and goals of behavior.

Conversely, attempting to explore underlying feelings during the early phase of the helping process is counterproductive. Uncovering feelings beyond the client's awareness before a working relationship is firmly established tends to mobilize opposition and may precipitate premature termination of the contact. Involuntary clients in a negotiated relationship may never desire such uncovering of deeper feelings and may find exploration of them to be intrusive (Ivanoff, Blythe, and Tripodi, 1994, p. 21).

Exercises in Identifying Surface and Underlying Feelings

In the following exercise, identify both the apparent surface feelings and the probable underlying feelings embodied in the client's message. Remember that most of the feelings in the messages are merely implied, as clients often do not use feeling words. As you complete the exercise, read each message and write down the feelings involved. Next, scan the lists of affective words and phrases to see whether you might improve your response. After you have responded to all four messages, check the feeling words and phrases you identified with those given at the end of the chapter. If the feelings you identified were similar in meaning to those identified in the answers, consider your responses to be accurate. If they were not, review the client messages for clues about the client's feelings that you overlooked.

Client Statements

1. *Elderly client*: I know my children have busy lives. It is hard for them to have time to call me.

   Apparent feelings:
   Probable deeper feelings:

2. *Lesbian client referring to partner who has recently come out to her family*: When I was at your brother's wedding and they wanted to take family pictures, nobody wanted me in the pictures. In fact nobody wanted to talk to me.

   Note that this is a quote from a client in the "Home for the Holidays" video connected to this chapter.

   Apparent feelings:
   Probable deeper feelings:

3. *Client*: When I was a teenager, I thought that when I was married and had my own children, I would never yell at them like my mother yelled at me. Yet, here I am doing the same things with Sonny. [*Tearful.*]
   Apparent feelings:
   Probable deeper feelings:

4. *African American client in child welfare system*: The system is against people like me. People think that we drink, beat our kids, lay up on welfare, and take drugs.

Apparent feelings:

Probable deeper feelings:

Exercises at the end of this chapter for formulating reciprocal empathic responses will also assist you in increasing your perceptiveness to feelings.

Accurately Conveying Empathy

Empathic responding is a fundamental, yet complex skill that requires systematic practice and extensive effort to achieve competency. Skill in empathic communication has no limit or ceiling; rather, this skill is always in the process of "becoming." In listening to their taped sessions, even highly skilled professionals discover feelings they overlooked. Many social workers, however, do not fully utilize or selectively employ empathic responding. They fail to grasp the versatility of this skill and its potency in influencing clients and fostering growth in moment-by-moment transactions.

In fact, some social workers dismiss the need for training in empathic responding, mistakenly believing themselves to already be empathic in their contacts with clients. Research findings indicate that beginning social work students relate at empathic levels considerably lower than the levels necessary to work effectively with clients (Fischer, 1978; Larsen, 1975).

These findings are not totally unexpected, of course, because comparatively few people are inherently helpful in the sense of relating naturally with high levels of empathy or any of the other core conditions. Although people achieve varying degrees of empathy, respect, and genuineness through their life experiences, attaining high levels of these skills requires rigorous training. Research scales that operationalize empathy conditions have been developed and validated in extensive research studies (Truax & Carkhuff, 1967). These scales, which specify levels of empathy along a continuum ranging from high- to low-level skills, represented a major breakthrough not only in operationalizing essential social worker skills but also in establishing a relationship between these skills and successful outcomes in practice.

The empathic communication scale has proved particularly helpful to social work educators in assessing pre- and post-levels of empathy of trainees in laboratory classes (Larsen & Hepworth, 1978; Wells, 1975). The scale has been further employed to help students distinguish between high- and low-level empathic responses and has been used by peers and instructors in group training to assess levels of students' responses. Students then receive guidance in reformulating low-level responses to bring them to higher levels.

The Carkhuff (1969) empathy scale, which consists of nine levels, has been widely used in training and research, and similar versions of this scale can be found in the literature. Although we have found nine-point scales valuable as training aids, they have proven somewhat confusing to students, who often have difficulty in making such fine distinctions between levels. For this reason, we have adapted the nine-level scale described by Hammond, Hepworth, and Smith (1977) by collapsing it to the five-level scale presented later in this section.

On this empathic communication scale, level 1 responses are generally made by social workers who are preoccupied with their own—rather than their clients'—frame of reference; for this reason, they completely fail to match the clients' feelings. At this low level of responding, social workers' responses are usually characterized by the ineffective communication styles identified in Chapter 7. Responses at level 2 convey an effort to understand but remain partially inaccurate or incomplete.

At level 3, the midpoint, social workers' responses essentially match the affect of their clients' surface feelings and expressions. This midpoint, widely referred to as "interchangeable" or "reciprocal" responding in the literature, is considered the "minimally facilitative level" at which an effective and viable process of helping can take place.

Above the midpoint, social workers' responses add noticeably to the surface feelings. At the highest level, they add significantly to the clients' expressions. At these higher levels of empathic responding, social workers accurately respond to clients' full range of feelings at their exact intensity and are "with" clients in their deepest moments. Level 4 and 5 empathic responses, which require the social worker to infer underlying feelings, involve mild to moderate interpretations.

Empathic Communication Scale

Level 1: Low Level of Empathic Responding

At level 1, the social worker communicates little or no awareness or understanding of even the most conspicuous of the client's feelings; the social worker's responses are irrelevant and often abrasive, hindering rather than facilitating communication. Operating from a personal frame of reference, the social worker changes the subject, argues, gives advice prematurely, lectures, or uses other ineffective styles that block communication, often diverting clients from their problems and fragmenting the helping process. Furthermore, the social worker's nonverbal responses are not appropriate to the mood and content of the client's statement.

When social workers relate at this low level, clients often become confused or defensive. They may react by discussing superficialities, arguing, disagreeing, changing the subject, or withdrawing into silence. Thus, the client's energies are diverted from exploration and/or work on problems.

Unfortunately, level one responses occur with some frequency in settings in which clients are involuntary, stigmatized, or considered deviant. Such responses may provoke client anger but pose few consequences for the practitioner unless there are norms that clients must be treated respectfully in all circumstances. These responses are shared not for the purpose of modeling them, but rather to alert you that if you see them occurring, or it occurs to you, it signals problems with the practitioner or the setting. It could just be a worker on a bad day; but worse if it has become a standard of practice that passes unnoticed. Consider the following example of a mother in the child welfare system who has recently completed a drug treatment program.

Client: I want to go into an after-care treatment program near my home that is culturally sensitive and allows me to keep my job.

Level 0 response: You should not be thinking about what is convenient for you but rather what might ultimately benefit your child by your being a safe parent for her. Your thinking here is symptomatic of the problem of why your child is in custody, and your chances of regaining custody are limited.

It is possible that practitioner might have valid reasons for wishing the client to consider a variety of options. Making the judgmental statement only makes the circumstances worse and makes it unlikely that the client will consider the worker's opinion.

Level 1 response: "I see that you want to find a program near your home."

This response is minimally facilitative, but at least avoids the judgmental statements of the previous example.

African American male: [*to child welfare worker*]: I don't trust you people. You do everything you can to keep me from getting back my son. I have done everything I am supposed to do, and you people always come up with something else.

Level 1 Responses

- *"Just carry out the case plan and you are likely to succeed."* (Giving advice.)
- *"Just think what would have happened if you had devoted more energy in the last year to carrying out your case plan: You would have been further along."* (Persuading with logical argument; negatively evaluating client's actions.)
- *"How did you get along with your last social worker?"* (Changing the subject.)
- *"Don't you think it will all work out in time?"* (Leading question, untimely reassurance.)
- *"Why, that's kind of an exaggeration. If you just work along with me, before you know it things will be better."* (Reassuring, consoling, giving advice.)
- *"I don't think you have a very positive attitude. If you had just taken responsibility for your own actions and completed your case plan, you wouldn't have gotten yourself into this situation."* (Judging and blaming client.)

The final response above could have actually been rated on a negative scale of empathic responding. That is, not only is the response not empathic, but it is actively attacking and judgmental. Instead of conveying empathy, it conveys antipathy. Social workers' frustration with clients who endanger others is understandable. Statements like the one above, however, greatly hinder further efforts to work with them in a collaborative fashion.

> You can see two versions of the same situation in the video "Domestic Violence and the Probation Officer" connected with this chapter. Note the client response to level 1 empathic responses in version one. Note also how the situation looks different when the practitioner employs higher levels of empathy in version two.

The preceding examples illustrate ineffective styles of communication used at this low level. Notice that messages reflect the social worker's own formulations concerning the client's problem; they do not capture the client's inner experiencing. Such responses stymie clients, blocking their flow of thought and producing negative feelings toward the social worker.

Level 2: Moderately Low Level of Empathic Responding

At level 2, the social worker responds to the surface message of the client but erroneously omits feelings or factual aspects of the message. The social worker may also inappropriately qualify feelings (e.g., "somewhat," "a little bit," "kind of") or may inaccurately interpret feelings (e.g., "angry" for "hurt," "tense" for "scared"). Responses may also emanate from the social worker's own conceptual formulations, which may be diagnostically accurate but not empathically attuned to the client's expressions. Although level 2 responses are only partially accurate, they do convey an effort to understand and, for this reason, do not completely block the client's communication or work on problems.

Level 2 Responses

- *"You'll just have to be patient. I can see you're upset."* The word *upset defines the client's feelings only vaguely, whereas feeling words such as* angry, furious, *and* discounted *more accurately reflect the client's inner experiencing.*
- *"You feel angry because your case plan has not been more successful to date. Maybe you are expecting too much too soon; there is a lot of time yet." The listener begins to accurately capture the client's feelings but then moves to an evaluative interpretation ("you expect too much too soon") and inappropriate reassurance.*
- *"You aren't pleased with your progress so far?" This response focuses on external, factual circumstances to the exclusion of the client's feelings or perceptions regarding the event in question.*
- *"You feel like things aren't going too well." This response contains no reference to the client's immediately apparent feelings. Beginning social workers often use the lead-in phrase "You feel like ..." without noticing that, in employing it, they have not captured the client's feelings.*
- *"You're disappointed because you haven't gotten your son back?" This response, although partially accurate, fails to capture the client's anger and distrust of the system, wondering whether any of his efforts are likely to succeed.*
- *"I can see you are angry and disappointed because your efforts haven't been more successful so far, but I think you may be expecting the system to work too quickly." Although the message has a strong beginning, the empathic nature of the response is* negated by the listener's explanation of the reason for the client's difficulties. This response represents a form of taking sides—that is, justifying the actions of the child welfare system by suggesting that too much is expected of it.

In the video "Getting Back to Shakopee," the practitioner had heard an account of uncomfortable relations with co-workers on the job. She summarizes and adds a level 2 empathic comment: "So just that I understand what you are talking about, you were working on your own project and Mary came over and added hers to yours and asked you to finish it for her? What did that do for you?" The empathy is implied in the practitioner's question, but it could have been more explicit.

The preceding responses illustrate many of the common errors made by social workers in responding empathically to client messages. Although some part of the messages may be accurate or helpful, all the responses in some way ignore or subtract from what the client is experiencing.

Level 3: Interchangeable or Reciprocal Level of Empathic Responding

The social worker's verbal and nonverbal responses at level 3 convey understanding and are essentially interchangeable with the client's obvious expressions, accurately reflecting factual aspects of the client's messages and surface feelings or state of being. Reciprocal responses do not appreciably add affect or reach beyond the surface feelings, nor do they subtract from the feeling and tone expressed.

Acknowledging the factual content of the client's message, although desirable, is not required; if included, this aspect of the message must be accurate. Level 3 responses facilitate further exploratory and problem-focused responses by the client. The beginning social worker does well in achieving skill in reciprocal empathic responding, which is an effective working level. This is the goal for appropriateness at this level; see examples in the Shakopee and Squeaky Wheel videos.

Level 3 Responses

- *"You're really angry about the slow progress in your case and are wondering whether your efforts are likely to succeed."*
- *"I can tell you feel very let down and are asking yourself, 'Will I ever get my son back?'"*

The video "Serving the Squeaky Wheel" contains a lengthy exchange in which the client, Molly, expresses her suspicion about what is written about her in social worker's case records. The practitioner responds, "I am hearing that it is a real sore point with you about what I write and think and what goes into the records about you." This response deals directly with her concern.

Essentially interchangeable, level 3 responses express accurately the immediately apparent emotions in the client's message. The content of the responses is also accurate, but deeper feelings and meanings are not added. The second response also illustrates a technique for conveying empathy that involves changing the reflection from the third to the first person, and speaking as if the social worker were the client.

Level 4: Moderately High Level of Empathic Responding

Responses at level 4 are somewhat additive, accurately identifying the client's implicit underlying feelings and/or aspects of the problem. The social worker's response illuminates subtle or veiled facets of the client's message, enabling the client to get in touch with somewhat deeper feelings and unexplored meanings and purposes of behavior. Level 4 responses thus are aimed at enhancing self-awareness.

Level 4 Responses

- *"You feel very frustrated with the lack of progress in getting your son back. You wonder whether there is any hope in working with a new worker and this system, which you feel hasn't been helping you."*

In the "Serving the Squeaky Wheel" video, the client, Molly, says that other people's conceptions of mental illness do not include her. The practitioner responds, "Let me see if I understand what you are saying: some people may think because you have a car and you speak up for yourself, that you are a very competent person who doesn't need any resources [Client: "There you go."] and if you ask for them [Client: "I am screwing the system."] that you are trying to take things that you are not entitled to. But your view is that you can have a car and speak up for yourself and still have other needs." This response not only conveys immediately apparent

feelings and content but also is noticeably additive in reflecting the client's deeper feelings. In this case, the client's immediate response—finishing the practitioner's sentences—indicates that the empathic response is perceived as accurate.

Level 5: High Level of Empathic Responding

Reflecting each emotional nuance, and using voice and intensity of expressions finely attuned to the client's moment-by-moment experiencing, the social worker accurately responds to the full range and intensity of both surface and underlying feelings and meanings at level 5. The social worker may connect current feelings and experiencing to previously expressed experiences or feelings, or may accurately identify implicit patterns, themes, or purposes. Responses may also identify implicit goals embodied in the client's message, which point out a promising direction for personal growth and pave the way for action. Responding empathically at this high level facilitates the client's exploration of feelings and problems in much greater breadth and depth than responding at lower levels. Conveying this level of empathy occurs rarely with inexperienced interviewers and only somewhat more often with highly experienced interviewers. The opportunity to respond at such depth is more likely to occur near the end of an interview and with clients who have become more voluntary.

Level 5 Responses

In the video "Serving the Squeaky Wheel" connected with this chapter, a developing theme is that Molly, a client with serious and persistent mental illness, acts, as she puts it, as a "greasy wheel," always advocating for herself and acting assertively, as she has been trained to do in many education programs. And yet those skills act as a "two- or three-edged sword" in that sometimes she is punished for this assertiveness. Reflecting these themes and Molly's language, the practitioner, Ron Rooney, says, "You just seem to be courageous in fighting battles and you have learned some skills in assertiveness, and as you say, that can be a two-edged or three-edged sword. Sometimes your assertiveness gets you what you want and sometimes your assertiveness causes some people to look at you as the squeaky wheel that has squeaked too much."

Exercises in Discriminating Levels of Empathic Responding

The following exercises ask you to rate responses for their level of empathy and are designed to assist you in refining your ability to determine the helpfulness of responses. These exercises will prepare you for subsequent practice in formulating your own empathic messages. Three client statements are given, followed by several possible responses. Using the empathic scale, rate each response. Rating messages will be less difficult if, using the list of affective words and phrases, you first identify the feelings contained in the client's message. After you have rated each response, compare your rating with those given at the end of the chapter. Referring to the rating scale, analyze the responses you rated inaccurately, trying to pinpoint the reason for the authors' ratings. Additional exercises are available on the CD-ROM or Web site connected with this chapter.

Client Statements

1. *Single woman, age 80 [to social worker concerning her request to move to an independent living complex provided for ambulatory elderly persons]:* Goodness, the more I think of moving, the more scared I get. I have neighbors here who look after me, and I won't know a soul there. I'm afraid I'll be all alone.

Level Responses

1. "It's pretty scary to you, leaving your neighbors and familiar surroundings. But there will be a lot of friendly people there and things to do. Besides, they fix one hot meal for you every day."
2. "Don't worry, you'll make friends in no time, and you'll wish you'd moved sooner."
3. "Did you sign those application papers I left with you a few days ago?"
4. "Just thinking about moving worries you because you'll be leaving your own neighborhood and friends. Even though your life would be much easier, you're unsure you'll be better off in other ways."
5. "So I gather in some ways you'd rather stay right where you are rather than gamble on a change."
6. "Lots of other people in the new apartments were just as scared as you before they moved, but I don't know a single one who's sorry now."
7. "It sounds as though you have some pretty mixed feelings about moving. Part of you wants to go because you could live more comfortably, but another part of you is afraid you'll feel alone and lost and wants to cling to people you know care about you."
8. "Are you saying we just ought to forget the whole thing?"

2. *Male, age 16 [in weekly visit to social work probation officer]:* I don't see the sense in having to come here every lousy week. I haven't been in any trouble now since I went to court a month ago. You should know by now you can trust me.

Level Responses

1. "A month isn't very long, you know. And how can I be sure you're staying out of trouble?"
2. "I gather you'd rather not have to see me. I can understand that, but the judge ordered it and you'd be in trouble with him if you didn't meet the conditions of your probation."
3. "Has it been a month since you went to court? I didn't think that it had been that long."
4. "You'd prefer not coming here and feel you've earned my trust."
5. "Having to come here each week gripes you, and I gather you're irritated with me for encouraging you to follow the judge's order."
6. "Look, you got yourself into this mess so don't complain to me if you don't like it. Maybe you'd like to talk the judge into changing his mind."
7. "It irritates you to have to come here each week. You'd like to get me off your back."
8. "You're confused about why you have to come here and wish you didn't have to."

3. *Group member [in hesitant, quiet voice]:* It's really hard for me to say what I want to say in this group. When I do start to talk, I get tongue-tied, and my heart starts beating faster and faster. I feel like some of you are critical of me.

Level Responses
(By Group Members or Group Leader)

1. "Yeah, I feel that same way sometimes, too."
2. "It is frightening to you to try to share your feelings with the group. Sounds like you find yourself at a loss for words and wonder what others are thinking of you."
3. "I know you're timid, but I think it's important that you make more of an effort to talk in the group, just like you're doing now. It's actually one of the responsibilities of being a group member."
4. "You get scared when you try to talk in the group."

5. "I sense that you're probably feeling pretty tense and tied up inside right now as you talk about the fear you've had in expressing yourself."
6. "Although you've been frightened of exposing yourself, I gather there's a part of you that wants to overcome that fear and become more actively involved with the rest of the group."
7. "What makes you think we're critical of you? You come across as a bit self-conscious, but that's no big deal."
8. "You remind me of the way I felt the first time I was in a group. I was so scared, I just looked at the floor most of the time."
9. "I wonder if we've done anything that came across as being critical of you."

4. A homeless client who has been referred to a housing program is completing an intake with the social worker when he is asked about what led to his losing his job. He responds, "Budget cuts, lays offs, and I did not have seniority."

Level Responses

1. "How did you feel about that?"
2. "So several things, including cuts, lay offs, and low seniority, contributed to your losing your job and contributed to your homelessness."
3. "How long have you been homeless?"
4. "Don't you think you have some responsibility for losing your job?"

Responding with Reciprocal Empathy

Reciprocal or interchangeable empathic responding (level 3) is a basic skill used throughout the helping process to acknowledge client messages and to encourage exploration of problems. In the initial phase, empathic responding serves a vital purpose in individual, conjoint, and group sessions: It facilitates the development of a working relationship and fosters the climate of understanding necessary to promote communication and self-disclosure. In this way, it sets the stage for deeper exploration of feelings during subsequent phases of the helping process.

Note that the benefits of making additive empathic responses at levels 4 and 5 are not contingent on the frequency of their usage. In fact, making one such response in a first or second interview may be helpful and appropriate. More frequent attempts presume a depth

of relationship that has not yet developed. Additive empathic responses often exceed the level of feelings and meanings expressed by clients during early sessions and are thus reserved, in large part, for the later phases of the helping process.

Because reciprocal responding is an essential skill used frequently to meet the objectives of the first phase of the helping process, we recommend that you first aim to achieve beginning mastery of responding at level 3. Extended practice of this skill should significantly increase your effectiveness in establishing viable helping relationships, interviewing, and gathering data. The remainder of this chapter provides guidelines and practice exercises that will help you in mastering reciprocal responding. Although responding at additive levels represents an extension of the skill of reciprocal responding, the former is an advanced skill that can be used in a variety of ways to achieve specific objectives. For this reason, it has been grouped with other change-oriented or "action" skills presented in Part 3 of the book.

Constructing Reciprocal Responses

To reach level 3 on the empathic scale, you must be able to formulate responses that accurately capture the content and the surface feelings in the client message. It is also important to frame the message so that you do not merely restate the client's message.

The following paradigm, which identifies the elements of an empathic or reflective message, has proven useful for conceptualizing and mastering the skill of empathic responding:

You feel_____ about_____ because_____.

                                          Accurately identifies or describes feelings

The response focuses exclusively on the client's message and does not reflect the social worker's conceptualizations.

The following excerpt from a session involving a social worker and a 17-year-old female illustrates the use of the preceding paradigm in constructing an empathic response:

Client: I can't talk to my father without feeling scared and crying. I'd like to be able to express myself and to disagree with him, but I just can't.

Social worker: It sounds as though you just feel panicky when you try to talk to your father. I gather you're discouraged because you'd like to feel comfortable with your dad and able to talk openly with him without falling apart.

Many times, client messages contain conflicting or contrasting emotions, such as the following: "I like taking drugs, but sometimes I worry about what they might do to me." In such cases, each contrasting feeling should be highlighted:

- *You feel _____, yet you also feel _____.*
- *I sense that you feel torn because while you find taking drugs enjoyable, you have nagging thoughts that they might be harmful to you.*[1]

Remember that to respond empathically at a reciprocal level, you must use language that your clients will readily understand. Abstract, intellectualized language and professional jargon create barriers to communication and should be avoided. It is also important to vary the language you use in responding. Many professionals tend to respond with stereotyped, repetitive speech patterns, commonly using a limited variety of communication leads to begin their empathic responses. Such leads as "You feel ..." and "I hear you saying ..." repeated over and over not only distract the client but also seem phony and contrived. This kind of stereotyped responding draws more attention to the social worker's technique than to his or her message.

The list of varied introductory phrases will help you expand your repertoire of possible responses. We encourage you to read the list aloud several times and to review it frequently while practicing the empathic communication training exercises in this chapter and in Chapter 17, which covers additive empathic responding. The reciprocal empathic response format ("You feel _____ because _____") is merely a training aid to assist you in focusing on the affect and content of client messages. The leads list will help you respond more naturally.

Exercises designed to help you to develop level 3 reciprocal empathic responses appear at the end of the chapter. Included in the exercises are a variety of client statements taken from actual work with individuals, groups, couples, and families in diverse settings.

In addition to completing the skill development exercises, we recommend that you record the number of empathic responses you employ in sessions over several weeks to determine the extent to which you are applying this skill. We also suggest that either you or a knowledgeable associate rate your responses and determine the mean level of empathic responding for each session. If you find (as most beginning social workers do) that you are underutilizing empathic responses or responding at low levels, you may wish to set a goal to improve your skill.

Leads for Empathic Responses

Could it be that ...	You're feeling ...
I wonder if ...	I'm not sure if I'm with you but ...
What I guess I'm hearing is ...	You appear to be feeling ...
Correct me if I'm wrong, but I'm sensing ...	It appears you feel ...
Perhaps you're feeling ...	Maybe you feel ...
Sometimes you think ...	Do you feel ...
Maybe this is a long shot, but ...	I'm not sure that I'm with you; do you mean ...
I'm not certain I understand; you're feeling ...	It seems that you ...
As I hear it, you ...	Is that what you mean?
Is that the way you feel?	What I think I'm hearing is ...
Let me see if I'm with you; you ...	I get the impression that ...
The message I'm getting is that ...	As I get it, you felt that ...
If I'm hearing you correctly ...	To me it's almost like you are saying ...
So, you're feeling ...	So, as you see it ...
You feel ...	I'm picking up that you ...
It sounds as though you are saying ...	I wonder if you're saying ...
I hear you saying ...	So, it seems to you ...
So, from where you sit ...	Right now you're feeling ...
I sense that you're feeling ...	You must have felt ...
Your message seems to be ...	Listening to you, it seems as if ...
I gather you're feeling ...	You convey a sense of ...

| If I'm catching what you say ... | As I think about what you say, it occurs to me you're feeling ... |
| What you're saying comes across to me as ... | From what you say, I gather you're feeling ... |

Employing Empathic Responding

In early sessions with the client, empathic responding should be used frequently as a method of developing rapport and "staying in touch" with the client. Responses should be couched in a tentative manner to allow for inaccuracies in the social worker's perception. Checking out the accuracy of responses with appropriate lead-in phrases such as "Let me see if I understand..." or "Did I hear you right?" is helpful in communicating a desire to understand and a willingness to correct misperceptions.

In initially using empathic responses, learners are often leery of the flood of emotions that sometimes occurs as the client, experiencing none of the usual barriers to communication, releases feelings that may have been pent up for months or years. It is important to understand that empathic responses have not "caused" such feelings but rather have facilitated their expression, thus clearing the way for the client to explore and to consider such feelings more rationally and objectively.

You may worry, as do many beginning social workers, about whether you will "damage" the client or disrupt the helping relationship if your empathic responses do not always accurately reflect the client's feelings. Perhaps even more important than accuracy, however, is the commitment to understand conveyed by your genuine efforts to perceive the client's experience. If you consistently demonstrate your goodwill and intent to help through attentive verbal and nonverbal responding, an occasional lack of understanding or faulty timing will not damage the client–social worker relationship. In fact, your efforts to clarify the client's message will usually enhance rather than detract from the helping process, particularly if you respond to corrective feedback in an open, non-defensive, and empathic manner.

Multiple Uses of Empathic Communication

Earlier in the chapter, we referred to the versatility of empathic communication. In this section, we delineate a number of ways in which you can employ reciprocal empathic responding.

Establishing Relationships with Clients in Initial Sessions

As discussed previously, the use of empathic responding actively demonstrates the social worker's keen awareness of clients' feelings and creates an atmosphere in which clients feel safe enough to risk exploring their personal thoughts and feelings. Numerous researchers have established that when social workers relate empathically, clients are more likely to continue contact than when little empathy is conveyed.

To employ empathy with maximal effectiveness in trans-cultural relationships, social workers must be sensitive to cultural factors. The importance of understanding cultural factors was documented almost 40 years ago by Mayer and Timms (1969), who studied clashes of perspectives between clients and social workers. Based on their findings, they concluded, "It seems that social workers start where the client is psychodynamically but they are insufficiently empathic in regard to cultural components" (p. 38).

Although empathic communication is important in bridging cultural gaps, it can be used to excess with many Asian Americans and Native Americans. Many members of these groups tend to be lower in emotional expressiveness than other client groups, and they may react with discomfort and confusion if a social worker relies too heavily on empathic communication. Nevertheless, it is important to "read between the lines" and to sensitively respond to troubling emotions that these clients do not usually express directly. Like other clients, they are likely to appreciate a social worker's sensitive awareness to the painful emotions associated with their difficulties.

We must reemphasize the importance of assuming a more directive, active, and structured stance with some Asian Americans. As Tsui and Schultz (1985) have clarified, "A purely empathetic, passive, nondirective approach serves only to confuse and alienate the [Asian] client" (p. 568). The same can be said of many Native American clients, based on their levels of acculturation.

In the videotape "Getting Back to Shakopee" linked with this chapter, the social worker, Dorothy, is working with a Native American client, Valerie, who appears guarded and apprehensive about contact with a social worker after referral by her employer. She appears worried that seeing a social worker might lead to a child welfare investigation. Dorothy makes many efforts to establish empathic and cultural linkages. A turning point appears to occur when Valerie discovers that Dorothy knows about an upcoming powwow and plans to attend.

Staying in Touch with Clients

Reciprocal empathic responding operationalizes the social work principle of "starting where the client is" and keeps social workers attuned to their clients' current feelings. Although he or she inevitably employs many other skills and techniques, the social worker constantly returns to empathic responding to keep in touch with the client. In that sense, empathic communication is a fundamental intervention and a prerequisite to the use of other interventions. Gendlin (1974) used the analogy of driving a car to illuminate the vital role of empathy in keeping in touch with clients. Driving involves much more than watching the road. A driver does many things, including steering, braking, signaling, and watching signs. One may glance at the scenery, visit with others, and think private thoughts, but watching the road must be accorded the highest priority.

When visibility becomes limited or hazards appear, all other activities must cease and the driver must attend exclusively to observing the road and potentially dangerous conditions. Just as some drivers fail to pay proper attention to their surroundings and become involved in accidents, so some social workers also fail to attend sufficiently to cultural differences and changes in clients' moods and reactions, mistakenly assuming they know their clients' frame of mind. As a consequence, social workers may fail to discern important feelings, and their clients may perceive them as disinterested or insensitive and subsequently disengage from the helping process.

Accurately Assessing Client Problems

The levels of empathy offered by social workers are likely to correlate with their clients' levels of self-exploration. That is, high-level empathic responding should increase clients' exploration of self and problems. As the social worker moves "with" clients by frequently using empathic responses in initial sessions, clients will begin to lay out their problems and to reveal events and relevant data. Figuratively speaking, clients then take social workers where they need to go by providing information crucial to making an accurate assessment. Such an approach contrasts sharply with sessions that emphasize history-taking and in which social workers, following their own agendas rather than the clients', spend unnecessary time asking hit-or-miss questions and gathering extraneous information.

Responding to Clients' Nonverbal Messages

Through their facial features, gestures, and body postures, clients often hint at feelings that they do not express verbally. In the course of a session, for instance, a client may become pensive, or he or she may show puzzlement, pain, or discomfort. In such instances, the social worker may convey understanding of the client's feeling state and verbalize the feeling explicitly through a reflective response that attends to the emotion suggested in the client's nonverbal expressions. For instance, in response to a client who has been sitting dejectedly with her head down for several minutes after having reported some bad grades, a social worker might say, "At this moment you seem to be feeling very sad and discouraged, perhaps even defeated." In group or conjoint sessions, the social worker might reflect the nonverbal messages of several, or all, of the members. For example, the social worker might say, "I sense some restlessness today, and we're having a hard time staying on our topic. I'm wondering if you're saying, 'We're not sure we want to deal with this problem today.' Am I reading the group correctly?"

Children are likely to communicate more nonverbally with unfamiliar adults such as social workers than they communicate in verbal ways. It can be useful to ask about such nonverbals and what they might mean. A child interacting with a toy, making limited eye contact, and making one-word replies to questions about how things are going at home may be communicating some things about how uncomfortable or unfamiliar he or she is with the process. Rather than force the child to explain what is happening in words, play therapy techniques have permitted children to tell a story, through actions, of what is occurring to them (Lukas, 1993).

Empathic responses that accurately tune into clients' nonverbal experiencing will usually prompt clients to begin exploring feelings they have been experiencing. Making explicit the nonverbal messages of clients is an important skill discussed in Chapters 6, Chapters 8, and Chapters 10 of this book.

Making Confrontations More Palatable

Confrontation is employed in the change-oriented phase to expand clients' awareness and to motivate them to action. It is most appropriate when clients are contemplating actions that are unlawful or that are dangerous to themselves or others. Confrontation is also appropriate when such actions conflict with the goals and values a client has chosen for himself or herself.

Of course, even well-timed confrontations may meet with varying degrees of receptiveness. Both concerns for the client's welfare and prudence dictate that the social worker determine the impact of a potential confrontation upon the client and implement a process for making such an intervention more palatable. This may be accomplished by employing empathic responses attuned to the client's reaction immediately following a confrontation. As social workers listen attentively and sensitively to their clients' expressions, the clients' defensiveness may abate. Indeed, clients often begin to process new information and think through and test the validity of their ideas, embracing those that fit and rejecting others that seem inapplicable. Guidelines for this important skill are presented in Chapter 17.

Blending confrontation and empathic responses is a particularly potent technique for managing group processes when the social worker must deal with a controversial issue or distractive behavior that is interfering with the work of the group.

Handling Obstacles Presented by Clients

Client opposition to what is happening in a session is sometimes healthy. What is often interpreted as unconscious resistance may, in fact, be a negative reaction to poor interviewing and intervention techniques used by the social worker or to client confusion, misunderstanding, or even inertia. For these reasons, it is important to carefully monitor clients' reactions and to deal directly and sensitively with their related feelings. Clients' verbal or nonverbal actions may comment indirectly on what is occurring in the helping process. For instance, a client may look at her watch and ask how long the session will last, shift her body position away from the social worker, begin tapping a foot, or stare out the window. When it appears that the client is disengaging from the session in this way, an empathic response that reflects the client's verbal and/or nonverbal message may effectively initiate discussion of what is occurring.

Social workers sometimes practice with highly verbal clients who talk rapidly and jump quickly from one topic to another. Overly verbal clients present a particular challenge to beginning social workers, who must often overcome the misconception that interrupting clients is rude. Because of this misconception, novice interviewers sometimes spend most of an initial session listening passively to highly verbal clients without providing any form or direction to the helping process. They may also allow clients to talk incessantly because they mistakenly view this as constructive work on problems. Quite the contrary, excess verbosity often keeps the session on a superficial level and interferes with problem identification and exploration. It may also indicate a more serious affective mental health problem.

It is important that social workers provide structure and direction to each session, thereby conveying an expectation that specific topics will be considered in depth. Much more will be said about this in later chapters. For now, we simply underscore the necessity of

using empathic responses with highly verbal clients as a preliminary strategy to slow the process and to provide some depth to the discussion.

For example, a social worker might interject or intervene with "I'd like to interrupt to check whether I'm understanding what you mean. As I get it, you're feeling ..." or "Before you talk about that topic, I would like to make sure I'm with you. You seem to be saying ..." or "Could we hold off discussing that for just a minute? I'd like to be sure I understand what you mean. Would you expand on the point you were just making?"

Managing Anger and Patterns of Violence

During individual or group sessions, clients (especially those who were not self-referred and may be involuntary clients) often experience surges of intense and conflicting feelings, such as anger, hurt, or disappointment. In such instances, empathic responding is a key tool for assisting them to work through those feelings. As empathic responses facilitate expanded expression of these feelings, clients engage in a process of venting, clarifying, and experiencing different feelings. Over time, they may achieve a mellowing of emotions and a more rational and thoughtful state of being.

When it is employed to focus sharply on clients' feelings, empathic responding efficiently manages and modifies strong emotions that represent obstacles to progress. As the social worker successfully handles such moments and clients experience increased self-awareness and cathartic benefits, the helping relationship is strengthened.

Empathic responding is particularly helpful in dealing with hostile clients and is indispensable when clients become angry with the social worker, as illustrated in the following client statement: "What you're doing to help me with my problems doesn't seem to be doing me any good. I don't know why I keep coming." At such moments, the social worker must resist the temptation to react defensively, because such a response will further antagonize the client and exacerbate the situation. Responding by challenging the client's perception, for instance, would damage the helping relationship. The social worker's responses should represent a genuine effort to understand the client's experiencing and feelings and to engage the client in fully exploring those feelings.

Involuntary clients sometimes become frustrated with the seemingly slow pace of progress toward goals and may feel that policies and individuals in the system are acting to thwart them. Empathizing with this anger is necessary before the social worker and client can collaborate productively and figure out how to make the system work toward client goals (Rooney & Chovanec, 2004).

Keeping this idea in mind, consider the impact of the following reciprocal empathic response: "You're very disappointed that things aren't better and are irritated with me, feeling that I should have been more helpful to you." This response accurately and nondefensively acknowledges the client's frustration with the situation and with the social worker. By itself, it would not be sufficient to calm the client's ire and to free the client to consider the problem more fully and rationally.

Carefully following the client's feelings and remaining sensitively attuned to the client's experiencing by employing empathic responses for several minutes usually assists both the social worker and the client to understand more clearly the strong feelings that prompted the client's outburst and to adequately assess the source of those feelings. Attending to the emotions expressed does not mean that the content is discounted. The social worker might, for example, follow the empathic response above by saying, "I'd like to explore more fully with you which parts of our work have not felt worthwhile to you."

When faced with angry clients in group and conjoint sessions, it is critical that the social worker empathically not only reflect the negative feelings and positions of the clients who are displaying the anger, but also reach for and reflect the feelings or observations of members who may be experiencing the situation differently. Utilizing empathic responses in this manner assists the social worker in gathering information that will elucidate the problem, helping angry members air and examine their feelings, and bringing out other points of view for the group's consideration. In addition, employing empathic responding at such moments encourages a more rational discussion of the issues involved in the problem and thus sets the stage for possible problem solving.

The principles just discussed also apply to clients who are prone to violent behavior. Such clients often come to the attention of social workers because they have abused their children and/or spouses. People who engage in violence often do so because they have underlying feelings of helplessness and frustration and because they lack skills and experience in coping with troubling situations in more constructive ways. Some have short fuses and weak emotional controls, and many come from backgrounds in which they vicariously learned violence as a mechanism of coping. Using empathy to defuse their intense anger and to tune into their frustrations is an important first step in working with such clients (Lane,

1986). Other clients may have difficulties with anger and express this emotion only when under the influence of alcohol or other substances. Helping them experience and ventilate anger when sober and in control is a major approach employed to assist such clients to learn constructive ways of coping with anger (Potter-Efron & Potter-Efron, 1992).

> Several parts of the "Serving the Squeaky Wheel" video deal with the client, Molly, expressing anger and frustration and the practitioner, Ron Rooney, attempting to respond empathically to that anger. In particular, Molly is frustrated with an abrupt replacement of her previous case worker by Rooney and insists on his proving his identity as a social worker. Note how this challenge is met. At other points, Molly scales her level of trust at below zero and attributes this to a history of distrust of social workers.

Utilizing Empathic Responses to Facilitate Group Discussions

Social workers may facilitate discussion of specific issues in conjoint or group sessions by first identifying a particular topic and then using empathic (or paraphrasing) responses to reflect the observations of various group members in relation to that topic. The social worker may also actively seek responses from members who have not contributed and then employ empathic responses (or paraphrases) to acknowledge their observations. Utilized frequently in this manner, empathic responding encourages (and reinforces) clients' participation in group discussions.

Teaching Clients to Respond Empathically

Clients often experience difficulties in their relationships because their styles of communication include many barriers that prevent them from accurately hearing messages or conveying understanding to others. An important task for the social worker involves teaching clients to respond empathically. This task is accomplished in part by modeling, which is generally recognized as a potent technique for promoting client change and growth. People who distort or ignore others' messages (e.g., in marital, family, and other close relationships) may benefit vicariously by observing the social worker listen effectively and respond empathically. Moreover, clients who are hard to reach or who have difficulties in expressing themselves may gradually learn to recognize their own emotions and to express themselves more fully as a result of the social worker's empathic responding.

Teaching empathic communication skills to clients also can entail assuming an educational role. Several approaches to assisting partners who are having serious conflicts rely on teaching both parties to gain and express empathy for each other. Social workers' roles as educators require them to intervene actively at opportune moments to enable their clients to respond empathically, particularly when they have ignored, discounted, or attacked the contributions of others in a session. With respect to this role, we suggest that social workers consider taking the following actions:

1. Teach clients the paradigm for empathic responding introduced in this chapter. If appropriate, ask them to engage briefly in a paired practice exercise similar to the one recommended for beginning social workers at the end of the chapter. Utilizing topics neutral to the relationship, have each person carefully listen to the other party for several minutes, and then reverse roles. Afterward, evaluate with participants the impact of the exercise on them.

2. Introduce clients to the list of affective words and phrases and to the leads list provided in this chapter. If appropriate, you may wish to have clients assume tasks during the week to broaden their feeling vocabulary similar to the tasks recommended for beginning social workers.

3. Intervene in sessions when clients ignore or fail to validate messages—a situation that occurs frequently during direct social work with couples, families, and groups. At those moments, interrupt the process in a facilitative fashion to ask the sender to repeat the message and the receiver to paraphrase or capture the essence of the former's message with fresh words, as illustrated in the following example:

16-year-old daughter: I don't like going to school. The teachers are a bunch of dweebs, and most of the kids laugh and make fun of me.

Mother: But you've got to go. If you'd just buckle down and study, school wouldn't be half so hard for you. I think …

Social worker: [*interrupting and speaking to mother*]: I can see that you have some real concerns about Janet's not going to school, but for a moment, I'm going to ask you to get in touch with what she just said to you by repeating it back to her.

Mother: [*looking at social worker*]: She said she doesn't like school.

Social worker: That's close, but turn and talk to Janet. See if you can identify what she's feeling.

Mother: [*turning to daughter*]: I guess it's pretty painful for you to go to school. And you don't like your teachers and you feel shut out and ridiculed by the kids.

Janet: [*tearfully*]: Yeah, that's it … it's really hard.

Notice that the mother did not respond empathically to her daughter's feelings until the social worker intervened and coached her. This example illustrates the importance of persevering in teaching clients to "hear" the messages of others, a point we cannot overemphasize. Clients often have considerable trouble mastering listening skills because habitual dysfunctional responses are difficult to discard. This is true even when clients are highly motivated to communicate more effectively and when social workers actively intervene to assist them.

4. Give positive feedback when you observe clients listening to each other or, as in the preceding example, when they respond to your coaching. In the example, the social worker might have praised the mother as follows: "I liked the way you responded, because your message accurately reflected what your daughter was experiencing. I think she felt you really understood what she was trying to say." It is also helpful to ask participants to discuss what they experienced during the exchange and to highlight positive feelings and observations.

Authenticity

Although many theorists agree that empathy and respect are vital to developing effective working relationships, they do not agree about the amount of openness or self-disclosure practitioners should offer. *Self-disclosure* refers to the sharing with the client of opinions, thoughts, feelings, reactions to the client, and personal experiences of the practitioner (Deal, 1999). Decisions about whether or when to self-disclose must be guided by a perception of benefit to the client, not the practitioner's need to share. As one client said, "My case worker wanted to tell me all about his weekend and his girlfriend and so on. And I said, 'TMI: too much information. I don't need to know this, and I don't want to know this.' I don't want to share this kind of information with him and don't want to know it from him." Clearly, this client did not perceive the benefit of this kind of personal sharing. Deal reports that although beginning practitioners frequently report engaging in self-disclosure, they seem less clear about the conditions under which it was appropriate to do so.

With respect to empirical evidence, numerous research studies cited by Truax and Mitchell (1971) and Gurman (1977) indicated that empathy, respect, and genuineness are correlated with positive outcomes. Critical analyses of these studies and conflicting findings from other research studies, however, have led experts to question these early findings and to conclude that "a more complex association exists between outcome and therapist 'skills' than originally hypothesized" (Parloff, Waskow, & Wolfe, 1978, p. 251).

Nevertheless, authenticity (also called genuineness) and the other facilitative conditions are still viewed as central to the helping process. *Authenticity* is defined as the sharing of self by relating in a natural, sincere, spontaneous, open, and genuine manner. Being authentic, or genuine, involves relating personally so that expressions are spontaneous rather than contrived. In addition, it means that social workers' verbalizations are congruent with their actual feelings and thoughts. Authentic social workers relate as real people, expressing their feelings and assuming responsibility for them rather than denying the feelings or blaming the client for causing them. Authenticity also involves being nondefensive and human enough to admit one's errors to clients. Realizing that they expect clients to lower their defenses and to relate openly (thereby increasing their vulnerability), social workers themselves must model humanness and openness and avoid hiding behind a mask of "professionalism."

Relating authentically does not mean that social workers indiscriminately disclose their feelings. Indeed, authentic expressions can be abrasive and destructive. Yalom and Lieberman (1971), for example, found in a study of encounter groups that attacks or rejections of group members by leaders or other members produced many psychological casualties. Social workers should thus relate authentically only when doing so is likely to further the therapeutic objectives. This qualification provides considerable latitude and is merely intended to constrain social workers from (1) relating abrasively (even though they may be expressing genuine feelings) and (2) meeting their own needs by focusing on their personal experiences and feelings rather than those of the client.

With respect to the first constraint, social workers must avoid misconstruing authenticity as granting free license to do whatever they wish, especially with respect to expressing hostility. The second constraint reiterates the importance of social workers' responding to clients' needs rather than their own. Moreover, when social workers share their feelings or experiences for a therapeutic purpose, they should immediately shift the focus back on the clients. Keep in mind that the purpose of relating authentically—whether with individuals, families, or groups—is to facilitate growth of clients, not to demonstrate one's own honesty or authenticity.

Types of Self-Disclosure

The aspect of authenticity denoted as self-disclosure has been variously defined by different authors (Chelune, 1979). For our discussion here, we define self-disclosure as the conscious and intentional revelation of information about oneself through both verbal expressions and nonverbal behaviors (e.g., smiling, grimacing, or shaking one's head in disbelief). Viewed from a therapeutic perspective, self-disclosure encourages clients to reciprocate with trust and openness.

Danish, D'Augelli, and Hauer (1980) have identified two types of self-disclosure, *self-involving statements* and *personal self-disclosing*. The former type includes messages that express the social worker's personal reaction to the client during the course of a session. Examples of self-involving statements follow:

- *"I'm impressed with the progress you've made this past week. You applied what we discussed last week and have made another step toward learning to control angry feelings."*
- *"I want to share my reaction to what you just said. I found myself feeling sad for you because you put yourself down unmercifully. I see you so differently from how you see yourself and find myself wishing I could somehow spare you the torment you inflict on yourself."*
- *"You know, as I think about the losses you've experienced this past year, I marvel you've done as well as you have. I'm not at all sure I'd have held together as well as you have."*

Personal self-disclosure messages, by contrast, center on struggles or problems the social worker is currently experiencing or has experienced that are similar to the client's problems. The following are examples of this type of self-disclosure:

- [To couple] *"As you talk about your problems with your children, it reminds me of similar difficulties I had with mine when they were that same age."* (The social worker goes on to relate his experience.)

- [To individual client] *"I think all of us struggle with that same fear to some degree. Earlier this week I ..."* (The social worker goes on to relate events in which she experienced similar fears.)

Research findings comparing the effects of different types of self-disclosure have been mixed. Given the inconclusive findings, social workers should use personal self-disclosure judiciously. They should also recognize cultural variations that may suggest that some relatively low-level self-disclosure may be necessary early in the helping process. Rosenthal-Gelman has reported in a study that Hispanic practitioners are more likely to engage in some self-disclosure at the beginning of contact with Hispanic clients, honoring the cultural norm of establishing a more personal contact (Rosenthal-Gelman, 2004). Logic suggests that self-disclosures of current problems may undermine the confidence of clients, who may well wonder how social workers can presume to help others when they haven't successfully resolved their own problems. Moreover, focusing on the social worker's problems diverts attention from the client, who may conclude that the social worker prefers to focus on his or her own problems. Self-involving disclosures, by contrast, appear to be of low risk and are relevant to the helping process.

> As noted in the "Getting Back to Shakopee" video, self-disclosure of cultural experiences by the practitioner, Dorothy, appears essential in beginning to develop trust and rapport with her client.

Timing and Intensity of Self-Disclosure

Yet another aspect of self-disclosure focuses on the timing and level of intensity of the social worker's sharing, ranging from superficial to highly personal statements. Social workers should avoid sharing personal feelings and experiences until they have established rapport and trust with their clients and the clients have, in turn, demonstrated readiness to engage on a more personal level. The danger in premature self-disclosure is that such responses can threaten clients and lead to emotional retreat at the very time when it is vital to reduce threat and defensiveness.

The danger is especially great with clients from other cultures who are unaccustomed to relating on an intense personal basis. Greater formality with less self-disclosure may be useful in cross-cultural transactions between Caucasian social workers and clients of color. With respect to Asian American clients, however, Tsui and Schultz (1985) indicate that self-disclosure by social workers may facilitate the development of rapport: Personal disclosure and an appropriate level of emotional expressiveness are often the most effective ways to put Asian clients at ease. Considering the generally low level of emotional expressiveness in Asian families, the therapist is, in effect, acting as a role model for the client, thereby showing the client how the appropriate expression of emotion facilitates the treatment process (Tsui and Schultz, 1985, p. 568). Asian American families, of course, are not homogenous, as their members differ in terms of their level of acculturation and familiarity with values such as self-disclosure.

As clients experience trust, social workers can appropriately relate with increased openness and spontaneity, assuming that their authentic responses are relevant to their clients' needs and do not shift the focus from the client for more than brief periods. Even when trust is strong, social workers should exercise only moderate self-disclosure—beyond a certain level, even authentic responses no longer facilitate the helping process (Truax & Carkhuff, 1964).

A Paradigm for Responding Authentically

Beginning social workers (and clients) may learn the skill of relating authentically more readily if they have a paradigm for formulating effective messages. This paradigm includes the four elements of an authentic message:

(1) "I" ( )	*About*	*Because*
(2) Specific feeling or wants	(3) Neutral description of event	(4) Impact of situation upon sender or others

The following example (Larsen, 1980), involving a social work student intern's response to a message from an institutionalized youth, illustrates the use of this paradigm. The student describes the situation: "Don and I had a tough go of it last week. I entered the living unit only to find that he was angry with me for some reason, and he proceeded to abuse me verbally all night long. This week, Don approached me to apologize."

Don: I'm really sorry about what happened the other night. I didn't mean nothing by it. You probably don't want nothing more to do with me.

Student: Well, you know, Don, I'm sorry it happened, too. I was really hurt and puzzled that night because I didn't understand where all your anger was coming from. You wouldn't talk to me about it, so I felt frustrated and I didn't quite know what to do or make of it. One of my real fears that night was that this was going to get in the way of our getting to know each other. I really didn't want to see that happen.

Note that the student uses all of the elements of the paradigm: identifying specific feelings (hurt, puzzlement, frustration, fear); describing the events that occurred in a neutral, nonblaming manner; and identifying the impact she feared these events might have upon the client–social worker relationship.

As you consider the paradigm, note that we are not recommending that you use it in a mechanistic and undeviating "I-feel-this-way-about …" response pattern. Rather, we suggest that you learn and combine the elements of the paradigm in a variety of ways as you practice constructing authentic messages. Later, as you incorporate authentic relating into your natural conversational repertoire, you will no longer need to refer to the paradigm.

Note that this paradigm is also applicable in teaching clients to respond authentically. We suggest that you present the paradigm to clients and guide them through several practice messages, assisting them to include all of the elements of the paradigm in their responses. For example:

Specific "I" Feelings	Description of Event	Impact
I get frustrated	when you keep reading the paper while I'm speaking	because I feel discounted and very unimportant to you.

It is important to stress with clients the need to use conversational language when they express authentic messages. Also emphasize, however, that they should talk about their own feelings and opinions. Otherwise, they may slip into accusatory forms of communication as they vary their messages.

Guidelines for Responding Authentically

As you practice authentic responding and teach clients to respond authentically in their encounters with others, we suggest you keep in mind the following guidelines related to the four elements of an authentic message.

1. *Personalize messages by using the pronoun "I."* When attempting to respond authentically, both social workers and clients commonly make the mistake of starting their statements with "You." This introduction tends to focus a response on the other person rather than on the sender's experiencing. In contrast, beginning messages with "I" encourages senders to own responsibility for their feelings and to personalize their statements.

Efforts by social workers to employ "I" statements when responding can profoundly affect the quality of group processes, increasing both the specificity of communications and the frequency with which their clients use "I" statements. As a general rule, groups (including couples and families) are likely to follow a social worker's communication style.

Just as groups tend to follow suit when social workers frequently use "I" messages, they may also imitate counterproductive behaviors of the social worker. That includes communicating in broad generalities, focusing on issues external to the individual, or relating to the group in an interrogative or confrontational manner. For this reason, the behavior of some social workers may not necessarily be a good model for clients to emulate in real life.

Social workers must be careful to model the skills they wish clients to acquire. They should master relating authentically to the extent that they automatically personalize their messages and constructively share their inner experiencing with clients. To facilitate personalizing messages, social workers can negotiate an agreement with individuals or groups specifying that clients will endeavor to incorporate the use of "I" statements in their conversational repertoires. Thereafter, it is critical to intervene consistently to assist clients to personalize their messages when they have not done so.

2. *Share feelings that lie at varying depths.* Social workers must reach for those feelings that underlie their immediate experiencing. Doing so is particularly vital when social workers experience strong negative feelings (e.g., dislike, anger, repulsion, disgust, boredom) toward a client, because an examination of the deeper aspects of feelings often discloses more positive feelings toward the client. Expressing these feelings preserves the client's self-esteem, whereas expressing superficial negative feelings often poses a threat to the client, creating defensiveness and anger.

For example, in expressing anger (and perhaps disgust) toward a client who is chronically late for appointments, the social worker may first connect his feelings of anger to feeling inconvenienced. In reaching for his deeper feelings, however, the social worker may discover that the annoyance derives from disappointment that the client is not fully committed to the helping process. At an even deeper level may lie hurt in not being more important to the client. Further introspection may also uncover a concern that the client is exhibiting similar behavior in other areas of life that could adversely affect his or her relationships with others.

The social worker may discover multiple (and sometimes conflicting) feelings that may be beneficially shared with the client, as illustrated in the following message:

Social worker [*To mother*]: I've been experiencing some feelings in the session I want to share with you because it may shed some light on what others may experience with you. I was wanting to tell you that it appears you often come to Robert's [the client's son] rescue in the session, and that sometimes you seem to protect him from the consequences of his own actions, but I held back and began to feel a slight knotting in my stomach. Then it hit me that I was afraid you'd be hurt and offended and that it might have a negative effect on our relationship. As I think about it just now, I'm aware that sometimes I feel I'm walking on eggshells with you. I don't like that because it puts distance between us. Another reason I don't like it is because I think I'm underestimating your ability to handle constructive feedback. I think you're stronger than you come across at times. [*Slight pause.*] Could you share what you're feeling just now about what I said?

Like prospective social workers, clients are prone to focus on one aspect of their experiencing to the exclusion of deeper and more complex emotions. Clients often have difficulty, in fact, pinpointing any feelings they are experiencing. In either case, social workers should persevere to help clients broaden their awareness of their emotions and to express them openly, as illustrated in the following exchange:

Social worker: When you told your wife you didn't want to take her to a movie and she said you were a "bump on a log"—that you never seemed to want to do anything with her—what feelings did you experience?[2]

Husband: I decided that if that's what she thought of me, that's what I'd be.

Social worker: Can you get in touch with what you were feeling? You told me a little bit about what you thought, but what's happening inside? Try to use feeling words to describe what you're experiencing.

Husband [*pause*]: I felt that if she was going to get on my back …

Social worker [*gently interrupting*]: Can you use a feeling word like "bad," or "hurt," or "put down"? What did you feel?

Husband: Okay. I felt annoyed.

Social worker: So you experienced a sense of irritation. Good. I'm pleased you could get in touch with that feeling. Now see if you can get to an even more basic feeling. Remember, as we've talked about before, anger is usually a surface feeling that camouflages other feelings. What was under your annoyance?

Husband: Uh, I'd say frustrated. I just didn't want to sit there and listen to her harp at me. She never quits.

Social worker: I would like to check out something with you. Right now, as you're talking about this, it seems you're experiencing a real sense of discouragement and perhaps even hopelessness about things ever changing. It's as though you've given up. Maybe that's part of what you were feeling Saturday.

Husband: Yeah, I just turn myself off. There doesn't seem to be anything I can do to make her happy.

Social worker: I'm glad that you can recognize the sense of despair you're feeling. I also appreciate your hanging in there with me for a minute to get in touch with some of your feelings. You seem to be a person whose feelings run deep, and sometimes expressing them may come hard for you. I'm wondering how you view yourself in that regard.

In the preceding excerpt, the social worker engaged in extensive coaching to assist the client in discovering his underlying feelings. Deeper than the feelings of annoyance and frustration the client identified lay the more basic emotions related to feeling hurt and being unimportant to his wife. By providing other spontaneous "training sessions," the social worker can help this client to identify his feelings more readily, to find the feeling words to express them, and to begin formulating "I" statements.

3. *Describe the situation or targeted behavior in neutral or descriptive terms.* In their messages, clients often omit references or make only vague references to the situations that prompted their responses. Moreover, they may convey their messages in a blaming manner, engendering defensiveness that overshadows other aspects of their self-disclosure. In either event, self-disclosure is minimal and respondents do not receive information that could otherwise be of considerable value.

Consider, for example, the low yield of information in the following messages:

- *"You're a nice person."*
- *"You should be more conscientious."*

- *"You're progressing well in your work."*
- *"You have a bad attitude."*

All of these messages lack supporting information that respondents need to identify specific aspects of their behavior that is competent and warrants recognition or is substandard. Social workers should assist parents, spouses, or others to provide higher-yield feedback by including behavioral references. Examples of such messages follow (they involve a parent talking to a 6-year-old girl):

- *"I've really appreciated all that you've done tonight by yourself. You picked up your toys, washed your hands before dinner, and ate dinner without dawdling. I'm so pleased."*
- *"I'm very disappointed with your behavior right now. You didn't change your clothes when you came home from school; you didn't feed the dog; and you haven't started your homework."*

Note in the last example that the parent sent an "I" message and owned the feelings of disappointment rather than attacking the child for being undependable.

When responding authentically, social workers should carefully describe specific events that prompted their responses, particularly when they wish to draw clients' attention to some aspect of their behavior or to a situation of which they may not be fully aware. The following·social worker's message illustrates this point:

Social worker: I need to share something with you that concerns me. Just a moment ago, I gave you feedback regarding the positive way I thought you handled a situation with your husband. [*Refers to specific behaviors manifested by client.*] When I did that, you seemed to discount my response by [*mentions specific behaviors*]. Actually, this is not the first time I have seen this happen. It appears to me that it is difficult for you to give yourself credit for the positive things you do and the progress you are making. This, in fact, may be one of the reasons that you get so discouraged at times. I wonder how you view your behavior in this regard.

Social workers constantly need to assess the specificity of their responses to ensure that they give clients the benefit of behaviorally specific feedback and provide positive modeling experiences for them. It is also vital to coach clients in giving specific feedback whenever they make sweeping generalizations and do not document the relationship between their responses and specific situations.

4. *Identify the specific impact of the problem situation or behavior on others.* Authentic messages often stop short of identifying the specific effects of the situation on the sender or on others, even though such information would be very appropriate and helpful. This element of an "I" message also increases the likelihood that the receiver will adjust or make changes, particularly if the sender demonstrates that the receiver's behavior is having a tangible effect on him or her.

Consider a social worker's authentic response to a male member of an adult group:

Social worker: "Sometimes I sense some impatience on your part to move on to other topics. [*Describes situation that just occurred, documenting specific messages and behavior.*] At times I find myself torn between responding to your urging us "to get on with it" or staying with a discussion that seems beneficial to the group. It may be that others in the group are experiencing similar mixed feelings and some of the pressure I feel.

Here the social worker first clarifies the tangible effects of the client's behavior on himself and then suggests that others may experience the behavior similarly. Given the social worker's approach, others in the group may be willing to give feedback as well. The client is then free to draw his own conclusions about the cause-and-effect relationship between his behaviors and the reactions of others and to decide whether he wishes to alter his way of relating in the group.

Social workers can identify how specific client behaviors negatively impact not only the social worker but also the clients themselves (e.g., "I'm concerned about [*specific behavior*] because it keeps you from achieving your goal"). Further, they may document how a client's behavior affects others (e.g., his wife) or the relationship between the client and another person (e.g., "It appears that your behavior creates distance between you and your son").

Clients often have difficulty in clarifying the impact of others' behavior on themselves. For example, a mother's message to her child, "I want you to play someplace else," establishes no reason for the request, nor does it specify the negative impact of the behavior on her. If the mother responds in an authentic manner, however, she clearly identifies the tangible effect of her child's behavior: "I'm having a hard time getting through the hallway because I keep stumbling over toys and having to go around you. I've almost fallen several times, and others might, too. I'm worried that someone might get hurt, so I'm asking you to move your toys to your room."

The preceding illustration underscores the point that when clients clarify how a situation affects them, their requests do not appear arbitrary and are more persuasive; hence, others are likely to make appropriate accommodations. We suspect that an important reason why many clients have not changed certain self-defeating behaviors before entering the helping process is that others have previously attacked or pressured them to change, rather than authentically and unabrasively imparting information that highlights how the clients' behavior strikes them. Others may have also attempted to prescribe behavioral changes that appear to be self-serving (e.g., "Come on, stop that sulking") instead of relating their feelings (e.g., "I'm concerned that you're down and unhappy; I'd like to help but I'm not sure how"). Such statements do not strike a responsive chord in clients, who may equate making changes with putting themselves under the control of others (by following their directives), thereby losing their autonomy.

In the following exchange, note how the social worker assists Carolyn, a group member, to personalize her statements and to clarify her reaction to the behavior of another member who has remained consistently silent throughout the first two sessions:

Carolyn: We've talked about needing to add new guidelines for the group as we go along. I think we ought to have a guideline that everyone should talk in the group. [*Observe that Carolyn has not personalized her message but has proposed a solution to meet a need she has not identified.*]

Social worker [*to Carolyn*]: The group may want to consider this guideline, but for a minute, can you get in touch with what you're experiencing and put it in the form of an "I" statement?

Carolyn: Well, all right. Janet hasn't talked at all for two solid weeks, and it's beginning to really irritate me.

Social worker: I'm wondering what else you may be experiencing besides irritation? [*Assists Carolyn to identify her feelings besides mild anger.*]

Carolyn: I guess I'm a little uneasy because I don't know where Janet stands. Maybe I'm afraid she's sitting in judgment of us—I mean, me. And I guess I feel cheated because I'd like to get to know her better, and right now I feel shut out by her.

Social worker: That response helps us to begin to get to the heart of the matter. Would you now express yourself directly to Janet? Tell her what you are

experiencing and, particularly, how her silence is affecting you.

Carolyn [*to Janet*]: I did wonder what you thought about me since I really opened up last week. And I do want to get to know you better. But, underneath all this, I'm concerned about you. You seem unhappy and alone, and that makes me uncomfortable—I don't like to think of your feeling that way. Frankly, I'd like to know how you feel about being in this group, and if you're uneasy about it, as you seem to be, I'd like to help you feel better somehow.

In the preceding example, the social worker assisted Carolyn to experience a broader range of feelings and to identify her reaction to Janet's silence. In response to the social worker's intervention, Carolyn also expressed more positive feelings than were evident in her initial message—a not infrequent occurrence when social workers encourage clients to explore deeper-level emotions.

Engaging one member in identifying specific reactions to the behavior of others provides a learning experience for the entire group, and members often expand their conversational repertoires to incorporate such facilitative responding. In fact, the extent to which social workers assist clients to acquire specific skills is correlated with the extent to which clients acquire those same skills.

Cues for Authentic Responding

The impetus for social workers to respond authentically may emanate from (1) clients' messages that request self-disclosure or (2) social workers' decisions to share perceptions and reactions they believe will be helpful. Next, we consider authentic responding that emanates from these two sources.

Authentic Responding Stimulated by Clients' Messages

Requests from Clients for Personal Information. Clients often confront students and social workers with questions aimed at soliciting personal information, such as "How old are you?", "Do you have any children?", "What is your religion?", "Are you married?", and "Are you a student?" It is natural for clients to be curious and to ask questions about a social worker in whom they are confiding, especially when their well-being and future are at stake.

Self-disclosing responses may or may not be appropriate, depending on the social worker's assessment of the client's motivation for asking a particular question. When questions appear to be prompted by a natural desire for information, such responses are often very appropriate. Seemingly innocuous questions, however, may camouflage deep concerns or troubling feelings. In such instances, providing an immediate answer may not be advisable because doing so may close the door to exploring and resolving clients' concerns and feelings (Strean, 1997). Clients are then left to struggle with their feelings alone, which may seriously impair progress or cause premature termination of the social work contact.

To illustrate, consider the following exchange from an initial session involving a 23-year-old student social worker and a 43-year-old woman who requested help in dealing with her marital problems:

Client: Are you married?
Student social worker: No, but I'm engaged. Why do you ask?
Client: Oh, I don't know. I just wondered.

Given the context of an older adult with a much younger student, the client's question was likely motivated by a concern that the student might lack life experience essential to understanding her marital difficulties or the competence needed to assist her in resolving them. In this instance, immediate authentic disclosure by the student was inappropriate because it did not facilitate exploration of the feelings underlying the client's inquiry.

Conversely, such an exchange may yield information vital to the helping process if the social worker avoids premature self-disclosure. It is sometimes very difficult to distinguish whether the questions of clients are motivated by a natural desire for information or by hidden concerns or feelings. As a rule of thumb, when you have questions about clients' motivation for making personal inquiries, *precede disclosures of views or feelings with either open-ended or empathic responses.* Responding in this manner significantly increases the probability that clients will reveal their underlying concerns. Notice what happens when the social worker utilizes an empathic response before responding authentically:

Client: Are you married?
Student social worker: I gather you're wondering if I can understand and help you with your difficulties in light of the fact that I'm much younger than you.
Client: Well, I guess I was thinking that. I hope it doesn't offend you.
Student social worker: To the contrary—I appreciate your frankness. It's natural that you want to have confidence in your counselor. I know there's a lot at stake for you. Tell me more about your concerns.

Here the student responded to the probable concern of the client and struck pay dirt. Such astuteness tends to foster confidence in clients and greatly facilitates the establishment of a therapeutic partnership. The fact that the student "leans into" the situation by inviting further exploration rather than skirting the issue may also be read by the client as an indicator of the student's own confidence in his or her ability to help. After fully exploring the client's concerns, the student can respond with an authentic response identifying personal qualifications:

Student social worker: I do want you to know that I believe I can be helpful to you. I have studied marriage counseling at some length, and I have counseled other clients whose difficulties were similar to your own. I also consult with my supervisor regularly.

Of course, the final judgment of my competence will rest with you. It will be important for us to discuss any feelings you may still have at the end of the interview as you make a decision about returning for future sessions.

Questions That Solicit the Social Worker's Perceptions. Clients may also pose questions that solicit the social worker's opinions, views, or feelings. Typical questions include "How do I compare to your other clients?", "Do you think I need help?", "Am I crazy?", and "Do you think there's any hope for me?" Such questions can pose a challenge for social workers, who must consider the motivation behind the question and judge whether to disclose their views or feelings immediately or to employ either an empathic or an open-ended response.

When social workers do disclose their perceptions, however, their responses must be congruent with their inner experiencing. In response to the question "Do you think there's any hope for me?" the social worker may congruently respond with a message that blends elements of empathy and authenticity:

Social worker: Your question tells me you're probably afraid that you're beyond help. Although you do have some difficult problems, I'm optimistic that if we work hard together things can improve. You've shown a number of strengths that should help you make changes, including [*reviews strengths*]. Of course, a lot will depend on whether you're willing to commit to making changes you think would improve your situation and to invest the time and effort necessary to achieve your goals. In that respect, you're in control of the situation and whether things change for the better. That fact is something that many people find encouraging to know.

It is not necessary to answer all questions of clients in the service of authenticity. If you feel uncomfortable about answering a personal question or deem it inadvisable to do so, you should feel free to decline answering. When doing so, it is important to explain your reason for not answering directly, again utilizing an authentic response. If a teenage client, for example, asks whether the social worker had sexual relations before she married, the social worker may respond as follows:

Social worker: I would rather not reveal that information to you, because it is a very private part of my life. Asking me took some risk on your part. I have an idea that your question probably has to do with a struggle you're having, although I could be wrong. I would appreciate your sharing your thoughts about what sparked your question.

The social worker should then utilize empathic responding and open-ended questions to explore the client's reaction and motivation for asking her question.

Authentic Responding Initiated by Social Workers

Authentic responding initiated by social workers may take several forms, which are considered next.

Disclosing Past Experiences. As previously indicated, self-disclosure should be sparingly used, brief, relevant to the client's concerns, and well timed. In relating to a particular client's struggle, a social worker might indicate, "I remember I felt very much like that when I was struggling with …" Social workers may also cite personal perceptions or experiences as reference points for clients—for example, "I think that is very normal behavior for a child. For instance, my five-year-old …" A fundamental guideline that applies to such situations is that social workers should be certain they are focusing on themselves to meet the therapeutic needs of their clients.

Sharing Perceptions, Ideas, Reactions, and Formulations. A key role of the social worker in the change-oriented phase of the helping process is to act as a "candid feedback system" by revealing personal thoughts and perceptions relevant to client problems (Hammond et al., 1977). Such responding is intended to further the change process in one or more of the following ways:

1. To heighten clients' awareness of dynamics that may play an important part in problems
2. To offer a different perspective regarding issues and events

3. To aid clients in conceptualizing the purposes of their behavior and feelings
4. To enlighten clients on how they affect others (including the social worker)
5. To bring clients' attention to cognitive and behavioral patterns (both functional and dysfunctional) that operate at either an individual or a group level
6. To share the social worker's here-and-now affective and physical reactions to clients' behavior or to processes that occur in the helping relationship
7. To share positive feedback concerning clients' strengths and growth

After responding authentically to achieve any of these purposes, it is vital to invite clients to express their own views and draw their own conclusions. *Owning* perceptions rather than using under-the-table methods to influence clients to adopt particular views or to change in ways deemed desirable by the social worker (e.g., "Don't you think you ought to consider …") relieves clients of the need to behave deviously or to defend themselves from the tyranny of views with which they do not agree.

Sharing perceptions with clients does involve some risk. In particular, clients may misinterpret the social worker's motives and feel criticized, put down, or rebuked. Clarifying the social worker's helpful intent before responding diminishes this risk somewhat. Nevertheless, it is critical to watch for clients' reactions that may indicate a response has struck an exposed nerve.

To avoid damaging the relationship (or to repair it), the social worker should be empathically attuned to the client's reaction to candid feedback, shifting the focus back to the client to determine the impact of the self-disclosure. If the client appears to have been emotionally wounded by the social worker's authentic response, the social worker can use empathic skills to elicit troubled feelings and to guide subsequent responses aimed at restoring the relationship's equilibrium. Expressions of concern and clarification of the goodwill intended by the social worker are also usually facilitative:

Social worker: I can see that what I shared with you hit you pretty hard—and that you're feeling put down right now. [*Client nods but avoids eye contact.*] I feel bad about that, because the last thing I'd want is to hurt you. Please tell me what you're feeling.

Openly (and Tactfully) Sharing Reactions When Put on the Spot. Clients sometimes create situations that put social workers under considerable pressure to respond to messages that bear directly on the relationship, such as when they accuse a social worker of being uninterested, unfeeling, irritated, displeased, critical, inappropriate, or incompetent. Clients may also ask pointed questions (sometimes before the relationship has been firmly established) that require immediate responses.

The first statement of one female client in an initial interview, for example, was "I'm gay. Does that make any difference to you?" In the opening moments of another session, a pregnant client asked the social worker, "How do you feel about abortion?" Over the years, students have reported numerous such situations that sorely tested their ability to respond facilitatively. In one instance, a male member of a group asked a female student leader for her photograph. In another case, an adolescent boy kept taking his shoes off and putting his feet (which smelled very bad) on the social worker's desk. In reflecting on your practice experience, you can undoubtedly cite instances in which the behavior of clients caused you to squirm or produced butterflies in your stomach.

Experiencing Discomfort in Sessions. Sometimes intense discomfort may indicate that something in the session is going awry and needs to be addressed. It is important to reflect on your discomfort, seeking to identify events that seem to be causing or exacerbating it (e.g., "I'm feeling very uneasy because I don't know how to respond when my client says things like 'You seem to be too busy to see me' or 'I'm not sure I'm worth your trouble' "). After privately exploring the reason for the discomfort, the social worker might respond as follows:

Social worker: I'd like to share some impressions about several things you've said in the last two sessions. [*Identifies client's statements.*] I sense you're feeling pretty unimportant—as though you don't count for much—and that perhaps you're imposing on me just by being here. I want you to know that I'm pleased you had the courage to seek help in the face of all the opposition from your family. It's also important to me that you know that I want to be helpful to you. I am concerned, however, that you feel you're imposing on me. Could you share more of those feelings with me?

Notice how the social worker specifically identifies the self-defeating thoughts and feelings and blends elements of empathy and authenticity in the response.

Other situations that put social workers on the spot include clients' angry attacks, as we discuss later in this chapter. Social workers must learn to respond authentically in such scenarios. Consider a situation in which an adolescent attacks a social worker in an initial interview, protesting, "I don't want to be here. You social workers are all losers." In such instances, social workers should share their reactions, as illustrated in the following response:

Social worker: It sounds as though you're really ticked off about having to see me and that your previous experiences with social workers have been bummers. I respect your feelings and don't want to pressure you to work with me. I am concerned and uncomfortable, however, because you apparently have lumped all social workers together and that makes me a loser in your eyes. If you close your mind to the possibility that we might accomplish something together, then the chances are pretty slim I can be helpful. I want you to know that I am interested in you and that I would like to know what you're up against.

Intertwining empathic and authentic responses in this manner often defuses clients' anger and encourages them to think more rationally about a situation.

Sharing Feelings When Clients' Behavior Is Unreasonable or Distressing. Although social workers should be able to take most client behaviors in stride, sometimes they may experience justifiable feelings of frustration, anger, or even hurt. In one case, a client acquired a social worker's home phone number from another source and began calling frequently about daily crisis situations, although discussions of these events could easily have waited until the next session. In another instance, a tipsy client called the social worker in the middle of the night "just to talk." In yet another case, an adolescent client let the air out of a social worker's automobile tires.

In such situations, social workers should share their feelings with clients—*if they believe they can do so constructively.* In the following recorded case example, note that the student social worker interweaves authentic and empathic responses in confronting a Latino youth in a correctional institution who had maintained he was innocent of hiding drugs that staff had found in his room. Believing the youth's story, the student went to bat for him, only to find out later that the client had lied. Somewhat uneasy at her first real confrontation, the student tries to formulate an authentic response.

In an interesting twist, the youth helps her to be "up-front" with him:

Student social worker: There's something I wanted to talk to you about, Randy … [*Stops to search for the right words.*]

Randy: Well, come out with it, then. Just lay it on me.

Student social worker: Well, remember last week when you got that incident report? You know, I really believed you were innocent. I was ready to go to the hearing and tell staff I was sure you were innocent and that the charge should be dropped. I guess I'm feeling kind of bad because when I talked to you, you told me you were innocent, and, well, that's not exactly the way it turned out.

Randy: You mean I lied to you. Go ahead and say it.

Student social worker: Well, yes, I guess I felt kind of hurt because I was hoping that maybe you had more trust in me than that.

Randy: Well, Susan, let me tell you something. Where I come from, that's not lying—that's what we call survival. Personally, I don't consider myself a liar. I just do what I need to do to get by. That's an old trick, but it just didn't work.

Student social worker: I hear you, Randy. I guess you're saying we're from two different worlds, and maybe we both define the same thing in different ways. I guess that with me being Anglo, you can't really expect me to understand what life has been like for you.

Several minutes later in the session, after the student has further explored the client's feelings, the following interchange occurs:

Student social worker: Randy, I want you to know a couple of things. The first thing is that when social workers work with clients, they must honor what they call confidentiality, so I can't share what we talk about without your permission in most cases. An exception to this relates to rule or law violations. I can't keep that confidential. The second thing is that I don't expect you to share everything with me. I know there are certain things you don't want to tell me, so rather than lying about something that I ask you about, maybe you can just tell me you don't want to tell me. Would you consider that?

Randy: Yeah, that's okay. [*Pause.*] Listen, Susan, I don't want you to go around thinking I'm a liar now. I'll tell you this, and you can take it for what it's worth, but this is the truth. That's the first time I've ever lied to you. But you may not believe that.

Student social worker: I do believe you, Randy. [*He seems a little relieved and there is a silence.*]

Randy: Well, Susan, that's a deal, then. I won't lie to you again, but if there's something I don't want to say, I'll tell you I don't want to say it.

Student social worker: Sounds good to me. [*Both start walking away.*] You know, Randy, I really want to see you get through this program and get out as fast as you can. I know it's hard starting over because of the incident with the drugs, but I think we can get you through. [*This seemed to have more impact on Randy than anything the social worker had said to him in a long time. The pleasure was visible on his face, and he broke into a big smile.*]

Noteworthy in this exchange is that the social worker relied almost exclusively on the skills of authenticity and empathy to bring the incident to a positive conclusion. Ignoring her feelings would have impaired the student's ability to relate facilitatively to the client and would have been destructive to the relationship. In contrast, focusing on the situation proved beneficial for both.

Sharing Feelings When Clients Give Positive Feedback. Social workers sometimes have difficulty responding receptively to clients' positive feedback about their own attributes and/or performance. We suggest that social workers model the same receptivity to positive feedback that they ask clients to demonstrate in their own lives, as illustrated in the following exchange:

Client: I don't know what I would have done without you. I'm just not sure I would have made it if you hadn't been there when I needed you. You've made such a difference in my life.

Social worker: I can sense your appreciation. I'm touched by your gratitude and pleased you are feeling so much more capable of coping with your situation. I want you to know, too, that even though I was there to help, your efforts have been the deciding factor in your growth.

Positive Feedback: A Form of Authentic Responding

Because positive feedback plays such a vital role in the change process, we have allocated a separate section in our attempt to do justice to this topic. Social workers often employ (or should employ) this skill in supplying information to clients about positive attributes or specific areas in which they demonstrate strengths, effective coping mechanisms, and incremental growth. In so doing, social workers enhance their clients' motivation to change and foster hope for the future.

Many opportune moments occur in the helping process when social workers experience warm or positive feelings toward clients because of the latter's actions or progress. When appropriate, social workers should share such feelings spontaneously with clients, as illustrated in the following messages:

- *"I'm pleased that you have what I consider exceptional ability to 'self-observe' your own behavior and to analyze the part you play in relationships. I think this strength will serve you well in solving the problems you've identified."*
- *"I've been touched several times in the group when I've noticed that, despite your grief over the loss of your husband, you've reached out to other members who needed support."*
- [To newly formed group]: *"In contrast to our first session, I've noticed that this week we haven't had trouble getting down to business and staying on task. I've been pleased as I've watched you develop group guidelines for the past 20 minutes with minimal assistance from me. I had the thought, 'This group is really moving.'"*

The first two messages acknowledge strengths of individuals. The third lauds a behavioral change the social worker has observed in a group process. Both types of messages sharply focus clients' attention on specific behaviors that facilitate the change process, ultimately increasing the frequency of such behaviors. When sent consistently, positive messages also have the long-range effect of helping clients who have low self-esteem to develop a more positive self-image. When positive feedback is employed to document the cause-and-effect relationship between their efforts and positive outcomes, clients also experience a sense of satisfaction, accomplishment, and control over their situation.

Positive feedback can have the additional effect of increasing clients' confidence in their own coping ability. We have occasionally had experiences with clients who were on the verge of falling apart when they came to a session but left feeling able to manage their problems for a while longer. We attribute their increased ability to function in part to authentic responses that documented and highlighted areas in which they were coping and successfully managing problems.

Taped sessions of students and social workers often reveal relatively few authentic responses that underscore clients' strengths or incremental growth. This lack of positive feedback is unfortunate because, in our experience, clients' rates of change often correlate with the extent to which social workers focus on these two vital areas. If social workers consistently focus on their clients' assets and the subtle positive changes that often occur in early sessions, clients will typically invest more effort in the change process. As the rate of change accelerates, social workers can in turn focus more extensively on clients' successes, identifying and reinforcing their strengths and functional coping behaviors.

Social workers face several challenges in accrediting clients' strengths and growth, including improving their own ability to recognize and express fleeting positive feelings when clients manifest strengths or progress. Social workers must also learn to document events so that they can provide information about specific positive behaviors. Another challenge and responsibility is to teach clients to give positive feedback to one another, strategies that we discuss in Chapter 15.

To increase your ability to discern client strengths, we recommend that you and your clients construct a profile of their resources. This task may be completed with individuals, couples, families, or groups, and preferably occurs early in the helping process. In individual sessions, the social worker should ask the client to identify and list all the strengths she or he can think of. The social worker also shares observations of the client's strengths, adding them to the list, which is kept for ongoing review to add further strengths as they are discovered.

With families, couples, or groups, social workers may follow a similar procedure in assessing the strengths of individual members, but they should ask other group members to share their perceptions of strengths with each member. The social worker might also ask couples, families, or groups to identify the strengths and incremental growth of the group per se periodically throughout the helping process. After clients have identified their personal strengths or the strengths of the group, the social worker should elicit observations regarding their reactions to the experience. Often they may mutually conclude that clients have many more strengths than they have realized. The social worker should also explore any discomfort experienced by clients as they identify strengths, with the goal of having them acknowledge more comfortably their positive attributes and personal resources.

We further suggest that you carefully observe processes early on in sessions. Note the subtle manifestations of strengths and positive behavioral changes, systematically recording these in your progress records. Record not only the strengths and incremental growth of clients, but also whether you (or group members) focused on those changes. Keep in mind that changes often occur very subtly within a single session. For instance, clients may begin to discuss problems more openly during a later part of a session, tentatively commit to work on problems they had refused to tackle earlier, show growing trust in the social worker by confiding high-risk information about themselves, or own responsibility for the first time regarding their part in their problems. Groups and families may likewise experience growth within short periods of time. It is vital to keep your antenna finely tuned to such changes so that you do not overlook clients' progress.

Relating Assertively to Clients

Another aspect of relating authentically entails relating assertively to clients when a situation warrants such behavior. There are myriad reasons for relating assertively. To inspire confidence and influence clients to follow their lead, social workers must relate in a manner that projects competence. This is especially important in the initial phase of the helping process. Clients often covertly test or check out social workers to determine whether they can understand their problems and appear competent to help them.

In conjoint or group sessions, clients may question whether the social worker is strong enough to protect them from destructive interactional processes that may occur in sessions. Indeed, family or group members generally will not fully share, risk, or commit to the helping process until they have answered this question affirmatively through consistent observation of assertive actions by the social worker.

If social workers are relaxed and demonstrate through decisive behavior that they are fully capable of handling clients' problems and of providing the necessary protection and structure to control potentially chaotic or volatile processes, clients will typically relax, muster hope, and begin to work on problems. If the social worker appears incapable of curtailing or circumventing dysfunctional processes that render clients vulnerable, clients will have justifiable doubts about whether they should be willing to place themselves in jeopardy and, consequently, may disengage from the helping process.

Skill in relating assertively is also prerequisite to initiating confrontation, a major technique that social workers employ to surmount opposition to change. But social workers must employ confrontation with sensitivity and finesse, because the risk of alienating clients by using this technique is high. All forms of assertiveness, in fact, must be conveyed in a context of goodwill and empathic regard for clients' feelings and self-esteem.

In this section, we identify guidelines that can help you to intervene assertively with clients.

Making Requests and Giving Directives

To assist clients to relate more easily and work constructively to solve their problems, social workers frequently must make requests of them. Some of these requests may involve relating in new ways during sessions. For example, social workers may ask clients to do any of the following:

1. Speak directly to each other rather than through the social worker.
2. Give feedback to others in the session.
3. Respond by checking out the meanings of others' messages, take a listening stance, or personalize messages.
4. Change the arrangement of chairs.
5. Role-play.
6. Make requests of others.
7. Take responsibility for responding in specified ways during sessions.
8. Agree to carry out defined tasks during the week.
9. Identify strengths or incremental growth for themselves or others in the group or family.

When making requests, it is important to express them firmly and decisively and to deliver them with assertive nonverbal behavior. Social workers often err by couching their requests in tentative language, thus conveying doubt to clients about whether they must comply with the requests. The contrast between messages delivered in tentative language and those phrased in firm language can be observed in the exchanges given in Table 5-1.

Many times social workers' requests of clients are actually *directives*, as are those under the column "Firm Requests" in Table 5-1. In essence, directives are declarative statements that place the burden on clients to object if they are uncomfortable, as the following message illustrates:

Social worker: Before you answer that question, please turn your chair toward your wife. [*Social worker leans over and helps client to adjust chair. Social worker speaks to wife.*] Will you please turn your chair, also, so that you can speak directly to your husband? Thank you. It's important that you be in full contact with each other while we talk.

TABLE-5-1 TENTATIVE VERSUS FIRM REQUESTS

TENTATIVE REQUESTS	FIRM REQUESTS
Would you mind if I interrupted …	I would like to pause for a moment …
Is it okay if we role-play?	I'd like you to role-play with me for a moment.
Excuse me, but don't you think you are getting off track?	I think we are getting off track. I'd like to return to the subject we were discussing just a minute ago.
Could we talk about something Kathy just said?	Let's go back to something Kathy just said. I think it is very important.

If the social worker had given these clients a choice (e.g., "Would you like to change your chairs?"), they might not have responded affirmatively. We suggest that when you want clients to behave differently in sessions, you simply state what you would like them to do. If clients verbally object to directives or manifest nonverbal behavior that may indicate that they have reservations about complying with a request, it is vital to respond empathically and to explore the basis of their opposition. Such exploration often resolves fears or misgivings, freeing clients to engage in requested behavior.

Maintaining Focus and Managing Interruptions

Maintaining focus is a vital task that takes considerable skill and assertiveness on the social worker's part. It is often essential to intervene verbally to focus or refocus processes when interruptions or distractions occur. Sometimes, social workers may also respond assertively on a nonverbal level to prevent members from interrupting important processes that may need to be brought to positive conclusion, as illustrated in the following excerpt from a family session:

Kim, age 14 [*in tears, talking angrily to her mother*]: You hardly ever listen. At home, you just always yell at us and go to your bedroom.

Mrs. R: I thought I was doing better than that …

Mr. R [*interrupting his wife to speak to social worker*]: I think it's hard for my wife because …

Social worker [*holds up hand to father in a "halt" position, while continuing to maintain eye contact with mother and daughter; speaks to Kim*]: I would like to stay with your statement for a moment. Kim, please tell your mother what you're experiencing right now.

Interrupting Dysfunctional Processes

Unseasoned social workers often permit dysfunctional processes to continue for long periods either because they lack knowledge of how to intervene or because they think they should wait until clients have completed a series of exchanges. In such instances, social workers fail to fulfill one of their major responsibilities—that is, to *guide and direct* processes and to influence participants to interact in more facilitative ways. Remember that clients often seek help because they cannot manage their destructive interactional processes. Thus, permitting them to engage at length in their usual patterns of arguing, cajoling, threatening, blaming, criticizing, and labeling each other merely exacerbates their problems. The social worker should intervene in such circumstances, teaching the clients more facilitative behaviors and guiding them to implement such behaviors in subsequent interactions.

If you decide to interrupt ongoing processes, do so decisively so that clients will listen to you or heed your directive. If you intervene nonassertively, your potential to influence clients (particularly aggressive clients) will suffer, because being able to interrupt a discussion successfully demonstrates your power or influence in the relationship (Parlee, 1979). If you permit clients to ignore or to circumvent your interventions to arrest dysfunctional processes, you yield control and assume a "cone-down" position in relationship to the client.

With respect to interrupting or intervening in processes, we advocate using assertive—not aggressive—behavior. You must be sensitive to the vested interests of clients, because even though you may regard certain processes as unproductive or destructive, clients may not. The timing of interruptions is therefore vital. If it is not critical to draw clients' attention to what is happening immediately, you can wait for a natural pause. If such a pause does not occur shortly, you should interrupt. You should *not* delay interrupting destructive interactional processes, however, as illustrated in the following excerpt:

Wife [*to social worker*]: I feel the children need to mind me, but every time I ask them to do something, he [*husband*] says they don't have to do it. I think we're just ruining our kids, and it's mostly his fault.

Husband: Oh—well—that shows how dumb you are.

Social worker: I'm going to interrupt you because find-ing fault with each other will only lead to mutual resentment.

In this exchange, the social worker intervenes to refocus the discussion after just two dysfunctional responses on the clients' part. If participants do not disengage imme-diately, the social worker will need to use body move-ments that interfere with communication pathways or, in extreme instances, an exclamation such as "Time out!" to interrupt behavior. When social workers have demonstrated their intent to intervene quickly and de-cisively, clients will usually comply immediately when asked to disengage.

"Leaning Into" Clients' Anger

We cannot overstate the importance of openly addres-sing clients' anger and complaints. It is not unusual to feel defensive and threatened when such anger arises. Many social workers, especially those who are working with involuntary clients who are alleged to have harmed others, are inclined to retaliate, conveying the message, "You have no right to your anger. You have brought this on yourself. Do it my way or suffer the con-sequences." Responding assertively to a client's anger does not mean that you become a doormat, accepting that anger passively and submissively. Unless social workers can handle themselves assertively and compe-tently in the face of such anger, they will lose the respect of most clients and thus their ability to help them. Fur-ther, clients may use their anger to influence and intim-idate social workers just as they have done with others.

To help you respond assertively in managing clients' anger, we offer the following suggestions:

- *Respond empathically to reflect clients' anger and, if possible, other underlying feelings (e.g., "I sense you're angry at me for _____ and perhaps disap-pointed about _____").*
- *Continue to explore the situation and the feelings of participants until you understand the nature of the events that inspired the angry feelings. During this exploration, you may find that the anger to-ward you dissipates and that clients begin to focus on themselves, assuming appropriate responsibility for their part in the situation at hand. The "real problem," as often happens, may not directly involve you.*
- *As you explore clients' anger, authentically express your feelings and reactions if it appears appropriate (e.g., "I didn't know you felt that way … I want to*

hear how I might have contributed to this situation. There may be some adjustments I'll want to make in my style of relating … I'm pleased that you shared your feelings with me.").
- *Apply a problem-solving approach (if appropriate) so that all concerned make adjustments to avoid similar occurrences or situations in the future.*
- *If a particular client expresses anger frequently and in a dysfunctional manner, you may also focus on the client's style of expressing anger, identify pro-blems that this communicative approach may cause him or her in relationships with others, and negoti-ate a goal of modifying this response pattern.*
- *In addition to empathizing with client anger, you can model assertive setting of personal limits and boundaries. For example, you might say, "I think that I have a good idea about how you are feeling about this situation and what you would like to be different about it. But I can't readily talk with you when you are so upset. Do you have a way of calming yourself down, or should we plan to meet again when you feel more in control of your emo-tions?" Alternatively, you might say, "I have pledged to do my part to listen to and respond to the issues you have raised. I am not willing to continue to be verbally abused, however."*

Saying No and Setting Limits

Many tasks that social workers perform on behalf of their clients are quite appropriate. For example, negoti-ating for clients and conferring with other parties and potential resources to supplement and facilitate client action are tasks that are rightly handled by social work-ers (Epstein, 1992, p. 208). In contracting with clients, however, social workers must occasionally decline re-quests or set limits. This step is sometimes difficult for beginning social workers to take, as they typically want to demonstrate their willingness to help others. Com-mitment to helping others is a desirable quality, but it must be tempered with judgment as to when acceding to clients' requests is in the best interests of both social worker and client.

Some clients may have had past experiences that led them to believe that social workers will do most of the work required out of sessions. However, clients are of-ten more likely to experience empowerment by increas-ing the scope of their actions than by having social workers perform tasks on their behalf that they can learn to do for themselves. Consequently, if social work-ers unthinkingly agree to take on responsibilities that clients can perform now or could perform in the future, they may reinforce passive client behavior.

Setting limits has special implications when social workers work with involuntary clients. Cingolani (1984) has noted that social workers engage in negotiated relationships with such clients. In negotiated relationships, social workers assume the roles of compromiser, mediator, and enforcer in addition to the more comfortable role of counselor. For example, when an involuntary client requests a "break" related to performance of a court order, the social worker must be clear about the client's choices and consequences of making those choices. He or she must also clarify what the client should expect from the social worker.

Rory [*member of domestic violence group*]: I don't think that it is fair that you report that I didn't meet for eight of the ten group sessions. I could not get off work for some of those sessions. I did all I could do.

Social worker: You did attend seven of the sessions, Rory, and made efforts to attend others. However, the contract you signed, which was presented in court, stated that you must complete eight sessions to be certified as completing the group. I do not have the power to change that court order. Should you decide to comply with the court order, I am willing to speak with your employer to urge him to work with you to arrange your schedule so that you can meet the court order.

In his response, the social worker made it clear that he would not evade the court order. At the same time, he assured Rory that if he chose to comply with the court order, the social worker would be willing to act as a mediator to assist him with difficulties in scheduling with the employer.

Being tactfully assertive is no easier for social workers with excessive needs to please others than it is for clients. These social workers have difficulty declining requests or setting limits when doing so is in the best interests of clients. Moreover, such social workers may benefit by setting tasks for themselves related to increasing their assertiveness. Participating in an assertiveness training group and delving into the popular literature on assertiveness may be highly beneficial as well.

Following are a few of the many situations in which you may need to decline requests of clients:

1. When clients invite you to participate with them socially
2. When clients ask you to grant them preferential status (e.g., set lower fees than are specified by policy)

3. When clients request physical intimacy
4. When clients ask you to intercede in a situation they should handle themselves
5. When clients request a special appointment after having broken a regular appointment for an invalid reason
6. When clients ask to borrow money
7. When clients request that you conceal information about violations of probation, parole, or institutional policy
8. When spouses request that you withhold information from their partners
9. When clients disclose plans to commit crimes or acts of violence against others
10. When clients ask you to report false information to an employer or other party

In addition to declining requests, you may need to set limits with clients in situations such as the following:

1. When clients make excessive telephone calls to you at home or the office
2. When clients cancel appointments without giving advance notice
3. When clients express emotions in abusive or violent ways
4. When clients habitually seek to go beyond designated ending points of sessions
5. When clients consistently fail to abide by contracts (e.g., not paying fees or missing numerous appointments)
6. When clients make sexual overtures toward you or other staff members
7. When clients come to sessions while intoxicated

Part of maturing professionally means learning to decline requests, set limits, and feel comfortable in so doing. As you gain experience, you will realize that you help clients as much by ensuring that they have reasonable expectations as you do by providing a concrete action for them. Modeled responses for refusing requests and for saying no to clients are found in the answers to the exercises designed to assist social workers to relate authentically and assertively.

Of course, social workers must also assert themselves effectively with other social workers and with members of other professions. Lacking experience and sometimes confidence, beginning social workers tend to be in awe of physicians, lawyers, psychologists, and more experienced social workers. Consequently, they may relate passively or may acquiesce in plans or demands that appear unsound or unreasonable. Although it is critical to remain open to the ideas of other professionals, beginning social workers should nevertheless risk expressing their own views and asserting their own rights. Otherwise, they may know more about a given client than other professionals but fail to contribute valuable information in joint case planning.

Beginning social workers should also set limits and assert their rights by refusing to accept unreasonable referrals and inappropriate assignments. Likewise, assertiveness may be required when other professionals deny resources to which clients are entitled, refer to clients with demeaning labels, or engage in unethical conduct. In fact, being assertive is critical when you act as a client advocate, a role discussed at length in Chapter 14.

Summary

This chapter prepared the way for you to communicate with clients and other persons on behalf of clients with appropriate empathy, assertiveness, and self-disclosure. Chapter 6 will build on these skills by developing your abilities in listening, focusing, and exploring. First, however, you should practice your new skills by completing the exercises in this chapter.

Related Online Content

Visit the *Direct Social Work Practice* companion Web site at *www.cengage.com/social_work/hepworth* for additional learning tools such as glossary terms, chapter outlines, relevant Web links, and chapter practice quizzes.

Exercises in Responding Authentically and Assertively

The following exercises will assist you in gaining skill in responding authentically and assertively. Read each situation and client message, and then formulate a written response as though you were the social worker in the situation presented. Compare your written responses with the modeled responses, keeping in mind that these models represent just a few of the many possible responses that would be appropriate.

You will find additional exercises that require authentic and assertive responding in Chapter 17 (in the confrontation exercises) and in Chapter 18 (in the exercises concerned with managing relational reactions and resistance).

Statements and Situations

1. *Marital partner* [*in third conjoint marital therapy session*]: It must be really nice being a marriage counselor—knowing just what to do and not having problems like ours.

2. *Female client, age 23* [*in first session*]: Some of my problems are related to my church's stand on birth control. Tell me, are you a Catholic?

3. *Client* [*fifth session*]: You look like you're having trouble staying awake. [*Social worker is drowsy from having taken an antihistamine for an allergy.*]

4. *Adult group member* [*to social worker in second session; group members have been struggling to determine the agenda for the session*]: I wish you'd tell us what we should talk about. Isn't that a group leader's function? We're just spinning our wheels.

5. *Male client* [*sixth session*]: Say, my wife and I are having a party next Wednesday. We'd like to have you and your wife come.

6. *Client* [*calls 3 hours before scheduled appointment*]: I've had the flu the past couple of days, but I feel like I'm getting over it. Do you think I should come today?

7. *Client* [*scheduled time for ending appointment has arrived, and social worker has already moved to end session; in previous sessions, client has tended to stay beyond designated ending time*]: What we were talking about reminded me of something I wanted to discuss today but forgot. I'd like to discuss it briefly, if you don't mind.

8. *Client* [*has just completed behavioral rehearsal involving talking with employer and played role beyond expectations of social worker*].

9. *Female client* [*tenth interview*]: I've really felt irritated with you during the week. When I brought up taking the correspondence course in art, all you could talk about was how some correspondence courses are ripoffs and that I could take courses at a college for less money. I knew that, but I've checked into this correspondence course, and it's well worth the money. You put me down, and I've resented it.

10. *Client* [*seventh session*]: You seem uptight today. Is something bothering you? [*Social worker has been under strain associated with recent death of a parent and assisting surviving parent, who has been distraught.*]

11. *Client* [*as the final session of successful therapy draws to a close*]: I really want to thank you for your help. You'll never know just how much help you've been. I felt like a sinking ship before I saw you. Now I feel I've got my head screwed on straight.

12. *Male delinquent on probation, age 15* [*first session*]: Before I tell you much, I need to know what happens to the information. Who else learns about me?

13. **Social worker** [*forgot to enter an appointment in daily schedule and, as a result, failed to keep a scheduled appointment with a client; realizing this the next day, she telephones her client.*]

Modeled Responses

1. [*Smiling.*] "Well, I must admit it's helpful. But I want you to know that marriage is no picnic for marriage counselors either. We have our rough spots, too. I have to work like everyone else to keep my marriage alive and growing."

2. "I gather you're wondering what my stand is and whether I can understand and accept your feelings. I've worked with many Catholics and have been able to understand their problems. Would it trouble you if I weren't Catholic?"

3. "You're very observant. I have been struggling with drowsiness these past few minutes, and I apologize for that. I had to take an antihistamine before lunch, and a side effect of the drug is wanting to sleep. I want you to know my drowsiness has nothing to do with you. If I move around a little, the drowsiness passes."

4. "I can sense your frustration and your desire to firm up an agenda. If I made the decision, though, it might not fit for many of you and I'd be taking over the group's prerogative. Perhaps it would be helpful if the group followed the decision-by-consensus approach we discussed in our first session."

5. "Thank you for the invitation. I'm flattered that you'd ask me. Although a part of me would like to come because it sounds like fun, I must decline your invitation. If I were to socialize with you while you're seeing me professionally, it would conflict with my role, and I couldn't be as helpful to you. I hope you can understand my not accepting."

6. "I appreciate your calling to let me know. I think it would be better to change our appointment until you're sure you've recovered. Quite frankly, I don't want to risk being exposed to the flu, which I hope you can understand. I have a time open on the day after tomorrow. I'll set it aside for you, if you'd like, in the event you're fully recovered by then."

7. "I'm sorry I don't have the time to discuss the matter today. Let's save it for next week, and I'll make a note that you wanted to explore this issue. We'll have to stop here today because I'm scheduled for another appointment."

8. "I want to share with you how impressed I was with how you asserted yourself and came across so positively. If you'd been with your boss, he'd have been impressed, too."

9. "I'm glad you shared those feelings with me. I can see I owe you an apology. You're right, I didn't explore whether you'd checked into the program, and I made some unwarranted assumptions. I guess I was overly concerned about your not being ripped off because I know others who have been by taking correspondence courses. But I can see I goofed because you had already looked into the course."

10. "Thank you for asking. Yes, I have been under some strain this past week. My mother died suddenly, which was a shock, and my father is taking it very hard. It's created a lot of pressure for me, but I think I can keep it from spilling over into our session. If I'm not able to focus on you, I will stop the session. Or if you don't feel that I'm fully with you, please let me know. I don't want to shortchange you."

11. "Thank you very much. As we finish, I want you to know how much I've enjoyed working with you. You've worked hard, and that's the primary reason you've made so much progress. I'm very interested in you and want to hear how your new job works out. Please keep in touch."

12. "Your question is a good one. I'd wonder the same thing if I were in your situation. I keep the information confidential as much as I can. We keep a file on you, of course, but I'm selective about what I put in it, and you have the right to check the file if you wish. I do meet with a supervisor, too, and we discuss how I can be of greatest help to clients. So I might share certain information with her, but she keeps it confidential. If you report violations of the law or the conditions of your probation, I can't assure you I'll keep that information confidential. I'm responsible to the court, and part of my responsibility is to see that you meet the conditions of your parole. I have to make reports to the judge about that. Could you share with me your specific concerns about confidentiality?"

13. "Mr. M, I'm very embarrassed to be calling you, because I realized just a few minutes ago I blew it yesterday. I forgot to enter my appointment with you in my schedule book last week and completely forgot about it. I hope you can accept my apology. I want you to know it had nothing to do with you."

Skill Development Exercises in Empathic Communication

The following exercises, which include a wide variety of actual client messages, will assist you in gaining mastery of reciprocal empathic responding (level 3). Read the client message and compose on paper an empathic response that captures the client's surface feelings. You may wish to use the paradigm, "You feel _____ about (or because) _____," in organizing your response before phrasing it in typical conversation language. Strive to make your responses fresh, varied, and spontaneous. To expand your repertoire of responses, we strongly encourage you to continue using the lists of affective words and phrases.

After formulating your response, compare it with the modeled response provided at the end of the exercises. Analyze the differences, paying particular attention to the various forms of responding and the elements that enhance the effectiveness of your own responses and the modeled responses.

Because this exercise includes 27 different client statements, we recommend that you not attempt to complete the entire exercise in one sitting, but rather work through it in several sessions. Consistent practice and careful scrutiny of your responses are essential in gaining mastery of this vital skill.

Client Statements

1. **Father of developmentally disabled child, age 14** [*who is becoming difficult to manage*]: We just don't know what to do with Henry. We've always wanted to take care of him, but we've reached the point where we're not sure it's doing any good for him or for us. Henry has grown so strong—we just can't restrain him anymore. He hit my wife last week when she wouldn't take him to the 7–11 late at night—I was out of town—and she's still bruised. She's afraid of him now, and I have to admit I'm getting that way, too.

2. **Latino** [*living in urban barrio*]: Our children do better in school if they teach Spanish, not just English. We're afraid our children are behind because they don't understand English so good. And we don't know how to help them. Our people have been trying to get a bilingual program, but the school board pays no attention to us.

3. **Female client, age 31**: Since my husband left town with another woman, I get lonely and depressed a lot of the time. I find myself wondering whether something is wrong with me or whether men just can't be trusted.

4. **Mother** [*to child welfare protective services worker on doorstep during initial home visit*]: Who'd want to make trouble for me by accusing me of not taking care of my kids? [*Tearfully.*] Maybe I'm not the best mother in the world, but I try. There are a lot of kids around here that aren't cared for as well as mine.

5. **Male ninth-grade student** [*to school social worker*]: I feel like I'm a real loser. In sports I've always had two left feet. When they choose up sides, I'm always the last one chosen. A couple of times they've actually got into a fight over who doesn't have to choose me.

6. **Member of abused women's group**: That last month I was living in mortal fear of Art. He'd get that hateful look in his eyes, and I'd know he was going to let me have it. The last time I was afraid he was going to kill me—and he might have, if his brother hadn't dropped in. I'm afraid to go back to him. But what do I do? I can't stay here much longer!

7. **Male, age 34** [*to marital therapist*]: Just once I'd like to show my wife I can accomplish something without her prodding me. That's why I haven't told her I'm coming to see you. If she knew it, she'd try to take charge and call all the shots.

8. **African American man** [*in a group session*]: All I want is to be accepted as a person. When I get hired, I want it to be for what I'm capable of doing—not just because of my skin color. That's as phony and degrading as not being hired because of my skin color. I just want to be accepted for who I am.

9. **Client in a state prison** [*to rehabilitation worker*]: They treat you like an animal in here—herd you around like a damn cow. I know I've got to do my time, but sometimes I feel like I can't stand it any longer—like something's building up in me that's going to explode.

10. **Client** [*to mental health worker*]: I don't have any pleasant memories of my childhood. It seems like just so much empty space. I can remember my father watching television and staring at me with a blank look—as though I didn't exist.

11. **Patient in hospital** [*to medical social worker*]: I know Dr. Brown is a skilled surgeon, and he tells me not to worry—that there's very little risk in this surgery. I know I should feel reassured, but to tell you the truth, I'm just plain panic-stricken.

12. **Female member, age 29** [*in marital therapy group*]: I'd like to know what it's like with the rest of you. Hugh and I get into nasty fights because I feel he doesn't help me when I really need help. He tells me there's no way he's going to do women's work! That really irritates me. I start feeling like I'm just supposed to be his slave.

13. **Male college student, age 21**: Francine says she's going to call me, but she never does—I have to do all the calling, or I probably wouldn't hear from her at all. It seems so one-sided. If I didn't need her so

much I'd ask her what kind of game she's playing. I wonder if she isn't pretty selfish.

14. ***White student, age 14*** [*to school social worker*]: To be really honest, I don't like the black kids in our school. They pretty much stay to themselves, and they aren't friendly to whites. I don't know what to expect or how to act around them. I'm antsy when they're around and—well, to be honest—I'm scared I'll do something they won't like and they'll jump me.

15. ***Single female, age 27*** [*to mental health worker*]: I've been taking this class on the joys of womanhood. Last time the subject was how to catch a man. I can see I've been doing a lot of things wrong. But I won't lower myself to playing games with men. If that's what it takes, I guess I'll always be single.

16. ***Married male, age 29*** [*to marital therapist*]: Sexually, I'm unfulfilled in my marriage. At times I've even had thoughts of trying sex with men. That idea kind of intrigues me. My wife and I can talk about sex all right, but it doesn't get better.

17. ***Married female, age 32*** [*to family social worker*]: I love my husband and children, and I don't know what I'd do without them. Yet on days like last Thursday, I feel I could just climb the walls. I want to run away from all of them and never come back.

18. ***Married blind female*** [*to other blind group members*]: You know, it really offends me when people praise me or make a fuss over me for doing something routine that anyone else could do. It makes me feel like I'm on exhibition. I want to be recognized for being competent—not for being blind.

19. ***Male teacher*** [*to mental health social worker*]: I have this thing about not being able to accept compliments. A friend told me about how much of a positive impact I've had on several students over the years. I couldn't accept that and feel good. My thought was, "You must be mistaken. I've never had that kind of effect on anyone."

20. ***Lesbian, age 26*** [*to private social worker*]: The girls at the office were talking about lesbians the other day and about how repulsive the very thought of lesbianism was to them. How do you think I felt?

21. ***Male member of alcoholics group***: I don't feel like I belong in this group. The rest of you seem to have better educations and better jobs. Hell, I only finished junior high, and I'm just a welder.

22. ***Male, age 30*** [*to private social worker*]: Sometimes I can't believe how pissed off I get over little things. When I lose a chess game, I go into orbit. First, I'm furious with myself for blundering. It's not like me to make rank blunders. I guess I feel humiliated, because I immediately want to start another game and get even with the other guy.

23. ***Male client, age 72*** [*to medical social worker*]: Since I had my heart attack, I've just had this feeling of foreboding—like my life's over, for all practical purposes. I feel like I'm just an invalid—of no use to myself or anyone else.

24. ***Child, age 15, in foster care*** [*to child welfare worker*]: I've had it with them [*the foster parents*]. They want me to work all the time—like I'm a slave or something. If you don't get me out of here, I'm going to run.

25. ***Family member, age 13*** [*in initial family group session*]: Yeah, I can tell you what I'd like to be different in our family. I'd like to feel that we care about each other, but it's not that way. Every time I go in the house, Mom nags me, and Dad doesn't say anything—he doesn't seem to care. Sometimes I feel there's no point in going home.

26. ***Married woman*** [*in initial interview with marital therapist*]: I think this is just a complete waste of time. I didn't want to come and wouldn't be here if my husband hadn't forced me. He's the one who should be here—not me.

27. ***Married woman*** [*in YWCA adult women's group*]: This past week I've felt really good about how things are going—like I've finally got my act together. I've handled my emotions better, and for the first time in a long time, I've felt like an intelligent human being.

Modeled Responses

1. "So you're really in a difficult situation. You've wanted to keep Henry at home, but in light of his recent aggressiveness and his increasing strength, you're becoming really frightened and wonder if other arrangements wouldn't be better for both you and him."

2. "I can see you're worried about how your children are doing in school and believe they need a bilingual program."

3. "It's been a real blow—your husband leaving you for another woman—and you've just felt so alone. And you find yourself dwelling on the painful question, 'Is something wrong with me, or is it that you just can't trust men?' "

4. "This is very upsetting for you. You seem to be saying that it's not fair being turned in when you believe you take care of your children. Please understand I'm not accusing you of neglecting your children. But I do have to investigate complaints. It may be that I'll be able to turn in a positive report. I hope so. But I do need to talk with you further. May I come in?"

5. "I gather you feel you really got shortchanged as far as athletic talents are concerned. It's humiliating to you to feel so left out and be the last guy chosen."

6. "It sounds as though you lived in terror that last month and literally feared for your life. You were wise to remove yourself when you did. A number of other women in the group have had similar experiences and are facing the same dilemma about what to do now. As group members, each of us can be helpful to other group members in thinking through what's the best course of action. In the meantime, you have a safe place to stay and some time to plan."

7. "Sounds like you get pretty annoyed, thinking about your wife's prodding and trying to take charge. I gather it's important right now that you prove to her and to yourself you can do something on your own."

8. "I gather you're fed up with having people relate to you because of your race instead of being accepted as an individual—as yourself."

9. "If I understand you, you feel degraded by the way you're treated—as though you're less than a human being. And that really gets to you—sometimes you find yourself seething with resentment that threatens to boil over."

10. "From what you say, I get a picture of you just feeling so all alone as you were growing up—as though you didn't feel very important to anyone, especially your father."

11. "So intellectually, you tell yourself not to worry, that you're in good hands. Still, on another level you have to admit you're terrified of that operation. [*Brief pause.*] Your fear is pretty natural, though. Most people who are honest with themselves experience fear. I'd be interested in hearing more about your fears."

12. "So the two of you get into some real struggles over differences in your views about what is reasonable of you to expect from Hugh. You seem to be saying you very much resent his refusal to pitch in—that it's not fair to have to carry the burden alone. Hugh, I'd be interested in hearing your views. Then we can hear how other members deal with this kind of situation."

13. "Sounds like part of you is saying that you have a right to expect more from Francine—that you don't feel good about always having to be the one to take the initiative. You also seem to feel you'd like to confront her with what she's doing, but you're uneasy about doing that because you don't want to risk losing her."

14. "So, you're uncomfortable around your black classmates and just don't know how to read them. I gather you kind of walk on eggshells when they're around for fear you'll blow it and they'll climb all over you."

15. "There is a lot of conflicting advice around these days about how men and women should relate to one another, and it is hard to figure out what to believe. You know you don't want to play games, yet that is what the class is telling you to do if you don't want to be single."

16. "Things don't get better despite your talks, and you get pretty discouraged. Sometimes you find yourself wondering if you'd get sexual fulfillment with men, and that appeals to you in some ways."

17. "So even though you care deeply for your family, there are days when you just feel so overwhelmed you'd like to buy a one-way ticket out of all the responsibility."

18. "Are you saying that you feel singled out and demeaned when people flatter you for doing things anyone could do? It ticks you off, and you wish people would recognize you for being competent—not being blind."

19. "In a way, you seem to be saying that you don't feel comfortable with compliments because you feel you don't really deserve them. It's like you feel you don't do anything worthy of a compliment."

20. "You must have felt extremely uncomfortable and resentful believing that they would condemn you if they knew. It must have been most painful for you."

21. "Ted, you seem to feel uncomfortable, as if you don't fit in with the other group members. I gather you're worried the rest of the members are more educated than you are and you're concerned they won't accept you."

22. "When you lose, lots of feelings surge through you: anger and disappointment with yourself for losing, loss of face, and an urgency to prove you can beat the other guy."

23. "So things look pretty grim to you right now—as though you have nothing to look forward to and are just washed up. And you're apprehensive that things might get worse rather than better."

24. "You sound pretty mad right now, and I can sense you feel there has to be a change. I'd like to hear more about exactly what has been happening."

25. "Am I getting it right—that you feel picked on by Mom and ignored by Dad? You'd like to feel that they really care about you. You'd also like family members to show for each other."

26. "You're feeling pretty angry with your husband for forcing you to come. I gather that you resent having to be here now and just don't see the need for it."

27. "That sounds great. You seem delighted with your progress—like you're really getting on top of things. And most of all you're liking yourself again."

Answers to Exercise in Identifying Surface and Underlying Feelings

1. *Apparent feelings*: unimportant, neglected, disappointed, hurt. *Probable deeper feelings*: rejected, abandoned, forsaken, deprived, lonely, depressed.
2. *Apparent feelings*: unloved, insecure, confused, embarrassed, left out or excluded. *Probable deeper feelings*: hurt, resentful, unvalued, rejected, taken for granted, degraded, doubting own desirability.
3. *Apparent feelings*: chagrined, disappointed in self, discouraged, letting children down, perplexed. *Probable deeper feelings*: guilty, inadequate, crummy, sense of failure, out of control, fear of damaging children.
4. *Apparent feelings*: frustrated, angry, bitter. *Probable deeper feelings*: depressed, discouraged, hopeless.

Answers to Exercises to Discriminate Levels of Empathic Responding

CLIENT STATEMENT

Client 1	
Response	Level
1.	2
2.	1
3.	1
4.	3
5.	2
6.	2
7.	4
8.	1

CLIENT STATEMENT

Client 2		Client 3	
Response	Level	Response	Level
1.	1	1.	1
2.	3	2.	4
3.	1	3.	2
4.	2	4.	2
5.	4	5.	5
6.	1	6.	1
7.	3	7.	2
8.	2	8.	2

Notes

1. Such highlighting of opposing feelings is a key technique for assisting clients in assessing their readiness for change in the motivational interviewing method (Miller and Rollnick, 2002).
2. In categorizing her husband as a "bump on a log," the wife makes a sweeping generalization that fits her husband's behavior into a mold. Although the social worker chose to keep the focus momentarily on the husband, it is important that he helps the couple to avoid labeling each other. Strategies for intervening when clients use labels are delineated in a later chapter.

Verbal Following, Exploring, and Focusing Skills

CHAPTER OVERVIEW

Chapter 6 introduces verbal following skills and their uses in exploring client concerns and focusing. These skills are the building blocks for social workers' efforts to communicate empathically with clients. In addition to being helpful in work with clients in micro practice, such skills are useful at the meso level in work on behalf of clients, through advocacy, and in work with colleagues and other professionals. This chapter also includes content on the CD-ROM accompanying the text.

Maintaining Psychological Contact with Clients and Exploring Their Problems

Verbal following involves the use of and, sometimes, blending of discrete skills that enable social workers to maintain psychological contact on a moment-by-moment basis with clients and to covey accurate understanding of their messages. Moreover, verbal following behavior takes into account two performance variables that are essential to satisfaction and continuance on the part of the client:

1. *Stimulus-response congruence.* The extent to which social workers' responses provide feedback to clients that their messages are accurately received.
2. *Content relevance.* The extent to which the content of social workers' responses is perceived by clients as relevant to their substantive concerns.

These variables were first conceptualized by Rosen (1972), who detailed empirical and theoretical support about how they related to client continuance. They received further validation as critical social worker behavioral responses in a study conducted by Duehn and Proctor (1977). Analyzing worker–client transactions, these authors found that social workers responded incongruently to clients' messages much more frequently with clients who terminated treatment prematurely than with clients who continued treatment. (Incongruent messages fail to provide immediate feedback to clients indicating that their messages have been received.) Further, social workers gave a lower proportion of responses that matched the content expectations of "discontinuers" than they did with "continuers." Duehn and Proctor concluded that responses that are relevant and that accurately attend to client messages gradually increase moment-by-moment client satisfaction with interactions in the interview. Conversely, continued use of questions and other responses that are not associated with previous client messages and that do not relate to the client's substantive concerns contribute to consistent client dissatisfaction. When client content expectations are not fulfilled, clients often prematurely discontinue treatment. In contrast, effective use of attending behaviors should enhance motivational congruence, or the fit between client motivation and social worker goals, a factor that is associated with better outcomes in social work effectiveness studies (Reid & Hanrahan, 1982). Employing responses that directly relate to client messages and concerns thus enhances client satisfaction, fosters continuance, and greatly contributes to the establishment of a viable working relationship.

Studies of how social work students learn the practice skills described in this book suggest that the skills can be taught and demonstrated successfully in simulated interviews (Sowers-Hoag & Thyer, 1985). However, generalization to field practice has not been conclusively demonstrated. For example, one study found that students in the field demonstrated increased skills in facilitation of empathy but not questioning or clarification skills (Carrillo, Gallant, & Thyer, 1995). Another study found that students in the field were more inclined to ask closed-ended questions and give advice than had been the emphasis in their training program (Kopp & Butterfield, 1985). A recent study found that while most of the practice skills of second-year students were not significantly more advanced than those of first-year students, the second-year students were better able to focus on tasks and goals compared with first-year students (Deal & Brintzenhofe-Szok, 2004).

Tsui and Schultz (1985) have emphasized the importance of explaining the relevance of questions to Asian Americans seen for mental health problems. In such cases, the social worker must explicitly educate the client about the purpose of questions regarding clinical history, previous treatment information, family background, and psychosocial stressors. The linkage of these issues to their current symptoms is not clear to many Asians or, indeed, to other clients. Many Asian clients conceive of mental distress as the result of physiological disorder or character flaws. This issue must be dealt with sensitively before any sensible therapeutic work can occur (Tsui & Schultz, 1985, pp. 567–568). Similarly, clients who are members of historically oppressed groups may perceive questions as interrogations not designed to help them with their own concerns, so the rationale for such questions must be explained.

> In the video "Getting Back to Shakopee, GBS" linked to this chapter, a continuing theme is Val's distrust of social workers and her fear that they may ask questions that will result in a child welfare investigation.

In addition to enabling social workers to maintain close psychological contact with clients, verbal following skills serve two other important functions in the helping process. First, they yield rich personal information, allowing social workers to explore clients' problems in depth. Second, they enable social workers to focus selectively on components of the clients' experiences and on dynamics in the helping process that facilitate positive client change.

The following pages introduce a variety of skills for verbally following and exploring clients' problems. Some of these skills are easily mastered. Others require more effort to acquire. The exercises in the body of the chapter will assist you in acquiring proficiency in these important skills. Although empathic responding is the most vital skill for verbally following clients' messages, we have not included it in this chapter because it was discussed in detail in Chapter 5. Later, however, we discuss the blending of empathic responses with other verbal following skills to bolster your ability in focusing on and fully exploring relevant client problems.

Verbal Following Skills

The discrete skills highlighted in this chapter include seven types of responses:

1. Furthering
2. Paraphrasing
3. Closed-ended responses
4. Open-ended responses
5. Seeking concreteness
6. Providing and maintaining focus
7. Summarizing

Furthering Responses

Furthering responses indicate social workers are listening attentively and encourage the client to verbalize. They are of two types: minimal prompts or accent responses.

Minimal Prompts

Minimal prompts signal the social worker's attentiveness and encourage the client to continue verbalizing. They can be either nonverbal or verbal.

Nonverbal minimal prompts consist of nodding the head, using facial expressions, or employing gestures that convey receptivity, interest, and commitment to understanding. They implicitly convey the message, "I am with you; please continue."

Verbal minimal prompts consist of brief messages that convey interest and encourage or request expanded verbalizations along the lines of the previous expressions by the client. These messages include "Yes," "I see," "But?", "Mm-mmm" (the so-called empathic grunt), "Tell me more," "And then what happened?", "And?", "Please go on," "Tell me more, please," and other similar brief messages that affirm the appropriateness of what the client has been saying and prompt him or her to continue.

Accent Responses

Accent responses (Hackney & Cormier, 1979) involve repeating, in a questioning tone of voice or with emphasis, a word or a short phrase. Suppose a client says, "I've really had it with the way my supervisor at work is treating me." The social worker might reply, "Had it?" This short response is intended to prompt further elaboration by the client.

Paraphrasing Responses

Paraphrasing involves using fresh words to restate the client's message concisely. Responses that paraphrase are more apt to focus on the cognitive aspects of client messages (i.e., emphasize situations, ideas, objects, or persons) than on the client's affective state, although reference may be made to obvious feelings. Four examples of paraphrasing follow.

Example 1

Elder client: I don't want to get into a living situation in which I will not be able to make choices on my own.

Social worker: So independence is a very important issue for you.

Example 2

Client: I went to the doctor today for a final checkup, and she said that I was doing fine.

Social worker: She gave you a clean bill of health, then.

Example 3

> ***Native American Client (from "GBS" video):*** The idea of a promotion makes me feel good; I could earn more money, the supervisor in that department is real nice, she respects me, we get along really good.
>
> ***Social worker:*** So you feel that you would get more support for you at work and for your family?

Example 4

Managed care utilization reviewer: We don't think that your patient's condition justifies the level of service that you recommend.

Social worker: So you feel that my documentation does not justify the need that I have recommended according to the approval guidelines you are working from.

Note that in Example 4, paraphrasing is used as part of the communication with a person whose opinion is important because it relates to delivering client services, the health insurance care manager (Strom-Gottfried, 1998a). When employed sparingly, paraphrasing may be interspersed with other facilitative responses to prompt client expression. Used to excess, however, paraphrasing produces a mimicking effect.

Paraphrasing is helpful when social workers want to bring focus to an idea or a situation for client consideration. In contrast, this technique is inappropriate when clients are preoccupied with feelings. In such cases, social workers need to relate with empathic responses that accurately capture clients' affect and assist them to reflect on and sort through their feelings. Sometimes social workers may choose to direct the discussion away from feelings for therapeutic purposes. For instance, a social worker might believe that a chronically depressed client who habitually expresses discouragement and disillusionment would benefit by focusing less on feelings and more on actions to alleviate the distress. When the social worker chooses to deemphasize feelings, paraphrases that reflect content are helpful and appropriate.

> In the video "Elder Grief Assessment, EGA" connected with this chapter, the practitioner asks a senior recently widowed client what she would like to see occur at the end of their work together. The client replies: "I would like to feel better myself, the house looking better, the yard looking better, I would like to go grocery shopping when I want to, get to the doctor without calling someone." The social worker, Kathy, summarizes empathically by saying, "You would like to remain independent."

Exercises in Paraphrasing

In the following exercises, formulate written responses that paraphrase the messages of clients and other persons. Remember, paraphrases usually reflect the cognitive aspects of messages rather than feelings. Modeled responses for these exercises appear at the end of the chapter. Note, however, that paraphrasing a client's or other person's comments does not mean that you agree with or condone those thoughts.

Client/Colleague Statements

1. ***Client:*** I can't talk to people. I just completely freeze up in a group.
2. ***Wife:*** I think that in the last few weeks I've been able to listen much more often to my husband and children.
3. ***Client:*** Whenever I get into an argument with my mother, I always end up losing. I guess I'm still afraid of her.
4. ***Husband:*** I just can't decide what to do. If I go ahead with the divorce, I'll probably lose custody of the kids—and I won't be able to see them very much. If I don't, though, I'll have to put up with the same old thing. I don't think my wife is going to change.

5. *Elder client:* It wasn't so difficult to adjust to this place because the people who run it are helpful and friendly and I am able to make contacts easily—I've always been a people person.

6. *Mother* [*speaking about daughter*]: When it comes right down to it, I think I'm to blame for a lot of her problems.

7. *Mother* [*participating in welfare-to-work program*]: I don't know how they can expect me to be a good mother and make school appointments, supervise my kids, and put in all these work hours.

8. *Member of treatment team:* I just don't see how putting more services into this family makes sense. The mother is not motivated, and the kids are better off away from her. This family has been messed up forever.

9. *Terminally ill cancer patient:* Some days I am really angry because I'm only 46 years old and there are so many more things I wanted to do. Other days, I feel kind of defeated, like this is what I get for smoking two packs of cigarettes a day for 25 years.

10. *Elementary school student:* Kids pick on me at school. They are mean. If they try to hurt me then I try to hurt them back.

Closed- and Open-Ended Responses

Generally used to elicit specific information, *closed-ended questions* define a topic and restrict the client's response to a few words or a simple yes or no answer. Typical examples of closed-ended questions follow:

- *"When did you obtain your divorce?"*
- *"Do you have any sexual difficulties in your marriage?"*
- *"When did you last have a physical examination?"*
- *"Is your health insurance Medicare?"*

Although closed-ended questions restrict the client and elicit limited information, in many instances these responses are both appropriate and helpful. Later in this chapter, we discuss how and when to use this type of response effectively.

In contrast to closed-ended responses, which circumscribe client messages, *open-ended questions* and statements invite expanded expression and leave the client free to express what seems most relevant and important. For example:

Social worker: You've mentioned your daughter. Tell me how she enters into your problem.

Client: I don't know what to do. Sometimes I think she is just pushing me so that she can go live with her father. When I ask her to help around the house, she won't, and says that she doesn't owe me anything. When I try to insist on her helping, it just ends up in an ugly scene without anything being accomplished. It makes me feel so helpless.

In this example, the social worker's open-ended question prompted the client to expand on the details of the problems with her daughter, including a description of her daughter's behavior, her own efforts to cope, and her present sense of defeat. The information contained in the message is typical of the richness of data obtained through open-ended responding.

In other circumstances, such as in the prior example of a telephone conversation with a managed care utilization reviewer, the social worker can use an open-ended question to attempt to explore common ground that can lead to a mutually beneficial resolution.

Social worker [*to managed care utilization reviewer*]: Can you clarify for me how appropriate coverage is determined for situations such as the one I have described?

Some open-ended responses are unstructured, leaving the topic to the client's choosing (e.g., "Tell me what you would like to discuss today" or "What else can you tell me about the problems that you're experiencing?"). Other open-ended responses are structured in that the social worker defines the topic to be discussed but leaves the client free to respond in any way that he or she wishes (e.g., "You've mentioned feeling ashamed about the incident that occurred between you and your son. I'd be interested in hearing more about that."). Still other open-ended responses fall along a continuum between structured and unstructured, because they give the client leeway to answer with a few words or to elaborate with more information (e.g., "How willing are you to do this?").

Social workers may formulate open-ended responses either by asking a question or by giving a polite command. Suppose a terminally ill cancer patient said, "The doctor thinks I could live about six or seven months now. It could be less; it could be more. It's just an educated guess, he told me." The social worker could respond by asking, "How are you feeling about that prognosis?" or "Would you tell me how you are feeling about that prognosis?" Polite commands have the same effect as direct questions in requesting information but are less forceful and involve greater finesse. Similar in nature are embedded questions that do not take the form of a question but embody a request for information.

Examples of embedded questions include "I'm curious about ...," "I'm wondering if ...," and "I'm interested in knowing ...." Open-ended questions often start with *what* or *how*. Why questions are often unproductive because they may ask for reasons, motives, or causes that are either obvious, obscure, or unknown to the client. Asking how ("How did that happen?") rather than why ("Why did that happen?") often elicits far richer information regarding client behavior and patterns.

> In the video "Home for the Holidays, HFH" the practitioner, Kim Strom-Gottfried, asks one partner about the experience of when she came out to her parents as a lesbian: "Let me ask a bit about the coming out conversation. Sounds like it was not an easy one, yet one you were able to have. Can you tell me a little bit more about that?"

Exercises in Identifying Closed- and Open-Ended Responses

The following exercises will assist you to differentiate between closed- and open-ended messages. Identify each statement with either a C for a closed-ended question or O for an open-ended question. Turn to the end of the chapter to check your answers.

1. "Did your mother ask you to see me because of the problem you had with the principal?"
2. "When John says that to you, what do you experience inside?"
3. "You said you're feeling fed up and you're just not sure that pursuing a reconciliation is worth your trouble. Could you elaborate?"
4. "When is your court date?"

Now read the following client messages and respond by writing open-ended responses to them. Avoid using *why* questions. Examples of open-ended responses to these messages appear at the end of the chapter.

Client Statements

1. *Client:* Whenever I'm in a group with Ralph, I find myself saying something that will let him know that I am smart, too.
2. *Client:* I always have had my parents telephone for me about appointments and other things I might mess up.
3. *Teenager* [*speaking of a previous probation counselor*]: He sure let me down. And I really trusted him. He knows a lot about me because I spilled my guts.

4. *Group nursing home administrator:* I think that we are going to have to move Gladys to another, more suitable kind of living arrangement. We aren't able to provide the kind of care that she needs.

The next sections of the book explain how you can blend open-ended and empathic responses to keep a discussion focused on a specific topic. In preparation for that, respond to the next two client messages by formulating an empathic response followed by an open-ended question that encourages the client to elaborate on the same topic.

5. *Unwed teenage girl seeking abortion* [*brought in by her mother, who wishes to discuss birth alternatives*]: I feel like you are all tied up with my mother, trying to talk me out of what I have decided to do.
6. *Client:* Life is such a hassle, and it doesn't seem to have any meaning or make sense. I just don't know whether I want to try figuring it out any longer.

The difference between closed-ended and open-ended responses may seem obvious to you, particularly if you completed the preceding exercises. It has been our experience, however, that beginning—and even seasoned—social workers have difficulty in actual sessions in determining whether their responses are open- or closed-ended, in observing the differential effect of these two types of responses in yielding rich and relevant data, and in deciding which of the two types of responses is appropriate at a given moment. We recommend, therefore, that as you converse with your associates, you practice drawing them out by employing open-ended responses and noting how they respond. We also recommend that you use the form provided at the end of the chapter to assess both the frequency and the appropriateness of your closed- and open-ended responses in several taped client sessions.

Discriminant Use of Closed- and Open-Ended Responses

Beginning social workers typically ask an excessive number of closed-ended questions, many of which block communication or are inefficient or irrelevant to the helping process. When this occurs, the session tends to take on the flavor of an interrogation, with the social worker bombarding the client with questions and taking responsibility for maintaining verbalization. Notice what happens in the following excerpt from a recording of a social worker interviewing an institutionalized youth.

Social worker: I met your mother yesterday. Did she come all the way from Colorado to see you?

Client: Yeah.

Social worker: It seems to me that she must really care about you to take the bus and make the trip up here to see you. Don't you think so?

Client: I suppose so.

Social worker: Did the visit with her go all right?

Client: Fine. We had a good time.

Social worker: You had said you were going to talk to her about a possible home visit. Did you do that?

Client: Yes.

When closed-ended responses are used to elicit information in lieu of open-ended responses, as in the preceding example, many more discrete interchanges will occur. However, the client's responses will be brief and the information yield will be markedly lower.

Open-ended responses often elicit the same data as closed-ended questions but draw out much more information and elaboration of the problem from the client. The following two examples contrast open-ended and closed-ended responses that address the same topic with a given client. To appreciate the differences in the richness of information yielded by these contrasting responses, compare the likely client responses elicited by such questions to the closed-ended questions used above.

Example 1

Closed-ended: "Did she come all the way from Colorado to see you?"

Open-ended: "Tell me about your visit with your mother."

Example 2

Closed-ended: "Did you talk with her about a possible home visit?"

Open-ended: "How did your mother respond when you talked about a possible home visit?"

Occasionally, beginning social workers use closed-ended questions to explore feelings, but responses from clients typically involve minimal self-disclosure, as might be expected. Rather than encourage expanded expression of feelings, closed-ended questions limit responses, as illustrated in the following example:

Social worker: Did you feel rejected when she turned down your invitation?

Client: Yeah.

Social worker: Have there been other times when you've felt rejected that way?

Client: Oh, yeah. Lots of times.

Social worker: When was the first time?

Client: Gee, that's hard to say.

Here, the social worker was leading the client here rather than finding out how she perceived the situation. Had the social worker employed empathic and open-ended responses to explore the feelings and thoughts associated with being rejected, the client would likely have revealed much more.

Because open-ended responses elicit more information than closed-ended ones, frequent use of the former technique increases the efficiency of data gathering. In fact, the richness of information revealed by the client is directly proportional to the frequency with which open-ended responses are employed. Frequent use of open-ended responses also fosters a smoothly flowing session; consistently asking closed-ended questions, by contrast, may result in a fragmented, discontinuous process.

Closed-ended questions are used chiefly to elicit essential factual information. Skillful social workers use closed-ended questions sparingly, because clients usually reveal extensive factual information spontaneously as they unfold their stories, aided by the social worker's open-ended and furthering responses. Although they are typically employed little during the first part of a session, closed questions are used more extensively later to elicit data that may have been omitted by clients, such as names and ages of children, place of employment, date of marriage, medical facts, and data regarding family or origin.

In obtaining this kind of factual data, the social worker can unobtrusively weave into the discussion closed-ended questions that directly pertain to the topic. For example, a client may relate certain marital problems that have existed for many years, and the social worker might ask parenthetically, "And you've been married for how many years?" Similarly, a parent may explain that a child began to have irregular attendance at school when the parent started to work 6 months ago, to which the social worker might respond, "I see. Incidentally, what type of work do you do?" It is vital, of course, to shift the focus back to the problem. If necessary, the social worker can easily maintain focus by using an open-ended response to pick up the thread of the discussion. For example, the social worker might comment, "You mentioned that Ernie began missing school when you started to work. I'd like to hear more about what was happening in your family at that time."

Because open-ended responses generally yield rich information, they are used throughout initial sessions. They are used most heavily, however, in the first portion of sessions to open up lines of communication and to invite clients to reveal problematic aspects of their lives. The following open-ended polite command is a typical opening message: "Could you tell me what you wish to discuss, and we can think about it together." Such responses convey interest in clients as well as respect for clients' abilities to relate their problems in their own way; as a consequence, they also contribute to the development of a working relationship.

As clients disclose certain problem areas, open-ended responses are extensively employed to elicit additional relevant information. Clients, for example, may reveal difficulties at work or in relationships with other family members. Open-ended responses like the following will elicit clarifying information:

- *"Tell me more about your problems at work."*
- *"I'd like to hear more about the circumstances when you were mugged coming home with the groceries."*

Open-ended responses can be used to enhance communication with collaterals, colleagues, and other professionals. For example, Strom-Gottfried suggests using effective communication skills in negotiation and communication between care providers and utilization reviewers. When a client has not been approved for a kind of service that the social worker has recommended, the social worker can attempt to join with the reviewer in identifying goals that both parties would embrace and request information in an open-ended fashion.

> *"I appreciate your concern that she gets the best available services and that her condition does not get worse. We are concerned with safety, as we know you are. Could you tell me more about how this protocol can help us assure her safety?" (Strom-Gottfried, 1998a, p. 398).*

It may sometimes be necessary to employ closed-ended questions extensively to draw out information if the client is unresponsive and withholds information or has limited conceptual and mental abilities. However, in the former case, it is vital to explore the client's immediate feelings about being in the session, which often are negative and impede verbal expression. Focusing on

and resolving negative feelings (discussed at length in Chapter 12) may pave the way to using open-ended responses to good advantage. Using closed-ended messages as a major interviewing tool early in sessions may be appropriate with some children, but the use of open-ended responses should be consistently tested as the relationship develops.

When you incorporate open-ended responses into your repertoire, you will experience a dramatic positive change in your interviewing style and confidence level. To assist you to develop skill in blending and balancing open-ended and closed-ended responses, we have provided a recording form to help you examine your own interviewing style (see Figure 6-1). Using this form, analyze several recorded individual, conjoint, or group sessions over a period of time to determine changes you are making in employing these two types of responses. The recording form will assist you in determining the extent to which you have used open- and closed-ended responses.

In addition, you may wish to review your work for the following purposes:

1. To determine when relevant data are missing and whether the information might have been more appropriately obtained through an open- or closed-ended response
2. To determine when your use of closed-ended questions was irrelevant or ineffective, or distracted from the data-gathering process
3. To practice formulating open-ended responses you might use instead of closed-ended responses to increase client participation and elicit richer data.

Seeking Concreteness

Many of us are inclined to think and talk in generalities and to use words that lack precision when speaking of our experiences ("How was your weekend?" "It was awesome"). To communicate one's feelings and experiences so that they are fully understood, however, a person must be able to respond concretely—that is, with specificity. Responding concretely means using words that describe in explicit terms specific experiences, behaviors, and feelings. As an example, in the following message, an intern supervisor expresses his experiencing in vague and general terms: "I thought you had a good interview." Alternatively, he might have described his experience in more precise language: "During your interview, I was impressed with the way you blended open-ended with closed-ended questions in a relaxed fashion."

SOCIAL WORKER'S RESPONSE	OPEN-ENDED RESPONSES	CLOSED-ENDED RESPONSES
1.		
2.		
3.		
4.		
5.		
6.		
7.		

Directions: Record your discrete open- and closed-ended responses and place a check in the appropriate column. Agency time constraints will dictate how often you can practice it.

FIG-6-1 Recording Form for Open- and Closed-Ended Responding Seeking Concreteness

To test your comprehension of the concept of concreteness, assess which of the following messages give descriptive information concerning what a client experiences:

1. "I have had a couple of accidents that would not have happened if I had full control of my hands. The results weren't that serious, but they could be."
2. "I'm uneasy right now because I don't know what to expect from counseling, and I'm afraid you might think that I really don't need it."
3. "You are a good girl, Susie."
4. "People don't seem to care whether other people have problems."
5. "My last social worker did not answer my calls."
6. "I really wonder if I'll be able to keep from crying and to find the words to tell my husband that it's all over—that I want a divorce."
7. "You did a good job."

You could probably readily identify which messages contained language that increased the specificity of the information conveyed by the client.

In developing competency as a social worker, one of your challenges is to consistently recognize clients' messages expressed in abstract and general terms and to assist them to reveal highly specific information related to feelings and experiences. Such information will assist you to make accurate assessments and, in turn, to plan interventions accordingly. A second challenge is to help clients learn how to respond more concretely

in their relationships with others—a task you will not be able to accomplish unless you are able to model the dimension of concreteness yourself. A third challenge is to describe your own experience in language that is precise and descriptive. It is not enough to recognize concrete messages; in addition, you must familiarize yourself with and practice responding concretely to the extent that it becomes a natural style of speaking and relating to others.

The remainder of our discussion on the skill of seeking concreteness is devoted to assisting you in meeting these three challenges.

Types of Responses That Facilitate Specificity of Expression by Clients

Social workers who fail to move beyond general and abstract messages often have little grasp of the specificity and meaning of a client's problem. Eliciting highly specific information that minimizes errors or misinterpretations, however, represents a formidable challenge. Clients typically present impressions, views, conclusions, and opinions that, despite efforts to be objective, are inevitably biased and distorted to some extent. As previously mentioned, clients are also prone to speak in generalities and to respond with imprecise language. As a consequence, their messages may be understood differently by different people.

To help you to conceptualize the various ways you may assist clients to respond more concretely, the following sections examine different facets of responses that seek concreteness:

1. Checking out perceptions
2. Clarifying the meaning of vague or unfamiliar terms
3. Exploring the basis of conclusions drawn by clients
4. Assisting clients to personalize their statements
5. Eliciting specific feelings
6. Focusing on the here and now, rather than on the distant past
7. Eliciting details related to clients' experiences
8. Eliciting details related to interactional behavior

In addition to discussing these aspects, this section includes 10 skill development exercises, which are designed to bring your comprehension of concreteness from the general and abstract to the specific and concrete.

Checking Out Perceptions

Responses that assist social workers to clarify and "check out" whether they have accurately heard clients' messages (e.g., "Do you mean ..." or "Are you saying ...") are vital in building rapport with clients and in communicating the desire to understand their problems. Such responses also minimize misperceptions or projections in the helping process. Clients benefit from social workers' efforts to understand, because clarifying responses assist clients in sharpening and reformulating their thinking about their own feelings and other concerns, thereby encouraging self-awareness and growth.

Sometimes, perception checking becomes necessary because clients' messages are incomplete, ambiguous, or complex. Occasionally, social workers may encounter clients who repetitively communicate in highly abstract or metaphorical styles, or clients whose thinking is scattered and whose messages just do not "track" or make sense. In such instances, social workers must spend an inordinate amount of time sorting through clients' messages and clarifying perceptions.

At other times, the need for clarification arises not because the client has conveyed confusing, faulty, or incomplete messages, but rather because the social worker has not fully attended to the client's message or comprehended its meaning. Fully attending throughout each moment of a session requires intense concentration. Of course, it is impossible to fully focus on and comprehend the essence of every message delivered in group and family meetings, where myriad transactions occur and competing communications bid for the social worker's attention.

It is important that you develop skill in using clarifying responses to elicit ongoing feedback regarding your perceptions and to acknowledge freely your need for clarification when you are confused or uncertain. Rather than reflecting personal or professional inadequacy, your efforts to accurately grasp the client's meaning and feelings will most likely be perceived as signs of your genuineness and your commitment to understand.

To check your perceptions, try asking simple questions that seek clarification or combining your request for clarification with a paraphrase or empathic response that reflects your perception of the client's message (e.g., "I think you were saying _____. Is that right?"). Examples of clarifying messages include the following:

- *"You seem to be really irritated, not only because he didn't respond when you asked him to help, but because he seemed to be deliberately trying to hurt you. Is that accurate?"*
- *"I'm not sure I'm following you. Let me see if I understand the order of the events you described ..."*
- *"Would you expand on what you are saying so that I can be sure that I understand what you mean?"*
- *"Could you go over that again, and perhaps give an illustration that might help me to understand?"*

- *In the video "Serving the Squeaky Wheel, SSW" the practitioner, Ron Rooney, asks Molly, the client with serious and persistent mental illness, "So you feel that other people's ideas about what mental illness means is not the same as yours?"*

- *"I'm confused. Let me try to restate what I think you're saying."*
- *"As a group, you seem to be divided in your approach to this matter. I'd like to summarize what I'm hearing, and I would then appreciate some input regarding whether I understand the various positions that have been expressed."*

In addition to clarifying their own perceptions, social workers need to assist clients in conjoint or group sessions to clarify their perceptions of the messages of others who are present. This may be accomplished in any of the following ways:

- By modeling *clarifying responses, which occurs naturally as social workers seek to check out their own perceptions of clients' messages.*
- By directing *clients to ask for clarification. Consider, for example, the following response by a social*

worker in a conjoint session: "You [mother] had a confused look on your face, and I'm not sure that you understood your daughter's point. Would you repeat back to her what you heard and then ask her if you understood correctly?"

- By teaching *clients how to clarify perceptions and by reinforcing their efforts to "check out" the messages of others, as illustrated in the following responses:*

  [To group]: *"One of the reasons families have communication problems is that members don't hear accurately what others are trying to say and, therefore, they often respond or react on the basis of incorrect or inadequate information. I would like to encourage all of you to frequently use what I call 'checking out' responses, such as 'I'm not sure what you meant. Were you saying …?', to clarify statements of others. As we go along, I'll point out instances in which I notice any of you using this kind of response."*

  [To family]: *"I'm wondering if you all noticed Jim 'checking' out what his dad said…. As you may recall, we talked about the importance of these kinds of responses earlier. [To father] I'm wondering, Bob, what you experienced when Jim did that?"*

Clarifying the Meaning of Vague or Unfamiliar Terms

In expressing themselves, clients often employ terms that have multiple meanings or use terms in idiosyncratic ways. For example, in the message, "The kids in this school are mean," the word *mean* may have different meanings to the social worker and the client. If the social worker does not identify what this term means to a particular client, he or she cannot be certain whether the client is referring to behavior that is violent, unfriendly, threatening, or something else. The precise meaning can be clarified by employing one of the following responses:

- *"Tell me about the way that some kids are mean in this school."*
- *"I am not sure I know what is happening when you say that some kids act in a mean way. Could you clarify that for me?"*
- *"Can you give me an example of something mean that has happened at this school?"*

Many other words also lack precision, so it is important to avoid assuming that the client means the same thing you mean when you employ a given term. For example, *codependent, irresponsible, selfish,* and *careless* conjure up meanings that vary according to the reference points of different persons. Exact meanings are best determined by asking for clarification or for examples of events in which the behavior alluded to actually occurred.

Exploring the Basis of Conclusions Drawn by Clients

Clients often present views or conclusions as though they are established facts. For example, the messages "I'm losing my mind" and "My partner doesn't love me anymore" include views or conclusions that the client has drawn. To accurately assess the client's difficulties, the social worker must elicit the information on which these views or conclusions are based. This information helps the social worker assess the thinking patterns of the client, which are powerful determinants of emotions and behavior. For example, a person who believes he or she is no longer loved will behave as though this belief represents reality. The social worker's role, of course, is to reveal distortions and to challenge erroneous conclusions in a facilitative manner.

The following responses would elicit clarification of the information that serves as the basis of the views and conclusions embodied in the messages cited earlier:

- *"How do you mean, losing your mind?"*
- *"How have you concluded that you're losing your mind?"*
- *"What leads you to believe your partner no longer loves you?"*

Note that entire groups may hold in common fixed beliefs that may not be helpful to them in attempting to better their situations. In such instances, the social worker faces the challenging task of assisting members to reflect upon and to analyze their views. For example, the social worker may need to help group members to assess conclusions or distortions like the following:

- *"We can't do anything about our problems. We are helpless and others are in control of our lives."*
- *"People in authority are out to get us."*
- *"Someone else is responsible for our problems."*
- *"They (members of another race, religion, group, etc.) are no good."*

In Chapter 13, we discuss the social worker's role in challenging distortions and erroneous conclusions and identify relevant techniques that may be used for this purpose.

Assisting Clients to Personalize Their Statements

The relative concreteness of a specific client message is related in part to the focus or subject of that message. Client messages fall into several different classes of topic focus (Cormier & Cormier, 1979), each of which emphasizes different information and leads into very different areas of discussion:

- Focus on self, *indicated by the subject "I" (e.g., "I'm disappointed that I wasn't able to keep the appointment")*
- Focus on others, *indicated by subjects such as "they," "people," "someone," or names of specific persons (e.g., "They haven't fulfilled their part of the bargain")*
- Focus on the group or mutual relationship between self and others, *indicated by the subject "we" (e.g., "We would like to do that")*
- Focus on content, *indicated by such subjects as events, institutions, situations, ideas (e.g., "School wasn't easy for me")*

Clients are more prone to focus on others or on content, or to speak of themselves as a part of a group rather than to personalize their statements by using "I" or other self-referent pronouns. This tendency is illustrated in the following messages: "Things just don't seem to be going right for me," "They don't like me," and "It's not easy for people to talk about their problems." In the last example, the client means that it is not easy for *her* to talk about *her* problems, yet she uses the term *people*, thereby generalizing the problem and obscuring her personal struggle.

In assisting clients to personalize statements, social workers have a three-part task:

1. Social workers must model, teach, and coach clients to use self-referent pronouns (*I, me*) in talking about their concerns and their own emotional response to those concerns. For example, in response to a vague client message that focuses on content rather than self ("Everything at home seems to be deteriorating"), the social worker might gently ask the client to reframe the message by starting the response with "I" and giving specific information about what she is experiencing. It is also helpful to teach clients the difference between messages that focus on self ("I think …," "I feel …," "I want …") and messages that are *other-related* ("It …," "Someone …").

2. Social workers must teach the difference between self-referent messages and subject-related messages (i.e., those dealing with objects, things, ideas, or situations). Although teaching clients to use self-referent

pronouns when talking about their concerns is a substantive task, clients derive major benefits from it. Indeed, not owning or taking responsibility for feelings and speaking about problems in generalities and abstractions are among the most prevalent causes of problems in communicating.

3. Social workers must focus frequently on the client and use the client's name or the pronoun *you*. Beginning social workers are apt to attend to client talk about other people, distant situations, the group at large, various escapades, or other events or content that give little information about self and the relationship between self and situations or people. In the following illustration, the social worker's response focuses on the situation rather than on the client:

Client: My kids want to shut me up in a nursing home.
Social worker: What makes you think that?

In contrast, the following message personalizes the client's concern and explicitly identifies the feelings she is experiencing:

Social worker: You worry that your children might be considering a nursing home for you. You want to be part of any decision about what would be a safe environment for you.

A social worker may employ various techniques to assist clients to personalize messages. In the preceding example, the social worker utilized an empathic response. In this instance, this skill is invaluable to the social worker in helping the client to focus on self. Recall that personalizing feelings is an inherent aspect of the paradigm for responding empathetically ("You feel about/because_____"). Thus, clients can make statements that omit self-referent pronouns, and by utilizing empathic responding, social workers may assist clients to "own" their feelings.

Eliciting Specific Feelings

Even when clients personalize their messages and express their feelings, social workers often need to elicit additional information to clarify what they are experiencing, because certain "feeling words" denote general feeling states rather than specific feelings. For example, in the message, "I'm really *upset* that I didn't get a raise," the word "upset" helps to clarify the client's general frame of mind but fails to specify the precise feeling. In this instance, "upset" may refer to feeling disappointed, discouraged, unappreciated, devalued, angry, resentful, or even incompetent or inadequate due to the failure to receive a raise. Until the social worker has elicited additional information, he or she cannot be sure of how the client actually experiences being "upset."

Other feeling words that lack specificity include *frustrated, uneasy, uncomfortable, troubled,* and *bothered.* When clients employ such words, you can pinpoint their feelings by using responses such as the following:

- *"How do you mean, 'upset'?"*
- *"I'd like to understand more about that feeling. Could you clarify what you mean by 'frustrated'?"*
- *"Can you say more about in what way you feel bothered?"*

Focusing on the Here and Now

Another aspect of concreteness takes the form of responses that shift the focus from the past to the present, the here and now. Messages that relate to the immediate present are high in concreteness, whereas those that center on the past are low in concreteness. Some clients (and social workers) are prone to discuss past feelings and events. Unfortunately, precious opportunities for promoting growth and understanding may slip through the fingers of social workers who fail to focus on emotions and experiences that unfold in the immediacy of the interview. Focusing on feelings as they occur will enable you to observe reactions and behavior firsthand, eliminating any bias and error caused by reporting feelings and experiences after the fact. Furthermore, the helpfulness of your feedback is greatly enhanced when this feedback relates to the client's immediate experience.

The following exchange demonstrates how to achieve concreteness in such situations:

Client [*choking up*]: When she told me it was all over, that she was in love with another man—well, I just felt—it's happened again. I felt totally alone, like there just wasn't anyone.

Social worker: That must have been terribly painful. [*Client nods; tears well up.*] I wonder if you're not having the same feeling just now—at this moment. [*Client nods agreement.*]

Not only do such instances provide direct access to the client's inner experience, but they also may produce lasting benefits as the client shares deep and painful emotions in the context of a warm, accepting, and supportive relationship. Here-and-now experiencing that involves emotions toward the social worker (e.g., anger, hurt, disappointment, affectional desires, fears) is known as *relational immediacy.* Skills pertinent to relational immediacy warrant separate consideration and are dealt with in Chapter 18.

Focusing on here-and-now experiencing with groups, couples, and families (a topic discussed at length in Chapter 15) is a particularly potent technique for assisting members of these systems to clear the air of pent-up feelings. Moreover, interventions that focus on the immediacy of feelings bring buried issues to the surface, paving the way for the social worker to assist members of these systems to clearly identify and explore their difficulties and (if appropriate) to engage in problem solving.

Eliciting Details Related to Clients' Experiences

As previously mentioned, one reason why concrete responses are essential is that clients often offer up vague statements regarding their experiences—for example, "Some people in this group don't want to change bad enough to put forth any effort." Compare this with the following concrete statement, in which the client assumes ownership of the problem and fills in details that clarify its nature:

Client: I'm concerned because I want to do something to work on my problems in this group, but when I do try to talk about them, you, John, make some sarcastic remark. It seems that then several of you [*gives names*] just laugh about it and someone changes the subject. I really feel ignored then and just go off into my own world.

Aside from assisting clients to personalize their messages and to "own" their feelings and problems, social workers must ask questions that elicit illuminating information concerning the client's experiencing, such as that illustrated in the preceding message. Questions that start with "how" or "what" are often helpful in assisting the client to give concrete data. For example, to the client message, "Some people in this group don't want to change bad enough to put forth any effort," the social worker might respond, "What have you seen happening in the group that leads you to this conclusion?"

Eliciting Details Related to Interactional Behavior

Concrete responses are also vital in accurately assessing interactional behavior. Such responses pinpoint what actually occurs in interactional events—that is, what circumstances preceded the events, what the participants said and did, what specific thoughts and feelings the client experienced, and what consequences followed the event. In other words, the social worker elicits details of what happened, rather than settling for clients' views and conclusions.

An example of a concrete response to a client message follows:

High school student: My teacher really lost it yesterday. She totally dissed me, and I hadn't done one thing to deserve it.

Social worker: That must have been very disappointing. Can you lay out for me the sequence of events—what led up to this situation, and what each of you said and did? To understand better what went wrong, I'd like to get the details as though I had been there and observed what happened.

In such cases, it is important to keep clients on topic by continuing to assist them to relate the events in question, using responses such as "Then what happened?", "What did you do next?", or "Then who said what?" If dysfunctional patterns become evident after exploring numerous events, social workers have a responsibility to share their observations with clients, to assist them to evaluate the effects of the patterned behavior, and to assess their motivation to change it.

Specificity of Expression by Social Workers

Seeking concreteness applies to the communication of both clients and social workers. In this role, you will frequently explain, clarify, give feedback, and share personal feelings and views with clients. As a social worker who has recently begun a formal professional educational program, you may be prone to speak with the vagueness and generality that characterize much of the communication of the lay public. When such vagueness occurs, clients and others may understandably misinterpret, draw erroneous conclusions, or experience confusion about the meaning of your messages.

Consider the lack of specificity in the following messages actually delivered by social workers:

- *"You seem to have a lot of pent-up hostility."*
- *"You really handled yourself well in the group today."*
- *"I think a lot of your difficulties stem from your self-image."*

Vague terms such as *hostility, handled yourself well,* and *self-image* may leave the client in a quandary as to what the social worker actually means. Moreover, in this style of communication, conclusions are presented without supporting information. As a result, the client must either accept them at face value, reject them as invalid, or speculate on the basis of the conclusions. Fortunately, some clients are sufficiently perceptive, inquisitive, and assertive to request greater specificity—but many others are not.

Contrast the preceding messages with how the social worker responds to the same situations with messages that have a high degree of specificity:

- *"I've noticed that you've become easily angered and frustrated several times as we've talked about ways you might work out child custody arrangements with your wife. This appears to be a very painful area for you. I would like to know just what you have been feeling."*

- *"I noticed that you responded several times in the group tonight, and I thought you offered some very helpful insight to Marjorie when you said…. I also noticed you seemed to be more at ease than in previous sessions."*

- *"We've talked about your tendency to feel inferior to other members of your family and to discount your own feelings and opinions in your contacts with them. I think that observation applies to the problem you're having with your sister that you just described. You've said you didn't want to go on the trip with her and her husband because they fight all the time, yet you feel you have to go because she is putting pressure on you. As in other instances, you appear to be drawing the conclusion that how you feel about the matter isn't important."*

- *In the video "HFH," the practitioner, Kim Strom-Gottfried, makes a specific observation that simultaneously provides feedback and suggests the meaning for a behavior (something we will explore further in chapter 17): "There is a dynamic here that is going on at many levels between the two of you as you sort out this holiday problem. And yet it sounds like it is part of a larger issue, in terms of conversations of how you put together this relationship with your family relationships."*

When social workers speak with specificity, clarify meanings, personalize statements, and document the sources of their conclusions, clients are much less likely to misinterpret or project their own feelings or thoughts. Clients like to be clear about what is expected of them and how they are perceived, as well as how and why social workers think and feel as they do about matters discussed in their sessions. Clients also learn vicariously to speak with greater specificity as social workers model sending concrete messages.

Both beginning and experienced social workers face the additional challenge of avoiding inappropriate use of jargon. Unfortunately, jargon has pervaded professional discourse and runs rampant in social work literature and case records. Its use confuses, rather than clarifies, meanings for clients. The careless use of jargon with colleagues also fosters stereotypical thinking and is therefore antithetical to the cardinal value of individualizing the client. Furthermore, labels tend to conjure up images of clients that vary from one social worker to another, thereby injecting a significant source of error into communication. Consider the lack of specificity in the following messages that are rich in jargon:

- *"Mrs. N manifests strong passive-aggressive tendencies."*
- *"Sean displayed adequate impulse control in the group and tested the leader's authority in a positive manner."*
- *"Hal needs assistance in gaining greater self-control."*
- *"The client shows some borderline characteristics."*
- *"The group members were able to respond to appropriate limits."*
- *"Ruth appears to be emotionally immature for an eighth-grader."*

To accurately convey information about clients to your colleagues, you must explicitly describe their behavior and document the sources of your conclusions. For example, with the vague message, "Ruth appears to be emotionally immature for an eighth-grader," consider how much more accurately another social worker would perceive your client if you conveyed information in the form of a concrete response: "The teacher says Ruth is quiet and stays to herself in school. She doesn't answer any questions in class unless directly called upon, and she often doesn't complete her assignments. She spends considerable time daydreaming or playing with objects." By describing behavior in this way, you avoid biasing your colleague's perceptions of clients by conveying either vague impressions or erroneous conclusions.

It has been our experience that mastery of the skill of communicating with specificity is gained only through extended and determined effort. The task becomes more complicated if you are not aware that your communication is vague. We recommend that you carefully and consistently monitor your recorded sessions and your everyday conversations with a view toward identifying instances in which you did or did not communicate with specificity. This kind of monitoring will enable you to set relevant goals for yourself and to chart your progress. We also recommend that you enlist your practicum instructor to provide feedback about your performance level on this vital skill.

Exercises in Seeking Concreteness

In the following exercises, you should formulate written responses that will elicit concrete data regarding clients' problems. You may wish to combine your responses with either an empathic response or a paraphrase. Reviewing the eight guidelines for seeking concreteness as you complete the exercise will assist you in developing effective responses and help you to clearly conceptualize the various dimensions of this skill as well. After you have finished the exercises, compare your responses with the modeled responses.

Client Statements

1. **Adolescent** [*speaking of his recent recommitment to a correctional institution*]: It really seems weird to be back here.
2. **Client:** You can't depend on friends; they'll stab you in the back every time.
3. **Client:** He's got a terrible temper—that's the way he is, and he'll never change.
4. **Client:** My supervisor is so insensitive, you can't believe it. All she thinks about are reports and deadlines.
5. **Client:** I was upset after I left your office last week. I felt you really didn't understand what I was saying and didn't care how I felt.
6. **Client**: My dad's 58 years old now, but I swear he still hasn't grown up. He always has a chip on his shoulder.
7. **Elder client:** My rheumatoid arthritis has affected my hands a lot. It gets to be kind of tricky when I'm handling pots and pans in the kitchen.
8. **Client:** I just have this uneasy feeling about going to the doctor. I guess I've really got a hang-up about it.
9. **African American student** [*to African American social worker*]: You ask why I don't talk to my teacher about why I'm late for school. I'll tell you why. Because she's white, that's why. She's got it in for us black students, and there's just no point talking to her. That's just the way it is.
10. **Client:** John doesn't give a damn about me. I could kick the bucket, and he wouldn't lose a wink of sleep.

Modeled Responses

1. "Can you tell me how it feels weird to you?"
2. "I gather you feel that your friends have let you down in the past. Could you give me a recent example in which this has happened?"
3. "Could you tell me more about what happens when he loses his temper with you?" or "You sound like you don't have much hope that he'll ever get control of his temper. How have you concluded he will never change?" [*A social worker might explore each aspect of the message separately.*]
4. "Could you give me some examples of how she is insensitive to you?"
5. "Sounds like you've been feeling hurt and disappointed over my reaction last week. I can sense you're struggling with those same feelings right now. Could you tell me what you're feeling at this moment?"
6. "It sounds as if you feel that your dad's way of communicating with you is unusual for someone his age. Could you recall some recent examples of times you've had difficulties with how he communicates with you?"
7. "It sounds as if the arthritis pain is aggravating and blocking what you normally do. When you say that handling the pots and pans is kind of tricky, can you tell me about recent examples of what has happened when you are cooking?"
8. "Think of going to the doctor just now. Let your feelings flow naturally. [*Pause.*] What goes on inside you—your thoughts and feelings?"
9. "So you see it as pretty hopeless. You feel pretty strongly about Ms. Wright. I'd be interested in hearing what's happened that has led you to the conclusion she's got it in for black students."
10. "So you feel as if you're nothing in his eyes. I'm wondering how you've reached that conclusion?"

Focusing: A Complex Skill

Skills in focusing are critical to your practice for several reasons. Because your time with clients is limited, it is critical to make the best use of each session by honing in on key topics. You are also responsible for guiding the helping process and avoiding wandering. Helping relationships should be characterized by sharp focus and continuity, unlike normal social relations. As social workers, we perform a valuable role by assisting clients to focus on their problems in greater depth and to maintain focus until they accomplish desired changes.

In addition, families and groups sometimes experience interactional difficulties that prevent them from focusing effectively on their problems. To enhance family and group functioning, social workers must be able to refocus the discussion whenever dysfunctional interactional processes cause families and groups to prematurely drift away from the topic at hand.

To assist you in learning how to focus effectively, we consider the three functions of focusing skills:

1. Selecting topics for exploration
2. Exploring topics in depth
3. Maintaining focus and keeping on topic

Knowledge of these functions will enable you to focus sharply on relevant topics and elicit sufficient data to formulate an accurate problem assessment—a prerequisite for competent practice.

Selecting Topics for Exploration

Areas relevant for exploration vary from situation to situation. However, clients who have contact with social workers in the same setting, such as in nursing homes, group homes, or child welfare agencies, may share many common concerns.

Before meeting with clients whose concerns differ from client populations with which you are familiar, you can prepare yourself to conduct an effective exploration by developing (in consultation with your practicum instructor or field supervisor) a list of relevant and promising problem areas to be explored. This preparation will help you avoid a mistake commonly made by some beginning social workers—namely, focusing on areas irrelevant to clients' problems and eliciting reams of information of questionable utility.

In your initial interview with an institutionalized youth, for example, you could more effectively select questions and responses if you knew in advance that you might explore the following areas:

1. Client's own perceptions of the concerns at hand
2. Client's perceived strengths and resources
3. Reasons for being institutionalized and brief history of past problems related to legal authority and to use of drugs and alcohol
4. Details regarding the client's relationships with individual family members, both as concerns and sources of support
5. Brief family history
6. School adjustment, including information about grades, problem subjects, areas of interest, and relationships with various teachers

7. Adjustment to institutional life, including relationships with peers and supervisors
8. Peer relationships outside the institution
9. Life goals and more short-term goals
10. Reaction to previous experiences with helpers
11. Attitude toward engaging in a working relationship to address concerns

Because the institutionalized youth is an involuntary client, part of this exploration would include the youth's understanding of which parts of his work are non-negotiable requirements, and which parts could be negotiated or free choices (Rooney, 2009).

Similarly, if you plan to interview a self-referred middle-aged woman whose major complaint is depression, the following topical areas could assist you in conducting an initial interview:

1. Concerns as she sees them, including the nature of depressive symptoms such as sleep patterns and appetite changes
2. Client's perceived strengths and resources
3. Health status, date of last physical examination, and medications being taken
4. Onset and duration of depression, previous depressive or manic episodes
5. Life events associated with onset of depression (especially losses)
6. Possible suicidal thoughts, intentions, or plans
7. Problematic thought patterns (e.g., self-devaluation, self-recrimination, guilt, worthlessness, helplessness, hopelessness)
8. Previous coping efforts, previous treatment
9. Quality of interpersonal relationships (e.g., interpersonal skills and deficiencies, conflicts and supports in marital and parent–child relationships)
10. Reactions of significant others to her depression
11. Support systems (adequacy and availability)
12. Daily activities
13. Sense of mastery versus feelings of inadequacy
14. Family history of depression or manic behavior

Because she is self-referred, this client is likely to be more voluntary than the institutionalized youth. You should therefore pay more attention to identifying the specific concerns that have led her to seek help.

As noted previously, problem areas vary, and outlines of probable topical areas likewise vary accordingly. Thus, a list of areas for exploration in an initial session with a couple seeking marriage counseling or with a group of alcoholics will include a number of items that differ from those in the first list (i.e., the areas

identified for the institutionalized youth). Note, however, that items 1, 2, and 8–11 would likely be included in all exploratory interviews with individual clients and would be equally applicable to preparatory interviews with prospective group members.

In using an outline, you should avoid following it rigidly or using it as a crutch; otherwise, you could potentially destroy the spontaneity of sessions and block clients from relating their stories in their own way. Instead, encourage your clients to discuss their problems freely while you play a facilitative role in exploring in greater depth any problems that emerge. In particular, you must use outlines flexibly—reordering the sequence of topics; modifying, adding, or deleting topics; or abandoning the outline altogether if using it hinders communication.

Of course, you cannot always anticipate fruitful topical areas. After all, although clients from the same population may share many commonalities, their problems inevitably have unique aspects. For this reason, it is important to review tapes of sessions with your practicum instructor or a field supervisor for the purpose of identifying other topical areas you should explore in future sessions.

Exploring Topics in Depth

A major facet of focusing is centering discussions on relevant topics to assure that exploration moves from generality and superficiality to greater depth and meaning. Social workers must have the skills needed to explore problems thoroughly, because their success in the helping process depends on their ability to obtain clear and accurate definitions of problems.

Selectively attending to specific topics is challenging for beginning social workers, who often wander in individual or group sessions, repeatedly skipping across the surface of vital areas of content and feelings, and eliciting largely superficial and sometimes distorted information. This tendency is illustrated in the following excerpt from a first session with an adolescent in a school setting:

Social worker: Tell me about your family.

Client: My father is ill and my mother is dead, so we live with my sister.

Social worker: How are things with you and your sister?

Client: Good. We get along fine. She treats me pretty good.

Social worker: How about your father?

Client: We get along pretty well. We have our problems, but most of the time things are okay. I don't really see him very much.

Social worker: Tell me about school. How are you getting along here?

Client: Well, I don't like it very well, but my grades are good enough to get me by.

Social worker: I notice you're new to our school this year. How did you do in the last school you attended?

By focusing superficially on the topics of family and school, this social worker misses opportunities to explore potential problem areas in the depth necessary to illuminate the client's situation. Not surprisingly, this exploration yielded little information of value, in large part because the social worker failed to employ responses that focused in depth on topical areas. In the next sections, we further delineate the skills that will considerably enhance a social worker's ability to maintain focus on specific areas.

Open-Ended Responses

Social workers may employ open-ended responses throughout individual, conjoint, and group sessions to focus unobtrusively on desired topics. Earlier we noted that some open-ended responses leave clients free to choose their own topics, whereas others focus on a topic but encourage clients to respond freely to that topic. The following examples, taken from an initial session with a mother of eight children who has depression, illustrate how social workers can employ open-ended responses to define topical areas that may yield a rich trove of information vital to grasping the dynamics of the client's problems.[1]

- *"What have you thought that you might like to accomplish in our work together?"*
- *"You've discussed many topics in the last few minutes. Could you pick the most important one and tell me more about it?"*
- *"You've mentioned that your oldest son doesn't come home after school as he did before and help you with the younger children. I would like to hear more about that."*
- *"Several times as you've mentioned your concern that your husband may leave you, your voice has trembled. I wonder if you could share what you are feeling."*
- *"You've indicated that your partner doesn't help you enough with the children. You also seem to be saying*

that you feel overwhelmed and inadequate in managing the children by yourself. Tell me what happens as you try to manage your children."
- *"You indicate that you have more problems with your 14-year-old daughter than with the other children. Tell me more about Janet and your problems with her."*

In the preceding examples, the social worker's open-ended questions and responses progressively moved the exploration from the general to the specific. Note also that each response or question defined a new topic for exploration.

To encourage in-depth exploration of the topics defined in this way, the social worker must blend open-ended questions with other facilitative verbal following responses that focus on and elicit expanded client expressions. After having defined a topical area by employing an open-ended response, for instance, the social worker might deepen the exploration by weaving other open-ended responses into the discussion. If the open-ended responses shift the focus to another area, however, the exploration suffers a setback. Note in the following exchange how the social worker's second open-ended response shifts the focus away from the client's message, which involves expression of intense feelings:

Social worker: You've said you're worried about retiring. I'd appreciate your sharing more about your concern. [*Open-ended response.*]

Client: I can't imagine not going to work every day. I feel at loose ends already, and I haven't even quit work. I'm afraid I just won't know what to do with myself.

Social worker: How do you imagine spending your time after retiring? [*Open-ended response.*]

Even though open-ended responses may draw out new information about clients' problems, they may not facilitate the helping process if they prematurely lead the client in a different direction. If social workers utilize open-ended or other types of responses that frequently change the topic, they will obtain information that is disjointed and fragmented. As a result, assessments will suffer from large gaps in the social worker's knowledge concerning clients' problems. As social workers formulate open-ended responses, they must be acutely aware of the direction that responses will take.

Seeking Concreteness

Earlier we discussed and illustrated the various facets of seeking concreteness. Because seeking concreteness enables social workers to move from the general to the specific and to explore topics in depth, it is a key focusing technique. We illustrate this ability in an excerpt from a session involving a client with a serious and persistent mental illness:

Client: I just don't have energy to do anything. This medicine really knocks me out.

Social worker: It sounds as if the side effects of your medication are of concern. Can you tell me specifically what those side effects have been?

By focusing in depth on topical areas, social workers are able to discern—and to assist clients to discern—problematic thoughts, behavior, and interaction. Subsequent sections consider how social workers can effectively focus on topical areas in exploratory sessions by blending concreteness with other focusing skills. In actuality, the majority of responses that social workers typically employ to establish and maintain focus are blends of various types of discrete responses.

Empathic Responding

Empathic responding serves a critical function by enabling social workers to focus in depth on troubling feelings, as illustrated in the next example:

Client: I can't imagine not going to work every day. I feel at loose ends already, and I haven't even quit work. I'm afraid I just won't know what to do with myself.

Social worker: You seem to be saying, "Even now, I'm apprehensive about retiring. I'm giving up something that has been very important to me, and I don't seem to have anything to replace it." I gather that feeling at loose ends, as you do, you worry that when you retire, you'll feel useless.

Client: I guess that's a large part of my problem. Sometimes I feel useless now. I just didn't take time over the years to develop any hobbies or to pursue any interests. I guess I don't think that I can do anything else.

Social worker: It sounds as if part of you feels hopeless about the future, as if you have done everything you can do. And yet I wonder if another part of you might think that it isn't too late to look into some new interests.

Client: I do dread moping around home with time on my hands. I can just see it now. My wife will want to keep me busy doing things around the house for her all the time. I've never liked to do that kind of thing. I suppose it is never too late to look into other interests. I have always wanted to write some things for fun, not just for work. You know, the memory goes at my age, but I have thought about just writing down some of the family stories.

Note how the client's problem continued to unfold as the social worker utilized empathic responding, revealing rich information in the process. The social worker also raises the possibility of new solutions, not just dwelling in the feelings of uselessness.

Blending Open-Ended, Empathic, and Concrete Responses to Maintain Focus

After employing open-ended responses to focus on a selected topic, social workers should use other responses to maintain focus on that topic. In the following excerpt, observe how the social worker employs both open-ended and empathic responses to explore problems in depth, thereby enabling the client to move to the heart of her struggle. Notice also the richness of the client's responses elicited by the blended messages.

Social worker: As you were speaking about your son, I sensed some pain and reluctance on your part to talk about him. I'd like to understand more about what you're feeling. Could you share with me what you are experiencing right now? [*Blended empathic and open-ended response that seeks concreteness.*]

Client: I guess I haven't felt too good about coming this morning. I almost called and canceled. I feel I should be able to handle these problems with Jim [*son*] myself. Coming here is like having to admit I'm no longer capable of coping with him.

Social worker: So you've had reservations about coming [*paraphrase*]—you feel you're admitting defeat and that perhaps you've failed or that you're inadequate—and that hurts. [*Empathic response.*]

Client: Well, yes, although I know that I need some help. It's just hard to admit it, I think. My biggest problem in this regard, however, is my husband. He feels much more strongly than I do that we should manage this problem ourselves, and he really disapproves of my coming in.

Social worker: So even though it's painful for you, you're convinced you need some assistance with Jim, but you're torn about coming here because of your husband's attitude. I'd be interested in hearing more about that. [*Blended empathic and open-ended response.*]

In the preceding example, the social worker initiated discussion of the client's here-and-now experiences through a blended open-ended and empathic response, following it with other empathic and blended responses to explore the client's feelings further. With the last response, the social worker narrowed the focus to a potential obstacle to the helping process (the husband's attitude toward therapy), which could also be explored in a similar manner.

Open-ended and empathic responses may also be blended to facilitate and encourage discussion from group members about a defined topic. For instance, after using an open-ended response to solicit group feedback regarding a specified topic ("I'm wondering how you feel about …"), the social worker can employ empathic or other facilitative responses to acknowledge the contribution of members who respond to the invitation to comment.

By utilizing open-ended responses, the social worker can successively reach for comments of individual members who have not contributed ("What do you think about …, Ray?").

In the next example, the social worker blends empathic and concrete responses to facilitate in-depth exploration. Notice how these blended responses yield behavioral referents of the problem. The empathic messages convey the social worker's sensitive awareness and concern for the client's distress. The open-ended and concrete responses focus on details of a recent event and yield valuable clues that the client's rejections by women may be associated with insensitive and inappropriate social behavior. Awareness of this behavior is a prelude to formulating relevant goals. Goals formulated in this way are highly relevant to the client.

Single male client, age 20: There has to be something wrong with me, or women wouldn't treat me like a leper. Sometimes I feel like I'm doomed to be alone the rest of my life. I'm not even sure why I came to see you. I think I'm beyond help.

Social worker: You sound like you've given up on yourself—as though you're utterly hopeless. At the same, it seems like part of you still clings to hope and wants to try. [*Empathic response.*]

Client: What else can I do? I can't go on like this, but I don't know how many more times I can get knocked down and get back up.

Social worker: I sense you feel deeply hurt and discouraged at those times. Could you give me a recent example of when you felt you were being knocked down? [*Blended empathic and concrete response.*]

Client: Well, a guy I work with got me a blind date for a dance. I took her, and it was a total disaster. I figured that she would at least let me take her home. After we got to the dance, she ignored me the whole night and danced with other guys. Then, to add insult to injury, she went home with one of them and didn't even have the decency to tell me. There I was, wondering what had happened to her.

Social worker: Besides feeling rejected, you must have been very mad. When did you first feel you weren't hitting it off with her? [*Blended empathic and concrete response.*]

Client: I guess it was when she lit up a cigarette while we were driving to the dance. I kidded her about how she was asking for lung cancer.

Social worker: I see. What was it about her reaction, then, that led you to believe you might not be in her good graces? [*Concrete response.*]

Client: Well, she didn't say anything. She just smoked her cigarette. I guess I really knew then that she was upset at me.

Social worker: As you look back at it now, what do you think you might have said to repair things at that point? [*Stimulating reflection about problem solving.*]

In the next example, observe how the social worker blends empathic and concrete responses to elicit details of interaction in an initial conjoint session. Such blending is a potent technique for eliciting specific and abundant information that bears directly on clients' problems. Responses that seek concreteness elicit details. In contrast, empathic responses enable social workers to stay attuned to clients' moment-by-moment experiencing, thereby focusing on feelings that may present obstacles to the exploration.

Social worker: You mentioned having difficulties communicating. I'd like you to give me an example of a time when you felt you weren't communicating effectively, and let's go through it step by step to see if we can understand more clearly what is happening.

Wife: Well, weekends are an example. Usually I want to go out and do something fun with the kids, but John just wants to stay home. He starts criticizing me for wanting to go, go, go.

Social worker: Could you give me a specific example? [*Seeking concreteness.*]

Wife: Okay. Last Saturday I wanted all of us to go out to eat and then to a movie, but John wanted to stay home and watch TV.

Social worker: Before we get into what John did, let's stay with you for a moment. There you are, really wanting to go to a movie—tell me exactly what you did. [*Seeking concreteness.*]

Wife: I think I said, "John, let's take the kids out to dinner and a movie."

Social worker: Okay. That's what you said. How did you say it? [*Seeking concreteness.*]

Wife: I expected him to say no, so I might not have said it the way I just did.

Social worker: Turn to John, and say it the way you may have said it then. [*Seeking concreteness.*]

Wife: Okay. [*Turning to husband.*] Couldn't we go out to a movie?

Social worker: There seems to be some doubt in your voice as to whether John wants to go out. [*Focusing observation.*]

Wife [*interrupting*]: I knew he wouldn't want to.

Social worker: So you assumed he wouldn't want to go. It's as though you already knew the answer. [*To husband.*] Does the way your wife asked the question check out with the way you remembered it? [*Husband nods.*]

Social worker: After your wife asked you about going to the movie, what did you do? [*Seeking concreteness.*]

Husband: I said, nope! I wanted to stay home and relax Saturday, and I felt we could do things at home.

Social worker: So your answer was short. Apparently you didn't give her information about why you didn't want to go but just said no. Is that right? [*Focusing observation.*]

Husband: That's right. I didn't think she wanted to go anyway—the way she asked.

Social worker: What were you experiencing when you said no? [*Seeking concreteness.*]

Husband: I guess I was just really tired. I have a lot of pressures from work, and I just need some time to relax. She doesn't understand that.

Social worker: You're saying, then, "I just needed some time to get away from it all," but I take it you had your doubts as to whether she could appreciate your feelings. [*Husband nods.*] [*Turning to wife.*] Now, after your husband said no, what did you do? [*Blended empathic and concrete response.*]

Wife: I think that I started talking to him about the way he just sits around the house.

Social worker: I sense that you felt hurt and somewhat discounted because John didn't respond the way you would have liked. [*Empathic response.*]

Wife [*nods*]: I didn't think he even cared what I wanted to do.

Social worker: Is it fair to conclude, then, that the way in which you handled your feelings was to criticize John rather than to say, "This is what is happening to me?" [*Wife nods.*] [*Seeking concreteness.*]

Social worker [*to husband*]: Back, then, to our example. What did you do when your wife criticized you? [*Seeking concreteness.*]

Husband: I guess I criticized her back. I told her she needed to stay home once in a while and get some work done.

In this series of exchanges, the social worker asked questions that enabled the couple to describe the sequence of their interaction in a way that elicited key details and provided insight into unspoken assumptions and messages.

Managing Obstacles to Focusing

Occasionally you may find that your efforts to focus selectively and to explore topical areas in depth do not yield pertinent information. Although you have a responsibility in such instances to assess the effectiveness of your own interviewing style, you should also analyze clients' styles of communicating to determine to what extent their behaviors are interfering with your focusing efforts. Many clients seek help because they have—but are not aware of—patterns of communications or behaviors that create difficulties in relationships. In addition, involuntary clients who do not yet perceive the relationship as helping may be inclined to avoid focusing. The following list highlights common types of client communications that may challenge your efforts to focus in individual, family, and group sessions:

- *Responding with "I don't know"*
- *Changing the subject or avoiding sensitive areas*
- *Rambling from topic to topic*
- *Intellectualizing or using abstract or general terms*
- *Diverting focus from the present to the past*
- *Responding to questions with questions*
- *Interrupting excessively*
- *Failing to express opinions when asked*
- *Producing excessive verbal output*
- *Using humor or sarcasm to evade topics or issues*
- *Verbally dominating the discussion*

You can easily see how individuals who did not seek help from a social worker and want to avoid focusing might use these kinds of methods to protect their privacy. With such involuntary clients, such behaviors are likely to indicate a low level of trust and a skepticism that contact with a social worker can be helpful. You can counter repetitive behaviors and communications that divert the focus from exploring problems by tactfully drawing them to clients' attention and by assisting clients to adopt behaviors that are compatible with practice objectives. In groups, social workers must assist group members to modify behaviors that repeatedly disrupt effective focusing and communication; otherwise, the groups will not move to the phase of group development in which most of the work related to solving problems is accomplished. Children as clients often respond at first contact in a limited, passive, non-expressive style. This might be interpreted as non-communicative behavior. In fact, such behavior is often what the children expect to be appropriate in interactions with strange authority figures (Hersen & Thomas, 2007; Lamb & Brown, 2006; Evans, 2004; Powell, Thomson, & Dietze, 1997).

Social workers may use many different techniques for managing and modifying client obstacles. These techniques include asking clients to communicate or behave differently; teaching, modeling for, and coaching clients to assume more effective communication styles; reinforcing facilitative responses; and selectively attending to functional behaviors.

Intervening to Help Clients Focus or Refocus

Communications that occur in group or conjoint sessions are not only complex, but may also be distractive or irrelevant. Consequently, the social worker's task of assisting members to explore the defined topics fully, rather than meander from subject to subject, is a challenging one. Related techniques that social workers can employ

include highlighting or clarifying issues and bringing clients' attention to a comment or matter that has been overlooked. In such instances, the objective is not necessarily to explore the topic (although an exploration may subsequently occur), but rather to stress or elucidate important content. The social worker focuses clients' attention on communications and/or events that occurred earlier in the session or immediately preceded the social worker's focusing response. This technique is used in the following messages:

- [To son in session with parents]: *"Ray, you made an important point a moment ago that I'm not sure your parents heard. Would you please repeat your comment?"*
- [To individual]: *"I would like to return to a remark made several moments ago when you said _____. I didn't want to interrupt then. I think perhaps the remark was important enough that we should return to it now."*
- [To family]: *"Something happened just a minute ago as we were talking. [Describes event.] We were involved in another discussion then, but I made a mental note of it because of how deeply it seemed to affect all of you at the time. I think we should consider what happened for just a moment."*
- [To group member]: *"John, as you were talking a moment ago, I wasn't sure what you meant by _____. Could you clarify that for me and for others in the group?"*
- [To group]: *"A few minutes ago, we were engrossed in a discussion about _____, yet we have moved away from that discussion to one that doesn't really seem to relate to our purpose for being here. I'm concerned about leaving the other subject hanging because you were working hard to find some solutions and appeared to be close to a breakthrough."*

Because of the complexity of communications in group and family sessions, some inefficiency in the focusing process is inescapable. Nevertheless, the social worker can sharpen the group's efforts to focus and encourage more efficient use of its time by teaching effective focusing behavior. We suggest that social workers actually explain the focusing role of the group and identify desirable focusing behaviors, such as attending, active listening, and asking open-ended questions. During this discussion, it is important to emphasize that by utilizing these skills, members will facilitate exploration of problems.

Social workers can encourage greater use of these skills by giving positive feedback to group or family members when they have adequately focused on a problem, thus reinforcing their efforts. Although group members usually experience some difficulty in learning how to focus, they should be able to delve deeply into problems by the third or fourth session, given sufficient guidance and education by social workers. Such efforts by social workers tend to accelerate movement of groups toward maturity, a phase in which members achieve maximum therapeutic benefits. A characteristic of a group in this phase, in fact, is that members explore issues in considerable depth rather than skim the surface of many topics.

Summarizing Responses

The technique of summarization embodies four distinct and yet related facets:

1. Highlighting key aspects of discussions of specific problems before changing the focus of the discussion
2. Making connections between relevant aspects of lengthy client messages
3. Reviewing major focal points of a session and tasks that clients plan to work on before the next session
4. Recapitulating the highlights of a previous session and reviewing clients' progress on tasks during the week for the purpose of providing focus and continuity between sessions

Although employed at different times and in different ways, each of these facets of summarization serves the common purpose of tying together functionally related elements that occur at different points in the helping process. They are considered in detail in the following sections.

Highlighting Key Aspects of Problems

During the phase of an initial session in which problems are explored in moderate depth, summarization can be effectively employed to tie together and highlight essential aspects of a problem before proceeding to explore additional problems. For example, the social worker might describe how the problem appears to be produced by the interplay of several factors, including external pressures, overt behavioral patterns, unfulfilled needs and wants, and covert thoughts and feelings. Connecting these key elements assists clients in gaining a more accurate and complete perspective of their problems.

Employed in this fashion, summarization involves fitting pieces of the problem together to form a coherent whole. Seeing the problem in a fresh and more accurate perspective often proves beneficial, because it expands clients' awareness and can generate hope and enthusiasm for tackling a problem that has hitherto seemed insurmountable.

Summarization that highlights problems is generally employed at a natural point in the session when the social worker believes that relevant aspects of the problem have been adequately explored and clients appear satisfied in having had the opportunity to express their concerns. The following example illustrates this type of summarization. In this case, the client, an 80-year-old widow, has been referred to a Services to Seniors program for exploration of alternative living arrangements because of her failing health, isolation, and recent falls. As the two have worked together to explore alternative living arrangements, the pair have identified several characteristics that would be important for the client in an improved living situation. Highlighting the salient factors, the social worker summarizes the results to this point:

Social worker: It sounds as if you are looking for a situation in which there is social interaction but your privacy is also important to you: You want to maintain your independence.

Summarizing responses of this type serve as a prelude to the process of formulating goals, as goals flow naturally from problem formulations. Moreover, highlighting various dimensions of the problem facilitates the subsequent identifications of subgoals and tasks that must be accomplished to achieve the overall goal. In the preceding example, to explore an improved living situation, the social worker would help the client analyze the specific form of privacy (whether living alone or with someone else) and the type of social interaction (how much and what kind of contact with others) she desires.

Summarizing salient aspects of problems is a valuable technique in sessions with groups, couples, and families. It enables the social worker to stop at timely moments and highlight the difficulties experienced by each participant. In a family session with a pregnant adolescent and her mother, for example, the social worker might make the following statements:

- [To pregnant adolescent]: *"You feel as if deciding what to do about this baby is your decision—it's your body and you have decided that an abortion is the best solution for you. You know that you have the legal right to make this decision and want to be supported in making it. You feel as if your mother wants to help but can't tell you what decision to make."*

- [To mother]: *"As you spoke, you seemed saddened and very anxious about this decision your daughter is making. You are saying, 'I care about my daughter, but I don't think she is mature enough to make this decision on her own.' As you have noted, women in your family have had a hard time conceiving, and you wish that she would consider other options besides abortion. So you feel a responsibility to your daughter, but also to this unborn baby and the family history of conceiving children."*

Such responses synthesize in concise and neutral language the needs, concerns, and problems of each participant for all other members of the session to hear. This type of summarization underscores the fact that all participants are struggling with and have responsibility for problems that are occurring, thus counteracting the tendency of families to view one person as the exclusive cause of family problems.

Summarizing Lengthy Messages

Clients' messages range from one word or one sentence to lengthy and sometimes rambling monologues. Although the meaning and significance of brief messages are often readily discernible, lengthy messages challenge the social worker to encapsulate and tie together diverse and complex elements. Linking the elements together often highlights and expands the significance and meaning of the client's message. For this reason, such messages represent one form of additive empathy, a skill discussed in Chapter 17.

Because lengthy client messages typically include emotions, thoughts, and descriptive content, you will need to determine how these dimensions relate to the focal point of the discussion. To illustrate, consider the following message of a mildly brain-damaged and socially withdrawn 16-year-old female—an only child who is extremely dependent on her overprotective but subtly rejecting mother:

Client: Mother tells me she loves me, but I find that hard to believe. Nothing I do ever pleases her; she yells at me when I refuse to wash my hair alone. But I can't do it right without her help. "When are you going to grow up?" she'll say. And she goes out with her friends and leaves me alone in that old house. She knows how scared I get when I have to stay home alone. But she says, "Nancy, I can't just baby-sit you all the time. I've got to do something for myself. Why don't you make some friends or watch TV or play your guitar? You've just got to quit

pitying yourself all the time." Does that sound like someone who loves you? I get so mad at her when she yells at me, it's all I can do to keep from killing her.

Embodied in the client's message are the following elements:

1. Wanting to be loved by her mother, yet feeling insecure and rejected at times
2. Feeling inadequate about performing certain tasks, such as washing her hair
3. Feeling extremely dependent upon her mother for certain services and companionship
4. Feeling afraid when her mother leaves her alone
5. Feeling hurt (implied) and resentful when her mother criticizes her or leaves her alone
6. Feeling intense anger and wanting to lash out when her mother yells at her

The following summarizing response ties these elements together:

Social worker: So you find your feelings toward your mother pulling you in different directions. You want her to love you, but you feel unloved and resent it when she criticizes you or leaves you alone. And you feel really torn because you depend on her in so many ways. Yet at times, you feel so angry you want to hurt her back for yelling at you. You'd like to have a smoother relationship without the strain.

In conjoint interviews or group sessions, summarization can also be used effectively to highlight and to tie together key elements and dynamics embodied in transactions, as illustrated in the following transaction and summarizing responses of a social worker:

In the conjoint interview entitled "HFH" on the CD-ROM connected with this chapter, partners who come to family treatment are in conflict about how open to be about their relationship to their families. Jackie comes from a family in which there is open communication. She is frustrated with the reticence to deal openly with feelings that is reflected in Anna's family. Kim, the practitioner, makes the following summarizing statement: "Often when we are forming new families and new couples we are torn between the families we come from and the new family we are creating. This can play out in logistical decisions about the holidays."

Occasionally, client messages may ramble to the extent that they contain numerous unrelated elements that cannot all be tied together. In such instances, your task is to extract and focus on those elements of the message that are most relevant to the thrust of the session at that point. When employed in this manner, summarization provides focus and direction to the session and averts aimless wandering. With clients whose thinking is loose or who ramble to avoid having to focus on unpleasant matters, you may need to interrupt to assure some semblance of focus and continuity. Otherwise, the interview will be disjointed and unproductive. Skills in maintaining focus and continuity are discussed later in this chapter and in Chapter 13.

Reviewing Focal Points of a Session

During the course of an individual, conjoint, or group session, it is common to focus on more than one problem and to discuss numerous factors associated with each problem. Toward the end of the first or second session, depending on the length of the initial exploration, summarization is employed to review key problems that have been discussed and to highlight themes and patterns related to these problems. Summarizing themes and patterns expands each client's awareness of dysfunctional patterns and his or her role in the difficulties identified (assuming the client affirms the validity of the summarization). In this way, use of this skill opens up promising avenues for growth and change.

In fact, through summarizing responses, social workers can review problematic themes and patterns that have emerged in their sessions and test clients' readiness to consider goals aimed at modifying these problematic patterns.

In the video "GBS" associated with this chapter, near the end of the session, Dorothy, the social worker, summarizes: "You have had a lot of stress at work with a poor performance review and anxiety that your co-workers are being rude to you over the possibility that you might get promoted. At home, you are dealing with your mother, who is living with you; your son and his girlfriend not working outside of the home and their baby; your daughter who helps take care of the little ones. All of the work of keeping up the household comes back to you. You are not eating, not sleeping very well, and have lost interest in some things you used to like to do."

Providing Focus and Continuity

The social worker can also use summarization at the beginning of an individual, group, or conjoint session to review work that clients have accomplished in the last session(s) and to set the stage for work in the present session. At the same time, the social worker may decide to identify a promising topic for discussion or to refresh clients' minds concerning work they wish to accomplish in that session. In addition, summarization can be employed periodically to synthesize salient points at the conclusion of a discussion or used at the end of the session to review the major focal points. In so doing, the social worker will need to place what was accomplished in the session within the broad perspective of the clients' goals. The social worker tries to consider how the salient content and movement manifested in each session fit into the larger whole. Only then are the social worker and clients likely to maintain a sense of direction and avoid needless delays caused by wandering and detours—problems that commonly occur when continuity within or between sessions is weak.

Used as a "wrap-up" when the allotted time for a session is nearly gone, summarization assists the social worker to draw a session to a natural conclusion. In addition to highlighting and linking together the key points of the session, the social worker reviews clients' plans for performing tasks before the next session. When the session ends with such a summarization, all participants should be clear about where they have been and where they are going in relation to the goals toward which their mutual efforts are directed.

Analyzing Your Verbal Following Skills

After taking frequency counts over a period of time of some of the major verbal following skills (empathy, concreteness, open-ended and closed-ended responses), you are ready to assess the extent to which you employ, blend, and balance these skills in relation to each other. On the form for recording verbal following (Figure 6-2), categorize each of your responses from a recorded session. As you analyze your relative use and blending of responses alone or with your practicum instructor, determine whether certain types of responses were used either too frequently or too sparingly. Think of steps that you might take to correct any imbalances in your utilization of skills for future sessions.

CLIENT MESSAGE	OPEN-ENDED RESPONSES	CLOSED-ENDED RESPONSES	EMPATHIC RESPONSES	LEVEL OF EMPATHY	CONCRETE RESPONSES	SUMMARIZING RESPONSES	OTHER TYPES OF RESPONSES
1.							
2.							
3.							
4.							
5.							
6.							
7.							

Directions: Categorize each of your responses from a recorded session. Where responses involve more than one category (blended responses), record them as a single response, but also check each category embodied in the response. Excluding the responses checked as "Other Type of Responses," analyze whether certain types of responses were utilized too frequently or too sparingly. Define tasks for yourself to correct imbalances in future sessions. Retain a copy of the form so that you can monitor your progress in mastering verbal following skills over an extended period of time.

FIG-6-2 Recording Form for Verbal Following Skills

Summary

This chapter has helped you learn how to explore, paraphrase, and appropriately use closed- and open-ended responses as a means of better focusing, following and summarizing in your social work practice. These skills may be applied both with clients and with other persons and colleagues, on behalf of clients. In Chapter 7, we will explore some common difficulties experienced by beginning social workers and some ways to overcome them.

Modeled Responses to Exercise in Paraphrasing

1. "You just get so uptight in a group you don't function."
2. "So you've made some real progress in tuning in to your husband and children."
3. "Because your fears really block you when you argue with your mother, you consistently come out on the short side."
4. "You're really torn and wonder if not seeing the children very often is too high a price to pay for a divorce. You seem pretty clear, though, that if you stay with her, there won't be any improvement."
5. "So people's helpfulness here and your own skills in meeting people have helped your adjustment here."
6. "So you see yourself as having contributed to many of her problems."
7. "It sounds as if you feel overloaded with conflicting parenting and work responsibilities."
8. "It sounds as if your experience causes you to doubt whether more services would be helpful. Could you tell me about your feeling that the mother is not motivated?"
9. "So sometimes you feel cheated by life and at other times that your illness is a consequence for your smoking history."
10. "So it sounds as if it has not been easy for you to relax and have friends in this school; when they have acted in a way that feels mean to you, you have felt a need to act to protect yourself."

Answers to Exercise in Identifying Closed- and Open-Ended Responses

Statement	Response
1	C
2	O
3	O
4	C

Modeled Open-Ended Responses

1. "Could you tell me more about your wanting to impress Ralph?"
2. "What are you afraid you'd do wrong?"
3. "Given your experience with that probation officer, how would you like your relationship with me to be?"
4. "So you feel that your facility cannot provide what Gladys needs. Can you describe the kind of care you believe she needs?"
5. "So you don't trust that I want to try to help you make what you feel will be the best decision. Can you tell me what I have done that has caused you to think that your mother and I are allies?"
6. "You sound as if you are at a pretty hopeless point right now. When you say you don't know if you want to keep trying to figure it out, can you tell me more about what you are thinking about doing?"

Notes

1. Note that several of these messages could also be categorized as seeking concreteness. Messages that seek concreteness and open-ended messages are not mutually exclusive; indeed, they often overlap to a considerable extent

Eliminating Counterproductive Communication Patterns

CHAPTER OVERVIEW

Chapter 7 explores communication difficulties that often arise in the practice of beginning (and many experienced) social workers and suggest some positive alternatives to these defective patterns. By becoming alert to these difficulties, beginning social workers can focus their attention on communicating in a positive fashion. In addition to applications in direct practice, the chapter provides numerous communication examples related to both meso and macro practice. As with the previous chapters, additional video examples are included in the accompanying CD-ROM.

Impacts of Counterproductive Communication Patterns

As a beginning social worker, you bring to your practice a desire to be helpful and a commitment to improve your own skills. That desire and commitment will not directly translate into flawless skills that ensure that all clients solve their problems and appreciate your abilities. Instead, you will inevitably make mistakes that cause you to wonder whether you will ever find complete success, at least without great effort. But take heart: Even the most successful social workers were once beginners, and learning from your mistakes is an integral part of your education. This chapter is geared toward helping you recognize and overcome nonverbal and verbal communication patterns that may inhibit the helping process.

The communication repertoires of aspiring social workers usually include halting beginning practice of new skills and some response patterns that inhibit the free flow of information and negatively affect helping relationships. Such responses impede progress each time they occur, eliciting, for example, defensiveness, hostility, or silence. Consistent use of such responses can block growth, precipitate premature terminations of contact, or cause deterioration in clients' functioning.

Nugent and Halvorson (1995) have demonstrated how differently worded active-listening responses may lead to different short-term client affective outcomes.

A recent study of beginning student practice, based on the analysis of 674 role-play videos completed by 396 BSW and 276 MSW students, revealed patterns of frequent errors, which will be reviewed below (Ragg, Okagbue-Reaves, & Piers, 2007).

Eliminating Nonverbal Barriers to Effective Communication

Nonverbal behaviors strongly influence interactions between people. The importance of this medium of communication is underscored by the fact that counselors' nonverbal interview behavior contributes significantly to ratings of counselor effectiveness. Nonverbal cues, which serve to confirm or to deny messages conveyed verbally, are in large part beyond the conscious awareness of participants. In fact, they may produce "leakage" by transmitting information that the sender did not intend to communicate to the receiver. Facial expressions—a blush, a sneer, or a look of shock or dismay, for example—convey much more about the social worker's attitude toward the client than what is said aloud. In fact, if there is a discrepancy between the social worker's verbal and nonverbal communication, the client is more likely to discredit the verbal message. Over time, people learn through myriad transactions with others that nonverbal cues more accurately indicate feelings than do spoken words.

Physical Attending

Beginning social workers are often relatively unaware of their nonverbal behaviors, and they may not have learned to consciously use these behaviors to advantage in conveying caring, understanding, and respect. Therefore, mastering physical attending—a basic skill critical to the helping process—is one of the social worker's first learning tasks. Physical attentiveness to another person is communicated by receptive behaviors, such as facing the client squarely, leaning forward, maintaining eye contact, and remaining relaxed.

Attending also requires social workers to be fully present—that is, to keep in moment-to-moment contact with the client through disciplined attention. Attending in a fully present, relaxed fashion is not to be expected with beginning social workers, who are typically anxious about what to do next, how to help, and how to avoid hurting clients. Such skill is more likely to evolve with greater experience after novice social workers have engaged in considerable observation of expert social workers, role-playing, and beginning interviews with clients.

Cultural Nuances of Nonverbal Cues

To consciously use nonverbal behaviors to full advantage in transcultural relationships, social workers must be aware that different cultural groups ascribe different meanings to certain nonverbal behaviors. Eye-to-eye contact, for example, is expected behavior among members of mainstream American culture. In fact, people who avoid eye-to-eye contact may be viewed as untrustworthy or evasive. Conversely, members of some Native American tribes regard direct gazing as an intrusion on privacy. It is important to observe and investigate the norms for gazing before employing eye-to-eye contact with members of some tribes (Gross, 1995).[1]

It is hazardous to make generalizations across ethnic groups, however. A recent study reported that Filipino students were more similar to white students than to Chinese students in relation to many attitudes, perceptions, and beliefs. Meanwhile, the same study showed that women were more similar to one another across ethnic groups than they were to men within their own group (Agbayani-Siewart, 2004).

With this proviso in mind, social workers should consider the possibility that Asian clients might view helping professionals as authorities who can solve their problems (often presented as physical symptoms) by providing advice. Because of this respect for authority, the Asian client may speak little unless spoken to by the social worker; the social worker, in turn, may mistakenly perceive the client's behavior as passive, silent, and ingratiating. Consequently, "long gaps of silence may occur as the client waits patiently for the therapist to structure the interview, take charge, and thus provide the solution" (Tsui & Schultz, 1985, p. 565). Such gaps in communication engender anxiety in both parties that may undermine the development of rapport and defeat the helping process. Further,

failure to correctly interpret the client's nonverbal behavior may lead the social worker to conclude erroneously that the client has flat affect (i.e., little emotionality). Given these potential hazards, social workers should consider being more active with Asian clients, including placing greater emphasis on clarifying role expectations.

Other Nonverbal Behaviors

Barriers that prevent the social worker from staying in psychological contact with the client can be caused by preoccupation with judgments or evaluations about the client or by inner pressures to find immediate solutions to the client's problems. Likewise, reduced focus on the client can result from being preoccupied with oneself while practicing new skills. Extraneous noise, a ringing phone, an inadequate interviewing room, or a lack of privacy can also interfere with the social worker's being psychologically present.

The social worker may convey a lack of concern for the client by displaying any of numerous undesirable behaviors and revealing postural cues. For example, staring vacantly, looking out the window, frequently glancing at the clock, yawning, and fidgeting suggest a lack of attention; trembling hands or rigid posture may communicate anger or anxiety. These and a host of other behavioral cues that convey messages such as inattention or disrespect are readily perceived by most clients, many of whom are highly sensitive to criticism or rejection in any form. Quite frankly, voluntary clients with sufficient

See the "Work with Probation Officer" video on the CD-ROM for an example of disrespectful nonverbal and verbal behavior, approximating level 0 empathy. Such examples are unfortunately not uncommon in settings dealing with persons who are alleged to have engaged in deviant behavior, such as violence against a partner, in which clients have low power, and the practitioner is under time pressure to complete an assessment. Note the practitioner calling the client's attention to time pressures and judging how little the client had accomplished in previous anger-management training. Fortunately, you are also able to link to example 7-2, which revisits the scenario in example 7-1 from a much more respectful perspective. Make a list of the practitioner behaviors you see in example 7-1 and contrast them with behaviors exhibited in example 7-2.

resources and self-esteem are not likely to accept social worker behavior that they consider disrespectful, nor should they. This leaves the social worker with just those involuntary clients with fewer choices, fewer resources, and lower self-esteem, who may believe that they have little recourse other than accepting such behavior.

Taking Inventory of Nonverbal Patterns of Responding

To assist you in taking inventory of your own styles of responding to clients, Table 7-1 identifies recommended and not recommended nonverbal behaviors. You will

TABLE-7-1 INVENTORY OF PRACTITIONER'S NONVERBAL COMMUNICATION

RECOMMENDED	NOT RECOMMENDED
Facial Expressions	
Direct eye contact (except when culturally proscribed)	Avoidance of eye contact
Warmth and concern reflected in facial expression	Staring of fixating on person or object
Eyes at same level as client's	Lifting eyebrow critically
Appropriately varied and animated facial expressions	Eye level higher or lower than client's
Mouth relaxed; occasional smiles	Nodding head excessively
	Yawning
	Frozen-on rigid facial expressions
	Inappropriate slight smile
	Pursing or biting lips
Posture	
Arms and hands moderately expressive; appropriate gestures	Rigid body position; arms tightly folded
Body leaning slightly forward; attentive but relaxed	Body turned at an angle to client
	Fidgeting with hands
	Squirming or rocking in chair
	Slouching or placing feet on desk
	Hand or fingers over mouth
	Pointing finger for emphasis
Voice	
Clearly audible but not loud	Mumbling or speaking inaudibly
Warmth in tone of voice	Monotonic voice
Voice modulated to reflect nuances of feeling and emotional tone of client messages	Halting speech
Moderate speech tempo	Frequent grammatical errors
	Prolonged silences
	Excessively animated speech
	Slow, rapid, or staccato speech
	Nervous laughter
	Consistent clearing of throat
	Speaking loudly
Physical Proximity	
Three to five feet between chairs	Excessive closeness or distance
	Talking across desk or other barrier

probably find that you have a mixed repertoire of nonverbal responses, some of which have the potential to enhance helping relationships and foster client progress. Other, less desirable behaviors of the beginning social worker may include nervousness that may block your clients from freely disclosing information and otherwise retard the flow of the helping process. You thus have a threefold task: (1) to assess your repetitive nonverbal behaviors; (2) to eliminate nonverbal styles that hinder effective communication; and (3) to sustain and perhaps increase desirable nonverbal behaviors.

At the end of this chapter, you will find a checklist intended for use in training or supervision to obtain feedback on nonverbal aspects of attending. Given the opportunity to review a videotape of your performance in actual or simulated interviews and/or to receive behaviorally specific feedback from supervisors and peers, you should be able to adequately master physical aspects of attending in a relatively brief time.

A review of your taped performance may reveal that you are already demonstrating some of the desirable physical attending behaviors listed in Table 7-1. You may also possess personal nonverbal mannerisms that are particularly helpful in establishing relationships with others, such as a friendly grin or a relaxed, easy manner. As you take inventory of your nonverbal behaviors, elicit feedback from others regarding these behaviors. When appropriate, increase the frequency of recommended behaviors that you have identified. In particular, try to cultivate the quality of warmth, which we discussed in Chapter 3.

As you review videotapes of your sessions, pay particular attention to your nonverbal responses at those moments when you experienced pressure or tension; this assessment will assist you in determining whether your responses were counterproductive. All beginning interviewers experience moments of discomfort in their first contacts with clients, and nonverbal behaviors serve as an index of their comfort level. To enhance your self-awareness of your own behavioral patterns, develop a list of the verbal and nonverbal behaviors you display when you are under pressure. When you review your videotaped sessions, you may notice that under pressure you respond with humor, fidget, change voice inflection, assume a rigid body posture, or manifest other nervous mannerisms. Making an effort to become aware of and to eliminate obvious signs of anxiety is an important step in achieving mastery of your nonverbal responding

In the video "Serving the Squeaky Wheel," the practitioner, Ron Rooney, was surprised by questions about his credentials when he became the new case manager for a client with serious and persistent mental illness. Notice how he responded at first with sarcasm and disgruntlement, before he recovered to consider how the client was in fact acting to protect herself from possible exploitation (see example in chapter 7 of the accompanying CD-ROM). Experienced practitioners also make mistakes. Hopefully, they recognize their errors and recover more quickly than is often possible for beginners.

Eliminating Verbal Barriers to Communication

Many types of ineffective verbal responses dissuade clients from exploring problems and sharing freely with the social worker. To understand why, we refer to reactance theory, which suggests that clients will act to protect valued freedoms (Brehm & Brehm, 1981). Such freedoms can include the freedom to have one's own opinions and the inclination to action. When such valued freedoms are threatened, clients will often withdraw, argue, or move to a superficial topic.

The following list identifies common verbal barriers that usually have an immediate negative effect on communications, thereby inhibiting clients from revealing pertinent information and working on problems:

1. Reassuring, sympathizing, consoling, or excusing
2. Advising and giving suggestions or solutions prematurely
3. Using sarcasm or employing humor that is distracting or makes light of clients' problems
4. Judging, criticizing, or placing blame
5. Trying to convince the client about the right point of view through logical arguments, lecturing, instructing, or arguing
6. Analyzing, diagnosing, or making glib or dogmatic interpretations
7. Threatening, warning, or counterattacking

The first three behaviors are mistakes that beginning practitioners commonly make across a variety of populations and settings, often reflecting the social worker's nervousness and an abounding desire to be immediately helpful. Numbers 3–7 are also common, but are more likely to occur when the social worker is working with "captive clients"—a situation in which there is a power differential and the client cannot readily escape. An underlying theme of these behaviors can be the social worker reflecting a sense of superiority over people whose behaviors or problem solving has been harmful to themselves or to others (as seen in example 7-1 on the CD-ROM).

Reassuring, Sympathizing, Consoling, or Excusing

- *"You'll feel better tomorrow."*
- *"Don't worry, things will work out."*
- *"You probably didn't do anything to aggravate the situation."*
- *"I really feel sorry for you."*

A pattern found in 90% of the taped interviews completed by beginning students was that they would reassure clients that their responses were normal and that they were not responsible for the difficulty they were concerned about (Ragg, Okagbue-Reaves, Piers, 2007). When used selectively and with justification, well-timed reassurance can engender much needed hope and support.[2] By glibly reassuring clients that "things will work out," "everybody has problems," or "things aren't as bleak as they seem," however, social workers avoid exploring clients' feelings of despair, anger, hopelessness, or helplessness. Situations faced by clients are often grim, with no immediate relief at hand. Rather than gloss over clients' feelings and seek to avoid discomfort, social workers must undertake to explore those distressing feelings and to assist clients in acknowledging painful realities. Beginning social workers need to convey that they hear and understand their clients' difficulties as they experience them. They will also want to convey hope while exploring prospects for change—albeit at the appropriate time in the dialogue.

Reassuring clients prematurely or without a genuine basis for hope often serves the purposes of social workers more than the purposes of clients and, in fact, may represent efforts by social workers to dissuade clients from revealing their troubling feelings. That is, reassurance may serve to restore the comfort level and equilibrium of social workers rather than to help clients. Instead of fostering hope, these glib statements convey a lack of understanding of clients' feelings and raise doubts about the authenticity of social workers. Clients may, in turn, react with thoughts such as "It's easy for you to say that, but you don't know how very frightened

I really am," or "You're just saying that so I'll feel better." In addition, responses that excuse clients (e.g., "You're not to blame") or sympathize with their position (e.g., "I can see exactly why you feel that way; I think I would probably have done the same thing") often have the effect of unwittingly reinforcing inappropriate behavior or reducing clients' anxiety and motivation to work on problems.

In place of inappropriate reassurance, a more positive and useful response can come from positive reframing, which does not discount concerns but places them in a different light. For example, in the video "Getting Back to Shakopee," the client, Val, begins to describe her concerns about a possible drug relapse. Rather than discount those concerns, the practitioner, Dorothy, asks a coping question about how Val has been managing to cope with the desire to relapse (see example on the CD-ROM).

Advising and Giving Suggestions or Solutions Prematurely

- *"I suggest that you move to a new place because you have had so many difficulties here."*
- *"I think you need to try a new approach with your daughter. Let me suggest that ..."*
- *"I think it would be best for you to try using time-out ..."*
- *"Because your partner is such a loser, why don't you try to create some new relationships with other people?"*

Another frequent pattern found in the Ragg, Okagbue-Reaves, and Piers (2007) study was that in 90% of the videos of beginning practitioners, they would appear at points to turn off from listening to the client and seem to be engaging in an internal dialogue related to formulating a solution to concerns raised. Such patterns may have been fostered in previous work positions and exchanges with friends in which the pattern was to move quickly to problem-solving solutions without grasping the larger situation. We do not mean to discount the practitioner's capacity to think about a problem and possible solutions. Rather, we want to stress the importance of waiting until the practitioner has fully grasped the situation and empathized with the client before moving into a mutual examination of alternatives. Little is known about the actual provision of advice in terms of its frequency or the circumstances in which it occurs (Brehm & Brehm, 1981). Clients often seek advice, and appropriately timed advice can be an important helping tool. Conversely, untimely advice may elicit opposition. Even when clients solicit advice in early phases of the helping process, they often react negatively when they receive it because the recommended solutions, which are invariably based on superficial information, often do not address their real needs. Further, because clients are frequently burdened and preoccupied with little-understood conflicts, feelings, and pressures, they are not ready to take action on their problems at this point. For these reasons, after offering premature advice, social workers may observe clients replying with responses such as "Yes, but I've already tried that," or "That won't work." In fact, these responses can serve as feedback clues that you may have slipped into the habit of giving premature advice.

While many clients seek advice from social workers because they see the practitioners as expert problem solvers, those social workers can (wrongly) seek to expedite problem solving by quickly comparing the current situation to other similar ones encountered in the past and recommending a solution that has worked for other clients. In such cases, social workers may feel pressure to provide quick answers or solutions for clients who unrealistically expect magical answers and instant relief from problems that have plagued them for long periods of time. Beginning social workers may also experience inner pressure to dispense solutions to clients' problems, mistakenly believing that their new role demands that they, like physicians, prescribe a treatment regimen. They thus run the risk of giving advice before they have conducted a thorough exploration of clients' problems. In reality, instead of dispensing wisdom, a major role of social workers is to create and shape processes with clients in which they engage in mutual discovery of problems and solutions—work that will take time and concentrated effort.

Beginning social workers who are working with nonvoluntary clients may feel justified in "strongly suggesting" their opinions because of the poor choices or problem solving they may presume landed these clients in their current predicament. As suggested in Chapter 4, social work practice does not have a place for judging clients: We may have to evaluate clients' performance and capabilities in certain circumstances, but that is not the same as judging them as people. Assisting clients through modeling and reinforcement of pro-social behavior is not the same as judging clients and imposing social workers' own opinions (Trotter, 2006).

The timing and form of recommendations are all-important in the helping process. Advice should be offered sparingly, and only after thoroughly exploring the problem and the client's ideas about possible solutions. At that point, the social worker may serve as a consultant, tentatively sharing ideas about solutions to supplement those developed by the client. Clients who try to pressure social workers to dispense knowledge prematurely are merely depriving themselves of the opportunity to develop effective solutions to these problems. In such circumstances, social workers should stress clients' roles in helping to discover and tailor solutions to fit their unique problems.

Clients may expect to receive early advice if social workers have not appropriately clarified roles and expectations about how mutual participation in generating possible solutions will further the growth and self-confidence of clients. Assuming a position of superiority and quickly providing solutions for problems without encouraging clients to think through the possible courses of action fosters dependency and stifles creative thinking. Freely dispensing advice also minimizes or ignores clients' strengths and potentials, and many clients tend to respond with inner resentment to such high-handed treatment. In addition, clients who have not been actively involved in planning their own courses of action may, in turn, lack motivation to implement the advice given by social workers. Moreover, when advice does not remedy a problem—as it often doesn't—clients may blame social workers and disown any responsibility for an unfavorable outcome.

Using Sarcasm or Employing Humor Inappropriately

- *"Did you get up on the wrong side of the bed?"*
- *"It seems to me that we've been through all this before."*
- *"You really fell for that line."*
- *"You think you have a problem."*

Humor can be helpful, bringing relief and sometimes perspective to work that might otherwise be tense and tedious. Pollio (1995) has suggested ways to determine appropriate use of humor. Similarly, van Wormer and Boes (1997) have described ways that humor permits social workers to continue to operate in the face of trauma. Using plays on words or noting a sense of the preposterous or incongruous can help social workers and clients face difficult situations. Situations can be put into perspective, with both social workers and clients appreciating incongruous outcomes. Humor can also allow clients to express emotions in safe, less emotionally charged ways (Dewayne, 1978). Kane (1995) describes the way humor in group work can facilitate work with persons afflicted with HIV. In group work, Caplan (1995) has described how facilitation of humor can create a necessary safety and comfort level in work with men who batter.

Excessive use of humor, however, can be distracting, keeping the content of the session on a superficial level and interfering with mutual objectives. Sarcasm often emanates from unrecognized hostility that tends to provoke counter-hostility in clients. Similarly, making a comment such as "you really win the prize for worst week" when a client recounts a series of crises and unfortunate incidents runs the risk of conveying that the difficulties are not taken seriously. A better response would be to empathize with the difficulties of the week and compliment the client on persisting to cope despite them.

Judging, Criticizing, or Placing Blame

- *"You're wrong about that."*
- *"Running away from home was a bad mistake."*
- *"One of your problems is that you're not willing to consider another point of view."*
- *"You're not thinking straight."*

Clients do not feel supported when they perceive the worker as critical, moralistic, and defensive rather than warm and respectful (Coady & Marziali, 1994; Eaton, Abeles & Gutfreund, 1993; Safran & Muran, 2000). Responses that evaluate and show disapproval can be detrimental to clients and to the helping process. Clients usually respond defensively and sometimes counterattack when they perceive criticism from social workers; some may simply cut off any meaningful communication with social workers. When they are intimidated by a social worker's greater expertise, some clients also accept negative evaluations as accurate reflections of their poor judgment or lack of worth or value. In making such negative judgments about clients, social workers violate the basic social work values of nonjudgmental attitude and acceptance.

Such responses are unlikely to be tolerated by voluntary, noncaptive clients with adequate self-esteem or enough power in the situation to have alternatives. Such clients are likely to "fire" you, speak to your supervisor, or put you on notice if you act in such

seemingly disrespectful ways. Others may shut down, perceiving you as having some power over them.

Involuntary clients often face what they believe to be dangerous consequences for not getting along with the social worker. Hence, some clients with substantial self-control and self-esteem may put up with such browbeating without comment. Others may respond in kind with attacks of their own that then appear in case records as evidence of client resistance.

If the social worker is concerned about danger to the client or to others, or about violations of the law, then he or she may ask a question to raise the client's awareness of consequences and alternatives. For example, the social worker might ask, "How do you look now at the consequences of running away from home?" or "How would this appear from your partner's point of view?"

Trying to Convince Clients about the Right Point of View through Logic, Lecturing, Instructing, or Arguing

- *"Let's look at the facts about drugs."*
- *"You have to take some responsibility for your life, you know."*
- *"Running away from home will only get you in more difficulty."*
- *"That attitude won't get you anywhere."*

Clients sometimes consider courses of action that social workers view as unsafe, illegal, or contrary to the client's goals. However, attempting to convince clients through arguing, instructing, and similar behavior often provokes a kind of boomerang effect—that is, clients are not only not convinced of the merits of the social worker's argument, but may also be more inclined to hold onto their beliefs than before. According to reactance theory, clients will attempt to defend their valued freedoms when these privileges are threatened (Brehm & Brehm, 1981). For some clients (especially adolescents, for whom independent thinking is associated with a particular developmental stage), deferring to or agreeing with social workers is tantamount to giving up their individuality or freedom. The challenge when working with such clients is to learn how to listen to and respect their perspective at the same time as you make sure that they are aware of alternatives and consequences. Compare the two ways of handling the same situation described below.

Teen parent client: I have decided to drop out of high school for now and get my cosmetology license.

Practitioner: Don't you know that dropping out of high school is going to hurt you and your children, both now and in the future? Are you willing to sacrifice hundreds of thousands of dollars less that you would earn over your lifetime for you and your children just to buy a few little knick-knacks now?

Teen parent client: But this is my life! My babies need things now! You don't know what it is like scraping by. You can't tell me what to do! You are not my momma! I know what is best for me and my children!

Rather than escalate into what has been called the confrontation-denial cycle (Murphy & Baxter, 1997), a better alternative is to respond to the teen parent client with an effort to understand her perspective, before exploring alternatives and consequences.

Teen parent client: I have decided to drop out of high school for now and get my cosmetology license.

Practitioner: So you have been going to high school for a while now with some success, and now you are considering that going in a different direction and getting your cosmetology license may work better for you. Tell me about that.

Teen parent client: Well, it is true that I have been working hard in high school. But I need more money now, not just far off in the future. My babies and I don't have enough to get by.

Practitioner: And you feel that getting a cosmetology license will help you do that.

Teen parent client: I do. I still want to finish high school and get my diploma. I know that I will earn more for my kids and myself with a diploma than if I don't finish. If I get my cosmetology degree, it will take a little longer to get my high school diploma, but I think I am up to it.

Practitioner: So your longer-term plan is still to get your high school diploma but just to delay it. You think that getting your cosmetology degree will help you and your kids get by better now. Are there any drawbacks to withdrawing from high school at this time?

Teen parent client: Only if I get distracted and don't return. I could kind of get out of the habit of going to school and I might be around people who haven't finished school.

Practitioner: Those are things to consider. How might you be sure that your withdrawal from high school was only temporary?

In the first example above, the practitioner attempts to vigorously persuade the client about the course of

action he or she deems wisest. Such efforts, while well meaning, often create power struggles, thereby perpetuating dynamics that have previously occurred in clients' personal relationships. By arguing, social workers ignore their clients' feelings and views, focusing instead on the social worker "being right"; this tactic may engender feelings of resentment, alienation, or hostility in clients. Such efforts are both unethical and ineffective.

Persuasion in the sense of helping clients to obtain accurate information with which to make informed decisions can be an ethical intervention. When clients contemplate actions that run contrary to their own goals, or will endanger themselves or others, then an effort to persuade can be an ethical intervention. Such efforts should not focus on the one "pet" solution of the social worker, however, but rather should assist the client in examining the advantages and disadvantages of several options, including those with which the social worker may disagree (Rooney, 2009). Hence, the effort is not to convince, but rather to assist clients in making informed decisions. By not attacking the client in example 2, the practitioner is able to support the client's right to make decisions for herself and to do so considering alternatives and consequences.

Analyzing, Diagnosing, or Making Glib or Dramatic Interpretations

- *"You're behaving that way because you're angry with your partner."*
- *"Your attitude may have kept you from giving their ideas a fair hearing."*
- *"You're acting in a passive-aggressive way."*
- *"You're really hostile today."*

When used sparingly and timed appropriately, interpretation of the dynamics of behavior can be a potent change-oriented skill (see Chapter 18). However, even accurate interpretations that focus on purposes or meanings of behavior substantially beyond clients' levels of conscious awareness tend to inspire client opposition and are doomed to failure.

When stated dogmatically (e.g., "I know what's wrong with you," or "how you feel," or "what your real motives are"), interpretations also present a threat to clients, causing them to feel exposed or trapped. When a glib interpretation is thrust upon them, clients often expend their energies disconfirming the interpretation, explaining themselves, or making angry rebuttals rather than working on the problem at hand.

Using social work jargon such as *fixation, transference, resistance, reinforcement, repression, passivity, neuroticism*, and a host of other terms to describe the behavior of clients in their presence is also destructive to the helping process. Indeed, it may confuse or bewilder clients and provoke opposition to change. These terms also oversimplify complex phenomena and psychic mechanisms and stereotype clients, thereby obliterating their uniqueness. In addition, these sweeping generalizations provide no operational definitions of clients' problems, nor do they suggest avenues for behavior modification. If clients accept social workers' restricted definitions of their problems, then they may define themselves in the same terms as those used by social workers (e.g., "I am a passive person" or "I have a schizoid personality"). This type of stereotypic labeling often causes clients to view themselves as "sick" and their situations as hopeless, providing them with a ready excuse for not working on their problems.

Threatening, Warning, or Counterattacking

- *"You'd better ... or else!"*
- *"If you don't ... you'll be sorry."*
- *"If you know what's good for you, you'll ..."*

Sometimes clients consider actions that would endanger themselves or others or are illegal. In such instances, alerting clients to the potential consequences of those actions is an ethical and appropriate intervention. Conversely, making threats of the sort described above often produces a kind of oppositional behavior that exacerbates an already strained situation.

Even the most well-intentioned social workers may occasionally bristle or respond defensively under the pressure of verbal abuse, accusatory or blaming responses, or challenges to their integrity, competence, motives, or authority. Social workers conducting group sessions with adolescents, for instance, can testify that the provocative behavior of this client population may defeat even the most herculean efforts to respond appropriately.

Whatever the dynamics behind clients' provocative behavior, responding defensively is counterproductive, as it may duplicate the destructive pattern of responses that clients have typically elicited and experienced from others. To achieve competence, therefore, you must learn to master your own natural defensive reactions and evolve effective ways of dealing with negative feelings.

Empathic communication, for example, produces a cathartic release of negative feelings, defusing a strained situation and permitting a more rational emotional exploration of factors that underlie clients' feelings. For example, to reply to a client, "You have difficult decisions to make, and are caught between alternatives that you don't consider very attractive; I wish you well in making a decision that you can live with in the future" can convey support and respect for the right to choose.

The negative effects of certain types of responses are not always immediately apparent because clients may not overtly demonstrate negative reactions at the time or because the retarding effect on the helping process cannot be observed in a single transaction. To assess the effect of responses, then, the social worker must determine the frequency with which he or she issues detrimental responses and evaluate the overall impact of those responses on the helping process. Frequent use of some types of responses by the social worker indicates the presence of counterproductive patterns of communication such as the following (note that this list is a continuation of the list of problematic social worker behaviors on page 158):

8. Stacking questions
9. Asking leading questions
10. Interrupting inappropriately or excessively
11. Dominating the interaction
12. Fostering safe social interaction
13. Responding infrequently
14. Parroting or overusing certain phrases or clichés
15. Dwelling on the remote past
16. Going on fishing expeditions

Individual responses that fall within these patterns may or may not be ineffective when employed occasionally. When they are employed extensively in lieu of using varied response patterns, however, they inhibit the natural flow of a session and limit the richness of information revealed. The sections that follow expand on each of these verbal barriers and detrimental social worker responses.

Stacking Questions

In exploring problems, social workers should use facilitative questions that assist clients to reveal detailed information about specific problem areas. Asking multiple questions at the same time, or *stacking*, diffuses the focus and confuses clients. Consider the vast amount of ground covered in the following messages:

- *"When you don't feel you have control of situations, what goes on inside of you? What do you think about? What do you do?"*
- *"Have you thought about where you are going to live? Is that one of your biggest concerns, or is there another that takes priority?"*

Stacking questions is a problem frequently encountered by beginning social work practitioners, who may feel an urgent need to help clients by providing many options all at one time. Adequately answering even one of the foregoing questions would require a client to give an extended response. Rather than focus on one question, however, clients often respond superficially and nonspecifically to the social worker's multiple inquiries, omitting important information in the process. Stacked questions thus have "low yield" and are unproductive and inefficient in gathering relevant information. Slowing down and asking one question at a time is preferable. If you have asked stacked questions (and all social workers have at many points), and the client hesitates in response, you can correct for the problem by repeating your preferred question.

Asking Leading Questions

Leading questions have hidden agendas designed to induce clients to agree with a particular view or to adopt a solution that social workers deem to be in clients' best interests. For example:

- *"Do you think you've really tried to get along with your partner?"*
- *"You don't really mean that, do you?"*
- *"Aren't you too young to move out on your own?"*
- *"Don't you think that arguing with your mother will provoke her to come down on you as she has done in the past?"*

In actuality, these types of questions often obscure legitimate concerns that social workers should discuss with clients. Social workers may conceal their feelings and opinions about such matters, however, and present them obliquely in the form of solutions (e.g., "Don't you think you ought to …") in the hope that leading questions will guide clients to desired conclusions. It is an error, however, to assume that clients will not see through such maneuvers. Indeed, clients often discern the social worker's motives and inwardly resist having views or directives imposed on them under the guise of leading questions. Nevertheless, to avoid conflict or controversy with social workers, they may express feeble agreement or simply divert the discussion to another topic.

By contrast, when social workers authentically assume responsibility for concerns they wish clients to consider, they enhance the likelihood that clients will respond receptively to their questions. In addition, they can raise questions that are not slanted to imply

the "correct" answer from the social worker's viewpoint. For example, "How have you attempted to reach agreement with your partner?" does not contain the hint about the "right" answer found in the first question given above. Similarly, the last question could be rephrased as follows: "I am not clear how you see arguing with your mother as likely to be more successful than it has proved in the past."

Interrupting Inappropriately or Excessively

Beginning social workers often worry excessively about covering all items on their own and their agency's agenda ("What will I tell my supervisor?"). To maintain focus on relevant problem areas, social workers must sometimes interrupt clients. To be effective, however, these interruptions must be purposeful, well timed, and smoothly executed. Interruptions may damage the helping process when they are abrupt or divert clients from exploring pertinent problem areas. Frequent untimely interruptions tend to annoy clients, stifle spontaneous expression, and hinder exploration of problems. Identifying and prioritizing key questions in advance with an outline can assist in avoiding this pattern.

Dominating the Interaction

At times, social workers may dominate the interaction by talking too much or by asking too many closed-ended questions, thus seizing the initiative for guiding discussions rather than placing this responsibility with clients. Other domineering behaviors by social workers include repeatedly offering advice, pressuring clients to improve, presenting lengthy arguments to convince clients, frequently interrupting, and so on. Some social workers are also prone to behave as though they are all-knowing, failing to convey respect for clients' points of view or capacities to solve problems. Such dogmatic and authoritarian behavior discourages clients from expressing themselves and fosters a one-up, one-down relationship in which clients feel at a great disadvantage and resent the social worker's supercilious demeanor.

Social workers should monitor the relative distribution of participation by all participants (including themselves) who are involved in individual, family, or group sessions. Although clients naturally vary in their levels of verbal participation and assertiveness, all group members should have equal opportunity to share information, concerns, and views in the helping process. Social workers have a responsibility to ensure that this opportunity is available to them.

As a general guideline, clients should consume more "speaking time" than social workers in the helping process, although during initial sessions with many Asian American clients, social workers must be more directive than they are with non-Asian clients, as discussed earlier. Sometimes social workers defeat practice objectives in group or conjoint sessions by dominating the interaction through such behaviors as speaking for members, focusing more on some members than on others, or giving speeches.

Even social workers who are not particularly verbal may dominate sessions that include reserved or nonassertive clients as a means of alleviating their own discomfort with silence and passivity. Although it is natural to be more active with reticent or withdrawn clients than with those who are more verbal, social workers must avoid seeming overbearing.

Using facilitative responses that draw clients out is an effective method of minimizing silence and passivity. When a review of one of your taped sessions reveals that you have monopolized the interaction, it is important that you explore the reasons for your behavior. Identify the specific responses that were authoritarian or domineering and the events that preceded those responses. Also, examine the clients' style of relating for clues regarding your own reactions, and analyze the feelings you were experiencing at the time. Based on your review and assessment of your performance, you should then plan a strategy for modifying your own style of relating by substituting facilitative responses for ineffective ones. You may also need to focus on and explore the passive or nonassertive behavior of clients with the objective of contracting with them to increase their participation in the helping process.

Fostering Safe Social Interaction

Channeling or keeping discussions focused on safe topics that exclude feelings and minimize self-disclosures is inimical to the helping process. Social chit-chat about the weather, news, hobbies, mutual interests or acquaintances, and the like tends to foster a social rather than a therapeutic relationship. In contrast to the lighter and more diffuse communication characteristic of a social relationship, helpful, growth-producing relationships feature sharp focus and high specificity. Another frequent pattern found in the Ragg, Okagbue-Reaves, and Piers (2007) study was that beginning practitioners would attempt to diffuse expressions of high emotion such as anger, dismay, or sadness rather than reflect them.

Parent: I have had about all I can take from these kids sometimes. They are so angry and disrespectful that it is all I can do to keep from blowing up at them.
Practitioner: Kids nowadays can be difficult.

A more appropriate response would be:

Practitioner: You sometimes feel so frustrated when your kids act disrespectfully that you want to do something about it, and it is hard to keep the lid on.

In general, safe social interaction in the helping process should be avoided. Two exceptions to this rule exist, however:

- *Discussion of safe topics may be utilized to assist children or adolescents to lower their defenses and risk increasing openness, thereby assisting social workers to cultivate a quasi-friend role with such clients.*
- *A brief discussion of conventional topics may be appropriate and helpful as part of the getting-acquainted or warm-up period of initial sessions or during early portions of subsequent sessions. A warm-up period is particularly important when you are engaging clients from ethnic groups for which such informal openings are the cultural norm, as discussed in Chapter 3.*

Even when you try to avoid inappropriate social interaction, however, some clients may resist your attempts to move the discussion to a topic that is relevant to the problems they are experiencing and to the purposes of the helping process. Techniques for managing such situations are found in Chapter 18 of the book. For now, simply note that it is appropriate for the social worker to bring up the agreed upon agenda within a few minutes of the beginning of the session.

Responding Infrequently

Monitoring the frequency of your responses in individual, conjoint, or group sessions is an important task. As a social worker, you have an ethical responsibility to utilize fully the limited contact time you have with clients in pursuing your practice objectives and promoting your clients' general well-being. Relatively inactive social workers, however, usually ignore fruitful moments that could be explored to promote clients' growth, and they may allow the focus of a session to stray to inappropriate or unproductive content. To be maximally helpful, social workers must structure the helping process by developing contracts with clients that specify the respective responsibilities of both sets of participants.

For their part, they engage clients in identifying and exploring problems, formulating goals, and delineating tasks to alleviate clients' difficulties.

Inactive social workers contribute to counterproductive processes and failures in problem solving. One deleterious effect, for example, is that clients lose confidence in social workers when they fail to intervene by helping clients with situations that are destructive to themselves or to others. In particular, clients' confidence is eroded if social workers fail to intervene when clients communicate destructively in conjoint or group sessions.

Although social workers' activity per se is important, the quality of their moment-by-moment responses is critical. Social workers significantly diminish their effectiveness by neglecting to utilize or by underutilizing facilitative responses.

Parroting or Overusing Certain Phrases or Clichés

Parroting a message irritates clients, who may issue a sharp rebuke to the social worker: "Well, yes, I just said that." Rather than merely repeating clients' words, social workers should use fresh language that captures the essence of clients' messages and places them in sharper perspective. In addition, social workers should refrain from punctuating their communications with superfluous phrases. The distracting effect of such phrases can be observed in the following message:

Social worker: You know, a lot of people wouldn't come in for help. It tells me, you know, that you realize that you have a problem, you know, and want to work on it. Do you know what I mean?

Frequent use of such phrases as "you know," "Okay?" ("Let's work on this task, okay?"), "and stuff" ("We went to town, and stuff"), or "that's neat" can annoy some clients (and social workers, for that matter). If used in excess, the same may be said of some of the faddish clichés that have permeated today's language—for example, "awesome," "sweet," "cool," "tight," or "dude."

In "Work with the Corning Family," Allie frequently uses the term "you guys" to refer to her husband and wife clients. We don't know how they respond to this plural term and whether they respond to it positively or negatively. What alternative terms could be used to refer to these clients?

Another mistake social workers sometimes make is trying to "overrelate" to youthful clients by using adolescent jargon to excess. Adolescents tend to perceive such communication as phony and the social worker as inauthentic, which hinders the development of a working relationship.

Dwelling on the Remote Past

Social workers' verbal responses may focus on the past, the present, or the future. Helping professionals differ regarding the amount of emphasis they believe should be accorded to gathering historical facts about clients. Focusing largely on the present is vital, however, because clients can change only their present circumstances, behaviors, and feelings. Permitting individuals, groups, couples, or families to dwell on the past may reinforce diversionary tactics they have employed to avoid dealing with painful aspects of their present difficulties and with the need for change.

Messages about the past may reveal feelings the client is currently experiencing related to the past. For example:

Client [*with trembling voice*]: He used to make me so angry.
Social worker: There was a time when he really infuriated you. As you think about the past, even now it seems to stir up some of the anger and hurt you felt.

As in this excerpt, changing a client's statement from past to present tense often yields rich information about clients' present feelings and problems. The same may be said of bringing future-oriented statements of clients to the present (e.g., "How do you feel now about the future event you're describing?"). As you see, it is not only possible but also often productive to shift the focus to the present experiencing of clients, even when historical facts are being elicited, in an effort to illuminate client problems.

Going on Fishing Expeditions

A danger that beginning (and many experienced) social workers face is pursuing content that is tangentially related to client concerns, issues of client and family safety, or legal mandates. Such content may relate to pet theories of social workers or agencies and be puzzling to clients. This kind of confusion may arise if the connection of these theories to the concerns that have brought clients into contact with the social worker is not clear. A wise precaution, therefore, would be to avoid taking clients into tangential areas if you cannot readily justify the rationale for that exploration. If the social worker feels that the exploration of new areas is relevant, then an explanation of its purpose is warranted.

Gauging the Effectiveness of Your Responses

The preceding discussion should assist you in identifying ineffective patterns of communication you may have been employing. Because most learners ask too many closed-ended questions, change the subject frequently, and recommend solutions before completing a thorough exploration of clients' problems, you should particularly watch for these patterns. In addition, you will need to monitor your interviewing style for idiosyncratic counterproductive patterns of responding.

The manual that is provided for instructors who use this book contains classroom exercises designed to assist students in recognizing and eliminating ineffective responses. Because identifying ineffective styles of interviewing requires selective focusing on the frequency and patterning of responses, you will also find it helpful to analyze extended segments of taped sessions using the form "Assessing Verbal Barriers to Communication," which is found at the end of this chapter.

One way of gauging the effectiveness of your responses is to carefully observe clients' reactions immediately following your responses. Because multiple clients are involved in group and family sessions, you will often receive varied verbal and nonverbal cues regarding the relative effectiveness of your responses when engaging clients in these systems.

As you assess your messages, keep in mind that a response is probably helpful if clients react in one of the following ways:

- *They continue to explore the problem or stay on the topic.*
- *They express pent-up emotions related to the problematic situation.*
- *They engage in deeper self-exploration and self-experiencing.*
- *They volunteer more personally relevant material spontaneously.*
- *They affirm the validity of your response either verbally or nonverbally.*

By contrast, a response may be too confrontational, poorly timed, or off target if clients react in one of the following ways:

- *They reject your response either verbally or nonverbally.*
- *They change the subject.*
- *They ignore the message.*
- *They appear mixed up or confused.*
- *They become more superficial, more impersonal, more emotionally detached, or more defensive.*
- *They argue or express anger rather than examine the relevance of the feelings involved.*

In analyzing social worker–client interactions, keep in mind that the participants mutually influence each other. Thus, a response by either person in an individual interview affects the expressions of the other person. In group and conjoint sessions, the communications of each person, including the social worker, affect the responses of all other participants. In a group situation, however, the influence of messages on the subsequent responses of other participants is sometimes difficult to detect because of the complexity of the communications.

Beginning interviewers often reinforce unproductive client responses by responding indiscriminately or haphazardly or by letting positive responses that support practice objectives or reflect growth pass without comment. For example, Ragg, Okagbue-Reaves, and Piers (2007) found that beginning practitioners would often respond to complex client responses by picking up on the final expression whether or not it was of particular significance in its context. A more productive response would be to reflect back the several themes you have heard. It is important that you, as a beginning social worker, monitor and review your moment-by-moment transactions with clients with a view toward not allowing ineffective or destructive communication to be perpetuated by yourself and your clients.

Although beginning social workers may experience ineffective patterns of communication in individual interviews, they are even more likely to encounter recurring problematic communications in groups or in conjoint sessions with spouses or family members. In fact, orchestrating an effective conjoint interview or group meeting often presents a stiff challenge to even advanced social workers because of clients' rampant use of ineffective communications, which may provoke intense anger, defensiveness, and confusion among family or group members.

In summary, your task is twofold: You must monitor, analyze, and eliminate your own ineffective responses while simultaneously observing, managing, and modifying ineffective responses by your clients. That's a rather tall order. Although modifying dysfunctional communications among clients requires advanced skill, you can eliminate your own barriers to effective communication in a relatively short time. You will make even faster progress if you also eliminate ineffective styles of responding and test out your new communication skills in your private life. Unfortunately, many social workers compartmentalize and limit their helping skills to their work with clients but continue to use ineffective communication styles with their professional colleagues, friends, and families.

Social workers who have not fully integrated the helping skills into their private lives typically do not relate as effectively to their clients as do social workers who have fully implemented and assimilated those skills as a part of their general style of relating. We are convinced that to adequately master these essential skills and to fully tap into their potential for assisting clients, social workers must promote their own interpersonal competence and personality integration, thereby modeling for their clients the self-actualized or fully functioning person. Pursuing this personal goal prepares social workers for one of their major roles: teaching new skills of communicating and relating to their clients.

The Challenge of Learning New Skills

Because of the unique nature of the helping process, establishing and maintaining a therapeutic relationship requires highly disciplined efforts on the social worker's part. Moment by moment, transaction by transaction, the social worker must sharply focus on the needs and problems of his or her clients. The success of each transaction is measured in terms of the social worker's adroitness in consciously applying specific skills to move the process toward the therapeutic objectives.

Interestingly, one of the major threats to learning new skills emanates from students' fear that in relinquishing their old styles of relating they are giving up an intangible, irreplaceable part of themselves. Similarly, students who have previously engaged in social work practice may experience fear related to the fact that they have developed methods or styles of relating that have influenced and "moved" clients in the past; abandoning these response patterns may mean surrendering a hard-won feeling of competency. These fears are often exacerbated when instruction and supervision in the classroom and practicum primarily strive to eliminate errors and ineffective interventions and responses rather than to develop new skills or enhance positive responses or interventions with clients. In such circumstances, students may receive considerable feedback about their errors but inadequate input regarding their effective responses or styles of relating. Consequently, they may feel vulnerable and stripped of their defenses (just as clients do) and experience more keenly the loss of something familiar.

As a beginning social worker, you must learn to openly and nondefensively receive constructive feedback about your ineffective or even destructive styles of relating or intervening. At the same time, you must take responsibility for eliciting positive feedback from educators and peers regarding your positive moment-by-moment responses. Remember that supervision time is limited and that the responsibility for utilizing that time effectively and for acquiring competency necessarily rests equally with you and your practicum instructor. It is also vital that you take steps to monitor your own growth systematically by reviewing audio- and videotapes, by counting your desirable and undesirable responses in client sessions, and by comparing your responses with the guidelines for constructing effective messages found in this book. Perhaps the single most important requirement for you in furthering your competency is to assume responsibility for advancing your own skill level by consistently monitoring your responses and practicing proven skills.

Most of the skills delineated in this book are not easy to master. In fact, competent social workers will spend years perfecting their ability to sensitively and fully attune themselves to the inner experiencing of their clients; in furthering their capacity to share their own experiencing in an authentic, helpful manner; and in developing a keen sense of timing in employing these and other skills.

In the months ahead, as you forge new patterns of responding and test your newly developed skills, you will inevitably experience growing pains—that is, a sense of disequilibrium as you struggle to respond in new ways and, at the same time, to relate warmly, naturally, and attentively to your clients. Sometimes,

ASSESSING VERBAL BARRIERS TO COMMUNICATION

Directions: In reviewing each 15-minute sample of taped interviews, tally your use of ineffective responses by placing marks in appropriate cells.

15-Minute Taped Samples	*1*	*2*	*3*	*4*
1. Reassuring, sympathizing, consoling, or excusing				
2. Advising and giving suggestions or solutions prematurely				
3. Using sarcasm or employing humor that is distracting or makes light of clients' problems				
4. Judging, criticizing, or placing blame				
5. Trying to convince the client about the right point of view through logical arguments, lecturing, instructing, or arguing				
6. Analyzing, diagnosing, or making glib or dogmatic interpretations				
7. Threatening, warning, or counterattacking				
8. Stacking questions				
9. Asking leading questions				
10. Interrupting inappropriately or excessively				
11. Dominating the interaction				
12. Fostering safe social interaction				
13. Responding infrequently				
14. Parroting or overusing certain phrases or clichés				
15. Dwelling on the remote past				
16. Going on fishing expeditions				
Other responses that impede communication. List:				

ASSESSING PHYSICAL ATTENDING BEHAVIORS

	Comments
1. Direct eye contact 0 1 2 3 4	
2. Warmth and concern reflected in facial expression 0 1 2 3 4	
3. Eyes at same level as client's 0 1 2 3 4	
4. Appropriately varied and animated facial expressions 0 1 2 3 4	
5. Arms and hands moderately expressive; appropriate gestures 0 1 2 3 4	
6. Body leaning slightly forward; attentive but relaxed 0 1 2 3 4	
7. Voice clearly audible but not loud 0 1 2 3 4	
8. Warmth in tone of voice 0 1 2 3 4	
9. Voice modulated to reflect nuances of feeling and emotional tone of client messages 0 1 2 3 4	
10. Moderate speech tempo 0 1 2 3 4	
11. Absence of distracting behaviors (fidgeting, yawning, gazing out window, looking at watch) 0 1 2 3 4	
12. Other 0 1 2 3 4	

Rating Scale:
0 = Poor, needs marked improvement.
1 = Weak, needs substantial improvement.
2 = Minimally acceptable, room for growth.
3 = Generally high level with a few lapses.
4 = Consistently high level.

you may feel that your responses are mechanistic and experience a keen sense of transparency: "The client will know that I'm not being real." If you work intensively to master specific skills, however, your awkwardness will gradually diminish, and you will eventually incorporate these skills naturally into your repertoire.

Summary

Chapter 7 outlined a series of nonverbal and verbal barriers to effective communication that are often experienced by beginning social workers. As you become alert to these potential obstacles and more skilled in applying more productive alternatives, you will become more confident in your progress. Chapter 8 asks you to apply your communication skills to one of the most important tasks you will face: conducting a multisystemic assessment.

Notes

1. It is important not to set up artificial dichotomies that do not represent actual behaviors. Emma Gross (1995) argues, for example, that too frequently writers have inappropriately generalized across Native American cultures.

2. Reassurance is best directed to clients' capabilities. Appropriate reassurance can be effectively conveyed through the skill of positive feedback, as described in Chapter 5.

CHAPTER 8

Assessment: Exploring and Understanding Problems and Strengths

CHAPTER OVERVIEW

Assessment involves gathering information and formulating it into a coherent picture of the client and his or her circumstances. Because assessments involve social workers' inferences about the nature and causes of clients' difficulties, they serve as the basis for the rest of their interactions with their clients—the goals they set, the interventions they enact, and the progress they evaluate. Chapter 8 focuses on the fundamentals of assessment and the strategies used in assessing the client's problem and strengths. Chapter 9 describes the characteristics that are taken into account when examining and portraying an individual's functioning and his or her relations with others and with the surrounding environment. The client's interpersonal functioning and the related social systems and environments are addressed in both Chapters 8 and 9. Chapter 10 describes the methods and concepts employed when assessing family functioning and interactions. Chapter 11 addresses the concepts for planning and assessing groups.

As a result of reading this chapter you will:

- Understand that assessments involve both gathering information and synthesizing it into a working hypothesis

- Learn the distinctions between assessment and diagnosis

- Know what the DSM-IV-TR is and how it is organized

- Understand how to capture client strengths and assets in assessment

- Recognize the elements of culturally competent assessments and the risks of ethnocentric assessments

- Identify the roles that knowledge and theories play in framing assessments

- Know the sources of data that may inform social workers' assessments

- Learn questions to bear in mind while conducting an assessment

- Be familiar with the various elements of problem analysis

The Multidimensionality of Assessment

Human problems—even those that appear to be simple at first glance—often involve a complex interplay of many factors. Rarely do sources of problems reside solely within an individual or within that individual's environment. Rather, *reciprocal interaction* occurs between a person and the external world. The person acts upon and responds to the external world, and the quality of those actions affects the external world's reactions (and vice versa). For example, a parent may complain about having poor communication with an adolescent, attributing the difficulty to the fact that the teenager is sullen and refuses to talk about most things. The adolescent, in turn, may complain that it is pointless to talk with the parent because the latter consistently pries, lectures, or criticizes. Each participant's complaint about the other may be accurate, but each unwittingly behaves in ways that have produced and now maintain their dysfunctional interaction. Thus, the behavior of neither person is the sole cause of the breakdown in communication in a simple cause-and-effect (linear) fashion. Rather, their reciprocal interaction produces the difficulty; the behavior of each is both cause and effect, depending on one's vantage point.

The multidimensionality of human problems is also a consequence of the fact that human beings are social creatures who depend on both other human beings and complex social institutions to meet their needs. Meeting basic needs such as food, housing, clothing, and medical care requires adequate economic means and the availability of goods and services. Meeting educational, social, and recreational needs requires interaction with societal institutions. Meeting needs to feel close to and loved by others, to have companionship, to experience a sense of belonging, and to experience sexual gratification requires satisfactory social relationships within one's intimate relationships, family, social network, and community. Likewise, the extent to which people experience self-esteem depends on certain individual psychological factors and the quality of feedback from other people.

In conducting an assessment, a social worker needs extensive knowledge about the client and the numerous systems (e.g., economic, legal, educational, medical, religious, social, interpersonal) that impinge upon the client system. Assessing the functioning of an individual entails evaluating various aspects of that person's functioning. For example, the social worker may need to consider dynamic interactions among the individual's biophysical, cognitive, emotional, cultural, behavioral, and motivational subsystems and the relationships of those interactions to the client's problems. When the client system is a couple or family, assessment entails paying attention to communications and patterns of interaction, as well as to each member of the system. Not every system and subsystem plays a significant role in the problems experienced by a given client situation. However, overlooking relevant systems will result in an assessment that is incomplete at best and irrelevant or erroneous at worst. Interventions based on poor assessments, therefore, may be ineffective, misdirected, or even harmful.

In summary, the client's needs and the helping agency's purpose and resources will influence your choices and priorities during the assessment. You must be sure to attend to the client's immediate concern, or presenting problem; identify any legal or safety issues that may alter your priorities; be attuned to the many ways that strengths and resources may appear in the case; and consider all of the sources of information you may call upon to arrive at your assessment. You must also recognize the many facets to be taken into account in a multidimensional assessment, as well as the reciprocal nature of interactions, which requires an assessment that goes beyond mere cause and effect. Finally, you must be alert to your own history, values, biases and behaviors that might interject subjectivity into your interactions with clients and in the assessment that results.

Defining Assessment: Process and Product

The word *assessment* can be defined in several ways. For example, it refers to a process occurring between practitioner and client, in which information is gathered, analyzed, and synthesized to provide a concise picture of the client and his or her needs and strengths. In settings in which social work is the primary profession, the social worker often makes the assessment independently or consults with colleagues or a member of another discipline in creating it. Typically, formal assessments may be completed in one or two sessions. These assessments also represent opportunities to determine whether the agency or individual social worker is best suited to address the client's needs and wants. The social worker may identify the client's eligibility for services (for example, based on his or her insurance coverage or other admission criteria) and make a referral to other resources if either the program or the social worker is not appropriate to meet the client's needs.

In settings in which social work is not the only or not the primary profession (often called *secondary* or *host settings*), the social worker may be a member of a clinical team (e.g., in mental health, schools, medical, and correctional settings), and the process of assessment may be the joint effort of a psychiatrist, social worker, psychologist, nurse, teacher, and perhaps members of other disciplines. In such settings, the social worker typically compiles a social history and contributes knowledge related to interpersonal and family dynamics. The assessment process may take longer due to the time required for all of the team members to complete their individual assessments and to reach a collective assessment during a group meeting.

The focus of the assessment is also influenced by the auspices in which it takes place and the theoretical orientation from which the social worker practices. While some data are common to all interviews, the focus of a particular interview and assessment formulation will vary according to the social worker's mission, theoretical framework, or other factors. For example, a social worker who is investigating an allegation of child endangerment will ask questions and draw conclusions related to the level of risk or potential for violence in the case. A social worker whose expertise lies in cognitive-behavioral theory will structure the assessment to address the effects of misconceptions or cognitive distortions on the client's feelings and actions. A clinician in a correctional setting will use different concepts and standards to categorize offenders and to determine risks and needs (Beyer & Balster, 2001). This does not mean that in any of those cases, the worker addresses *only* those issues, but rather that the questions asked and the conclusions drawn will be narrowed by the social worker's mission, theory, setting and clinical focus.

Social workers engage in the process of assessment from the beginning of their contacts with the client and through the relationship's termination, which may occur weeks, months, or even years later. Thus, assessment is a fluid and dynamic process that involves receiving, analyzing, and synthesizing new information as it emerges during the entire course of a given case. In the first session, the social worker generally elicits abundant information; he or she must then assess the information's meaning and significance as the client–social worker interaction unfolds. This moment-by-moment assessment guides the social worker in deciding which information is salient and merits deeper exploration and which is less relevant to understanding the individual and the presenting problem. After gathering sufficient information to illuminate the situation, the social worker analyzes it and, in collaboration with the client, integrates the data into a tentative formulation of the problem. Many potential clients do not proceed with the social worker beyond this point. If their concerns can be best handled through a referral to other resources, if they do not meet eligibility criteria, or if they choose not to continue the relationship, contact often stops here.

Should the social worker and the client continue the contact, assessment continues as well, although it is not a central focus of the work. Clients often disclose new information as problem solving progresses, casting the original evaluation in a new light. Sometimes this new perspective emerges as the natural result of coming to know the client better. In other cases, clients may withhold vital information until they are certain that the social worker is trustworthy and capable. As a result, preliminary assessments often prove inaccurate and must be discarded or drastically revised.

Note that the term *assessment* also refers to the written products that result from the process of understanding the client. As a product, assessment involves an actual formulation or statement *at a given time* regarding the nature of clients' problems, resources, and other related factors. A formal assessment requires analysis and synthesis of relevant data into a working definition of the problem. It identifies associated factors and clarifies how they interact to produce and maintain the problem. Because assessments must constantly be updated and revised, it is helpful to think of an assessment as *a complex working hypothesis based on the most current data available.*

Written assessments range from comprehensive psychosocial reports to brief analyses about very specific issues, such as the client's mental status, substance use, capacity for self-care, or suicidal risk. An assessment may summarize progress on a case or provide a comprehensive overview of the client to facilitate his or her transfer to another resource or termination of the case.

The scope and focus of the written product and of the assessment itself will vary depending on three factors: the *role* of the social worker, the *setting* in which he or she works, and the *needs* presented by the client. For example, a school social worker's assessment of an elementary school student may focus on the history and pattern of disruptive behaviors in the classroom, as well as on the classroom environment itself. A social worker in a family services agency seeing the same child may focus more broadly on the child's developmental history and his or her family's dynamics, as well as on the troubling classroom behavior. A worker evaluating the child's eligibility to be paired with an adult mentor would look at family income and other information as well as the child's existing social systems to determine his or her capacity to benefit from the match. To use another example, a hospital social worker whose focus is discharge planning may evaluate a client's readiness to leave the hospital after heart surgery and determine the services and information needed to make the return home successful. A social worker in a community health or mental health agency may assess the same client to determine the impact of the disease and the surgery on the client's emotional well-being and on his or her marital relationship. A social worker in a vocational setting may focus the assessment on the client's readiness to return to work and the job accommodations needed to facilitate that transition.

While the social worker's setting will lead to focused assessment on particular issues pertinent to that setting, certain priorities in assessment influence all social work settings. Without prioritization, workers run the risk of conducting unbalanced, inefficient, or misdirected evaluations. Initially, three issues should be assessed in all situations:

1. *What does the client see as his or her primary problems or concerns?* Sometimes referred to as "starting where the client is," this question highlights social work's emphasis on client self-determination and commitment to assisting clients (where legal, ethical, and possible) to reach their own goals. Practically speaking, sharing concerns helps alleviate the client of some of the burdens and apprehensions that brought him or her to the interview.

2. *What (if any) current or impending legal mandates must the client and social worker consider?* If the client is mandated to receive services or faces other legal concerns, this factor may shape the nature of the assessment and the way the client presents himself or herself. Therefore, it is important to "get this

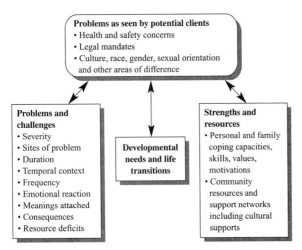

FIG-8-1 Overview: Areas for Attention in Assessing Strengths and Problems

issue on the table" at the outset. For example, an adult protection worker must assess the risk of abuse, neglect, or other danger to an elderly client, whether or not the client shares those concerns.

3. *What (if any) potentially serious health or safety concerns might require the social worker's and client's attention?* Social workers must be alert to health problems and other conditions that may place clients at risk. These issues may be central to the client's presenting problem, or they may indicate a danger that requires immediate intervention by the worker. While the profession places high value on client self-determination, social workers must act—even if it means overruling the client's wishes—in situations that present "serious, foreseeable, and imminent harm" (NASW, 1999, p. 7).

After addressing these three fundamental questions, the social worker goes on to explore the client's functioning, interactions with his or her environment, problems and challenges, strengths and resources, developmental needs and life transitions, and key systems related to the case. The remainder of this chapter and Chapter 9 further delineate how each of these areas is assessed (see Figure 8-1).

Assessment and Diagnosis

It is important at this point to clarify the difference between diagnoses and assessments. *Diagnoses* are labels or terms that may be applied to an individual or his or her situation. A diagnosis provides a shorthand categorization based on specifically defined criteria. It can reflect a medical condition (e.g., "end-stage renal disease," "diabetes"), mental disorder (e.g., "depression," "agoraphobia"), or other classification (e.g., "mild retardation," "emotionally and behaviorally disturbed," "learning disabled"). Diagnostic labels serve many purposes. For example, they provide a language through which professionals and patients can communicate about a commonly understood constellation of symptoms. The use of accepted diagnostic terminology facilitates research on problems, identification of appropriate treatments or medications, and linkages among people with similar problems. For example, diagnosing a set of troubling behaviors as "bi-polar disorder" helps the client, his or her physician, and social worker to identify necessary medication and therapeutic services. The diagnosis may comfort the client by helping "put a name to" the experiences he or she has been having. It may also help the client learn more about the disease, locate support groups, and stay abreast of developments in understanding the disorder.

But diagnoses have their difficulties, too. Although such labels provide an expedient way of describing complex problems, they never tell the whole story. Diagnoses can become self-fulfilling prophecies, wherein clients, their families, and their helpers begin to define the client only in terms of the diagnostic label. This distinction is captured in the difference between saying "Joe is schizophrenic," "Joe has schizophrenia," or "Joe is a person with schizophrenia." While these labels carry a lot of power, they can sometimes be bestowed in error (the result of misdiagnosis or a diagnosis that changes over time), and they may obscure important information about the client's difficulties and capacities. Referring to a client as "mildly retarded," for example, may speak only to that individual's score on an IQ test—not to his or her level of daily functioning, interests, goals, joys, and challenges.

At this point, assessment steps in. Assessments describe the symptoms that support a particular diagnosis, but they go further to help us understand the client's history and background, the effect of the symptoms on the client, the available support and resources to manage the problem, and so on. In other words, diagnoses may result from assessments, but they tell only part of the story.

The Diagnostic and Statistical Manual (DSM-IV-TR)

The *Diagnostic and Statistical Manual* (*DSM-IV-TR*) is an important tool for understanding and formulating mental and emotional disorders (American Psychiatric Association, 2000). It is linked to *The International Statistical Classification of Diseases and Related Health*

Problems, 10th Revision (ICD-10), a commonly used system to codify health and mental health disorders, symptoms, social circumstances, and causes of injury or illnesses (Munson, 2002). Diagnostic systems such as the *DSM-IV-TR* have come under fire for a number of reasons, including excessive focus on individual pathologies over strengths and societal and environmental problems. Critics suggest that the manual is time- and culture-bound, throwing the validity of the categorizations in dispute. Some find the use of the *DSM* to be particularly incongruent with social work, in light of the history and focus of the profession (Kirk & Kutchins, 1992).

Criticisms notwithstanding, the *DSM-IV-TR* is widely used by professionals and consumers; the diagnoses and assessments are often required for insurance reimbursement and other forms of payment for services, and many social workers work with clients who have received mental health diagnoses, whether or not the social worker him- or herself actually gave the diagnosis.

You will need specialized knowledge and training in order to be thoroughly familiar with the *DSM-IV-TR* system and apply it to the complexities of human behavior and emotion. This section is intended only to provide foundation knowledge, acquaint you with the features of the classification system, and to serve as a reference point for discussions in Chapter 9 about prominent cognitive and affective diagnoses.

The *DSM-IV-TR* uses a *multiaxial* system, in which coding on five axes provides diagnostic and functional information.

Axis I   Clinical syndromes (e.g., sleep, anxiety, eating, and mood disorders; schizophrenia; disorders usually first evident in infancy, childhood or adolescence; and substance-related disorders)
    Other conditions that may be a focus of clinical attention (e.g., relational problems, problems related to abuse and neglect, psychological factors affecting a medical condition)

Axis II   Personality disorders (e.g., borderline, antisocial, narcissistic, obsessive-compulsive, schizoid, paranoid)
    Mental retardation

Axis III   Physical disorders (e.g., diabetes, chronic obstructive pulmonary disease, hypertension). Clinicians must note the source of this information, for example "patient report" or "physician referral"

Axis IV   Psychological and environmental problems, or "PEPs" (e.g., educational problems, problems related to interaction with the legal system/crime, housing problems)

Axis V   Global Assessment of Functioning, or "GAF scores" (a 1–100 scale on which the professional assigns a numeric score of psychological, social, and occupational functioning at the time of evaluation; the time frame is noted in parentheses next to the score. Zero is used to indicate insufficient information to assign a GAF score) (Bloom, Fischer, & Orme, 2006)

In the *DSM-IV-TR* system, disorders are assigned a 3–5 digit code wherein digits after the decimal point specify the severity and course of the disorder. Therefore, 296.21 would represent Major Depressive disorder, Single Episode, Mild (Munson, 2002). For each disorder, the manual uses a standardized format to present relevant information. The sections address current knowledge on:

- *Diagnostic features*
- *Subtypes/specifiers*
- *Recording procedures*
- *Associated features and disorders*
- *Specific culture, gender, and age features*
- *Prevalence*
- *Course*
- *Familial patterns*
- *Differential diagnosis*
- *Diagnostic criteria*

The manual attempts to be strictly descriptive of the conditions it covers. It does not use a specific theoretical framework, recommend appropriate treatments, or address the causation (or etiology) of a disorder, except in unique circumstances. Resources such as Kaplan & Sadock (2007), the *DSM-IV-TR Casebook* (Gibbon, 1995), and the *DSM-IV-TR* itself (American Psychiatric Association, 2000) are helpful materials to prepare for regular use of the manual and for developing the clinical acumen for making and using diagnoses.

Culturally Competent Assessment

This book discusses many cultural factors related to various aspects of the helping process. In this section, we focus on general cultural factors that have relevance for the process of assessment. Here, we emphasize culture as it relates not only to racial or ethnic groups, but also to other groups (e.g., gay, lesbian, bisexual, transgendered, hearing impaired, elderly, and persons in recovery) that reflect distinct cultural attributes. Culturally competent assessment requires knowledge of cultural norms, acculturation, and language differences;

the ability to differentiate between individual and culturally linked attributes; the initiative to seek out needed information so that evaluations are not biased and services are culturally appropriate; and an understanding of the ways that cultural differences may reveal themselves in the assessment process.

Cultures vary widely in their prescribed patterns of child-rearing, communication, family member roles, mate selection, and care of the aged—to name just a few areas of differentiation. For example, to whom would you properly address concerns in a Latino family about a child's truancy? What are normative dating patterns in the gay and lesbian communities? At what age is it proper to allow a child to babysit for younger siblings? What are appropriate expectations for independence for a young adult with Down syndrome? How might Laotian parents view their child's educational aspirations?

Knowledge of your client's cultural norms is indispensable when the client's cultural background differs markedly from your own. Without such knowledge, you may make serious errors in assessing both individual and interpersonal systems, because patterns that are functional in one cultural context may prove problematic in another, and vice versa. Such errors in assessment may potentially lead to culturally insensitive interventions that may aggravate rather than diminish clients' problems. The necessary knowledge about cultural norms is not easy to obtain, however. It requires a baseline understanding of areas of difference and histories and risks of oppression experienced by different groups, self-examination for biases and prejudices, and ongoing conversation with clients and other key informants (Gilbert, 2003; Smith, 2004).

This last piece is important because of the considerable variations that occur within ethnic groups. Making overgeneralizations about members of any group may obscure (rather than clarify) the meanings of individual behavior. For example, more than 400 different tribal groups of Native Americans live in the United States, and these groups speak more than 250 distinct languages (Edwards, 1983). Comparisons of Plains tribes with Native Americans of the Southwest have revealed sharply contrasting cultural patterns and patterns of individual behavior as well as marked differences in the incidence of certain social problems (May, Hymbaugh, Aase, & Samet, 1983). Similarly significant heterogeneity exists within every racial and cultural group.

Even where homogeneity exists in cultural subgroups, wide variations also exist among individuals. As a consequence, being knowledgeable about the cultural characteristics of a given group is necessary but not sufficient for understanding the behavior of individual members of the groups. The task confronting practitioners, therefore, is to differentiate between behavior that is culturally mediated and behavior that is a product of individual personality. In-depth knowledge about a given cultural group helps in making such distinctions. When in doubt, however, practitioners are advised to consult with well-informed and cooperative members of the culture in question.

In assessing the functioning of someone from an ethnic minority, it is important to consider the degree to which he or she experiences a goodness of fit with the culture in which he or she is situated. Ethnic minority clients are actually members of two cultures (or perhaps more, depending on their identities and differences in the parents' families of origin), so their functioning must be considered in relationship to both their culture of origin and the majority culture. Clients from the same ethnic group may vary widely in the degree of their acculturation or their comfort with biculturalism due to several factors—for example, the number of generations that have passed since the original emigration, the degree of socialization, and interactions with the majority culture. Consider these possibilities for distinguishing individual members of an ethnic minority:

1. The degree of commonality between the two cultures with regard to norms, values, beliefs, perceptions, and the like
2. The availability of cultural translators, mediators, and models
3. The amount and type (positive or negative) of feedback provided by each culture regarding attempts to produce normative behaviors
4. The conceptual style and problem-solving approach of the minority individual and his or her mesh with the prevalent or valued styles of the majority culture
5. The individual's degree of bilingualism
6. The degree of dissimilarity in physical appearance from the majority culture, such as skin color, facial features, and so forth (De Anda, 1984, p. 102)

Members of nondominant groups may experience psychological difficulties as a result of trying to identify with the dominant group while being treated in a prejudiced or racist manner by members of the group they aspire to join (Mayadas, Ramanathan, & Suarez., 1998–1999). Other difficulties may emerge from conflicting values between cultures. For example, majority persons may not distinguish between Jamaicans, Sudanese, Liberians and African Americans, categorizing all on the basis of skin tone or other features rather than culture.

Amish men or women who choose to leave the faith may find themselves caught between two worlds and accepted in neither (McGoldrick, Giordano, & Pearce, 1996). A lesbian whose religious faith condemns homosexuality may have difficulty reconciling her two worlds. These examples support the need for social workers to assess the biculturalism of clients, to sensitize themselves to various cultures, to encourage clients to maintain ties to their cultural roots, and to understand the complexities of interacting with other cultures. Cultural self-awareness is likewise important for social workers themselves, as that knowledge will help them understand and serve their clients better (Gilbert, 2003).

A client's degree of bilingualism is important for his or her acculturation and for the social worker when conducting an assessment. In settings where no multilingual services are available, non–English-speaking clients may have great difficulty in formulating and explaining their problems. Even for clients who have a strong command of English, care providers "should be aware that the foundational thought structures through which the client processes the world will likely be in the primary language, with English language interpretations only a rough equivalent of the original. Subtle shifts in meaning can create confusion, frustration and even fear in the client or the client's family" (Ratliff, 1996, pp. 170–171). An interpreter may be called in to bridge the language gap. Even when one is used, however, the social worker should recognize that interpretations may merely approximate what the client is attempting to convey. If an interpreter is not available, it is important to speak in simple terms and to proceed at a slower pace. Clients need ample time to process messages, and practitioners must exercise care in checking out whether clients have grasped the intended meaning of their messages and whether they have truly understood what the client is trying to express.

The use of interpreters is also an important issue to consider when working with deaf clients (Santos, 1995). The primary language used by many deaf people is American Sign Language (ASL), which is a unique and separate language from English, not merely a visual translation of English. Interpreters are often a necessity for deaf clients to communicate effectively with hearing social workers; at the same time, social workers should bear in mind that concepts may not be easily transferred from ASL to English. For this reason, they should take time to ensure that concepts are being accurately understood on both ends. Social workers working with deaf clients who use ASL should also apply the factors mentioned earlier for adjusting to differences in spoken

language to make sure that they do not become barriers to effective treatment.

Another issue for assessment is considering how the client's fluency in English may contribute to the presenting problem (e.g., the school is angry at the parents for not coming to teacher conferences when, in fact, the family didn't understand that they were required to do so). Language differences can block access to essential community resources (especially for clients isolated from their cultural reference groups) and limit access to information through newspapers, computers, radio, and television. These obstacles, therefore, may produce social isolation and deprive people of information essential to locating and utilizing essential resources.

Clients from cultural groups that have endured a history of marginalization, oppression, and prejudice may approach helping agencies (and their representatives) with skepticism and even hostility. The possible reasons underlying this posture should be factored into the assessment process and findings. You can address anger and apprehensions by being genuine, trustworthy, and committed to the client's best interests (Harper & Lantz, 1996; Rooney, 1992). This interaction may be facilitated if the client and practitioner have some degree of cultural similarity. Of course, even when the social worker and client share a cultural background, they may differ in other important ways, such as values, education, socioeconomic status, and level of acculturation.

Cross-cultural contact also occurs between minority practitioners and clients from the majority culture. While the minority practitioner is usually more familiar with the majority culture than the majority practitioner is with minority cultures, clients often challenge the credibility of minority practitioners (Hardy, 1993; Proctor & Davis, 1994). The client may assign credibility to a social worker because of his or her education, position, role, age, gender, and other factors emphasized in the client's culture—that is, because of factors over which a practitioner has little control. Credibility can also be achieved, however, when clients have favorable experiences with social workers that foster respect, confidence, trust, and hope (Harper & Lantz, 1996); who address areas of difference in a straightforward manner; and who seek to learn about the client's culture by asking the client.

Emphasizing Strengths in Assessments

Clients typically seek social work services for help with problems or difficulties. As a result, the assessment typically focuses on the problem—sometimes with an overemphasis on client pathology and dysfunction at the expense of strengths, capacities, and achievements whose recognition might help provide a fuller understanding of the client. In addition, research suggests that many social workers underestimate client strengths.

Perhaps this negativism stems from a historical emphasis on client deficits (Saleeby, 1997), which viewed clients as fragile or dysfunctional, and the professional's job as "fixing" the problem or person. Some assessments are negative because they reflect troubling attitudes, values, or burnout on the part of the social worker, who may hold the client in contempt. An avoidance of strengths may also stem from eligibility requirements that require the client to look problem laden so as to qualify for (or continue to receive) services (Frager, 2000). That is, the funding for services, whether it comes through insurance reimbursement or government contracts, may be based on the client's difficulties and level of impairment. Emphasizing clients' strengths in a case report may cause utilization reviewers to question whether services are needed at all.

This tendency to focus on pathology has several important ramifications. First, to tap client strengths effectively, practitioners must be sensitive to them and skillful in utilizing them to accomplish case goals. Second, social workers who fail to account for strengths and selectively attend to pathology are ill equipped to determine the client's potential for growth and the steps needed to get there. Third, a large proportion of clients need help in enhancing their self-esteem. Troubled by self-doubts, feelings of inadequacy, or worthlessness, their lack of self-confidence and self-respect underlies many destructive cognitive, emotional, and behavioral patterns, including fears of failure, depression, social withdrawal, alcoholism, and hypersensitivity to criticism—to name just a few. To assist clients to view themselves more positively, social workers and their agencies must first view their clients more positively.

To emphasize strengths and empowerment in the assessment process, Cowger makes three suggestions to social workers:

1. Give preeminence to the *client's* understanding of the facts.
2. Discover what the client wants.
3. Assess personal and environmental strengths on multiple levels (1994, p. 265).

Cowger (1994) has developed a two-dimensional matrix framework for assessment that can assist social workers in attending to both needs and strengths. On the vertical axis, potential strengths and resources are depicted at one end and potential deficits, challenges, and obstacles are shown at the other end. The horizontal axis ranges from environmental (family and community) to individual factors. This framework prods

Ideas in Action

The following section applies Cowger's matrix to the case of Jackie and Anna, featured in the video "Home for the Holidays."

Strengths or Resources
Quadrant 1 – Environmental Factors
- Anna and Jackie are both in contact with, and value, their immediate and extended family. Anna's hesitancy to discuss the couple's relationship, in spite of the conflict it causes, demonstrates her desire to remain connected to her family of origin.
- Anna and Jackie are both employed. Anna owns her own business.

Quadrant 2 – Personal Factors
- Anna and Jackie's intimate relationship and friendship is a source of strength and joy for both of them. Their willingness to attend conjoint sessions and create assignments at the end of the first meeting attests to their appreciation of their partnership.

- Anna has a bold personality and is not afraid to stand up for herself, demanding the respect she deserves.
- Jackie is thoughtful and deliberate. She considers all of the consequences of her actions.

Deficit, Obstacle, or Challenge
Quadrant 3 – Environmental Factors
- Anna's parents are uncomfortable talking about their daughter's intimate relationship with another woman.
- Anna's work schedule is busy and her days are full. She is often drained when she comes home and lacks the energy to connect with Jackie.

Quadrant 4 – Personal Factors
- Anna is prone to social withdrawal. She avoids conflict with her parents and Jackie.
- Jackie appears impatient to Anna. Her communication style comes off as "pushy."

FIG-8-2 Framework for Assessment

SOURCE: Adapted from Charles D. Cowger, Assessment of Client Strengths. In D. Saleeby, *The Strengths Perspective in Social Work Practice* (2nd ed.) (Figure 5.2, p. 69). Boston: Allyn & Bacon. Reprinted by permission of Allyn & Bacon.

us to move beyond the frequent preoccupation with personal deficits (*quadrant 4*), to include personal strengths and environmental strengths and obstacles (Cowger, 1992). Figure 8-2 demonstrates this framework and highlights two facts: A useful assessment is not limited to either deficits or strengths, and both the environmental and personal dimensions are important. Use of all four quadrants provides information that can help in pursuing the client's goals, while remaining mindful of obstacles and challenges.

The following list emphasizes strengths that may be overlooked or taken for granted during assessment. Cultivating your sensitivity to these strengths will help you be attuned to others as they emerge:

1. Facing problems and seeking help, rather than denying or otherwise avoiding confronting them
2. Taking a risk by sharing problems with the social worker—a stranger
3. Persevering under difficult circumstances
4. Being resourceful and creative in making the most out of limited resources
5. Seeking to further knowledge, education, and skills
6. Expressing caring feelings to family members and friends
7. Asserting one's rights rather than submitting to injustice
8. Being responsible in work or financial obligations
9. Seeking to understand the needs and feelings of others

10. Having the capacity for introspection or for examining situations by considering different perspectives
11. Demonstrating the capacity for self-control
12. Being able to function effectively in stressful situations
13. Demonstrating the ability to consider alternative courses of actions and the needs of others when solving problems

The Role of Knowledge and Theory in Assessments

"What you see depends on what you look for." This saying captures the roles that knowledge and theory play in shaping the questions that are asked in assessment and the hypotheses that result. Competent, evidence-based practice requires that assessments are informed by problem-specific knowledge (O'Hare, 2005, p. 7). As a result, you would consider the nature of the problem presented by the client at intake (e.g., explosive anger, sadness, parent–child conflict, truancy) and refer to available research to identify the factors that contribute to, sustain, and ameliorate those problems. This knowledge would help you to know the relevant data to be collected during assessment and the formulations that result. For example, the literature might suggest that truancy is caused by a poor fit between the student's needs and the classroom environment or the teacher's attitude and methods. Or it might stem from chaos at home in which children are not woken up for school, prepared for the day, or even expected to attend. Poor school attendance may come from poor performance as a result of vision or hearing problems, attention deficits, or learning disabilities. It may also arise from shame on the child's part about hygiene, dress, worthiness, or bullying and other negative peer experiences. Regardless of the factors involved, there is rarely a strictly linear, cause-and-effect explanation for truancy. Instead, the influence of some factors (e.g., poor vision or hearing) leads to behaviors (acting out or truancy) that distance the child from peers, irritate the teacher, and lead to a withdrawal by the student that puts him or her even further behind, and in turn more likely to act out or withdraw further. An understanding of the research and theories on human behavior will help focus the assessment on those elements that are involved in a particular client's difficulties.

The demand for evidence-based assessments may make it appear that you have to do a research paper or literature review for every client. While this would be too onerous, do not underestimate the importance of thorough research; the costs of poorly directed assessments and interventions are extensive. They range from client discouragement and wasted professional and agency resources to perhaps even harm, if the resulting services are negligent. To the extent that you and your organization specialize in particular problems or populations, the knowledge gained from research done for any one case can be called on for similar cases. And, with increased access to electronic resources and reference guides that summarize the best available evidence in a variety of areas, it has become much easier to find and evaluate existing knowledge[1] (Bloom, Fischer, & Orme, 2006; O'Hare, 2005; Thyer & Wodarski, 1998; Wodarski & Thyer; 1998).

As with available knowledge, theories shape assessments. Some theories have a selective influence as concepts associated with that theory are adopted for more general use. For example, multidimensional assessments make use of concepts drawn from the fields of ego psychology, such as reality testing, judgment, and coping mechanisms, and concepts prominent in object relations theory, such as attachment and interpersonal relationship patterns. Most assessments address patterns in thought, behaviors and actions, interpersonal relationships, affect, and role transitions, though they may not be targeted toward the provision of interpersonal therapy (IPT). In addition, assessments typically utilize concepts such as risk and resilience and empowerment and strengths, even if the assessment is not wholly organized around those frameworks.

Some theoretical orientations play a greater role in the structure of the assessment and the conclusions that are drawn. For example, *brief, solution-focused therapy* is one model that is encountered in a variety of settings. This model is based on a number of assumptions—for example, that small changes can lead to larger changes, that focusing on the present can help the client tap into unused capacities and generate creative alternatives, and that paying attention to solutions is more relevant than focusing on problems. While solution-building questions may be used with other frameworks, an assessment guided by this practice model will utilize:

Seeking exceptions: Questions that determine when the problem does not exist or does not occur. The answer may refer to different sites, times, or contexts. Exploration then asks the client to elaborate on what is different in those incidents and what other factors might cause it to be different.

Scaling the problem: This involves asking the client to estimate, on a scale of 1 to 10, the severity of the problem. The response can help in tracking changes over time, open up the opportunity to ask what accounts for the current level of difficulty or relief, and determine what it might take to move from the current level to a higher point on the scale.

Scaling motivation is similar to scaling problems or concerns. It involves asking clients to estimate the degree to which they feel hopeful about resolution, or perhaps the degree to which they have given up hope. How would they rate their commitment to working on the problem?

The *miracle question* helps the practitioner to determine the client's priorities and to operationalize the areas for change. Essentially, the social worker asks, "If, while you were asleep, a miracle occurred and your problem was solved, how would things be different when you woke up?" This technique helps the client envision the positive results of the change process and elicits important information for structuring specific behavioral interventions (Jordan & Franklin, 2003).

As with other assessment tools, the key to successful use of these techniques lies in the sensitivity and timing with which they are employed. For example, asking the miracle question prematurely may lead the client to believe that you are not listening or are minimizing his or her distress. Typically, these questions may be prefaced by statements acknowledging the client's concern—for example, "I know your son's misbehavior has been troubling to you, but I wonder if there are times when he does follow your directions?" Sensitivity is also demonstrated through inflection or tone of voice, eye contact, and other nonverbal methods of attending that assure the client of your attention and regard.

Other theoretical orientations with demonstrable efficacy will shape the entire assessment. For example, cognitive theories suggest that thoughts mediate emotions and actions (Beck 1995; Ellis, 1963; Lantz, 1996). Therefore, assessments derived from these theories would focus on the nature of the client's thoughts and schemas (cognitive patterns), causal attributions, the basis for the client's beliefs, and antecedent thoughts in problematic situations (Walsh, 2006). Behavioral theories suggest that actions and emotions are created, maintained, "and extinguished through principles of learning" (Walsh, 2006, p. 107). As such, the assessment focuses on the conditions surrounding troubling behaviors, the conditions that reinforce the behavior, and the consequences and secondary gains that might result. Questions to address this sequence include:

- *When do you experience the behavior?*
- *Where do you experience the behavior?*
- *How long does the behavior usually last?*
- *What happens immediately after the behavior occurs?*
- *What bodily reactions do you experience with the behavior?*
- *What do the people around you usually do when the behavior is happening?*
- *What happened afterward that was pleasant?* (Bertolino & O'Hanlon, 2002; Cormier, Nurius, & Osborn, 2009; Walsh, 2006)

The intent of these questions is to create a hypothesis about what triggers and reinforces the behavior in order to construct a plan involving new reinforcement patterns and a system for measuring change.

Naturally, there are cautions about the degree to which existing knowledge or theories influence assessment. While they are helpful in predicting and explaining client behaviors and in structuring assessments and interventions, when applied too rigidly, they may oversimplify the problem and objectify the individual client (Walsh, 2006). Poorly tested theories and beliefs may be given greater weight and prominence than they deserve. Frameworks may be improperly applied to populations that differ markedly from those on which the framework was tested. Adhering to a single preferred framework may obscure other relevant factors in the case, blind the practitioner to limits in existing theory or knowledge, and inhibit him or her from pursuing promising new knowledge and interventions. Critical thinking and proper training are required so that professionals can effectively evaluate and apply frameworks to enhance client services (O'Hare, 2005).

Sources of Information

Where do social workers get the information on which to base their assessment? Numerous sources can be used individually or in combination. The following are the most common:

1. Background sheets or other forms that clients complete
2. Interviews with clients (i.e., accounts of problems, history, views, thoughts, events, and the like)
3. Direct observation of nonverbal behavior
4. Direct observation of interaction between partners, family members, and group members
5. Collateral information from relatives, friends, physicians, teachers, employers, and other professionals
6. Tests or assessment instruments
7. Personal experiences of the practitioner based on direct interaction with clients

The *information obtained from client interviews* is usually the primary source of assessment information. The skills described in Chapters 5 and 6 for structuring and conducting effective interviews will help in establishing a trusting relationship and acquiring the information needed for assessment. It is important to respect clients' feelings and reports, to use empathy to convey understanding, to probe for depth, and to check with the client to ensure that your understanding is accurate. Interviews with child clients may be enhanced or facilitated by use of instruments (McConaughy & Achenbach, 1994; Schaffer, 1992) and by play, drawing and other techniques. As with other information sources, verbal reports often need to be augmented because faulty recall, biases, mistrust, and limited self-awareness on the part of clients may not present a wholly accurate picture.

Direct observation of nonverbal behavior adds information about emotional states and reactions such as anger, hurt, embarrassment, and fear. To use these sources of data, the social worker must be attentive to nonverbal cues, such as tone of voice, tears, clenched fists, vocal tremors, quivering hands, a tightened jaw, pursed lips, variations of expression, and gestures; he or she must link these behaviors to the topic or theme during which they arise. The social worker may share these observations in the moment ("Your whole body deflated when you were telling me what she said") or note them to be included with other data ("The client's voice softened and he had tears in his eyes when talking about his wife's illness").

Observations of interactions between spouses or partners, family members, and group members are also often enlightening. Social workers frequently are amazed at the striking differences between clients' reports of their relationships and the behaviors they actually demonstrate in those relationships. A social worker may observe a father interacting with his daughter, impatiently telling her "I know you can do better"; in an earlier session, however, the father may have described his behavior to her as "encouraging." Direct observation may reveal that his words are encouraging while his tone and gestures are not.

Observation can occur in natural settings (e.g., a child in the classroom, adults in a group setting, or a family as they answer a worker's question in session). Home visits are a particularly helpful forum for observation. One major benefit of in-home, family-based services is the opportunity to observe the family's lived experiences firsthand rather than rely on secondhand accounts (Ronnau & Marlow, 1995; Strom-Gottfried, 2009). Observing clients' living conditions typically reveals resources and challenges that would otherwise not come to light.

Social workers can also employ *enactment* to observe interactions firsthand rather than rely on verbal report. With this technique, clients reenact an event during a session. Participants are instructed to recreate the situation exactly as it occurred, using the same words, gestures, and tones of voice as in the actual event. You might explain: "To understand what produced the difficulties in the situation you just described, I'd like you to recreate it here in our session. By seeing what both of you do and say, and how you do it, I can get an accurate picture of what actually happens. I'd like you to replay the situation exactly as it happened. Use the same words, gestures, and tone of voice as you did originally. Now, where were you when it happened, and how did it start?" To counteract the temptation to create a favorable impression, the social worker can ask each participant afterward about the extent to which the behaviors demonstrated in the enactment correspond with the behaviors that occurred in actual situations.

Enactment can also be used in contrived situations to see how a couple or family members interact in situations that involve decision making, planning, role negotiation, child discipline, or similar activities. Social workers will need to exercise their creativity in designing situations likely to generate and clarify the types of interaction that they wish to observe. Another form of enactment involves the use of symbolic interactions— for example, through the use of dolls, games, or other forms of expressive or play therapy (Jordan & Hickerson, 2003).

Remember, however, that direct observation is subject to perceptual errors by the observer. Take care when drawing conclusions from your observations. Scrutinize how congruent your conclusions are with the information acquired from other sources. Despite the flaws, information from various forms of direct observation adds significantly to that gained from verbal reports.

Client self-monitoring is a potent source of information (Kopp, 1989). It produces a rich and quantifiable body of data and empowers the client by turning him or her into a collaborator in the assessment process. In self-monitoring, clients track symptoms on logs or in journals, write descriptions, and record feelings, behaviors, and thoughts associated with particular times, events, symptoms, or difficulties. The first step in self-monitoring is to recognize the occurrence of the event (e.g., signs that lead to anxiety attacks, temper tantrums by children, episodes of drinking or overeating). Using self-anchored rating scales (Jordan & Franklin, 2003) or simple counting measures, clients and/or those around them can keep a record of the frequency or intensity of a behavior. How often was Joe late for school? How severe was Joan's anxiety in the morning, at noon, and in the evening? Which nights did Ralph have particular difficulty sleeping? Did this difficulty relate to events during the day, medications, stresses, or anything he ate or drank?

A major advantage of self-monitoring is that the process itself requires the monitor to focus attention on patterns. As a result, clients gain insights into their situations and the circumstances surrounding their successes or setbacks. As they discuss their recorded observations, they may "spontaneously operationalize goals and suggest ideas for change" (Kopp, 1989, p. 278). The process of recording also assists in evaluation, because progress can be tracked more precisely by examining data that show a reduction of problematic behaviors or feelings and an increase in desirable characteristics.

Another source for assessment data is *collateral contacts*—that is, information provided by relatives, friends, teachers, physicians, child care providers, and others who possess essential insights about relevant aspects of clients' lives. Collateral sources are of particular importance when, because of developmental capacity or functioning, the client's ability to generate information may be limited or distorted. For example, parents, guardians and other caregivers are often the primary source of information about a child's history, functioning, resources, and challenges. Similarly, assessments of clients with memory impairment or cognitive limitations will be enhanced by the data that collaterals (family members, caregivers, or friends) can provide.

Social workers must exercise discretion when deciding that such information is needed and in obtaining it. Clients can assist in this effort by suggesting collateral contacts that may provide useful information; their written consent (through agency "release of information" forms) is required prior to making contact with these sources.

In weighing the validity of information obtained from collateral sources, it is important to consider the nature of their relationship with the client and the ways in which that might influence these contacts' perspectives. For example, members of the immediate family may be emotionally involved or exhausted by the client's difficulties and unconsciously skew their reports accordingly. For example, studies indicate that elderly clients may overrate their functional capacity while families underrate it, and nurses' evaluations fall somewhere in the middle (Gallo, 2005). Individuals who have something to gain or to lose from pending case decisions (e.g., custody of a child, residential placement) may be less credible as collaterals than individuals who do not have a conflict of interest or are further removed from case situations. Conversely, individuals who have limited contact with the client (such as other service providers) may have narrowed or otherwise skewed views of the client's situation. As with other sources of information, input from collateral contacts must be critically viewed and weighed against other information in the case.

Another possible source of information consists of various *assessment instruments*, including psychological tests, screening instruments, and assessment tools. Some of these tests are administered by professionals, such as psychologists or educators, who have undergone special training in the administration and scoring of such assessment tools. In these cases, social workers might receive reports of the testing and incorporate the findings into their psychosocial assessments or treatment plans. Examples of these instruments include intelligence tests such as the Wechsler Adult Intelligence Scale, 3rd edition (WAIS-III) or the Wechsler Intelligence Scale for Children, 3rd edition (WISC-III) (Lukas, 1993), or instruments to assess personality disorders and other mental health problems, such as the Million Multiaxial Clinical Inventory-III (MCMI-III) (Millon & Davis, 1997), the Minnesota Multiphasic Personality Inventory (MMPI-II) (Hathaway & McKinley, 1989), or the Primary Care Evaluation of Mental Health Disorders (PRIME-MD) (Spitzer et al., 1994).

Some instruments are designed for use by social workers and allied professionals. Examples include the WALMYR Assessment Scales, which can be used to measure depression, self-esteem, clinical stress, anxiety, alcohol involvement, peer relations, sexual attitudes, homophobia, marital satisfaction, sexual satisfaction, nonphysical abuse of partners, and a variety of other clinical phenomena.[2] The Multi-Problem Screening Inventory (MPSI) is a computer-based multidimensional self-report measure that helps practitioners to better assess and understand the severity or magnitude of client problems across 27 different areas of personal and social functioning. The completed instrument helps both the client and the social worker evaluate areas of difficulty and determine the relative severity of difficulties in the various life areas. In addition to providing for better accuracy and efficiency, these and other computerized instruments simplify the tracking of results over time and assist in gathering data for determining case progress.

Instruments such as the Burns Depression Checklist (Burns, 1995), the Beck Depression Inventory (Beck, Rush, Shaw, & Emery, 1979), the Zung Self-Rating Depression Scale (Zung, 1965), and the Beck Scale for Suicidal Ideation (Range & Knott, 1997) have well-established validity and reliability, can be effectively administered and scored by clinicians from a variety of professions, and can assist practitioners in evaluating the seriousness of a client's condition.

Other instruments to measure alcohol or drug impairment may be conducted by the social worker, self-administered by the client, or computer administered (Abbott & Wood, 2000). Commonly used tools include the Michigan Alcoholism Screening Test (MAST) (Pokorny, Miller, & Kaplan, 1972; Selzer, 1971), and the Drug Abuse Screening Test (DAST) (Gavin, Ross, & Skinner, 1989). Some instruments use mnemonic devices to structure assessment questions. For example, the CAGE (Project Cork, n.d.) consists of four items in which an affirmative answer to any single question is highly correlated to alcohol dependence:

1. Have you ever felt you should **C**ut down on your drinking?
2. Have people **A**nnoyed you by criticizing your drinking?
3. Have you ever felt bad or **G**uilty about your drinking?
4. Have you had an **E**ye opener first thing in the morning to steady your nerves or get rid of a hangover? (www.projectcork.org/clinical_tools/html/CAGE.html)

Similarly, the CRAFFT utilizes six questions to assess problematic alcohol use in adolescents (Knight, Sherritt, Shrier, Harris, & Chang, 2002). In this test, affirmative answers to two items would indicate the need for further examination of the youth's involvement with alcohol and other drugs.

1. Have you ever ridden in a **C**ar driven by someone (including yourself) who was high or had been using alcohol or drugs?

2. Do you ever use alcohol or drugs to **R**elax, feel better about yourself, or fit in?
3. Do you ever use alcohol or drugs while you are by yourself, **A**lone?
4. Do you ever **F**orget things you did while using alcohol or drugs?
5. Do your **F**amily or Friends ever tell you that you should cut down on your drinking or drug use?
6. Have you ever gotten into **T**rouble while you were using alcohol or drugs?
   (CRAFFT, n.d.)

Other tools may be helpful for identifying clients' strengths and needs, when used within the context of an assessment interview (Burns, Lawlor & Craig, 2004; VanHook, Berkman, & Dunkle, 1996). Examples include the Older Americans Resources and Services Questionnaire (OARS), which provides information about the client's functioning across a variety of domains, including economic and social resources and activities of daily living (George & Fillenbaum, 1990). Other tools can be applied to a range of client populations to measure variables such as social functioning, caregiver burden, well-being, mental health, and social networks, and still others may be used in the evaluation of specific syndromes, such as post-traumatic stress disorder, conduct disorders, or anxiety (O'Hare, 2005; Parks & Novelli, 2000; Sauter & Franklin, 1998; Thompson, 1989; Wodarski & Thyer, 1998).

Tests and screening instruments are useful and expedient methods of quantifying data and behaviors. They are also essential components in evidence-based practice in that they "enhance the reliability and validity of the assessment and provide a baseline for monitoring and evaluation" (O'Hare, 2005, p. 7). As a consequence, scales and measures play an important role in case planning and intervention selection. To use these tools effectively, however, practitioners must be well grounded in knowledge of test theory and in the characteristics of specific tests. Many instruments, for example, have biases, low reliability, and poor validity; some are ill suited for certain clients and thus should be used with extreme caution. To avoid the danger of misusing these tools, social workers should thoroughly understand any instruments they are using or recommending, and seek consultation in the interpretation of tests administered by other professionals. Sources such as Bloom, Fischer, and Orme (2006), Fischer and Corcoran (2006, 2007), Thyer and Wodarski (1998), and Wodarski and Thyer (1998) can acquaint social workers with an array of available instruments and their proper use.

A final source of information for assessment is the social worker's *personal experience* based on direct interaction with clients. You will react in different ways to different clients, and these insights may prove useful in understanding how others respond to them. For example, you may view certain clients as being withdrawn, personable, dependent, caring, manipulative, seductive, assertive, overbearing, or determined. For instance, a client who reports that others take him for granted and place unreasonable demands upon him may appear to you to be self-deprecating and go to great lengths to please you. These experiences may provide you with clues about the nature of his complaint that others take advantage of him.

Some cautions are warranted with using this method. Clients may not behave with the social worker as they do with other people. Apprehension, involuntariness, and the desire to make a good impression may all skew the client's presentation of himself or herself. Also, initial impressions can be misleading and must be confirmed by additional contact with the client or other sources of information. All human beings' impressions are subjective and may be influenced by our own interpersonal patterns and perceptions. Your perceptions of and reactions to clients will be affected by your own life experiences. Before drawing even tentative conclusions, scrutinize your reactions to identify possible biases, distorted perceptions, or actions on your part that may have contributed to clients' behavior. For example, confrontational behavior on your part may spur a defensive response by the client. Perhaps the response reveals more about your actions than it represents the client's typical way of relating. Social constructions and personal experience may lead us to identify a client's acts and statements as "stubborn" vs. "determined," "arrogant" vs. "confident," or "submissive" vs. "cooperative." Self-awareness is indispensable to drawing valid conclusions from your interactions with clients.

Assessments that draw from multiple sources of data can provide a thorough, accurate, and helpful representation of the client's history, strengths, and challenges. However, workers must be attuned to the advantages and disadvantages inherent in different types of input and weigh those carefully in creating a comprehensive picture of the client system.

Questions to Answer in Problem Assessment

Good practice suggests that you use a variety of communication methods to encourage the client to tell his or her story. Therefore, the following questions are not intended to be *asked* in the assessment, but instead are meant to be used as a *guide* or *checklist* to ensure that you have not overlooked a significant factor in your assessment of the problem. What are the clients' concerns and problems as they and other concerned parties perceive them?

1. Are any current or impending legal mandates relevant to the situation?
2. Do any serious health or safety issues need attention?
3. What are specific indications of the problem? How is it manifesting itself?
4. What persons and systems are involved in the problem(s)?
5. How do the participants and/or systems interact to produce and maintain the problem(s)?
6. What unmet needs and/or wants are involved?
7. What developmental stage or life transition is entailed in the problem(s)?
8. How severe is the problem, and how does it affect the participants?
9. What meanings do clients ascribe to the problem(s)?
10. Where do the problematic behaviors occur?
11. When do the problematic behaviors occur?
12. What is the frequency of the problematic behaviors?
13. What is the duration of the problem(s)? Why is the client seeking help now?
14. What are the consequences of the problem?
15. Have other issues (e.g., alcohol or substance abuse, physical or sexual abuse) affected the functioning of the client or family members?
16. What are the clients' emotional reactions to the problem(s)?
17. How have the clients attempted to cope with the problem, and what are the required skills to resolve the problem?
18. What are the clients' skills, strengths, and resources?
19. How do ethnocultural, societal, and social class factors bear on the problem(s)?
20. What support systems exist or need to be created for the clients?
21. What external resources do clients need?

Questions 1–3 should serve as preliminary inquiries so that the social worker learns whether any prevailing issues may guide the direction of the interview. Questions 4–17 pertain to further specification of problems. They do not imply that a problem focus takes priority over explorations of strengths and resources (covered by questions 18–22). As suggested in the strengths matrix depicted in Figure 8-2, assessment of abilities, resources, and limitations or challenges is required for a full assessment.

Getting Started

After opening social amenities and an explanation of the direction and length of the interview, you should begin by exploring the client's concerns. Sometimes this question is a simple, open-ended inquiry: "Mrs. Smith, what brings you in to see me today?" or "I'm glad you came in. How can I help you?" Questions such as these allow the client an opportunity to express his or her concerns and help give direction to the questions that will follow.

At this point, the worker must be attentive to other issues that may alter the direction of the interview, at least at the outset. If the client's request for service is nonvoluntary, and particularly if it results from a legal mandate (e.g., part of probation, the consequence of a child maltreatment complaint), then the nature of the mandate, referring information, and the client's perception of the referral will frame the early part of the first interview.

A further consideration at the first interview is whether any danger exists that the client might do harm to himself or herself or to others. Some referrals— for example, in emergency services—clearly involve the risk for harm, which should be discussed and evaluated at the outset. In other instances, the risk may be more subtle. For example, a client may open an interview by saying, "I'm at the end of my rope…. I can't take it any longer." The social worker should respond to this opening by probing further: "Can you tell me more…?" or "When you say you can't take it, what do you mean by that?" If further information raises the social worker's concerns about the danger for suicidal or aggressive behavior, more specific questioning should follow, geared toward assessing the lethality of the situation.

Whatever the client's presenting problem, if shared information gives rise to safety concerns, the social worker must redirect the interview to focus on the degree of danger. If the threats to safety are minor or manageable, the practitioner may resume the interview's focus on the issues that brought the client in for service. However, if the mini-assessment reveals serious or imminent risk to the client or others, the focus of the session must be on ensuring safety rather than continuing the more general assessment.

Chapter 9 describes the process for conducting a suicide lethality assessment. Morrison (1995), Houston-Vega, Nuehring, & Daguio (1997), and Lukas (1993) offer additional guidelines for interviewing around issues of danger and assessing the degree of risk in various situations. Such texts can be useful resources for learning more about the topic.

Identifying the Problem, Its Expressions, and Other Critical Concerns

Your initial contacts with clients will concentrate on uncovering the sources of their problems and engaging them in planning appropriate remedial measures. People typically seek help because they have exhausted their coping efforts and/or lack resources required for satisfactory living. They have often found that, despite their most earnest efforts, their coping efforts are futile or seem to only aggravate the problem.

Problem identification takes a somewhat different course when the client has been referred or mandated to receive service. Referred clients may approach services willingly, even if those services were prompted by the suggestion of a professional, friend, or family member. However, many referred clients acquiesce passively because someone else thinks that they "need help." Their initiation of contact does not necessarily imply willingness to accept services. Sometimes when clients are referred by others, the referral source (often a doctor, employer, family member, or school official) has a view of the problem and recommendations for a treatment plan. It is important to clarify with clients that they can choose to work on problems of concern to them, not necessarily the concerns identified by the referral source.

Meanwhile, involuntary clients are at a later point on the continuum of voluntarism, reluctantly seeking help because of coercion from family members or some official power structure. Involuntary clients often do not perceive themselves as having problems or they portray pressure from the referral source as the problem. They may send the message: "I don't know why I should have to come. My wife (boss, parent) is the one with the problems. She's the one who should be here." When the source of motivation lies outside the client, it is more difficult to identify the parameters of the problem. After attempting to understand and reduce the client's negativism about being pressured to seek help, you should engage the client in an exploration of his or her life situation. The goals are to determine whether areas of dissatisfaction or interest on the client's part

can be identified and used as a source of motivation. When and if the client acknowledges a problem, the boundaries of the problem will become clear, and the exploration can then proceed in a typical fashion.

Another variation on involuntariness may stem from culturally derived attitudes toward help seeking. For example, the underutilization of (or "resistance" to) mental health services by Asian Americans may have its origins in several cultural themes. For example, an acceptance of "fate" may lead to "quiescence in the face of unpleasant life situations" (Yamashiro & Matsuoka, 1997, p. 178). A culture's tradition of arranged marriages may discourage the pursuit of formal assistance for problems that could reflect poorly on the suitability of a prospective spouse. Given the ways that religion and culture shape the perception of problems and therefore the methods chosen to address them, it is little wonder that many people seek assistance first from "informal" helpers, such as spiritual leaders, community or clan leaders, or traditional healers. In light of reluctance to seek help outside the family or culture, the social worker might encounter shame and apprehension during an initial interview. It is important to understand that this may not be the client's typical presentation of self and that establishing rapport and trust may be slow and require both sensitivity and empathy. While the client may have appeared for services reluctantly, the strength required to take this step should be acknowledged.

When asked to describe their problems or concerns, clients often respond by giving a general account of their problems. The description typically involves a deficiency of something needed (e.g., health care, adequate income or housing, companionship, harmonious family relationships, self-esteem) or an excess of something that is not desired (e.g., fear, guilt, temper outbursts, marital or parent–child conflict, or addiction). In either event, the issue often results in feelings of disequilibrium, tension, and apprehension. The emotions themselves are often a prominent part of the problem configuration, which is one reason why empathic communication is such a vital skill during the interview process.

This understanding of the *presenting problem* is significant because it reflects the client's immediate perceptions of the problem and is the impetus for seeking help. It is distinct from the *problem for work*. The issues that bring the client and the social worker together initially may not, in fact, be the issues that serve as the focus of goals and interventions later in the relationship. The problem for work may differ from the original or presenting problem for a number of reasons. As the helping process progresses, the development of greater information, insights, and trust may mean that factors are revealed that change the focus of work and goals for service. This does not mean, however, that you should disregard the problems that brought clients to you in the first place. The assessment process will reveal to you and the client whether the problem for work differs from the one that brought the client to your service.

The presenting problem is important because it suggests areas to be explored in assessment. If the difficulty described by parents involves their adolescent's truancy and rebellious behavior, for example, the exploration will include the family, school, and peer systems. As the exploration proceeds, it may also prove useful to explore the parental system if difficulty in the marital relationship appears to be negatively affecting the parent–child relationship. If learning difficulties appear to contribute to the truancy, the cognitive and perceptual subsystems of the adolescent may need to be assessed as part of the problem. The presenting problem thus identifies systems that are constituent parts of the predicament and suggests the resources needed to ameliorate it.

The Interaction of Other People or Systems

The presenting problem and the exploration that follows usually identify key individuals, groups, or organizations that are participants in the client's difficulties. An accurate assessment must consider all of these elements and determine how they interact. Furthermore, an effective plan of intervention should take these same elements into account, even though it is not always feasible to involve everyone who is a participant in a given problematic situation.

To understand more fully how the client(s) and other involved systems interact to produce and maintain the problem, you must elicit specific information about the functioning and interaction of these various systems. Clients commonly engage in transactions with the following systems:

1. The family and extended family or kinship network
2. The social network (friends, neighbors, coworkers, religious leaders and associates, club members, and cultural groups)
3. Public institutions (educational, recreational, law enforcement and protection, mental health, social service, health care, employment, economic security, legal and judicial, and various governmental agencies)
4. Personal service providers (doctor, dentist, barber or hairdresser, bartender, auto mechanic, landlord, banker)
5. Religious/spiritual belief system

Understanding how the interaction of these elements plays out in your client's particular situation requires detailed information about the behavior of all participants, including what they say and do before, during, and after problematic events. This specific information will help you and the client illuminate circumstances associated with the client's difficulties, the way that each system affects and is affected by others, and consequences of events that tend to perpetuate problematic behavior.

Certain circumstances or behaviors typically precede problematic behavior. One family member may say or do something that precipitates an angry, defensive, or hurt reaction by another. Pressure from the landlord about past due rent may result in tension and impatience between family members. A child's outburst in the classroom may follow certain stimuli. Events that precede problematic behavior are referred to as *antecedents*. Antecedents often give valuable clues about the behavior of one participant that may provoke or offend another participant, thereby triggering a negative reaction, followed by a counter negative reaction, thus setting the problematic situation in motion.

In addition to finding out about the circumstances surrounding troubling episodes, it is important to learn about the consequences or outcomes associated with problematic behaviors. These results may shed light on factors that perpetuate or reinforce the client's difficulties.

Analyzing the antecedents of problematic behavior, describing the behavior in specific terms, and assessing the consequences or effects of the problematic behavior provide a powerful means of identifying factors that motivate dysfunctional behavior and are appropriate targets of interventions. This straightforward approach to analyzing the functional significance of behavior is termed the *ABC model* (A = antecedent, B = behavior, C = consequence) (Ellis, 2001). Although it is far less simple than it may seem, the ABC model provides a coherent and practical approach to understanding problems, the systems involved, and the roles they play.

Assessing Developmental Needs and Wants

As we noted earlier, clients' problems commonly involve unmet needs and wants that derive from a poor fit between these needs and the resources available. Determining unmet needs, then, is the first step in identifying which resources must be tapped or developed. If resources are available but clients have been unable to avail themselves of those resources, it is important to determine the barriers to utilization. Some people, for example, may suffer from loneliness not because of an absence of support systems but because their interpersonal behavior alienates others and leaves them isolated. Or their loneliness may stem from shame or other feelings that keep them from asking for assistance from family or friends. Still other clients may *appear* to have emotional support available from family or others, but closer exploration may reveal that these potential resources are unresponsive to clients' needs. Reasons for the unresponsiveness typically involve reciprocal unsatisfactory transactions between the participants. The task in such instances is to assess the nature of the negative transactions and to attempt to modify them to the benefit of the participants.

Human *needs* include the universal necessities (adequate nutrition, safety, clothing, housing, and health care). They are critical and must be at least partially met for human beings to survive and maintain sound physical and mental well-being. As we use the term, *wants* consist of strong desires that motivate behavior and that, when fulfilled, enhance satisfaction and well-being. Although fulfillment of wants is not essential to survival, some wants develop a compelling nature, rivaling needs in their intensity. For illustrative purposes, we provide the following list of examples of typical wants involved in presenting problems.

Typical Wants Involved in Presenting Problems

- *To have less family conflict*
- *To feel valued by one's spouse or partner*
- *To be self-supporting*
- *To achieve greater companionship in marriage or relationship*
- *To gain more self-confidence*
- *To have more freedom*
- *To control one's temper*
- *To overcome depression*
- *To have more friends*
- *To be included in decision making*
- *To get discharged from an institution*
- *To make a difficult decision*
- *To master fear or anxiety*
- *To cope with children more effectively*

In determining clients' unmet needs and wants, it is essential to consider the developmental stage of the individual client, couple, or family. For example, the psychological needs of an adolescent—for acceptance by peers, sufficient freedom to develop increasing independence, and development of a stable identity (including a sexual identity)—differ markedly from the typical needs of elderly persons—for health care, adequate income, social relationships, and meaningful activities. As with individuals, families go through developmental phases that include both tasks to be mastered and needs that must be met if the family is to provide a climate conducive to the development and well-being of its members.[3]

Although clients' presenting problems often reveal obvious needs and wants (e.g., "Our unemployment benefits have expired and we have no income"), sometimes the social worker must infer what is lacking. Presenting problems may reveal only what is troubling clients on the surface, and careful exploration and empathic "tuning in" are required to identify unmet needs and wants. A couple, for example, may initially complain that they disagree over virtually everything and fight constantly. From this information, one could safely conclude that the pair wants a more harmonious relationship. Exploring their feelings on a deeper level, however, may reveal that their ongoing disputes are actually a manifestation of unmet needs of both partners for expressions of love, caring, appreciation, or increased companionship.

The process of translating complaints and problems into needs and wants is often helpful to clients, who may have dwelled on difficulties or blamed others and have not thought in terms of their own specific needs and wants. The presenting problem of one client was that her husband was married to his job and spent little time with her. The social worker responded, "I gather then you're feeling left out of his life and want to feel important to him and valued by him." The client replied, "You know, I hadn't thought of it that way, but that's exactly what I've been feeling." The practitioner then encouraged her to express this need directly to her husband, which she did. He listened attentively and responded with genuine concern. The occasion was the first time she had expressed her needs directly. Previously, her messages had been sighs, silence, or complaints, and her husband's usual response had been defensive withdrawal.

Identifying needs and wants also serves as a prelude to the process of negotiating goals. Expressing goals in terms that address needs and wants enhances the motivation of clients to work toward goal attainment, as the payoff for goal-oriented efforts is readily apparent to them.

Of course, some desires are unrealistic when assessed against the capacity of the client and/or opportunities in the social environment. Moreover, wanting to achieve a desired goal is not the same as being willing to expend the time and effort and to endure the discomfort required to attain that goal. These matters warrant extensive consideration and are central topics in Chapter 12.

Stresses Associated with Life Transitions

In addition to developmental stages that typically correspond to age ranges, individuals and families commonly must adapt to other major transitions that are less age specific. Your assessment should take into account whether the client's difficulties are related to such a transition and, if so, which aspects of the transition are sources of concern. Some transitions (e.g., geographical moves and immigrations, divorce, and untimely widowhood) can occur during virtually any stage of development. Many of these transitions can be traumatic and the adaptations required may temporarily overwhelm the coping capacities of individuals or families. Transitions that are involuntary or abrupt (a home is destroyed by fire) and separations (from a person, homeland, or familiar role) are highly stressful for most persons and often temporarily impair social functioning.

The person's history, concurrent strengths and resources, and past successful coping can all affect the adaptation to these transitions. The environment plays a crucial role as well. People with strong support networks (e.g., close relationships with family, kin, friends, and neighbors) generally have less difficulty in adapting to traumatic changes than do those who lack strong support systems. Assessments and interventions related to transitional periods, therefore, should consider the availability or lack of essential support systems.

The following are major transitions that may beset adults:

Role Changes	
Work, career choices	Retirement
Health impairment	Separation and divorce
Parenthood	Institutionalization
Post-parenthood years	Single parenthood
Geographic moves and migrations	Death of a spouse or partner
Marriage or partnership commitment	Military deployments

In addition to these transitions, other milestones affect specialized groups. For example, gay and lesbian persons have difficult decisions to make about to whom and under what conditions they will reveal their sexual identities (Cain, 1991a, 1991b); furthermore, they may need to create procedures and rituals for events (e.g., marriage, divorce, and end-of-life decisions) from which they are legally excluded because of their sexual orientations. A child whose parents are divorcing may experience a loss of friends and change of school along with the disruption of his or her family structure. Life events such as graduations, weddings, and holidays may be more emotionally charged and take on greater complexity when there has been divorce or remarriage in the family of origin. The parents and siblings of individuals with severe illnesses or disabilities may experience repeated "losses" if joyous milestones such as sleepovers, graduations, dating, proms, marriage, and parenthood are not available to their loved ones. Retirement may not represent a time of release and relaxation if it is accompanied by poverty, poor health, or new responsibilities such as caring for ill family members or raising grandchildren (Gibson, 1999).

Clearly, life transitions can be differentially affected by individual circumstances, culture, socio-economic status, and other factors. Social workers must be sensitive to these differences and take care not to make assumptions about the importance of a transitional event or developmental milestone.

Severity of the Problem

Assessment of the severity of problems is necessary to determine whether clients have the capacity to continue functioning in the community or whether hospitalization or other strong supportive or protective measures are needed. When functioning is temporarily impaired by extreme anxiety and loss of emotional control, such as when people experience acute post-traumatic stress disorder, short-term hospitalization may be required. The acuteness of the situation will necessarily influence your appraisal of the client's stress, the frequency of sessions, and the speed at which you need to mobilize support systems.

Meanings That Clients Ascribe to Problems

The next element of assessment involves understanding and describing the client's perceptions and definitions of the problem. The meanings people place on events ("meaning attributions") are as important as the events themselves, because they influence the way people respond to their difficulties. For example, a parent might attribute his son's suicide attempt to his grounding the boy earlier in the week. The meaning in a job loss might entail feeling individual shame and failure versus seeing the layoff as a part of a poor economy and organizational downsizing. In both of the preceding meaning attributions, personal guilt might keep the client from seeking help from support systems that could otherwise assist him or her in dealing with the problem. You, your clients, other participants in problems, and external observers thus may view problem situations in widely varying ways.

Determining these views is an important feature of assessment. Exploratory questions such as the following may help elicit the client's meaning attributions:

- *"What do you make of his behavior?"*
- *"What were the reasons (for your parents grounding you)?"*
- *"What conclusions have you drawn about (why your landlord evicted you)?"*
- *"What are your views (as to why you didn't get a promotion)?"*

Discovering meaning attributions is also vital because these beliefs about cause and effect can be powerful and may represent barriers to change. The following examples demonstrate distorted attributions (Hurvitz, 1975):

1. *Pseudoscientific explanations:* "My family has the gene for lung cancer. I know I'll get it, and there's nothing we can do about it."
2. *Psychological labeling:* "Mother is senile; she can't be given a choice in this matter."
3. *Fixed beliefs about others:* "She'll never change. She never has. I think we're wasting our time and money on counseling."
4. *Unchangeable factors:* "I've never been an affectionate person. It's just not in my character."
5. *Reference to "fixed" religious or philosophical principles, natural laws, or social forces:* "Sure, I already have as many children as I want. But I don't really have a choice. The church says that birth control is against God's will."
6. *Assertion based on presumed laws of human nature:* "All children tell lies at that age. It's just natural. I did when I was a kid."

Fortunately, many attributions are not fixed: people are capable of cognitive flexibility and are open—even eager—to examine their role in problematic situations and want to modify their behavior. When obstacles such as those listed above are encountered, however, it is vital to explore and resolve them before attempting to negotiate change-oriented goals or to implement interventions.

Sites of Problematic Behaviors

Determining *where* problematic behavior occurs may provide clues about which factors trigger it. For example, children may throw tantrums in certain locations but not in others. As a result of repeated experiences, they soon learn to discriminate where certain behaviors are tolerated and where they are not. Adults may experience anxiety or depression in certain environmental contexts but not in others. One couple, for example, invariably experienced a breakdown in communication in the home of one spouse's parents. Some children have difficulty following directions at school but not at home, or vice versa. Determining where problematic behavior occurs will assist you in identifying areas that warrant further exploration and in pinpointing factors associated with the behavior in question.

Identifying where problematic behavior *does not* occur is also valuable, because it provides clues about the features that might help in alleviating the problem and identify situations in which the client experiences relief from difficulties. For example, a child may act out in certain classes at school but not in all of them. What is happening in the incident-free classes that might explain the absence of symptoms or difficulties there? How can it be replicated in other classes? A client in residential treatment may gain temporary respite from overwhelming anxiety by visiting a cherished aunt on weekends. In other instances, clients may gain permanent relief from intolerable stress by changing employment, discontinuing college, or moving out of relationships when tension or other unpleasant feeling states are experienced exclusively in these contexts.

Temporal Context of Problematic Behaviors

Determining *when* problematic behaviors occur often yields valuable clues about factors at play in clients' problems. The onset of a depressive episode, for example, may coincide with the time of year when a loved one died or when a divorce occurred. Family problems may occur when one parent returns from work or travel, at bedtime for the children, at mealtimes, when visitations are beginning or ending, or when children are (or should be) getting ready for school. Similarly, couples may experience severe conflict when one partner is working the midnight shift, after participation by either partner in activities that exclude the other, or when one or both drink at parties. These clues can shed light on the patterns of clients' difficulties, indicate areas for further exploration, and lead to helpful interventions.

Frequency of Problematic Behaviors

The frequency of problematic behavior provides an index to both the pervasiveness of a problem and its effects on the participants. As with the site and timing of symptoms, information on frequency helps you to assess the context in which problems arise and the pattern they follow in the client's life. Services for clients who experience their problems on a more or less ongoing basis may need to be more intensive than for clients whose symptoms are intermittent or less frequent. Determining the frequency of problematic behaviors thus helps to clarify the degree of difficulty and the extent to which it impairs the daily functioning of clients and their families.

Assessing the frequency of problematic behaviors also provides a baseline against which to measure behaviors targeted for change. Making subsequent comparisons of the frequency of the targeted behaviors enables you to evaluate the efficacy of your interventions, as discussed in Chapter 13.

Duration of the Problem

Another important dimension vital to assessing problems relates to the history of the problem—namely, *how long* it has existed. Knowing when the problem developed and under what circumstances assists in further evaluating the degree of the problem, unraveling psychosocial factors associated with the problem, determining the source of motivation to seek assistance, and planning appropriate interventions. Often significant changes in individuals' life situations, including even seemingly positive ones, may disrupt clients' equilibrium to the extent that they cannot adapt to changes. An unplanned pregnancy, loss of employment, job promotion, severe illness, birth of a first child, move to a new city, death of a loved one, divorce, retirement, severe disappointment—these and many other life events may cause severe stresses. Careful exploration of the duration of problems often discloses such antecedents to current difficulties.

Events that immediately precede decisions to seek help are particularly informative. Sometimes referred to as *precipitating events*, these antecedents often yield valuable clues about critical stresses that might otherwise be overlooked. Clients often report that their problems have existed longer than a year. Why they chose to ask for help at a particular time is not readily apparent, but uncovering this information may cast their problems in a somewhat different light. For example, a parent who complained about his teenage daughter's longstanding rebelliousness did not seek assistance until he became aware (1 week before calling the agency) that she was engaging in an intimate relationship with a man 6 years her senior. The precipitating event is significant to the call for help and would not have been disclosed had the practitioner not sought to answer the critical question of why they were seeking help at this particular time.

In some instances, clients may not be fully aware of their reasons initiating the contact, and it may be necessary to explore what events or emotional experiences occurred shortly before their decision to seek help. Determining the duration of problems is also vital in assessing clients' levels of functioning and in planning appropriate interventions. This exploration may reveal that a client's adjustment has been marginal for many years and that the immediate problem is simply an exacerbation of long-term multiple problems. In other instances, the onset of a problem may be acute, and clients may have functioned at an adequate or high level for many years. In the first instance, modest goals and long-term intermittent service may be indicated; in the second instance, short-term crisis intervention may suffice to restore clients to their previous level of functioning.

Other Issues Affecting Client Functioning

Numerous other circumstances and conditions can affect the problem that the client is presenting and his or her capacity to address it. For this reason, it is often wise to explore specifically the client's use of alcohol or other substances, exposure to abuse or violence, the presence of health problems, depression or other mental health problems, and use of prescription medication.

Questions to probe into these areas should be a standard element of the initial interview. As such, they can be asked in a straightforward and nonjudgmental fashion. For example, opening questions might include the following:

- *"Now, I'd like to know about some of your habits. First, in an average month, on how many days do you have at least one drink of alcohol?"*
- *"Have you ever used street drugs of any sort?"*
- *"Have you had any major illnesses in the past?"*
- *"Are you currently experiencing any health problems?"*
- *"What medications do you take?"*
- *"How do these medications work for you?"*
- *"Have you been in situations recently or in the past where you were harmed by someone or where you witnessed others being hurt?"*

The answers you receive to these questions will determine which follow-up questions you ask. In some circumstances, you may ask for more specific information—for example, to determine the degree of impairment due to drug and alcohol use or whether the client is able to afford medication and is taking them as prescribed. At a minimum, you will want to learn how the client views these issues in light of the presenting problem. For example, you might ask these follow-up questions:

- *"How has the difficulty sleeping affected your ability to care for your kids?"*
- *"What role do you see your alcohol use playing in this marital conflict?"*
- *"Did the change of medication occur at the same time these other difficulties began?"*
- *"I wonder if the run-in with the bullies has anything to do with you skipping school lately?"*

Depending on the setting and purpose of the interview and on the information gathered, the social worker may focus the interview specifically on the client's medical history, abuse, substance use, or mental health. Further information on these assessments is included in Chapter 9. Lukas (1993) and Morrison (1995) also offer particularly good advice for conducting these kinds of specialized assessments.

Clients' Emotional Reactions to Problems

When people encounter problems in daily living, they typically experience emotional reactions to those problems. It is important to explore and assess these reactions for three major reasons.

First, people often gain relief simply by expressing troubling emotions related to their problems. Common reactions to problem situations are worry, agitation, resentment, hurt, fear, and feeling overwhelmed, helpless, or hopeless. Being able to ventilate such emotions in the presence of an understanding and concerned person is a source of great comfort. Releasing pent-up feelings often has the effect of relieving oneself of a heavy burden. In fact, expressing emotions may have a liberating effect for persons who tend to be out of touch with their emotions and have not acknowledged to themselves or others that they even have troubled feelings.

Second, because emotions strongly influence behavior, the emotional reactions of some people impel them to behave in ways that exacerbate or contribute to their difficulties. In some instances, in fact, people create new difficulties as a result of emotionally reactive behavior. In the heat of anger, a non-custodial parent may lash out at a child or former spouse. Burdened by financial concerns, an individual may become impatient and verbally abusive, behaving in ways that frighten, offend, or alienate employers, customers, or family members. An adult experiencing unremitting grief may cut himself or herself off from loved ones who "cannot stand" to see him or her cry. Powerful emotional reactions may thus be an integral part of the overall problem configuration.

Third, intense reactions often become primary problems, overshadowing the antecedent problematic situation. For example, some people develop severe depressive reactions associated with their life problems. A mother may become depressed over an unwed daughter's pregnancy; a man may react with anxiety to unemployment or retirement; and culturally dislocated persons may become depressed following relocation, even though they may have fled intolerable conditions in their homeland. Other individuals may react to problematic events by experiencing feelings of helplessness or panic that cause virtual paralysis. In such instances, interventions must address the overwhelming emotional reactions as well as the situation that triggered them.

Coping Efforts and Needed Skills

Perhaps surprisingly, the social worker can learn more about clients' difficulties by determining how they have attempted to cope with their problems. The coping methods that clients employ give valuable clues about their levels of stress and of functioning. Exploration may reveal that a client has few coping skills, but rather relies upon rigid patterns that are unhelpful or cause further problems. Some clients follow avoidance patterns—for example, immersing themselves in tasks or work, withdrawing, or numbing or fortifying themselves with drugs or alcohol. Other clients attempt to cope with interpersonal problems by resorting to aggressive, domineering behavior or by placating other participants or becoming submissive. Still other clients demonstrate flexible and effective coping patterns but collapse under unusually high levels of stress. By contrast, other clients depend heavily on others to manage difficulties for them.

Likewise, approaches to problem solving vary among cultures. The stereotypical middle-class American strategy values an individually focused, analytical-cognitive approach (De Anda, 1984). Other cultures, however, embrace approaches based on group values about coping with problems. All cultures exert pressures on individuals to follow prescribed solutions for a given problem, and developing new or creative solutions may be discouraged or frowned upon. Deviating from cultural expectations for coping or problem solving may add to the client's distress.

Exploring how clients have attempted to cope with problems sometimes reveals that they have struggled effectively with similar problems in the past but are no longer able to do so. In such instances, it is important to explore carefully what has changed. For example, a person may have been able to cope with the demands of one supervisor but not with a new one who is more critical and aloof or who is of a different generation, race, or gender than the client. The client's typical ability to cope may also be affected by changes in functioning. Severely depressed clients, for example, commonly overestimate the difficulty of their problems and underestimate their coping abilities. Some clients are able to cope effectively in one setting but not in another. Thus, by exploring the different circumstances, meaning attributions, and emotional reactions of clients, you should be able to identify subtle differences that account for the varied effectiveness of your clients' coping patterns in different contexts.

Another aspect of assessment is the task of identifying the skills that clients need to ameliorate their difficulties. This information enables you to negotiate appropriate and feasible goals aimed at developing skills. To improve parent–child relationships, for example, clients may need to develop listening and negotiating skills. Socially inhibited clients may need to learn skills in approaching others, introducing themselves, and engaging in conversation. To enhance couples' relationships, partners often need to learn communication and conflict management skills. To cope effectively with people who tend to exploit them, still other clients must acquire assertiveness skills.

Cultural, Societal, and Social Class Factors

As we noted earlier, ethnocultural factors influence what kinds of problems people experience, how they feel about requesting assistance, how they communicate, how they perceive the role of the professional person, and how they view various approaches to solving problems. It is therefore vital that you be knowledgeable about these factors and competent in responding to them. Your assessment of clients' life situations, needs, and strengths must be viewed through the lens of cultural competence (Rooney & Bibus, 1995). What does this mean in practice? Some examples follow:

- *A client emigrating from Mexico, Africa, Asia, or Eastern Europe may display psychological distress that is directly related to the migration or refugee experience. Beyond this consideration, a social worker who understands the ramifications of immigration may need to be sensitive to the special issues that may arise for refugees or others whose immigration was made under forced or dire circumstances (Mayadas et al., 1998–1999).*

- *An interview with an older person experiencing isolation should take into account that hearing difficulties, death or illness of peers, housing and economic status, and other factors may impede the client's ability to partake in social activities.*

- *Racial and ethnic stereotypes may lead to differences in the way that minority youth and majority youth are perceived when accused of juvenile crimes. Similarly, detrimental experiences with authority figures and institutional racism may affect the way that these clients interact with the social worker (Bridges & Steen, 1998).*

- *A young woman is persistently late for appointments, which her social worker interprets as a sign of resistance and poor organizational skills. In fact, the young woman must make child care arrangements and take three buses to reach the mental health clinic. Rather than indicating shortcomings, her arrival at appointments (even late) is a sign of persistence and precise organization.*

- *An elderly couple living on a remote farm may become isolated, refuse to allow visitors in the home, and deny any problems in functioning out of fear that they will be forced to leave their home for an institutional placement.*

Workers must possess cultural sensitivity and the capacity to take many perspectives when viewing client's situations and drawing conclusions about them. Chapter 9 addresses these skills as they apply to individual and environmental factors.

External Resources Needed

When clients request services, you must determine (1) whether the services requested match the functions of the agency and (2) whether the staff possesses the skills required to provide high-quality service. If not, a referral is needed to assure that the client receives the highest quality service to match the needs presented. Referrals may also be required to complement services within your agency or to obtain a specialized assessment that will be factored into your services (e.g., "Are the multiple medications that Mrs. Jones is taking causing her recent cognitive problems?", "Are there neurological causes for John's outbursts?"). In such instances, the practitioner performs a broker or case manager role, which requires knowledge of community resources (or at least knowledge of how to obtain relevant information). Fortunately, many large communities have community resource information centers that can prove highly valuable to both clients and professionals in locating needed resources. Remember that irrespective of the presenting problem, clients may benefit from help in a variety of areas—from financial assistance, transportation, and health care to child or elder care, recreation, and job training.

In certain instances, in addition to the public and private resources available in your community, you should consider two other major resources that may be less visible forms of assistance. The first is self-help groups, where members look to themselves for mutual aid and social support. In particular, the Internet has expanded the reach of such groups across geographic distances on a round-the-clock basis (Fingeld, 2000). The second resource is natural support systems, including relatives, friends, neighbors, coworkers, and close associates from school, social groups, or one's faith community. Some therapists have developed innovative ways of tapping these support systems collectively through an intervention termed *network therapy*. These clinicians contend that much of the dysfunctional behavior labeled as mental illness actually derives from feelings of alienation from one's natural social network, which consists of all human relationships that are significant in a person's life, including natural support systems. In network therapy, these practitioners mobilize 40 to 50 significant people who are willing to come

together in a period of crisis for one or more members of the network. The goal is to unite their efforts in tightening the social network of relationships for the purpose of offering support, reassurance, and solidarity to troubled members and other members of the social network. Mobilizing social networks is in keeping with the best traditions of social work.

In instances of cultural dislocation, natural support systems may be limited to the family, and practitioners may need to mobilize other potential resources in the community (Hulewat, 1996). Assisting refugees poses a particular challenge, because a cultural reference group may not be available in some communities. A language barrier may create another obstacle, and practitioners may need to search for interpreters and other interested parties who can assist these families in locating housing, gaining employment, learning the language, adapting to an alien culture, and developing social support systems.

In still other instances, people's environments may be virtually devoid of natural support systems. Consequently, environmental changes may be necessary to accomplish a better fit between needs and resources, a topic we consider at greater length in Chapter 9.

Assessing Children and Older Adults

Social workers are often employed in settings serving children and older adults. Assessments with these groups utilize many of the skills and concepts noted elsewhere in this chapter and in earlier sections. However, elderly clients and child clients also present unique requirements because of their respective life stages and circumstances. This section is intended to acquaint you with some of the considerations that will shape assessments with these populations.

Because children and older adults often present for service in relation to systems of which they are already a part (e.g., hospitals, schools, families, assisted living facilities), your assessment may be bounded by those systems. This can present a challenge for creating an integrated assessment, as several caregivers, agencies, and professionals may hold pieces of the puzzle while none possesses the mandate or capacity to put all of the pieces together.

Similarly, children and older adults typically appear for service because someone else has identified a concern. These referral sources may include parents or guardians, caregivers, teachers, neighbors, or health care providers. This factor does not automatically mean that the client will be resistant, but rather indicates that he or she may disagree about the presence or nature of the problem or be unmotivated to address it.

Maltreatment

Older adults and children are both at particular risk for maltreatment at the hands of caregivers. Therefore, it is important for professionals to understand the principles for detecting abuse or neglect and their responsibilities for reporting it. For both minors and older adults mistreatment can be categorized into four areas: neglect, physical abuse, sexual abuse, and emotional or verbal abuse. For elderly persons, a fifth category would be financial exploitation (Bergeron & Gray, 2003). The specific definitions of various forms of abuse vary by jurisdiction (Rathbone-McCuan, 2008; Wells, 2008). Sometimes abusive individuals or their victims will forthrightly report abuse to the social worker. More commonly it is covered by fear, confusion, and shame, and thus the professional must be alert to signs of abuse, such as:

- Physical injuries: *Burns, bruises, cuts, or broken bones for which there is no satisfactory or credible explanation; injuries to the head and face*
- Lack of physical care: *Malnourishment, poor hygiene, unmet medical or dental needs*
- Unusual behaviors: *Sudden changes, withdrawal, aggression, sexualized behavior, self-harm, guarded or fearful behavior at the mention of or in the presence of caregiver*
- Financial irregularities: *For the older client, includes missing money or valuables, unpaid bills, coerced spending (Lukas, 1993; Mayo Clinic, 2007).*

Social workers (including student workers) are mandated to report suspicions of child abuse to designated child protective agencies; most jurisdictions also compel workers to report elder abuse, although it may be voluntary in some regions. All professionals should know the steps required in their setting and state for making an abuse report. Referring the case to agencies that have the mandate and expertise to investigate maltreatment is the best way to assure that proper legal and biopsychosocial interventions are brought to bear in the case.

Data Sources and Interviewing Techniques

In working with children and older adults, particularly the frail elderly, you may need to rely more than usual on certain data sources (e.g., collateral contacts or observations) and less than usual on other sources (e.g., the client's verbal reports). A trusting relationship with the client's primary caregivers will be vital to your access to the client and will dramatically affect the rapport you achieve with him or her. Depending on the child's level of development or the older adult's capacities, he or she may have difficulty helping you construct the problem analysis or identify strengths or coping methods. Other data sources, such as interviews with collateral contacts (teachers, family members, service providers, institutional caregivers), may be essential in completing a satisfactory assessment, although, as noted earlier, these can be open to various distortions.

Child assessments may also require new skills, such as the use of drawings, board games, dolls, or puppets as sources of information for the assessment. The way that the child approaches these activities can be as telling as the information they reveal (Webb, 1996). For example, are the child's interests and skills age-appropriate? What mood is reflected in the child's play, and is it frequently encountered? Do themes in the child's play relate to possible areas of distress? How often do those themes recur? How does the child relate to you and to adversity (the end of play or a "wrong move" in a game)? How well can the child focus on the task? Clearly, in this context, play is not a random activity meant for the child's distraction or enjoyment. Instead, you must use it purposefully and be attentive to the implications of various facets of the experience. Your impressions of the significance and meaning of the play activities should be evaluated on the basis of other sources of information.

A *developmental assessment* may be particularly relevant for understanding the child's history and current situation. With this type of assessment, a parent or other caregiver provides information about the circumstances of the child's delivery, birth, and infancy; achievement of developmental milestones; family atmosphere; interests; and significant life transitions (Jordan & Hickerson, 2003; Lukas, 1993; Webb, 1996). This information helps form impressions about the child's experiences and life events, especially as they may relate to his or her current functioning. As with other forms of assessment, you must organize and interpret what you discover from all sources so as to paint a meaningful picture of the child's history, strengths, and needs; this assessment will then serve as the basis of your goals and interventions.

Screening instruments intended specifically for child clients or problems associated with childhood may also be useful. Some involve the child as a participant–respondent while others are completed by the parent or guardian in reference to the child. The Denver Developmental Screening for Children (DDST-II) (Frankenburg, Dodds, Archer, Shapiro & Bresnick, 1992) is used with children up to age six to determine whether development is in the normal range and to offer early identification of neurological and other problems. The kit utilizes props such as a tennis ball, doll, a zippered bag and a pencil for drawing to test personal and social functioning (self-care, getting along with others), fine motor skills (eye-hand coordination, manipulation of small objects), language (hearing and understanding), and gross motor skills (sitting, walking, jumping).

Comprehensive, competent assessments for geriatric clients involve items that go beyond the typical multidimensional assessment. For example, functional assessments would address the client's ability to perform various tasks, typically, *activities of daily living* (ADLs)—those things required for independent living such as dressing, hygiene, feeding, and mobility. Instrumental ADLs (IADLs) involve measuring the client's ability to perform more intricate tasks such as managing money, taking medicine properly, housework, shopping, and meal preparation (Gallo, 2005). Because some of the IADL skills may be traditionally performed by one gender or another, you should ascertain the client's baseline functioning in these areas before concluding that there are deficits or declines in IADLs. In that driving is a complex skill, an area of significant risk, a powerful symbol of independence, and an emotionally charged issue, assessment of capacity in this area is a specialized and important aspect of functioning (Gallo, 2005).

The use of *physical examinations* and health histories takes on particular importance in assessment of elderly clients. These assessments must take into account the impact of limitations in vision and hearing, restricted mobility and reaction times, pain management, and medication and disease interactions. Gallo and Bogner note that "the presenting complaint may involve the most vulnerable organ system rather than the organ system expected. For example, congestive heart failure may present as delirium" (2005, p. 9). Sexual functioning is another element of assessments that is commonly overlooked in elderly clients. Specialized and comprehensive evaluations require interdisciplinary teams with expertise in geriatric care.

As with other issues and populations, standardized tools are effective in evaluating the needs and functioning of older adults. Examples include the Determination of Need Assessment (DONA) (Paveza, Prohaska,

Hagopian, & Cohen, 1989), the Instrumental Activities of Daily Living Screen (Gallo, 2005), and the Katz Index of Activities of Daily Living (Katz, 1963). Tests like theDirect Assessment of Functioning Scale (DAFS) (Lowenstein et al., 1989) and the Physical Performance Test (Reuben & Siu, 1990; Rozzini, Frisoni, Bianchetti, Zanetti, & Trabucchi, 1993) require clients to demonstrate or simulate basic tasks such as climbing stairs, lifting a book and placing it on a shelf, writing, making a telephone call, brushing teeth, telling time, and eating. Other tests focus on the presence and severity of dementia, querying caregivers about the frequency with which the client shouts, laughs, or makes accusations inappropriately, wanders aimlessly, smokes carelessly, leaves the stove on, appears disheveled, is disoriented in familiar surroundings, and so on (Gallo, 2005).

For both very young and very old clients, direct observation of functioning may yield more reliable results than either self-reports or information from collateral sources. Specialized expertise is required to ensure that assessments are properly conducted and interpreted for these and other especially vulnerable populations.

Summary

Chapter 8 introduced the knowledge and skills entailed in multidimensional assessment. A psychiatric diagnosis may be part of, but is not the same as, a social work assessment. The discussion in this chapter emphasized strengths and resources in assessments. A framework for prioritizing what must be done in assessment was presented, along with the components of the problem exploration and application to specific sub populations. In Chapter 9, we consider the assessment of intrapersonal and environmental systems and the terms and concepts used to describe their functioning.

Skill Development Exercises in Exploring Strengths and Problems

On April 16, 2007, 23-year-old Seung-Hui Cho killed 32 people on the campus of Virginia Tech University before turning the gun on himself. In the months leading up to the murders, Cho had numerous encounters with mental health professionals. He had been declared an "imminent danger to self or others as a result of mental illness" on a temporary detention order from a Virginia District Court. Two students had filed complaints against him for bizarre phone calls and emails he had sent. Another student, his former roommate, called campus police stating that Cho could be suicidal. A poetry professor at the school recalled that he was "menacing" in class and other students stopped attending after he began photographing them. This professor later removed Cho from her class and worked with him one-on-one. She also reported that the content of his poems and other writings was disturbing and seemed to have an underlying threat.

A South Korean national, Cho moved with his family to the United States at the age of eight. As a youngster, he had been diagnosed with depression and selective mutism, a condition associated with social anxiety, and had received therapy and special education services as a result. He had been a successful elementary school student, but by middle school he was apparently subject to mockery from fellow students due to his speech abnormalities, his accent, and his isolation.

Imagine you worked in a setting where Seung-Hui Cho presented for service at age 10, 15, or 22, and address the following questions.

1. What sources of information would you use to better understand your client, his problems and his strengths?
2. What cross-cultural issues should you be aware of in this case?
3. What questions would you ask as part of problem analysis?
4. What transitional and developmental issues might be of particular interest?
5. What role would your client's diagnoses play in your assessment?

6. What environmental and interpersonal interactions are relevant in this case?
7. What consultation would be helpful to you in completing this assessment?

Related Online Content

Visit the *Direct Social Work Practice* companion Web site at *www.cengage.com/social_work/hepworth* for additional learning tools such as glossary terms, chapter outlines, relevant Web links, and chapter practice quizzes.

Notes

1. See the US Department of Health and Human Services Substance Abuse and Mental Health Services Administration Web site, mentalhealth.samhsa.gov/cmhs/communitysupport/toolkits/about.asp, and the North Carolina Evidence Based Practice Center (www.ncebpcenter.org) for toolkits, workbooks, and other resources for evidence-based practice in an array of problem areas.
2. For more information, consult WALMYR Publishing Company, P.O. Box 12217, Tallahassee, FL 32317. (850) 383-0970. E-mail: scales@walmyr.com. Or visit www.walmyr.com.
3. For resources on family development and norms across cultures, we suggest Congress (2002), Corcoran (2000), Lum (1996), and McGoldrick et al. (1996).

Assessment: Intrapersonal, Interpersonal, and Environmental Factors

CHAPTER OVERVIEW

Chapter 9 reviews three key aspects of a comprehensive assessment: those things going on within the client (physically, emotionally, cognitively), those things going on within the client's environment (physical and social), and the transactions between the two. The chapter introduces these areas for examination and helps you develop an understanding of the difficulties and the assets to consider in these systems. It also discusses how culture affects these factors and offers guidance for understanding these effects when the social worker and client come from different backgrounds. As a result of reading this chapter, you will:

- Understand how assessments capture the reciprocal nature of client systems

- Learn the elements of intrapersonal functioning, including physical, emotional, cognitive, spiritual, and environmental factors

- Know the questions to ask to assess substance use and the common drugs of abuse

- Learn the diagnostic criteria for common thought and affective disorders

- Appreciate the elements of a mental status exam and how one looks in writing

- Understand how to evaluate suicide risk

- Know the do's and don'ts for writing assessments and observe an example

The Interaction of Multiple Systems in Human Problems

Problems, strengths, and resources encountered in direct social work practice result from interactions among intrapersonal, interpersonal, and environmental systems. Difficulties are rarely confined to one of these systems, however, because a functional imbalance in one system typically contributes to an imbalance in others. For example, individual difficulties (e.g., feelings of worthlessness and depression) invariably influence how one relates to other people; interpersonal difficulties (e.g., job strain) likewise affect individual functioning. Similarly, environmental deficits (e.g., inadequate housing, hostile working conditions, or social isolation) affect individual and interpersonal functioning.

The reciprocal effects among the three major systems, of course, are not limited to the negative effects of functional imbalance and system deficits. Assets, strengths, and resources also have reciprocal *positive* effects. A supportive environment may partially compensate for intrapersonal difficulties; similarly, strong interpersonal relationships may provide positive experiences that more than offset an otherwise impoverished environment. Figure 9-1 depicts the range of elements to be considered in assessing individual and environmental functioning.

Intrapersonal Systems

A comprehensive assessment of the individual considers a variety of elements, including biophysical, cognitive/perceptual, emotional, behavioral, cultural, and motivational factors and the ways that these interact with people and institutions in the individual's environment. Keeping this in mind, the social worker's assessment and written products may focus more sharply on some of these areas than others, depending on the nature of the client's difficulties, the reason for the assessment, and the setting in which the assessment is taking place. It is important to remember, however, that an assessment is just a "snapshot" of the client system's functioning at any given point in time. As we noted in

INTRAPERSONAL SYSTEMS

Biophysical Functioning
  Physical characteristics and presentation
  Physical health

Assessing Use and Abuse of Medications, Alcohol, and Drugs
  Alcohol use and abuse
  Use and abuse of other substances
  Dual diagnosis: comorbid addictive and mental disorders

Assessing Cognitive/Perceptual Functioning
  Intellectual functioning
  Judgment
  Reality testing
  Coherence
  Cognitive flexibility
  Values
  Misconceptions
  Self-concept
  Assessing thought disorders

Assessing Emotional Functioning
  Emotional control
  Range of emotions
  Appropriateness of affect
  Assessing affective disorders
    Bipolar disorder
    Major depressive disorder
    Suicidal risk
    Depression and suicidal risk with children and adolescents

Assessing Behavioral Functioning

Assessing Motivation

Assessing Environmental Systems
  Physical environment
  Social support systems
  Spirituality and affiliation with a faith community

FIG-9-1 Overview: Areas for Attention in Assessing Intrapersonal Functioning

Chapter 8, the social worker's beliefs and actions and the client's feelings about seeking help may distort the assessment at any given point. For all of these reasons, care and respect are required when collecting and synthesizing assessment information into a working hypothesis for intervention.

Biophysical Functioning

Biophysical functioning encompasses physical characteristics, health factors, and genetic factors, as well as the use and abuse of drugs and alcohol.

Physical Characteristics and Presentation

People's physical characteristics and appearance may be either assets or liabilities. In many cultures, physical attractiveness is highly valued, and unattractive or odd people may be disadvantaged in terms of their social desirability, employment opportunities, or marriageability. It is thus important to be observant of distinguishing physical characteristics that may affect social functioning. Particular attributes that merit attention include body build, dental health, posture, facial features, gait, and any physical anomalies that may create positive or negative perceptions about the client, affect his or her self-image, or pose a social liability.

How people present themselves is worthy of note. People who walk slowly, display stooped posture, talk slowly and without animation, lack spontaneity, and show minimal changes in facial expression may be depressed, in pain, or over-medicated. Dress and grooming often reveal much about a person's morale, values, and standard of living. The standard for assessing appearance is generally whether the dress is appropriate for the setting. Is the client barefoot in near-freezing weather or wearing a helmet and overcoat in the summer sun? Is the client dressed seductively, in pajamas, or "overdressed" for an appointment with the social worker? While attending to these questions, social workers should take care in the conclusions they reach. Westermeyer (1993) notes that the determination of "appropriateness" is greatly influenced by the interviewer's cultural background and values. A "disheveled" appearance may indicate poverty, carelessness, or the "rock star" fashion. Being clothed in bright colors may indicate mania or simply an affiliation with a cultural group that favors that particular form of dress (Morrison, 1995; Othmer & Othmer, 1989). As with other elements of assessment, your description of what you observe ("collared shirt, dress pants, clean-shaven") should be separate from your assessment of it ("well-groomed and appropriately dressed").

Other important factors associated with appearance include hand tremors, facial tics, rigid or constantly shifting posture, and tense muscles of the face, hands, and arms. Sometimes these characteristics reflect the presence of an illness or physical problem. Such physical signs may also indicate a high degree of tension or anxiety, warranting exploration by the social worker. During the assessment, an effective social worker will determine whether the anxiety displayed is normative for the given situation or whether it is excessive and might reveal an area for further discussion.

Physical Health

Ill health can contribute to depression, sexual difficulties, irritability, low energy, restlessness, anxiety, poor concentration, and a host of other problems. It is therefore important for social workers to routinely consider their clients' state of health as they explore these individuals' situations. One of the first assessment activities is to determine if clients are under medical care and when they last had a medical examination. Social workers should rule out medical sources of difficulties by referring clients for physical evaluations, when appropriate, before attributing problems solely to psychosocial factors. They should also be cautious and avoid drawing premature conclusions about the sources of problems when there is even a remote possibility that medical factors may be involved.

A variety of biophysical factors can affect cognitive, behavioral, and emotional functioning in individuals. For example, a history of child malnutrition has been linked to attention deficits, poor social skills, and emotional problems that may continue to affect children even after they become adequately nourished (Johnson, 1989). Nutritional deficits can also cause dementia in elderly people; however, some of this cognitive decline may be reversed if it is treated early enough (Naleppa, 1999). Encephalitis, which has been shown to cause brain damage, can lead to symptoms of attention deficit disorder (Johnson, 1989). Hormone levels also affect behavioral and emotional functioning—for example, high testosterone levels have been correlated with high levels of aggression (Rowe, Maughan, Worthman, Costello, & Angold, 2004).

Assessing the health of clients is especially important with groups known to underutilize medical care. Some may have a greater-than-average need for health care due to their specific conditions, while others may simply have more difficulty accessing basic care. People in these groups may also be more vulnerable to disease due to poor nutrition, dangerous environmental conditions, and the lack of preventive services (Buss & Gillanders, 1997; Ensign, 1998; Jang, Lee, & Woo, 1998; Suarez & Siefert, 1998; Zechetmayr, 1997). Assessments should determine whether the individual's access to care is limited by affordability, availability, or acceptability (Julia, 1996).

Whether care is *affordable* depends on whether the client has health insurance coverage and whether he or she can pay for the services not covered by insurance. Approximately 44 million people in the United States lack basic health insurance. Even those who do have coverage may be unable or reluctant to pursue care, given the cost of medications, deductibles, and co-payments not covered by insurance. Concerns about costs may lead clients to delay basic care until the situation worsens to a dangerous level or to the point where even more expensive interventions are required. Individuals with extensive or chronic health problems, such as those with AIDS, may find that hospitalization and drug costs outstrip both their insurance coverage and their income, thereby affecting even those with considerable financial assets and high-paying jobs.

Availability refers not only to the location of health care services, but also the hours they are available, the transportation needed to reach them, and the adequacy of the facilities and personnel to meet the client's needs (Mokuau & Fong, 1994). If the nearest after-hours health care resource is a hospital emergency room, it may be the facility of choice for a desperate mother, even if the health concern (e.g., a child's ear infection) might be better addressed in another setting.

Acceptability refers to the extent to which the health services are compatible with the client's cultural values and traditions. Chapter 8 discussed the importance of understanding how culture may affect the client's interpretation of his or her problems. An important task in intrapersonal assessment involves determining clients' views about the causes of illness, physical aberrations, disabling conditions, and mental symptoms, because their expectations regarding diagnoses and treatment may differ sharply from those presented by Western health care professionals (Yamamoto, Silva, Justice, Chang, & Leong, 1993) and their rejection of these formulations may be misinterpreted as noncompliance or resistance (Al-Krenawi, 1998). For these reasons, all practitioners should be knowledgeable about the significance of caregivers, folk healers, and shamans for clients from an array of cultural groups (Canda, 1983).

Beyond differences in beliefs, differences arise related to peoples' comfort in accepting care. New immigrants may have limited knowledge of Western medical care and of the complex health care provider systems in the United States, and they may be reticent to seek care because of concerns about their documentation and fears of deportation (Congress, 1994). The use of indigenous healers or bilingual and bicultural staff can enhance the acceptability of health care to these individuals.

A health assessment may also entail gathering information about illnesses in the client's family. A genogram may be helpful in capturing this information. This tool, which is similar to a family tree, graphically depicts relationships within the family, dates of births and deaths, illnesses, and other significant life events. It reveals patterns across generations of which even the client may not have been aware (Andrews, 2001; McGoldrick, 1985). You may also find out about family history simply by asking the client. For example, you might ask, "Has anyone else in your family ever had an eating disorder?", "Is there a history of substance abuse in your family?" or "How have other relatives died?" This information helps in assessing the client's understanding of and experience with a problem. It may also identify the need for a referral for specialized information and counseling related to genetically linked disorders (Waltman, 1996).[1]

Assessing Use and Abuse of Medications, Alcohol, and Drugs

An accurate understanding of a client's biophysical functioning must include information on his or her use of both legal and illicit drugs. First, it is important to determine which prescribed and over-the-counter medications the client is taking, whether he or she is taking them as prescribed, and whether they are having the intended effect. Another reason for evaluating drug use is that even beneficial drugs can produce side effects that affect the functioning of various biopsychosocial systems. An array of common reactions such as drowsiness, changes in sexual functioning, muscle rigidity, disorientation, inertia, and stomach pains may result from inappropriate combinations of prescription drugs or as troubling side effects of single medications (Denison, 2003). Finally, questioning in this area is important because the client may report a variety of conditions,

from confusion to sleeplessness, which may necessitate a referral for evaluation and medication.

Alcohol is another form of legal drug, but its abuse can severely impair health, disrupt or destroy family life, and create serious community problems. Conservatively estimated to afflict 9 to 10 million Americans, alcoholism can occur in any culture, although it may be more prevalent in some than in others. Alcoholism is also associated with high incidences of suicide, homicide, child abuse, and partner violence.

Like alcohol abuse, the misuse of illicit drugs may have detrimental consequences for both the user and his or her family, and it brings further problems due to its status as a banned or illegal substance. For example, users may engage in dangerous or illegal activities (such as prostitution or theft) to support their habits. In addition, variations in the purity of the drugs used or the methods of administration (i.e., sharing needles) may expose users to risks beyond those associated with the drug itself. The following sections introduce the areas for concern related to alcohol and drug abuse and the strategies for effectively assessing use and dependence.

Alcohol Use and Abuse

Chapter 8 contains information on the Michigan Alcoholism Screening Test (MAST) and other instruments for assessing alcohol use. Other questions for substance abuse assessment are included in Table 9-1. Understanding a client's alcohol use is essential for a number of reasons. Clearly, problematic use may be related to other problems in work, school, and family functioning. Even moderate use may be a sign of escape or self-medication and lead to impaired decision making and risky behavior, such as driving while intoxicated.

Alcoholism can be distinguished from heavy drinking in that it causes distress and disruption in the life of the person with alcohol dependency, as well as in the lives of members of that person's social and support systems (Goodwin & Gabrielli, 1997). Alcoholism is marked by a preoccupation with making sure that the amount of alcohol necessary for intoxication remains accessible at all times. As a result, individuals may affiliate with other heavy drinkers in an attempt to escape observation. As alcoholism advances, the signs tend to become more concealed, as the user hides bottles or other "evidence," drinks alone, and covers up drinking binges. Feelings of guilt and anxiety over the behavior begin to appear, which usually leads to more drinking in

TABLE-9-1 INTERVIEWING FOR SUBSTANCE ABUSE POTENTIAL

THE FIRST SIX QUESTIONS WILL HELP GUIDE THE DIRECTION OF YOUR INTERVIEW, THE QUESTIONS YOU ASK, AND YOUR FURTHER ASSESSMENT.

1. Do you—or did you ever—smoke cigarettes? For how long? How many per day?
2. Do you drink?
3. What do you drink? (Beer, wine, liquor?)
4. Do you take any prescription medications regularly? How do they make you feel?
5. Do you use any over-the-counter medications regularly? How do they make you feel?
6. Have you ever used any illegal drug?
7. When was the last time you had a drink/used?
8. How much did you have to drink/use?
9. When was the last time before that?
10. How much did you have?
11. Do you always drink/use approximately the same amount? If not, is the amount increasing or decreasing?
12. (If it is increasing) Does that concern you?
13. Do most of your friends drink/use?
14. Do (or did) your parents drink/use?
15. Have you ever been concerned that you might have a drinking/drug problem?
16. Has anyone else ever suggested to you that you have (or had) a drinking/drug problem?
17. How does drinking/using help you?
18. Do other people report that you become more careless, or angry, or out of control when you have been drinking/using?
19. Do you drink/use to "get away from your troubles?"
20. What troubles are you trying to get away from?
21. Are you aware of any way in which drinking/using is interfering with your work?
22. Are you having any difficulties or conflict with your spouse or partner because of drinking/using?
23. Are you having financial difficulties? Are they related in any way to your drinking/using?
24. Have you ever tried to stop drinking/using? How?

SOURCE: From *Where to Start and What to Ask: An Assessment Handbook* by Susan Lukas. Copyright © 1993 by Susan Lukas. Used by permission of W. W. Norton & Company, Inc.

an effort to escape the negative feelings, which in turn leads to an intensification of the negative feelings.

Females who abuse alcohol present a somewhat different profile. They are more likely to abuse prescription drugs as well, to consume substances in isolation, and to have had the onset of abuse after a traumatic event such as incest or racial or domestic violence (Nelson-Zlupko, Kauffman, & Dore, 1995). Women are less likely than men to enter and complete treatment programs, because obstacles to treatment often include social stigma associated with alcoholism and a lack of available transportation and child care while in treatment (Yaffe, Jenson, & Howard, 1995).

Another serious problem associated with alcohol abuse involves adverse effects on offspring produced by the mother's alcohol consumption during pregnancy.[2]

The potential effects range from full-blown fetal alcohol syndrome (FAS) to fetal alcohol effects (FAE). Because of these risks, social workers should routinely question women about their use of alcohol during pregnancy, gathering a history of consumption of beer, wine, and liquor (focusing on frequency, quantity, and variability).

Use and Abuse of Other Substances

People abuse many types of drugs. Because immediate care may be essential in instances of acute drug intoxication, and because abusers often attempt to conceal their use of drugs, it is important that practitioners recognize the signs of abuse of commonly used drugs. Table 9-2 categorizes the most commonly abused drugs and their indications. In addition to those signs of abuse

TABLE-9-2

TYPE OF DRUG	TYPICAL INDICATIONS	COMMERCIAL/STREET NAME
1. Central nervous system depressants (alcohol, sedative–hypnotics, benzodiazepines, barbiturates, flunitrazepam, methaqualone)	Intoxicated behavior with/without odor, staggering or stumbling, "nodding off" at work, slurred speech, dilated pupils, difficulty concentrating	(barbiturates) *Amytal, Nembutal, Seconal, Phenobarbital*: barbs, reds, red birds, phennies, tooies, yellows, yellow jackets (benzodiazapines) *Ativan, Halcion, Librium, Valium, Xanax*: candy, downers, sleeping pills, tranks (flunitrazepam) *Rohypnol*: forget-me pill, Mexican Valium, R2, Roche, roofies, roofinol, rope, rophies (methaqualone) *Quaalude, Sopor, Parest*: ludes, mandrex, quad, quay
2. Central nervous system stimulants (amphetamines, methamphetamine, MDMA, methylphenidate, nicotine)	Excessively active, increased alertness, euphoric, irritable, argumentative, nervous, long periods without eating or sleeping, weight loss	(amphetamine) *Biphetamine, Dexedrine*: bennies, black beauties, crosses, hearts, LA turnaround, speed, truck drivers, uppers (MDMA) Adam, clarity, ecstasy, Eve, lover's speed, peace, STP, X, XTC (methamphetamine) *Desoxyn*: chalk, crank, crystal, fire, glass, go fast, ice, meth, speed (methylphenidate) *Ritalin*: JIF, MPH, R-ball, Skippy, the smart drug, vitamin R (nicotine) cigarettes, cigars, smokeless tobacco, snuff, spit tobacco, bidis, chew
3. Cocaine and crack (also CNS)	Energetic, euphoric, fixed and dilated pupils, relatively quick or slow heart beat, euphoria quickly replaced by anxiety, irritability and/or depression, some times accompanied by hallucinations and paranoid delusions	*Cocaine hydrochloride*: blow, bump, C, candy, Charlie, coke, crack, flake, rock, snow, toot
4. Opiates (codeine, fentanyl, opium, heroin, morphine, oxycodone HCL, hydrocodone bitartrate, acetamethophin)	Euphoric, scars from injecting drugs, fixed and constricted pupils, frequent scratching, loss of appetite (but frequently eat sweets); may have sniffles, red and watering eyes, nausea and vomiting, constipation, and cough until another "fix," lethargic, drowsy, and alternate between dozing and awakening ("nodding")	(codeine) *Empirin with Codeine, Fiorinal with Codeine, Robitussin A-C, Tylenol with Codeine*: Captain Cody, Cody, schoolboy; (with glutethimide) doors & fours, loads, pancakes and syrup (fentanyl) *Actiq, Duragesic, Sublimaze*: Apache, China girl, China white, dance fever, friend, goodfella, jackpot, murder 8, TNT, Tango and Cash (heroin) *diacetylmorphine*: brown sugar, dope, H, horse, junk, skag, skunk, smack, white horse (morphine) *Roxanol, Duramorph*: M, Miss Emma, monkey, white stuff (opium) *laudanum, paregoric*: big O, black stuff, block, gum, hop (oxycodone HCL) *OxyContin*: Oxy, O.C., killer (hydrocodone bitarate, acetametaphine) *Vicodin*: vike, Watson-387
5. Cannabinoid (marijuana, hashish)	In early stages, may be euphoric or anxious and appear animated, speaking rapidly and loudly with bursts of laughter; pupils may be blood-shot; may have distorted perceptions such as increased sense of taste or smell; reduced short-term memory; lowered coordination and increased reaction time; increased appetite; in later stages, may be drowsy	(marijuana) blunt, dope, ganja, grass, herb, joints, Mary Jane, pot, reefer, sinsemilla, skunk, weed (hashish) boom, chronic, gangster, hash, hash oil, hemp

TABLE-9-2 (Continued)

TYPE OF DRUG	TYPICAL INDICATIONS	COMMERCIAL/STREET NAME
6. Hallucinogens (LSD, STP, DOM, mescaline, psilocybin, DTM, DET)	Behavior and mood vary widely, may sit or recline quietly in trancelike stare or appear fearful or even terrified; dilated pupils in some cases; may experience nausea, chills, flushes, dizziness, irregular breathing, extreme lability, sweating, or trembling of hands; may experience changes in sense of sight, hearing, touch, smell, and time	(LSD) lysergic acid diethylamide: acid, blotter, boomers, cubes, microdot, yellow sunshines (mescaline) buttons, cactus, mesc, peyote (psilocybin) magic mushroom, purple passion, shrooms
7. Inhalants and volatile hydrocarbons (chloroform, nail polish remover, metallic paints, carbon tetrachloride, amyl nitrate, butyl, isobutyl, nitrous oxide, lighter fluid, fluoride-based sprays)	Reduced inhibitions, euphoria, dizziness, slurred speech, unsteady gait, giddiness, drowsiness, nystagmus (constant involuntary eye movement), weight loss, depression, memory impairment	Solvents (paint thinners, gasoline, glues), gases (butane, propane, aerosol propellants, nitrous oxide), nitrites (isoamyl, isobutyl, cyclohexyl): laughing gas, poppers, snappers, whippets
8. Anabolic and androgenic steroids	Increased muscle strength and reduced body mass, acne, aggression, changes to libido and mood, competitiveness, and combativeness	*Anadrol, Oxandrin, Durabolin, Depo-Testosterone, Equipoise*: roids, juice

Lowinson, J. H. Ruiz, P., Millman, R. B., & Langrod, J. G. (Eds.). (2004). *Substance Abuse: A Comprehensive Textbook* (4th ed.). Philadelphia, PA: Lippincott, Williams & Wilkins.

National Institute on Drug Abuse. (2008, January 2). *Commonly Abused Drugs*. Retrieved June 30, 2008, from http://www.drugabuse.gov/DrugPages/DrugsofAbuse.html

of specific drugs, common general indications include the following:

- *Changes in attendance at work or school*
- *Decrease in normal capabilities (e.g., work performance, efficiency, habits)*
- *Poor physical appearance, neglect of dress and personal hygiene*
- *Use of sunglasses to conceal dilated or constricted pupils and to compensate for inability to adjust to sunlight*
- *Unusual efforts to cover arms and hide needle marks*
- *Association with known drug users*
- *Involvement in illegal or dangerous activities to secure drugs*

In assessing the possibility of drug abuse, it is important to elicit information not only from the suspected abuser (who may not be a reliable reporter for a number of reasons) but also from people who are familiar with the habits and lifestyle of the individual. Likewise, the social worker should assess problems of drug abuse from a systems perspective. Explorations of family

relationships, for example, often reveal that drug abusers feel alienated from other family members. Moreover, family members often unwittingly contribute to the problems of both alcoholics and drug abusers. Consequently, many professionals regard problems of drug abuse as manifestations of dysfunction within the family system. Keep in mind that drug abusers both affect and are affected by the family system.

Dual Diagnosis: Addictive and Mental Disorders

Because alcohol and other drug abuse problems can co-occur with a variety of health and mental health problems (known as *comorbidity*), accurate assessment is important for proper treatment planning. As Lehman (1996) suggests, several combinations of factors must be taken into account:

- *The type and extent of the substance use disorder*
- *The type of mental disorder(s) and the related severity and duration*
- *The presence of related medical problems*

- *Comorbid disability or other social problems resulting from use, such as correctional system involvement, poverty, or homelessness*

Depending on the combination of factors that affect them, clients may have particular difficulty seeking out and adhering to treatment programs. Furthermore, an understanding of the reciprocal interaction of these factors may affect your assessment and resulting intervention. For example, some psychiatric problems may emerge as a result of substance use (e.g., paranoia or depression). Social problems such as joblessness or incarceration may limit the client's access to needed treatment for substance abuse. Problems such as personality disorders may impede the development of a trusting and effective treatment relationship.

Using Interviewing Skills to Assess Substance Use

Social workers are often involved with substance users before they have actually acknowledged a problem or sought help for it (Barber, 1995). It may be difficult to be nonjudgmental when the user denies that illicit or licit substances are a problem and attempts to conceal the abuse by blaming others, lying, arguing, distorting, attempting to intimidate, diverting the interview focus, or verbally attacking the social worker. Despite these aversive behaviors, the social worker needs to express empathy and sensitivity to the client's feelings, recognizing that such behaviors are often a subterfuge behind which lie embarrassment, hopelessness, shame, ambivalence, and anger.

When asking about alcohol use, be forthright in explaining why you are pursuing that line of questioning. Vague questions tend to support the client's evasions and yield unproductive responses. The questions listed in Table 9-1 should be asked in a direct and compassionate manner. They address the extent and effects of the client's substance use, and the impact on his or her environment.

Assessing Cognitive/ Perceptual Functioning

Assessing how clients perceive their worlds is critically important, because people's perceptions of others, themselves, and events largely determine how they feel and respond to life's experiences in general and to their problematic situations in particular. Recall from Chapter 8 that the meanings or interpretations of events—rather than the events themselves—motivate human beings to behave as they do. Every person's world of experience is unique. Perceptions of identical events or circumstances thus vary widely according to the complex interaction of belief systems, values, attitude, state of mind, and self-concept, all of which in turn are highly idiosyncratic. It follows, then, that to understand and to influence human behavior you must first be knowledgeable about how people think. Our thought patterns are influenced by intellectual functioning, judgment, reality testing, coherence, cognitive flexibility, values, beliefs, self-concept, cultural belief system, and the dynamic interaction among cognitions, emotions, and behaviors that influence social functioning. In the following sections, we briefly consider each of these factors.

Intellectual Functioning

Understanding the intellectual capacity of clients is essential for a variety of reasons. Your assessment of the client's intellectual functioning will allow you to adjust your verbal expressions to a level that the client can readily comprehend, and it will help you in assessing strengths and difficulties, negotiating goals, and planning tasks commensurate with his or her capacities. In most instances, a rough estimate of level of intellectual functioning will suffice. In making this assessment, you may want to consider the client's ability to grasp abstract ideas, to express himself or herself, and to analyze or think logically. Additional criteria include level of educational achievement and vocabulary employed, although these factors must be considered in relationship to the client's previous educational opportunities, primary language, or learning difficulties, because normal or high intellectual capacity may be masked by these and other features.

When clients have marked intellectual limitations, your communications should include easily understood words and avoid abstract explanations. To avoid embarrassment, many people will pretend that they understand when, in fact, they do not. Therefore, you should make keen observations and actively seek feedback to determine whether the client has grasped your intended meaning. You can also assist the client by using multiple, concrete examples to convey complex ideas.

When a client's presentation is inconsistent with his or her known intellectual achievement, it may reveal an area for further investigation. For example, have the client's capacities been affected by illness, medications, a head injury, or the use of substances?

Judgment

Some people who have adequate or even keen intellect may nevertheless encounter severe difficulties in life because they suffer deficiencies in judgment. Clients with poor judgment may get themselves into one jam after another. Examples of problems in judgment include consistently living beyond one's means, becoming involved in "get rich quick" schemes without carefully exploring the possible ramifications, quitting jobs impulsively, leaving small children unattended, moving in with a partner with little knowledge of that person, failing to safeguard or maintain personal property, and squandering resources.

Deficiencies in judgment generally come to light when you explore in detail clients' problems and the patterns surrounding them. You may find that a client acts with little forethought, fails to consider the probable consequences of his or her actions, or engages in wishful thinking that things will somehow magically work out. With other clients, dysfunctional coping patterns may lead predictably to unfavorable outcomes. Because they fail to learn from their past mistakes, these individuals appear to be driven by intense impulses that overpower consideration of the consequences of their actions. Impulse-driven clients may lash out at authority figures, write bad checks, misuse credit cards, or do other things that provide immediate gratification but ultimately lead to loss of jobs, arrest, or other adverse consequences.

Reality Testing

Reality testing is a critical index to a person's mental health. Strong functioning on this dimension means meeting the following criteria:

1. Being properly oriented to time, place, person, and situation
2. Reaching appropriate conclusions about cause-and-effect relationships
3. Perceiving external events and discerning the intentions of others with reasonable accuracy
4. Differentiating one's own thoughts and feelings from those of others

Clients who are markedly disoriented may be severely mentally disturbed, under the influence of drugs, or suffering from a pathological brain syndrome. Disorientation is usually easily identifiable, but when doubt exists, questions about the date, day of the week, current events that are common knowledge, and recent events in the client's life will usually clarify the matter. Clients who are disoriented typically respond inappropriately, sometimes giving bizarre answers. For example, in responding to a question about his daily activities, a recluse reported that he consulted with the White House about foreign policy.

Some clients who do not have thought disorders may still have poor reality testing, choosing to blame circumstances and events rather than take personal responsibility for their actions (Rooney, 1992). For example, one man who stole an automobile externalized responsibility for his behavior by blaming the owner for leaving the keys in the car. Some clients blame their employers for losing their jobs, even though they habitually missed work for invalid reasons. Still others attribute their difficulties to fate, claiming that it decreed them to be losers. Whatever the sources of these problems with reality testing, they serve as impediments to motivation and meaningful change. Conversely, when clients take appropriate responsibility for their actions, that ownership should be considered an area of strength.

Perceptual patterns that involve distortions of external events are fairly common but may cause difficulties, particularly in interpersonal relationships. *Mild distortions* may be associated with stereotypical perceptions (e.g., "All social workers are liberals" or "The only interest men have in women is sexual"). *Moderate distortions* often involve marked misinterpretations of the motives of others and may severely impair interpersonal relationships (e.g., "My boss told me I was doing a good job and that there is an opportunity to be promoted to a job in another department; he's only saying that to get rid of me" or "My wife says she wants to take an evening class, but I know what she really wants . . . to meet other men"). In instances of *extreme distortions*, individuals may have *delusions* or false beliefs—for example, that others plan to harm them. On rare occasions, people suffering delusions may take violent actions to protect themselves from their imagined persecutors.

Dysfunction in reality testing of psychotic proportions is involved when clients "hear" voices or other sounds (*auditory hallucinations*) or see things that are not there (*visual hallucinations*). These individuals lack the capacity to distinguish between thoughts and beliefs that emanate from themselves and those that originate from external sources. As a consequence, they may present a danger to themselves or others when acting in response to such commands. Social workers must be able to recognize such severe cognitive dysfunction and respond with referrals for medication, protection, and/or hospitalization.

Coherence

Social workers occasionally encounter clients who demonstrate major thought disorders, which are characterized by rambling and incoherent speech. For example, successive thoughts may be highly fragmented and disconnected from one another, a phenomenon referred to as *looseness of association* or *derailment* in the thought processes. As Morrison puts it, the practitioner "can understand the sequence of the words, but the direction they take seems to be governed not by logic but by rhymes, puns or other rules that might be apparent to the patient but mean nothing to you" (1995, p. 113). Another form of derailment is *flight of ideas*, in which the client's response seems to "take off" based on a particular word or thought, unrelated to logical progression or the original point of the communication.

These difficulties in coherence may be indicative of mania or thought disorders such as schizophrenia. Incoherence, of course, may also be produced by acute drug intoxication, so practitioners should be careful to rule out this possibility.

Cognitive Flexibility

Receptiveness to new ideas and the ability to analyze many facets of problematic situations are conducive not only to effective problem solving but also to general adaptability. People with cognitive flexibility generally seek to grow, to understand the part they play in their difficulties, and to understand others; these individuals can also ask for assistance without perceiving such a request to be an admission of weakness or failure. Many people, however, are rigid and unyielding in their beliefs, and their inflexibility poses a major obstacle to progress in the helping process.

A common pattern of cognitive inflexibility is thinking in absolute terms (e.g., a person is good or evil, a success or a failure, responsible or irresponsible—there are no in-betweens). People who think this way are prone to criticize others who fail to measure up to their stringent standards. Because they can be difficult to live with, many of these individuals appear at social agencies because of relationship problems, workplace conflict, or parent–child disputes. Improvement often requires helping them examine the destructive impact of their rigidity, broaden their perspectives of themselves and others, and "loosen up" in general.

Negative cognitive sets also include biases and stereotypes that impede relationship building or cooperation with members of certain groups (e.g., authority figures, ethnic groups, and the opposite sex) as individuals.

Severely depressed clients often have another form of "tunnel vision," viewing themselves as helpless or worthless and the future as dismal and hopeless. When they are lost in the depths of illness, these clients may selectively attend to their own negative attributes, have difficulty feeling good about themselves, and struggle with being open to other options.

Values

Values are an integral part of the cognitive-perceptual subsystem, because they strongly influence human behavior and often play a key role in the problems presented for work. For this reason, you should seek to identify your clients' values, assess the role those values play in their difficulties, and consider ways in which clients' values can be deployed to create incentives for change. Your ethical responsibility to respect the client's right to maintain his or her values and to make choices consistent with them requires you to become aware of those values. Because values result from our cultural conditioning, understanding the client's cultural reference group is important, particularly if it differs from your own. For example, traditional Native American values—(1) harmony with nature versus mastery of nature, (2) orientation to the present versus orientation to the present and future, (3) orientation to "being" activity versus orientation to "doing" activity, and (4) primacy of family and group goals versus primacy of individual goals (DuBray, 1985)—would be significant both in assessing Native American clients and in crafting appropriate interventions for their problems. Understanding the individual *within* his or her culture is critical, however, because people adopt values on a continuum, with considerable diversity occurring among people within any given race, faith, culture, or community (Gross, 1995).

Value conflicts often lay at the heart of clients' difficulties—for example, when an individual is torn between a desire for independence on the one hand and loyalty to his or her family on the other hand. Value conflicts may also be central to difficulties between people. Parents and children may disagree about dress, behavior, or responsibilities. Partners may hold different beliefs about how chores should be divided, how finances should be handled, or how they should relate to each person's family of origin.

Being aware of clients' values also aids you in using those values to create incentives for changing dysfunctional behavior—for example, when clients express strong values yet behave in direct opposition to those values. *Cognitive dissonance* may result when clients discover inconsistencies between their values and behaviors. Examining these contradictions can help reveal whether this tension is problematic and self-defeating. As an example, consider an individual coming to terms with his homosexuality within a religious faith that condemns his sexual orientation. Tension, confusion, and distress can result as this client and others attempt to reconcile disparate beliefs. The social worker may help by identifying and labeling the cognitive dissonance and working with the client to reconcile the differences or create options so that they are no longer mutually exclusive.

Examples of questions that will clarify clients' values follow:

- *"You say you believe your parents are old-fashioned about sex. What are your beliefs?"*
- *"If you could be married to an ideal wife, what would she be like?"*
- [*To a couple*]: *"What are your beliefs about how couples should make decisions?"*
- *"So you feel you're not succeeding in life. To you, what does being successful involve?"*

Misconceptions

Cognitive theory holds that beliefs are important mediators of both emotions and actions (Ellis, 1962; Lantz, 1996). It makes sense, then, that mistaken beliefs can be related to problems in functioning. Sometimes, beliefs are not misconceptions, but rather are unhelpful, if accurate, conceptions. Examples of common destructive beliefs and contrasting functional beliefs include: "The world is a dog-eat-dog place; no one really cares about anyone except themselves" versus "There are all kinds of people in the world, including those who are ruthless and those who are caring; I need to seek out the latter and strive to be a caring person myself"; or "All people in authority use their power to exploit and control others" versus "People in authority vary widely—some exploit and control others, while others are benevolent; I must reserve judgment, or I will indiscriminately resent all authority figures."

It is important to identify misconceptions and their sources so as to create a comprehensive assessment. Depending on how central these beliefs are to the client's problems, the goals for work that follow may involve modifying key misconceptions, thereby paving the way to behavioral change. As with other areas, client strengths may derive from the *absence* of misconceptions, and from the ability to accurately, constructively,

or positively perceive and construe events and motivations.

Self-Concept

Convictions, beliefs, and ideas about the self have been generally recognized as one of the most crucial determinants of human behavior. Thus, there are strengths in having good self-esteem and in being realistically aware of one's positive attributes, accomplishments, and potential as well as one's limitations and deficiencies. A healthy person can accept limitations as a natural part of human fallibility without being distressed or discouraged. People with high self-esteem, in fact, can joke about their limitations and failings.

Many people, however, are tormented with feelings of worthlessness, inadequacy, and helplessness. These and similarly self-critical feelings pervade their functioning in diverse negative ways, including the following:

- *Underachieving in life because of imagined deficiencies*
- *Passing up opportunities because of fears of failing*
- *Avoiding social relationships because of fears of being rejected*
- *Permitting oneself to be taken for granted and exploited by others*
- *Excessive drinking or drug use to fortify oneself because of feelings of inadequacy*
- *Devaluing or discrediting one's worthwhile achievements*
- *Failing to defend one's rights*

Often clients will spontaneously discuss how they view themselves, or their description of patterns of difficulty may imply damaged self-concept. An open-ended query, such as "Tell me how you see yourself," will often elicit rich information. Because many people have not actually given much thought to the matter, they may hesitate or appear perplexed. An additional query, such as "Just what comes into your head when you think about the sort of person you are?" is usually all that is needed to prompt the client to respond.

Assessing Emotional Functioning

Emotions are affected by cognitions and powerfully influence behavior. People who seek help often do so because they have experienced strong emotions or a sense that their emotions are out of control. Some clients, for example, are emotionally volatile and engage

Box 9-1 Cognitive or Thought Disorders

As you assess cognitive functioning, you may note signs and symptoms of thought disorders and developmental delays. Three particular disorders to be alert to are mental retardation, schizophrenia, and dementia.

Mental retardation is typically diagnosed in infancy or childhood. It is defined as lower-than-average intelligence and "significant limitations in adaptive functioning in at least two of the following skill areas: communication, self-care, home living, social/interpersonal skills, use of community resources, self-direction, functional academic skills, work, leisure, health and safety" (American Psychiatric Association, 2000, p. 41). General intellectual functioning is appraised using standardized tests, and other measurement instruments may be used to assess the client's adaptive functioning, or ability to meet common life demands. Four levels of mental retardation are distinguished: mild, moderate, severe, and profound.

Schizophrenia is a psychotic disorder that causes marked impairment in social, educational, and occupational functioning. Its onset typically occurs during adolescence or young adulthood, and development of the disorder may be abrupt or gradual. It is signified by a combination of *positive and negative symptoms*. In this context, these terms do not refer to whether something is good or bad, but rather to the presence or absence of normal functions. For example, positive symptoms of schizophrenia "include distortions in thought content (delusions), perception (hallucinations), language and thought processes (disorganized speech), and self-monitoring of behavior (grossly disorganized or catatonic behavior)" (American Psychiatric Association, 2000, p. 299). Negative symptoms include flattened affect, restricted speech, and *avolition*, or limited initiation of goal-directed behavior.

Dementia is characterized by "multiple cognitive deficits that include memory impairment and at least one of the following: *aphasia* (deterioration in language functioning), *apraxia* (difficulty with motor activities), *agnosia* (failure to recognize familiar objects), or *disturbance in executive functioning* (abstract thinking, and planning, sequencing, and ceasing complex activities)" (American Psychiatric Association, 2000, p. 148). These deficits must be of a sufficient severity to affect one's daily functioning to warrant a diagnosis of dementia.

Treatment of individuals with these diagnoses is specialized and varied, but may include use of medication as well as vocational, residential, and case management services. Understanding the features of these and other cognitive/thought disorders will assist you in better understanding clients, in planning appropriate treatment, and in understanding how your role with clients meshes with that of other service providers.

in aggressive behavior while in the heat of anger. Others are emotionally unstable, struggling to stay afloat in a turbulent sea of feelings. Some people become emotionally distraught as the result of stress associated with the death of a loved one, divorce, severe disappointment, or another blow to self-esteem. Still others are pulled in different directions by opposing feelings and seek help to resolve their emotional dilemmas. To assist you in assessing emotional functioning, the following sections examine vital aspects of this dimension and the related terms and concepts.

Emotional Control

People vary widely in the degree of control they exercise over their emotions, ranging from *emotional constriction* to *emotional excesses*. Individuals who are experiencing constriction may appear unexpressive and withholding in relationships. Because they are out of touch with their emotions, they do not appear to permit themselves to feel joy, hurt, enthusiasm, vulnerability, and other emotions that might otherwise invest life with zest and meaning. These individuals may be comfortable intellectualizing but retreat from expressing or discussing feelings. They often favorably impress others with their intellectual styles, but sometimes have difficulties maintaining close relationships because their emotional detachment thwarts them from fulfilling the needs of others for intimacy and emotional stimulation.

People with emotional excesses may have a "short fuse," losing control and reacting intensely to even mild provocations. This behavior may involve rages and escalate to interpersonal violence. Excesses can also include other emotions such as irritability, crying, panic, despondency, helplessness, or giddiness. The key in assessing whether the emotional response is excessive entails determining whether it is appropriate and proportionate to the stimulus.

Your assessment may stem from your personal observation of the client, feedback from collateral contacts, or the client's own report of his or her response to a situation. As always, your appraisal of the appropriateness of the response must factor in the client's culture and the nature of his or her relationship with you. Both may lead you to misjudge the client's normal emotional response and what is considered "appropriate" emotional regulation.

Cultures vary widely in their approved patterns of emotional expression.[3] Nevertheless, emotional health in any culture shares one criterion: It means having control over the emotions to the extent that one is not overwhelmed by them. Emotionally healthy persons also enjoy the freedom of experiencing and expressing emotions appropriately. Likewise, strengths include the ability to bear painful emotions without denying or masking feelings or being incapacitated by them. Emotionally healthy persons are able to discern the emotional states of others, empathize, and discuss painful emotions openly without feeling unduly uncomfortable—recognizing, of course, that a certain amount of discomfort is natural. Finally, the ability to mutually share deeply personal feelings in intimate relationships is also considered an asset.

Range of Emotions

Another aspect of emotional functioning involves the ability to experience and to express a wide range of emotions that befits the vast array of situations that humans encounter. Some individuals' emotional experiencing remains confined to a limited range, which often causes interpersonal difficulties. For example, if one partner has difficulty expressing tender emotions, the other partner may feel rejected, insecure, or deprived of deserved affection.

Some individuals are unable to feel joy or to express many pleasurable emotions, a dysfunction referred to as *anhedonia*. Still others have been conditioned to block out their angry feelings, blame themselves, or placate others when friction develops in relationships. Because of this blocking of natural emotions, they may experience extreme tension or physiological symptoms such as asthma, colitis, and headaches when they face situations that normally would engender anger or sadness. Finally, some people, to protect themselves from unbearable emotions, develop psychic mechanisms early in life that block them from experiencing rejection, loneliness, and hurt. Often this blockage is reflected by a compensatory facade of toughness and indifference, combined with verbal expressions such as "I don't need anyone" and "No one can hurt me." Whatever its source, a blocked or limited range of emotions may affect the client's difficulties and thus represent a goal for work.

Emotionally healthy people experience the full gamut of human emotions within normal limits of intensity and duration. The capacity to experience joy, grief, exhilaration, disappointment, and the rest of the full spectrum of emotions is, therefore, an area of strength.

Appropriateness of Affect

Direct observation of clients' affect (emotionality) usually reveals valuable information about their emotional functioning. Some anxiety or mild apprehension is natural in initial sessions (especially for involuntary clients and those referred by others), as contrasted to intense apprehension and tension at one extreme or complete relaxation at the other. Healthy functioning involves spontaneously experiencing and expressing emotion appropriate to the context and the material being discussed. The ability to laugh, to cry, and to express hurt, discouragement, anger, and pleasure when these feelings match the mood of the session constitutes an area of strength. Such spontaneity indicates that clients are in touch with their emotions and can express them appropriately.

Inordinate apprehension—often demonstrated by muscle tension, constant fidgeting or shifts in posture, hand wringing, lip-biting, and similar behaviors— usually indicates that a client is fearful, suspicious, or exceptionally uncomfortable in unfamiliar interpersonal situations. Such extreme tension may be expected in involuntary situations. In other cases, it may be characteristic of a client's demeanor in other contexts.

Clients who appear completely relaxed and express themselves freely in a circumstance that would normally evoke apprehension or anxiety may reflect a denial of a problem and or a lack of motivation to engage in the problem-solving process. Further, a charming demeanor may reflect the client's skill in projecting a favorable image when it is advantageous to do so. In some situations, such as in sales or promotional work, this kind of charm may be an asset; in other circumstances, it may be a coping style developed to conceal the individual's insecurity, self-centeredness, and manipulation or exploitation of others.

Emotional blunting is what the term suggests: a muffled or apathetic response to material that would typically evoke a stronger response (e.g., happiness, despair, anger). For example, emotionally blunted clients may discuss, in a detached and matter-of-fact manner, traumatic life events or conditions such as the murder of one parent by another, deprivation, or physical and/or sexual abuse. Emotional blunting can be indicative of a severe mental disorder, a sign of drug misuse, or a side effect of medications, so it always warrants special attention.

Inappropriate affect can also appear in other forms, such as laughing when discussing a painful event (gallows laughter) or smiling constantly regardless of what is being discussed. Elation or euphoria that is incongruent with the individual's life situation, combined with constant and rapid shifts from one topic to another (flight of ideas), irritability, expansive ideas, and constant motion, also suggests mania.

In transcultural work, appropriateness of affect must be considered in light of cultural differences. According to Lum (1996), minority clients may feel uncomfortable with nonminority social workers but mask their emotions as a protective measure, or they may control painful emotions according to culturally prescribed norms. Measures to assure appropriate interpretation of client affect include understanding the features of the client's culture, consulting others familiar with the culture or the client, and evaluating the client's current presentation with his or her demeanor in the past.

Affective Disorders

The DSM-IV-TR (American Psychiatric Association, 2000) contains extensive information on the criteria for diagnosing affective disorders (i.e., disorders of mood). Of particular importance for the beginning direct social worker are *bipolar disorders* (known formerly as manic-depressive illness) and *unipolar/major affective disorders* (such as severe depression). Treatment of clients with these diagnoses generally includes medication (often with concurrent cognitive or interpersonal psychotherapy). These diagnoses provide direction in treatment planning. Moreover, they can often be linked to suicidal ideation and other serious risk factors.

Bipolar Disorder

The dominant feature of bipolar disorder is the presence of manic episodes (mania) with intervening periods of depression. Among the symptoms of mania are "a distinct period of abnormally and persistently elevated, expansive or irritable mood ..." (American Psychiatric Association, 2000, p. 362) and at least three of the following:

- *Inflated self-esteem or grandiosity*
- *Decreased need for sleep*
- *More talkative than usual or pressure to keep talking*
- *Flight of ideas or subjective experience that thoughts are racing*

- *Distractibility*
- *Increase in goal-directed activity (either socially, at work or school, or sexually) or psychomotor agitation*
- *Excessive involvement in pleasurable activities with a high potential for painful consequences, such as unrestrained buying sprees, sexual indiscretions, or foolish business investments*

Full-blown manic episodes require that symptoms be sufficiently severe to cause marked impairment in job performance or relationships, or to necessitate hospitalization to protect patients or others from harm.

If exploration seems to indicate a client has the disorder, immediate psychiatric consultation is needed for two reasons: (1) to determine whether hospitalization is needed and (2) to determine the need for medication. Bipolar disorder is biogenetic, and various compounds containing lithium carbonate may produce remarkable results in stabilizing and maintaining affected individuals. Close medical supervision is required, however, because commonly used medications for this disorder have a relatively narrow margin of safety.

Major Depressive Disorder

Major depressive disorder, in which affected individuals experience recurrent episodes of depressed mood, is far more common than bipolar disorder. Major depression differs from the "blues" in that *dysphoria* (painful emotions) and the absence of pleasure in previously enjoyable activities (anhedonia) are present. The painful emotions commonly are related to anxiety, mental anguish, an extreme sense of guilt (often over what appear to be relatively minor offenses), and restlessness (agitation).

To be assigned a diagnosis of major depressive episode, a person must have evidenced depressed mood and loss of interest or pleasure as well as at least five of the following nine symptoms for at least 2 weeks (American Psychiatric Association, 2000, pp. 375–376):

- *Depressed mood for most of the day, nearly every day*
- *Markedly diminished interest or pleasure in all, or almost all, activities*
- *Significant weight loss or weight gain when not dieting or decrease or increase in appetite*
- *Insomnia or hypersomnia*
- *Psychomotor agitation or retardation*
- *Fatigue or loss of energy*
- *Feelings of worthlessness, or excessive or inappropriate guilt*

- *Diminished ability to think or concentrate, or indecisiveness*
- *Recurrent thoughts of death or suicidal ideation or attempts*

As noted in Chapter 8, a number of scales are available to assess the presence and degree of depression. When assessment reveals that clients are moderately or severely depressed, psychiatric consultation is indicated to determine the need for medication and/or hospitalization. Antidepressant medications have proven to be effective in accelerating recovery from depression and work synergistically with cognitive or interpersonal psychotherapy.[4]

In assessing depression, it is important to identify which factors precipitated the depressive episode. If an important loss or series of losses has occurred, it may be difficult to differentiate between depression and complicated bereavement. While depression and mourning may share certain characteristics such as intense sadness and sleep and appetite disturbances, grief reactions generally do not include the diminished self-esteem and guilt often observed in depression. "That is, the people who have lost someone do not regard themselves less because of such a loss or if they do, it tends to be only for a brief time. And if the survivors of the deceased experience guilt, it is usually guilt associated with some specific aspect of the loss rather than a general, overall sense of culpability" (Worden, 1991, p. 30).

Suicidal Risk

Not all individuals with depressive symptoms are suicidal and not all suicidal individuals are depressed. Nevertheless, whenever clients exhibit depressive symptoms or hopelessness, it is critical to evaluate suicidal risk so that precautionary measures can be taken when indicated. With adults, the following factors are associated with high risk of suicide:

- *Feelings of despair and hopelessness*
- *Previous suicidal attempts*
- *Concrete, available, and lethal plans to commit suicide (when, where, and how)*
- *Family history of suicide*
- *Perseveration about suicide*
- *Lack of support systems, and other forms of isolation*
- *Feelings of worthlessness*
- *Belief that others would be better off if the client were dead*
- *Advanced age (especially for white males)*
- *Substance abuse*

When a client indicates, directly or indirectly, that he or she may be considering suicide, it is essential that you address those concerns through careful and direct questioning. You may begin by stating, "You sound pretty hopeless right now; I wonder if you might also be thinking of harming yourself?" or "When you say 'They'll be sorry' when you're gone, I wonder if that means you're thinking of committing suicide?" An affirmative answer to these probes should be followed with a frank and calm discussion of the client's thoughts about suicide. Has the client considered how he or she might do it? When? What means would be used? Are those means accessible? In asking these questions, you are trying to determine not only the lethality of the client's plans but also the specificity. If a client has a well-thought-out plan in mind, the risk of suicide is potentially greater. An understanding of the client's history, especially with regard to the risk factors mentioned and previous suicide attempts, will also help you decide the degree of danger and the level of intervention required. In addition, standardized scales can be used to evaluate suicidal risk.[5]

Ideas in Action

In the videotaped interviews with Josephine, the worker, Kathy, inquires about the recent death of Josephine's husband. Noting signs of grief and depression, Kathy probes further about past coping, sleep patterns, eating, weight loss, substance use, energy level, hobbies and interests, social contacts, and mood. She also asks the client to walk her through a typical day. Ultimately, she explains and administers a brief depression inventory, the Geriatric Depression Scale (GDS) (Yesavage et al., 1983), and provides a booklet about grief. In the follow-up session, Kathy educates Josephine about the phases of grief and describes the results of the depression evaluation, with a typical score at 5 and Josephine's score at 12 ("off the chart"). As a result, Kathy recommends consideration of medication, a physician consultation regarding insomnia, and counseling, from a widow-to-widow program on grief or from a professional.

When the client's responses indicate a potentially lethal attempt, it is appropriate to mobilize client support systems and arrange for psychiatric evaluation and/or hospitalization if needed. Such steps provide a measure of security for the client who may feel unable to control his or her impulses or who may become overwhelmed with despair.

Depression and Suicidal Risk with Children and Adolescents

Children and adolescents may experience depression just as adults do, and suicide can be a risk with these groups. It is estimated that 500,000 young people between ages 15 and 24 attempt suicide each year and nearly 5,000 children and youth (age 5 to 24) kill themselves each year. In fact, suicide is the third leading cause of death for those in the 15-to 24–year-old age bracket (CDC, 2005; McIntosh, 2003). The World Health Organization (WHO) reports global statistics, noting that in the past 45 years suicide rates have grown 60% worldwide and that suicide is the third leading cause of death for those between the ages of 15 and 44 (WHO, 2008).

Clearly, it is important to recognize the symptoms of depression in adolescents and the behavioral manifestations that may be reported by peers, siblings, parents, or teachers. Common symptoms of depression in adolescents include the following:

- *Loss of interest in activities the youth previously enjoyed (anhedonia)*
- *Depressed mood*
- *Significant weight loss or gain*
- *Insomnia or hypersomnia*
- *Psychomotor agitation or retardation*
- *Fatigue or loss of energy*
- *Feelings of hopelessness, worthlessness, guilt, and self-reproach*
- *Indecisiveness or decreased ability to concentrate*
- *Suicide ideation, threats, or attempts*
- *Recurring thoughts of death*

Childhood depression does not differ markedly from depression in adolescence; the behaviors manifested and the intensity of feelings are similar, once developmental differences are taken into consideration (Wenar, 1994; Birmaher et al., 2004). One major difference between childhood and adolescent depression appears when comparing prevalence rates between the sexes. The prevalence of depression is approximately the same in boys and girls in middle childhood, but

beginning in adolescence twice as many females suffer from depression as males (Kauffman, 1997; Hankin et al., 1998). Also, adolescent girls diagnosed with depression report more feelings of anxiety and inadequacy in middle childhood, whereas adolescent boys report more aggressive and antisocial feelings (Wenar, 1994; Leadbeater, Kupermic, Blatt, & Hertzog, 1999).

Because parents, coaches, and friends often do not realize the child or adolescent is depressed, it is important to alert them to the following potentially troublesome symptoms (American Association of Suicidology, 2004; Gold, 1986):

- *Deterioration in personal habits*
- *Decline in school achievement*
- *Marked increase in sadness, moodiness, and sudden tearful reactions*
- *Loss of appetite*
- *Use of drugs or alcohol*
- *Talk of death or dying (even in a joking manner)*
- *Withdrawal from friends and family*
- *Making final arrangements, such as giving away valued possessions*
- *Sudden or unexplained departure from past behaviors (from shy to thrill seeking or from outgoing to sullen and withdrawn)*

Specific subgroups may experience additional, unique risk factors related to their particular gender, race or ethnicity, or sexual orientation and the ways that these interact with the environments around them (Macgowan, 2004). Given the tempestuousness typical of adolescence, it may be difficult to distinguish any warning signs from normative actions and behavior. Cautious practice would suggest taking changes such as these seriously, rather than minimizing them or writing them off as "typical teen behavior." Whether or not they are indicative of depression, changes in behavior and patterns such as these indicate that something is going on that is worthy of adult attention, as well as professional consultation and evaluation.

Suicidal risk is highest when the adolescent, in addition to exhibiting the aforementioned symptoms of severe depression, shows feelings of hopelessness, has recently experienced a death of a loved one, has severe conflict with parents, has lost a close relationship with a key peer or a love interest, and lacks a support system. Brent and colleagues indicate that "interpersonal conflict, especially with parents, is one of the most commonly reported precipitants for completed and attempted suicides" (1993, p. 185). Other studies have indicated that moderate to heavy drinking or drug abuse is implicated in as many as 50% of adolescent suicides (Fowler, Rich, & Young, 1986; Rowan, 2001).

While completed suicides and suicide attempts are more common among adolescents (with adolescent males completing more suicides and adolescent females attempting more suicides), the number of younger children completing and attempting suicide is increasing (Kauffman, 1997). Therefore, it is important to be cognizant of depressed behavior and signs of suicide ideation in children as well as adolescents. Warning signs of suicide ideation in younger children are similar to those discussed for adolescents, albeit translated to the appropriate developmental level. When faced with a young client who is considering suicide, social workers should use the same lethality assessment questions discussed earlier for work with adults. In addition, assessment tools geared to evaluating suicide risk in children and adolescents are available, such as the Children's Depression Scale (Kovacs, 1992) and the Johns Hopkins Depression Scale (Joshi, Capozzoli, & Coyle, 1990).

Depression and Suicidal Risk with Older Adults

In addition to the signs noted above for depression and suicidal ideation, older adults warrant particular attention in screening for these conditions. Approximately 20% of all suicides in the USA are committed by the elderly, though they constitute only 10% of the population, and white males over the age of 65 are more likely to commit suicide than any other age group (Brown, Bruce, Pearson, & the PROSPECT Study Group, 2001; Hester, 2004; Yin, 2006). Particular risk factors for older persons include isolation, ill health, hopelessness, and functional and social losses. Further, older clients may be reluctant to appear for mental health services and psychiatric conditions may be overlooked by primary care providers and loved ones, or minimized as typical features of aging. Commonly used instruments to assess depression, such as the Geriatric Depression Scale, may provide insufficient screening for suicidal ideation (Heisel, Flett, Duberstein, & Lyness, 2005). The assessment of suicidality in elder clients requires particular discernment to distinguish among suicidal intent and the awareness of morality or preparedness for death which may be hallmarks of that developmental phase (Heisel & Flett, 2006).

Zivin and Kales (2008) point out that the approach clinicians take to explain depression and antidepressants to patients can have a significant impact on their adherence to their medication regime. However, they also state that doctors often lack the time or training to give effective explanations. Zivin and Kales also note that though anti-depressants can be effective in treating depression in older adults, 40 to 75 percent do not take their anti-depressants as directed or at all. They argue that older adults who present as treatment-resistant may instead simply be non-compliant with their anti-depressants. Elders may intentionally not take their anti-depressants out of fear of becoming dependant, over concerns that the medicine will prevent them from feeling natural sadness, or because they do not recognize their depression as a medical condition. Other seniors may forget to take their anti-depressants or misunderstand dosage instructions, especially if they have cognitive impairment and no caregiver to assist them with medications. Some seniors are reluctant to take their anti-depressants because they fear they will negatively interact with other medications. Other risk factors for being non-compliant with medications include taking three or more other medications, having diagnoses of both depression and anxiety, dependence on substances, having a caregiver who does not believe depression is a medical condition, lack of social support, and an inability to pay for medications. While spirituality can often aid elders in dealing with mental health issues, at times faith can have a negative effect on depression. Some elders may feel that they do not need medical treatment because God can heal them and others might interpret their depression as a punishment from God (Zivin & Kales, 2008).[6]

Assessing Behavioral Functioning

In direct social work practice, change efforts frequently target behavioral patterns that impair the client's social functioning. As you assess behavior, it is important to keep in mind that one person's behavior does not influence another person's behavior in simple linear fashion. Rather, a circular process takes place, in which the behavior of all participants reciprocally affects and shapes the behavior of other participants.

Because behavioral change is commonly the focus of social work interventions, you must be skillful in discerning and assessing both dysfunctional and functional patterns of behavior. In individual sessions, you can directly observe clients' social and communication patterns as well as some personal habits and traits. In conjoint interviews and group sessions, you can observe these behavioral patterns as well as the effects that these actions have on others.

In assessing behavior, it is helpful to think of problems as consisting of excesses or deficiencies. For excesses-related problems, interventions aim to *diminish* or *eliminate* the behaviors, such as temper outbursts, too much talking, arguing, competition, and consumptive excesses (e.g., food, alcohol, sex, gambling, or shopping). For behavioral deficiencies, when assessment reveals the absence of needed skills, interventions aim to help clients *acquire* the skills and behaviors to function more effectively. For example, a client's behavioral repertoire may not include skills in expressing feelings directly, engaging in social conversation, listening to others, solving problems, managing finances, planning nutritional meals, being a responsive sexual partner, or handling conflict.

In addition to identifying dysfunctional behavioral patterns, it is important to be aware of those behaviors that are effective and represent strengths. To assist you in assessing both dysfunctional and functional patterns of behavior, Table 9-3 lists numerous patterns

TABLE-9-3 BEHAVIORAL PATTERNS

DIMENSIONS OF BEHAVIOR	DYSFUNCTIONAL PATTERNS	FUNCTIONAL PATTERNS (STRENGTHS)
Power/control	Autocratic, overbearing, aggressive, ruthless, demanding, domineering, controlling, passive submissive; excludes others from decision making	Democratic, cooperative, assertive; includes others in decision making, stands up for own rights
Nurturance/support	Self-centered, critical, rejecting, withholding, demeaning, distant, punitive, fault-finding, self-serving, insensitive to or unconcerned about others	Caring, approving, giving, empathic, encouraging, patient, generous, altruistic, warm, accepting, supportive, interested in others
Responsibility	Undependable, erratic; avoids responsibility, places pleasure before responsibility, externalizes responsibility for problems, neglects maintenance of personal property	Dependable, steady, consistent, reliable, follows through, accepts responsibility, owns part in problems, maintains personal property
Social skills	Abrasive, caustic, irritable, insensitive, aloof, reclusive, sarcastic, querulous, withdrawn, self-conscious, ingratiating, lacks social delicacy	Outgoing, poised, personable, verbally fluent, sociable, witty, courteous, engaging, cooperative, assertive, spontaneous, respectful to others, sensitive to feelings of others, has sense of propriety
Coping patterns	Rigid, impulsive, rebellious; avoids facing problems, uses alcohol or drugs when under stress, becomes panicky, lashes out at others, sulks	Flexible; faces problems, considers and weighs alternatives, anticipates consequences, maintains equilibrium, seeks growth, consults others for suggestions, negotiates and compromises
Personal habits	Disorganized, dilatory, devious, dishonest, compulsive, overly fastidious, impulsive, manifests poor personal hygiene, has consumption excesses, has irritating mannerisms	Planful, organized, flexible, clean, efficient, patient, self-disciplined, well groomed, honest, open, sincere, temperate, considerate, even dispositioned, punctual
Communication	Mumbles, complains excessively, nags, talks excessively, interrupts others, tunes others out, stammers, yells when angry, withholds views, defensive, monotonic, argumentative, taciturn, verbally abusive	Listens attentively, speaks fluently, expresses views, shares feelings, uses feedback, expresses self spontaneously, considers others' viewpoints, speaks audibly and within tolerable limits
Accomplishment	Unmotivated, aimless, nonproductive, easily discouraged, easily distracted, underachieving, lacks initiative, seldom completes endeavors, workaholic, slave to work	Ambitious, industrious, self-starting, independent, resourceful, persevering, successful in endeavors, seeks to advance or improve situations
Affectionate/sexual	Unaffectionate, reserved, distant, sexually inhibited, promiscuous, lacking sexual desire, engages in deviant sexual behaviour	Warm, loving, affectionate, demonstrative, sexually responsive (appropriately)

of individual behavior. The behavioral categories in Table 9-3 do not include dysfunctional patterns of interaction between two or more persons in couples, family, and group contexts, as these are addressed in later chapters in this book. Instead, the list focuses on those patterns that most frequently create interpersonal difficulties.

As you review Table 9-3, you may question whether some of the patterns are functional or dysfunctional. This determination, of course, depends on the situational context within which the behavior occurs. Aggressive behavior may serve a self-protective function in a hostile environment but may be dysfunctional in family relationships or in the workplace. Your evaluation, then, must take context into account, and consider the effect of the behavior on the client's environment and success in functioning.

Note that Table 9-3 includes many adjectives and verbs that are very general and are subject to different interpretations. In assessing behavior, it is vital to specify actual problem behaviors. For example, rather than assess a client's behavior as "abrasive," a social worker might describe the behaviors leading to that conclusion—"the client constantly interrupts his fellow workers, insults them by telling them they are misinformed, and boasts about his own knowledge and achievements." It is easier for you and the client to focus your change efforts when detrimental behavior is specified and operationalized.

An adequate assessment of behavior, of course, goes beyond merely identifying dysfunctional behaviors. You must also determine the antecedents of behaviors, when, where, and how frequently they occur, and identify the consequences of the behaviors. Further, you should explore thoughts that precede, accompany, and follow the behavior, as well as the nature of and intensity of emotions associated with the behavior.

Assessing Motivation

As introduced in Chapter 8, evaluating and enhancing client motivation are integral parts of the assessment process. When working with family members or groups, social workers are likely to encounter a range of motivation levels within a single client system. Clients who do not believe that they can influence their environments may demonstrate a kind of *learned helplessness*, a passive resignation that their lives are out of their hands. Others may be at different phases in their readiness to change. Prochaska and DiClemente (1986)

suggest a five-stage model for change: *precontemplation, contemplation, determination, action*, and *maintenance*. The initial stage is characterized by a lack of awareness of the need for change. In the contemplation stage, the client recognizes his or her problem and the consequences that result. In the determination phase, the client is committed to action and works with the clinician to develop a plan for change. Action and maintenance implement the changes identified and take steps to avoid problem recurrence.

To assess motivation, the social worker needs to understand the person, his or her perception of the environment, and the process by which he or she has decided to seek help. Motivation, of course, is a dynamic force that is strongly influenced by ongoing interaction with the environment, including interaction with the social worker. *Motivational interviewing* is a specialized, person-centered method for addressing ambivalence and enhancing motivation (Moyers & Rollnick, 2002). In this framework, client-worker interactions are dominated by OARS, an acronym for **o**pen-ended questions, **a**ffirmations, **r**eflective listening, and **s**ummarizing. Motivational interviewing also employs specific attitudes and techniques to reduce and defuse resistance. Motivation is enhanced by developing and highlighting discrepancies, for example, within a client's statements or between the client's current situation and the one he or she aspires to (Wagner & Conners, 2008).

Assessing Environmental Systems

After evaluating the history and pattern of the presenting problem and various facets of individual functioning, the social worker must assess the client in the context of his or her environment. In this, the assessment focuses on the *transactions* between the two, or the *goodness of fit* between the person and his or her environment. Problem-solving efforts may be directed toward assisting people to adapt to their environments (e.g., training them in interpersonal skills), altering environments to more adequately meet the needs of clients (e.g., enhancing both the attractiveness of a nursing home and the quality of its activities), or a combination of the two (e.g., enhancing the interpersonal skills of a withdrawn, chronically ill person and moving that person to a more stimulating environment). This part of assessment, then, goes beyond the evaluation of resources described in Chapter 8 to take a holistic view of the client's environment and examines the adequacy of various aspects of the environment to meet the client's needs. The concepts of affordability, availability, and accessibility (introduced earlier in this chapter in regard to health care) provide a useful framework for examining transactions with other facets of the environment and targeting the nature of strengths and barriers in those transactions.

In assessing environments, you should give the highest priority to those aspects that are most salient to the client's individual situation. The adequacy of the environment depends on the client's life stage, physical and mental health, interests, aspirations, and other resources. For example, a family may not be concerned about living in a highly polluted area unless one of the children suffers from asthma that is exacerbated by the physical environment. Another family may not worry about the availability of day treatment programs for an adult child with mental retardation until a crisis (e.g., death of a parent or need to return to work) forces them to look outside the family for accessible, affordable services.

You should tailor your assessments of clients' environments to their varied life situations, weighing the individual's unique needs against the availability of essential resources and opportunities within their environments. In addition to noting the limitations or problems posed by inadequate physical or social environments, acknowledge the strengths at play in the client's life—the importance of a stable, accessible, affordable residence or the value of a support system that mobilizes in times of trouble.

The following list describes basic environmental needs; you can employ this list in evaluating the adequacy of your client's environments:

1. A physical environment that is adequate, is stable, and fosters the client's health and safety (this includes housing as well as surroundings that are free of toxins and other health risks)
2. Adequate social support systems (e.g., family, relatives, friends, neighbors, organized groups)
3. Affiliation with a meaningful and responsive faith community
4. Access to timely, appropriate, affordable health care (including vaccinations, physicians, dentists, medications, and nursing homes)
5. Access to safe, reliable, affordable child and elder care services
6. Access to recreational facilities
7. Transportation—to work, socialize, utilize resources, and exercise rights as a citizen

8. Adequate housing that provides ample space, sanitation, privacy, and safety from hazards and pollution (both air and noise)
9. Adequate police and fire protection and a reasonable degree of security
10. Safe and healthful work conditions
11. Adequate financial resources to purchase essential resources
12. Adequate nutritional intake
13. Predictable living arrangements with caring others (especially for children)
14. Opportunities for education and self-fulfillment
15. Access to legal assistance
16. Employment opportunities

We will address the first three areas—physical environment, social support systems, and faith community—in depth, in light of their particular importance for client functioning. This discussion may also help you to generalize some of the complexities of environmental assessment to the other 13 areas.

Physical Environment

Physical environment refers to the stability and adequacy of one's physical surroundings and whether the environment fosters or jeopardizes the client's health and safety. A safe environment is free of threats such as personal or property crimes. Assessing health and safety factors includes considering sanitation, space, and heat. Extended families may be crammed into small homes or apartments without adequate beds and bedding, homes may not be designed for running water or indoor toilets, or access to water may be broken or shut off. Inadequate heat or air conditioning can exacerbate existing health conditions and lead to danger during periods of bad weather. Further, families may take steps to heat their residences (such as with ovens or makeshift fires) that can create further health dangers. Sanitation may be compromised by insect or rodent infestations or by owner or landlord negligence in conforming to building standards and maintaining plumbing. The home may be located in areas with exposure to toxic materials or poor air quality.

For an elderly client, an assessment of the physical environment should also consider whether the person's living situation meets the client's health and safety needs (Gallo et al., 2005; Rauch, 1993). If an elderly person lives alone, does the home have adequate resources for the individual to meet his or her functional needs? Can the client use bathroom and kitchen appliances to conduct his or her daily activities? Does clutter contribute to the client's confusion or risk (e.g., not being able to find bills or stumbling over stacked newspapers)? Is the home a safe environment, or do some aspects of the building (e.g., stairs or loose carpeting) pose a danger to less mobile clients? If the client resides in an institution, are there mementos of home and personal items that bring comfort to the individual? Tools described in Chapter 8, such as the Instrumental Activities of Daily Living Screen (Gallo, 2005) and Direct Assessment of Functioning Scale (DAFS) (Lowenstein et al., 1989) can assess functional ability, screen for and address risk factors, and evaluate changes in functioning.

When the environment poses dangers to clients or exacerbates other problems, steps must be taken to improve living conditions. Because of the geographic ties and the scarcity of adequate low-cost housing, moving to a better neighborhood or a safer home may not be feasible. Some groups, such as the elderly, may qualify for subsidized housing facilities, which provide both adequate housing and social opportunities. You may also help clients to access home improvement, heating assistance, and other programs to enhance their living conditions. When other parties are responsible for detrimental environmental conditions, social workers should assist clients in undertaking advocacy actions to address these problems or in organizing with other neighbors to lobby for change and develop "block watch" or other mutual aid services.

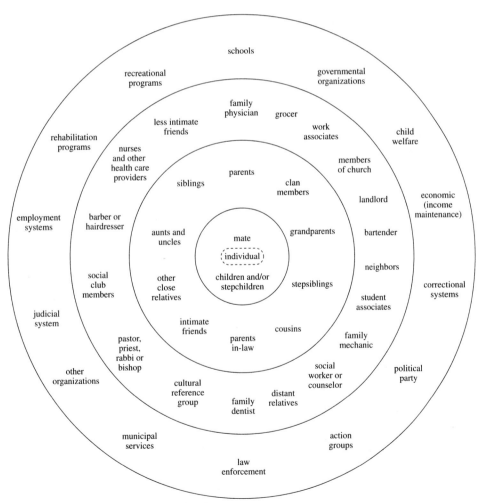

FIG-9-2 Diagram of Ecological Social Systems

Social Support Systems

Embodied in the earlier list of resources are social systems that provide needed goods and services. Diverse social support systems either are part of the problem configuration or represent resources needed to improve the client's quality of life. To enable you to identify pertinent social systems, Figure 9-2 depicts interrelationships between individuals and families and other systems (Hartman, 1994).

Systems that are central in a person's life appear in the center of the diagram in Figure 9-2. These systems typically play key roles as both sources of difficulties and resources that may be tapped or modified in problem solving. Moving from the center to the periphery in the areas encompassed by the concentric circles are systems that are progressively farther removed from individuals and their families. There are exceptions, of course, such as when an individual feels closer to an intimate friend or a pastor than to family members. Moreover, if clients' situations require frequent contacts with institutions or organizations (e.g., child protective services, income maintenance programs, and judicial systems), those institutions will no longer occupy a peripheral position because of how dramatically they affect individuals and families at such times. The intensity of affiliation with extended family or kinship networks may vary by cultural group and reflect the effects of migration and cultural dislocation (Jilek, 1982; Kumabe et al., 1985; Mwanza, 1990; Ponce, 1980; Sotomayor, 1991; Sue, 1981). Reciprocal interactions thus change across time, and diagrams depicting these interactions should be viewed as snapshots that remain accurate only within limited time frames.

The challenge in diagramming clients' social networks is to include the salient boundaries of the clients' situation and to specify how the systems interact, fail to interact, or are needed to interact in response to clients' needs. One useful tool is the *eco-map*, which identifies and organizes relevant environmental factors outside of the individual or family context. Eco-maps are useful in clarifying the supports and stresses in the client's environment, revealing patterns such as social isolation, conflicts, or unresponsive social systems. They also show the direction in which resources flow (for example, if the client gives but does not receive support).

The eco-map can be completed by the worker following discussion with the client or in tandem with the client (Strom-Gottfried, 1999b). In it, the client system (individual, couple, or family) are in the middle

circle and the systems relevant to their lives appear in the surrounding circles. The nature of positive interactions, negative interactions, or needed resources can be depicted by using colored lines to connect the individual or other family members to pertinent systems, where different colors represent positive, negative, or needed connections and interactions with those systems. If colored lines do not appeal to you, then you can use different types of lines—single, double, broken, wavy, dotted, or cross-hatched—to characterize the relationships and the flow of resources among the systems.

Social support systems (SSSs) are increasingly recognized as playing a crucial role in determining the level of social functioning. Theorists have long recognized the critical importance of a nurturing environment to healthy development of infants and children, but it is now clear that adults also have vital needs that can be met only through affiliation with supportive systems. What benefits accrue from involvement with SSSs?

1. Attachment, provided by close relationships that give a sense of security and sense of belonging
2. Social integration, provided by memberships in a network of people who share interests and values
3. The opportunity to nurture others, which provides incentive to endure in the face of adversity
4. Physical care when persons are unable to care for themselves due to illness, incapacity, or severe disability
5. Validation of personal worth (which promotes self-esteem), provided by family and colleagues
6. A sense of reliable alliance, provided primarily by kin
7. Guidance, child care, financial aid, and other assistance in coping with difficulties as well as crises

Consequently, the lack of adequate SSSs is considered an area of vulnerability and may represent a source of distress, whereas adequate SSSs reduce the effects of stressful situations and facilitate successful adaptation. Knowing what the SSSs are and what roles they play with clients is essential for assessment and may even be the focus of interventions that tap into the potential of dormant SSSs or mobilize new ones.

Members of certain groups may have particular need for enhanced SSSs, or may be especially vulnerable due to limited or blocked SSSs:

- *The elderly (Berkman et al. 1999)*
- *Abused or neglected children (Brissette-Chapman, 1997)*

- *Teenage parents (Barth & Schinke, 1984; Brindis, Barth, & Loomis, 1987; De Anda & Becerra, 1984)*
- *Persons with AIDS (Indyk, Belville, Lachapelle, Gordon, & Dewart, 1993)*
- *Widows and widowers (Lieberman & Videka-Sherman, 1986)*
- *Persons with severe mental illness, and their families (Zipple & Spaniol, 1987; Rapp, 1998)*
- *The terminally ill (Arnowitz, Brunswick, & Kaplan, 1983)*
- *Persons with disabilities (Hill, Rotegard, & Bruininks, 1984; Mackelprang & Hepworth, 1987)*
- *Persons who experience geographical and/or cultural dislocation as refugees and immigrants (Hulewat, 1996)*

The reasons for diminished social supports may vary by group, and each presents challenging opportunities to social workers when collaborating to develop natural support networks and to plan service delivery systems that respond to the individual's unique needs. In some vulnerable groups, you may find that other, more experienced and sophisticated members of the group are willing to assist "newcomers" to find their way through the maze of bureaucratic structures. Indigenous nonprofessionals have also been employed as staff members to serve as client advocates, provide direct outreach, organize disenfranchised people for social action, and assume the role of advocate or interpreter (in both language and policy).

Within some cultures and geographic regions, the extended family may provide an extensive network of support and assistance in crisis situations. There may also be cultural variations in the person to whom one turns for assistance with life problems. In many Native American tribal groups, for example, members actively seek counsel from elders (Hull, 1982) while Southeast Asian immigrants may seek assistance from clan leaders, shamans, or herbalists, depending on the nature of the difficulty. Similar examples of specialized supports abound in other cultures and communities.

To this point, we have highlighted the positive aspects of SSSs. It is also important to note that some SSSs may foster and sustain problems in functioning. For example, overprotective parents may stunt the development of competence, autonomy, and personal responsibility in their children. Street gangs and other antisocial peer groups may foster violence and criminality, even as they provide a sense of belonging and affiliation. Friends or family may ridicule or sabotage a person's aspirations, thereby undermining that individual's confidence and capacity for success.

You should be aware of the various social networks at play in a client's life, and assess the roles that those SSSs play in the person's difficulties or in his or her ability to overcome such problems. Sometimes, a negative support system can be counteracted by the development of prosocial or positive networks. At other times, the system itself may be the focus of intervention, as you strive to make the members aware of their roles in the client's problems and progress.

A number of instruments have been developed to assess SSSs; one that is especially practical for social workers is the Social Network Grid (Tracy & Whittaker, 1990). This instrument yields the following information:

1. Key persons in clients' social networks
2. Areas of life in which the support occurs
3. Specified types of support provided by each person
4. The degree to which support persons are critical
5. Whether the support is reciprocal or unidirectional
6. The degree of personal closeness
7. The frequency of contacts
8. Length of the relationship

Completion of the grid, for which Tracy and Whittaker provide explicit instructions, yields rich information for both the practitioner and the client and helps provide direction for intervention.

Spirituality and Affiliation with a Faith Community

The issue of one's spirituality and its expression actually transcends the categories of individual functioning and environmental systems. Spirituality can shape beliefs and provide strength during times of adversity, and the link to a faith community can be a tangible source of assistance and social support. While we have placed our discussion of this issue within the context of assessing environmental systems, we will address assessment of faith more broadly.

Canda (1997) differentiates between spirituality and religion, suggesting that *spirituality* is the totality of the human experience that cannot be broken into individual components, whereas *religion* is the socially sanctioned institution based on those spiritual practices and beliefs. Sherwood (1998) also distinguishes between spirituality and religion, wherein the former reflects the "human search for transcendence, meaning and connectedness beyond the self" and "religion refers to a more formal embodiment of spirituality into relatively specific belief systems, organizations and structures" (p. 80). He cites a typology by Ressler wherein persons may fall into one of four categories: spiritual and nonreligious; religious and dispirited; dispirited and nonreligious; and spiritual and religious. A "spiritual assessment," then, may help the worker to better understand the client's belief system and resources.

Questions such as "What are your sources of strength and hope?", "How do you express your spirituality?", "Do you identify with a particular religion or faith?", and "Is your religious faith helpful to you?" can begin to elicit information as the foundation to seeking further understanding about the client's beliefs. Authors such as Hodge (2005), Sherwood (1998), Ortiz and Langer (2002), and Ellor, Netting, and Thibault (1999) offer a variety of guides for gathering information about both clients' spiritual beliefs and religious affiliations.

Why is it important to understand the role of religion and spirituality in the lives of your clients? As Ratliff (1996) notes in discussing health care settings,

Religious beliefs may dictate food choices, clothing styles, customs of birthing and dying, etiquette in the sick room, use of modern conveniences, invasive procedures, organ donation, reception, use of blood products, certain diagnostic tests, gynecological procedures, spiritual influences on or control of sickness and healing, the wearing of protective devices or tattoos, and the need for prayers and rituals performed by various religious specialists. (p. 171)

At times, religious issues may be central to the presenting problems clients bring to service. For example, parents may disagree about the spiritual upbringing of their children; couples may be at odds over the proper roles of women and men; families may be in conflict about behaviors proscribed by certain religions, such as premarital sex, contraceptive use, alcohol use, divorce, or homosexuality (Meystedt, 1984).

As Thibault, Ellor, and Netting (1991), conceptualize it, spirituality involves three relevant areas: cognitive (the meaning given to past, current, and personal events), affective (one's inner life and sense of connectedness to a larger reality), and behavioral (the way in which beliefs are affirmed, such as through group worship or individual prayer). Thus, spiritual beliefs may affect the client's response to adversity, the coping methods employed, the sources of support available (e.g., the faith community may form a helpful social network), and the array of appropriate interventions available. Particularly when clients have experienced disaster or unimaginable traumas, the exploration of suffering, good and evil, shame and guilt, and forgiveness can be a central part of the change process. As Ellor et al. (1999) and others suggest, social workers must be aware of their own spiritual journey and understand the appropriate handling of spiritual content, depending on the setting, focus, and client population involved. Social workers are also advised to involve clergy or leaders of other faiths to work jointly in addressing the personal and spiritual crises faced by clients (Grame et al., 1999).

Written Assessments

The assessment phase is a critical part of the helping process. It provides the foundation on which goals and interventions are based. It is also an ongoing part of the helping process, as appraisals are reconsidered and revised based on new information and understanding. As a written product, assessments may be done at intake, following a period of interviews and evaluations, and at the time of transfer or termination (a summary assessment). They may be brief and targeted (such as an assessment for referral), a detailed report for the court or another entity, or a comprehensive biopsychosocial assessment. Whichever form it takes, several standards must be followed to craft a sound document that clearly conveys accurate information and credible depictions of the client (Kagle, 2002).

1. *Remember your purpose and audience.* These will help you decide what should be included and maintain that focus. Know the standards and expectations that apply in your work setting, and understand the needs of those who will review your document.

2. *Be precise, accurate, and legible.* It is important that any data you include be accurate. Erroneous information can take on a life of its own if what you write is taken as fact by others. If you are unclear on a point, or if you have gathered conflicting information, note that in your report.

Document your sources of information and specify the basis for any conclusions and the criteria on which a decision was based (for example, to refer the client to another agency, to recommend a custody placement, or to conclude that suicidal risk was slight).

Present essential information in a coherent manner. An assessment is intended to be a synthesis of information from a variety of sources, including observation, documents, collateral contacts, and client interviews.

Organizing that material so that it paints a comprehensive picture of the client's situation, strengths, and challenges at that particular moment is not easy. Avoid going off on tangents or piling up excessive details that derail the clarity of your document. Keep details that illustrate your point, document your actions, or substantiate your conclusions.

3. *Avoid the use of labels, subjective terminology, and jargon.* In assessing the social functioning of individuals, social workers often make global judgments—for example, "At best, this person's level of functioning is marginal." Such a sweeping statement has limited usefulness, because it fails to specify areas in which the client's functioning is marginal and it emphasizes

deficits. Instead of using labels ("Alice is a kleptomaniac"), use the client's own reports or substantiate your conclusion ("Alice reports a 3-year history of shoplifting on a weekly basis" or "Alice has been arrested five times for theft and appears unable to resist the compulsion to steal small items on a regular basis"). You should be factual and descriptive, as opposed to relying on labels and subjective terms.

Take care to create a document that demonstrates respect for your client. Should he or she read it, would it be considered a fair characterization of the client's presentation of self, life circumstances, assets, and needs? For help in honing your skills and expanding your assessment vocabulary, consult resources

Date of Assessment: 11/15/08

Background

Josephine is a Caucasian female, estimated to be in her late 70s, who lost her husband to a heart attack six months ago. The attack was unexpected and hence his death was sudden. Josephine met with Kathy, a social worker from Family Services, on two occasions (9-2-08 and 9-9-08) to share background and assessment information and to formulate goals and objectives to direct her adjustment to living alone.

Mental Status Exam

On both occasions, the interview was held in Josephine's home. She was dressed in a housecoat for the first meeting, a blouse and slacks for the second. Her hair was styled and neat. She appeared her stated age, was alert and aware of her surroundings, yet acted somewhat disengaged and uninterested, particularly in the first interview. She was physically still for most of the time that the worker spent with her, looking down at the table the two were seated at. Occasionally Josephine moved her hand back and forth over the table, and also changed her position in her chair intermittently.

Josephine showed no deficit in memory or concentration. Her self-report of memory functioning, offered during a depression screening administered by the worker, does not indicate deficits. Josephine showed evidence of sound judgment, agreeing that engaging in new activities and adopting healthy eating habits would improve her mood and health. Additionally, when asked what she would do in case of a fire in her kitchen, she responded, "Call 911." She was oriented

to time, place, person, and situation and had no deficit in reality testing.

Josephine's speech was quiet and at times somber. She was brief and direct in her answers to the worker's questions. These speech characteristics match Josephine's mood and affect. She reported feeling depleted of energy, experiencing a lack of interest in activities, and having trouble sleeping. Her lack of energy has led to her neglecting her doctor's dietary recommendations. Josephine carried a depressed affect that varied appropriately to the conversation and, at times, brightened. She scored in the high range on a depression inventory.

Josephine followed the worker's questions. Her thoughts focused on improving her mood and diet and arranging for services to allow her to remain in her home. Josephine appeared overwhelmed at times, though reported understanding what the worker was saying.

Josephine showed no evidence of cognitive distortions or hallucinations. She was cooperative in the interviews and showed flexibility of thought by agreeing to consider the suggested interventions. Josephine reported feeling that there was hope in her future, that in the past she had found redemptive aspects of persevering through challenging times, and that her children represent her purpose in life.

Biophysical Considerations

Health

Josephine was diagnosed with high blood pressure and prescribed two medications for this condition. She is also prescribed a third medicine to help lower her cholesterol. Her doctor told her a couple of years ago that she is borderline diabetic. She acknowledged that she could do more to care for this condition by preparing healthier meals. Josephine reported that she no longer drives, making her dependent on her daughter to go to the grocery store. Additionally, she stated, "I don't feel like cooking. I just grab what there is." She has lost 10 pounds in the past six months.

Josephine is also dependent on others for transportation to her doctor, whom she has seen for 20 years, for her monthly visits. Josephine reported some hearing loss. She is able to read and reports that she does quite a bit, with the use of glasses.

Josephine reported trouble getting to sleep at night, but she has been sleeping a few hours each afternoon. She does not have a prescription to help her sleep, though sometimes she takes an over-the-counter sleep aid.

Josephine mentioned that she used to walk regularly for exercise, but has not been doing any exercise lately as she lacks the motivation, stating, "I don't have any energy." She reported no recent falls or accidents.

Josephine does not report using alcohol. She stopped smoking cigarettes five years ago.

She rates her overall health as "fair," which is poorer than her self-assessment of a year ago, which was "good."

Social Factors

Josephine is the lone survivor in her family of origin. Her two brothers passed soon after World War II and her sister died a few years ago. She mentioned that this fact, compounded with the death of her husband, amplifies her sense of isolation.

Josephine was married to her husband for several decades; they met on a blind date after World War II. She has three children, a daughter who lives close by and another daughter and son who live out of state. She is now dependent on her daughter for transportation, because her husband did the driving when he was alive. This is an uncomfortable situation, as Josephine reports feeling like she imposes on her daughter yet does not have an alternative to get to appointments and shop for groceries.

Josephine and her husband both retired after age 65. Josephine worked in retail, her husband in insurance. Since retirement, the couple traveled and visited with their grandchildren. As of her husband's death, Josephine reported she has not been involved in normal social activities due to her lack of energy and motivation. Her neighbor has visited once and offered to drive her to church, which Josephine declined but will reassess in the future.

Legal/Financial

Josephine reported that she owns her house and paid for her husband's funeral. She receives Social Security, though she will receive less than she used to as a result of recalculations after her husband's death. She characterized her income as just "adequate."

Josephine is unable to care for the house by herself. Her husband was responsible for the yard work, and she states she is not strong enough to complete it alone. She reported lacking the energy to do laundry and housework and is considering the possibility of receiving assistance with household chores.

Josephine reported that she would like to remain at home until she can no longer live alone. She is open to the idea of moving in the future.

Mood

Josephine repeatedly referred to her lack of interest, motivation, and energy caused by her grieving for her husband. She noted that her past coping methods involved connecting with people close to her. With the loss of her husband, she has lost her confidant. Josephine has not received counseling or therapy in the past.

Josephine correlated her mood to her lack of activities, reporting that she does not go out often, attends to her appearance less than she used to, and does not complete household chores.

Josephine scored high on a depression inventory. The worker recommended passing on these results to her physician and speaking to him about antidepressant medication.

Josephine does not report loss of hope or purpose. She stated, "I do think there is hope," and "My life has a purpose...I have wonderful children." She did not relate any suicidal ideation or thoughts of hurting herself. In her second interview, Josephine was asked to respond to a battery of questions designed to assess spirituality. Her answers were genuinely positive and life-affirming. Notably, she indicated that the most important thing in her life at present is "to feel better."

Conclusion

The sudden and recent death of Josephine's husband has resulted in financial changes, increased role demands, social withdrawal, and changes in nutrition, sleep patterns, and emotional functioning. Symptoms of grief and depression both contribute to these problems and affect Josephine's ability to reach out for assistance or participate in church and other previously valued activities. She has a clean, safe, and stable home environment and numerous relationships of a long duration with family, friends, and her physician. She is interested in better understanding her situation, consulting her physician and receiving services to assist with transportation, grief, home care, meals, and other issues.

such as Norris (1999), Zuckerman (1997), and Kagle (1991).

The accompanying example incorporates the concepts described in this chapter into a written assessment based on the videotaped interviews with Josephine. Two other examples of written assessments are available on this text's companion Web site.

Case Notes

In addition to more comprehensive assessments, direct practitioners record information in client charts based on each meeting or contact with the client, and after significant contacts about the case, such as the receipt of test results or information from a collateral contact. Record-keeping policies are often specific to the setting. For example, in schools, social work notes would be kept separate from the child's educational record; in some settings notes are dictated, and in others handwritten. Well-crafted case notes "provide accountability, corroborate the delivery of appropriate services and support clinical decisions" (Cameron & Turtle-Song, 2002, p. 1). Although there are many different practices in record keeping, one commonly used practice is worthy of attention. SOAP notes refer to subjective observations, objective data, assessments and plans (Kettenbach, 2003). A variation on this, DAP, combines subjective and objecting information under one heading, data. These *progress notes* refer back to the most recent assessment, problem list, and treatment plan. The "subjective" section has information shared by the client or significant others, such as recent events, emotions, changes in health or well-being, changes in attitude, functioning, or mental status. Information in this section is typically paraphrased and presented as, for example, "The client reports…", "The patient's mother states…", "She indicates…", or "Patient's husband complains of…." Direct client quotes should be kept to a minimum (Cameron & Turtle-Song, 2002).

The "objective" section in SOAP notes should be factual, precise, and descriptive, based on your observations or written material, and presented in quantifiable terms—factors that "can be seen, heard, smelled, counted or measured" (Cameron & Turtle-Song, 2002,

p. 2). In progress notes, the advice for writing proper assessments applies: avoid conclusions, judgments, and jargon and substitute descriptions that would lead to such conclusions with more objective commentary. Rather than saying, "The client was resistant," an objective statement might read, "The client arrived 20 minutes late, sat with her coat on and her arms folded, and did not make eye contact with this writer."

The "assessment" portion of SOAP notes is the place to include diagnoses, judgments, and clinical impressions, based on both the subjective and objective data that precede the assessment. The last section, "plan," addresses following appointments, next steps, referrals planned, and actions expected of both the client and the worker. Each SOAP entry should begin with the date and end with the worker's name, credentials title, and signature. Entries should be completed as soon as possible after the actual contact to ensure they are accurate and up-to-date.

Summary

This chapter discussed assessment of physical, cognitive/perceptual, emotional, and behavioral functioning, as well as motivation and cultural and environmental factors. Although each of these factors was presented as a discrete entity here, these factors are neither independent nor static. Rather, the various functions and factors interact dynamically over time and, from the initial contact, the practitioner is a part of that dynamic interaction. Each factor is therefore subject to change, and the social worker's task is not only to assess the dynamic interplay of these multiple factors but also to instigate changes that are feasible and consonant with clients' goals.

Assessment involves synthesizing relevant factors into a working hypothesis about the nature of problems and their contributory causes. You need not be concerned in every case with assessing all of the dimensions identified thus far. Indeed, an assessment should be a concise statement that embodies only the most pertinent factors.

This chapter's scope was limited to intrapersonal and environmental dimensions. It excluded conjoint, family, and group systems, not because they are unimportant components of people's social environments, but rather because they generally are the hub of people's social environments. To work effectively with interpersonal systems, however, requires an extensive body of knowledge about these systems. Therefore, we devote the next two chapters to assessing couple and family systems and therapeutic groups.

Skill Development Exercises in Assessment

Review the opening session with Irwin and Angela Corning and address the following questions.

1. What words would you use to describe them across the following variables?
   a. Appearance (Posture, Attire, Psychomotor functioning)
   b. Cognitive Functioning (Memory Concentration, Judgment, Reality Testing, Coherence, Cognitive Flexibility, Misconceptions, Sensory Perceptions)
   c. Affective Functioning (Predominant mood, Variability, Range and Intensity of Affect)
   d. Values and Self-Concept
   e. Attitude Toward the Interviewer
2. Are there any areas in which you lack information? How would you go about getting the information in a subsequent session?
3. To what extent might the nature of the interview and the worker's style and characteristics have affected the clients' presentation of themselves in the session?
4. Now, compare your findings with those of a classmate. How much congruence is there in your assessments? What might account for areas of difference?
5. How do your descriptions compare with the assessment of the Cornings on this text's Web site?
6. What conclusions can you draw about the skills, values and knowledge needed to write effective, accurate assessments?

Related Online Content

Visit the *Direct Social Work Practice* companion Web site at *www.cengage.com/social_work/hepworth* for additional learning tools such as glossary terms, chapter outlines, relevant web links, and chapter practice quizzes.

Notes

1. Bernhardt and Rauch (1993) offer an informative guide for social workers interested in learning more about the genetic basis for illnesses and about conducting genetic family histories.
2. See Steinmetz (1992) for an article about FAS, including photographs comparing a normal fetus with one damaged by excessive alcohol consumption by the mother. Detailed information about FAS and FAE has been presented in articles by Giunta and Streissguth (1988) and Anderson and Grant (1984).
3. For example, individuals from Jewish, Greek, Lebanese, or Italian cultures may express emotions more freely, particularly within their families, than might those from Scandinavian, English, or east Indian cultures (McGoldrick, Giordano, & Pearce, 1996). Latinos also tend to be animated, and may vary in emotional expressiveness when switching languages from Spanish to English (Queralt, 1984).
4. See Walsh and Bentley (2002) for further information on psychotropic medications, their effects, and side effects.
5. The Hopelessness Scale (Beck, Resnik, & Lettieri, 1974), the Scale for Suicide Ideation (Beck, Kovacs, & Weissman, 1979), the Suicide Probability Scale (Cull & Gill, 1991), the Chronological Assessment of Suicide Events (Shea, 1998), and the Training Institute for Suicide Assessment and Clinical Interviewing, http://www.suicideassessment.com/home.html. Range and Knott (1997) offer a comprehensive evaluation of these and 17 other suicide assessment instruments.
6. Article summary by Kate Brockett.

CHAPTER **10**

Assessing Family Functioning in Diverse Family and Cultural Contexts

CHAPTER OVERVIEW

Chapter 10 focuses on family dimensions of the assessment phase of the helping process. Practice with families as discussed in this chapter emphasizes both a "cultural variant" and a "family variant" perspective, so that families are assessed within their own idiosyncratic context. Within this framework, *family* is conceptualized as a dynamic and transactional social system in which each of its constituent parts and subsystems interact with one another in a predictable, organized fashion. Because families as social systems interact with, influence, and are influenced by other systems in the social environment, these factors are discussed as well.

Social Work Practice with Families

Social work from its historical beginnings has been concerned with the family as a unit and as a focus of intervention. Nichols and Schwartz (2004) trace social work's contributions to families back to the friendly visitors of the Charity Organization Societies (COS), led by Mary Richmond in the early 20th century. These family caseworkers met with families in their homes, and, in effect, their work marked the beginning of outreach and home-based family services. Richmond's conceptualization of the family as a social system is considered to have been the vanguard of "family's therapy's ecological approach, long before systems theory was introduced" (Nichols & Schwartz, 2004, p. 17). Her classic 1917 text, *Social Diagnosis*, introduced the family as a treatment unit and clarified the family as a social system.

While the focus on the family as a system remains intact, social work practice with families has continued to evolve, integrating post-modern family-centered methods, for example, narrative, social constructionist, feminist, and solution-focused, each of which has made significant contributions to practice with families.

As a social system, the family interacts with and is influenced by other systems. Therefore, practice with families has also been influenced by perspectives and models that include attention to the situational, relational, or environmental stressors and the multiple systems in which families interact (Boyd-Franklin & Bry, 2000; Constable & Lee, 2004; Kilpatrick & Holland, 2006). In the social justice and relational justice framework, family systems' focus is on assessing families in the broader context and structures of society; in particular, the influence that economics, politics, inequality, oppression, and trauma have on family functioning (Boyd-Franklin & Bry, 2000; Constable & Lee, 2004; Dietz, 2000; Finn & Jacobson, 2003a; McGoldrick, 1998; Vera & Speight, 2003; Walsh, 1996).

Defining Family

During the last several decades how families were defined emphasized legal, economic, religious, and political interests or some combination thereof. In some instances, nostalgic references to the 1950s-era family described a family form that is no longer dominant or practical in view of the diverse configurations of today's families (Fredriksen-Goldsen & Scharlach, 2001; Walsh, 1996). Recognizing and valuing other family forms, although often times controversial, does not intentionally distract from or devalue the traditional family. Instead, diverse family forms add to the rich opportunities in which individuals experience a sense of belonging, loyalty, reciprocal care, and interrelatedness. Moreover, as social workers, our awareness of the ways in which people are nurtured emotionally and are stable and socially connected ultimately facilitates practice with families (McGoldrick, 1998).

In view of the diverse family forms that exist, how families themselves define their members is best articulated by the family. Following are some of the ways in which the variability and choices of family membership are achieved.

- *Marriage, which may be an arranged marriage*
- *Remarriage; recoupling after separation, or blended family*
- *Birth, adoption, foster care, or legal custody*
- *Commitment or created, the latter of which involves a relational network of supportive friends*
- *Informal relationship, biological and nonbiological kin, friends, social networks within communities and/or cultural groups*
- *Nannies or other surrogates in the family*

Households may consist of single or two parents, who may also be of the same sex. Families may be multigenerational (Fredriksen-Goldsen & Scharlach, 2001; Okun, 1996; Sue, 2006; Crosson-Tower, 2004; Carter & McGoldrick, 1999a; Weston, 1991). In addition, there are a significant number of families consisting of grandparents and grandchildren, in which the grandparents have legal custody or an informal arrangement with the children's parents (Gibson, 1999; Burnette, 1999; Jimenez, 2002). In reports issued by the American Association of Retired Persons (AARP) based on data from the 2000 census, 2.4 million families consisted of children living with a grandparent (American Assoication of Retired Persons, 2007; Goyer, 2006). Clearly, family configurations can be as diverse as family membership. The more critical concern, and thus the focus of practice, is the extent to which the family has the capacity to perform the essential functions that contribute to the development of its members.

Family Functions

Irrespective of their form, families share both a history and a future and experience the lifecycle together. The family performs certain functions and has certain responsibilities to and for its members unlike any other social system. Families perform the essential function of attending to the social and educational needs, health and well-being, and mutual care of its members (Hartman, 1981; Meyer, 1990; Okun, 1996; Sue, 2006). Families perform functions that are rarely replicated in other systems and therefore are considered to be the

preferred arrangement for minors. For example, when it has been necessary to remove a child from his or her biological home, the preferred placement is with kin or a foster family rather than an institution. It is largely through the family that character is formed, attachments are developed, vital roles are learned, and members are socialized for participation in their subculture and the larger society. Constable and Lee characterize the family as "the basic informal welfare system in any society" (2004, p. 9).

All families have distinct patterns of relating, decision making, rules, scripts, and a division of roles and labor. The manner in which these functions are implemented, and by whom, may be influenced by cultural or racial preferences, socioeconomic status, and available resources. Available resources or the lack thereof can determine roles and responsibilities. In single-parent families or when both parents are employed, roles and responsibilities can be more dispersed. For example, children, extended kin, or friends in the family network may assume responsibilities essential to maintaining the family system. Cultural traditions are also influential; in Hispanic or Latino families there are prominent *familismo* roles of honor and respect that are independent of legal or nonlegal familial status (Sue, 2006).

As Meyer (1990), in advocating for the celebration of diverse families, stated, it is a "phenomenon of our times that people have discovered so many ways" in which individuals make up a family system. As a result, a variety of members may carry out the different functions that nurture the well-being and development of it members. Of course, the diversity of families makes it more likely that you as a social worker will have contact with variant family and cultural forms. Within a broader definition of family, forms are less important than how the family functions, the relational patterns the family exhibits, and their relationship with the social environment.

Given the nature of modern families, and because of the varying family needs and circumstances, how should you as a social worker approach the daunting task of working with families? Appreciating diverse family forms is critical, but you may encounter families in which, irrespective of the family forms, family dynamics have an adverse effect on individuals. Not all family environments are nurturing, and some members may lack the skills, resources, or capacity to foster the development and well-being of all family members. Kilpatrick and Holland (2006), in describing Level 1 families, call attention to a multiplicity of factors, for example, resources, psychological and environmental needs that these families may lack. You may be challenged by family situations in which a member is gravely ill, or encounter child, partner, spousal, or elder abuse. In these and other situations, family functioning is undermined, and families experience enormous physical and psychological distress (McKenry & Price, 2000). Not all environments in which the family interacts are *enabling* in that the support and growth opportunities necessary for member development and functioning is constrained. There are also those environments in which internal and external conditions are *entrapping* because they adversely impact the family's ability to perform all or some of its functions (Kilpatrick & Holland, 2006; Saleebey, 1996, 2004).

Discomfort can arise when you encounter a family that is vastly different from your own and whose norms are inconsistent with your values as well as those reflected in the dominant society. For example, consider an unmarried teen parent family living in the household of the young father's parents. Based on your own experience, your first thought might be, "The couple is too young to have, care for and support a baby." You may feel inadequate to deal with the customs of families of a different race or culture. Levels of intimacy and attachment are culturally dependent, and the Western perspective may not be prominent in other cultures. For example, Okun, Fried, and Okun (1999) point to the fact that in cultures where marriages are arranged, attachment and feelings about a mother-in-law may be considered unimportant. The norm however of holding her in a position of honor includes certain nonnegotiable obligations. Feeling uncomfortable or challenged and having certain biases based on your worldview is to be expected. When you are faced with differences, being clear about your personal and professional biases is an essential first step toward resolution of internal conflict. Moreover, it is crucial that you avoid concluding that the unfamiliar is evidence of deviance (Hartman, 1981; Meyer, 1990; Walsh, 1996).

In unfamiliar family territory, the central task is to assess families through the lenses of their particular level of functioning, needs, strengths, resilience, migratory status, and the lifecycle (Hernandez & McGoldrick, 1999l; Kilpatrick & Holland, 2006; Silberberg, 2001). In doing so, you have an opportunity to honor the narratives of cultural and family variants, which allows for more collaborative practice. Hartman (1981) articulated the essence of collaborative practice in asserting that social workers should determine the extent to which their practice is "sensitive and responsive" to families.

To illustrate Hartman's point of view, the following situation, in which the teenaged parents are residing in the home of the father's family is revisited.

Case Example

A school social worker became involved with the families because the teenaged mother was required to attend an alternative school for pregnant teens. At age 16 years, neither teen was of legal age to be married. Each set of parents were unhappy about the pregnancy. The initial parent–child and family–family interactions were marked by conflict. Both families, while low-income, were adamant about not wanting the young couple to rely on "public aid," for which the teen mother and the unborn child were potentially eligible. Further, both families wanted to ensure the well-being of their grandchild and also that the youth completed high school. Relying on their preferences as central to working with the families, the social worker assisted them in facilitating a solution. In essence, the young couple would live in the paternal parent home; however, both of their parents would provide resources and support. This arrangement provided a stable living environment, child care, financial assistance, and parental role models. It also took into account the youth's developmental stage and the unexpected lifecycle phase of the families, while supporting their dual role as developing individuals and parents.

Collaborative practice as illustrated by the social worker's actions in this case seems especially pertinent to this particular family system. Specifically, a relevant question posed by Hartman (1981) for social workers to consider is: "*Does our practice involve families to the fullest extent possible in defining the problems and creating solutions, or does it replace a family function in a situation where with help, the family itself could meet the needs of its members?*" How was this perspective applied in this case? The social worker saw her role as engaging the families in developing solutions that addressed parental concerns for both the youth and the unborn child. Similarly, Hartman encourages social workers to query the extent to which their practice with families is "*based on an understanding that people are part of current and intergenerational family system and that these human connections are powerful, persistent and essential to the welfare of the individual.*"

Both questions frame the essence of collaborative practice with families while respecting their decisions and strengths. Collaborative practice as a framework has broad implications for families in general, yet guides social workers to reflect upon those indigenous patterns and perceptions that influence help-seeking behavior within diverse groups (Constable & Lee, 2004; Green, 1999; Hartman, 1981; Hirayama, Hirayma & Cetingok, 1993; Laird, 1993; Poulin, 2000).[1]

Family Stressors

A family event stressor is described by McKenry and Price (2000, p. 6) as "anything that provokes change or some aspect of change, such as boundaries, structures, goals, roles or values, each of which can result in stress." Stressors have tended to be categorized as either *normative* (e.g., marriage) or *nonnormative* (e.g., an accident). An additional dichotomy, according to these authors, is whether or not the stressor changes the family system.

Normative stressors and life cycle transitions are a part of family life. Stressors may also include internal family dynamics, such as inadequate communication skills, or external factors, for example, racial or economic discrimination that marginalize families. Both dynamics can encroach on family functioning. How families cope with and adapt may depend on their resources, strengths, or resilience, bolstered by family networks and social supports and spirituality and relational caregiving.

Normative stressors of a different type occurs in some families, especially those who, by virtue of their differences, frequently encounter a hostile or indifferent environment in the course of their everyday lives. For example, gay and lesbian families face a legal labyrinth with respect to medical and child care, power of attorney, family benefits, and civil rights regarding relational commitment. Indifference may be built into the structure of public policy; for example, the lack of national health insurance limits access to affordable health care for a significant number of families. In practice, indifference can occur with certain families when professionals perceive the family as functioning outside of acceptable norms. In consequence, these families are often labeled and stigmatized.

As social systems, families are not isolated. In light of this, the next section discusses public policy, poverty, work, and family issues as factors that influence families and contribute to both normative and nonnormative stressors that some families face.

Public Policy

All families are subject to the influence of public policies; for example, requirements that minors attend school until they reach a certain age and are immunized against communicable diseases. Public policy can be a source of stress for some families, especially poor families. The extent to which public policy responds—or fails to respond—to the needs of these families or empower, support, or strengthen them, is a concern. The *"family values"* and *"personal responsibility"* emphasis of both the Clinton and George W. Bush administrations effectively changed the longstanding social contract with disadvantaged families in the United States. New inequities and the resulting challenges received scant attention; instead the support for families in the new century appeared to be more symbolic than substantive. For example the pro-marriage proposal advanced by the Bush administration urged poor single-parent women, to get married. This proposal was in contrast to the stance of diminishing the government's role in the lives of families, the exception being, apparently, if the family is poor (Locke, 2001).

In essence, the concepts of family values and personal responsibility were shifts away from the much-maligned Great Society programs family policies of the 1960s, which were intended to rectify structural inequities and were the source of great debates. Unfortunately, the debates about the merits of shifts in public policy as reported by the media tended to be dichotomous. Liberals, in essence, were portrayed as champions of sustained support for families and unapologetic about what they perceived as the role of government. In contrast, fiscal and social conservatives reportedly believed that these programs were counterproductive and sought to restrain their growth and costs. At the heart of the arguments, neither of which is an absolute, is the struggle to reconcile the role of government and its responsibilities to citizens with the roles and responsibilities of states, individuals, families, and communities.

Perhaps the most pervasive sentiment behind the welfare reform and personal responsibility initiatives is the public attitude of not wanting someone to live off "my hard work and earnings." Another factor that fuels the opposition to family support, in which the theme of personal responsibility is able to thrive, is the portrayal of undeserving families. The image that the public sees and hears thorough political and media messages is that of large, multigenerational minorities, mostly African American, living off the state—when in fact minorities as a whole are not the only families on welfare. Segal (2007) reports, for example, that of those who receive welfare benefits, whites account for 31%, African Americans 38%, and Hispanics 24%.

For the most part, the prevailing belief about families on welfare is that they are lacking in personal responsibility and that their lives are outside the boundaries of acceptable societal standards. Further, they are viewed as chaotic, drug-involved, and prone to engaging in irresponsible and risky behaviors (Jenkins, 2007; Rank & Hirschl, 2002). Of course, such images create strong feelings among those who perceive welfare as a crutch for a marginal segment of the population. Although welfare recipients may include these families, there are many more families who make use of the supports on a short-term basis. The beneficiaries of government-supported programs are in fact far broader than either scenario. Rank and Hirschl (2002) concluded that two-thirds of the American population between 20 and 65 years of age will at some point live in a household that receives benefits from a means-tested welfare program.

Poverty

Poverty in the United States and the global community is an enduring source of stress for a significant number of families. Income disparities are evident in the 2004 Congressional Budget Office Report, which showed stagnant earnings for the bottom one-fifth of the population, while income for the top percent increased by more than 63 percent. Middle-class families fared somewhat better, realizing a gain of 23 percent (Leonhardt, 2007). Overall, median incomes increased; however, low-income Americans did not realize significant gains. Almost all presidential administrations have proposed solutions to resolve persistent poverty in the United States. None, of course, have equaled the anti-poverty initiatives under the Johnson administration during the 1960s. Other solutions have included, for example, the Earned Income Tax Credit (ETC) initiated during the Nixon Administration. Asset development, a promising initiative, has been promoted as a remedy; for example, home ownership or loans to start a small business to help families transition out of poverty (Oliver & Shapiro, 2007; Yunus, 2007). Yunus (2007) however, believes that exclusionary policies in the United States are a major obstacle because they limit the accumulation of assets and punish work activity of welfare recipients. Yunus advocates that instead of reducing

benefits as a result of additional income, recipients should be allowed to earn and save while receiving assistance, thereby enabling them to eventually improve their economic status.

Another solution championed by some policymakers and advocates for the poor was a change in the minimum wage. Advocates for an increase in the minimum wage, which did occurr in 2007, have persistently advanced this policy change as a means to address poverty. The increase, the first in 10 years, increased wages from $5.15 an hour to $5.85. Subsequent increases are due to take effect over the next several years (Cummings, 2007). Not all job classes are covered, however, for example, seasonal workers or those who care for the children of others (e.g., babysitters or nannies). Also, similar to welfare benefits, wages vary by geographical region. Not all states had to increase their minimum wage because hourly wages already exceeded the federal minimum. In other states, in which the hourly wage was at or below the federal standard, adjustments were made. The downside to the increased minimum wage is the fact that many employers decided to trim their workforce.

Even with the wage increase, unfortunately, many minimum-wage earners lack health care and other benefits. Data released by the federal government in 2007 reported that fewer people lived in poverty, the number of Americans without health insurance changed only slightly (Peterson, 2007). Rising health insurance costs, even when provided by the employer, affects all families. In 2006, the U.S. Census Bureau reported that 2 million Americans lost their private health insurance coverage, because employers could no longer afford the expense or because they lost their jobs. For many families, losing employment means they also lose insurance, because they are ineligible for public insurance programs. For other familes, many could not afford private insurance premiums which on average is $12, 500 per year.

The impetus to restrain the expansion of family-supportive social programs became a front-and-center issue during the debates about the State Children's Insurance Program (SCHIP). The measure, proposed by moderate, conservative and liberal advocates and bipartisan members of Congress would have added 3.8 million children to the 6 million already covered. Created by Congress in 1997, the program provides insurance coverage for children whose family incomes are too great for Medicaid but insufficient to pay for private insurance. Under the expansion, access would have been extended to children in families upon the death of a parent, when a parent lost their job, or when an employer discontinued health care coverage.

Despite the bipartisan support, President Bush reasoned that because the measure was an expansion it was "a big step in the direction of government-controlled medicine." Further he asserted that a program expansion would represent a growth in "government programs that substituted government solutions for private sector options" (Healey, 2007). How were children and families affected? Those families with children who are eligible for Medicaid are unlikely to experience a difference. But for families outside of eligibility guidelines it may mean that children do not receive preventive health care—for example, immunizations and routine dental care. Instead, their families will perhaps continue to rely on emergency room-only care. Employers are also affected as parents miss work and their productivity is lower. Family policy advocates had high hopes for the program's expansion. The measure, however, was vetoed by President Bush. The veto was supported by critics who were concerned about extending this benefit to middle-income families.

Who are the Poor and Why?

Debates about why people are poor range from assertions that the manner in which poverty is measured is deeply flawed—specifically, that the poverty lines are too high—to the argument that there is a culture of poverty—specifically, that it is a matter of will—to an emphasis on the structural inequities of society (Greenberg, 2007; Miller & Øyen, 1996; Segal, 2007; Wilson, 1997). Segal (2007) noting the life-experience distance between welfare recipients and policy makers, as well as between that of low and high wage earners, can lead to a lack of *social empathy*. Social empathy requires a visualization of self in the position of others, a nonjudgmental attitude that seeks to understand the realities and circumstances of those who are different from oneself. It is an essential part of understanding the lives of those with whom you, as a social worker, may have limited personal contact.

In examining "who are the poor," it is useful to look at various categories of poor people. Categories of poor families include those who rely on Temporary Assistance to Needy Families (TANF) or disability benefits, the *"diligent"* working poor, and an often unnoticed group referred to as the *"missing class."*

For the families, who receive Temporary Assistance to Needy Families (TANF) under welfare reform had their benefits changed, reduced or eliminated, and these measures varied from state to state. For those families who remained eligible, the level of benefits did little to reduce poverty. Questions were raised about the ethics and values of the changes as well as the extent to which they sustained a sufficient minimum standard of living (Albert, 2000; Collins, Stevens & Lane, 2000; Withorn, 1998).

The poverty spectrum also includes those families described as the *"diligent and still poor"* (Spriggs, 2007, p A6). Within these families, some of whom are well-educated, there is at least one family member who is employed full time, but even with the earned income the family still lives under the poverty line (Reisch, 2002; Segal, 2007; Spriggs, 2007).

Another group, which Newman and Chen (2007) identified as the *"missing class,"* are those families who unlike the poor are ineligible for benefits or government assistance. The earned income of these families, in the range of $40,000, is approximately 100% to 200% above federal poverty income guidelines for a family of four. Hence they do not qualify for the Earned Income Tax Credit (ETC) or other government assistance benefits. It is estimated that 34 million families are considered poor, while this group consist of about 53 million families. Like the poor, nonetheless, these families tend to live in neighborhoods with few resources, and their children attend inadequate schools.

Impact on Children

The debate over the pros and cons of who is poor, the reasons for poverty, and who is responsible will likely continue throughout our lifetime. What we know is that living in poverty can be a constant stressor that affects family stability and mobility and limits the family's ability to meet basic needs. It influences where families live, including the conditions of the housing where the family resides, the education that children receive, and the safety of the neighborhood in which they live. Poverty is strongly associated with out-of-home care for children living in urban areas (Barth, Wildfire, & Green, 2006; Rodenburg, 2004: Roberts, 2002). The influence of poverty on child development is documented in the literature. But as Brooks-Gunn and Duncan (1997) and Costello, Compton, Keeler, and Angold (2003) found, family income has the greatest impact on child development, irrespective of the family structure. Because of the fact that children are reported as being the most affected, Sengupta (2001) has raised two critical questions:

- *"Must so many children in the nation grow up poor?"*
- *"Is this the best that the United States can do?"*

In response to these questions, and specifically whether the United States could do better, Sengupta (2001) cites three confounding factors:

- *The relationship between the labor markets and the government*
- *The hands-off posture of the government with respect to families*
- *The tenacious manner in which politicians and the public hold on to the ideal of individuality and [income] redistribution*

Until recently, the issue of poverty and its effects on families had essentially disappeared from the political radar screen, including presidential campaigns. Nor had much attention been paid to the economic struggles of the middle-class. There are hopeful signs as both the public and the private sector, including private foundations and coordinated fund drives have made ending poverty high priority on their agendas.

Life Transitions and Separations

In the normal course of family life, people join together, perhaps including children and adolescents who move toward independence and eventually leave home as young adults. Families deal with life course transitions, such as death in the family, divorce and separation, and other significant events. There are also many families who experience transitions that exceed and exacerbate those generally associated with the life cycle. For example, traumatic events such as Hurricanes Rita and Katrina, floods and earthquakes in various parts of the country and the world, devastated entire communities. Because of the magnitude of these extraordinary disruptions, family functions out of necessity had to be assumed by private and public organizations, including those at the state and federal level.

Extraordinary Family Transitions

There are other intemperate transitions that families experience that have a profound affect on the family system, for example, military or legally induced family separations. Stressors faced by families when a member was called to military duty during the Gulf War, discussed by Black (1993), are also pertinent to the war in Iraq. The two armed conflicts are similar, in that the majority of those on duty are members of National Guard or Reserve Units. As such, individuals in these units may live with their families in different parts of the country rather than on military bases. Therefore, their families are more geographically dispersed and

may lack the supportive network of other military families, and professional assistance is provided by civil rather than military personnel. The lack of geographical proximity of military families to each other can be especially difficult for children because among their peers they may not know other children who have a parent on duty in the armed services. Children in these situations may experience uncertainty and anger and be especially sensitive to the emotions and moods of the nonmilitary parent.

Deployment, and in some instances, redeployment, causes stressors for the nonmilitary adult family member who has had to adapt to the reallocation of roles and responsibilities, changes in income status, managing the day-to-day family tasks, combined with concerns about a spouse's safety in a hostile environment (Williams, 2007). The stress of deployment as reported by the American Medical Association has resulted in an increase in child abuse and neglect in military families (Williams, 2007). While technology has enabled families to stay in touch, the reintegration of a family member into the family system can also create stressful dynamics. A major task for the family system is managing the dynamics or the reentry, especially as the absent member attempts to regain their position in the family.

In the post-September 11 era, the United States, in an effort to protect its borders, increased enforcement of immigration laws, thereby creating many family stressors, and in some cases separating families. For example, the U.S. Department of Homeland Security ended the protected status of Liberians, many of whom had been in the United States for 20 years (Brown, 2007). Many feared the break-up of their families, especially those with U.S-born children. Families anxiously awaited the result of the debates of the Liberian Refugee Immigration Act, 2007, which did extend their stay but did not provide for permanent resident status.

The enforcement of the 1996 immigration laws prompted increased surveillance and deportations that resulted in the break-up of many families. Of particular interest were those immigrants who had the status of aliens who had entered the United States without legal documentation. National attention was focused on raids in six Midwestern states at meat-packing plants, in which agents reportedly "arrested first and asked questions later" (Hopfensperger, 2007). Children were often left in day-care centers or at home, unaware of their parents' situation. In some instances, a parent was deported. Advocates decrying the level of trauma and anxiety experienced by the children as a result, argued that immigration agents should focus on terrorists. Futher, advocates maintained that foreign-born workers and their families, mainly those from Mexico and Latin American countries, had "taken center stage in the national drama" with respect to security concerns (Tienda, 2007). Added to the concerns about national security were those voices who argued that undocumented and illegal immigrants decreased wages and displaced U.S. workers and did not pay taxes (Tienda, 2007). Assertions about depressed wages and displaced workers are not well documented. However, these individuals do pay taxes under assigned identification numbers and many become homeowners. In fact, lenders reported that despite the nationally increasing rate of mortgage failures, immigrant families rarely defaulted on their home loans (Jordan, 2007). Even so, public sentiment was mixed. Although wage and job related concerns were prominent, as were concerns about the separtation of children from parents, others asserted that laws should observed. For this group, deportations were caused by irresponsible parental behavior. As stated by one immigration agent when asked about the impact on families, "It's not the law that is dividing families; instead it is poor decisions by the parents" (Hopfensberger, 2007). Whatever we believe about these families and immigration policies, we cannot ignore the level of stress and the impact on family as a result of the sudden implementation of immigration policies.

Work and Family

Families in all socioeconomic strata experience stressors. Findings from a national survey conducted by the Search Institute (2002) suggested that a cross section of parents, at all socioeconomic levels feel the need for community support and for work–family balance. The world of work and the state of the economy continue to be significant stressors for families (Ostroff and Atwater, 2003; Ehrenreich, 2001). Barbara Ehrenreich's *Nickled and Dimed* (2001) called attention to the plight of low-wage earners, some of whom were homeless because their earnings were insufficient to afford housing.

All members of U.S. society are affected by these situations and benefit when they improve. Changes in the state of the economy may affect some groups more than others. During the last recession, U.S. unemployment was highest in the Hispanic and African American communities. For example, Hispanic American women, due to their concentration in low-wage, low-skilled jobs, are vulnerable when shifts in the economy result in high rates of unemployment (Solis & Corchado, 2002). According to Ostroff and Atwater (2003), gender—despite improvements in the labor market—remains a major determinant of earning power. Women, even at managerial levels, are paid less than their male peers, as well as the male employees whom they supervise. The disparities in the earning power of many women means that retirement is a greater obstacle for them (Hawthorne, 2007).

The average American spends more time engaged in work activities than in family or leisure activities when one factors in staying late at work or bringing work home. Yet, the George W. Bush administration, with the support of segments of the business community, opposed legislation that would extend overtime benefits to millions of workers. In 2008, Congress, under Democratic leadership, in a move that baffled many observers voted to reduce provisions under the Family and Medical Leave Act for federal employees. The intent of this act was to help families deal with the competing demands of work and family obligations. Opponents noted that the United States already lags behind most other countries in this and other family–work supportive measures.

Employers over time have adopted more family-friendly work policies. In many organizations, about 60 percent of working mothers are employed part-time. This arrangement is considered to be ideal as they manage work and family life. Technology allows many professional men and women to work from their homes, use flex-time and have a shorter onsite work week. It is also encouraging that 73 percent of work organizations have policies that support professional career breaks for family reasons (Palmer, 2007).

Welfare-to-work programs brought many poor women into the workplace. These women had to juggle the same work and family demands as other employed mothers, in addition to adjusting or readjusting to a work environment. Generally, these mothers were concerned about "doing a good job, and the fit between work and family" (DeBord, Canu, & Kerpelman, 2000). A majority of these women reported being satisfied with their jobs. In fact, many worked longer hours to meet the economic needs of their family. The availability of family and community supports, for example child care, was a contributing factor to their ability to maintain their employment and to achieve a balance between work and family.

Child care remains a controversial issue in the United States, perhaps dating back to the days when the role of women was primarily in the home. If women worked, employers and policymakers reasoned that they would eventually leave their jobs if necessary to attend to needs in the home. Currently, the only families who receive child care assistance are those involved in welfare-to-work programs. Even for them, according to Collins (2007), this benefit can be lost when they become employed outside the program. For middle-class families, the annual cost of child care can be up to $12,000. Yet the average child care worker, most of whom are female, earned about $8.78 per hour, which is barely sufficient to support their own families.

Middle-income families face pressures despite their healthy level of income. For the most part, their income will prove insufficient in the event of a major emergency, and they typically have inadequate savings for retirement. Moreover, the net worth of households within an income range of $20,000 to $80,000 largely grew as a result of an increased valuation of their homes, rather than any increase in wages (Crenshaw, 2003). In October 2003, *The Washington Post* reported that highly skilled workers were able to find jobs in such growth fields as health care. Conversely, many of the manufacturing jobs, which are often the most readily available to blue-collar workers, were eliminated or outsourced abroad.

The discussion of the these normative and nonnormative stressors for families illustrates Constable and Lee's (2004) assertion that families today may have less control over their functioning than did their ancestors, for whom family interventions occurred only when they "demonstrated gross inadequacies" (p. 58). Tensions in families, whether created by public policy, poverty, transitions or separations, or conflicts between work and family, are extra-familial sources of stress. They affect family functioning as well as the ability to carry out family roles and responsibilities. In working with families, be aware of the extent to which work (or lack of work), public policy, and other environmental factors support or burden family well-being and hinder access to resources (Zimmerman, 1995; Vosler, 1990). Also, you should be aware that extreme stress might occur in minority or culturally diverse families whose configuration, values, or beliefs clash with those of the dominant work culture.

Resilience in Families

Every family, despite the stressors, strains and trauma it faces, has strengths, displays an enormous amount of resilience, and has resources that can help its members survive (McCubbin, 1988; McCubbin & McCubbin, 1988; Silberberg, 2001; Simon, Murphy & Smith, 2005; Walsh, 1996). The fact that families cope with and survive poverty, oppressive forces, and extraordinary transitions is a testimonial to their resilience.

On a day-to-day basis, adults and minors leave and return home and they perform various tasks that maintain the family system. In a report of the finding of a national youth survey conducted by the Associated Press/MTV, irrespective of family circumstances a majority of respondents reported that being with family "brings them joy." These findings reinforce the primacy of family even in today's rapidly changing world. Families continue to celebrate rites of passage that emphasize their continuity. For example, the Quinceañero marks an adolescent girl's entry into adulthood in Hispanic families. Numerous other rituals focusing on the possibilities of future generations are observed in immigrant, African American, Native American, and Southeast Asian communities, including religious, coming-of-age, spiritual, or naming ceremonies. Indeed, almost every family, irrespective of its culture, race, or class, has some way of marking and celebrating individual and family passages. The family system, even when it differs from the traditional configuration, has demonstrated a capacity to adapt to a vast range of environmental challenges. Signs of hope attesting to the resilience of families are evident in family celebrations and rituals, as well as family activism.

One sign that families are seeking to regain control of their time and relationships is the emergence of movements such as "Putting Families First." This grassroots movement, which was initiated by family social scientist William Doherty at the University of Minnesota, quickly gained national momentum. Other hopeful signs include the efforts of advocates who are diligently trying to force policymakers to craft more, not less, family friendly policies.

A Systems Framework for Assessing Family Functioning

A primary characteristic of any system is that all of its parts are engaged in transactions. There is interdependence between systems and their component parts. As a consequence, whatever affects that system—albeit internal or external, normative or nonnormative—affects the whole to some extent. In general systems thinking, the system as a whole (i.e., the family) is greater than the sum of its component parts (i.e., subsystems). Systems constantly exchange information with other systems. Families, like other systems, manage inputs from thorough boundary maintenance. When faced with inputs, a system may seek to ensure stability or equilibrium, change, or remain in a steady state, and in some instances, become factionalized (Martin & O'Connor, 1989).

The systems framework is useful for assessing families in that the focus may be on the relational and inter-action patterns, dynamics that are internal to the family system. At the same this framework allows for an assessment of the influence of larger systems on the family. For example, a complete family assessment should include both mezzo- and micro-level factors such as communication styles, culture, and family inter-actions and dynamics. Assessment questions might also be raised about whether internal family dynamics are precipitated by or maintained by macro-level factors, such as socioeconomic status; institutionalized discrim-ination or bigotry; the experience of refugee, migrant, or immigrant status; and the state of the overall economy.

As an example, consider the micro, mezzo, and macro dynamics in a family in the following case.

Case Example

The father has recently lost his job and now works part-time as a handyman and part-time for a ven-dor that sells beverages during sports events. The mother in the family has a full-time job cleaning houses. Because of the drop in the father's income, she has taken a part-time job in the evenings, leav-ing an older child to care for the household. In your initial contact with the family, they describe con-flict in their relationship as a primary concern. The mother also states that when the father is not work-ing, he sits on the couch watching television and drinking beer, leaving her and the older child to do most of the work around the house. As a result, the mother and father constantly argue about child care, household tasks, and finances. The older child, who was formerly a good student, is currently having problems in school and has been reported to the school truancy officer for skipping classes. As you read the descriptions of the assessment instruments in Table 10-1, reflect upon which of these instruments might be used to assess this family.

Family Assessment Instruments

Several tools are available to aid the assessment pro-cess. These tools and their authors are summarized in Table 10-1.

In addition to the multidimensional assessment pro-cess outlined in Chapter 8, you may review the instru-ments in the table to further your understanding of assessing family dynamics, internal and external rela-tionships, and stressors. In some instances, you will find it beneficial to combine assessment tools so that you can develop a more complete picture of the family. In using these tools to guide the assessment, they can facilitate your engaging the family in the process.

- *The Clinical Assessment Package for Assessing Risks and Strengths (CASPARS) developed by Gilgun (1994, 2001), for families receiving mental health and child welfare services, responds to related concerns. Specifically, CASPARS measures both risks and protective factors related to family relationships, peer relationships, and sexuality.*
- *The Culturalgram (Congress, 1994) is a useful tool for assessing family dimensions in the context of*

TABLE-10-1 FAMILY ASSESSMENT TOOLS

TOOL	AUTHOR(S)
Clinical Assessment Package for Assessing Risks and Strengths (CASPARS)	Gilgun (1994, 2001)
Culturalgram	Congress (1994)
Ecomap	Hartman & Laird (1983)
Family Assessment Wheel	Mailick & Vigilante (1997)
Genogram	McGoldrick & Gerson (1985)
Integrative Model by Level of Need	Kilpatrick & Cleveland (1993)
Multisystems	Boyd-Franklin & Bry (2000)
Social Support Network Map	Tracy & Whittaker (1990)

culture, because *"the systems view limits important cultural considerations"* (Green, 1999, p. 8).

- *The Ecomap enables you to focus on the social context of families and interactions between the family and the larger society (Hartman & Laird, 1983).*
- *The Family Assessment Wheel allows you to examine the sociopolitical and cultural context of the family experience (Mailick & Vigilante, 1997).*
- *The Genogram assesses internal family functioning, including mapping family structure, family history, and showing relationships (McGoldrick & Gerson, 1985).*
- *The Integrative Model by Level of Need, developed by Kilpatrick and Cleveland (1993), recognizes five levels of family need and functioning. The model is discussed and illustrated in Kilpatrick and Holland (2006). A Level 1 family's needs, for example, are related to basic survival, such as food, shelter, and medical care. Assessments of families at this level would therefore focus on their needs strengths and basic resources needed. In contrast, a Level 3 family has succeeded in satisfying its basic needs, so the assessment would focus on relationships, boundaries, alliances, and communication skills (Kilpatrick & Holland, 2006).*
- *The Multisystems approach developed by Boyd-Franklin & Bry (2000) is derived from structural behavioral family therapy but is also applicable to social work practice with families. This approach recognizes that assessment and intervention goals involve families as well as the systems external to the family that affect and serve as resources to families.*
- *The Social Support Network Map examines the structure and quality of the family's interconnected relationships and social supports (Tracy & Whittaker, 1990).*

Hirayama, Hirayama, and Cetingok (1993) suggest both the Ecomap and the Genogram as useful tools in assisting refugees to understand patterns of social relationships and communication shifts associated with the tensions of immigrant and refugee relocation.

Strengths-Based and Risk Assessments

In addition to Gilgun's assessment package (1994; 2001), other strengths-based measures for families and children include the *Family Functioning Style Scale (FSSS)* and the *Family Resources Scale (FRS)*. Both allow you to include strengths in your assessment of families and to consider a range of family functioning (i.e., capabilities). ROPES, a similar instrument cited in

Jordan and Franklin (2003), considers family *resources, options, possibilities, exceptions,* and *solutions* (hence the instrument's name). New initiatives in child welfare—for example, alternative or differential response teams—are designed to balance families' risks and strengths, with interventions consisting of services for families instead of out-of-home placement.[2]

Often social workers are called upon to assess risks in families—for instance, in cases involving child neglect and abuse, probation, and family violence. *Risk assessments* are standardized structured actuarial tools that specify indicators and scores in an attempt to predict the probability of future behaviors or maltreatment. Risks can be either enduring or transient. Assessment tools, however, tend to emphasize enduring risks, for which an intervention is warranted. Even in cases involving enduring risks, you should strive to conduct a balanced assessment, including micro-, mezzo-, and macro-level strengths, protective factors, and resilience. In this way, risks are not overly emphasized at the expense of strengths and contributing environmental factors. Because there can be difficulty in finding the right tool for a family or its problem, multi-screening inventory tools may be more appropriate for assessing family strengths and stressors (Hudson & McMurtry, 1997).

Systems Concepts

Families, like other systems, are divided into subsystems such as parents, siblings, grandparents or extended biological and nonbiological kin who join together to perform various family functions. Members of the family system influence and are influenced by every other member. The family creates a system that has unique properties, that is governed by both implicit and explicit rules that specify roles, power structures, and communication styles. Within the family system there are preferred ways of problem solving, decision making, and negotiating. Roles, power structure, and communication patterns are the dynamic processes of the system and its interrelated and interdependent constituent parts.[3]

Because the family is a unique system, using the systems framework will enable social workers to analyze and assess the content and processes of families as well as external influences. In the interest of addressing the importance of family assessment in which formal family therapy is neither requested nor provided by the agency, we illustrate family assessment systems concepts and their application to the Diaz family and a couple, Mr. and Mrs. Barkley. The first takes place in a health care setting.[4]

Case Example

Carlos Diaz, 66, lives with his 16-year-old son John in a subsidized apartment on the second floor of a three-story building. Mr. Diaz is diabetic, is visually impaired but not legally blind, and has a history of heavy alcohol use, though he has abstained from alcohol for the last 7 years. Mr. Diaz's companion of 18 years, Ann Mercy, recently died of a massive stroke. She had provided emotional support, given Mr. Diaz his insulin injections, and managed the household. Mr. Diaz has difficulty walking, has fallen several times in the past year, and is now hesitant to leave his apartment. In addition to John, Mr. Diaz has eight children from an earlier marriage who live in nearby suburbs, though only one, Maria, calls him regularly. Mr. Diaz's physician considers his current living arrangement to be dangerous because of the need for Mr. Diaz to climb stairs. The physician is also concerned about his capacity to administer his own insulin. A medical social worker convenes a family meeting with Mr. Diaz, John, his son John, daughter Maria and stepdaughter Anita.

Application of Systems Concepts

Problems occur in a person or family and situation context. In this case example, the problems occur in part because of Mr. Diaz's living situation, his access to alternative living environments, and the availability of a continuum of care that might include in-home supports. Mr. Diaz's income and health insurance coverage will also influence the alternatives available to the family. Such systems factors should always be accorded prominence to avoid assumptions that problems are caused by factors internal to the family system. In this case, both internal and external factors impinge upon and disrupt family functioning and influence family dynamics. When families experience a disruption, like that faced by the Diaz family, family dynamics are often directed toward restoring equilibrium. Table 10-2

summarizes the system concepts considered in this and the Barkley couple case.

Family Homeostasis

Homeostasis is a systems concept that describes the function of a system to maintain or preserve equilibrium or balance. When faced with a disruption, a system tends to try to regulate and maintain system cohesion. For example, it may try to maintain the status quo in response to family transitions in the life cycle or stressors associated with acculturation or environmental events. As systems, families develop mechanisms that serve to maintain balance (i.e., homeostasis) in their structure and operations. They may restrict the interactional repertoires of members to a limited range of familiar behaviors and develop mechanisms for restoring equilibrium whenever it is threatened (in much the same way that the thermostat of a heating system governs the temperature of a home).

The death of a family member (in this case, Ann Mercy) is one of the factors that disrupted the Diaz family's equilibrium. In effect, previously established patterns and expectations—for example, Mr. Diaz's role as the head of the family and his ability to care for himself and John—have been called into question because of his physical condition.

Several factors are playing out in this case. Mr. Diaz rejects the physician's assessment and that of his family regarding his capacity. Atchey notes that "it is common for the elderly to feel a lower power as a result of social limitations imposed by others' perceptions of physical conditions as well as the limitations of the condition itself" (1991, p. 79). Another factor is the intergenerational conflicts in the Diaz case. Intergenerational conflicts may also occur around issues of care taking, dependency, or a decline in health, especially with the loss of a spouse. Finally, Mr. Diaz's behavior may be seen as an attempt to restore family equilibrium in the family system by asserting his independence and protecting his role. Minuchin (1974) speaks of this tendency of families to maintain preferred patterns as long as possible and to offer resistance to change beyond a certain range of specific behaviors:

Alternative patterns are available within the system. But any deviation that goes beyond the system's threshold of tolerance elicits mechanisms, which reestablish the accustomed range. When situations of

TABLE-10-2 SYSTEMS CONCEPTS APPLICATIONS TO FAMILIES

Family Homeostasis

Family Rules

Content and Process Levels of Family Interactions

system disequilibrium arise, it is common for family members to feel that other members are not fulfilling their obligations. Calls for family loyalty and guilt producing maneuvers then appear. (p. 52)

When the medical social worker convenes the Diaz family, she recognizes that the previous state of equilibrium in Mr. Diaz's life and health care has been disrupted by the death of Ann Mercy. Maria is concerned about Mr. Diaz's capacity to care for himself and his son John. Ann Mercy's daughter, Anita (from a previous marriage), has taken Ann Mercy's possessions, including a washing machine, without Mr. Diaz's knowledge or approval which was an additional disruptive dynamic. Mr. Diaz fears that his children want to place him in a nursing home and to remove John from his care. He states emphatically that he can administer his own insulin and can cook, clean, and vacuum, although he has not done these tasks. Mr. Diaz's wishes can be seen as an effort to protect his independence and restore as much of the family equilibrium as possible. Meanwhile, other family members (except John) and his doctor doubt his capacity to assume these duties. These dynamics, including those stemming from family rules about behavior, play a decisive role in the family's interactions.

Family Rules

Family homeostasis is maintained to the extent that all members of the family adhere to a limited number of rules or implicit agreements that prescribe the rights, duties, and range of appropriate behaviors within the family. Rules are formulas for relationships, and are guides for scripts, conduct and interactions in the family. They represent a set of prescriptive behaviors that define relationships and organize the ways in which family members interact. Implicit rules (i.e., unwritten, covert laws governing behavior) are often beyond the participants' level of awareness; thus they must be inferred from observing family interactions and communications. Examples of implicit rules that dictate the behavior of members in relation to family issues include the following:

- *"Dad has the final word"* (a rule observed in the Diaz family).
- *"You know that your parents expect us for the holidays."*
- *"Children don't talk back to their parents."*
- *"Children are not involved in the affairs of adults."*
- *"Avoid saying what you really feel."*

- *"Elderly parents are cared for by their children."*
- *"In this house, we respect the privacy of other family members."*
- *"Don't talk about unpleasant things or feelings."*
- *"Private family matters are not talked about in public."*

Families do, of course, formulate rules that are openly recognized and explicitly stated, such as the following:

- *"That gangsta rap is not coming in this house."*
- *"We don't allow children to play violent video games."*
- *"It doesn't matter who has a tattoo, you're not getting one."*
- *"Children are limited to two hours of TV per day."*
- *"There will be no swearing in this house."*
- *"Who told you that you could go to the mall?"*

In assessing family systems, you are interested in the implicit rules that guide a family's actions and the extent that they have a disruptive effect. Because these rules are unwritten, their impact on the lives of families often goes unrecognized, or when recognized, unspoken. In consequence, members become caught in situations in which their behavior is dictated by forces of which they are unaware. By adhering to such "rules," family members often perpetuate and reinforce the very problematic behavior of which they complain. For example, teenagers often complain about parental pressures, yet they often persist in the behavior that prompts the parental response.

Although rules govern the processes of families, they differ drastically from one culture to another and from one family to another. Examples of culturally or racially based rules that govern family processes include the following:

- *"Do not bring attention to yourself."*
- *"Respect your elders."*
- *"Avoid shaming your family at all costs."*
- *"Bring honor to your family."*
- *"The duty of children is to listen and obey."*
- *"Loyalty to the family is expected."*
- *"Elders in the family are wise."*
- *"Share what you have with your relatives."*
- *"A wife's duty is to her husband and his family."*
- *"Respect authority."*

These rules may differ significantly from the typical family rules in Western society, which tend to stress competitiveness, assertiveness, individualism, and limited obligations beyond the nuclear family. Yet some may not exclusively be based on culture or race. Some may even seem outdated, as the U.S. society has tended to move toward a more egalitarian position in interactions between age groups. Two of these rules appear to be influencing the Hispanic Diaz family:

- *Respect your elders.*
- *The duty of children is to listen and obey.*

Mr. Diaz perceives the violation of these rules as a threat to his autonomy as the family decision maker and his role as head of the family. Reactions to these rules on the part of the various family members contribute to the family dynamics and impede attempts by the social worker to move the family toward consensus and problem solving.

Functional and Rigid Rules

The implicit rules or "norms" found in a family system may be either functional or rigid in that they may occur in a situational context. Examples of rules that may have consequences for families include the following:

- *"Dad can express his needs and wants, but other members of the family (mother, grandmother, siblings) can't express theirs unless they are in agreement with those of Dad."*
- *"Be careful what you say around Mom. She will get upset."*
- *"Self-control is a sign of strength so don't let people see your weaknesses."*
- *"Avoid serious discussions of family problems."*
- *"Don't take responsibility for your own behavior. Always put the blame on someone else."*
- *"Don't be different from other family members."*
- *"It is important to win all arguments."*
- *"Don't raise your voice."*

If rules are functional, they enable the family to respond flexibly to environmental stress, to individual needs, and to the needs of the family unit. Functional rules provide the family with opportunities to explore solutions, thereby contributing to the development of capable, adaptive, and healthy family members within the family system. Rules that permit the system to respond flexibly are optimal. Examples of functional rules that facilitate and open and flexible climate in the family include the following:

- *"Everyone's ideas and feedback are important."*
- *"Family members don't always have to agree or to like the same things."*

- *"It is okay to talk about any feelings—disappointments, fears, anger, or achievements."*
- *"Family members should work out their disagreements with other family members."*
- *"It is okay to admit mistakes; others in the family will understand and support you."*

As you observe family processes, keep in mind that all families have functional and facilitative rules as well as rigid rules. The latter can however, undermine positive family dynamics. But, facilitative rules allow the family to "work out disagreements," or to observe that "everyone's ideas are important." Variations in both types of rule can of course occur depending on the age and cognitive ability of minors in the family.

Identifying both types of rules is critical to making a balanced assessment of family functioning. Generally, family systems operate according to a relatively small set of rules governing relationships and behavior. Your understanding of family rules will enhance your assessment of the situation. Because families are rule-governed, many behaviors or communications you observe are likely to be stylized or patterned. Be alert to repetitive sequences of behavior in all areas of family life; behaviors that are crucial to the operations of the family will appear over and over. As a result, you will have many opportunities to observe stylized behavior that is an integral part of the family's functioning. Because culture may play a decisive role in family rules, you should avoid assessing family rules using indices that may be relevant to native U.S. families. Also, some racial and ethnic families in the U.S. may function optimally with rules that are opposite of those previously described (Okun, Fried, & Okun, 1999).

In the Diaz family, the social worker observed that two rules, "Dad has the final say" and "respect your elders," posed difficulties for problem solving. Given an opportunity to contribute, others in the family suggested potential solutions in support of Mr. Diaz's desire for independence. The role of the social worker in this case was to establish a climate in which members expressed their concerns without blaming other members or assuming defensiveness or polarized positions. For this turnaround to occur, the neutrality of the social worker was important.

Cautions about Assessing Rules

Perceptions about whether rules are rigid or dysfunctional warrant further words of caution. In this case example, the rules observed by Mr. Diaz formed the basis for norms stating that parents are to be obeyed and have status. His assertion of his parental status coupled with his limited capacity to care for himself and John, although in conflict with the views of his daughter, is a culturally derived expectation. Likewise, with Anita's unwillingness to honor the family rules you would want to explore whether the basis of her behavior stems from intergenerational tension (current or historical, adult, child–parent), whether the tension is between traditional norms, and the degree of acculturation (child reared in the United States and parent born in another country) (McAdoo, 1993, p. 11).

A labeling of rules as rigid by U.S. standards may, in fact, be biased when applied to certain racial or cultural groups. Rules should therefore be explored in the context of culture and identity, including the culture of same-sex families and the family's origins. Because it is almost impossible to be attentive to all the nuances of race and culture without making generalizations, asking the client about the role of culture or race may provide the "most direct and accurate information about cultural realities" (Caple, Salcido, & di Cecco, 1995, p.162; McAdoo, 1993). Okun, Fried & Okun (1999). Spitalnick and McNair (2005) also point to identity as a cultural component and therefore an important consideration in working with same-sex couples. Irrespective of the type, rules serve a purpose in the family system in that they govern behavior and socialize members to family expectations. In times of crisis, rules provide structure that may in fact keep the family from spiraling out of control.

Violation of Rules

When rules are violated, new behaviors are introduced into its system. In response, the family may resort to habitual modes of a previous state of equilibrium, thereby keeping the system "on track." These modes often take the form of feedback or admonitions to members, filled with "shoulds," "oughts," and "don'ts" intended to modify or eliminate behaviors that deviate from the norm. For example, "You should have asked me if you could go to the mall." This statement indicates that a rule has been broken. Specifically, going to the mall was without parental permission. Family members, by using threats, anger, guilt, or other such forms of behavior, may also counteract irregularities in the system. For example, "I guess that it does not matter what I think," may be intended to induce guilt or express anger. Responses to violations of rules may be observed in nonverbal behaviors, for example, hand or eye gestures, facial expressions, silence, or exaggerated sighs. To help you grasp the effectiveness of a system in

limiting or eliminating proscribed behaviors, note the pressure exerted by Mr. Diaz on his stepdaughter to adhere to the rule of "Dad has the final say":

Anita: I have taken Mom's things, including the washing machine, because they were hers. She bought them. I want things to remember her by, and she said I could have them.

Mr. Diaz: You have no right to come in here and take things that belonged to your mother and me. You show no respect for your stepfather.

Anita: You were often a burden to Mom with your drinking and providing for your insulin. It is clear that you can't take care of John and something has to be done. You are not my father.

Mr. Diaz: You cannot come into this house and decide how things will be done. [He turns away and stops speaking to Anita]

Anita: If you don't agree, I can go to court to get custody of John.

In the preceding scene, Anita and Mr. Diaz disagree about the rule that "Dad has the final say," in part because Anita does not consider Mr. Diaz to be her father. If the family has a rule that anger may not be expressed overtly—for example, in a physically or verbally aggressive manner—family members may stop speaking and ignore an offending member until the latter offers an apology. The family's rule about anger is unclear, but it may be assumed that Anita has violated an implicit rule, which Mr. Diaz perceives as a sign of disrespect.

The previous examples of rules may remind you of incidents in your own nuclear or extended family in which your behavior was regulated, reinforced, or extinguished by the response of other family members. As you contemplate your own experiences, perhaps you can begin to appreciate more fully the powerful influence of the family in shaping the lives and behaviors of clients, even years after they have physically departed from their families of origin.

Flexibility of Rules

The opportunity to influence rules or to develop new rules varies widely from family to family. Optimally, families will have rules that permit the system to respond flexibly to change and to evolve new rules compatible with changing needs and developmental stage of family members. In contrast, rigid rules prevent members from modifying their behavior over time in response to changing circumstances and pressures, thus crystallizing relationships and stereotyping roles.

With respect to flexibility of rules, Becvar and Becvar (2000a) discuss the concepts of morphostasis and morphogenesis. *Morphostasis* describes a system's tendency toward stability, a state of dynamic equilibrium. *Morphogenesis* refers to the system-enhancing behavior that allows for growth, creativity, innovation, and change (p. 68). For a system to find and maintain balance, it must be able to remain stable in the context of change and to change in the context of stability (Becvar & Becvar, 2000a). Optimally, system rules will allow for a change when it is necessary to meet individual and family needs. As you assess family systems, then, you must not only identify a family's rules and operations, but also determine the degree of flexibility (or rigidity) of the rules and of the system itself. This may be observed in part by assessing the degree of difficulty that a family experiences in adjusting and maintaining a dynamic state of balance in response to potential developments that occur during its life cycle, such as individual maturation, emancipation of adolescents, marriage, birth, retirement, aging, and death.

Pressures on families from rules can change over the life span. The ongoing developmental changes in minors may cause them to press for redefinition of family rules or pursue interests and values alien to those embraced by the family. Rules that govern the behavior of minors are modified when they become adults. Elders, however, accustomed to a certain set of rules vis-à-vis their status, may be disinclined to accept modifications. Further, it is often difficult for elders to cope with situations in which they feel acted upon by rules set forth by their adult children, professionals, or institutions. These dynamics cause "disequilibrium within the family system, a sense of loss, and perhaps a feeling of strangeness until new transactional patterns restore family balance" (Goldenberg & Goldenberg, 1991, p. 40).

In addition to assessing the stresses on rules caused by developmental changes and internal events (inner forces), the social worker must assess the extent to which a family's rules allow the system to respond flexibly to dynamic societal stresses (outer forces), such as loss of a job, concerns about neighborhood safety, relocation of the family, occurrence of a natural disaster, or uprooting of the family experienced by immigrants or refugees. Families concerned about neighborhood safety, or minority families, for example may adopt rigid rules that function as protective factors to minimize risks. For immigrants or refugee families, further complicating dynamics are the vast contrasts between their rules and those of the Western culture. The process of immigration and cultural transition requires a large number of life changes over a short period of time—for example, material, economic, and educational changes; changes in roles; and the loss of extended family, support systems, and familiar environments (Green, 1999). Rules that these families may adopt may be a mix of the new and old cultures.

Responding successfully to inner and outer stresses requires constant transformation of the rules and behaviors of family members to accommodate ongoing changes while maintaining family continuity. Families often seek help because of an accumulation of events that have strained the coping ability of the entire family or of individual members. Even when these changes are for the better, they may overwhelm the coping mechanisms and resilience of individual members or an entire family system.

Most families have rules that do allow the system to respond readily to dynamic inner and outer forces. Indeed, the "normal" family or optimally functioning family may actually be an atypical phenomenon. The Diaz family may fall in the midrange of this continuum, because they have both rigid and functional rules. The rule that "Dad has the final say" is a rigid rule with Mr. Diaz's family insofar as it seems to be observed by his biological children, but not Anita. However, the rule that "Taking care of family members is a primary obligation" is functional in that it has meant that both Maria and John, two of Mr. Diaz's biological children, wish to assist him in continuing to live independently and safely. Maria, for example, offers to help her father find a first-floor apartment near her and to join with John in learning how to administer his insulin.

Mapping Rules

As you assess rules, you might, in collaboration with the family, devise a map in which the family indicates the status and function of rules. In this way, families can decide which rules are functional and facilitative, or rigid, or culturally based. In this way, you are engaging the family in the assessment and also you gain a better understanding of the family in its own context.

Content and Process Levels of Family Interactions

In addition to identifying family rules, it is important for social workers to understand the concepts of *content* and *process* levels of interaction, the third system concept in Table 10-2. Suppose that the following scenario occurs in your office in a family agency as you conduct the initial interview with Mr. and Mrs. Barkley.

Case Example

In response to your inquiry about the problems they are experiencing, Mr. Barkley glances at his wife and then indicates that she has been depressed and "sick" for some time. He states that the couple has come to your agency seeking help for "her" problem. As you look at Mrs. Barkley, she nods in agreement.

You are concerned at this moment with not only with what the couple is saying to you (the content of the discussion); at the same time, you are keenly interested in assessing the underlying intent or meaning of messages. Further, you observe the manner in which the spouses relate or behave as they talk about the problem. In other words, you are observant of the process *that occurs and the* content. *You make mental note of the fact that the husband—with tacit approval from the wife—speaks for his wife and that the wife is the identified problem. Both spouses appear to disregard any impact of the problem on the husband, any possible part he might play in reinforcing or exacerbating his wife's depression or problematic behavior, or problems he might be experiencing. With respect to roles, the wife is presented as the "problem person" and the husband as the social worker's "consultant." Several important interactional behaviors thus occurred at the process level in the initial session, revealing information about the manner in which the spouses define their problem and how they relate, and pointing to promising avenues for exploration in assessing their problems.*

Families' roles and rules are often revealed at the process level, but may be ignored by you as you selectively attend to what clients are "saying." For this reason, using your observational skills to attend to what people are doing as they discuss problems is crucial to assessing and intervening effectively in family systems. Otherwise, in this case you could easily become caught up at the content level by continuing to explore the etiology of Mrs. Barkley's "depression." The husband maintains his role as information-giver and Mrs. Barkley is the passive, identified client, while all involved ignore the stylized behaviors of the couple that may play a vital part in the problem. Family relationships form reciprocal repetitive patterns and have *circular* rather than *linear* motion. Carter and McGoldrick (1999b) caution

social workers against cause-and—effect thinking, which asks why and looks for someone to blame. Instead, they suggest, "identifying patterns and tracing their flow" may prove useful, because family patterns "once established, are perpetuated by everyone involved in them, although not all have equal power or influence" (p. 437).

Before leaving this case, consider whether or not, cultural norms may have dictated that Mr. Barkley act as the spokesperson for the couple and the manner in which her symptoms are discussed. In this second scenario, Mr. Barkley describes Mrs. Barkley as being restless and as having headaches and frightening dreams that prevent her from sleeping. While the content and process of their interaction is similar to the previous couple, in this situation the *content* level may pertain to how depression is culturally described. The *process* level also has a cultural component, in that Mr. Barkley serves as the spokesperson. Think about how you could draw Mrs. Barkley into the conversation, taking care to respect the culturally derived status and role relationship between the couple. You might ask Mr. Barkley if it is permissible to direct exploratory questions to the wife, explaining that hearing from her will improve your understanding of their concerns. In this way, you show the couple that you respect their family structure and cultural norms. You might also inquire about how their own culture would deal with the situation as Mr. Barkley has described it, as well as what prompted the couple's decision to seek help.

Sequences of Interaction

To assess families adequately, paying attention to the sequences of interaction that occur between members is important. All families play out scenarios or a series of transactions in which they manifest redundancies in behavior and communication, some of which may be culturally derived (e.g., as illustrated in the second Barkley family example). Analysis of interactional sequences may reveal coping patterns that are utilized by individuals or by the entire family system. Observation of interactional sequences may yield rich information concerning communication styles, the behaviors of individuals, and the manner in which all family members reinforce counterproductive interactions.

To illustrate how this works, consider the following excerpt taken from the first minutes of a session with the Diaz family. In this example, Mr. Diaz, daughter Maria, son John, and stepdaughter Anita demonstrate the sequential behaviors that have a powerful impact on the family system. The medical social worker involved with this family has convened a family group conference to consider health and safety alternatives for Mr. Diaz.

Anita [*to social worker*]: Carlos can't maintain himself or John. John runs wild, with no appropriate adult supervision, and Carlos can't take care of himself now that Mother has died [*Anita looks earnestly at the social worker, but signals distance by using Mr. Diaz's first name. Mr. Diaz sits stolidly, arms folded, glowering straight ahead*].

Maria [*to social worker*]: Dad is having trouble with John and hasn't taken care of himself all these years with Ann Mercy doing the cooking and cleaning and injecting his insulin [*To Mr. Diaz.*] Dad, I respect you and want to help you in any way, but things just can't continue like they are. [*attempting to reason with her father*].

Mr. Diaz [*to social worker*]: These children "no tienen respeto." They don't give me the respect they should give me the father of this family. They want to put me in a nursing home and take John away from me [*appealing to the social work to notice the unfair, disrespectful way that he is being treated*].

Anita: Maybe that would be for the best, since you can't take care of yourself or John [*triumphant facial expression resembling a smile*].

Maria [*showing frustration, explains to social worker*]: Dad is used to having his own way and we do respect him—at least I do—but he won't listen to how some things have to change.

Mr. Diaz: Maria, you have been a good daughter, and I am surprised at your behavior. I would think that you would stick by your father if anyone would.

John: Dad, you know I stick by you. And I can help with some things, too. I want to stay with you. We have been getting along okay, and I want to be a good son and take care of you [*attempting to establish equilibrium by supporting the father*].

Anita: John, you have been running in the streets, in trouble with the law, taking money from your father. You are no help to him, and he can't be a good parent to you [*reasserting her position*].

Maria: John, I know you want to help, and you are close to your dad. But you have made a lot of problems for him, and I, too, wonder if you can take care of him or he can take care of you.

In this excerpt, the family plays out a discordant, yet repetitive thematic interaction that, with slight variation, can be observed over and over in their transactions. Families may discuss an endless variety of topics or content issues, but their processes often have a limited number of familiar behaviors. It is as though the family is involved in a screenplay, and once the curtain is raised, all members participate in the scenario according to the family script. It is important to understand that this family script has no beginnings or endings; that is, anyone may initiate the scenario by enacting his or her "lines." The rest of the family members almost invariably follow their habitual styles of relating, editing their individual scripts slightly to fit different versions of the scene being acted out by the family. In these scenes, the subjects discussed will vary, but the roles taken by individual family members and the styles of communicating and behaving that perpetuate the scenario fluctuates very little.

In the preceding scenario, notice the sequencing of the transactions that took place:

1. Anita speaks forthrightly about her concerns about John and Mr. Diaz's capacity for parenting him because of Mr. Diaz's medical condition. Responding nonverbally (*folding his arms and glowering*), Mr. Diaz declines to participate openly (*a patterned behavior when there is disagreement*).
2. Maria affirms some of Anita's concerns but also speaks directly to her father, affirming her respect for him as father and head of the family.
3. Mr. Diaz asserts that his children "no tienen respeto" and that their motivation is to put him away.
4. Anita does not deny that a nursing home might be the best solution.
5. Maria reasserts her respect for her father, yet notes that some things must change.
6. Mr. Diaz addresses Maria and questions whether she is, in fact, showing proper respect for him as her father.
7. John joins the fray and tries to identify himself as a good son with "respeto," which adds another dimension to the transactions.
8. Anita puts John in his place by doubting whether he has acted as a good son or whether Mr. Diaz can be a good parent to him.
9. Maria supports John's desire to be a good son but agrees that there are persistent problems with Mr. Diaz and his care of John.

In observing this and other similar scenarios of the Diaz family, you can identify patterned behaviors and "rules" governing family sequenced interactions that may not be apparent when observing single transactions. For example:

- *Anita, perhaps because she is a stepdaughter, does not acknowledge the family rule of "respeto" and challenges Mr. Diaz's wishes and capabilities. In fact, she calls him by his first name.*
- *Maria does acknowledge Mr. Diaz's place in the family and tries to show appropriate respect while acknowledging that problems do exist.*
- *John attempts to forge a strong coalition with Mr. Diaz by identifying his wishes to maintain the current situation.*
- *Mr. Diaz addresses the social worker and Maria, ignoring Anita, who has violated a family rule.*
- *Anita and Mr. Diaz invariably disagree.*
- *Maria attempts to mediate, affirming Mr. Diaz's position and the rule, while acknowledging problems.*

As the social worker in this situation, your first impulse might be to shout "Stop!" In reality, observing the interaction responses in family allows you to focus interventions strategically on the family's limited number of processes. Analyzing the rules, processes, content, and patterns in the interactions provided the social worker with multiple entry points for intervening and to assist the family in coming to a decision. For example, there is the agreement between the stepsisters (Maria and Anita) that Mr. Diaz cannot continue to live his life as he has in the past and that change is required. Mr. Diaz's role is not altogether clear at this point, but he understands and eventually reluctantly agrees that he needs help in maintaining his independence and caring for himself and John. It is obvious, that *he*, in particular his clinging to rigid rules, is the focus of the family's problem, rather than his physical condition. An alliance is formed between the parent–child subsystem consisting of Mr. Diaz and John, who are allied as the two males in the family and protective of each other, and between the two stepsisters. In working with the family, the social worker had two major tasks:

- *Focusing members' attention on Mr. Diaz's needs related to his physical condition.*
- *Engaging members in discussion that facilitates problem solving around this issue.*

Even so, family rules and patterns are playing a part in the problem and its potential resolution, and therefore must be addressed.

Employing "Circular" Explanations of Behavior

To this point, the discussion is focused on the interactions and dynamics of the Diaz family from a systems framework. The repetitive interactional patterns and the reciprocal influence of all actors in the family system were emphasized. In this discussion, the concept of *circular causality* was applied, demonstrating that each member's behavior becomes a stimulus to all other involved members of the system.

The concept of circular behavior stands in contrast to a *linear explanation* of the causes of behavior. In a linear explanation, event A causes event B; event B causes event C; and so forth. To illustrate the difference between these two conceptual frameworks for viewing the causality of behavior, the Diaz family is once again considered.

- *In a linear explanation of behavior, one would say, "When Anita attacks Mr. Diaz, he defends himself."*
- *A circular explanation of behavior would take the following form: "When Anita attacks Mr. Diaz, he defends himself, and Maria acts to mediate, supporting both Mr. Diaz and Anita.*
- *The mediation is not accepted, thus the charges and countercharges between Anita and Mr. Diaz continue, with John attempting to ally himself with his father."*

Nichols and Schwartz (1998) underscore the point that *circular* and *linear* concepts of causality reflect contrasting approaches in assessing and intervening in family processes. The circular explanation is systemic and is systems-oriented—not only because it offers a more adequate description of behavior, but also because it offers a greater number of alternatives for intervention. In the preceding example, if the social worker had operated from a linear orientation, she would have intervened to stop Anita from attacking Mr. Diaz. Instead, she referenced the circular explanation, focusing on the sequence of behavior, targeting the entire circular patterns for intervention.

Examining the role of the external factors, such as the level of insurance coverage, also prompted the social worker to assist family members in exploring environmental constraints and solutions that might affect the goal of Mr. Diaz continuing to live independently. By addressing mezzo- and macro-level factors, the resource assistance and family supports necessary to achieve this goal was clarified.

By emphasizing circular influences in your interviewing style in the assessment process, you may observe three types of differences that may be useful to explore:

- *Differences between individuals (e.g., "Anita gets angry the most.")*
- *Differences between relationships (e.g., "What is the difference between the way Mr. Diaz treats Anita compared to how he treats Maria?")*
- *Differences between time periods (e.g., "How did she get along with Mr. Diaz last year as compared to now?")*

By orienting the assessment to solicit information regarding differences, you should be able to elicit relevant data more efficiently than if you tried to obtain linear descriptions. Linear explanations focus on the action–reaction cycles—that is, assigning responsibility or blame to one or more members whose problematic behavior is conspicuous. If you are attuned only to the repetitive nature of linear interactions, you may sharply reduce your ability to help family members reframe their behaviors and move away from counterproductive patterned interactions.

Family members also tend to explain behavior using a linear orientation, often assigning arbitrary beginnings and endings to sequences of interaction in ways that define other members as villains and themselves as victims. Mr. Diaz, for instance, viewed himself as an innocent victim of Anita's disrespectful behavior. Further, he perceived her as the person who had upset the family system. In situations of this nature, a task is to counteract the linear perspective of one person as the initiator and the other person as the reactor. You can explain systems concepts emphasizing the role, responsibility, and reciprocity of all family members in maintaining and developing functional interactions and problem solving. In the interest of problem solving, you can also share your observations so that each member can reflect on his or her role in the situation. Your ultimate goal is to create a climate in which family members' thoughtful (rather than reactive) responses become the norm.

With the Diaz family and Mr. and Mrs. Barkley, the systems concepts of homeostasis, rules and sequences, and patterns of interaction, including linear and circular communications, were applied. Family rules in the Diaz family were emphasized in that they had a tremendous influence on the other transactions in the family. In further assessing this family, you might utilize one of the family strengths assessment tools to explore potential resources, and the family's social support network, both of which might include viable alternatives that would support Mr. Diaz's desire to live independently and to care for John.

Assessing Problems Using the Systems Framework

The utilization of a systems perspective on family problems has implications for gathering relevant data in the assessment process. Many clients—even those designated as troubled by other family members—see themselves as victims of the actions of others or of external forces over which they have no control. When families initially seek help, they are often prepared to "complain" or be the informant about those who are "causing" their problems. Because of their selective perception of the "causes" of events, these individuals often do not offer information that assists social workers in formulating a clear picture of how these problems may be reinforced and exacerbated either by the identified client or by others in the family system. They may also omit details with regard to other systems or events that influence the problems that they are experiencing. As a consequence, it is important that you have a conceptual framework and accompanying skills with which to identify themes within the family's processes and to elicit relevant data about the family system. Otherwise, you may unwittingly adopt a family member's definition of "who has the problem," focus interventions on changing the behavior of these selected persons, and neglect the influence of other family members and events.

Although systemic patterns of interaction that restrict and mold clients' behavior are woven throughout the fabric of many family problems, you often do not have the opportunity of observing these interactions firsthand. Family members, for instance, may refuse service or be absent or unavailable. In the Diaz case, Anita lived in another city and was available only briefly. It was unclear whether she would be involved with the family beyond the family conference as a participant in problem solving. In some cases, a family member may describe problems that he or she is experiencing in relationships with family members or with significant others who are not present. In other situations, a family member may be reluctant to participate.

When you cannot directly observe interactional and problem-solving processes, you then face the important task of eliciting highly specific information from family members. This is best accomplished by carefully exploring a number of critical incidents that illustrate the problem, before, during, and after; the context in which the problem occurred; and its duration and frequency. Further, you will want to explore how the family has coped, the extent to which other systems are involved, their attempts to resolve the situation, as well as resources and strengths. In instances in which family relationships are identified as a concern, you will want to identify underlying family patterns, establish the sequences of discrete transactions, and elicit descriptive information about the behaviors and communications of all involved. Given that clients tend to summarize critical incidents ("The teacher called and said that Shondra was messing up in school"), possibly omitting critical details (her father was recently sentenced to prison for five years). It is helpful to explain to families that you are searching for each discrete event or transaction that occurred in any critical incident targeted for exploration.

You can begin by asking family members to give a descriptive account of an event so that you see what happened as clearly as if you had been present. As members provide this descriptive information, you can also observe family relationships. In observing the interactions between family members, you can identify key interaction patterns and the nature of alignments among various subsystems of the family (e.g., parents, siblings, grandparents, and other kin). In such explorations, it is not uncommon to discover that other persons (e.g., an older sibling, stepparents, grandparents) and other systems play significant roles in contributing to or resolving the family's problem. Based on information gained through your exploration of family affiliative ties and rules, you will often need to redefine and expand the problem system to include more actors than were originally identified.

In assisting families to understand the need for an overall assessment of the family, it is helpful to explain that the family is a "system," stressing that the entire family is affected by, and may even exacerbate, problems experienced by one member. Exploring with each family member the ways in which they are affected by the problem can help them to understand what you mean by the family as a system. Parents of youth who are in involved with juvenile court, for example, may be at their wit's end and simply want the child out of their hair for a time. Often, they may say, "Take him. I can't do anything with him anymore; he doesn't listen to me. Maybe time away from home will change his attitude."

Tears, guilt, and fears about what is happening to the child and the family may punctuate their tirade, despite their anger. Redefining the problem as a family issue invokes both relief and fears. Note, however, that this approach works only to the extent to which you are nonaccusatory and nonjudgmental, because parents or other family members often interpret the problem with minors as a failure on their part.

Dimensions of Family Assessment

Having discussed the application of system concepts in the Diaz and Barkley families, this next section describes family assessment. Table 10-3 highlights the dimensions of assessment, some of which includes systems concepts, that can be used as guidelines for exploring and organizing the massive amount of data you will gather in working with families. These dimensions will assist you in assessing interactions and evaluating aspects of family operations—a critical preliminary step when planning interventions in solving family problems. Keep in mind that you can augment your assessment by appropriately using the assessment tools described in Table 10-1.

The dimensions to formulate family assessments and plan interventions, utilize the following guidelines.

1. *Identify the dimensions that are most relevant to your clients.* Although the dimensions apply to the processes of couples and families, some may not be pertinent given the presenting complaint and the nature of the

TABLE-10-3 DIMENSIONS OF FAMILY ASSESSMENT

Family context
Family strengths
Boundaries and boundary maintenance
Family power structure
Family decision-making processes
Family goals
Family myths and cognitive patterns
Family roles
Communication styles of family members
Family life cycle

help requested by the family. For example, a family may seek help because of stress caused by providing care for an elderly relative living in their home. Your initial exploration may reveal no major concerns in the relative's functioning (e.g., decision making) as a contributing factor to the family's problem. Thus, you would narrow the assessment to an exploration of the specific problem identified by the family—in this case, caregiver-related stress.

2. *Use the dimensions to guide your exploration of family behavior.* After the first session, review the dimensions and develop relevant questions to further your exploration in subsequent sessions. For example, how has the family handled or coped with problems? How does the family communicate with each other and other patterns of interaction?

3. *Use the dimensions as guidelines for organizing new data into themes and patterns.* Determine the family's or couple's rules or habitual ways of relating in relation to *each* relevant dimension. For example, ask about the family's rules in relation to decision making, roles and power structure, and family goals.

4. *Based on the relevant dimensions, develop a written profile of behaviors of individual members within the system.* For example, with respect to the dimension of communication, a family member may tend to paraphrase messages of others and personalize statements. The same person may be prone to interrupt and to talk excessively, thus monopolizing the session. Developing a profile of behaviors for each family member will provide a framework not only for assessing behaviors but also for planning interventions.

5. *Employ this dimension to assess relevant behaviors of the entire family, developing a profile of salient functional and problematic behaviors that are manifested by the system itself.* For the dimension of communication, functional behaviors of a family may include listening responses and responses that acknowledge the contributions of others (e.g., "You did a good job"). In contrast, responses observed in the same family that may include labeling of members (e.g., you are dumb") or frequent responses of anger directed toward other members are counterproductive.

Family Context

Factors involved in assessing family context include culture, race, socioeconomic class, family form, sexual orientation, and experiences of oppression and discrimination. Recall also the earlier discussion of normative

and nonnormative (e.g., public policy, poverty) family stressors. The extent to which external stressors influence family functioning or have an effect on the family system is an essential part of the assessment process. Families learn to live in a context, often coping with situations that over time may disrupt the family system and diminish family well-being.

The dimension of family context entails simply mapping family life and family functioning to external forces such as relational and social justice. The Ecomap is a tool that can assist you and the family to identify external stressors. In assessing family context with a newly arrived immigrant family, for example, you could use the Culturalgram or the Family Assessment Wheel to assess the family's relative functioning with its situation and to identify stressors associated with the loss of their cultural reference group (Congress, 1994; Mailick & Vigilante, 1997).

Family context may also involve assessing a family's relative social status and oppressive forces acting on them. Oppression is a justice matter, and as such moves beyond simply assessing external forces. It requires the "unmasking of oppressive forces" that affect family functioning (Carniol, 1992). Examples of questions that can guide assessments with an emphasis on social justice are as follows:

- *Is the problem that a family is facing related to their marginalized status in the social environment? (Carniol, 1992).*
- *Is there a relationship between family problems and oppressive forces, for example, structural inequities? (Guadalupe & Lum, 2005; Rooney, 2009; Van Voorhis, 1998).*
- *What is the level of family alienation within the social environment? (Van Voorhis, 1998).*
- *How does the family's narrative inform you of their experience with oppression? (Saleebey, 1996).*
- *Do assumptions about family deviance minimize the effects of oppression and perpetuate the dominant normative narrative about families? (Weinberg, 2006).*

The assessment dimension of family context would also focus on the extent to which the family has access to basic resources, such as food, health care, housing, financial aid, or job training and their ability to secure such resources (Kilpatrick & Holland, 2006; Vosler, 1990). Assisting families to meet their survival needs must take precedence, in fact, over interventions to change family dynamics or to teach communication or parenting skills (Kilpatrick & Holland, 2006). Often, families who lack basic resources are in a crisis, for example, a family who is homeless. Therefore, assessment and intervention strategies related to, for example, communication skills are simply not relevant to this family at this point in their life. This dimension may, however, become relevant when their dire need for basic sustenance is satisfied.

Family Form

Family context also involves family form, in which the task of gathering data and assessing families is paramount to accurately viewing the family within the sphere of its various cultural and family nuances. As discussed earlier, assumptions about family composition and type are often based on traditional definitions of family. Families have evolved from the post–World War II ideal of the two-parent, one-wage-earner unit (Walsh, 1996). For some families, this ideal was never a reality. For example, in a majority of poor and minority families, women have almost always worked outside the home.

Although the form of families may differ dramatically, the external systems of the dominant culture typically still exert considerable influence on family functioning. Carter and McGoldrick (1999a) note, for example, that gay and lesbian couples experience harassment, violence, and the denial of "key legal protections and entitlements" (p. 352). This lack of protection, along with the lack of roles and language for gay or lesbian families, are not only stressors, of course, but it should be noted that these families are "vulnerable to intrusion and invalidation" (Slater, 1995). Minorities who are gay or lesbian face additional difficulties of racial discrimination and may have access to fewer resources because of the stigma of their sexual orientation in their communities. Moreover, limited social support for gay and lesbian youth is available, and in many instances these young people experience both family and social isolation (Morrow, 1993).

It is vital, then, that social workers include the larger contextual issues (e.g., race, culture, class, gender, sexual orientation) and their influence in the assessment of families. In gathering contextual information you are able to develop a working knowledge of the family in its own reality. This knowledge will include culture, biculturalism, ethnic status, language, social class, customs, history, and sexual orientation—all factors that may affect families and the problems they experience. In engaging families to filter out the extent to

which these factors are important, you can emphasize what Norton (1978) and McPhatter (1991) call a "*dual perspective.*" This perspective involves "the conscious and systematic process of perceiving, understanding and comparing simultaneously the values and attitudes of the larger societal system with those of the client's immediate family and community system" and is a vital construct in assessing the social context of a family's presenting problems (McPhatter, 1991, pp. 14–15). In their elaboration on the context of diverse families, Kilpatrick and Holland (2003) maintain that the "dual perspective fosters problem resolution in tune with distinct values and community customs" (pp. 40–41). This perspective recognizes that families are members of two systems, one of "which is dominant or sustaining and the other, the nurturing system. Attention to the influence of both systems is important" (pp. 40–41).

Utilizing the dual perspective helps to identify the points of conflict between the family and larger systems, such as in an assessment of same-sex couples. These couples live in the context of "homophobia" in the larger culture, defined operationally as the fear and hatred of same-sex intimacy and love. As a consequence, these couples may risk job loss, freedom, access to benefits, custody of children, and the ability to jointly purchase homes if they are explicitly identified as a couple. A dual perspective is a necessity for assessing the rich variety of family cultures, because family behavior can be understood in the larger cultural context in which it is embedded. Such a perspective also will prevent you from relying on broad generalizations about particular groups, considering behavior patterns or lifestyles as indicators of dysfunction (Green, 1999; McAdoo, 1993). In utilizing a dual perspective, social workers can view the functionality of a family's behavior within the context of what is "normal" for that particular family's culture.

Numerous authors have cautioned social workers about imposing their own cultural views on the families they serve. Such errors may cause social workers to intervene in ways that are actually disruptive to the family system. For instance, terms such as *enmeshment, fusion,* and *undifferentiated ego mass* may be inappropriate when describing the interdependence observed in some families (Berg & Jaya, 1993; Bernal & Flores-Ortiz, 1982; Boyd-Franklin, 1989a; Flores & Carey, 2000; Okun, Fried, & Okun, 1999). Similarly, although women have a shared history of discrimination, gender when combined with race or ethnicity may not be assumed to be the most important factor for women of color because their lives are also shaped by other realities of oppression (Brown & Root, 1990).

Contextual family factors may also be influenced by narrow definitions of family, personal bias, or oppression. A narrow perspective on family form, for example, presents difficulties for gay or lesbian families because their perspective of "family" means caring, committed, and intimate relationships over time. Native families may also be misunderstood. For instance, the effects of poverty, discrimination, culture, and a collective remembered history have shaped Native American attitudes toward child welfare, social workers, and other professionals. In failing to appreciate the family context emphasized in their culture you may unintentionally use assessment dimension guidelines in a way that has limited relevance to the family situation.

Diversity within Groups

Family context also has a cultural component that may not only influence help-seeking behavior, but also determine how problems are defined. For example, because of perceptions of mental illness and such diseases' negative connotations for self and the family, different cultural groups may respond to assistance that focuses on the cognitive, rather than the emotional, aspects of family difficulties (Sue, 2006; Hirayama, Hirayama, & Cetingok, 1993). In many Native American families, the extended family structure has been important to economic, social, and spiritual survival. As a consequence, your not understanding the Native American practice of consulting with the family about important decisions and reliance on family input for a course of action can cause alienation between you and the family (Horesji, Heavy Runner, & Pablo 1992). Moreover, the principle of self-determination may have a different meaning for some cultural or ethnic groups. Ewalt and Mokuau (1996), for example, suggest that the term may have greater meaning for interests and obligation to an entire group than in the notion of individualism and autonomy.

In working with families who are ethnically or racially diverse, Green (1999) suggests that a basic dimension of cultural competence is identifying what is salient about a client's culture and honestly addressing this factor (p. 37). As an exemplar, Green presents a case described by Rooney and Bibus (1996) and involving a Native American family (p. 43). In this case, Rooney and Bibus integrate the lenses of culture as a critical context in addressing difficulties with parental

substance abuse. In utilizing the culturally defined definition of family, other relatives and tribal members are viewed as resources for the children in the family while the parents receive treatment. Context in this case also takes into account the historical experience of Native Americans when children were systematically separated from their families and tribal connections.

To facilitate an assessment of context with diverse families, Lum (2004) and Chau (1990) have developed practice assessment dimensions in which psychosocial and socio-environmental factors affect clients—for example, oppression and powerlessness. Lum (2004) also identifies the spiritual dimension as being important. These dimensions may be integrated so that social workers are ethnically sensitive throughout the helping process.

It is not possible for you to understand the cultural nuances and their implications in every diverse family. Unfortunately, when you have acquired knowledge of various groups, you face an increased danger of stereotyping. As a social worker, you may feel caught between wanting to be sensitive and culturally competent, and yet experiencing resentment when you are lectured about the importance of understanding racial and cultural differences. At the risk of adding to this tension, we feel that it is important to discuss aspects of culture and race that are important considerations in the overall assessment of family context.

- *Recognize that members of various groups may differ considerably from profiles or descriptions of typical behaviors. This point is particularly important for members of minority groups.*
- *Understand that there are vast differences in race, language, and culture within groups designated as racial or ethnic minorities (Green, 1999). Spanish-speaking people, for example, share some aspects of Hispanic or Latino heritage such as a similar language, however may be differ in other ways depending on their country of origin.*
- *Be aware that members of diverse cultures differ with respect to social class and nationalities. Caple, Salicido, and di Cecco (1995), Hirayama, Hirayama, and Centigok (1993), McAdoo (1993), and Sue (2006) are among the writers who inform us that all group members do not necessarily embrace the normative values of their particular group. Accordingly, differences may be observed along intergenerational lines (as in the case of family rules*

in the Diaz family) and be based on the evolving degree of acculturation.

- *With respect to acculturation, children may adapt to new cultures at a much more rapid pace than their parents because of their exposure to the dominant culture through school, and perhaps because they have no or few years of contact with their culture of origin (Caple, Salcido, & di Cecco, 1995; Hirayama, Hirayama, & Cetingok, 1993).*
- *The values of cultural groups are not fixed but continually evolving. As a consequence, variations may occur within families and reflect their stage in the acculturation process.*

As a means to sort out cultural variations and nuances, McAdoo (1993) suggests using your acquired knowledge to formulate a hypothesis and then exploring the extent to which this information is relevant in a particular family's situation. The implications of these observations are critical and unique for each family system. Therefore, we must be able to individualize each family within its cultural context.

Immigrant and Refugee Status

As you assess the context of families from various cultural groups, you must be aware of the extent to which a family may struggle with efforts to maintain the values and norms of its country of origin while adapting selectively to aspects of American society. When working with such families, it is advisable to obtain information about the family's migration history and look for continuing stresses placed on the family by its efforts to accommodate two (and sometimes more) cultures. Depending on their country of origin, some immigrants and refugees will be more educated and less poor. Nevertheless, all ethnic minority groups in the United States who have migrated or come as refugees face issues related to acculturation. As McGoldrick, Giordano, and Pearce (1996) observe, family values and identity may be retained for several generations after the migration experience and continue to influence the family's outlook, life cycle, and development. Indeed, this experience often preempts the completion of family developmental tasks, and it may require the reconstruction of social networks that have been diminished as a result of leaving the family's cultural reference group.

Rooney (1997) emphasized the dilemma that immigrant and refugee families face in a society that can be both welcoming and hostile. Employers, for example, see such individuals as a source of labor. Yet as the

workforce has become more diverse, workplace policies have not kept pace with family concerns and may constrain an employee's ability to fulfill traditional role obligations. The pressure to conform may distract or delay the new worker's ability to find a place in the employment organization's culture, resulting in stress in the family system. Language is yet another source of conflict, as reflected in U.S. society's indifference to bilingualism and antipluralistic public policy. In the late 1990s, for example, several states passed legislation that made English their official language. In addition, societal expectations assume that immigrants and refugees will act, speak, and dress like the majority population. Tensions exist in the interactions between native born citizens and immigrant groups, and between racial minority and immigrant groups (Rooney, 1997, p. 316). Most often, these tensions are related to jobs, resources, and language and are played out in schools and neighborhoods. More recently, conflicts and tensions have occurred in countries other than the United States.

The essence of systems thinking relative to family context is seeing patterns in which external forces such racism, classism, poverty, work pressures, and homophobia may be referred to as "extra-familial obstacles" (Nichols & Schwartz, 1998, p. 135). While all families encounter obstacles in their transactions with the other social systems, these obstacles may disproportionately affect more-diverse families, adding stressors that affect their functioning and the resources available to them. Hopefully, the discussion of family context will increase your understanding of the relevance of this dimension in the assessment process.

Family Strengths

All families have a range of individual member and group strengths that you should identify during the assessment process (Cowger, 1997; Early & GlenMaye, 2000). In their diverse family and cultural variants, families show strengths in the ability to create supportive networks, interact with a society that may not understand or be indifferent to them, cope with stressful transitions and policies that perceive them as inadequate or undeserving. Yet they still continue on.

Acknowledging strengths in families is not an easy task. Many agencies, professionals, policymakers and funding sources, because of the deeply entrenched focus on pathology, have yet to embrace family strengths. Clients themselves are not always comfortable with a strengths focus. In the process of seeking help, they have been socialized to articulate their needs or problems in exchange for services and often must do so to establish their eligibility for those services. Highlighting what is going right and what is working in families is difficult under these circumstances, and you may need to educate families to focus on their strengths. Assessing and accrediting the strengths inherent in the family system require the deliberate and disciplined effort of all involved.

Even though identifying and utilizing strengths is consistent with the values and principles of the social work profession, according to Jordan and Franklin (2003), the strengths perspective is more of a "philosophical stance than a set of defining assessment and practice skills" (p. 29). The perspective continues to evolve and social workers are encouraged to adopt strengths as a frame of reference in problem solving with clients and in the language that they use (McMillen, Morris & Sherraden, 2004). On the part of the professional, it is also an attitude that informs interactions with clients. Often the dichotomy rests between perceiving oneself as a helper and collaborator, a situation in which client strengths are acknowledged and utilized and clients are thought to be capable of making their own decisions. The other side is perceiving oneself as a hall-monitor or enforcer, in which case, clients with problems are simply told what to do.

A focus on strengths does not preclude paying attention to problems or risks. Instead, strengths are recognized as important to resolving problems. Assessing strengths in families may be oriented toward the future—that is, highlighting goals, aspirations, hopes, and dreams beyond the current difficulties that the family is experiencing. Strengths observed in the Diaz family, despite their patterned behavior was their commitment to helping their father continue to live on his own with supports. Further, an assessment includes current functioning, and aspects of the family climate such as spirituality or religion, coping with adversity, adapting to changes, and resilience (Early & GlenMaye, 2000; Walsh, 1996). Strengths may take the form of protective factors that are external to the family—for example, connections to a larger social network. The strengths perspective is based on the empowerment and humanistic notion that people can change and grow (Jordan & Franklin, 2003). In short, strengths are integral resources in the helping process.

In your assessment, you need to pay particular attention to the strengths of families from various cultural or racial groups, many of whom have been disadvantaged by historic discrimination or, in the case of political refugees, extreme losses. The hopefulness of refugees or immigrants may be affected by their circumstances. Although they may feel demoralized and powerless, they have demonstrated an amazing capacity to survive. Providing these families with an opportunity to tell their story will reinforce the notion of family strengths, even in the most difficult circumstances.

Assessment questions that explore family strengths and resources focus on the following topics:

- *Family traditions, rituals celebrations*
- *Communications*
- *Shared goals*
- *Loyalty*
- *Patterns of help-seeking behavior*
- *Hardiness, coping and resilience in times of adversity*
- *Information about how a problem would be handled in the particular family or its community*
- *Individuals or institutions that the family may turn to in times of difficulty*
- *Family capacities, adaptations, hopes, dreams, or aspirations*

Although these questions are useful with all families, they may have particular relevance to minority groups as a means to identify and observe strengths. Also, as you work with families, in the absences of such a tool in your agency, you can develop your own strengths assessment questions and integrate them into your practice.

Boundaries and Boundary Maintenance of Family Systems

Boundaries, a central concept in family systems theories, can be likened to abstract dividers that function: (1) between and among other systems, or subsystems within the family, and (2) between the family and the environment.

Boundaries may change over time as the family system and its members experience various developmental levels. For example, when a child begins school, the boundaries of the family systems willingly expand to permit interactions with the educational system. Conversely, entry into the family by a juvenile probation officer may be met with reactions, yet the family system by necessity may reluctantly accommodate this intrusion.

In adapting Bertalanffy's general systems theory, Martin and O'Connor (1989) conclude that all systems are open and interdependent with their environment. Within this framework, no system is ever truly closed.

It does, however, selectively respond, permit, screen, or reject inputs, in the form of information, people, or events, through the boundary maintenance function. Conceptualizing the family as an open system allows you to examine the family system's boundaries and boundary maintenance. You can determine the extent to which the family is an *included* system—specifically, its connection to other kin, the community, and membership with other groups. The Social Support Network Map assessment tool can assist you in this regard.

External Family Boundary Maintenance

Because systems are part of still larger systems, families necessarily engage in diverse transactions with the environment. At the same time, they differ widely in the degree to which they are accepting of transactions with other systems which can depend on the flexibility of their boundaries. By "flexibility," we mean the extent to which outsiders are permitted or invited to enter the family system, and members of the family are allowed to invest emotionally and engage in relationships outside the family. Flexibility also involves the extent to which information and materials are exchanged with the environment. Individuals are given the freedom to regulate their interactions external to the family as long as they do not adversely affect other family members or violate the family norms. Those who hold authority in families (e.g., the parental subsystem) perform the bounding functions in such a way that they create discrete family space that exists apart from the larger space of the neighborhood and community. Bounding functions may also be observed in larger family systems such as a clan, in which family is defined in a much broader context.

A family system with thick boundaries is characterized by strict regulation that limits its transactions with the external environment and restricts incoming and outgoing people, objects, information, and ideas. Thick boundaries preserve territoriality, protect the family from undesired intrusions, safeguard privacy, and, in some instances, foster secrets. Authorities in such a family or clan maintain tight control of traffic at the system's perimeter, and the bounding function is rarely relinquished or shared with outsiders or even with family members who have not been assigned the role of performing bounding functions. This form of boundary maintenance is not necessarily a reason for concern, except when there is evidence of harm to family members.

When assessing the bounding patterns of families, it is essential to consider the family's unique style, strengths, and needs. Families may have more flexible boundaries with extended family members, perhaps including well-defined obligations and responsibilities to one another. Conversely, those boundaries may appear less flexible when external influences intrude upon family traditions and values and are seen as a source of conflict or disruption to the family system. At still other times, the family may change to accommodate new inputs over the course of the life cycle or during transitions. Immigrant families, for example, are generally open to new information as they make the transition to a new society. Simultaneously, they may erect boundaries in an effort to screen out what they deem to be undesirable aspects of the new culture. An article in the September 4, 2003, edition of *The New York Times Sunday Magazine* illustrates this point. Entitled "For Schooling, a Reverse Emigration to Africa," tells the story of immigrant Ghanaian parents who send their children back to Ghana so that the children can avoid negative elements in U.S. society.

In another case, a dominant theme of immigrant parents participating in a series of focus groups related to the extent that formal institutions are able to cross family boundaries. The parents were confused about interventions from child protective services and they expressed dismay that schools could teach certain content without seeking parental permission. They were also concerned about the influences of the media and popular culture on their children that were inconsistent with their values and beliefs. Above all, they experienced a loss of respect, and a sense of powerlessness in their parental roles. As one parent indicated, "When I tell my child to do or not do something and he doesn't like it, he will tell me, 'I am going to call 911 and report you.' "[5]

Knowledge of the boundaries and boundary maintenance functions of the family should assist you in identifying the bounding patterns of families you encounter in practice. Bear in mind that the discussion here has emphasized prototypes that may guide you in assessing the bounding patterns of families. In actual practice, your assessment should consider each family's unique style of transacting with the environment and give credibility to the reality of their experience.

Internal Boundaries and Family Subsystems

Assessing the bounding patterns in blended families or families in which parents share custody may prove to be particularly difficult. Children caught in these situations often have to adapt to the expectations, rules, or norms of two households. For them, boundary ambiguity arises as they navigate between parental households and in interactions with each parent. Intergenerational or stepparent boundaries may be problematic and result in conflict. In the Diaz family, for example, the role of Anita (the stepdaughter) in the family's decision making about her brother John and stepfather was unclear. Completing family Genograms, in which you and the family diagram the family's history and constellation over several generations, can provide important data on bounding patterns when working with any type of family (Kilpatrick & Holland, 2006). In the Diaz family, the Genogram would portray relationships between family members; information about previous marriages, divorces, or deaths; and details about the family life cycle, including changes in the children's living arrangements. In summary, the Genogram provides a picture of where family members have been and who was involved, as well as which relational interactions need to be resolved.

Family Subsystems and Coalitions

All families develop networks of coexisting subsystems formed on the basis of gender, interest, generation, or functions that must be performed for the family's survival (Minuchin, 1974). Members of a family may simultaneously belong to numerous subsystems, entering into separate and reciprocal relationships with other members of the nuclear family, depending on the subsystems they share in common (e.g., parents, mother/daughter, brother/sister, father/son), or with the extended family (e.g., grandmother/granddaughter, uncle/nephew, mother/son-in-law). Each subsystem can be thought of as a natural coalition between participating members. Of course, many of the coalitions or alliances that families form can be situation-related and temporary in nature. For example, a teenager may be able to enlist her mother's support in asking her father's permission for a special privilege. A grandmother living in a home may voice disagreement with her daughter and son-in-law regarding his discipline of children, thus temporarily forming a coalition with the children. Such passing alliances are characteristic of temporary subsystems. A situational alliance occurred between the Diaz stepsisters, as well as between John and Mr. Diaz.

Other subsystems—especially partners or spouses, parental, and sibling subsystems—are more enduring in nature. According to Minuchin (1974), the formation of stable, well-defined coalitions between members of these vital subsystems is critical to the well-being and health of the family. Unless there is a strong and endur-

ing coalition between parents, for instance, conflict will reverberate throughout a family, and children may be co-opted into one faction or another as parents struggle for power and control. In general, the boundaries of these three subsystems must be clear and defined well enough to allow members sufficient differentiation to carry out functions without undue interference (Minuchin, 1974). At the same time, they must be permeable enough to allow contact and exchange of resources between members of the subsystem. Minuchin points out that the clarity of the subsystem boundaries has far more significance in determining family functioning than the composition of the family's subsystem. For instance, a parental subsystem that consists of a grandmother and an adult parent-child may function perfectly adequately.

The relative integrity of the boundaries of the spouse, parental, and sibling subsystems is determined by related family rules. A mother clearly defines the boundary of a parental subsystem, for instance, by telling the oldest child not to interfere when she is talking to a younger child about assigned chores that the child has left undone. The message, or "rule," then, is that children are not in a parenting role with their siblings. The mother, however, may delegate parental responsibility to an older child when she leaves the home. In this instance, the "rules" regarding who does the parenting and under what circumstances clearly delineate the boundaries of the parental and sibling subsystems.

Cultural and Family Variants

Culture and race play a critical role in many family subsystems. For example, traditionally many Native American tribes did not consider people to be functional adults until they reached their mid-fifties or became a grandparent. For this reason grandparents were assigned the child-rearing responsibilities. Thus the parenting subsystem included grandparents and grandchildren, rather than parents and their own children. Similar arrangements may be found in other minority-group families, whereby a variety of adults may perform the function of a parent, and in which there is a distribution of family roles and tasks (Boyd-Franklin, 1989a; Carter & McGoldrick, 1999a; McAdoo, 1993; Okun, Fried & Okun, 1999).

The clarity of boundaries within a family is a useful parameter for evaluating family functioning. Minuchin (1974) conceives of all families as falling somewhere along a continuum of extremes in boundary functioning, where the opposite poles are disengagement (diffuse boundaries) and enmeshment (inappropriately rigid boundaries). Family closeness in an enmeshed family system is defined as everyone thinking and feeling alike. Membership in such families requires a major sacrifice of autonomy, thereby discouraging members from exploration, independent action, and problem solving. In contrast, members of disengaged families tolerate a wide range of individual variations by members but are apt to lack feelings of family solidarity, loyalty, and a sense of belonging. Individuals in such families find it difficult to give or to get support from other family members.

Family organization in such systems is unstable and chaotic, and it may become factionalized, with leadership shifting on a moment-to-moment basis. Members often develop individual bounding patterns or become disengaged from the larger family. Yet, when a member of this kind of family experiences high-level stresses that significantly affect other members, this tension will typically activate the family's supportive systems. Otherwise, these systems tend not to respond even when a response is appropriate—for example, parents may not become concerned when an adolescent stays out all night. At the enmeshed end of the continuum, one member's behavior immediately affects others, echoing throughout the family system. Parents accustomed to the adolescent staying at home will respond to any variations with excessive speed and intensity—becoming very angry, for instance, when the adolescent does go out and gets in trouble with the police.

Enmeshment and disengagement are not necessarily dysfunctional processes. Indeed, they may have little or no relevance for some cultural, racial, or socioeconomic groups. According to Minuchin (1974), every family experiences some enmeshment or disengagement between its subsystems as the family passes through various developmental phases. During a family's early developmental years, for instance, a caretaker and young children may represent an enmeshed subsystem. A cultural variant however, is that children may be attached to more than one caretaker. Adolescents gradually disengage from the parental–child subsystem, as they move toward independence and perhaps prepare to leave home. Of course, each of these notions has a cultural variant and may not be a relevant expectation in some cultures. For example, in some cultures, adolescents may be married, although they will live in their own family. In others, young adults live with their families until they are married. Therefore, fluid roles, bonding patterns, and rules as framed in Western society may not signal an enmeshed or disengaged style of relating. Sharing the parental bed until a certain age or sleeping in the same room with parents has been at the center of legal and child development debates in the United States. However, it is a common practice in other cultures (Fontes, 2005). In the United States, many middle-class mothers prefer this arrangement as well; however, there are concerns from the medical profession related to risk to a co-sleeping infant.

Social workers are advised to assess relationships in a cultural context, paying particular attention to culturally derived subsystems or coalitions between family members and patterns of relating (Okun, Fried & Okun, 1999). Cross-generational coalitions that are based on gender can in fact influence cultural solutions (McGoldrick, 1998).

One last word of caution is in order. Social workers would be well advised to closely examine the notion of the "parentified child." This all-inclusive, generally negative term is used to describe a child who has responsibilities or performs roles believed to be beyond dominant normative expectations. In some families, parents out of necessity may delegate responsibilities to a child. Morever, in many cultures, the notion of ages and stages of childhood is not observed and children perform a variety of functions that are critical to maintaining the family system. For some rural farming families and those at the lower end of the socioeconomic spectrum worldwide, children may participate in the division of labor in the household as a matter of survival. Obviously, when compared to Western culture's preferred perception of childhood, this may not be an ideal situation. Such cases warrant your attention if the role of the child exceeds the limits of safety, if a parent or other supervising adult is unavailable for a prolonged period of time, or if children are performing duties that affect their growth and well-being. Even so, you may assume an educational rather than a punitive role with parents, ensuring that they understand that the issue at hand is the health and safety of the child, rather the structural arrangements in the family system.

Relationships in Disengaged Families

Some families can be described as disengaged, that is, members operate separately and apart from the family system to an extent that exceeds the notion of individualism. In these families, some members may form coalitions, but these alliances are apt to be fragile and short-lived, based on immediate gratification of individual needs. Because of the transitory nature of such coalitions, members will likely abandon relationships once their needs are satisfied or an alliance no longer serves their purposes. In such families, the relative lack of opportunity to sustain stable alliances typically proves detrimental to the growth needs of individuals. In the resulting "disconnectedness" of this transactional family style, members become isolated and alienated from one another. Disconnected family members often form relationships and loyalties outside the family unit in an attempt to meet their needs.

In assessing the various structural arrangements of a family, attend to those alignments between family members and outsiders that tug at family loyalties and cause acute family stress. For example, a grandparent living outside the home may take the side of children in family disputes and provide a refuge for them. While this action can be consoling to the children, it may also interfere with the ability of the parents and children to work out their difficulties. Of course, relationships between family members and grandparents or other relatives are not necessarily a disruptive force. Grandparents and other relatives may perform vital supportive functions and roles in families. Further, their involvement can be a significant connection for children, and they may be a primary resource for the transmission of family history, values, and beliefs.

There are times when professional intervention can unwittingly reinforce disengagement in families when they connect with one family member, rather than with the family system as a whole. This problem may be exacerbated in especially troubled families, in which there is a tendency to rescue a member (often a child) from dysfunctional family dynamics. In one case, for example, the mother with a history of substance abuse complained—appropriately so—that the social worker routinely came to her home and picked up her daughter, and she had no idea what they were doing or what they discussed. The social worker's rationale for focusing on the daughter was that she had little hope of the mother changing, and that the daughter needed a positive influence in her life. In attending to the message from the mother, the social worker could have seized on her complaint as a means to engage her. In fact, the mother's complaint suggested that she wanted to be involved. The dynamic of "rescuing" is often associated with social workers in high-stress job situations, such as child protective services, substance abuse, and family violence programs. Highly stressed parents may also disengage by assigning their parental role to a social worker by telling the child, "If you don't go to school, I am going to call your social worker." In either case,

it is advisable to assess these dynamics and work to reconnect members to the family system.

External Family Disengagement

In light of the earlier discussion about family boundaries and oppression, you should also consider whether the entire family system is disengaged from the social environment. Bounding patterns, for example, may represent a family's decision to be separate from all or some values and beliefs contrary to their own. Oppression, in fact, separates and marginalizes some families, treating them as outsiders. Over time, these families may adapt actions, codes of conduct, and behaviors as a means of coping with being so alienated. With little or no reciprocity between these families and the larger environment, their marginalized status is reinforced.

Family Power Structure

Aspects of power may be defined as psychological, economic, and social. The focus of the discussion here deals primarily with power as a dynamic process within the family system. Recall that in the systems framework the family as a system interacts with and is influenced by other systems. Thus, power may serve as an external factor that influences power as a dimension within the family. Zimmerman (1995) for example, points to "the differences in male and female power and the results of policies and programs that disadvantage women" (p. 207). Miller (1994) calls our attention to historical events that influence family structure, gender roles, and even courtship and marriage. Further, Miller asserts, "the family's construction of power is shaped in a context of neighborhood and community" (p. 224). The relevance of power is evident in political processes, occupational opportunities, social class, race and ethnicity, and policies that "differentially affect the fortunes of families" (Miller, 1994, p. 224). In analyzing the power of policies and political structures on family functioning, Lewis, Skyles, and Crosbie-Burnett (2000) point to the "allocation of goods and services that have differentially affected education, health, hunger, family structure and functioning, and life expectancy," especially among families of color and low-income families.

Families may experience a lack of power as a result of classism, bigotry, prejudice, discrimination, or historical oppression that has been institutionalized into the formal and informal fabric of society. Examples include social policies that define "family" as being limited to a nuclear family configuration, essentially excluding extended family and significant nonbiological kin. Lack of power can take the form of marginalized status, and further in the denial of basic resources, for example, access to economic, health, and housing opportunities. According to Okun, Fried, and Okun (1999), women of all cultures have limited power because of oppressive scripted role expectations. They also point to the experience of powerlessness for males in some racial groups as a result of oppression and inequality, which can lead to turmoil in the family.

Power also resides in the position of the social worker, the politician, and the social welfare organization. Their ability to define family needs or functioning can determine the level of services a family may receive or whether they receive any services at all. In assessing power as it relates to families, we believe that the systems external to the family represent an important dimension. These external vestiges of power influence family functioning and well-being irrespective of power differentials in the family structure.

Elements of Power within the Family System

Having alerted you to some of the external issues related to power, we now turn to the process of assessing power within the family system. All families develop a power structure. Because of this structure, the family system directs and maintains the behaviors of individuals with acceptable limits and includes leadership roles that ensure family maintenance. Parental subsystems, for example, use the power vested in their roles to socialize, establish rules, and shape the behaviors of minors in the family system.

One element of power relates to the capacity of dominant family members to impose their preferred interpretations or viewpoints on other members, in effect denying a meaning or reality other than their own (Kilpatrick & Holland, 1999, p. 29). This exercise of power has disruptive consequences for the family, because members feel pressured to experience, speak about, or react to events or situations in the manner prescribed by the dominant member. Dominant members have power in determining the boundaries of the family system in situations involving family violence or child abuse. In some families, culture, customs, or traditions are enforced even though some members may question their value. They may cooperate to avoid conflict, however, thereby allowing the family to maintain a perception of balance. For example, Okun, Fried, and Okun (1999) discussed the tensions that can occur in immigrant families when authority is challenged by younger members who have been exposed to more egalitarian relationships. At other time, a family member may undermine power by their covert behaviors.

When all members do not embrace this power structure, conflict can result. Power may also be leveraged in the form of scapegoating—a dynamic that focuses the attention and energy of the family on a particular member.

Power is a socially constructed dynamic that varies according to such factors as culture as well as preferences within the family system. In assessing power, you should listen to family members, allowing them to tell their stories so that you may better understand the nature of this dynamic in their family. In the family system, power may be held both covertly and openly. For instance, one individual may be formally acknowledged as the central figure in the family and thus have more power in family decision making. In traditional Western culture, at one point in time, this status was generally associated with the economic resources of the male. Even so, other, less visible members or subsystems held significant power in the family.

Distribution and Balance of Power

Families are often viewed as having a single, monolithic power structure, but this is not always true. In some modern families, one individual may be the primary decision maker in some situations; in other families, other members may participate equally. Although on a surface level the male may be the central family figure, you should explore the extent to which he actually dominates family decision to avoid making a premature assessment. Keep in mind that power may shift depending on the situation or family structure. Today's families are more diverse in both form and structure, causing some traditional roles to become eroded and others to evolve in their stead. In same-sex couples, for example, power roles are often shared. Other sources of power may emerge within the family as a result of family coalitions or subsystems. For example, a strong alliance may exist between a child and grandparents or between a parent and child. In addition, extended kin, clan, tribal, or family and friendships networks may hold power that becomes apparent during family decision making.

The extent to which children are able to influence decisions made by the parental subsystem or assume the decisive role illustrates their role in the family's power structure. Parental subsystems hold power, and they appropriately exert influence over children. Yet, on a situational basis, a parent may delegate parental authority and include children in family decision-making. Situational shifts in power occur as the result of both inner and outer forces—for example, loss of employment, decline of a member's health, life-cycle changes, or opposition to family rules. In immigrant or refugee families where the English language is secondary, a minor child may interpret for parents. This form of power is temporary and must not be construed as the child holding power beyond the particular situation.

Notably, power can shift in divorce and remarriage. Adult factors associated with holding more power include which parent has custody of the children, level of education, or income. Sometimes custody may be distributed equally through joint arrangement. In the past, laws have generally given women more power in custody decisions, except in lesbian unions where societal discrimination takes precedence. Even in these unions, the biological mother is granted custody by the court and joint custody is not an option unless the other partner has legally adopted the minor. Interpersonal alliances tend to change in remarriage, separation and divorce, and grandparents or a same-sex partner may lose or gain power. In a single-parent family system, power shifts may produce conflict when the parent exercises their role of authority with an adolescent of the opposite gender. Finally, children in a divorce and remarriage situation may acquire more power than they previously held when both parents resided in the same household.

Multicultural Perspectives

Although almost all cultures tend to view males as central power figures, generalizations about power may be based on limited knowledge of the power nuances in different cultures. Many cultures are male oriented, so that females may appear to lack power in the traditional sense. The preceding section explored the question of who holds power and under what circumstances. In such assessments, caution is advised when making assumptions, especially when dealing with diverse groups.

For instance, groups may differ in their gender-role definitions, expectations, and responsibilities, yet these roles may not be uniformly constructed as lacking in power. Women, grandparents, aunts or uncles, and other significant individuals included in the family system may have considerable power in the family. Elders, for example, have powerful roles in some Latino or Hispanic, Asian American, African American and immigrant families and communities. In some Latino families, the existence of male dominance and female subordination as a cultural ideal ignores the norm of "hembrismo" or "marianismo," which emphasizes the status of the mother (Hines, Garcia-Preto, McGoldrick,

Almeida, & Weltman, 1992). The covert power held by women in some cultures, despite what may be observed as their subservient status, is referred to by Rotunno and McGoldrick (1982) as a paradox: What is observed as a cultural female script does not diminish the powerful role these women play in the family system. Therefore, in assessing power the distribution of power is to be understanding of the family's cultural and situational frame of reference, which includes covert and overt factors as well the power of individuals.

Assessing Power

As the result of many complex factors, including industrialization, higher levels of female education, increased rates of female employment, the contributions of the feminist perspective, and the equal rights movement, families in Western society appear to be moving toward more egalitarian definitions of male and female roles. At the same time, many families continue to experience stress because of the difficulties in trying to resolve discrepancies between traditional and egalitarian definitions of male–female roles. As immigrant families enter the United States, they may face the same issues.

The balance or distribution of power can be disrupted when families encounter stressful situations (e.g., loss of a job, changes in health or mental health, a traumatic event), resulting in the realignment of the family's power base. In fact, the emotional impact of stressors and the tumultuous upheaval can lead family members to struggle for power and control. In a transitional situation, this tension may greatly contribute to a family's difficulties. In assessing the distribution of power in the family system, it is important to:

- *Determine how power has been distributed in the family in the past and whether changing conditions of the family are threatening the established power base (McGoldrick, 1998; Okun, Fried & Okun, 1999).*
- *Determine whether the distribution of power is gender-specific out of the necessity for the family to survive in a hostile environment (Okun, Fried & Okun, 1999).*
- *Assess the extent to which the family systems allow power to be flexibly reallocated and permit roles to be adjusted to meet the demands of changing circumstances.*
- *Determine how members view the distribution of power in the family. Even if it is distributed unequally, family members may be satisfied with the arrangement.*

A number of factors, then, are addressed when social workers and families assess the power base and the manner in which power is distributed: who holds the "balance of power"; who, if anyone, is the formally designated leader; to what extent power is covertly held by members who have aligned to form a power bloc; and to what extent covert power accrues to individual members who are manifesting extreme symptoms in the family. The role of a family's culture in determining the distribution of power is also considered. Unless power dynamics and distribution play a significant role in family problems, it is inappropriate to attempt to make adjustments in this area.

Keep in mind that power in families may shift on a situational basis, and power can be distributed among many members on some level and at different times. Sometimes families' struggles over power may result in destructive coalitions that are evident in those families' processes. Also remember that all families must address power issues and allocate power in some manner. It is the functionality of the power structure in meeting individual psychological needs and promoting the health of the system that must be determined when assessing this dimension of family functioning. Assessment questions that address the functionality of the power structure include the following:

- *Does the family's power structure (even when it is unfamiliar to you), allow the system to carry out its maintenance functions in an orderly manner?*
- *Are members in competition for power, causing the power base to shift as they compete for power?*
- *Does the power base reside within the executive subsystem or within covert coalitions in the family?*
- *Are members of the family satisfied with the relative distribution of power?*
- *Does the power structure allow the family to honor and maintain its cultural heritage?*
- *How does culture influence the power structure in the family?*
- *To what extent have external conditions necessitated power adjustments in the family?*

Family Decision-Making Processes

The family's style of decision making is closely tied to its power dimension. Families range along a continuum of the extreme of leaderless families in which no one has sufficient power to determine and direct activities or organize decision making, to families in which absolute power to make decisions is rigidly held by one member.

Although effective deliberation and decision making are considered to be important in maintaining the well-being of the system, most families do not consciously select a modus operandi for making family decisions. Rather, the family's style of decision making usually evolves in its formative stages of development and is often patterned after decision-making approaches modeled by parents in the families or culture of origin. In some instances, persistent conflicts experienced by families can be traced back to the inability to resolve, at a covert level, incompatible expectations (emanating from role models they have experienced) regarding the distribution of power and the manner in which decisions should be made in the family. As children are added to the system, they may be pulled into the situation, as neither parent is fully successful in wrestling power from the other.

Of course, approaches to decision making may change over the course of the family life cycle. Young children, for example, have fewer opportunities to fulfill the decider role. As they become adolescents and young adults, they may have more input into family decisions. Nonetheless, the parental subsystem retains the right of making final decisions. For some families, decision making may extend beyond the immediate family, reflecting the practices based on family tradition, race, or culture. In the traditional Hmong community, for example, decision making about health matters and the use of Western medicine requires the consultation and approval of esteemed individuals in the clan. Cultural norms also play a role in decision making. A Native American colleague who is a member of the Upper Sioux, Lakota Tribe, advised that decisions are made based on their influence on the future. Given the many variants of culture and the options for distribution of power that may exist in a family, decision making may shift on a situational basis and be influenced by other factors.

In the assessment of decision making in the family, the overall goal is to determine the extent to which decisions facilitate family well-being, disrupt the family system, or promote conflict. Prolonged or unresolved conflict may factionalize the family unit and prompt some members to disengage. To assess the decision-making processes found in families, it is important to understand the elements that are inherent in effective problem solving with family systems. The following guidelines for effective decision making were adapted from Satir (1967), with additional notations of some general cultural variants, since they also influence this process.

1. *Decision making requires open feedback and self-expression among family members.* This includes skills in compromise, agreeing to disagree, or taking turns to negotiate and resolve differences. Culturally derived roles and scripts may not support feedback. Members provide feedback only when asked or minors are not involved in family decisions.

2. *Members should be able to say what they think and feel without fearing conflict* between themselves and others in the family. Conflict as defined by U.S. standards may in fact be the manner in which individuals in other cultures habitually interact. In fact, it is expected and tolerated in some cultures, and can include "raised voices and insults." In other cultures, non-verbal cues my signal conflict, and in others, "people are expected to become emotional and it is not necessary that everyone agrees" (McGoldrick, 1998; Okun, Fried & Okun, 1999, pp. 40-44).

3. *Without open feedback and self-expression, decision-making processes will be unresponsive to the needs of individual family members* that emerge as the system goes through transitional developmental phases that demand adaptation to internal and external stresses and crises.

4. *Decision making requires a philosophical or attitudinal set on the part of each family member that all members of the system "count"*—that is, the family must agree that each member's needs will be taken into consideration in decision making that will affect another member.

5. *Members think in terms of needs rather than solutions which is consistent with the systems perspective.* It is also consistent with some cultures in which the needs and interests of the collective takes precedence over those of the individual. In essence, decision making may include negotiation and compromise rather than struggles around competing needs.

6. *Family members need to be able to generate alternatives.* This activity closely parallels group brainstorming, in which members generate options, no matter how far fetched, without facing criticism or censorship. Individuals manifest this skill when they draw from a repertoire of ideas that are not merely variations on a single theme but rather different categories of solutions to a given problem. In the assessment process, then, one of your tasks may be to determine to what extent families identify alternatives in contrast to quarreling over competing solutions.

7. *Family members must able to process and weigh alternatives.* Decisions may be made in families after gathering information, receiving input from members, and deliberating on the options. Alternatively, they may be made impulsively without gathering or weighing relevant information or without considering the needs of family members in relation to possible solutions.

8. Effective decision making *requires that the family organize itself so as to carry out decisions by assigning tasks to individual members.* Cultural variants may include, age and gender roles, and responsibilities and power. Planning to implement a decision is just as important as making the decision initially. Considerations also include whether the family system is so disorganized that making and implementing decision is difficult. The process may also break down at the implementation stage because members lack motivation to carry out decisions because their input was not elicited or considered.

9. *Effective decision making requires room for negotiation and adjustment of earlier decisions based on new information and emerging individual and family needs.* Some systems, of course, are much more responsive and flexible to change than others.

Assessing Family Decision-Making

In assessing the family's decision-making style, you should elicit information and view the processes and potential cultural variants you observe in relation to the preceding guidelines. Bear in mind that you are looking for both functional and disruptive patterns in each of the assessment. In addition, note that the decision-making skills described here represent optimal family functioning as perceived and encouraged in Western culture. These skills may not be observed or desirable in some families, and they may not be fully developed even in families with roots in Western culture. For example, the indicators of effective decision making may vary among racial or cultural families in which there is a preserved hierarchy in roles and power. They may also vary in same-sex couple families, in which there may be less conflict about decisions because the relationship does not precisely mirror that of heterosexual families.

Decision making, as a key to autonomous functioning of the family unit, is not an ideal in all families. Such skills may not be considered to be important in families from different ethnic backgrounds. Many cultural groups have no frame of reference for "joint decision making" and, in fact, espouse cultural values that stand in direct contradiction to the methods of decision making discussed here. Including family members in decision making and assuring that the needs of all are satisfied is a Western ideal advocated by helping professionals and social scientists. Although this book indicates that families need to learn decision-making skills, you must assess whether introducing these skills to family members facilitates or disrupts family functioning. In the latter instance, a disruption can disturb deeply engrained and culturally sanctioned patterns of behavior. Hence, collaboration with families in this part of the assessment process is essential.

Consider the case of a young Somali woman who is currently living with her parents. She would like to move into her own apartment so that she is closer to the university where she attends classes. In assessing the resources available for this move, she described a family situation in which she and other family members were expected to contribute a portion of their earnings to family members still living in Somalia. The social worker who presented the situation in case consultation believed that this expectation affected the well-being of the client, "shortchanging the direction that she wanted to take in her life." Further that the decision to contribute to the family well-being, prohibited the young woman from moving out and living independently.

Examining this situation through the lens of Western values—namely, autonomy and independence—the social worker asserted the right of the young woman to manage her own money. Intervention in this situation by the social worker without consideration for the context of the family's cultural values and norms was potentially disruptive to this family system. This situation represents a clash between the values of two cultures. Such cases require social workers to work with clients in such a way that does not isolate them from the family system and their community. Familiar with the community and its leaders, the social worker sought the advice and assistance from key individuals the Somali community, who allowed that the young woman should finish her education, but living on her own and not supporting the family decision was not an option. The resolution of the situation they further advised was a matter for the family to decide.

Decision making as a family process is neither uniform nor universal. Indeed, similar to power, this dimension has considerable variations. Some styles may share common elements, however. In a study by McAdoo (1993), few differences distinguished the decision-making responses of African Americans and their white counterparts of similar socioeconomic status. The study results did reveal that African Americans of lower socioeconomic status who had fewer resources

tended to be more cooperative than other groups in their relationships and decision-making patterns. Thus, McAdoo stresses the importance of recognizing family context in understanding decision-making and broader relational patterns. In particular, cooperation may be a value because it results in lower-income African Americans helping one another to "survive and thrive within the American community" (p. 119). This value or sense of obligation is clearly not specific to African Americans, as it is also evident in other ethnic or racial groups.

Family Goals

The family is a social group in which members typically cooperate and coordinate their efforts so as to achieve certain goals. Family members may talk to each other about goals, and children may express a preference, similar to decision making and power, family goals are generally established by the parental subsystem. Families may establish goals in one of two ways. First, they may adopt and have in common goals consistent with those of the larger society—for example, socializing children, transferring major cultural patterns, and meeting certain personal, nurturing, and safety needs of family members. Second, partners may bring individual goals with them into the family, perhaps based on preferences of their family or culture of origin.

Goals that families adopt and support, may be openly recognized or embraced by its members or they may be covert and beyond the family's awareness. "We want to put all the kids through college" and "It is important for the young to know the old ways" are examples of explicit goals. Covert or unrecognized goals also have a profound influence on a family system. In a competitive society, a covert goal may drive a family's striving toward being at the top of the social ladder, which in turn influences individual member behavior. At the same time, families who are new arrivals to Western society may want their children to maximize opportunities, but also maintain connection to and honor their traditional roots. The first goal related to opportunities is explicit; the other is unspoken, yet understood by family members.

When families are in crisis, the systems' goals and their ordering often become more apparent, for at these times families may be forced to choose between competing goals and values. For example, a wide variety of responses would be observed if one were to study a number of families confronted with a sudden and drastic reduction in income. When faced with expenditures of its limited financial resources, a family may, for example, decide that maintaining an adequate diet for the children is a priority. In a study that examined definitions of child neglect, the participants reported that when their funds were limited, they chose food and clothing for their children over, for example, a bed with a frame. As a result, the sleeping arrangement for a child may be a mattress on the floor. Their reasoning for such decisions and others had to do with their avoiding an intervention by child protection services, especially if their children went to school hungry or wore clothes that called attention to themselves (Rooney, Neathery, & Suzek, 1997).

Family goals and the ways in which they are carried out can also conflict with societal and professional expectations. Consider the case of a single mother whose priority goal is to move her family to a better and safer neighborhood. To accomplish this goal, she holds down two jobs, one of which is the evening shift in a convenience store adjacent to the apartment building in which the family lives. To the 12-year-old child she has delegated the responsibility of caring for the younger siblings, ages 6 and 8. This arrangement has generally worked, and the mother checks on the children during her break. One night, a neighbor reports to the authorities that the children are home alone, which results in an intervention from child protection services. The mother is devastated, angry, and confused. To her this arrangement is reasonable as it allows her to reach the goal of moving the family to a better neighborhood. The manner in which she seeks to reach the goal, however, is perceived as irresponsible and problematic, because the children lacked adult supervision. The mother's actions are understandable in light of her aspirations for her family, especially when they are understood in the context in which they were developed. As the social worker in this case, understanding the context of the mother's action is important in the assessment. Further, by focusing on her aspiration (a strength) you would assist the mother to obtain the necessary resources, for example a different child care arrangement, in support of her goal.

In most families, members vary in regard to the goals each considers important and the value each attaches to common goals. As in any system, a family functions best when there is a consensus concerning the majority of family goals. In the preceding case, the older child understood the mother's goal, even though she may not have been involved in the decision. The mother as the parental subsystem may not have felt the need to involve her minor children in how to reach her goal,

and she had determined their needs herself. In general, however, depending on the capacity of family members, there should be an opportunity for them to have input in and be able to negotiate goals in consideration of the unique needs, aims, and wishes of individuals. While family goals may vary and can break down in times of crisis, family goals represent a strength that may be used as a resource in problem solving. Many patterns of interaction in families evolve in part to achieve goals. If you examine the family's interactions without considering the goals of the system, you may miss the meaning of patterns that you identify.

In summary, the following questions are intended to assist you in assessing family goals for both strengths and difficulties:

- *Are goals that guide the family group clear to all members?*
- *To what extent are members aware of the family's overriding goals?*
- *Is there a shared consensus among members regarding major goals and the priorities assigned to these goals?*
- *Has the family experienced conflict because of a lack of consensus regarding the primary goals of individual family members?*
- *Do goals held in common by the family meet the needs of individual members and promote the well-being of the whole?*
- *To what extent are patterns of interaction related to covert goals within the family?*
- *Do external pressures influence family goals?*
- *To what extent are family goals signs of strengths and hopes for the future?*

To the extent that goals are clear, that consensus exists regarding major goals, and that goals serve the needs and interests of the individual members and the whole, the family manifests key strengths on this assessment dimension. To reiterate what has been a recurring theme throughout this chapter: social workers must view the family within its own cultural and family variant to avoid the hazard of only assessing the family against those dimensions deemed desirable in Western culture. Also, to avoid biased evaluations, it is important not to view a family as deficient simply because the means used to achieve its goals may not conform to the ideals and resources of the mainstream culture as was the instance in the case example. Rather, it is important to determine the specific goals of the family and to assess and support them in their appropriate context.

Family Myths and Cognitive Patterns

Family rules were emphasizes earlier in this chapter, in particular the way in which they spread throughout all aspects of family life. Rules have both a behavioral component and a cognitive component. That is, the behaviors manifested by family members flow from, and are inextricably related to, shared perceptions or myths about one another, the family unit, and the world at large. These shared perceptions may be congruent with the views of neutral outside observers or may be distortions of reality—in other words, ill-founded, self-deceptive, well-systematized beliefs uncritically held by members. Such distortions are often part of the beliefs or myths subscribed to by the family that help shape, maintain, and justify goals, decision-making interactional patterns and relationships. The following case illustrates this point.

Case Example

Over the past four years, 10-year-old Jeffrey's interactions with his teachers have been consistently conflicted because of his open defiance of classroom rules, argumentative behavior, and physical skirmishes with other children. Responding to these problems, his parents attempted to make decisions about Jeffrey that were consistent with their goal of providing him with an excellent education. Supporting each other in this goal, they had changed Jeffrey's enrollment from one school to another three times during the past five years. Both parents share the cognitive set that "The teachers do not try to understand Jeffrey." Given this perceptual set, they regard each school contact as a battleground in which they must argue, protest, protect their rights, and defend their son. Continually overbearing, their confrontational style has alienated school personnel, pushing them to take extreme stands on issues that might otherwise be mutually negotiated. The parents' constant negative and angry comments at home regarding Jeffrey's teachers and his school reinforce his disruptive classroom behavior.

In the preceding case example, the behaviors and cognitive processes of the family are mutually reinforcing. The myth—"Jeffrey is okay, the school is unreasonable"—in essence determines predictable negative responses from school personnel. In turn, the family's negative encounters with the school officials reinforce and confirm their perceptions that the world is dangerous and that school personnel are inattentive to their son's needs and cannot be trusted. Sometimes, systems are in fact unresponsive to client's needs. They too may have constructed myths (e.g., "poor or minority parents are unreliable") and these myths inform their interactions with families. In either case you should assess the context of family relationships with these systems so as to obtain a complete picture of these transactions.

Social cognitions play a role in how individuals and families interpret and remember information, and how they categorize internal and external events. These thematically organized categories are referred to as "cognitive schema" (Berlin & Marsh, 1993, p. 5). In a general sense, schemas are generalizations that may be utilized to process information about attributes, guide perceptions (e.g., Jeffrey's parents) and influence cognition. Imagine, for example, the cognitions that may be held about people with certain attributes, such as people or certain groups who receive financial assistance from the government. Other myths are the basis for such perceptions as "certain groups are more capable than others." In addition, seeing a group of youth with certain physical attributes and who are dressed in a certain style may cue perceptions of them as being members of a violent gang. Stored memories derived from schemas can be an integral part of the shared experience of families from a particular homogeneous group. For example, it may be difficult for African Americans who share a history of racial discrimination and oppression to distinguish when race is not a dynamic in interracial social situations or in encounters with the police. The Native American community, having experienced multiple historic traumas, can be especially sensitive and suspicious of professional helpers (Hand, 2006). Other groups, in particular immigrants who may be unfamiliar with formal helping institutions, may be wary of encounters with a multiplicity of strange and bureaucratic organizations.

Berlin and Marsh (1993) maintain that the cognitions associated with schemas may persist long after a particular event or episode has occurred. Not all schemas are problematic, of course. The important thing to remember is that a schema functions as a heuristic device that allows an individual to take a shortcut when processing information. When cognitions based on schemas are challenged, the result is cognitive dissonance; thus they are not easily replaced. Schemas can also function as both internal and external bounding patterns of the family.

Potentially damaging to development are the persistent beliefs or myths within a family that single out one member as being different or deviant from the group. Beliefs and myths within a cognitive set can result in the assignment of irreversible labels, such as "sick," "bad," "crazy," or "lazy," or a family member may become a scapegoat for the family, carrying the blame for all of its problems. This pattern of interaction obscures the fact that other members also bear responsibility for difficult transactions and communications. Attributes thought to be positive can also fuel myths and beliefs; for example, "handsome," "smart," and "ambitious" can be as burdensome as negative labels and may also separate and estrange members from one another. For example, such labels may cause other family members to resent the inordinate amount of attention, praise, and recognition accorded to that individual. Whether positive or negative, labels stereotype roles of family members, causing other members to relate to them on the basis of a presumed single characteristic and overlooking a wide range of attributes, attitudes, and strengths. In effect, myths and beliefs and the accompanying labels only serve to limit the behavioral options available to an individual member as well as others within the family.

Family Roles

Family roles may be thought of as being complementary and reciprocal, and family members as being differentiated into social roles within the family system. Role theory, when applied to the family system, suggests that each person in a family fulfills many roles that are integrated into the family's structure and that represent certain expected, permitted, or forbidden behaviors. According to Nichols and Schwartz (1998), family roles are not independent of each other. Rather, role behavior involves two or more persons engaging in reciprocal transactions. Roles within the family system may be assigned on the basis of legal or chronological status or cultural and societal scripts. In many families, role assignments are based on gender. At the same time, as with power and decision making, roles may be flexible and diffused throughout the family system.

Roles and role expectations are learned through the process of social interactions, and they can be based on status or gender. Role status locates the individual in a particular social position. In contrast, the role that an individual fills in the family system has specific attitudes—that is, behaviors that are expected of people in that particular situation.

In sorting out roles in the family system, individual role behavior may be *enacted, prescribed*, or *perceived* (Longres, 1995). In the enacted role, a mother may, for example, engage in the actual behaviors expected of her position in the family. A prescribed role is influenced by the expectations that others hold for the individual; those expectations may be influenced by societal or cultural preferences. For example, a major premise of attachment theory is that bonding between a mother and a child is important. Yet, as we have learned from other cultures, children bond with and are attached to a range of adults in their lives. Perceived role behavior focuses on the expectations held by others about a person who is filling that role. In a family's interaction with a bank officer, for example, a male may always be presumed to be the primary decision maker in the family and the head of the household.

Roles are both learned and accrued. The role of parent, for example, is accrued and also learned from others and through experience. Similarly, the various roles that exist between couples in a relationship are learned based on interactions over time. Satisfaction with the respective role behavior between individuals indicates a level of harmony in an interpersonal relationship. Janzen and Harris (1997) refer to "harmonized" interpersonal roles as independent–dependent relationships. In addition, roles may be either *complementary* or *symmetrical*. An example of a complementary independent–dependent role is the relationship that exists between parents and their children in which the needs of both are fulfilled. In contrast, symmetrical relationships are equal, as in the case of a couple in which each partner shares family chores, decision making, and child-rearing duties. Roles for the most part are not static, but rather evolve as a result of interactions and negotiation. As a consequence, they often defy traditional stereotypical role behaviors. In actuality, role relationships in most families operate along a continuum and may be characterized as complementary, quid pro quo, or symmetrical.

Life transitions and conflict often demand changes, flexibility, and modifications in role behavior. A family may experience *role transition* difficulties in making the necessary adjustments when an elderly relative comes to live in their home, for instance. The elderly parent may experience difficulties in adjusting to becoming dependent on adult children. Another significant change for some parents is adjusting to the void when children leave the home. Conflict in the family may occur when individuals become dissatisfied with their roles, when there is disagreement about roles, or when individuals holding certain roles become overburdened. Parents, for example, may disagree about discipline:

One parent may overdiscipline children, while the other may have a more permissive style of parenting.

Interrole conflict can occur when an individual is faced with competing and multiple role obligations, especially when two or more roles are incompatible. In exploring the concerns of employed women, Rooney (1997) found that women, whether single or married, experienced difficulties with their management of multiple roles. Excessive role demands as described by the women in this study amounted to feeling caught between juggling multiple roles—for example, wife or partner, mother, daughter, employee, and often caretaker for an elderly parent. Multiple role taking, compliance with gender-based roles, and time pressures were complicated by such factors as the separation of work and family, unresponsive workplace policies, and lack of time for self. The women in the study also reported feeling interpersonal conflict, diminished physical stamina, and concerns for their physical health, which had detrimental effects on their job performance and on their lives.

Minority women experienced similarly arranged gender divisions of labor stressors. In addition, gender-based role division carried the adjoining weight of strong cultural norms explicit to gender role expectancies. For single mothers, the absence of another parent meant that they had to assume both the male and female roles in the family system. Also single, never-married women reported that other family members expected them to be the primary caretakers for elderly family members. A point to consider with minority families is the fact that interrole conflict may occur in their transactions with the larger community—for example, a cultural expectation of caring for the elderly, or being responsible for family in a broader sense.

Intrarole tensions may emerge in the family when contradictions between role performances arise. Imagine a child who has broad responsibilities in the family, yet is expected to be obedient. Also reflect on the potential for conflict between two individuals who contribute to the economic interest of the family, yet are not equal participants in making decisions about how the family spends its money. The latter example may of course be complementary or quid pro quo. Nevertheless, if both individuals are not satisfied with the arrangement, tensions can occur.

Understanding the distribution of roles within the family, the way in which these roles are defined, and role conflict are important elements in the assessment of the role dimension. Because each culture or family configuration may have its own definitions of roles, social workers must also determine and assess the goodness of fit with the needs of family members. Assessment then must consider how well members are satisfied with respective roles and, if a member is dissatisfied, whether the family is amenable to modifying or changing determined roles.

Communication Styles of Family Members

One theme that cuts across many cultural groups is that of patterns discouraging the open expression of feelings. Although Western culture emphasizes the value that openness and honesty are the best, the reality is that most people have considerable difficulty in asserting themselves or in confronting others, particularly in ways that are facilitative. Another issue which transcends culture, and may be generational, is the multiple ways that people communicate with each other. Youth, for example, as did every other generation of young people, use words, phrases, short cuts, and abbreviations in their communications repertoire. This generation is more likely to use and rely on e-mail, text messaging, and/or personal web pages as a primary means of interacting with each other. While these modes of communicating are not problematic, they may not conform to some of the conventional communication rules. For example using "I" statements or the use of incomplete sentences, dramatic interpretations and informality are communication modes that are generally thought of as communication barriers.

Problems experienced by families from diverse groups, then, may partially arise because of cultural norms about openness. Before attempting to make a change, you must first determine whether the family's communication patterns and styles negatively affect members' relationships and further whether change is desirable. If a member agrees with the need for change, you may be able to move forward with this individual, but the two of you would weigh the cultural implications associated with making such a change. Whether or not family communication patterns are culturally influenced or otherwise determined, they may be faulty, causing significant problems for family members. In assessing the impact of a family's communication styles, you must be aware of the complexities of communication and be prepared to assess the function of members' communication styles and other relevant factors.

To illustrate the communication and other assessment dimensions, Ideas in Action presents the case of Jackie and Anna in "Home for the Holidays." The CD-ROM version of this interview has information that is relevant to this chapter and Chapter 15.

Congruence and Clarity of Communication

Family members convey messages through both verbal and nonverbal channels and qualify those messages through other verbal and nonverbal messages; congruency is when there is correspondence between both aspects of the communication. Congruence and clarity may also be related to a goal to which not all family members agree. For example, Anna would like Jackie to broach the subject of her sexuality with her parents. The content of her message is clear, but Jackie and Anna's goals are dissimilar. As you watch the interview with the social worker, how would you describe the congruency of Anna's message?

In observing communication styles, a task of the social worker is to assess the *congruency* of communications. According to Satir (1967) and other communication theorists, messages may be qualified at any one of three communication levels:

> *Verbal level.* When people explain the intent of their messages, they are speaking at a meta-communication level. For example, the implied message in Anna's insistence that Jackie talk to her parents is "If you really cared about my feelings, you would stand up to your parents about our relationship." Contradictory communications occur when two or more oppositional messages are sent in sequence via the same verbal channel. For example, Anna to Jackie regarding Jackie's discomfort in talking to her parents about her sexuality: "You should follow my advice—you need to make your own decisions."
>
> *Nonverbal level.* People qualify their communications through many nonverbal modes, including gesture, facial expressions, tone of voice, posture, and intensity of eye contact. Nonverbal messages

Ideas in Action

Home for the Holidays

Jackie and Anna scheduled the session at Jackie's request. Both women are Caucasian and appear to be close in age (25–35 years old). Jackie, a chef, owns the restaurant where she works.

The couple has been together for five years and have lived together for the past year. They initiated couples' therapy because of disagreements about their holiday plans. They both would like to spend the time together. Jackie, however, feels pulled to visit her family during the holidays because they live in another state and she has not seen them in a while. Anna states that she does not feel completely comfortable at the home of Jackie's parents. She perceives them as distant and avoiding meaningful contact because of their discomfort with their relationship. In fact, when they attended a family wedding, Anna was not invited to stand with the family when pictures were taken.

Jackie recently came out to her parents as a lesbian. When she disclosed to them that she was moving in with her significant other, Anna, her parents were quiet and took up other activities. This withdrawal behavior is normalized in Jackie's family. She explained that in her family, "there is little outward expression and we don't make a big deal about everything." Nonetheless, Jackie did recognize her parent's discomfort with her sexuality. Anna acknowledged a difference between their family styles, remarking that in her family "there were no secrets and that everyone's state of affairs was open for discussion." Anna would like Jackie to broach the subject of her sexuality with her parents a second time to "strengthen the connection between Jackie and her parents, to hasten Jackie's parents' acceptance of our relationship."

When asked to explore the meaning that this conversation would hold for her, Jackie expressed feeling pushed by the request and that it felt like an ultimatum. For Jackie, there was "too much at stake for her to risk another conversation" with her parents at this time. In her mind, the worst-case scenario being that her parents would shut her out. Hearing Jackie's interpretation of the request as an ultimatum and the pressure that Jackie was feeling, Anna clarified and softened her position. To Anna, the conversation "would help Jackie open up more." Anna also stated that as is the case in her family of origin, "Jackie does not communicate at home."

Concerning their plans for the holiday, Anna agreed to go to Jackie's house. The two made plans to cook a meal together for the family and to give gifts from both of them, as a sign of unity. Jackie agreed to consider plans to hold hands with Anna at dinner; she requested time to discuss this at the next session. Their overall goal is to improve their communication with each other.

may reinforce verbal messages (Anna is welcomed in the home as a guest) which contradicts or modifies their verbal message ("You can visit, but we are not obliged to welcome you as significant in Jackie's life"). Also consider the wedding scene in which Jackie and Anna attend together, but Anna is not included in the family's photos.

Contextual level. The situation in which communication occurs reinforces or disqualifies the verbal and nonverbal expressions of a speaker. For example, Jackie feels punished by what she perceives as a "right now" ultimatum from Anna, but as she turns to Anna, she observes a softening in Anna's expression and her tone. The context or situation in which Anna sends the message to Jackie qualifies her verbal expression. In other instances, nonverbal expressions will have an opposite affect, when there is a mismatch between the content of the verbal and nonverbal message.

Functional communicators identify discrepancies between levels of communication and seek clarification when a person's words and expressions are incongruent. Vital to assessment, then, is the task of ascertaining the extent to which there is *congruence* between the verbal, nonverbal, and contextual levels of messages on the part of individuals in the family system. In addition to considering the congruence of communications, it is important to assess the *clarity* of messages. The term *mystification* (Laing, 1965) describes how some families befuddle or mask communications and obscure the nature and source of disagreements and conflicts in their relationships. Mystification of communications can be accomplished by myriad kinds of maneuvers, including disqualifying another person's experience (Anna to Jackie, "You need to talk to your parents"). In this statement, Anna does not seem to respect Jackie's reluctance to talk to her parents, thereby disqualifying her feelings. Other maneuvers can include addressing responses to no one in particular even though the intent of the speaker is to convey a message to a certain person, using evasive responses that effectively obscure knowledge of the speaker, or utilizing sarcastic responses that have multiple meanings. Some couples use their children or pets to convey messages to each other.

Family rules, interactions, and communication patterns often accompany couples and play out in their relationship with each other. For example, Anna states, "In my family there are no secrets, every one's state of affairs is open for discussion." Jackie on the other hand wishes to maintain homeostasis in her family by adhering to the family rule of "We don't make a big deal about everything." Clearly Jackie and Anna have had prior conversations about their relationship and the response from Jackie's parents. They are in different stages of coming out. In their sequence of interactions, Anna appears to perceive Jackie and her family as the problem in their relationship. For example, Anna pushes Jackie to talk to her parents again, which in her mind is a premium in their relationship. Jackie is understandably reluctant to do so and the repetitive interactional circle is complete.

Barriers to Communication

In Chapter 7, we identified a number of barriers to communication that, when utilized by social workers block client communications and hamper the therapeutic progress. Likewise, family members often repetitively respond with these and similar responses in their communications with others, thereby preventing meaningful exchanges and creating tension in relationships. Response categories that represent obstacles to open communications, in that they prevent genuine dialogue in relationships, are highlighted in Table 10-4.

The assessment of communication barriers also includes nonverbal behaviors—for instance, glaring, turning away from a family member, fidgeting, shifting posture, pointing a finger, or using facial expressions that show disgust or disdain. Nonverbal behaviors also present obstacles to communication when there are discrepancies between verbal and nonverbal levels of communication.

TABLE-10-4 COMMUNICATION BARRIERS

Prematurely shifting the subject or avoiding topics

Asking excessive questions, dominating interactions

Sympathizing, excusing, or giving reassurance or advice

Mind reading, diagnosing, interpreting, or overgeneralizing

Dwelling on negative historical events in a relationship

Making negative evaluations, blaming, name-calling, or criticizing

Directing, threatening, admonishing

Using caustic humor, excessive kidding, or teasing

Focusing conversations on oneself

All families have communication barriers within their conversational repertoires. Members of some families, however, monitor their own communications and adjust their manner when their response to has an adverse impact on another person. As you observe the communication styles of families, it is important to assess three issues:

- *The presence of patterned negative communications.*
- *The pervasiveness of such negative patterns.*
- *The relative ability of individual members of the system to modify communication styles.*

In addition to assessing the preceding factors, it is vital to ascertain the various combinations of communication styles that occur repetitively as individual members of the family system relate and react to one another. For instance, one individual may frequently dominate, criticize, attack or accuse the other, whereas the other may defend, apologize, placate, or agree.

In an exchange in which one member continues to attack or accuse another member, the other tends to continue to defend his or her position, thus manifesting a *"fault–defend"* pattern of communication. Attacks or accusations generally take the form of "You never ..." in which case the other defends him- or herself by providing examples that contradict the accusation. In such situations, even though the topic of conflict or the content of the discussion may change, the manner in which couples or family members relate to each other and orchestrate their scenario remains unchanged. Further, repetitions of the same type of partner-to-partner interchanges will be manifested across many other areas of the couple's interaction. The thematic configurations that occur in families' or couples' communication tend to be limited, but they reinforce tensions in the relationships. Your task as the social worker is to assist them to recognize that their ways of communicating represent a thematic pattern. For instance, rather than allowing them to follow the fault–defend pattern, you might assist them to understand the sequence of their interactions and help them learn reciprocal or symmetrical patterns of expressing feelings or complaints, so that issues can be resolved.

Receiver Skills

In assisting couples or families to learn different ways of communicating, focusing on how they send and receive messages is useful, helping them to develop skills for sending and receiving messages in a manner that facilitates their communications.

A critical dimension of communication is the degree of receptivity or openness of family members to the inner thoughts and feelings of other members in the system. Receptivity is manifested by the use of certain receiving skills, which will be discussed shortly. Again, a caution: These skills are in keeping with Western traditions, and therefore may be inconsistent with the preferences of some racial or ethnic groups.

Before considering these skills, it should be stressed that a majority of families operate along a continuum with respect to their skills in verbal and nonverbal responses. You may observe response patterns in some families that convey understanding and demonstrate respect for the sender's message. In other families, the reactions of members may take appear to be a form of ridicule, negative evaluations, or depreciation of character, yet is not an indication of a problem. Still in other families, members may engage in "dual monologues"; that is, they communicate simultaneously, which to the casual observer might appear to be a free-for-all. Family members may also use words, sayings, or gestures specific to their family or reference group. In general, facilitative receiver skills invite, welcome, and acknowledge the views and perceptions of others. For example, free-for-all conversations invite, even encourage responses, but not in the way that may be the most familiar to you. In such situations, family members feel free to express agreement or disagreement, even though doing so may sometimes spark conflict. Facilitative responses that convey understanding and acceptance include the following:

- *Physical attending (i.e., direct eye contact, receptive body posture, hand gestures, attentive facial expressions)*
- *"Listening" or paraphrasing responses by family members that restate in fresh words the essence of a speaker's message (e.g., "Man, you said..." or as a youth might say, "I feel you")*
- *Responses by receivers of messages that elicit clarification of messages (e.g., "Tell me again, I'm not sure what you meant." or "Am I right in assuming you meant ...?)*
- *Brief responses that prompt further elaboration by the speaker (e.g., "Oh," "I see," "Tell me more")*

Sender Skills

Another dimension of communication is the extent to which members of families can share their inner thoughts and feelings with others in the system. Becvar and Becvar (2000b, p. 274) refer to this quality as the ability of individual family members to express themselves clearly as feeling, thinking, acting, valuable, and separate individuals and to take responsibility for their thoughts, feelings, and actions. Operationalized, "I" messages are messages phrased in the first person that openly and congruently reveal either pleasant or unpleasant feelings, thoughts, or reactions experienced by the speaker ("I feel …," "I think …," "I want …"). For the social worker, an essential task is to help families create a climate in which members can be candid, open, and congruent in their communications.

This climate stands in sharp contrast to the situation in which family communications are characteristically indirect, vague, and guarded and individuals fail to take responsibility for their feelings, thoughts, or participation in events. Rather than "I" messages, these family members are likely to use "you" messages that obscure or deny responsibility, or that attribute responsibility for the feelings to others (e.g., "You've got me so rattled, I forgot"). Such messages are barriers to communication, and are often replete with injunctions ("shoulds" and "oughts") concerning another's behavior or negatively evaluate the receiver of the message (e.g., "You shouldn't feel that way").

In assessing the communication styles of families, you can help them keep track of the extent to which individual members (and the group as a whole) utilize facilitative communication skills. A simple grid with the relevant indicators can be developed and responses can be rated as a plus or minus by other family members.

Responses That Acknowledge Strength and Achievement and Accredit Growth

Critical to the development of self-confidence in individual family members are messages from others that consistently validate the person's worth and potential. In observing patterns in which the communication repertoires are characterized by constant negative messages (e.g., putdowns, attacks, or criticism) or otherwise humiliate or invalidate the experience of others you should intervene to alter these patterns. Family members caught in a cycle can, when given the opportunity, focus on positive attributes of members, rather than on deficiencies. The essential thrust of your work is to increase the family's capacity to acknowledge strengths and achievements, and to create an atmosphere that facilitates their communication skills and interactions. It is also wise to keep in mind that family transitions or internal and external stressors

may, in fact, challenge even previously effective communication skills.

Family Life Cycle

The family life cycle is the final dimension of family assessment. It encompasses the developmental stages through which families as a whole must pass. Based on the seminal work of Duvall (1977) and other theorists, Carter and McGoldrick (1988) developed a conceptual framework of the life cycle of the middle-class American family. This model, which focuses on the entire three- or four-generational system as it moves through time, includes both predictable development events (e.g., birth, marriage, retirement) and unpredictable events that may disrupt the life-cycle process (e.g., untimely death, birth of a developmentally delayed child, divorce, chronic illness, war).

Carter and McGoldrick (1988) identified six stages of family development, all of which address nodal events related to the comings and goings of family members over time:

1. Unattached young adult
2. New couple
3. Family with young children
4. Family with adolescents
5. Family that is launching children
6. Family in later life

To master these stages, families must successfully complete certain tasks. The unattached young adult, for example, must differentiate from the family of origin and become a "self" before joining with another person to form a new family system. The new couple and the families of origin must renegotiate their relationships with one another. The family with young children must find the delicate balance between over- and under-parenting. In all of these stages, problems are most likely to appear when an interruption or dislocation in the unfolding family life cycle occurs, signaling that the family is "stuck" and having difficulty moving through the transition to its next phase.

Variations in the life cycle are, of course, highly likely to occur in today's world. Families can change, readjust, and cope with stressful transitions, both normative and nonnormative that occur with in the life cycle span (McKenry & Price, 2000). In the modern life cycle of families, as Meyer (1990) notes, the ground rules have changed as far as the timing and sequence of events are concerned. In much of our society, education, work, love, marriage, childbirth, and retirement are now out of synch. Older adults return to school; adult children live with their parents; and childbirth is no longer within the exclusive realm of the traditional family form. Because of various changes, one life cycle phase may not necessarily progress in a linear fashion. In this world, life events are not preordained. Instead, they are more likely to be atomistic, mixed-and-matched responses to self-definition and opportunity (Meyer, 1990, p. 12).

Variations also occur in the family life cycle among cultures. Every culture marks off stages of living, each with its appropriate expectations, defining what it means to be a man or woman, to be young, to grow up and leave home, to get married and have children, and to grow old and die. Exploring the meaning of the life cycle with diverse families is particularly critical to determine important milestones from their perspective. Cultural variants that have a negative connotation in Western society include the legal versus the culturally derived age for marriage, family responsibilities and roles for children. Families from other countries may, therefore, experience adverse reactions to practices that were common in their country of origin. Recall the earlier case example of the young Somali woman, in which the social worker felt that her family obligations prevented her from living independently and thus had the potential to create a disruptive family dynamic. Carter and McGoldrick (1999b) emphasize that culture plays an important role in family progression and life-cycle expectations. Therefore, culture is an essential dimension in the assessment of family functioning at a particular development stage in the life cycle.

Summary

This chapter introduced systems concepts and dimensions that will facilitate your assessment of families. Families are not made up of equals, nor do they reflect in their totality the preferred norms of functioning. The systems perspective is useful for understanding family context, processes, interaction, and structure and in assessing both internal and external factors that contribute to or hamper family functioning. As social systems, families influence and are influenced by every member. They create their own implicit rules, power structure, forms of communication, and patterns of negotiating and problem solving. They also influence and are influenced by transactions in the larger social environment.

Irrespective of their configuration, composition, class, race, or ethnicity, families play an essential role in meeting the needs of their constituent members.

The task of assessing family functioning has never been more challenging than it is today, because of the changing definition of the family as well as the greater diversity of racial and ethnic groups in the United States. It is vitally important that we as social workers respect family and cultural variants with respect to leadership, hierarchy, decision-making processes, patterns of interactions and communication styles.

As a final note, we want to emphasize that for the most part the dimensions of assessment discussed in this chapter have evolved from a Western perspective with regard to the family system and its functioning. The extent to which all aspects of these dimensions may be observed among diverse groups is not well documented in the literature. As such, family context (i.e., culture) may be a highly salient factor in the assessment process with diverse families, as it may determine to a large extent the family's rules, roles, bounding, or communication patterns as well as the family's experience with other social systems.

Related Online Content

Visit the *Direct Social Work Practice* companion Web site at *www.cengage.com/social_work/hepworth* for additional learning tools such as glossary terms, chapter outlines, relevant Web links, and chapter practice quizzes.

Skill Development Exercises

1. What are the preferred conversational styles in your family?
2. Describe the different forms of power in your family and identify who the holders are. Specify whether or not the power in your family, in whatever form, is culturally constructed.
3. Reflecting on marginalized families that you have worked with, write a brief response to the assertion in this chapter that oppression is a normative experience for some families.
4. Review the guidelines for effective decision making and assess your own family's adherence to these guidelines. If appropriate, identify cultural variants.
5. Put yourself in the position of a teen mother who is meeting with a social worker for the first time. What would you like to be the starting point in your initial contact?
6. Develop a set of questions or indicators that you could use to assess family strengths.

7. Focusing on problems versus strengths is an ongoing discussion in the social work profession. What is your opinion of this issue?

8. Think of ways in which the strengths of clients may have a minor or major role in your experience with agencies, funding resources, and policy makers. How would you articulate the strengths perspective to any one or all of these organizations?

9. Think of a case that you are currently involved with. Now consider the relevant systems concepts that are applicable to the case.

10. Describe how boundary maintenance, internal and external, operates in your family.

11. As you observe the interactions between Jackie and Anna, identify the barriers to communication using Table 10-4.

12. Discuss how public policy has the potential to influence social work practice with diverse and/or poor families.

13. Reflect on the concept of social empathy. How would you apply this concept in your work with families?

14. How are decisions made in your family and who is involved in the process?

Notes

1. For further reading on family diversity, Demo, D. D., Allen, K. R., & Fine, M. A. (Eds.). (1996). *The Handbook of Family Diversity*. New York: Oxford University Press is recommended. Also, *Child Welfare Journal* (2005) Volume LXXXIV, Number 5, is a special issue devoted to working with immigrants and refugees in child welfare. Fontes (2005) is an excellent resource on child abuse and culture.

2. Jordan and Franklin (2003) is a resource for further study on family assessment tools. Refer also to Fontes (2005) and Dubowitz and DePanfilis (Eds.). (2000). *Handbook for Child Protection Practice. Sage Publications.*

3. Although our discussion centers largely on families, the concepts presented are pertinent to couples as well.

4. The social worker in this case was Marilyn Luptak, Ph.D., while she was a doctoral student at the University of Minnesota.

5. The focus group leader was Patience Togo, Ph. D., while she was a doctoral student at the University of Minnesota. The focus groups were a part of an agency's initiative to develop responsive services identified by diverse groups.

CHAPTER 11

Forming and Assessing Social Work Groups

CHAPTER OVERVIEW

Groups instill hope and encouragement, universalize experiences, break down isolation, and allow members to experience altruism and the satisfaction of helping others (Pack-Brown, Whittington-Clark, and Parker, 1998). In groups, clients grapple with existential questions, learn coping skills for life experiences, and experience healing through cohesion and mutuality. These powerful features are common to an array of well-designed and well-executed treatment groups (Reid, K.E., 2002). Groups can provide a powerful mechanism for change, whether they are used as the only intervention or in conjunction with individual counseling, family work, or other treatments

Social workers plan and lead groups in a variety of settings and with an array of populations. This chapter describes essential processes in developing the purpose of the group, forming and structuring the group, and conducting appropriate assessments with a variety of group types. Specifically, you will develop knowledge in:

* The distinctions between task and treatment groups and different group subtypes

* The steps in planning groups

* The steps in recruiting and screening group members

* Developing individual and group goals

* Identifying individual and group patterns in behaviors and communications

* Understanding the ethical considerations in group work

* The application of group concepts to a case example

Social workers frequently practice with groups. Barker (2003) defines group work as occurring when "small numbers of people who share similar interests or common problems convene regularly and engage in activities designed to achieve certain objectives" (p. 404). Thus, social work practice with groups is goal-directed. It may focus on helping individuals to make changes—for example, through *treatment groups* that attempt to enhance the socioemotional well-being of members through the provision of social skills,

education, and therapy. Group goals may also focus on the group as a whole as a unit of change or the group as a mechanism for influencing the others. Examples include *task groups*, such as committees, treatment teams, and task forces that seek the completion of a project or development of a product.

Whichever type of group the social worker leads, he or she must: (1) create a group that can effectively serve the purpose for which it was designed; (2) accurately assess individual and group dynamics; and (3) intervene effectively to modify processes that are affecting the group's achievement of its goals.

The success or failure of a group frequently rests on the groundwork that takes place before the group even meets. The social worker must thoughtfully and skillfully visualize a group and determine its purpose, structure, and composition. Without careful forethought in creating group structure and atmosphere, all assessment and intervention efforts will be jeopardized by the lack of a firm foundation. This chapter provides a framework that will enable you to effectively form groups and accurately assess group processes. It lays the foundation for effective group interventions, the subject of Chapter 16. In both group work chapters you will see references to the HEART (Healthy Eating, Attitudes, Relationships and Thoughts) group for teenage girls who are overweight. In these chapters, you will meet the members and read transcripts that demonstrate how the group progresses through the phases of development and the joys and struggles that accompany them. Before focusing on these objectives, though, we briefly discuss the types of groups that social workers create and lead in their practice settings.

Classification of Groups

Social workers are typically associated with two types of groups: *treatment groups* and *task groups*. Each of these categories, in turn, has several subtypes. Stated broadly, the purpose of treatment groups is to meet members' socioemotional needs. Task groups, by contrast, are established to "accomplish a task, carry out a mandate, or produce a product" (Toseland & Rivas, 2009, p. 14). Treatment and task groups can be distinguished in a number of basic ways. In treatment groups, communications are open and members are encouraged to actively interact. In task groups, communications are more structured and focus on the discussion of a particular issue or agenda item. Member roles in treatment groups evolve as a result of interaction; in task groups, they may be assigned (e.g., facilitator, minutes-taker). Procedures in treatment groups may be flexible or formal, depending on the group; task groups usually follow formal agendas and rules.

In addition, treatment and task groups differ with respect to self-disclosure, confidentiality, and evaluation. In treatment groups, self-disclosure is expected to be high, proceedings are kept within the group, and group success is based on individual members' success in meeting the treatment goals. In task groups, self-disclosure is low, proceedings may be private or open to the public, and the success of the group is based on members' accomplishing a task, fulfilling a particular charge, or producing a result.

Toseland and Rivas (2009) further refine their classification of treatment groups by describing subtypes that are characterized by their unique purposes.

1. *Support groups* help members cope with life stresses by revitalizing coping skills so that they can more effectively adapt to life events (e.g., schoolchildren meeting to discuss the effect of divorce, people with cancer discussing the effects of the disease and how to cope with it) (Magen & Glajchen, 1999).

2. *Educational groups* have the primary purpose of helping members learn about themselves and their society (e.g., an adolescent sexuality group, a diabetes management group, a heart attack recovery group).

3. *Growth groups* stress self-improvement, offering members opportunities to expand their capabilities and self-awareness and make personal changes (e.g., personal development group or a communication enhancement group for couples). Growth groups focus on promoting socioemotional health rather than alleviating socioemotional deficits.

4. *Therapy groups* help members change their behavior, cope with or ameliorate their personal problems, or rehabilitate themselves after a social or health trauma (e.g., a drug addiction group, an anger management group, a dialectical behavior therapy group for persons diagnosed with personality disorders). While support and growth are also emphasized, therapy groups primarily focus on remediation and rehabilitation.

5. *Socialization groups* facilitate transitions through developmental stages, from one role or environment to another, through improved interpersonal relationships or social skills. Such groups often employ program activities, structured exercises, role plays, and the like (e.g., a social club for formerly institutionalized persons, a social skills group for children who have difficulty making friends).

These groups meet in a variety of public and private settings serving both voluntary and involuntary clients. For example, today's social workers are exploring connections with clients who cannot meet in the same physical place through the use of telephone and online groups (Carr, 2004; Fingeld, 2000; Meier, 1997; Rounds, Galinsky, & Stevens, 1991; Schopler, Galinsky, & Abell, 1997). Social workers also find that groups are useful for supporting people who may traditionally have been marginalized by society, such as people of color, gay/lesbian/bisexual/transgendered (GLBT) individuals, the elderly, and those with stigmatizing illnesses (Miller, 1997; Pack-Brown, Whittington-Clark, & Parker, 1998; Peters, 1997; Salmon & Graziano, 2004; Saulnier, 1997; Schopler, Galinsky, Davis, & Despard, 1996; Subramian, Hernandez, & Martinez, 1995). Involuntary clients, such as perpetrators of domestic violence and adolescents in correctional settings, may also benefit from the mutuality found in groups (Rooney & Chovanec, 2004; Goodman, 1997; Thomas & Caplan, 1997). Groups can also be used as a method for increasing intergroup understanding and conflict reduction—for example, between clashing racial and ethnic groups (Bargal, 2004).

Some group types overlap as they are designed to meet multiple purposes. For example, Bradshaw (1996) describes groups for persons with schizophrenia that simultaneously provide therapy, have a major educational component, and provide support. Groups to assist gay men who are acting as caregivers for others with AIDS provide support as well as education and resources exchange (Getzel, 1991). A men's cooking group at a community center is intended to educate members, prepare them with skills, and provide socialization for the members, all of whom are widowed or newly divorced (Northen & Kurland, 2001). A group of teens convened after the shootings at Columbine High School helped to facilitate intergenerational communication and allowed youth the opportunity to articulate their fears and needs, in contrast to safety measures instituted by authorities without their input (Malekoff, 2006). Such groups offer the opportunity for social reform in the midst of individual change.

In *self-help groups*, members have central shared concerns, such as coping with addiction, cancer, or obesity. These groups are distinguished from treatment and task groups by the fact that the self-help group is led by nonprofessionals who are managing the same issues as members of the group, even though a social worker or other professional may have aided in the development or sponsorship of the group. Self-help groups emphasize interpersonal support and the creation of an environment in which individuals may retake charge of their lives. Such groups offer resources and support for such shared problems as addictions, aggressive behavior, mental illness, disabilities, the death of a child, gambling, weight control, family violence, sexual orientation, and AIDS, among others. It is the social worker's task to offer support and consultation to such groups without taking them over. For example, in a self-help group for Temporary Aid for Needy Families (TANF) recipients, the social service provider's role was to initiate the group, assist a member to become the group facilitator, and evaluate the group's effectiveness. Other members took active roles on tasks such as advertising, recruitment, supportive contact between meetings, and outreach to inform agencies of the group (Anderson-Butcher, Khairallah, & Race-Bigelow, 2004).

Task groups are generally organized into three different types (Toseland & Rivas, 2009):

- *Those that are created to meet client needs (treatment teams, case conferences, staff development committees)*
- *Those that are intended to meet organizational needs (committees, cabinets, boards)*
- *Those that address community needs (social action groups, coalitions, delegate assemblies)*

Traditionally, task and treatment groups have involved face-to-face meetings of group members, and the preponderance of groups today fit that model. However, with technological advances, groups can be convened electronically in synchronous (real time) or asynchronous (anytime) formats (Meier, 2006). As such, the groups can meet through written internet postings and discussion forums, as well as teleconference or videoconference capacities, where phones or computer-mounted cameras bring members together. Technology-mediated groups pose unique advantages

and challenges in service delivery, which will be noted throughout this chapter and Chapter 16. While group types may differ, several underlying principles are common to all forms of group work practice. We will begin with the common features of creating and assessing treatment groups before proceeding to task groups.

Formation of Treatment Groups

The success or failure of a treatment group rests to a large extent on the thoughtful creation of the group and the careful selection and preparation of members for the group experience. In this section, you will learn the steps needed to foster a positive group outcome.

Determining the Need for the Group

The decision to offer services through groups can arise from a number of origins. Some agencies adopt group-based services as their primarily modality, because of ideological or practice considerations, or as a strategy to meet efficiency or cost-containment targets. Sometimes practitioners or agencies determine that groups are needed based on the problems that clusters of clients are presenting and the evidence that group modalities are the most effective means for addressing the problem. Sometimes group work is indicated when existing groups require social work interventions, for example, in school or community settings where violence or racial conflicts are threatening the safety of the learning environment. Social workers may initiate needs assessments based on observations that one or more individual clients have needs that could be addressed through mutual aid with others facing the same challenges (Toseland & Rivas, 2009). As a result, workers might contact colleagues in their own or other agencies to substantiate the need, begin recruitment, or advertise the group.

Establishing the Group Purpose

Clarifying the overall purpose of a group is vital, because the group's objectives influence all the processes that follow, including recruiting and selecting members, deciding on the group's duration, identifying its size and content, and determining meeting location and time. Kurland and Salmon (1998) describe several common problems to avoid in developing an appropriate group purpose.

1. Group purposes are promoted without adequate consideration of client need. That is, the purpose may make sense to the prospective leaders or the agency, but not to the potential clients. For example, clients may be assembled because they share a status, such as having a serious and persistent illness and living independently. From the viewpoint of these potential clients, a purpose that relates to a commonly perceived need such as recreation or socializing may be more attractive than grouping by status.

2. The purpose of the group is confused with the content. For example, the group's purpose is described in terms of what the members will do in the group—their activities—rather than the outcome toward which those activities are directed.

3. The purpose of the group is stated too generally, so that it is vague and meaningless to potential members and provides little direction to prospective leaders.

4. Leaders are reluctant to share their perceptions about the purpose, leaving members to wonder why they are there or to grapple with the issue alone.

5. The group is formed with a "public" purpose that conflicts with its actual hidden purpose. For example, prospective members may not know the basis on which they were contacted to become part of a group. Potential clients may be invited to join on the basis of the fact that they overuse prescription drugs, yet this commonality is not shared with them.

6. Group purposes may be misunderstood as static rather than dynamic (adjusting to the evolving desires and needs of the members).

General group purposes may include overarching goals such as the following:

- *To provide a forum for discussion and education whereby divorced women with small children who live in a rural area may explore and seek solutions to common problems, such as a sense of alienation, scarcity of resources, and lack of opportunities for adult companionship*
- *To provide an opportunity for lesbians with problems of alcoholism to explore their marginalization and environmental context as a means for creating coping responses to alcoholism (Saulnier, 1997)*
- *To participate in decision making that affects the quality of life in a nursing home by establishing a governing council for residents*

- *"To teach young probationers how to protect their physical safety and avoid rearrest by adopting prosocial thinking and actions" (Goodman, Getzel, & Ford, 1996, p. 375)*
- *"To enhance the development of personal and racial identity as well as professional advancement" of African American women (Pack-Brown, Whittington-Clark, & Parker, 1998, p. xi)*

The overall purpose of a planned group should be established by the social worker in consultation with agency administrators and potential clients prior to forming the group; the goals subsequently negotiated by the group should reflect the perspectives of those three stakeholders.

The Agency's and Social Worker's Perspectives

Because of the agency's key role in determining and perhaps influencing the group's purpose, social workers must ensure that the agency's objectives are reflected in the group's overall purpose and the agency must ensure that the leader selected will be appropriate for the group's intent and target population (Northen & Kurland, 2001). However, the agency and the social worker may not always share a common perspective regarding desired goals for a new group. Differences between the views of the agency and social worker may arise, for instance, because of the latter's personal or professional orientation or because of preferences of either the agency or the social worker for particular theories, ideologies, or techniques not espoused by the other party. For example, one of the authors of this book was asked to form a group of women in an outpatient mental health setting who were perceived to overuse tranquilizers. Rather than focus on the negative identity of "drug abuser," the author formed a women's growth group. That growth was defined as including reduction of inappropriate use of drugs.

In the pre-formation period, then, social workers must be clear about their own objectives for a proposed group and must engage in dialogue with administrators, staff and potential clients to elicit their views concerning the prospective group. If the agency's goals differ from the social worker's goals, those involved must negotiate a general group purpose that is agreeable to both parties. Failing to do so may lead to ambiguity in the group, send mixed messages, and triangulate its members.

The Client's Perspective

The potential member of a group wants some questions answered: "Why should I join this group? What is in it for me? What will it do for me? Will it help me?" (Kurland & Salmon, 1998, pp. 7–8). The potential voluntary group member wants these questions settled before deciding whether to join a group and, later, whether to continue attending. The potential member who is mandated or pressured to attend also wants to know the answers to these questions, even if the consequences of failure to join or attend are more punishing for this individual than they would be for the voluntary client.

At the point of entry into a group, the client's goals may differ considerably from those of either the agency or the social worker. Schopler and Galinsky (1974) note that the client's goals may be influenced by many internal or external forces, such as the expectations of others and the client's personal comfort, motivation, and past experiences in group settings. During group formation, the social worker must carefully explore clients' expectations of the group; help them to develop individual and collective goals that are realistically achievable; and negotiate between individual, group, and agency purposes. For example, several members of the HEART group for overweight teen girls joined because their relatives insisted they do so. As such, the leader should acknowledge members' goal of avoiding conflict or coercion from family members as a condition for participation in the group. Alongside these goals, members may have individual goals, such as controlling unhealthy eating behaviors, seeking advice and support from others in similar situations, improving self-esteem, addressing interpersonal difficulties with parents and peers, reducing symptoms of depression and anxiety, and learning weight-loss techniques pertaining to diet and exercise. Even entirely voluntary groups operate best when the leader's and the members' purposes are compatible or when the purposes of the two diverge but the social worker goes along with the group's purpose. Conversely, when the social worker insists on goals that are incompatible with members' needs and wishes, the groups may prematurely dissolve or become more preoccupied with conflict than their purpose.

Deciding on Leadership

Once the group's purpose is established, group planners must consider whether individual or co-leadership will be necessary to assist the group in meeting its aims. Many types of groups benefit from co-leadership. Having two leaders can provide additional eyes and ears for the group, with one leader specifically attending to content and the other taking note of the process and meta-messages by group members. Co-leaders bring different perspectives, backgrounds, and personalities to the group process, which can appeal to a wider array of members than a single leader might. They can also use their interactions to model effective communication and problem solving (Jacobs, Masson, & Harvill, 1998). In addition, two leaders can keep a watchful eye on each other, providing feedback and noting patterns where individual facilitators' needs and motives may impede effective management of the group (Corey, Corey, Callanan, & Russell, 2004).

Sometimes co-leadership is necessary for practical reasons. With two leaders, one can check on a member who has left the room or has been asked to take time out, while the other continues working with the group. Co-leadership can provide continuity if illness or another emergency on the part of one leader might otherwise result in cancellation of a session. With some populations, two leaders may help send a message of authority in an otherwise disruptive group; they may also provide a sense of physical safety and protection from liability by their very presence (Carrell, 2000). In some groups, such as those for men accused of partner violence, mixed-gender co-leaders can provide "deliberate and strategic modeling of alternative forms of male–female interactions" (Nosko & Wallace, 1997, p. 5).

Of course, co-leadership is sometimes impractical because of the costs involved and the time needed to coordinate roles, plan the group sessions, and debrief together. In managing the cost concern, some agencies utilize volunteers or "program graduates"—consumers who have had group training and can bring personal experiences to the group process.

Co-leaders who work together on a regular basis may find increased efficiencies as they formulate a common "curriculum" for the group and develop comfort and rapport with each other. Such coordination is essential to avoid disruptive rivalries from occurring or to prevent members from pitting the co-leaders against each other (Northen & Kurland, 2001). As Levine and Dang (1979) note, "co-therapists constitute an inner group that must work through its own process while facilitating the progress of the larger group" (p. 175). Borrowing from Paulson, Burroughs, and Gelb, Nosko, and Wallace (1997) suggest three ground rules for effective co-leadership: "establish a common theoretical orientation; agree on the identification and handling of problems; and agree on what constitutes the appropriate quantity and quality of each leader's participation" (p. 7). Because characteristics such as gender and race affect personal interactions and are reflected in power dynamics and status expectations, co-leaders must deliberately share all group functions and roles (such as confrontation and support). In doing so, they model equality, undo damaging expectations that members may hold, and help the group adopt the same norms of fairness and flexibility outside of members' stereotyped notions.

Establishing Specific Individual and Group Goals

After establishing an overall purpose and convening the group, the social worker engages members in formulating specific goals at both individual and group levels. Individual goals embody the hopes and objectives of members as they enter the group. Group goals, by contrast, "are the emergent product of the interaction of all participants together, the organizer and the members, as they express their ideas and feelings about the reasons for the existence of the group and its anticipated outcomes" (Hartford, 1971, p. 139).

The following list gives examples of specific goals that may be formulated at either individual or group levels:

1. To identify my strengths and to give and receive positive feedback about challenges and areas of growth for myself and others
2. To identify my self-defeating behaviors and replace them with more constructive behaviors
3. To develop problem-solving skills that enhance decision making in my personal life and apply them to specific problems
4. To relate to others more honestly and address conflict more comfortably
5. To become free from external imperatives—that is, "shoulds," "oughts," and "musts"
6. To learn employment skills that will assist me in getting a better job
7. To learn and practice skills in making friends
8. To lose weight by understanding and managing my eating patterns
9. To understand barriers to effective service delivery and create program changes to reduce those barriers for consumers
10. To plan a conference that will energize, excite, and educate participants about new advances in services to elders

Conducting a Preliminary Interview

Before convening a group, social workers often meet individually with potential group members for the purpose of screening members, establishing rapport, exploring relevant concerns, formulating initial contracts with those motivated to join the group, and clarifying limits and options for involuntary clients. Individual interviews are essential to providing effective group composition; they ensure that the members are selected according to predetermined criteria and possess the behavioral or personality attributes needed for them to make effective use of the group experience.

When creating a group of involuntary clients (e.g., court-referred adolescents or parents referred to meet child protective service mandates), these interviews are a vital first step in clarifying options and assisting potential members to identify acknowledged as well as attributed problems. In rural areas, preliminary interviews provide an opportunity to notify potential members that others they know might attend; in doing so, the group leader can address any concerns that this group composition provokes. With groups from diverse ethnic or racial groups, pre-group orientation can use a rationale congruent with cultural beliefs to socialize prospective members to the treatment process, help them understand what to expect, reduce apprehension, and learn how best to participate (Pack-Brown, Whittington-Clark, & Parker, 1998; Subramian, Hernandez, & Martinez, 1995).

There are several advantages to having pre-group meetings with potential members:

- *They help leaders obtain information that may prove valuable in selecting and directing interventions in early sessions. Without these early meetings, such information might not emerge until several weeks into the group's sessions.*
- *Preliminary interviews enable social workers to enter the initial group sessions with a previously established relationship with each member—a distinct advantage given that leaders must attend to multiple communication processes at both individual and group levels.*
- *Previous knowledge facilitates the leader's understanding of the members' behaviors and allows the leader to focus more fully on group processes and the task of assisting members to develop relationships with one another. For example, the leaders in one bereavement support group knew from initial interviews that two members had lost loved ones*

in a traumatic fashion through homicide. This information alerted them to these members' unique concerns and needs and fostered a connection between the two participants who shared a common experience.

- *Establishing rapport with the leader is also beneficial for members, in that it enables them to feel more at ease and to open up more readily in the first meeting.*

Social workers should focus on the following in preliminary interviews:

1. *Orient potential members to proposed goals and purposes of the group*, its content and structure, the leader's philosophy and style in managing group processes, and the roles of the leader and group members. This is also a good time to identify ground rules, such as attendance, confidentiality, the appropriateness of relating to members outside the group, and so on (Yalom, 1995). With involuntary groups, you must distinguish between nonnegotiable rules and policies, such as attendance expectations and general themes to be discussed, and negotiable norms and procedures, such as arrangements for breaks, food, and selection of particular topics and their order.

   In preliminary meetings, you should also elicit each client's reactions and suggestions on ways that the group might better meet his or her unique needs. Orientation should also include a sharing of the time and place of meetings, length of sessions, and the like. In addition, the social worker may wish to emphasize commonalities that the client may share with other persons considering group membership, such as problems, interests, concerns, or objectives.

2. *Elicit information on the client's prior group experiences*, including the nature of the client's relationship with the leader and other members, his or her style of relating in the previous group, the goals that he or she accomplished, and the personal growth that was achieved. Social workers should anticipate negative reactions from involuntary group members, recognize them as being expected, and yet emphasize ways that these clients can make use of their decision to participate in the group to reach both the mandated goals and their own goals.

3. *Elicit, explore, and clarify the clients' problems*, and identify those that are appropriate for the proposed group. In some instances, either because clients are reluctant to participate in the group or because their problems appear to be more appropriately handled through other treatment modalities or community agencies, you may need to refer them to other resources. For example, to determine whether family treatment may be more appropriate than group work, Garvin (1981) suggests using three criteria:

   a. Is the problem maintained by processes operating in the family as a system?

   b. How will the family respond to changes the individual may choose to make, and will these responses support or retard such changes?

   c. Does the individual wish to involve the family, and is the family amenable to such involvement?" (p. 74)

4. *Explore the client's hopes, aspirations, and expectations* regarding the proposed group (e.g., "What would you like to be different in your life as a result of your attending this group?").

5. *Identify specific goals that the client wishes to accomplish*, discussing whether these goals can be attained through the proposed group, and determining the client's views as to whether the group is an appropriate vehicle for resolving personal problems. With involuntary groups, sharing personal goals that prior members have chosen, in addition to mandated goals, may make the group more attractive to the reluctant member.

6. *Mutually develop a profile of the client's strengths and attributes*, and determine any that the client might like to enhance through work in the group.

7. *Identify and explore potential obstacles* to participation in or benefiting from the group, including reservations the client may have about attending the group. Obstacles may include shyness or discomfort in group situations, opposition from significant others about entering the group, a heavy schedule that might preclude attending all group meetings, or problems in transportation or child care. In addition to exploring these barriers to group membership, the social worker and client may generate possible alternatives or determine whether the obstacles are so difficult to overcome that participation is unwise at this time.

8. *Ensure that screening for the group is a two-way process.* Potential members should have the opportunity to interview the group leader and determine whether the group is appropriate for their problems and interests and whether the relationship with the leader will likely facilitate a successful outcome.

Deciding on Group Composition

Composition refers to the selection of members for the group. On occasion, composition may be predetermined—for example, when the group consists of all residents in a group home, all patients preparing for discharge, or all motorists referred to alcohol treatment due to charges of driving while intoxicated. In rural areas or other settings, the leader may work with a naturally formed group, which has already developed around a common problem, rather than recruit and create a new group (Gumpert & Saltman, 1998).

When the leader is responsible for deciding the group composition, the overriding factor in selecting members is whether a candidate is motivated to make changes and is willing to expend the necessary effort to be a productive group member. Another key factor is the likelihood of that person being compatible with other members in the group. Social workers also usually consider the following issues in determining the composition of groups: sex, age, marital status, intellectual ability, education, socioeconomic status, ego strength, and type of problem (Flapan & Fenchal, 1987).

Homogeneity versus heterogeneity of these characteristics is a vital issue in creating a group. Significant homogeneity in personal characteristics and purpose for joining the group is necessary to facilitate communication and group cohesion. Without such commonality, members will have little basis for interacting with one another. Toseland and Rivas (2009), for example, identify levels of education, cultural background, degree of expertise relative to the group task, and communication ability as characteristics vital to creating group homogeneity. Sometimes, the group's purpose will influence the decision for similarity along certain characteristics. For example, there are advantages to creating female-only groups for women who have chemical dependencies, as their issues often differ from those of men (Nelson-Zlupko, Kauffman, & Dore, 1995). Likewise, a group for those charged with domestic violence might contain members of a single sex due to the nature of the issues involved. In cognitive-behavioral groups for troubled youth, similarity in age and socioemotional development is essential to avoid dominance by older members who are less mature (Rose, 1998).

Conversely, some diversity among members with respect to coping skills, life experience, and levels of expertise fosters learning and introduces members to differing viewpoints, lifestyles, ways of communicating, and problem-solving skills. To attain the desired outcomes of support, learning, and mutual aid, a treatment group, for example, might include members from different cultures, social classes, occupations, or geographic areas. Heterogeneity is also vital in task group membership so that the group has sufficient resources to fulfill its responsibilities and efficiently divide the labor when dealing with complex tasks (Toseland & Rivas, 2009). The challenge in any type of group is to attain a workable balance between differences and similarities of members, given the group's purpose.

Corey (1990) cautions against including members in voluntary groups whose behavior or pathology is extreme, inasmuch as some people reduce the available energy of the group for productive work and interfere significantly in the development of group cohesion.[1] This is particularly true of individuals who have a need to monopolize and dominate, hostile people or aggressive people with a need to act out, and people who are extremely self-centered and who seek a group as an audience. Others who are generally less likely to benefit from most groups are people who are in a state of extreme crisis, who are suicidal, who are highly suspicious, or who are lacking in ego strength and prone to fragmented and bizarre behavior (Milgram & Rubin, 1992, p. 89).

A decision to include or exclude a client has a lot to do with the purposes of the group. For example, a person with alcoholism might be excluded from a personal growth group but appropriately included in a homogeneous group of individuals who suffer from various types of addictions. Oppositional behavior may be a common denominator in some groups, such as those formed to address domestic violence and drug addiction (Milgram & Rubin, 1992); in such cases, this behavior would not be a criterion for exclusion, but rather a central problem for work. An older woman raising her grandchildren might find little benefit in a parenting group where the focus is on education for first-time parents. This does not mean that the grandparent is not in need of group assistance, but rather that it is important for her needs to be congruent with the group purpose and composition.

Garvin (1987) warns against including in a treatment group a member who is very different from the others, for the danger is that this person "will be perceived as undesirable or, in sociological terms, deviant by the other members" (p. 65). Differences in socioeconomic status, age, race, problem history, or cognitive abilities may lead to the individual's discomfort and difficulty in affiliating with the group. It may also produce member behaviors that isolate or scapegoat the person. "Outliers" should be avoided, both for the satisfaction of the individual and for the health of the group. When group composition could potentially lead to the isolation of a member, Garvin (1987) recommends enrolling another member who "is either similar to the person in question or who is somewhere in the 'middle,' thus creating a continuum of member characteristics" (p. 65) and assisting in establishing the members' affiliation and comfort.

Open versus Closed Groups

Groups may have either an *open* format, in which the group remains open to enrolling new members, or a *closed* format, in which no new members are added once the group gets under way. Typically, groups that are open or closed in terms of admitting new members are also open or closed in regard to their duration. Alcoholics Anonymous and Weight Watchers are examples of open-ended and open-membership groups A 10-week medication management group and a 5-week social skills group would be examples of closed-membership, closed-ended groups.

Open-ended groups are generally used for helping clients cope with transitions and crises, providing support, acting as a means for assessment, and facilitating outreach (Schopler & Galinsky, 1981). Having open-ended groups ensures that a group is immediately available at a time of crisis. An open format itself presents different models (Henry, 1988; Reid, 1991), including the *drop-in* (*or drop-out*) *model* in which members are self-selecting, entry criteria are very broad, and members attend whenever they wish for an indefinite period. In the *replacement model*, the leader immediately identifies someone to fill a group vacancy. In the *re-formed model*, group members contract to attend for a set period of time, during which no new members are added but original members may drop out. At the end of the contract period, a new group is formed consisting of some old and some new members.

The choice of format depends on the purpose of the group, the setting, and the population served. An open format provides the opportunity for new members to bring fresh perspectives to the group and offers immediate support for those in need, who come when they need to and stay as long as they choose. At the same time, the instability of this format discourages members from developing the trust and confidence to openly share and explore their problems—a strong feature of the closed-ended group. Frequent changes of membership may also disrupt the work of the open-ended group, although the developmental patterns in such groups vary according to how many new members enter and the frequency of turnover (Galinsky & Schopler, 1989). Leaders of open-ended groups need to be attuned to clients being at different places in the group process and to be able to work with core members to carry forward the particular group's traditions (Schopler & Galinsky, 1981).

Advantages associated with a closed group include higher group morale, greater predictability for role behaviors, and an increased sense of cooperation among members. Disadvantages are that the group may not be open to members when potential participants are ready to make use of it and that, if too many members drop out, the group process will be drastically affected by the high rate of attrition.

Determining Group Size and Location

The size of the group depends in large part on its purpose, the age of clients, the type of problems to be explored, and the needs of members. Seven to 10 members is usually an optimal number for a group with an emphasis on close relationships (Reid, 2002). Bertcher and Maple (1985) suggest that the group should be small enough to allow it to achieve its purpose, yet large enough to ensure that members have a satisfying experience. As such, educational and task groups may accommodate larger numbers of members than would therapy and support groups, where cohesion is central to the group progress.

The location of group meetings should be selected with convenience and image in mind. *Image* speaks to the impression that the site makes on members—the message it conveys that may attract them to the group or make them uncomfortable in attending. For example, a parenting group held at a school building may not be attractive to potential members if their own experiences with education or with the particular school system have been unfavorable. A parenting group that meets at a local YMCA/YWCA or community center may be perceived as comfortable to members who are used to going there for their children's sports or other community events.

Convenience refers to the accessibility of the site for those people whom the group chooses to attract. For example, is the site readily accessible to a public transportation line for those who do not own automobiles? Is it safe, with plenty of parking, and easy to find for those who may be uncomfortable venturing out at night? Social workers who are familiar with a community might make note of the "participation patterns" of residents, as these may reveal neutral locations for meetings (Gumpert & Saltman, 1998).

Leaders may have little choice over the meeting location if the sponsoring agency's site must be used. Those planning groups should take the image and accessibility of the location into account, however, when recruiting prospective members or when diagnosing problems in group membership.

Setting the Frequency and Duration of Meetings

Closed groups benefit from having a termination date at the outset, which encourages productive work. Regarding the possible lifespan of a group, Corey (1990) notes: "The duration varies from group to group, depending on the type of group and the population. The group should be long enough to allow for cohesion and productive work yet not so long that the group seems to drag on interminably" (p. 92). For a time-limited therapy group, Reid (1991) recommends approximately 20 sessions, stating that this length provides adequate time for cohesiveness and a sense of trust to develop. Others might suggest that a 20-session limit is not feasible; that attrition and other obligations may erode participation; and that shortening this length as Reid suggests may lead to an unwarranted sense of failure. Shorter durations, during which attendance can be assured, may leave clients "wanting more" but with a sense of accomplishment and goal achievement at the group's conclusion. In general, short-term groups vary between 1 and 12 sessions, with the shorter-duration groups being targeted at crisis situations, anxiety alleviation, and educational programs (Northen & Kurland, 2001).

Formulating Group Guidelines

Developing consensus concerning guidelines for behavior (e.g., staying on task, adhering to confidentiality) among members is a vital aspect of contracting in the initial phase of the group. Some group guidelines, especially when clients are involuntary, cannot be determined by consensus. Wherever possible, however, voluntary agreement should be sought on as many group guidelines as possible. In formulating guidelines with the group, the social worker takes the first step in shaping the group's evolving processes to create a "working group" capable of achieving specific objectives. Unfortunately, attempts to formulate guidelines often fail to achieve this intended effect for three major reasons.

First, the social worker may establish parameters *for* the group, merely informing members of behavioral expectations to which they are expected to adhere. While non-negotiable requirements such as attendance are often part of involuntary groups, overemphasis on such control may convey the message, "This is my group, and this is how I expect you to behave in it." Such a message may negate later actions by the social worker to encourage members to assume responsibility for the group. Without consensus among members concerning desirable group guidelines, power struggles and disagreements may ensue. Further, members may not feel bound by what they consider the "leader's rules" and may deliberately test them, creating a counterproductive scenario.

Second, the social worker may discuss group guidelines only superficially and neglect either to identify or to obtain the group's commitment to them. This is unfortunate, because the extent to which members understand what these parameters mean will influence the extent to which they conform to them.

Third, just because the group adopts viable guidelines for behavior does not mean that members will subsequently conform to them. Establishing group ground rules merely sets guideposts against which members may measure their current behavior. For negotiated behaviors to become normative, leaders must consistently intervene to assist members in adhering to guidelines and in considering discrepancies between contracted and actual behaviors.

Because formulating guidelines is a critical process that substantially influences the success of a group, we offer the following suggestions to assist you in this aspect of group process:

1. If there are non-negotiable expectations (e.g., no smoking policies or rules forbidding contact between members outside sessions), you should present the rules, explain their rationale, and encourage discussion of them (Behroozi, 1992). Confidentiality is often a non-negotiable rule. The rationale for ensuring that issues discussed in the group will not be shared outside the group should be explained.

2. Introduce the group to the concept of *decision by consensus* on all negotiable items (explained later in this section), and solicit agreement concerning adoption of this method for making decisions *prior* to formulating group guidelines.

3. Ask group members to share their vision of the kind of group they would like to have by responding to

the following statement: "I would like this group to be a place where I could ...." Reach for responses from all members. Once this has been achieved, summarize the collective thinking of the group. Offer your own views of supportive group structure that assists members to work on individual problems or to achieve group objectives.

4. Ask members to identify guidelines for behavior in the group that will assist them to achieve the kind of group structure and atmosphere they desire. You may wish to brainstorm possible guidelines at this point, adding your suggestions. Then, through group consensus, choose those that seem most appropriate.

Group Format

In addition to determining the group purpose, goals, composition, duration, and other elements, leaders must attend to the group *structure,* or how the time in the group will be used to most effectively meet the needs of participants. In research on interventions in rural groups, Gumpert and Saltman (1998) found that worker interventions were determined by the group purpose (reported by 98% of respondents), by a recent incident or event in the group (reported by 61%), by agency expectations (46%), and by the group curriculum (28%).

The following activities will assist you and your members to focus your energies so as to achieve therapeutic objectives effectively and efficiently.

1. Define group and individual goals in behavioral terms and rank them according to priority.
2. Develop an overall plan that organizes the work to be done within the number of sessions allocated by the group to achieve its goals. The leader (or coleaders) should have done preliminary work on this plan while designing the group.
3. Specify behavioral tasks (homework) to be accomplished outside the group each week that will assist individuals to make the desired changes.
4. Achieve agreement among members concerning the weekly format and agenda—that is, how time will

be allocated each week to achieve the group's goals. For instance, a group might allocate its weekly 1.5 hours to the format shown in Table 11-1.

The group leader is responsible for developing the format and presenting it and the rationale to the group. Although input and mutuality are important, group members are typically ill equipped, due to their own pain or lack of group experience, to give meaningful input in creating group structure. They may, however, respond with concerns or preferences about the format offered, and may be better able to offer input as the group evolves.

The result should be a clearly conceptualized format that provides the means for evaluating the ongoing process experienced by group members. Regardless of the treatment modality utilized, clients have a right to accountability in the form of continuing and concrete feedback concerning their progress. The structure adopted by your group should also be flexible enough to accommodate differing group processes and the unique needs of members. To ensure its continued functionality, review the format periodically throughout the life of the group.

Group Decision Making

Effective deliberation and decision making are critical in determining the productivity and success of a group. This is particularly true of task groups. To achieve its objectives, every group ultimately develops methods of making decisions. Left to their own devices, however, groups may evolve counterproductive decision-making processes. Some groups, for example, permit the power for making decisions to be vested in a few members, "counting in" some members and "counting out" others. This pattern perpetuates conflict and intrigue in the group, causing unrest and resentments that divert energies from productive tasks and block developmental progress. Other groups learn problem solving through extended trial-and-error, gradually gaining from their mistakes, although often contributing to frustration and discontent in the process.

TABLE-11-1 EXAMPLE OF A GROUP FORMAT

15 MINUTES	1 HOUR	15 MINUTES
Check-in Reviewing and monitoring tasks	Focusing on relevant content (presentation and discussion). Mutual problem solving. Formulating tasks Plan for the week	Summarizing plan for the week Evaluating group session

Most groups can quickly learn to adopt a model of decision by consensus, given effective leadership in educating the group. Further, equipping groups with an effective decision-making model in the early stages of development can expedite group process and assist members to more readily achieve an advanced level of group functioning. The decision-by-consensus method can be taught early in the first group session according to the following sequence:

1. Explain that groups need a decision-making method that gives each person an equal vote and "counts everyone in."
2. Gain group acceptance of this method of making decisions.
3. Explain steps for effective decision making (these steps are discussed in Chapter 13).
4. Identify the leader's function in assisting the group to make decisions that meet the needs of all members.
5. Use the decision-by-consensus approach in setting up the initial contract and focus explicitly on the process to enhance group awareness of the use of this approach.

Additional Group Issues to Address

This section provides guidelines for 11 issues that are pertinent to treatment groups, although each guideline's applicability depends on the specific focus of the group.

Help-Giving/Help-Seeking Roles Groups formed to assist individuals with personal problems benefit from clarification of what might be termed *help-giving* and *help-seeking* roles. Although the two terms are self-explanatory, you may wish to assist the group to operationalize these roles by considering the behaviors embodied in them. The help-seeking role, for example, incorporates such behaviors as making direct requests for input, authentically sharing one's feelings, being open to feedback, and demonstrating willingness to test new approaches to problems. The help-giving role involves such behaviors as listening attentively, refraining from criticism, clarifying perceptions, summarizing, maintaining focus on the problem, and pinpointing strengths and incremental growth.

The leader should give special attention to the issue of advice in the help-giving role, and emphasize the necessity of carefully exploring fellow members' personal problems before attempting to solve them. Otherwise, groups tend to move quickly to giving advice and offering evaluative suggestions about what a member "ought" or "ought not" to do. You can further help

the group to appropriately adopt the two roles by highlighting instances in which members have performed well in either of these helping roles.

Visitors A group convened for treatment purposes should develop explicit guidelines specifying whether and under what conditions visitors may attend group meetings. Depending on the group purpose or structure (open or closed), visitors can detrimentally affect group processes by causing members to refrain from sharing feelings and problems openly, by threatening the confidentiality of the proceedings, or by creating resentment toward the individual who invited the visitor and thereby violated the integrity of the group. Anticipating with members the possible effects of visitors on the group and establishing procedures and conditions under which visitors may attend sessions can avert group turmoil as well as embarrassment for individual members.

New Members Procedures for adding and orienting new members may need to be established. In some cases, the group leader may reserve the prerogative of selecting members. In other instances, the leader may permit the group to choose new members, with the understanding that those choices should be based on certain criteria and that the group should achieve consensus regarding potential members. In either case, procedures for adding new members and the importance of the group's role in orienting those entrants should be clarified. As mentioned earlier, adding new members in an open-ended group should occur in a planned way, considering the stage of development of the group.

Individual Contacts with the Social Worker Whether you encourage or discourage individual contacts with members outside the group depends on the purpose of the group and the anticipated consequences or benefits of such contacts. In some cases, individual contacts serve to promote group objectives. For example, in a correctional setting, planned meetings with an adolescent between sessions may provide opportunities to focus on troubling actions in the group, support strengths, and develop an individual contract with the youth to modify behaviors. In the case of couples' groups, however, individual contacts initiated by one partner may be a bid to form an alliance with the social worker against the other partner (or may be perceived as such by the partner who did not initiate the contact). If you have questions regarding the advisability of having individual contacts outside the group, you should thoroughly discuss these with a supervisor and address guidelines for contact with group members.

Member Contacts Outside the Group The practice literature contains differing views on this topic. Shulman (2009) explains that group sessions are but one activity in clients' lives and that therefore it is unreasonable to expect members to follow rules that extend outside the temporal and special boundaries of the group. Shulman (2009) also notes that the nature and benefit of collaborative support is limited if members are forbidden to make contact outside of session.

Toseland and Rivas (2009) list possible drawbacks to contact between members outside the group, including diversions from the group's goal, the effect of coalitions on the other members' interactions in the group, and arguments stemming from the dissolution of an alliance or friendship formed outside the group.

Yalom (1995) acknowledges both therapeutic benefits and pitfalls of contacts outside the group. His analysis reveals that outside group contact should be disclosed to the entire group, as clandestine contacts risk harming group unity. Sexual relationships between members is discouraged, as the connection between partners will surpass the connection that either feel for the remaining group members (Yalom, 1995).

Care for Space and Cleanup Making group decisions regarding care of the room (e.g., food, furniture, trash) and cleanup (before having to contend with a messy room) encourages members to assume responsibility for the group space. Otherwise, resentments may fester, and subgroups destructive to group cohesiveness may form when some members feel responsible for cleanup and others do not.

Use of Recorders The social worker should always ask for the group's permission before making audio or video recordings of a group session (NASW, 1999). Before asking for such a decision, you should provide information concerning the manner in which the recording will be utilized outside the session. Reservations regarding recording the session should be thoroughly aired, and the group's wishes should be respected.

The organization sponsoring the group will determine the written records that should be kept, their format, and the content needed. In any event, you should take care not to record identifying information about other group members in an individual member's record.

Eating, Drinking, and Smoking Opinions vary among group leaders concerning these activities in groups. Some groups and leaders believe that they distract from group process; others regard them as relaxing and actually beneficial to group operation. Some groups may intentionally provide meals as an incentive to encourage group attendance (Wood, 2007). You may wish to elicit views from members concerning these activities and develop guidelines with the group that meet member needs, conform to organization or building policies, and facilitate group progress.

A related issue is the use of profanity in the group. Some social workers believe that group members should be allowed to use whatever language they choose in expressing themselves. However, profanity may be offensive to some participants, and the group may wish to develop guidelines concerning this matter. If it appears that the leader might be the only one offended, he or she needs to be aware that imposing the leader's preferences as a guideline might inhibit the group.

Attendance Discussing the problems that irregular attendance can pose for a group before the fact and soliciting commitments from members to attend regularly can do much to solidify group attendance in future group sessions. Involuntary groups often have attendance policies that permit a limited number of absences and late arrivals. Late arrivals and early departures by group members can typically be minimized if the group develops norms about this behavior in advance and if the leader starts and ends meetings promptly. Exceptions may be needed, of course, to accommodate crises affecting the schedules of members or to extend the session to complete an urgent item of business if the group concurs. However, individual and group exceptions to time norms should be rare.

Programming Sometimes, group formats include activities or exercises. In "addition to discussion, content from games, play, structured exercises, role-playing, art, drama, guided imagery, cooking, hobbies, and other forms of creative self-expression are used to build group bonds and enhance the potential of the group to achieve group tasks and individual and social change" (Garvin & Galisky, 2008, Programming section, para. 1). Domestic violence or substance abuse groups may use psychoeducational programming, children's groups may use activities or field trips (Rose, 1998; Ross, 1997), and cognitive-behavioral groups may use role plays and mnemonic devices to remind members of options for problem solving (Goodman, Getzel, & Ford, 1996). It is essential that the activities selected relate directly to the group's purpose. Any such activities should be prefaced and concluded by discussions or debriefing that ties the activities to the group's goals and evaluates the effectiveness of the experience.

With increased attention in the profession devoted to evidence-based practices, manualized curricula have been developed which detail the sequence, content, and activities for various types of groups. There are several advantages of these programmed approaches. They help to focus treatment, advance systematized practices, and support research on interventions. However, those who oppose manual-based practice are concerned that they promote paternalistic, one-size-fits-all approaches instead of the organic, empowerment-based changes that arise from members' and workers' dynamic interactions (Wood, 2007). A further concern is that they may be misused by workers who adopt curricula without supervision or sufficient appreciation for group dynamics and in the absence of group facilitation skills. Clearly, there is a balance between "intuitive practice at one pole and standardized practice at the other" (Galinsky, Terzian and Fraser, 2006, p. 13). Knowledgeable workers can integrate tested programming ideas with practice wisdom and emerging group needs to achieve group and individual purposes.

Touching   The sensitive nature of some group topics may lead to expressions of emotion, such as crying or angry outbursts. It is important to have group guidelines that provide physical safety for members (e.g., "no hitting"). It is also important to set a climate of emotional safety, to sanction the appropriate expression of feelings. Some group guidelines prohibit members from touching one another with hugs or other signs of physical comfort. Sometimes these rules are included to protect members from unwanted or uncomfortable advances. Other groups maintain that touch is a "feeling stopper" when one is tearful, and insist that group members can display their empathy in other ways— through words or through eye contact and attention to the other, for example. Whatever the group's policy, it is important to explain the expectation and the rationale, and to address member concerns, rather than impose the guideline unilaterally.

Guidelines are helpful only to the extent that they expedite the development of the group and further the achievement of the group's goals. They should be reviewed periodically to assess their functionality in relationship to the group's stage of development. Outdated guidelines should be discarded or reformulated. When the group's behavior is incompatible with the group guidelines, the leader would be wise to describe what

is happening in the group (or request that members do so) and, after thoroughly reviewing the situation, ask the group to consider whether the guideline in question is still viable. If used judiciously, this strategy not only helps the group to reassess its guidelines but also places responsibility for monitoring adherence to those guidelines with the group, where it belongs. Leaders who unwittingly assume the role of "enforcer" place themselves in an untenable position, because group members tend to struggle against what they perceive as authoritarian control on the leader's part.

Assessing Group Processes

In group assessment, social workers must attend to processes that occur at both the individual and the group levels, including emerging themes or patterns, in an effort to enhance the functioning of individuals and the group as a whole. This section describes the procedures for accurately assessing the processes for both individuals and groups. A systems framework facilitates the identification and impact of such patterns. Instruments may also help in the identification and quantification of group processes and outcomes. For example, Macgowan (1997) has developed a group work engagement measure (GEM) that combines measures of attendance, satisfaction, perceived group helpfulness, group cohesion, and interaction.

A Systems Framework for Assessing Groups

Like families, groups are social systems characterized by repetitive patterns. All social systems share an important principle—namely, that persons who compose a given system gradually limit their behaviors to a relatively narrow range of patterned responses as they interact with others within that system. Groups thus evolve implicit rules or norms that govern behaviors, shape patterns, and regulate internal operations.

A systems framework helps leaders to assess group processes; they can attend to the repetitive interactions of members, infer rules that govern those interactions, and weigh the functionality of those rules and patterns. For example, a group may develop a habit in which one person's complaints receive a great deal of attention while others' concerns are dismissed. The "rules" leading to such a pattern may be that "if the group didn't attend to Joe, he might drop out or become angry" or "Joe is hurting more than anyone else" or "Joe's issues resonate with those of others, so he deserves the additional attention, whereas the other concerns that are raised aren't shared concerns and don't deserve group time." This pattern may result in the disenfranchisement of the members who feel marginalized, or it may lead to relief that some members can recede while the spotlight is on Joe. More constructively, the other members may concur that Joe's issues are symptomatic of the group and thus be glad that he is bringing them to the surface for discussion.

Conceptualizing and organizing group processes into response patterns enables leaders to make systematic, ongoing, and relevant assessments. This knowledge can help "make sense" of seemingly random and chaotic interactions and bring comfort to group leaders, who may otherwise feel that they are floundering in sessions. In addition to identifying patterned behaviors, leaders must concurrently attend to individual and group behaviors. Observing processes at both levels is difficult, however, and workers sometimes become discouraged when they realize they attended more to individual dynamics than to group dynamics (or the converse), resulting in vague or incomplete assessment formulations. Recognizing this dilemma, we discuss strategies for accurately assessing both individual and group patterns in the remainder of this chapter.

Assessing Individuals' Patterned Behaviors

Some of the patterned behaviors that group members display are *functional*—that is, they enhance the well-being of individual members and the quality of group relationships. Other patterned behaviors are *dysfunctional*—that is, they erode the capacities of members and are destructive to relationships and group cohesion. Sometimes, people join groups specifically because some of their patterned behaviors are producing distress in their interpersonal relationships. At times, though, members are not aware of the patterned nature of their behavior, or of the impact it has on their ability to achieve their goals. A major role of leaders in groups, then, is to aid members to become aware of their patterned behavioral responses, to determine the effects of these responses on themselves and others, and to choose whether to change such responses. To carry out this role, leaders must formulate a profile of the recurring responses of each member, utilizing the concepts of *content* and *process*, which we discussed earlier in this book. Recall that content refers to verbal statements and related topics that members discuss, whereas process involves the ways members relate or behave as they interact in the group and discuss content. Consider the following description of a member's behavior in two initial group sessions:

In the first group meeting, June moved her chair close to the leader's chair. June complimented the leader when giving her introduction to the group and made a point to verbalize her agreement with several of the leader's statements. In the subsequent meetings, June again sat next to the leader and offered advice to other group members, referring to opinions she thought were jointly held by her and the leader. Later, June tried to initiate a conversation with the leader concerning what she regarded as negative behavior of another group member in front of that member and the rest of the group.

It is at the process level that leaders discover many of the patterned behavioral responses of individuals. The preceding case example revealed June's possible patterned or *thematic behaviors*. For example, we might infer that June is jockeying to establish an exclusive relationship with the leader and bidding for an informal position of co-leader in the group. Viewed alone, none of June's discrete behaviors provides sufficient information to justify drawing a conclusion about a possible response pattern. Viewed collectively, however, the repetitive responses warrant inferring that a pattern does, in fact, exist, and may create difficulty for June in the group and in other aspects of her life.

Identifying Roles of Group Members

In identifying patterned responses of individuals, leaders also need to attend to the various roles that members assume in the group. For example, members may assume *leadership roles* that are *formal* (explicitly sanctioned by the group) or *informal* (emerging as a result of group needs). Further, a group may have several members who serve different functions or who head rival subgroups.

Some members may assume *task-related* or *instrumental roles* that facilitate the group's efforts to define problems, implement problem-solving strategies, and carry out tasks. These members may propose goals or actions, suggest procedures, request pertinent facts, clarify issues, or offer an alternative or conclusion for the group to consider. Other members may adopt *maintenance* roles that are oriented to altering, maintaining, and strengthening the group's functioning. Members who take on such roles may offer compromises, encourage and support the contributions of others, or suggest group standards. Some members may emerge as spokespersons around concerns of the group or enact other *expressive* roles. Rather than confront such a person as a negative influence, it is often useful to consider whether, in fact, that person is bringing to the fore issues that have been discussed outside of the group or that are lingering below the surface in group sessions. In short, that person may be acting as an informal group leader who can be joined in seeking to make the group succeed (Breton, 1985). Still other members may assume self-serving roles by seeking to meet their own needs at the expense of the group. Such members may attack the group or its values, stubbornly resist the group's wishes, continually disagree with or interrupt others, assert authority or superiority, display lack of involvement, pursue extraneous subjects, or find various ways to call attention to themselves.

Members may also carry labels assigned by other members, such as "clown," "critic," "uncommitted," "lazy," "dumb," "silent one," "rebel," "over-reactor," or "good mother." Such labeling stereotypes members, making it difficult for them to relinquish the set of expected behaviors or to change their way of relating to the group. Hartford (1971) elaborates:

> For instance, the person who has become the clown may not be able to make a serious and substantial contribution to the group because, regardless of what he says, everyone laughs. If one person has established a high status as the initiator, others may not be able to initiate for fear of threatening his position. If one has established himself in a dependency role in a pair or subgroup, he may not be able to function freely until he gets cues from his subgroup partner. (p. 218)

One or more members may also be assigned the role of scapegoat, bearing the burden of responsibility for the group's problems and the brunt of consistent negative responses from other members. Such individuals may attract the marginalized role because they are socially awkward and repeatedly make social blunders in futile attempts to elicit positive responses from others (Balgopal & Vassil, 1983; Klein, 1970). Or they may assume this role because they fail to recognize nonverbal cues that facilitate interaction in the group and thus behave without regard to the subtle nuances that govern the behavior of other members (Balgopal & Vassil, 1983; Beck, 1974). Individuals may also unknowingly perpetuate the scapegoat role they have assumed in their nuclear families, workplaces, schools, or social systems. Although group scapegoats demonstrate repetitive dysfunctional behaviors that attract the hostility of the group, the presence of the role signals a group phenomenon (and pattern) whose maintenance requires the tacit cooperation of all members.

Individuals may also assume the role of an isolate, which is characterized by the individual being ignored by the group, not reaching out to others, or doing so but being rejected. Sometimes this lack of affiliation may arise from poor social skills or values, interests, and beliefs that set the individual apart from the other group members (Hartford, 1971). The isolate differs from the scapegoat in that the latter gets attention, even if it is negative, whereas the former is simply disregarded. Some members, of course, assume roles that strengthen relationships and enhance group functioning. By highlighting these positive behaviors, leaders may boost members' self-esteem and place the spotlight on behaviors that other members may fruitfully emulate.

It is important to identify all of the roles that members assume because those roles profoundly affect the group's capacity to respond to the individual needs of members and its ability to fulfill the treatment objectives. Identifying roles is also vital because members tend to play out in treatment groups the same roles that they assume in other social contexts. Members need to understand the impact of functional and dysfunctional roles on themselves and others.

Developing Profiles of Individual Behavior

During assessment, group leaders need to develop accurate behavioral profiles of each individual. To carry out this function, leaders must record functional and dysfunctional responses that members displayed in initial sessions. Operating from a strengths perspective, it is important to record and acknowledge functional behaviors such as the following:

Functional Behaviors

1. Expresses caring for group members or significant others
2. Demonstrates organizational or leadership ability
3. Expresses her/himself clearly
4. Cooperates with and supports others
5. Assists in maintaining focus and helping the group accomplish its purposes
6. Expresses feelings openly and congruently
7. Accurately perceives what others say (beyond surface meanings) and conveys understanding to them
8. Responds openly and positively to constructive feedback
9. Works within guidelines established by the group
10. "Owns" responsibility for behavior

11. Risks and works to change self
12. Counts in others by considering their opinions, including them in decision making, or valuing their differences
13. Participates in discussions and assists others to join in
14. Gives positive feedback to others concerning their strengths and growth
15. Acknowledges his or her own strengths and growth
16. Expresses humor constructively
17. Supports others nonverbally

Dysfunctional Behaviors

1. Interrupts, speaks for others, or rejects others' ideas
2. Placates or patronizes
3. Belittles, criticizes, or expresses sarcasm
4. Argues, blames, attacks, or engages in name-calling
5. Verbally dominates group "air time"
6. Gives advice prematurely
7. Expresses disgust and disapproval nonverbally
8. Talks too much, talks too loudly, or whispers
9. Withdraws, assumes the role of spectator, ignores others, or shows disinterest
10. Talks about tangential topics or sidetracks the group in other ways
11. Displays distracting physical movements
12. Is physically aggressive or "horses" around
13. Clowns, mimics, or makes fun of others
14. Aligns with others to form destructive subgroups
15. Intellectualizes or diagnoses (e.g., "I know what's wrong with you")
16. Avoids focusing on self or withholds feelings and concerns pertinent to personal problems

These behaviors can also be tracked by client self-reports or by peer observation within the group. In either case, the data may be captured through charts, logs, diaries or journals, self-anchored rating scales or observations, which can be naturalistic; through role plays and simulations; or through analysis of videotapes of group process (Toseland & Rivas, 2009).

Table 11-2 is a record of the HEART young women's support group that illustrates how leaders can develop accurate behavioral profiles of each member by keeping track of the members' functional and dysfunctional behaviors. The profile of behaviors in Table 11-2 identifies specific responses by individuals in the group but does not necessarily identify their *patterned or stylized*

behaviors. Recording the specific responses of individuals at each session, however, aids in identifying over time recurring behaviors and roles members are assuming. For example, a glance at Table 11-2 suggests that Liz is vulnerable to becoming an isolate in the group.

In addition to direct observation, information about the behavioral styles of members can be obtained from many other sources. In the formation phase of the group, for example, social workers can elicit pertinent data in preliminary interviews with the prospective member or from family members, agency records, or other professionals who have referred members to the group. Within the group, leaders may glean substantial data concerning patterned behavior of members by carefully attending and exploring members' descriptions of their problems and interactions with others.

Identifying Individuals' Growth

Because growth occurs in subtle and diverse forms, a major role of leaders is to document (and to assist the group to document) the incremental growth of each member. To sharpen your ability to observe individuals' growth, we suggest that you develop a record-keeping format that provides a column for notations concerning the growth that members demonstrate from one session to the next or across several sessions. Without such a documentation system, it is easy to overlook significant changes and thus miss vital opportunities to substantiate the direct relationship between member's efforts to change and the positive results they attain.

The Impact of Culture

Assessment of individual functioning, of course, must take group members' cultural backgrounds into account. Tsui and Schultz (1988) stress that "the group norms comprising the so-called therapeutic milieu are actually Caucasian group norms that, in themselves, resist intrusion and disruption from minority cultures" (p. 137). Individuals from other cultures living in a majority culture different from their own are influenced by that majority culture in unique ways and may vary in their degree of acculturation. The behavior of a minority group member might be significantly influenced by cultural norms about sharing personal material with strangers, speaking up before others, offering answers, or advising other members. Assessment of group interactions must occur in light of knowledge about each member's culture and his or her individual characteristics within that culture. As with individual practice, group workers must be careful not to discredit behavior they do not understand, behavior that may arise from

TABLE-11-2 EXAMPLES OF BEHAVIORAL PROFILES OF HEART GROUP MEMBERS

NAME	DESCRIPTIVE ATTRIBUTES	FUNCTIONAL BEHAVIOR	DYSFUNCTIONAL BEHAVIOR
Amelia	15 years old Lives with both parents and one sister Artistic, plays tennis	Participated often in the group Asked pertinent questions of other members Offered to take on maintenance tasks for the group Volunteered an idea for a warm-up exercise for the group	Challenged the leader's motivation and ability to facilitate the group Hesitates to focus on self
Liz	16 years old Lives with both parents Only child Reports intense depression and anxiety	Expressed feelings clearly Attentive Expressed desire to change	Withdrawn, speaks infrequently in the group
Maggie	16 years old Lives with both parents Only child Student body President	Expressed ambivalence about attending group Participated often, and made positive contributions to the group Took a risk, by sharing personal concerns about relating to peers	Sometimes off topic, pursued extraneous lines of questioning Confronts bluntly Experiences difficulty talking about self
Amber	17 years old Lives with parents and grandmother Only child Plays first base on varsity softball team	Joined in discussions, and supported others appropriately Recognized concerns and strengths with regards to self-esteem Acknowledged the possibility for change	Teased another member Made some distracting comments
June	16 years old Lives with mother Brother diagnosed with diabetes Participates in several activities: library club, band, and volunteers at the animal shelter and convalescent center	Initiated group discussion of several topics Outgoing and spontaneous Adds energy to group	At times interrupted others in the group Dominates "air time" Attempts to ally herself with the facilitator
Jen	15 years old Lives with both parents Recently moved, is new at her school Used to play volleyball, holds part-time job in a fast food restaurant	Attentive in group Discussed hurtful messages she receives from her parents Acknowledged change as a result of her participation in group	Speaks infrequently Expressed sense of hopelessness about change

the member's upbringing, or attempts to cope with the current environment and the stress and strain of adaptation (Chau, 1993; Mason, Benjamin, & Lewis, 1996; Pack-Brown, Whittington-Clark, & Parker, 1998).

Assessing Individuals' Cognitive Patterns

Just as group members develop patterned ways of behaving, so do they develop patterned cognitions—that is, typical or habituated ways of perceiving and thinking about themselves, other persons, and the world around

them. Such patterned cognitions are revealed in the form of silent mental speech or internal dialogue that individuals utilize to define the meaning of life events. To use an analogy, it is as though various types of events in a person's life trigger a tape recording in his or her mind that automatically repeats the same messages over and over, coloring the person's perceptions of events and determining his or her reality. Examples of negative internal dialogue that tend to create problems for group members include repeated messages such as "I'm a failure," "No one wants to hear what I have to say,"

"The other people in this group are stupid", and "Other people are better than I am."

Patterned cognitions and behavior are inextricably related and reciprocally reinforce each other. The following case example of a group member's problem illustrates the link between cognitions and behavior and the insidious effect that negative cognitions may have on a client's life.

Case Example

Amber, a 17-year-old high school student, joined a therapy group for teenage girls who are overweight. She reported experiencing low self-esteem, especially with regard to her body. She stated that she lacked confidence when interacting with boys and while changing clothes for gym and softball practice. Amber also discussed difficulties shopping with her friends, stating, "I can't fit into any of the clothes there, and I really want to because they're really cute clothes and it kinda makes me feel out of the loop with my friends."

In contrast to these moments of insecurity, Amber informed the group that there were times when she felt good about herself. Because of her skill at softball, she experienced a boost in confidence when playing on the team. Additionally, Amber stated that she received positive attention from her peers, particularly boys, at dance parties. "You know, at parties and things, whenever rap songs come on about fat girls and fat booties everyone looks to me and I get to dance in front of everybody ... I feel good when the attention is on me."

Amber's cognitions relate to her desire for acceptance by her peers. Although she recognizes positive aspects of herself and has been successful in putting her skills to use, she continues to seek approval from others, although on their terms. Her thoughts can be summarized as "I'm not good enough as I am" and "People will like me if I act how they want me to." In group, Amber discovered that these thoughts contribute to her feelings of low self-esteem, and explored other ways of thinking. She stated, "They call me bootylicious sometimes. I like that because it makes me stand out from them, but maybe I'd appreciate another nickname that didn't have to do with my body."

Because patterned behavioral and cognitive responses are inextricably interwoven and perpetuate

each other, leaders must be able to intervene in groups to modify dysfunctional cognitions. Prior to intervening, however, leaders must fine-tune their perceptions to identify the thematic cognitions that lie behind members' verbal statements. The following statements, for example, reveal conclusions members have drawn about themselves and others:

> ***Male teen in group on adjusting to divorce in the family:*** *I can't tell how I feel. (If I am honest my parents will reject me or I will hurt their feelings.)*
> ***Member of job-preparedness group:*** *The economy is so bad nobody is hiring. (My situation is hopeless and out of my control.)*
> ***Member of bereavement group:*** *Sometimes I lost my patience when mother soiled herself. I shouldn't have shouted at her. (I am a bad daughter/caregiver.)*
> ***Teen girl in HEART group:*** *If you accept yourself, then you just say, "Okay. I'm resigning myself to being fat forever." (I do not like the way I am, yet I am not confident that I can change.)*

You can record the cognitive themes or patterns of members in the same manner that you observe and record their functional and problematic behavioral responses. Returning to the example of the women's support group profiled in Table 11-2, note the cognitive responses of several members recorded by the leader in the same session, as illustrated in Table 11-3.

Social workers can help group members identify cognitive patterns during problem exploration by asking questions such as "When that happened, what did you say to yourself?", "What conclusions do you draw about others under those circumstances?", or "What kind of self-talk do you remember before your anxiety level rose?" Leaders can also teach groups to recognize symptoms of patterned cognitions. As the group grasps the significance of internal dialogue and attends to cognitive patterns expressed by members, leaders should reinforce the group's growth by giving members descriptive feedback concerning their accomplishments.

Assessing Groups' Patterned Behaviors

Beyond attending to the ritualized behaviors of individual members, group workers must be alert to the patterns of the group as a whole. To heighten your awareness of functional and dysfunctional patterned group behaviors, we provide contrasting examples in Table 11-4.

TABLE-11-3 EXAMPLES OF COGNITIVE RESPONSES MADE BY SOME HEART GROUP MEMBERS

NAME	FUNCTIONAL COGNITIONS	PROBLEMATIC COGNITIONS
Amelia	It's okay to risk talking about feelings. Other people will usually treat those feelings with respect and be responsive. I'm willing to risk by staying in this group because I know I need help.	I've been hurt by the past. I don't think I'll ever get over it. I will always blame myself for what happened.
June	I care about other people. I want to help them. I can do things to make myself feel better. I can get help from this group.	I can't stop myself from talking so much. I always do that when I get anxious. People in this group may not like me.
Maggie	I have personal strengths. There are good things about me; I'm a leader. I can take care of myself.	My ideas, beliefs, positions are right; those of other people are wrong. I have to be right (or others won't respect me). You can't trust other people; they will hurt you if they can. The less you disclose about yourself, the better.

The functional behaviors in the table are characteristic of a mature therapeutic group. These facilitative group behaviors may also emerge in the *initial* stages of development, although their appearance may be fleeting as the group tackles early developmental tasks, such as building trust and defining common interests and goals. Brief or short-lived positive behaviors that are revealed early in the life of a group include the following:

- *The group "faces up to" a problem and makes a necessary modification or adjustment.*
- *The group responds positively the first time a member takes a risk by revealing a personal problem.*
- *Members of the group are supportive toward other members or demonstrate investment in the group.*
- *The group works harmoniously for a period of time.*
- *Members effectively make a decision together.*
- *Members adhere to specific group guidelines, such as maintaining focus on work to be accomplished.*
- *Members give positive feedback to another member or observe positive ways the group has worked together.*
- *The group responsibly confronts a member who is dominating interaction or interfering in some way with the group accomplishing its task.*
- *Members pitch in to clean up after a group session.*

This list of positive behaviors is by no means exhaustive. Once social workers fine-tune their observational skills to register positive group behavior, they will catch glimpses of many newly developing behaviors that enhance a group's functioning. Social workers can then intervene in a timely fashion to note these positive

features and reinforce their continued use (Larsen, 1980).

The group may also display transitory negative behaviors in initial sessions. Many of these behaviors are to be expected in the early phases of group development. Their appearance may signal evolving group patterns that are not firmly "set" in the group's interactional repertoire. Counterproductive behaviors that may evolve into patterns include any of the examples of dysfunctional behavior listed in Table 11-4.

Just as we have suggested that you employ a written system to record the functional and dysfunctional responses of individual members, we also recommend using the same type of record-keeping system to track the functional and dysfunctional behaviors of the group itself, adding a column to record the growth or changes that you note in the group's behavior. For example, using the categories that you wish to track, you might develop a chart like the one depicted for individuals in Table 11-2.

Assessing Group Alliances

As members of new groups find other members with compatible attitudes, interests, and responses, they develop patterns of affiliation and relationship with these members. As Hartford (1971) points out, subgroup formations may include pairs, triads, and foursomes. Foursomes generally divide into two pairs, but sometimes shift to three- and one-member subgroups. Groups as large as five may operate as a total unit, but generally these groups begin to develop subdivisions influencing "who addresses whom, who sits together, who comes and leaves together, and even who may meet or talk together outside of the group" (Hartford, 1971, p. 204).

TABLE-11-4 EXAMPLES OF GROUP BEHAVIORS

FUNCTIONAL GROUP BEHAVIOR	PROBLEMATIC GROUP BEHAVIOR
• Members openly communicate personal feelings and attitudes and anticipate that other members will be helpful.	• Members talk on a superficial level and are cautious about revealing their feelings and opinions.
• Members listen carefully to one another and give all ideas a fair hearing.	• Members are readily critical and evaluative of each other; they rarely acknowledge or listen to contributions from others.
• Decisions are reached through group consensus after considering everyone's views and feelings. Members make efforts to incorporate the views of dissenters rather than to dominate or override these views.	• Dominant members count out other members in decision making; members make decisions prematurely without identifying or weighing possible alternatives.
• Members recognize and give feedback regarding strengths and growth of other members.	• Members focus heavily on negatives and rarely accredit positive behaviors of others.
• Members recognize the uniqueness of each individual and encourage participation in different and complementary ways.	• Members are critical of differences in others, viewing them as a threat.
• Members take turns speaking. Members use "I" messages to speak for themselves, readily owning their own feelings and positions on matters.	• Members compete for the chance to speak, often interrupting one another.
• Members encourage others to speak for themselves.	• Members do not personalize their messages but rather use indirect forms of communication to express their feelings and positions.
• Members adhere to the guidelines for behavior established in initial sessions.	• Members speak for others.
• The group is concerned about its own operations and addresses obstacles that prevent individual members from fully participating or the group from achieving its objectives.	• Members display disruptive behaviors incompatible with group guidelines. Members resist talking about the here and now or addressing personal or group problems. Examples of distracting behaviors include fidgeting, whispering, or reading while others are talking.
• Members assume responsibility for the group's functioning and success. Members also express their caring for others.	• Members show unwillingness to accept responsibility for themselves or the success of the group and tend to blame the leader when things are not going well.
• The group shows its commitment by staying on task, assuming group assignments, and working out problems that impair group functioning.	• Members dwell on past exploits and experiences and talk about issues extraneous to the group's purpose.
• Members concentrate on the present and what they can do to change themselves.	• Members focus on others rather than on themselves.
• Members are sensitive to the needs and feelings of others and readily give emotional support.	• Members show little awareness of the needs and feelings of others; emotional investment in others is limited.

The subgroupings that invariably develop do not necessarily impair group functioning. Group members, in fact, often derive strength and support from subgroups that enhance their participation and investment in the larger group. Indeed, it is through the process of establishing subgroups, or natural coalitions, that group members achieve true intimacy. Problems may arise in groups, however, when members develop exclusive subgroups that disallow intimate relationships with other group members or inhibit members from supporting the goals of the larger group. Subgroups that meet online or in person outside of group sessions can have a

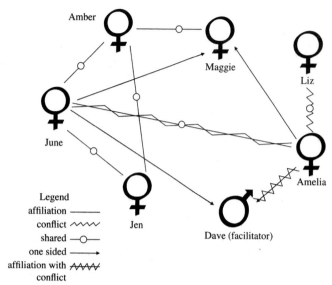

FIG-11-1 Sociogram

particularly pernicious effect on the functioning of the group as a whole. Competing factions can often impede or destroy a group.

To work effectively with groups, leaders must be skilled in identifying subdivisions and assessing their impact on the group. To recognize these subdivisions, leaders may wish to construct a sociogram of group alignments. Credited to Moreno and Jennings (Jennings, 1950), a sociogram graphically depicts patterned affiliations and relationships between group members by using symbols for people and interactions. Figure 11-1 illustrates a sociogram that captures the predominant connections, attractions, and repulsions among members of the HEART group during the fifth session in which the teens discussed the challenges of fitting in with current fashions and peers.

Sociograms are representations of group alliances *at a given point*, because alliances inevitably shift and change, particularly in the early stages of group development. Charting the transitory bonds that occur early in group life can prove valuable to leaders in deciding where and when to intervene to modify, enhance, or stabilize relationships between members.

We suggest that you construct a sociogram of members' interactions after every session until you are confident that group relationships have stabilized in positive ways that support the group's therapeutic objectives. Be creative with your sociograms. Perhaps you might use different colors to show communications or relationships, or place members closer together or farther apart on the sociogram to convey emotional

closeness or distance. Avoid trying to capture in a single sociogram the exact nature of all the relationships each member has with every other member of the group, as the drawing will become overly complicated. Rather, depict only the major subgroupings and identify the relationships in which major attractions or repulsions are occurring.

Assessing Power and Decision-Making Styles

Like families, groups develop ways of distributing power among members. To ensure that their needs are not discounted, some members may make bids for power and disparage other members. Others tend to discount themselves and permit more aggressive members to dominate the group. Still others value power and actively pursue it as an end in itself. When their members are involved in power struggles, groups may initially fail to make decisions on an equitable basis.

Some subgroups may try to eliminate opposing factions from the group or align themselves with other members or subgroups in a bid to increase their power. Groups, in fact, are sometimes torn apart and meet their demise because unresolved power issues prevent the group from meeting the needs of some members (Smokowski, Rose, & Bacallao, 2001).

When social workers assess groups, they need to identify the current capacity of members to share power and resources equally among themselves and to implement problem-solving steps that ensure "win-win" solutions.

Leaders must help the group make each member count if the group is to advance through stages of development into maturity. You can accelerate the group's progress through these stages by assuming a facilitative role in teaching and modeling effective decision making and by assisting the group to adopt explicit guidelines for making decisions in the initial sessions.

Assessing Group Norms, Values, and Cohesion

To understand a group, the social worker must assess its norms, values, and cohesion. Imbedded in the norms, or ways of operating, are the members' implicit expectations and beliefs about how they or others should behave under given circumstances. The interplay of these values and the emergence of constructive group norms affect the group's capacity to develop cohesion and mutual aid.

Norms

Norms are regulatory mechanisms that give groups a measure of stability and predictability by letting members know what they can expect from the group and from one another. Norms may define the *specific* behaviors that are appropriate or permissible for individuals, or they may define the *range* of behaviors that are acceptable in the group. Group norms represent the internalization of the guidelines discussed earlier in this chapter.

Groups develop formal and informal sanctions to reduce behaviors that are considered deviant and to return the system to its prior equilibrium. For example, an implicit group norm may be that other group members may not challenge the opinions of the informal leader. If a new group member treads on this norm by questioning the opinion of the informal leader, other members may side with the informal leader against the "upstart," pressuring him or her to back away.

People often learn about the norms of particular groups by observing situations in which norms have been violated. Toseland and Rivas (2009) note that as group members watch the behavior of other members they reward some behaviors and punish others. Once members realize that sanctions are applied to certain behaviors, they usually attempt to adapt their behavior to avoid disapproval or punishment.

The extent to which members adhere to norms varies. Some norms are flexible or weakly held, and the psychological "costs" to members of violation are low or nonexistent. In the HEART group, speaking out of order, or while another person is speaking, is understood as undesirable, yet often goes unchecked by the

members during their sessions together. In other instances, the group's investment in norms is significant and group reaction is severe when members violate them. The members of the HEART group vigilantly uphold their shared agreement to be respectful in group. Members who put others on the spot or criticize brusquely are reproached without delay. The relative status of members—that is, the evaluation or ranking of each member's position in the group relative to the others—also determines the extent to which members adhere to norms. Toseland, Jones, and Gelles (2006) observe that low-status members are the least likely to conform to group norms because they have little to lose by deviating. Such behavior is less likely if the member has hopes of gaining a higher status. Medium-status group members tend to conform to group norms so that they can retain their status and perhaps gain a higher status. High-status members generally conform to valued group norms when they are establishing their position. At the same time, because of their elevated position, high-status members have more freedom to deviate from accepted norms.

Norms may or may not support the treatment objectives of a group and should be assessed in terms of whether they are beneficial or detrimental to the well-being of members and the overall treatment objectives of the group. Table 11-5 provides examples of both functional and problematic norms.

All groups develop norms, and once certain norms are adopted, they influence the group's response to situations and determine the extent to which the group offers its members therapeutic experiences. A major role for the leader, then, is to identify evolving group norms and influence them in ways that create a positive climate for cohesion and change. Discerning norms is often difficult, however, because they are subtly embedded in the group process and can be inferred only from the behavior occurring in the group. Leaders may be able to identify norms by asking themselves key questions such as the following:

1. What subjects can and cannot be talked about in the group?
2. What kinds of emotional expressions are allowed in the group?
3. What is the group's pattern with regard to working on problems or staying on task?
4. Do group members consider it their own responsibility or the leader's responsibility to make the group's experience successful?
5. What is the group's stance toward the leader?

TABLE-11-5 EXAMPLES OF GROUP NORMS

FUNCTIONAL	PROBLEMATIC
• Take a risk by spontaneously revealing personal content about yourself. • Treat the leader with respect and seriously consider the leader's input. • Focus on working out personal problems. • Allow members equal opportunity to participate in group discussions or to become the focus of the group. • Talk about any subject pertinent to your problem. • Communicate directly other group members. • Talk about obstacles that get in the way of achieving the group's goals.	• Keep the discussion centered on superficial topics; avoid taking risks or self-disclosing. • Play the game "Let's get the leader." Harass, criticize, or complain about the leader whenever the opportunity arises. • Spend time complaining about problems and don't commit the energy necessary to work them out. • Let aggressive members dominate the group. • Don't talk about emotionally charged or delicate subjects. • Direct comments to the leader. • Ignore obstacles and avoid talking about group problems.

6. What is the group's attitude toward feedback?
7. How does the group view the contributions of individual members? What kind of labels and roles does the group assign to them?

These questions also enable the leader to improve his or her observations of redundant or patterned behaviors exhibited by members. This is a vital point, because *patterned behaviors are always undergirded by supporting norms.*

Another strategy for identifying norms is to explain the concept of norms to group members and to ask them to identify the guiding "rules" that influence their behavior in the group. This strategy forces members to bring to a conscious level the group norms that are developing and to make choices in favor of those that advance the group's goals. It is also an important topic for the leader who is joining an existing group to consider.

Values

In addition to norms, every treatment group will create a set of values held in common by all or most of the group's members that include ideas, beliefs, ideologies, or theories about the truth, right or wrong, good or bad, and beautiful, ugly, or inappropriate (Hartford, 1971). Examples of such values include the following:

- *This is a "good" group and worth our commitment and investment of time. (Alternatively, this is a "dumb" group, and we're not going to get anything out of it.)*
- *It is "bad" to betray confidences to outsiders.*

- *People who belong to different groups (e.g., authorities or individuals of a different race, religion, or status) are "bad" or inferior.*
- *It is undesirable to show feelings in the group.*
- *It is fun to try to outwit authority figures (particularly applicable to groups of adolescents or offenders).*

Just as the group's "choice" of norms significantly affects its capacity to offer a therapeutic milieu, so does the group's "choice" of values. Similar to norms, values can be categorized as functional or dysfunctional when viewed in light of the group's therapeutic objectives. Values that encourage work on personal problems or self-disclosure, acceptance of others, and a positive attitude toward the group, for example, are functional to the group's development. By contrast, values that discourage self-disclosure, create barriers in relationships or negative attitudes toward the group, or prevent members from working on problems are obviously unhelpful.

Cohesion

In the initial phases of the group's life, leaders must also assess and foster the development of cohesion in groups. Defined as the degree to which members are attracted to one another, cohesion is correlated, under certain conditions, to productivity, participation in and out of the group, self-disclosure, risk taking, attendance, and other vital concerns (Rose, 1989; Stokes, 1983). Cohesion in groups positively affects members' satisfaction and personal adjustment. Greater cohesiveness leads to increased self-esteem, more willingness to listen to others, freer expression of feeling, better reality testing, higher self-confidence, and more effective use of other members' evaluations in enhancing a member's own development (Toseland & Rivas, 2009; Yalom, 1985).

Cohesion is inextricably linked to the development of norms in a beginning group. Norms that may potentially interfere with both group formation and cohesion include irregular attendance, frequent tardiness, pairing off, changing membership, excessive interpersonal aggression, excessive dependence on the leader, dominance of interaction by a few members, and general passivity in the interaction (Rose, 1989). Research on negative group experiences indicates that the individuals who are damaged by the group may be those very members who are too timid to help contribute to group rules and thus have little investment in the norms that have been negotiated between the leader and more vocal members (Smokowski, Rose, & Bacallao, 2001). These detrimental norms require the attention of both the leader and the group members, because the failure to address them discourages group development and jeopardizes the group itself.

Formation of Task Groups

We move now from consideration of treatment groups to task groups. Although many of the same issues considered with treatment groups also apply to task groups, this section focuses on planning and beginning task groups. Task groups are organized to meet client, organizational, and community needs (Toseland & Rivas, 2009). Among the various types of task groups are teams, treatment conferences, and staff development groups. Task groups may also be formed to meet organizational needs such as committees, cabinets, and boards of directors. Task groups instituted to meet community needs include social action groups, coalitions, and delegate councils (Toseland & Rivas, 2009). All of these groups focus on producing products, developing policies, and making decisions rather than on enhancing the personal growth of members (Ephross & Vassil, 1988).

Important early tasks in forming and assessing task groups are planning for the group and structuring initial sessions to address the purpose of the group.

Planning for Task Groups

Whereas members of treatment groups are recruited for the specific purpose that prompted the group's formation, membership in task groups may be constrained by organizational bylaws or dictated by organizational structure (Toseland & Rivas, 2009). For example, members of a delegate council may be elected by constituents, and an organization may decide who should participate in a treatment conference by the professional role needed (e.g., speech therapist, teacher, social worker, behavior specialist). Task group composition may be voluntary, by appointment, or by election, and should be responsive to the group's purpose and goals. For example, a treatment conference may have the purpose of coordinating the efforts of members of a team involved in serving a particular client or family. An ad hoc committee may be recruited to work on a fundraising event for an agency. A board of directors is appointed or elected to provide guidance and accountability to an organization. A community crime prevention panel may consist of volunteers from the neighborhood who are especially concerned about this issue.

The initiation of a task group and the determination of its purpose may come from many sources. For example, a staff member might propose a delegate council in a halfway house, the director of an agency might propose a committee to develop better agency communications, or residents of a housing development might suggest a social action group to deal with poor housing conditions.

Members of any task group should have the interest, information, skills, and power needed to accomplish the purpose of the group. The specific purpose of the group suggests sources for its membership. For example, a group formed to study how managed care affects service delivery might include consumers, providers, and representatives from insurance groups and regulatory agencies. A group formed to plan a new teen pregnancy program might include teen parents, health care providers, teachers, public health researchers, and child welfare workers.

Membership should be large enough and sufficiently diverse to represent the major constituencies affected by the problem being targeted, and participants should possess adequate skills and knowledge for addressing the group's purposes. As with treatment groups, organizers should ensure that no individual is an isolate. For example, a special education advisory committee should not consist of a group of professionals plus a token parent. When consumers or those whose personal experience is valuable to the task group's purpose are included, multiple representatives should be recruited for the group and, if possible, should serve as representatives of other consumers. For example, in a committee on mental health reform, multiple consumers and parents might be involved and some should represent groups, such as the National Alliance for the Mentally Ill. Taking these steps will help enhance the comfort, power, and legitimacy of group members.

Quality planning in this stage is reflected by accurately and clearly communicating the group's purposes and expectations to prospective members. The level of clarity achieved has important implications for whether those prospective members decide to attend and, later, how well they perform the functions of the group.

As with treatment groups, task groups may be open or closed in time and in membership. Formal boards or committees generally are ongoing but have structures that provide for the rotation of membership in and out of the group, allowing for "staggered" changes to assure continuity. Other groups may be time limited and relatively closed in membership (e.g., a task force to review an incident where a resident was injured, a committee to plan an agency's anniversary celebration). Other groups may be ongoing but have closed membership (e.g., an ethics committee that hears different cases each month, as brought to them by members of the hospital staff).

Beginning the Task Group

The agenda for a beginning session of a task group is similar to that for a treatment group. It includes facilitating introductions, clarifying the purpose of the group, discussing ground rules, helping members feel a part of the group, setting goals, and anticipating obstacles (Toseland & Rivas, 2009). An opening statement, including the agency's function and mission as it relates to the group purpose, should be shared so that members will understand why they have been called together. Members can then be assisted to find commonalities in their concerns and experiences and to identify shared goals for group participation. Some members may know one another from previous roles and have positive or negative preconceptions from that past. "Ice breakers" and other introductory activities can be used to facilitate communication and identify experiences and resources that members possess (Dossick & Shea, 1995; Gibbs, 1995).

Developing group rules and concurrence on decision making (e.g., majority rule, consensus) then follows. A common rule involves adherence to confidentiality, as premature or distorted release of information might hinder the work and destroy the cohesion of the group. Other rules in task groups usually include expectations about attendance and preparation, and structural issues such as timing of meetings, submission of agenda items, and effective communications (Levi, 2007).

Task groups then proceed to goal setting. Such goals always include those mandated by the external purpose of the group, such as reviewing managed care arrangements in the agency, planning a conference, implementing new regulations on confidentiality, or coordinating care. In addition, the group may generate its own goals—for example, generating a list of best practices in achieving its purpose or tailoring its response to the group's purpose based on the specific talents and assets available in the group.

As with treatment groups, task group members may take on or be assigned formal (e.g., secretary, chairperson, treasurer) and informal roles (e.g., timekeeper, devil's advocate, instrumental leader, expressive leader). Whether these roles are constructive depends on how they are enacted and the extent to which they help the group fulfill its purpose. As with other types of groups, assessing the behaviors of individual members and the group as a whole will help identify functional and dysfunctional patterns. Table 11-4 and Table 11-5 include many attributes that apply to task groups as well as to treatment groups.

Other parallels with treatment groups include the evolution of subgroups, norms, cohesion, and the role of members' status in group dynamics. As with treatment groups, these phenomena can play either destructive or positive roles in the group's development. For example, a faction within a task group may form a voting bloc that inhibits the full participation of all members or hijacks the democratic decision making of the group. Members' roles and statuses outside the group may play out in their behaviors and relationships in the group. The agency director may be used to deferential treatment and expect that from fellow group members. Professionals may be dismissive of (or overly solicitous of) the input of consumer representatives on a committee. Counterproductive norms may include: "attendance is optional," "my opinion doesn't matter," "we never get anything done," or "no one comes prepared." Constructive norms about attendance, respect, full participation, and honesty can help the group effectively and efficiently achieve its purpose. While developing cohesion is less crucial in task groups, the presence of socioemotional ties between members will help with the meaning, commitment, and participation members give to the group process.

Ethics in Practice with Groups

The values and ethical standards introduced in Chapter 4 apply to social work practice with systems of all sizes. However, the nature of in-person and online groups presents particular challenges for interpreting and applying ethical standards. In this chapter we will focus on five particular areas: informed consent, confidentiality, self-determination, competence, and nondiscrimination.

Informed consent involves explaining in clear and understandable language the potential risks and anticipated benefits of service, the limits of confidentiality, the consequences of service refusal, and other policies and considerations that will shape the course of treatment. This should be done as early as feasible in the helping process so that the client can agree to (or decline) those conditions before service commences. Sometimes informed consent is a verbal agreement that is documented in the case record, but more commonly it takes the form of a written document that is acknowledged by both the social worker and client. A common tension in informed consent is the perception by professionals that if they provide a thorough accounting of risks, benefits, and limitations, clients will balk at agreeing to those terms, or they will agree but be overly guarded in what they share with the worker. From the consumer's perspective, though, it is vital to understand from the outset what the "rules of the game" will be, to avoid surprises and to support self-determination. Therefore, it is important to alert clients to the limits of confidentiality—for example, that the worker will need to act on suspicions of child endangerment or potential harm to the client or others—before the client unknowingly divulges such events. Other elements of informed consent depend on the client, setting, and services. For example, parents of minor clients may have the right to review treatment records or to receive updates on services, so those limits should be explained to clients at the outset. People who are receiving services involuntarily may face consequences if they do not attend or cooperate with services, thus those ramifications should be explained. People in time-limited services or programs with a particular focus may be notified at the beginning that the program only addresses certain issues or utilizes a particular type of intervention. For example, in the HEART group for teen girls with obesity, the worker described how the group might fit with (or differ from) the members' expectations: "We won't be doing exercises together or focusing on good eating habits, though sometimes you might trade ideas about those things. Mostly, we'll talk about what it is like for you, what some of the struggles are in losing weight, and how you can help each other understand and overcome those barriers."

In groups, an important part of informed consent involves articulating the expectations and limits of confidentiality. The worker must explain his or her commitment to members' privacy and the legal and ethical limits of that promise. The worker must also involve the group in discussing confidentiality, what it means, and how the commitment to each others' privacy will be reinforced. For example, this was the dialogue in the HEART group:

First Session

Dave (facilitator): Good evening everyone and thank you for joining this group. I am glad to see you all again, and I want to start this session by saying a few words about housekeeping things, about how I'd like the group to go, or what I'd like to see us get out of the group, and also talk about confidentiality requirements for this setting.

So to begin, I hope that we can create a safe space for you all to talk about any concerns that you have about symptoms of depression or anxiety and concerns you have about being overweight and about behaviors that might contribute to that for you. I would like for us to decide how we are going to accomplish that as a group; it's a process that we call consensus decision making. So, together we'll come up with the rules for how we're going to operate for the next 12 weeks that will determine how business is conducted, how each member takes time, and how we support each other and interact to make this group work. As a consideration for everybody and as required by law, everything that happens in the group has to stay in the group. You are allowed to talk about what you say in group outside, but we're not allowed to talk about anybody else's business outside of the group. I'd like to see, just by the nods of your heads, that this is something that you understand and agree with. One exception to that rule is that if I find that someone appears to be in danger either from somebody else or in danger of harming themselves; then I have a duty to report that, to keep everybody safe. And I would like to know that everybody understands and is comfortable with that. Okay, terrific.

As a way to start then I'd like to ask you to introduce yourselves to the group. I'm okay to take a volunteer if somebody wants to volunteer to go first, otherwise I'll need to choose somebody. Would anybody like to lead and introduce themselves to the rest of the group?

Amelia: I'll start.

Dave: Terrific Amelia. Go ahead.

Amelia: Okay. Can I actually ask a question?

Dave: Of course.

Amelia: When you say you have to tell people if you're going to hurt yourself, what if you've already hurt yourself—is that an issue that you would have to tell?

Dave: I would want to know if you currently feel like you're not safe physically. If you're in harm's way, however that may happen, I have to take steps to keep you safe, even if that means breaking our confidentiality agreement.

June: So if I say, Maggie told me, "Oh you can eat wraps in this certain place and they're good for you," I shouldn't tell that to anybody?

Dave: You shouldn't tell anybody that Maggie told you that.

June: Okay. I can say that wraps are good.

Dave: You can say that. I'm particularly focused on personal information about members of the group. So information about eating and exercise and dieting you can share; just don't say who said it.

Amelia: So, like, what's said in group, stays in group, right?

Dave: Yes, that's it.

While group workers endeavor to extract and enforce agreements about privacy, informed consent requires facilitators to acknowledge that they cannot control the actions of other members of the group. As the NASW Code of Ethics (1999) states:

> *When social workers provide counseling services to families, couples, or groups, social workers should seek agreement among the parties involved concerning each individual's right to confidentiality and obligation to preserve the confidentiality of information shared by others. Social workers should inform participants in family, couples, or group counseling that social workers cannot guarantee that all participants will honor such agreements. (1.07f)*
>
> *Social workers should inform clients involved in family, couples, marital, or group counseling of the social worker's, employer's, and agency's policy concerning the social worker's disclosure of confidential information among the parties involved in the counseling. (1.07g)*

This can lead to ethical dilemmas as group facilitators try to balance standards on self-determination, confidentiality, safety, and informed consent. Such a dilemma emerged for Dave facilitating the HEART group when the group was talking about the challenges of peer acceptance and Amber talked about "hooking up" with boys who would later reject her. The group, all older teens but still legal minors, had not discussed the bounds of confidentiality or their parents' and guardians' rights to information. The resulting dilemma for Dave was whether to alert Amber and the others to the possibility that he might need to divulge such risky behavior. In the moment, he decided to let the group focus on the problem Amber was raising, though he shared his dilemma with his supervisor after the session. From that consultation, he decided that he needed to discuss with the group their parent's expectations and how their questions about the group might be handled. He reiterated his intention to alert adult caregivers if he felt members in the group were in danger, and engaged the girls in a discussion about what kinds of things parents had a right to know, including binging and purging behavior, risky sexual activity, and drug and alcohol use. The girls clearly expected privacy when they shared about things they had done in the past (cutting behavior, casual sex, sneaking food) and when they shared about things that "normal teens do, but parents might not like," such as drinking. However, they agreed that it was their responsibility to be honest about their thoughts and actions and Dave's responsibility to assure their safety if he felt they were doing or planning on doing something that could bring immediate harm.

In individual contacts with the girls' parents and caregivers, Dave reaffirmed the boundaries of confidentiality and sought their consent. For example, "As June's mom, you have a right to look at her records and learn about her treatment, but it is our experience that group members need to trust that we'll support their privacy, if they are to bring up the things they are experiencing and feeling most deeply. I'll certainly alert you, or expect June to tell you, if she is putting herself or someone else at risk, but I hope you'll trust me to make that call, knowing that she will share a great deal of personal information that she may want me to keep private. Will that be okay with you?"

These already complex issues can be exacerbated in online and other electronically-facilitated groups. Facilitators must take steps to confirm the identity of participants and reduce risks posed by severely distressed members, minors, or participants who misrepresent themselves and their problems. Some steps to address this include posting agency policies and informed consent procedures on the Web site so that prospective group members can review them in advance of applying for the group. During the recruitment phase, facilitators are urged to contact prospective members in person to assess suitability for the group and determine how and where the individual will be accessing the group (Meier, 2006). This conversation also provides the opportunity to address another ethical concern, upholding the integrity of written communications and protecting others' privacy. Preliminary discussions with group members should address whether their computer is secure from use by others, their capacity for privacy during group phone calls, and expectations about confidentiality. All members of technology-mediated groups should sign and discuss informed consent statements indicating that they understand the expectations and limits of confidentiality.

While ethical practice demands that all group leaders must be competent in both the issues under discussion in the group and group processes themselves, social workers facilitating electronic groups must be familiar with the challenges of the particular medium (Northen, 2006). For example, this means being skilled in interpreting phone-only communications and mastering expression in instant messaging and online formats (Meier, 2006) and understanding the complexities that can arise in this novel and evolving form of service. Beyond the specialized competence required for technology-enhanced groups, the general standards of professional competence in group work demand that workers:

- *Avoid using techniques with which they are unfamiliar*
- *Understand group processes, dynamics, and skills, even if using manualized curricula (Galinsky, Terzian, & Fraser, 2006)*
- *Respect group members and avoid creating conditions in which members are bullied, coerced, or manipulated*
- *Provide supportive and respectful confrontations when they are required*
- *Put the needs of group members ahead of their own (Corey, Corey, & Callanan, 2007)*
- *Help members to differentiate their personal needs from collective, community needs*
- *"Operationalize values of democracy and self-determination in task group process" (Congress & Lynn, 1997, p. 72).*

A final set of ethical dilemmas for group leaders arises in balancing group composition considerations with values and ethics that emphasize nondiscrimination (Fluhr, 2004). For example, in creating the HEART group, a decision was made to limit membership to girls, ages 15–17, with the rationale that developmental differences would be too great if older or younger members were allowed, and that a mixed-sex group would impede the members' comfort and depth of sharing about crucial issues such as body image, peer relationships, dating, and so on. These are appropriate decisions, driven by the purpose and nature of the group. However, composition decisions naturally exclude certain people on the basis of gender, age, problem profile and other characteristics. Is this unethical? Such decisions are legitimate if they are made for appropriate clinical reasons, taking into account the need for, purpose of, and goals of the group. Consternation about exclusion can be addressed by creating parallel groups to address unmet needs or excluded populations (overweight teen boys, for example). Of course, competent professionals must always be mindful of their own prejudices, and ensure that they are not veiling biases in an indefensible rationale.

Summary

This chapter presented guidelines for assessing and beginning treatment groups and task groups. We addressed considerations in structuring the group, such as format (open or closed), size, frequency, duration, and composition. We used a systems framework to examine the intersection of individual needs and behaviors and with those of the group as a whole. We discussed common concerns for members at the outset of a group and the strategies for introducing and assessing group guidelines, norms, and values. Chapter 12 turns to considerations of how to build on the social worker's assessment knowledge to construct workable contracts with individuals. We will return to consideration of groups in Chapter 16.

Related Online Content

Visit the *Direct Social Work Practice* companion Web site at www.cengage.com/social_work/hepworth for additional learning tools such as glossary terms, chapter outlines, relevant Web links, and chapter practice quizzes.

Skills Development Exercises in Planning Groups

Imagine that you are planning a group to address one of the following populations or problems:

1. People charged with domestic violence
2. Diabetic middle school students
3. Teenage fathers
4. Families of people with schizophrenia
5. Elementary school children who have been exposed to family or community violence
6. Parents and community members who wish to change a school policy on suspensions

7. Elderly residents recently admitted to a nursing home
8. 7th- and 8th-grade "outcasts" who have no friends
9. Teens who want to start a Gay–Straight Alliance in their high school
10. Pre-marital couples
11. Widows
12. People concerned about bullying in a school

Using the guidelines in this chapter, determine:

a. The name you will give the group
b. The type of group
c. A one-sentence statement of purpose
d. The size of the group
e. The length, structure, and format
f. The location where you will meet
g. Important factors in group composition
h. How you will recruit and screen members

Notes

1. Magen and Glajchen (1999) report that members of 12 different cancer support groups ranked cohesion, hope, and altruism as important factors in their satisfaction with the group process.

Developing Goals and Formulating a Contract

CHAPTER OVERVIEW

Chapter 12 elaborates on Phase I by focusing on the knowledge and skills necessary for the development of goals and the agreement to work together. Goals and the contract are products that flow from the assessment process as discussed in Chapters 8, 9, 10, and 11. First, the chapter discusses the purpose and development of goals. Developing goals with voluntary and involuntary clients and minors is also emphasized. The remainder of the chapter is devoted to mutually formulating the contract or service agreement and measuring progress.

Goals

Goals as a strategy for achieving outcomes are central to the work in systematic process-oriented approaches such as the helping process discussed in this text. Goals are also prominent in the Task-Centered and Crisis Intervention models and Cognitive Restructuring, which, along with the Solution-Focused approach are discussed as change-oriented strategies in Chapter 13. In Solution Focused, however, outcomes are formulated as solutions rather than goal attainment. Whether these strategies make use of goals or promoting solutions, the ultimate intent of each is to change or reduce a critical priority concern expressed by the individual or family, or in the case of an involuntary client to meet the requirement of the legal mandate.

The Purpose and Function of Goals

Goals specify what is to be accomplished. It may be useful to imagine goals as a road map, proceeding from *Point A*, the priority concern as the starting point, to *Point B*, the desired outcome, the end point or final destination. Once goals are established, the objectives and incremental steps to their attainment may be thought of as mileage markers. Within each mileage marker there may be short-term goals developed, for example, reaching a certain point by the end of the day.

Goals evolve from the priority target concern expressed by the client or contained in the legal mandate. In your work with clients, goals facilitate the destination point in which the specific condition, need, status, behavior, or functioning expressed by the client or the legal mandate has changed. Indeed, as you listen to the wants and needs of the voluntary client you are engaging in preliminary goal selection. The needs of non-voluntary, or involuntary, clients have been established by a referral or a court order. For this group of clients, goals specify the corrective action that is required. Even so, involuntary or non-voluntary clients may express needs that are different from or overlap with those goals identified in the mandate or referral. In the course of your assessment conversation with clients, they may indeed identify need concerns for which they would like assistance.

Linking Goals to Target Concerns

Goals function best when they are linked to a specific target concern and have a clear performance standard (Corwin, 2002; Huxtable, 2004; Ribner & Knei-Paz, 2002; Varlas, 2005). This connection is illustrated in the assessment summary of Margaret in the following case example and in Table 12-1. Goal Setting and Motivation Theories and Motivation Interviewing strategies suggest general, vague, or unspecified goals and unclear performance standards, and subject clients to an experience in which their confidence and capacity is challenged (Miller & Rollnick, 2002; Oettingen, Bulgarella, Henderson & Gollwitzer, 2004). Think about setting a goal for yourself, for example, to lose weight. While the general goal is clear, the specific amount of weight that you want to lose is unclear. But a goal of losing 10 pounds is specific, and can be used by you to incrementally assess your performance.

TABLE-12-1 LINKAGE BETWEEN ASSESSMENT, TARGET CONCERN, AND GOALS

ASSESSMENT SUMMARY	TARGET CONCERN	GOALS
Margaret, age 87, feels unable to remain in her home because of concerns for her safety. She wants to maintain her independence and is reluctant to leave her home. She realizes that she needs assistance and is open to the option of moving to an assisted-living complex.	Margaret is concerned about her ability to continue to live safely in her own home.	To live in a safe environment. To maintain her independence.

Case Example

Margaret is an 87-year-old voluntary client of a community-based senior center. She currently resides in her own home. Her husband is deceased and her four adult children live in other states. During the assessment phase she talked about concerns about her safety. Specifically, she defined her safety concerns as a diminished capacity to complete activities of daily living, as well as needing resources and supports to maintain a level of cleanliness in her home. Because she no longer feels sufficiently comfortable to drive, she also has transportation needs. Margaret prefers to remain in her own home because she believes that she will lose the limited independence that she now has. She has thought about home health services, but after listening to her friends who are conflicted about the benefit she is ambivalent about this resource. In fact, her friends have tended to emphasize that their freedom is constrained by the scheduled visits. She recounted that one friend complained, "You have to get up and out of bed, and there are times when just don't feel like having people in your house everyday." Margaret, after a lengthy discussion about possible options, agreed to visit assisted-living facilities. She and the social worker developed a list of questions and observations that could be used to rank each facility. Her overall goal is to live in a safe environment where she has access to needed services and supports.

Elderly people like Margaret and her friends have complex social, psychological, and biological needs. But, they are often are reluctant to have their lives transformed, so it can become a trade-off between accepting help and remaining in charge of their lives. Note, for example, that Margaret wanted to balance her need for safety with her desire to maintain a level of independence.

In addition to facilitating the movement between points A and B, specifically linking goals to target concerns, goals serve the following functions:

- *Ensure that you and the client are in agreement, where possible, about outcomes to be achieved.*
- *Provide direction, focus, and continuity to the helping process and prevent wandering.*
- *Facilitate the development and selection of appropriate strategies and interventions.*
- *Assist social workers and clients to monitor progress.*
- *Serve as the outcome criteria in evaluating the effectiveness of specific interventions and of the helping process.*

How well goals are defined in measurable language increases their success. In Margaret's case, she and the social worker agreed that the target concern was safety. The plan to visit facilities was developed and provided the focus and direction of their work together. They also discussed the option of her remaining in her home with resource supports. She also had a secondary goal of maintaining her independence. Because the two goals were specific, they were also measurable. Attainment of these goals, along with tasks or objectives to achieve them, could be tracked to answer the ultimate question of whether Margaret found the desired housing arrangement.

There are times when a goal that is developed between you and the client involve utilizing the resources of another agency. For example, Margaret's goal required the resources available through a senior housing facility. If she decides to remain in her home, other agencies such as home health services, including cleaning services, and perhaps home-delivered meals will provide the essential supports she needs. It is also quite possible that informal arrangements with neighbors, family members, or community organizations could augment the formal services.

Program Objectives and Goals

Goals are found in institutional or agency mission statements. Indeed, professionals may be attracted to work at an agency because of its mission. Program objectives flow from mission statements and inform how resources are utilized. Objectives may further specify the particular needs or a problem and the manner in which they will be addressed. Objectives statements may focus on micro (individual), mezzo (family/group), or macro (system/environmental) issues. In general, they function to guide an organization's services and specify expected program outcomes. Public schools, for example have as a primary charge to educate and socialize minors with the expectation that they become productive citizens. Offering counseling and support services to individuals who have been in prison to "reintegrate in the community" is an example of a micro-level program objective. Program objectives may direct agency resources to address mezzo-level issues, for example, "to reduce the number of homeless families with children by assisting them to find affordable housing." A macro-level program objective of an agency might be to "end poverty by pursuing legislation that would increase the earned income of a segment of the population."

Organizations may clarify their missions and program objectives in such a way to further distinguish themselves from other service providers. An agency's program might articulate its mission objective as providing "culturally specific services that strengthen ties to the community." Another may define its programs as responding to the "needs of gay, lesbian, bisexual, and transgender youth in a safe and supporting environment." In these instances, the mission and the program objectives of these agencies address a specific population. Thus, clients may voluntarily seek these services, and some may be referred because of an identified or agreed-upon need. In instances in which clients seek out a particular agency, self-selection is a key element. Even so, the fit between their needs and the agency's services needs to be determined (Gardner, 2000). Moreover, clients will want to participate in the development of goals to ensure that the agencies respond to their unique concerns as well as the decisions about how their goals are achieved.

Self-selection with respect to an agency's services is constrained by clients' status, specifically whether the client is involuntary or nonvoluntary. With respect to the latter, residents of a nursing home facility may have been pressured by their family or their level of functioning to move into a facility, and as such they are non-voluntary. These facilities have standardized evidenced-based templates that assess competencies and establish treatment regimes. The overall goal is to ensure the maximum functioning of the residents and their quality of life. Depending on the level of a resident's cognitive and physical functioning, individual goal plans are set forth and reviewed in care conferences, with or without the resident. When the latter is the case, care plans can be developed by staff in consultation with family members. Nonvoluntary status also applies to minors who are referred to groups or remedial learning classrooms with parental consent. The minor is generally not involved in goal setting. In the case of the remedial learning classroom, a team of professionals develops the goals for the Individual Education Plan (IEP) for the minor based on state and federal guidelines.

There are institutions whose mission is to protect the public, in which case the client base is involuntary. For these institutions, their purpose and function can be found in federal policy and state statutes. Individuals become involved with these institutions because they have broken a law. One example is juvenile offender rehabilitation, restitution, diversion, or programs (Ellis & Sowers, 2001; Strom-Gottfried, 2008). The program objectives are included in individual behavioral contracts that specify behaviors in need of change, responsibilities, and potential consequences for noncompliance (Ellis & Sowers, 2001). Federal and state laws and policies also influence child welfare, child protection services, and specifically the health and well-being of minors. Accordingly, this objective is reflected in the case plan goals of the parents or legal guardians of the minor. Similarly, a program objective for a domestic violence program in which participants are court-ordered may require them to "increase their awareness of individual cues that trigger anger" as an indicator of a successful client and program outcome.

Keep in mind that institutional and agency program objectives are, in addition to their mission or mandate, are influenced by funding streams, including that of federal, state, and private organizations. For example, agencies may have a purchase of service agreement (POS), or they may respond to a request for proposals (RFP) initiated by a county, state, or federal government. Agencies may also have state or federal grants to provide services to particular populations. Further, agencies may tailor their programs to annual priorities established by coordinating fund organizations like the United Way. Private foundations may also seek agencies to provide programs and services to specific populations or that address a specific issue, such as assisting new immigrants to adjust to and transition into their new environment. These funding sources may outline the program objectives to be established and the outcomes to be met.

Goals and program objectives are often used interchangeably to indicate expected outcomes. To distinguish agency program objectives from individual goals, it may be useful to think of objectives as statements that indicate expected program outcomes. Goals, however, as discussed in this text refer to outcomes sought by clients. To further distinguish between objectives and goals, program objectives describe outcomes that are expected for all clients. To avoid, however, the one-size-fits-all approach, you may need to selectively include the program objectives in the case or treatment plan as they pertain to the unique situation of each client.

Factors That Influence the Development of Goals

Client Participation

Goal pursuits begin with a need or want expressed by the client, or in the instance of nonvoluntary or involuntary status adapting to a goal assigned by someone else. You should not expect the development of goals to be a neatly defined linear process. Listening to client's stories takes time, and several options may need to be explored prior to deciding upon a specific goal. This is time well spent. There are two types of experts in the goal development process—the client and you:

Social Worker: As the social worker, your expertise, knowledge and skills are used to assist clients to define and specify goals in measurable language, as well as to help them to assess feasibility and identify potential barriers.

Client: The client is the foremost expert in articulating what they would like to be different. Their stories provide context, specifically the "when, with whom and under what circumstances target behaviors occur" (Murphy & Dillon, 1998, p. 183).

Whether context involves interpersonal, intrapersonal, or family relationships or external social systems, it is vital to understanding client situations. As Marsh (2002) reminds us, having clients identify their concerns and the changes they wish to make supports the axiom of "starting where the client is" (p. 341). Both voluntary and involuntary clients are motivated by a

process in which they are self-involved and, further, one in which they need to perceive the procedures as being just (Greenberg & Tyler, 1987). In contrast, their lack of involvement has implications for self-definition, self-efficacy, and motivation (Bandura, 1997; Boehm & Staples, 2004; Gondolla, 2004; Meyer, 2001; Wright, Greenberg & Brehm, 2004). Clients' participation in the development of goals is essential to their empowerment and sense of efficacy as they cope with a difficult situation (Smith & Marsh, 2002; Meyer, 2001). Participation is a basic social justice principal (Finn & Jacobson, 2003b), which clarifies that "clients have a right to their reality, and to have their reality be a part of their service provisions" (pp. 128–129).

Sensitivity to the views of clients is especially important in cross-cultural, social justice, and anti-oppression practice (Al-Krenawi & Graham, 2000; Dietz, 2000; Finn & Jacobson, 2003; Guadalupe & Lum, 2005; Jordan & Franklin, 2003; Lee, 2003; Lum, 2004; Paz, 2002; Sue, 2006; Vera & Speight, 2003; Weaver, 2004). Recall the Diaz case (Chapter 10), in which respect to the father's role as head of the household was a cultural force. Thus the interfamilial interaction was informed by cultural expectations of member behavior, with rules and roles. The social worker's access to this information could only be gained through the family's participation.

Like the Diaz case, diverse individuals and families experience tensions that can be characterized as interpersonal in nature. But it is not uncommon that the concerns of diverse individuals involve multiple external systems and adverse environmental interactions. Without the participation of these clients, goals can be developed that are counterproductive to their interests and which reinforce clients' marginal status and their experience of oppression (Dietz, 2000; Finn & Jacobson, 2003a; Sue, 2006; Vera & Speight, 2003). Listening to the stories of diverse clients facilitates their participation and ensures that goals are consistent with their reality, their culture and their experience. In this way, you are not asserting the preeminence of the expert role and further reinforcing the experience of inequality and oppression (Clifford & Burke, 2005; Guadalupe & Lum, 2005; Pollack, 2004; G. D. Rooney, 2009; Weinberg, 2006).

Values and Beliefs

Goals are by their nature intended to facilitate change. Clarifying the values and beliefs of clients is consistent with the "ethics of participation," the starting point with clients and your understanding of their reality (Finn and Jacobson, 2003b; Marsh, 2002). Studies have shown that conventional behaviors, lifestyles, and values are different in impoverished communities (Dunlap, Golub & Johnson, 2006). The tendency has been to treat different beliefs and values in these communities as unconventional or oppositional without recognition of their context. As such, diverse values and beliefs may be perceived as problematic, and the holder is considered to be an outsider. You should be mindful of the fact that ethical problems can occur when there are differences between your values and those of the client with regard to a goal. There is an inherent ethical conflict, specifically a tension between autonomy and paternalism, when the goals that you may have for a client are favored over those of the client. In truth, clients make choices and have values that are consistent with their circumstances and world view, as well as the resources available to them (Orme, 2002; Pollack, 2004; Weinberg, 2006)

Value Inherent in Goal Setting

Sue (2006, p. 135) issues a cautionary note about goals, asserting that the process is value laden. He maintains that "there are certain values reflected in the goal setting process" that may be counter to the experience and beliefs of clients. The process, for example, assumes that clients, including minors, both understand, believe in, and value setting goals. Clients faced with the rigor and stress of everyday life may fail to see how goals can alter their situation. Further, Sue (2006) remarks that the expectation of client participation and the process of developing goals assumes the voluntary YAVIS (young, articulate, verbal, intelligent, and successful) client. This image can create the potential for discrimination against those who are less socially connected. Examples include culturally diverse groups, those who speak a second language or dialects, people of lower socioeconomic status, and elderly or minor clients with diminished cognitive capacity (James & Gilliland, 2005; Sue, 2006). Also, an emphasis on individuals or the nuclear family may result in goals that express a value in which the focus is on self-determination and autonomy. James and Gilliland (2005), citing the work of Hall (1976), distinguish between low and high context cultures. Whereas in the former, individual aspirations conform to Western norms, the reverse is true in high-context cultures. Specifically, in high-context cultures, individual aspirations and esteem are derived from and are interdependent with the reference cultural group.

Family Involvement

Knowledge of group values and beliefs and cultural preferences are important considerations in the goal-setting process, as well as in goal attainment. Yet you should not assume their prominence as a hard-and-fast rule for all clients. Nor should the involvement of the client's family or social network be ignored. Whether the family or other supportive networks are to be involved is a decision to be made by the client. In this way, you are respecting his or her preference, be it based on culture, family form, or status. The attainment of goals for minors in most instances will require family support and in some cases other individuals or systems with whom the minor is involved. For example, goals related to school performance may require that the minor's teachers are involved. When a parent has become overwhelmed with the behavior of a minor, they may demand that their offspring be "fixed" by the professional. In these instances, extra effort may be required to encourage parental participation.

There is evidence that the positive support of the family or significant others can facilitate goal attainment. Rittner and Dozier (2000), for example, examined the effectiveness of court-mandated substance abuse services in preventing the reoccurrence of drug use. Their research acknowledged the power of the court mandate; however, the supportive involvement of family members was as important. Other works have shown that family involvement provided a cultural frame of reference that was essential to developing goals that were consistent with the values and beliefs of a particular group (Gardner, 2000; Hodge & Nadir, 2008; James & Gilliland, 2005; Lum, 2004, 2007; Sarkisian & Gerstel, 2004; Sue, 2006). Hodge (2004), Potocky-Tripodi (2002), Wong (2007), and Sue (2006) are among the writers who emphasize the importance of family participation in decisions about health and mental health treatment plans for ethnic groups, immigrants, and refugees. A deciding factor for lesbian women in selecting a mental health or health care provider was whether their partners could be involved (Saulnier, 2002). Family group conferencing decision making is a child welfare strategy that has been shown to be an effective means to ensure support for the well-being of minors. The integration of family and cultural preferences is crucial to the success of this strategy (MacGowan, Pennell, Carlton-LaNey & Weil, 2004).

The support of family members for goal attainment is not definite and several factors may need to be explored. Support can depend on the nature of prior and existing relationships. Tensions between individuals, and tensions and unresolved issues within the family, can diminish the potential of family support. Changes in the behavior of an individual can challenge existing family dynamics and require a change in how members relate to one another. Also, in some instances you may find that families are burdened by their own needs, stressors, or limited resources or that their goodwill has been exhausted. Family members may also evoke a quid pro quo, in essence giving conditions under which they will provide support. Moreover, the desired outcome sought by an individual may be inconsistent with their culture and its perspectives on behavior, including the act of seeking help from an outsider (Fredriksen, 1999; Williams, 2006; Wong, 2007). Even under the best of circumstances, there are situations in which a client's goal conflicts with family values and therefore support is unavailable.

Case Example

Christa recently graduated from high school with honors. She had planned to attend a local community college where she intended to study photography. She recently learned that she was pregnant. Her parents, upset over the fact that she is pregnant and unmarried, insisted that she leave their home. For several weeks, Christa couch-surfed at the homes of various friends. Currently, she is living with an aunt, the only family member with whom she feels comfortable. Her priority goal is to find stable housing during the pregnancy and to have access to prenatal care. Beyond this point she is unclear about what to do. She questions whether she can care for a baby on her own. Further, she states that her parents would never accept a decision of having an abortion and she herself is ambivalent about this option. Marriage is out of the question, as the father of the baby left for college and has made it clear that he is out of the picture.

Her support systems are limited, beyond the housing support of her aunt. Prior to becoming pregnant, she had strong relationships with her parents and the parents of her boyfriend. Her boyfriend made it clear that she could not tell his parents about the pregnancy. Although the threat of potential harm from him was ruled out, Christa is reluctant to involve his family, believing that it is best to move on. With her aunt, she is living in a safe and supportive environment, but needs to find a place to live by the end of the month because the aunt has accepted a new job in California. Because the aunt is moving away, Christa is anxious and scared about becoming homeless. Her parents are a tenuous resource, but there are

significant value tensions that cannot be ignored. It is unclear whether the parents are willing to support Christa's goal of safe, stable housing, preferably with them.

With this goal as a focus, Walt the social worker obtained Christa's permission to talk with her mother about the possibility of her moving home.

Phone call with mother:

Social Worker: Hello, may I speak to Christa's mother?

Mother: I am her mother, who is this?

Social Worker: My name is Walt. I am a social worker who is working with your daughter.

Mother: You mean to tell me that social workers support girls who go out and sleep around?

Social Worker: Not exactly, but I am working with your daughter to help her find a safe place to live during her pregnancy.

Mother: Well, I knew she was at my sister's house and I believe she is doing fine. We surely don't need or want you. Besides, what does she want from us? We didn't betray our family's values or get her pregnant without being married. She went and did that all on her own!

Socials Worker: I understand that you feel this way about the situation. I also respect your concern that she betrayed your family. She acknowledges that she made a mistake, but needs and wants your help and guidance. One of the goals that we set up together was for Christa to have safe and stable housing while she is pregnant. She would like to meet with you and her father to talk about returning home. Would you and your husband be willing to meet with her?

With Walt acting as a mediator between Christa and her mother, eventually the mother agreed to a meeting, but asserted that she could not "speak for the father."

What about the social worker's values and beliefs in this situation? The conversation between Walt and Christa's mother seems pretty straightforward. Nonetheless, in presenting the case for consultation, Walt, recognized that his own values and parental experience had the potential to intrude upon this situation. He acknowledged that he had very strong feelings about Christa's situation and her parent's reaction. He stated, "I really had to hold back to keep from saying to the mother to live in the modern world." Having supportive parents as a gay male, he could not imagine circumstances in which parents would withhold support from a child. Note, however, that in the conversation with the mother, he was careful not to dismiss the influence of the family values in their decision. Yet for him, Christa faced a major turning point in her life that required the support of her parents. Certainly he understood that her parents were disappointed and that Christa's situation was inconsistent with their values about marriage and pregnancy. In his opinion, however, their values were hardly a valid reason for "turning her out of her home."

There are also times when social proximity or social distance can influence attitudes about clients (Clifford & Burke, 2005; Weinberg. 2006). In this case, social proximity was a factor. Walt was a recent MSW graduate, and his being relatively close in age to Christa raised the possibility for him to become over-involved in the case. Self-evaluation is a demand of ethical practice. Like Walt, you should critically examine your values, your cultural, political or religious beliefs, and your biases, paying careful attention to whether your experience becomes a force in the goal-setting process.

Environmental Conditions

Environmental resources and supports or the lack thereof should be assessed in the goal development process. Attributes such as age, race, gender, class, and sexual orientation and structural inequality are factors that can influence the capacity to attain goals irrespective of client motivation. Helping a low-income couple to obtain subsidized housing, for example, may be constrained by geographical location or the limited number of available federal funds for subsidized housing. Discrimination in housing, employment, and institutional lending patterns is illegal, yet there are subtle forms that exist that pose barriers to low-income and minority clients (Fernandez, 2007). Many of the problems experienced by minority persons can have a debilitating psychological effect (Dietz, 2000; Guadalupe & Lum, 2005; Pollack, 2004; Sue, 2006). As such, clients may be unable to marshal the energy required to engage in developing goals. For example, low-income women, disadvantaged by poverty, race, or ethnic minority status were found to experience depression at a higher level when compared to the general population (Grote, Zuckhoff, Swartz, Bledsoe & Giebel 2008). In addition, agency mission or resources and public policy may constrain individual or family goals. Initiatives such as the Defense of Marriage Act curtail the basic civil rights of gay and lesbian parents with respect to child visitation, adoption, or becoming foster patents (Fredriksen, 1999). The assets of the elderly or low-income families may be a decisive factor in the determination of eligibility for state or federal benefits. In many instances structural inequality that limits resources makes it impractical for diverse groups to survive and thrive.

Involuntary Status

Involuntary status may mean that the client is reluctant to participate in a process in which they perceive themselves as having limited power and control. The experience of having both problem and solution externally defined can exaggerate feelings of being marginalized (Lum, 2004; G. D. Rooney, 2009; Sue, 2006). A second aspect of involuntary status is that of being different by reason of birth. Few people would choose to be outside of the mainstream of society, a situation in which there are certain risks and fewer benefits (G. D. Rooney, 2009). Reluctance, distrust, and suspicion may be increased in that the goals are set forth by an external authority for both groups, especially when based on perceived deficits. The fact that individuals or families from minority groups are often referred to seek help under pressure and mandates often adds to the tension in your working relationship with them (R. H. Rooney, 2009).

Starting where the client is, albeit that the individual or family is constrained by an external authority, is equally important in your work with involuntary clients. Of course, eliciting their participation in developing goals that they themselves have not chosen can be a challenge. Initially, you may need to address their concerns and feelings about mandated goals in which they have had limited or no participation in defining the problem. In spite of these dynamics, involuntary clients have a right be heard and to articulate their view of their situation, as well as participate in the decisions about how to achieve goals or solutions (DeJong & Berg, 2001).

Types of Goals

Goals may involve changes in both *overt* and *covert* behaviors. An overt goal for Christa, for example, was finding stable housing during her pregnancy, preferably with her family. A covert goal would involve reducing her fear of becoming homeless as a means to diminish her stress. The systems or subsystems involved will also influence the feasibility and type of goals to be developed. For example, Christa's parents figured prominently in whether she could achieve her goal of returning home during her pregnancy. Another system included a clinic in which she could receive prenatal care for herself and her unborn child. Systems and subsystems that are the focus for change also determine the type of goal to be developed and who will be involved. For example, a goal to improve the conditions of a playground in a neighborhood may include parents and city or county officials. Individual goals may also focus on intrapersonal subsystems as well as interactions with the social and physical environment.

Goals may initially be expressed in broad terms, for example, changes in *cognitive and emotional functioning* or *behavior*. Consider an individual who is facing eviction for failure to pay their rent of time. An example of behavioral changes would be to increase frequency of paying rent on time. The behavior goal may be combined with one that requires a change in cognitive functioning, if the reason for late payment was "forgetting when the rent is due."

Goals may be further categorized by their type and their function. When the target system is a couple, family, or group, goals typically involve changes on the part of all the relevant participants in the system. In these larger systems, *shared goals* are those that are held in common and agreed upon by members of the system. For example, after brainstorming ways in which members in a group could assist each other, members may agree to use positive and supportive messages with one another. The distinguishing feature of shared goals is that all participants agree to act in such a way.

TABLE-12-2 GUIDELINES FOR SELECTING AND DEFINING GOALS

Goals must be related to results sought by voluntary clients

Strategies for developing goals with involuntary clients

Goals must be defined in explicit and measurable terms

Goals must be feasible

Goals should be commensurate with knowledge and skills of the Practitioner

Goal should be stated in positive terms that emphasize growth

Avoid agreeing with goals about which you have major reservations

Goals should be consistent with function of the agency

Reciprocal goals have some elements of a shared goal in that they are also developed with the parties involved. With reciprocal goals, all involved agree upon exchanges of different behavior and to act or respond to each other in a different manner. In some instances, a reciprocal goal may be a precursor to developing other goals. Anita, the daughter, and Mr. Diaz, for example, eventually agreed to listen to each other without interrupting. Reciprocal goals tend to be *quid pro quo* in nature; that is, each person agrees to modify his or her personal behavior contingent upon the other person making a corresponding behavioral change. "I will listen to you without interrupting, if you will also listen to me." Adhering to this reciprocal goal, Anita and Mr. Diaz, in Chapter 10 and the other family members could then devote their energy to developing a goal with respect to Mr. Diaz health care needs and his desire to remain independent.

Guidelines for Selecting and Defining Goals

The process of selecting and defining goals will differ depending on whether the client is voluntary or involuntary. Because the dynamics between you and the client are different in each case, the following discussion highlights the distinction between voluntary and involuntary clients. With the voluntary client, both you and the client are engaged in the process together. Conversely, with involuntary clients, a goal has been defined for them. Further, the authority attributed to your role with each client group is different. Hence, your relationship with the involuntary client may involve tensions, and can be vastly different from the voluntary collaboration. Table 12-2 summarizes the criteria upon which decisions about selecting and defining goals.

Goals Must Relate to the Desired Results Sought by Voluntary Clients

With the voluntary client, the psychological authority attributed to you, the social worker is generally positive. However, some clients may have been hesitant to seek professional help. Their reluctance may be influenced by cultural norms, their belief that their situation is too difficult, or they may simply be embarrassed. Yet they may have exhausted other possibilities. By the time you have reached the point of developing goals (having earlier worked on their feelings and established rapport) their perception of you is based on trust. Therefore, their perception of your goodwill has a positive influence on the collaborative nature of your relationship. Even so, for voluntary clients to be motivated and emotionally invested they must believe that the outcome of working with you will address and ultimately alter their concerns (Lum, 2004; Marsh, 2002; Meyer, 2001; Smith & Marsh, 2002). Collaborating with clients in developing and selecting goals does not mean that you, as the social worker, should assume a passive role. To the contrary, many clients often will want your guidance. You should, however balance sharing your professional expertise and responsibility with focusing on the primary concerns presented by the client.

Strategies of Selecting and Defining Goals with Involuntary Clients

Unlike the voluntary client who is motivated to seek help by the weight of an identified concern, the involvement of the involuntary client often results in a different set of dynamics. Perhaps the most volatile issues for them in their suspicion, mistrust, and reactance is that goals for them are constructed around perceived deficits (Lum, 2004; R. H. Rooney, 2009; Sue, 2006). Initially, the involuntary client's reaction may be emotion-focused, centered on the explicit authority granted to you by the legal mandate. Other dynamics can emerge in particular with involuntary clients who are also a member of a minority group. Their fears may be heightened by their perception of your authority; their compliance, prescriptive goals, by a sense of powerlessness and of being further marginalized (DeJong & Berg, 2001; G. D. Rooney, 2009; R. H. Rooney, 2009).

In defining goals with this client group, your understanding of and empathy with these dynamics, including being attuned to their emotions, is critical to reducing reactance and facilitating their engagement. In addition to the interactional dynamics between you and involuntary clients, you should be mindful of the fact that members of minority groups are overrepresented among those clients who are involuntary, even though their numbers may be smaller overall in the client population. Minority group members and involuntary clients share certain attributes; for example, tensions related to external control versus personal control, marginal status, constrained self-determination, and lack of power. Because of this overlap of status these attributes can be a forceful relational dynamic when combined with the authority vested in you by the mandate (G. D. Rooney, 2009).

Strategies for work with involuntary clients were first developed by Rooney (1992) based on his work with

TABLE-12-3 STRATEGIES FOR WORK WITH INVOLUNTARY CLIENTS

Motivational Congruence
Agreeable Mandate
Let's Make a Deal
Getting Rid of the Mandate

involuntary minors and parents involved in child protection. These strategies, which are summarized in Table 12-3, may be used to facilitate the development of goals with this client group as well as to encourage their participation.

Prior to reading about the strategies, you might imagine walking into a new required class for which the instructor had determined that your goal should be to perform at the highest level. At this point, the course content and performance standards are unfamiliar, and you might question the authority of the instructor to establish such a goal. Because the goal has been set without consideration for either you as an individual or involving your participation, you most likely would become anxious, fearful and discouraged. Because the class is required, you might consider enrolling in section taught by another instructor. Assuming that you decided to stay in the class, what could the instructor do or say that would motivate you to achieve the goal?

Exploring the "intensity of motivation theory," Gendolla (2004) raises a question that is pertinent to you, the involuntary student, and the involuntary client. The question is whether people "automatically mobilize maximal effort in goal pursuits when their achievement has direct implications for the self-esteem, self-direction and personal interest?" (p. 2005). The potential of motivating involuntary clients to respond to imposed goals has implications for their self-determination and autonomy in the change effort. The advantage of the strategies is that they focus on specific change while engaging the client in the instrumental behavioral change required by the mandate.

Motivational Congruence

The principle of "starting where the client is," is equally important with involuntary clients. Exploration should include their view of the problem described by the court. According to DeJong and Berg (2001), congruence is possible when mandated clients are able to "take control by describing the mandated situation themselves" (p. 364). When given the opportunity, involuntary clients will express their opinion of problems or situations that resulted in the mandate. In this way, self-definition and involvement in the process can be a motivation factor, by virtue of the fact that their view is solicited and heard.

Clients may describe their circumstances and the situation in great detail, including expressing their anger, frustration, and sense of outrage. In child welfare, a parent can be sensitive to goals established as a risk assessment relative to indicators of harm and acceptable norms of parenting. The definition of the client as irresponsible is a serious one and may be inconsistent with the parent's view of themselves and their perspective of the problem. Mandates and risk assessment are not structured in a way that aids in understanding the circumstances of a behavior or act. Instead, the focus is on the outcome of an act or behavior, and goals that focus on corrective action. For example, leaving children at home alone for a period of time to go to a party is a legitimate concern of the child protective service and the court. The court is unconcerned about the circumstances, only that the well-being of the children has been compromised by the behavior of the parent.

Two central questions emerge with respect to achieving motivational congruence:

- *What are the concerns of the parent in this situation?*
- *Is it possible that leaving a child at home alone, unsupervised, is also a parental concern?*

Motivational congruence as illustrated in Figure 12-1 is possible when the target goals of the court and client are compatible. In essence, there is agreement between the parent, the court and you as the social worker about the supervision of the children when the parent is not at home. Goals that are consistent with parental needs and wants are more likely to succeed and, because of their involvement, have a longer-lasting change. The reverse may be true in cases where the client's motivation is primarily devoted to escaping punishments or gaining rewards or the parent's capacity is severely impaired.

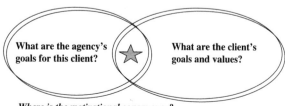

Where is the motivational congruence?
Are there opportunities for meaningful choices?

FIG-12-1 Motivational Congruence

Agreeable Mandate

It is likely that the circumstances in which the behavior occurred, that is leaving children unsupervised, will explain the client's view of the problem. The court, of course, is not privy to nor interested in this information. As such, the client's view is likely to diverge from that of the legal authority that mandated the contact. Without the opportunity to tell their story in court, a parent is most likely to resent being perceived as neglectful and further may believe that the court does not understand or care about their situation. Hence for them, it is a question of fairness in both the process and the outcome (Greenberg & Tyler, 1987).

The *agreeable mandate* strategy entails a search for common ground that bridges the differing views of the client and that of the court (DeJong & Berg, 2001; R. H. Rooney, 2009). Pursuing the agreeable mandate may also involve reframing the definition of the problem in such a way that it adequately addresses the concerns identified in the mandate or referral source while simultaneously responding to the concerns of the client. Reframing is a useful technique for reducing reactance, facilitating a workable agreement, and increasing the client's motivation. This strategy may be combined with motivational interviewing and motivational congruence. Let's consider the example of a participant in a treatment group for men who batter. The participant may reject the descriptive language used by the professional group leader, for example, "perpetrator," or the pressure to admit that he is abusive as the starting point for behavior change. But he may agree to a goal of improving his relationship with his spouse in which the focus is on how this can be accomplished. Motivational interviewing can also provide the client with the opportunity for self-reflection. For example, if one of the men (or several) disagree that they have a problem handling their anger, you might ask them to consider how their expression of anger impacts those around them.

Let's Make a Deal

Negotiating goals with involuntary clients can include a bargaining strategy, or *"Let's make a deal."* Essentially, the private concerns of the involuntary client are combined with the problem that precipitated the mandate or referral. To illustrate, let's return to the mother who left her children alone while she went to a party in the neighborhood. While she was away, there was a small fire in the apartment, and the older child called the fire department. When the firefighters discovered that the children were home alone, they reported the situation to child protection and the children were moved to a temporary shelter. The mother was angry, stating, "They had no right to take my kids. It is hard to always be stuck at home and not have time for myself." The problem from the perspective of child protective services is that the "children were left unsupervised, and further the fire presented a dangerous situation." In this case, the deal could be that you would address the mother's need to have time for herself if she would agree to work on resolving the issue of supervision for the children. The efficacy of this strategy is derived from your willingness to offer a payoff that is meaningful to the client, thus creating an incentive for her to be involved in developing problem-solving goals.

Getting Rid of the Mandate

With some involuntary clients, none of the preceding strategies is viable. In these cases, the only recourse left is to appeal to clients' desire to be free of the restraints imposed by the mandate or referral source. This strategy appeals to the client's motivation of *getting rid of the mandate or outside pressure* (R. H. Rooney, 2009; Jordan & Franklin, 2003). The case of the unsupervised children can be used to illustrate this: She feels misunderstood and angry, and she rejects the notion that she has neglected her parental responsibility: "I love my kids, I am all they have." She reports the incident as a one-time event, necessitated by "feeling as if I was going to lose my mind being cooped up in the house with these kids all the time." She is clear that her primary motivation is to "get you people out of my hair," and to escape what she considers an adversarial and invasive presence in her life. If the overall goal is child safety and the return of the children to the home, then incremental steps may be developed with her that satisfy both the mandate and her desire to be rid of oversight from child protective services. In essence, all parties concerned have a shared goal; specifically, the return of the children to the home, albeit when certain requirements are met.

Motivating change talk and the selection of goals becomes possible when the relationship between you and the involuntary client is collaborative rather than coercive (Miller & Rollnick, 2002). Motivational interviewing uses empathy rather than blame. Blaming and arguing with clients to get acceptance of the mandate or to comply, and using your authority to coerce them, is generally counterproductive and likely to result in reactance. For example, with the mother in the above example, paraphrasing with empathy would include a statement such as, "It must difficult to be a single parent, working all day and then coming home to...." This statement conveys to the mother that you have an understanding of her situation, and that you are not sitting in judgment of her as a person.

Each of the discussed strategies appeals to the client's self interest and his or her involvement in the process of change. Motivational congruence and the deal strategy counter the notion that certain clients are opposed to change. Instead, both the client and you have the advantage of exploring common ground in which mandated goals can be defined and achieved. With the agreeable mandate strategy, for example, an involuntary client may transition through the stages of change, moving from being involuntary to a level of voluntary status. In stages of change, goals may emerge as a result of self-evaluation as a client progresses from the stage of pre-contemplation ("Leaving the children at home one time was not a problem") to contemplation ("I am willing to look at the harm that resulted from leaving the children unsupervised"). In the pre-contemplation stage, the male who batters might deny that his behavior is abusive by saying, for example, "I had little choice, she was in my face." At the contemplation stage, he might say, "I am willing to look at my behavior," at which point self-reflection and self-evaluation become goals of examining "the effects of my behavior on self and significant others."

Clients may argue for the status quo, discount, minimize, or excuse their behavior (Miller & Rollnick, 2002). Perhaps you might think that talking about change or the strategies for change shift the focus away from clients' behavior. Research has shown, however, that a focus on a specific cognition or behavior can be a mediator between actions and change, ultimately increasing the frequency of desired behaviors (Nichols, 2006). In addition, how you respond to the client can create cognitive consonance or dissonance, which can predict change. For example, when the mother says, "This was the only time that I left the kids at home by themselves," an inductive open-ended response might be, "What do others say is about leaving the kids at home?" or "When the children were home alone this one time, what happened?"

Goals Should Be Defined in Explicit and Measurable Terms

To provide direction in the helping process, clients' goals must be defined in explicit and measurable terms. Explicitly defined measurable goal statements clarify the who, what, and under what circumstances of the desired outcome (Bloom, Fischer & Orme, 2003). Examples of explicit measurable goals are:

> "The children will be supervised when the mother goes out for the evening."
> "Christa will obtain prenatal care for herself and her unborn child."
> "Mr. Diaz will administer his insulin under the supervision of a home health aide."
> "Participants in the social skills group will learn and practice listening skills in the classroom."

In each of the examples, you can readily document and measure goal progress and goal achievement. For example, did Christa obtain prenatal care? You can also measure whether the participants in the social skills group improve their listening skills. Further measurement procedures for the skills group participants would assess the individual level of improvement by comparing the pre-group baseline to the post group performance in the classroom.

Appropriately stated, specific and measurable goals will specify both overt and covert changes. By way of illustration, consider Terrence, who is habitually late for school, usually arriving after attendance is taken in his homeroom. Attendance records verify that he has been absent from school fifteen times within the last month. He claims to have difficulty waking up in the morning, and then he often is late getting up, because he does not

Client/Family:	Staff:		
Statement of Concern:			
Goal Statement:			Goal #__
General Tasks:			
Identify Strengths/Resources:		Identify Potential Barriers/Obstacles:	
Tasks/Steps–Participant:		Tasks/Steps–Staff:	

Date:	Progress Notes:	Staff
Goal Status Summary: C__ PC__ NC__ (Need summary explanation)		

FIG-12-2 Case Progress Notes

like to go to school. An overt goal would be for "Terrence to get out of bed when he hears the alarm." This goal may be observed by others and precise measurement is possible. A covert change might include "increasing his positive thoughts about school." This goal can also be recorded and is measurable, albeit only by Terrence. It may also be more difficult for him to achieve at the current time because of his feelings about school. At any rate, measures of covert behavior are subject to error as a result of inconsistent self-monitoring and the effects of self-monitoring on the target behavior. For example, Terrence may forget to record his thoughts, and after a time, he may find the task tedious and he may claim that his thoughts about school are unrelated to his attendance.

In either instance, the case record and/or SOAP (subjective, objective, assessment and plan) notes provide for documenting, maintaining focus, and assisting you to monitor and measure progress. Establishing a baseline with Terrence—for example, the number of days that he has been on time for school, as well as the number of days that he as attended school—would be recorded in the case record. This information can also be used in the termination phase in the evaluation of outcomes. Although agencies typically have their own forms for recording progress, we provide an example, which is illustrated in Figure 12-2. Note that both strengths and obstacles are recorded, as well as steps or tasks for both the client and the staff. The status of the goals may also be noted, indicating whether they have been completed or partially completed.

Also, giving clients a copy of the goals that you have written, or having them record their goals, including involuntary clients, lessens the power differences and fosters a more collaborative relationship. Many experienced social workers provide clients with a folder that contains goal statements, tasks, and case notes, to help them keep track of goals and their progress.

Partializing Goals

Even goals formulated with a high level of specificity often are complex and involve multiple actions that must be completed in a logical sequence. Because of this complexity, clients may feel overwhelmed and intimidated when facing the prospect of tackling goal implementation. For these reasons, it is important that you partialize their ultimate goals into constituent parts. Partializing is not a new technique in social work practice. Indeed, the technique has long been a basic tenet of social work practice theory (Perlman, 1957, pp. 147–149). It is consistent with the social work commitment to empowerment, especially in facilitating clients' ability to make decisions and to achieve desired outcomes. When goals are partialized, they are dissected into manageable portions. Clients are better able to develop discrete corrective or problem-solving actions (general and specific tasks), giving them a sense of efficacy that ultimately leads to goal accomplishment.

Goals and General Tasks. Goals represent the desired outcome, but as expressed by clients and legal mandates they may be articulated at various levels of abstraction or general terms. Rarely are individuals able to go from zero to sixty in their efforts to achieve goals. For this reason, general tasks are developed as instrumental strategies to further partialize goals (Reid, 1992). General tasks are the basis of *objectives or specific tasks*. Whether phrased as specific tasks or objectives, the essential function of both is that they indicate the action steps to be taken and developed to achieve goals. For example, attaining your degree in social work is a specific goal. But, it is important to distinguish this goal, which represents the desired outcome, from general tasks. Instrumental strategies in the form of general tasks related to obtaining your social work degree may be to obtain financial assistance, attend classes on a regular basis, and complete required assignments, as well as additional tasks such as arranging for child care and transportation.

Table 12-4 distinguishes between goals and general tasks so as to further assist you to discriminate between global and explicit goals. The table is intended to help you to conceptualize the relationship that exists between goals and general tasks. Included in the table are goals that involve both overt and covert behaviors. Notice that explicit goals refer to specific behaviors or environmental changes that suggest the nature of the corresponding intervention.

General tasks may also be categorized in a broad sense as either *discrete* or *ongoing* (or continuous). Discrete general tasks consist of one-time actions or changes that resolve or ameliorate problems. Examples include obtaining a needed resource (e.g., housing or medical care), making a major decision (e.g., deciding to adopt a child), or making a change in one's environment (e.g., moving into an assisted-living complex). Ongoing general tasks involve actions that are continuous and repetitive and rely on incremental progress toward the *ultimate or global* goal. For example, registration for classes is a discrete task, attending classes on a regular basis is an ongoing, incremental task toward obtaining the degree (ultimate goal).

TABLE-12-4 GOALS AND GENERAL TASKS

GOALS	GENERAL TASKS
Increase control over emotions	1. Reduce frequency of anger outbursts by being aware of cues that elicit anger; increase use of internal dialogue to decrease anger
Improve social relations	2. Approach others and initiate and maintain conversation by using listening skills and minimal furthering responses
Enhance interactions with social environment	3. Explore living arrangements in a center for elderly persons that provides outside activities
Enhance self-confidence	4. Focus on strengths and positive attributes and qualities; express self-approval
Improve parenting skills	5. Demonstrate competence in planning and preparing nutritious meals and maintaining adequate sanitary and hygienic conditions
Increase social participation in group sitations	6. Initiate discussion, providing personal views and by asking questions in group discussions
Improve communication skills	7. Listen without interrupting when interacting with others.
Minimize conflict with peers	8. Learn conflict resolution skills
Express anger in a constructive manner	9. Learn alternative ways of expressing anger
Engage in one of the responsibilities in my case plan.	10. Attend school on a regular basis.

In defining explicit goals and ongoing general tasks, a part of this process involves identifying the level of the desired change. With goals that involve ongoing behavior, growth is potentially infinite, so it is desirable to determine the extent of the change or the scope of the solution sought by the client or mandate; for example, "The children will be supervised when the parent goes out for the evening." The advantage of specifying the desired levels of change is that you and the client mutually agree to the ends sought by the latter. As another example, consider the social skills group in which the goal was to increase listening skills in the classroom. Within this global group goal, each student will no doubt aspire to varying levels of goal attainment and each would have a different behavior baseline. Your role is to assist each individual to develop a goal that is consistent with their expected and desired level of goal attainment. In using a baseline for each group participant, the two of you are able to specify, monitor, and measure individual levels of progress.

Goals Must Be Feasible

People prefer to choose or adopt goals that are feasible and desirable based on their assessment of their capacity for goal attainment (Bandura, 1997; Oettingen, Bulgarella, Henderson & Gollwitzer, 2004). Selecting unachievable goals sets up clients for failure that can result in discouragement ("Why bother?"), disillusionment ("The situation is hopeless"), or a sense of defeat ("Nothing ever changes").

Most clients, motivated by self-direction, are capable of accomplishing the goals they set for themselves, so it is important to affirm their sense of self by reinforcing the validity of those goals. But at the same time, clients may choose goals that are more difficult to attain than they had originally imagined. You may encounter clients who have grandiose or impractical aspirations or who may pay scant attention to personal or environmental limitations. Faced with this dilemma, first your ethical obligation is to engage the client in a discussion about feasibility. Ethical persuasion is similar to, but not the same as, informed consent. Ethical persuasion involves exploring alternatives and a review of advantages and disadvantages of a decision (Miller & Rollinick, 2002; R. H. Rooney, 2009). Caution should be exercised however. You should not assume a paternalistic or beneficent expert role, or in the case of the involuntary client, the position of the authority vested in you by a mandate. Central questions related to the feasibility of goals may include the following:

- *How can I affirm a client's goal and reinforce and support their motivation without participating in a potential situation in which they might become discouraged?*

- *How can I assist the client to partialize goals and to develop incremental tasks or objectives so that their goals can be realistically be achieved?*
- *What are realistic and measurable expectations as to what can feasibly be achieved within a given time period?*

Goal attainment in the best of circumstances, however, requires more than a force of will. Arda, for example, believes that she can complete a nurse practitioner program in less than the scheduled time. At the same time, consideration must be given to the fact that she is a mother, wife, a caretaker for an elderly immigrant parent, and she is employed full-time. She perceives completing the program as her contribution to increasing the economic stability of her family. Affirming and supporting Arda's goal while assessing its feasibility is a balancing act. Therefore, in suggesting a modification to her goal, she needs to perceive that your suggestion increases her ability to achieve her goal. You should explain that the intent is not to change her goal and to reinforce your support. Instead in discussing feasibility with her, the two of you can realistically appraise what can be accomplished given her other commitments.

Involuntary Clients' Mandated Case Plans

The feasibility of goals, in particular those involving involuntary clients, can be especially difficult to manage. Feasibility also involves the clients' confidence in their ability to achieve goals, which may not possible unless goals are specific and defined. Mandated goals can be vague and may involve unrealistic expectations about what clients can accomplish in a given time frame. Goals set forth in a mandate case plan may resemble a *"kitchen sink"* (i.e., the plans include "everything but the kitchen sink"). Essentially, case plans may be established without a priority ranking and outline numerous changes that the client is required to make. Goals achievement may also commit the client to simultaneous involvement with numerous other service providers, each of which may establish their own program objectives and related outcomes. A situation in which multiple service providers are involved, and the services lack coordination, can unintentionally create difficulties for the client. As one client, mandated to seek drug treatment, submit to weekly urine analysis (UAs), attend parenting classes, and find employment queried, "How am I supposed to find a job when I spent so much time running around

seeing all of you people?" Further, she asked, "When I find a job, nobody is going to let me to miss a lot of work. How am I gonna tell my supervisor that I have leave work to go pee in a cup?"

The *"cookie cutter"* approach involves program objectives that are applied uniformly to the case plans of clients. The assumption is that the client population has the same or similar needs and therefore that program objectives need not be selectively applied to the client's unique situation. For example, if a client is court-ordered to a parenting class, focusing on the specific skills that a parent is expected to learn, within a certain time period, would probably have greater appeal to the client. For example, for a parent who lacks knowledge about preparing nutritious meals for her children, specific goals might be:

1. Upon completion of the parent class, the parent will have learned about the major food groups.
2. Prepare meals using foods from three of the five food groups during the next week.

Assessing the feasibility of both the kitchen sink or cookie cutter goals is especially important because they can add to the tension that a client experiences. For example, resources that a client needs may be limited or unavailable; however, the "clock" continues to tick. Given this scenario, some clients may resign themselves to failure and drop out. For others, their motivation can be diminished; while others perceive the situation as unjust. Goal attainment that requires extraordinary effort and for which feasibility is uncertain causes an undue hardship for the client (Wright, Greenberg & Brehm, 2004).

In addition to the previous questions posed, which were related to feasibility, there are other questions that should be answered with regard to goals that have been mandated for the involuntary client.

- *Can the required goals be attained within the time limits?*
- *When the client expresses frustration, is this viewed as a lack of motivation or opposition?*
- *What is the level of progress that would satisfy the court?*
- *Does the client have the resources to achieve the goal?*
- *Are there interpersonal, intrapersonal, or environmental barriers to goal attainment?*
- *What are opportunities and challenges, in the client's relationships; for example, the receptiveness and capacity of significant others to change?*

In working with involuntary clients, you can feel caught between your ethical obligation to the client and to the authority of the court. Moreover, responding to mandates or other pressures requires the compliance of both you and the client. It is your ethical responsibility to increase the likelihood that a client is able to achieve mandated goals. Thus, you can assume responsibility for helping the client to prioritize and manage the various goal requirements.

Prioritizing goals involves identifying a definite case plan period by focusing on legal mandates of the greatest significance (e.g., child safety). It may require that you act as a mediator between the client and the county or state staff person who has responsibility for oversight and reporting to the court. Part of your role may also include advocacy on behalf of the client, requesting that the court consider constraints or barriers to goal achievement, reporting the progress that has been made, and seeking the court's permission to prioritize any remaining goals. For example, "The parent has completed the drug treatment program and her UAs have been clear for six months." In this way the court is informed that progress has occurred, but additional time is needed for the parent to, for example, find a job. Your advocacy role enables the parent to have a reasonable opportunity to develop and demonstrate the skills and capacities needed to resolve the other concerns related to the mandate.

Goals Should Be Commensurate with the Knowledge and Skill of the Practitioner

Certain problems and goals require a high level of expertise, for example, child sexual abuse. It is your legal and ethical responsibility to the client and to the profession that you engage in practice within the scope of you knowledge, ability, and skill (Reamer, 2001). Practice beyond your scope can result in harm to the client and pose a liability for you and your agency. The National Association of Social Worker's (NASW) Code of Ethics provides clear direction with regard to engaging in practice beyond your scope of practice and competence.

Secondary Supervision

Alternatively, *secondary supervision* can provide you with access to a qualified professional, making it possible for you to contract for goals beyond your scope under their guidance or consultation (Strom-Gottfried, 2007; Caspi & Reid, 2002; Reamer, 1998). Secondary supervision is restricted to a specific case, and is therefore different from the *supervisor of record*. Whereas the secondary or consultant provides guidance with regard to a particular area of practice expertise, the supervisor of record performs the functions required by the employing organization. Secondary supervision as an alternative arrangement generally involves a contract between the expert and the agency. In some instances, you may contract for supervision on your own. This arrangement, however, requires the approval of your agency supervisor, as this individual is ultimately responsible for oversight of your work (Strom-Gottfried, 2007).

Of course, using secondary supervision assumes that this resource is available in your particular geographical area. Although advances in technology have made it possible to access secondary supervision or consultation remotely, all parties involved must take precautions to protect client confidentiality (Loewenberg, Dolgoff & Harrington, 2005; Panos, Panos, Cox, Roby & Matheson, 2002; Reamer, 1998). When secondary supervision is not an option, you may consider working with a client under specific restricted conditions:

- *First, you should explain to the client the limitations of your competence with regard to their goal. Advising a client of your limitations allows them to decide on an informed basis whether to continue with their contact with you.*
- *Second, you must evaluate whether or not developing goals in an area where you lack expertise places the client or others at risk.*

Each of the discussed options offers considerations to be carefully evaluated against the potential risks to the client and to your agency. Also, undertaking alternative arrangements and engaging in practice beyond your scope (as defined by legal regulation in your state or province) pose a risk to you (Reamer, 1998; Strom-Gottfried, 2007). In general, it is ethical and legal to engage in practice that is commensurate with your scope and competence, and to refer clients who require service beyond your competence or that of your agency to a qualified professional (Reamer, 1998).

Goals Should Be Stated in Positive Terms That Emphasize Growth

Goals should emphasize growth, highlighting the benefits or gains to the client as a result of their attainment. In formulating goal statements, stipulating negative behaviors that must be eliminated tends to draw attention to what clients must give up, thereby emphasizing deficits in their behavior. For example, "Veronica's interactions with her peers need improvement so that she can attend the spring festival." What do you notice about this goal? Interactions with her peers lacks definition. In addition, the focus is on the negative aspects of her behavior, which, without improvement, result in punishment. Rewriting this goal as a positive and specific might be "Veronica will learn conflict resolution skills so that she is able to improve her interactions with her peers."

Consider the case plan for a father who was recently released from prison and regained custody of his children. Shortly after his release he is reported for excessive discipline of an older child. The case plan read: "*Parent will demonstrate understanding of his inability to manage stress and anger, and the resulting tendency to use punishment, resulting in physical abuse of the child.*" The father wanted help and he recognized that as a result of being in prison for ten years, he lacked some parenting skills. The image of him reflected in the case plan, that of an angry, abusive, and uncaring parent, needed to be reconciled with his self-image that he was "trying to do the right thing." His reaction is not uncommon. In fact, people tend to react to negative evaluations of their behavior or situations. Also, when goals are vague, a lack of understanding of what is expected can increase a client's psychological stress and anxiety. In working with him to complete the case plan, it would be important for you to reinforce the positives of his behavior. Psychologically, defining goals positively that have clear performance standards tends to enhance client motivation and to mitigate conscious or unconscious opposition to change (Bloom, Fischer & Orme, 2003; Miller & Rollnick, 2002). Table 12-5 contains examples of contrasting negative and positive goal statements.

Avoid Agreeing to Goals about which You Have Major Reservations

Increasingly, professionals are asserting their right to serve or not serve clients because of religious or moral beliefs despite ethical codes that emphasize the primacy of client's rights, autonomy, and self-determination. There are also instances when you may be faced with a tension between ethical and legal responsibility. For example, confidential information provided by an immigrant client, for whom you have an ethical and fiduciary obligation, may be in conflict with state and federal laws.

Social Worker Values and Goal Tensions

Clients may have goals that are incompatible with your values. Values, of course, are highly individualized, yet you can have reservations about providing services to clients with whom you do not share common ground. You may also have experienced a situation in which you may have evaluated a client's situation using the lens of your own life experiences and values. For example, a social worker whose caseload is composed of poor and minority clients recognized that when she made home visits, she had to be careful to avoid assessing clients' home environments based on her own childhood experiences. This social worker was often uncomfortable in homes in which she perceived the parenting to be "less structured," as well as those that were not as clean as she would have preferred.

Should you find yourself in a situation in which your beliefs have the potential to intrude upon your fiduciary obligation to the client, what is an appropriate course of action? Some situations may of course tax

TABLE-12-5 NEGATIVE AND POSITIVE GOAL STATEMENTS

NEGATIVE	POSITIVE
Reduce the incidence of criticism among family members	Increase family members' awareness of one another's strengths and increase the frequency of positive messages
Eliminate conflict between family members	Communicate specific disagreements promptly and address them in a constructive manner
Prevent formation of coalitions and nonparticipatory behavior by group members	Unite the efforts of the group in working collectively and draw each member into participation
Discontinue the frequency of drinking binges	Achieve ever-increasing periods of sobriety, taking one day at a time
Refrain from running away from home	Talk about concerns with parents as an alternative option to running away from home
Decrease the use of physical punishment	Apply new ways of disciplining children, such as utilizing "time out," for self and child
Reduce incidents of abusive behavior	Walk away from situations that arouse anger

your ability to work with some clients. In these situations, you should be aware of the primacy of the client's rights, and the professional nature of the client–social worker relationship. Specifically, this means that your personal values should not dictate how you work with clients.

Referrals as a Resource

Ethical practice demands that you refer the client to another professional or agency, providing an honest and nonjudgmental explanation to the client. Cases in which you have strong reservations about the work to be done or the individuals involved pose an ethical dilemma for which you will need to seek supervision or consultation (Strom-Gottfried, 2007). Continuing to work with clients in circumstances where you disagree with their goals is an issue of their rights to effective treatment and their rights to self-determination. In situations where you have reservations, the first thing that may come to mind is, "I will refer the case," which can be a viable option in some cases. But if this resource is unavailable, it is useful if the kind of help you can provide is stated up front, and then other goals may be negotiated. For example, "I can help you with your goal of retaining custody of your son by submitting a report about our work together to the family court judge. But, on the basis of the information that you shared with me, I am unable to assist you in proving that the child's father is irresponsible."

Ethical and Legal Tensions

There are those times in which you may decline to assist a client with a particular goal for legal and ethical reasons. For example, goals that involve a threat of harm the client or others, which of course is neither ethical nor legal. You may also face a situation in which ethical and legal choices are in conflict. Responding to the legal choice may in your opinion be unjust and undermine your ethical obligation to the client (Kutchins, 1991; Reamer, 2005). Feasibility of goals can also be influenced by both legal and ethical concerns. The social worker in the following case was confronted with such a situation. Further, adherence to an ethical principle of primary responsibility to the client was in conflict with the law and posed a legal risk to the social worker and the client. Cultural norms were an additional tension in the case.

Case Example

A mother who had been a victim of political torture in Liberia escaped to a neighboring country with her children and her mother. After living in a refugee camp for two years, the woman, under the Liberian Immigration Act, obtained a permit that allowed her to come to the United States. She was in the process of completing the paperwork so that her children and her mother could immigrate to the United States as well. This process required DNA reports for the children as well as their birth records, which the mother was able to provide for two of the children. When asked by the Legal Aid attorney whether the third and youngest child was her child, the mother replied yes. Actually, the family had found the child abandoned and had taken her in as a member of the family. Although not biologically related, in Liberia this child was considered to be the mother's child because she had cared for the child. The social worker assisting the mother knew the status of this child, and felt uncomfortable with the information that the mother had provided to the attorney. When the attorney left the room, the social worker expressed her concern and the mother became upset, telling the social worker to "remove herself from the case if she could not be more supportive."

The mother's ultimate goals were for her family to come to the United States to live, and eventually for all members of the family to become citizens. This goal and whether it was feasible had both a legal and an ethical implications for the social worker. She was confronted with several difficult choices, between her responsibility to the client, the client's right to autonomy, and the right to confidentiality and compliance with the law. Observing the ethical obligations however, has legal implications. Although somewhat intimidated by the mother's reaction, the social worker explained the legal consequences for the family of providing false information to the attorney and to the Immigration and Naturalization Service (INS) (INS has since been renamed Immigration and Customs Enforcement). Also, she explained that being a party to the deception had legal implications for her as the social worker, because she knew the information about the youngest child was false. She further explained that while she was sensitive to the Liberian culture's definition of "family," she would not be able to continue working with the mother unless she agreed to tell the truth about this child. Instead, she proposed helping the mother explain the child's status to the attorney and on the immigration forms, in an effort to resolve the matter.

In a review of this case during a peer consultation session, some staff believed this to be primarily a legal issue because the child did not meet the legal requirement of being a biological family member. Others, including the social worker presenting the case, viewed the situation differently. For them, it was within the ethical role of the social worker to assist the Legal Aid Attorney to understand the cultural context within which this child was considered to be a member of this family. Knowledge of a client's culture in the provision of services is also an ethical principle, and social workers are expected to use their knowledge to explain the functions of behavior within a cultural context (NSAW Code of Ethics, Standard 1.05). Of course, you may imagine that this case example represents an exceptional situation. But, increasingly, as social workers have contact with diverse clients, they are likely to encounter situations that require them to act as cultural interpreters and advocates.

Goals Must Be Consistent with the Functions of the Agency

Explorations of clients' problems, wants, and desired changes may be incompatible with the agency's mission, function and program objectives. For example, a family services agency may not provide vocational counseling. Similarly, in hospital settings, an assessment of the client's needs may indicate problems that require services beyond the scope of the hospital's primary function and length of stay. For example, hospitals generally do not provide family counseling, except in specific situations (e.g., grief and loss) and only then on a short-term basis while an individual is an inpatient. Should clients needs not match or exceed agency function, it is appropriate for you to assist the client in obtaining the needed services through referral to an appropriate agency. To facilitate the referral, it is often useful to make the call while the client is with you. Afterwards, a followup phone call from you to the client confirms that the client has been connected and is satisfied with the referral.

Applying Goal Development Guidelines with Minors

Instances in which minors are involved with professionals include parent–child conflict, the involvement of the family system, school referrals, juvenile authorities or the court, parental behavior, a crisis, or parents seeking help for problematic behavior. In addition, parents or legal guardians may set academic or extra-curricular performance goals for their children. A social worker who has worked extensively with minors once remarked that "starting where the client is" absolutely applies to this population. Rarely are minors in contact with helping professionals of their own accord. Further, she noted, "Their contact is usually associated with some type of formal or informal mandate, in which an adult has framed goals for them. It is therefore essential to talk with minors, because the goals of the adult involved and that of the minor may be vastly different." To elaborate on this point, consider a situation in which a child has been removed from his or her biological home. The goal of the social worker as required by law is the safety and well-being of the child. Minors may not always understand or trust the helping motives of adults, even when they are in a vulnerable situation; hence in response to his removal, a child stated, "I want to be with my family." In this type of situation, as well as others in which a minor may feel acted upon, the challenge is to reconcile the goals of the minor and the multiple systems involved.

Earlier in this chapter, the factors discussed that influence goals are also applicable to minors. The following are additional considerations for developing goals with minors.

Eliciting the Minors' Understanding of the Goal and Their Point of View of the Problem, and Using this Information to Assist Them to Develop Goals Minors arrive at the point of helping with their own story, whether it involves conflict with a parent in which the goal might be to create a context for joint collaboration, or a referral from an authority with whom the minor is involved; for example, a teacher. When minors are referred or mandated by parents or another authority, their histories, more often than not, tend to be articulated by the adults who have developed them to address such attributes as "at risk, defiant, inattentive in school," or descriptors of their family or community life such as single-parent household or dysfunctional community.

Listening to the minor's narrative is a starting point in establishing an atmosphere in which goals or solutions can be developed (Davis, 2005; Fontes, 2005; McKenzie, 2005; Morgan, 2000; White & Morgan, 2006; Smith & Nylund, 1997). In the literature, a narrative-oriented approach, in which open-ended questions are encouraged, allows minors of all ages to tell their story based on their experience and perception of the world in which they interact. For example, make note of the various reasons for their behavior given by the boys in the following example, in which the experienced social worker mentioned earlier is facilitating the development of goals in a social skills group. The overall goal established by the school is appropriate classroom behavior.

School-based Group Example

The group is a year-long, school-based social skills group for elementary school-aged boys. Encouraging the boys to talk and participate was time consuming and challenging, and generally this process required several group sessions. The boys were involuntary, having been sent to the group by their teachers for disruptive classroom behavior. After the settling-in period, the social worker asked the boys to describe their understanding of why they were sent to the group. Another question, which the social worker considered as critical, was allowing time for the boys to express their feelings about being in the group. Minors, depending on their age, cognitive capacity and emotional intelligence may not readily express their feelings unless they are asked. In this group, given the opportunity, some expressed that the group was "stupid." Others were resentful, embarrassed, or anxious about participating in a group that was perceived as a group for "problem kids." Some also perceived the group as "better than having to sit in the classroom." Feelings also emerged when each boy was asked to tell why he thought he had been sent to the group:

"The teacher does not like me."
"The teacher is always mad about something."
"Because I sometimes play around in class."
"The teacher does not like _____ kids" [snickering among group members], followed by a side comment, "Shut up, boy."
"I was telling my friend about the gunshots around my house last night."

Responding to the individual comments of each boy, the social worker was able to obtain their understanding of why they believed that were in the group. For example, responding to the "the teacher does not like me" statement, she respected his view without judging. But in follow-up to the statement, she asked, "What do you think would make the teacher like you?", to which the boy replied, "If I paid attention in class." After a round of similar questions to each

participant, she asked the group about how to make the group comfortable: "Getting something for coming"—specifically, what was the incentive for their participation—was a unanimous response. To make the group successful, each boy was asked to write or draw a picture about what they wanted to get out of the group.

The social worker commented that "school-based groups often are a window into the family and community life of group participants, which is specially challenging. You often hear about parts of their lives that have little to do with the purpose of the group, but, in fact, these parts do matter. They are informative of what happens in their lives outside of school and often explain their behavior in the classroom." For example, the reason given by one boy, "I was telling my friend about the gunshots around my house last night." Later, when asked about his goals, the boy reluctantly said, "I want my family to be safe." This event in the mind of a minor of this age is perhaps exciting information to share, but you can also observe his anxiety and fear of the experience as well. Behavior that is identified as disruptive can be a way in which minors act out and cope with the trauma in their lives.

Schools out of necessity establish structure and rules for behavior to meet their educational objectives. Huffine (2006) notes, however, that "blaming youth for their behaviors may be easier than addressing the social ills" that influence behavior (p. 15). Three questions are relevant to the comment of the group participant who stated, "The teacher does not like _____ kids." Is this an attempt on his part to legitimize his behavior in the classroom? The cognitions, perceptions, and feelings of young minors influence their self-definition and self-evaluation relative to the outside world. Second, what are the relational dynamics between the boy and the teacher? The final question to be considered is, "What has been his life experience that has led him to conclude that this teacher (and perhaps others) doesn't like kids with certain physical attributes?"

The language associated with goals, their purpose, function, and type is meaningless to a majority of elementary school-aged minors. Even so, when asked, a majority of the boys identified a goal behavior that they could do, in response to the social worker's question, "What could you do differently so that you are able to remain in the classroom?" Because behavior change was an essential goal established by the school and for continuing group participation, the question and the boys' responses were important to the development of goals. Using their desire to remain in the classroom as a motivator, the specific behavior-change goals were clarified. Further, open-ended questions enabled the social worker and the boys to create mutuality, in which the group and individual goals could be achieved. The group participants also developed reciprocal goals in support of behavioral guidelines within the group. For example, "Waiting your turn to talk, not hitting or making fun of each other or making gestures or noises when another member was speaking" were rules suggested by the participants. These behaviors in the classroom were among the reasons that they were referred to the group, according to the social worker. Without this arrangement, the group time would have been counterproductive.

Is the minor voluntary or involuntary? Voluntary or involuntary status can, as is the case with adult clients, make a difference in the dynamics of the contact. Voluntariness can of course progress along a continuum. In work with family systems, minors may be involved; nonetheless the force behind the contact is parental authority. Even when minors are voluntary, they may feel that seeking help portrays them as being less than adequate (Lindsey, Korr, Broitman, Bone, Green & Leaf, 2006; Teyber, 2006).

Minors who are involuntary, either because of a referral or mandate (which they may perceive as being one and the same), may be reluctant to participate and set goals (Erford, 2003). Their feelings should be recognized as valid, relative to their self-definition, especially within the peer group. Yet, helping minors understand how their thoughts, feelings, and behaviors affect themselves and others and establishing ownership for goals is encouraged. For example, the social worker asked, "What could you do differently so that the teacher would allow you to stay in the classroom?" By this question, the social worker enables the participants to focus on their behavior and their own goals for behavioral change.

Among the strategies for work with involuntary clients, all are applicable to involuntary minors. Motivational congruence and motivational interviewing may be especially pertinent to this group, but you should consider their appropriateness to the minor's developmental stage. Note that in the group, motivational congruence—that is, the boys wanted to be in the classroom, as do the teacher and the school. This fit facilitated the goals that were developed.

Definition and specificity of the behavior to be changed. In general, minors respond to clearly defined and measurable goals and objectives or tasks in which

they are involved. Criteria for developing clear goals with minors cited by Corwin (2002) and Huxtable (2004) are:

1. emphasize the behavior that is to occur
2. define the conditions in which the change is to occur
3. the expected level of goal performance within a specific timeline

The following example illustrates how this process works.

Goal 1: By the end of the first mid-year school term, Veronica will use the conflict resolution skills she has learned when she is in a difficult situation with her peers.

Goal 2: In a situation in which conflict resolution skills are not working, Veronica will walk away from the situation.

Goals should always be tailored to individual needs; therefore, the participation of the minor is important. For example, the second goal was developed by Veronica, based on her concern about whether she could immediately accomplish the first goal. In addition, Veronica had concerns about how she would feel about herself when she walked away; thus, a self-talk goal was developed in which she would affirm herself and the action that she had taken.

With minors, the relationship between setting goals and outcomes is not always a straight line process. Goals can be partialized and tasks or objectives clarified so that they are more manageable as progress proceeds toward an ultimate goal. In addition to goals that are clearly defined, specific, feasible and measurable, a number of other factors, have particular relevance to this population:

- *A sense of self-direction, particularly with adolescents who tend to react to being told what to do and how to act.*
- *Linking goals to something that the minors want for themselves.*
- *The minor's sense of their ability to achieve goals.*
- *Their involvement in establishing evaluative measures.*
- *Regular feedback about their performance, at regular intervals, and honoring the progress that has been made. Praising their efforts as well as goal attainment.*
- *Their sense of satisfaction with their performance, including having minors talk about how they accomplish a goal.*

- *Providing the opportunity for them to measure their progress and praise themselves.*
- *Identifying strengths and protective factors; for example, the support of family or significant others in the minor's life.*

Huxtable (2004) and Morgan (2000) suggest using visual aids, metaphors, stories, and games to facilitate goal development. Using a creative metaphor, Huxtable (2004) for example, encourages motivation by likening goals to "a race to the finish line, to appeal to a minor who likes cars" (p. 3). The goal-development process is optimal when the words, phrases, and language of the minor are used rather than professional or institutional jargon.

In settings in which behavioral contracts are used, for example, in schools, residential settings, or juvenile detention centers, minors may not be involved in establishing their goals. These contracts specify goals and expected outcomes, contingency rewards, and consequences (Ellis & Sowers, 2001). You can however, assist minors to meet the expectations by engaging them in devising ways in which goals can be achieved.

Age and stage of development, cognitive ability. Davis (2005) notes that "telling stories is a natural ways for minors to communicate," and further that storytelling inspires them to be "confident about their own perceptions." From these stories, goals may be developed. Decisions about goals, however, are dependent on a minor's stage of development, cognitive and moral ability, and their ability to give consent (Note: informed consent and minors is discussed in Chapter 13).

In developing goals with minors, their reaction tends to be situation specific. In very young minors, for example in an abuse situation, a referral from a teacher or conflict in the family, the minor can feel vulnerable and subject to self-blame, anxiety and fear (Fontes, 2005; McKenzie, 2005).

Minors develop scripts about themselves, rooted in culture, family rules, and styles of problem solving. Any one of these factors can influence goal development. At almost any stage of development, consideration must be given to the power differences between you and the minor. Younger minors, even those who are involuntary, are sensitive to power, how they are evaluated by others, and have a tendency to want to please.

Older minors, in particular adolescents, may be capable of making decisions, but tend to be fiercely protective of their identity, independence, and autonomous locus of control. At this stage, in particular if the minor is involuntary, it can be important to appeal to

their future-oriented focus regarding the choices that they make. Sensitivity to and empathizing with the stress and multiple mood behaviors that minors experience can be especially useful, as illustrated in the following case situation.

Case Example

Case records show that Bettina, aged 17, was removed from home along with her siblings when she was 6 years of age. She has experience multiple placements, and at age 15 she was on the run and pregnant.

A majority of the entries in her case record describe her as alternatively hostile, rude, uncooperative, cooperative, contrite, and motivated. She has lived in the group home for a year. Because of her behavior, staff in the home routinely initiate punishment for rule violations.

Bettina's Story

"I don't like people telling me what to do [independence, separating from adults]. I know my own mind [identity, external locus of control]! Everyone is always watching me [sensitivity to control], the mistakes that I make, like I care what they think. You know what I'm saying? Sometimes I get confused and scared [stress], but then my worker says, 'Bettina you can do it!' Then we talk about stuff [exploring range of future possibilities], like what I want to do. I want to become emancipated and live on my own.

The other day when I was angry and cursing, although she had made an appointment with me, I had taken my baby to see his Daddy. She was not happy that she had driven across town to see me and I was not there. So I started cursing as soon as she opened the door [reactive to potential of punishment]. She let me go on for awhile and then she asked me, 'What is going on in your head right now?' and I just started crying [sensitivity to feelings/empathy, listening to presentation of self and expression of feelings]."

The multiple issues occurring in this situation with Bettina are shown in brackets. Bettina's desire and hence her goal is to become independent. Anything that seems to stand in the way of this goal causes her to react. When the social worker was interviewed, she emphasized that empathy rather than confrontation was an important factor in turning this situation around, so goals could be accomplished. Other staff tended to be put off by Bettina's behavior and would refuse to interact with her other than to issue a punishment. At this point, Bettina would react, and may or may not comply with the sanction. From this example, you can see the importance of understanding developmental stages in setting goals with minors.

Process of Negotiating Goals

Table 12-6 summarizes the steps that are involved in the negotiation of goals with clients, including those who are involuntary. The steps may be implemented in following sequence, or the sequence may be being adapted to the unique circumstances of each case. For example, a client may not be prepared to negotiate goals because they may not fully understand their function and purpose. In which case, an explanation would have precedence over determining readiness. If, however, the client confirms his or her readiness, then you would proceed to the next step of explaining the purpose and function of goals.

Determine Clients' Readiness for Goal Negotiation

At this stage in the process, voluntary clients are generally ready to get on with the business of resolving their concerns. Assessing whether a client is prepared to identify specific goals may begin with a summary of priority concerns; for example, "We've talked about your concerns about living in transitional housing." Summarization as used here is intended to clarify agreement, which enables you and the client to move to the next step of negotiating goals. In confirming readiness, you could ask: "I wonder if you are prepared at this point to focus on moving from transitional housing, or would you like to

---

TABLE-12-6 PROCESS OF NEGOTIATING GOALS

Determine client's readiness for goal negotiation—Voluntary and Involuntary clients

Explain the purpose and function of goals

Jointly select appropriate goals

Define goals explicitly and specify level of change

Determine potentials barriers to goal attainment and discuss benefits and risks

Assist clients to make a clear choice about committing themselves to specific goals

Rank order of goals according to client's priorities

---

provide additional information?" If the client responds that moving from transitional housing is the goal, you are ready to move ahead. On the other hand, should the client respond, "I think so," or "maybe," this is a signal that the client is ambivalent or hesitant about the goal. Determining readiness is essential because clients can be at different starting points and have varying levels of confidence (Miller & Rollnick, 2002). The source of their ambivalence may relate to a lack of confidence in their ability to change themselves or their circumstances, each of which can be explored.

Readiness of Involuntary Clients

Determining an involuntary client's readiness for negotiating goals may be a critical first step. In addition, educating these clients, both minors and adults, about the purpose and function of goals can create an atmosphere in which the negotiation can occur. This discussion may significantly change the tone of the contact and their reaction to mandated goals. Goals should focus on the specific behavior or conditions to be changed so that involuntary clients (adults or minors) understand what is expected of them. Points to be considered in the negotiation of goals are illustrated in the following statements:

- **Review the Mandate:** *"The court has identified a problem that needs to be resolved."* Review the mandate and specify *what is expected: "The court requires that you participate in a parent training group and that you have an assessment of your parenting skills after you complete the program."*
- **Specificity:** *"The court expects that the parent training sessions will help you learn to set limits with your children and to learn other methods of discipline."* Explaining the intent of goals to clients provides specificity and indicates that they will be able to retain some control over their lives.
- **Level of Freedom:** *"You do, however, have a choice. You can choose among the various parenting programs on an approved list."*
- **Client's Viewpoint:** *"Your view of the problem as well as your other concerns that you may have are also important."* For goals to be relevant to the client and their situation, contextual meaning is important. *"It would be useful for me to hear from you how you came to be involved in the court."*
- **Involving Client in Setting Goal:** *"I'd like for you to suggest ways in which you could meet the requirements of the court."*

- *Measuring Progress:* *"I will keep a record of your* progress *in learning skills in the parenting class and will include this information in my reports to the court."* This statement clarifies for the client the focus of the mandate and the importance of demonstrating progress to prevent further action by the court.

What is accomplished by reviewing the mandate as well as the other suggestions in the statements? Essentially, as your review the mandate you specify the change required by the court. In soliciting their point of view, you provide the client with an opportunity to explain his or her understanding of the situation and describe the circumstances. In this way, you can respond to the client's viewpoint and explore goals important to the client in addition to those defined by the mandate. "The court requires that the children are supervised when you go out for the evening. I also understand that you need to find childcare." Allowing the client to choose from available parenting programs gives them a choice by which they can be motivated and empowered, ultimately ensuring their participation. A clear indication of about how their progress will be measured as well as how this information will be used can diffuse their anxiety. Clients should also be informed of requirements of the parenting groups. For example, the program may also stipulate that participants "attend a certain number of classes" and that they "actively participate." These requirements would need to be included in the client's goal statement as well as the timelines imposed by the court.

In working with involuntary clients, the process of negotiating goals may include those that are important to the client. For example, "As you know, the court would like to see changes in your parenting. In addition to the changes ordered by the court, would you also like to discuss changes that you would like to make on your own?"

Explain the Purpose and Function of Goals

Many elements of the helping process are educational. "Goals and objectives" are generally terminology used within the professional community. When goals are discussed, a client is apt to simply express what they want to be different or what they would like to do. Clients may also have questions about goals. A minor for example might ask, "What do I need a goal for? Involuntary clients most often raise the question, "What do I have to do? When clients understand the purpose and function of goals, they are more likely to appreciate their significance. A brief explanation which complements the

socialization process as discussed in Chapter 5 is generally all that is required. This socialization process may be especially pertinent to work with minors.

Explaining the purpose and function of goals may be a particularly critical step with individuals for whom the Western structure and formal helping systems may be unfamiliar (Potocky-Tripodi, 2002). In explaining the purpose of goals to all clients, you will want to emphasize that selected goals represent the changes that are most important to them. The explanation should clarify the function of goals by stressing the following point: Specifically, "goals provide direction and the focus of our work together and make sure we stay on track." Explanations to a young minor may need to include tangible results; for example, "You will be able to return to the classroom."

Your explanation, of course, should emphasize the importance of clients' participation and their ultimate authority in selecting voluntary goals, even though you may have some ideas to contribute. For example, "I have some ideas, but it is important for you to tell me which goals are important to you." Eliciting this information ensures that both you and your clients are trying to accomplish the same results. With involuntary clients, a similar explanation may be used; however, the emphasis is on complying with the goals of the mandate. The language used with voluntary or involuntary clients in explaining goals is important. What should be made clear to them is that goals represent a plan of action by which their concerns or those of the mandate can be resolved.

Jointly Select Appropriate Goals

Voluntary clients are generally capable of identifying most or all of the goals and general tasks that they believe will resolve their problems. There may be instances when because of your external vantage point goals will occur to you that they may have overlooked or omitted. Consequently, you may make suggestions about goals for the client's consideration, explaining your reasoning and making reference to their priority concern.

As clients verbalize goals, you may need to seek clarification, paraphrase, or suggest rewording a goal to clarify meaning and specificity. In paraphrasing, be cautious about taking liberties with what clients have said and obtain their approval of rewordings by reading to them what you have written. Suppose that Mrs. Lenora Johnson, an elderly African American client who has been referred for depression, states, "I'd like to not feel blue." You would write what she has said, and then seek clarification by asking her to describe what she means so that you understand "feeling blue" in her terms and determine whether it is consistent with symptoms of depression. Also, unless this client has indicated otherwise, she should be addressed as Mrs. Johnson, rather than Lenora. As the U.S. society has become more informal and egalitarian we have tended to discard traditional ways of addressing people. Some elderly persons may take exception to this informality and in some communities and cultures using first names is considered disrespectful.

At this point, it is also useful to ask the client about their expectations about when goals are achieved. The following questions are examples of clarifying expectations:

Social Worker: "What would be different for you and your children when you move from transitional to permanent housing?"

Client: "There are too many people under one roof. The place is noisy, you have to go to bed at a certain time and my children would be able to play outside, instead of being cooped up in a building. It would just be less stressful."

Social Worker: "If your family could be the way you would like it to be, how would each of you behave differently?"

Parent: "I think that we would all respect each other more, be caring and supportive."

Minor: I wouldn't feel scared when my parents are yelling at each other, and my brother would not pick on me as much."

Social Worker: "When you complete the parent training program, what would you imagine would be different in your relationship with your children?"

Client: "Oh, I don't know, maybe I would learn how to be less stressed out. Sometimes, I ignore what my kids are doing and then they get on my nerves and I blow up at them. Maybe I will learn how to do things with them and be more relaxed. I think that my kids would like this."

Social Worker: "When you say that you would like to not feel blue, tell me what it would be like for you to not have this feeling?"

Client: I think that I would have more energy, visit my grandchildren, and when they ask, "How are you doing Grandmama?" I could truthfully tell them that I feel good."

Notice that each message asks clients to clarify their expectations and also their desired level of change, which paves the way to the next step of defining goals explicitly.

If clients have difficulty identifying goals, you can prompt them by referring to needs and wants they identified during the exploration and assessment process and suggest that they consider related changes. To illustrate prompting, we return to the case of the Diaz family (Chapter 10). Recall that Mr. Diaz reported that he wanted to maintain some independence in his living arrangements and medical regimen.

Social worker: When you talked about your feeling that your family wanted to limit your freedom, you said that you could administer your own medication with help. At this point, can we talk about working toward getting the kind of assistance necessary that would make your administering your insulin possible?

As with most clients, Mr. Diaz's statement in Chapter 10 as summarized by the social worker includes emotional content that could have derailed the process of goal selection. The social worker's statement effectively summarized a key issue and helped Mr. Diaz to focus on his particular goal.

Define Goals Explicitly and Specifying Level of Change

After jointly deciding on specific goals and clarifying expectations, the next step is to define and refine them to determine the level of change desired by the client or that is required by the mandate. With respect to determining the desired level of change, you can use messages similar to the following:

Social Worker: You said that you want a better relationship with your wife and that you are tired of being hauled off by the police. What are the specific changes that you can make that will improve your relationship with your wife and avoid contact with the police?

Client: I would just walk away when she is in my face and I would not hit her. We would talk when both of us aren't so mad at each other.

Specifying a desired level of change is a facet of defining goals explicitly. The goal and the level of change should be congruent with the client situation. With goals that involve ongoing behavior, growth is potentially infinite.

Determine Potential Barriers to Goal Attainment and Discuss Potential Benefits and Risks

The importance of feasibility was previously discussed at length under guidelines for developing goals. Exploring potential barriers moves beyond, but includes, feasibility, and involves identifying concrete examples, events, or circumstances that could undermine goal achievement. To illustrate, we return to an earlier example of a client's expectations.

Social Worker: You said that when your wife is in your face, you plan to walk away and to avoid hitting her. I believe that you are committed to this goal because you want to improve your relationship with her. Can you think of what might prevent you from walking away?

Client: Well, at first it might be hard, especially if she keeps yapping at me or if she follows me out the door, screaming her fool head off, embarrassing me in front of everybody. I guess if this happens, I could just keep on walking. Most of all I will not hit her, because I don't want to deal with the police.

A discussion of the benefits of attaining goals tends to enhance clients' commitment and sustained their efforts. Clients, according to a social worker, often feel "relieved, energized, or giddy" about the benefits of the change that they have envisioned. Another benefit identified by the client that energized his goal of not hitting his wife: "I don't want my kids to be afraid of me anymore." Enthusiasm or relief about benefits of achieving goals may however overshadow or give superficial attention to risks or negative consequences.

Social Worker: So the benefit of walking away is that the police will not be called because you have hit your wife. Are there also possible risks to your doing so?

Client: Well, if it is at night when this happens, and the kids are asleep, they will be left home by themselves. If they start crying, a neighbor will call the police.

Prudent practice requires that you discuss benefits and potential risks with clients. Reviewing potential obstacles and risks is intended to help clients think in advance about events or situations that might influence their ability to attain their goals. A further discussion between you and the client can include planning for alternative responses to barriers. Discussions about potential barriers may also indicate that a goal is not feasible. In which case, a more feasible goal should be developed.

You are also obligated to assist clients in assessing the possible risks associated with attaining goals. In particular, changes in behaviors might evoke ambivalent feelings and both positive and negative consequences. The husband in the above situation may, for example, have mixed feelings about his loss of power if he relinquishes his abusive behavior. Although he may benefit from not having his children afraid of him, he may experience the emotionally negative consequence of refraining from old behavior on the way to developing a different response.

Assist Clients to Make a Choice about Committing Themselves to Specific Goals

After exploring the potential barriers, benefits, and risks of pursuing specific goals, the next step is to reach a decision about making a commitment to strive to attain the goals in question. In most instances, benefits are likely to outweigh risks, and clients will demonstrate their readiness to contract to work toward their goals. A simple but effective means to assess clients' willingness to change is to ask them to rate their readiness on a scale from 1 to 10, where 1 represents "extremely uncertain and not at all ready" and 10 represents "optimistic, eager to start, and totally committed." Asking the husband, for example, on a scale of 1 to 10, how willing are you to commit to the goal of improving your relationship with your wife? A readiness factor in the range of 6–8 usually indicates a sufficient willingness to proceed with the contracting process. In contrast, if he indicated a readiness level of 5 or lower, this score would mean that he is unprepared to proceed. If such was the case, you might ask him to visualize which of his goals would bring immediate relief or change.

Occasionally, clients are ambivalent, which suggests that you need to explore their reservations further. In these cases, we recommend that you respect clients' misgivings and refrain from attempting to convince them to immediately sign on to the goals identified. At the same time, it is important to identify the basis for their misgivings (e.g., an adolescent bully may hesitate to pursue a goal of avoiding conflict because he may appear to be timid in front of peers; an immigrant family may fear that moving away from their community will result in a loss of cultural ties). In these situations, you should explore the extent to which their concerns are an important dynamic affecting the problem. With the adolescent bully, for example, this might mean exploring with him whether conflict with his peers is the reason for his multiple school suspensions and his mandate to attend an anger management class. As a next step, you might ask whether his fear of appearing to be timid is a good enough reason for not accomplishing the goal of decreasing school suspensions.

In instances where a client is ambivalent, developing intermediate goals may be possible. With the adolescent, the two of you could agree to resolve his concerns by negotiating an intermediate goal before moving on, perhaps by exploring the importance (i.e., in the client's reality) of being bold rather than timid. Negotiating an intermediate goal in this way reduces the threat to the primary goal of decreasing the number of school suspensions and can increase his readiness to enter into a working contract. The negotiated intermediate goal in this case would involve his agreement to attend a conflict resolution group whereby he could learn conflict resolution skills.

With involuntary clients, commitment to mandated goals is not expected to be in the highest range. You should anticipate, respect, and appreciate their reactance to the mandates. In many cases, involuntary clients may want help, but not in the way it is offered or for the reason it is offered. This may especially be true if the goal emphasizes deficiencies or behavioral compliance. For example, in the adolescent's case, tension may arise between the mandated goal of attending a conflict resolution class and his belief that not backing down in a confrontation is necessary for survival.

While you empathize with his feelings and the pressures he experiences because of the mandate you can emphasize that he has the freedom to choose the approach to attaining the goal. He may, for example, be given the option to attend a conflict resolution class with other adolescents who live in his neighborhood. He also should be aware that he has the option to reject working on the goal and to risk the consequences of this choice (R.H. Rooney, 2009). You are obligated to advise clients about the potential consequences of their actions and to ensure that, in fact, they are making an informed choice. Involuntary client status does not diminish the right of self-determination, yet it is your ethical responsibility to advise them of the risks associated with their chosen course of action and to help them work through their concerns related to the mandate.

Encountering reactance as exhibited by an involuntary client's appraisal of his or her situation can be very frustrating. You may become the target of clients' anger, especially when they do not perceive your authority as being separate from the court's. In the face of hostility, anger, and sometimes abusive language, it is easy to simply give up on the client and rely on the old adage that people will only change when they are ready or have suffered enough. As disconcerting as these dynamics may be, you are encouraged to depersonalize the experience. In doing so, you are able to focus on exploring the feelings and frustrations underlying the client's reaction. Moreover, a client's hostile reaction may be countered by highlighting potential benefits and the opportunity for growth as a result of working on mandate goals. The following example illustrates the social worker's exploration of the parent's beliefs, feelings, and ambivalence about attending court-ordered parenting classes, while emphasizing that working on this goal has a potential benefit to the client concerned:

Social worker: I respect your claim that you do not need parenting skills. I also understand your feelings about the court telling you how to deal with your kids. You said that your mother was a parent, that your grandmother was a parent, and that you learned from them. But, there seems to be a problem in the way that you discipline your children. For example, hitting a child with a belt that leaves multiple marks on their body is a problem. Your mother and grandmother may have used this method, but it is a concern that has to be resolved.

Client: Yeah, but it didn't hurt me and my brothers and sisters, we all turned out okay! None of us are doing drugs or are in jail!

Social Worker: I understand that this is what you believe, and that you feel that you and your brothers and sisters are doing okay. When we talked about your circumstance and your frustrations with being a single parent, you said that you felt stressed out a great deal of the time.

Client: Yeah, that's right. These kids do get on my nerves a lot, and I feel bad after I hit one of them. So tell me, how is attending a parenting class going to help me?

Social Worker: Are you willing to consider that by attending the parenting class you might gain skills in setting limits with your children without hitting them, and relieve some of the stress that you have in dealing with them?

Rank Goals According to Clients' Priorities

Following the identification of and the client's commitment to specific goals, it can be helpful to rank those goals in order of their priority. The purpose of identifying high-priority goals is to ensure that beginning change efforts are directed toward the goals of utmost importance to clients. Depending on the nature of the goals, the developmental stage, the resources available to the client, and the time required, settling on no more than three goals is advisable.. When mandated goals are included, these can also be prioritized because simultaneous efforts to achieve all goals may not be possible. In addition, some goals will necessarily have greater consequences than others. Participating in a drug treatment program, for example, may take priority over a goal of returning to school. Prioritizing goals further supports the client's commitment and participation, thereby enhancing his or her motivation to work on goal attainment. When working with larger systems you might create a list of goals for both the individuals and the systems involved, and then rank them for each person and the system. Where there are differences between the rankings, your help is needed to assist all parties to negotiate the final rankings.

As a lead-in to the ranking process when the client is voluntary, the following is an example of a summary message that can be used:

Social worker: So far, we have talked about several concerns. You mentioned the desire to move from transitional housing. You also want your children to have a quiet place to study in the current housing situation. Now that you've settled upon these goals, how would you rank them according to priority? Of these goals, we should start with the goal most important to you, the one on which you will focus your energy at this point. Then you can rank the others as you see fit. We'll get to all of the goals in time, but we want to start with the most important one.

With involuntary clients, you might use a message like this:

Social worker: While we have reached an agreement about which goals are most important to you, we also need to give priority to the goal established by the court. As you have said, you want the court out of your life. Your court order states that you need to complete a parenting class immediately, so this has to be a top priority. You also said that you feel isolated and exhausted by the demands of caring for four children and want to have time for yourself. We should also think about your desire to complete a degree at the local community college. Are you able to say which of these goals you would like to work on first?

As illustrated in the above scenario and the following case there are instances in which you may be able to work toward achieving a mandated goal and the client's own goals simultaneously.

Case Example

William, 16, a repeat truant from school, has recently become involved with a group of other truants who were reported for stealing at a local convenience store. Because this was a first offense for William, the judge ordered him to attend school on a regular basis, and to have no unexcused absences. A probation officer would monitor his attendance, and his failure to comply with the judge's order would result in his being sent to a juvenile detention center for 90 days. During the initial session with the social worker, William indicated that he was unlikely to attend school because he thought school was "lame" and that he was not learning anything of value to what he wanted to do in his life. When asked to explain his assertion, he stated that he would like to learn how to play the guitar and that guitar lessons were not offered by the school. Also, learning to play the guitar was important to William as he was interested in joining the youth musical ministry group in his parish. His goal of learning to play the guitar was not, of course, consistent with the mandate, nor was it clear that learning to play the guitar would improve his attendance.

William, who is 16 years old, in addition to being an involuntary client, has a strong reaction to authority—not unusual for people in his age group. At this developmental stage, independence and exploring identity are both developmental tasks. Yet asserting their independence often means conflicted relationships with authority.

Creative solutions are useful with minors, especially those that allow them to save face, as well as to feel empowered and involved. The social worker found a music teacher at the school who was willing to give William guitar lessons after school. But the teacher stipulated that William had to be a student in good standing. The social worker and William negotiated a goal plan that specified that if he attended school on a regular basis, he would receive guitar lessons. The importance of this intermediary or transitional goal, specifically learning to play the guitar, made William more amenable to attending school.

You might question this *quid pro quo* goal arrangement, and instead insist on a behavioral change; specifically, that William attend school as ordered by the court. In fact, the social worker encountered other staff in the school with similar opinions. You might also attempt to coerce William to attend, or persuade him by pointing out that responding to the court mandate was in his best interest. Given his developmental stage, the context that frames his perception of school, and what he valued, he is unlikely to do so if you use this approach.

Decisions, when working with minors, can be influenced by utilitarian ethics, in which case consideration would be given to the overall outcome. For example, rather than attending school, consider the trajectory of his life, should he remain a truant. Instead of pursuing prosocial behavior that is supported by his association with the parish music youth group, he continues his involvement with truant peers. A peer reference group, when weighed against adult authority is important to youth at this stage of development. Thus his peer relational needs may outweigh the consequence of his non-compliance with the court order. The social worker's action facilitated the development of a problem-solving goal.

When the target system involves more than one person, different members may naturally accord different priorities to goals. Consistent school attendance was ranked by the court as the priority goal. The mandate, however, did not specify how the goal was to be achieved. Presumably the court, his parents and teachers, and the social worker shared a goal of William attending school. His parents, neither of whom completed high school, hoped that he would go to college. In the long term, for them, school was valued more than his learning to play the guitar. Therefore, the social worker met with the parents so that they understood the rationale for the arrangement that he had negotiated with William and the music teacher.

In this scenario, the parents also had a reciprocal role in ensuring that the goal of attending school was accomplished. Similarly, if the target system is a couple, a group, an organization, or a family, it is desirable to have goals that pertain both to individuals and to the larger system.

Measurement and Evaluation

Measurement of the outcomes of interventions with clients is an essential component of direct practice. Once goals have been developed, agreed upon, and explicitly defined, jointly deciding with the client how progress will be measured and recorded is a logical next step. Measurement involves the precise definition of what is to be changed, and it clarifies the observations to be made that indicate progress toward the identified goal (Bloom, Fischer & Orme 2003). For example, the goal of regular school attendance for William could be measured by attendance records and parental and self-reports.

Evaluation, by comparison, assesses the effectiveness of the intervention in relationship to the goal. In the case of William, enabling him to take guitar lessons is the intervention. To assess the effectiveness on this intervention, you and William could use an AB Single Subject Design that recorded school attendance prior to his taking guitar lessons and then monitor his attendance after the intervention was introduced. Change is often incremental, and clients should be encouraged to identify indicators or levels of desired change. For example, because William has not had a record of attending school on a regular basis, you might establish an incremental change of attending school four out of five days each week.

Evaluation is an ongoing process, occurring at various levels of the intervention or action taken to rectify a target concern. The process also informs both you and the client of progress (or lack of progress) and indicates whether the intervention is producing the intended results (Berlin & Marsh, 1993). Evaluation is, of course, an integral element in the termination process, as discussed in Chapter 19. Poulin (2004) suggests that the process of evaluation "can help motivate clients, and further their resolve to make progress" (2000, p. 142). He poses several questions that may assist the social worker to "take stock" when monitoring an intervention:

- *Are we making progress?*
- *Is the intervention working?*
- *Do I need to try another approach?*

Measurement and evaluation in social welfare organizations pose a real challenge because of the environmental complexities of both the organizations involved and the clients they serve. Demands for accountability from funding sources, third-party payers, managed care, and administrators have nonetheless increasingly required organizations to gather evidence proving the efficacy of their work with clients. Both social welfare organizations and social workers have responded to these demands by developing programmatic outcomes for clients, along with information systems that increase their ability to track the impact of services with regard to the desired outcomes (Gardner, 2000; Lewis, Lewis, Packard & Souflee, 2001). Measures of success used by organizations tend to be reported in the aggregated statistical data and are therefore different from the case-by-case monitoring and effectiveness questions required of the individual social worker. In evaluating the outcomes of program objectives, an organization's questions might be the number of "homeless families with children found affordable housing."

Evaluation methods have evolved to include the extent to which interventions influence both intermediate and final outcomes (DePoy & Gilson, 2003). In the final analysis, evaluation assists you to answer the essential questions related to the effectiveness of intervention strategies and to document changes in client conditions (Bloom, Fischer & Orme, 2003; Corcoran & Gingerich, 1994). This information is critical to the feedback loop so that it can improve both the social worker's and the program's effectiveness and ensure ethical practice.

Methods of Evaluation and Measuring Progress

This section provides an overview of both quantitative and qualitative methods that may be used to measure progress and to evaluate outcomes. Irrespective of the method used, the following components are considered to be fundamental to this process:

- *Identification of the specific problem or behavior to be changed*
- *Specific, measurable, and feasible goals*
- *Matching goal and measurement procedures*
- *Maintenance of a systematic record of relevant information*
- *Evaluation of intermediate and final outcomes*

The first three factors were discussed earlier in this chapter. As indicated earlier, this information and the progress toward goals should be systematically recorded in the case record. The information in the case progress or SOAP notes, as well as other information discussed in this section, will allow both you and your client to track the client's progress over the course of the contract. If progress falls short, then goals should be reviewed or renegotiated as needed.

Involving Clients in Monitoring Progress

Feedback from clients regarding their progress and their satisfaction with the services that they have received is an important aspect of measuring and monitoring progress. For example, diverse clients might be asked whether their experience with you and the agency was culturally sensitive and what could be improved. The importance of involving clients as collaborators in measuring and monitoring their progress is summarized in the following points.

1. By eliciting clients' views of their progress or by comparing their latest rates of the target behavior with the baseline, you maintain focus on goals and enhance the continuity of change efforts.
2. Clients gain perspective in determining where they stand in relationship not only to their ultimate goals but also to their pretreatment level of functioning. Observing incremental progress toward goals tends to sustain motivation and to enhance confidence in the helping process and in the social worker.
3. Eliciting clients' feelings and views regarding their progress enables social workers to detect and to work through feelings of disappointment and discouragement that may impede future progress and lead to premature termination.
4. Clients can provide feedback on the efficacy of an intervention change strategy and whether an approach has yielded positive results within a reasonable period of time.
5. Indications of marked progress toward goal attainment alert social workers to possible readiness by clients to shift the focus to another goal or to consider planning for termination if all goals have been achieved.

Overall, the methods for monitoring, assessing and evaluating progress should be consistent with the agreement negotiated in the contracting or treatment planning. Progress toward goals should be monitored every two to three sessions at a minimum.

Evaluation Resources

Numerous computerized information systems are available that can assist you with collecting and evaluating information. A number of standardized instruments are also available, some of which use computers to track progress over time (Hudson, 1990, 1996; Springer & Franklin, 2003). Standardized measures, including those employing computer-assisted technologies, have several advantages. As summarized by Bloom, Fischer and Orme (2003) and Streeter and Franklin (2003), they are uniform in both administration and scoring procedures and outcome results. In addition, the measures have undergone rigorous research procedures, being tested on a large representative sample (p. 98). A number of resources provide extensive information and examples of scales, questionnaires, and information systems, both qualitative and quantitative that measure, for example, depression, social skills, child well-being, mental and health status, and the functioning of families, children, and adults.

Cautions and Strengths

While you should not feel dissuaded from using standardized instruments for evaluation and monitoring progress, a discussion about their strengths and limitations is warranted. There are evidence-based tools that may be used for certain problems. Evidence-based resources are not the same as measures of effectiveness and monitoring progress. Their use can, however, assist you to assess, evaluate, and monitor, for example, behavioral change, health status, and child well-being. A notable limitation of standardized instruments is that tools may focus on problems rather than strengths, resources, or situational factors; thus the kind of information collected is limited (Berlin & Marsh, 1993; Jordan & Franklin, 2003; Vosler, 1990). For example, completing a structured risk assessment may confirm that risks exist. Yet the narrow band of questions tends to focus solely on assessing risk factors and ignores ecological, environmental, or other interactions that may contribute to the underlying situation. Kagle asserts that standardized instruments have the tendency to emphasize the "credibility of science, and the practitioner as the expert" (1994, p. 96). Further, she states that the results may place members of socioeconomic, cultural, and sexual minority groups at greater risk of appearing more "deviant or troubled."

Fortunately, there has been an increased recognition of the limitation of standardized tools, which have resulted in tools that assess client strengths. The Clinical Assessment Package for Assessing Client Risks and Strengths (CASPARS) developed by Gilgun (1999, 2001) is an example of one such instrument. This assessment tool attempts to capture and weigh both risks and strengths, and in doing so provides a more complete picture of the client's situation. In this respect, CASPARS is consistent with social work practice and the multidimensional assessment process.

Despite the fact that standardized measures may have involved a representative sample during their development, few evaluation/monitoring instruments take into account differences related to culture, race, ethnicity, or language. For example, the words, symptoms, or expressions used to describe depression as well as the attitudes toward illness are different in different populations.

Recall the words of Mrs. Johnson, the elderly African American client mentioned earlier: "I'd like to not feel blue." In immigrant or refugee groups, cultural norms, beliefs, and language may not have an explanation for feelings, so symptoms of depression may be reported as a physical condition (Kagle, 1994; Potocky-Tripodi, 2002). Finally, standardized instruments, even those with established reliability and validity, may not be appropriate for use with certain populations or directly related to the goals of a specific client concern.

These factors discussed should not totally preclude the use of standardized instruments in your practice. In utilizing standardized tools effectively, however, you would need to have used them previously in the assessment process in order to measure and evaluate change. When choosing resources for measuring progress and evaluating outcomes, you should be sure to match the methods selected with the client situation and need. You may also find that a standardized instrument enables you to assess a client's situation and evaluate outcomes in a more systematic and complete manner. In deciding whether an instrument is appropriate, Jordan and Franklin suggest that you consider the ethical question of whether the tool provides the means "to assess and serve the clients better" (2003, p. 128).

In instances where an available evaluation tool is inappropriate or no tool exists, you and a client can agree to develop scales or measures tailored to their specific conditions (Collins, Kayser, & Platt, 1994; Jordan & Franklin, 1995, 2003). One example is illustrated in Figure 12-3. This goal and task form is developed jointly by you and the client and allows each of you to track the intermediate and overall progress toward the goal. Tasks as instrumental strategies and goal attainment strategies can also be evaluated. For example, to assess whether tasks or action steps were completed, as well as the extent to which they affected the status of the goal.

Although an evaluation method devised by you and the client is tailored to the client's situation, the essential evaluation questions should be considered. Overall, any tools used should inform the effectiveness of your practice. This information can be aggregated with other client information to provide you with data relevant your practice as a whole and also that of agency program objectives.

Quantitative Measurements

Quantitative evaluation embodies the use of procedures that measure the frequency and/or severity of target problems. Measurements taken before implementing

Name: _____

Statement of Problem/Condition to Be Changed: _____

_____

Goal
Statement: _____

General
Tasks: _____

_____

Potential
Barriers: _____ _____ _____ _____

Benefits: _____ _____ _____ _____

Specific Tasks (steps to be taken to achieve goal):

	Completion Date	Review Date	Outcome Code
1. _____	_____	_____	_____
2. _____	_____	_____	_____
3. _____	_____	_____	_____

Outcome Codes

Tasks and Goal Status [ ] C (completed) [ ] P (partially completed) [ ] NC (not completed)

FIG-12-3 Sample Goal and Task Form

change-oriented interventions are termed *baseline* measures because they provide a baseline against which measures of progress and measures at termination and follow-up can be compared. These comparisons thus provide quantitative data that make it possible to evaluate the efficacy of work with clients. The single subject design is one example that can be used in a variety of settings, including mental health, family, and private practice. The method can be adapted so that you can integrate evaluation as a key element in your practice. Recall, the suggestion was made that an AB design could be used to track William's school attendance prior to and after the intervention.[2]

Measuring Overt Behaviors

Baseline measures can analyze either overt or covert behaviors. Overt behaviors are observable and, as such, lend themselves to frequency counts. For example, group members who have negotiated a shared goal of increasing the frequency of positive messages sent to one another. You would instruct them to keep a tally of the number of such messages conveyed during group sessions. The session averages would then serve as a baseline against which progress could be measured. Similar baselines can be determined for target behaviors such as increasing the number of times that a student

raised her hand before speaking in class or spoke up in social situations or expressed feelings. Such measures quantify behaviors and make it possible to ascertain both weekly progress and ultimate outcomes of change efforts. In addition, clients can observe even small incremental changes, a factor that sustains hope and motivation.

Clients, observers, or you may perform frequency counts. This can also be done when the target behavior occurs in family or group sessions. Baselines obtained through self-monitoring, however, are not true measurements of behavior under "no treatment" conditions, because self-monitoring itself often produces therapeutic effects. For example, monitoring the rate of a desired behavior (i.e., raising one's hand before speaking) may, in fact, act to increase the frequency of that behavior. Similarly, measuring the rate of negative behavior may influence a client to reduce its frequency.

The effects of self-monitoring on the target behavior are termed *reactive effects*. When viewed by a researcher, reactive effects represent a source of contamination that confounds the effects of the interventions being tested. From your viewpoint, however, self-monitoring may be employed *as an intervention* precisely because reactive effects tend to increase or decrease certain target behaviors. Although desired changes that result from self-monitoring may be either positive or negative behaviors, emphasizing positive behaviors is preferable because doing so focuses on strengths related to goals. It may be useful to use multiple measures or observations, of which self-monitoring is just one measure. For example, the teacher in the classroom situation may also serve as a source of information with respect to the frequency of a student raising his hand prior to speaking in class. Another measure could involve the number of times the student is referred to the "time-out" room for being disruptive in the classroom.

When baseline measures focus on current overt behaviors, repeated frequency counts across specified time intervals are typically used. The time intervals selected should be those during which the highest incidence of behavioral excesses occurs or times at which positive behaviors are desired. It is also important to obtain measures under relatively consistent conditions. Otherwise, the measure may not be representative or reflect the true picture accurately (Bloom, Fischer & Orme, 2003).

Retrospective Estimates of Baseline Behaviors

Baseline measurements are obtained before change-oriented interventions are implemented, either by having clients make retrospective estimates of the incidence of behaviors targeted for change or by obtaining data before the next session. Although it is less accurate, the former method often is preferable because change-oriented efforts need not be deferred pending the gathering of baseline data. This is a key advantage, because acute problems or a crisis may demand immediate attention and delaying the intervention for even one week may not be advisable. However, delaying interventions for one week while gathering baseline data in general does not create undue difficulty, and the resultant data are likely to be far more reliable than clients' estimates.

When determining the baseline of target behavior by retrospective estimates, it is common practice to ask the client to estimate the incidence of the behavior across a specified time interval, which may range from a few minutes to one day, depending on the usual frequency of the target behaviors. Time intervals selected for frequent behaviors, such as nervous mannerisms (tapping a pencil on a desk), should be relatively short (e.g., 15-minute intervals). For relatively infrequent behaviors, such as speaking up in social situations, intervals may involve several hours or days.

Measuring Covert Behaviors

Baseline data can also be obtained for covert behaviors, such as an emotional state of "feeling blue," and thoughts or feelings. Clients can make frequency counts of targeted thoughts or rate degrees of emotional states. To illustrate, we return to the case of Mrs. Johnson. You and this client would develop a five- or seven-point scale that represents varying levels of internal states, ranging from total absence of feeling or thoughts at one extreme to maximal intensity at the other extreme. Where goals involve altering feelings, such as anger, depression, loneliness, or anxiety, it is desirable to construct self-anchoring scales that denote various levels of an internal state. To "anchor" such scales, ask a client to imagine experiencing the extreme degrees of the given internal state and to describe what they experience. You can then use these descriptions to define at least the extremes and the midpoint of the scale. Developing scales in this manner quantifies internal states in a unique manner for each client. In constructing self-anchoring scales, it is important to avoid mixing different types of internal states: Even though emotions such as "happy" and "sad" appear to belong on the same continuum, they are qualitatively different, and mixing them will result in confusion. Figure 12-4 depicts a seven-point anchored scale.

Self-Anchored Scales

Clients can use self-anchoring scales to record the extent of troubling internal states across specified time intervals (e.g., three times daily for seven days) in much the same way that they take frequency counts of overt behaviors. In both instances, clients keep tallies of the target behaviors. A minimum of ten separate measures is generally necessary to discern patterns among data, but urgent needs for intervention sometimes require that you settle for fewer readings. For example, the client, Mrs. Johnson, could complete the scale to record the varying levels and circumstances in which she was "feeling blue" and when she did not experience these feelings.

1	2	3	4	5	6	7
Least anxious (calm, relaxed, serene)		Moderately anxious (tense, uptight, but still-functioning with effort)			Most anxious (muscles taut, cannot concentrate or sit still, could "climb the wall")	

FIG-12-4 Example of a Self-Anchored Scale

The self-anchored scale is also useful for monitoring incremental change. In the range of most to least anxious, you and the client will want to explore events or situations that appear to trigger an anxiety response, providing additional descriptive information. With young minors, pictures or graphic illustrations may be used or you might ask the child to draw or express their own indicators.

Guidelines for Obtaining Baseline Measures

When you are using baseline measures, it is vital to maximize the reliability and validity of your measurements (Bloom, Fischer & Orme, 2003; Berlin & Marsh, 1993). Otherwise, your baseline measures and subsequent comparisons with those measures will be flawed and will lead to inappropriate conclusions. Adhering to the following guidelines will assist you in maximizing the reliability and validity of the data collected:

1. *Define the target of measurement in clear and operational terms.* Reliability is enhanced when the behavior (overt or covert) targeted for change is specifically defined. For example, measurements of compliments given to a partner are more reliable than general measurements of positive communications, because the client must make fewer inferences when measuring the former than when counting the latter instances.

2. *Be sure your measures relate directly and specifically to the goals targeted for change.* Otherwise, the validity of your measurements both at the baseline and at subsequent points will be highly suspect. For example, when a client's goal is increasing social skills, indicators of social skills should be used as measurement targets. Likewise, if a parent is to attend parenting classes to learn parenting skills, the measures should be devised that directly specify observable behavioral changes. Similarly, measures of violent behavior and alcohol abuse should correspond to the frequency of angry outbursts (or control of anger in provocative situations) and consumption of alcohol (or periods of abstinence), respectively.

3. *Use multiple measures and instruments when necessary.* Clients typically present with more than one problem, and individual problems may involve several dimensions. For example, flat affect, fatigue, irritability, and anxiety are all frequently indicators of depression. A client may also present with goals related to increasing self-confidence or improving their social skills, which would require the use of multiple measures and instruments to track.

4. *Measures should be obtained under relatively consistent conditions.* Otherwise, changes may reflect differences in conditions or environmental stimuli, rather than variations in goal-related behaviors. For example, if a child's difficulty is that she does not talk while she is at preschool, measuring changes in this behavior while the child is at home, in church, or in other settings may be informative, but it is not as helpful as the indications of change at preschool, where the behavior primarily occurs.

5. *Baseline measures are not relevant when clients present with discrete goals.* Evaluating the efficacy of helping efforts in such instances is clear-cut, because either a client has accomplished a goal or they have not. For example, with a goal of getting a job, the job seeker is either successful or not successful. By contrast, progress toward ongoing goals is incremental and not subject to fixed limits, as in the case of completing a job application. Employing baseline measures and periodic measures, therefore, effectively enables both you and the client to monitor incremental changes. Consider the following baseline measure for an ongoing goal: "Justin will sit in his seat and keep his hands on his desk during English class." If Justin's baseline indicated that he is out of his seat (off task) 25 times per week, then improvement to 15 times per week would be significant.

Measuring with Self-Administered Scales

Self-administered scales are also useful for obtaining baseline data. Many psychological scales are available, but the WALMYR assessment scales (Hudson, 1992) are especially useful for social workers. Designed by Hudson and fellow social workers, the 22 separate scales (see Chapter 8) tap into many of the dimensions relevant to social worker practice. Their ease of administration, scoring, and interpretation, as well as acceptable reliability and validity, are among the advantages of these scales.

Self-administered scales may also be used to quantify target problems. Although they are somewhat subjective and less precise than behavioral counts, they are particularly useful in measuring covert behavioral states (e.g., anxiety, depression, self-esteem, clinical stress) and clients' perceptions of their interpersonal relationships. Like tools to measure overt behaviors, selected scales can be administered before implementing treatment and thereafter at periodic intervals to monitor progress and to assess outcomes at termination and follow-up.

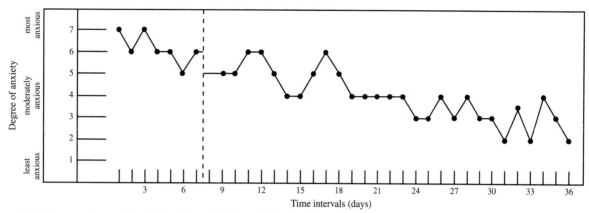

FIG-12-5 Example of a Graph Recording the Extent of Anxiety during Baseline and Intervention Periods

Interestingly, unlike behavioral self-monitoring (e.g., counting behaviors or thoughts), subjective self-reporting through self-administered instruments is less likely to produce reactive effects (Applegate, 1992).

After obtaining baseline measures of targets of change, the next step is to transfer the data to a graph on which the horizontal axis denotes time intervals (days or weeks) and the vertical axis denotes the frequency or severity of target behaviors. Simple to construct, such a graph makes it possible to observe the progress of clients and the efficacy of interventions. Figure 12-5 depicts the incidence of anxiety before and during the implementation of change via such a graph.

In Figure 12-5, note that the baseline period was seven days and the time interval selected for self-monitoring was one day. Interventions to reduce anxiety were implemented over a period of four weeks. As illustrated in the graph, the client experienced some ups and downs (as usually occurs), but marked progress was nevertheless achieved.

In monitoring progress by taking repeated measures, it is critical to use the same procedures and instruments used in obtaining the baseline measures. Otherwise, meaningful comparisons cannot be made. It is also important to adhere to the guidelines for measurement listed in the preceding section. Repeated measurement of the same behavior at equal intervals enables practitioners not only to assess progress but also to determine variability in clients' behavior and to assess the effects of changes in the clients' life situation. For example, by charting measures of depression and increased social skills from week to week, it becomes possible to discern either positive or negative changes that correspond to concurrent stressful or positive life events. In this way,

graphs of measured changes enable clients both to view evidence of their progress and to gain awareness of how particular life or environmental events contribute to their emotional states or behaviors.

Monitoring Progress with Quantitative Measurements

Monitoring progress has several other advantages. Measures establish indicators, and monitoring tells both the client and you when goals have been accomplished, the relationship can be terminated, or the court mandate has been satisfied. For example, when observable behaviors related to parenting skills have improved to the degree that they conform to explicit indicators, termination is justified. Regular school attendance beyond the initial baseline measure is yet another indication for termination. Similarly, termination is indicated when measurements of depression have changed to the range of non-clinical depression. Results of monitoring can also substantiate progress and be used to justify continued coverage by third-party payers and in reports to the court in the case of mandated clients. For clients, monitoring provides evidence of change, assuring them that they are not destined to remain forever involved with the social worker or agency. A final and critical advantage of monitoring is that if interventions are not achieving measurable results after a reasonable period, you can explore the reasons for this lack of progress and negotiate the use of different interventions.

Receptivity of Clients to Measurement

You may feel hesitate to ask clients to engage in self-monitoring or to complete self-report instruments because of your concern that they will resist or react in a negative manner. Research studies by Applegate (1992) and Campbell (1988, 1990) indicate that such concerns are not justified. These researchers found that clients generally were receptive to formal evaluation procedures. In fact, Campbell found that clients preferred being involved in evaluation of their progress. In addition, clients preferred "the use of some type of systematic data collection over the reliance on social worker's opinion as the sole mean of evaluating practice effectiveness" (Campbell, 1988, p. 22). Finally, practitioners were able to accurately assess clients' feelings about different types of evaluation procedures (Campbell, 1990).

Qualitative Measurement

Qualitative measurement methods have emerged as a viable option for monitoring progress and evaluation. Qualitative measures are consistent with narrative and social constructivism approaches. Hence qualitative methods may be especially useful with minors in that they focus on the subjective experience and personal stories (Andrews & Ben-Arieh, 1999; Morgan, 2000). Qualitative evaluation measures have significant advantages for monitoring progress, depending on the information that you are seeking. When combined with quantitative measures, a more complete picture of the intervention and the contextual conditions of the change emerges (Holbrook, 1995; Shamai, 2003). Although the literature on the utilization of qualitative measures remains limited, we nonetheless think that it is important to acquaint you with the information that is available.

Qualitative methods differ in their philosophical, theoretical, and stylistic orientation from quantitative methods (Jordan & Franklin, 1995, 2003; Shamai, 2003). The process of data collection is more open-ended and allows clients to express their own reality and experience. In the assessment and evaluation process, the goal is to explore the individual's (or family's or group's) experience, frame of reference, beliefs, values, and cultural realities. In essence, the client is considered to be the key informant or expert regarding his or her problem and the desired change (Crabtree & Miller, 1992; Jordan & Franklin, 1995, 2003). Gilgun (1994) has suggested that qualitative measurements' focus on client perception makes for a good fit with social work values emphasizing self-determination. Cultural factors may also be included. For example, the findings of a study that examined the use of hospice care by African Americans revealed a difference in values that was a barrier to hospice utilization (Reese, Ahern, Nair, O'Faire & Warren, 1999).

In evaluating progress or outcomes using qualitative methods, you attempt to understand the change from their clients' viewpoint. Information obtained from clients provides the context for and the dimensions of their concerns. In this sense, qualitative measures provide you with insight into the interaction or combination of factors that contribute to change. This descriptive information may be expressed in words, graphs, pictures, diagrams, or narratives. For example, in the structural approach to family therapy, symbols are used to create a visual map of family relationships and interaction patterns. Narratives provided by the family and individual members at the points of change (even change that is incremental) in patterns of interaction highlight the dynamics or events associated with the change. That the minor increased the number of times that she raised her hand before speaking in class is attributed to the fact that the teacher responded to her in a positive manner. The information could also be graphically summarized, noting change over time.

Some critics have questioned the reliability and validity of qualitative measurement methods. The aim of qualitative information, however, is to ensure credibility, dependability, and confirmability (Crabtree & Miller, 1992; Jordan & Franklin, 1995, 2003). Like quantitative methods, qualitative measurements require systematic observation and may involve multiple points of triangulated observations. For example, triangulation would include client self-reports, your observations, and data from other relevant systems. The triangulation of data replication establishes the credibility of information and guards against bias.

Two methods that may be used to measure and monitor change are logical analysis effects and informative events, or critical incidences. They are discussed in the next two subsections.

Logical Analysis Effects

The case of William, the truant from school discussed earlier in this chapter, will be used to illustrate the use of the logical analysis effects method. Recall that William was ordered by the court to attend school rather than be placed in a juvenile detention center. However, William thought school was "lame." As a result, William may either continue to miss a significant number of days or fail to go to school. The arrangement between the social worker and the music teacher simultaneously responded to the goal of the court and William's goal of learning to play the guitar. After several weeks, William reported that he had missed fewer days in school, and the majority of his absences were excused.

Davis and Reid (1988) describe logical analysis effects as establishing a linkage among context, intervention, and change. In William's case, the intervention was arranging for him to receive guitar lessons. To track this change, you would need to establish that his improved school attendance resulted from this intervention. Descriptive information could be obtained by collecting and charting William's pre- and post-intervention attendance, combined with self- and parent reports, and the attendance record. The pertinent question here is: Specifically, what was the effect of the guitar lessons on William's school attendance?

Informative Events or Critical Incidences

Informative events or critical incidences refer to intended or unintended gains that can be attributed to a particular event or action. These events or actions are also referred to as "therapeutic effects" or "turning points" in that they contributed significantly to a goal, thereby changing the status of the target problem (Davis & Reid, 1988; Shamai, 2003). You and a client might agree that the completion of a certain task was instrumental in the attainment of a goal. Successful completion of a task—for example, continuously paying rent on time—means that the individual will not face eviction. Also, you and clients can identify an event or set of circumstances that contributed to goal attainment. William and the social worker identified his being able to take guitar lessons as a turning point for William in his school attendance. Clients may be asked to pinpoint intervention strategies in terms of the most and least helpful. Greater weight may be assigned to those strategies about which you and the client agree.

Therapeutic effects or critical incidences enable clients to put feelings and emotional thoughts into words. For example, being in a group session that allowed mothers to reflect upon and discuss their grief and sadness about the removal of their children from the home was acknowledged by them as marking a change in their ability to move toward reunification with a child or children. Previously, many of the mothers had stored-up feelings of anxiety, fear, and even ambivalence about the return of their children to their care. When asked by the social worker leading the group "What made a difference," the majority of the mothers agreed that the discussion helped them to voice their emotions. Several participants expressed that by releasing their feelings they were able to concentrate on moving toward reunification. Morgan (2000, p. 91) suggests that significant turning points should be celebrated. A certificate highlights such turning points by naming the problem and the alternative story that emerged. For example, certificates for the mothers in the above group might note their movement from self-doubt to confidence or from guilt or shame to freedom from these feelings.

Combining Methods for Measuring and Evaluating Program Objectives

Programs objectives were discussed earlier relative to client outcomes. While each of the methods discussed are qualitative, and their intent is to capture the client's narrative about change, you may want to combine them with quantitative methods for purposes of program evaluation (Padgett, 2004; Rubin & Babbie, 2005; Weiss, 1998). For example, in attributing or tracking the outcomes of specific intervention strategies, questions posed might be whether participants in parenting classes learned new skills (pre/post type measure) and at what point the new skills changed; for example, their interactions with their children improved (logical analysis or turning point). Each method will provide you with different information; specifically quantitative measures provide you with statistical information and qualitative information enriches the data by giving you access to the client's evaluative story.

Although measuring change is not generally associated with tasks groups, isolating particular events or actions can be adapted to these situations. For example, task group members can be asked to evaluate a meeting by noting an event or discussion that facilitated the group accomplishing its work.

Monitoring Progress with Qualitative Measurements

Monitoring progress need not be an ordeal for you, and existing assessment tools may be utilized to measure progress or change in the target problem. Think about the eco-map, which is an assessment tool that examines the relationship between a family and other social systems. It helps both the client and the social worker identify areas of tension as well as potential resources. For evaluation purposes, the eco-map may also be used in a pre- and post-intervention fashion to graphically track change, assuming that the tension lines were identified as targets. In Figure 12-6a, for example, credit card debt was identified as a major stressor in the Strong family. The family identified paying off their debt as a priority, and the social worker referred them to a consumer credit counselor. After the family had worked with this counselor, they and the social worker charted the change. In Figure 12-6b, the tenuous relationship initially reported by the family has changed to a strong resource relationship following the intervention of consumer credit counseling. Of course, this change occurred incrementally. Over time, it might be useful to insert one or more lines to credit card debt to demonstrate the progression or change.

The aim of qualitative methods in monitoring progress and assessing outcomes is to understand the individual's or family's experience and the meaning that this experience holds for them (Witkin, 1993). For the Strong family in Figure 12-6, reducing their level of credit card debt meant that they could begin saving to buy a house. In completing the eco-map with the family, the social worker learned about the family's desire to buy a home, once they were able to manage their debt. Using qualitative methods in this case, the family's narrative provided insight into the interaction or combination of factors that contributed to their desired change. Numbers (i.e., quantitative data) represent descriptive information that is informative about change, or the reduction of symptoms; thus, statistical data fulfill an important function. Statistical data, however, cannot provide the contextual narratives associated with qualitative data. The most salient characteristic of qualitative evaluation methods is that the data adds "a human texture to statistical data," thereby increasing our understanding of progress" (Shamai, 2003).

To Measure or Not to Measure

Monitoring client progress and measuring change is central to your ethical practice as a social worker. The process informs you and the client about the effectiveness of an intervention strategy as well providing you with evaluative information about your own practice. Moreover, the monitoring and measuring of progress informs the movement toward eventual termination.

As previously discussed, measurement and monitoring progress may be accomplished by using either qualitative or quantitative methods, or a combination of the two. Monitoring progress may take the form of notes made in case records, in session reviews, and evaluations. Measurement can be accomplished by using pre- or post-designs, rating or behavioral scales, graphs or grids, or reflective methods (e.g., informative events or incidences). Monitoring and measuring progress with young minors can be facilitated by using pictures, stories, and conversation-related feelings (Morgan, 2000).

Behavioral Contracts and Goal Attainment Scales

Your practice agency setting may, however, have its own methods for measuring outcomes. Schools and residential or juvenile facilities tend to use behavioral contracts that stipulate how progress is measured or goal attainment scales. Goal attainment scales generally have indicators that identify a target event, and measurement before and after an intervention. Observations are

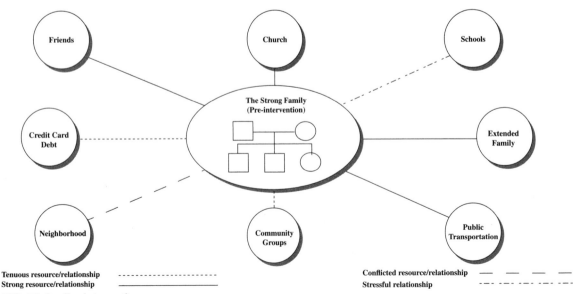

FIG-12-6a Pre-intervention eco-map

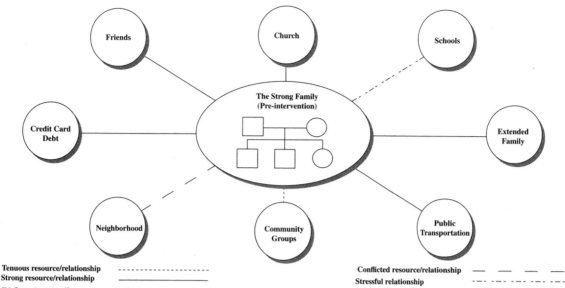

Tenuous resource/relationship   - - - - - - - - - - - - - - - - - -
Strong resource/relationship   ——————————

Conflicted resource/relationship   — — — — —
Stressful relationship   - — - — - — - — - — - —

FIG-12-6b Post-intervention eco-map

weighted along an outcome scale of most to least favorable outcome, an expected level, and performance that is better than expected or anticipated.

In essence, procedures that you use to monitor progress should be implemented in a systematic manner that informs you of the effectiveness of an intervention strategy. In addition, a criterion for the method chosen is the extent to which the measure is compatible and consistent with the goal. A goal of avoiding eviction, for example is tracked differently than a goal of "not feeling blue."

Client Participation

Client participation, an integral factor in the goal negotiation and development process, should be maintained at the measurement stage as well. Participation may mean that measures and monitoring procedures are culturally relevant and consistent with clients' values and beliefs (Potocky-Tripodi, 2002). Not only should clients be involved, they should understand and be receptive to measurement and monitoring.

Lum (2004) and Jayaratne (1994) emphasize involving clients in establishing systematic evaluation procedures to "give voice" to their perspective and therefore be a means of empowerment. Kagle (1994) supports including clients' perspectives because by doing so it creates a balance of the power held by the social worker and the client. Kagle (1994) further asserts that clients' involvement and perspectives lessen the impact of systematic methods, which "casts clients' viewpoints as

being less scientific" (p. 98). These points of view are consistent with the empowerment and collaborative nature of the social worker–client relationship that are emphasized throughout this book.

In deciding which method is appropriate, Jordan and Franklin (2003) suggest that social workers pose the ethical question of how you can "assess and serve the client better" (p. 128). Regardless of whether you use qualitative or quantitative methods or some combination of each method, you should always attend to the central question: How is change systematically measured and recorded?

Contracts

Goals focus the work that is to be completed between you and the client. Contracts are tools in which the agreement between you and the client is outlined. Depending on the practice setting, contracts may also be referred to as service agreements, behavioral contracts, or case or treatment plans. A contract, and hence your work with a client, may be influenced by a court order or referral source when the client is involuntary. Contracts should not be confused with legal mandates or case plans, although elements of both may be included as you develop an agreement to work together. The legal mandate or case plan outlines the concern upon which the contract is based and specifies the expected outcome. But, it can also include concerns and goals that are important to the client. Program objectives may also be included in contracts or agreements. For example, the *Behavioral Treatment Agreement* found at the end of this chapter includes both individual change and requirements that address program objectives.

In addition to contracts, case plans, including behavioral and treatment plans, may be developed that are more short term in nature. For example, you might develop a *child safety plan* that specifies that a parent will call a relative when his or her frustration reaches a point at which they would usually hit their child. This agreement identifies the potential behavior and also specifies a resource for the parent under specific circumstances. For example, "When I feel frustrated, I will call my mother and talk it out with her." A short-term safety agreement might also be reached with a client in an emotional crisis in which the client agrees to refrain from harmful behavior: "I will pay attention to the psychological cues that tell me that I am at risk for harming myself." Further, the agreement could include that the client make an appointment with a professional. The safety plan is signed by the social worker and the client.

Other types of short-term agreements include the *contingency* (quid pro quo) and *good-faith* contracts. Used in cognitive-behavioral family therapy, a contingency contract identifies a desired behavior change on the part of all parties involved. Its fulfillment is contingent on each individual's behavior in response to the other parties' behavior (Nichols & Schwartz, 2004). In a good-faith contract, the parties involved agree to change their behavior independently of one another. This type of contract may be used in a social-behavioral skills group and a behavioral parenting training group.

The Rationale for Contracts

Contracting is the natural culmination of the assessment phase and the introduction of the change-oriented (goal attainment) phases. Key ingredients outline the purpose and focus of your work with clients as well as mutual accountability. They also describe the goals to be achieved and the means of accomplishing them. In some practice settings they may clarify the role of the client and social worker, as well as establish the conditions under which assistance is provided. Contracts are also consistent with the requirements of record keeping and informed consent (Reamer, 1998; Strom-Goffried, 2007)

Developing a contract or service agreement with clients may require an explanation of the purpose and rationale for the contract. Explanations may be particularly important for clients who are hesitant to sign a

document without fully understanding its purpose. Involuntary clients may be suspicious or distrustful, perceiving the contract as infringing on their freedom by committing them to behaviors of which they may disagree. For minors, regardless of their age and developmental stage, the concept of a contract may be a totally alien concept. In settings in which his or her choice of whether or not to work with you is limited, specifying the required change and your role in supporting the minor to achieve goals, as well as clarifying rewards and benefits, can be especially important.

Formal and Informal Contracts

Contract or service agreements can be developed with varying degrees of formality. Public agencies often require written service agreements in the form of case plans or behavioral contracts signed by clients. *Written contracts* provide space for entering the particular concerns or problems of a client situation and listing the expected intervention outcomes. Safety plans are almost always written and they are a ready resource for clients in a crisis. Under normal circumstances, you and the client both sign the contract, giving it much the same weight as a legal document. Some private agencies prefer *service agreements* to contracts, believing that contracts are more appropriate for administrative purposes than for client–professional relationships.

Students often ask whether written or verbal contracts are preferable. For some social workers, the rationale for using a written contract is that it provides a tangible reference to the commitments between themselves and their clients. In this way, the potential for a misunderstanding is minimized. Other social workers prefer *verbal contracts* that include all of the same provisions but lack the formality, sterility, and finality of a written contract. A third option is to utilize a partially verbal and partially written contract, with the latter including the basics of problems and goals identified, role expectations, time limits, and provisions for revision. With minors, either verbal or written or some combination thereof may be appropriate. Whether the contract is verbal or written, at a minimum, clients should understand what is to be accomplished in your work with them. If contracts or agreements are verbal, questions may arise later with regard to informed consent. With verbal contracts, the client should be given a written copy of this information.

As with all other pertinent documents, a written contract or a description of the verbal agreement is included in the case record. Although a contract can be changed, and may not be considered to be legally binding (a fact that should be emphasized to clients), you must outline the work to be done, thereby ensuring that clients are informed and that you have their consent. Otherwise, clients may believe they are justified in filing suit for malpractice if they do not achieve their goals (Reamer, 1998; Houston-Vega, Nuehring & Daguio (1997).

Developing Contracts

Contracting is the final discrete activity of Phase I of the helping process. Generally, contracts should include certain elements which form the basis of the Agreement for Service found at the end of this chapter. The following is a brief discussion of each element.

Goals to be Accomplished

First and foremost, the goals to be accomplished in relation to the target concern are ranked by priority, as goals provide the focus for work over the course of ongoing sessions. At the same time, goals are fluid and can be expanded or modified as situations change and new information emerges that has a bearing on the initial goals. Of course, there must be a valid reason for changing goals. At this stage, a continuous shifting of target concern and goals may signal that the client is not ready to proceed.

Roles of Participants

In Chapter 5, the process of socialization related to the client and practitioner roles is discussed. These roles may need to be revisited during the contracting process. Role clarification may be especially pertinent with involuntary clients who have a mandated case or treatment plan for which their compliance is required. In which case, your role and that of the client are specified in writing. Whether the client is voluntary or involuntary, the identification of roles affirms the mutual accountability and commitment of all parties, including that of the agency involved.

Further socialization about the purpose of contract roles may be required with certain clients. For some clients, trust may emerge as an issue, despite the heretofore positive dynamics of your relationship with them. Involuntary clients may feel particularly vulnerable and ambivalent when asked to sign a contract and perceive their doing so as one more indication of being pressured or controlled and an infringement on their freedom. Potocky-Tripodi (2002) points out that some immigrants or refugees may experience fear and apprehension about contracts depending on their perceptions

and past experiences. Hence, the contract may be "perceived as an instrument of authoritarian coercion" (p. 167). Minors may also feel vulnerable, which may require you to review what is expected of them and how you will assist them. For example, "I have written down that I will help you return to the classroom" or "Your role is to attend group sessions and to learn different ways of behaving in the classroom." In all instances, taking the time to explain the function and purpose of contracts and the client's role will facilitate the client remaining active in the process.

Interventions or Techniques to Be Employed

This aspect of the contract involves specifying the interventions and techniques that will be implemented in order to accomplish the stated goals. During initial contracting, it is often possible to identify interventions only on a somewhat global level. For example, group or family sessions may involve a combination of strategies. In some instances, depending on the identified goals, you and the client can discuss intervention strategies with greater specificity. For example, decreasing or eliminating irrational thoughts, beliefs, and fears (cognitive restructuring); and developing skills (e.g., communication, assertiveness, problem solving, and conflict resolution). In cases where you are the case manager, you would also indicate if a referral source would be the primary agent in assisting a client to meet a particular goal (e.g., finding housing). Whenever you consider implementing interventions it is vital to discuss them with clients, providing a brief overview of the intervention to elicit clients' reactions and to gain their consent. Bear in mind, however, that contracting is an ongoing process, and therefore subject to change.

Time Frame and Frequency and Length of Sessions

Specifying the time frame, frequency, and length of sessions is an integral part the contract. Most people tend to intensify their efforts to accomplish a given goal or task when a deadline exists. Just consider the last-minute cramming that students do before an examination! A time frame stated in the contract counters the human tendency to procrastinate. Yet another argument that supports the development of a definite time frame is the fact that most of the gains that are achieved occur early in the change process. In work with families, Nichols and Schwartz (2004) note that historically treatment has been established as brief and within a limited time period, based on the rationale that change occurs quickly, if it occurs at all. Moreover, whatever the intended length, most contact with clients turns out to be relatively brief, the median duration of which is between five and six sessions (Corwin, 2002; Reid & Shyne, 1969).

On the whole, clients respond favorably to services that are offered when they need them the most and when they experience relief from their problems. This is not to say that clients will not seek help for concrete or daily living concerns that they may have. But, time-limited contracts may be valued by them because they make a distinction between talking and actual change, and within this particular time frame the focus is on a specific concern. Questions have been raised about the brevity associated with time limits. Are time-limited contracts, for example, effective with racial and ethnic groups? Some theorists believe that time limits are inconsistent with perspectives of time held by some minority groups (Devore & Schlesinger, 1999; Green, 1999; Logan, Freeman & McRoy, 1990). Other theorists cite outcome studies that emphasize that time-limited contracts are preferable with racial and ethnic minority clients, because they focus on immediate, concrete concerns. Examples included Devore and Schlesinger (1999), Ramos and Garvin (2003) and James (2008). They note that in stressful situations, persons of color respond best to a present- and action-oriented approach. Corwin (2002), citing the work of Koss and Shiang (1994) and Sue and Sue (1990), points out the advantages of time-limited, brief treatment by noting that these approaches are "congruent with how many minority clients understand and utilize mental health and social services" (p. 10). Of course it would be presumptuous to assert hard-and-fast rules about a relationship between time limits and minority status. As highlighted in the previous discussion, brief contact with a specific focus appears to be a pattern with a majority of clients, irrespective of their status.

A second question relates to whether time limits are appropriate to all client populations and situations. Certainly, time-limited contracts may be inappropriate in some instances. For example, as an outpatient mental health case manager your responsibility can be ongoing, hence time limits may be impractical. Nonetheless, you may find that time-limited contracts may be used with circumscribed problems of living or concrete needs are defined as goals. In these instances, time-limited contracts can be effective when they are divided into multiple short-term contracts related to specific problems and episodes. A brief contract may, for example, involve a safety agreement, or finding housing.

Decisions about specified time frames may be imposed on the work to be completed between you and clients. Managed care demands (specifically the brevity of the period in which outcomes are expected to be achieved) have dramatically influenced practice in both the private and the public sectors of social welfare services. In addition, agency resources, purchase of service (POS) contracts, funders, public policy, or the courts may stipulate a time frame and the duration of contact. In child welfare, for example, under the Adoption and Safe Family Act, 1997, parents are required to meet their case plan goals within a definitive time period. Time pressures resulted in tensions for many parents. For some, this pressure was a decisive factor in eventual reunification with their children. For example, often there was little or no consideration as to whether services were available nor if the services could be obtained within the required time frame. These time limits must be included in contracts that you develop with clients. Within the contract, you can help clients with the ticking of the clock by assisting them to focus their efforts on responding to the most pressing concerns.

The helping process as presented in this text relies on the time frame being brief. The time period used is that which is commonly associated with the task-centered social work model, in which specific target concerns and goals are identified. The action-oriented emphasis in the model can foster a mindset that is conducive to change in which an expectancy of a change in the target concern has a positive effect on self-direction and motivation.

Research conducted within various settings and with various groups, including minors, supports the efficacy of 6 to 12 sessions conducted over a time span of two to four months. The flexibility inherent in this time frame, however, means that you can negotiate with the client regarding the specific number of sessions to be undertaken (Nichols & Swartz, 2004).

Frequency and Duration of Sessions

In most agencies, weekly sessions are the norm, although more frequent sessions may be required in cases that need intensive support and monitoring. For example, child welfare/child protective services, job-training programs, outpatient drug treatment, services for the frail elderly, and school truancy or homeless youth programs can require daily contact. Provisions can also be made in contracts for spacing sessions farther apart during the termination phase of the helping process.

There are few solid guidelines as to the amount of time for sessions. Agencies generally have established guidelines for the billable hour, which tends to be 50 minutes. Conversely, if your setting is a public agency, for example, in child and family or protective services, time spent is only a part of what you do. You can spend considerable time arranging for and monitoring visitations between parents and children, home visits, crisis problem-solving, and teaching parenting skills. The duration of sessions is also influenced by the client. Because some children, adolescents, and elderly clients have difficulty tolerating long sessions, shorter and more frequent sessions are more practical. Frequency and duration of sessions are also influenced by settings requirements (e.g., school, hospital, correctional facility). For example, in a hospital setting, your contact may last 15 or 20 minutes, depending on the condition of the patient and the goals to be achieved. Also, your contact is limited to while the person is an inpatient. For school-based groups, the duration and length of sessions may require a structured time frame and may be influenced by concerns teachers have about out-of-classroom time.

Means of Monitoring Progress

At this stage of the contracting process, previous discussions between you and the client focused on the specific methods that will be used to monitor progress. Thus a brief review is all that may be needed. Within the contract, you may cite the specific means that will be used to monitor progress. For example, when baseline measures on target problems have been obtained, you would explain that the same measuring device would be used at specified intervals to note change in the target problem. If baseline data are not available, a crude method of quantifying progress is to ask clients to rate their progress on a scale of 1 to 10, where 1 represents no progress and 10 represents complete achievement of a given goal. Comparing their ratings from one session to the next gives a rough estimate of clients' progress.

In addition, when a narrative progress review is a part of each session, it can serve the function of monitoring progress. For example, if you have used the Goal and Task Form (Figure 12-3) you and the client would review tasks and the status of goals. You and the client may have opted for using scales or calibrated drawings of thermometers with a scale from 1 to 10, where a colored marker indicates progress on the chart. Visual methods of monitoring progress are particularly appealing to young children.

The frequency of monitoring may be negotiated with the client, and whichever method that is chosen, devoting time in at least every other session to review progress is advisable. Of course, you can be flexible, but no more than three sessions should pass between discussions of progress. Less frequent monitoring dilutes the growth and benefits achieved and the focus on desired changes.

Stipulations for Renegotiating the Contract

Contracting within a brief time frame assumes that when goals are met, that is a change, or that significant reduction in the target problem will occur. Contracting continues during the entire helping process. Renegotiating a contract with clients can occur when their circumstances change or new facts emerge and thereby the process evolves. For this reason, it is important to clarify for clients that conditions in the contract are subject to renegotiation at any time. Above all, the contract should be continually reviewed and updated to ensure its relevance and fit. You should explain that you and the client may request modifications in the contract. This explanation highlights and enhances mutuality in the helping process. When contracting with involuntary clients, any circumstances that would cause a unilateral change in the contract (e.g., evidence of new legal violations) should be specified.

Housekeeping Items

Talking with clients about such issues as provisions for canceling or changing scheduled sessions and financial arrangements can be awkward and at best mundane, but are necessary. Many agencies have printed material on such topics as fee schedules, the expectation of prompt payment of fees, and changes in appointments. In making home visits, nothing is more frustrating than showing up for an agreed-upon appointment time only to find that the client or family is not at home or is unavailable or unprepared for the visit. You should have the same expectations of yourself. Whether contact with a client is in your office or in their home, clients should be able to rely on your being available and attentive to their concerns. Of course, there are legitimate reasons that you or a client can have for changing or canceling an appointment. Discussing the "what ifs" in advance clarifies the expectations of you and the client about attending sessions and being available and prevents misunderstandings.

Perhaps discussing fees may be the most awkward for you, and uncomfortable for the client. Your discomfort is understandable given that your basic instinct as a social worker is to help people. Even so, most private agencies have policies that require payment for services, and the majority of clients expect to pay, albeit on a sliding-scale fee arrangement. In addition, insurance providers often have co-payment requirements for services.

Financial arrangements, where required, are a fundamental part of the professional agreement between you and the client. A component of a social worker's competency is being able to effectively discuss financial arrangements, openly and without apology, when payment of services is expected. When clients fail to pay fees according to the contract, you should explore the matter with them promptly. Avoidance and procrastination just make matters worse, and may result in you developing negative feelings toward the client. Moreover, a failure to pay fees may derive from the client's passive, negative feelings toward the practitioner, financial strains, or irresponsibility in meeting obligations, each of which merits immediate attention.

There are situations in which there are exceptions to a discussion about fees. Examples in which fees are not prominent include purchase of service agreement contracts with your agency or if the service is funded by a grant. This would also include services provided to minors in school settings. When the client is a minor in an agency setting any discussion about fees is a conversation between you and the minor's parent or legal guardian.

Sample Contracts

To assist you in developing contracts, we have included sample contracts at the end of this chapter (see pages 347–351). Each contract includes most of the components discussed in preceding sections, although some are emphasized more than others. Elements of the first contract, "Agreement for Professional Services," were adapted from Houston-Vega, Nuehring and Daguio (1997). This informative resource includes sample contracts for individuals, families, and groups, as well as ethical guidelines for social workers and guidelines for managing malpractice risks. In using any of the contracts or agreements, you should clear them with your agency supervisor.

An "Agreement for Professional Services" contract is presented in outline form. An outline is used as the particular elements were detailed in an earlier discussion about the general elements of a contract. The agreement for the social worker is much more detailed, committed to observing ethical standards of practice.

The second contract was developed to be used with participants of the agency "the back door" (DeLine, 2000). This agency is committed to helping homeless and runaway youth get off the streets. It outlines the

program objective and the services the agency provides. In addition, the role of youth clients is amplified, because the focus is exclusively on how they will use the agency's services to alter their situation. The goal of the contract is to identify priorities and the most manageable tasks. For additional information on the back door, and their use of contracts, you can access the agency's Web site: *www.infor@buildingdoorways.org*.

The remaining examples illustrate a treatment plan and two behavioral contracts. One is used in a county mental health center with men in a domestic violence program. Note that program requirements and objectives are a part of each client's treatment plan. The other details the elements of a type of behavioral contract for a juvenile justice facility and for use in school settings. Each detail the specific behaviors to be changed, adapted from Ellis and Sowers (2001).

Summary

This chapter focused on goals, their purpose and function, their measurement, and the contract or service agreement as essential elements of the helping process. Also, goals were distinguished from program objectives, although the latter may be included as they pertain to a client's situation. General objectives or specific tasks were discussed as instrumental strategies for goal attainment. As you reflect on the chapter, it might be useful to think of goals as global, whereas general and specific tasks are akin to the objectives that you as a student would develop in field contracts. General and specific tasks (objectives) are measurable and represent the manner in which an outcome will be achieved. For example, suppose you have decided that you wish to increase your practice skills as a part of your field contract. Your general tasks would include observing your supervisor and other social workers when they interview clients, and then carrying out your own interviews. From that general task, you would develop specific tasks (objectives), also measurable, which you would complete in order to accomplish your ultimate goal of increasing your direct practice skills.

Students and even seasoned social workers often have difficulty in developing specific, measurable goals and their ability to do so requires practice. In training sessions related to goal development, we have encouraged participants to develop goals for themselves as a means of refining their skills. After reading this chapter, we hope that you feel more comfortable with your knowledge of the skills needed in negotiating and developing goals with clients of all ages.

Agreement for Professional Services

Name(s) of Client(s) _____ Name _____

Address _____ City _____ State _____ ZIP Code _____

Outline for the agreement to work collaboratively in achieving goals, and joint planning in carrying out activities for the achieving goals.

   I. **Problem(s) or/Concern(s):** Defined and Specified

  II. **Prioritized Goals & General Tasks:**

    Goals _____ General tasks _____

    _____ _____

 III. Conditions under which goals might change or revised for others added.

  IV. **Time Limits Applicable to Case:** Time frame that may influence the rate at which goals may need to be accomplished or where significant progress toward goals may need to be documented.

   V. **Sessions:** Meeting times, frequency and durations, location, beginning and ending dates, and the total number of sessions.

  VI. **Who is involved:** Individual, couple or family, group or a combination?

 VII. **Fees:** For service and method and arrangement of payment.

VIII. **Evaluation:** How progress will be monitored and measured, including client participation, evaluating progress each session by reviewing the goal plan, and the steps taken to achieve goals and final evaluation at termination.

  IX. **Reports and Records:** Confidentiality of records and consent of Release of Information. Specifies who will receive reports about progress (e.g., court, third-party payer, referral source).

   X. **Requirements of Mandated Reporting:**

  XI. **Agreement:** Affirmation of the review of the terms of the agreement, and that an understanding that the agreement can be renegotiated at any time.

Signature (Client/Family/Group Member)

Name _____ Name _____ Date _____

 XII. **Social Worker:**

    a) I agree to work collaboratively with _____ to achieve the goals outlined in this service agreement and others that we may subsequently agree upon.

    b) I agree to adhere to the conduct that _____ agency expects of its staff and to abide by the regulatory laws and ethical codes that govern my professional conduct.

    c) I have provided a copy of agency information about the rights of clients, available agency services, and information about the agency.

    d) I have read the above terms of the service agreement, and pledge to do my best to assist the client(s) to achieve the goals listed and others that we may subsequently agree upon.

Professional's Signature: _____

Date: _____

the back door
MAKING CHANGE

Name: _____ **Date:** _____

File #: _____

☐ Housing   ☐ Planning   ☐ Drugs/Alcohol
☐ Employment   ☐ Volunteering   ☐ Problem Solving
☐ Education   ☐ Finances   ☐ Identification
☐ Personal   ☐ Leadership   ☐ Legal
     ☐ Other

CONTRACT STEP: _____ Step#: _____

WHAT I WANT TO WORK ON TODAY (i.e., WHERE I AM TODAY IN MY LIFE):
_____
_____

WHAT RESULT(S) I WOULD LIKE TO SEE (i.e., WHERE I WOULD LIKE TO BE):
_____
_____

WHAT I NEED TO MAKE IT WORK:
_____
_____

MY STEPS:
1 _____
2 _____
3 _____
4 _____

Contractor: _____ Paid by: _____

The following principles & questions reflect how *the back door* hopes to work. Please take time to think about how they worked for you in THIS contract step.
1. Principle: INTEGRITY/DIGNITY
   How did contracting this step contribute positively to your self esteem?
2. Principle: LIFE IS SUCH THAT THINGS DO NOT ALWAYS WORK
   In attempting the above step how did you find this to be so?
3. Principle: ACCEPTANCE WITHOUT JUDGMENT OR PREJUDICE
   How did contracting this step allow you to experience positive input from another person?
4. Principle: FORGIVENESS: EVERY DAY IS A NEW DAY
   How did contracting this step give you the freedom to learn from the past and try again?
5. Principle: PEOPLE WHO LISTEN TO EACH OTHER LEARN FROM EACH OTHER
   How did planning/working on this step help you to understand another person's point of view?
6. Principle: ALL ACTIONS/CHOICES AFFECT OTHER PEOPLE
   Did your working on this step have any effect on other people in your life?

Source: Used by permission of *the back door* © 2000.

Sample Treatment Plan

Areas of Concern	Short-Term Goals/Objectives	Long-Term Goals	Treatment Plan

Adpated from Springer, D.W. (2002). Treatment planning with adolescents. In A.R. Roberts & J.J. Green (Eds.). *Social Worker's Desk Reference.* New York: Oxford University Press.

In the factors that can influence the development of goals, client participation and consideration of their values and beliefs was affirmed for both voluntary and involuntary clients. Clients live in a context, in which their value and belief systems and their worldview narratives are all perspectives that cannot be obtained without their participation. Goal development should also take into account challenges that result from clients' socioeconomic status, race, culture, or issues related to minority status. While the focus of your contact with clients revolves around expressed needs or wants, or in the case of involuntary clients a need that is externally defined, clients have strengths that if channeled help them to reach their goals. Finally, assumptions about the dynamics in your relationship with the voluntary client are unlikely to apply when goals are developed with involuntary clients, whether adults or minors. Nevertheless, there are certain considerations and strategies that can facilitate work with involuntary minors and adults.

This chapter also emphasized the importance of monitoring progress and measurement and evaluation, whether the method used was quantitative or qualitative. Irrespective of method, measurement requires systematic and oftentimes multiple points of observation. Remember that goals flow directly from and relate specifically to the target problem or concern. Thus, the measure selected to monitor and evaluate

progress must also be consistent with goal-related behaviors or conditions. In general, the essential evaluation question is: Did change occur and, if so, in what way? In addition to seeking an answer for you, this question is universally one that is of utmost importance to funding resources, agencies, and third-party payers. In addition, ethical practice demands that you as a social worker can demonstrate that what you do with clients is effective.

The contract examples provided in this chapter are intended as guides that may be adapted to particular situations or settings. Depending on the developmental age and stage of minors and client situations, a certain form may be more appropriate than another. Settings and client situations or status may dictate the inclusion of some elements over others. Regardless of the form that a contract might take, it should define the work to be completed between you and the client. Thus, it should have clarity about goals, roles, and expectations, and include the structured time frame in which the collaborative work is to be completed and evaluated.

Skill Development Exercises

1. Develop a goal for yourself. Assess the feasibility of your goal, potential barriers, and risks and benefits.

Behavioral Treatment Agreement

Name _____ Client # _____ Date _____ Therapist _____

1. Progress

Summary _____

_____

2. New Treatment Goals

1. Increased awareness of individual cues that trigger getting angry
2. Increased awareness of nonabusive alternative ways of expressing anger
3. Increased use of support networks
4. Accepting responsibility for past abusive behavior

3. Plan

Attend 18 educational themes/complete 9 tasks

4. Outcomes

1. Side effects of treatment discussed ☐ yes ☐ no
2. Outcomes of treatment discussed ☐ yes ☐ no
3. Treatment options discussed ☐ yes ☐ no
4. Cost of treatment explained to client ☐ yes ☐ no
5. Client and staff rights form provided to client ☐ yes ☐ no
6. Is client considering:
    Chemotherapy ☐ yes ☐ no
    Hospitalization ☐ yes ☐ no
    Other medical treatment ☐ yes ☐ no

If the answer is yes to any of the above, the physician or consulting psychiatrist shall inform the client of the treatment alternatives, the effects of the medical procedures, and the possible side effects.

All clinical services shall be provided according to the individual treatment plan.

5. Expected Duration of Treatment

18 weeks/dependent on task completion. You need to begin completing the required tasks within the first 4 weeks of the program

6. Frequency of Treatment

Weekly

7. Collateral Resources and Referrals

_____

I understand the terms of this treatment agreement as well as my responsibilities in implementing the same. I have received a copy of this treatment plan.

Client _____ Date _____

Therapist _____ Date _____

Clinical Director _____ Date _____

Source: Used by permission. © MHC.

Sample Behavioral Contract

Name _____

Date _____

Responsibilities (activities, counseling sessions, behaviors to avoid):

Privileges (outlines privileges associated with meeting responsibilities):

Bonuses (meeting requirements for a certain time period):

Sanctions (circumstances in which privileges are lost, and possible action if requirements are not met):

Monitoring (identifies who is responsible for monitoring whether requirements are met):

Client's Signature _____

Social Worker's Signature _____

Adapted from Ellis & Sowers (2001). Juvenile Justice Practice

---

Also, determine which of the measurement and evaluation procedures that were discussed in the chapter you would use to observe goal attainment.

2. Using the same goal that you developed for yourself, rate your level of readiness. Now develop general and specific tasks or objectives that will help you meet your goal.

3. Reread the case of Bettina, the adolescent parent in the group home. What is your reaction to the staff pattern of punishment, based on what you have read about the client's sense of self-definition, self-direction, and motivation?

4. Review motivational congruence as a strategy for working with involuntary clients and think about ways in which you could make use of this strategy.

5. What are values that you hold that have the potential to create tension between what you believe and the goals that a client might want to pursue? Other than using a referral resource, which may or may not be

an option, how would you deal with the differences between you and the client?

Notes

1. In addition to the procedures for measurement and monitoring discussed in this book, we recommend Jordan and Franklin (2003), Bloom, Fischer and Orme (2003), and Corcoran and Fischer (1999) for more in-depth information on standardized instruments and methods to evaluate practice.

2. For those interested in further study on single-subject research, informative resources are Bloom, Fischer and Orme (1999, 2003), Corcoran and Fischer (1999), and Thyer (2001). These texts are informative resources and describe a wide variety of methods that may be used to evaluate practice. *Internet Resource: Evidence-based practice: Young Children with Challenging Behavior.*

PART 3

The Change-Oriented Phase

13 Planning and Implementing Change-Oriented Strategies

14 Developing Resources, Planning, Organizing and Advocacy as Intervention Strategies

15 Enhancing Family Relationships

16 Intervening in Social Work Groups

17 Additive Empathy, Interpretation, and Confrontation

18 Managing Barriers to Change

After formulating a contract, service agreement or treatment plan, the social worker and the client begin Phase II of the helping process—the goal attainment or change-oriented phase. In Phase II, social workers and clients plan and implement strategies to accomplish goals related to the identified problems or concerns. Implementing these strategies involves employing interventions and techniques specified in the contract and contracting to use others as indicated by changing circumstances. Before considering these factors further, however, a preview of Part 3 is in order.

Chapter 13 begins with a discussion of planning goal attainment strategies and includes change-oriented practice approaches. Crisis intervention is a model that is related to the task-centered system but is applied in somewhat more specific situations. Cognitive restructuring, a technique used in cognitive-behavioral therapy. It is useful for addressing the cognitive component of diverse problems and may be employed in conjunction with other interventions. In keeping with the focus on brief, time-limited practice in this book, however, we have included a discussion of the solution-focused approach. The tenets and techniques of the solution-focused approach are compatible with the task-centered, crisis intervention, and cognitive restructuring approaches to practice. The four approaches, empirically grounded, are used broadly in social work practice with individuals and families. Given the large number of treatment models in the helping professions and an even larger number of specific interventions, it is not possible to examine all of them in a single volume.[1]

Chapter 14 focuses on macro practice; its coverage is enriched by case examples from social workers addressing environmental or institutional barriers in which macro-level interventions were indicated.

In Chapter 15, the family interventions introduced build on the material from Chapter 10 on family assessment. Similarly, Chapter 16 presents group interventions, which build on Chapter 11's discussion of group formation and assessment. Techniques employed to expand self-awareness and to pave the way to change (additive empathy, interpretation, and confrontation) are considered in Chapter 17. Part 3 concludes with Chapter 18, which introduces skills in managing barriers to change.

CHAPTER 13

Planning and Implementing Change-Oriented Strategies

CHAPTER OVERVIEW

Thus far, you have learned the knowledge and skills needed to complete a multidimensional assessment, develop goals, formulate a contract or treatment plan, and methods for monitoring and measuring progress. Chapter 13 continues the processes of helping by focusing on change-oriented strategies that may be used to alter the target problem or concern and promote solutions.

Change-Oriented Approaches

Chapter 12 discussed guidelines and criteria for developing goals. The step beyond this point requires that you plan and select an intervention approach. Four approaches are introduced in this chapter that serve this purpose. They can be use in collaboration with clients to help them achieve their goals or respond to a mandate. In addition, their use is based on empirical studies and empirically based techniques or scales. Research studies have demonstrated the effectiveness of these approaches with diverse populations and settings, including minors.

The four approaches are:

- *The Task-Centered System*
- *Crisis Intervention*
- *Cognitive Restructuring*
- *Solution-Focused*

The task-centered and crisis intervention models and cognitive restructuring are problem-solving approaches. As such, problems or concerns or behaviors are specified and assessed with regard to context, frequency, duration, antecedents, and the system or systems involved. As the name implies, the solution-focused approach departs from a problem focus and has a more deliberate emphasis on solutions to problems. It is primarily focused on how symptoms and

exceptions are manifested in a client's life. Hence, exceptions to the problem as presented by the client are emphasized and minimal time is spent exploring the specifics of context in which the problem occurs, its antecedents, and the problem's frequency and duration.

All four approaches are organized around the systematic interpersonal and structural elements of the helping process, which is divided into the distinct phases of engagement, assessment, intervention, and termination and evaluation. At the intervention or change-oriented phase, they may be used in your work with individuals, families, and groups. They adhere to the principles of social work practice, which emphasize mobilizing individuals and families toward positive action that demonstrates that change can occur. Within each approach, clients' strengths are emphasized, which increases clients' self-efficacy, a critical element of empowerment. Hence, these four approaches are compatible with the helping process discussed in this text thus far.[1]

The four approaches are also consistent with systematic generalist-eclectic practice as articulated by Coady and Lehmann (2008, p. 5); the elements are as follows:

- *A person and environment focus that is informed by ecological theory*
- *An emphasis on establishing a positive helping relationship and empowerment as well as a holistic multilevel assessment, including a focus on diversity, oppression, and strengths*
- *A problem-solving model that provides structure and guidelines for work with clients*
- *Flexibility in the use of problem-solving methods that allows a choice among a range of theories and techniques based on their compatibility with each client's situation*

Planning Goal Attainment Strategies

In planning intervention strategies, choose an intervention that makes sense to both you and the client and which is relevant to the situation. The operative word that facilitates this process is *matching*. That is, the intervention selected should ideally respond to the following questions adapted from Cournoyer (1991):

- *What is the problem and what are the goals?*
- *Is the approach relevant and appropriate to the person, family, or group?*
- *Is the approach compatible with the basic values and ethics of social work?*
- *What empirical or conceptual evidence supports the effectiveness of the approach?*
- *Am I sufficiently knowledgeable and skilled enough in this approach to use with others?*

What is the Problem and What are the Goals?

In the assessment phase, you gained a picture of the person, his or her situation, and the problem. To achieve expected outcomes, interventions must be directed to the problem specified by the client or the mandate, as well the systems that are implicated in the problem. With minors, their problems often will involve the family, educational, and perhaps the juvenile justice systems. The coordination of these various systems relative to the problem and the goals is not a small task. After goals have been agreed upon, or in the case of the involuntary client, identified, the intervention approach selected should match the problem. The approach should also be feasible for facilitating change and goal attainment. The four change-oriented approaches discussed in this text may be used with voluntary or involuntary individuals, families, or groups, including minors. Your method selection, however, requires an understanding of circumstances, the nature of the problem, the goals, and timing.

The task-centered model has been shown to be effective with interpersonal concerns, family problems, emotional distress, drug use, mental health and health-related concerns, transitions, and inadequate resources (Reid, 1992). The approach is not suitable for clients who are in need of an insight-oriented intervention. Ramos and Tolson (2008) suggest that the basic thrust of the approach is incompatible with mandated clients who refuse help or who are unable to identify changes

that they wish to make. Of course, you might consider whether any approach without modification can effectively respond to such dynamics. Similar to task-centered, the solution-focused approach is action-oriented and uses a series of strategic questions to identify solutions for a range of problems clients' may present (Trepper, Dolan, McCollum, & Nelson, 2006). It is, however, not advisable to use the solution-focused "miracle question" (see below) in and of itself as an intervention. For example, in the initial crisis stage, the crisis intervention strategies such as attending to the client's emotional state would take precedence over using the miracle question.

The crisis and cognitive behavioral approaches—in particular, cognitive restructuring are indicated when a certain set of conditions and circumstances exist. Crisis intervention responds to situations in which clients experience an event or situation that exceeds their capacity to function and cope (James, 2008). Cognitive restructuring, a procedure of the cognitive behavioral therapy is focus on changing clients' problematic thought patterns, self-statements and behaviors. Cognitive behavioral therapy has been shown to be effective in treating depression, certain behavioral problems, interpersonal problems, trauma situations, and in assisting minors and youth to improve their skills (Cormier & Nurius, 2003; James, 2008; Smagner & Sullivan, 2005). Even so, a more integrative cognitive approach in which you attend to micro and macro factors that contribute and sustain problematic cognitions can be more effective (Berlin, 2001); for example, if the cognitive procedure of restructuring appears to be advisable with a client presenting with depression. But if you have assessed that her depression is influenced by the impoverished physical and social environment in which she lives, then the procedure as a stand-alone intervention would be inappropriate. Because life situations can affect how people respond, an effort to replace or alter the client's thought processes would require that you also address the related physical and social environmental factors.

There may be instances in which the client's problem and related goals call for a combination of micro, mezzo, and macro strategies. At other times, you may use techniques or strategies from each approach, depending on your knowledge and skill level.

Is the Approach Appropriate to the Person, Family, or Group?

Because clients vary in their levels of cognitive, social, and psychological development, gender, age, and stage in life, you must consider these factors when choosing intervention strategies. No doubt you have been exposed to this content in your human behavior courses, thus a lengthy discussion of interventions appropriate for all developmental and life-cycle phases here would be excessive. You should, however, make use of this knowledge in planning and selecting intervention strategies. *An overarching question to consider is whether the approach is appropriate to developmental and lifecycle stage, transitional or situational dynamics, and minority status?*

Child Development and Family Lifecycle

Developmental age and stage are critical factors that should inform the selection and planning of intervention strategies with and for minors. A developmental perspective according to Spoth, Guyll, Chao & Molgaard (2003) is important in the prevention of and intervention with problems or risky behaviors among both minority and nonminority adolescents. The perspective can also inform whether adaptations or modifications of an approach are needed. Very young children, for example, typically lack the cognitive capacity to think abstractly. Therefore, you may need to include play, imagery, interactive structured group activities, psychoeducational groups, or mutual storytelling (Nader & Mello, 2008; Morgan, 2000). For example, a younger minor when asked what they wish to be different is generally able to draw pre- and post-faces to indicate their current feelings and how they would feel differently after their situation has changed. School-aged minors, particularly in middle childhood, are influenced by self-evaluation, the evaluation of others and their own sense of mastery (Hutchison, 2003). Hence, the use of task, consistent with the task-centered or solution-focused approaches, both of which can reinforce and support their sense of self, may be advisable.

Substantive developmental issues for adolescents is that of establishing identity, including racial, cultural, and sexual identity, and asserting their independence. In some case, these issues are at the center of interpersonal relational conflicts between parents and reactions to other authority figures or the systems with whom they interact. Yet, these developmental tasks for youth in immigrant or refugee families can become exaggerated in immigrant families where neither a separate identity or independence is a normative value. Tensions can occur between the youth and their families, in particular when the youth embraces customs that differ from cultural expectations.

Although significant differences may exist between subgroups, you should also be aware of culturally derived developmental expectations. Not all cultural or racial groups mark development according to the normative Western expectations (Garcia Coll, Akerman & Cicchetti, 2000; Garcia Coll, Lamberty, Jenkins, McAdoo, Crinic, Wasik, & Valesquez Garcia, 1996; Ogbu, 1997, 1994). Farmer (1999) points to the need to understand minors who are immigrants or refugees with respect to their stage of acculturation and relational and developmental needs. In a powerful example of an immigrant youth's gang involvement Farmer (1999), using the Human Behavior in the Social Environment (HBSE) framework, examines the youth's behavior in the context of an immigrant environment and the developmental and social needs that are satisfied by the group.

Special consideration is warranted when a minor's contact with you is involuntary. For example, school suspensions, parental incarceration, placement in an institutional setting or outside of the home are situations that have particular implications for a minor's reaction; in the context of their developmental age and stage. The situation of young minors in placement, for example, raises concerns about attachment and loss not only to the parent, but also other family members and the community. Mandated contact can cause fear, a sense of failure, and concerns about their status and self-evaluation in young children. Older minors using the attitudinal weapons at their disposal may react with anger and at a minimum refuse to cooperate. Moreover, the needs of minors are especially acute when a parent is incarcerated (Enos, 2008). These types of situations are crisis-oriented, and as such, the emotional state of the minor may initially need to be addressed.

Family life-cycle theory marks developmental phases for families and delineates certain tasks to be completed (Carter & McGoldrick, 1999). Over the course of the life cycle, family needs and circumstances vary; therefore, interventions must consider the family's level of functioning, strengths, and migratory status (Kilpatrick & Holland, 1999; Hernandez & McGoldrick, 1999). Family life cycle and child development theories assume an orderly progression of development according to Western norms. A particular assumption in both, for example, is that youth will eventually separate from their parents and form peer and intimate relationships beyond the family system.

Stressful Transitions

Difficulties for individuals and families often occur in conjunction with overwhelming stresses precipitated by life transitions or situational events. Stressful transitions involve birth, death, marriage, divorce, the coming of age of a minor, relocating to a new country, active military duty during armed conflict, or a change in role. Extreme situations such as exposure to violence or dramatic events such as a natural disaster can diminish coping capacity and can affect both physical and emotional health (James & Gilliland, 2001). The spill-over, for example, from ongoing marital conflict can affect the stress level of minors and influence their behavior (McHale & Cowan, 1996).

Over the course of the life cycle, middle-aged and older adults may experience situational stress when their role in the family, work life, or the community is diminished. In instances where physical limitations are a concern, these transitions can be stressful for the individual and their family. For example, ongoing care-taking responsibilities of a minor or elderly relative who is ill pose a particular challenge. Aging is a normative event in the life-cycle transition. Popular media images of aging range from the happily retired, active individual or couple, or the offspring or spouse who is concerned about an elderly person's need for constant care. In truth, neither image tells the entire story. Hence, interventions should consider an individual's level of cognitive and physical functioning along a developmental continuum. Other central questions are whether an intervention is consistent with the aging client's stage of life, their role in the family system and life cycle, their life experiences, and current perspectives on life.

Of course, people cope and function with varying levels of stress including the normative, transitional, or adverse events that can occur at various stages in the family life cycle. Consider the simultaneous pride and stress felt by parents when their young adult college graduate relocates to another state. At the other end of this spectrum (an all-too-frequent occurrence in low income families of color) is the remorse and grief of the family when facing the adversity of a youth or young adult sentenced to a lengthy prison sentence (Shane, 2007).

The ability to cope with transitions and adversity depends of such factors as cognition, adaptability, resilience, strength, emotional and physical status, and the adequacy of social and institutional resources (Berlin, 1996; McMillen, 1999). In addition, the ego strengths of individual and family members, cohesion, communication patterns, and commitment among members may determine how they cope, as will interactions beyond the family, such as social support networks (Berlin, 1996; Janzen & Harris, 1997; McMillen, 1999). At the

same time, you should be aware of the fact that different cultures react differently and assign different levels of importance to crisis or transitions. For example, for some groups, death is a time of celebration; for others, it is a time of great mourning and sacred rituals (Hines, Preto, McGoldrick, Almeida, & Weltman, 1999).

According to Levinson's (1996) "seasons of life," transitions are normative life cycle occurrences. Although transitions may alter development, they may also result in a "turning point" in the lives of individuals and families. Consider a 67-year-old couple who upon the death of their daughter gained custody of her children. As they grieved their loss, the situation represented an opportunity, despite the strain and stress of becoming parents all over again.

Minority Groups

The problems and concerns of people of color and other minority groups, including those with disabilities, different sexual orientation, and economic status may require intervention strategies at the micro, mezzo and macro level. In this discussion, the central questions that can guide your selection of an intervention approach with minority clients are summarized as follows:

- *Is the approach flexible enough that it can be adapted to, and respects the cultural beliefs, values, and worldview of diverse groups?*

Green (1999) informs us that "help-seeking behavior" is embedded in a cultural context as well as influenced by the experience of minorities with helping professionals and society (pp. 50–51). Exploring the client's cultural context may include considering gender relations, position in the family, and community. For some groups, helping may, in fact, necessitate a blending of Western and traditional healing systems (Al-Krenawi & Graham 2000; Sue, 2006). Kung (2003) explored the help-seeking behaviors of Chinese Americans and concluded that the act of asking for help—whether formally or informally—has different meanings in different cultures, although the behavior may be influenced by the degree of acculturation. For Asians, according to Kung (2003), personal or emotional problems may not be perceived as important, but instead are considered as personal thoughts, lack of willpower, or failure of self-control (p. 111). The impetus to solve one's own problem is a common phenomenon in many minority and cultural communities, as is the drive to repress feelings and emotions so as not to be characterized as vulnerable or a cultural anomaly (Sue, 2006; Potocky-Tripodi, 2002; Green, 1999; Nadler, 1996; Mau & Jepson, 1990).

Help-seeking behavior is inevitably guided by culture, acculturation, historical experiences, subjective perceptions, and interpersonal deliberations related to the cost-benefit trade-off of seeking help (Nadler, 1996). For example, when presented with an intervention approach, a client's cost-benefit deliberation may be whether the approach allows them to retain their sense of self. The idea of change can be threatening for clients who have limited or no prior experience with formal systems or if the experience involved forceful tactics. Potocky-Tripodi (2002) explains that many immigrants and refugees have had limited contact with formal helping systems before their current contact with the social worker and, furthermore, this contact may have been repressive.[2]

Intervention approaches that call for change from the familiar to the unfamiliar—for example, child rearing practices and beliefs that are customary to a particular group—can present a particular challenge. One couple from a West African country involved with child protection services spoke of the difficulty of unlearning ways of thinking; for example, the ways of disciplining of their children, the custom of arranged marriages, and their loss of position in their community. For their young daughter, the contact was less traumatic. She did, however, emphasize concerns about losing contact with important people in her life; for example, she said, "I miss my grandparents."

When planning interventions with minority clients, another consideration is the extent to which the approach is amenable to the involvement of family. Family ties and relationships have tended to be a source of emotional and concrete support for diverse groups; as such, their inclusion may be critical to goal attainment (Asai & Kameoka, 2005; Chan, Chan & Lou, 2002; Congress, 2002; Green, 1999; Rothman, Gant & Hnat, 1985; Fuentes, 2002; Hodge, 2005; Potocky-Tripodi, 2002). Of course, the inclusion of family members or resource networks needs the agreement of the client. Within particular ethnic groups, grandparents or other esteemed elders using traditional healing practices based on spiritual or religious practices may be included. In this case, the approach needs to be significantly flexible so as to honor and respect these traditions (Gelman, 2004; Hand, 2006; Waites, MacGowan, Pennell, Carlton-LaNey & Weil, 2004; Voss, Douville, Little Soldier & Twiss, 1999; Voss, Douville, Little Soldier & White Hat, 1999).

At this point you might ask, "How am I supposed to help diverse individuals with whom I have contact as a social worker?" Green (1999) refers us to the "discovery procedure" in planning interventions with racial or ethnic minority persons. *Discovery* means to solicit clients' views of the problem at hand; the related symbolic, cultural, and social nuances of their concerns; and their ideas about what should be done to remedy their difficulties. Clients' suggestions will be in harmony with their beliefs, values, and religion or spirituality (Farmer, 1999). Determining clients' worldviews through discovery allows you to implement interventions that clients will perceive as relevant, and to frame the rationale for selecting them in terms that make sense to clients.

- *Does the approach address the sociopolitical climate as a factor in creating and sustaining the client's problem?*

Minority and poor clients, many of whom are involuntary, often face insurmountable odds in their everyday lives as a result of limited resources, pressures to conform to dominant societal norms, marginalized status, and constrained self-determination. Even so, they have strengths, and over time they have been able to cope with adversity (Sousa, Ribeiro & Rodriques, 2006). For lesbian couples, for example, oppression is a tremendous stressor, yet they often exhibit significant resilience (Connolly, 2006).

In order to be effective, intervention approaches must address problems faced by ethnic/racial minority persons and should include attention to the person-in-environment. This means that the approach must take into account the psychosocial and socio-environmental aspects of the problem within the minority experience (Sue, 2006; Lum, 2004; Hurdle, 2002; Potocky-Tripodi, 2002). Moreover, you must weigh the extent to which factors such as race, class, gender, sexual orientation, and the accompanying issues of oppression, toxic environments, and powerlessness have influenced the problem (Dietz, 2000; Green, 1999; Guadalupe & Lum, 2005; Lum, 2004; Pollack, 2004; Rooney, G. D., 2009; Sue, 2006; Spitalnick & McNair, 2005; Van Voorhis, 1998).

Societal presumptions about people, their competence, or lifestyles are oppressive forces that individuals, families, and groups contend with on a daily basis. In most instances, overt acts of discrimination and bigotry have diminished as a result of laws, except in the case of gay and lesbian people. Laws, however, cannot mandate positive interpersonal and social behavior, especially covert interactions. Covert interactions are those subtle acts in the form of microaggression in which people are treated differently based on their race, sexual orientation, ethnicity, ability, or status (Sue, Capodilupo, Torino, Bucceri, Holder, Nadal, & Esquilin, 2007). As such these acts are assaults on cognitive, physical, and psychological functioning.

The nuances of microaggreesion remind people of their status and for the most part are invisible to non-minorities. They also tend to deny with explanations that question the validity of the minority experience. An act of microaggression is typified by an account from the successful African American actor Danny Glover. Referring to his race, irrespective of his achievements, as a lifelong stressor, Glover asserts that "Every day of my life I walk with the idea that I am black, no matter how successful I am" (2004). In many instances, you could insert another minority group member's experience into Glover's statement.

Societal interactions are not the only arena in which minority persons may encounter disparate treatment. Sue et al. (2007), Sue (2006), Hodge (2005), and Palmer and Kaufman (2003) maintain that bias, assumptions about competence or pathology, the distribution of resources and benefits and the exclusion of clients' worldview are often evident in interactions between professionals and clients. Savner (2000) points to evidence of professional bias and differential treatment of African American and Hispanic women leaving welfare. The women reported that information about job opportunities, child care assistance, and support for their educational aspirations was routinely withheld. Whereas workers tended to support and encourage white women to complete their education, African American women reported "being talked to any kind of way" and being told to get a job, as completing a GED was "not what this program is about" (p. 4). This situation should cause you to query whether an intervention approach contributes to or inhibits a client's ability to achieve a stated goal, and further whether the strategy contains prescriptive or formulaic notions about what the client's goals should be. These issues have implications for ethical practice, in particular the principles of dignity and worth and ethics of self-determination, along with related concerns of beneficence, coercion, and paternalism.

What Empirical or Conceptual Evidence Supports the Effectiveness of the Approach?

In planning, matching interventions to problems is a task that is facilitated when empirical evidence has demonstrated that a certain approach is effective for a specified problem or population. You should be able to answer the central question regarding the effectiveness of an approach with specific populations, in particular settings, with diverse populations. Evidence of effectiveness can also be determined by your own deliberate evaluation of your own practice, which would include seeking information from the client. Ideally, measures of progress and effectiveness were developed in collaboration with the client, as they are key informants about what did and did not work. This information is a feedback loop that can be used to inform your practice.

Empirical evidence in support of a particular approach should also specify its effectiveness with respect to client's status, developmental stage, cognitive ability, and consistency with culture and values and beliefs. Each of the four approaches has empirical support for a range of client problems, including minors, and with diverse groups. This information is summarized in the discussion of each approach. You will also note, however, that there is evidence that adaptations and modifications with certain groups were required.

In addition to the empirical support for the four approaches, increasingly research and evaluation studies have provided social workers with comprehensive empirical knowledge they can use to determine the effectiveness of specific intervention approaches. The emergence of evidence-based practice represents significant progress in this regard (Corcoran, 2000a; Corcoran & Fisher, 1999; Jordan & Franklin, 2003). *The Journal of Research on Social Work Practice* has made a significant contribution to evidence-based social work practice, and *The Journal of Evidence-Based Social Work* and *Evaluation in Clinical Practice* promise to do the same.

Is the Approach Compatible with Basic Values and Ethics of Social Work?

An effective intervention approach is one that has the most promise for achieving goals identified by the client or the mandate. It also requires empirical evidence that supports the approach with whom, under what circumstances, and what were the results. In addition, in your selection of a particular approach, you are ethically responsible for having sufficient knowledge and skills to use the approach to resolve a particular client problem.

Social work ethics and values, in conjunction with knowledge and skills, guide decisions about the approach to be implemented. Chapter 4 discussed social work values and ethics extensively, and you may wish to review the chapter as you think about their application to change-oriented strategies. For example, in school settings, your work is linked to the multiple systems to which the minor is connected (Berman-Rossi & Rossi, 1990). Ethical issues can arise when school personnel want to know about the nature of your work with a student. Kutchins (1991) suggests that "unless there is an important legally recognized reason for the professional to convey information about a case," the client has the power to decide "what can be discussed about their situation" (p. 110). Confidentiality can also be an issue when an intervention discussion takes place in the home or in institutional settings such as a hospital or residential facility. When making a home visit, removing an agency identification badge is an additional step that can be taken by you to ensure confidentiality.

Two specific ethical standards are applicable in the selection and intervention approach. A key question to be answered is:

- *Does the approach safeguard clients' rights to self-determination?*

Self-determination as applied to intervention approaches is the extent to which the client is self-directed by their maximal involvement in intervention decisions. Promoting self-determination requires that clients are empowered to fully participate in decisions that will resolve their situation. You might ask, "What if the client has limitations such as in language, cognitive, or mental or physical capacity that can hamper their ability to make self-directed decisions?" In completing the multidimensional assessment, you should be informed about the client's capacities and adjust the approach accordingly. But, people with different capacities are not without strengths. While they may unable to make decisions about some aspects of their lives, their limitations are not the sum total of who they are, nor does it mean that they are unable to process task-specific information. In such cases, you would identify possible decisions and provide them with options. For example, "If we select this approach to resolve your concern, it would mean that you and I would develop tasks that you think would best change your situation."

Fostering self-determination may be particularly challenging with minors, involuntary clients, and when parents, agencies or professionals acting as proxies presume that a client or a client population lacks the capacity for self-direction and for making decisions. Best interest, in many instances, has become a means to sacrifice self-determination, and instead professionals act in a paternalistic manner. The defining question in this regard is what is the justification for a decision that ignores the client's rights? Of course, self-determination is not an unabridged right, for example, in the case of the involuntary client as their rights are constrained by a mandate. Nonetheless, the involuntary client has the right to exercise self-determination without being subjected to coercion or beneficent authority. Because mandates are an intrusion into the private life of an involuntary client, feelings about their loss of freedom may interfere and result in a reactive-based judgment. Hence, they may focus less on their rights and instead comply with what you to tell them to do in order to regain control over their life.

Some clients will not accept the notion of self-determination, believing instead that their marginalized status has destined them to a life of constrained choices. As such, their involuntary status fuels their perception. Yet, your efforts to promote self-direction can be critical at this stage, beginning with your encouraging the client to participate in their case or treatment plan and alerting them to the ways in which they are able to be self-directed (R. H. Rooney, 1992; 2009). The ethical-legal typology developed by Reamer (2005) and Rooney, (1992; 2009) can be a useful screening tool to determine whether an approach is relevant to a client situation. For example, an approach with an involuntary client may be advised legally; however, its use may not be ethical with a particular client at a given point in time.

Self-determination in crisis situations requires that the professional have an awareness of self as well as cultural preference or customs and expressions of emotions. Sommers-Flannagan (2007) and Fullerton and Ursano (2005) emphasize that in crisis situations there is a strong desire to help. This desire, however, can interfere with ethical principles. Therefore, professionals assisting clients in crisis situations should examine their own motives and reactions. They should also be alert to the dynamic of transference so as to avoid circumventing the outcome that the client seeks.

Minors

The issue of the right to self-determination with minors is complicated. In most states, minors are presumed to have limited decision-making capacity; therefore, it is the responsibility of parents or legal guardians to act as their proxy (Strom-Gottfried, 2008). Developmental stage, reasoning, and cognitive capacity are also significant factors that influence a minor's capacity for decision making and self-direction. Minors who are immigrants may be unfamiliar with the ideals of self-determination and consent and they can become anxious or fearful about being asked to make a choice

(Congress & Lynn, 1994). In addition, decisions by minors may be outside of the realm of cultural expectations. Nonetheless, you should not assume that a minor cannot make choices because in general they are able to express how they feel and what they want with respect to their best interest. Your task is to provide the opportunity for them to participate in intervention planning, which includes your explaining potential risks using words that they understand (Green, Duncan, Barnes & Oberklaid, 2003; Strom-Gottfried, 2008). Recall the behavioral intervention school-based group discussed in Chapter 12 in which the social worker encouraged active participation by asking boys about their understanding as to why they were referred to the group. Afterwards she explained to the group her understanding of the referral, citing specific behavioral concerns voiced by their teachers. The boys could then decide whether to stay in the group and consider the risks and benefits of their choice.

Non-Western Perspective

The ethical principle of self-determination is taken for granted in Western society, but it examines a community and sociocultural context. The ideals of autonomy, self-direction, and independence are values that are in sharp contrast to the beliefs of particular cultures. The freedom and success of the individual among Muslims, for example, is understood in terms of group or community success (Hodge & Nadir, 2008). Indeed, for some cultural groups, family, which can include a spiritual leader, relatives, or an entire community will have a prominent role in intervention decisions (Palmer & Kaufman, 2003; Hodge 2005). In these situations, honoring client self-determination may simply be respecting their decisions, especially when they are consistent with the values of the client and his or her community.

- *Can the approach and the rationale for its use be explained to clients in a way that they are able to make an informed decision and give or decline consent?*

Ensuring that clients understand and consent to an approach is essential to ethical collaborative practice. So that clients are fully informed, you should explain the approach in language that they understand and provide them with information about the benefits or risks, including evidence of effectiveness of an approach. This same information should be provided to involuntary clients, even though they lack the freedom to refuse services. They can however be given information about their options and the consequences or their choices.

Similar to self-determination, the ability to give consent is informed by developmental stage, cognitive ability, and reasoning. In particular, informed consent presumes that adult clients not only understand a proposed approach, but are also competent to weigh potential outcomes. Strom-Gottfried (2008, pp. 55–62), cites five developmental factors to be considered in facilitating informed consent with minors:

- Information *is provided in age appropriate, informal language so that the minor is able to understand the approach.*
- Understanding *involves your presenting information in consideration of the age of the minor and his or her "developmental capacity" for comprehension.*
- Competence *in making informed decisions about an approach requires the ability to understand and reason so that a preference can be articulated. Therefore the age and cognitive capacity of the minor are critical, as are social, emotional, cultural, and environmental factors.*
- Voluntariness *refers to freedom from coercion or manipulation in decision making. With minors, decisions can be influenced by a power imbalance between the parent, the social worker, or in the case of involuntary status the court or an institutional placement. Each of these factors can affect decision making. For example, a minor placed out of the home for parental behavior is involuntary and may be emotionally conflicted about their home life and their placement.*
- Reasoning *involves an understanding and the ability to make a choice about the information that is provided, which will vary by age and cognitive ability. Autonomy and self-direction should be supported, however, and social workers should take the extra steps when necessary to assist minors to articulate their views on matters that affect them.*

Competence to give consent can vary with the age of minors and can be abridged in institutional and residential settings where treatment or case plan protocols guide intervention decisions. Further, parents or legal guardians are presumed to act in the best interest of minors, and therefore they are able to give consent (Berman-Rossi & Rossi, 1990) Even so, you should provide minors with an explanation in a language that they are able to understand. Minors, while unable to provide consent, can be asked whether they assent; that is an "affirmative agreement" when a parent has given permission to an approach (Strom-Gottfried, 2008, p. 62).

Am I Sufficiently Knowledgeable and Skilled Enough in this Approach?

The complexities of clients' problems often necessitate having knowledge of different approaches and techniques, and being skillful in how you use them. Eclectic practice does not mean that you select a little bit of this and that from various interventions. Ethically, you must consider if an approach is right for this client at this time, and further, whether you are have the requisite knowledge and skills to·implement the approach.

Models & Techniques of Practice

This section discusses the major tenets and theoretical frameworks of each approach, their implications for practice with diverse populations, including involuntary clients and minors, and their strengths and limitations.

The Task-Centered System

The task-centered system is a social work model developed by social workers William Reid and Laura Epstein. The model's contribution to social work practice is the focus on problems of concern to the client and its emphasis on tasks and the collaborative responsibilities between the client and the social worker.

Tenets of the Task-Centered Approach

The Task centered approach was developed by William Reid and Laura Epstein as a social work practice model. The direction of the approach with regard to goal attainment is both systematic and efficient. Termination begins at the point of contact, facilitated by specific goals and the completion of tasks. The model emerged when the prevailing view of the resistant client and open-ended models were the norm in social work and allied disciplines. Within a brief time-limited period, the model attempts to "reduce problems in living," including those related to interpersonal conflict, difficulties in social relations or role performance, reactive emotional distress, inadequate resources, or difficulties with organizations (Ramos & Tolson, 2008; Reid & Epstein, 1972; Reid, 1992; Epstein, 1992).

Central themes of this approach are that people are capable of solving their own problems and that it is important to work on problems that are identified by the client. Clients' identification of priority concerns and the collaborative relationship are empowering aspects of the model.

Theoretical Framework

Research by Reid and Shyne (1969) informed the development of the approach as an action-oriented model in which problem solving activities occurred within a limited time frame. This research demonstrated that brief focused contact and the conscious use of time limits were as effective as those strategies that required a longer time period. The development of the model was also influenced by Studt's (1968) conception of the efficacy of tasks and structural aspects of Perlman's (1957) problem-solving model. The use of tasks is consistent with Bandura's (1997) research related to self-efficacy. Tasks are intended to facilitate a client's sense that through their effort, "success is eventually possible" (Reid, 1992, p. 59).

The task-centered system is designed to be eclectic. Reid (1992), however, stresses selecting research based theories and interventions. With this in mind, you are able to make use of various theories that are relevant to the client situation (Ramos & Tolson, 2008; Reid, 1992). For example, cognitive restructuring can inform task strategies when feelings, anxieties, and fears are influenced by beliefs or irrational thought patterns (Reid, 1992). Still, Reid cautions that you should first determine that the client's emotional state is consistent with cognitive theory, rather than stressors caused by environmental events or conditions or a crisis situation. In addition the task-centered model allows for the advent of a crisis, in which techniques from the crisis intervention approach may be used.

Empirical Evidence and Uses of the Task-Centered Model

The task-centered system has been adapted to various settings in which social workers practice, and its efficacy has been empirically established with many different client populations, including families, organizations, and communities (Parihar, 1994; Ramarkrishman, Balgopal, & Petts, 1994, 2008; Reid & Fortune, 2002; Pomeroy, Rubin, & Walker, 1995; Reid, 1987, 1997a; Tolson, Reid, & Garvin, 1994). Adaptations of the task-centered approach have been tested in most settings in which social workers practice, including mental health, health care, and family practice (Alley & Brown, 2002; Fortune, 1985; Reid, 1987, 1992, 1997a, 2000) and case management with elderly clients (Neleppa & Reid, 2000).

Examples of application of the model with minors include schools and residential facilities (Bailey-Dempsey & Reid, 1996; Pazaratz, 2000; Reid & Bailey-Dempsey, 1995; Reid, Epstein, Brown, Tolson, &

Rooney, 1980). Effectiveness of task-centered practice has been demonstrated with groups (Lo, 2005; Pomeroy, Rubin, & Walker, 1995; Garvin, 1987; Larsen & Mitchell, 1980) and in supervision and staff development (Caspi & Reid, 2002). Using the task-centered model as a guiding framework (R. H., 1992; 1981) expanded application of the model to include social work practice with involuntary clients in child welfare and minors in a school setting.

Application with Diverse Groups

Ramos and Tolson (2008, p. 286) cite the fact that the task-centered model has been used in agencies in which the client base consists of clients who are from "poor, minority and ethnocultural groups." The model is thought to be sensitive to the experience of minority clients because of its emphasis on the right of clients to identify concerns and the use of tasks to empower clients who are marginalized, lack power, and are oppressed (Ramos & Garvin, 2003; Boyd-Franklin, 1989a). The model also responds to issues characterized by Sue (2006) as "barriers to multicultural clinical practice" because of its explicit acceptance of the client's view of the problem and its action orientation, rather than insightful talking. When faced with day-to-day concerns related to survival, poor or minority clients place more value on concrete actions that respond to their here-and-now needs. In their evaluation of various models of practice, Devore and Schlesinger (1999) conclude that the basic principles of the task-centered system are a "major thrust" in ethnically sensitive practice (p. 121). Because of the model's accommodation of different worldviews it has been translated into several languages and is used outside of the United States in different settings (Ramos & Toseland, 2008).

Procedures of the Task-Centered Model

Figure 13-1 presents an overview of this model. The initial phase begins with the client assuming the primary role in the identification and prioritization of target problems. It is recommended that priority concerns and goals be limited to a maximum of three within a particular time frame. Goals are agreed upon and general and specific tasks are developed to achieve goal attainment. Termination begins with the first session, in keeping with the model's action-oriented, brief time frame. Clients agree to work with you for a particular number of sessions (e.g., six to eight weeks), although there is an

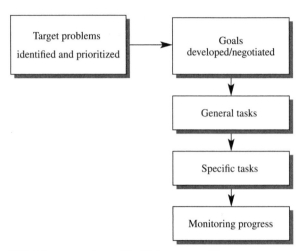

FIG-13-1 Overview of the Task-Centered System

opportunity to extend contact or negotiate a new contract for a different problem. Progress is monitored in each session as the client moves toward termination.

Developing General Tasks

As illustrated in Figure 13-1, when you and the client have identified a target problem and related goals, you are ready to develop general tasks. Recall from the discussion in Chapter 12 related to partialized goals using general tasks. General tasks consist of discrete actions to be undertaken by the client and, in some instances, by you the social worker. Each general task has specific tasks that direct the incremental steps to achieve goals. The following case situations illustrate the target problem, goals, and the general tasks associated with them.

Target Problem 1. Agnes, age 6, Cody, age 8, and Jennifer, age 10, were removed from the custody of their parents because of the unsanitary conditions of the home environment and nutritional neglect. The judge's order states that the children can be returned home when the parents show evidence that the home environment has changed and does not represent a health hazard to the children and that they are provided with regular meals.

Goal: Regain custody of children removed from their home.

As the social worker in this case, you and the parents discuss the conditions that must be met to regain custody of the children. These conditions are reflected in the development of the following general tasks.

General Tasks

1. Improve the sanitary conditions of the home environment.

2. Develop and follow a routine housekeeping schedule in collaboration with the social worker.
3. Develop and implement acceptable nutritional standards using the five food groups appropriate to the age of the children.

Target Problem 2. Justin, age 17, became homeless when his stepfather demanded that he immediately leave home after he came out to the family about his sexual orientation. For the past six months he has alternatively slept under a bridge, in an adult shelter which he dislikes and feels unsafe in, or in an abandoned building that serves as a "flop house" with other homeless youth. As a group, the youth gather on busy street corners and beg for money and food.

Goal 2. To obtain employment so that he can have the means to secure safe and affordable housing.

As the social worker in a youth housing program, you and Justin partialized his goal into the following general tasks.

General Tasks

1. Obtain information about job opportunities.
2. Work with the program's housing coordinator to identify resources for housing options.
3. Enroll in the independent living skills classes provided by the youth program.

Partializing Group or Family Goals

The same processes pertain to a family or a group. In such cases, family or group members are involved in formulating relevant general tasks to accomplish their identified objective. In the following situations a group and a family develop goals and general tasks. In the first situation, residents develop general tasks that will address their target concerns about the conditions of the apartment building where they live. In the second situation, a family living in a transitional housing facility makes plans to move to a permanent residence.

Target Problem 3. Residents of the Logan Square Apartment Complex are concerned about sanitation code violations that the landlord has ignored. He has also ignored their requests for improved conditions, so a small group of residents is ready to take action.

Goal 3. Influence the landlord to maintain city housing code sanitation standards in an apartment complex. The general tasks associated with this goal are described below.

General Tasks

1. Talk with other tenants and mobilize an action group.
2. Plan meetings of the tenants to enlist leaders and develop strategies.
3. Explore resources for obtaining legal representation.
4. Present a formal grievance to the landlord and express the group's intention of pursuing legal means if necessary to force him to make needed improvements.
5. File a complaint with the health department and initiate court action, if necessary.

During the meeting with a group of residents, the members suggested the above general tasks. With such an extensive list, it may be important to ask the group to prioritize general tasks so that they are not involved in a series of simultaneous actions.

Target Problem 4. Mr. and Mrs. Corning, an interracial couple, and their three children, Teshida (age 12), Henri (age 10), and Katrina (18 months) are homeless. Currently, they are living in a family transitional housing facility. Mr. Corning lost his job eight months ago when the county agency where he worked for as a maintenance specialist hired a private contractor to reduce their labor costs. Mrs. Corning is employed in the evenings as a maid at a hotel. Prior to becoming homeless, the family had a comfortable living, owned their home, and they were pleased with the neighborhood and their children's school. When Mr. Corning became unemployed, the couple was unable to pay their bills or maintain their mortgage payment. Initially, the family lived with Mrs. Corning's sister's family.

Both Mr. and Mrs. Corning are concerned about the impact of their stressful situation on their children. To make matters worse, the school reports that Teshida and Henri are having difficulty at school. Both parents feel, however, that the school situation will be resolved once the family is stable. Their preference is to purchase another home, but they realize that at this point they will need to move into an apartment until their financial situation has improved.

Goals

1. Move from transitional housing facility into an apartment.
2. Find employment for Mr. Corning.

The Corning family is faced with two competing needs. They had hoped that Mr. Corning would find employment that would give the family the financial resources to make the move into another house. But at this point, they are eager to move, and therefore are willing to live in an apartment. They identify moving from the housing facility as their priority goal.

They believe that the move will lessen their stress and provide a more stable environment for the children. Mr. Corning can in the meantime continue to look for employment.

General Tasks

1. Meet with the transitional housing case manager to obtain information about affordable three-bedroom apartments.
2. Plan to visit apartments located in the general area where they want to live.
3. Identify schools in the area for the children.
4. Develop a budget.

General Tasks for the Social Worker

From these examples, it is apparent that general tasks involve actions by the client. Yet general tasks can also require actions of you, on their behalf. In the situations involving the parents, as the social worker, you could agree to obtain a nutrition chart for them by contacting the public health department. As the housing coordinator you may undertake the task of locating housing resource options for Justin. In the third example, you may explore possible legal resources, possibly involving representatives of the Logan Square tenants' group in talking with legal aid.

Initially, general tasks may be disconnected and they may not follow a logical sequence. Therefore, they will need to be prioritized by you and the client. Think about the situation in which the goal of the parents was to regain custody of their children. It would be important to determine which of the general tasks are most significant in moving toward this goal, thereby focusing their beginning change efforts on this general task. If timing is critical to regaining custody, then a priority general task might be that the parents concentrate on improving the home environment. Of course, the parents may be unable to begin work on the general task of developing a housekeeping schedule immediately, but they may be able to draft a schedule to review during your next scheduled home visit. With the resident group, mobilizing other residents might be the first step and other general tasks would be prioritized

accordingly. It is important to settle on tasks for which the benefit is obvious and which have a good chance of success for the client. Success with one task encourages clients' confidence in their ability to tackle another task.

Developing Specific Tasks

Even general tasks can prove to be overwhelming to some clients. Thus, the process of partializing continues with the development of specific tasks. The key to the task-centered system is to divide general tasks into specific agreements about which actions the client and you as the social worker will attempt between one session and the next. Specific tasks related to the previously outlined general tasks are illustrated in the following examples.

Goal 1. Regain custody of children removed from their parents because of the condition of their living environment and neglect.

General Task

Improve the sanitary conditions in the home environment.

Specific Tasks

1. Get rid of old magazines and newspapers and unused household items.
2. Obtain the necessary cleaning products and equipment for cleaning the house.
3. Develop and maintain a daily/weekly cleaning schedule.

It may be that each specific task will need to be further broken down into subtasks. For example, if the parents are unfamiliar with cleaning products, subtask may involve reading the product labels so that they understand how to use them. What if the parents are unable to afford cleaning products? This issue would need to be addressed, and perhaps obtaining the needed resources would be a task for you as the social worker to complete.

Goal 3. Influence the landlord to maintain city housing code sanitation standards in an apartment-housing complex.

General Task

Plan meetings of the tenants to elect leaders and develop strategies.

Specific Tasks

1. Send notices to all residents about the purpose of the meetings.
2. Talk to residents about their specific concerns.
3. Plan meetings during a time when a majority of the residents are available.
4. Post announcements of the meeting date, time and place in residents' common areas.

Goals. The Corning family will move from transitional housing facility into an apartment.

General Task

Meet with the transitional housing case manager to obtain information about affordable three-bedroom apartments.

Specific Tasks

1. Schedule a meeting with housing coordinator within the next week.
2. Use the housing information list to review together potential housing options.

Specific tasks may consist of either behavioral or cognitive actions that require effort and perhaps discomfort on the client's part. The following examples illustrate specific behavioral and cognitive tasks.

Behavioral Tasks
Justin

- *Telephone the employment center for information about available jobs in the metropolitan area.*
- *Develop a summary of work experience and abilities.*
- *Study the independent skills manual each day for a specified length of time.*

Parents of Agnes, Cody, and Jennifer

- *Follow the schedule for completing household tasks.*

Logan Square Group

- *Keep other residents informed of the improvements in the housing code violations that the landlord has made in the complex.*

Cognitive Tasks
Justin

- *Practice interview skills with employment counselor.*
- *Take notes on learning from independent living skills manual.*

Parents of Agnes, Cody and Jennifer

- *Review the major food pyramid and include this information in daily meal planning.*

Notice that both general and specific tasks are stated in terms of positive behaviors that clients are to complete. Positively framed tasks highlight growth and gains. Clients tend to be more enthusiastic about tasks oriented to growth and achievement, and accomplishing such tasks often motivates them to undertake even further changes. In contrast, tasks that specify eliminating negative behaviors focus exclusively on what clients must give up.

Partializing goals into general tasks and ultimately into specific tasks can consume a substantial amount of time. Also, the preparation for accomplishing one or more specific tasks can take time. Also, when multiple tasks are developed, it is important to focus on and plan implementation of at least one task before concluding a session. In fact, many clients are eager to get started and welcome "homework assignments." Mrs. Corning for example, asked what the couple could do before the next session. By mutually identifying tasks and planning their implementation in each session, time spent from one session to the next can sharpen the focus on action-oriented steps that facilitate progress.

Brainstorming Task Alternatives

Essential tasks are often readily apparent. Further, because clients are experts about their situation, their decisions are invaluable in developing tasks. They are usually committed to tasks that they identify on their own. As with goals, if such tasks are feasible and realistic, they should be supported. For example, the Corning couple wanted to simultaneously work on moving from transitional housing and finding a job. During the brainstorming session, Mr. Corning suggested a task which involved him exploring an apprenticeship program as a means to obtain employment. With some clients, however, if tasks are less readily apparent to them, you can brainstorm with them to identify a range of alternatives.

Brainstorming is the creative process of mutually focusing efforts on generating a broad range of possible options from which the individual, family or group may choose. Brainstorming can be particularly useful with minors to encourage their ownership of possible actions. However, you may need to initiate the process. Most clients will be generally receptive to your suggestions of tasks. In addition, Reid (2000; 1978) found that there was little difference in the rate with which clients' accomplished tasks suggested by the social worker when compared to those they proposed themselves.

When you suggest tasks during the brainstorming process, however, it is critical to check with the clients to ensure that they agree with and are committed to those tasks. You should be sensitive to nonverbal reactions to your ideas. Commitment and a willingness to engage in tasks are indicators of follow-through by the client (Reid, 1978). In some instances, especially with minors and involuntary clients, you may be tempted to assign tasks. For the most part, clients of all ages and status unlikely to be motivated or receptive to assigned tasks. Assigning tasks, whether in the form of providing advice or giving a directive, have a lesser likelihood of being implemented by clients (Reid, 1997a). Also, you are likely to encounter behavior in the form of reactance with involuntary clients. Reactance theory suggests that individuals are inclined to protect valued freedoms when they perceive that they have limited choices or when choices are imposed on them (Brehm & Brehm, 1981; Miller & Rollnick, 2002). But don't confuse a healthy assertion of individuality with opposition to change.

Dynamics associated with brainstorming tasks within groups or families can require an active facilitation role on your part. Group or family members may assist others by suggesting additional options, some of which may limit of constrain choice. For example, family or group members may quickly suggest tasks that they think other members should complete. In these situations, you should protect individual members' right to choose, without pressure, which tasks they will undertake and, indeed, if they will complete any.

Task Implementation Sequence

After agreeing on one or more tasks, the next step is to assist clients in planning and preparing to implement each task. When skillfully executed, this process augments clients' motivation for undertaking tasks and substantially enhances the probability of successful outcomes. The *task implementation sequence* (TIS) as described by Reid (1975; 2000), involves a sequence of discrete steps. These steps, which are summarized in Table 13-1, encompass major ingredients generally associated with successful change efforts. The results of research findings suggest that clients were more successful in accomplishing tasks when TIS was implemented than when it was not (Reid, 1975; 2000). Although Reid recommends that the TIS be applied systematically, he cautions that you should be sufficiently

---

TABLE-13-1 TASK IMPLEMENTATION SEQUENCE (TIS)

1. Enhance the client's commitment to carry out tasks.
2. Plan the details of carrying out tasks.
3. Analyze and resolve obstacles.
4. Rehearse or practice behaviors involved in tasks.
5. Summarize the task plan.

---

flexible so as to permit adaptation to the sequence appropriate to the circumstances of each case. The Task Implementation Sequence has been modified and adapted to different situations and groups. For example, it has been applied to case management (Neleppa & Reid, 2000), and applied in organizations (Tolson, Reid, & Garvin, 1994), and educational supervision (Caspi & Reid, 2002).

It would be simplistic to assume that merely agreeing to carry out a task ensures that the client has the knowledge, resources, courage, interpersonal skill, or emotional readiness to successfully implement a task. You will notice that the sequence considers clients' motivation, a review of potential obstacles to task completion, and provides for rewards or incentives for task completion. Each step in the sequence is intended to increase a successful outcome. With this rationale in mind, the steps in the sequence are summarized.

Enhance the Client's Commitment to Carry Out a Task

Step 1 in the sequence is directly aimed at enhancing clients' motivation to carry out a task. This step involves clarifying the relevance of tasks to clients' goals and identifying their potential benefits. To follow through with tasks, clients must perceive that the potential gains outweigh the potential costs (including anxiety and fear) associated with risking a new behavior or dealing with a changed situation. Because change is difficult, exploring apprehension, discomfort, and uncertainty is especially critical when clients' motivation to carry out a given task is questionable.

It is advisable to begin implementing step 1 of the TIS by asking clients to identify benefits they will gain by successfully accomplishing the task. In many instances, the potential gains of carrying out a task are obvious, and it would be pointless to dwell on this step. For example, for Justin and Mr. Corning, the gain of obtaining information about employment opportunities is evident. But in group situations, for example the residents of Logan Square, it must be apparent to all members that their tasks will result in improvement in the code violations and a change in the landlord's behavior. In an involuntary client situation, like the parents of Agnes, Cody, and Jennifer, a discussion of benefits may be essential to their motivation. Specifically, the completion of task will result on their regaining custody of their children.

In addition to highlighting benefits, you should engage clients in assessing potential risks and barriers to task completion. In work with groups, you can facilitate a discussion of the benefits and risks of individual goals by eliciting suggestions from other group members. For example, Justin's goal was to achieve independent living, yet he was anxious about living on his own and about finding a job. Members of the independent living skills group in which he was a participant gave voice to some of his concerns. As peer consultants, group members who had experienced feelings similar to Justin's made suggestions based on their own experiences. For example, several group members had suggestions about "how to dress," to avoid the risk of being turned down from a job. Preferably, ideas from members should be solicited after the individual considering a potential change has had an opportunity to contemplate the relative benefits and risks in assuming a task on their own.

Rewards and Incentives for Adult Clients.   In enhancing clients' motivation to change ingrained behaviors, it is sometimes necessary to create immediate incentives by planning tangible rewards for carrying out planned actions. The parents of Agnes, Cody, and Jennifer had a long-established pattern of allowing the kids to eat whatever they wanted, rather than preparing meals. The mother wanted to lose weight, but stated that she "lacked the willpower" to do so.

To enable her to experience success in exercising self-control, the social worker asked her to think about her weight loss and the preparation of balanced nutritious meals for the children as a step toward losing weight. As a further reward, the social worker suggested that the mother identify something she wanted to buy for herself. However, to actually make the purchase, she would need to prepare meals from four of the five food groups on a daily basis otherwise she would forfeit her right to purchase a dress at the local consignment shop. The mother was excited by this challenge and agreed to share it with her husband, whose knowledge of her agreement would be an additional motivating force. If she successfully completed the task, she would realize another incentive—the fact that she had the capacity to consciously exercise willpower.

Rewarding oneself (self-reinforcement), as illustrated in the example, can increase one's motivation for completing a task. Rewards and incentives are particularly relevant when a change in behavior or cognition is associated with the choice of pain over pleasure, such as relinquishing one's free time to engage in activities that may be perceived as unattractive (e.g., studying, household chores). Possible rewards should be identified by assessing each client's unique situation and should be realistically within reach.

Rewards and Incentives for Minors.   Rewards can motivate and create incentives for children to complete tasks, such as finishing homework assignments, minimizing rivalry with siblings, being respectful to teachers, raising a hand and waiting to be called upon in class, or doing household chores. In addition to negotiating tasks with children, you can establish complementary tasks with parents or other significant persons in their lives. The intent of rewards is to help children to complete tasks toward modifying problematic behavioral patterns.

When you create incentives with children, it is important during the early stages of change to reward them immediately, preferably as soon as they perform desired behaviors. Also, reward small changes. Otherwise, children tend to become discouraged and give up, believing they cannot meet the expected standards. Adults often naively assume that elaborate long-range rewards (e.g., get a bicycle in June, go on a field trip) are sufficient incentives. In reality, time does not hold the same meaning for young children as it does for adults. If it is now September, then getting a bicycle in June probably will not sustain their motivation. Even for older children, a smaller reward given soon after the behavior is a far more effective incentive.

In setting up tasks with accompanying incentives or rewards for minors, follow these guidelines:

- *Frame tasks so that children understand what they are to do and when they are to do it is explicitly defined. Also, specify the time frame and the conditions under which the task is to be performed (e.g., every 2 hours, twice daily, each Wednesday, once an hour for the next 4 days).*
- *Designate what can be earned for exhibiting the specific target behavior, and establish a method for tracking the behavior (e.g., each time the child responds appropriately by raising his or her hand in*

class before speaking, responding to requests to clean his or her room). It is useful to construct this system of tracking methods and rewards in conjunction with the child.

- *Invite children to choose the type of reward they wish to earn, because they will choose rewards that have maximal value as incentives.*
- *Establish rewards for specified periods of time (e.g., if the child raises his or her hand for 4 of the 5 days in a week's class, he or she will be able to read a story and earn points toward something the child values.) Whenever possible, it is important to offer relationship rewards, rather than monetary or material items. Relationship rewards involve things such as going to the mall or spending time with friends or other significant individuals.*
- *Provide a bonus for consistent achievements of tasks over an extended period of time.*
- *Encourage task completion by providing consistent and positive feedback, or developing visual indicators that mark the child's progress on tasks as motivators.*

Plan the Details of Carrying Out Tasks

This step, the second one in the sequence is vital in assisting clients to prepare themselves for all of the actions inherent in a task. Most tasks consist of a series of actions to be carried out sequentially, and they may involve both cognitive and behavioral subtasks. For example, before carrying out an overt action, such as requesting repairs from a landlord or undergoing a medical examination, it may be beneficial for clients to prepare themselves psychologically. Preparation may involve a review of potential benefits, addressing and resolving fears by realistically appraising the situation. For individual clients, you may want to help them reflect on past successes, or focus on their spirituality or faith. By including cognitive strategies in this step, you are assisting clients to cope with their ambivalence or apprehension over implementing new actions.

Planning overt actions requires considering the real-life details. For example, the Corning couple discussed whether or not to take their children with them while they looked for an apartment. If they went during the early part of the day, the two older children would be in school. In the evenings, they would need to take all three children, which might be difficult as they would need to use public transportation, which can be a difficult situation with three children. In addition, they would need bus fare for themselves and the older

children. By addressing the details involved in completing the task, there is a greater chance for success. Moreover, by planning and discussing discrete actions with clients you are able to observe cues about their misgivings, fears, or lack of skill, each of which must be addressed.

The Social Worker's Role in Task Planning. Sometimes task planning may involve tasks to be carried out by the social worker; however, these tasks are coordinated with the client's actions. Clients may also wonder about what your role in task planning. Mrs. Corning, for example, asked the social worker, "What kinds of things do you do? I'm not clear about how you can help us." In planning the details of tasks, a social worker's tasks can be developed when he or she has ready access to resources or information that will facilitate client work. In the Corning case, the social worker agreed to obtain information about financial assistance for families moving from transitional housing. If the client could benefit from eventually being able to carry out the task on his or her own, it will be useful for the client and the social worker to walk through the steps together. In some instances, social workers may accompany or arrange for someone else to accompany the client during the performance of a task. In a group or family situation, the social worker can engage a group or family member to assist in the planning of carrying out actions.

Conditions for Tasks. Planning the details of tasks also involves specifying the conditions under which each task will be carried out. For example, a sixth-grade student who constantly disturbs his peers, speaks without raising his hand, and irritates his teacher through boisterous teasing behavior may accept the following task: listen attentively when the teacher is speaking during the 1-hour math class and raise his hand three times to answer questions during that time. He agrees to carry out this task each day for the next 5 days. Although he exhibits the problematic behavior in other classes, the math class and time frames identified are the conditions in which the behavioral tasks are to occur. While the goal is to eventually change his behavior in all classes, it would be unrealistic to expect a drastic and immediate new behavior.

Why specify the conditions and time for implementing tasks in such detail? When these points are left vague, clients (and social workers) tend to procrastinate, leaving little time to effectively implement the requisite actions. Also, focusing on behaviors in the math class further partializes the change effort for the sixth-grader. In determining a time frame, his input should be elicited regarding the amount of time he feels is needed to accomplish a specific task.

In selecting and planning tasks pertaining to *ongoing* goals, you should observe an additional caution. Because progress on such goals is incremental, it is vital to begin with tasks that are within the clients' capacity to achieve. In the previous classroom situation, for example, a goal of having the student raise his hand for 5 straight days may be difficult for him to achieve. However, a goal of raising his hand in math class for 3 out of 5 days may, with positive feedback from the teacher, be more attainable. His chances of later completing tasks (5 out of 5 days) are greater if he succeeds in implementing the initial task. Conversely, if he experiences failure on the initial tasks, his confidence and courage may decline, making him reluctant to assume future tasks. Reducing his boisterous behavior may be a much more difficult task, in particular, if the benefit of this behavior is reinforcing attention from peers, which he values. It is thus preferable to have the first task be easy—for example, raising his hand before speaking in class.

Analyze and Resolve Obstacles

Based on recognition of the inevitability of barriers that impede change, this step is aimed at acknowledging and addressing these forces. When implementing this step, you and the client deliberately anticipate and analyze obstacles that have the potential to influence task accomplishment. In the classroom situation previously described, for example, it would be useful to explore potential obstacles to attentive listening such as social, physical or psychological barriers.

In Justin's case, making a telephone call to inquire about available jobs appears to be a relatively simple task. But an obstacle, such as whether Justin has the resources to complete this task is a potential difficulty that should be addressed. Eamon & Zhang (2006) for example, found that social work students failed to assess economic resources as a barrier that prevented client from completing tasks. A caveat should be observed, however: A simple action for some people, such as making a phone call may prove difficult for others depending on their level of confidence, cognitive capacity or social ability. In addition, fears and cognitions can pose formidable barriers to accomplishing a task and require careful exploration so that they do not impede progress. For example, Mr. Corning: Although he was eager to find employment, his confidence was hampered by the experience of "being laid off" and his

perception of being a failure because of his belief that "a man ought to provide for his family."

When tasks are complex, obstacles likewise tend to be complex and difficult to identify and resolve. Tasks that involve changes in patterns of interpersonal relationships tend to be multifaceted, encompassing subsidiary but prerequisite intrapersonal tasks as well as a mastery of certain interpersonal skills. Successfully resisting the impulse to engage in boisterous behavior by the sixth-grader in the classroom may, for example, involve powerful fears about being rejected by what is to him an important social group and appearing to be "lame." Change for him involved not only mastering new behaviors, it also meant changing his patterned behavior of relating in the classroom environment.

Identifying Potential Barriers and Obstacles. Clients vary in their capacity to anticipate obstacles. Overlooking or underestimating the impact of barriers can delay or cause needless difficulties in the accomplishment of tasks and lead to outright failure. With continuous engagement and collaboration, however, you can identify possible obstacles to completing a planned course of action. You can safeguard clients' self-efficacy by explaining that obstacles are common and by sharing observations that you have regarding potential obstacles. With the sixth-grader, the two of you would brainstorm scenarios that could hamper his capacity to raise his hand before speaking in class. What if, for example, he raised his hand and the teacher did not call on him? What would he do if he was eager to answer a question posed by the teacher, and someone else was quicker than he in responding? In reviewing different scenarios with him, potential obstacles are identified and possible responses are clarified in advance. This discussion in effect maximizes his opportunity to engage in the targeted behavior.

Psychological barriers to accomplishing tasks are often encountered regardless of the nature of the target problem. Applying for a job, changing classroom behavior, talking to a judge, and expressing intimate feelings are all tasks that are charged with strong emotions, and therefore seem threatening to some people. A prerequisite to the successful accomplishment of a task, therefore, may be a subsidiary task of neutralizing emotions. This can be accomplished (often in a brief amount of time) by eliciting and clarifying the client's apprehension, rationally analyzing it, and modeling and rehearsing the behavior required to implement the task successfully. Any time and effort that are invested in the exploration of obstacles are likely to pay dividends in the form of clients achieving a higher rate of success in accomplishing tasks. Consider the economy of this process, as failure to complete tasks further extends the time required for successful problem solving.

Addressing Barriers and Obstacles.   After identifying obstacles to task implementation, you must next assist the client in overcoming them. The barriers encountered most frequently include deficiencies in social skills, and misconceptions and irrational fears associated with performing tasks. The former is a formidable barrier that must be overcome, because the client may lack the skill and experience to know how to carry out a task. Some clients (especially minors) are afraid of bungling a task and appearing ridiculous. Undertaking the task thus is perceived as placing the client's self-efficacy in jeopardy. Modeling and behavioral rehearsal in sessions may encourage and teach the skills necessary to carry out interpersonal tasks.

Cognitions—specifically, misconceptions and irrational beliefs about self, stereotypic perceptions of others, and intense apprehensions based on distorted consequences of actions—represent major obstacles to task completion. Cognitive theorists present a compelling case to the effect that the quality and intensity of emotions experienced in a given situation are largely determined by the perceptions and attributions or meaning associated with that situation. Inordinate fear and apprehension, for example, signal that something is amiss in the client's patterns of thought. Mr. Corning for example, when explaining the couple's situation, showed that he was preoccupied with his personal struggle related to his job loss. "Nothing is comfortable about this situation," he asserted at one point. Further, he believes that the company that gained the "county cleaning contract would employ people who were not legal citizens," depriving him and others of jobs.

Your task is to elicit the problematic emotions, to identify their cognitive sources, and to assist clients in aligning their thoughts and feelings with reality. Removing this barrier usually enables them to move several points higher on the readiness scale.

Assessing Clients' Readiness to Begin Tasks.   You should be alert to nonverbal behaviors as potential obstacles or as possible indicators of clients' apprehension about undertaking a task. When you detect such reactions, you should further explore the presence of this nonverbal barrier. At one point, Mr. Corning, for example, appears to be annoyed and remains mostly quiet unless prompted by the social worker or Mrs. Corning. When asked about his willingness to develop tasks, he states, "I am ready to do something, instead of sitting

here talking, I could be out looking for a job or a place for my family to live. So, let's get on with it."

Assessing clients' readiness to engage in mutually negotiated tasks is critical to successful task implementation. Their readiness, however, should not be confused with feeling comfortable; it is neither realistic nor desirable to expect clients to feel altogether comfortable with the task. A certain amount of tension and anxiety is to be expected. Tension and anxiety nonetheless can act to positively motivate clients to risk the the new behavior embodied in the task. Inordinate anxiety, by contrast, may be a major deterrent to undertaking a task as it can impair a client's capacity to attempt the task. Obviously, when clients report that they did not carry out a task, you should consider the possibility that the task was developed prematurely and whether unforeseen barriers to its completion emerged. Another possible explanation for failure to complete tasks is that the client was inadequately prepared or not committed to the task. These and other factors are discussed later in this chapter.

Clients' readiness for implementing tasks can be gauged by asking them to rate their readiness on a scale from 1 to 10, where 1 represents a lack of readiness and 10 indicates that the client is ready to go. When clients rate their readiness on the low end of this scale, their reticence must be explored. To ease any lingering concerns, you can assure them that a certain amount of apprehension is natural and that relief may come as a by-product of successful implementation of the task. You can provide support by expressing confidence in the client's ability to successfully implement the task and by conveying an expectation that the planned actions will be carried out.

An explanation and support are important especially when clients are hesitant to the point of postponing taking actions. Clearly, when you have reached the point of developing and planning for tasks, hesitations on the part of clients can be frustrating. But exploring the reasons for a low rating on the readiness scale will often uncover vital information concerning potential obstacles that should be addressed, including reservations about completing the task.

Rehearse or Practice Behaviors Involved in Tasks

Certain tasks involve skills that clients lack or behaviors with which they have had little or no experience. Step 4 of the TIS is aimed at assisting clients to gain the experience and mastery in performing behaviors essential to task accomplishment. Bandura (1977) builds a strong case for mastery which has been documented by research. Specifically, he asserts, that that the degree of an individual's positive expectation in their ability to perform, will in effect determine how much effort they will expend, and how long they will persist in the face of obstacles or aversive circumstances. It follows that a major goal of the helping process is to enhance clients' sense of self-efficacy, which is accrued through successful task completion. Successful experience, even in simulated situations fosters the belief that the individual has the ability to carry out a task effectively. An expectation of success is vital, as Bandura (1977) has indicated: "The strength of people's convictions in their own effectiveness is likely to affect whether they will even try to cope with given situations" (p. 193).

Research evidence cited by Bandura (1977, p. 195) indicates that, once established, self-efficacy and skills tend to be transferred by individuals to other situations including those which they had previously avoided. According to Bandura, people receive information about self-efficacy from four sources:

- Performance accomplishments: *Major methods of increasing self-efficacy through performance accomplishment include assisting clients to master essential behaviors through modeling, behavior rehearsal, and guided practice, all of which we discuss at length later in this chapter. An example of performance accomplishment would be assisting the sixth-grader to master specific communication skills during an actual session.*
- Vicarious experience: *Insight may be gained by observing others demonstrate target behaviors or perform threatening activities without experiencing adverse consequences and can also generate confidence and expectations in clients. Efficacy expectations based on observing you or others model desired behaviors or receiving reassurance is useful. Observing others, however, is clearly not as powerful as the sense of self-efficacy that results from the client successfully completing a task.*
- Verbal persuasion: *Raises outcome expectations rather than enhancing self-efficacy per se. Information about one's capabilities based on perceptions and assumptions that one can also perform competently is, however, quite persuasive and provides concrete evidence of self-efficacy.*
- Emotional arousal: *A source of information about self-efficacy based on the fact that the perceived level of emotional arousal affects how people perform. Clients who are extremely anxious or fearful about performing a new behavior are unlikely to have*

sufficient confidence that they can perform the behavior competently. Interventions directed toward reducing anxiety or fear or toward persuading clients to believe they are not fearful or anxious are generally ineffective. Evidence cited by Bandura (1977) indicates that to be effective, reductions in emotional arousal must be genuine and not based on deceptive feedback aimed at assuring clients they are not anxious when, in fact, they are anxious. Emotional arousal obviously is an undependable source of self-efficacy because it is not related to actual evidence of capability. Indeed, perceived self-competence tends to reduce emotional arousal rather than the converse.

Of these four sources, performance accomplishment is especially influential because it is based on personal mastery experience.

Increasing Self-Efficacy through Behavioral Rehearsal, Modeling, and Role-Play. Having defined the sources of information about self-efficacy, behavioral rehearsal when indicated can be an important next step. Used in an actual session, behavioral rehearsal assists clients to practice new coping patterns under your guidance. Indications for using this technique include situations that clients feel inadequately prepared to confront a situation or when clients are uneasy or appear overwhelmed by the prospects of carrying out a given task. This technique is an effective way of assisting clients to develop the requisite skills and diminish the threat posed by the action. Such tasks usually involve interacting with significant other people with whom strain already exists or is expected to develop as a result of the planned actions.

Role-playing is the most common mode of behavioral rehearsal. Before engaging clients in rehearsal of desired behaviors, however, you can use role-playing to have clients demonstrate their initial levels of skills. In this way, you can model skills that build on clients' existing skills. Modeling behavior that clients are expected to perform before actually having them rehearse the behavior can be effective when the behavior is unfamiliar to them, or when the client is anxious or concerned about how others will perceive his or her behavior. Modeling through role-play has been amply documented to be an effective means of enabling clients to learn vicariously new modes of behavior and of reducing anxieties or other concerns.

When modeling a particular behavior, ask the client to play the role of the *other* person involved in the real-life difficulty and, in doing so, simulate as accurately as possible the anticipated behavior to be encountered in the actual situation. In the following case example, the social worker successfully assisted a client to overcome perceived obstacles using role-play.

Case Example

The client had lost his job because the chicken processing plant in the small town where he lived relocated its operations to another state. Although he had contact with potential employers, he was anxious about approaching them regarding a job. Both his father and his grandfather had worked at the chicken processing plant, so when he applied to work there after high school, few questions were asked. Now, however, there were issues in his past that the client felt might deter a potential employer from hiring him.

To address his concerns, the social worker acted out the role of the client, with the client assuming the role of a potential employer. In this role, the client was able to pose the questions that he feared he might be asked, as well as explore his qualifications for potential jobs. The role-playing enabled the social worker to model appropriate behavioral responses to questions that might otherwise overwhelm the client. After the role-playing, they discussed what happened, focusing on the client's behavioral and cognitive reactions. The social worker also found it beneficial to explain her rationale for particular responses and to share difficulties she experienced with particular questions. In assuming the role of the client in an interaction with a potential employer, the social worker gained new insights and a fuller appreciation of the difficulties the client expected to encounter.

After completing a modeling exercise, the client and the social worker moved to the next step. They reversed roles, so that the client was able to rehearse the actual target behavior. When the social worker assumed the role of a potential employer, she acted out the anticipated behavior of an employer, including tone of voice, facial expressions, gestures, choice of words, and provocative behavior as role-played earlier by the client. The client's responses to the simulated behavior provided an opportunity for the social worker to make corrective suggestions, and to provide reinforcement and encouragement.

Role-playing and behavioral rehearsal are techniques that can increase a client's capacity to tackle situations in real life. Indeed, potential barriers or obstacles can best be assessed and resolved by observing behaviors that occurred during the behavior rehearsal and role-play. Most importantly, clients' confidence to carry out tasks is enhanced by this technique.

Behavioral rehearsal need not be confined to sessions. It is often productive to encourage clients to continue rehearsing target behaviors on their own by pretending to be involved in real-life encounters. Also, modeling and behavioral rehearsal need not be restricted to social workers and individual clients. Members of a group or family session can model effective and realistic coping for each other. Indeed, a rule of thumb in conducting group role-playing sessions is to tap into members' resources for coping in a help-giving role.

If modeling proves ineffective, an interim strategy could focus on implementing *coping efforts* rather than achieving *mastery*. Coping emphasizes the struggles that a person might expect to experience in performing the behavior or activity. Emphasizing coping lessens anxiety and, hence, the threat of having to perform without making a mistake.

Modeling need not be limited to overt behaviors. Many clients will benefit from modeling of covert behaviors because this strategy can help them to overcome cognitive barriers to task accomplishment. Covert modeling involves expressing aloud thoughts and feelings associated with manifest difficulties and restructuring thoughts in a way that is more productive for dealing with or coping with problems. As with modeling of overt behavior, covert modeling could emphasize coping rather than mastery. As clients mobilize the efficacy, energy, and courage gained through behavioral rehearsal, they prepare themselves to confront problematic situations directly with a more realistic perspective.

Guided Practice. Closely related to behavioral rehearsal, guided practice is another technique to aid task accomplishment. It differs from behavioral rehearsal in that it consists of in vivo rather than simulated behavior. Using guided practice as a mode of intervention, you assist clients to gain mastery of target behaviors by observing and coaching them as they actually engage in the target behaviors. For example, in family sessions, you can observe interactions and subsequently assist family members to master problem-solving or conflict resolution skills. As you observe problematic behavior firsthand, you can provide immediate feedback. Such on-the-spot interventions enable you to clarify what is occurring as well as coach clients in engaging in more productive behavior.

Summarize the Task Plan

Implementation of this final step of the TIS involves reviewing the various actions that clients must engage in to accomplish a task. This step, which takes place in the concluding segment of an individual, family, or group session, enables clients to leave the session with a clear understanding of what they are to do, in what sequence, and under what conditions. To enable clients to gain maximum benefit from this step, you ask them to review the details of their task implementation plan, including strategies discussed for dealing with potential obstacles. By eliciting clients' details of their plans, you can determine whether certain aspects of the plan need to be clarified. It is often useful to begin by describing your own plans to complete tasks in a specified time frame: "I have agreed to contact the public health nurse by our meeting next week." In follow-up, you would request the client to review and summarize their plans: "What are your plans for cleaning the house by our next session?"

Many clients find it beneficial for you to prepare a list of agreed-upon tasks. Some clients prefer to write their own lists. In either case it is useful for both you and the client to have a copy of the agreed upon tasks. A copy is also included in the case record or SOAP notes. This information can be used to monitor and review progress as well as in evaluation at the termination phase.

After summarizing the plan for task implementation, it is appropriate to terminate the session. An effective way of closing the session is to express support for clients' plans and an expectation that they will implement the assigned tasks. It is recommended that you devote the beginning of the next session to task review and progress.

Maintaining Focus and Continuity

The strength of the task-centered system lies in its focus on change through task accomplishment and its systematic format that promotes continuity of change efforts. Individual sessions are sharply focused, and continuity is maintained from one session to the next. Each session begins with a review of clients' experiences in implementing tasks that were agreed upon during the previous session. The task form introduced in Chapter 12 (Figure 12-2 on page 315) enables both you and the client to monitor progress. Social workers in the case examples included in this section report that the task form is not merely a useful guide for task development, but also a helpful tool for reviewing the status of tasks at the beginning of each session. They also affirmed the benefit of giving clients a copy of the form because it

helped them to focus on activities to be implemented between sessions. It was also a visual reminder that they were making progress. Minors especially liked the idea of checking-off tasks that they had completed.

In addition to maintaining focus and continuity, there are two other major objectives (and benefits) of discussing clients' experiences in implementing tasks. First, both clients and you can identify ways in which clients can further improve their effectiveness in performing newly developed behaviors. This discussion may enhance clients' comfort in coping with problematic situations and suggest additional activities in the session to refine their skills. Second, you can explore clients' perceptions of the tasks' effects on others and clients' feelings as they implemented the tasks. This discussion provides an opportunity to identify additional work to be done and prepares the ground for mutually planning future tasks.

In reviewing task accomplishments, it is critical to elicit the details about the conditions, actions, or behaviors that assisted clients in achieving a task. Even when tasks have been only partially completed, it is important to connect the results achieved to clients' efforts. Highlighting that clients have more control than they had previously realized is a powerful force for increasing their sense of self-efficacy.

After completing a review of task implementation, social workers and clients should mutually plan additional tasks that will enable clients to make more progress toward their final goals. In addition to following the steps previously delineated for defining tasks, it is important in working toward accomplishment of *ongoing goals* to plan tasks that involve incremental changes and build on one another. Planning tasks that are graded in difficulty improves clients' chances of success and tends to increase their motivation to exert greater efforts in the change process. To illustrate the gradual progression in developing tasks, recall the client who was seeking employment after the plant closure. His initial task involved contacting potential employers to find out about available jobs. After talking with potential employers by phone, as a next step he would complete applications at those employers where jobs were available. An additional next step may involve the client following up by phone to determine the status of his applications.

Failure to Complete Tasks

In actual practice, progress may not be as smooth as the preceding example implies. Maintaining focus and continuity can become derailed when tasks are not completed. Clients may fail to carry out tasks for a variety of reasons, some of which are summarized in Figure 13-2. In the figure, the reasons for low task performance are classified into two categories: reasons related to specific tasks; and reasons related to the target problem.

Performance Problems Related to the Task

Occasionally, unforeseen circumstances or unanticipated obstacles such as the unavailability of others necessary to complete the task or a crisis may preclude task accomplishment between sessions. In this case tasks are carried over to the next week. In other cases, the failure to complete tasks may stem from a lack of commitment, the emergence of more pressing problems, negative reactions to the social worker or to the group, vague or unspecified tasks, or inadequate preparation. In any event, the reasons for a failure to complete the task should be explored. Also, the factors that block implementation should be identified and resolved. The caveat, of course, is that both the social worker and the client agree that the specified task remains valid. If the task is not valid, it is important to shift the focus to more relevant tasks.

Occurrence of a Crisis.   Although it is advisable to be flexible in shifting focus, it is equally important to avoid allowing crises to dominate change efforts. For those clients who live from crisis to crisis, it is often beneficial for them in the larger scheme of their lives to maintain focus on tasks through to completion. Certain situations may dictate taking a brief detour of course of action, especially when the failure to complete tasks in the focal situation is related to overriding problems a client has not yet revealed. Some clients disclose only relatively minor difficulties during initial interviews and defer

discussing more thorny problems until they feel more comfortable with the social worker. Hence, the initial tasks may not be valid in that they do not relate to the clients' paramount concerns. In such cases, it is appropriate to shift the focus to more urgent difficulties and to formulate new goals and tasks accordingly. It is important, however, to clarify whether the shift in focus is a reinforcing a pattern of avoidance.

Lack of Commitment.   Clients may sometimes fail to complete tasks because of a lack of commitment. Reid (1977, 1997a, 2000) has documented this factor as a statistically significant predictor of task progress on a consistent basis. A lack of commitment should not be confused with a lack of readiness. In the former case, the willingness to change is absent. In the latter case, clients possess the willingness but are blocked from acting by other barriers.

One frequent cause of a lack of commitment to undertake interpersonal tasks is a covert unwillingness to own one's part of a problem. "I would raise my hand if the teacher would call on me," is an example of paying lip service to carrying out a specific task but subsequently making excuses for not doing so. Inwardly, unwilling clients may blame others for their behavior and passively wait for others to initiate corrective actions. In family situations, when a commitment is weak, or blame is involved, it is important to explore further the interactions between all involved so as to clarify which part of the difficulty is owned by each individual. The technique of confrontation may also be used to help clients recognize their responsibility for maintaining the undesirable status quo when they dawdle and wait for others to change. If clients exhibit a continued hesitancy to work on tasks, it is appropriate to explore their willingness to change using ethical confrontation which is discussed in Chapter 17.

A lack of commitment to carry out specific tasks is frequently a dynamic in practice with involuntary clients. Their reactions may also reflect the fact that their problem is attributed, rather than acknowledged (e.g., the judge believes that I have a drinking problem). In other instances, clients may not fully appreciate the consequences of failing to address the requirements of a mandated problem. In these instances, it is your responsibility to engage such clients by acknowledging and respecting their reactions, and by creating an incentive for change. Persistent failure to carry out tasks, however, belies expressed intentions; inaction certainly speaks louder than words, and the benefits of continuing to work with the client should be carefully weighed.

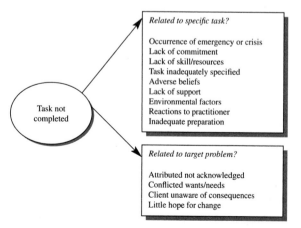

FIG-13-2 Reasons for Low Task Performance

Planning and Implementing Change-Oriented Strategies 377

Of course, what may initially appear to be clients' lack of commitment may actually reflect their focus on other, more pressing concerns. Clients with multiple problems that have stretched their coping skills to the limit may experience difficulties that supersede the target problem. Such situations require judicious handling, because both social worker and client face a difficult decision. It is important to be flexible and to shift focus when emerging problems demand immediate attention. When a client constantly shifts from one issue to another, he or she should be made aware of the consequence of making minimal progress on a target problem.

Unspecified or Vaguely Specified Tasks. Frequently clients fail to complete tasks because those tasks are vague or inadequately specified—that is, the client did not understand what to do. In other cases, failure may result from clients' adverse beliefs. For example, some parents hesitate to utilize reward systems, believing that parents should not barter with children (Rooney, 1992, p. 241). In practice with families or couples, individual members may renege on their commitments to carry out tasks because each party does not trust the other members to carry out their part of the bargain. Further, individuals may gather "evidence" that others are uncommitted to the agreed-upon task, in an effort to justify their own noncompletion of tasks. Adequate preparation for an initial task with couples or families may entail the exploration of the trust and developing a contract stating that each individual will strictly monitor his or her own task performance regardless of whether the other person does or does not.

Lack of Support. When a client's problems involve another system—and especially when the behaviors of others impose on identified problems—relevant individuals should be involved in supporting task accomplishment. For example, the teacher of the sixth-grader should be encouraged to call on him when he raises his hand, or give him an indication that she will so in time. Sometimes families will accommodate change in individual members, at other times family dynamics can conspire to defeat efforts to change or modify behavior. Rather than change, the family opts to maintain a sense of equilibrium, essentially preferring the comfort of the familiar. Families may also exhibit pervasive interactional patterns that make it extremely difficult for members to change without great cost unless adjustments are made in the entire system. Although involving all family members in such situations is difficult, their participation is essential in sessions to assess individual needs

and to garner their support for the individual's goal and task planning.

Stage of group development is a factor that plays a role when the social worker is assisting groups to assume tasks. Group members have difficulty accomplishing significant change-oriented tasks in the first two stages of group development. In these stages, members generally test out the social worker, other group members, and the group itself, while simultaneously attempting to find their own positions. Thus, they sometimes have little psychic energy or commitment to accomplish individual or group tasks. For this reason, tasks should be kept simple, and accomplishing them should not require an inordinate investment of effort by members. For instance, requiring a newly formed group of delinquent adolescents in a correctional facility to change their antagonistic behavior toward staff or peers before they are "emotionally committed" to the purposes of the group is doomed to failure. Conversely, asking members to complete small tasks during the week so that the group might participate in an attractive activity may be more appealing.

Negative Reactions to the Social Worker. Negative reactions to the social worker may also block task accomplishment. Reactions can result for example when tasks are arbitrarily assigned. Assigning tasks tends to activate negative feelings in clients akin to those experienced toward a parent or another authority figure.

Negative reaction to a social worker who has failed to complete a task on behalf of the client is another factor that may block task accomplishment. For example, a client expressed her frustration with a social worker thus: "She keeps telling me that she is going to call the job resource center, and week after week, she tells me that she was so busy." Progress is also impeded when the social worker neglects to review the client's experience in implementing a task, is unorganized or appears unprepared for the session, or changes the focus to other topics before actually seeing previous efforts through to completion. Such shifts disrupt the continuity of change efforts and foster "drift," which dilutes and prolongs the helping process. Clients may also have strong reactions to both verbal and nonverbal cues sent by the social worker, particularly if they perceive a lack of empathy, attentiveness, or positive regard on the social worker's part, or the interaction is highly confrontational.

Inadequate Preparation. A final factor sometimes involved in failures either to attempt or to implement tasks is inadequate preparation. The skills needed to complete a task may be overestimated, or the time needed to completing a task may be underestimated. Actually, it is better for clients not to attempt tasks than to attempt them and fail because they are unprepared. In the former instance, the impact on self-confidence is usually minimal, and additional efforts can adequately prepare them. Failure, by contrast, may undermine clients' confidence in the helping process.

Even when preparation has been adequate, successful outcomes of task efforts are not guaranteed. Unanticipated reactions of others, ineffectual task performance, panic reactions, inappropriate task selection based on inaccurate assessment and adverse circumstances may all block goal attainment. To avoid or minimize undue discouragement of clients when results are negative, you should interpret such results not as failures but as indications of the need for additional information and further task planning. Indeed, negative results sometimes serve a constructive purpose by further informing you of the dynamics underlying problems, thereby enabling you and the client review the assessment of the target problem, and related goals and tasks.

Performance Problems Related to the Target Problem

Issues related to low task performance with regard to the target problem can occur when the problem is attributed to, rather than acknowledged by, the client. This situation frequently occurs when clients are mandated (involuntary) or coerced (nonvoluntary) to seek help. Furthermore, if goals and tasks have already been determined by an outside authority, involuntary or nonvoluntary clients may be reluctant to seek help for a problem that they have not acknowledged: "I don't have a drug problem. Sometimes I do a little meth [methamphetamine] with my buddies, but that don't mean that I'm a drug head."

In other instances, failure to perform a required task may stem from the client's lack of understanding about the consequences of their failure. For example, completing a chemical dependency treatment program and providing clean urinalysis samples (UAs) when tested is a requirement of being able to return to work. In some cases, clients may have coped with a problem for so long, and seen their own efforts to resolve the issue fail so many times, that they lack hope. Clients may then agree to undertake certain tasks without having any confidence that they have the capacity to alter their situation (e.g., "I tried to break away from the gang, but they kept coming at me"). Any of these circumstances will require concerted effort on your part to assist clients to gain the momentum to move forward. These types of situations may be an opportunity to use role-play or behavioral rehearsal.

Monitoring Progress

One way of maintaining focus and continuity is to regularly monitor progress made toward goal attainment. Although measuring and monitoring progress was discussed in Chapter 12, the following objectives relate to a systematic review of progress specific to the task-centered approach.

1. Once tasks have been identified and agreed upon, time in each session is devoted to a review of progress. In this process both client and social worker are able to document which tasks have been completed, and the extent to which the target problem has changed.

2. During the review process, if tasks have not been completed or had the intended effect on the target problem, reasons for low task performance are explored. When necessary, tasks can be renegotiated or new ones developed.

3. The task and goal form helps clients to observe their incremental progress toward their ultimate goal.

4. Clients' views of their progress, change or lack thereof can be documented using a rating scale. Ratings can be done on a weekly basis to maintain focus on goals and enhance the continuity of change efforts. Tasks are marked as completed, in progress, or incomplete in the case record and are reviewed accordingly.

5. The completion of tasks are indications of progress toward goal attainment and the move toward termination.

Overall, maintaining a change focus on the target problem and goals is accomplished by the continuous development of tasks. This process provides immediate feedback of gains as well as alerting the client and social worker about potential adjustments that need to be made. Ultimately, measuring and monitoring progress should clarify the status of the identified target problem and related goals.

Strengths & Limitations

The task-centered approach is an empirically based model of a planned short-term problem-solving approach, developed within social work. With more than 30 years of development, the efficacy of the model is supported by empirical evidence and has demonstrated an effective application with diverse client situations and in diverse and international settings

(Ramos & Garvin, 2003; Ramos & Tolson, 2008; Reid, 2000, 1996, 1997). The emphasis on taking action on problems acknowledged by clients is appealing to racial and ethnic minorities (Boyd-Franklin, 1989a; Devore & Schlesinger, 1999; Lum, 2004).

The model honors both strengths and empowerment by allowing clients' to define the problem, the acceptance of their judgment about goals and tasks, and their participation in measuring progress. Tasks are instrumental in mobilizing action by the social worker and the client to resolve the target concern. To increase clients' self efficacy and opportunity of mastery, obstacles are identified once tasks are developed. Session reviews of tasks allow for the systematic monitoring of progress. When tasks are not completed, the reasons for low task performance are reviewed and new tasks can be developed. The major components of task accomplishment, namely, preparation, implementation, and follow-up, are foundational in all of the specific change-oriented interventions (Hoyt, 2000).

Critics have suggested that the approach is too structured and that a therapeutic relationship with clients is unlikely to develop in such a brief period. The model, therefore, is not feasible with certain types of clients and problem situations. For example, time limits, a central tenet of the model, may not be compatible with clients who seek an insight-oriented approach or ongoing support (Ramos & Tolson, 2008). Nevertheless, many of the tactics of the system can be employed to increase the efficiency of other types of interventions. Progress can often be accelerated in open-ended interventions; for example, by maintaining a sharp focus on an identified task and continuity which are key aspects of the system.

Ramos and Tolson (2008) suggest that involuntary clients, especially those who refuse to identify a change or refuse present a particular challenge, are not considered to be good candidates for the approach. Of course, a central question might be, whether any approach will work with such clients. Building on the basic thrust of the model, specifically the clients' view of the mandate and task implementation strategies R. H. Rooney (1992), has demonstrated its applicability to involuntary clients. In his work, Rooney found that these strategies had the potential to reduce reactance, and engage the client.

Crisis Intervention

The crisis intervention model discussed in this text is the equilibrium model, which is based on basic crisis theory. Knowledge of this practice approach is considered to be "essential for competent social work practice" (Knox & Roberts, 2008). Depending on the nature of the crisis and the systems involved, it may be necessary for you to address the crisis situation at the micro, mezzo, and macro levels (Gelman & Mirabito, 2005). Although members of multiple disciplines played an important role in developing crisis theory, social workers have been responsible for advancing practice methods, theory, and skills and for formulating strategies for responding to crises (Bell, 1995; Fast, 2003; Komar, 1994; Lukton, 1982; Parad & Parad, 1990).

The model utilizes tasks similar to task-centered and solution-focused approaches and is similarly oriented toward the future. While aspects of task-centered and solution-focused practice are intended to restore functioning to a nonproblematic state, restoring equilibrium is a particular focus of crisis intervention. Specifically, crisis intervention differs from other brief treatment approaches in that its goal is to "recognize and correct temporary affective, behavioral and cognitive distortions as a result of a traumatic event" (James, 2008, p. 11).

Tenets of the Crisis Intervention Equilibrium Model

The crisis equilibrium model is the basic intervention approach to crisis intervention. It is designed to reduce stress, relieve symptoms, restore functioning, and prevent further deterioration. Promptness of response and the importance of intervening immediately is the basic thrust of the model. Timely intervention is considered to be critical to prevent deterioration in functioning. It is during the acute period that people are most likely to be receptive to an intervention. Key elements of the model are assessing the nature of the crisis, identifying priority concerns, and developing limited goals.

The assessment is rapid and the orientation is focused on the here-and-now. In this respect, it differs from the process outlined in Chapter 8. Nevertheless, you will recognize that similar dimensions are involved. Assessment in the crisis situation, as outlined by James (2008), involves determining the following:

- *The severity of the crisis*
- *The client's current emotional status and level of mobility/immobility*
- *Alternatives, coping mechanisms, support systems, and other available resources*
- *The client's level of lethality; specifically, is the client a danger to self or others?*

James (2008) cites the Triage Assessment System developed by Meyer, Williams, Otten, and Schmidt (1991) as a "fast" and efficient way to assess and "obtain a real time estimate of what is occurring with a client" (pp. 43–48). This three-dimensional assessment scheme provides a framework for you to assess the client's *affective, behavioral, and emotional* functioning, the severity of the situation, and to plan the appropriate intervention strategy. Where possible, you would also compare the Triage Assessment System results to determine the functioning level of the client in these domains prior to the crisis (James, 2008).

Definition and Stages of Crisis

A crisis may be a challenge, loss, a threat or traumatic event. A *crisis* as defined by James (2008, p. 3) is "a perception of an event or situation as an intolerable difficulty that exceeds the resources or coping mechanism of the person." Prolonged, crisis-related stress has the potential to severely affect cognitive, behavioral, and physical functioning.

In your work with clients, you have no doubt assisted clients to deal with crisis situations. These situations may have ranged from everyday occurrences—for example, job loss, death, eviction, divorce, domestic violence, or child abuse and neglect, crime or relocation—to more extreme situations such as a natural disaster. Crisis situations inevitably have a subjective element, because people's perceptions and coping capacities vary widely. Crises such as threats, loss, or transitions that are severely stressful and overwhelming for one client, may be manageable, for another.

Referencing the case situation of the Corning family, you will recall that job loss set in motion a series of events that were considered to be a significant threat to the family's stability. Yet Mr. and Mrs. Corning were able to work with the social worker to establish goals. In contrast, revealing his sexual orientation to his family, no doubt a dreaded high-anxiety event, resulted in Justin becoming homeless, creating a crisis situation and additional stressors. Refugees, immigrants, and migrants may simultaneously experience transitional loss, hazards, and threats as a result of leaving their homeland, networks, and culture. An additional challenge for them is to adjust to the extent considered desirable to the cultural norms and values and language of another country. At the same time, relocation can be an opportunity, in spite of the loss of valued status and family ties.

At the core of the definition of basic crisis intervention theory is the assumption of *the big event*, in which immediate assistance is critical. There are segments of the population, however, in which threats can result in an ongoing crisis state. Consider, for example, the hypervigilance of people who have entered the United States or another country without the proper papers; or the very real threats experienced by gay and lesbian individuals as a result of hate crimes, brutal beatings, and even murder. Intense anxiety and threats and potential harm are also pervasive in some poor minority communities. Residents of these communities are often faced with violence, negative encounters with the police, poverty-related stressors, and inadequate services or resources. For these segments of the population, crisis dynamics are not closely associated with the "big event"; instead, they are woven into the fabric of everyday life. Ultimately, these factors undermine the individual and community sense of self and organization and produce a steady state of disequilibrium.

Emotional and psychosocial crisis resulting from the traumatic experience of combat military personnel, specifically post-traumatic stress disorder (PTSD), can pose a lifetime risk for the individual (Halpern & Tramontin, 2007; James, 2008). Traumatic stress-related symptoms may also be observed in professionals, especially those who work in highly stressful, emotionally charged situations (Bell, 2003; Curry, 2007; Knight, 2006; O'Halloran & Linton, 2000).

Traumatic events in the United States, such as the bombing of the federal office building in Oklahoma City and the September 11, 2001, terrorist attacks profoundly affected the communities in which they occurred. Incidents of this magnitude are relatively new for the U.S. public. All citizens of the country were exposed to the trauma by constant media coverage (Belkin, 1999). In other parts of the world, political or armed conflicts and instability are common in everyday life. These situations, along with the occurrence of devastating natural disasters, constitute ongoing crisis situations. In each of these circumstances, you might expect to find entire communities who feel particularly vulnerable and experience prolonged anxieties, physical, emotional, and cognitive distress, as well as an overall sense of grief and diminished coping capacity.

Crisis Reactions

A *crisis reaction* may be described as any event or situation that upsets "normal psychic balance" (Lum, 2004, p. 272) to the extent that the individual's sense of equilibrium is severely challenged. For example, many individuals and families were so traumatized by the September 11 attacks that the benefit of any intervention with them was diminished by a sense of denial and numbing similar to that encountered in combat situations. Thus, a basic thrust of crisis work, specifically promptness of response to reduce distress and restore equilibrium, proved in many cases to be ineffective.

Crisis intervention theory posits that people's reactions typically go through several stages, although theorists differ as to whether three or four stages are involved. The following description is a synthesis of stages identified by various authors (Caplan, 1964; James & Gilliland, 2001; Okun, 2002).

> Stage 1: The initial tension is accompanied by shock and perhaps even denial of the crisis-provoking event.
> Stage 2: To reduce the tension, the individual attempts to utilize his or her usual emergency problem-solving skills. If these skills fail to result in the lessening of their tension, the stress level will become heightened.
> Stage 3: The individual experiences severe tension, feels confused, overwhelmed, helpless, angry, or perhaps acutely depressed. The length of this phase varies according to the nature of the hazardous event, the strengths and coping capacities of the person, and the degree of responsiveness from social support systems.

Patterns associated with these stages may be characterized as disorganization, recovery, and reorganization (Lum, 2004; Parad and Parad, 1990, 2006; Roberts, 1990, 2005). People's reactions to a crisis will vary and they may not progress through the stages in a linear fashion. At the point of contact clients may present at different crisis stages; therefore, it is important that you assess their functioning, coping, and adaptation capacity. The potential exists for clients to cope in ways that are either adaptive or maladaptive. You should be aware, however, that prolonged stress may exceed their coping capacity and usual problem solving, so much so that they are unable to effectively handle the stressors. Achieving equilibrium for some may depend on the extent to which their strengths, resilience, and social supports are mobilized. In these instances, the individual can perhaps achieve a higher level of functioning. As suggested by James (2008), the crisis may evoke a positive change *opportunity*. Specifically, an individual's reaction to a crisis may be to seek help and be motivated to succeed, thereby using the opportunity to their benefit (James, 2008). For

others, the level of tension and feelings of being overwhelmed can escalate and their coping patterns may reach a level of *danger*. Danger is evident when restoring equilibrium is not immediately possible because the individual is unable to function, in which case additional assistance is required (James, 2008).

Duration of Contact

Typically, crisis work is limited in its duration, occurring within a time period spanning 4 to 8 weeks, although some clients or situations may require a longer time period. It is expected that active and intensely focused work in a brief time period will assist people to achieve a degree of pre-crisis functioning. The duration of contact may depend on the type of services offered by your agency and the crisis situation. Ultimately, the time required to resolve a crisis depends on the stress level; the individual's ego strengths, social supports, and resources; and whether the crisis is acute or chronic.

Your contact with clients may be daily, in an office, at a shelter, or in the home, especially during the acute crisis period. Interventions range from a single-session, telephone intervention to comprehensive services with groups, families, and entire communities (Fast, 2003; Gibar, 1992; James & Gilliland, 2001; West, Mercer, & Altheimer, 1993).

Several factors guide the time limited contact duration:

- *The focus is on the here-and-now. Hence, no attempt is made to deal with either pre-crisis personality dysfunction or intrapsychic conflict, although attention to these symptoms may be required.*
- *Goals are limited to alleviating distress and assisting clients to regain equilibrium.*
- *Tasks are identified and task performance is intended to help clients achieve a new state of equilibrium.*

Although you may actively direct and define tasks, you should encourage clients to participate to the extent that they are capable of doing so. Obviously, clients' ability to actively participate and perform tasks may be limited during periods of severe emotional distress, but may increase as the distress subsides.

Considerations for Minors

Minors are among the individuals, for example, the elderly, persons with a disability or serious mental illness, that are more vulnerable and at risk to crisis or traumatic events (Halpern & Tramontin, 2007; James, 2008). Schwartz and Perry (1994) were among the first to add to the knowledge base for minors with regard to post-traumatic stress disorder (PTSD) by focusing specifically on their response. Their work integrated neurodevelopmental and psychosocial aspects of trauma, and makes a distinction between the adaptations of adults and those of children.

The *Diagnostic and Statistical Manual for Mental Disorders (DSM)* in its fourth edition (*DSM-IV-TR*) is thought to be a limited resource as a diagnostic tool for young children because it requires "verbal descriptions of a subjective mood state," which may be beyond the communication skills for younger children (James, 2008, p. 163). Work by Terr (1995) as discussed by James (2008, p. 163) established Type I and Type II categories related to childhood trauma.

Type I involves a single and distinct traumatic experience in which "symptoms and signs" are manifested. For example, with Type I trauma, the minor can display "fully detailed etched-in memories, misperceptions, cognitive reappraisals and reasons of the event." Type II, in contrast, is the result of longstanding and repeated trauma. According to James (2008), the minor's psyche develops defensive and coping strategies. Behaviorally, the potential exists for the minor to identify with and mimic aggression or use denial, self-numbing or self-injury as a means to cope. Prominent coping emotions may be expressed by an absence of feelings or by rage or depression.

A high incidence of childhood depression was found to exist in a study by Lindsey, Korr, Broitman, Bone, Green and Leaf (2006) in minors who resided in highly urban communities. Their findings may indicate that the group of minors in the study that may well fit within the Type II category. Similarly, the prevalence of violence exposure described by Voisin (2007) in which minors experience violence as a victim, a witness, or hear about violent situations is consistent with the Type II behaviors and emotions.

The results of trauma experienced by minors have a cumulative or differential effect. Maschi (2006) examined the relationship between delinquency and violence exposure focusing on physical abuse, physical or sexual assault, or witnessing violence. Results showed that adolescents who experience violence were at risk for delinquency. Maschi (2006) and Voisin (2007) reached a similar conclusion. Based on this data, it would appear to be prudent for schools and agencies serving minors to include in their assessments explorations of inclusive trauma and stress factors.

For minors, a traumatic event has the potential to disrupt biological, social, and cognitive development.

Age can make a significant difference in how minors respond. In very young children, Zeira, Astor, and Benbenishty (2003) for example, found that fear and perceived threats of school violence, which affected school attendance, were more prominent among younger children. The Type I crisis seems to best fit with an initial response proposed by Halpern and Tramontin (2007) in which the focus is to stabilize the minor within the situation. Thus, the initial response may in fact be restoring the pre-crisis state of their caregivers [and community] so that they can help the minor after exposure to a traumatic event.

To direct the assessment and the potential for post-traumatic impact Korol, Green and Grace (1999) emphasize developmental ecological framework. The premise of this framework is that the developmental stage and the environment within which the minor operates are interrelated (James, 2008). Within this framework, four attributes described below were identified by Korol, et al. (1999) to guide the intervention with minors. The four attributes, based on research findings are summarized by Halpern & Tramontin (2007, pp. 149–150).

- Characteristics of the stressors, *including the perception of threat related to the event, physical proximity to the event, duration and intensity.*
- Characteristics of the minor. *Developmental stage, gender and vulnerability play a significant role in how a minor experiences a threat, as well as psychological or behavioral problems that existed prior to the threat.*
- The minor's efforts to cope. *Limited research precludes generalizations about resources that may "buffer" negative outcomes for minors. Generally, a minor with good communications skills, a sense of self and internal locus of control and average intelligence are indicators of a positive outcome.*
- Characteristics of the post-disaster environment. *The minor's reaction to the post-environment is strengthened by the presence of social supports from significant others and resources. These factors can reduce stress, act as protective factors and mediate the impact of a disaster.*

The Interactive Trauma/Grief-Focused Therapy (IT/G-FT) model is another approach to address the post-effects on minors following exposure to trauma (Nader & Mello, 2008). Eclectic in nature, the model utilizes theories relevant to the situation, including psychodynamic and cognitive behavioral approaches. Using the narratives, emotions, cognitions, and memories of the minor, the goals of this approach are to assist them to recover and to regain the healthy aspects of pre-crisis functioning. This model may be used in Type I or Type II situations, including with past trauma.

The stages of crisis and the reaction may differ with minors. They may, for example, need additional help in understanding their crisis reaction and in developing problem-solving skills. The Triage System assessment can be especially important in determining the cognition and behaviors of minors as a result of the crisis. Cognitively, a crisis event can increase minors' sense of vulnerability and their perceptions of a lack of power. Behavioral responses to an event may involve the minor's coping by role-playing an all-powerful action figure (Knox & Roberts, 2008).

The equilibrium model, consistent with generalist practice, is appropriate for minors and may in some instances be combined with psycho-educational groups. Common themes within this model stress the importance of family as a resource and, where possible, the school and the community. They also emphasize the need for you to understand child development and the effects of trauma. Elements of the equilibrium model can inform a first response to Type II trauma. You should however, pursue additional resources beyond the scope of this text if the population with which you are involved consists of minors who fit within this category.

Benefits of a Crisis

Much of the literature has tended to focus on the adverse effects of crises on people. Not surprisingly, then, interventions and strategies, while incorporating strengths, coping, and social support, have sought to restore functioning to the pre-crisis level. Some theorists and researchers suggest that negative events may actually promote growth in the aftermath of a crisis (Caplan, 1964; Halpern & Tramontin, 2007; James, 2008; McMillen & Fischer, 1998; McMillen, Zuravin, & Rideout, 1995; McMillen, Smith, & Fischer, 1997; Joseph, Williams, & Yule, 1993). Note however, that the findings are specific to adult populations.

Building on prior research as well as the notion of benefit advanced by Caplan (1964), McMillen and Fisher (1998) explored the perceived harm and benefits with individuals who had experienced a negative event. In fact, people did report some benefits from negative events in the form of positive life changes. Among the benefits perceived by the study subjects were self-efficacy, spirituality, faith in people, compassion, and an increase in community closeness. According to McMillen and Fisher (1998), the perceived benefit

varied in relationship to the perceived harm, symptoms triggered by the event or situation, and the type of support or assistance received.

The McMillen and Fisher study results were significant for two reasons:

- *The deficit approach to psychosocial consequences appears to influence how human services professionals view their clients and how clients view their experience. Specifically, professionals may tend to focus on the trauma alone, whereas clients may view the situation or event through multiple lenses.*
- *In understanding the positive benefits that accrue from crises, professionals are able to construct interventions that strengthen these factors and increase successful outcomes.*

These findings also emphasize the subjective nature of the crisis experience as a key element in crisis intervention. Likewise, they point to the need for you to fully assess the affective, behavioral, and cognitive capacities of clients, which include their perceptions of harm or benefit. This information would be included in your assessment of their post-crisis level of functioning.

Theoretical Framework

Parad (1965), Caplan (1964), and Golan (1981) were early and significant contributors to basic crisis intervention theory, delineating the nature of crises, stages, and intervention strategies for crisis resolution. Lukton (1982) further developed practice theory and skills for social workers. Early crisis intervention theory focused on grief and loss reactions and maturational or biopsychosocial crisis at various developmental stages. Role transitions, or traumatic or accidental life events were also among the crisis situations that could occur (Lindemann, 1944, 1956; Rapoport, 1967). Strategies tended to reflect this paradigm, so early tenets and theory were generally psychoanalytic in nature. Therefore, consideration for environmental and situational factors as contributors to crisis and crisis reactions were not as prominent as they are today.

Over time, other theories have evolved, and basic crisis theory as a single theory may be incapable of explaining the human response to trauma (Knox & Roberts, 2008; James, 2008). Crisis theories and the related models are influenced by, for example, ego psychology and developmental, cognitive behavioral, chaos, and ecological systems theories. In expanding the tenets of crisis intervention theory, Okun (2002) and James (2008) more broadly defined the context in

TABLE-13-2 EXPANDED CRISIS THEORY

THEORY	ASSUMPTIONS
Psychoanalytic	The experience of disequilibrium for an individual in a crisis state can be understood by examining unconscious thought patterns and prior emotional experiences, and by assisting clients to "gain insight into the dynamics and causes of their problems."
Ecosystems	Fundamental concepts of systems theory—for example, the interaction and interdependence between individuals and the environment, and "between people and events"—are used to explore interpersonal relationships (e.g., in the family system) as well as social and environmental forces that give rise to a crisis situation or event.
Adaptational	A crisis is stressful and disruptive. It can adversely affect biological, psychological, and social functioning, and it may produce disturbed emotions, impaired functioning, and maladaptive behaviors. This theory is based on the "premise that a person's crisis will recede when maladaptive coping behaviors are changed to adaptive behaviors, therefore moving to a more positive mode of functioning."
Interpersonal	A crisis emerges and persists when individual validation is influenced by the evaluation of others, and is dependent on this evaluation. Referred to as "conferring their locus on control," on an external source, the crisis will continue until the individual gains a sense of self-efficacy over his or her life by taking action.
Chaos	Situations are less predictable, shifting, emerging, and complex. Solutions may be based on trial and error as people attempt to cope. May involve "false starts, temporary failures, dead ends, creativity and innovation."

SOURCE: From JAMES, "Crisis Intervention Strategies", 6E. © 2008 Wadsworth, a part of Cengage Learning, Inc. Reproduced by permission. www.cengage.com/permissions.

which a crisis may occur and, in doing so, expanded the underlying theoretical framework of crisis work. Expanded crisis theories and their focus as delineated by James (2008) are summarized in Table 13-2.

Types of Crisis

In differentiating the various types of crises, Okun (2002) has integrated a composite of theoretical frameworks, which, as Lum (2004, p. 272) suggests, "helps to differentiate incidents and events more accurately." Okun's (2002, p. 245) six categories of crises are summarized as follows:

1. *Dispositional Crisis:* Occurs when an individual lacks the information needed to make a decision.
2. *Anticipated Life Transition:* Normative life and developmental events such as marriage, divorce, changing jobs or careers, entering into a different stage of life (e.g., midlife or aging).
3. *Traumatic Stress:* Situations that are imposed on an individual by circumstances or events out of his or her control, and that emotionally overwhelms the individual. Examples include unexpected death, sudden loss, rape, receiving health status information, and illness.
4. *Maturational/Developmental Crisis:* Crucial transitions and points in the lifespan process that mark significant developmental changes, such as midlife

crisis, leaving home as a young adult, adolescent identity, and independence.
5. *Psychopathological Crisis:* An emotional crisis that is precipitated by a preexisting psychopathology and emerges during a time of distress because of situational or environmental factors related to transitions, trauma, or developmental age.
6. *Psychiatric Emergency:* Occurs when an individual's functioning becomes severely impaired such that he or she is incapable of performing daily living functions, poses a danger to self and others, or sometimes both.

Understanding the type of crisis, the perception of threat, the harm to or vulnerability of those involved, and the client's affective, emotional, and behavioral functioning will assist you to respond and plan appropriate interventions. Otherwise, your intervention strategy may have little or no value to the client.

Application with Diverse Groups

An advantage of crisis intervention strategies is their use with different populations (Knox & Roberts, 2008). Lum (2004) asserts that crisis intervention as a generalist practice approach has "universal application to people of color" (p. 272). This assertion is based on the fact that people of color "often experience personal and environmental crisis" and in many instances have "exhausted community and family resources" prior to seeking professional help (p. 273). In some instances, patterns of help-seeking behavior and historically based anxieties about formal helping can delay contact, which can mean that a crisis has reached a chronic state. In addition, influenced by culture, different communities may respond and cope differently to a traumatic event (Halpern & Tramontin, 2007).

James (2008) acknowledges that crisis intervention along with other dominant practice strategies is specific to Western assumptions, noting that the majority of the world is unfamiliar with these ideals. It is possible that the social constructionist view that clinical categories focus on such factors and normalcy, while omitting such cultural factors, for example, faith or injustice, has merit (Freud, 1999; Silvo, 2000). In the aftermath of Hurricane Katrina, unavoidable questions about inequality and justice were raised with respect to the crisis response for the citizens of the 9th Ward in New Orleans. You might, however, question whether the response to this particular segment of the population was the result of systemic structural barriers rather than shortcomings of the crisis model. The nature of this traumatic event certainly overwhelmed and profoundly affected the coping capacity of those involved.

Although research and literature related to crisis intervention strategies with regard to culture, gender, and racial groups is limited, there are works that have advanced our knowledge base. Examples include the work of Congress (2000) and Potocki-Tripodi (2002) with culturally diverse and immigrant families and Cornelius, Simpson, Ting, Wiggins and Lipford (2003) and Ligon (1997) with African Americans. Halpern & Tramontin (2007) amplify how culturally derived perceptions can influence expectations of crisis reactions in particular Asian communities. They point to the reaction in these communities which tend to differ from those in Western societies. In working with immigrants and refugees, Potocky-Tripodi (2002) suggests that while crisis intervention strategies are appropriate, ideally they should be implemented as preventive measures prior to the resettlement stage. Congress (2002, 2000) identifies common precipitants of crisis among immigrants and refugees; namely, intergenerational conflicts, changes in roles, unemployment, and interactions with formal institutions in which crisis strategies are appropriate. Ligon (1997) departs somewhat from the equilibrium model, relying instead on cultural and ecological systems perspectives integrated with empowerment. Using this framework to resolve the crisis of a young adult African American female, Ligon demonstrated its potential merit with other populations of color and individuals with serious health or mental health concerns (Potocky-Tripodi, 2002; Lum, 2004; Poindexter, 1997). Poindexter (1997) makes the point that for HIV-infected individuals, the experience may involve a series of crises. Learning of the disease is a precipitating event; yet as the condition progresses, multiple crises—social, situational, and developmental—can occur simultaneously. Poindexter's work, along with that of Ell (1995) and Potocky-Tripodi (2002), is significant in that it helps us to move beyond certain assumptions about the episodic nature of crises and to understand the evolving stages of certain crisis situations.

Crisis intervention, like other practice models, calls for multicultural helping that includes self-knowledge, awareness of bias, knowledge of the status and culture of diverse groups, and the willingness to use alternative strategies appropriate to the client's culture and situation (James, 2008; Sue, 2006). Perhaps the most important factor for you to recognize is that crisis work like any other problem solving strategy should include the worldview of the client, the meaning that they ascribe to the situation, and their patterns of coping and preferences for resolution. In this regard, combining aspects of the social constructionist approach can advance your understanding of the cultural perspective of the client.

Process and Procedures of Crisis Intervention

The processes and procedures of the six-step crisis intervention model that was initially developed by Gilliland (1982) are illustrated in Figure 13-3. The steps can be used for systematically intervening in a crisis situation.[3] Also, the steps are consistent with the eclectic problem solving approach (James, 2008). The figure also outlines the fundamental skills and the range of actions required for you to take in a crisis situation. Procedures for implementing the model, as illustrated in Figure 13-3, are applied to the case of Lia, a pregnant teen. Cultural tensions related to her pregnancy are also discussed.

Step 1: Define the Problem

As a social worker in a crisis situation, you must determine the unique meaning of a crisis and severity of the situation to the client. Having clients talk about the meaning and significance of the crisis can be a relieving cathartic process and thus be highly therapeutic for them. Gathering this information provides you with essential information about how the client defines their problem.

ASSESSING:
Overarching, continuous, and dynamically ongoing throughout the crisis; evaluating the client's present and past situational crises in terms of the client's ability to cope, personal threat, mobility or immobility, and making a judgment regarding type of action needed by the crisis worker. (See crisis worker's action continuum, below.)

Listening	Acting
↓	↓
LISTENING: Attending, observing, understanding, and responding with empathy, genuineness, respect, acceptance, nonjudgment, and caring.	ACTING: Becoming involved in the intervention at a nondirective, collaborative, or directive level, according to the assessed needs of the client and the availability of environmental supports.
1. *Define the problem.* Explore and define the problem from the client's point of view. Use active listening, including open-ended questions. Attend to both verbal and nonverbal messages of the client.	4. *Examine alternatives.* Assist client in exploring the choices he or she has available to him or her now. Facilitate a search for immediate situational supports, coping mechanisms, and positive thinking.
2. *Ensure client safety.* Assess lethality, criticality, immobility, or seriousness of threat to the client's physical and psychological safety. Assess both the client's internal events and the situation surrounding the client, and, if necessary, ensure that the client is made aware of alternatives to impulsive, self-destructive actions.	5. *Make plans.* Assist client in developing a realistic short-term plan that identifies additional resources and provides coping mechanisms—definite action steps that the client can own and comprehend.
3. *Provide support. Communicate* to the client that the crisis worker is a valid support person. Demonstrate (by words, voice, and body language) a caring, positive, nonpossessive, nonjudgmental, acceptant, personal involvement with the client.	6. *Obtain commitment.* Help client commit himself or herself to definite, positive action steps that the client can own and realistically accomplish or accept.

Crisis Worker's Action Continuum

Crisis worker is nondirective   Crisis worker is collaborative   Crisis worker is directive

(Threshold varies from client to client)   (Threshold varies from client to client)

Client is mobile   Client is partially mobile   Client is immobile

The crisis worker's level of action/involvement may be anywhere on the continuum according to a valid and realistic assessment of the client's level of mobility/immobility.

FIG-13-3 The Six-Step Model of Crisis Intervention
SOURCE: From JAMES, "Crisis Intervention Strategies", 6E. © 2008 Wadsworth, a part of Cengage Learning, Inc. Reproduced by permission. www.cengage.com/permissions.

Cultural factors and status are equally essential in assessing clients' problem definitions and reactions to crisis situations. Situations deemed to be crises vary widely from one culture to another, as do the reactions to them. Interventions work best when they include cultural values, beliefs, and rituals (e.g., spiritual healing, circles of care) as critical reference points.

Case Example

The problem as presented by Lia, age 17 years, was that she was pregnant and unmarried. During the school year she participated in a school-based teen group for female students. On the day of the referral, during group Lia became so emotionally distraught that the teen group leader took her aside to talk with her individually. Lia told her that she was pregnant and that she was in trouble with her family as a result. The group leader referred her to a social worker at the community health/mental center.

During the first session with Lia, the social worker's initial tasks in this session were twofold:

- *Assess and alleviate Lia's emotional distress*
- *Elicit Lia's definition of the problem*

Assess and alleviate Lia's emotional distress: *During the initial interview Lia was crying, had trouble breathing, and expressed concern about whether the social worker could understand her situation. Further, by assessing Lia's emotional state, the social worker gained an understanding of the magnitude of her distress in relationship to the problem. Her emotional distress became even more significant when she indicated that she had thought of suicide. In addition, she stated that she had shared her feelings in conversations with her 12-year-old brother.*

In focusing on Lia's emotions, the social worker, responding empathically, listened to her talk about her feelings. She also learned that she had talked about suicide, which prompted an immediate referral to the center's mental health services. In addition, Lia had concerns about the safety and well-being of both herself and her unborn child. Although she had missed several days of school, she had continued her involvement with the teen group, which was a hopeful sign.

Eliciting the client's definition of the problem: *Lia's problem as she defined it was being pregnant* and unmarried, which was further complicated by cultural norms. The extremity of the situation escalated when Lia talked about the response from her family. From the perspective of her family, Lia's pregnancy, without her being married, brought shame to them. Upon learning that she was pregnant, her father had dismissed her from the family. He refused to talk to others, or allow other family members to do so. The fact that Lia faced social ostracism, loss of face, a disconnection from her family and members of the clan added to her distress.

Clearly, being pregnant and unmarried was worrisome to Lia, but she believed that she could cope with her situation and had some ideas about how to do so. Her family's definition of the problem, however, was grounded in the context of cultural norms and expectations. Unwed pregnancy requires considerable adaptation in most cultures, but may pose an extreme challenge for first-generation immigrant families. Lia's situation presented a multi-level problem, as defined by her and by her family and community. In gathering the information, the social worker understood the various factors that contributed to the crisis and her distress.

Step 2: Ensure Client Safety

Ensuring client safety is the first and foremost concern in crisis intervention and an ongoing consideration (James and Gilliland, 2001; James, 2008). Safety involves deliberate steps to minimize the "physical and psychological" danger to the client or others (James, 2008). The social worker requested, and Lia agreed to complete, a depression scale. The results of the test confirmed the necessity of making the referral to mental health services for an evaluation.

Because Lia had spoken of considering suicide, the social worker developed an immediate safety plan contract with her; with each party identifying resources, including a crisis hotline that Lia could call when her feelings reached the level at which she had contemplated harming herself.

In the assessment of her affective, cognitive, and behavioral domains, Lia's scores were moderate. In addition, she displayed some coping behaviors, namely, that she often volunteered for the closing shift at work and then walked to her sister's home to spend the night to avoid going home. In addition, while she missed school, she continued to participate in the teen group, which was another sign of her coping. Furthermore, the fact that she was concerned about the well-being of her

unborn child was an indication of her future-oriented thinking. The social worker focused on this concern in order to minimize the threat of self harm. An additional safety concern was the fact that Lia was walking to her sister's house late at night after work, so she and the social worker explored other transportation alternatives. In assessing the three domains, the social worker was able to observe Lia's adaptive and coping capacities. She also learned about family resources that could be tapped into to alleviate Lia's distress and help to ensure her safety.

Step 3: Provide Support

Within this step, the objective of the social worker was to identify Lia's social support systems, because mobilizing a helping network can be enormously helpful as part of crisis intervention. Social supports may include friends, relatives, and in some cases institutional programs that care about the client and that can provide comfort and compassion (James & Gilliland, 2001).

As Lia and the social worker explored potential support resources, several were identified: her sister and an aunt, as well as certain clan members who were sympathetic to her situation. These resources were also included in the safety plan. A school-based group for pregnant teens was identified as a new resource. In a supportive role, the social worker walked with her to the appointment with the psychiatrist and introduced her to the social worker in the healthy baby program at the center. She also arranged a daily check-in schedule with Lia.

Step 4: Examine Alternatives

In this step, both the social worker and Lia explored courses of action appropriate to her situation. Of course, some choices that they considered were better than others, and it was important that they were selective in prioritizing available options. Ideally, alternatives are considered to the extent to which they are:

- *Situational supports, involving people who care about what happens to the client*
- *Coping mechanisms, represented by actions, behaviors, or environmental resources that clients may use to get past the crisis situation*
- *Positive and constructive thinking patterns that effectively alter how the client views the problem, thereby lessening the level of stress and anxiety*

Lia had actually thought of alternatives, yet was sufficiently immobilized emotionally that she had not acted upon them. For example, in response to the threat from her father to change the locks on the doors, effectively forcing her out of the house, she considered moving in with her sister or aunt (*situational supports*) until after her child was born. Afterwards, she would be 18 years of age and able to live independently. Instead of acting on this option, however, she planned to wait until her parents were asleep or at work, and appeal to her siblings (*coping mechanism*) to let her in the house. She had depended on her siblings in the past to let her into the house when she had stayed out too late with her boyfriend. Relying on this choice was a short-term solution at best, and posed greater risks for both Lia and her siblings.

A more viable alternative suggested by the social worker involved Lia moving into a transitional housing complex for pregnant teens, located near her high school and job (*positive constructive thinking and action*). Program services offered in the housing complex included transportation to prenatal visits, group counseling, independent living skills classes, and assistance in finding permanent housing. Although she was initially reluctant, Lia agreed to consider this option. At times you may be better able to plan alternatives with clients and alter their thinking when they understand their point of view. For example, Lia's qualms about the pregnant teen housing program reflected her desire to remain with, or at least near, her family and community.

Of course there were additional alternatives to consider in stabilizing the situation. You should however, be aware that multiple options for a client in crisis can be overwhelming. Therefore, the alternatives that you and the client consider should be "realistic" to the situation (James, 2008). In Lia's case, two options were considered: moving in with her aunt on a short-term basis and the housing program for pregnant teens. She chose the housing program because of the services available. She and the social worker, however, also discussed ways in which she could have some contact with her family.

Step 5: Making Plans
Planning and contracting flow from the previous steps and involve the same elements as were described in Chapter 12. In this step, Lia and the social worker agreed on specific action steps or tasks as well as time limits. General and specific tasks, will, of course, vary according to the nature of the crisis situation and the unique characteristics of each person and/or family.

In developing and negotiating task, the social worker solicited Lia's views on what she believed would help her function at a level of pre-crisis equilibrium. Together they identified her safety as a priority in planning. They also identified tasks that needed to be

accomplished so that she could eventually move in to the pregnant teen housing program.

Lia's concern about her estrangement from her parents was also a central issue. The social worker asked Lia to consider writing a letter of apology to her parents, inquiring about the cultural appropriateness of such a gesture. Lia was unsure about writing the letter, but agreed to talk with her aunt. Lia was also encouraged to think about ways in which she could resume some form of contact with her family and the clan. Their planning would involve the aunt and the sister as supportive resources.

There are times during this step, when your interaction with a client requires you to be directive. For example, the idea of writing a letter to her family was the social worker's idea. James and Gilliand (2001), however, caution against your "benevolently imposing" a plan on clients. Instead, you should strive to find a balance between being directive and giving the client autonomy, encouraging and reinforcing independent actions whenever feasible. As it turned out, Lia thought the idea was a good one, yet she was unsure about the impact that the letter might have. Nonetheless, writing the letter might provide her with some relief.

Step 6: Obtaining Commitment
Completing tasks, which flow directly from the previous step, are considered to be essential to a client's mastery of crisis situations. In the sixth and final step, Lia and the social worker committed to collaboratively engage in specific, intentional, and positive tasks steps designed to restore her to level of pre-crisis functioning.

After a week, Lia agreed to pursue the plan of moving into the housing program for pregnant teens. In the interim, she would explore living with her sister or her aunt, perhaps dividing her time between the two of them. Tasks were also developed that would ensure her safety. Agreed-upon tasks involved the following:

Lia

- *Call the 24-hour crisis line or other supports when she was feeling overwhelmed*
- *Talk to her sister or aunt about moving in with one of them*
- *Visit the pregnant teen housing program*
- *Explore ways to have contact with family members*
- *Continue to attend the school-based teen group*

Social Worker

- *Provide Lia with information on the pregnant teen housing program prior to her visit*

- *Accompany Lia on her visit to the housing program*
- *Obtain information about financial support for Lia and her unborn child*

Anticipatory Guidance

In addition to completing the six steps of the model, you may also find anticipatory guidance to be a useful activity with clients. This activity has preventive implications. It involves assisting clients to anticipate future crisis situations and to plan coping strategies that will prepare them to face future stresses. Focusing on the potential of future stressors is essentially exploring "what if" scenarios. In this regard, the social worker and Lia discussed potential ways in which she could cope in the event that, despite her best efforts, her family continued to isolate her because of her pregnancy. They also talked about the eventual, but normative, stress of the birth of her baby, living independently, and the resources that were available to her. In their discussion, the social worker helped Lia to focus on her problem-solving, coping, and adaptation skills in her current situation. For example, her volunteering to work the late shift to avoid going home. While this raised other concerns, specifically, walking alone late at night, it also shows her problem-solving and adaptation capacities.

In using anticipatory guidance, it is important that you do not convey an expectation that a client will always be able to independently manage crisis situations in the future. Even though you reassure clients of their skills and help them to anticipate future scenarios, you should clarify that you or another professional are available if they need future help.

Strengths and Limitations

The basic crisis intervention model involves a structured, time-limited series of steps utilizing techniques that are guided by basic crisis theory. The initial intervention phase has three strategic objectives: (1) to relieve the client's emotional distress, (2) to complete an assessment of the client's cognitive, behavioral, and emotional functioning, and (3) to plan the strategy of intervention, focusing on relevant tasks the client must perform.

Much of the theory upon which the equilibrium model is based assumes that people experience an event or situation that alters their usual patterns of living. Therefore, the goal of the intervention is to restore their pre-crisis functioning. Other techniques, for example, cognitive restructuring and reframing, especially with

minors, can augment crisis strategies to lessen feelings that somehow the situation was their fault.

Over time, in recognition that no one theory is capable of defining or explanting a crisis, expanded theories and models have influenced a classification of different kinds of crises and trauma and crisis responses. Models have also evolved that have emphasized the need to respond to clients' crisis needs differently in consideration of developmental stage. Promising research has demonstrated the effectiveness of crisis strategies with diverse populations by integrating assumptions from other crisis theories. Likewise, crisis theory includes trauma and disaster in its definition of a crisis, for which it is necessary to implement strategies that respond to the needs of entire communities and groups. These contributions are significant in that they advance our understanding and ability to differentiate crisis work.

While there is consensus about the definition of a crisis, it is understood that what actually constitutes a crisis may be individually and culturally defined. Perceptions of a crisis may vary based on associated threats, individual cognitions, and the significance of the situation, ego strengths, coping capacity, and problem-solving skills. In some instances, people may perceive and articulate positive benefits that emerge as a result of a negative experience. Of course, a perception of benefit may be limited by the nature and severity of the crisis, the developmental stage of minors, as well as the resources and supports that are available at an opportune time.

The model retains the assumption of a crisis as an episodic, time-limited event. As such, responding to the stress and distress of individuals, communities, or groups is at this level. Specifically, crisis professionals aim to relieve emotional distress and develop a plan of action that will restore individuals to a pre-crisis level of functioning. Furthermore, there is the assumption that certain behaviors and cognitive tasks must be mastered.

Ell (1995) challenges the assumption that a crisis is necessarily time-limited as well as the notion of homeostasis- specifically, the ability to achieve equilibrium. According to Ell, these assumptions are not valid for individuals, and perhaps entire communities, that experience chronic and constant stress. Crisis intervention for example, does not address living continuously in stressful environments, structural and socio-environmental threats nor the historical trauma of prolonged discrimination and inequality. Indeed, it is quite possible that individuals and entire communities face daily trauma situations resulting in their living in a constant state of disequilibrium or vulnerability. In many instances, in poor and minority communities, the crisis intervention point of entry is the hospital emergency room or the police station, and may result in a *Diagnostic and Statistical Manual (DSM)* classification. It is quite possible that not all of the stages of crisis reactions occur in these communities. Indeed, people in these situations may lack the power or resources to problem solve. For example, an individual's initial response to gang, police or politically motivated violence may be shock or denial. From this point, according to the crisis reaction stages, they may become angry, overwhelmed, or hopeless or depressed. In prolonged crisis situations, where normal problem-solving skills are inadequate, and in which coping skills have been exhausted, there is the potential for individuals to become numb, experience severe depression, and to remain at this stage. Thus, as suggested by Ell (1995), the notion of the time-limited crisis is not always applicable, and the potential to restore equilibrium may be neither feasible nor realistic.

The efficacy of crisis intervention strategies with diverse populations and in diverse settings is not diminished by these observations. These possibilities do suggest, however, that an assessment of socio-environmental factors and their impact on cognitive, affective, and behavioral functioning is indicated. In addition, you should recognize that even though the potential exists to restore the individual's sense of self-efficacy, the notion of time-limited episodes may not be universally applicable in all crisis situations.

Understanding basic crisis theory provides you with a framework for working with both adults and minors. The steps of the equilibrium/disequilibrium model are derived from basic crisis theory. The assessment of the cognitive, affective, and behavioral domains enables you to determine the level of distress a client is experiencing. Further, assessing these domains provides you with information with respect to the level of functioning and whether clients are immobilized by their distress. The model is consistent with generalist practice and utilizes the practice values, knowledge, and skills with which you are already familiar.

Cognitive Restructuring

Cognitive restructuring is a therapeutic process derived from cognitive-behavioral therapy (CBT). Also referred to as cognitive replacement, cognitive restructuring is "considered to be the cornerstone of cognitive behavioral approaches" (Cormier & Nurius, 2003, p. 435) Intervention techniques in cognitive behavioral therapy are designed to help individuals modify their beliefs, faulty thought patterns or perceptions, and destructive verbalizations, thereby leading to changes in behavior. An assumption of cognitive restructuring is that people often manifest cognitive distortions—that is, irrational thoughts derived from negative schemas that lead to unrealistic interpretations of people, events, or circumstances. Frequently, although clients may be aware of their faulty thinking, they may lack the emotional strength to alter their schematic patterns.

Theoretical Framework

For you to fully appreciate the foundation of cognitive restructuring, it is important that you understand the theories upon which the technique is based. According to cognitive theorists, most social and behavioral problems or dysfunction are directly related to the misconceptions that people hold about themselves, other people, and various life situations (J. Beck, 1995; Dobson & Dozioss, 2001). The early and historic work of Ellis (1962), Beck (1976), and others in this arena led to cognitive theories and techniques that can be applied directly and systematically to problems of cognitive dysfunction. Ellis's (1962) seminal work, *Reason and Emotion in Psychotherapy*, explicated the theory underlying rational-emotive therapy (RET). Perhaps the most significant is *The Cognitive Therapy of Depression* (Beck, Rush, Shaw, & Emery, 1979), which is widely recognized as the definitive work on treatment of depression.

The classical work of Pavlov (1927) related to conditioning and the operant conditioning studies of Skinner (1974) are prominent in the theoretical framework of cognitive behavioral therapy (Cobb, 2008). Learning as a primary focus is influenced by Bandura's (1986) social learning theory. According to social learning theory, thoughts and emotions are best understood in the context of behaviors associated with cognition or cognitive processes as well as the extent to which individuals adapt and respond to different stimuli and make self-judgments. Increasingly, cognitive behavioralists include social constructionists' perspectives of the specific realities of different clients, and unique behaviors relative to their culture, beliefs, and worldview (Cobb, 2008; Cormier & Nurius, 2003).

In the 1960s, behavioral theory and methods were introduced by Edwin Thomas at the University of Michigan (Gambrill, 1995). Berlin's (2001) *Clinical Social Work Practice: A Cognitive-Integrative Approach*, is a significant contribution to adapting cognitive behavioral therapy to social work.

Tenets of Cognitive Behavioral Therapy-Cognitive Restructuring

In general, the goal of cognitive behavioral intervention strategies is to increase the client's cognitive and behavioral skills so as to enhance his or her functioning. Restructuring is a cognitive procedure that aims to change a client's thoughts, feelings, or overt behaviors that contribute to and maintain problem behavior. To be effective in using cognitive restructuring and other procedures of the cognitive behavioral approach, you must be skilled in assessing cognitive functioning and in applying appropriate interventions. (See assessing cognitive functioning and patterns in Chapters 9 and 11.)[4]

Cognitive behavioral theory is based on the assumption that people construct their own reality. It is within the realm of processing information that people assess and make judgments that fit into their cognitive schema.

The basic tenets of the cognitive-behavioral theory are:

Thinking is a primary determinant of behavior and involves statements that people say to themselves. This inner dialogue, rather than unconscious forces, is the key to understanding behavior. To fully grasp this first major tenet, you must clearly differentiate thinking from feeling, as confusing feelings with thoughts tend to create confusion in communication. This confusion can be observed in messages such as "I feel our marriage is on the rocks," or "I feel nobody cares about me." Here, the use of the word *feel* does not actually identify feelings, but rather embodies views, thoughts, or beliefs. *Thoughts* per se are devoid of feelings, although they are often accompanied by and generate feelings or emotions. *Feelings* consist of emotions, such as sadness, joy, disappointment, and exhilaration (recall the examples of feelings listed in the list of affective words and phrases in Chapter 5).

Cognitions affect behavior, which is manifested in behavioral responses. Behavioral responses are a function of the cognitive processes of attention, retention, production, and motivation, as well as of rewarding or unrewarding consequences (Bandura, 1986). Cognitions that lead to cognitive distortions or faulty thinking can be monitored and changed.

Behavioral Change involves assisting clients to make constructive changes by focusing on their misconceptions and the extent to which they produce or contribute to their problems. The thrust of this tenet is that changes in behavior can be accomplished by changing the way in which people think. In identifying distortions and faulty thoughts and behaviors, new patterns of thinking can be learned.

With clients whose behaviors are generally rooted in misconceptions and faulty logic, the tenets can be valid. You should, of course, temper the assumptions of the tenets in recognition of the fact that other factors contribute to the ways in which people think and process information, for example, inadequate resources or adverse environments. Also, you should not assume that cognitions are necessarily faulty given the realities of culture and sociopolitical structures and social interactions in which class race, gender, or sexual orientation are major issues. Berlin (2001) and Pollack (2004) explain that the context in which people live has a significant impact on their thinking and cognitions, and therefore, the relationship between cognition and context should not be minimized or overlooked.

What are Cognitive Distortions?

Beck (1967), in separating thinking from cognition, identified automatic thoughts and cognitive distortions as factors for which cognitive restructuring is indicated. The processing of information for most of us is automatic as our minds attempt to navigate and narrate our interactions and environment. Problems occur when automatic thoughts are consistently distorted because of ingrained beliefs and faulty reasoning. Cognitive distortions are irrational, but they make logical sense to the individual. Moreover, they maintain negative thinking and reinforce negative emotions. The most common categories of distortions and negative thinking patterns conceptualized by Beck (1975) and summarized by Leahy and Holland (2000) and Walsh (2006) are as follows:

- All or Nothing Thinking *involves seeing things as all or nothing scenarios, and in most instances the glass is always half empty. "I wanted to do well on the exam, and now that I didn't I will never get into graduate school." "If I don't smoke stuff [dope] with my friends they won't hang with me again." "Unless we know the background of these clients, we won't be able to help them." In these statements, you may see the similarities between this thinking and catastrophizing and overgeneralizing.*
- Blaming *stems from perceiving others as the source of negative feelings or emotions, and therefore one avoids taking responsibility. "I feel so stressed out because a driver cut in front of me on the way home." "Her snippy attitude about going shopping with me put me in a bad mood."*

- Catastrophizing *is the belief that if a particular event or situation occurs, the results would be unbearable, effectively influencing your sense of self-worth.* "I need to study all the time, because if I don't get the highest grade possible in the exam, I will lose my financial aid and return home a failure."
- Discounting Positives *is the tendency to disqualify or minimize the good things that you or others do, and instead treats a positive as a negative.* "My friends said that I looked great in my dress I got at the secondhand store, but really, they were just being nice to me because they feel sorry for me that I don't have money." "Of the forty people at my presentation, two said that I was boring."
- Emotional Reasoning *guides your interpretation based on how you feel, rather than reality. Interpretations and beliefs are facts bolstered by negative emotions which are assumed to reflect reality.* "If I feel stuck [stupid] in social situations, then that's really who I am."
- Inability to disconfirm *functions very much like a barricade in that you are unable to accept any information that is inconsistent with your beliefs or negative thoughts. For example, if your sister with whom you frequently argue says that she is willing to keep your kids any other night except tonight because she has an appointment, your mental response may be,* "That's not the real reason. She has never liked me or my kids." *Here you discount the fact that she has on numerous other occasions cared for your children.*
- Judgment Focus *involves the perception of self and others or events as good or bad, excellent or awful. Rather than describing, accepting, or attempting to understand what is happening or considering alternative possibilities, your quick assessment of a situation or individual is either good or bad.* "I know that when I show up at the party people won't talk to me." *In some instance, you may establish arbitrary standards by which you measure yourself, only to find that you are unable to perform at this level.* "I won't do well in the class no matter how hard I try," *is an example of a self-defeating judgment statement, as is* "Everyone else is a good student, but not me." *A judgment in contrast to one that is self-defeating is an assumption that a presentation was good because* "a lot of people came."
- Jumping to Conclusions *assumes a negative when there may be limited supporting evidence. Assumptions may also take the form of mind reading and fortune telling based on a prediction of a negative* outcome. "If I don't agree to watch her children, she will be upset with me. I don't want to risk having her be angry with me."
- Mind Reading *assumes that you know what people think or will do in response to you.* "There's no point in my asking my daughter to visit me more often. She will just see it as my attempt to get attention or embarrass her. If I bring up the topic, she and I will end up in an argument; besides, she is busy with her own family."
- Negative (Mental) Filtering *results in mentally singling out bad events and ignoring the positives.* "As I was standing in the hallway at work, this kid bumped into me, you know, they are all like that. I was so angry. Then he turned around and apologized, but I pretended not to hear him. He should have apologized sooner." *In some instances, negative filters are linked to overgeneralizations about people or events.*
- Overgeneralizations or globalization *involve perceiving isolated events and using them to reach broad conclusions.* "Today, when I raised my hand in class, the instructor called on another student. He never calls on me." *Labeling is another form of overgeneralizing in which a negative label is attached to self or others based on a single incident.* "I am not a very good student, so he does not value my opinion." "He is a lousy instructor otherwise he would help everyone [me]."
- Personalizing *assumes that you had a role in or that you are responsible for a negative situation, assuming that the results were in your control.* "We were close friends and then she was called to active duty and we lost contact." *When applied to others, it is very much like blaming.* "She could have written to me while she was away." "The party that I planned in the park was a failure because it rained and people left early."
- Regret Orientation *is generally focused on the past,* "If I had worked harder, I could have gotten a better grade." "I had a chance for a better job, if I had been willing to relocate to a different city."
- Should Statements *are about self-failure or judgments about others relative to how things should be.* "I should be able to take the bus on my own when I work late." "My sister ought to be willing to care for my child when I am working late." *Should statements as judgments about others generally cause resentment and anger.* "My sister has a husband, so she doesn't really understand how hard it is for me as a single parent."

- Unfair Comparisons *measure self with others who you believe have desirable attributes. "She is prettier than I am." "Everybody in the class is smarter than me." Unfair comparisons can also lead to should or shouldn't statements when comparing self to others; for example, "Even if she is prettier than me, she shouldn't wear that color lip gloss."*
- What ifs *is the tendency for you to continually question yourself about the potential for events or the catastrophe that might happen. "I would go to the doctor to have her look at the mole on my back, but what if she finds that I am really sick?" "What if I tell my sister that I can't watch her kids tonight and she gets upset with me and she refuses to talk to me ever again?"*

In each of the above categories you are able to see how distorted and negative thoughts fit within an individual's cognitive schema. Schemas, either positive or negative, are the memory patterns that an individual uses to organize information (Berlin, 2001; Cormier & Nurius, 2003; McQuaide & Ehrenreich, 1997). Nonetheless, whether they emanate from a strengths or deficit orientation, schemas are shortcuts in thinking. Rather than processing information, the individual quickly accesses repeatable content in their mind set, without further evaluating events or interactions. Because they represent ingrained beliefs it is often difficult for people to hear or process divergent information and they may experience cognitive dissonance if they do.

The activation of negative thinking or schema can be the result of external or internal events that are adaptive or maladaptive. It is the latter, that becomes the focus of attention in your work with clients. Consider the encounter in the hallway when the youth bumped into the woman. Her automatic thought was, "They are all like that." Even though he apologized, her memory pattern, that is her global thinking about "they," was already operating in full force. As a result, she was unable to process the apology as new information and alter her cognition of the event. This event could have been triggered by a negative past experience or simply be the result of her ingrained biased thinking. If we were to examine this same situation from the internal thought vantage point, context would involve assessing her mood at the time of the incident and the extent to which it influenced her cognition and behavior. In either case, it is important that you first determine the context and the type of situation that trigger and maintain problematic behavior (Cormier & Nurius, 2003; Berlin, 2001). Further, whereas negative filtering about self and others has emotional content, blaming statements may be related to mood at a particular point in time. By the same token, negative thoughts may be grounded in the individual's reality, however irrational they may appear to be. Hence your focus should be on how external and internal stimuli that lead to cognitive errors are actual distortions or an individual's misunderstanding of his or her experiences. Keep in mind that negative thoughts and schemas do not represent the whole person. People generally are able to go about their daily lives until such time that an external or internal event ignites a particular thought pattern, upon which their reality is constructed.

Circumstances in which information is processed and the resulting related behaviors can be activated as schemas in an adaptive or maladaptive form (Cormier & Nurius, 2003). Considerations include culturally derived interpretations, developmental stage, and status. In some cultures, a positive is expressing admiration to an esteemed individual, for example, "What a beautiful sweater." In response, the individual replies as dictated by his culture, "Take it, with my gratitude." But you unaware of this norm, process the exchange through your mental filter, based on norms of Western society. Therefore, you might interpret the gesture as a negative, because you are embarrassed and uncomfortable, perhaps perceiving the exchange to be inappropriate between a male and a female. For the individual, however, his position demands this response, as it reinforces his status, specifically his ability to give away the sweater.

You should also be mindful of the fact that marginalized and oppressed people and involuntary clients are often perceived as negative thinkers with distorted realities. Yet if they continually encounter events or situations based on the reality of their experiences, can we be sure that they are actually discrepancies, without further examination? As difficult as it may be for us to acknowledge truths that may be different from our own, the focus on making change is that ultimately it is meaningful to the client, rather than what we may consider to be an acceptable pattern of thinking and behaving.

Empirical Evidence and Uses of Cognitive Restructuring

Cognitive restructuring techniques are particularly relevant for treating problems associated with low self-esteem; distorted perceptions in interpersonal relations; unrealistic expectations of self, others, and life in general; irrational fears, panic, anxiety, and depression;

control of anger and other impulses; and lack of assertiveness (Cormier & Nurius, 2003; Walsh, 2006). Selected studies have demonstrated the range of cognitive restructuring components in treating anger (Dahlen & Deffenbacher, 2000), impulse control associated with child abuse and gambling (Sharpe & Tarrier, 1992), and substance abuse and relapse (Bakker, Ward, Cryer, & Hudson, 1997; Steigerwold & Stone, 1999). Cognitive restructuring was shown as effective in the treatment of social phobia and anxiety (Feeny, 2004), spousal caregiver support groups (Gendron, Poitras, Dastoor, & Perodeau, 1996), and in increasing the self-efficacy and reducing social anxiety in adolescents (Rheingold, Herbert & Franklin, 2003; Guadiano & Herbert, 2006) and in crisis or trauma situations (Glancy & Saini, 2005; Jaycox, Zoellner & Foa, 2002). The procedure is often blended with other interventions (e.g., modeling, behavioral rehearsal, imagery, psychoeducation), because combinations of interventions are believed to be more potent than single interventions in producing change (Corcoran, 2002).

Utilization with Minors

In comparison to adult populations, there are fewer studies that show evidence of effectiveness and the use of cognitive restructuring with minors. When combined with other strategies, for example, narrative and enactive performance-based procedures, cognitive restructuring can be effective with younger children. Graham (1998) notes that for children, distortions in thinking can affect their social and interpersonal skills. The works of Giacola, Mezzich, Clark and Tarter (1999) Liau, Barriga and Gibbs (1998) and Rudolph and Clark (2001) emphasize assessing the context in which the child's behavior occurs.

Several studies found contextual variations among minors with respect to cognitive distortions. Young children with depressive and aggressive symptoms, for example, may exaggerate accounts of true negatives, raising the question as to whether their cognitions were distorted or were expressions of their actual reality (Rudolph, & Clark, 2001). With older minors, in particular those who are engaged in antisocial behaviors, cognitive distortions may be used as self-servicing explanations for their behavior (Liau, Barriga and Gibbs, 1998). Giacola, Mezzich, Clark, and Tarter (1999) suggest that unfortunately, distortions and negative self-talk exhibited by minors may not be fully explored by professionals. Instead, their behavior is often interpreted as oppositional defiant behavior, attention deficit or conduct disorder. In a further exploration of the adolescents, however, the thought patterns and negative self-talk of participants in the study were linked to harsh punishment and excessive criticism in the home life. Collectively, these studies highlight the need to assist minors to distinguish between feelings and cognitions, in view of their circumstances and symptoms.

Studies specific to anger control in minors include Seay, Fee, Holloway & Giesen, 2003; Sukhodolsky, Kassinore, & Gorman; 2004; Tate, 2001. Tate emphasizes peer influence and positive cognitive restructuring in schools, instead of strategies that are intended to control and rehabilitate and maintain adult-imposed order. Sukhodolsky, et al. (2001) found the procedure to be more effective with older adolescents than with younger children, especially when the former did not have a prior history of violent behavior. Seay, Fee, Holloway and Giesen, 2003, report improvement in anger control when specific behavior was targeted, accompanied by practicing different responses. Bailey (2001), citing the importance of the involvement of family and the school, discussed cognitive restructuring as effective when age-appropriate strategies are used.

Application of Cognitive Restructuring with Diverse Groups

The worldview and social psychological processes that shape minority perceptions and resulting thoughts or experiences are different from the majority culture. There is a need to look at different groups because history and context can influence cognitive processes and development. Work completed by Shih & Sanchez (2005) examined the role of identity among youth who have multiple identities with respect to cognition. Multiple identities, they assert, shape how individuals view their world as well as how they adjust to the real world of rejection and discrimination. Hence, as you examine distortions or negative thought patterns you should not assume that individual's cognitions and thought patterns are necessarily irrational.

At the practice level, cognitive restructuring is widely used in correctional institutions in which the majority of inmates are members of minority groups. Based on the belief that change is needed in the criminal mindset, cognitive procedures are intended to reduce recidivism. The assumption is that a patterned way of thinking essentially short circuits the ability to think in a logical manner and to use reason to make decisions. As a therapeutic intervention, the goal is to alter criminal thought processes, by restructuring or replacing them with more acceptable patterns. Pollack (2004), in critiquing cognitive procedures, explains that they tend to overlook or deemphasize the influence of environmental and structural inequities. Potocky-Tripodi (2002), however, suggests that under specific circumstances cognitive restructuring as "supportive" counseling may help immigrants and refugees with their maladaptive thoughts and increase their coping skills in intercultural situations.

Hays (1995), as cited in Cormier and Nurius (2003), in critiquing cognitive restructuring with multicultural groups, observes that this "approach supports the status quo of mainstream society" (p. 437). Cognitive models tend to presume that negative views of self and the world represent cognitive distortions of the environment. But, standardized beliefs inherent in cognitive restructuring relate to how people should perceive and react to their world require and suggest a monolithic majority society. To a large extent this is true, as the rules and standards of behaving and acting are embedded in institutional and societal structures. With this in mind, you should be aware that cognition and thoughts expressed by different groups when measured by majority culture can be considered highly irregular behavior. In using the procedure, an adaptation is in order so that it is responsive and does not oppress or punish differences.

Culturally compatible adaptations and modifications of cognitive procedures are illustrated in studies with Chinese Americans (Chen & Davenport, 2005), Latino clients (Organista, Dwyer & Azocar, 1993), Native Americans (Renfrey, 1992) and Muslims (Hodge & Nadir, 2008). Still, you should observe that the preferences, spirituality, beliefs, and self-perceptions that give purpose and direction to what people think and feel are constructed by culture and within the context of their environment (Bandura, 1988; Berlin, 2001; Bronfenbrenner, 1989). For example, Renfrey (1992) combined Native American religious ceremonies with cognitive procedures, and Hodge and Nadir (2008) advocate for adaptations to achieve a congruence between individual self-statements that are consistent with the beliefs of Muslims.

While there is a need to study different groups in their context and its influence on cognitive processes and development, there are research studies with respect to the efficacy of cognitive restructuring with different racial and cultural groups. Selected examples include interventions with African American women smokers (Ahijevych & Wewers, 1993); low-income African American woman in group treatment (Kohn, Oden, Munoz, Leavitt, & Robinson, 2002); and in addressing race-related stressors among Asian American

Pacific Islanders in the military (Loo, Ueda, & Morton, 2007). Work by Kuehlwein (1992), Ussher (1990), and Wolfe (1992) reported positive results with gay and lesbian clients. The procedure used as a component of treatment with women effectively helped them gain a sense of power in confronting cultural messages of ideal physical attributes (Srebnik & Saltzberg, 1994; Brown, 1994).

Use of the procedure with minors includes cognitive restructuring as an intervention to reduce HIV risk among African American adolescents (St Lawrence, Brasfield, Jefferson, O'Bannon & Shirley, 1995). Another study provides evidence of the effectiveness of cognitive restructuring with abused African American adolescents (Lesure-Lester, 2002). Reseach related to the efficacy of cognitive restructuring with diverse groups is limited. The studies discussed here have demonstrated that adaptations in language, culture and specific group circumstances can result in cognitive restructuring's being an effective intervention strategy with diverse groups.

Procedure of Cognitive Restructuring

The primary goal of cognitive restructuring is to alter thoughts, feelings associated with thought processes, and the accompanying self-statements or behaviors. Cognitive restructuring is particularly useful in assisting clients to gain awareness of self-defeating thoughts and misconceptions that impair their personal functioning and to replace them with beliefs and behaviors that are aligned with reality.

Several discrete steps are involved in cognitive restructuring. Although different authors may vary slightly in how they define these steps, the similarities between their models are far greater than the differences. These steps, as summarized in Table 13-3, have been adapted from those identified by Goldfried (1977), and Cormier and Nurius (2003).

Case Example

The case situation is used to demonstrate the steps of cognitive restructuring with an adolescent whose goal is to increase his comfort level in expressing himself in peer social situations at school. He reports that he is fearful of joining peer groups at lunchtime because he believes that they see him as being stuck [stupid]. Because of his fears, he will at times join a group, but not talk. When others in the group don't talk to him, he perceives their behavior as evidence of his being excluded.

TABLE-13-3 STEPS IN COGNITIVE RESTRUCTURING

1. Assist clients in accepting that their self-statements determine their emotional reactions to events. (Tool: explanation and treatment rationale)

2. Assist clients in identifying dysfunctional beliefs and thought patterns. (Tool: self-monitoring)

3. Assist clients in identifying situations involving dysfunctional cognitions.

4. Assist clients in replacing dysfunctional cognitions with functional self-statements.

5. Assist clients in identifying rewards and incentives for successful coping efforts.

1. *Assist clients in accepting that their self-statements, assumptions, and beliefs largely mediate their emotional reactions to life's events.* In this first step it is important to provide clients with an explanation and rationale for cognitive restructuring as an intervention procedure. The power difference between you and the clients is likely to become heightened when you present a goal of changing how they perceive themselves. Mistrust and suspicion may be particularly acute with minors, members of a racial or ethnic group, and involuntary clients.

Explanation of Cognitive Restructuring

Social worker: As I understand what you have said so far, you want to be a part of a group during the lunch period, but you are afraid of what others will think about you. But, you also stated that you want to be a part of the group and to talk. So that you may achieve this goal, we first need to determine what happens inside you that maintains your fears. This will involve your becoming aware of thoughts you experience in these situations—in other words, what you say to yourself before, during, and after you join a group. Generally, our thoughts occur automatically, and often we aren't fully aware of many of them. Becoming aware of self-defeating thoughts, assumptions, and beliefs is an important first step in replacing them with others that serve you better.

Social Worker's Use of Self in Explaining Cognitive Restructuring

To guide you in assisting clients to understand cognitive restructuring, the following example demonstrates how the social worker used self to explain the technique

to the adolescent. As illustrated in the following dialogue, the social worker draws upon his own experience to illustrate ways of thinking and responding to a situation. In doing so, he demonstrated to the adolescent how cognitions mediate emotions and thinking.

Social worker: What you think determines in large measure what you feel and do? For example, recently I bought a used car. My friend told me that I was stupid, or to use your word, stuck, because I bought a used car instead of a new one. I could have made various meanings or self-statements related to his message, each of which results in different feelings and actions. Consider the potential responses that I might have made to my friend's comment:

Response 1: *He's probably right; he's a bright guy, and I respect his judgment. Why didn't I think of buying a used car? He thinks that I am stupid.*

If I think that he is right, then my feelings and statements about myself are negative and I may not like my new car as much.

Response 2: *Who does he think he is, calling me stupid? He's the one who's stupid. What a jerk!*

If I think that, I'll feel angry and defensive and I may get in an argument over which one of us is right.

Response 3: *It's apparent that my friend and I have different ideas about cars. He's entitled to his opinion, although I don't agree with him and I feel good about buying the new car. I don't like his referring to my choice as stupid, though. There's no point in getting bent out of shape over it, but I think I'll let him know how I feel about what he said to me.*

If I think these thoughts, I'm less likely to experience negative feelings about myself. I'll feel good about my actions despite the other person's difference of opinion, and I won't be unduly influenced by his lack of sensitivity.

The social worker then adds that other responses could be made, but these three should suffice to make the point. He then points out that the task at hand is to enable the adolescent to master his fears, and to explore together his self-statements and how they affect his feelings and behavior. In using a self example, he is able to pinpoint how thoughts and beliefs can cause difficulties as well as how the cognitive restructuring will help the two of them to begin working on developing other thoughts that are realistic and consistent with his goal.

When the rationale for cognitive restructuring is presented in a simple, straightforward manner, the majority of clients will agree to proceed. Nevertheless, it is important to elicit their reactions to your explanation and allow time for discussion and questions. You should not proceed with cognitive restructuring until clients have indicated that they are receptive to and are committed to your implementing the intervention. Commitment is necessary because clients may resist changing their beliefs when they feel they are being coerced to adopt your beliefs or those of another person.

2. *Assist clients in identifying self-statements, beliefs and patterns of thoughts that underlie their problems.* Once clients accept the proposition that thoughts and beliefs mediate emotional reactions, your next task is to assist them to examine those personal thoughts and beliefs that pertain to their difficulties. This step requires detailed exploration of events related to problematic situations and their antecedents, with particular emphasis on cognitions that accompany distressing emotions. For example, some clients may attribute their problems to fate, inherent personal attributes, and other forces beyond their control. In identifying key misconceptions, both you and the client need to agree on the beliefs that will be the focus of change.

You can begin the process of exploration by focusing on problematic events that occurred during the preceding week or on events surrounding a problem the client has targeted for change. As you mutually explore these events, you should elicit specific details regarding the client's overt behaviors, cognitions (i.e., self-statements and images), and emotional reactions. Focusing on all three aspects helps you and the client to see the connections between them and to understand the role of cognitions in mediating feelings and behaviors. As clients identify their self-statements and beliefs, they will become increasingly aware that automatic thoughts and beliefs they have not subjected to critical analysis act as powerful determinants of their behavior. This, in turn, increases their receptivity and motivation to work on tasks that seek to liberate them from counterproductive thoughts, misconceptions, and beliefs.

As you and the client further explore the situation, you will be able to *identify thoughts and feelings that occur before, during, and after events*. To elicit self-statements, ask the client to recreate the situation just as it unfolded, recalling exactly what he or she thought, felt, and did. For example, with the adolescent, the social worker asked him to describe his thoughts and feelings when he joined the group. If reflection had proven to be difficult for him, the social worker could ask him to close his eyes and *run a movie* of his

thoughts and feelings prior to, during, and after the problematic event.

By listening to the adolescent, as he described his thoughts, the social worker was able to pinpoint cognitive sets that predisposed him to experience certain emotions and to behave in predictable ways. To illustrate, consider the self-statements that the social worker elicited from him about joining peers in the school lunchroom:

- *"I'm outey [out of here—disappear]. Straight up [the truth is], I'm not sure I want to join the others. If I do, I'll just cool [sit] there and feel that they be [are] hating [left out] on me."*
- *"If I show, they'll dis me [disrespect me] about something."*
- *"I'd better show [join in]; otherwise, they will be hollering at me later about some other stuff. I'm outey, straight up."*
- *"I'm cool" [okay].*

Given these self-statements, the adolescent clearly felt uneasy and apprehensive about joining his peers. These thoughts predisposed him to enter the situation programmed for defeat. In addition to his self debate, when he recreated the situation his nonverbal cues—for example, his physical posture—spoke volumes. The social worker was able to observe that his self-defeating statements not only dominated his thinking, they also contributed to his presentation of self within the group.

Exploration of self-statements during events often reveals that thoughts maintain self-defeating feelings and behaviors and drastically reduce personal effectiveness. For example, the adolescent tended to dwell on his fears and was vigilant to the possible negative reactions of others. As a result, he was unable to *tune in* fully to conversations or to express himself in a way that created favorable impressions. In other words, he found it difficult to be fully present and involved because of his self-consciousness and fears about exposing his imagined personal inadequacies.

To illustrate the destructive impact of his thoughts, let us again consider his self-statements in the lunch group with his peers:

- *"Well, here I am, just like always, I am being dissed [disrespected, left out of the conversation]."*
- *"I wish I had the low, low [something interesting to say], but my life's ain't about doing anything [uninteresting]. What's up with this? They ain't interested in any low [ideas, information] that I might put out [say]."*

- *"Go figure, they're wondering why I even show [join them]. I don't add anything to the group. I cool, I out of here [I don't add anything to the group]."*

It is apparent from these and other like self-statements that the adolescent is dwelling on self-defeating thoughts. Because he thinks of himself as having little or nothing to offer, he behaves accordingly, and he feels unwanted and unworthy to actively participate. His preoccupation with these thoughts and assumptions about himself effectively blocks him from engaging with his peers.

Clients' self-statements and feelings following events reveal the impact of earlier thoughts and behaviors on subsequent feelings, highlighting further the mediating function of cognitions. Moreover, the conclusions that clients draw about the outcomes of events indicate whether they are able to focus on positive aspects of their behavior and to identify challenges for further growth or whether they merely perceive an event as the latest in a long series of failures caused by their personal inadequacies. The meanings that clients draw from events, of course, powerfully shape their attitudes and feelings toward future events. Consider the thoughts and feelings of the adolescent as he describes his encounter with the group:

- *"I out man [blew it again]. I'm too threw [I'm finished; I might as well quit trying]. This ain't real for sure [no use kidding myself; I just can't talk with others]."*
- *"It ain't like that [they didn't really try to include me]. They be hating on me [it's obvious they could care less about me]. They'd probably be pleased if I didn't join them tomorrow."*
- *"This is whack [uncomfortable; I won't eat lunch with them anymore]. I don't enjoy it, and I'm sure they don't either. Tomorrow I outey [eat by myself], for shiddley [for sure]."*

Clearly, his feelings and thoughts have led to a sense of failure. Without intervention into his circular self-defeating thought patterns, he may tend to withdraw even further and perhaps become depressed.

The following questions can be used to challenge clients to assess the rationality of their beliefs and self-statements:

- *Asking them how they reached certain conclusions*
- *Challenging them to present evidence supporting dysfunctional views or beliefs*
- *Challenging the logic of beliefs that magnify feared consequences of certain actions*

To assist the adolescent to assess the rationality of his conclusions, for example, the social worker responded as follows:

Social worker: So did someone "dis" you when you joined the group? What did they say that made you think that they were "hating" on you?

Through guided practice, the social worker provides the adolescent with the impetus to critically examine the validity of his thoughts. As illustrated in the following example, clients may not immediately acknowledge the irrationality of certain beliefs, especially those that are deeply embedded in their belief systems:

Adolescent client: Well, you see, this girl, I got the low [perception, idea], by the way she was looking at me, straight-up, this was whack [not good].

Clients can tenaciously cling to key misconceptions and argue persuasively about their validity. You must therefore be prepared to challenge or "dispute" such irrational beliefs and to persist in assisting clients to recognize the costs or disadvantages associated with not relinquishing these beliefs. At this point, the social worker prompts the adolescent to consider the relationships between his thoughts and his goal.

Social worker: Well, if you continue think that joining in with the group is whack, and you continue to be "outey," how will this affect your goal of joining with a group during the lunch period?

The following client self-statements and the social worker's responses further illustrates ways that can direct clients to analyze the validity of their statements.

Student Preparing for Exam
Self-statement:
- *"I've got to study every available moment. If I don't get the highest score on that test, it will be just awful."*

Social worker responses:
- *"Let's just suppose for a moment you really bombed on the test. What would it really mean for you?"*

Relative Caring for Children
Self-statement:
- *"I don't want to care for her children, but if I don't she'll be furious. I don't want to risk displeasing her and get her angry at me."*

Social worker responses:
- *"How have you concluded she'd be furious?"*

Elderly Client Concerned about Visits

Self-statement:

- *"There's no point in my asking my daughter to come and visit me more often. She will just see it as my attempting to get attention and trying to embarrass her. If I bring up the topic, we will just end up in an argument. She's busy with her job and her own family."*

Social worker responses:

- *"Sounds like you've convinced yourself that your daughter would not understand that you would like to see her more often. Have you explained this to her?"*

Clusters of misconceptions are commonly associated with problematic behavior. Often it is possible for you to discern such patterns of thoughts within one session by closely following feelings and eliciting accompanying thoughts. Table 13-4 provides our conception of belief clusters typically associated with unreasonable self-expectations.

By identifying clusters or patterns of misconceptions, you can direct your efforts to the theme common to all of them, rather than dealing with each misconception as a separate entity. The cluster of statements of the elderly client concerned about her daughter's visiting pattern, for example, is characteristic of jumping to conclusions or setting unrealistic expectations for oneself and others. Focusing on the central themes presented of self-statements allows you to conserve your efforts, because the related misconceptions are often slight derivatives of the central one.

3. Assist clients in identifying situations that engender dysfunctional cognitions. Pinpointing places where stressful events occur, key persons involved, and situations that involve demeaning oneself in the face of self-expectations enables you and the client to develop tasks and coping strategies that are tailored to those specific situations.

Self-monitoring between sessions is a concrete way for clients to measure and recognize cognitions related to their difficulties and problematic events. They are also able to become increasingly aware of the pervasive nature of their thoughts and the need to actively cope with them. Self-monitoring thus expands self-awareness and paves the way for later coping efforts.

To facilitate self-monitoring, with the adolescent, the social worker asked him to keep daily logs to record information, as illustrated in Figure 13-4. In the log, the adolescent recorded the situation, his feelings, beliefs, and self-statements.

Daily self-monitoring is a valuable tool because the logs focus a client's efforts between sessions; clarify the connections between cognitions and feelings; and provide information about the prevalence and intensity of thoughts, images, and feelings. In this case, keeping a daily log stimulated the adolescent to logically examine his thoughts.

Social Worker: After completing a week of logs, did you find anything out about yourself and the way that you think and behaved when you are with a group?

Adolescent Client: Yeah, I could see that I was whacked [out of bounds], and when I was scared I acted stuck. Then I wanted to be out of there before they dissed me.

To prevent clients from feeling overwhelmed by the task of keeping a log, you might suggest they initially limit their recording to events related to those identified during the session and that they record only about three such events each day. Otherwise, they may experience this task as a burden. As other counterproductive patterns of thoughts emerge during sessions, the focus of self-monitoring can be shifted as necessary.

TABLE-13-4 BELIEFS AND SELF-EXPECTATIONS

BELIEFS	SELF-EXPECTATIONS
Beliefs about oneself	I am usually not very good at anything that I do.
	My accomplishments aren't that significant, anyone could have done it.
Beliefs about others' perceptions and expectations of oneself	My partner dismisses my opinion, because I am not very smart.
	When I compare myself with others, I never quite measure up.
Expectations of oneself	At work, I feel I must perform better than others in my unit.
	I should be able to do lots of things and perform at a high level.
Expectations of others	She should understand how I feel without my having to tell her. My children should want to visit me.

Date: Tuesday, September 6, 2008		
Situation or Event	**Feelings** (Rate rationality from 1 to 10)	**Beliefs or Self-Statements** (Rate intensity from 1 to 10)
1. Joined group at lunch time	Scared (7) Stuck (7)	They will dis me, this is whack (6)
2. No one said anything to me; I didn't say anything	I'm outey (4); afraid to join in (8); disgusted with self (7)	I should speak up (9); they will ignore me and I'd be embarrassed (2); it is not worth the hassle (3)

FIG-13-4 Daily Log for Adolescent

In addition to situations and events, explorations of cognitions and self-monitoring can include images, as they may also play a key role in mediating emotions. As you and the client review completed log sheets and continue to identify problematic feelings and cognitions associated with stressful events, it is important to note recurring situations or themes. Recurring themes for the adolescent, for example, was his fear about being left out.

4. Assist clients in substituting functional self-statements for self-defeating cognitions. As clients expand their awareness of their dysfunctional thoughts, beliefs, and images, your goal is to help them recognize how their thought patterns produce negative emotional reactions. Another goal is to help them cope as they begin to learn new patterns. Coping strategies typically consist of self-statements that are both realistic and effective in eliminating negative emotional reactions and self-defeating behaviors. Although functional self-statements foster courage and facilitate active coping efforts, they are not completely idealistic. That is, they do not ignore the struggles inherent in shifting from habitual, ingrained patterns of thinking, feeling, and behaving to new patterns. Instead, coping self-statements embody recognition of the difficulties and anxiety inherent in risking new behavior. To introduce the adolescent to coping self-statements, the social worker explained and modeled positive self-statements:

Social worker: Now that you've identified your key self-defeating beliefs and thoughts, we're going to focus on how to replace them with new self-statements. It

will take a lot of hard work on your part, but as you practice new self-statements, you'll find that they will become more and more natural allowing you to rely less on old ways of thinking.

After providing this explanation to the adolescent, the social worker modeled coping self-statements that the adolescent could substitute for self-defeating thoughts and beliefs. In the exercise, he assumed the role of the adolescent, expressing his thoughts as he might when coping with the target situation.

Social Worker as Adolescent client: I know a part of me wants to avoid being dis [the discomfort of socializing]. I feel whack [scared], but it's not going to get any better by being outey [withdrawing]. "I don't have to low [talk] a lot to be part of the group. If I tune [listen] to the others and get my mind off myself, I can be cool [involve myself more].

Notice how the social worker modeled the potential struggle going on within the adolescent rather than modeling "mastery" self-statements. This is important because coping self-statements must closely reflect a client's actual experience, whereas mastery self-statements do not. Moreover, the former convey empathy for and understanding of the client's struggle, which in turn inspires greater confidence in the process and in the social worker. As an alternative self-statement, the social worker proposed the following:

Social worker: Yes, you might think: "I can't expect them to include me in their conversations. It would be nice if they did, but if they're going to do so, I'll have to be responsible for including myself. It's better than withdrawing and feeling out of it."

After modeling coping self-statements, it is appropriate to ask whether the client feels ready to practice similar behavior. To enhance the effectiveness of guided practice, you could suggest that clients close their eyes and picture themselves in the exact situation they will be in *before* engaging in the targeted behavior. When they report they have succeeded in capturing this situation, ask them to think aloud the thoughts they typically experience when contemplating the targeted behavior. Then ask them to substitute coping thoughts, coaching them as needed. Give positive feedback and encouragement when they produce reinforcing self statements independently, even though they may continue to struggle with conflicting thoughts. You may also expect that clients will express doubt and uncertainty about their ability to master new patterns of thinking. If they do, explain that most people experience misgivings as they experiment with new ways of thinking. Continue to practice with them until they feel relatively comfortable in their ability to generate new self-statements.

When the client demonstrates increased confidence in employing coping self-statements before entering a target situation, you can shift to a strategy of self-statements *during* the time the client is actually in the target situation. Again, model coping self-statements, as done here with the adolescent client:

Social Worker as Adolescent: Okay, I'm feeling anxious. That's to be expected. I can still pay attention and show interest in the group. I can tune [communicate] by nodding my head, laughing when someone says something funny and not feeling that this is whack. When I feel more comfortable, I can join in by asking for clarification if I want to know more. This is another way to show interest. If I have some take on the subject they're discussing, I think that my opinions are worth as much as theirs. Go ahead, take a chance and express them, but look at others as I talk.

Following the modeling exercise, the social worker asked the youth to describe his feelings about what had happened so far. Inquiring about feelings is important; for example, had the modeling resulted in the youth becoming anxious, uncomfortable, or skeptical, the social worker would need to deal with these feelings before proceeding further. Because he had demonstrated the ability to generate positive self-statements in the *during* phase, the social worker asked him to rehearse self-statements in the *after* phase of the contact.

Again, it is important for the social worker to model and have the client rehearse reinforcing statements. Here are some examples:

Social Worker as Adolescent: "Well, I did it. I stuck it out and even said a couple of things. That's a step in the right direction."

- *Adolescent Statement:* "*No one played me [ignored me] when I sat down with the group. Man, it was hot [good] maybe I'm not stuck [stupid] so bad after all. Even though I was on ten [anxious] it was 100 percent real [good], it was so fire that it snuck upon me [even better than I expected]. It's a rap, [accomplishment].*"

To further assist clients in utilizing positive statements, it is beneficial to negotiate them as tasks between sessions. Between-session tasks foster autonomy and

independent action by clients. But don't rush them, because undue pressure may be perceived as threatening or discouraging. You may use the readiness scale (defined earlier in this chapter) as a gauge.

Continued self-monitoring by clients is essential as they implement this step of the cognitive restructuring process. Maintaining a daily log, similar to the format suggested in Figure 13-4, is also important. As the adolescent progresses, a fourth column could be added, titled *"Rational or Positive Coping Self-Statements."* Filling in this column should facilitate active reinforcing statements as they replace self-defeating ones.

Another technique that helps clients to cope with automatic dysfunctional self-statements is to encourage them, upon first awareness of such thoughts, to nip them in the bud. You might suggest that their first awareness of such thoughts is a flashing yellow signal, indicating caution and that they need to replace their thoughts immediately. One option involves *having a talk with oneself.* During their self-dialogue, positive thoughts can be substituted.

Substituting coping self-statements for self-defeating thoughts or misconceptions forms the heart of cognitive restructuring. Because they tend to be automatic and deeply embedded, however, dysfunctional thoughts tend to persist. As a result, clients sometimes become discouraged when they do not achieve quick mastery of this step. It is important to explain that step 4 may extend across a number of weeks. Should clients become discouraged with their progress, you can reassure them by explaining that change occurs gradually and that a satisfactory degree of mastery is generally achieved over time.

5. *Assist clients in rewarding themselves for successful coping efforts.* For clients who attend only to their failures and shortcomings and rarely, if ever, give themselves positive feedback, step 5 in cognitive restructuring is especially important. To reinforce their new statements and behaviors, you should explain the rationale for giving oneself credit for progress.

Social worker: So you joined the group. That exciting, given where you started. It's important to learn to give yourself credit for your accomplishments. What are your thoughts on how you would like to celebrate?

Adolescent: Well, it's a done deal as far as I am concerned. I even sent a text to a girl in the group, and she wrote back "r u ok, SPK."

Social Worker: Well, that is a good thing! I also want you to think about rewarding statements that you can make to yourself. I'm going to pretend that I am you. I'll say aloud self-statements you might think about to give yourself credit.

- *"I wasn't sure that I was up to it but I did it!"*
- *"I backed off. I dismissed my negative thoughts and stayed in the game!"*

Social Worker: Now what would you say to yourself?

Adolescent: Like I told you man, it's a rap. Everything is cool, maybe I'll go to a movie.

For some clients, formulating and rewarding positive self-statements may be difficult and they may feel awkward or self-conscious. Adults may be more readily able to think about rewards than minors. When clients are reluctant, empathic understanding and encouragement on your part will usually prompt them to try this exercise. Some clients, like the adolescent, may want to focus only on the overall outcome. For example, he has achieved his goal of joining a lunchroom group, plus a bonus of a text message exchange with a female in the group. But, it is important that you review a client's progress with them and provide positive feedback by identifying the small and often subtle incremental signs of growth over time. By way of review, you can also encourage clients to review their self-monitoring logs and credit their record of their daily successes. Their doing so acts as a powerful reinforcement.

Strengths, Limitations, and Cautions

Cognitive restructuring is an effective procedure that has been implemented to address a range of problems. It is particularly useful in altering perceptions, distorted beliefs, and thought patterns that result in negative or self-defeating behaviors. As a process, it is also compatible with crisis intervention, the task-centered system, and solution-focused treatment. The "miracle question" a solution-focused technique, may, indeed, motivate clients to address problematic behaviors and encourage them to formulate specific change behavioral goals. For the adolescent in the case situations, for example, the miracle question may have helped him to imagine his being accepted by the peer group.

In assisting clients to make changes, however, social workers must not mistakenly assume that clients will be able to perform new behaviors solely as a result of changes in their cognitions or beliefs. In reality, they may lack cognitive and social skills, and require instruction and

practice before they can effectively perform new behaviors. Cognitive restructuring removes cognitive barriers to change and fosters a willingness to risk new behaviors, but it does not always equip clients with the skills required to perform those new behaviors. In addition, as noted by Vodde and Gallant (2002), simply changing one's story does not ensure a certain outcome, given the presence of very real constraints such as oppression, adverse social forces, and lack of power. Without an acknowledgment of these factors, minority clients, for example, may potentially perceive cognitive restructuring as just another form of social control and ideological domination. Client opposition or reactance to cognitive restructuring may result from a failure on the part of the social worker to understand these externalizing factors.

The worldview and social psychological processes that shape minority perceptions and resulting thoughts or experiences are different from those noted with the majority culture. Hays (1995), as cited in Cormier and Nurius (2003), in critiquing cognitive restructuring with multicultural groups, observes that this approach supports the status quo of mainstream society and suggests that standardized beliefs exist about how people should perceive and react to their world. Thus, according to Hays, cognitive restructuring has the potential to place blame on the individual when, in fact, the client's perceptions, beliefs, and behaviors may accurately reflect injustices experienced by that person. Herein lies a central challenge to using cognitive restructuring with minority group and involuntary clients. Attempts to reshape the thought patterns and perceptions so as to reflect a construction of a different pattern in contrast to their actual experience may be perceived as a threat.

Involuntary clients who are minority adolescents encountered in school settings are often labeled as oppositional defiant. Despite their style of dress, behavior, language, and choice of music, these clients may respond to interventions based on cognitive and social learning theories of vicarious capability and modeling. Indeed, modeling or observational learning procedures of cognitive restructuring may hold promise when working with such individuals because these strategies may be perceived as less threatening, especially if the focus is on a specific behavior, rather than the perceptions or experiences of the whole person.

Of course, some minority group members have mastered a dual frame of reference that is selectively congruent with dominant views and beliefs. For these individuals, cognitive restructuring may be a useful intervention procedure. Similarly, this approach may be beneficial when thoughts or beliefs are derived from interpersonal relations within groups—for example, the adolescent client in the peer group situation. In either case, use of cognitive restructuring strategies with minorities requires an orientation to the realities of their experience, beliefs, and values.

Finally, although cognitive theorists attribute most dysfunctional emotional and behavioral patterns to mistaken beliefs, these are by no means the only causes. Dysfunctions may be produced by numerous biophysical problems, including brain injury, neurological disorders, thyroid imbalance, blood sugar imbalance, circulatory disorders associated with aging, ingestion of toxic substances, malnutrition, and other forms of chemical imbalance. Consequently, these possibilities should be considered before undertaking cognitive restructuring.

Solution-focused Brief Treatment

Solution-focused is a postmodern, constructivist approach with a unique focus on resolving client's concerns (Murray & Murray, 2004). It grew out of Steve de Shazer and Imsoo Kim Berg and their associates' work at the Brief Family Therapy Center in Milwaukee, Wisconsin (Nichols & Schwartz, 2004; Trepper, Dolan, McCollum & Nelson, 2006). It was influenced by the views of Milton Erickson, who believed that people were constrained by the social construction of their problems. A basic assumption is that people have untapped unconscious resources, which can be released by shifting their perspectives. In this regard, the approach integrates aspects of cognitive restructuring. Mainly, as the professional you have an active role in first "helping clients to question self-defeating constructions," and then assisting them to construct "new and more productive perspectives" (Nichols & Schwartz, 2004, p. 101). Work with clients is facilitated by having them identify and prioritize solutions. Like the task-centered system the solution-focused approach is based on the premise that change can occur over a brief period of time.[5]

Tenets of Solution-Focused

The approach has emerged over the past 20 years as a strategy for working with adults, minors, families, including clients who are involuntary. In the view of de Shazer and Berg, traditional practice was saturated with an emphasis on problems, often without regard to client's strengths and capacities (DeJong & Berg, 1998). Although clients may begin with a problem statement, a key belief is that problems and analysis does not necessarily predict a client's ability to problem solve (Corcoran, 2008). Further the approach emphasizes that solutions and problems are not necessarily connected. Therefore, it is preferable to engage clients in developing solutions rather than assessing and discovering how problems developed or were perpetuated (Koob, 2003; Nichols & Schwartz, 2004).

Oriented toward the future, rather the past, the solution-focused treatment approach asserts that clients have a right to determine their desired outcomes. Moreover, it is believed that change occurs in a relatively brief time period, especially when clients are empowered and motivated to use their expertise to construct solutions. Your role is to listen, to absorb information that clients provide, and subsequently guide them toward solutions utilizing the "language of change" (De Jong & Berg, 2002, p. 49). Lee (2003) believes that these principles are motivating factors that strengthen the viability of the solution-focused approach in cross-cultural practice.

Theoretical Framework

The solution-focused approach borrows from social constructivists the belief that people use language to create their reality (de Shazer & Berg, 1993). Reality is constructed by culture and context, as well as perceptions and life experiences, thus an absolute truth does not exist (Murray & Murray, 2004). For example, truths about normative functioning or development are a phenomenon that has been imposed by professionals, which may have little relationship to the reality of the client's situation (Freud, 1999; Nichols & Schwartz, 2004). Therefore, it is more important for you to understand the way in which clients construct the meaning of their experiences and relationships. The approach also draws from cognitive-behavioral theory the assumption that cognitions guide language and behavior.

Empirical Evidence and Uses of Solution-Focused Strategies

Solution-focused brief treatment is utilized in a variety of settings and with diverse populations, including involuntary clients (Berg & Kelly, 2000; Corcoran,

2008; DeJong & Berg, 2001; Tohn & Oshlag, 1996; Trepper, et al., 2006). Ingersoll-Dayton, Schroepfer, and Pryce (1999) found that a focus on positive attributes of nursing home residents with dementia, rather than their behavioral problems, changed interactions between the residents and the staff. Murray and Murray (2004) used the approach in premarital counseling to assist couples to build a vision for the marriage. The efficacy of solution-focused approach has also been demonstrated in couples' therapy by McCollum and Trepper (2001) and Nelson and Kelly (2001).

Exception-based solutions were found to be more successful when compared with attempts to stop or change the abusive behavior of male participants (Corcoran & Franklin, 1998). Similar results occurred in a treatment group of male domestic violence offenders. In working with these men, Lee, Greene, and Rheinscheld's (1999) results showed that empowering the men to identify solutions to their behavior was more effective than focusing on their violent behavior. Another study involved women in abusive relationships. This work combined solution-focused strategies with other approaches as a means to help the participants move away from their "problem-saturated" focus and to engage them in solutions (McQuaide, 1996). Their narratives were analyzed using techniques derived from psychodynamic and cognitive-behavioral approaches, but the solution-focused narratives were the basis for changing the clients' emotional states (McQuaide, 1996).

Utilization with Minors

In school settings with children and adolescents, scaling and miracle questions were used to explore feelings, develop behavioral goals, and encourage positive behaviors (Corcoran & Stephenson, 2000; Franklin & Streeter, 2004; Springer, Lynch, & Rubin, 2000). Using an ecological framework, Teal (2000) describes teachers, parents, and school counselors as resources and as co-creators of solutions to classroom behavioral problems. Similarly, for children who were assigned to social skills training groups, parents have become involved in developing solutions as a means to address behavioral problems (Watkins & Kurtz, 2001). Studies have also shown the approach to be effective in helping minors to improve their social social skills and in responding to classroom management and school-related behavior problems (Cook & Kaffenberger, 2003; Gingerich & Eisengard, 2000; Gingerich & Wabeke, 2001). Additional work with adolescents includes using the solution-focused approach with juvenile offenders and treatment with difficult adolescents (Corcoran, 1997;

Selekman, 2005) and mixed strategies, including tasks and cognitive-behavioral group intervention, with pregnant and parenting adolescents (Harris & Franklin, 2003). Exception and scaling questions were found to be effective in fostering behavioral changes of high-risk youth, juvenile offenders, and high-risk middle and high school students referred for academic or behavioral problems (Corcoran, 1998, 1997).

Application with Diverse Groups

Critiques of the solution-focused approach point to a lack of attention on the diversity of clients (Corcoran, 2008). Dermer, Hemesath and Russell (1998) praised the approach for its explicit attention to competence and strengths, but, they believe that it fails to address gender-related power differences. For example, they might argue that despite a change in the narrative of men and women in abusive relationships, the change lacked sufficient attention to the narrative power differences.

The solution-focused approach, nonetheless, is considered to be responsive to diverse groups, because its basic thrust emphasizes the expert narrative and language of clients. Proponents assert that because the professionals respect and honor the distinct cultural background of clients, the approach is consistent with the demands of multicultural practice with individual clients in social service agencies (DeJong & Berg, 2002; Pichot & Dolan, 2003; Trepper, et al., 2006). The results of previously cited work in schools, child protection agencies, and with juvenile offenders and involuntary clients, of which a majority were members of diverse groups, is promising.

Solution-Focused Procedures and Techniques

A series of questions which follows the stages of helping, specifically, engagement, assessment, goal setting, intervention, and termination are used in this approach. *Well-formed goals* drive the plans for actions that are important to the client, feasible, and usually the beginning of something (Corcoran, 2008; DeJong & Miller, 1995; Tohn & Oshlag, 1996). Goal setting begins as soon as you have contact with the client (Berg, 1994). In the development of goals, solutions sought by the client are framed on the basis of exceptions. For example, clients are asked about the absence of the problem and it is on this basis that the work toward solutions is formed.

Typical interview questions that engage the client's capacity to think about the future and identify solutions include the following queries adapted from Lipchik (2002) and de Shazer & Berg (1993):

1. How will you know when your problem is solved?
2. What will be different when the problem is solved?
3. What signs will indicate to you that you don't have to see me any longer?
4. Can you describe what will be different in terms of your behavior, thoughts, or feelings?
5. What signs will indicate to you that others involved in this situation are behaving, thinking, or feeling differently?

Four questions typically guide the assessment, goal-setting, and intervention process. The various types of interview questions used to move clients toward specific goals and to think of solutions are summarized in Table 13-5. The Corning family's goal to move from transitional housing to an apartment is used to illustrate how each question type can be used.

Scaling questions solicit the client's assessment of progress or readiness to complete a well-formed goal; this helps you and the client gauge readiness to attempt a well-formed goal about leaving home. For example, asking Mr. and Mrs. Corning, "On a scale of 1 to 10, how ready do you feel to talk about moving out of transitional housing?" In addition to assessing readiness, scaling questions can also identify behaviors and resources that are needed to achieve goals (Corcoran, 2008; Trepper, et al., 2006). For the Cornings, in view of Mr. Corning's employment status, their resource needs meant that Mrs. Corning would be required to work additional hours so that the family would have money for rent.

Scaling questions may also be used to avert a client from returning to problematic behaviors and to develop specific behavioral indicators along a continuum. For example, a client might be asked to assess the potential of a relapse with alcohol: "On a scale of 1 to 10, where 1 is 'there is no chance I will relapse' and 10 is 'I feel like having a drink as soon as I leave here,' where would you rate yourself?" Use of the scaling question in this way helps to determine what kinds of goals might prove useful in moving the risk to a lower and safer level.

TABLE-13-5 SOLUTION-FOCUSED QUESTIONS

Scaling

Coping

Exceptions

Miracle

Also, if this client indicated that he was at the lower end of the scale with respect to a relapse, you would point to the progress that he has already made.

Coping questions capture the resources and strengths that clients have used previously when dealing with issues. For example, you might ask the Cornings, "In the past, when you attempted to find housing, what were some of the things that you tried that worked?" Coping questions credit the prior efforts of clients, and are intended to clarify and energize their strengths and capacities. Focusing on strengths can also reinforce the positives of a client's coping: "In view of the chaos that you described in the transitional housing facility, please tell me how you have managed to find time to be actively involved with your children?"

Another procedure, *exception questions, are* considered to be the core of the intervention (Corcoran, 2008). Designed to diminish the problem focus, these questions assist clients to identity when their current situation did not exist (Bertolino & O'Hanlon, 2002: DeJong & Berg, 2002; Trepper, et al., 2006; Shoham, Rohrbaugh & Patterson, 1995). For example, in addressing Mr. and Mrs. Corning, "What was it like when you owned your home and lived in a neighborhood of your own choosing?" Their concerns about the difficulties that the older children were currently experiencing in school might be might be addressed as, "How did the children do in school before the family moved into the transitional housing facility?"

The exception question also advances the client's ability to externalize or separate themselves from the problem by building upon their strengths and resources (Corcoran, 2008). Mr. Corning, for example, had expressed a firm belief that "a man should provide for his family." Your response would emphasize that he had done so up until the time he had lost his job. In essence, by reframing you address his self-defeating statement.

Exception questions can also encourage the exploration of past or current behaviors, effectively helping clients to discover clues to solutions within their own experience. For example, in situations involving parent–adolescent conflict, each would be asked to think of times in which they had interacted, either now or in the past, without conflict and have enjoyed each other.

Finally, *miracle questions* draw attention to what could be different and what would need to change to reach a desired state (Corcoran, 2008; Koob, 2003; Lipchik, 2002). Koob (2003) cites research that concludes that having a positive vision about the future is a motivating force. In responding to miracle questions, clients identify goals related to where they would like to see themselves tomorrow, imagining how things would look if, by a miracle, the problem disappeared overnight. For Mr. Corning, the miracle was "having a fulltime job," and that the "family would live in a mixed race neighborhood in which the children would feel comfortable." They both laughed when Mrs. Corning playfully added, "A three bedroom house with a white picket fence and a garden." Their responses in essence shaped the work to be completed between them and the social worker and the collaborative construction of change-oriented solutions.

Tasks

Formula tasks are used to accomplish goals identified by the miracle questions in a proactive manner (homework assignment). For example, a social worker might direct a couple who are experiencing conflict in their relationship to engage in *exceptions*, such as talking more with each other when they are not in conflict. Other formula tasks may require a parent and teen to make observations—for example, "Before the next session, observe your interactions, and focus on those interactions that you would like to continue." The Corning couple might also be assigned *prediction tasks*, in which they are asked to predict the status of their problem, for better or for worse, tomorrow (de Shazer, 1988).

In the solution-focused approach, three types of individuals are identified: *customers, complainants, or visitors* (Corcoran, 2008; Jordan & Franklin, 2003). The individual or family who is willing to make a commitment to change is called the *customer*. Therefore, the series of questions and the tasks to be completed are directed to them. Those individuals who identify a concern but do not see themselves as part of the problem or solution are called *complainants*. A person who is willing to be minimally or peripherally involved but is not invested in the change effort is referred to as a *visitor*. These distinctions allow you to identify where potential clients stand relative to their commitment to change and their ownership of concerns. In distinguishing the various types of individuals, the social worker can focus the change effort on the concerns identified by the customer. There may be instances however, when it is advisable to engage the complainant or visitor, if only to ensure that they do not interfere with the customer's efforts.

Strengths and Limitations

The solution-focused approach involves practical techniques and procedures that can be readily learned

by you that are applicable in many situations. For example, miracle questions encourage clients to deliberate and become invested in a future vision. The particular emphasis on clients' strengths and positive attributes are also significant contributions with respect to the image of clients and their capacities. The solution-focused approach affirms that change—albeit even small gains—can occur over a brief period of time. The potential of rapid change encourages clients to focus on and utilize their strengths and resources and their optimism about the future.

How the solution-focused approach is used in the future will depend in part on the results of studies analyzing when and how the approach is best applied. The body of evidence supporting the solution-focused approach is growing but is not yet robust as a result of methodological and design concerns (Corcoran, 2008). As the approach has matured, promising empirical evidence have shown its efficacy with diverse populations and with the variety of problems presented by clients (Trepper, et al., 2006). Previously discussed studies have also demonstrated the effectiveness of using certain questions with specific populations, including minors. For example, the use of the miracle exception question was found to be successful resolving problematic classroom behavior (Corcoran & Stephenson, 2000; Franklin & Streeter, 2004; Springer, Lynch & Rubin, 2000).

Particular aspects of the process and procedures of the approach have been criticized. Both critics and proponents of the solution-focused approach have questioned whether the approach is, in fact, collaborative as opposed to being more directive in nature, in particular, the assigning of tasks and the emphasis on solutions (Wylie, 1990; Lipchik, 1997; O'Hanlon, 1996). In addition, research conducted by family therapists using the approach, for example, revealed discrepancies between clients' experiences and the observations made by their therapists related to outcomes (Metcalf, Thomas, Duncan, Miller, & Hubble, 1996). Storm (1991) and Lipchik (1997) maintain as a result of their work that the primary focus on adherence to solutions was disconcerting for some clients. Specifically, the positive thrust of the approach prevented them from discussing their real concerns and influenced clients to explore solutions and to avoid talking about their problems. The latter of which is believed to have limited value (Efran & Schenker, 1993). Similarly, the limited attention on behaviors and not on feelings ignores the connection between cognitions (Lipchick, 2002). These critiques, however, in many respects ignore the fact that clients seeking help are socialized to talk about and describe their problems in great detail in exchange for services.

Some critics have suggested that the simplicity and practicality of some of the solution-focused techniques may lead in some cases to a "cookbook" adoption of techniques, ignoring the relational dynamics between the professional and the client. As noted by Lipchik (1997), collaboration that keeps the "axles turning" as well as the "speed and success of solution construction depend on the therapist's ability to stay connected with the client's reality throughout the course of therapy" (p. 329). In fact, Metcalf et al. (1996) found that therapists had a tendency to focus on techniques, whereas clients were more concerned with their relationship with the professional.

Professionals who work in environments that are frequently if not at least problem-focused, are pathology-focused. In consequence, they found the solution-focused approach to be challenging (Trotter, 1999). For example, clients involved in the legal system are typically required to demonstrate that problems have been resolved or dangers have been reduced. Of course, the same is true for problem-solving approaches in these systems, as strengths and empowerment often tend to be ignored.

The approach is relatively silent, however, regarding situations in which the social worker is a public agency employee. For example, the solution-focused approach respects the role of "visitors" to treatment who have not chosen contact and hence have no expectations for their involvement. As a public agency worker, you may have mandated involvement with a client such that, you are charged with completing the requirements of a court order whether or not the "visitor" wishes to have contact. In spite of the pressures of a mandate in a situation, for example, a child placed outside of their home, the miracle or scaling questions may clarify for the parent the behaviors, actions, and resources required for reunification instead of focusing exclusively on the events that prompted removal of the child. Some social workers have also suggested that by not focusing on the problematic events, you are attempting to remedy a situation that may not be fully understood.

While the research and literature regarding involuntary clients is limited, the use of solution-focused procedures has demonstrated success with this often-neglected and marginalized client group (Berg & Kelly, 2000; Corcoran, 1997; Corcoran, 1999; De Jong & Berg, 2001; Tohn & Oshlag, 1999). The involvement of an involuntary client can be enhanced by combining solution-focused procedures with motivational congruence and motivational interviewing (Dejong & Berg. 2001; Lewis & Osborn, 2004; Miller & Rollnick, 2002; Tohn & Oshlag, 1999). Using these techniques, the involuntary client is encouraged to provide their version of the situation and the circumstances that led to the mandated contact.

The approach supports the client's construction of their reality, which is an essential factor in interactions with diverse groups. In this regard, the expertise of the professional is minimized, as is the opportunity to rely on basic stereotypes and generalizations. On this basis, well-informed goals are more likely to be relevant to the client. At the same time, the assignment of tasks by the professional would appear to be more directive than collaborative. For example, the assignment of generic formula tasks involving homework assignments raises concerns about the individualization of the task plan and the fit with the client's circumstances. Another concern relates to scaling questions and tasks in that the approach does not provide for a review of potential personal and environmental obstacles that may interfere with desired behaviors or the completion of tasks.

The solution-focused approach offers a positive approach for working with clients. The ease in learning and practical aspects of solution-focused procedures such as coping, scaling, exception, and miracle questions are attractive adjuncts to much of social work practice. The emphasis on engaging clients in talk about solutions—not just problems—is an empowering method that should be expanded in social work practice. The various types of questions are also compatible with other approaches. For example, the scaling question can reinforce a commitment to change, and a miracle query can facilitate the development of goals. At the same time, crisis situations require the judicious use of the various questions. For example, the miracle question may be used to help a client reframe their situation, but not when the client exhibits acute distress or danger (James, 2008).

The commitment to client empowerment, a focus on strengths and client capacities toward improving their situations and reaching solutions is a significant contribution. The assumption of client competence is a value consistent with social work's commitment to self-determination. However, having faith in and wishing to support client capacities should not lead us to assume that clients, in fact, have within them the solutions to all difficulties. In fact, some clients may lack sufficient cognitive skills and resources or face sociopolitical barriers that impact their ability to actually achieve their miracle. As Chapters 8 and 9 attest, practice need not focus exclusively on either problems and deficits or strengths and resources. Rather, in helping clients, an appraisal of each, including risks and protective factors, is important in developing a realistic view of a client's situation and systems involved (McMillen, Morris & Sherraden, 2004).

Summary

With the exception of solution-focused brief treatment , the approaches discussed in the chapter are problem-solving models. They are similar in that the focus is primarily on the present, they are time-limited, and they emphasize clients' capacity to change and grow through autonomous independent action.

Research studies have shown brief, time-limited approaches to be as effective as those that require a longer time period (Reid & Shyne, 1969; Wells, 1994; Wells & Gianetti, 1990; Corwin, 2002). The efficacy of brief, time-limited approaches is that their scope is on target problems or behaviors, and specific goals are developed that address the problem or behavior. The conscious use of time is considered to be productive in that specific goals make the best use of brief contact (Corwin, 2002; Hoyt, 2000; Reid, 1996).

Increasing the power of the client to participate in and influence change in their lives is a salient characteristic of the four approaches. Whereas, task-centered practice, crisis intervention, and cognitive restructuring seek to empower clients through systematic and collaborative problem-solving, the solution-focused approach aims to provide empowerment through the construction of solutions. Empowerment, for example, is evident in the task-centered approach by its emphasis on accepting the client's identification of their target concern and their participation in developing tasks and goals. Similarly the "scaling" and "miracle" questions in the solution-focused approach achieve this goal. The assumption is that clients know what they want and have a right to, and that they have the capacity to solve their own problems (DeJong & Berg, 2002; Reid & Epstein, 1972).

A deliberate emphasis on clients' strengths in recognition of the critical social work principle that "people have the capacity to change and grow," is also prominent in each approach. Strengths and resilience are foremost in the exploration of prior coping and adaptations, resources, and emotional stability in the crisis intervention and task-centered approaches. The recognition of how clients have coped and what they have done in the past effectively builds on their skills and resources. In solution-focused practice, clients are encouraged to reflect on exceptions to the problem and the problem as defined in a situational rather than an individual context. Cognitive restructuring recognizes the strength of the individual's capacity for self-direction and manages their beliefs through the development of self-talk, coping statements, and self-reliance.

Whether constructed around problems or solutions, each of the approaches begins with a clear description of the client's concern. Goals or solutions flow from the problem or concern identified by the client or, in the case of involuntary clients, from the mandate. The focus of tasks, as utilized during the brief time period, is not to change the client or their lives, but rather to alleviate their current distress or stress and to improve their functioning. It has been our experience that people who come in contact with social workers are seeking relief. The very act of developing goals or envisioning solutions, taking action, and being able to see movement is an empowering experience. Clients are invariably energized and motivated when they see incremental progress toward an outcome.

There is significant overlap in the theoretical perspectives and strategies of the four approaches. For example, cognitive-behavioral and social learning theories influence the task-centered system, crisis intervention and the solution-focused approaches. Cognitive Restructuring is also used in task-centered practice to address client's beliefs and in crisis intervention, depending on the nature of the crisis (Reid, 1992; James & Gilliland, 2001). The overlapping strategies and perspectives of each approach provide the flexibility of being able to draw upon and adapt the change process to various theories of human behavior, needs, environment, and lifestyles. Of course, each approach has limitations, and for certain populations an adaptation or modification may be required. Nevertheless, each has merit in that these interventions are brief, are action-oriented, and focus on specific goals for change.

Empirical support for each of the approaches, including with diverse populations, age groups, and in diverse settings was summarized in the section in which the approach was discussed. With solution-focused practice, the empirical evidence continues to evolve. Therefore, selecting the most suitable intervention strategy requires consideration of the problem and goal, developmental stages, racial, or cultural beliefs, customs and values, and environmental factors.

Trends and Challenges in Problem-Solving Intervention Approaches

When initially introduced by Perlman (1957), the problem-solving model was an attempt to focus social work practice on the psychosocial challenges of daily living common to social work constituents. During the past several years, discussions have occurred with regard to a problem orientation versus a more strengths orientation with individuals, families, or communities (Sarkisian & Gerstel, 2004; Early & GlenMaye, 2000; McMillen, Morris & Sherraden, 2004).

In their evolution, helping or problem-solving approaches have not remained static. Integrating systems and ecological theories and human development and behavior, problem-solving approaches have moved in a direction that separates clients from their problem by assessing the person and their situation in addition to problem analysis. This movement has been augmented by the inclusion of the strengths perspective, client empowerment, and an emphasis on culture and the cultural competence of social worker. These factors have influenced the assessment and goal development process, intervention strategies, and the professional language used to describe clients (Saleebey, 1996, 2002). The role of the social worker as the expert in determining clients' needs has lessened and as a result the relationship with clients has become empowerment-oriented and more collaborative. The recognition and utilization of clients' strengths represents an important shift in social work practice and supports the profession's principle of dignity and worth.

Client empowerment has become a constructive influence that has informed best practices in problem-solving approaches. As considered by Parsons (2002), Lee (2001), Salzar (1997) and Staples (1990) empowerment is both a process and an outcome. The process of empowerment actively encourages clients' participation in decisions about their lives (Gutierrez, Parsons, & Cox, 1998; Saleeby, 1992, 1997, 2002). Building on the principle of "starting where the client is," clients' narratives and their participation are emphasized in all phases of the problem-solving process. This principle is also observed in the inclusion of cultural preferences and diverse world views. Attention is also paid to whether problems have occurred because a client lacks resources and or has a diminished sense of self (Greene, Lee, Hoffpauir, 2005). In general, empowerment is akin to self-direction and self-efficacy in that the outcome is

that clients gain a sense of control over their situation in a process in which they participated. Dunlap, Golub & Johnson (2006) note however, that empowerment of clients may be severely constrained as a result of poverty and other sociopolitical factors.

Empowerment and strengths are interpersonal and structural dynamic in the problem-solving relationship between the client and the social worker. Even so, the structure of an organization which guides the relationship with clients may not reflect an appreciation of the criticality of empowerment. In order for the professional to act to empower clients, the culture of the organization must also demonstrate this commitment (Linhorst, Hamilton, Young, & Eckert, 2002). The same applies to strengths, which can be hampered by agency practices (Marsh, 2003).

Few people wake up one morning and decide to seek the help of a social worker. For many, their problem-solving capacity has been exhausted or they are pressured or mandated to seek help. Still others have contact with social workers because of the advent of a crisis, while others are disempowered due to a lack of resources, ongoing stressors, environmental conditions, and marginalized status. Certainly, people have contact with social workers for a variety of reasons, but as a social worker, you need not focus solely on problem reduction activities or solely on strengths (McMillen, Morris & Sherraden, 2004; Farmer, 1999).

As the population becomes older and more diverse, in spite of intervention strategies that promote strengths and empowerment and recognize culture, additional research is needed to clarify the effectiveness of problem-solving approaches with diverse groups. For example, Morell (2003) discusses empowerment from a feminist, disability perspective with regard to aging women. Chapin and Cox (2001) further suggest a change in the basic assumptions of the dominant paradigm with respect to the problems of frail elderly to a more strengths–empowerment orientation. Dunlap, Golub & Johnson (2006) explore the constraints of empowering African American families living in poverty.

Problem-solving models and methods include guiding principles that stress the need to understand the environmental and sociopolitical factors that contribute to and sustain problems that clients face. The requisite knowledge base for practice in this regard includes cultural competence, understanding oppression, and an ecological view of human behavior and functioning. Few guidelines, however, exists that intentionally guide practice social workers as to how to incorporate their knowledge of oppression into practice

(Dietz, 2000; Pollack, 2004; G. D. Rooney, 2009; Van Voorhis, 1998). Herein lies the challenge which in many respects cannot be limited to a focus on clients' strengths or problems. In recognition of the sociopolitical and socio-environmental challenges that a majority of social work's constituents face, a central question is to what extent are problem-solving approaches effective with respect to addressing oppression as a forceful and dynamic reality in the lives of clients.

Skill Development Exercises

1. Using the Corning case, select both a task-centered and a solution-focused approach as a change-oriented strategy and assess the merits of each approach in this case. In what way could you combine aspects of both approaches in this case?
2. A mother who has been sanctioned for failing to comply with the welfare-to-work rule tells you that her caseworker is "out to get her." What additional information or factors would you need to determine how you would react to the client's statement?
3. You are the social worker for a minor in a residential treatment program. How would you determine if the >minor is able to give consent for his treatment plan?
4. Review Lipchik's (2002) solution-focused questions and answer the questions based on a current concern that you have. Also, indicate how you would use scaling, coping, exceptions, and the miracle question.
5. Using the same situation that you have identified, develop a goal and general and specific tasks in the task-centered approach. Indicate how you would measure goal attainment.
6. Choose one of the cognitive distortion statements that apply to you. What strategies would you use to modify your thinking?

Related Online Content

Visit the *Direct Social Work Practice* companion Web site at www.cengage.com/social_work/hepworth for additional learning tools such as glossary terms, chapter outlines, relevant Web links, and chapter practice quizzes.

Notes

1. For additional information on brief treatment models, see Corwin (2002), Roberts & Greene (2002), Wells & Gianette (1990), and Walsh (2006).
2. Potocky-Tripodi (2002) has written an informative text on "best practices" for social work with immigrants and refugees.
3. For additional information on models and crisis intervention practice, see Parad & Parad (1990, 2006), Roberts (2000), Roberts (2005) the *Crisis Intervention Handbook: Assessment, Treatment and Intervention (3rd. ed.)* and Okun (2002). Suggested resources for crisis strategies with minors include the *Journal of Traumatic, Violence and Abuse* and the *Journal of Aggression Maltreatment and Trauma*. For more extensive information on the early definition and development and a critique of crisis intervention strategies, see Aguilera & Messick (1982), Golan (1978), Puryear (1979), Caplan (1964), and Lukton (1982). For evidence-based approaches to trauma intervention, see Cohen (2003).
4. Cormier and Nurius (2003) is highly recommended as a resource for more comprehensive information on change strategies and skills in cognitive-behavioral therapy and cognitive restructuring. Another resource includes Bergin and Garfield (2004), *Handbook of Psychotherapy and Behavioral Change*. See also Beck's *Handbook of Cognitive-Behavioral Therapies* (2005) for a review of the current state of cognitive therapy. For cognitive therapy specific to children, Reinecke, Dattilio & Freeman (2003) is an excellent resource. Walen, DiGuiseppe & Wessler (1980) present and illustrate earlier comprehensive strategies for disputing beliefs.
5. Chapin, R., Nelson-Becker, H. & MacMillan, K. (2006). Strengths-based and solution-focused approaches to practice. In Berkman, B. & D'Ambruson, S. (Eds.) *Handbook of Social Work in Health and Aging.* New York: Oxford University Press.

Developing Resources, Organizing, Planning, and Advocacy as Intervention Strategies

CHAPTER OVERVIEW

Chapter 14 transitions from direct practice intervention approaches to macro-level change strategies. Case examples provided by students and practicing social workers are used to demonstrate macro practice. The chapter concludes with a discussion of service coordination and collaboration at the macro level and general guidelines for evaluating outcomes.

Social Work's Commitment

Brueggemann (2006) and Schneider and Lester (2001) trace the historical commitment of the profession to the ideal of improving the human condition through social reform, social justice, and equality. These long-standing ideals have become principles that are reflected in the National Association of Social Workers (NASW) Code of Ethics and the Council of Social Work Educational Standards (CSWE) for the professional educational preparation of social workers. Guided by the ethical principles of NASW, social workers have a primary obligation of enhancing the welfare of individuals, improving social conditions through resources development and planning and engaging in social action (NASW, 1996). Promoting social and economic justice and improving social conditions, including populations at risk, are overarching principles articulated in Educational Policy and Accreditation Standards (EPAS) of CSWE. These principles underscore the profession's commitment "to advance human rights and social and economic justice" and the educational preparation of social workers to "engage in policy practice to advance social and

economic well-being, and to deliver effective social work services" (CSWE, 2008, pp. 5–6).

Similarly, global standards that frame the core purpose of international social work stress social action, political action, and advocacy, "to facilitate the inclusion of marginalized, socially excluded, dispossessed, and vulnerable at-risk groups of people" (Global Standards for Social Work Education and Training, 2004, p. 3). Fundamental among the principles of international social work are respect for diverse beliefs, traditions, and cultures as well as regard for human rights and social justice. These principles are also articulated in the NASW Standards for Cultural Competence in Social Work Practice (NASW, 2001).

Responding to needs, social conditions through the development of resources, advocacy and social action, and organizing with an emphasis on social justice and equality is hardly the exclusive domain of the social work profession. Other professions, organizations, and faith communities act as change agents and address some or all of the same concerns as those of the social work profession. However, social work has accepted as its mandate as a focus on the person-in-the-environment, economic and social justice, oppression, and equality. In addition, the principles of social work mandate intolerance for systems that create and maintain social conditions that result in personal problems. Urging the profession to go a step further in its social justice agenda, Hodge (2007) points to the need of the profession to advocate for a *Universal Declaration of Human Rights*, in particular, for religious freedom and an end to religious persecution on a national and global level.

Defining Macro Practice

By definition, macro practice has as its focus problems and conditions at the systems rather than the individual level. In essence, social problems and social conditions are the targets of intervention, underscored by the premise that seeing and intervening in the whole picture can ultimately change and improve the lives of people (Parsons, Jorgensen & Hernandez, 1988, 1994; Long, Tice & Morrison, 2006).

As characterized by Brueggemann (2006, p. 7), macro social work is the "practice of helping people solve social problems and make social change at the community, organizational, societal and global levels" (p. 3). Similarly, Breton (2006), White and Epston (1990), and Saleebey (2004) emphasize broad environmental concerns and social conditions that create and sustain problems experienced by individuals. According to these authors, the social worker has a duty to assist clients to externalize problems and conditions beyond the individual level. Reminiscent of the Settlement House Movement, Breton (2006) asserts "there is a dialectical relationship between social change and personal change" (p. 34).

Recall the case examples of Justin and Mr. Corning in Chapter 13. Their plights typify those of millions of Americans as well as citizens in other countries. The 2007 Office of Juvenile Justice and Delinquency Prevention in the U.S. Department of Justice report estimates that there are 1,682,900 homeless and runaway youth in the United States (National Coalition for the Homeless, 2007). Primary reasons for youth homelessness are economic, family, and residential instability; family conflict; and a lack affordable housing (Ferguson, 2007). Of the estimated 1.6 million homeless youth, the National Gay and Lesbian Task Force Policy Institute reports that like Justin, 20 to 40% of youth identity as lesbian, gay, bisexual or transgender (Ray, 2007). Likewise, Mr. Corning is among those Americans who lost their jobs in 2008. Job loss, according to a 2008 mid-year report by the Department of Labor, is expected to affect an unprecedented 8.5 million Americans (Aversa, 2008). As organizations adjust to an uncertain economy, trimming labor costs is among the first steps to be considered.

Both Justin and Mr. Corning are representatives of a whole picture. Therefore, helping individuals and families to change requires recognition of the broader context in which problems occur and the social and environmental factors that contribute to and sustain problems. This issue of unemployment and underemployment is not unique to the United States. For example, seeking economic opportunity, nearly one-tenth of the population of the Philippines works overseas (Mydans, 2004). Economic opportunity seekers include immigrant or migrant workers; many are undocumented, so their vulnerability to injustice and unequal treatment goes unobserved. Their numbers may also be uncounted for in times of natural disasters or political conflicts (as was the case after the September 11, 2001, disaster, for example). The countries from which these men and women emigrate rely on these workers to fuel their economies by providing ongoing financial support to family members in their countries of origin. At the same time, neither their home countries nor U.S. laws protect these immigrants and migrants against exploitation.

The blending of micro and macro strategies deemphasizes the distinction between the two practice arenas. Instead, both strategies should be considered as dual and interlocking, the public and the private, in responding to clients' needs and conditions (Long, Tice & Morrison, 2006).

Linking Micro and Macro Practice

Macro activities are professionally guided interventions, beyond the individual level. But it is at the individual level that social conditions and problems often emerge. In the course of direct practice interactions with clients social workers have the opportunity to observe the impact of these conditions on groups of clients (Netting, Kettner & McMurtry, 2004). Problems experienced by individual clients can lead to a broader question: To what extent is the individual client's situation reflective of a larger group experience? In essence, micro-level observations can inform you of adverse conditions that are common among groups and communities for which macro strategies are required to rectify. Figure 14-1

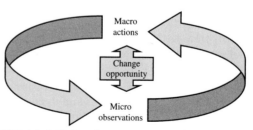

FIG-14-1 Linkage between Micro and Macro Practice

provides a perspective on the linkage between micro and macro practice. This linkage is illustrated by a program initiated by a county health and human services agency staff who, during weekly reviews of their cases, observed common concerns among families served by the agency.

Case Example

Staff of a county health and human services organization found that the nonpayment of child support by fathers was a significant and recurring theme in their child and family welfare cases. The failure to pay child support, in turn, negatively impacted families who were struggling with limited financial resources, some of whom were at risk for becoming involved with child protective services. In addition, nonpayment of child support was frequently reported as a source of interpersonal tension between the custodial and noncustodial parents. The county board was adamant about pursuing the fathers for payment of their debts because a majority of the members viewed the families affected by this problem as a financial drain on county resources.

Focus groups with the fathers were convened to explore issues related to the nonpayment of child support. The dominant themes that emerged from the groups included unemployment, underemployment, and a lack of low-skill-level employment opportunities in the county. The group participants also identified the metro area's inadequate public transportation as an additional complicating factor.

Using the results of the focus group discussion, staff devised a number of simultaneous actions to resolve the issue of nonpayment of child support. To address the fathers' concerns about jobs, educational job skills were developed, which included recruiting local employers to provide apprenticeship opportunities, thereby enabling the fathers to develop employable skills. Perceiving the problem as one in which the community should also be invested, staff enlisted the help of key individuals and civic groups to help locate or create jobs, provide transportation, for example, ride-share, or donating cars so that the fathers could take advantage of opportunities in the greater metropolitan area.

On a policy level, staff advocated for the fathers, making presentations to the county board and the courts, to explain the situations faced by the nonpaying fathers.

Ultimately, they persuaded the county board and the courts to support a less disciplinary and punitive approach toward the fathers. Undoubtedly, some fathers were shirking their parental responsibility. However, by taking action that empowered those fathers who had the desire but not the means to provide for their children, the staff reframed the problem and the problem arena. In doing so, they developed resources and influenced policy as advocates on behalf to the client group. In pursuing a macro-level strategy, the health and human services staff agency was able to achieve the county's goal: that the fathers paid child support. This action effectively bridged micro- and macro-practice strategies by addressing the external social and economic conditions that perpetuated individual problems (Vodde & Gallant, 2002; White & Epston, 1990; Parsons, Jorgenson & Hernandez, 1994).

Macro Practice Activities

As macro-level change agents, social workers use a range of social work roles (e.g., educator, enabler, mediator, advocate, resource developer, and broker). Netting, Kettner, and McMurtry (2004) identify the professional titles associated with these roles as including supervisor, manager, program coordinator, planner, policy analyst, and community organizer. The county staff discussed in the previous example involved the roles of educator (teaching job skills), resource developer (apprenticeships and transportation services), and broker and policy advocate (explaining the circumstances of the fathers to the county board, and advocating for a more sensitive policy). Jansson (2003) argues that social workers have a "moral obligation" to engage in "policy sensitive" and policy-related advocacy because of the "unique positions" that social workers "occupy in organizations" (p.36). Also, as demonstrated in the county agency's response, organizations can take the lead as change agents equally as well as individual social workers (Rothman, Erlich & Tropman, 2001; Brueggemann, 2006; Netting et al., 2004).

When the county staff engaged in change, they targeted system-level change, involving larger entities such as organizations, the community, and the population affected. Their systematic approach, as illustrated by Figure 14-2, was consistent with the macro-level change episode and the three overlapping focal points: the problem, the population, and the change arena envisioned by Netting, Kettner, and McMurtry (2004).

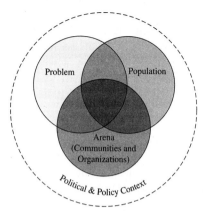

FIG-14-2 Macro Practice Conceptual Framework: Understanding Problem, Population, and Arena
SOURCE: From Netting, *Social Work Macro Practice*, 3rd ed. Reproduced by permission Pearson Education, Inc.

Intervention Strategies

Many different forms of interventions are used to change conditions, improve environments, and respond to needs found within organizations, groups, or communities. A full discussion of the various macro-level strategies is beyond the scope of this practice foundation of this text. Instead, we will focus our discussion on selected general strategies that emphasize the following method and strategies of macro-level interventions:

- *Developing and supplementing resources*
- *Utilizing and enhancing support systems*
- *Advocacy and social action*
- *Social planning and organizing*
- *Improving institutional environments*
- *Service coordination and interorganizational collaboration*

Prior to a discussion of the specific intervention listed above, the following section focuses on empowerment and strengths and analyzing social problems as significant aspects of macro practice.

Empowerment and Strengths

Empowerment means that groups or communities can act to prevent problems, gain or regain the capacity to interact with the social environment, and expand the resources available to meet their needs (Gutierrez, GlenMaye & Delois, 1995; Long, Tice & Morrison, 2006; Weil, 1996). Thereby, as a process, empowerment

actively engages people in decisions about their well-being, potential, life satisfaction, and the outcome of realizing to the extent possible, control over their lives. Empowerment, according to Long, Tice and Morrison (2006), also promotes social and economic justice when communities and groups are able to secure resources that have a positive influence on their lives. As social workers, we must respond to the needs and interests identified by groups or communities in ways that will assist them to realize their hopes, dreams, and aspirations and builds on their strengths.

Why the focus on empowerment and strength? Constituents of social work may include individuals, groups, and entire communities who lack the power of self-determination. Indeed, the powerless are more likely to have government agencies and public policy exert significant authority in their lives. Public policy examples include welfare programs, child protection services, educational systems, immigration and naturalization services, housing authorities, police protection, and transportation agencies. Transportation decisions can make a difference in the mobility of the elderly and the poor, which, when combined, constitutes a powerless group. In a large metropolitan area in Texas, for example, neighborhood bus stops were relocated, which made them less accessible to the largely poor and minority elderly residents. Elderly residents, many of whom lived alone, were dependent on the bus and the light rail to do their shopping and getting to community or church social activities. The relocation of the bus stops came as a surprise to the community, and when challenged, officials stated that "there was little public response from this group." Further the official noted that "electronic messages were sent to individuals in the neighborhood." When asked, how many residents received the message, the official was uncertain. Moreover, relying on electronic mail as the primary method of communication, represented unequal access to the medium by which the information was delivered.

The empowerment perspective assumes that issues of power (and powerlessness) are inextricably linked to the experiences of oppression, which are most frequently experienced by racial and ethnic minority groups and communities. Embedded in the experiences of most minority groups is a history of discrimination, stigma, and oppression. Certain vulnerable groups may exhibit a limited sense of individual or collective self-efficacy coupled with a pervasive sense of powerlessness and hopelessness to alter their circumstances. Nonetheless, the strengths perspective "encourages and respects community and individual stories," views them as "resourceful and resilient," and works in "collaboration with them to achieve a range of possibilities" (Long, Tice & Morrison 2006, p. 34). Moreover, enhancing a sense of power is closely linked to developing competence, self-efficacy, support systems, and the belief that individual actions or actions in concert with others can alter or improve situations or conditions (Carter, 2000; White & Epston, 1990).

Although groups or communities may lack power and experience poor congruency between themselves, their needs, and the social environment, strengths—for example, natural helping networks and support systems exist in all communities and groups. Unfortunately, in some instances, the strengths of groups and communities may become taxed in the face of overwhelming needs and be obscured or eroded by oppressive and discriminatory forces. Even so, valuing the community's or group's definitions of problems and building on their strengths to forge a collaborative helping relationship are critical aspects of the empowerment process (Gutierrez & Lewis, 1999; Long, Tice & Morrison, 2006; Saleebey, 2004; Van Voorhis & Hostetter, 2006).

In essence, your role as a social worker in the empowerment process is to "help individuals develop the capacity to change their situations" (Gutierrez & Ortega, 1991, p. 25). Gutierrez (1994) suggests that in addition to increasing self-efficacy and developing new skills, empowerment includes the development of a critical consciousness about the causes of injustice. When combined strengths and empowerment are forces that enable communities and groups to develop, own and govern their self-efficacy. In this environment, the shape and influence of the change effort is directed by active community leadership (Weil, 1996; Van Voorhis & Hostetter, 2006).

Analyzing Social Problems and Conditions

Practice at all levels interacts with and is influenced by forces external to the profession, including societal values, laws, and policies. The experiences of people, especially those without power, and the conditions they face should prompt all social workers to analyze social problems and conditions using the lens of social justice and to assess whether civil and human rights are being violated. Armed with this knowledge, social workers and social welfare organizations should assume proactive roles in providing the leadership for addressing policies and legislation that adversely impact groups and communities.

The following questions, which are adapted from the work of Finn and Jacobson (2003b), can be used in this analysis from a macro perspective.

- *What are the social justice issues affecting the people with whom I work?*
- *What are the particular values expressed for groups and communities when resources are distributed in our society?*

In addition to these questions, social workers should query:

- *Who is affected by policy decisions and in what way?*
- *Does the policy or legislation have a disparate impact on a particular segment of the population?*

To these questions, we add a core question from the FrameWorks Institute:

- *Who and what is responsible for the problem?*

The FrameWorks Institute is a nonprofit organization that provides training for professionals and other advocates in "thinking strategically" about social problems and reframing issues that appeal to basic societal values when communicating with policy-makers or the public. You may obtain additional information about the institute by accessing its Web site (www.frameworksinstitute.org).

Values and the Distribution of Resources

To a large extent, social welfare services continue to be directed primarily toward individual change (Breton, 2006; Brueggemann, 2006; Long, Tice & Morrison, 2006). This focus has been reinforced over the last two decades by the emphasis on personal responsibility and at the expense of social justice (Linhorst, 2002). As noted by Breton (2006), the financial resource entities upon which social welfare organizations depend are rarely interested in social action. Further, Breton asserts that professional and social welfare organizations are "locked into a path dependency paradigm." Specifically, "the therapeutic process of individual change," tends to emphasize goals and values" that are acceptable to society. Breton (2006) and Abramovitz (2005) also offer practical arguments and examples that articulate that a shift to a more group-oriented activist approach to social problems, inequality, and social justice over the therapeutic approach, indeed has costs to the organization and the profession.

Adherence to the values that have influenced the distribution of resources prompted Specht and Courtney (1994) to admonish the profession for moving away from its historical roots. Some of course would argue differently, pointing to the sustained commitment of social work embodied in the ethical principles of the National Association of Social Workers and the educational standards of the Council on Social Work Education. Others might argue that social advocacy and social action are too radical, hence the mission of the profession is to help individuals cope, in spite of the environmental challenges that they face. Breton (2006, p. 33) suggests that engaging in social action and advocacy does not mean that we as social workers become "revolutionaries." Social action is however exemplified in the lobbying and advocacy efforts implemented by NASW to address the resource needs of low-income families and Medicare reimbursement.

Who is Affected by Policy Decisions and in What Way?

Following Breton's assertion, let's examine ways in which social workers can have influence with regard to policies that affect the services that clients receive. The Personal Responsibility and Work Opportunity Reconciliation Act of 1996 (PRWORA), which reformed the system of public welfare, and the Adoption and Safe Family Act of 1997 (ASFA), are examples of policy decisions that affected large segments of social work constituents. The PRWORA requires the head of the family receiving welfare assistance to become employed within 2 years and sets a 60-month lifetime limit on receiving assistance. At the same time, the ASFA emphasized greater scrutiny of poor families' ability to care for their children but did not take into account the removal of some of the safeguards by the PRWORA.

Undoubtedly, there was a need to reexamine both the public welfare and the child welfare systems, but the competing and conflicting demands of these two concurrent pieces of legislation resulted in many families experiencing system-level difficulties in meeting requirements and timelines. Ultimately, the burden of the corrective action undertaken in both welfare reform and child welfare reform fell on individuals. The assumption made in child welfare policy was that neglectful parents' lack of parental responsibility was the primary culprit when they failed to meet the timelines required to achieve family reunification or permanency. However, the review of the delays in permanency and reunification failed to consider the possibility that the excess time that a child remained in care resulted from an overloaded, under funded and fragmented system. In much the same manner, a core belief driving welfare reform was that people receiving public assistance

lacked motivation to work. In reality, the previous policy disallowed those receiving benefits from being employed. Some research suggests a relationship between welfare reform and increased reports of child maltreatment and neglect, in that there was a significant increase in such reports (Courtney, 1999; Hutson, 2001).

Disparate Impact and Social Justice

Implementation of policy often has had an uneven impact on segments of the population, and in particular on minority communities, giving rise to questions about justice and inequality. Because of social worker's routine contact with clients affected by welfare reform, we have access to data that can be used to inform policymakers of the realities of their lives.

Leaving welfare, as many recipients did, and not returning was not as easy policymakers imagined. For example, Anderson, Halter and Gryzlak (2004), using Chicago as an example, found that unstable and low-wage jobs, the high concentration of recipients in large urban areas, and a lack of supportive services were contributing factors that influenced the ability of welfare recipients to become or remain financially self-sufficient. Disputing the popular image of the unmotivated, self-satisfied welfare recipient, their findings also showed that recipients were on the whole dissatisfied with their economic situation and the stigma attached to being on welfare. Thus, these findings suggest that it was not simply a matter of aspirations dissimilar from those of the larger society or personal responsibility. Instead the women faced the very real presence of structural and economic barriers and environmental deprivation. Interviews with welfare recipients conducted by Banerjee (2002) substantiated these and other barriers, for example, limited or no work experience or job training. In addition, under the "new federalism," states can decide how to distribute resources and what services to provide; for example, whether or not to provide funds for child care, and if provided, for how long. Trends under the new federalism that influenced tax and spending decisions ultimately had an impact on the level of client services available through non-profit organizations, county, and state programs (Abramovitz, 2005; Linhorst, 2002).

Given the reality of fewer services, the increase in the volume of cases, and the state of the economy (which influences the availability of jobs), are the sanctions and penalties against those who are unable to achieve work just? In fact, many social workers report that their work with clients has little to do with professional practice, such as developing or helping clients find resources. Because of federal and state compliance mandates and performance benchmarks for agencies and client compliance the social worker were concerned that their role was more akin to that of a compliance officer or investigator, and less of that of a professional helper (Abramovitz, 2005).

As another example, consider the Adoption and Safe Family Act. This legislation was intended to move children to permanent homes. Specific timelines were enacted to ensure that children did not languish within the child welfare system. For instance, parents were given 12 months to achieve reunification. Some states, such as Minnesota and Vermont, elected an even shorter timeline depending on the age of the child. Workers and advocates questioned the wisdom of the abbreviated time period, as well as the justice of concurrent planning. Concurrent planning involves the simultaneous planning of reunification and adoption as a permanent outcome (Curtis and Denby, 2004). Justice concerns centered on the fact that resources were available to potential foster/adoptive parents but not uniformly so for the biological parent. An additional justice issue related to the fact that the restrictive timelines resulted in an increase in the termination of parental rights.

The implementation of this law disproportionately struck some segments of African American communities and families, because the majority of the children involved in the child welfare system were children of color, in particular, African Americans (Curtis & Denby, 2004; Morton, 1999). Roberts (2002) likens the child welfare system to apartheid, the effects of which constitute "group harm" because entire communities experience the impact. In fact, in large urban communities, the intervention of child welfare and child protection services may be traced to specific ZIP codes primarily populated by poor and minority families. In large part, according to Chipungu and Bent-Goodley (2003, p. 9), the child welfare system has become a "safety net for poor children" funded by Title IV-E, rather the provision of services and resources to support and sustain the family system.

Equality and justice issues emerge on several levels. First and perhaps foremost are the uncertain outcomes of out-of-home placement when measured against established health and well-being standards. States receive funding based on the number of placements, and once a child is placed, there is little or no follow-up to determine child well-being (Munroe, 2004).

Indeed, it is the perception of many advocates in minority communities that out-of-home placement is a first step in the disruption of a minor's life, and a precursor to juvenile justice system. Eventually, advocates maintain that the youth transition to adult corrections or become homeless. You might question the social justice of this negative trajectory of outcomes. As noted by a county welfare administrator, "In spite of the fact that everyone in the system [child welfare] wants to do the right thing, there is still an unwillingness to look critically at whether what we are doing makes a difference in a concrete way" (Robinson, 2000).

Pervasive poverty, including homelessness, is among the reasons that a majority of African American and other children of color are placed out of the home, giving rise to the question of whether poor families should lose their children because of their economic circumstances or whether there is a need for greater economic supports for poor families. An additional complicating factor is that under the current child welfare–child protection system, there is little distinction made between child neglect and child abuse. Hence, poverty-related neglect, a primary reason that families of color have contact with child protective services, is treated in the same criminalized and stigmatized fashion as egregious harm associated with child abuse. Wulczyn & Lery (2007), raising the question about "whether parents have the resources to protect children," suggest that placement decisions take into account both human and social capital, including the skill set of parents for raising their children, the services available in the community, and the availability of supportive community networks.

Who and What Is Responsible for the Problem?

This question is perhaps the most difficult to answer. Inherent in the previously discussed legislative policies is the notion of personal responsibility as opposed to that of society's responsibility to ensure equality and the well-being of all citizens. On balance, the former, specifically, personal and parental responsibility, appears to have in many ways overshadowed the latter. We know that poverty and the related stressors continue to play a role in social problems—in particular, child development, family stability, health, and mental health status. A study conducted by Rank and Hirschl (1999) traced poverty over the lifespan and suggested that minorities—in particular, poor African Americans—are likely to remain impoverished throughout their lifetime. Brooks-Gunn and Duncan (1997) discuss the prevalence of poverty within third-generation minority and immigrant groups.

The harmful effects of prolonged exposure to poverty and stressful life events on child and adolescent development has been well documented in the literature (e.g., Freeman & Dyers, 1993; Icard, Longres & Spenser, 1999; Jose, Caffassso & D'Anna, 1994; McLoyd, 1997; Mosley & Lex, 1999; Smith & Carlson, 1997). It is the children in families who are most apt to be affected by welfare reform, out-of-home placements, and exhibit mental health concerns. Findings from a study that examined the relationship between poverty and psychopathology (specifically, behavioral symptoms identified in *DSM-IV*) is of interest. The results suggested that improved family income had a "major effect on children's psychiatric disorders" (Costello, Compton, Keeler, & Angold 2003, p. 2023). Similarly, behavioral symptoms such as oppositional defiant behavior previously diagnosed for children in these families significantly decreased when family income improved, effectively moving them out of poverty.

Poor families and even entire communities experience chronic stressors in their everyday lives because they lack the minimum resources required to meet their basic needs (Tolan & Gorman-Smith, 1997). In the article "Enough to Make You Sick," Epstein (2003) vividly describes life in "America's rundown urban neighborhoods," noting that illnesses normally associated with old age are showing up in young, inner-city residents. A parent interviewed for the article described her life as "you wake up stressed, you go to sleep stressed." In his portrayal of the stark ecological realities of inner-city life, *There Are No Children Here*, Alex Kotlowitz (1991) described a situation in which 1,000 new appliances were found waterlogged and infested with rodents in the storage area of a public housing project despite the fact that a majority of the residents did not have adequate appliances. While Kotlowitz's and Epstein's accounts are about single families, the stories of these families are the unfortunate truths of groups of families—indeed, entire communities—who live, cope, and survive in circumstances beyond their control.

Analyzing problems and conditions from a macro perspective provides an opportunity for social workers to give voice to the powerless by framing issues so that the public becomes invested in the problem. Does the public, for example, appreciate that a costly child welfare system has uncertain or poor outcomes? What would be the response of the public if they knew that sanctions and penalties are applied to welfare recipients for failing to comply with the 60-month timelines without regard to their circumstances—for example,

a disabled parent or child, or the state of the economy? Without becoming revolutionaries, social workers can evaluate and monitor the impact of legislation such as AFSA and PWORA, and act on behalf of client groups by taking an active role in articulating the circumstances of clients. Seeking information regarding the impact, outcome and effectiveness of policies and their implementation is justice work (Breton, 2006; Linhorst, 2002).

The preceding discussion identified conditions and policy trends that demand the attention of social work and a focus on problem-solving at the macro level. Of course, the climate for taking action is not always conducive or favorable. Indeed, with increasing frequency, the context in which social welfare services are delivered is framed by a series of rules, policies, and procedures (RPPs); legislative and court mandates; and managed-care directives. Social workers often experience pressures that demand their compliance, and that of their clients, at the expense of their professional knowledge and discretion. Nonetheless, it is important for social workers to remain grounded in the historical roots of their profession, and to feel compelled to promote social and economic justice, and advocate for social change when the well-being of class is severely compromised.

When initially formulated, policies and legislative mandates may be intended to be neutral with respect to race, class, gender, culture, or sexual orientation, only to have a disparate impact on certain groups when they are actually implemented. In recognition of this fact, we as social workers should understand and be able to articulate the impact of legislation or court mandates, policies, and "therapeutic jurisprudence" on our constituent groups (Alexander, 2003; Madden & Wayne, 2003; Wexler, 1992).

Developing and Supplementing Resources

In some instances, resource needs that address social problems or conditions are obvious. For example, low-income individuals and families need affordable housing. Working families in all economic strata need affordable child care and some need child care assistance. Overtime, shelters for women in transition from abusive relationships and food banks have become permanent services in response to obvious resource needs. As the population ages, the resource needs of the elderly will increase as well as the needs of their caregivers.

Developing new resources is indicated when it is apparent that a significant number of people within a given ecological boundary have needs that are not met, or for which matching resources are not available. Regular, meaningful contact with individuals, families, and groups places you in a strategic position to identify the resources needs. Resource development may include working with policy-makers, civic groups, and administrators of social welfare organizations to educate and create an awareness of social conditions for which resources are needed.

Whether the goal is to develop resources, deliver useful services, or influence social policies, a starting point is an understanding and documenting of the nature of resource needs. Questions that may be posed to guide the development of resources for which data should be gathered include:

- *What are the resource needs of a particular group?*
- *How would client groups describe their resource needs?*
- *Are there unmet needs or gaps in services?*
- *What are barriers to the utilization of existing resources?*
- *Are the services that are provided effective?*

Answers to these questions suggest the manner in which you would obtain the relevant information. You should also be aware that client groups may identify needs that are different from your own ideas. Tools for understanding resource needs include mapping, specifically using organizational or government statistical data, and conducting a needs assessment. Inviting client groups to articulate their resource needs can be accomplished by group interviews using critical or participatory action research models (DePoy, Hartman & Haslett, 1999; Reese, Ahern, Nair, O'Faire & Warren, 1999). Descriptive examples and the implementation of each of these methods are described below.

- Mapping *involves the use of geographic information system to track problems of interest to social workers (Hillier, 2007). Accessing data about homeless youth in an area of Los Angeles, for example, led Ferguson (2007) to implement the Social Enterprise Intervention Model (SEI) as a resource intervention strategy that focused on service-related needs, employment training, and mental health resources. The overall intent was to help youth to transition from "street life." As a new resource, the intervention model contrasts with the traditional outreach approach of providing services for youth because it promotes*

economic stability, changing the risky behavior, and providing mental health services.

- Needs assessment *is one method in which information may be gathered to identify unmet resource needs. According to Rubin & Babbie (2005), you must first determine whether the resource is intended to respond to a* normative *or a* demand *need. Normative needs are compared to a specific community's experience with the normal experience of other communities. Examples are parks or recreational facilities, transportation, or mental or health services. In other words, assets that you would expect to find in a thriving community. Conversely, demand needs relate to needs required of a particular community and perhaps address a particular concern. For example, a parent living in a low-income neighborhood may press for public space in which the children are able to play. Depending on the situation, demand needs may overlap with normative needs. For example, if other neighborhoods indeed have public play spaces, then the demand need as identified by the low-income parents is normative. Gathering information through conducting a needs assessment may involve individual or group interviews, questionnaires, community forums with key informants, and a targeted group.*

Homan (2008), issues a cautionary note about needs assessments. The intent is to discover unmet or undeclared needs, but without producing a "catalog of maladies." Noting that all communities have resource capabilities, the overall intent of the needs assessment, according to Homan (2008) and Lewis, Lewis, Packard and Souflee (2001), should be to assist the community and determine if there is a need for action in order to address its resource needs.

Consistent with the design of the needs assessment proposed by Zastrow (2003), in particular, clarifying the unmet needs of the community of interest and examining the range of needs, work completed by students in a macro practice evaluation class provides rich examples of how the method can be used. One assessment included a review of case records and client interviews to ascertain whether a gap existed in the resource needs identified at intake, and whether the same needs remained a concern at termination. Another student's project focused on aging gay and lesbian individuals in rural areas of a state. Through individual interviews the student identified unmet resource needs for this specific segment of the population. Similarly, another student project involved interviews with metro area seniors to identify their range of transportation needs. The results of the assessment in the rural gay and lesbian population and the senior citizens were used by agencies serving these groups to develop resources. There are times when the needs assessment can be directed toward identifying the knowledge and skill needs that staff have so they are better able to assist clients. Using research on asset accumulation, which is suggested as a means to reduce poverty, one student sought to clarify the educational needs of staff about asset accumulation so that they could counsel families on establishing Individual Development Accounts (IDA).

- *Homeless Against Homelessness is a group of homeless individuals. They worked with a social worker to conduct an assessment or resource needs of other homeless individuals. The social worker combined facets of the critical action research framework with the needs assessment. Participatory action research involves the governance, composition, and active participation of stakeholders throughout the project (Depoy, Hartman & Haslett, 1999). In this case, the active stakeholders were the homeless individuals who actually designed the project and conducted the assessment interviews. As key informants, they were essential to the development of interview questions that were relevant to the population, and which could easily be administered on the street. The ultimate goal of the group was to document the resource needs of homeless individuals and families. The findings were submitted to the city/county commission on homelessness.*
- *Observing the low participation of ethnic and racial minorities in using hospice services as a resource, Reese, Ahern, Nair, O'Faire and Warren (1999) describe a participatory action research project with a group of African American ministers as key informants. The goal of the project was to identify cultural and institutional barriers that prevented African Americans from using hospice care as a resource.*

These examples represent ways in which you can verify, document, and aggregate resource needs with the intent of promoting the development of responsive services within your agency and among policy makers. In some instances, additional measures such as social action or advocacy may be needed and which might require a coalition of agencies and professional in order to influence the expected outcomes. For example, the Homeless Against Homelessness group formed a coalition with other groups as collective advocates for the

homeless, and also taught homeless individuals how to engage in effective self-advocacy.

Supplementing Existing Resources

Needs for resources vary according to specific concerns and differ substantially from one community or population to another. For example, you might imagine that the resource needs of aging gay and lesbian individuals in rural areas to be different from their urban peers. In some instances, existing resources may be inadequate for the level of need, in which case resources need to be supplemented. Factors such as stigmatization and dominant values and beliefs often clash with the realities of need, however, and may unintentionally reinforce oppression and denial of access to needed resources. An overview of the social condition of homelessness illustrates this point.

Views of the homeless, in which individuals are characterized as lazy, immoral, or possessing other attributes of depravity resemble nineteenth-century thought (McChesney, 1995). Becoming homeless is not a random event. Being poor is significant risk factor; however the current (2008) mortgage crisis has resulted in an unprecedented increase in homelessness among middle-income families. This trend has tempered the prevailing view of the homeless, yet to a large extent, the plight of the homeless continues to be ignored, especially the economic and social contributing factors. The following scenarios are known to contribute to being or becoming homeless:

- *Poverty is a primary factor for families becoming homeless, which extends to the ability to find and maintain affordable housing. Many families have exhausted or overextended informal networks and have few alternatives (McChesney, 1995).*
- *Families displaced from circumstances beyond their control such as natural disasters, fires, or apartment buildings in which numerous code violations by landlords force municipal officials to declare the space uninhabitable.*
- *Although the minimum wage has increased, studies have confirmed that the low skilled and disadvantaged and those in economically depressed areas are the most likely to lose jobs as a result of the minimum wage mandate (Kreutzer, 2008).*
- *In rural and suburban areas that have limited housing options, the issue of homelessness has not been sufficiently acknowledged or discussed, making it difficult to determine the composition of this*

geographical group (McChesney, 1995; Gershel, Bogard, McConnell & Schwartz, 1996).

- *Limited affordable and aging housing stock in inner cities has reduced the housing options for the poor. When combined with the phasing out of governmental subsidy programs intended to counter the effects of a lack of affordable housing, low-income families had fewer options. Many low-income families depended on Section 8, federal subsidy program vouchers that enabled them to pay private market rent, as a safety net against becoming homeless. In 2004, in a seeming contradiction of the Bush administration's mandate to end long-term homelessness, the U.S. Department of Housing and Urban Development announced retroactive budget cuts to the Section 8 Housing Choice program. This action converged with the trend among landlords to discontinue accepting Section 8 vouchers and a resurgence of urban regentrification, effectively lessening the availability of affordable housing.*
- *As reported by the Child Welfare League of America, children account for a large percentage of the homeless in the United States; yet children do not exist apart from their families. In urban areas, a majority of the homeless are families rather than individuals, and most are African American.*
- *Youth leaving their homes for a variety of reasons increasingly represent yet another significant portion of the homeless population. Homeless youth constitute a highly vulnerable population that presents a wide range of problems and needs. They include runaways, throwaways, youth in conflict with their parents, and youth who have aged out of the child welfare system without essential supports (Ferguson, 2007; Kurtz, Lindsey, Jarvis & Nakerud, 2000; Kurtz, Kurtz & Jarvis, 1991; Nord & Ludloff, 1995; Ray, 2007).*

Although the homeless are a homogenous group in that they share a need for shelter and food, the demographics of the homeless differ in both composition and geography, as reported in a regional research study conducted in the southeastern states in which most of the homeless youth lacked stable and supportive families. Living arrangements for the homeless also vary (McChesney, 1995; Gerstel, Bogard, McConnell & Schwartz, 1996). Being homeless may mean making frequent moves between shelters and transitional housing facilities. Some individuals may be living on the streets, while others live in shelters or with a series of family or friends. Irrespective of the various entry points to

homelessness status, the resources for this population are clearly inadequate and contribute to further problems. For example, homeless families are at risk for intervention by child protective services. Homeless youth are often victimized by violence and may engage in illegal and risky behaviors (e.g., prostitution) to support themselves (Ferguson, 2007). Whether a homeless family or youth is able to exit from this status greatly depends on the availability and accessibility to substantial institutional and governmental supports (McChesney, 1995; Piliavin, Wright, Mare & Westerfelt, 1996).

In some cases, as illustrated in the following example, existing resources were inadequate to meet either demand or normative resource needs. In response to the needs of the growing homeless population a group of social workers began working with community and homeless groups with the goal of supplementing existing resources. They also simultaneously advocated for the homeless, which included influencing legislative and policy initiatives to end homelessness. Unfortunately, while the group achieved its overall goal of augmenting resources (a demand need) for the homeless, an oversight in planning the change effort resulted in difficulties with a key group.

Case Example

Social workers, staff and residents from a homeless shelter convened with a group of community, religious, and business leaders to explore the possibility of expanding available shelter beds. A proposal to use churches throughout the city for "bed only" space was developed and presented to the Social Justice Committees of the various churches. Several churches agreed to the proposal, and minimal opposition was encountered from the business community, city officials, and neighborhoods in which the churches were located.

However, all involved neglected to elicit the views of a key group—the parents and the staff of a day-care center housed in one of the churches. Believing that they had included all of the critical stakeholders, the social workers were unprepared for the most vocal opposition that came from day-care parents. Parental concerns centered on child safety and fears about the presence of homeless men in close proximity to their children.

In conceptualizing change, good intentions—no matter how noble and practical—may often prove to be insufficient. In the evaluative debriefing sessions, the social workers learned a point emphasized by Rothman, Erlich and Tropman (2001) and Homan (2008). Specifically, that it is important to explore potential barriers such as ideological conflicts, fears, and value conflicts that members of a community might have to a proposed change. In this situation, the day-care center parents and staff were not involved in the initial discussion and, therefore, their concerns were not adequately addressed. In the end, the church in which the center was located withdrew their support of the proposal as a result of the parents, but the membership remained committed to the overall goal of the initiative.

Despite the set-back, the case example emphasizes the way in which social workers can work closely with community leaders, civic or religious groups and elected officials. Coordinating these various groups requires the social worker to fill the roles of broker, mediator, and enabler. Another success of the case is that social workers were able to act in concert with others in the community to document the demand resource needs of the homeless population in their particular locale.

The group recognized that developing additional shelter space was at best, an interim solution to a growing problem. Intermediary efforts are by no means a substitute for advocacy, and long-range planning and action are required when a particular issue affects a significant number of people or the community as a whole. Toward this end, the shelter staff, social workers and the various church committees formed a coalition that lobbied and educated elected officials about the plight of the homeless, in hope of influencing long range solutions. The coalition also actively focused on larger systemic issues—for example, advocating for affordable housing, "living wage jobs," and improved public transportation so that shelter residents would gain access to jobs in suburban communities.

Mobilizing Community Resources

Mobilizing existing resources can address concrete needs, but resources can vary depending on the community and the situation. For example, rural communities may have fewer formal resources, and those that do exist are often taxed beyond their limits. There is a tendency to construct an idealized positive image of the rustic rural community, in which informal networks exist and seamlessly meet all needs—in essence,

"neighbor helping neighbor." In contrast, large urban areas can generate an image of faceless, nameless people who rarely interact or assist each other; hence the residents in urban areas are more dependent on formalized resources.

Neither image is entirely accurate, even though they are often magnified in conversations, there are certain situations that arouse an emotional and altruistic response in people, irrespective of where they live. During Hurricane Katrina and the floods in Midwestern states, neighbors and volunteers, some of whom traveled great distances, lent a helping hand. Even so, informal helping could not replace the formal systems that were necessary to deal with situations of this magnitude. When inequality exist in the distribution of resources, poorer communities are more vulnerable. In these communities, the organized mobilization of resource is required beyond that of informal helping. For example, the 9th Ward of New Orleans highlights how sustained economic and racial inequality can render a community less capable of mobilizing resources. The lack of response on the part of elected officials was a betrayal of the resource mobilization upon which all citizens should be able to rely.

Homan (2008, p. 187), citing the Pew Partnership for Civic Change (2001), reports that 90% of Americans "believe that working with others is the way to solve community problems." Primary factors were "knowing what to do," "having a linkage to the community," and "a strong cultural or ethnic identity." Indeed, Homan asserts that people are the most valuable resource and that a majority are willing to become and remain involved when asked. He suggests that people are likely to become involved when a four-step process is followed (p. 188):

- *Contact people*
- *Give them a reason to join*
- *Ask them to join*
- *Maintain their involvement*

Project Homeless Connect, "a one-stop model for delivering services to people experiencing homelessness," is a coordinated partnership effort to mobilize resources. This project was initiated by staff and social workers in a homeless shelter. Initially intended to provide essential resources for people without shelter, many of whom were living under bridges. The effort has expanded over time to provide resources to poor families who may or may not be homeless. The major emphasis of the program however remains on providing resources to the homeless. During the course of the two-day event, homeless persons are able to take showers, see health and mental health professionals, meet with housing and benefit specialists, and receive concrete goods, for example, backpacks, toothbrushes, and clothing. Note Homan's steps in the announcement that is sent to former and potential volunteers:

Project Homeless Connect

Greetings!

We Need Your Help!

Ending Homelessness, one person at a time. Project Homeless Connect is a one-stop model for delivering services to people experiencing homelessness. Hennepin County and the City of Minneapolis partner with service providers, businesses, citizens and faith communities to bring multiple resources to one location where people can find the help they need. These services include: housing providers, employment specialists, medical and mental health care, eye care, haircuts, transportation assistance and food and clothing.

December Success

Thanks to the wonderful work of 500 volunteers and 100 service providers, and over 1200 men, women and children. The last event was a great success:

- *1500 meals were served*
- *221 people received immediate medical care*
- *42 received dental care*
- *443 were given vouchers for shoes*
- *62 new voice mail numbers were established so that people could receive messages about work and housing*
- *300 were able to have free haircuts*
- *473 received employment referrals*
- *157 housing applications were submitted, with 6 people placed in housing on the day of the event, and 12 more in the following days*
- *36 veteran contacts were made*

700 Hundred Volunteers Needed

My reason for writing is to ask you to help at the upcoming event. With even more participation expected this year, we need at least 700 volunteers to make this another success. The Convention Center will be set up with tables, rooms and areas for the various services available and volunteers will assist guests in connecting with the assistance that they need or request. Volunteers must be 18 years of age or older.

Sign up to Volunteer

To volunteer, click below on the Click here to Volunteer box. Please also choose a training date. Share this e-mail with anyone who is interested in helping us reach our goal. You may go directly to our Web site to volunteer to help to end homelessness.

We are counting on you. Won't you connect? Thank you.

_____

_____

Describing the event as a one-day opportunity, volunteers are alerted to the time that they are being asked to participate. In this communication, former volunteers are encouraged to remain involved by documenting and personalizing the success of the previous event, which would also be attractive to new recruits. Further, former volunteers can attribute the success to their contribution of time, skills and talent. This information also appeals to new volunteers and provides them with concrete reasons to participate in a variety of ways. For example, as volunteers they could be involved on the day of the event or donate cash or their services. Volunteer training was available which provided an incentive for potential recruits who may have been reluctant to become involved, believing that they lacked the necessary skills.

Although this announcement was sent by e-mail, volunteers are actively recruited from community groups and businesses and informal networks, for example, book clubs, athletic facilities and fraternal groups. Overall, the communication is a strong appeal, beginning with the first sentence, "We need your help," and in essence engages volunteers as active stakeholders in addressing the needs of the homeless population in their community. Direct appeals such as this have the potential to engage the altruistic instincts and basic values of potential volunteers, many of whom desire equality and dignity for the disenfranchised, but are unaware of how to do it.

Developing Resources with Diverse Groups

It is critical for social workers to familiarize themselves with the cultural nuances, values, norms, and political structures of various groups while they are developing or supplementing supportive systems or networks within a community. The tendency to generalize information about certain groups may potentially lead to conflicts, because there may actually be status and power differences or clan or religious differences within groups, even among those who may share the same country of origin.

Many non-Western cultures are characterized as valuing interdependence and collectivism over the more Western post-industrial trait of independence (Greenfield, 1994; Ogbu, 1994). This tendency would suggest that social support resources are more readily available in immigrant or refugee communities. In some cases, this belief leads to a useful framework for understanding cultural influences or pressures and social and economic arrangements in these communities. Nevertheless, social workers must recognize that length of stay, the extent of acculturation, within-group power structures, and clan or kinship ties may ultimately influence social support systems.

For example, domestic violence may thrive when a code of silence prevails in a particular community. Oliver Williams, Executive Director of the Institute on Domestic Violence in the African American Community, interviewed in the May 2002 issue of *Essence* magazine, asserts that "often, abused Black women do not believe that the police are there to protect them," while others are reluctant for "fear of the consequences their partner may suffer at the hands of the police." In other communities, silence may be related to cultural norms that pose barriers to utilizing resources. For example, a social worker seeking to help immigrant women who were abused by their husbands found that the women's community was sympathetic to the issue. At the same time, fear of the husband's status in the community, cultural norms and relationships between clans prevented others from providing a safe haven for these women. Moreover, in some instances, perceptions in a community of what constituted an abusive relationship is inconsistent with definitions of abuse in Western societies. This point is not to suggest that women in this situation are content, but rather to demonstrate the way in which cultural and role expectations can influence the provision of resources. In another situation, a social worker urged a woman to seek refuge in a women's shelter (rather than relying on the community to help resolve a marital conflict); as a result, the woman became isolated. Intervention strategies must always be informed by and remain sensitive to how particular communities resolve situations and, wherever possible, those strategies should be supported. These types of situations often present ethical and legal dilemmas for social workers, particularly when there is evidence of flagrant harm. The two examples used in this discussion are not intended to suggest that domestic abuse is more prevalent in communities of color or immigrant communities. Rather, they are simply used as examples to emphasize the necessity of understanding the structure and culture and political realities of different communities.

These examples as well as others provided by Hirayama, Hirayama and Cetingok (1992), Green (1999) and Sue (2006) highlight the fact that diverse groups may differ in their definition of a problem and therefore may not respond to the same resources developed to address a particular concern. As Hirayama et al. (1992) and Potocky-Tripodi (2002) note, although immigrants, migrants, and refugees experience reactive depression, they may not access mental health services because of a negative perception of the "mental illness" label. Similarly, cultural beliefs and perceptions may influence the extent to which some Hispanics access mental health services (Green, 1999; Malgady & Zayas, 2001; Sue, 2006). An individual's reluctance to articulate concerns may also be influenced by the threat of stigmatization or reinforcing the negative perceptions of his or her community by the larger society.

Utilizing and Enhancing Support Systems

Relatives, neighbors, and congregations are natural ecological structures, and as such may offer support needed by a variety of groups. Although support networks were common in pre-industrialization communities, they are virtually an untapped resource in post-industrial Western society, especially with the advent of more formal social welfare systems. In exploring the dynamics of help, Bertha Reynolds (1951) stressed, "people seem to look upon taking and giving help as they do any other activity of life" (p. 16).

Social supports or kinship networks exist in almost all groups and communities, even those in which residents experience chronic stressors as well as positive and negative life events. Residents of most communities demonstrate a tremendous amount of resilience, coping skills, and the capacity to help others in times of need. For example, low-income single mothers in a community-based research group that sought to define "neglect" reported that "sometimes the best thing that you can do for somebody is to be their friend" (Rooney, Neathery & Suzek, 1997, p. 19). Although the interactions between the women was limited to the research project, they quickly developed relationships, many of which were fostered by listening to each other stories. For example, one group of mothers initiated a child care cooperative and a "mother's night out" program to provide much-needed respite for single, overburdened mothers and their children.

Kinship care and support systems such as church and neighborhood groups or networks also serve as community-level protective factors (Testa, 2002; Gibson, 1999; Haight, 1998; Tracy & Whittaker, 1990; Jackson, 1998; Brookins, Peterson & Brooks, 1997). In fact, kinship studies (e.g., the placement of children with kin) found that the utilization of informal resources lasts longer and is more supportive of the child's cultural, racial or ethnic identity. Kinship care also supported and sustained familial connections, and was relatively stable in comparison to nonkin placements (Hegar, 1999; Danzy & Jackson, 1997). Community-level care may be inspired when people become aware of a particular situation for which a resource response is needed. McRoy (2003), for example, describes the action of a church in a small town in Texas, where the minister led the congregation in adopting African American children. The movement, called "Saving a Generation," resulted in more than 50 children being adopted.

Relatives, friends and neighbors are support systems that can be activated when support is needed and in times of adversity. Professionals and organizations can and do provide support, in response to a variety of situations. But neither the professional nor the organization can or should replace natural support and resource systems.

Community Support Systems and Networks

While modern social welfare services have tended to remove or become a substitute for the natural helping that has sustained people over time, there is a rich history detailing the contributions of Jewish, Catholic, Protestant, fraternal, and civic groups as mutual aid societies in support of individuals and families.

Furthermore, reliance on indigenous networks and community support was critical for economic and social survival among historically oppressed groups. In addition, members of minority groups have traditionally been reluctant to seek assistance from outside of their communities because they had demeaning, impersonal, or negative experiences with formal social welfare organizations or because services were not available to them as a result of discriminatory practices (Green, 1999; Lum, 2004; Sue, 2006).

A series of examples can provide a few glimpses into various group traditions and values related to support systems and their resource potential. (Of course, these examples represent general observations that may not be pertinent to all members of the particular group.) Horejsi, Heavy Runner and Pablo (1992) note that persistent poverty among Native Americans has resulted in a norm of sharing concrete resources. Tribal gaming has energized this tradition, by providing housing, social and mental health services and educational and economic opportunities for tribal members using profits from the casinos. In African American and Hispanic communities, the strength and survival of families and groups have often been dependent on strong kinship ties, flexibility in family membership, and connections to the church as a social and economic resource. In the African American community, for example, the legacy of helping includes the building of institutions of higher education, care for orphaned children, and establishment of widows' pensions and insurance societies. Other communities of color likewise have a long history of formal and informal human services—witness the Buddhist mutual aid associations and social services in Asian communities (Canda & Phaobtong, 1992). In an interview with a Somali student, one of this book's authors learned that religious teaching prevented the accumulation of personal wealth. The student emphasized the fact that family groups tended to pool their resources for the collective community. For example, if an individual develops a business, it is understood that the profits were for the support of a number of families and for the benefit the community.

Informal networks and natural support systems can act as both resources and preventive measures. Wendy Auslander, of Washington University in Saint Louis, investigated the effects of culture on health, using natural support systems (Mays, 2003). The project's goal was to find ways to teach healthy eating habits to African American women who were considered to be at risk for diabetes. The project used inner-city women who were trained as nutritional counselors. The findings showed that women at risk for the onset of diabetes, were most receptive when the information about diabetes was provided by peers, neighbors, or friends. Auslander also found that the natural support networks in the communities in which the women lived were well developed, and they were interconnected at various levels. These factors were instrumental in developing a very efficient and effective means to achieve changes in the eating habits of the targeted group of women.

Similar results were reported in Montgomery County, Maryland, with "Barber's Cuttin Cancer Out." This project was initiated by the Maryland Department of Health and Human Services in partnership with local barbershops. As barber shops are gathering places in many African American communities, they were a natural place to educate men about cancer and to address some of the barriers that prevented the men from seeking oncology screening (Mallory, 2004).

Organizations as Support Systems

Organizations can also act as support systems, particularly for people who are in the midst of a transition. The American Red Cross is an example of a formal organization that assists communities in times of disaster. Examples of supportive systems include transitional housing, shelters for battered women, work environment policies that are responsive to family demands, workplaces that offer classes for individuals for whom English is a second language and programs that promote health and wellness for employees. Other organizations that function as support systems include Habitat for Humanity, an organization devoted to building affordable housing for low-income families; the National Doula Society, which provides indigenous or professional helpers to women during birth and delivery; Alzheimer's disease groups for caretakers; Parents, Family, and Friends of Lesbians and Gays (PFLAG), an organization founded by a parent of a gay man; and the National Alliance for the Mentally Ill (NAMI), which consists of family members and consumers of mental health services.

Case Example

An innovative residential reunification and permanency program for youth in out-of-home placements illustrates how one human services organization built support into its program design. The agency was concerned about the significant numbers of African American males between the ages of 12 and 17 who had multiple stays in its shelter system;

these youth seemed destined to remain adrift or cycle through various foster home placements and institutions. The goal of the program was to move the youth in this population toward stability and permanency, through reunification with the family, living with a relative, or independent living in the community.

In the development stage of the program, groups of youth in the shelter were interviewed to obtain their views of their situation and to determine the need for resources to support the goal of reunification and permanency. As a result of the interviews two additional components, were added, specifically, home visits and respite care.

Home visits facilitated the youth's gradual reentry into the family system as well as their transition into the community. This component recognized that the transition from institution to a home environment could pose difficulties for families. Further the visit allows staff to asses resource needs and potential tensions. Respite care was intended to be supportive and preventative. In addition to maintaining residential beds, the agency set aside respite beds that could be used for up to 72 hours by the youth and family in times when youth–family conflicts are a crisis. As an alternative to a stay in the facility, the youth could stay for a brief period with kin or a member of the community network. During the respite period, kin or community members were involved in the effort to resolve the difficulty and avoid another placement.

Following the first complete year of implementation, evaluation sessions were conducted with youth, parents, and relatives participating in the program. Home visits and respite care were identified by the participants as the most helpful aspects of the program. They also viewed the ongoing support that families received from the agency as a positive. One parent offered a particularly poignant commentary on the level of support: "The staff held our family's hand until we could go it alone."

This program is an example of a macro-level intervention with a focus on developing a response that would alter the situation of a particular group. Using county statistical data, and its own experience as a shelter provider, the agency determined that the current short-term shelter arrangement perpetuated a continuous cycle for youth in the shelter system. As a result, shelter youth rarely achieved stability or permanence, and a majority were eventually disconnected from their families and community. The program was intended to reverse the destructive pattern of continuous and reoccurring shelter placements.

In developing this program, the organization perceived its goal as innovative and its role as supportive. This support was integrated with the work of natural support systems (e.g., relatives, mentors, and community networks), each of which played a critical role in achieving the ultimate program goals of stability, reunification, and permanency for shelter youth. The shift in the agency's program focus required gathering information about the plight of youth who seemed destined have repeat stays at various shelters and to move from shelter to shelter. Statistical data compiled by the agency included a profile of the youth as a group, as well as the number of days spent in the shelter system. This information was then used to advocate for a different approach, which necessitated convincing other organizations, funding sources, county officials, the community, and, in some instances, shelter staff of the program's potential.

Immigrant and Refugee Groups

Immigrant or refugee groups have particular needs for organizational social support and resources. Geographic relocation is, in and of itself, traumatic. While formal organizations and civic, social, and governmental agencies provide assistance, these services cannot make up for the cultural isolation, discontinuity, or occupational concerns. In addition, some groups may be unfamiliar with formal services or assistance from the government and therefore may not seek the services to which they are entitled.

Undocumented individuals are ineligible for government programs and may also be underserved by civic groups or churches. They have needs unique to their status—for example, fear of deportation and exploitation as cheap labor. Consider what happened when a group of hotel employees consisting of both legal and undocumented individuals attempted to join the local union. The hotel's management retaliated by calling immigration authorities. This action mobilized numerous community and professional groups, and the issue was successfully resolved. Increasingly, social workers will be involved in the workplace as organizations seek to respond to their needs for a viable labor force. Social work practice in the workplace may resemble the period at the beginning of the

twentieth century, referred to as welfare capitalism, when social workers played an active role in developing organizational supports and resources while advocating for the needs of a largely immigrant workforce (Brandes, 1976).

Children are often included as undocumented individuals, although some may have been born in the United States and are therefore entitled to services. Unfortunately, many families remain reluctant to seek or utilize services even for children who are entitled to services for fear of calling attention to themselves. A case of a social worker who was asked for consultation illustrates this point. In this case, the social worker was employed in a Hispanic agency that had a purchase-of-service contract to serve the Spanish-speaking population, including providing child welfare services.

Case Example

This case involved a widowed mother with three children; the two younger children had been born in the United States. The mother and her eldest child were undocumented. The mother and father had originally come to the United States 5 years earlier to work in sugar beet fields in the Midwest. They later moved to a larger city, where the father obtained a job with a roofing company. Two years prior to the referral to the agency, the father died as a result of an accident at a construction site.

The eldest child's teacher reported the family to the agency's child and family services unit for maltreatment because the child appeared to be malnourished. An investigation concluded that a charge of maltreatment was unsubstantiated, and that the basis of the child's condition was medical. When the social worker explained the child's need for medical care, the mother understood the need, but was fearful that the family would be reported to immigration authorities and subsequently deported. After assuring the mother of confidentiality and receiving her permission to act, the social worker presented the situation to the development officer of a local private children's hospital. Within a few days, she received a call from a pediatrician on staff, who agreed to evaluate the child and provide the necessary medical care.

In pursuing resources for this family, the social worker learned that the hospital board viewed outreach to the immigrant community as a part of the hospital's mission. Thus, while the intervention focused primarily on the needs of one family, the social worker efforts resulted in a resource for the larger community. The social worker was invited to become a member of a hospital community task group charged with making recommendations regarding responding to the medical needs of the community, especially prenatal and infant care programs and infant loss support groups—needs previously identified by the local Hispanic community.

Cautions and Advice

Building on the natural helping systems of communities or groups recognizes strengths and resilience, which may thrive despite the chronic stressors and adverse life events. Social supports and relational networks are protective factors that may buffer and extend coping capacity. As highlighted in the previous examples, agencies can also be supportive resource systems especially when their services are responsive to social conditions and client concerns.

Caution is advised when working with these networks, however. When utilizing or developing social support systems, you should not favor one type over the other. For example, groups or communities may act as supplemental resources, but they may be limited in their scope. Reliance on these resources may prevent people from accessing formal services to which they may be entitled. Informal resources should not be strained, be exhausted, or cause a hardship to the providers. In addition, informal resources lacked the capacity to sustain long-term solutions to social problems. A more integrated approach that would address the several concerns raised in the preceding discussion would be an arrangement that would coordinate formal and informal resources.

In some segments of society, social support and social networks may play a critical role, yet be difficult to develop. For example, persons in controlled therapeutic environments, prison environments, or institutional group placements may be psychologically and sometimes geographically isolated from the larger community. Even in the best of situations, contact with relatives, neighbors, or friends may remain grossly inadequate. Although the objective is for these individuals to eventually return to the community, connections to the community are rarely an integral part of services. These situations provide social workers with opportunities to develop social support and networks through connections with the community for these individuals, as well as to create supportive networks among individuals within institutions.

Advocacy and Social Action

The social work profession has a long and proud tradition of advocacy and social action leading to social reform. Indeed, Stuart (1999) characterizes the focus on the person and the environment as "linking of clients and social policy as a distinctive contribution of the social work profession" (p. 335). Haynes and Mickelson (2000) trace the involvement of social workers during the development of some of the more enlightened and humane social policies in both the nineteenth and twentieth centuries. Practice, especially in the African American community, involved advocacy and social action that focused on the "private troubles of individuals and the larger policy issues that affected them" (Carlton-LaNey, 1999). Diverse individuals and groups of social workers have been devoted activists and advocates, often acting in concert with grassroots or minority civic groups. For example, social workers supported the United Farm Workers, the Equal Rights Amendment, the National Welfare Rights Organization, and the Civil Rights Movement, by either joining in the activities of these groups directly or providing expert testimony. More recently, the president of the NASW responded to the Abu Ghraib prison situation in Iraq by sending a letter to the Senate Armed Services Committee, "demanding the U.S. Congress take steps to end the abuse of prisoners of war in Iraq" (Stoesen, 2004).

Despite this rich history, social work has not always been attentive to the sociopolitical and historical mandates of the profession. In tracing the "cycles of social work practice," Franklin (1990) concluded that social work practice changes to reflect the dominant views and ideologies of the times. At some times, the profession has focused on social action and environmental factors; at other times, the focus has been on the individual. In their book *Unfaithful Angels*, Specht and Courtney (1994) ignited a debate about the profession's goals with regard to the role of social workers as advocates and initiators of change. This argument has roots in the "emergence of two separate and interacting movements" from which the profession evolved—specifically, the Charity Organization Societies and the Settlement Houses. Some have perceived that social work has failed to maintain a leadership role in social efforts over time (Haynes & Mickelson, 2000). Nevertheless, the Council on Social Work Education, the National Association of Social Workers, the International Association of Schools of Social Workers, and the International Federation of Social Workers have affirmed their support for social action

and social advocacy. For a more compr[ehensive]
historical account of the profession'[s]
with advocacy and social action, we [...]
1999 Centennial Issue of *Social Worl*[k]

Policies and Legislation

On a day-to-day basis, social[...]
vast array of social policies a[nd...]
advocacy and social action[...]
this chapter, the Adoption [...]
and the Personal Work Opp[...]
Act, 1996 were discussed[...]
influence social work pr[...]
cerns about equality ar[...]
had profound and di[...]
segments of the pop[...]
minorities, and chil[...]

These policies [...]
1990's policy deb[...]
servative Reagar[...]
ment adopted a[...]
both the phil[...]
Cuts or redu[...]
stemming f[...]
social polic[...]
example, t[...]
mandate[...]
of famil[...]
Mickel[...]
mean[...]
ply [...]
of [...]
ad[...]
c[...]

[...]r
[...]ty,
[...]ion
[...]s and
[...]new
[...]ts sim-
[...]lves out
[...]ures were
[...]passionate
[...]asures also
[...]military per-
[...]n attempts to
[...]ertime pay for

[...]wentieth century,
[...]gislative policy, as
[...]he focus was main-
[...]relationship between
[...]rime, and in spite of
the ac[...] [...]ures of incarceration.
Nonetheless, [...] [indu]stry grew, as did the
incarceration of min[...] [m]ales. Under the Clinton
administration, comprehensive legislation such as the
Personal Responsibility and Work Opportunity Act
of 1996 dramatically changed child care provisions,
the Food Stamp Program, Supplemental Security

for legal immigrants, nutrition
[...], education, and welfare funding
[...]ocky-Tripodi, 2002; Haynes &
[...]hneider & Netting, 1999).

[a]nd the Personal Work [a]nd Reconciliation Act

[...]) has questioned the ethics of welfare
[...]l as the lack of discussion among both
[...]conservative politicians about the conse-
[...] the revised federal entitlement program
[...] The perception that the primary goal of the
[...]lation was a reduction in caseload as opposed
[...]uction in poverty raised new ethical questions:

[...]ave people actually left poverty?
[...]re children, for whom welfare was actually in-
tended, living healthier lives?

Interviews with social workers and agency adminis-
[tr]ators raised additional ethical concerns related to the
[l]egislation's compliance and mandates (Abramovitz,
2005). Staff interviewed perceived themselves as being
caught between the demands of professional ethical
practice and mandates that required client compliance.
For example, the "work first mandate" meant that participants were not allowed to pursue or continue educational opportunities (Banerjee, 2002).

The NASW Code of Ethics guides social workers to
protect the rights of clients to make their own decisions.
Staff in these agencies however, believed that government mandates and penalties forced them to "push
clients to make decisions that were not in their
best interest," and posed a risk to client "autonomy"
(p. 181). Moreover, because agency contracts were
performance-based, social workers felt that they often
had to ignore client's choices in order to meet the demands for maintaining the numbers needed to justify
the continuation of the contract. Ethical tension also
emerged with regard to protecting client confidentiality
because of reporting requirements. For example, if a
family member was given money as a gift, this information needed to be reported. By reporting the gift, staff
were aware that their doing so would jeopardize the
family's cash income and benefits.

The ethical issues highlighted in the previous discussion had an impact on human and civil rights and basic
dignity—both important to the values of social work.
They promoted an intrusion into family life, including
the initiative that perceived marriage as value added for
the poor. For example, in writing for *The New York Times*,
Barbara Ehrenreich (2004) questioned how marriage

could resolve poverty because it is the number one problem for the low-income population. Ehrenreich suggested that since people tend to marry within their social class, a female welfare recipient would have to marry 2.3 men to exit poverty. The policy, to entice low-income marriage and education was financed at the level of $200 million. Ironically, it came about during a time when the Bush administration planned cuts in housing subsidies, more stringent requirements for welfare recipients, and a reduction in welfare programs.

Cause Advocacy and Social Action

After reading about the state of affairs with respect to selected policies and legislation and their impact on poor families, you might wonder, "What can I do?" You may already have been a case advocate—that is, working with and on behalf of a client to ensure that they receive those benefits and services to which they are entitled and that safeguard their dignity. This aspect of advocacy closely corresponds to one dictionary definition of an *advocate* as "one who pleads the cause of another." Cause advocacy and social action include this key element; however, confronting the effects of legislation and policies cannot rely on the effort of a single social worker. But as Sherraden, Slosar & Sherraden (2002) propose, the shift in policymaking from the federal to the state level is an opportunity for collaborative policy advocacy and organizers to include researchers, practitioners, advocates, and students on behalf of clients.

Another opportunity for you to act is through NASW collaboration with social work programs in sponsoring "Social Work Day at the Capital," during which there is an opportunity for you to meet with, discuss policy, and influence elected officials. The results of research findings can also inform and influence policy. Rice (1998), for example, integrates research and advocacy, using the results of a study with welfare participants related to their experiences with welfare reform legislation to report to the state legislature. Also recall that the Homeless Against Homelessness advocacy group presented the results of their interviews to the county commissioner.

Social workers are often involved in cause advocacy as private individuals and through their membership in professional associations, such as the Child Welfare League of America, Influence, and the National Association of Social Workers' PACE Committee. In addition, some national organizations, such as Family Service of America, engage in advocacy in their work with local client, civic, and citizens' groups. You may have received a phone call or e-mail asking you to contact elected officials about a particular piece of legislation for the benefit of a client group.

Advocacy and Social Action Defined

Proposing a new definition of advocacy, Schneider and Lester (2001) define social work advocacy as the *"exclusive and mutual representation of a client(s) or cause in a forum, attempting to systematically influence decision making in an unfair and unresponsive system."* Barker (1996) defined *social action* as "a coordinated effort to achieve institutional change to meet a need, solve a social problem, correct any injustices or enhance the quality of human life" (p. 350). Both advocacy and social action are inherently political. Hyde (1996), referring to a major tenet of feminist organizing and advocacy, suggests that the "the personal is political."

By integrating *advocacy and social action* we have adapted elements from each to form a unified definition, because there are often instances in which advocacy and social action are combined to achieve the desired results. Together, they represent a process of affecting or initiating change either with or on behalf of client groups to:

- *obtain services or resources that would not otherwise be provided*
- *modify or influence policies or practices that adversely affect groups or communities*
- *promote legislation or policies that will result in the provision of requisite resources or services.*

Models of advocacy are defined and discussed by Haynes and Mickelson (2000) and Freddolino, Moxley and Hyduk (2004). These authors stress that using particular models are important because they guide the intervention and the strategies used. We refer you to these informative resources as guides.

Indications for Advocacy or Social Action

Advocacy and social action may be appropriate when there are conditions or problems that affect a group or community, including the following:

1. When services or benefits to which people are entitled are denied to a group or community.
2. When services or practices are dehumanizing, confrontational, or coercive.
3. When discriminatory practices or policies occur because of race, gender, sexual orientation, religion, culture, family form, or other factors.

4. When gaps in services or benefits cause undue hardship or contribute to dysfunction.
5. When people lack representation or participation in decisions that affect their lives.
6. When governmental or agency policies and procedures, or community or workplace practices adversely affect or target groups of people.
7. When a significant group of people have common needs for which resources are unavailable.
8. When clients are denied basic civil or legal rights.

Other circumstances for which advocacy or social action may be indicated include situations in which a group or community is unable to act effectively on their own behalf. These situations may involve persons who are institutionalized, children in need of protection, or those who have a need for immediate services or benefits because of a crisis situation or cannot act as self-advocates because of their legal status.

Competence and Skills

Skills that are used in direct practice can translate to advocacy and social action (Breton, 2006) But, Schneider and Lester (2001, p.71) emphasize that advocacy is not problem solving in the tradition of direct practice problem-solving models. In contrast to the problem-solving process, "advocacy requires particular actions, such are representation, influencing and the use of a forum" to bring about specific change.

Specific skills required in advocacy or social action include policy analysis, group facilitation and communication, and competency in negotiation and the analysis of multidimensional and systematic information. Let's say for example that you are approached to represent and act on behalf a group of mothers who believe that the placement of their children was unjust. Undoubtedly, you posses characteristic of an advocate, that is, you are action-oriented, opposed to injustice, and upon hearing their stories, inaction on your part, in your opinion is not an option (Schneider & Lester, 2001). Nonetheless, before acting, you are advised to analyze the circumstances of individual situations, and become familiar with the state and federal policies and the systems involved. Situations of injustice arouse emotions and can incite anger as those affected, including the advocate, are rarely neutral. However, an analysis will help you and the group that you intend to represent to avoid making premature and erroneous conclusions that may lead to undesired or embarrassing consequences. Can you assume for example, that all of the mothers were treated unfairly?

Assuming that the situation indicates that advocacy or social action is desirable, a decision would be made as to how the group wanted to proceed. Further action may necessitate extending membership in the group as well as building a coalition with others who are affected by or are interested in the problem. Group facilitation, negotiation, consensus building, and organizing skills are essential in coalition building. To gather support for an intended action, information that documents the problem, the population affected, and in what way is critical. Recall the earlier case example of the reunification and permanency program. The agency relied on statistical data to document the pervasiveness of the problems associated with the cycling of youth through the shelter system.

Advocacy and Ethical Principles

Both advocacy and social action assume a wide range of social work roles and skills, each of which observes the values and ethics of the profession as guiding principles. Advocacy and social action embodies values and ethical principles that the social work profession has embraced, such as dignity and worth, self-determination, and giving voice to the powerless (Schneider & Lester, 2001). But, advocacy and social action may at times constitute a delicate balance between self-determination and beneficence. Ezell (2001) calls attention to this dilemma, citing the conflict that can occur in deciding "whether to empower clients to advocate for themselves or to represent them" (p. 45). Schneider and Lester (2001) provide guidance in their definition of advocacy. The relationship between the social worker and the client group is *mutual*, which means observing their interdependence and reciprocity in collaborative decision-making and planning. In other words, you are working with and representing the client.

A potential dilemma with respect to self-determination is that some clients may not wish to assert their rights in the face of formidable opposition. Advocates do not "dominate or set the agenda" (Schneider & Lester, 2001). Regardless of the decisions that a client group might make, you are ethically bound to respect their decision. In essence, the advocacy or social action effort should go no further than the client group wishes to go.

As in direct practice, you have a responsibility to explore potential barriers and the possible adversarial or negative consequences to advocacy and social action activities with clients. Implementing advocacy and social action typically creates a certain amount of strain and tension; moreover, a positive outcome cannot always be assured. What if, for example a landlord under pressure from a resident action group decided to ignore building code violations, at which point the city might condemn the building, displacing the residents. Discussing possible consequences or barriers not only allows for the planning of alternative strategies, but also ensures that clients are well educated about the pros and cons, leaving the final decision in their hands.

Clients should also be made aware of the risks and limitations to advocacy and social action. Rothman (1999) cautions community practitioners about the potential for opposition and obstacles to social action and organizing activities, including "institutions that block needed improvements in education, housing, employment and law enforcement." He further states that "change advocates have to keep in mind that elites will lash out when they perceive that their interests are challenged." To deal with this resistance, advocates should "calculate" their ability and that of their client group to sustain, remain focused, and defend themselves against counterattacks (p. 10). The example of the agency program to reunify youth with their families and prevent their continuous cycling through the shelter system was, in many respects, social action. The program represented a marked departure from business as usual and when implemented, threatened the resources of other agencies that served this population. In consequence, the agency encountered considerable opposition from other shelter providers and their opposition effectively derailed the implementation of the program for a considerable period of time.

Techniques and Steps of Advocacy and Social Action

Targets of advocacy or social action may be individuals (e.g., a landlord or public official) or organizations or divisions of government (e.g., on behalf of or with families affected by public policy). Approaches to situations vary considerably according to the target system, but all require a thorough understanding of how organizations or communities are structured and function, how the legislative and rule-making processes work, and an appreciation for organizational politics (Alexander, 2003; Homan, 2008; Roberts 2000; Rothman, 1991).

Advocacy can involve different levels of assertive intensity, ranging from discussion and education to a high level of social action and organizing, for example, protests. Sosin and Callum (1983) have developed a

useful typology of advocacy that assists practitioners in planning appropriate advocacy actions. Along with the models discussed by Haynes and Mickelson (2000) and Freddolino, Moxley and Hyduk (2004), Sosin and Callum's (1983) typology can help determine the opportunities that exist, and the techniques or strategies to be used and at what level. As a rule of thumb, you should rely on the use of the techniques that are required to achieve a given objective. Deciding which technique to use depends on the nature and analysis of the problem, the wishes of the group or community, the nature of the action and the political climate. Although militant action may be required in some instances, this approach should be utilized with great discretion, because the short-term gains may not outweigh the long-term negative images, the response from the public and the potential for fractured relationships.

Effective social action and advocacy require a rational, planned approach incorporating the following steps:

1. Analyze the problem or condition.
2. Systematically gather information and complete an analysis of the people, structure, system, or policy to be changed.
3. Assess both the driving forces that may promote change and the forces that may conceivably resist or inhibit change.
4. Identify specific goals, eliciting a broad range of viewpoints within the client group.
5. Carefully match techniques or strategies to the desired outcome.
6. Make a feasible schedule for implementing the plan of action.
7. Incorporate in the plan a feedback process for evaluating the changes that the action stimulates.

In addition to these steps and the skills and competencies discussed previously, three other ingredients are required to ensure effective social action and class advocacy: a *genuine* concern for that cause, the ability to keep the cause in *focus*, and *tenacity*. Successful advocates have a thorough understanding of how their government and systems are organized and changed. Blind emotion may work a few times, but maintaining a successful, sustained advocacy and action requires know-how. In many instances, class advocacy and social action are best described as a marathon rather than a race. As noted some years ago by John Gardner, a leader of the Common Cause organization, "The first requirement for effective citizen action is stamina."

Finally, the manner in which an issue is presented may make a substantial difference. The FrameWorks

Institute suggests translating messages about what can be done to address social problems into language that engages ordinary people and advances their interest in policy and program solutions. Questions that facilitate formulating the institute's "strategic frame analysis" are illustrated in the following examples:

- *What shapes public opinion about a particular social condition or problem, for example, issues that affect children, families, and poor people?*
- *What role do [can] the media play?*
- *How do policy-makers gauge public opinion?*

Answering these questions can facilitate advocacy and social action. Further the questions may assist you to sharpen your message to a specific group about a specific problem, and perhaps to effectively communicate about social conditions framed by the tenets of social justice.

Different Perspectives of Social Justice

You should be aware of the fact that the term social justice as articulated by the social work profession—specifically, promoting economic and social equality and defending the rights of disenfranchised and oppressed people—is not a universal viewpoint. Barusch (2002) argues that social justice is defined differently depending on the philosophical orientation of the audience, public opinion, and the framers of social policy. For example, presented with the idea that the mandate and compliance requirement for welfare recipients is unjust, libertarian values, according to Barusch, would perhaps stress the "distribution of benefits on the basis of production." Conversely, liberals tend to be utilitarian in their thinking (e.g., the greatest good for the greatest number of people) and therefore, place emphasis on "economic liberty and political equality for all" (p. 15). Differing viewpoints, however, can find common ground on particular issues and labels should not prevent you from exploring opportunities for involving certain individuals or coalition building. Recognition of this fact might lead you, as suggested by one of the strategic frame questions, to explore how opinions about a particular were influenced. Also, consider that people are complex and their perspectives can range from liberal, moderate or conservative depending on the issue at hand. Understanding the basis of different philosophies is, however, essential. The knowledge of the ideological and political context in which social problems and policies are framed can inform your analysis of the forces that may promote or inhibit change.

Community Organization

Community organizing's primary goal according to Hardina (2004) is social transformation. Similar to advocacy and social action, community organizing is action-oriented on a larger scale, intended to effect social change in which "neighborhood organizations, associations, faith communities join together to address social problems in their community" (Brueggemann, 2006, p. 204). Further, it is an arena in which participants "develop their own solutions, advance their own needs or build capacity" in partnership with private or governmental organizations (Bruggemann, 2006; Weil & Gamble, 1995).

Models and Strategies of Community Intervention

Models of community organizing and intervention and their basic means of influence are described by Rothman, Erlich and Tropman (2001) and Carter (2000). The most frequently referred to methods or strategies for organizing communities are summarized in Table 14-1.

Locality development seeks to build relationships within the community and enhance community integration and capacity thorough broad participation. Locality development supports empowerment in that the community is actively involved in defining its problem and determining goals (Cnaan & Rothman, 1986). In Quebec, Canada, locality development relied on natural helping networks and lay citizens in analyzing problems and planning remedial measures (Gulati & Guest, 1990). Users of services were considered to be partners as opposed to client–consumers. They facilitated the integration and coordination of programs and services and prevention efforts in their community. The flexibility in organizational structure and decentralized administration enabled the local communities to develop programs that respond to their unique needs.

TABLE-14-1 STRATEGIES AND METHODS OF COMMUNITY INTERVENTION

Locality Development
Social Action
Social Planning
Capacity Building

Social Action as a community organization strategy is similar in its approach as previously discussed under advocacy. It is the action on the part of communities to advocate, so that institutions and decision makers address unfairness in resource distribution (e.g., the relocation of bus routes that disadvantaged a specific population), remedy the imbalance of power through neighborhood associations or concerned citizens (e.g., the coordinated efforts of seniors, relatives, and senior citizen advocates), and solve problems or conditions identified by the community.

Social Planning as a strategy relies on experts, consultants, and technical assistance for solving problems (Rothman & Tropman, 1987). These individuals generally work with community leaders and the focus of their work is to expand, develop, and coordinate social policies and social services (Carter, 2000, p. 81). Unlike locality development, participation by the larger community is limited.

Capacity building has as its main focus, increasing the ability of a community to act on its own behalf, make decisions, and direct its own actions (Hannah, 2006). This approach takes exception to the assumption that expert or governmental interventions are a primary means to achieve a solution to a community problem. Instead, the community develops its own agenda and the work to be completed is directed "from the inside out" (Rivera & Erlich, 1998, p. 68). Organizing efforts under the auspices of Communities United to Rebuild Neighborhoods (CURN) in Chicago is an example in which residents worked together to resolve their community concerns. They focused on the collective community strengths, and individual talents at all age levels, believing that these attributes were central to the change effort, and therefore should be identified, energized, and deployed.

Within each of the first two methods, activities may support coalition building and evolve into political and social action or social movements capable of influencing social planning. In some instances, they may overlap or be employed simultaneously (Carter, 2000; Hyde, 1996: Rothman, 1995). Carter (2000), for example, discusses how coalition building evolved into effective political and social action in responding to the inaction of the Department of Justice during the 28 reported incidents of arson in African American churches in 1996. Agents were initially non-responsive, and their treatment of the congregations and their leadership was "insensitive and accusatory," laced with undertones of disrespect. But by challenging the inaction of the agents and that of the United States Justice Department about

the cause of the fires, the community realized their self-efficacy as a group which bolstered their coming together and taking action.

Irrespective of the method or the agenda, planning and organizing is directed by the community or its leadership. Social planners, for example, as experts should address the concerns of the community. Hannah, (2006) notes that community capacity initiatives must be able to gain and maintain involvement of the community which is possible if the initiative has community support. An advantage of locality development is that it reinforces empowerment and the broad community's reality and experiences, and therefore meets the sustainability criteria. As described by O'Melia and Miley (2002), empowerment is socially constructed, taking into account the social processes and the reciprocal interaction between the two domains in approaches to problem solving. Social planning and policy development, in contrast, rely on the technical process of addressing problems conducted by experts.

Steps and Skills of Community Intervention

Theorists conceptualize community organizing in different ways, outlining different stages that vary according to the levels of elaboration of relevant tasks. Rothman, Erlich and Tropman, (1995) and Rothman (1999) use a six-phase process to address community concerns:

1. Identification of need, condition, or problem as framed by the community
2. Definition and clarification of the need, condition or problem
3. Systematic process of obtaining information
4. Analysis of the information
5. Development and implementation of a plan of action
6. Terminal actions and evaluation of outcome or effects

This process may not be entirely linear, because the emergence of new information may require alternative action, including making a new start or reframing strategies and tactics (Rothman, Erlich & Tropman, 1999). In any event, maintaining focus is important and this schema of activities will assist in this regard. As Homan (1999, p.160) points out, you should keep in mind that organizing to promote change "involves more than just fixing a specific problem." Further, in advancing and empowering the capacity of the community, productive organizing includes the intent to increase the capability of people to respond meaningfully and effectively in the face of future challenges.

Organizing Skills

Working with communities and implementing organizing strategies make use of similar skills associated with direct practice. For example, the ability to establish rapport with diverse groups, genuineness and empathy, and communication skills. Because the work involves groups or communities, skills in group facilitation, fostering interpersonal relationships, and managing group dynamics are also essential. Homan (2008) adds to the skill base, emphasizing a balance between the objective and subjective, self-awareness, patience, focus, and timing. Other skills and competencies include those embodied in policy analysis, research methods and the management of data.

Organizing and Planning with Diverse Groups

Rivera and Erlich (1998), in analyzing models of community development or organizing, rebuff the assumption that prevailing models (i.e., locality development, social planning, and social action) are color-blind and therefore applicable in any community. They conclude that additional factors must be included when working with communities of color:

- *Racial, ethnic, and cultural aspects of the community*
- *Implications of this uniqueness in particular communities*
- *The empowerment process and the development of a critical consciousness*

Rivera and Erlich's work is intended to guide our thinking in planning and organizing and, in fact, represents a significant contribution to organizing strategies. Heretofore, methods had an implicit assumption that good intentions sufficed in community interventions and that, unlike direct practice, considerations of the race, ethnicity, and culture in this work were secondary. The three levels of contact as conceptualized by Rivera and Erlich (1998) for entry into communities facilitate a greater understanding of work with diverse groups and of the roles beyond those traditionally considered in social work. Table 14-2 outlines these three levels.

This schema provides an opportunity to rethink approaches to communities as well as the classical view of communities. Even the most impoverished communities have strengths, formal helping networks, and informal helping networks, and they are best able to identify their concerns. In instances where communities may lack the know-how or power for achieving resolution, social workers participate in community initiatives as partners. In addition, agencies may adopt an alternative approach such as the one initiated in Quebec (Gulati and Guest, 1990). By taking this alternative approach, agencies become more flexible in how they deliver services and which services are delivered, because they relied on the unique perceptions of each community for guidance. This approach has merit in that it appears to combine locality development with social planning, and thus may have appeal to diverse communities.

In addition to the paradigm advocated by Rivera and Erlich (1998), we propose contact with key informants or individuals who can act as cultural guides as a means to facilitate entry into communities. At the third point of entry level into the community, for example, as an "outsider," you would be cautious in making assumptions about universal values, beliefs, and instead be sensitive to the cultural traditions to guide preferences. Home ownership among some immigrants, for example,

TABLE-14-2 LEVELS OF COMMUNITY CONTACT

ENTRY LEVEL	CHARACTERISTICS
Primary	Requires that an individual has the same racial, cultural, and linguistic background as the community. The community is open to and respects this individual.
Secondary	The individual need not be a member of the same racial, ethnic, or cultural group, but should be closely aligned and sensitive to community needs. He or she may serve as a liaison to the broader community, and facilitate contact with institutions outside the community.
Tertiary	The individual is an "outsider," yet shares the community's concerns. The practitioner's skills and access to power—rather than his or her ethnic, racial, or cultural identity—are valued assets.

SOURCE: Adapted from Rivera and Erlich (1998).

lags behind the rates seen for other groups. In part, this discrepancy may be attributed to differences in income levels, lending practices of financial institutions, and suspicions about governmental agencies. Of course, lending practices and discrimination are areas in which social workers can assist communities to organize. It is advisable however, that you educate yourself about values and attitudes so that you understand their influence in community decisions. For example, as reported by Serres (2004), language and traditions may prevent home ownership. Hence it would be unproductive to attempt to organize this community around the lending practices of local banks or mortgage companies. The Hmong language lacks words for "mortgage" and "credit." In some cultures, religious beliefs forbid the payment of interest associated with debt. For example, in the Somalian community, there are several factors that act as an aversion to owning property. Religious views are one example, as the Koran speaks against paying or receiving interest. Also, Somalis, as predominately nomadic people, are accustomed to being mobile and thus perceive home ownership to be a burden. Moreover, many in the United States hope to return to their homeland.

Impressions or assumptions about other communities can also be imperfect. Shannon, Kleiniewski and Cross (2002) caution us against contrasting the "rosy picture" of rural communities as close-knit, family-centered enclaves with the view of urban communities as disorganized, chaotic, and impersonal. In fact, rural communities have a number of problems, including poor living conditions, racial and class conflicts, and challenges that are similar to those faced by their urban counterparts (e.g., transportation, unemployment, funding for schools, and affordable housing). According to Shannon et al., traditional urban neighborhood patterns may have changed, but these residents remain more likely than their rural counterparts to have a broader reach into the outside world—for example, through employment, mass transit ties and relationships between neighborhoods, and friends or family members who live elsewhere. Likewise, you should be aware of the fact that suburban communities rarely resemble the familiar sitcom family in a neighborhood that lacks diversity. Population trends show that suburban communities are becoming increasing diverse because they tend to be the geographical choice of new immigrants.

These examples are by no means exclusive, but rather illustrate the complexities of diversity of people and communities and the influence of their beliefs or values in defining need. Acceptable ways of doing things are normative strengths of communities and they clarify a community's unique patterns and characteristics. Thus, it is incumbent on you to take into account each community's particular political, economic, interpersonal, and power relationships, as well as its strengths and resources.

Strengths may be identified by eliciting the views of the community; however, viewpoints can vary. For example, there were contrasting views between residents of a community and those of a church's congregation located in the community. Both groups were interested in organizing to address local community concerns, but each group had different perceptions of the community. Church members, the majority of whom were nonresidents, viewed the urban neighborhood as fragmented, poor, crime-ridden, and unsafe. Conversely, residents described their community as close-knit and they emphasized such positive features as ease of access to public transportation, the various cultural institutions located in the community, and the historical significance of many of the older houses. But, like the congregation, the resident group was concerned about crime and police protection. As you might imagine, settling on a direction and building consensus with respect to the issues around which the two groups could partner, took a took a considerable amount of time. Eventually the two groups, each of whom valued the various cultural institutions in the community, settled on organizing to preserve them. The success of this effort led to the two groups developing a plan to address their concerns about crime and police protection.

Ethical Issues in Community Organizing

It is the groups or associations within communities that are best able to identify their needs and plan solutions. As social workers, we can become involved in their efforts as advocates, change agents, and planners, using our skills, knowledge, and values grounded in principles of social justice and empowerment to help groups and communities to achieve their goals. An ongoing question—and perhaps an ethical dilemma (posed by Ezell, 2001)—for advocates and change agents is when to act on behalf of the community and when to provide the skills and resources that will allow clients to represent themselves. Of course there are times when a division of labor directs tasks that you as a social worker will complete and others that will be implemented by a community member or leader. Your completion of certain tasks may be because you have ease of access to resources and knowledge or skills that facilitate task completion. For example, as a professional, you may be able to attend meetings, prepare reports, deal with established and formidable institutions, or make contacts that may be inaccessible to groups or communities. Yet, these scenarios suggest strategic reflection on your part. Specifically, does the planned action call for joint efforts? By acting alone, will you disempower your clients? Can clients do or speak for themselves? If not, what skills are required to assist them? (Ezell, 2001).

Hardina (2004), points out that community organizing and its methods address issues that are not directly covered in the social work Code of Ethics. For example, the Code does not address dual relationships between the organizer and community residents. Nor does the Code address the choice of tactics that an organizer might use. To the first point, specifically dual relationships, in the Rivera and Erlich (1998), schema, at entry level one, you are a member of the community as well as an organizer. Because you are a part of the community, there may have been numerous other occasions in which you have interacted with other residents, socially and politically. However, being involved in this way with community members could be perceived as a violation of the Code (Hardina, 2004). Just as with advocacy and social action, community organizers should observe self-determination; the community should be informed and consent to the tactics to be used, as well as understand the risks and benefits. Hardina (2004) suggests that if the ethical principle and subsequent dilemma is not obvious, the organizer should use the Ethical Rule Screen proposed by Loewenburg, Dolgoff and Harrington (1996, 2005). For example, "protection of life" or "privacy and confidentiality" must be weighed when considering a forceful tactic that may place people at risk. In addition, Reisch and Lowe (2002), as discussed by Hardina (2004, p. 600), have proposed a useful Ethical Decision-Making Framework for community organizers. In this series of steps, Reisch and Lowe propose that the social worker organizers should:

- *Identify the ethical principles that apply to the situation at hand.*
- *Collect additional information necessary to examine the ethical dilemma in question.*
- *Identify the relevant ethical values and/or rules that apply to the ethical problem.*
- *Identify any potential conflicts of interest and the people who are likely to benefit from such conflict.*
- *Identify ethical rules and rank them in terms of importance.*
- *Determine the consequences of applying different ethical rules or ranking these rules differently.*

Improving Institutional Environments

Social welfare organizations are organized to provide a service, information, benefits, or goods. They are formal social systems with multiple constituents and dynamic arenas in which client eligibility for services is determined and the resources vital to the organization's existence are distributed. The culture of organizations includes core values and purposes as portrayed in mission statements, leadership styles, and assumptions and rituals. Schein (1985) describes organizational culture as follows:

> *A pattern of basic assumptions—invented, discovered, or developed by a given group as it learns to cope with its problems of external adaptation and internal integration—that has worked well enough to be considered valid and therefore to be taught to new members as the correct way to perceive, think and feel in relation to those problems. (p. 9)*

Change within Organizations

Organizational change refers to "modifications in how the organization functions, who its members and leaders are, what form the organization takes, how it allocates it resources, or transitions in the type of strategy the organization pursues to achieve its goals" (Condrey, Facer & Hamilton, 2005, p. 223). Proehl (2001) notes for example, that organizations are influenced by external forces such as the state of the economy. Similar to Sherraden, Slosar and Sherraden (2002), Proehl believes that the political and legislative initiatives that shifted fiscal decision making to states provide opportunities for influence. Welfare reform, for example, has had a significant impact on both public and private organizations, their internal operations, staff functions and job satisfaction, and goals and resources (Abramovitz, 2005; Condrey, Facer & Hamilton, 2005). The federal requirements for the implementation of specific performance standards, for example, is among the adjustments that agencies had to make so that they could monitor and report the work-related activities of recipients.

Many non-profit organizations and some social workers have struggled with the mandated goals of welfare reform (PWORA). At issue for many were requirements which were counter to their mission and the values of the social work profession. At the same time, the leadership and culture of the organization enabled some organizations to respond to these pressures in ways that were less disruptive and more beneficial to the organization (Condrey, Faces & Hamilton, 2005).

Change strategies within organizations require an understanding and analysis of organizational structure, function, culture, and resource environment. Martin and O'Connor (1989) analyze the social welfare organization using systems theory. Their conceptual schema offers a conceptual scheme for understanding social welfare organizations as open systems. In this framework, the focus is on the organizations':

- *Relations with the environment*
- *Internal structures and processes*
- *Dilemmas associated with a conflicting—indeed, sometimes hostile—social, cultural, and political-economic environment*

Netting, Kettner, and McMurtry (2004) provide guidelines for analyzing change efforts in social welfare organizations; we refer you to their work for further elaboration of this process.

Change Strategies

Netting et al. (2004) suggest two types of macro-level changes in organizations:

- *improve resources provided to clients*
- *enhance the organization's working environment so that personnel can perform more efficiently and effectively, thus improving services to clients.*

Brager and Holloway (1978) have outlined organizational change as focusing on three areas: people-focused change, technological change, and structural change. Changes may take the form of a policy, a program, or the initiation of a project and by the organization positioning itself as a learning organization (Kettner, Daley & Nichols, 1985; Senge, 1990, 1994).

Organizational Learning and Learning Organizations

Organizational learning and the learning organizations offer an approach to effect organizational change.

A *learning organization* is a process that enables members of the organization to periodically review performance and make adjustments to improve it. It is also considered to be a relevant factor in the quality of staff work life, with respect to job design and performance awards (Lewis, Lewis, Packard & Souflee, 2001; Morgan, 1997). A learning organization positions itself so that it can continuously review and revise its operations, purposes, and objectives so as to ensure the quality of the organizational experience for clients and staff. Questions that might be posed include:

- *How is work done?*
- *What are the outcomes of this work?*

Through this process the organization has an opportunity to reflect on its strengths and limitations, so that it can develop strategies that enhance the former and address the latter.

While organizational learning and the learning organization are often discussed as a single concept, the *learning organization*, as defined by Senge (1990, 1994) and Morgan (1997), essentially speaks to the ecology of the organization. That is, it refers to a particular type of organization and its ability to scan, anticipate, and respond to environmental changes. The learning organization develops capacities that empower members to question and challenge operating norms and assumptions, thereby ensuring its stability and promoting its evolution through strategic responses and direction (Morgan, 1997). In contrast, *organizational learning* emphasizes a set of activities pertinent to the organization's internal operations and the interdependence among its various units.

Both organizational learning and the learning organization require a supportive environment, in which the organization's culture fosters dialogue, open communication and feedback. One county human health and human services agency, under the leadership of its director, initiated a series of "community dialogues" among staff to position itself as a learning organization and a shared vision to facilitate organizational learning. For example, how well did the various units serving families coordinate and work together? Recall the example of the fathers and child support introduced at the beginning to this chapter. It was during a staff community dialogue session that the idea for this program was developed. Lewis et al. (2001) encourage the adoption of the learning organization as a way to create opportunities for growth in human service organizations.

Organizational Environments

The quality of the organizational environment and the values of the organization as experienced by clients are important aspects of service delivery. In this section we consider ways of changing or enhancing three major facets of institutional environments: staff, policies and practices, and programs.

Staff

The organization's staff forms the heart of an organization's environment. The staffing mix of an organization includes professionals who have regular contact with clients; support personnel; and administrative personnel. Administrative personnel—specifically, managers and supervisors—direct, monitor, coordinate, evaluate, and bear the responsibility for the oversight of overall organizational operations. In the organization's highly interdependent environment, each position is critical to achieving its mission. To a large extent, staff behavior is governed by a mix of internal and external factors, including professional orientations, ethical codes and standards, licensing or regulatory boards, union contracts, funding sources, the media, and the public.

When an organization's staff are dedicated, caring, and responsive to clients' needs, as well as congenial with one another, the environment tends to be conducive to the growth and well-being of all concerned. To be optimally effective, an organization's culture should promote staff empowerment and a commitment to deliver high-quality client services. Among the factors that characterize a healthy organizational culture and climate are open communication, a willingness to deal with conflict, flexibility and risk taking, a sense of interdependence and cohesiveness, and respect for boundaries. Although the creation of an organization's environment is within the domain of organizational leadership, it is the responsibility of all staffing levels.

Hackman and Oldham (1976, 1980) have conceptualized the most elaborate and widely accepted theories of job design and motivation as contributing to the overall psychological states of meaningfulness, staff responses, morale, and job satisfaction of staff. They have identified five core characteristics:

- *Task identity*
- *Task significance*
- *Skill variety*
- *Job feedback*
- *Autonomy*

Task identity, task significance, and skill variety add to the feeling that work is meaningful. Feedback with regard to one's job performance provides information about the results achieved, thereby acting as both a developmental and a motivating factor. Autonomy inspires a sense of responsibility for one's own work, the outcomes of this work, and the work of the team. Empowerment, which is implicit in autonomy, works in much the same way as self-determination does for clients. Just as clients may terminate social work contact when their interests and needs are ignored, so a lack of staff empowerment may affect job performance, reduce productivity, and contribute to more rapid turnover.

Change may be indicated when dynamics within the organization—whether stemming from conflicting professional orientations, competing ideologies, diversity, or controversies over values—that create tensions that affect job satisfaction, morale, and identity. These dynamics have the potential to spill over into interactions with clients. If these conflicts are left unresolved, staff members may react in ways that are counterproductive to the goals and purpose of the organization. Organizational environments with rigid rules, a lack of autonomy, and resistance to change become "psyche prisons" (Morgan, 1997). In sharp contrast to the growth found in the learning organization, staff in organizations perceived as psyche prisons frequently feel trapped in a construction of reality and a preferred way of thinking.

The extent to which staffs are empowered and are able to participate in work-related decisions makes a significant difference in the extent to which they feel valued. Likewise, these characteristics influence how much they engage in pro-social or extra-role behavior. Problem solving is also impacted by staff-related issues. For example, one social worker recounted how staff attempts to address concerns in his organization resulted in a manager stating, "If staff were involved in decision making, there would be no reason for upper management." When staff input was later solicited about ways to decrease indirect service expenditures, not surprisingly they showed little interest in the problem or its resolution. This situation is perhaps unique in that most organizations, having recognized the importance of developing an organizational culture that is conductive to change, encourage staff to identify needed changes. Many organizations also have mechanisms whereby proposals for change can be suggested and initiated. Finally, large human services organizations, in an effort to provide for greater staff participation in decision making and improve services, have become less hierarchical and more decentralized by implementing total quality management teams (Martin, 1993; Lewis et al., 2001).

Clients are affected by organizational environments in much the same way as staff. Clients reap the benefits when staff are motivated and treated as autonomous, yet interdependent, knowledgeable professionals. Conversely, they experience the residual effects when the opposite is true. The experience of clients may also reflect individual staff behaviors (i.e., the impaired professional) or failure to respect their right to be treated with dignity and having worth.

Of course, staff in the best of organizational environments will experience stress and frustrations when their work is constrained by limited resources, skewed funding priorities, and constant exposure to the "magnitude and complexities of client's problems" (Kirk & Koeske, 1995). Does work with families who have multiple needs and are involved with multiple agencies, in a managed care environment, with pressures further exacerbated by public policy, timelines, or compliance mandates, sound familiar? For example, social workers and other professionals who work in programs serving youth are often frustrated in this regard. Their frustrations are related to individualized program objectives and county funding that ignore an ecological or family system perspective, but instead focus on resolving specific problems (e.g., truancy). At the same time, work with the family as a whole was neither considered nor reimbursed.

We raise these points for discussion because funding priorities and organizational environments (i.e., climate and culture) are factors that affect staff morale, performance, and job satisfaction. These factors also affect the experiences of clients, as well as the quality of the services they receive.

Staff as Agents of Change

Although social workers may be very adept in advocating for clients, developing resources or support networks, and organizing, they are often reticent or feel unable to influence or propose changes within their own organizations. In some instances, they may identify organizational concerns in a hierarchical fashion, and therefore conclude that the impetus for change or resolutions resides in the management domain. In some instances, and with certain problems, this view may be valid. For example, staff performance or budgetary problems are ultimately the responsibility of management.

Nonetheless, we encourage you to assess situations, to present your concerns and ideas in a systematic manner, and to actively participate in change efforts. Because of the close interactions that take place between staff and clients, managers and administrators rely on those at the street-level to alert them to the dynamics that might affect the work environment and client well-being. Assuming responsibility for and participating in change is the essence of staff empowerment; and participation in change efforts is consistent with the ethical principles of the social work profession. The skills and competencies relevant in interventions with clients, as well as macro practice strategies, are pertinent to organizational change. Further, initiating change at the organizational level requires that you act as an organizational diagnostician and facilitator/expediter.

To be an effective change agent, you must have the knowledge and skills that will enable you to analyze the organization as well as the risks and benefits of the proposed change. Your analysis should provide clarity about the need for change. If service delivery is a concern, will your proposal, for example, improve the situation? (Brager and Holloway, 1978; Netting, Kettner & McMurtry, 2004). In addition, does your analysis suggest a change in a policy, or the development of a project or program? (Kettner, Daley & Nichols, 1985).

Risks, Benefits and Opposition

Promoting change in organizations is a complex process, and organizational opposition to change is perhaps as common as that found in families, individuals, and groups. Organizations are systems that seek to maintain equilibrium, and therefore, you may encounter opposition to proposals for change. Opposition may arise in response to proposals that challenge or exceed the capacity of the organization to implement proposals due to resource constraints or ideological differences. Likewise, proposals that would significantly change the purpose, mission, and goals of the organization may spur resistance. But, extending an agency's hours of operation may be considered to be a peripheral change, and have little or no effect on organizational goals or mission. In contrast, programmatic changes, which alter a program's objectives, have greater effects on organizational depth.

Frey (1990) has developed a useful framework with which you can assess organizational opposition. In assessing the potential benefits and to minimize opposition to a proposal, it is important to obtain the input of four groups:

• *Clients, including the extent to which the proposed change offers direct benefits to this group and will effectively alter and enhance the services they receive*

- *Administrators, who ultimately have legitimate authority for accepting the proposal and providing the resources for implementation*
- *Supervisors or staff, who will have responsibility for planning and/or overseeing implementation*
- *Staff persons, who ultimately carry out the change or are affected by it, once it is implemented*

By considering the impact of the potential change on each group, you can weigh benefits against detrimental effects and can plan strategies to counter reactions and resistance when the former (i.e., the benefits) clearly and substantially outweigh the latter.

Frey (1990) also suggest that you weigh risk, benefits and opposition by assessing whether your proposal is one in which can be characterized as "high risk" as characterized by the following:

- *Substantial costs to the organization—for example, purchasing expensive equipment or creating new units*
- *Actions that must be adopted in their entirety rather than implemented in stages*
- *Radical ideas that are in conflict with the dominant values of the organization, its members, or the public*

The following example describes a successful low-risk proposal initiated by a social worker; in particular, the proposal is consistent with the goals of the organization and does not involve costly changes. The change was consistent with the Netting et al.'s (2004), change strategy of "enhancing the organization's working environment so that personnel can perform more efficiently and effectively, thus improving services to clients."

Case Example

The primary client group served by the agency was individuals for whom English was their second language (ESL population). The agency provided counseling, educational programs, and services to assist clients in applying for financial assistance benefits. However, a majority of clients had difficulty in completing the financial assistance applications, despite the fact that the applications had been translated into several different languages. The particular problem documented by the social worker was the amount of staff time required (which far exceeded the contact hours allowed) to assist individuals or families in completing the forms. Incomplete applications resulted in the need for additional appointments and delays in establishing clients' eligibility.

To rectify this situation, the social worker proposed convening instructional groups scheduled at different times during the week instead of staff appointments with individuals or families. She envisioned that using a group format and the services of volunteers would respond to two concerns. First, use of groups would mitigate staff concerns related to scheduling and excessive contact hours. Second, recruiting agency clients who had successfully completed the forms to serve as volunteer helpers would ensure that clients, especially new arrivals, became connected to a social network.

The success of this proposal was attributed to the fact that the change did not require substantial organizational expenditures. Nor did it radically compromise the organization's goals and mission. In fact, rather than taxing organizational resources, it redeployed resources in a more efficient manner. By using a group approach and taking advantage of volunteers, the social worker's proposal augmented the agency's ability to serve this ESL population. Staff responded favorably, as it effectively addressed their frustrations about the time they spent in assisting individuals and families to complete the financial forms.

In general, proposals that fit with an organization's ideology, resource capacity, and potential are likely to win the support of a significant number of members and, therefore, are more likely to succeed. Of course, irrespective of its nature, change is often met with skepticism and resistance. Indeed, the social worker's proposal encountered some opposition. In response, the social worker documented the cost-benefit ratio to the organization (which satisfied administrators) and clarified the benefits for staff (their time would be freed so that they could accomplish other tasks). To build support for her proposal, the social worker spoke with co-workers, especially those who were most affected by the need to reschedule appointments for the purpose of completing the eligibility forms. The social worker met with other staff even though they were not directly involved in the ESL program, she recognized that their support would facilitate acceptance. A final point illustrated in this situation is individual staff were favorable to the proposal because they perceived it as either benign or a benefit to their position and function.

Policies and Practices

Social workers are in strategic positions in agencies and institutions to evaluate the impact of organizational policies, procedures, and practices on service delivery because of their close contact with clients. When certain organizational practices or policies impede service delivery or block the agency from fulfilling its mission in an optimal fashion, they are well positioned to identify the barriers and proposed changes. In this role, they function as organizational diagnostician/facilitator, mediator, expediter, and advocate.

In this section, the focus highlights three areas in which organizational policies and practices act as barriers to service delivery:

- *Policies or practices that fail to promote client dignity and worth*
- *Institutionalized racism and discrimination*
- *A lack of cultural competence at the organizational level*
- *Institutional programs*

Before beginning the discussion of the factors listed above, the following questions can assist you in critiquing policies and practices in your organization.

Examining Organizational Policies and Practices

The extents to which organizational policies and practice promote social justice, support client self-determination, and adhere to the principles of empowerment and strengths are lenses through which you can examine agency policies and practices. G.D. Rooney (2000) has developed an exercise for students designed to examine the values and ethics reflected in organizational policy decisions and practice. Policies or practices that lend themselves to a review include criteria for determining eligibility for services, rules that govern clients' behavior in residential or institutional settings, policies related to access to services, and procedures for developing treatment plans. Rooney (2000) outlines the following key points to consider when assessing organizational policies or practices:

1. What are the origins, ideology, and values that appear to have influenced the policy?
2. What are the intended and unintended consequences of the policy's application?
3. To what extent are the policy and its expectations of clients influenced by societal ideology (e.g., the worthy and unworthy poor), social control, or compliance?
4. What is the image of clients and practitioners portrayed by the policy?

5. What does the policy or practice demand of clients and practitioners?
6. How do clients react to the practice or policy?
7. To what extent do the policy and its procedures support or constrain social work values, ethics, and social justice concerns?

Unfortunately, some organizations may have dysfunctional policies or may engage in practices or have policies that create barriers to delivering services fully and effectively. The implementation of such policies may, in fact, deny resources to clients to which clients' are entitled or certain clients may receive services that are of lesser quality than others receive. In responding to their resource environment, agency practice can also be influenced by public policy, as discussed in the earlier example of welfare reform.

The series of questions for assessing organizational policies and practices developed by Rooney is intended to provide social workers with guidelines so that they may critique the effects of policy on clients and service delivery. Many students who have completed this assessment have reported the emergence of insightful questions.

Questions raised by students include the following:

- *In working with involuntary clients, does the policy or practice require clients to be compliant, such that the social worker's role becomes that of an enforcer?*
- *How do you reconcile unintended consequences of the implementation of rules?*
- *When clients have a strong reaction to a policy or practice, are there mechanisms in place so that the organization can respond to their concerns?*
- *Do policies and practices provide an image of clients that promotes dignity and worth, and acknowledges strengths as well as problems?*
- *How does the policy or practice ensure equal access to and equality of services? In particular, does the policy or practice provide differential treatment for one client group at the expense of another group?*

Many times, policies and practices are intended to help organizations manage limited resources and to ensure their distribution to those in need. For example, rules limiting the number of times a family can access a food bank are critical to preserving resources, thereby ensuring that help will be available to the greatest number of clients possible. At the same time, these limits convey the idea that clients may be dishonest or take advantage of the program. Policies may be considered to be dysfunctional when they intend to ensure compliance but unduly burden clients, and when procedures are implemented such that the potential for cheating takes precedence over service provisions.

Promoting Dignity and Worth

Human services organizations have the best of intentions when it comes to serving clients. Yet, in many ways, promoting service delivery in ways that enhance clients' dignity remains a challenge. These difficulties may be related to the images portrayed of clients in public policy, the media, or funding resources; organizational practices; and the actions of individual professionals. In some cases, organizations may strip clients of their dignity by requiring them to go to unreasonable lengths, for example, to establish eligibility for concrete aid or services. A vignette entitled "Four Pennies to My Name" is a powerful illustration of one client's perspective of this experience as she attempted to comply with the eligibility requirements for financial assistance (Compton & Galaway, 1994)

Staff Behavior and Attitudes

Clients' dignity may also be compromised if you are habitually tardy for appointments, cancel or frequently change scheduled appointments, or do not extend common courtesies. It is unfortunate when prior negative experiences (e.g., clients have been degraded or humiliated by the actions of staff persons, by breaches of confidentiality, or by demeaning procedures) dissuade individuals from accepting or seeking available services. Even worse, some staff persons may be either openly or subtly judgmental of clients, making remarks about their morality, veracity, character, or worthiness to receive assistance. Still other staff members may be brusque or rude, or they may intrude unjustifiably into deeply personal aspects of clients' lives, needlessly subjecting them to embarrassment and humiliation. You may also encounter a situation that leads you to question a colleague's competence and to consider whether their behavior with clients is a result of their impairment. These behaviors can evolve from bad personal behavior into an organizational issue when supervisors, managers, and staff allow them to go unchallenged. In addition, such behaviors are inhumane and unethical practice (e.g., NASW Code, 2000, Standards, 2.09, 2.10 and 2.11).

Beyond the organizational response, social workers who are aware of behavior by others that compromise client dignity and worth should comply with the ethical standards. Speaking with the colleague is a first step, and further discussion may involve the organization's administration. If necessary you can pursue filing a complaint with the appropriate licensing board and professional organization. You may be thinking to yourself at this point that these are dramatic extreme measures. Further, you may question the benefits or risks associated with your becoming involved. *Whistle blowing*, is discussed by Greene and Latting (2004) as a form of advocacy to be implemented when client's rights are ignored or in situations that represent a serious threat to their well-being and dignity. Of course, the act of whistle blowing has consequences for you and the organization, which is a primary reason that most people are reluctant to report wrongful acts or behaviors. Many question their perceptions or motives, or are fearful of losing status and relationships as well as loss of their employment. In summarizing the research on whistle blowing, Greene and Latting (2004, pp. 220-221) have identified characteristics that you can use to assess your potential action. Whistle-blowers have integrity if they are

- *Motivated by their altruism, and their actions are to the benefit of those being wronged*
- *Utilitarian, with a high level of moral development, and are driven by their sense of integrity and social [professional] responsibility to speak out, even under symbolic or literal pressures to keep silent*
- *Seem uninterested in tailoring their behavior to conform to particular situations and behave consistently across situations*
- *Allow their own attitudes and beliefs to guide them and refuse to lie or cover up*
- *Well-educated, hold professional or managerial positions, and keep well-documented records of that they perceive to be abuse or waste*

Privacy and Dignity and Worth

Another organizational issue related to dignity and worth is inadequate provisions for privacy in the physical space of the organization, such that interviews with clients (either by telephone or in person) are conducted in view of or within earshot of others. Many large public agencies are faced with limited space and increasing numbers of clients and thus struggle to ensure that both staff and clients are comfortable in the organizational environment. Hospital social workers often point to the lack of privacy in rooms shared by two patients, although social workers report being creative in addressing this concern. One social worker, for example, meets with a patient in a shared room, when the other patient is absent. Measures initiated by organizations to address this issue include home visits, smaller satellite offices in communities with proximity to target populations, and contracting with community-based agencies.

Organizational Safety Measures

Angry clients, concerns for safety, and threats of violence have prompted both public and private organizations to install metal detectors through which visitors and clients must pass, and the use of private guards or off-duty police to minimize risks to staff and clients. In responding to this very real concern, organizations must be aware of both the implied image conveyed of clients, and how clients experience the organization. One of this book's authors paid a visit to a Social Security Administration office located in a low-income neighborhood on behalf of a client; this visit illustrated all too well how demeaning an experience can be when a person perceives a lack of power in the face of authority. Entry into the Social Security office required that security personnel examine the content of the author's purse and briefcase. The author then had to pass through a metal detector. The experience was further exacerbated by the impersonal attitudes of the three officers, who asked what the author perceived to be rather personal questions.

While administrators and staff may regard this practice as routine and essential for managing risks and providing a safe work environment, they should be aware of the message and the power afforded to individuals who are not associated with the mission and goals of the organization. The first impulse of the author—and one surely experienced by clients—was to argue against the search and demand an explanation for it. She also wondered whether she would have been subjected to the same experience if she had chosen to visit an office in a different part of the city. Broad legal questions have been raised about the legitimacy and authority of private security personnel in the public domain. Realistically, although some view their presence as another form of oppression and social control, this practice is unlikely to go away. Nonetheless, social workers in organizations can play a key role in humanizing these situations by providing interpersonal and human relations skills for security personnel, and in developing criteria for the hiring and training of these individuals. When practices such as this result in clients being treated in an indiscriminate manner, without regard for their dignity, social workers must act to call attention to the policy's effects and advocate for change.

Institutionalized Racism and Discrimination

Racism and discrimination are embedded in the fabric of our society to such a pervasive extent that many people fail to recognize their many manifestations. Institutional racism often affects service delivery and availability of resources and opportunities in subtle ways. Therefore, it is vital that administrators and social workers be sensitized to its manifestations, especially in the allocation of resources and service delivery to clients. The effects of institutional racism range across the entire developmental span, beginning with prenatal care and continuing through services for the elderly, and beyond—even to burial arrangements. Racism and discrimination pervade our educational, legal, economic, and political institutions; determine employment opportunities; influence the how clients' situations are perceived, and may constrain access to health care and mental health services.

Social workers have an ethical responsibility to work toward (1) obliterating institutional racism in organizational policies and practices and (2) enhancing cultural competence. These are worthy goals, of course, but also represent formidable challenges. The first step toward meeting these challenges is developing awareness of possible traces of racist attitudes within oneself and the influence on your practice. Social workers must also analyze and address public policies and those of other social welfare agencies to ensure that all people are treated equitably.

The NASW Code (e.g., 4.02) speaks directly to the social worker's responsibility with regard to discrimination. Abramovitz (2005) cites the differences by race with respect to PWORA sanctions. Minority women, for example, were treated more harshly, and more likely to be sanctioned than their white counterparts. In some instances, racism and discrimination may not be as obvious. Rodenborg (2004), for example, refers to an indirect discrimination effect in child welfare agencies in which decisions about limited resources, or the lack thereof, did not respond to the needs of poor families. Examples included housing, jobs, or education needed to preserve the family or prevent child out-of-home placement. Differences in what services are provided, although not intentionally discriminatory, can in fact have the same effect. In a comparison between poor minority and poor nonminority families with the same problems, for example, Morton (1999) and Chipungu and Bent-Goodley (2003) have emphasized the fact that poor families of color are more likely to have their children placed, whereas poor nonminority families are more likely to receive preservation services.

Of course, these differences can be accounted for by analyzing the problems of the families. Nonminority poor families often present with problems related to parent–child conflicts, for which services may be readily available. Poor minority families on the other hand, often enter the child welfare system as a result of poverty-related neglect, for which there may be fewer resources. Although intended to enhance uniform decisions, indirect discrimination and the disparate placement of children of color may be linked to structured decision-making tools. These tools may be inherently biased against minority families, because many of the risk factors assessed are structural family vulnerabilities rather than protective factors emphasized by Halpern (1990) and Roberts (2002). These various scenarios call for an analysis by administrators and social workers to ensure that the so-called color-blind nature of policies and procedures, including those mandated in public policy, are not biased and discriminatory.

Persons of color are more likely to be receive a diagnosis of schizophrenia, a referral through the legal system, or social services in which they are often involuntary, in which the treatment approach can be coercive (Allen, 2007; Barnes, 2008; Richman, Kohn-Woods & Williams, 2007; Allen, 2007). Wolf (1991) and Barnes (2008), for example, describe problems encountered by African Americans in mental health settings and emergency rooms, in which standardized diagnostic manuals are used to classify and label behaviors. A study by Barnes showed that African Americans are more likely to be over diagnosed with schizophrenia or bipolar and depressive mood disorders, without regard for demographic variables. In consequence, clients were often treated with the wrong psychotropic medication. According to Longres and Torrecilha (1992), Whaley (1998), and Wolf (1991), in most instances a relationship exists between the client's race and the diagnostic or social labels applied to that person. That is, in their encounters with systems, minorities are often labeled pathological without regard to their ecological circumstances or needs. Malgady and Zayas (2001) and Walker and Stanton (2000) elaborate on this point with regard to Hispanics. They emphasize that while the *DSM-IV* includes culturally bound syndromes and ethnic and cultural consideration, it does not have a theoretical basis upon which culturally sensitive diagnosis can be made.

Increasingly, social workers, parents and community activists are voicing concerns about what they perceive as subtle forms of institutional racism in school settings. Specifically, they are concerned about the disproportionate number of suspensions of minority children and the frequent assignments of children to segregated instructional groups. The direct effect of these practices is an assault on the self-efficacy and confidence of minority children (Williams, 1990). These practices have a group effect as well, because the majority of those involved in suspensions and segregated groups are children of color—in particular, African American males.

Cultural Competence: A Macro Perspective. As noted earlier in this book, cultural competence is an issue in the interaction between clients and social workers who are different by virtue of their race, language, and culture. Cultural competence is typically discussed at this level in the social work literature. Although cultural competence requires the commitment, competence, and effort of the entire organization, external factors (e.g., public policy) may affect the organization's ability to make a commitment to cultural competence. At the macro level, we discuss two components of cultural competence that go beyond social workers: organizational competence and public policy.

Organizational Competence. The cultural competence of an organization is not a matter limited to the sensitivity and awareness of staff, or the assignment of staff who work with a particular racial or cultural group, nor is it limited to printed materials and organizational practices (Nybell & Gray, 2004; Fong & Gibbs, 1995). Striving for cultural competence within an organization as outlined by Nybell and Gray (2004) requires an agency to take steps outlined as follows:

- *A review of organizational policies and practice*
- *Assessing the organization's standing in communities of color*
- *Attention to how equitably the resources are allocated, in particular the programs or services that consists of a disproportionate number of poor clients and clients of color*
- *An assessment of staffing patterns, in particular, who is hired, what positions are held by whom, and who is promoted, or terminated*
- *Examining the distribution of power, focusing on who benefits and who is excluded*
- *Examining the narrative structures that inform agency practices, public relations, fundraisers, and board members*
- *An analysis of the decision-making process, who is involved, including clients, in such matters as agency location, allocation of resources, and who has access to this process.*

Of course, organizational change often results in conflict and the risks and benefits of proposals must be considered (Chesler, 1994b; Fry, 1990). However, cultural competence at the levels proposed by Nybell and Gray (2004) requires that the organization's leadership have a commitment to achieving cultural competence.

Organizational Strategies to Achieve Cultural Competence

Cultural competence and its assumptions were intended to address issues related to racism, bias, and discrimination by increasing culturally sensitive interventions in recognition of the fact that "traditional forms of practice were often ineffective with and sometimes oppressive to ethnic minority clients" (Rodgers & Potocky, 1997, p. 391). To be effective, organizations must embrace cultural sensitivity and competence and demonstrate their commitment through their policies and practices (Chesler, 1994a; Chesler, 1994b). Both public and private organizations have attempted to accommodate diverse populations by hiring professionals or community staff who represents a target group. Public agencies have also developed purchase-of-service (POS) contracts with ethnic or race-specific community-based agencies. The assumption is that these individuals and agencies are more likely to identify with their clients, and have a greater understanding of the group experience.

This practice initiative, while useful on one level in nonminority agencies, in effect creates an agency within an agency. This practice raises other concerns for consideration:

- *In essence, the ethnic or racial representative is solely responsible for clients with whom they share demographic characteristic, and therefore may rarely have the opportunity to work with other clients.*
- *When representative staff provide services only to one client group, other staff may ignore and are limited their exposure to clients who are different, further perpetuating racial inequality.*
- *The practice limits the organization's ability to expose all clients to diverse professionals.*
- *Representative staff assigned on the basis of their race, culture, or sexual orientation, are often overwhelmed by the volume of work, which can include responding to the demands of representing their community.*

The NASW Standard for Cultural Competence in Social Work Practice speaks to the issue of overload, asserting that the "special skills and knowledge that bicultural and bilingual staff bring to the profession" should compensated, rather than exploited (2001, p. 26). This issue should be addressed at the organizational level, because it has implications related to workload, morale, and unintentional discrimination.

The practice of hiring same-race or same-culture staff in organizations evolved out of a very real need to have a diversity of color, language, and understanding in organizations where the majority of staff members were white. At the same time, this practice is inadequate as a means to achieve organizational cultural competence. Of course, not everyone would agree with this assessment, with many pointing out that same-race or same-culture staffs provide important services to their communities. This is a valid argument, but at best it is an interim solution. On another level, however, while same-race or same-culture staff members can be empathetic, many express frustration that they are rarely able to alter the policies that affect their clients and their situations. Another matter that has emerged from talks with clients and supervisors is the fact that minority staff often perceives that they need to apply policies more harshly, so as not to appear too lenient or unprofessional when compared to their nonminority counterparts.

Resources and Tools

Tools and resources exist so that organizations can analyze their competence. The Child Welfare League of America (1990) for example, has developed a Cultural Competence Self-Assessment Instrument, which provides guidance to organizations in assessing and developing cultural competence at all levels of the organization. For social workers, Strom-Gottfried and Morrissey (2000) have developed an organizational audit, which assesses agency policies and practices as well as organizational strengths and effectiveness with respect to diversity.

Another resource for assessing both organizational leadership and social workers was developed by Cross, Bazron, Dennis, and Issacs (1989). Using specific indicators, this resource describes a continuum of organizational cultural competence. At a midpoint on this continuum is the practice of implementing policies that could be described as "color blind" and lacking sensitivity to their effects on minorities. One extreme indicator on the continuum is that agencies have culturally destructive policies. As an example, Cross et al. (1989) discuss policies and practices used in boarding schools in the early twentieth century that had the express purpose of eliminating Native American culture. At the other extreme of Cross et al.'s continuum is culturally sensitive and competent practice, which actively seeks to provide services relevant to various minority client populations. In general, the various levels provide a means for organizations to examine their policies and practices so as to determine their differential impact on populations served and to encourage proactive development of culturally sensitive policies.

Public Policy. Cultural competence comprises a set of behaviors and skills that have implications at the level of both the individual social worker and the organization. In both instances, competence must be supported and reinforced in agency practices. With few exceptions, the literature has emphasized cultural competence in the interactions between clients and practitioners (Weaver, 2004). Unfortunately, few guidelines beyond the standard policy analysis questions (who is affected and in what way) exist for analyzing cultural competence in public policy.

A culturally competent social worker cannot always ensure that clients will not experience racism or bias in public policy. In fact, in the face of public policy, organizations and social workers are often at a disadvantage, irrespective of the level of cultural competence they have attained. What is the basis of this assertion? Bias is inherent in most policies, even though their intent is to be neutral with respect to race, class, culture, and gender. Yet, as discussed in the example in this chapter related to racism and inequality in education and child welfare services, policies as implemented often have disparate effects on certain segments of the population.

Public policy has tended to take a narrow view of the culturally or racially determined dynamics that influence how people function. Further, public policy has paid little attention to how family networks and relationships are defined within diverse groups. For example, services for the elderly, mental health services and child welfare services are structured around the Western concept of the nuclear family, rather than a broad kinship network. Services for the elderly include provisions for assistance either in nursing homes or in-home care, both of which are based on the assumption of nuclear family support. Thus, while resources are available for biological kin to provide care and support, church members, neighbors, and other non relatives are deemed ineligible. Informal kinship arrangements, such as those found in many minority communities, also go unrecognized in public policy. In the child welfare situation, for example, relatives as well as non-relatives have often assumed responsibility for children; nevertheless, these individuals are unable to access resources unless they formally adopt the children. The concept of formally adopting a relative, while it has certain legal safeguards, is perceived differently in minority communities.

Van Soest and Garcia (2003) suggest that cultural competence at the public policy level is an issue of social justice. As such, administrators and social workers, acting as advocates are required to confront aspects of policies that are inherently biased and that have disparate and oppressive effects on various segments of the population. As Weaver (2004) asserts, "the social justice aspect of cultural competence is often obscured by cultural competence conceptualized and highly focused on individual interaction." In effect, this focus means that analyzing the cultural relevance of public policy has been ignored. Conclusions drawn by Voss, Douville, Little Soldier, and Twiss (1999), speaking to policies related to Native Americans, are relevant in this broader context. Specifically, these authors claim that when "social policies and interventions are not inclusive of cultural dynamics, they "rigidly enforce a kind of clinical colonialism" (p. 233).

In light of this discussion, we would add another dimension to the definition of cultural competence for the organization and the social worker. Given that laws and public policy influence service provisions—in particular, who is served—a stronger focus on and analysis of public policy are as crucial to cultural competence as are organizational practices and the social worker–client interaction. This analysis should examine the effects as well as the extent to which public policies and laws are culturally relevant or incompetent, such that they lead to different treatment of different groups or to discrimination. Organizations should also proactively examine the implementation of policies within their own practices to ensure that they are not, in fact, acting as a party to social injustice. Finally, procedural justice demands that leaders of organizations position themselves with and/or on behalf of their constituents, so that the needs of diverse groups are articulated to policy-makers, thereby ensuring that public policy is indeed culturally relevant. Distributive justice, the aspect of justice in which social workers agencies and social workers are most often engaged, may be compromised without an articulation of the needs of diverse groups. Only through the three-prong efforts of social workers, organizational leadership, and client groups can the tenets of cultural competence and equality in public policy and services ultimately be achieved.

Institutional Programs

Programs are the final facet to be addressed in improving the institutional or organizational environment. The program of an institution is crucial to the effective functioning of its clients. Organizations as social systems erect a set of policies and rules that govern the behavior of clients and staff. The rules maintain the equilibrium of the organization so that it is able to operate in an organized predictable manner. Stimulating, constructive, and growth-promoting programs enhance client functioning, whereas custodial care in which clients are not involved in decisions about their lives can be disempowering and foster apathy and in some, it can create reactance. Moreover, institutional environments where even the most routine resident behavior is governed by rules constitute unproductive environments that often inspire challenges to the rules and lead to swift punishment of clients.

An important factor in institutional programming is the extent to which clients or residents can exercise choice and control in their daily living and can participate in their treatment plans. To enhance choice and control, progressive residential programs encourage democratic participation in governance of the institution and allow choice where feasible in how residents spend their time and use their resources. When this is not the case, both residents and staff may experience the residual effects of discord. For example, an adult group home resident, referred to the social work case manager because he was "acting out," complained that he did not like having cigarettes and money rationed to him by staff; he felt that this practice suggested he was incapable of making his own decisions. A common complaint you may have heard in adolescent group homes or from other institutional residents is their dislike of the point system in which they lose points or privileges for failing to comply with rules (e.g., failing to comply with "lights out" orders, or exhibiting independent behaviors). Many perceive these systems as further limiting their already limited choices. Often, failure to respond to complaints of this nature escalates in the form of more assertive or aggressive behaviors on their part which leads to disciplinary action.

Prisons are institutions in which rules and the compliance to rules is strictly enforced. Yet aspects of programs within these environments have become increasingly more humane through the efforts of volunteer groups and special visitation days for minors whose parents are incarcerated (Ardittti, 2008). These efforts effectively link the incarcerated to the outside world. Volunteers are invaluable resources in that they teach skills in which those in prison can achieve a sense of mastery and connectedness. Special visitation days for minors help them maintain their parental attachment, but the physical space provided and the location of the prison can be a factor in the family's ability to visit (Christian, 2005; Enos, 2008; From, 2008). With an increase in the number of women in prisons, advocates are calling for more family-friendly policies, citing the impact on minors, for example, that it is punishing for them when they lose contact with their mothers or fathers because of their incarceration. Attention is also called to the impact of the Adoption and Safe Family Act, 1997, in which the mandatory timelines make the termination of parental rights an inevitable outcome for many incarcerated parents (Genty, 2008).

Obviously, many other factors come into play in ensuring that programs provide opportunities for social interaction as well as cultivate a connectedness. Of course, institutional rules governing behavior are among the ways in which organizations maintain order in their operations. Nevertheless, you should be sensitive to your client's needs and should act as an advocate when the organizational programs oppress and adversely affect the client's well-being.

Principles important to social work, for example, empowerment, self-determination, strengths and self-efficacy can be constrained in institutions. Certain vulnerable groups who are marginalized and lack power or hope are particularly in need for you to act as an advocate so that their environment can be improved. Empowerment and self-efficacy are also achieved when residents are able to exercise control over their lives and their environment to the best of their capacity, given organizational constraints. Institutional environments are most effective when they empower clients by including them in decisions that affect their lives and that enable them to gain or regain the capacity to interact with the environment. A sense of power is closely linked to competence, self-esteem, and the belief that individual actions or actions in concert with and supported by other systems can lead to improvement in one's life situation. These attributes or factors, in turn, are reciprocally influenced by the quality of the environment.

Empowerment as an aspect of the organization's own culture works in much the same way as for residents, as was described for staff earlier in this chapter. Nutritive environments that produce strong goodness of fit between individuals' needs and corresponding resources foster positive attributes, behaviors, and morale. Conversely, poor goodness of fit caused by major environmental deficiencies, rules, and inflexibility tends to produce powerlessness, reactance, and in some instances depression and poor morale on the part of residents.

Service Coordination and Interorganizational Collaboration

Social welfare organizations have always interacted through referrals, purchase-of-service (POS) agreements, and sometimes sharing space in a central community service center. Arrangements of this nature and the content of their relationship may be described as discretionary in that interactions occur on an ad hoc basis, with each organization maintaining its own resources, capabilities, goals, and mission.

Within the last several years, concerns related to service fragmentation, duplication, the complexities of social problems, and the managed care environment have influenced more formal organizational relationships. In addition, concerns about improving the quality and availability of services have resulted in an increased demand for interdependence between social welfare organizations. Funding initiatives and formal mandates from both local and federal agencies have also served as an impetus for more formal linkages between agencies in the form of coordination or collaborations. Much of the thinking behind this movement has been that effective relationships between organizations are

often needed to enhance aspects of the environment of a group of clients who share a common condition. In addition, non-profit organizations are experiencing the need to initiate interorganizational relationships with other non-profits and governmental agencies as a result of welfare reform (Reisch & Sommerfeld, 2003).

When services are uncoordinated between the various agencies involved, the lack of coordination can result in fragmented services or duplications and can cause an unmanageable hardship on clients. The experience of clients (see Figure 14-3) is perhaps the most telling with regard to service fragmentation and duplication. In Figure 14-3, the family consists of a mother who is developmentally delayed and her three daughters; the father is deceased. The family was referred for services soon after the father died. This referral led to others, so that eventually the family was involved with 12 service providers.

Each of the service agency teams involved with this family had its own goals, many of which were contradictory, conflicting, or competing, and which were responsible for adding stress to the family system. For instance, two agencies provided parent support or parenting services. Parenting support was also the reason the volunteer became involved with the family as well as family treatment teams from different agencies. Individual family members have their own therapists and are involved with other service providers as a result of referrals. In addition to the overwhelming number of providers, the lack of coordination and duplication of efforts fragmented the family system.

A crisis developed for the family when the condition of their housing required them to relocate. This particular family—which is far more representative than we

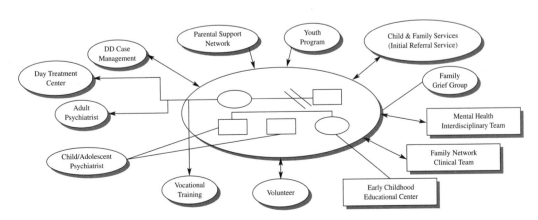

FIG-14-3 Service Fragmentation and Duplication

would like to admit—was spending more than 50 hours per week in appointments with the various agencies involved in their case. When the mother cancelled appointments to look for housing, several of the service agencies reported that she was resistant to change or lacked initiative to make progress; some threatened to withdraw their services. Instead of encouraging the family's problem-solving efforts, the providers' actions inhibited independent thought and action. Both the family and a social worker involved in this situation were extremely frustrated by the service providers' failure to acknowledge the family's housing crisis.

Types of coordination and collaboration between organizations include interdisciplinary or multidisciplinary teams, joint planning or programming, and case management. For example, many school districts are using interdisciplinary teams to address school truancy. These teams consist of staff from a group of organizations that have an interest in this issue. Multidisciplinary teams staffed by mental health and medical professionals are another form of collaborative practice. The use of teams as a form of collaborative practice is beyond the scope of this book, so we refer you to the literature for more on this topic (e.g., Lim & Adleman, 1997; Rothman, 1994; Glisson, 1994). In addition, Congress (1999) and Reamer (1998a) articulate the ethical standards, dilemmas, and principles related to interdisciplinary collaboration for social workers who are functioning as members of interdisciplinary teams.

Organizational Relationships

The relationship between organizations ranges from cooperation as the least formal arrangement to collaboration, in which a new entity or newly created professional roles can emerge. *Cooperation, coordination*, and *collaboration*, are often used interchangeably to describe a relationship between organizations, but the nature of the relationship is different, with respect to function, structure, and durability.

Cooperation among organizations is informal, without a defined structure or planning effort that supports and assists each organization to meet goals that are specific to the individual stakeholders. Organizations share information with each other, but each organization retains their authority and autonomy (Graham, 1999; Reilly, 2001).

Coordination, more formal in nature, seeks to improve service to clients and to address community or target population concerns. Through planning and some division of labor, the coordinated effort offers a range of services, bridges service gaps, or implements policies that are too broad for one agency to achieve alone (Alter & Hage, 1992; Beatrice, 1990; Alexander, 1991; Reilly, 2001). Within this context, the collective behavior of the organizations involved may be conceptualized as a social action system, in which interdependent processes, tasks, and functions emerge through a division of task and labor between the members of the coordinated effort. Although the organizations may join together in a coordinated effort and share compatible goals, they remain separate and continue to function independently. At the federal level, coordinated services are often designed to effect system change, program development, or implement service innovations (Alter & Hage, 1992).

Coordination provides a range of options for the coordination of services. For example, an individual coordinator, a coordinating unit, or an organization may act as the leader of this effort. The function of this individual, unit, or agency is to "coordinate the decisions, activities of an inter-organizational system with respect to a given area, issue, problem or program" (Alexander, 1991, p. 217). This management of services or resources is meant to provide an effective, integrated mix of services for groups or communities.

A critical issue in service coordination is that the agencies involved should share a common priority—for example, "to strengthen family shelter and transitional housing capacity in the state" (Beatrice, 1990). This arrangement requires that each organization contribute the elements necessary to achieve the joint goal (Rothman, 1994).

Case Management

Macro level case management is a form of service coordination because it involves the development and coordination of resources and services as system-level interventions to address complex social issues or target groups. Case management, a type of service coordination, reflects the blending of micro and macro systems, in which the essence of ecological practice comes to life. Case management is not a unitary type of service, and the literature contains varied conceptualizations of micro and macro case management (e.g., Walsh, 2000; Solomon & Draine, 1996; Patterson & Lee, 1998; Rose, 1992; Rothman, 1994; Austin, 1990; Moore, 1990; Roberts-DeGennaro, 1987). In health care settings, case management functions can include utilization review, program management, and locating and coordinating a defined group of services for a specific group of people. Capitman, MacAdam, and Yee (1988) have identified program types and models of case management in health care settings. All models, however, share a basic premise: Case management serves to link clients with essential resources and services.

As a macro strategy, case management functions to locate, organize, coordinate, monitor, and evaluate services at a systems level. Staff in administrative units generally perform these tasks. Large state agencies and managed care providers have units in which staff administer and coordinate services for a target group. At this level, service coordination can involve contracts with designated care providers or information and referral services. Rarely are these administrative units directly involved with clients; instead, they have a relationship with the service delivery agency. Although case management may vary in terms of its goals and settings, Rothman (1991), Holt (2002), Naleppa and Reid (2000), and Kane, Penrod, Davidson, Moscovice, and Rich (1991) emphasize that case management always includes the following characteristics:

- *Screening*
- *Multidimensional assessment*
- *Care planning*
- *Implementation*
- *Monitoring the progress and adequacy of services*
- *Reassessment at fixed intervals*
- *Outcome evaluation/termination*

Collaboration involves a much more elaborate process and more formal planning. It is a situation in which two separate organizations come together to achieve a mutual goal, thus forming a more "durable relationship." (Reilly, 2001, p. 55) Described by Reilly (2001) and Reitan (1998), the relationship that evolves between agencies is both a process and a product of the collaborative arrangement. Perhaps you are most familiar with the collaboration between your social work program and the community agency in which you are a student intern. In practice settings, you may also be familiar with the term "wraparound services," which is used to describe a relationship between agencies. However, this type of service is more client and case specific coordination in that groups of agencies work together with the family, community, and other systems to address the needs of individual clients.

Unlike service coordination, in which the goals and missions of the organizations remain separate, collaboration involves creating a shared vision and developing new goals. Thus, the organizational members determine the new venture's mission and authority. Ownership and control of the project are balanced; risks and benefits are shared and mutual. Mattesisch and Monsey (1992) define organizational collaboration as follows:

> *A mutually beneficial well defined relationship entered into by two or more organizations to achieve common goals. This relationship includes a commitment to: a definition of mutual relationships and goals; a jointly developed structure and shared responsibility; mutual authority and accountability for success; and sharing of resources and rewards. (p. 7)*

Organizational collaboration resembles one aspect of service coordination in that it draws upon the collective strength, knowledge, and expertise of each member organization to achieve through joint effort more than a single organization working alone can accomplish. Other assumptions of collaboration include the delivery of efficient and effective services, a reduction in staff costs, and the ability to address the total needs of a client group. In this respect, organizational collaboration is consistent with the trends described earlier in this chapter as well as the emergence of a more holistic framework in human services.

Collaboration can also involve the development of innovative approaches utilizing intervention and practice research (Hasenfeld & Furman, 1994; Galinsky, Turnbull, Meglin, & Wilner, 1993), macro level case management to improve the flow and form of services that clients receive (Rothman, 1994), the development of social policy (Beatrice, 1990), and the development of practice knowledge shared by researchers and practitioners (Hess & Mullen, 1995). Graham and Barter (1999, pp. 9–10) have identified four phases of collaboration, which are summarized in Table 14-2.

Several authors have outlined the antecedents, conditions, and factors that facilitate successful organizational collaboration (Graham & Barter, 1999; Sandfort, 1999; Reitan, 1998; Brunner, 1991). As Table 14-3 makes clear, collaborative relationships require a blending of resources, a relational system in which joint goals are created, joint decision making, and the creation of a new structure to accomplish the mutually determined goals (Alexander, 1991; Graham & Barter, 1999; Sandfort, 1999; Reilly, 2001; Reitan, 1998). It means that organizations are willing to relinquish their old ways of conducting business and to redefine roles: "Collaboration assumes the inevitability of conflicting ideas and differential power relationships as well as the necessity for compromise, continued advocacy for a position, and the knowledge and skills to differentiate between the two" (Graham & Barter, 1999, p. 10). The dynamics of

TABLE-14-3 PHASES OF COLLABORATION

1. Problem setting in which stakeholders within a domain are identified with mutual acknowledgment and common definition of issues
2. Agreement on direction and common values that guide individual pursuits and purposes, including expectations of outcome
3. Implementation of the plan and skills—for example, conferring, consulting, cooperation, and understanding the interdependence between the various professional orientations involved
4. Creation of a long-term structure that enables the collaboration to sustain, evaluate, and nurture the collaborative effort over time

SOURCE: Adapted from Graham and Barter (1999).

creating and sustaining the collaborative relationship are illustrated in the following case example.

Collaboration: A Case Example

One example of a successful collaborative effort between organizations that involves an initiative that joined staff from a community youth services agency with a group of county probation officers. Both organizations were interested in addressing the recidivism rate of youth offenders. Resources to ensure the development of the newly created organization combined budgetary allocations from both the agency and the county. Staff and managers were responsible for developing the organization's mission and goals, developing joint interventions and strategies, and creating case plans for youth.

Although members of the collaboration had a shared vision, actually coming together posed some difficulties. Concerns centered on issues of trust among staff as well as trust within the community based on community perceptions of probation officers. In particular, staff from the community agency had working relationships with families that tended to be more family and community oriented than the relationships between the families and the probation officers. For example, the agency staff, in their role as advocates for youth, had experienced adversarial relationships with probation officers. Another level of concern had to do with loss of autonomy, decision-making abilities, and communication. Probation officers, for example, were reluctant to relinquish their authority over case plans and decisions about expectations for the youth. *Differences in salaries, both actual and perceived, were also complicating factors.*

The issues highlighted in this example are among those identified by Mattesisch and Monsey (1992), Meyers (1993), and Sandfort (1999) as influencing the formation of a successful collaboration. Many of the concerns related to this initiative were resolved over time as the two groups worked to refine their vision, develop problem-solving skills, and improve their relationships.

Critical to creating and sustaining organizational efforts are the communication and problem-solving processes that participants use to establish goals, objectives, roles, decision-making procedures, and conflict resolution procedures. Sandfort (1999), in describing the structural impediments that affected the collaboration between a private and a public agency, suggests that the culture and beliefs of each organization as well as the prior relationships that existed between staff play an important part in determining how effectively front-line staff will ultimately be able to work together. Having one organization in the collaborative team designated as the administrative or fiscal agent, which is often a requirement of funders, can be another source of tension.

While no one model can ensure collaboration in all situations, the importance of having a shared vision about service delivery, the outcomes that participants wish to achieve, and the dynamics involved in forging a relationship should not be underestimated. In a climate of shrinking resources and in some instances organizational decline, the pooled resources that result from organizational alliances draw on the multiple capabilities that collaboration makes available. Social workers can play an important role in both the development and implementation process. First, through their contact with client groups, they can identify areas where new initiatives are needed. Second, in the implementation process, social workers can play a valuable role in problem solving and facilitating group processes. They can also assist with practices that ensure clients' rights and confidentiality, which can be an issue as organizations share information with each other about clients or client groups. For example, tensions in coordination and collaborative arrangements often stem from member organizations' struggles over how much information to share. Finally, social workers can use their skills to manage the collective actions and to deal with beliefs that organizations may have about each other. These skills are especially critical when the parties need to resolve philosophical differences about how clients are viewed or treated as was the case in the alliance between community staff and probation officers. In this role, the social worker acts as a mediator and advocate.

Macro Practice Evaluation

Each of the macro-level strategies discussed in this chapter lends itself to a variety of procedures for which outcomes may be assessed. Evaluation seeks to assess the extent to which the change effort and the strategies employed were successful. For example, evaluation of efforts to expand the number of beds for the homeless (discussed earlier in this chapter) would measure whether new beds were added through the recruitment of churches and would count the number of new beds available. With the father's group, the county staff would measure the number of jobs obtained and retained, and whether the employment of the fathers resulted in ongoing child support payments. Further analysis might involve examining a change in status of the families who received child support. Here, the evaluation focuses on the overall outcome.

Because evaluation also examines process, another aspect of the evaluation is to examine how the outcome was achieved—for example, the strategies used to recruit churches. Soliciting feedback from the church groups and participants is one way to obtain this information, such as asking participants to rate the appeal of specific recruitment literature or presentations. Did, for example, congregations respond more favorably to a presentation during worship service when compared with an announcement in the church bulletin or e-mail newsletter? Collecting this information helps to determine which strategies were the most effective, under what conditions, and with which populations.

A pre- and post-intervention rating scale measuring the change in problem status may be applied in situations involving social action and advocacy (e.g., Single Subject Design, scales). Change can be measured on an incremental basis, after a particular action technique, and at the end of the project. You may also decide to collect qualitative information along with statistical data. For example, in an interview format, community and congregation members could provide descriptive information regarding improved relationships between the police and a community. The evaluation may be implemented as a summative or formative process and include both qualitative and quantitative data (Weiss, 1998). For example, in conducting a needs assessment, you might question the extent that needs were being met, or if new resources are required by using a survey and also group interviews.

Several innovative approaches hold promise for enhancing the effectiveness of developing and planning community programs. The first approach utilizes the methodology of developmental or intervention research (Comer, Meier & Galinsky, 2004; Rothman & Thomas, 1994; Thomas, 1989). Developmental research is a rigorous, systematic, and distinctive methodology consisting of techniques and methods taken from other fields and disciplines. Its methodology relies on social research and model development and is sufficiently flexible to accommodate the unpredictable and uncontrolled conditions in most practice settings (Comer, Meier & Galinsky, 2004). Using this approach allows for strategies, models, or programs to be tested, and then modified based on the results.

To see how this process works, recall the earlier example in which an agency developed a program for youth who had repeated stays in the shelter system. Home visits while the youth were still in the residential phase of the program were identified as a critical factor in moving the youth toward reunification with their families. After a period of time, the program was examined using qualitative and quantitative data on the number of home visits, resources required, events that had disrupted the visit, and interviews with the youth, parents, and other kin. These data enabled the agency to direct its resources toward achieving the second goal of the program—permanency for the youth. As a result of the feedback, respite care and community intervention were added to the program. Specifically, it was learned that reintegration into the family system required additional support for the families to avoid further placement

Evaluation—whatever its form—requires clearly specified goals and objectives in measurable terms. In general, evaluation is an ongoing process for which it is important to establish indicators at the beginning of the intervention. The process involves continuous, systematic monitoring of the intervention's impact, which requires development and implementation of techniques of data management. Systematic analysis of data allows you to determine, for example, if the program activity or intervention is being implemented as planned and whether it is accomplishing the stated program goals. Conducting evaluation requires skills in selecting an appropriate research design, techniques of measurement, and analysis of data. The specific details of the various methods utilized are beyond the scope of this book. The requisite knowledge needed to implement the evaluation process is commonly discussed in research courses.

Empowerment, whether thorough organizing, social action, or improving institutional programs has been a consistent theme throughout this chapter. In keeping with the empowerment theme, we stress the importance of including client groups in the evaluation process. They should be involved in establishing success indicators as well as in evaluating the outcomes including whether in fact they perceived themselves to have been empowered (Gutierrez, Parsons, & Cox, 1998; Lum, 2004; Secret, Jordan & Ford, 1999).[2]

Summary

This chapter emphasized the range of roles filled by social workers who are acting as change agents at the macro level. Today's social, economic, demographic, and political trends present numerous opportunities for action and intervention at the macro practice level. In talking to social workers in preparation for writing this chapter, we were impressed with the breadth and depth of macro practice strategies they used. The social workers saw their practice as holistic and were comfortable employing a range of strategies to help people resolve problems or change social conditions. As one social worker stated, "It would be difficult to ask people to change without also addressing the circumstances and conditions that contribute to their situations." The person and environment focus reflected in this statement, in essence, frames the fundamental tenets and foundation of macro practice.

Related Online Content

Visit the *Direct Social Work Practice* companion Web site at www.cengage.com/social_work/hepworth for additional learning tools such as glossary terms, chapter outlines, relevant Web links, and chapter practice quizzes.

Skill Development Exercises

1. Assess the organizational policies or practices using the questions identified by Rooney.

2. Using Figure 14-1, reflect upon the potential benefit of linking an individual client situation that you have worked with to a change effort at the macro level.

3. Choose a public policy or social problem. How would you describe your position on either one or both? Would you say that you are a liberal (conservative, moderate, or radical) a conservative (fiscal, religious, or social) or a centrist? Think about how your identified position influences your thinking about the policy or problem.

4. Describe how client dignity and worth is fostered in your agency.

5. Think about the potential ways in which social work practice is influenced by public policy.

6. Using Figure 14-3 and the situation described, think about a case that you have in which the various professionals or agencies involved lack coordination. What could be done to improve the situation?

7. Rate your current position of each of Hackman and Oldham's core characteristics of job design and motivation.

8. Identify a change that you would like to make in your agency. Identify the risks, benefits, and potential opposition to your change proposal.

9. Using Rivera and Erlich's Level of Community Contact, what steps would you take in working with a community at each level? What are potential ethical issues at each level?

10. Reflect upon the organizational cultural competence factors discussed by Nybell and Gray (2004). How would you measure your agency using these factors?

Notes

1. The authors wish to thank the many social workers and agencies that provided the rich examples of macro-level intervention strategies discussed in this chapter.
2. For additional information, we refer you to Gutierrez, Parsons, and Cox (1998) for examples of facilitating empowerment through evaluation. Also, refer to the *Handbook of Community Practice* and the *Journal of Community Practice*.

CHAPTER 15

Enhancing Family Relationships

CHAPTER OVERVIEW

Chapter 15 builds on the family assessment skills you learned in Chapter 10, by describing skills in enhancing family functioning and relationships. The emphasis on the family as a social unit continues, in particular, the ways in which internal and external factors influence family relationships and interactions. Using case examples, particular attention is paid to cultural and family variants in a systems and ecological context.

Approaches to Work with Families

Social workers are involved with families in a variety of settings and for diverse purposes (Reid, 1985). This work encompasses a range of interventions ranging from mezzo to macro strategies; for example, assisting a family to prepare for the discharge of a member from an institution, helping a mother to take action so that her child is returned from foster care, conducting crisis-oriented interviews with families following a disaster, or mediating a conflict situation with a housing complex manager.

Family relationships and interactions are often punctuated and strained by numerous factors. Family life transitions, structural arrangements, patterns of communication, and roles (including role definition, overload, and strain) are but a few sources that contribute to family relational dynamics. Concepts related to family structure are rooted in family transaction patterns, interpersonal boundaries, and arrangements between subsystems. Process-oriented approaches tend to focus on the nature of family dynamics and their patterned interactions, including communication skills, and cause-and-effect sequences. Intervention strategies and goals—whether the focus is on family structure or family processes—have as their primary aim to alter relationship and interaction patterns so as to support the well-being of all family members.

Intervening in the family system is intended to "change the family, and in doing so, change the life of each of its members" (Nichols & Schwartz, 1998, p. 6). A variety of process-oriented and structural transaction approaches are used by social workers to accomplish this goal:

- Cognitive behavioral family therapy *is based on the work of Ellis (1978) and Beck (1976). The focus is on behavior and cognition, the intent of which is to help the family to modify specific patterns and learn new behaviors. Learning new behavior is expected to alter the process of circular or reciprocal sequences of behavior (Becvar & Becvar, 2000a; Nichols, 2006).*
- Communication *as an intervention approach aims to regulate and modify family communication patterns and alter communicational styles to promote positive interactions and family relationships (Satir, 1967). Expanding on experiential family therapy (Whitaker, 1958), Satir's (1972) aim was to reverse family complaints about each other, to find solutions, and to have members focus on the positive. Her work augmented that of communication therapists Jackson and Weakland (1961), who believed that the family unit was implicated in the family problems and that all families developed patterns of communicating, some of which were problematic.*
- Family systems, *developed by Murray Bowen (1960), seeks to reduce anxiety and symptoms by resolving multigenerational issues that intrude upon an individual's ability to balance emotional and intellectual functioning, intimacy and autonomy, and interpersonal relations (Goldenberg & Goldenberg, 2004). Major techniques include the Genogram a tool used to depict relationships and help family members use "I" positions. Family members are also encouraged to understand their own role and that of extended family members as part of family problems (Nichols, 2006).*
- Solution-Focused, *practice with families emerged from the work of de Shazer and Berg. The approach was developed as an alternative to problem focus therapy in which the focus of treatment was on the*

family's failed attempts to solve problems. The solution-focused approach directs the energy of the family or couple toward exceptions to the problem and ultimately its solutions (de Shazer & Berg, 1993: Berg, 1994). A core assumption of the approach is that solutions and exceptions create new narratives and they serve as potent forces that motivate people toward change.

- Structural family therapy, *developed by Minuchin, is intended to strengthen current family relationships, interactions, and transactional patterns. The approach emphasizes the "wholeness" of the family—that is, its hierarchical organization and the interdependent functioning of subsystems (Goldenberg & Goldenberg, 2004, p. 212; Minuchin, 1974). Because of its primary focus on improving family relationships, structural therapy pays attention to boundaries, alignments in the family system, and power, using the resources and power inherent in families to effect change.*

- Task-centered work *with families follows the basic tenets and procedures as work with individuals. The focus with families is the on the resolution of specific concerns acknowledged by the family unit (Reid & Fortune, 1985). The model draws from the relevant contributions of other theoretical frameworks of family therapy—for example, the communications, structural, and behaviorist approaches. Family problems tend to be framed as interactional in nature; potential goals and tasks are developed by family members for the unit as a whole and/or for individual members (Reid, 1996). Increasing the family's ability to work together is a key element of the task-centered approach. Family sessions may involve, for example, role-play to help members accomplish this goal.*

More recently, approaches to work with families have encouraged us to rethink earlier assumptions about what constitutes healthy or normal family development and functioning. Post-modern approaches, for example, narrative and social constructivists as well as feminists' literature, emphasize an attention to diversity and pluralism. In concert with this thinking, post-modern approaches have encouraged a diminished focus on absolute objective truths and the role and authority of the family therapist as paramount to family change. Narrative or interpretative reality and social construction, in contrast, are approaches in which the family and professional are collaborative and conversational. The goal of the conversation between family members and the

therapist is to help families create new meaning and viewpoints about their problems (Hartman, 1981; Nichols 2006; Nichols & Schwartz, 1998).

This chapter draws upon a cross section of family practice approaches and intervention techniques that you can use to help families improve their functioning, interactions and relationships. Interventions and techniques, of course, flow from the multidimensional assessment and emphasize family and cultural variants and the assessment dimensions discussed in Chapter 10. Mastering the content of this chapter and practicing relevant skills will advance your competence in the following areas:

- *Initial contact with couples, families, and parents*
- *Orchestrating the initial session and engaging families (voluntary, referred, or mandated) in the helping process*
- *Assisting families to enhance their interactions by increasing communication skills*
- *Modifying family interactions*
- *Modifying family rules*
- *Assisting family members to disengage from conflict*
- *Modifying misconceptions and distorted cognitions that impair interactions*
- *Modifying family alignments*

Although the interventions and techniques discussed in this chapter are applied to couples and families, most are also relevant to work with treatment groups, a topic discussed in Chapter 16. By way of review, you may also want to reread Chapter 10's discussion of how families define the relevant members of its system, family rules, boundaries, and communication styles that frame family interaction patterns. Also, recall that the family is a system within the larger social system. As a consequence, family context and hence family functioning, interaction, and relational patterns may be influenced by external factors. Family processes and structure may also be embedded in cultural values and norms, so conventional techniques used to intervene with families may not match the needs of diverse families. Some of these factors are highlighted in this chapter, as well as ecologically based concerns.

Initial Contacts

Enhancing the functioning and relationships of couples and family systems requires you to be skilled in engaging members and in focusing on the family as a whole. Generally, when seeking help, families or couples tend to not think in a systems framework. Instead, they often identify a concern, and perhaps target the behavior of another member as primary to their difficulties. Thus, it is important to manage initial contacts in ways that encourage work with relevant members of the family system, rather than settle prematurely on a problem identified in an individual's request for service. This section describes ways of handling the initial contacts that lay the groundwork for implementing the intervention strategies discussed later in this chapter.

Managing Initial Contact with Couples and Families

Most often, a member of a family initiates the initial request for service. Depending on the practice setting or the nature of a referral, the initial contact may occur in the home, in a school, institutional setting, over the telephone, or in your office. Generally, in an agency the upfront work, including the scheduled appointment, whether in the office or the home, has been completed in the intake process. The objectives of the initial session are influenced by the factors highlighted in the following discussion.

- Initial contact with a family member. *When the initial contact involves a family member alone, the session with this individual should be short and focused to avoid becoming entangled in the individual's perception of the family's problem. Ask the family member to describe the problem briefly, and empathically respond to their messages. This strategy not only helps establish rapport, but also yields important information. In addition, elicit information that will help you determine who else is involved in the problem. When you believe you have begun to establish rapport and have heard the presenting complaint, summarize the individual's view of the problem, his or her relevant feelings, and emphasize that person's needs or wants.*

- Referral. *In cases in which the contact is the result of a referral, for example, from a teacher, the conversation is also brief because the referral is but one source of information. Share the referral source information with the family, but emphasize that the family is a credible source about their problem. In much the same way as with a single family member's perception of a problem, you want to avoid becoming influenced by the referral's source view of the problem.*

- Agreement. *Reaching an agreement is the focus of the initial session and deciding who will attend future sessions when contact has been initiated by one family member. When an individual presents the family's concern, it is important to establish rapport with him or her as the initiator of the request for service. Wright and Anderson (1998) call our attention to attachment skills, which essentially concern "connecting" to this individual so that he or she feels heard and their concern has been validated. In sessions beyond the initial contact, you will want to emphasize that in the future, all family members are to be involved. An example of an exception is an identified child-related problem, in which case one or both parents may attend the initial session without the child (or children). Of course they may be instances in which parents will object to the child's exclusion ("He needs to be here, too!"). There may also be unusual circumstances (a crisis) in which the minor may be in danger, and therefore immediate action is required. When a situation (e.g. a child previously described) or circumstance dictate excluding other family members from the initial contact, convey the message that you will want to see these individuals in future sessions. For example, in a situation where an adult daughter has initiated contact out of her concern for an aging parent, the parent would be involved in future sessions.*

- Mandated contact. *In the instance of mandated contact, share the circumstances of the mandate, including the expressed purpose and goals stated in the mandate. You should clarify choices that the potential client may make, including whether to meet all or some of the requirements. In this session, you will want to identify topics to be addressed in this meeting. Before concluding the session, discuss with the client any requirements that will affect their choices, including applicable time limits.*

- Unavailable family member. *When a family member complains of problems involving another member, but insists that the individual is not available, you may agree to see an individual alone at first. You would, however, indicate that a next step would be to schedule an individual interview with the other person, thus giving him or her "equal time." Because people differ in their opinions, seeing each member individually allows you to obtain a balanced view of the problem. Some clients will comply with requests, but others may offer explanations such as "My husband works odd hours," "She won't come," or*

"He's not the one with the problem." These messages can reflect a reluctance to include other members, or perhaps the unwillingness of other members to become engaged and participate in resolving difficulties.

These dynamics can only be clarified by your having contact with the reportedly unwilling family member or members. But first, the situation should be further explored with the individual who initiated the contact and an explanation provided as illustrated by the social worker in the following statement:

Social worker: In helping people with the kinds of problems you've described, it is helpful to have other family members come for sessions. It has been my experience that when some members of the family have problems, other members are affected, and they also experience stress and discomfort. Equally important, changes in one member may require changes and adjustments in other family members. People accomplish change more frequently when all family members work together. For this reason, it will be important that other family members are involved.

When a family member emphatically states that they do not want to involve certain or any family members in the initial session, their reasoning should be respected. If their position is not subsequently modified, you may arrange to include any family members whom the individual is willing to include. Should a member continue to maintain that other members are unwilling or unable to become involved, ask him or her permission to contact those persons directly. If you gain permission (as will usually happen), you can telephone the individual, using a message similar to the following, after introducing yourself and stating the purpose of the call:

Social worker: As you know, [caller's name] has contacted me concerning problems involving your family. I understand that you are unavailable, but I thought I would give you a call to ask you to join us. Your participation would be extremely helpful, and I am interested in your perspective on the family's problem as well as hearing your ideas about how it can be resolved. Would you available for an appointment, say, at 4:00 P.M. next Wednesday?

In the best-case scenario, the individual will agree to your request. Some people, however, may react less favorably, and you will need to explore their response. Subsequently, you could ask the person to participate in *at least one* session, yet respect his or her decision should they decline

to do so. Exerting pressure may alienate the individual and the underlying dynamics can destroy future opportunities to obtain his or her involvement. With skillful handling, most often you will be able to dissolve strong opposition. There may, of course, be valid reasons for the absence of some family members. For example, minors are generally excluded from family sessions that focus on issues between their parents.

Initial Contacts in Other Settings

Because social work practice with families takes place in a variety of settings, the initial contact may not follow the scenarios we have outlined here. For example, your initial contact may take place in the family's home. This contact may be voluntary or involuntary. In the latter case, you may need to manage problematic involuntary client–social worker dynamics. In any event, home visits require making arrangements with families to ensure that sessions will be free of interruptions, especially when the family has small children. During home visits, you may encounter other family members or friends, in which case privacy and confidentiality issues need to be discussed and resolved. For example, a social worker sought consultation on whether he should have proceeded with the initial session with a family in the presence of an unidentified elderly man. This individual clearly held an esteemed position in the family. In fact, the father would often look for nonverbal cues from the man before responding to the social worker. In this case, it was decided that the social worker should have asked whether or not it was appropriate for him to be introduced to the elderly man and inquired about his role in the family.

In some situations, a key family member may be willing, but unavailable, as occurred in a case in which the mother was incarcerated. Despite being in prison, the mother wanted to remain connected to her husband and children. Therefore, the initial and all subsequent family sessions were arranged at the prison. The social worker at the facility arranged transportation to the prison for the family. Also, she had to navigate the system's rules for visitation, comply with visitation time limits, and ensure that the mother adhered to certain rules of conduct so that she could participate in the family sessions.

The requirements of other systems involved in this case—namely, child protective services and the probation officer—also had to be met. For example, the child protection social worker had to be present during the initial and subsequent family sessions, as the mother was not allowed to have unsupervised visits with her newborn child. Also, child protection was moving to terminate the mother's parental rights for the newborn because she had experienced a relapse while she was on probation for drug use; furthermore, her sentence exceeded the concurrent planning time frame for reunification. The situation was further complicated because the father of the older children was not the father of the newborn, yet he was willing to obtain custody of his stepchild. The management of the initial contact and of subsequent family sessions required the social worker in this case to assist the family to develop specific goals, within a limited time frame, as well as to coordinate with the other systems involved.

What happens during the initial session, assuming all parties are willing and involved? During the initial session with a family or couple, it is important to outline the purpose of the session, provide an explanation of the work to be completed. In this session, you would also review client confidentiality rights, and discuss how you will work with the couple or family together. To illustrate, the case of Anna and Jackie in "Home for the Holidays" introduced in Chapter 10, is used. In this case, Jackie had called to request the initial session and Anna agreed to meet with the social worker. Recall that Anna and Jackie have been in a relationship for a number of years, but had recently moved in together. They initiated couples' therapy because of disagreements about their holiday plans. They both want to spend the time together, but Jackie would prefer to visit her parents; however, Anna does not feel completely comfortable with Jackie's family. Jackie had recently "come out" to her parents, but is reluctant to pursue the topic in greater detail with them. In the initial session which can be viewed on the CD-Rom, the social worker explains her role and her expectations for the initial session.

As you view the session, note that the social worker began the conversation by acknowledging that Jackie had initiated the contact. She summarizes the reason for the contact provided by Jackie and by doing so, it is clear to both Anna and Jackie the reason for the request for service. Specifically, the couple was struggling with whether or not to spend the upcoming holiday with Jackie's parents. Afterwards she moved to socialize Anna and Jackie about the helping process, including what she hoped could be accomplished in this initial session. In explaining the goal of the first session and her role, the social worker also clarified that the session would be a safe place for each to discuss their concerns, and that she would work with them together.

Managing Initial Contacts with Parents

Initial sessions with parents (legal guardian or foster parent) should involve other persons who perform or share the executive parental function in the household, for example, a grandparent. Children may be included in subsequent sessions. Seeing parents alone initially gives you more time to become acquainted with the problems of the family and, on the basis of known information, to plan strategies for engaging the child.

Establishing rapport with parents. By having an initial session with parents, you are able to establish rapport with them and, where indicated, influence their behavior in future sessions that include the children. The behavior and style of relating of some parents may be so engrained and adversarial that initial attempts to see everyone together would prove to be disastrous. Further, having an initial session with parents alone enables you to clarify the systemic nature of problem; specifically, that the problem does not belong to the child alone.

Coaching parents. Interviewing parents first in an initial session also enables you to coach them about how best to bring an identified child into the helping process. For example, in talking to the child, they should clarify that the *family* is having a problem, rather than indicating that the family is having problems *with the child*. In addition, they should provide a general explanation of what the child can expect in the session. In doing so, they should be alert to any reservations that the child might have about coming to the session.

Establishing Concerns as a Family Problem. When meeting with parents or other individuals who perform this role in initial sessions for which a child is the identified problem, you will need to explore the basis of their belief. Depending on how the parents have communicated about the problem in front of the child, you may expect that in parent–child sessions the child will be defensive and perhaps oppose or be unenthusiastic about being involved. You can take some pressure off the minor by engaging all members in a discussion of changes they would like to make in resolving the *family's* problem. This strategy is also appropriate when an adult family member has been designated as the source of a problem.

Creating a safe place for the child. When parents bring a child to the initial session, you may need to coach them about how to behave constructively. For example, suggest to parents that they assist you in creating a climate that is conducive to open communication. If indicated, you would also ask them to refrain from repetitive blaming messages ("He continues to mess up in school, and hang around the wrong people"), and request that they focus on positive behaviors ("He was a helper this past summer in a program for kids in the park"). Using a technique from solution-focused treatment, you might divert the parent's attention to those instances of exceptions—for example, when "messing up in school" does *not* occur.

Allowing children to tell their story. In the initial session, you should provide an opportunity for the child to tell her or his story. Doing so allows you to hear directly from the minor, without being persuaded (as the child may perceive it) by information provided by the parents. Equally important, in giving the minor this time and space, you are establishing rapport and a level of trust with him or her. At the same time, you should be careful to avoid subordinating the parent's executive function or giving the impression that you are forming an alliance with the minor. In some cultures, for example, inviting minors to voice their concerns is unacceptable and perceived to be inappropriate role behavior. But there are instances when interviewing a minor alone is required—for example, in a situation of reported child maltreatment or sexual abuse. If culture permits, and there is no indication of the minor's need for protection, you can interview him or her either with the parents present or alone. A younger child may be more comfortable in the presence of parents; however, an adolescent may prefer to be seen alone.

Irrespective of whether minors are seen in the initial session with parents or alone, time set aside during the last part of the session is reserved for seeing all family members together. At this time, you will want to reemphasize the systemic nature of the minors' problem and assist all members to formulate individual and family goals.

Orchestrating the Initial Family or Couple Session

The goal of bringing the family together is to identify the problem at hand by eliciting the viewpoints of the various family members. The initial session, whether it occurs in the office or in the home, is referred to as the *social* or *joining stage* (Nichols & Schwartz, 1998; Boyd-Franklin, 1989a). In this stage, it is important to establish rapport and build an alliance with the family. It is useful to restate the reason for the voluntary contact ("Jackie contacted me because the two of you disagree about your holiday plans") to gather information about the family and to listen to their perspectives on

the problem. If the family's contact has been referred or mandated, then you acknowledge this fact—for example, "Katie's teacher referred the family to our agency because...."

In facilitating the *social* or *joining stage*, your tasks are twofold:

- *Ensure that each family member can voice his or her opinion without interruptions from other family members.*
- *Encourage family members to listen so that other members feel understood and accepted.*

You can further facilitate this stage by adopting an attitude of inquiry, for example, "What can I learn from and about this family that will help me work with them?"

The initial session with families is crucial. Clients' experiences during this session determine in large measure whether they will join with you and contract to work toward specified goals or solutions. Moreover, they may perceive the initial session as a prototype of the helping process. To lay a solid foundation for future work with families, it is important that you accomplish a number of objectives. The objectives as discussed are summarized in Table 15-1. You may use these objectives as a guide in both planning for and evaluating initial sessions.

Note that these objectives are essentially the same as those identified in earlier chapters of this book. In the following sections, however, we explain how to accomplish them in work with families. This discussion will also assist you in consolidating the knowledge and skills that have been presented earlier in this book.

1. *Establish a personal relationship with individual members and an alliance with the family as a group.* In working with couples or families (or groups), social workers have a twofold task of establishing personal relationships with each individual while developing a "connectedness" with the family as a unit. To cultivate relationships with family members, you use *socializing*, a technique that involves brief *social chitchat* at the beginning of the session to reduce tension. Joining or coupling techniques to expedite entry in to the family system must respect culture, family form, family rules, and the current level of functioning. You may also find that using the family's language and idioms—for example, "He's messing up in school," facilitates your connection to the family. Appropriate self-disclosure can also be facilitative, especially when such statements establish similarities or parallels between you and the family. You can further connect to the family by conveying your acceptance, and by engaging them in identifying their strengths.

TABLE-15-1 ORCHESTRATING THE INITIAL FAMILY OR COUPLE SESSION

- Establish a personal relationship with individual members and an alliance with the family as a group
- Clarify expectations and explore reservations about the helping process, including potential dynamics of minority status and culture
- Clarify roles and the nature of the helping process
- Clarify choices about participation
- Elicit the family's perception of the problem
- Identify wants and needs of family members
- Define the problem as a family problem
- Emphasize family strengths
- Ask questions to elicit information about patterned behaviors of the family
- Draw family members' attention to repetitive communications and discuss whether they want to change patterns
- Begin to assist family members to relate to one another in more positive ways
- Establish individual and family goals or solutions
- Gauge the motivation of family members to have future session and negotiate contract
- Negotiate tasks to be accomplished during the week
- End the session by summarizing points discussed and solutions and progress achieved

Conveying acceptance and offering support may be especially critical to vulnerable family members.

In the initial session, empathic responding can be particularly useful in establishing rapport with a member who appears to be reserved or reluctant to be involved. For instance, when a member does participate spontaneously, you can attempt to draw them into the session: "Tamika, we haven't heard from you about how you felt when you learned you were coming to see a social worker. Would you tell us how you felt?" You can then respond empathically to what she says or does. For example, if Tamika responded, "I thought that it would be a waste of time," and that the reason she is not involved is because she is "bored," an empathetic response might be; "Yes, I can understand why you would feel this way. At your age, I'm sure that I would have felt the same." Such an empathic message shows genuine interest that can cause reserved family members to become more active. Conversely, if Tamika's lack of involvement is related to family dynamics rather than to her feelings, you will need to be mindful of the potential risks of encouraging her to express an opinion. In either case, you should endeavor to distribute time and attention somewhat equally among members, to highlight individual strengths, and to intervene when one member dominates the conversation or when the session involves members' communicating blaming, shaming or put-down messages.

Finally, effectively connecting with families requires that you understand and have appreciation and empathy for the sociopolitical and cultural context of the family and for the family's collective strengths and competencies. Often, it is these attributes that have enabled the family to function in spite of their difficulties.

2. *Clarify expectations and explore reservations about the helping process.* Family members have varying and often distorted perceptions of the helping process and may have misgivings about participating in sessions (e.g., "a waste of time," "talking won't help"). To identify obstacles to full participation (which is a prerequisite to establishing a viable contract), you should elicit the responses of all family members to questions such as the following:

- *"What were your concerns about meeting with me?"*
- *"What did you hope might happen in our meetings together?"*
- *"What were your fears about what might happen in this meeting today?"*

Questions of a more specific nature are useful to help family members express their concerns, as illustrated in the following examples:

- *"Are you concerned that your family might be judged?"*

- *"In your community, how would others deal with this problem?"*
- *"Does seeking help from someone outside of your family make you feel uncomfortable?"*
- *"In what way do you think that I can be of help to your family?"*

As you explore reservations, concerns, and even hopes from each family member, you can broaden the focus to the family by asking, "I'm wondering if others share the same or similar concerns as…?" As members acknowledge similar feelings, they may begin to realize that despite their feelings, as a unit they share certain concerns in common. For example, family members might have individual positions on rigid family rules, but they all have anxieties about less income due to job loss.

In pursuing the issue of the reluctant or unwilling family member, you should remain sensitive to cultural norms. For example, you should be cautious in interpreting inactivity as reluctance. Some individuals may prefer to observe processes before they engage or participate. Culture may also influence expressions of feelings, hence some families may be baffled by *feeling* questions. Culture aside, certain family members will continue to have strong reservations about meeting with you. You can address their reluctance by asking them one or all of the following questions and addressing their subsequent responses:

- *"Would you imagine for a moment how you would like things to be different in your family?"*
- *"What, if anything, would make you feel better about participating?"*
- *"Given your concerns, are you willing to stay for the remainder of the session and decide at the conclusion whether to continue?"*

A willingness to negotiate the terms under which clients participate and your acknowledgment of their right of choice can reduce their reluctance to the point that they will agree to continue. For example, you might ask a person to attend a family session, but emphasize that the individual is not obligated to participate. Further, you may say to the reluctant member that they need not talk; the person can just be physically present in the session. This invitation diminishes the pressure on the person to contribute. Additional dynamics can be expected, and hence reluctance when an individual has been singled out as the problem. Their reluctance may be a protective function, rather than representing

opposition to change, especially if they feel ganged up on by other family members.

The Dynamics of Minority Status and Culture in Exploring Reservations

Minority status and culture are additional factors that may cause a family or family member to have reservations about seeking help. Families may fear "what might happen" if their problems are brought out into the open (Nichols & Schwartz, 1998, p. 132). Boyd-Franklin (1989a) and Lum (2004) explain that the historical experience of minority families and their being perceived as "unhealthy" may cause these families to hide their problems until they escalate to a point of crisis. Indeed, the experiences of other family members and entire communities may reinforce this silence. The unspoken rule of keeping family secrets can be more pronounced in minority families because of the value placed on privacy, or a sense of shame about involving an outsider in family matters. Flores and Carey (2000) note, for instance, that the comfort level of Hispanic families is increased when they do not feel the need to be defensive about their culture. Lum (2004, p. 153) emphasizes the importance of "confianza," the art of establishing mutual trust in the helping relationship as a means to address the concerns of people of color.

Reservations about attending family sessions may be a particular issue among ethnic minority families in which some members are undocumented or residing illegally in the United States (Pierce & Elisme, 1997; Fong, 1997; Falicov, 1996). In addition, immigrant or refugee families may be unfamiliar with formal helping systems (Potocky-Tripodi, 2002). Moreover, poor minority and gay or lesbian families have good reasons for their apprehensions and anxieties about seeking help. Wright and Anderson (1998) suggest that in actively tuning into the family, you might pose the question, "What is it like being with the client [family]?" especially during the initial session (p. 202). In effect, you are tuning in to and evaluating whether your reactions will enter into the session. You are also actively attempting to understand the family's frame of reference. To this self-assessment review, consider including two additional questions: "What is it like to be this family?" and "What does it mean to this family to seek professional help?" The answers to these questions will help you show sensitivity in your initial interactions with the family and to understand their experience in seeking help. To lessen the family concerns or reservations about the contact with you, it can be useful for you to affirm the protective function of reluctance, whether in a family member or the family system as a whole as a measure of safety for the family.

3. *Clarify roles and the nature of the helping process.* In exploring misgivings and reservations, you should educate families about the nature of the helping process, and clarify both your own and their roles. In educating families about the helping process, your objective is to create an atmosphere and structure where problem solving can occur. Role clarification is also addressed toward the end of the initial session in which an initial contract is negotiated.

4. *Clarify choices about participation in the helping process.* In the instance of referred contact, you can reiterate that the family is free to decide whether further contact with you will meet their needs and, if so, what to work on, regardless of the concerns of the referring source. If contact is mandated, it is necessary to clarify what you are required to do (e.g., submit a report to the court) and the parameters of required contact. In addition to mandated concerns, you can advise families that they can choose to deal with other problems of concern to them.

5. *Elicit the family's perception of the problems.* In initiating discussion of problems, social workers ask questions such as "Why did you decide to seek help?"(in the case of voluntary contact), "What changes do you want to achieve?" or "How could things be better in the family?" Eliciting the family's view of the problem is equally important in involuntary or referred contacts. In such cases, the mandate or referral has been summarized, but families are encouraged to tell their story: "Your family was required by the juvenile court judge to have contact with our agency because Juan was reported to the school truancy officer for missing school. This is the information that I have, but I still need to hear from you why you believe you are here." No doubt, Juan and his parents both have a point of view, which may be similar or vastly different. Because each person has his or her own viewpoint about the problem and its solution, your task is to move the family toward reaching a consensus that they can all support.

In sessions with a family or a couple, you will want to be aware of differences in interpretation and the various family roles within the family with respect to issues of gender, power, and boundaries. In addition, Rosenblatt (1994) urges us to pay attention to the language and metaphors used by the family as they describe their concerns. In particular, how family members expressing their views reflects their culture, their realities, and the meaning assigned to the family experience. The family experience includes exploring spirituality or religion in the life of the family (Anderson & Worthen, 1997).

6. *Identify needs and wants of family members.* As you engage the family in a discussion of problems, listen for needs that are inherent in their messages as illustrated in the family session with a foster mother and an adolescent parent (Ideas in Action). The social worker begins with a summary explanation of her understanding of the contact. Then she invites both the foster mother who initiated the contact and the adolescent parent to share their perception of the problem. You can view the session which takes place in the foster home on the CD-Rom, Part 1, Adolescent Parent & Foster Mother.

During the initial discussions of needs and wants as expressed by Janet and Twanna, the social worker strives to respect the rights of the foster mother while at the same time, creating a safe place for the adolescent to express her views. Also, she summarized the situation and empathized with the potential developmental conflict that is occurring with Twanna. That is, Twanna is a mother, but her desire as an adolescent of being with friends is developmentally appropriate. In fact, her main reason for not coming home at the expected time is because she wants to "hang out with her friends." Further, she reasoned that "I know that Janet is here, it's not like I am leaving my baby alone." At the same time, the social worker acknowledged Janet's unspoken need that her caring for the child is not taken for granted by Twanna. Janet's belief is that Twanna should bond with the child, because she, Janet, "will not be there in the future." This situation is a balancing act, as the social worker does not want to convey the

Ideas in Action

Janet is the foster mother of Twanna and her two-year-old child. Their relationship has generally been good. Janet cares for the child and her doing so allows Twanna to attend school and obtain a high school diploma. Janet called the social worker because she is frustrated, as lately Twanna has returned home after school later than expected. Janet has bonded with the two-year-old; however, she believes that it is important for Twanna to spend more time with her child. She reports that the situation is "affecting the entire relationship between the two of them."

perception that the needs of one person have priority and that she will support that person's position alone. She then summarized the concerns identified by Janet and Twanna and asked them to identify what they would like to see changed. In preparation for problem solving, the objective was to pinpoint the conflict and to have the two of them explore options that would meet both of their needs. One option considered by Twanna, for example, was "I could call if I am going to be late." By identifying and highlighting common needs, the social worker was able to focus the intervention on the similarities rather than the differences and to help Janet and Twanna develop goals and tasks that the could mutually work toward to improve their relationship. The session concluded with the two of them having reached several critical agreements.

7. *Define the problem as a family problem.* Earlier in the chapter, we highlighted the type of messages you can use in clarifying the systemic nature of problems. Continue to maintain this position stance throughout the family session, emphasizing that every member's perspective is important; that family members can do much to support the change efforts of other family members; that all members will need to make adjustments to alleviate the family's stress; and that the family can do much to increase the quality of relationships and the support that each member receives from others.

Despite your efforts to define problems as belonging to the family, you will often encounter a persistent tendency of some members to blame others. In these situations, your tasks are to:

- Monitor *your own performance to ensure that you do not collude with family members in labeling others as problems, and thus holding them responsible for the family's difficulties.*
- Model *the circular orientation to causality of behavior and emphasize that family members reciprocally influence one another in ways that perpetuate patterns of interaction.*

In the case of Janet and Twanna, the patterned interaction between the two consisted of Janet becoming frustrated because Twanna failed to return home at the agreed-upon time. In turn, Twanna reasoned that Janet was there to care for the child, so it was not neglectful behavior on her part. Neither had talked about what they really wanted, and their interactions ended up with both being dissatisfied, which further contributed to the problem.

Although Janet attributed their strained relationship to Twanna's behavior, she was careful not to label it. In fact, she stated, "I understand that she wants to be with her friends." Unfortunately, this level of generosity is not always present in families as there is a tendency to label behavior. In these instances, you can move to counteract patterns of attributing blame by using the technique of delabeling. Rather than focusing on a member's perception of behavior, *delabeling* emphasizes the reciprocal nature of the problem. Use of the technique can also set the stage for each member to identify positive behaviors that each would like from the other. Consider the following example in which the social worker poses a series of questions to a mother and son. The two individuals have a history of blaming messages that are counterproductive to their communicating with each other.

Case Example

John is a young man with mental illness. He has decided to move out of a group home and live independently with his girlfriend of several years. His mother, Mrs. G., is adamant that the move is a "stupid" decision and insists that he is incapable of living independently. Rather than turning to the son, the social worker utilized the following questions to focus on the mother's participation in the problematic situation:

- *"You've said that John doesn't listen to you about your concerns related to his plans. When you discuss your concerns with John how do you approach him?"*
- *"When John says he doesn't want to talk to you about his decision, how do you respond?*
- *How does John's reluctance to talk to you affect you and your relationship with him?"*

After posing questions to the mother, the social worker then divided questions between the mother and the son to explore the son's participation in the identified problem by asking the following questions:

- *"John, how does your mother approach you when she wants to discuss her concerns?"*
- *"What is your reaction to her approach?"*
- *"What might she do differently that would make you want to talk to her about your plans?"*

In this case, both mother and son were receptive, so the social worker helped them formulate reciprocal tasks that each could work on during the week to minimize the conflict in their relationship. Their reciprocal tasks were intended to change the dynamics of their interaction by changing their own behavior or responses to each other. For example, the mother would refrain from labeling John's plan as "stupid," and John agreed to listen to her concerns.

8. *Emphasize individual and family strengths.* In work with families, you can highlight family strengths and protective factors on two levels: the strengths of individual members and the strengths of the family as a whole. At the individual level, you may observe the strengths and resources of members during the session, drawing them to the attention of the family (e.g., "Twanna is a good student"). At the family level, you can report on the strengths you have observed in the way members operate as a group (Janet and Twanna have a good relationship). Protective factors and strengths include the presence of a supportive network as well as resources and characteristics of family members that contribute to and sustain the family unit. Examples of strengths-oriented statements follow:

- *"In your family, it is my sense that even though there are problems, you seem to be very loyal to each other."*
- *"Anna, your family's getting together for the holidays seems to connect members to each other."*
- *"Anna and Jackie, your relationship appears to be strong, despite the difficulties that Jackie has experienced with your family."*
- *"Janet, by taking care of Twanna's child while she goes to school shows that you are very supportive of her goal to obtain a high school diploma."*

Family strengths and protective factors may also be utilized to communicate a focus on the future. In particular, the hopes, dreams, talents, or capacities of individual members and the family as a whole are means to energize the family to resolve current difficulties. While a goal in the initial session is to move the family toward reaching a consensus on their concerns, it is the strength of the family—rather than the problem itself—that will ultimately enable them to resolve their difficulties. By exploring coping patterns with previous difficulties, experiences with positive episodes or past successes, and hopes and dreams for family life, you can activate family strengths, and note their resilience in support of their capacity to change (Weick & Saleebey, 1995).

9. *Ask questions to elicit information about the patterned behaviors and structure of the family.* For example, you might ask these questions:

- *"What brought the family here? Who made the decision, and what was the process of deciding to seek help?"*
- *"How are decisions usually made in the family?"*
- *"Who is most likely to argue in the family? The least likely? With whom?"*
- *"Who is the most likely to support other family members? The least likely?"*

Base your questions about family patterns and structure on the dimensions of the assessment. In cases where your race or culture is different from that of the family, asking questions related to race or culture is appropriate:

- *"What are the traditional ways in which families in your culture have approached this issue?"*
- *"How does your family express anger?"*
- *"Is expressing anger acceptable in your household?"*
- *"Are other people in your community involved in making decisions in your family?"*

Asking questions such as these will aid you in entering the family's frame of reference and allow the family to articulate the extent to which their culture or race is a critical element in the family's experience.

10. *Draw attention to repetitive communications.* Once these behaviors are identified, you can discuss whether the family wishes to change these patterns. If counterproductive communications occur during the initial session (as they frequently do), you can intervene to counteract their influence—for example, by translating a blaming message into a neutral one and by empathically reflecting the feelings and wants of the sender of the message. Or, when one family member speaks for another, you can intervene to elicit the views of the latter. Assisting families to improve their communication patterns occurs over time, so in the initial session your task is simply to begin this process. As the initial session proceeds, you can begin to draw counterproductive communications to the family's attention through responses such as the following:

- *"I observed [describes behavior and situation] occurring between family members. How do you see the situation?"*
- *"Did you notice a reaction from other family members as you talked about …?"*

Ideas in Action

As you watch the session with Anna and Jackie, note the repetitive patterns in their interactions and in their communications. For example, Anna makes the assertion, "Jackie does not talk about things." Jackie counters from a fault-defend position: "In your family, everything is open for discussion." Also, pay particular attention to their body language. The social worker then poses a critical intervention question: "To what extent is this symbolic of other issues in your relationship?" Anna, smiling, nods, and her arms are folded; Jackie appears to be very uncomfortable and remains silent. "See," Anna says, "this is what happens."

Questions such as these help clients to become aware of potentially counterproductive communication patterns.

You can also stimulate family members to analyze their behaviors further and to consider whether they wish to modify such communication patterns. This can be accomplished by asking clients questions similar to the following:

- *"How would you like to address these concerns?"*
- *"How would you like to solve these problems?"*
- *"How would you like to relate differently?"*
- *"How would behaving differently change your relationship?"*
- *"Given the problem your behavior creates in the relationship, how important is it to you to change the behavior?"*

Utilizing this line of exploration in initial and subsequent sessions, you can assist family members to define for themselves the relative functionality of behavior and to decide whether they wish to change it. If they choose to modify their behavior, you can negotiate relevant goals that will guide their efforts (and yours) in the helping process. To illustrate repetitive communication patterns, we refer you to the CD-Rom, Home for the Holidays.

11. *Begin helping members to relate to one another in more positive ways.* To begin this process, you would highlight counterproductive patterns: "Mrs. G, when you referred to John's plan as stupid, did you notice his reaction? How might you express your concern to him in a different manner?" Strategies for accomplishing this objective are discussed in greater detail later in this chapter. At the same time, you should communicate hope that the family can change by assisting individual members to see how they can reduce pressures, thereby allowing them to relate to one another in a more positive manner.

12. *Establish individual and family goals based on your earlier exploration of wants and needs.* Goals that flow from this exploration include individual goals, family goals, and goals that pertain to subsystems (e.g., Anna and Jackie want to spend the holiday together). You might also facilitate members to identify family goals by exploring answers to the "miracle question" (de Shazer 1988, p. 5): "Janet and Twanna, suppose that one night, while you were asleep, a miracle happened. When you awaken, how would the tension in your relationship have changed?" When asked this question, even the most troubled couples or families are able to describe a "new" miracle relationship. This vision and other desired conditions that they identify could then become goal statements, guiding efforts of both the family and the social worker.

13. *Gauge the interest of family members in returning for future sessions and negotiate a contract.* Because family members may not always reveal their feelings openly, never assume that all members want to return for another session (even if you were successful in engaging members and sparking their interest in working on problems). You will also want to assess the difference between the attitudes of participants at the beginning and at the end of the session. Ask about reservations that participants may still have about engaging in the helping process. In the case of a reluctant member, check with this individual about their commitment to future sessions. Note that it may take a number of sessions before they decide to participate fully or to commit to making change. As an alternative to their participation, you might ask him or her to consider the ways in which they can support other members or at least not block their change efforts. If family members are sufficiently motivated to continue family sessions, a next step is to identify who will be involved, and negotiate the contract (refer to Chapter 12). Other important elements of the contract discussion include any time limits that may be imposed by, for example, a referral source, court mandate, or third-party payer.

14. *Negotiate tasks to be accomplished during the week.* Although tasks were discussed at length in Chapter 13, we reemphasize that tasks should directly relate to goals

identified by individual members or by the family system. Assisting the family to explore and decide upon steps that can be taken during the week aids in focusing their attention on problem resolution. A task for Janet and Twanna, for example, was to schedule a time to meet together. At this point, you will also want to explore potential barriers. Twanna's task is to return home at the agreed-upon time, and to call if she is going to be late. The social worker then asked her to consider what might prevent her from completing this task.

15. *End the session by summarizing the problems discussed and the goals, tasks, and progress achieved.* Wrapping up the session by summarizing major topics, goals, and tasks highlights what has been accomplished in the session and is another means to encourage hope and to increase the momentum of change efforts.

Intervening with Families: Cultural and Ecological Perspectives

In intervening with clients of a different ethnicity, social workers must strive to be culturally sensitive in their approach, modifying as necessary the expectations espoused as universal norms for family functioning. They must also be aware of the potential intrusion of their own bias into the helping process. A study by Lavee (1997), for example, revealed "noticeable differences" between how social workers and clients defined a healthy marriage. Professionals tended to focus more on process indicators such as cooperation and communication, whereas clients tended to place greater emphasis on love, understanding, and family cohesion. Different emphases on the quality of family life, marital relationships, or problem definition may be a function of cultural and class differences between social workers and clients.

Your sensitivity to culture and the acquisition of knowledge that will prepare you to be culturally competent are ongoing learning processes. While certain factors may be germane to various cultural or racial groups, it is important that you clarify specific content and its relevance to a family's culture, subculture, or race. Goldenberg and Goldenberg (2000) suggest that learning about specific cultures requires social workers to assess the extent to which families identify with their ethnic or cultural background and to ascertain how much their background plays a role in the presenting family concern. Toward this end, "therapists must try to distinguish family patterns that are universal (common to a wide variety of families), culture-specific (common to a particular group) or idiosyncratic (unique to this particular family)" (p. 52). Patterns in family interactions may vary, of course, and your understanding this fact essentially minimizes a tendency to formulate generalizations about family dynamics. Identification with a particular culture or race may be a peripheral issue for some families. In other instances, it may be useful to help families determine how culturally specific behavior affects the problem at hand (Flores & Carey, 2000).

Note that culture should not be used as an excuse to minimize or overlook family behavior or relationships that are damaging or harmful to the family or individuals. With these words of caution in mind, we highlight factors that may be considerations when initiating interventions with families who are diverse with respect to culture or race.

Differences in Communication Styles

Because there are differences in the speech patterns in non-native English speakers, in many situations it may be more important to focus on process rather than content. In many Native American tribes, for example, there may be a "pause time"—a period signaling when one person has finished and another can begin speaking. Discomfort with this silence may result in your interrupting the Native American speaker. Individuals from some groups may be more demonstrative in both verbal and nonverbal language; others who are unaccustomed to seeking outside help may appear to be passive, because of a sense of shame or suspicion in their encounter with professional helpers (Fong, 1997; Pierce & Elisme, 1997; Berg & Jaya 1993; Boyd-Franklin, 1989a).

Studies that examined conflict resolution, emotional expression, and means of coping with stress conducted by Mackey and O'Brien (1998) and Choi (1997) revealed differences in communication styles based on gender and ethnicity. Emotions are complex experiences, expressing reactions to past, present, and future events. The person's worldview frames the emotional experience, as does his or her language. The range of words and language that many of us use daily to describe emotions may, in fact, be unfamiliar to or have a different connotation for diverse groups. Moreover, it is important that you examine your own communication style and assess how it is informed by your own cultural preferences.

In facilitating communication styles and differences, techniques and strategies from postmodern family practice models may be used. For example, the narrative and social constructionist approaches emphasize a more conversational, collaborative approach, allowing for a dialogue that is more meaningful to the client, as well as facilitating communication between client and social worker (Laird, 1993). Sue (2006) also draws attention to *high and low context communications*. In low-context cultures, for example, the United States, there is a greater emphasis on verbal messages as well an orientation toward the individual. In contrast, high-context cultures rely on nonverbal expressions and group identification and a shared understanding between the communicators. Of course, there are exceptions; for example, Sue notes that African Americans tend to be high-context communicators even though they live in the United States. Differences in meaning of words in other cultures may be subject to misinterpretation. For example, saying "no" may actually mean "yes" (e.g., Arab or Asian), although these are words that are taken for their literal meaning in Western societies (Sue, 2006).

Hierarchical Considerations

Depending on the age–sex hierarchies in some cultures, you are advised to address questions to, for example, the father, then the mother, then other adults, and finally the older and younger children. Grandparents or other elders in the family may actually be held in greater esteem than parents and figure prominently in the family's hierarchical arrangement. Caution is particularly advised in working with immigrant families where a child who has greater proficiency in the English language and is used as an interpreter in interviews with parents. You should be sensitive to the fact that the child's role in this instance may undermine traditional roles in the family and result in tensions between parents and their children (Ho, 1987; Pierce & Elisme, 1997). Beyond being sensitive, being empathetic and exploring the parents' feelings are means by which you reinforce your understanding of their role. In addition, when clients come from a culture in which chronological age and familial hierarchy play a significant role (e.g., Asian Indian and African American families), open dialogue between parents and children may be viewed as insolent or disrespectful (Segal, 1991; Carter & McGoldrick, 1999a). Also note that what may appear to you to be hierarchically

defined roles in the family may instead be complementary. Flores and Carey (2000), in counteracting the popular notion of machismo dominance in Hispanic families, emphasize this point. Specifically, the father functions as the authoritarian, protective figure in the family; the mother's role is complementary to that of the father in that she is expected to be expressive, caring, and nurturing. As you join with the family, it is best to ask questions, seek their preferences, and explore their rules with respect to family order and hierarchy.

Authority of the Social Worker

Many Asian Americans and Pacific Islanders do not understand the social worker's role and may confuse him or her with a physician. Nevertheless, observes Ho (1987), members of these groups will perceive you as a knowledgeable expert who will guide them in the proper course of action. Thus, you will need to take a more directive role rather than a more passive role in working with such families. Social workers should not hesitate to discuss their professional background, because these families need assurance that you are more powerful than their illnesses or family problems and will "cure" them with competent know-how. When writing notes, you should be aware that writing and documenting—while necessary for creating case or SOAP notes—may reinforce perceptions of the unequal power balance between you and the family (Flores & Carey, 2000; Boyd-Franklin, 1989a). To alleviate clients' concerns, you will find it helpful to explain their purpose, standards of confidentiality, and requirements for information that may involve an identified third party.

When working with African American clients, your perceived authority also reflects your use of first names with families and social distance. Robinson (1989) recommends that you use last names until invited by clients to do otherwise: "The racial importance of first names is magnified for the black client because of the historical tradition of calling black people by their first names in situations in which first names would not be permitted if both participants were white" (p. 328). Berg and Jaya (1993) also note that addressing Asian American elders by their first names may inhibit establishing a positive therapeutic alliance. Similar to African Americans and Asian Americans, the use of last names is appropriate in the introductory stage with Mexicans (Flores & Corey, 2000).

An informal and egalitarian approach, which is second nature to many Americans, is actually considered improper in many cultures. For example, Mexican Americans typically expect their initial encounter with you to be quite formal, polite, and reserved, with the social worker taking the initiative in solving the family's problem (Janzen & Harris, 1997; Sue, 2006). Passivity among immigrants, for example, may stem from their social and political status in the United States, a distrust of helpers, and a fear about expressing their true feelings to figures of authority (Potocky-Tripodi, 2003; Pierce & Elisme, 1997). While direct questioning, the informal use of language and expectations of full disclosure may diminish trust, Devore & Schlesinger (1999) suggest using empathy as a facilitative means to form an alliance.

Aponte (1982) perhaps summarizes these issues best by stating that power and authority are critical elements of the family–social worker relationship, especially for ethnic or racial groups. Most diverse families perceive the social worker as acting in his or her professional role rather than fulfilling a social role, therefore, they represent the majority society. Within this context, the social worker symbolizes the larger society's power, values, and standards. Because of the authority that is assigned to you as a professional, it is important to explicitly recognize families as decision makers and experts on their situation, and to ensure that you have their informed consent before proceeding further (Palmer & Kaufman, 2003).

Engaging the Family

Techniques for engaging or joining are particularly crucial when working with diverse families. Listening in context—especially allowing the family to present their story in their own way—and being mindful of the communication process are key concerns. For example, you should be aware of differences in communication styles, the cultural context of seeking help outside of the family, and the family's perceptions of your own and your agency's authority. While knowledge of culture is not guaranteed to provide you with an advantage in working with a particular family, exploring the relevance of cultural meanings of particular groups can facilitate the process of engagement (Janzen & Harris, 1997).

Engaging the family may also include accounting for extended family members in the process of joining, whether or not they participate in family sessions. Boyd-Franklin (1989a), in stressing the importance of the joining stage with African American families, points to the crucial linkage between engagement and problem solving. The former process enables you to establish credibility and trust with the family, and move to goals and problem solving. In the engagement phase, your entry into the family system is greatly enhanced by your respect for the problem as identified by the family. Finally, in the initial session, be aware that minority families tend to respond more favorably to brief intervention strategies that are directed toward taking action and implementing solutions (Lum, 2004; Corwin, 2002; Berg & Jaya, 1993; Boyd-Franklin, 1989a). Subsequent to engagement, then, it would be prudent for you and the family to specify and agree upon a time frame for the treatment.

Families from diverse backgrounds may feel more welcome in agencies where objects and symbols of their culture are visible in offices and waiting rooms. Home visits may be invaluable in the engagement stage with some families, because such visits afford you with an opportunity to observe and assess a family in its natural environment (Berg, 1994). Visits to the home may also allow you to learn about and observe the practices of families and important members of the family network. You will have an opportunity to convey your interest in the family by inquiring about portraits, cultural objects, and other items of interest. In visits to the home, "remember that you are on the client's home turf," caution Boyd-Franklin and Bry (2000), which means that you should remain flexible and show deference to the rules and structure of the family and the order of the household (p. 39). Even so, some family members may resent or resist involvement in the initial session, and they may cite culture as a defense against joining (Flores & Carey, 2000).

In instances where the family has been referred for treatment, members may be angry and resentful of this intrusion. Be mindful of the fact that most minority families tend to be involuntary help-seekers. If you represent an agency that they feel has power and authority over their lives, this "baggage" will affect their reaction to you. In situations where these dynamics have a significant impact, it is suggested that you avoid personalizing this experience and move quickly to acknowledge, accept, and validate clients' feelings (Berg, 1994; R. H. Rooney, 2009).

Finally, engaging diverse families is facilitated when you understand the cultural relevance of terminology describing family dynamics and structure. Autonomy and self-differentiation, for example, when considered in a sociopolitical or cultural context, may be neither desired nor expected.

Understanding Families Using an Ecological Perspective

Culture and race are merely two factors in the ecological schema of practice with families. Other salient factors include religion, gender, class, family form or status, and work and family concerns. To demonstrate sensitivity to multisystems influences and clarify their relationship to family concerns, you must also focus on the family and their environmental interactions. In doing so, you are exploring the extent to which these factors affect family relationships and interaction patterns. For example, work and family pressures may intrude upon parental ability to fulfill role functions within the family, producing role overload, conflict, and strain (Fredriksen-Golden & Scharlach, 2001; Marlow, 1993; G. D. Rooney, 1997). The ideal of egalitarian roles for men and women is becoming more evident in both rural and urban families in the United States as well as in the cultural schema of other countries. Even so, women for the most part still manage multiple roles—wife, daughter, mother, parent, employee. Acculturation may mean that gender roles are in transition, yet adaptation to the new roles may become a source of tension in much the same way that parent–adolescent conflict intensifies, thereby resulting in stressors within the family system.

For poor families, meeting immediate survival and resource needs may take precedence over pursuing more insight-oriented approaches (Kilpatrick & Holland, 2006). The family context–environment interaction may include intervening to address problems of housing, financial assistance, school–child conflicts, and unresponsive social institutions. Social support networks such as the extended family, tribe or clan, or other key people may be included in the discussion to reduce dysfunctional interactions and to increase concrete support for the family. A failure on your part to focus on family–environmental interactions may cause you to have an incomplete understanding of family functioning and hence to develop interventions that emphasize pathology over strengths. For example, dysfunctional interactions may emerge in immigrant families resulting from their attempts to cope with adjustment-related stressors or problems. In emphasizing this possibility, a study by Fong (1997) links spousal or child abuse to the stress-related adjustment problems among Chinese immigrants.

Flores and Carey (2000) note that many well-established approaches to work with families remain "silent" on issues of social justice, oppression, and the marginalization inherent in the minority experience. Until recently, the same was true regarding issues that are important to women. Thanks to the fuller understanding of families produced by feminists' evaluation of family practice approaches, social workers at a minimum should be acutely aware of the need to be sensitive to age, gender, and patriarchy. Goldenberg and Goldenberg (2000) emphasize that gender sensitivity does not mean merely being nonsexist. Instead, they suggest that gender-sensitive practice is proactive and deliberate in helping women move beyond the limitations imposed by social and political barriers (pp. 50–51). For minority women, the combination of gender with race or culture adds yet another series of social and political barriers. For this reason, you should not assume that minority women perceive their gender as the more prominent factor, when compared to race or ethnicity.

To help you appreciate the ecological context of families, we consider the cases of Twanna and Janet and Anna and Jackie.

Twanna, the Adolescent Mother

Negative societal attitudes and conditions can also pose environmental challenges and threats to families and thus influence the family system. For example, society almost always views single-mother families from a deficit perspective. They are held accountable for their perceived mistakes and for being responsible for their situation, rather than their strength as a viable family form being recognized. The age of the single mother adds an additional tension. As parents, adolescents are often treated like adults and children simultaneously, and society demands that they comply with their parental obligation; yet, societal institutions tend to play the forceful role of a parent.

At age 17, Twanna, an older adolescent, is also a single mother. Prior to coming to live with Janet, she had been placed since age 8 with three other foster families. As she grew older, and especially after she became pregnant, she was no longer welcome in the last family. Out-of-wedlock births, especially among adolescents and teens, remain taboo and the young women are stigmatized. In fact, her previous foster parents were outraged and embarrassed by her pregnancy and requested her removal from their home. As Weinberg (2006) notes, young single mothers often "represent a number of marginalized categories": they are young, female, impoverished, racial or ethnic minorities, from lower- or working-class families, and most of all they have children outside of the institution of marriage. In their marginalized status, these young women have often experienced a number of failures to support them—from their families, the education system, and in some instances their community. In Twanna's case, she is also vulnerable due to an additional marginal category, that of being a ward of the state. Her biological mother had been judged to be inadequate, hence she became a ward, and her child now also has the same status. Until she came to live with Janet in her home, Twanna's support system consisted of a series of child welfare workers.

Twanna has other challenges related to her developmental stage and that of her child. In many respects, the wants and needs associated with their developmental journey have certain similarities, summarized in the comparisons below.

TWANNA	CHILD
Identity and independence	Autonomy
Intimacy	Nurturing
Self-efficacy	Self-esteem
Attachment	Attachment
Relationships	Social interactions

Developmentally, however, they vary, as a young child needs consistency and the adolescent is in the process of exploration and experimentation. While adolescents search for their identity, separate and apart from their families and through their peers, the young child's sense of self is gained through their interactions with his or her caretaker. In Twanna's case, she is attempting to meet her own needs and those of her child, which without the support of Janet could result in role strain and overload. The social worker noted this conflict in her summary statement to Twanna: "What you are saying is that you understand that you are responsible for your child, but that you also need to be with your friends."

In the broader scheme of things, changes in the bonds between an adolescent seeking greater autonomy and his or her adult caretakers may require changes in interactions and communication patterns (Baer, 1999). As a foster parent, Janet makes certain demands that are consistent with her role as a parent, aspects of which include her obligation to ensure the well-being of Twanna and her child. According to Weinberg (2006), helping minors who are also parents is a balancing act between being a disciplinarian and an emancipator. It is not uncommon for parents to establish protective boundaries, which may include anxieties about both peers and the neighborhood and undertaking intense monitoring (Jarrett, 1995). Recall that Janet wanted to meet Twanna's friends so she "could get to know them." This family unit is, however, different from the normative family structure, and the rules of the state set a certain tone. For example, as a family unit, their interactions may be primarily with professionals, and the supportive family networks of kin and friends are not a given. In many respects, Janet and Twanna are attempting to establish functional family rules without the benefit of role models pertinent to their family configuration.

Gay and lesbian families are largely ignored as a viable family. Hence their internal family stress is a given as they attempt to navigate in an often hostile and indifferent social environment. Popular television programs have featured gay and lesbian individuals, and to some extent same-sex couples. Rarely, however, have these programs spotlighted the reality of the challenges and stressors of being different. For example, concerns voiced among lesbian mothers related to reactions toward their children and the family's experiences in their interactions with the larger community represent a case in point (Hare, 1994).

Anna and Jackie, a Lesbian Couple

Anna and Jackie are in a relationship that is disqualified in a society in which the legal and romantic norms emphasize the bond between males and females (Bepko & Johnson, 2000; McKenry & Price, 2006). As young adults, Anna and Jackie are involved in an age-appropriate developmental task, that of being in an intimate relationship. Forming a relationship requires new adaptations to roles and tasks; for example, realigning with family and establishing their own relationship. In the family life cycle, coupling is welcomed and celebrated by parents as a significant milestone in the lives of their children. Conversely, societal, and in some cases familial, attitudes deny couples the identity of same-sex unions. Thus, these uncelebrated committed relationships are without social supports.

The very act of "coming out" to one's family can create family strain and in some instances sever family ties. For example, Jackie and Anna are in different places with respect to claiming their identities as lesbians and as a couple. Anna family's appears to be comfortable with her sexuality. Jackie has taken a first step by coming out to her family; however, she is unwilling to press the issue with her family because she fears their response. At this stage in her relationship with Anna, Jackie contents herself with the fact that her parents "were quiet and took up other activities" when she told them of her intent to move in with Anna. As noted by Bepko and Johnson (2000), gay and lesbian individuals have different attitudes about how "out" they want to be with their families and in society. With their families, they may experience a conflict with respect to the direction of their loyalty. Without family support, external cultural stressors on same-sex couples can be more pronounced (Connolly, 2006).

The preceding examples highlight but a few of the many cultural dynamics and ecological factors to which social workers must attend in working with diverse families and in intervening in family functioning and relational dynamics. Fitting practice and intervention strategies to the ecology of a particular family is a complicated process that requires a multidimensional assessment; this assessment must include examination of the myriad internal and external factors that shape family life. You are urged to use your knowledge of culture, race, gender, sexual orientation, and sociopolitical issues as a lens through which to view families. The considerable diversity encountered among families may mean that some factors have greater relevance than others. For some families, culture or race may be peripheral to their identity, yet they may retain essential attributes that guide their family life. Acquiring sensitivity to gender, sexual orientation, and racial and cultural preferences can be achieved by facilitating the family narratives, taking an active and genuine interest in their story, and collaborating with the family to resolve their concerns.

Intervening with Families: Focusing on the Future

Families are often overwhelmed, frustrated, and perhaps saturated with their problems when you encounter them. Your responsibility as a social worker is to create a safe structure and climate in which family concern can be raised and to assist the family to move toward change. One major obstacle to change is the propensity of couples or families to focus on what they do not have or what is not working, rather than on what they would like *in the future.* Solution-focused therapy is a brief treatment approach that addresses problems in the present and inspires a future orientation beginning with the initial contact. Using miracle or scaling questions (two

solution-focused techniques), you might ask the family, "What would you like to do about the future?" or "How would you know that your family members have improved their communications with one another?" Scaling questions (e.g., "When you called for an appointment with me, your family was in trouble. Imagine how you might feel on a scale of 1 to 10 after you have achieved your goal.") are useful in helping families to reframe their problems and feel more in control of their lives.

Focusing on the future can serve as a guiding principle for helping families and social workers. The following examples are hypothetical statements related to the two previous cases:

- *A discussion that can lead quickly to consideration of what each person is willing to do to prevent a recurrence of an event, interaction, tension or argument* in the future. *For example, Twanna's statement,* "I will come home after school and be ready to take care of my baby" *and Janet's statement,* "It would be okay for her to invite her friends to the house."
- *Complaints or criticisms can be translated into information about how changes in others might affect the family* in the future. *Recipients can also give information: Anna to Jackie,* "You need to have the conversation again with your family." *Jackie to Anna,* "This is what you could do in the future *that would help me do what you are suggesting."*
- *Breakdowns in communication can be analyzed from a future-oriented point of view: Social worker to Anna and Jackie, after observing their interactions,* "What can you learn from what just happened that you can apply* in the future?"
- *Conflicts of interest and needs and wants can cause families to engage in "win-win" problem solving: Social worker to Twanna and Janet,* "How can you resolve the problem right now so we can feel good about your relationship* in the future?"

"Opting for the future," when adopted as a philosophy and guideline by families and social workers, removes the blame from their interaction. The future, not the past, is seen as more relevant. The future is fresh, hopeful, and untainted by tensions or stressors. Opting for the future, of course, requires that each family member commit to attending only to what *he or she* will do in the future, rather than monitoring the activities of the other person. You can increase families' focus on the future by putting problem talk on hold and by always starting sessions with a question regarding their successes in achieving goals or tasks, and by creating fresh, positive ways of interacting. Complementing this approach, Weiner-Davis (1992) teaches clients to focus on the "exceptional times" to determine what is working and why, and then encourages them to turn productive behaviors into habits. Focusing on exceptions diminishes problems, because identifying what they *can* do is infinitely more hopeful and empowering to them than noting what they *cannot* do. It also demonstrates to families that they are changeable and that seemingly fixed traits are fluid. Finally, focusing on exceptions supplies clients with a blueprint for describing exactly what they need to do the next time a particular situation occurs.

Communication Patterns and Styles

Communication approaches to families consist of teaching family members the rules of clear communication. Theorists believe that the patterns that family members use to communicate with one another are often interpreted in various ways, and are often punctuated by faulty cognitions and perceptions. What the sender believes is the message is not necessarily what the receiver understands the message to be. A difficult relationship between sender and receiver can also strain or distort the message.

Giving and Receiving Feedback

Positive feedback from significant others (i.e., expressions of caring, approval, encouragement, affection, appreciation, and other forms of positive attention) nourish morale, emotional security, confidence, and the feeling of being valued by others. Thus, increasing positive feedback fosters the well-being of individuals and harmonious family relationships. To enable family members to increase positive feedback, social workers must have skills in the following areas:

- *Engaging clients in assessing the extent to which they give and receive positive feedback*
- *Educating clients about the vital role of positive feedback*
- *Cultivating positive cognitive sets*
- *Enabling clients to give and receive positive feedback*

In the following sections, each of these skills is discussed.

Engaging Clients in Assessing How Well They Give and Receive Positive Feedback

Destructive communication patterns often result from strained relationships, so that the family system eventually becomes unbalanced. Communication theorists view the family as a functional system that depends on two communication processes: negative and positive feedback. They also believe that all behavior is communication. Thus, they view the social worker's role as being to help the family change the process of family interactions.

You can assist families and individual members to directly explore dimensions of communication by assessing how often and in what manner they convey positive feedback to significant others. Questions you might ask in couple or family sessions to achieve this end include the following:

- *"How do you send messages that let family members [or your partner] know that you care about them?"*
- *"How frequently do you send such messages?"*
- *"How often do you give feedback to others concerning their positive actions?"*

In instances of severe couple or family breakdown, members may acknowledge that they send positive messages infrequently or not at all. In some instances, they may actually have tepid positive feelings, but they usually experience more than they express. Besides exploring how couples or family members convey positive feedback, you can explore their desires to receive increased feedback from one another. Discussing how family members send positive messages or to what extent they desire increased positive feedback can open up channels for positive communication and improve relationships that have been stuck in a cycle of repetitive arguments, criticisms, blaming, and put-down messages.

Educating Clients about the Vital Role of Positive Feedback

As family members communicate about their needs to receive positive feedback, they will begin to appreciate the significance of this dimension in interpersonal relationships. You can further expand their awareness by explaining why positive feedback is crucial to family interactions. The logic behind increasing positive feedback is straightforward. Teaching clients to express their needs involves assisting them to send personalized messages in which they own their feelings and needs.

The following are examples of messages that explicitly express a need for positive feedback:

- *Partner: When we were talking about plans for my mother, I didn't interrupt you. I wish you would notice when I do something different.*
- *Adolescent: I felt discouraged when I showed you my grades yesterday. I really worked hard this term, and the only thing you seemed to notice was the one B. It didn't seem to matter that the rest were A's.*

In each of these statements, the speaker used "I" to personalize his or her messages. Each message also clearly indicates what the speaker is seeking from the other person. When messages are less clear, they may lead to a further breakdown in communications. You can intervene in these situations by using the technique of *on-the-spot interventions*. When using this technique, you coach clients to formulate clear messages that express their feelings and needs as illustrated in the following exchange. It begins with a message from a wife, who is seeking positive feedback from her husband, but what she wants from him is unclear.

Ruth [to husband]: I worked really hard at picking up around the house before people arrived, but the only thing you noticed was what I had not done—like the comment you made about fingerprints on the bathroom door.

Carl [to Ruth]: Well, let's face it, the fingerprints were there and as you yourself admitted it.

Social worker: Carl, Ruth was expressing what is important to her in the relationship, and I don't want her point to get lost in an argument. Ruth, think for a moment about what you said. What is it you are asking of Carl?

Ruth [after pausing]: Do you mean his not noticing what I do?

Social worker: In a way, yes. Would you like for Carl to let you know you're appreciated for what you had done?

In this scenario, Ruth has shared important information—namely, the need to feel valued. People want to receive positive feedback for what they are and what they do. Interactions that continuously focus on negative results may leave an individual feeling discouraged and insecure, and as a consequence relationships suffer.

In instructing Ruth and Carl about the importance of positive feedback, the social worker used this opportunity to allow them to practice communicating in a different manner.

Social worker: Ruth, I'd like you to start over and express that you want positive feedback from Carl. This time, however send an "I" message so that it is clear what you want from him.

Ruth [hesitating]: I hope that I can. Carl, I need to hear from you about the things that I do well and not only about what is wrong.

Initially, clients may feel timid about expressing their feelings clearly. The second part of helping family members to communicate is by assisting them to listen attentively. Asking Carl to repeat what he heard in Ruth's message is one way to emphasize listening for content. Because all individuals may not always express their needs openly and clearly, family members may need to go beyond just listening. That is, they may need to become *attuned* to needs expressed in the form of complaints, questions, and the attitudes of others. *Tuning in* also involves alerting others to pay attention to nonverbal messages and what those messages communicate about feelings.

Because it is difficult for family members to be attuned to the needs inherent in the messages of others, you should take advantage of "teachable moments" to help them to learn this skill, as illustrated in the preceding situation. Specifically, the social worker encouraged Ruth to express her need for positive feedback from Carl. Also, when the social worker focused on Ruth, she played a facilitative role in prompting her to express herself directly to Carl. The social worker likewise had Carl provide feedback to Ruth, thus performing a critical role in *facilitating positive interaction between the couple*. This is a crucial point. Serving as a catalyst, the social worker helped Carl and Ruth learn new communication skills by having them *actually engage in positive interaction*, which is an effective mode of learning.

Cultivating Positive Cognitive Sets

Before family members can provide positive feedback, they must first be able to acknowledge the strengths, positive attributes, and actions of others. Some will be attuned to these qualities, while others will habitually perceive weaknesses and flaws. Cognitive sets can consist of distorted assumptions or automatic thoughts from other relationships—that is, thoughts derived from negative schemas that are not based in reality, yet function to sustain dysfunctional relationships (Collins, Kayser, & Platt, 1994; Berlin & Marsh, 1993). In essence, schemas are problematic when the individual has an unrealistic or faulty view of the world. Thus, their behavior in interacting with others is influenced by their distortions. A key point is recognizing that attitudes, thoughts, and expectations are generally intertwined with emotions.

Using the cognitive-behavioral approach, the social worker attempts to improve family interactions by helping individual family members alter cognitive distortions and learn new behaviors. The social worker focuses on bringing negative cognitive sets that influence thoughts, feelings, and actions to the attention of family members, ultimately helping them learn to focus on positive behaviors. Strategies for accomplishing these tasks are described next.

Sensitizing Couples to Positive Cognitive Sets

You can set the stage for helping families and couples to develop positive cognitive sets by negotiating a *contingency contract*. The contingency contract identifies desirable behavior change between two parties and explicit rules for interaction, specifying that they agree to exchange positive rewarding behavior with each other (Becvar & Becvar, 2000a). Based on the theory of social exchange, cognitive behaviorists maintain that behavior exchange adhere to a norm of reciprocity. Specifically, negative or positive behavior from one person will induce reciprocal behavior from others. Using the contingency contract, you can actively intervene in the early stages of the helping process to highlight strengths and growth and to help clients incorporate "attention to positives" as part of their normative behavior. Families can develop their own set of positive indicators for desirable behavior change along with reciprocal goals. Generally, you would review progress on these indicators with the family (or couple) each week.

Reviewing Progress and Accrediting Incremental Growth

Social workers can also increase a family's sensitivity to positives by engaging members in briefly reviewing at the end of each session the work that has been accomplished and by observing incremental growth. To highlight incremental growth, ask members to contrast their current functioning with their functioning at an earlier time, as illustrated in the following message:

Social worker: This is our fourth session. Let's begin by identifying the changes the family has made in the way you communicate with each other. We can then contrast this change with how you were communicating in the first session. For now, I will hold my observations, but when you are done, I will add my own observations to the changes that you have identified.

Employing Tasks to Enhance Cognitive Sets

Negotiating tasks that family members can implement between sessions can facilitate the development of positive cognitive sets. For example, to further expand family members' or couples' awareness of the frequency with which they provide positive feedback, you might ask them to keep a daily tally of the number of positive messages they send to one another. They should also note the reciprocal behaviors of other members as a result of their actions. This practice not only enables family members and the social worker to gain a clear picture of their performance on this dimension, but also establishes baselines that can be used later to assess their progress. Without explicitly planning to do so, family members often increase the frequency of the desired behavior during the monitoring period. By systematically focusing on the positive attributes of others, clients can gradually achieve more positive cognitive sets. Of course, the ultimate reinforcement derives from improved interactions with others.

Enabling Clients to Give and Receive Positive Feedback

To assist families to learn to convey positive feedback, you can teach them to personalize their messages and guide them in giving positive feedback to others. Timely use of role-play as an educational intervention assists family members to form positive messages and to develop the skills needed to share their experiences in an authentic manner. When negative situations of some intensity have gone on for an extended period, you may also need to help some family members learn how to accept and trust positive feedback.

After completing these activities, family members are ready to work on the ultimate goal—increasing their rates of positive feedback. You can assist them by negotiating tasks that specify providing positive feedback at higher levels. Families, of course, must consent to tasks and determine the rate of positive feedback they seek to achieve. Family members can review their baseline information (gathered earlier through monitoring), and can be encouraged to set a daily rate that "stretches" them beyond their usual level. For example, an adolescent whose mean baseline daily rate in giving positive feedback to his father is 0.8 might select an initial task of giving positive feedback twice daily. He would then gradually increase the number of positive messages until he reached a self-selected optimal rate of five times daily.

As some family members implement the task of increasing positive feedback, they may inappropriately engage in insincere positive expressions. You should caution against this behavior, as such expressions are counterproductive for both the sender and the receiver.

In planning with family members to implement tasks, it is important to adhere to the task implementation sequence (TIS). In part, this exercise involves anticipating obstacles, including the two most common. First, family members who have been inhibited in expressing feelings may initially report discomfort: "It just doesn't come naturally to me." Second, other family members may respond unfavorably to an increased level of positive feedback and question the sender's sincerity, especially if this is a new behavior: "I wonder what she wants from me now?" You can assist family members to deal with others' skepticism by modeling, by having them rehearse appropriate coping behavior (including asserting the sincerity of their efforts), and by emphasizing the necessity of changing their behavior despite the obstacles. As with any tasks, you should plan to review progress in subsequent sessions and to explore favorable reactions and any difficulties that family members encountered.

Many of the strategies previously mentioned as instrumental in helping families give and receive positive feedback are applicable to couples and parents as well. Therefore, we will only briefly identify some additional tasks that may be used with couples and parents. One technique that you can employ to increase positive interactions between couples involves a strategy discussed by Stuart (1980) and Collins, Kayser, and Platt (1994). That is, both partners are asked to identify desired actions or behaviors: "Exactly what would you like your partner to do as a means of showing that he or she cares for you?" After giving each spouse or partner an opportunity to identify desired actions, you can ask each to develop a task directed toward engaging in a specified behavior identified by the other party. It may be useful to have them develop and prioritize a list of desirable positive behaviors. A reinforcing aspect of such tasks occurs when each person gives feedback and expresses appreciation when the other engages in the desired behavior.

Before negotiating tasks with parents to increase positive feedback to minors, you can request that parents list behaviors of each child. You can then ask parents to choose the behaviors they would most like to change, cautioning them that the process is gradual, rather than all or nothing. The next step is to negotiate a task that involves parents giving positive feedback at opportune times during the week when the specified behavior is *not* occurring—for example, when the child is *not* fighting with a sibling. Further, you should instruct parents to give positive feedback when children manifest behaviors that parents would like them to demonstrate *in place of the targeted behaviors*—for example, when the minor *has* told the truth. Parents may be understandably reluctant to agree to this strategy, especially if continual nagging or threats of punishment have been their only means for getting the child to engage in desirable behavior. In such instances, you will need to motivate children to comply by establishing with the parents an agreement under which children may earn certain rewards in exchange for specified behavior.

Because parental attention to children's behavior is a potent force for aggravating, modifying or reinforcing behavior, their mastery of the skill related to positive feedback is important. Oftentimes, when minors behave as expected, parents unfortunately take their behavior for granted. But they need to know what they are *already* doing that pleases their parents. When used consistently by parents, messages such as these have a significant effect in shaping and cultivating desired behavior. If parents want their children to assume particular behaviors, they must give them positive feedback when those behaviors occur. Note the reinforcing property of the following parental messages:

- *"I really appreciate your taking the time to visit your grandmother, and so does she."*
- *"Thank you for telling me the truth when I asked if you were smoking cigarettes."*

Parents must also be aware of their own behavior as it relates to vicarious learning and modeling. Specifically, children learn behavior including the consequences by observing other people and events.

In addition to providing positive messages and tangible rewards that reinforce desired behavior, tasks that involve incremental change and subsequent reinforcement are particularly useful with young children. Referred to as *successive approximation*, tasks involve incremental change and act as a shaping process that divides the desired behavior into subparts, providing contingencies and rewards until the whole of the desired behavior is achieved. Thus, if having a child sit quietly at her desk, pay attention to the teacher, raise her hand and wait to be called upon before speaking are targeted behaviors, parents might initially reward "sitting" as the first subpart of the whole (Becvar & Becvar, 2000a, p. 262).

Intervening with Families: Strategies to Modify Interactions

Interactional difficulties that families commonly present include repetitive arguments; struggles over power and authority; developmental conflicts associated with dependence to independence, or interdependence; dissension in making decisions; friction associated with discrepant role perceptions and fulfillments; and other forms of faulty communication. Interpersonal conflicts tend to be redundant; that is, in relations with others, individuals repeat over and over again various types of interactions that predictably lead to the same negative consequences. To assist you in helping families in developing more functional patterns of communication and interaction, we delineate guidelines and techniques that you can use in persuading them to modify their dysfunctional interactions. We draw from techniques used by cognitive-behavioral, structural, family systems, and communication theories as well as task-centered family practice. Note that teaching communication skills to family members is a vital aspect of modifying dysfunctional communications.

Metacommunication

To modify dysfunctional communication, family members must discuss their communication patterns, analyze their behaviors and emotional reactions, and consider the effects of the interaction on their relationship. Such discussions are termed *metacommunication*, because they involve "communication about communication." When you discuss with families a communication that has just occurred they are also engaging in metacommunication. Indeed, much of couple, family, and group therapy focus on metacommunication. Likewise, when you discuss relational reactions that occur in the context of the helping relationship, you are clarifying the meanings of messages and actions. Still other examples of metacommunication are messages that clarify intentions (e.g., "I'm teasing you" or "I want to

talk with you because I feel bad about the strain between us") or messages that "check out" or seek clarification of others' messages that are vague or ambiguous (e.g., "I'm not sure what you mean by that" or "Let me see if I understood what you were saying"). Metacommunications contain both verbal and nonverbal content. The content of a non verbal message is established through the tone of voice and body language, further shaping and defining the intent of the message and the relationship between those involved.

Skills in metacommunications play an important role in effective communications because they avoid needless misunderstandings (by checking out the meanings of messages) and provide feedback that enables others to make choices about modifying offensive or abrasive communication styles. Moreover, conflicts in relationships are kept at a minimum level of antagonism or disruption. A major role for the social worker, therefore, is to assist clients to learn to metacommunicate in a productive manner.

Although skills in assisting people to metacommunicate are important with all client systems, they are especially critical in working with families who manifest dysfunctional patterns of communication, including frequent use of incongruent and double-bind messages and messages within a message messages. Such families seldom clarify meanings or attend to the effects that their messages have on one another.

The following example illustrates use of metacommunication to enhance communication between Anna and Jackie.

Anna: "Jackie does not talk to her family about anything. In my family, everything is an open book. Just like her family, Jackie doesn't talk" [*Disconfirming Jackie as a separate person with different needs*].

Jackie: "I do talk to my family. I told them about us moving in together. Sometimes when I come home from work, I am tired, I don't want to talk. I think your family talks too much about everything."

Anna: "She doesn't talk to them anything about being gay." [*Assigning fault; disconfirming Jackie's message*].

Jackie: "It's not my responsibility." [*Defends position*].

Social worker: [*Interrupts to avert another disconfirming message from Anna*] "Jackie, how does it make you feel when Anna compares her family to your family?" [*Encouraging metacommunication; intervening to counter Anna acting as Jackie's spokesperson.*]

In the preceding exchange, the social worker actively intervened to prevent the interaction from following its usual unproductive course. As you can imagine, the circular and sequence interaction could go on forever without resolution. The social worker acted to intervene in the situation by not permitting Anna to act as Jackie's spokesperson in which she assigns motives to Jackie's behavior. Further, by involving them in a discussion about how comparisons between the two families are disconfirming to Jackie, Anna can begin to understand how these behaviors affect her and Jackie's relationship. Recognizing that Anna was conveying a message within a message, the social worker asked her, *"What meaning does Jackie's conversation with her parents have for you?"* For Anna, Jackie's conversation with her parents is a way of confirming their relationship. She has not directly said so previously, hence the message within the message. The social worker further clarified how each can modify their patterns of communication, thereby initiating corrective processes. Of course, such interventions must occur over a period of time if they are to produce enduring changes.

Modifying Family Rules

Family rules govern the range of behavior in the family system and the sequence of interactions or reactions to a particular event. Rules are a means by which the family system maintains its equilibrium. Dysfunctional family rules, however, can severely impair the functioning of family members. Because family rules are often covert, it follows that changes can occur only by bringing them into the open. You can assist family members to acknowledge and consider the effects of rules on family interactions. To illustrate, we return to Anna and Jackie in which the focus of the conversation is on family communication styles and family rules. The social worker shares her observation about the differences between their families and makes the point that family rules and communication styles influence the interactions in relationships. To begin to resolve the conflict about these differences, she asked, "Does Jackie's family have to be like your family?" By encouraging them to openly discuss family of origin rules; they can begin to consider rules that might better serve their relationship needs.

With families, it can be useful to have them make a list of apparent and unspoken rules so that you and they can understand how the family operates. You can prepare families to consider rules by introducing them to the concept, as illustrated in the following message:

Social worker: As we begin to work on problems the family is experiencing, we need to know more about how your family operates. Every family has some rules or understandings about how members are to behave. Sometimes these rules are easy to spot. For example, each person is to clear his or her own plate after a meal is a rule that all members of a family might be expected to follow. This is an apparent rule because every member of the family could easily tell me what is expected of them at the end of the meal. But the family's behavior is also governed by other rules that are less easy to identify. Even though members follow these rules, they are often unaware that they exist. I'm going to ask you some questions that will help you to understand these two kinds of rules better and to identify some of the ones that operate in your family. For example, you can ask family members to list some apparent rules, coaching them as needed, by asking questions such as "What are your rules about school work?" (or watching television or household chores, friends). Once family members have identified some of their common and readily apparent rules, you can then lead them into a discussion of implicit rules. For example, you might ask family members to identify family rules about showing anger or positive feelings or to explore decision-making or power (e.g., "Who do the kids go to in the family when they want something?"). The intent of these questions is not to engage in a lengthy exploration of rules, but rather to illustrate how hidden rules can influence family behavior, stressing that certain rules may hamper their interactions.

Consider the social worker's role in this regard in the following excerpt from a third session with Mr. and Mrs. Johnson and their three daughters, in which the social worker assisted the family to identify how hidden rules influence their patterned interactions:

Martha [age 14]: You took the red jersey again, right out of my closet—and you didn't ask. That really gripes me.

Cynthia [age 15]: You took the Britney Spears CD last week, and you still have it. What's up with that?

Mr. Johnson: In this family, we share, and you girls should know this.

Social worker: This seems to be a family rule. What does that mean in this family?

Mr. Johnson: It means that we have a limited amount of money to spend on extras, so we buy things for the girls to use together and no one person owns the things we buy. Besides, the girls are expected to share because they are so close in age and like similar things.

Social worker: So, what happens when there is a disagreement about a particular item?

Martha: I got mad at Cynthia, and I told her so.

Social worker [to Cynthia]: Then what did you do?

Cynthia: I told Martha she didn't have any right to complain because she wasn't sharing things either.

Social worker: Cynthia and Martha, the two of you were engaged in what is referred to as blaming messages; do you see it the same way? [*Girls nod.*]

[To Mr. Johnson] I wonder if you remember what you did when Cynthia and Martha were arguing.

Mr. Johnson: I was trying to get them to stop arguing and yelling at each other and reminding them that they are expected to share.

Social worker [exploring hidden rule]: Is everyone in the family aware of the expectation of sharing? I'd like to begin by asking a few questions, to see if you can figure out what the rules are in your family. Are you willing to explore this further?

[To 13-year-old Jennifer] You weren't involved in this argument. Do you argue with anyone in the family?

Jennifer [laughs]: My mother and Martha, but mainly my mother.

Social worker: When you get in an argument with your mother, what happens?

Jennifer: If my dad is home, he tries to stop it. Sometimes he tells my mother to go upstairs, and he'll talk to me.

Social worker [to Mrs. Johnson]: When your husband stops an argument between the girls, or you and one of the girls, what do you do?

Mrs. Johnson: Sometimes I let him deal with the problem with Jennifer or one of the other girls. But when he gets involved like that, it makes me so furious that sometimes he and I end up in a fight ourselves.

Social worker: We need to do a lot more work to understand what happens in such situations, but for the moment, let's see, Mr. Johnson, if you can put your finger on the rule.

Mr. Johnson: I guess I'm always trying to stop everyone from fighting and arguing in the family. I expect the girls to share and get along with each other, and not cause their mother grief.

Social worker: It does appear that you are the family's mediator. I would think that would be a very difficult role to play.

Mr. Johnson: Well, there are no rewards for it, I can tell you that!

Social worker: There's more to the rule. Who lets the father be the mediator?

Mrs. Johnson: We all do.

Social worker: That's right. It isn't the father's rule; it's the family's rule. It takes the rest of the family to argue and the father to break up the fights.

Many avenues could be explored in this scenario, but the social worker chose to narrow the focus by assisting the family to identify one of its major rules, for example, the expectation to share. She also addressed the rule that specifies the father's role of mediator in disputes. After further exploring specific patterned interactions of the family, the social worker introduced the following questions to help the family to weigh whether they wish to continue relating under the old rules.

TO FATHER

- *"How effective are you in actually stopping the girls and their mother from fighting?"*
- *"What are your worst fears about what might occur in the family if you didn't play that role?'*
- *"Would you like to free yourself from the role of being the family mediator?"*

TO OTHER FAMILY MEMBERS

- *"Do you want the father to continue to be the third party in your arguments?"*
- *"What are the risks to your relationship if he discontinued playing the role of mediator?"*
- *"Do you want to work out your own disputes?"*

Questions such as these focus the attention of all members on their patterned interactions and encourage them to determine the *function* of the behavior in the system.

Next, the social worker had the major task of assisting the family to modify their rules, by teaching them new skills for resolving disagreements. The social worker also needed to coach the father in declining the role of mediator and the girls and their mother in requesting that he let them manage their own conflicts.

On-the-Spot Interventions

On-the-spot interventions are a potent way of modifying patterns of interaction by intervening immediately when metacommunications occur between couples or family members. For example, the social worker uses the technique to stop the repetitive pattern in the communications between Anna and Jackie. On-the-spot interventions are also appropriate when:

- *A client send fuzzy or abrasive messages*
- *The receiver of a message distort its meanings*
- *A receiver of a message fails to respond appropriately to important messages or feelings*
- *The occurrence of destructive interaction occurs as a result of a message.*

In implementing on-the-spot interventions, you would focus on the destructive effects of the preceding communication, labeling the type of communication so that family members can subsequently identify their own dysfunctional behavior. In using the intervention, you also need to teach and guide family members in how to engage in more effective ways of communicating.

Teaching and guiding family members toward more effective ways of communication is illustrated in the following example. The social worker intervenes in a "*blind alley*" argument, one that cannot be resolved because neither party can be proved right or wrong.

Husband: I distinctly remember telling you to buy some deodorant when you went to the store.

Wife: You just think that you did, but you didn't. I'd have remembered if you said anything about it.

Husband: No, you just didn't remember. I told you for sure, and you're shifting the blame.

Wife [with obvious irritation]: Like hell you did! You're the one who forgot to tell me, and I don't appreciate your telling me I forgot.

Social worker: Can we stop for a moment and consider what's happening between you? Each of you has a

different recollection of what happened, and there's no way of determining who's right and who's wrong. You are involved in what I call a *blind alley* argument because you can't resolve it. You just end up arguing over who's right and feeling resentful because you're convinced the other person is wrong. That doesn't help you solve your problem; it just creates conflict in your relationship. Let's go back and start over. Are you willing to allow me to show you both a more effective way of dealing with this situation?

Alternatively, after labeling and intervening in the interaction and guiding the couple to communicate constructively, you might challenge the couple (or family members) to identify their behavior and to modify it accordingly. For example, interrupt their interactions with a statement like this: "Wait a minute! Think about what you're doing just now and where it's going to lead you if you continue." In modifying patterns, the intermediate objective is for family members to recognize and decrease their counterproductive behavior, and to substitute newly gained communication skills for the harmful communication style. The ultimate goal, of course, is for family members to *eliminate* the counterproductive processes through concentrated efforts between sessions.

Guidelines for Making On-the-Spot Interventions

1. *Focus on process rather than content.* For you to be infinitely more helpful to family members, you must focus on their interaction processes rather than on the content of their conflicts. Conflicts typically are manifested over content issues, but *how* family members interact in dealing with the focal point of a conflict is far more important. As the "blind alley argument" example illustrated, the issue of who is right in a given dispute is usually trivial when compared to the destructive effects of the processes. Thus, you should usually deemphasize the topics of disputes and focus instead on helping family members to listen attentively and respectfully, to own feelings and their responsibility in problems. Ultimately, you will want to teach them how to compromise, to disengage from competitive interaction, and to engage in conflict resolution.

2. *Give feedback that is descriptive and neutral rather than general or evaluative.* As you intervene, it is important that you present feedback in a neutral manner that does not fault family members but rather allows them to pinpoint specific behaviors that produce

difficulties. Feedback that evaluates their behavior produces defensiveness; overly general feedback fails to focus on behavior that needs to be changed.

To illustrate, consider a situation in which a man glares at his wife and says, "I've had it with going to your parents' house. You spend all the time while we are there talking with your mother, and I do not feel included or welcomed in the conversation. You can go by yourself in the future." A *general and evaluative message* would take the following form:

Social worker: "Garth, that message was an example of poor communication. Try again to send a better one."

The following message is *neutral and behaviorally specific*:

Social worker: "Garth, I noticed that when you just spoke to Barbara, you glared at her and sent a *you* message that focused on what you thought she was doing wrong. I watched Barbara as you spoke, and noticed that she frowned and seemed to be angry. I'd like you to get some feedback from Barbara about how your message affected her. Barbara, would you share with Garth what you experienced as he talked?"

In the summary of what has occurred, the social worker indicates that Garth's message to Barbara was problematic, but he avoids making an evaluative judgment. Moreover, by describing specific behavior and eliciting feedback about its impact, the social worker enhances the possibility that Garth will be receptive to examining his behavior and to modifying it. Note also that this message highlights the interaction of *both* participants, as specified in the following guideline.

3. *Balance interventions to divide responsibility.* When more than one family member is involved in sessions, you must achieve a delicate balance while avoiding the appearance of singling out one person as being the sole cause of interpersonal difficulties. Otherwise, that person may feel that you and other family members are taking sides and blaming. By focusing on all relevant actors, you can distribute responsibility, model fairness, and avoid alienating one person. Moreover, although one person may contribute more to problems than others, all members of a system generally contribute to difficulties in some degree.

The following example illustrates the technique of balancing in a situation in which the husband and wife are at odds with each other over caring for their baby and the amount of time the husband spends at work:

Social worker: Both of you seem to have some feelings and concerns that are legitimate, but for some reason you seem to be stuck and unable to work things out.

[*To wife*] You resent your husband not doing his part in child care so you can go ahead with the plan you agreed to about going back to work part-time.

[*To husband*] You feel that because you are on a new job, now is not the time to ask for time off for child care.

[*To both*] I'd like to explore what the two of you can do to make things better for each other.

In this example, the social worker responds empathically to the feelings of both husband and wife, thereby validating the feelings of each. In so doing, the social worker remains neutral rather than siding with or against either of the participants. The empathic responses also soften the impact of the social worker's messages.

Here are two more guidelines for making on-the-spot interventions into dysfunctional patterns:

1. Balance interventions equally between family members in much the same way as the social worker in the previous example divided responsibility for the couple's interactions. Because diverse interactions occur among family members, you must make choices about intervening in processes until all members have had an opportunity to focus on their concerns.

2. Direct messages from family members to one another, because couples and family members need to learn to communicate effectively with each other. Your role is to facilitate effective communication between them rather than to act as an intermediary. Family members do not learn the essential skills in communicating with one another by talking through you. Therefore, you should redirect messages to the parties whom they concern. For example, use a message such as "Would you tell your son how you feel about his being in trouble with juvenile corrections, please?"

When people are angry, they may express messages that are hostile, blaming, or critical, exacerbating an already difficult situation. Before redirecting messages, therefore, you must consider the likely consequences of the ensuing interaction. As you redirect such messages, you should actively intervene to facilitate positive interaction:

- *Coach family members to own their feelings:* "I am really angry with you for getting this family involved with the police."

- *Translate complaints into requests for change:* "I wish you would stay in school and stop hanging around with the neighborhood dropouts."
- *Metacommunicate by clarifying positive intentions:* "I want you to stay in school because I want your life to be better than mine."

Of course, these messages will be more effective when speakers' nonverbal behaviors are consistent with their message. For example, unless there is a cultural imperative observed in the family, when family members are speaking they should face one another and maintain eye contact. You may need to interrupt and direct them as illustrated in the following message:

Social worker: Cassandra, please stop for just a moment. You were talking to me, not to Jamal. Will you please start again, but this time talk and look directly at him?

Assisting Clients to Disengage from Conflict

One of the most common and harmful types of interaction within families involves arguments that quickly escalate, producing anger and resentment between participants. When sustained over time, these interactions may eventually involve other family members and subsystems. More often than not, the family system becomes factionalized, and individual efforts to regain equilibrium may result in further conflict. The content issues involved are generally secondary to the fact that on a process level each participant is struggling to avoid being one-down, which would mean losing face or yielding power to the other participants.

When one person's behavior (Twanna) results in conflict within the family, a central task is to challenge this linear thinking by asking others about their roles in creating or maintaining the problem. The situation between Janet and Twanna has not reached a crisis point, but if left unresolved, it has all of the key ingredients to escalate and impact the gains that the two of them have made. To view this session with Janet, Twanna and the social worker, go to Part 2, Adolescent Parent and Foster Mother.

Although the process of disengagement is easy to learn, it is not simple to apply. Many family members have nearly always responded in a reactive competitive pattern. In many ways, Janet is competing with Twanna as the child's parent. She reasons that the child does not have tantrums with her because she is the more familiar caretaker. Janet is also sending a mixed message to Twanna. Specifically, to act as the child's parent, but if Janet does not approve, she intervenes in the situation. Note that the social worker remarked that Janet wants Twanna to take a more active parenting role, but is not quite ready to play a secondary role. She also asked Janet, "Does the baby throw tantrums with you?" as a means to highlight the conflict between the two parenting styles. Even so, the strength of their relationship had improved. For example, Janet begins the session by praising Twanna for keeping her agreement about coming home and caring for her child.

To assist family members to avoid competitive struggles, you can emphasize that everyone loses in competitive situations or arguments and that negative feelings or emotional estrangement is likely to be a result (e.g., Twanna's withdrawal, slamming the door). It is also vital to stress that safeguarding mutual respect is far more important than winning. The concept of disengaging from conflict simply means that family members avoid escalating arguments by declining to participate further. A graceful way in which people can disengage is by making a comment similar to the following: "Listen,

Ideas in Action

A call from Twanna has resulted in a second family session with the social worker. Twanna is frustrated because of the differences in the parenting styles. The primary issue is that Janet is much more permissive with the child, yet she expects Twanna to be more involved as the child's mother. Twanna tends to rely on rules of behavior when interacting with the child, for example, no candy before meals. Although Janet wants Twanna to be more involved, she is not ready to entirely give over parenting responsibility to Twanna. She also maintains that the child is not accustomed to her mother telling her what to do. When Twanna, for example, refuses to allow the child to have candy, the child "throws a temper tantrum." Janet responds immediately to the child's distress signals, maintaining that "She's just a baby." When Janet takes over, Twanna's response has been to retreat to her room, slam the door, and listen to music using a headset to drown out the noise. When asked by the social worker how she felt about the situation, Twanna responded, "Janet made her this way, so she can deal with it." She also admits that she does not know how to handle the tantrums and would like Janet to teach her.

it doesn't really matter who's right. If we argue, we just get mad at each other, and I don't want that to happen." Teaching family members to evaluate their behavior and its effects on others is another strategy: "How do the children react when the two of you are having an argument?" You can further assist family members to avoid conflict between sessions by teaching them to develop code words that signal the need to disengage or reframe their message. Sentences or questions such as "When you do … ," "How could you think … ," "Did you think … ," "I know that you won't … ," "You never … ," "Don't tell me what to do … ," and "Why did you …" are generally powerful prompts, along with labeling, that set the stage for conflict.

Negotiating tasks for applying disengagement in interactions between sessions can help family members transfer these skills to their daily lives. Of course, family members may be incapable of intervening to disengage conflict in some instances—for example, in domestic violence situations where there is a threat or the actuality of physical harm. In these situations, you can teach family members—especially children—to call for help as well as to develop a safety plan.

Conflict resolution strategies may vary based on differences in both gender and ethnicity (Mackey & O'Brien, 1998; Berg & Jaya, 1993). Being aware of these differences will assist you in choosing intervention strategies that recognize how these factors affect the family's behavior. Berg and Jaya (1993) note that in Asian families, concerns are viewed as "our problems," emphasizing the interdependence between family members. This example suggests that you should explore the family narrative regarding how conflict is managed in the family's particular culture as well as the attached meanings or feelings. By doing so, you are able to engage members in formulating an effective intervention strategy.

In fact, understanding the family narrative with respect to conflict may yield benefits with all families, irrespective of their culture or ethnicity. Each family has its own style of communicating (e.g., Jackie, "We don't make a big deal of things"; Anna, "We talk about everything"). In some families, everyone talks simultaneously and makes outrageous statements; other members may remain passive during this display. Perhaps yelling or name-calling is a norm, as are demonstrative hand gestures, apparent threats, and a hostile or belligerent tone of voice. Be sensitive to the fact that these interactions in family communication styles are not necessarily evidence of destructive relating patterns, especially if they are not your own family's style. Observing the family and

inquiring about their preferred patterns of relating will enable you to assess family members' communication styles, and avoid drawing conclusions about their functional or dysfunctional status.

Modifying Complementary Interactions

Relationships, as described by communication theorists and without attributing a value to either descriptor, are either symmetrical or complementary (Becvar & Becvar, 2000a). *Symmetrical relationships* are thought to be more of an egalitarian arrangement. In contrast, the parties in *complementary relationships* have developed an exchange as a means for avoiding conflict, resolving differences, and creating a workable relationship.

Preferences for relationship patterns may be culturally derived and are considered to reflect a practical division of roles and responsibilities. Therefore, it is important that you avoid concluding that these patterns are an issue unless the family has indicated otherwise.

Note, however, that a complementary type of relationship may prove to be a concern to one or both partners. Frustrations may stem from role overload or strain, limitations imposed by role expectations, and disagreements related to decision making. One partner may grow to resent what she or he perceives as dominance. In such a case, the relationship may become *asymmetrical*, and one person may engage in passive resistance behavior or openly challenge the other. Moreover, an individual who is weary of the exchange may devalue the other party, or disengage, ultimately resenting his or her lack of involvement. In either event, harmful interactions are likely to occur, culminating in the participants seeking professional help.

In modifying dysfunctional complementary relationships, it is important to work with couples and family members to adopt changes that will bring their relationships into balance, assuming that they have chosen this goal. As part of this work, you may assist members to develop agreements that involve reciprocal changes.

Negotiating Agreements for Reciprocal Changes

In family or couple sessions, you can facilitate changes in specific behaviors by assisting one member to develop an agreement if another person will agree to make a reciprocal change. In this kind of *quid pro quo contract*, a member agrees to disengage from conflict if the other party agrees to avoid using code words that always prompt a negative response. Individuals are receptive to making changes when other parties agree to make reciprocal changes for two reasons. First, people are more prone to give when they know they are getting something in return. Second, when all involved parties agree to make changes, no single person loses face by appearing to be the sole cause of an interactional problem.

Contracting for reciprocal changes can be a powerful means of inducing change. Another advantage of reciprocal contracting is that it counters the tendency to wait for others to initiate changes. Still another benefit is that in working on reciprocal tasks all parties become *mutually* involved in a change venture. This mutual involvement may spark collaboration in other dimensions of their relationships—an important gain where interactions have been largely dysfunctional rather than collaborative.

Family members are unlikely to be able to implement reciprocal contracts if they have not moved beyond competitive bickering and blaming one another for their problems. For this reason, we recommend deferring use of this technique (unless clients spontaneously begin to negotiate) until you have assisted them to listen attentively to one another, and to change the tone of their interactions. It is also essential that participants demonstrate a commitment to improving their relationship. As Becvar and Becvar (2000a) point out, if family members view their own or others' changes as emanating primarily from meeting the stipulations of an agreement, rather than as a way to improve their relationship, they are likely to devalue the changes. Therefore, you will want to ask family members to explicitly clarify that improving their relationship is the primary factor motivating their willingness to make changes.

The following are examples of reciprocal agreements that could have been utilized in previous examples from this chapter. You may use them as a guide in assisting families to develop their own agreements:

- *Jackie agrees to talk with her family, if Anna stops pushing and allows her to do so when she is ready.*
- *Janet will refrain from interfering with Twanna's parenting and agrees to help her strengthen her bonds her child.*
- *Cynthia and Martha will not get into an argument if the other does not keep shared items for an extended period of time.*
- *Anna agrees to communicate her feelings, if Jackie agrees to accept that there are times she is too tired to talk.*

In developing reciprocal contracts, it is wise to allow family members to make their own proposals. By so doing, they become invested in the proposed changes. Moreover, they often generate innovative and constructive ideas, based on their knowledge of their particular family, that might not occur to you. To facilitate families in making proposals, you can use a message such as the following: "It's clear that each of you is unhappy with the situation. Perhaps this is a good time for you to develop ideas about what you could do to improve the situation." You could then prompt them to think about reciprocal actions.

As you mutually consider proposals, it is important to explore potential barriers and guard against the tendency to undertake overly ambitious actions. Initial task exchanges in reciprocal agreements should be relatively simple and likely to succeed, especially when intense conflict has marked interactions. When a feasible reciprocal proposal has been agreed upon, you can assist family members to reach a further agreement that specifies the tasks each member will complete prior to the next session. In developing and planning to implement these tasks, follow the steps of the TIS (outlined in Chapter 13). As you plan task implementation with family members or couples, stress that each person must exercise *good faith* in carrying out his or her part of the contract, as illustrated in the following message:

Social worker: You have agreed to make the changes we've discussed in an effort to improve the situation for everyone. To make these changes successful, however, each of you will need to carry out your part—no matter what the other person does. Waiting for the other person to carry out his or her part first, may result in neither of you making a move by the time of our next session. Remember, failure by the other person to honor the contract is no excuse for you to do likewise. If the other person doesn't keep to the agreement, you can take satisfaction in knowing that you did your part.

Stressing the individual responsibility of all family members to fulfill their respective commitments, as in the preceding message, counters the tendency of clients to justify their inaction in subsequent sessions by asserting, "He (or she) didn't carry out his part. I knew this would happen, so I didn't do my part either." If one or more family members have not fulfilled their parts of the agreement, you can focus on obstacles that prevented them from doing so. When the results have been favorable, you can focus on this experience to set the stage for exploring additional ways of achieving further positive interaction.

Intervening with Families: Modifying Misconceptions and Distorted Perceptions

Cognitions are often the basis for erroneous beliefs that produce dissatisfaction in couple and family relationships. Left unresolved, resentment towards others can become fertile ground for repetitive dysfunctional interaction. Unrealistic expectations of others and myths are two other forms of misconceptions that contribute to interactional problems. As with rules, unrealistic expectations often are not always obvious, so you may have to clarify them by asking family members' about their expectations of one another. Myths are similar to rules in that they govern family operations by shaping beliefs and expectations that can profoundly influence interactions in couple and family relationships.

To diminish misconceptions and dispel myths, bring them out in the open, using empathy to help family members recognize their distorted perceptions. Misconceptions and myths generally protect people from having to face the reality of their cognitions and perceptions. Therefore, attempts to change them can be perceived as threatening. Seldom are they relinquished without a struggle, because introducing an alternative perspective or new information that is contrary to beliefs creates cognitive dissonance. In addition, making essential change entails resolving fears, not the least of which is risking the consequences of learning and implementing new behavior. In these instances your empathetic response to fears and ambivalence and providing emotional support can be the impetus for people to change.

To illustrate, consider a family in which an adolescent, age 17, is experiencing extreme tension and anxiety as a result of parental expectations. During family sessions, it becomes apparent that the parents expect him to be a top student so that he can become a doctor. It is also obvious that the parents embrace the generalized myth "If you try hard enough, you can become anything you want." In an effort to reduce the pressure on the son, dispel the myth as it applies to him, and modify the parents' expectations, the social worker meets separately with the parents. The following excerpt is taken from that session.

Social worker: I've been very concerned that Gary has been making an almost superhuman effort to do well in chemistry and physics but he is not doing well in these subjects. It is my impression that he feels pressured to become a doctor, and that one reason he's so anxious is that he doesn't believe that he can do better despite his best efforts. It's important to him to have you think well of him. But his is falling short even though he continues to drive himself.

Father: Poof! Of course he is working hard. Why shouldn't he? He can become a doctor if he really wants to and continues to apply himself. You know, I could have been a doctor, but what did I do? I goofed off. I don't want Gary to repeat my mistake. He should recognize that he has opportunities that neither his mother nor I had.

Social worker: I sense your concern and care for Gary. Is it your perception that he is goofing off? I understand that both of you share the belief people can do anything they want. This message has been clear to Gary, and he's blaming himself because he's not making it, no matter how hard he tries.

Mother: Don't you think anyone can succeed in anything if they try hard enough?

Social worker: Actually, this belief is inconsistent with what I know about differences between people. Each of us has different aptitudes, talents, and learning styles. Some people are able to handle types of work that require dexterity. Others are able to visualize spatial relationships. Everyone has certain aptitudes, types of intelligence, and limitations. What's important in deciding a future career is discovering what our own aptitudes are and making choices that match them. I wonder if each of you can identify talents and limitations that you have?

Observe that as the social worker addressed the family myth, he highlighted the adverse impact of the myths on Gary. This tactic switched the focus from the abstract to the concrete and provided the parents with an opportunity to review and evaluate their beliefs. The social worker then further attempted to invalidate the myth by asking them to apply it to themselves.

No doubt, you will frequently encounter families who have distorted perceptions of one another that contribute to repetitive dysfunctional interactions. Recall from Chapter 13 that labeling the behaviors of others is a common source of cognitive and perceptual distortions. Labeling is like wearing a blinder because it places people in a certain frame, thereby limiting their attributes and behaviors to fit the framed image. In effect, the frame effectively obscures other qualities, so that in dealing with an individual, a person simply has to rely on their preexisting cognitions or perceptions without having to think.

Myths that distort individual or family perceptions can extend beyond those that influence internal family dynamics. They are also linked to discrimination, bigotry, and negative schemas engrained in societal and institutional perceptions and in attitudes held about certain groups. Distortions can be so embedded that for the individual they further warrant further critique. Instead they become the generalized narrative that informs what people believe about others. For example, criticizing the intelligence or performance of children of color on standardized achievement tests; drawing conclusions about youth based on their style of dress or music preferences; insisting that immigrants act, dress, and speak in a certain way that is comfortable for mainstream society; and avoiding or having adverse reactions to people who are different by virtue of their physical attributes, sexual orientation, language, or customs. These macro-level perceptions and distortions can influence where families choose to live, how they perceive their safety, and with whom children are allowed to interact.

When you observe myths and distortions about others operating in families, you have a responsibility to address them in the same manner as you would in intervening in family dynamics, because they affect the families toward whom this behavior is directed. They are also a source of stress and strain for those who hold these beliefs, infusing negativity in their interactions. A word of caution is in order, however: In focusing on the impact of labeling, myths, and distorted perceptions, either in interfamilial or extra-familial interactions, take care to describe the process rather than label the client.

Intervening with Families: Modifying Family Alignments

All families develop patterns of affiliation between members that either enhance or impair opportunities for individual growth or the family's ability to carry out survival functions. The functional structure—that is, the family's invisible or covert set of demands or code of behavior—reflects and regulates family functioning and determines transactional patterns (Minuchin, 1974). In this section, we draw upon structural approach techniques to guide intervention strategies when family functioning is impaired by dysfunctional alignments.

According to the structural approach, well-functioning families are hierarchically organized and feature a cohesive executive parental subsystem and age-appropriate roles, responsibilities, and privileges for children. Interventions to modify alignments are generally indicated in the following circumstances:

- *Bonds are weak between spouses, other individuals who form the parental subsystem, or other family members.*
- *Enmeshed alliances—that is, rigid or overly restrictive boundaries between members—limit appropriate bonds with other members (or outsiders).*
- *Two members of a family attempt to cope with dissatisfaction or conflict in their relationship by forming a coalition with a third family member, a phenomenon known as* triangulation.
- *Family members are disengaged or alienated from one another, tending to go their own ways, with little reliance on each other for emotional support.*
- *Members of the family have formed alliances with persons outside the immediate family (e.g., friends and relatives) that interfere with performing appropriate family roles or providing appropriate emotional support to other family members.*

In intervening to modify alignments, *structural mapping* may be used to delineate family boundaries and to highlight and modify interactions and transactional patterns. Structural mapping identifies symptoms that may be exhibited by an individual family member as an expression of difficulties in the family system. The structure of the family is revealed by who talks to whom, and in what way; that is in an unfavorable or favorable position; and how intense the family's transactions are. The goal of the structural approach is to change family structures by altering boundaries and by realigning subsystems to enhance family functioning. Interventions are thus devised to achieve the following goals:

- Develop alliances, cultivate new alliances, or strengthen underdeveloped relationships. *For example, a social worker might assist a new stepfather and stepson to explore ways that they can develop a relationship or the social worker might help a parent* who has been in prison to strengthen emotional bonds to his or her children.

- Reinforce an alliance, *by acting to maintain the alliance or to amplify its scope and/or strength. For instance, a social worker might assist a single parent to increase his or her ability to operate as an effective executive subsystem (e.g., Twanna).*
- Differentiate individuals and subsystems. *For example, a social worker might help a mother who gives most of her attention to a newborn infant to understand the need for supervision of older children, and to invest some of her emotional energy in them. Also, Janet and Twanna's child are a subsystem.*
- Increase family interactions *in disengaged families to make boundaries more permeable by changing the way in which members relate to one another.*
- Help family members accommodate changing circumstances or transitions *by decreasing rigid structures or rules that are no longer viable. For example, as a child reaches adolescence, the social worker might help the parents revise their expectations of the child's behavior so as to accommodate this developmental change.*

As can be surmised from these examples, structural problems may arise when the family structure is unable to adequately adjust to changing circumstances. Changing circumstances may be the result of external environmental forces, stressful transitions or dynamics internal to the family system. Before you intervene, it is important to understand the structural change as unique to the family's situation and make clear the nature of the structural dysfunction. Thus, the family should be involved in determining whether and in what ways such changes should take place.

Your first task in this respect is to assist family members to observe the nature of their alignments. This may be accomplished by asking general questions that stimulate family members to consider their alignments:

- *"If you had a difficult problem and needed help, whom would you seek out in the family (tribe or clan)?"*
- *"Sometimes members of a family feel closer to some members than to others and may pair up or group together. Which members of your family, if any, group together?"*
- *"In most families, members argue to some extent. With whom do you argue? With whom do other members argue?"*

- *"Is there one person in the family who is considered to be a favorite?"*
- *[To parents] "When you make a decision, do you feel that your decision is supported by the other parent? Are other people involved in your decisions?"*

You can also bring alignments and coalitions to the family's attention as they are manifested in family sessions:

- *"Martha, it seems that you're the center of the family. Most of the conversation seems to be directed through you, while other family members, with the exception of Joe, appear to be observers to the discussion."*
- *"Janet, in your description of how you spend your day, it appears that the baby receives a great deal of your attention."*
- *[To Twanna] "When you are upset, who do you talk to about how you feel?"*
- *"I noticed that each of you identified the same individual on your map. Can you tell me about this person and his (or her) role in your family?"*

As family members become aware of their alignments, you can assist them in considering whether they wish to become closer to others and to identify obstacles that could prevent this movement from happening. Family alignments may, in fact, involve "complex extended patterns or configurations" (Boyd-Franklin, 1989, p. 124). Members of the various configurations may include clan or tribal members, extended kin, friends, or individuals from the family's religious or spiritual community, such as a minister, shaman, rabbi, monk, medicine person, or priest. Be mindful of the fact that any of these people (or a combination of them) may be involved in family structural arrangements. As a consequence, it may be necessary to explore relationships and alignments beyond the immediate family system.

Family sculpting is a technique used in experiential family practice models for assisting family members to analyze and observe their alliances and to make decisions concerning possible changes. This technique allows family members to communicate spatial family system relationships in a nonverbal tableau, to discern alignments, and to recognize the need to realign their relationships. A variation of this technique is to have family members portray historical and current family relationships using the Genogram.

In family sculpting, family members are instructed to use rectangles in their drawing to represent each person in the family (Nichols, 2006). Rectangles can be of any size and located anywhere on a sheet of paper. You can coach family members to position the rectangles in ways that depict relative closeness and distance among family members as well as perceptions of power. After family members have completed their drawings, you would ask participants to draw family relationships as they would *like* them to be on the other side of the paper. In a subsequent discussion, you would ask members in turn to share their drawings of existing family relationships.

The benefit of the expressive exercise is that family members can observe the nature of their alignments and the emotional closeness and distance in their relationships with others. Invite family members to comment on their observations, based on hypothetical responses from an earlier situation in the chapter:

- *"It appears that Martha and I are quite close to each other, but that Jennifer doesn't feel as close to Martha as I do."*
- *"Jennifer and I seem to have the least conflict with each other."*
- *"We all seem to be close to Grandmother Maggie."*

After each family member has an opportunity to make their observations, you can ask them to explain their second drawings, which show how they would like family relationships to be. During this discussion, you can highlight the desired changes, assist individuals to formulate goals that reflect changes they would like to make, and identify "exceptional" times—for example, when Jennifer and Martha are not in conflict with each other.

A family sculpting or structural mapping exercises can also be used with parents to strengthen parental coalitions and mark generational boundaries. For example, does one parent triangulate with a child or children, or permit them to intrude into the parental subsystem? Does the father act as a mediator in family conflicts? Does one parent have the final say? The hazard associated with this alignment is that children may become adept at playing one parent against the other. In these instances, parental divisiveness is fostered, and in consequence, relationships between the children and the "excluded" parent are strained. In the case of the mother who expends a majority of her emotional energy on a newborn, emotional bonds and loyalty between her and her other children and family members may be lacking.

Developing cohesiveness, unity, and more effective alignments is a challenge that often confronts two families who have joined together—for example, when in the development of a relationship between a new stepfather and a stepson. Because these factors are apt to be present in foster or adoptive families, your attention to alliances and cohesiveness is equally important in such cases, especially when there are biological children in the home.

In situations where two families have joined together, you can assist parents to analyze whether differences or lack of agreement about their parenting styles is a factor in parent–child alignments. Hare (1994) urges us to be mindful of the fact that in lesbian families, issues related to two families joining together and parenting styles are not dissimilar to those problems faced by heterosexual families. Strategies for strengthening parental coalitions may include negotiating "united front" agreements in parent–child transactions requiring decision making and/or disciplinary actions (unless, of course, the other partner is truly hurtful or abusive to the child). Finally, assisting families to realign themselves and forge new alliances is particularly important in instances in which there has been a disruption in the family system. For example, when a child who has been placed outside of the home is reunified with the family, or when a parent or other key members has been absent from the family's life for an extended period of time.

Summary

This chapter focused on intervention techniques and strategies that may be used to strengthen families' or couples' relationships. These strategies discussed utilized techniques from a variety of approaches, for solution-focused, task-centered and family systems. Each approach shares the view of the family as a social system, and thus the intervention strategies focus on change in the family as a social unit. To a beginning social worker, using the various techniques may appear to be a daunting challenge. You are encouraged to seek supervision and consultation in applying them. To further enhance your knowledge and skills, you can use the references cited in this chapter.

In implementing the intervention strategies discussed in this chapter, we caution you against making assumptions about what constitutes "normal" family functioning. You should examine family functioning, communication patterns, and alignments in light of each family's particular culture, race, structure, and social class. Solution-focused family practice reminds us that attempts to identify families as functional or dysfunctional are inherently flawed. Instead, in using this approach, you assist the family to envision solutions and diminish the focus on problems. Those social workers operating in a framework of social constructionist or narrative therapy also find it unproductive to characterize or label families as functional or dysfunctional, preferring instead to honor the unique story of each family. We further urge that an appraisal of family ethnicity, race, configuration and sexual orientation must be factored into any assessment and intervention strategies.

Any approach that you may utilize in intervening with families requires systematic application of techniques and strategies, ongoing monitoring, and evaluation of the results. Research as summarized by Nichols and Swartz (1998) points to positive outcomes when specific problems are treated in a systematic manner.

Chapter 13 detailed the importance of matching intervention strategies to clients' goals and the client system. This chapter amplified this point, as well as pointing out the need for matching the intervention with the specific problem, developmental stages, and ethnocultural factors, taking into account internal family functioning and the external factors that may influence the family system.

Skill Development Exercises

1. Identify some examples of verbal or nonverbal metacommunications that you have used.
2. Describe how an unspoken rule in your family governs the behavior of family members.
3. From your observation of the session with Anna and Jackie ("Home for the Holidays"), describe how the social worker uses the technique of on-the spot intervention.
4. List three societal beliefs, and reflect upon how these beliefs may affect the families that you work with.
5. Choose several classmates to role-play a family situation. Acting as the social worker, facilitate the *joining* stage in the initial contact session.
6. Using the same family situation, identify the needs and wants expressed by each family member. What questions would you ask to help members identify their concerns?
7. In a family session in which one member is identified as being the problem, how would you proceed with the family?

Related Online Content

Visit the *Direct Social Work Practice* companion Web site at www.cengage.com/social_work/hepworth for additional learning tools such as glossary terms, chapter outlines, relevant Web links, and chapter practice quizzes.

CHAPTER 16

Intervening in Social Work Groups

CHAPTER OVERVIEW

This chapter builds on the skills introduced in Chapter 11 for forming and composing task, treatment, and support groups. This chapter addresses the stages of group development and skills needed to intervene effectively throughout group processes. At the completion of it you will:

- Be familiar with the phases through which groups progress and the features of each stage

- Understand the skills and knowledge needed to effectively intervene at each stage

- Observe the ways that these concepts reveal themselves in the dialogue of the HEART group

- Understand common worker errors at different phases of group process

- Be familiar with emerging issues in group work

- Understand how concepts on group interventions apply to task groups.

In any group with social work goals, it is the task of the leader to intervene so that the group can achieve those goals. In treatment groups, the leader's role is particularly complex, requiring in-depth, balanced interventions to assist the growth of both individuals and the group as a whole. To add to the complexity of this role, the leader must be astute in sorting through the maze of multilevel communication to bring meaning to the group's experience, to shape the group's therapeutic character, and to provide direction and focus to the group's processes at critical moments. Finally, the leader must formulate all interventions within the context of the stages of development through which a group progresses to reach full maturity. Similarly, in a task group, the leader plays a variety of facilitative roles in assisting the group to meet its objectives. This chapter focuses primarily on treatment groups, but provides additional content on task groups in the final section.

Because the leader's interventions are inextricably related to the group's stage of development, we begin at that point.

Stages of Group Development

All groups go through natural stages of development, although the pace and complexity of each stage may vary. Your understanding of these stages is essential in anticipating and addressing the behaviors that characterize each phase, so that the group's objectives can ultimately be met. You are also responsible for removing obstacles that threaten to derail the group's development and hinder the success of individual members. In doing so, you must make strategic, informed choices regarding your input and actions across the lifespan of the group.

Without knowledge of the group's stage of development, you may be prone to making errors, such as expecting group members to begin in-depth explorations in initial sessions or concluding that you have failed if the group exhibits the discord that is typical of early development. Leaders may also overlook positive behaviors that indicate that the group is approaching a more mature stage of development, or they may fail to intervene at critical periods to assist the group's evolution (for example, encouraging them to "stay on task," to "count in" all members in decision making, to foster free expression of feelings, or to adopt many other behaviors that are hallmarks of a seasoned group).

Various models of group development offer frameworks for organizing your observations about the group and its characteristics, themes, and behaviors. All of these models identify progressive steps in group development, although they may organize these steps into four, five, or even six stages. Some theorists have noted variations in group stages based on the gender of group members. For example, Schiller (1997) has noted that groups composed of women may emphasize intimacy for a longer period and come to power and control later in the group's history. Berman-Rossi and Kelly (2000) suggest that stages of group development are influenced by variables such as attendance patterns, worker skills, group content, gender and other member characteristics. Open-ended groups and those with turbulent changes in membership may not move through these phases in a linear fashion and may require more time at formative stages if cohesion is slow to develop (Galinsky & Schopler, 1989). In this chapter, we will use the classic model developed by Garland, Jones, and Kolodny (1965), which delineates five stages:[1]

1. Preaffiliation
2. Power and control
3. Intimacy
4. Differentiation
5. Separation

Stage 1. Preaffiliation: Approach and Avoidance Behavior

As anyone who has ever experienced the first day of a new class can attest, the initial stage of group development is characterized by members exhibiting *approach/avoidance* behavior. Apprehensions about becoming involved in the group are reflected in members' reluctance to volunteer answers to questions, to interact with others, and to support program activities and events. Hesitancy to participate is also shown by silence or tentative speech, as when members are occupied by their own problems and the feelings of uneasiness and apprehension that emanate from their first encounter with the group. Often fearful and suspicious, members may be sensitive to the responses of others, fearing possible domination, aggression, isolation, rejection, and hostility.

At this *forming* stage (Tuckman, 1963), participant behavior is wary, sometimes even provocative, as members assess possible social threats and attempt to discern the kinds of behaviors the group wants and expects. Members also tend to identify one another in terms of each individual's status and roles and to engage in social rituals, stereotyped introductions, and detailed intellectual discussions rather than in-depth or highly revealing conversation (Berman-Rossi & Kelly, 2000). They may be uncertain about the group's purpose and the benefits it may bring to them.

At times, members may employ testing behaviors to "size up" other members, to test the group's limits, to

find out how competent the leader is, and to determine to what extent the leader will safeguard the rights of members and protect them from feared hurt and humiliation. Members may also move tentatively toward the group as they seek to find common ground with other members, search for viable roles, and seek approval, acceptance, and respect. Much of the initial communication in the group is directed toward the leader, and some members may openly demand that the social worker pursue a "take charge" approach, making decisions regarding group issues and structure and issuing prompt directives to control the behavior of members.

Preaffiliation in the HEART Group

The HEART group, introduced in Chapter 11, is designed to assist teen girls who have overweight. In this chapter, trascripts from the group are used to illustrate client statements and worker responses that are indicative of various phases of the group process.

Dave: Thank you to everyone for sharing your progress from last week. I would like to do this at the beginning of each session because I think it helps to bring us together and to create a space where you feel safe and energized to share and give each other support. I'm wondering if, based on how things went today, anybody has other ideas of how to make this opening ritual go better for them? Does anybody have any ideas about making improvements to what we're doing? Or can you tell me how it went for you today?

Amelia: Well, I think that check-in kinda depends on what your mood is. Like, I'm in a kind of okay mood today so my check-in is more positive, but like, Liz is kinda being bitchy, you know? And so maybe she's really had a bad day or whatever. So I think to have something that everybody does instead of just a check-in, I don't know, it's just really different for everybody, depending on how you're feeling.

Dave: How you're going to interact in group, depends on how you're doing on that day.

Amelia: Yeah.

Dave: You know something I heard you say, Amelia, was that you felt that Liz was "bitchy," to use your word, and I want to check in with Liz to see how she received that, or how she heard that. So I'm wondering Liz, when Amelia said that, what came to mind?

Liz: It hurts my feelings because I thought people were talking about me all the time anyway, and then I come to this place, where everybody is supposed to be happy, and like me, and you call me bitchy. I think *that's* bitchy.

Amelia: Sorry.

Dave: Amelia, I think what you were saying was that during her introduction you heard that Liz was having a bad day. How does that sound?

Amelia: Yeah.

June: She didn't say you were a bitch, she said bitch-*y*, like kinda. I don't think she meant it in a mean way.

Liz: Well, that's how I took it, so I think that matters more than what you think you heard.

Dave: And June I would actually agree with Liz on that point. How someone hears what you're saying, matters as much as, or maybe more than, what you meant to say. One of the benefits of participating in group is having experiences like these to learn about how other people perceive you.

Stage 2. Power and Control: A Time of Transition

The first stage of group development merges imperceptibly into the second stage as members, having determined that the group experience is potentially safe and rewarding and worth the preliminary emotional investment, shift their concerns to matters related to autonomy, power, and control. The frame of reference for this *storming* (Tuckman, 1963) stage is that of *transition*—that is, members must endure the ambiguity and turmoil of change from a non-intimate to an intimate system of relationships while they try to increase the understandability and predictability.

After dealing with the struggle of whether they "belong" in the group, members now become occupied with how they "rank" in relation to other members. Turning to others like themselves for support and protection, members create subgroups and a hierarchy of statuses, or social "pecking order" (Yalom, 1995). Gradually, the processes of the group become stylized as various factions emerge and relationships solidify. Conflicts between opposing subgroups often occur in this stage, and members may team up to express anger toward the leader, other authority figures, or outsiders. Failed competition for favored status with the social worker may also produce hostility toward the group leader (Yalom, 1995).

Disenchantment with the group may reveal itself through hostility, withdrawal, or confusion about the group's purposes. Verbal abuse, attacks, and rejection of lower-status members may occur as well, and isolated members of the group who do not have the protection of a subgroup may stop attending. Attrition in membership may also occur if individuals find outside pursuits more attractive than the conflicted group experience. In fact, this depleted membership may put the group's very survival in jeopardy.

Power and Control in the HEART Group

June: You know Dave, I don't mean to be disrespectful, and I think this is a good discussion, but I just wonder, are we the first group you've done?

Dave: I've done a few others.

Maggie: With girls?

Dave: A few with girls.

Maggie: Like our age?

Dave: Some.

June: Like, fat?

Dave: Well, I've worked with adults and teenagers with overweight. I'm curious, June, why do you ask?

June: Because you're the only skinny person here. And you're the only boy.

Amelia: Mmhmm.

June: See now nobody else dares to say anything.

Liz: Don't you think that maybe if he's skinny, maybe he can teach us some things?

Maggie: Yeah, but what does he know about what we're going through?

June: I mean, he knows boys.

Amelia: He's probably always been thin. He has no idea probably, you probably have no idea, what we've been through.

Dave: I'm hearing you say that you don't believe I can identify with you.

Amelia: Well, you're a boy, you're skinny, I'm a girl, and I'm fat.

June: And he's older.

Amelia: Yeah.

Amber: And he's probably always had girlfriends, I've never had a boyfriend.

Amelia: Do you have a girlfriend now?

Dave: I'd rather not answer that question.

Maggie: Why? We talk about our boyfriends and friends, I mean we're telling you stuff.

Dave: Actually, I think, you're also telling each other stuff, and the group is about you…

Amelia: And you.

Dave: My role here is to help the group along, and if I take up time with my relationships…

Amelia: So you have one.

Dave: As I said, I'd rather not address it Amelia, but if I take up time with my business then it robs the group…

June [*to Amelia*]: I mean he can't be your boyfriend if he's your worker. [*taunting*]

Dave: No, I can't date anyone in the group.

Amelia: I don't want to date you, oh my god!

Maggie: Sure…

Amelia: Don't even, you're so full of yourself! I like girls anyway.

Dave: The other thing I want to say is that I can learn from you and follow your concerns, solutions, and your strategies for dealing with some of the things that you're up against right now. I hope that in my role as facilitator I can help all of you to help yourselves and even though I'm neither overweight nor a girl.

Stage 3. Intimacy: Developing a Familial Frame of Reference

Having clarified and resolved many of the issues related to personal autonomy, initiative, and power, the group moves from the "pre-intimate" power and control stage to that of intimacy. As the group enters this *norming* (Tuckman, 1963) stage, conflicts fade, personal involvement between members intensifies, and members display a growing recognition of the significance of the group experience. Members also experience an increase in morale and "we-ness," a deepening commitment to the group's purpose, and heightened motivation to carry out plans and tasks that support the group's objectives. Mutual trust increases as members begin to

acknowledge one another's uniqueness, spontaneously disclose feelings and problems, and seek the opinion of the group. To achieve this desired intimacy, however, group participants may suppress negative feelings that could produce conflict between themselves and others. In contrast to earlier sessions, they express genuine concern for absent members and may reach out to invite them to return to the group.

During this stage of development, a group "character" emerges as the group evolves its own culture, style, and values. Clear norms are established, based on personal interests, affection, and other positive forces. Roles also take shape as members find ways to contribute to the group and leadership patterns become firmly settled. The frame of reference for members is a familial one, as members liken their group experience to their experience with their own nuclear families, occasionally referring to other members as siblings or to the leader as the "mother" or "father" of the group.

How groups experience this stage depends on factors such as how regularly members attend group sessions, whether the group is open or closed, and how much member turnover occurs (Berman-Rossi & Kelly, 2000; Galinsky & Schopler, 1989). In groups that endure frequent transitions, it is important to develop rituals to help the members achieve a sense of cohesion so that they can move successfully to later stages.

Intimacy in the HEART Group

Amber: I was kind of down the other day. I went to the Fairmont Mall with my friends, and we were going to all the good stores like Abercrombie & Fitch, and Hollister, and American Eagle, that's one of my favorites…

June: And Bebe.

Amber: Yeah, and uh, all my friends were trying on the clothes, and I can't fit into any of the clothes there, but I really want to because they're really cute clothes. It makes me feel kind of out of the loop with my friends; do you guys have that problem too?

Amelia: Totally.

Amber: I can't shop at the same stores my friends shop at.

June: Yeah, I just mostly end up wearing sweats and T-shirts, you know, because…but you can't wear that everywhere.

Amber: Uh-huh.

Liz: Sometime I feel like I lost my friends because they all wear those cute outfits and they all share clothes and I couldn't relate anymore so we quit hanging out.

June: The peasant ones make you look pregnant if they come right under your boobs…

Dave: Amber, one of the things I want to ask you is what kind of feedback or what kind of support would you like right now?

Amber: I guess I just want to see if there are people in this group that felt that way sometimes, like if they didn't fit in with their friends sometimes that way.

Dave: Does anybody else have a similar experience as Amber does?

Amelia: I do. Yeah, like, I feel like when I go shopping with my mom I can try on the clothes that really fit me, but if I'm with my friends I have to stay on the rack that they're on. I'm taller than most of them, and I'm fat, and they're like super skinny. So when they try on clothes, I feel like I need to choose clothes from that rack too. So then, I don't know, I can't believe I'm saying this, but like, I'll buy the clothes and, you know, pretend that they fit, and then make my mom take them back. So, I hear ya.

June: Like last summer when I lost five pounds I thought, "I can get into those jeans," and then my friends said I was muffin-top 'cuz like my fat was hanging over.

Maggie: Your friends said that to you?

June: Well, you know, other kids in the band and stuff. And, well, I don't think they're trying to be mean they just, you know, maybe the jeans didn't look as good as I thought…

Dave: This is a difficulty and a concern for many of you. When you're at school or with your friends, you want to look your best, and you want to fit in.

Amber: I feel left out, um, before softball practice and games when we have to change in the locker rooms, sometimes I take my uniform into the bathroom stall; all the other girls change out in the locker room openly and I just don't feel that comfortable doing that.

June: Do they pick on you, like give you a flab grab or anything?

Amber: No, they're pretty nice, um, I just always feel like they're looking at me.

Amelia: Like you know you're different.

Amber: Yeah.

June: Are you the biggest person on the team?

Amber: Yeah.

Amelia: But you're pretty muscular.

Amber: Thanks.

Amelia: You're welcome.

Stage 4. Differentiation: Developing Group Identity and an Internal Frame of Reference

The fourth stage of group development is marked by cohesion and harmony as members come to terms with intimacy and make choices to draw closer to others in the group. In this *performing* stage (Tuckman, 1963), group-centered operations are achieved and a dynamic balance between individual and group needs evolves. Members, who participate in different and complementary ways, experience greater freedom of personal expression and come to feel genuinely accepted and valued as their feelings and ideas are validated by other members of the group. Gradually, the group becomes a mutual-aid system in which members spontaneously give emotional support in proportion to the needs of each individual.

In experiencing this newfound freedom and intimacy, members begin to perceive the group experience as unique. Indeed, as the group creates its own mores and structure, in a sense it becomes its own frame of reference. Customs and traditional ways of operating emerge, and the group may adopt a "club" name or insignia that reflects its purpose. The group's energy is channeled into working toward purposes and carrying out tasks that are clearly understood and accepted. New roles—more flexible and functional than those originally envisioned—are developed to support the group's activity, and organizational structures (e.g., officers, dues, attendance expectations, rules) may evolve. Status hierarchies also tend to be less rigid, and members may assume leadership roles spontaneously as the need for particular expertise or abilities arises.

By the time the group reaches the differentiation stage, members have accumulated experience in "working through problems" and have gained skill in analyzing their own feelings and the feelings of others, in communicating their needs and positions effectively, in offering support to others, and in grasping the complex interrelationships that have developed in the group. Having become conscious about the group's operations, members bring conflict out into the open and identify obstacles that impede their progress. All decisions are ultimately the unanimous response of the group and are strictly respected. Disagreements are not suppressed or overridden by premature group action; instead, the group carefully considers the positions of any dissenters and attempts to resolve differences and to achieve consensus among members. New entrants serve as catalysts and may express their amazement at the insight shared by veteran members, who in turn become increasingly convinced of the group experience's value.

Members may now publicize their group meetings among peers, whereas previously membership in the group may have been linked with secret feelings of shame. Secure in their roles and relationships within the group, members may become interested in meeting with other groups or in bringing in outside culture.

Differentiation in the HEART Group

Amber: So you gonna ask him?

Maggie: Ask him what?

June: Like is he just being a user. Using you.

Maggie: You know sometimes, I think he was just curious about stuff and that's sometimes why we maybe hooked up, you know? So maybe he was using me.

Jen: Well, what are you going to do the next time he tries to hook up with you?

Maggie: Smack him. I mean, not really! But I would say no. I'm not gonna…I don't know, maybe I will, 'cuz it's not all that bad. Awkward! Sorry, Dave. It's not all that bad when it happens.

June: I wouldn't know.

Liz: Nah, me neither.

Maggie: Maybe that's all I'm going to get, I don't know.

Dave: All you're going to get as far as the relationship with him, or…

Maggie: With him, or others; if all guys think like that, I should maybe just take what's there.

Amber: That's all I've gotten.

June: Like guys who only want to be with you in private and not in public?

Maggie: That's the guy, that's him!

June: Well, that sucks!

Maggie: It does.

Dave: So, does that sound like something that you want to have in your lives?

June: I don't think so. I mean I'm not in the situation, but if a guy's only going to want to be with me when no one else is around, then he doesn't really value me and he's just using me.

Stage 5. Separation: Breaking Away

During the last, *adjourning*, phase of group development, members begin to separate, loosening the intense bonds often established with other members and with the leader, and searching for new resources and ties to satisfy their needs. Group members are likely to experience a broad range of feelings about leaving the group. Indeed, the approach of group termination may set off a number of reactions, the diversity of which is reminiscent of the approach/avoidance maneuvers displayed in stage 1. Members may again feel anxiety, this time in relation to moving apart and breaking bonds that have been formed. There may be outbursts of anger against the leader and other members at the thought of the group ending, the reappearance of quarrels that were previously settled, and increased dependence on the leader. Denial of the positive meaning of the group experience is not uncommon. These separation reactions may appear in flashes or clusters as members attempt to reconcile their positive feelings about the group with feelings of abandonment, rejection, or apprehension over the group's ending.

As we will discuss further in Chapter 19, termination is also a time of evaluation, of contemplation of the work achieved, and of consolidation of learning. It is a time of finishing unfinished business, of getting and giving focused feedback, and of savoring the good times and the close relationships gained in the group.[2] Members, who have often begun to pull back their group investments and to put more energy into outside interests, speak of their fears, hopes, and concerns about the future and about one another. There is often discussion of how to apply what has been learned in the group to other situations and talk of reunions or follow-up meetings (Toseland & Rivas, 2009).

The Leader's Role in the Stages of Group Development

As suggested earlier, the role of the leader shifts and changes with the evolution of the group. Referring to earlier work by Lang (1972), Henry (1992) conceptualizes the leader as enacting certain roles and occupying different locations throughout the group's lifespan. The shifting *role* of leader exists along a continuum that ranges from primary to variable to facilitative, depending on the needs, capacities, and characteristics of the group's membership and its stage of development. Likewise, the leader occupies a *location* in the group that may be cast along a continuum ranging from central to pivotal to peripheral, depending again on the same variables. Research on damaging experiences in therapeutic groups indicates that group leaders' behaviors (e.g., confrontation, monopolizing, criticizing) or inaction (e.g., lack of support, lack of structure) play a primary role in group casualties or dropouts (Smokowski, Rose, & Bacallao, 2001).

The leader's role—a primary one at the outset of the group—is to select candidates for the group. Likewise, the leader is in a central location at this phase of group development, in that he or she recruits members and determines the group's purpose, structure, location, and duration. The leader retains this primacy and centrality before the group convenes, as he or she brings structure to the group, plans its content and function, conducts pre-group interviews, and negotiates reciprocal contracts with each prospective member. This set of role and location conditions prevails throughout the beginning phase of the group. During this stage, the leader initiates and directs group discussion, encourages participation, and begins blending the individual contracts with members into a mutual group contract.

As the group evolves to a new level of connectedness, the leader intentionally takes a variable role and occupies a pivotal location with respect to the group. According to Henry (1992):

> As the worker steps back from the central location and primary role, the members begin to supplant some of what the worker has been doing. In the vernacular of cinematography, the worker fades out as the group system comes up. However, because the group's (internal and external) systems are not yet stabilized at full functioning capacity, the worker needs to let the process run at its own speed and sometimes needs to move back in to help keep the system afloat. This is

> why the worker's role is referred to as variable, and the worker's location as pivotal. This role and location will be part of the mutual contract that is being negotiated at this time. (p. 34)

Henry notes that the leader's variable role and pivotal location continue in the group during the conflict/disequilibrium stage (stage 2, "power and control," in Garland, Jones, and Kolodny's terminology). When the group enters its maintenance or working phase (stages 3 and 4, "intimacy" and "differentiation"), the leader assumes a facilitative role and occupies a peripheral location. Inasmuch as the group has achieved full capacity to govern itself, the leader fulfills a resource role rather than assuming a primary role.

As the group moves into its separation or termination phase (stage 5), the leader once again returns to a primary role and central location to support the divesting of members, who are launching their own independent courses. In this role the leader aids the group in working through any regression to earlier stages of development and assures the successful ending of the group.

Table 16-1 illustrates the evolution of the leader's focus as a group advances through the various stages of development. Information contained in the table comes from a variety of sources, including Garland, Jones, and Kolodny (1965), Rose (1989), Henry (1992), and Corey and Corey (1992).

Intervention into Structural Elements of a Group

The primacy of the leader's role and the centrality of the leader's location are related at one level to the ability of members to assume responsibility for the group's treatment functions. At another level, these leader positions are related to the relative need to intervene to shape the group's therapeutic character, thereby creating a vehicle for members' change. In that respect, across the various stages of group development, the leader pays particular attention to shaping the following group elements:

- *Cohesion*
- *Normative structure*
- *Role structure*
- *Subgroup structure*
- *Leadership structure*

In fact, the evolution of these structures over time encompasses the phenomenon of group development

TABLE-16-1 STAGES, DYNAMICS, AND LEADER FOCUS

STAGE	DYNAMICS	LEADER FOCUS
Preaffiliation	Arm's-length exploration	Observes and assesses
	Approach/avoidance	Clarifies group objectives
	Issues of trust, preliminary commitment	Establishes group guidelines
	Intellectualization of problems	Encourages development of personal goals
	Interaction based on superficial attributes or experiences	Clarifies aspirations and expectations of members
	Protection of self; low-risk behavior	Encourages discussion of fears, ambivalence
	Milling around	Gently invites trust
	Sizing up of leader and other members	Gives support; allows distance
	Formulation of individual and group goals	Facilitates exploration
	Leader viewed as responsible for group	Provides group structure
	Member evaluation as to whether group is safe and meets needs	Contracts for help-seeking, help-giving roles
		Facilitates linkages among members
	Fear of self-disclosure, rejection	Models careful listening
	Uncertainty regarding group purpose	Focuses on resistance
	Little commitment to goals or group	Assures opportunities for participation
Power and control	Rebellion; power struggles	Protects safety of individuals and property
	Political alignments forged to increase power	Clarifies power struggle
	Issues of status, ranking, and influence	Turns issues back to group
	Complaints regarding group structure, process	Encourages expression and acceptance of differences
	Challenges to leader's roles	Facilitates clear, direct, nonabrasive communication
	Emergence of informal leadership, factional leaders	
	Individual autonomy; everybody for himself/herself	Examines nonproductive group processes
	Dysfunctional group roles	Examines cognitive distortions
	Normative and membership crisis; drop-out danger high	Facilitates member evaluation of dissident subgroups
	Testing of leader; other group members	Holds group accountable for decision by consensus
	Dependence on leader	
	Group experimentation in managing own affairs	Clarifies that conflict, power struggles are normal
	Program breakdown at times; low planning	Encourages norms consistent with therapeutic group
	Feedback highly critical	Consistently acknowledges strengths, accomplishments
		Nondefensively deals with challenges to leadership
		Focuses on the "here and now"
Intimacy	Intensified personal involvement	Encourages leadership
	Sharing of self, materials	Assumes flexible role as group vacillates
	Striving to meet others' needs	Aids sharper focus on individual goals
	Awareness of significance of the group experience	Encourages deeper-level exploration, feedback
	Personality growth and change	Encourages acknowledgment, support of differences
	Mutual revelation, risk taking	Guides work of group
	Beginning commitment to decision by consensus	Encourages experimentation with different roles
	Beginning work on cognitive restructuring	Encourages use of new skills inside and outside group
	Importance of goals verbalized	
		Assists members to assume responsibility for change

TABLE-16-1 (Continued)

	Growing ability to govern group independently	Gives consistent feedback regarding successes
	Dissipation of emotional turmoil	Reduces own activity
	Member initiation of topics	
	Constructive feedback	
Differentiation	Here-and-now focus	Emphasizes achievement of goals, exchange of skills
	High level of trust, cohesion	Supports group's self-governance
	Free expression of feelings	Promotes behaviors that increase cohesion
	Mutual aid	Provides balance between support, confrontation
	Full acceptance of differences	Encourages conversion of insight into action
	Group viewed as unique	Interprets; explores common themes
	Clarity of group purpose	Universalizes themes
	Feelings of security; belonging; "we" spirit	Encourages deeper-level exploration of problems
	Differentiated roles	Assures review of goals, task completion
	Group self-directed	Stimulates individual and group growth
	Intensive work on cognitions	Supports application of new behaviors outside group
	Goal-oriented behaviour	
	Work outside of group to achieve personal goals	
	Members feel empowered	
	Communication open, spontaneous	
	Self-confrontation	
Separation	Review and evaluation	Prepares for letting go
	Development of outlets outside group	Facilitates evaluation and feelings about termination
	Stabilizing and generalizing	Reviews individual and group progress
	Projecting toward future	Redirects energy of individuals away from group and toward self process
	Recognition of personal, interpersonal growth	Enables individuals to disconnect
	Sadness and anxiety over reality of separation	Encourages resolution of unfinished business
	Expression of fears, hopes, and others' anxiety for self	Reinforces changes made by individuals
	Some denial, regression	Administers evaluation instruments
	Moving apart, distancing	
	Less intense interaction	
	Plans as to how to continue progress outside group	
	Talk of reunions, follow-up	

(Rose, 1989; Yalom, 1995). Because of their importance, these elements are considered successively in the sections that follow.

Fostering Cohesion

Cohesion plays a central role in group success, and leaders play a key role in developing this positive force. The leader forges connections among group members and tries to expand the interpersonal networks of subgroup members, so that they relate to other people outside their subgroup. Further, the leader encourages cohesive behaviors by "pointing out who is present and who is absent, by making reference to 'we' and 'us' and 'our,' and by including the groups as a whole in his or her remarks in group sessions" (Henry, 1992, p. 167).

Leaders also encourage the development of cohesion by commenting on and reinforcing positive group-building behaviors as they occur. Henry (1992) identifies signs of cohesiveness that leaders might highlight. For example, attraction to the group is indicated when participants inquire about missing members, return to the group after absences or conflicts, take others' opinions into account in decision making, and seek increased responsibility for the group's operations. Although these indicators of cohesion are earmarks of advanced stages of group development, they may also make fleeting appearances early in a group, and should be explicitly acknowledged when they do.

Leaders also increase the attractiveness and cohesion in groups by facilitating high levels of interaction; by aiding members to successfully achieve goals, fulfill expectations, and meet needs; and by providing opportunities for prestige and access to rewards and resources that individual members alone could not obtain (Toseland & Rivas, 2009).

Ironically, these efforts at developing cohesion may be reversed during the termination phase:

Members must be helped to become less attracted to the group and, when appropriate, more attracted to alternative relationships. The worker, therefore, also reverses the application of principles for attaining group cohesion. For example, instead of increasing the frequency with which members have contact with one another, this may be reduced by having meetings less often and/or for a shorter time. … The worker may place less emphasis on resolving conflicts within the group and may not call attention to commonalities of experiences or attitudes except as those relate to ways of coping with termination. This may not be true in group psychotherapy, when this type of process is maintained until the very end. (Garvin, 1987, p. 222)

Addressing Group Norms

Chapter 11 introduced strategies to facilitate the development of constructive group norms. However, counterproductive norms may also emerge. For example, the group may split into several self-serving factions or subgroups that compete for control. Members may develop a habit of socializing rather than focusing on legitimate group tasks. Some participants may repeatedly cast others as scapegoats, harassing those members and blaming them for various group ills. In these and countless other ways, groups may develop negative behaviors that undermine their ability to coalesce and aid each other in reaching their goals.

As described in Chapter 11, leaders must observe evolving group behavior and determine whether these emerging patterns undermine or support the group's purposes. Once leaders have determined the impact of emerging patterns, they may then intervene to nurture functional group

behaviors and to assist participants to modify behaviors that are destructive to individuals or to the group.

The facilitator sets the stage for a therapeutic atmosphere and a "working group" by establishing an explicit contract with members in initial sessions that includes normative guideposts for the group. Along the way, the leader helps the group identify and articulate norms they wish the group to follow. Once decided, the guidelines should be recorded and revisited regularly, and the leader should take an active role in helping members consistently adhere to them. Some groups will even list them on a board that is posted in the meeting room, or on a laminated page for members' workbooks. Sample guidelines follow:

- *Make group decisions by consensus.*
- *Personalize communications by using "I statements" (e.g., "I (think) (feel) (want)…").*
- *Keep the group's focus on its task and mission.*
- *Keep discussions focused primarily on the present or future rather than the past.*
- *Avoid "gossiping."*
- *Share the "airtime" so all members can participate.*
- *Take responsibility for concerns about how the group is going by bringing them to others' attention.*

Norm Setting in the HEART Group

Dave: June, to come back to a point that you mentioned before, there is a guideline that I like, which is to encourage people to participate. Because a good group is one where everyone contributes and so I wonder the best way to say that—do the best you can, or…

June: Don't talk twice till everybody's talked once?

Dave: Well, I…

Liz: I disagree.

June: I'm just putting it out there. I don't know.

Dave: Liz, let's hear why you disagree.

Liz: Sometimes I'm just not in … I just don't want to contribute, I don't feel like talking.

Dave: And it might be too structured, then June, to say to Liz "we've all talked once and now you have to go." It might make the group unsafe for Liz, for the rule to be so measured out like that.

June: So I don't know what the rule should be.

Amelia: How about we all, like, try our best to actively participate.

Maggie: But don't call me out.

Jen: And actively participate doesn't necessarily mean talking, just paying attention.

Dave: That's a good point, Jen.

June: No sleeping in the group.

Maggie: Yeah, stay awake.

Amelia: If I'm talking about, like, pouring out my soul, and you're over there, like clearly thinking about something else or doodling or, you know, thinking about whatever, like, it shows on your face. You know what I mean guys?

Dave: And that's probably covered by one of the rules we already mentioned, which is "Be respectful." So "no sleeping" June, I think, comes under be respectful.

June: Okay.

Dave: And, Amelia, I like the idea of encouraging participation—what did you say? "Try as hard as we can … Do our best"?

Amelia: Do our best to participate actively.

Dave: How does everybody feel about that? [Agreement].

In addition to generating structural guidelines that pave the way for the adoption of therapeutic norms, leaders may aid members in adopting the following personal guidelines, adapted from Corey and Corey (2002):

- *Help establish trust. Initiate discussions of personal issues rather than waiting for someone else to make the first move.*
- *Express persistent feelings. Rather than bury feelings of boredom, anger, or disappointment, share your feelings about the group process.*
- *Decide how much to disclose. You are in charge of what, how much, and when you share personal issues.*
- *Be an active participant, not an observer. Share reactions to what others are saying in the group rather than remaining an unknown entity and thus a possible object of others' flawed observations.*
- *Listen closely and discriminately. Do not accept others' feedback wholesale or reject it outright, but decide for yourself what does and does not apply to you.*
- *Pay attention to consistent feedback. If a message has been received from a variety of sources, it may be valid.*
- *Focus on self. Talk about your role in problems; avoid blaming and focusing on extraneous situations or people outside of the group.*

The leader often intervenes to remind people of these individual-level norms or to point out when they are being violated. In established groups, members will also speak up to hold one another accountable. Ultimately, eventually, the locus of control for enforcing individual and group norms should reside with the members rather than with the leader (Carrell, 2000).

Intervening with Members' Roles

Roles are closely related to norms, as Toseland and Rivas (2009) explain:

> *Whereas norms are shared expectations held, to some extent, by everyone in the group, roles are shared expectations about the functions of individuals in the group. Unlike norms, which define behavior in a wide range of situations, roles define behavior in relation to a specific function or task that the group member is expected to perform.* (p. 68)

Within the group, roles include formal positions (e.g., chairperson or secretary) and informal positions created through group interactions (e.g., mediator, clown, rebel, initiator, or scapegoat). Like norms, roles may help fulfill group functions or meet individual treatment aims. Leaders must be attuned to the development of countertherapeutic roles and address them as they arise. For example, a member who avoids conflict or intimacy might make jokes to keep discussion at a superficial level, or a member who struggles to be taken seriously may make distracting or ridiculous comments, thereby reinforcing this destructive role. Yalom discusses the effect of "the monopolist" (1995, p. 369), who, perhaps due to anxiety, talks excessively, taking up airtime and turning the group mood into one of frustration.

The key when facing counterproductive roles is to encourage members to be self-observant, assure that they do not become locked into dysfunctional roles, and empower other participants to confront the member about the role and its impact. As Garvin notes:

> *The "clown" may wish to behave more seriously, the "mediator" to take sides, and passive people to function assertively. The worker, being cognizant of roles that are created out of group interactions, will attend to those that impede either the attainment of individual goals or the creation of an effective group.* (1986, p. 112)

Dysfunctional role performance is a critical choice point for intervention. One means of intervening is to use a technique developed by Garvin (1986) to identify informal roles occupied by group participants. Leaders administer a questionnaire asking members to "vote" on who (if anyone) fulfills group roles such as referee, expert, humorist, nurturer, spokesperson, and "devil's advocate." The discussion that results from this exercise can powerfully influence both members' awareness and the group process. Another technique is to simply describe a specific role that a member seems to have assumed and to ask that member for observations regarding the accuracy of that assessment. Preface this observation by asking the member if he or she would like group feedback. Doing so reduces defensiveness and gives the member appropriate control over the situation.

Another aspect of role performance involves aiding members in role attainment—that is, enabling them to fulfill the requirements of roles that they aspire to or are already in, such as student, parent, leader, spouse, employee, friend, or retired person. In doing so, the leader helps members assess their own interactions, practice the skills needed for their roles, and apply new ways of approaching and enacting those roles. Groups can assist members in these tasks through role-playing, through giving feedback, and through sharing personal examples. Some groups may be designed to specifically address the development of social skills (LeCroy, 2002). Chapter 13 offers further examples of change through behavioral rehearsal and skill development.

Addressing Subgroups

Subgroups inevitably emerge and exist in groups, affecting them in numerous ways. Subgroups may both hinder and enhance group process. Negative subgroups, like cliques, can raise issues of loyalty and exclusion in the group, challenge the leader's authority, and fragment communication as members of a subgroup talk among themselves and divert their energies from the whole group to the subset. The leader can modify the impact of such subgroups by taking these steps:

1. Initiating discussion of the reasons for the formation of the dissident subgroups and their impact on the group as a whole. This discussion may reveal the difficulties that they create for goal setting, communication, interaction, and decision making.
2. Neutralizing the effects of negative subgroups through programming or structuring. The leader, for example, might challenge dissident subgroups to work toward a common goal, change seating arrangements, use a "round robin" approach to get feedback from all members, assign members from different subgroups to work on common group

tasks, or use programming materials or exercises to separate subgroup members (Carrell, 2000).
3. Creating safe positions or roles for marginal members of the group that require minimal activity but at the same time involves them in a group activity (Balgopal & Vassil, 1983).
4. Helping powerful subgroups or individuals to relinquish power or to use it sparingly in the interest of other members. This may be accomplished by encouraging concern for others in the group and by enabling members to grasp the possibility that domination of others might be destructive to themselves (Garvin, 1987).
5. Appointing powerless members to roles that carry power, such as arranging for group activities, securing resources for the group, or fulfilling significant roles (e.g., observer, chairperson, or secretary).
6. Finding means to "connect" with dissident subgroups and to demonstrate a concern for their wants (Garvin, 1987).
7. Providing ways for subgroups to attain legitimate power by creating useful roles and tasks in the group.

Purposeful Use of the Leadership Role

The leader's role in a group can be described as a set of behaviors that facilitate the attainment of group and individual goals and ensure the maintenance of the group. Ultimately, the leader "puts him/herself out of business" by gradually distributing leadership functions to members as the group matures, while continuing to attend to the work of the group (Rose, 1989, p. 260).

Helping members to assume leadership behaviors is important for three reasons. First, members develop vital skills that they can transfer to other social groups, where leadership is usually highly valued. Second, the more that members exercise leadership, the more likely they are to become invested in the group. Third, performance of leadership activities enhances the perceived power or self-efficacy of members, who often experience powerlessness in a wide array of social situations (Rose, 1989).

Leaders may expedite the distribution of power by taking four steps (Shulman, 1984):

1. Encouraging member-to-member rather than member-to-leader communications
2. Asking for members' input into the agenda for the meeting and the direction the group should take in future meetings
3. Supporting indigenous leadership when members make their first tentative attempts at exerting their own influence on the group

4. Encouraging attempts at mutual sharing and mutual aid among group members during the first meeting

Group leadership problems occur when individuals or vying subgroups attempt to usurp the reins of power. Challenges to leadership (or lack of it) are, in fact, an inherent part of the group's struggle over control, division of responsibility, and decision making (Corey & Corey, 2002). It is important not to interpret these efforts as negative, because they may actually help the group succeed by calling attention to issues or roles that are important to individual members (Hurley, 1984). Examples of messages that illustrate control issues follow:

- *I don't want to talk just because you want me to talk. I learn just as much by listening and observing.*
- *There are several people in here who always get the attention. No matter what I do, I just don't seem to get recognized, especially by the leaders.*
- *You should pay more attention to Paul. He's been crying several times, and you haven't been taking care of him.*

The facilitator might respond to such a challenge by empathically exploring the statement, thanking the member for speaking up, eliciting feedback from other members regarding leadership style, and asking nondefensively for input (e.g., "Thanks for speaking up about that. What would you have me do differently?"). Corey and Corey (1992) also recommend responding authentically. They note that leaders must be self-aware when challenged and avoid focusing on "problem members" or difficult situations, rather than on how they are affected personally when group processes go awry:

> Typically, leaders have a range of feelings: being threatened by what they perceive as a challenge to their leadership role; anger over the members' lack of cooperation and enthusiasm; feelings of inadequacy to the point of wondering if they are qualified to lead groups; resentment toward several of the members, whom they label as some type of problem; and anxiety over the slow pace of the group, with a desire to stir things up so that there is some action. (Corey & Corey, 1992, p. 155)

By ignoring their reactions, leaders leave themselves out of the interactions that occur in the group. Instead, Corey and Corey (1992) urge leaders to model:

> a "direct" style of dealing with conflict and resistance. ... Your own thoughts, feelings and observations can be the most powerful resource you have in dealing

> with defensive behavior. When you share what you are feeling and thinking about what is going on in the group—in such a way as not to blame and criticize the members for deficiencies—you are letting the members experience an honest and constructive interaction with you. (p. 155)

By consistently responding authentically, even when challenged or under attack, the leader encourages the group to adopt this mode of representing self—one that is vital to members dealing effectively with the inevitable differences they encounter among themselves.

Interventions Across Stages of Group Development

As previously mentioned, a leader's role must always be pursued within the framework of the group's stages of development. Thomas and Caplan (1999) suggest a wheel metaphor for leadership. That is, the leader takes a particularly active role in getting the "wheel spinning," then gradually provides a "lighter touch," and finally reduces that role as the group gathers its own momentum, while still standing by to assure that events or digressions don't throw the wheel off track. These authors identify three key intervention techniques that leaders must employ over the life of the group:

- Process, *attending to both individuals' processes in addressing problems and the process for the group as a whole*
- Linking, *or helping members see the common themes in the issues raised, thereby building the reciprocity and mutuality essential to self-worth and group cohesion*
- Inclusion, *or tactics to engage reluctant members with the group.*

Social workers must also take care not to make errors that inhibit group development and process. Thomas and Caplan (1999) identify some of the most common mistakes. These mistakes include:

- *Doing one-on-one work in the context of the group. This practice inhibits the mutual aid that is the hallmark of group work*
- *Having such a rigid agenda that members cannot pursue emerging themes or otherwise own the group process*
- *Scapegoating or attacking individual members. This behavior inhibits others' involvement by sending a message that the group is not a safe place*

- *Overemphasizing content and failing to universalize themes so that all members can benefit from and relate to the experience of other members*
- *Ridiculing members or discounting some members' need to be heard*
- *Lecturing the group. This practice disempowers members and inhibits group investment and momentum*
- *Failing to address offensive comments or colluding with members around inappropriate, anti-authoritarian, racist, or sexist statements.*

It may be helpful to think of the preceding list as behaviors that stop the evolution of the group or send it veering off course. The following sections detail key aspects of *effective* group work, examining the leader's role across the group phases identified in Garland, Jones, and Kolodny's (1965) model.

Common Mistakes: Overemphasizing Content and Lecturing in the HEART Group

Dave: I want us to think about the word "fat" and to think about if that's an appropriate word to use to describe ourselves.

Liz: Not you, you're skinny.

Dave: When I speak to people who have been called fat, or who refer to themselves that way, I use the term, "person with overweight." And that's the way I talk about it. None of us are guaranteed to keep the bodies we have. Whether we like them or not, our bodies can always change. So I say people have overweight, because it's descriptive of a moment in time, rather than an enduring quality that someone possesses.

Amelia: My psychiatrist calls, um, says that I have a disordered relationship with food. [*the group laughs*]

Dave: What does that mean?

Amelia: Means I'm fat, I don't know! [*more laughter*]

Dave: Well, let's look at the words together then. What is disordered?

Amelia: Fat. I don't know, like not right, dysfunctional, not cool.

June: Out of order.

Amelia: Out of order. Yes, I'm out of order with food.

Dave: What do you think about that? Do you agree or disagree?

Amelia: I don't know; whatever, it makes sense to me.

Dave: What about it makes sense?

Amelia: Well, it's kind of a nice way of saying, I'm fat.

Dave: When I hear that phrase, it sounds to me as though your psychiatrist is telling you that you're using food for reasons other than nutrition.

Amelia: Yeah, maybe.

Interventions in the Preaffiliation Stage

As discussed in Chapter 11, pre-group individual interviews will serve as orientation for potential members of the group. In initial sessions the leader can prepare members for the experiences to come by explaining the basics of group process—for example, the stages of development through which the group will pass, ways to create a therapeutic working environment, behaviors and attitudes characteristic of an effective group, the importance of establishing and adhering to guidelines that lend structure and purpose to the group, and the importance of committing to "win-win" decisions regarding group matters. Research, in fact, suggests that direct instruction or teaching regarding group processes tends to facilitate a group's development during its early stages (Corey & Corey, 2002; Dies, 1983).

Leaders must also intervene to address the initial concerns of members. In early sessions, members will probably be tentative about expressing what they hope to get from the group. Most also experience fear and apprehension regarding the group experience. They worry about many things: how they will be perceived by other members, whether they will be pressured to talk, whether they will be misunderstood or look foolish, whether they will be at risk of verbal attack, and whether they want to go through a change process at all. The leader may address and allay these anxieties by acknowledging the presence of mixed feelings or by asking all members to share their feelings about coming to the initial group session. For example, the leader might ask members to rate their feelings about being present in the group at that moment on a scale of 1 to 10, where 1 represents "I don't want to be here" and 10 represents "I'm completely at ease with being in the group." The leader could then invite discussion about reasons behind the various scores.

In focusing on members' fears, leaders need to draw out all members' feelings and reactions, validate the importance of their fully disclosing feelings, and emphasize the need for the group to be a safe place in which such issues can be expressed openly. Finally, leaders should elicit suggestions for a group structure that will address member fears, out of which may flow the formulation of relevant group guidelines.

Leaders can measure the progress of a new group in addressing initial member concerns by administering a questionnaire developed by Rose (1989). This instrument contains items to which members can respond by circling a point on a scale. Examples of items include the following:

- *How useful was today's session for you?*
- *Describe your involvement in today's session.*
- *Rate the extent of your self-disclosure of relevant information about yourself or your problem.*
- *How important to you were the problems or situations you discussed (or others discussed) in the group today?*
- *Circle all the words that best describe you at today's session (e.g., excited, bored, depressed, interested, comfortable).*
- *How satisfied were you with today's session?*

In initial sessions, facilitators must repeatedly review basic information regarding the group's purpose, the manner in which the group will be conducted, and its ground rules. Reid (1991) emphasizes that none of this information should surprise members. However, reiteration is necessary because "in the beginning, members are often so preoccupied that they do not comprehend the group's purpose, their particular role, the worker's role, and what will be expected of them" (Reid, 1991, p. 205). Making sure that all members are "on the same page" helps to prevent these issues from erupting later in the life of the group.

In preliminary interviews, members contract with the leader for general goals they would like to achieve. In the initial group sessions, the leader must then blend these individual goals with the group's collective goals. Along the way, the binding contract expands from a reciprocal one between leader and individuals to a mutual contract between individuals and group. In the first meeting, the leader engages "all persons present in a discussion that establishes a group way of functioning yet allows each person's initial objectives to be addressed" (Henry, 1992, p. 80). Henry, who views finding common ground as "an unfolding process," utilizes what she calls a "Goal Questionnaire" to facilitate formulation of the mutual contract. On this questionnaire are two questions to which members respond in writing:

1. Why do you think all of you are here together?
2. What are you going to try to accomplish together?

Discussion of responses gives the group a beginning point from which to proceed.

In the contractual process of initial sessions, leaders also aid members to refine their general goals. An example from the HEART group illustrates the role of the leader in seeking concreteness to clarify global goals:

Seeking Concreteness

Dave: At our last session, I asked each of you to share what you'd like to get out of the group individually. I'd like to take some of our time today to think of group goals. What would you like to accomplish together?

Amelia: To lose weight.

Dave: I hope that happens for all of you, and that the group is a source of support to you in pursuing your weight loss goals; but losing weight is more of an individual goal.

Liz: Follow the group rules?

Dave: Tell us more…

Liz: Well, like, respect each other and actively participate.

Dave: Following the group guidelines will help you to reach your group goals, but…

Amber: I'd like to know how other people deal with the stuff I go through.

June: Yeah, like how to keep your mom off your back!

Dave: Okay, good. It sounds like a group goal is for you all to share experiences. Are there any others?

Amelia: Sometimes I just want somebody to listen, you know? I don't know, I know I shouldn't be eating so much, but then I do, and it makes me feel bad. I thought it would help to be around other people who, like, might know how I'm feeling.

Jen: Yeah, I thought that too.

Dave: So far, I've heard two suggestions for group goals. One is to share experiences and the other, which Amelia just mentioned, is to listen to each other and support one another, especially when it comes to feeling sad or worried.

The leader also keeps accomplishment of goals at the forefront of the group's work. Through bibliotherapy, journaling, and mindfulness, members can read, write, and reflect on the themes they are addressing and the insights they have achieved during and between group sessions (Corey, 1990). Session time may be allocated for discussing these insights, thereby reinforcing the value of continuing work between sessions.

Paying attention to the way each session opens and concludes is important for maximizing member productivity and satisfaction. Corey and Corey (2002) encourage leaders to draw from the following procedures in opening meetings:

1. Give members a brief opportunity to say what they want from the upcoming session.
2. Invite members to share their accomplishments since the last session.
3. Elicit feedback regarding the group's last session and give any reflections you have of the session.

To bring meetings to a close, Corey and Corey (2002) emphasize the need to summarize and integrate the group experience by following these procedures:

1. Ask members what it was like for them to be in the group today.
2. Invite members to identify briefly what they're learning about themselves through their experience in the group. Are they getting what they want? If not, what would they be willing to do to get it?
3. Ask members whether there are any topics, questions, or problems they would like to explore in the next session.
4. Ask members to indicate what they would be willing to do outside of the session to practice new skills.

Incorporating group rituals into the structure of sessions increases the continuity that flows from meeting to meeting. Examples include check-in as a ritual to start each session, structured refreshment breaks, and closing meditations or readings (Subramian, Hernandez, & Martinez, 1995). Such continuity heightens the transfer of insights and new behaviors from the group session into daily life.

Interventions in the Power and Control Stage

In stage 2 of group development, the group enters a period in which its dynamics, tone, and atmosphere are often conflict-ridden, although some groups may need encouragement to address underlying conflicts that threaten the health of the group (Schiller, 1997). Groups may be beset by problems in dealing with divisions among individuals and subgroups; complaints

and unrest over group goals, processes, and structure; and challenges to leadership. At the same time, the group is trying out its capacity to manage its own affairs. The leader is responsible for guiding the group through this stormy period so that it remains intact and demonstrates an emerging capacity to cope with individual differences and to manage its own governance. Leaders can employ several strategies in carrying out this responsibility: minimize changes, encourage balanced feedback, increase effective communication, and develop therapeutic group norms.

Minimize Changes

During the "power and control" stage, groups with a closed format are particularly susceptible to inner and outer stressors such as a change of leader, a move to a new meeting place, the addition or loss of members, or a change in the meeting time. Traumatic events such as a runaway, a death, an incidence of physical violence in an institutional setting, or acutely disturbing political or natural events at the community or national level may also significantly affect a group at this stage.

Although such changes or events can be upsetting to a group at any stage of development, they are particularly difficult to manage in stage 2. At this point, members have not yet become invested in the group to an appreciable extent and thus may become easily disenchanted. Adding new members or changing the group's leader is particularly stressful, causing members to raise their defenses because there are risks involved in revealing themselves when either the leader or a member is an unknown entity. The loss of a leader can also prove inordinately traumatic to members who have difficulty investing in relationships, affirming their stance that trusting others just brings disappointment.

In addition, making a significant change in the group structure without group involvement may cause members to conclude that the leader or agency has disregard for the impact of such decisions on the group and that the group is not important. Although changes are sometimes unavoidable, it behooves leaders to keep them to a minimum, to prepare members in advance whenever possible, and to aid them to "work through" their feelings when change is necessary.

Encourage Balanced Feedback

In stage 2 of group development, leaders must ensure that feedback is balanced. As they observe that group members are tentatively moving into their first authentic encounters, leaders should intervene in negative interactions to draw the group's attention to the need to provide balanced feedback. They thus remind members of the provision in the contract for focusing on positives as well as negatives. The following excerpt from an early group session with adult members illustrates this point.

Gary [*to Wayne, in irritated voice*]: Why do you keep grilling me with questions like that? I feel like I'm being interrogated.

Wayne: I didn't know I was coming across like that. Frankly, I just wanted to get to know you better.

Leader [*to Wayne*]: You said in the first session that you'd like to use the group as a way of getting feedback about how you come across to others. I'm wondering if this might be a time for that?

Wayne: Yeah. I don't know what's coming, but I really think I do need to know more about how you all see me. I was really surprised at what Gary said.

Leader [*to Wayne*]: Good. I can understand you may have reservations, but I'm also pleased that you're willing to take a risk this early in the group.

[*To group*] Because this is the group's first experience in giving feedback to members, I'd like to remind you of the contract not only to help members identify problems but also to share positive observations you may have. As you do so, I'd like you to personalize your statements. I'll help you do so.

Group members' first experiences in giving feedback to one another are crucial in setting the tone for all that follows in the group. By guiding members' first cautious efforts to drop their facades and to engage at an intimate level, the leader enables the group to experience success and incorporate attention to positives as a part of its character. As individuals come to trust that the group will attend to positives as well as negatives, they will often increase their level of participation and take the initiative in soliciting group feedback.

In addition to encouraging positive feedback for individuals, leaders can elicit examples of behaviors observed during a session that support the group's work in accomplishing its tasks. Such behaviors may include being willing to participate in discussions, to answer questions, and to risk revealing oneself; showing support to others; speaking in turn; giving full attention to the task at hand; accepting differing values, beliefs, and opinions; and recognizing significant individual and group breakthroughs. The leader can also highlight the *absence* of destructive behaviors that might have occurred earlier (e.g., whispering, fidgeting, introducing tangential topics, dominating, or verbally and physically pestering other members).

In addition, the leader must assist members to hear, acknowledge, and accept positive feedback, as illustrated in the following example:

Kim [*to Pat*]: I know you get discouraged sometimes, but I admire the fact you can manage four children by yourself and still work. I don't think I could ever manage that in a million years.

Pat: I don't always manage it. Actually, I don't do near enough for my children.

Leader: I hear you saying, Pat, that you feel inadequate as a mother—and I'll ask you in a moment whether you'd like to return to those feelings—but right now would you reflect on what you just did?

Pat: I guess I blew off Kim's compliment. I didn't feel I deserved it.

Leader: I wonder if others of you have responded in a similar way when someone has told you something positive.

The last response broadens the focus to include the experience of other group members, which may lead into a discussion of the difficulties that individuals sometimes encounter in accepting and internalizing positive feedback. The leader may also wish to help individuals or the entire group to identify dysfunctional cognitive patterns that underlie their discomfort in receiving positive messages (e.g., "I have to do things perfectly" or "If they knew me better, they'd realize I'm no good"). Identifying the disconfirming cognitions represents a first step toward replacing them with more accepting messages ("I do a good job considering all I have responsibility for" or "My group sees another side of me that I don't let myself acknowledge").

Increase Effective Communication

Achieving success during the "power and control" phase requires moment-by-moment interventions to increase the chances of effective communication. Previous chapters have described five basic relationship skills that, when possessed by clients, significantly increase their personal efficacy and ability to create satisfying relationships:

- *Positive feedback*
- *Empathic listening (the receiver skill)*

- *Authentic responding (the sender skill)*
- *Problem solving and decision making*
- *Requesting (a skill for expressing one's needs)*

Other facets of communication enable members to relate effectively as a group, such as taking turns in talking; learning how to explore problems before offering solutions; speaking for themselves, not others; and speaking directly to the person for whom the message is intended. In addition, members can learn to distinguish between effective and ineffective ways of responding and can include improving their communication repertoire as one of their individual goals for work.

Leaders increase the probability that members will adopt these effective communication skills by heavily utilizing and modeling these skills themselves. In addition, leaders aid the acquisition of skills by assuming the role of "coach" and intervening to shape the display of communications in the group, as illustrated in the following examples:

- [Eliminating negative communications] *"I'd like you to shy away from labeling, judging, lecturing, criticism, sarcasm, 'shoulds' and 'oughts,' and the words 'always' and 'never.' As we discussed in our group contract, try to give self-reports rather than indirect messages that put down or judge another person."*
- [Personalizing messages] *"That was an example of a 'you' message. I'd like you to try again, this time by starting out with the pronoun 'I.' Try to identify your feelings, or what you want or need."*
- [Talking in turn] *"Right now, several of you are speaking at the same time. Try to hold to the guideline that we all speak in turn. Your observations are too important to miss."*
- [Speaking directly to each other] *"Right now, you're speaking to the group, but I think your message is meant for Fred. If so, then it would be better to talk directly to him."*
- [Exploratory questions] *"Switching from closed- to open-ended questions right now could help Liz to tell her story in her own way."* (The leader explains the difference between these two modes of questioning.)
- [Listening] *"Try to really hear what she's saying. Help her to let out her feelings and to get to the source of the problem."*
- [Problem exploration versus problem solving] *"When the group offers advice too quickly, folks can't share their deeper-level feelings or reveal a*

problem in its entirety. We may need to allow Richard five to ten minutes to share his concerns before the group offers any observations. The timing of advice is critical as we try to help members share and solve problems."
- [Authenticity] *"Could you take a risk and tell the group what you're feeling at this very moment? I can see you choking up, and I think it would be good for the group to know what you're experiencing."*
- [Requesting] *"You've just made a complaint about the group. On the flip side of any complaint is a request. Tell the group what would help. Make a request."*

Intervening moment by moment to shape the communications of members, as in the instances illustrated here, increases the therapeutic potential of a group.

Stage 2 of group development may also present a challenge when the group has co-leadership. The presence of two leaders may increase members' defensiveness as they seek to erect boundaries that protect them from the influence presented by two leaders. Members may also attempt to split the leaders by exploiting disagreements or differences between them or by affiliating with one leader and working against the other. Clarity of purpose, preparation for these maneuvers, and strong communication can help co-leaders resist these efforts when they emerge (Nosko & Wallace, 1997).

Create Therapeutic Norms

As mentioned earlier, leaders must be concerned about the nature of the norms that evolve in the group. Many of the group patterns form in the "power and control" stage. The leader can intervene then to shape the power structure, the stylistic communications of the group, and the ways in which the group chooses to negotiate and solve problems.

In shaping the group's therapeutic norms, leaders need to intervene, for example, in the following instances:

- *When socializing or distracting behavior substantially interferes with the group's task*
- *When one or more members monopolize the group's airtime*
- *When one or more members are "out of step" with the group process and/or experience strong feelings such as hurt, anger, disgust, disappointment, or disapproval*

- *When several members or the entire group begin to talk about one member*
- *When a member's behavior is incompatible with the governing guidelines set by the group*
- *When participants intellectualize about emotion-laden material*
- *When one or more members display hostility through jokes, sarcasm, or criticism, or when they interrogate, scapegoat, or gang up on a single member*
- *When the group offers advice or suggestions without first encouraging a member to fully explore a problem*
- *When there is silence or withdrawal by one or more members or the group itself seems to be "shut down"*
- *When a member adopts a "co-leader" role.*

When problems such as these emerge, the leader must focus the group's attention on what is occurring in the "here and now." Leaders may simply document what they see by describing specific behaviors or the progression of events that have occurred and then request group input. Once the group focuses on the problem, the leader should facilitate discussion and problem solving rather than take decisive action on his or her own. Ultimately, the responsibility for resolution needs to rest with the group.

In regard to turning issues back to the group, Henry (1992) notes:

> *When the members are vying for ownership of the group, the wisest intervention for the worker is to join their struggle and to put issues and decisions back to them. The worker does not wholly give up her or his power, but holds back from what had previously been a more directive and active performance. (p. 148)*

However, as Henry (1992) acknowledges, at the end of a particularly conflict-filled episode or session, leaders need to intervene with a proposal to process what has occurred and to lead that processing. In such instances, leaders do not simply turn issues back to the group but opt, in the interest of closure and resolution, to "clarify what information people carry away from the confrontation, and to see what level of discomfort people are experiencing" (p. 151).

Although leaders need to avoid reaching premature closure on heated issues in a group, they must intervene immediately to refocus the process when group members criticize, label, or "cut down" others, or when they argue among themselves. Leaders may assume—

incorrectly—that letting members verbally "fight it out" when they have conflicts is cathartic or helpful. In fact, ample research indicates that aggression begets aggression and that not intervening in conflict merely encourages members to continue venting their anger in the same fashion. A leader's passive stance could allow conflict to escalate to the point that it turns into harmful verbal or physical altercations. In instances of serious disruption, a leader's lack of intervention may "prove" to members who are scrutinizing the leader's behavior that it is dangerous to take risks in the group because the leader will not protect them (Smokowski, Rose, & Bacallao, 2001).

It is vital that leaders intervene assertively when dysfunctional group processes arise. Otherwise, they will be in a "one-down" position in the group and lose their ability to effect change. Leaders must be willing to respond decisively when significant group disruption occurs, using physical and verbal measures as needed, such as clapping their hands loudly, standing up, speaking louder than group members, or putting themselves between members who are arguing.

Interventions should generally focus on group-related matters (rather than on individual attitudes or behaviors), because it is rare that the destructive or self-defeating behavior of an individual or subset will not affect the entire system. In fact, some problematic behaviors may be fostered or reinforced by the group as a whole. Focusing interventions on a pair, a trio, a foursome, or the group also avoids singling out one person or inadvertently "siding" with one segment of clients over others.

Consider, for instance, the following leader intervention in an adolescent group: "Mark and Jeannie, you're whispering again and interrupting the group. We need your attention." This message places the responsibility for the distracting behavior solely upon the two members and does not take into account what is happening with the group. In this instance, the leader's message is more likely to reinforce negative behavior than to encourage positive change for the following reasons:

- *It may polarize the group by aligning the leader with members who are irritated by this behavior ("the good guys") and against the two offending members ("the bad guys").*
- *The leader's solution ("We need your attention") circumvents group handling or problem solving of the matter.*
- *The leader's blunt intervention fails to attend to the message inherent in the problem behavior: "This group does not meet our needs at the moment." In*

fact, this view may be shared but not expressed by other members.

A guideline to formulating interventions that confront dysfunctional behavior is that the behavior must be analyzed in the context of the group process, with the leader considering how such behavior affects and is affected by group members. This approach is illustrated by the following message to the same situation:

Leader: I'm concerned about what is happening right now. Several of you are not participating; some of you are whispering; one of you is writing notes; a few of you are involved in the discussion. As individuals, you appear to be at different places with the group, and I'd like to check out what each of you is experiencing right now.

This message focuses on all group members, neutrally describes behavior that is occurring, and encourages the group process. By not imposing a solution on the group, the leader assumes a facilitative rather than an authoritarian role; the latter is the "kiss of death" for productive group discussion.

Interventions in the Intimacy and Differentiation Stages

Stages 3 ("intimacy") and 4 ("differentiation") of group development constitute the group's working phase. In the initial stages of a group's evolution, the critical issues at stake focused on trust versus mistrust, the struggle for power, and self-focus versus focus on others. In the working phase, however, issues shift to those of disclosure versus anonymity, honesty versus game playing, spontaneity versus control, acceptance versus rejection, cohesion versus fragmentation, and responsibility versus blaming (Corey & Corey, 2002).

In the working phase, leaders continue to promote conditions that aid members to make healthy choices in resolving issues by straightforwardly addressing and resolving conflict, openly disclosing personal problems, taking responsibility for their problems, and making pro-group choices. Thanks to the relaxed stance that characterizes this phase, leaders have more opportunities to intensify therapeutic group conditions. They may focus on refining feedback processes—for example, coaching members to give immediate feedback, to make such feedback specific rather than global, to render feedback in nonjudgmental ways, and to give feedback regarding strengths as well as problem behaviors (Corey & Corey, 2002).

Leaders can also enhance individual and group growth by focusing on the universality of underlying issues, feelings, and needs that members seem to share:

The circumstances leading to hurt and disappointment may be very different from person to person or from culture to culture. But the resulting emotions have a universal quality. Although we may not speak the same language or come from the same society, we are connected through our feelings of joy and pain. It is when group members no longer get lost in the details of daily experiences and instead share their deeper struggles with these universal human themes that a group is most cohesive. (Corey & Corey, 1992, p. 209)

Common themes identified by Corey and Corey include (1992):

fears of rejection, feelings of loneliness and abandonment, feeling of inferiority and failure to live up to others' expectations, painful memories, guilt and remorse over what they have and have not done, discovery that their worst enemy lives within them, need for and fear of intimacy, feelings about sexual identity and sexual performance, and unfinished business with their parents. (p. 210)

This list is not exhaustive, note Corey and Corey, but "merely a sample of the universal human issues that participants recognize and explore with each other as the group progresses" (p. 210).

During these middle phases of group development, group members can participate in a number of activities to work on individual and commonly held goals. Such activities may reduce stress and encourage pleasure and creativity; assist the leader in assessment as members are observed while "doing" rather than "saying"; facilitate communication, problem solving, and rapport among members; and help members develop skills and competence in decision making (Northen & Kurland, 2001). Nevil, Beatty, and Moxley (1997) suggest a variety of structured activities and socialization games that can be employed to improve interpersonal skills, increase social awareness, and enhance prosocial competence. While intended for use with persons with disabilities, many of these exercises can be adapted for use with a variety of populations. Other authors note their effectiveness with diverse populations, such as those of Hispanic heritage (Delgado, 1983) and Native Americans (Edwards, Edwards, Davies, & Eddy, 1987).

One element of a structured program targeting delinquency reduction consists of multifamily group meetings in which 8 to 10 families meet for eight weekly sessions lasting 2 1/2 hours each. In the meetings, family members sit together at designated tables, share a meal, and engage in "structured, fun, interactive" (McDonald, 2002, p. 719) activities that enhance communication skills, strengthen relationships, and facilitate networking among the families.

While art therapy and other expressive techniques generally require specialized training, reviewing resources such as Ross (1997) and Rose (1998) can acquaint social workers with the principles for applying these techniques in groups to address issues related to aggressive behavior, self-esteem, body image, and awareness of emotions. With all groups, the leader must take the group's purpose, stage of development, and member characteristics into account when selecting and implementing an experiential exercise or activity (Wright, 1999).

In the working phase, leaders also support a continuing trend toward differentiation, in which members establish their uniqueness and separateness from others. Leaders do not create these expressions of differences but rather stimulate or advance them. For example, the leader may note when a member reveals:

a heretofore hidden talent, or access to a resource that was previously believed inaccessible, or possession of a needed skill or perspective. A member may articulate a previously unspoken need, or offer an interpretation not thought of by the others, or pose a question that catalyzes or synthesizes a piece of the group's work. (Henry, 1992, p. 183)

The working phase is a time of intensive focus on achieving members' goals. Much of the group's work during this phase is devoted to carrying out contracts developed in the group's initial sessions. Members may have lost sight of their individual goals, so a major leadership role involves confirming goals periodically and promoting organized and systematic efforts to work on them.

The leader assumes the ongoing responsibility of monitoring the time allocated to each member to work on goals. Toseland and Rivas (2009) suggest that the leader help each member to work in turn. If a group spends considerable time aiding one member to achieve his or her individual goals, the leader should generalize the concepts developed in this effort to other members so that everyone benefits. The leader should also encourage participants to share relevant personal experiences with the member receiving help, thus establishing a norm for mutual aid. In addition, he or she should check on the progress of members who did not receive due attention and encourage their participation in the next session.

Finally, the leader should establish a systematic method of monitoring treatment goals and tasks in sessions. Without such procedures, monitoring may be haphazard and focus on only those members who are more assertive and highly involved; members who are less assertive or resistant will not receive the same attention. Without systematic monitoring, tasks to be completed between sessions may not receive the proper follow-up. As Toseland and Rivas (2009) suggest, group members may become frustrated when they have completed "homework" between sessions and have no opportunity to report on the results. The expectation of a weekly progress report helps increase motivation to work toward goals between sessions, reduces the necessity of reminding members of their contract agreements, and aids them in gaining a sense of independence and accomplishment.

In the working phase, leaders continue to encourage members to analyze the rationality of their thoughts and beliefs that maintain or exacerbate dysfunctional behaviors. According to Toseland and Rivas (2009), group members may:

(1) overgeneralize from an event, (2) selectively focus on portions of an event, (3) take too much responsibility for events that are beyond their control, (4) think of the worst possible consequence of future events, (5) engage in either/or dichotomous thinking, and (6) assume that because certain events have led to particular consequences in the past they will automatically lead to the same consequences if they reoccur in the future. (p. 288)[3]

Unhelpful Thoughts from the HEART Group: Selectively Focusing

June: Well, I just don't believe anybody that says high school's your best years, you know.

Amelia: My sister's in college, she says that college is the coolest.

Amber: I'm looking forward to college.

Amelia: Me too.

Jen: But I have another three years until I get there. How am I going to survive three years of people making fun of me?

Liz: How do you think college is going to be any different anyway? You have to go be in a dorm where you have to shower in front of people; then, it's not going to be any better.

June: I think I'll just work.

Maggie: Not go to college? My parents would kill me.

June: My parents would be relieved because then they wouldn't have to pay for it.

Dave: I'd like to pose a question to the group. What would be one thing to change about your mindset? What thought could you change that might help you get through high school or shopping or gym? What would be one thought?

Amber: That I don't have to be just like my friends.

Dave: How would that help?

Amber: That would make me feel better about not shopping at the same stores and wearing the same clothes and having the boyfriends that they have, but still being able to hang out with them in other situations.

Interventions in the Termination Stage

Termination is a difficult stage for members who have invested heavily in the group; have experienced intensive support, encouragement, and understanding; and have received effective aid for their problems. Leaders must be sensitive to the mixed feelings engendered by termination and carefully intervene to assist the group to come to an effective close. Chapter 19 identifies significant termination issues and change-maintenance strategies that may be utilized with clients in facilitating termination and generalizing changes to the outside world. Here, we address aspects of the leader's role that are specific to facilitating planned endings in groups.

Leaders may assist group members in completing their "commencement" proceedings (Mahler, 1969) by adopting strategies such as the following:

- *Ensure that the issues and concerns worked on by the group resemble those that members will encounter outside the group. Assure that the group is a place where members get honest feedback about how their behavior is likely to be received outside the group and a setting where they may obtain help in coping with those reactions (Toseland & Rivas, 2009).*
- *Refer to a variety of situations and settings throughout the group experience to aid members to practice and acquire skills, thereby better preparing*

them for the multifaceted situations they will inevitably encounter outside the group (Toseland & Rivas, 2009).

- *Facilitate members' discussion of how they will respond to possible setbacks in an unsympathetic environment. Build member confidence in existing coping skills and abilities to solve problems independently. Also, teach therapeutic principles that underlie intervention methods, such as those inherent in assertiveness, effective communication, or problem solving (Toseland & Rivas, 2009).*
- *Share your reactions to endings as a way of helping members to identify their own conflicted feelings and any sense of abandonment, anger, sadness, or loss.*
- *Reinforce members' positive feelings about themselves and the group, including the potency that comes from realizing that they are capable of accomplishing goals and assuming responsibility for their own lives; the sense of satisfaction, pride, and usefulness in being able to help others; and the sense of growth and of accomplishment that comes from successfully completing the group experience (Lieberman & Borman, 1979; Toseland & Rivas, 2009).*
- *Increase review and integration of learning by helping members to put into words what has transpired between themselves and the group from the first to the final session and what they have learned about themselves and others. Solicit information about what members were satisfied and unsatisfied within the group and ways in which sessions could have had greater impact. Ask members to spontaneously recall moments of conflict and pain as well as moments of closeness, warmth, humor, and joy in the group (Corey & Corey, 1992).*
- *Several sessions before termination, suggest that members consider using the remaining time to complete their own agenda. For example, ask, "If this were the last session, how would you feel about what you have done, and what would you wish you had done differently?" (Corey & Corey, 2002, p. 261).*
- *Facilitate the completion of unfinished business between members. One technique involves an exercise in which each person, in turn, says in a few short phrases, "What I really liked was the way you ... (supply a specific behavior exchanged between the persons, such as 'always gave me credit when I could finally say something that was hard for me to say'),"* and then, *"But I wish we ... (supplying a specific wish for a behavioral exchange between the two*

persons that did not occur, such as 'had made more opportunities to talk to each other more directly')" (Henry, 1992, p. 124). Note that this and other closure exercises should not be used to generate new issues but rather to bring resolution to the present situation.

- *Encourage members to identify areas for future work once the group concludes. Consider asking members to formulate their own individual change contracts, which may be referred to once the group ends, and invite each member to review his or her contract with the group (Corey & Corey, 2002).*

- *Engage individual members in relating how they have perceived themselves in the group, what the group has meant to them, and how they have grown. Ask the other members to give feedback regarding how they have perceived and felt about each person, including measured feedback that helps members strengthen the perceptions that they gained during the course of the group (e.g., "One of the things I like best about you is...," "One way I see you blocking your strengths is...," or "A few things that I hope you'll remember are...") (Corey, 1990, p. 512).*

- *Use evaluative measures to determine the effectiveness of the group and the leader's interventions. Such measures have the following benefits: (1) They address the leader's professional concerns about the specific effects of interventions; (2) they help workers improve their leadership skills; (3) they demonstrate the group's efficacy to agencies or funding sources; (4) they help leaders assess individual members' and the group's progress in accomplishing agreed-upon objectives; (5) they allow members to express their satisfactions and dissatisfactions with the group; and (6) they help leaders develop knowledge that can be generalized to future groups and other leaders (Reid, 1991; Toseland & Rivas, 2009).*

New Developments in Social Work with Groups

Contemporary developments in group work include increased attention to evaluating groups' effectiveness, the application of group techniques to new populations and new problem areas, and the use of technology in the delivery of group work services. We will address each in turn.

Like other areas of social work practice, group interventions face increased scrutiny to determine the efficacy of certain processes and the outcomes. Tolman and Molidor's (1994) review of research on social work with groups indicates that group work evaluation is growing ever more sophisticated and that multiple measures are being employed to determine group efficacy. For example, in addition to undertaking evaluation at the termination phase, more than one-third of the groups studied by Tolman and Molidor (1994) used follow-up measures to determine whether earlier gains had been maintained. These authors note, however, that while it is important to examine outcomes, the evaluative challenge lies in isolating those elements of group process that actually contributed to those outcomes.

Increasingly, curricula for group interventions include measurement instruments to assist in understanding both baseline and outcome measures. For example, in groups consisting of adolescents and preteens, Rose (1998) suggests using a variety of methods and sources of data, including standardized ratings by parents and teachers; self-monitoring or self-reports through checklists, logs, questionnaires, or sentence completion; observation of in-group behavior; performance during role-plays or simulations; sociometric evaluations; goal attainment scaling; and knowledge tests. Anderson-Butcher, Khairallah, and Race-Bigelow (2004) suggest that qualitative interviews may be used to ascertain client outcomes and to identify the characteristics of effective self-help groups. Magen's (2004) review of measurement issues in group evaluation offers guidance for effective selection of outcome and process measures.

At termination, members and the leader may all record their satisfaction with the group and their sense of its effectiveness. Members may respond to open-ended questions or a structured checklist, either of which may inquire about the changes the group brought about in the participant's life or relationships, the techniques used that had the greatest and least impact, perceptions of the leader, and so on (Corey, Corey, Callanan, & Russell, 2004). These authors also recommend that the leader keep a journal to evaluate group progress over time, note his or her reactions at various points, keep track of techniques or materials used and the perceived outcomes, and share self-insights that emerged during the life of the group.

Group services are also being applied to novel populations and problems. For example, building on the success of groups with gay and lesbian adolescents and with middle-aged persons in the coming-out process, Getzel (1998) notes that life review and socialization groups may serve as a promising resource for elder

GLBT persons. Others note that groups can be effective in addressing health issues, supporting treatment compliance and reducing treatment dropouts. These goals are met as members share feelings about their illnesses and medications, offer mutual aid, empathize with one another's experiences and side effects, break through isolation and grief, and generate strategies for self-care (Miller & Mason, 2001).

There is also increased interest in the use of social work groups for empowerment. For example, Lewis (1991) notes the influences of feminist theory and liberation theology as resources for empowerment-focused social group work. Feminist theory is egalitarian, is participatory, and validates each person's life experiences in context. By contrast, liberation theology focuses on the participation in economic and political action by those persons who are most vulnerable to injustice (Lewis, 1991). For example, Cox has described how female welfare recipients have begun to advocate for themselves with social services and other agencies through participation in empowerment-oriented groups (1991). A feminist-orientation to group therapy for women survivors of sexual trauma capitalizes on women's relational abilities to address feelings of mistrust, and to repair and develop socialization and emotional regulation skills (Rittenhouse, 1997; Fallot & Harris, 2002).

As new theories of change and new treatment modalities emerge, they will also be applied to work with groups. For example, evolving solution-focused interventions have been applied to groups in an array of situations, including recovery from sexual abuse, improving parenting skills, and resolving symptoms of anxiety and depression (Metcalf, 1998). Multifamily groups, composed of family members who share a common concern, have proved useful for addressing severe and persistent psychiatric disorders (McFarlane, 2002) and the risk for child abuse and neglect (Burford & Pennell, 2004; Meezan & O'Keefe, 1998), among other issues (Vakalah & Khajak, 2000).

In applying group work concepts to practice in rural areas, Gumpert and Saltman (1998) identified several challenges that warrant leaders' attention:

- *Cultural factors*—for example, distrust of confidentiality assurances, strong values of self-reliance, and suspicion of outsiders
- *Geographic factors*—for example, distance, weather and travel conditions, and difficulty finding a convenient location
- *Demographic factors*—for example, insufficient numbers of individuals with similar difficulties,

resource problems such as the lack of public transportation, insufficient child care, and too few potential group leaders.

Attention is also turning to the application of group work concepts to groups that meet only for a single session. For example, in interdisciplinary case meetings, membership shifts based on which professionals are involved with the particular case. In critical incident debriefing groups, professions intervene to assist people affected by a traumatic event—for example, after a workplace shooting (Reynolds & Jones, 1996). Some concepts used in the single-session groups—purpose, contracting, and worker roles—are variations on those used in groups of longer duration. Others—composition, member roles, norms, and group stages—may be less germane to single-session groups.

As described in Chapter 11, social workers are utilizing technological advances to enhance the delivery of services to clients through groups. Persons who are home-bound or who find attendance at agency settings difficult may be able to experience the support and benefit of groups through the medium of telephone, e-mail, or the Internet (Harris, 1999; Hollander, 2001). Online group facilitators must assure through informed consent that members understand the risks and benefits of such a model. The nature of typed, asynchronous communication means that members have more control and time for reflection as they craft their responses. In addition, they can participate in the virtual group at their convenience (Fingeld, 2000) and with a high degree of anonymity (Meier, 2002). However, participation may be stymied by Internet provider system problems and by trust issues, especially with "lurkers" (those who read e-mail but do not post to the group) and with participants' actual level of engagement with the process.

Leaders who work with these new technologies must be more active in guiding the process and drawing out implications for feelings and tone that are masked by the communication medium. This effort may require development of conventions or signals for indicating emotions in content (Schopler, Galinsky, & Abell, 1997). As access to such media increases, social workers must take advantage of technology to reach groups who cannot be reached by conventional means, as well as those individuals who may be reluctant to participate in face-to-face meetings. Technology-mediated groups are also well-suited for people seeking support on a 24/7 basis, such as grieving parents who may log in to share feelings and seek help at any hour of the day or night

(Edwards, 2007). Webcasts, conference calls, and other technology-enhanced methods are appropriate for task groups, to save time and travel costs, access expert consultation, and efficiently respond to crises and evolving circumstances in the practice environment.

Work with Task Groups

As described earlier, a significant aspect of professional social work practice is performance in task and work groups. In contrast to treatment groups, task groups try to accomplish a purpose, produce a product, or develop policies. You are likely to participate in task groups throughout your career, starting with group projects for class, continuing as a staff member, and eventually serving as a leader of such groups in your practice. As with treatment groups, task groups may have open or closed membership and they may be time-limited or open-ended. Members take on formal and informal roles, and the execution of these roles can facilitate or impede the group's success. Task groups may be composed of professionals, community members, clients, or a mixture of these parties, depending on the group's purpose and the way that members are recruited and assigned.

Effective task groups do not rely solely on the skills of the formal group leader. For example, as members of such groups, social workers are often effective participants in interdisciplinary teams thanks to their knowledge of group processes (Abramson, 2002). They can offer particular assistance in task groups in identifying which needs the group can meet, getting members involved, and paying attention to stages of development (including managing conflict during each stage).

Problem Identification

Leaders can help groups effectively identify problems that the group is capable of solving, that are within the group's domain, and that, among the many problems that could potentially be chosen, would provide a meaningful focus. During this process, the leader (or chairperson, or facilitator) should help the group avoid responding prematurely with solutions before the problem is well defined. In specifying appropriate problems and goals, the group can employ techniques such as brainstorming and nominal group techniques to consider an array of possibilities before selecting a focus. *Brainstorming* involves generating and expressing a variety of opinions without evaluating them. In the *nominal group* technique, members first privately list potential problems. The group then takes one potential problem from each member until all are listed. Finally, it evaluates and ranks those potential problems as a group (Toseland & Rivas, 2009).

Groups must also determine the strategies that will support effective decision making. Some procedures may be prescribed. For example, the charter of the group may require certain periods for commentary, use of clearly specified rules on who can vote, and adherence to Robert's Rules of Order. Other groups may determine their own norms, such as decision by consensus or majority rule.

Getting Members Involved

Task group membership may be voluntary (a neighborhood task force on crime), appointed (a coalition consisting of representatives of homeless shelters), elected (a board of directors), or determined by roles (an interdisciplinary team consisting of all professionals serving a particular family). To the maximum extent possible, the membership should possess the skills and resources needed to accomplish the purpose for which the group was convened. For example, if a committee concerned about crime had no law enforcement personnel as members, it might seek out someone to fill that niche. As with therapeutic groups, those convening task groups should be alert to the characteristics of potential members and ensure that no member will be an isolate or an outlier. This consideration is particularly important when service consumers or their family members fill representative roles in a group consisting largely of professionals and service providers. Multiple representatives from consumer or family organizations should be included in committee membership, thereby ensuring that they are empowered and that their positions move beyond a token role.

All members of the group need to have a clear understanding of the functions of the group, to have input into the agenda and decision making. Each session or meeting should be carefully planned and designed to take advantage of the time and talents available (Tropman & Morningstar, 1995). Roles can be assigned such that members will have to depend on each other to get the work of the group accomplished (Toseland & Rivas, 2009). Background papers often need to be circulated in advance to get all members to the appropriate level of information. It is often helpful to conduct the brainstorming or ice-breaking exercises in small groups to facilitate member interaction. Recognition of the particular skills, experiences, and perspectives that different members bring can also facilitate more confident sharing by new members.

Enhancing Awareness of Stages of Development

The stages of group development observed in treatment settings will also occur in task groups, albeit not in a linear fashion. Instead, some issues will recur, taking the group back to revisit earlier stages. In the preaffiliation stage, individuals enter with varying hopes for the group because common goals have not yet been established.

Early identity development in the group may be affected by preexisting relationships among group members, who may know or work with each other in other capacities. Depending on the quality of these past experiences, friction may be carried over into the new group, or trust and comfort may facilitate rapid movement into the work of the group. In either case, it is essential that individuals with existing relationships not form subgroups, as these splinter groups or voting blocs may diminish the comfort and cohesion of all members of the group.

The "power and control" phase (stage 2) in task groups often features competition over which programs or ideas the group will adopt. Conflict about ideas is to be expected—indeed, it should be encouraged if options are to be generated and thoroughly explored. All too often, task groups avoid conflict by evading thorny issues, sometimes even tabling an issue despite the availability of enough facts to make a decision. Establishing norms in which differing options are sought and evaluated on their own merits will aid the group in accomplishing its objectives. Leaders should attempt to stimulate idea-related conflict while managing and controlling personality-related conflict. Failure to achieve this balance may result in the marginalization of potential contributors and a less complete product. Without such healthy conflict, there is always the danger of "groupthink," a condition in which alternative views or options are not expressed or taken seriously. Leaders (and members) can assist others to express the rationale behind particular opinions, clarifying what information needs to be developed to answer questions raised in the course of the conflict.

Group leaders and members can use the communication skills described earlier in this book to reframe communications, thereby making them understandable to all parties, as well as to reflect, probe, seek concreteness, and summarize what is being heard. Facilitators can contribute to the creation of a productive working atmosphere by conveying that each member has something to contribute and by maintaining civility such that no member—or his or her ideas—is allowed to be degraded (Toseland & Rivas, 2009).

Termination in task groups may occur when individual members leave or when the group disbands. "Commencement" in task groups is often overlooked, as members experience relief at the reduction of the demands on their time and their group-related responsibilities, and perhaps satisfaction in successfully achieving their goal. Nevertheless, it is important to evaluate what worked and what did not work well in the group process, to acknowledge the contributions of time and effort made be group members, and to share gratitude about the roles that facilitated group success.

Summary

This chapter focused on the knowledge and skills you will need to effectively intervene in social work task and treatment groups. We addressed the stages of group development and the common member and group characteristics that arise with each phase, illustrating the leadership roles and skills necessary for an effective group experience. We examined the ethical implications of group work and reviewed novel or emerging areas of group work, including practice in rural settings, online groups, and task groups with mixed membership of consumers and professionals. For groups to be successful, leaders must thoughtfully apply the concepts of group formation, and flexibly use their role and interventions to suit the needs of the individuals and the group as a whole, from inception to termination.

Related Online Content

Visit the *Direct Social Work Practice* companion website at www.cengage.com/social_work/hepworth for additional learning tools such as glossary terms, chapter outlines, relevant Web links, and chapter practice quizzes.

Skills Development Exercises in Group Interventions

To assist you in developing group work skills, we have provided a number of exercises with modeled responses. Imagine that you are the facilitator and formulate a response that addresses the member's and group's needs, given the phase and type of group. We have drawn the statements from two types of groups. One is an interdisciplinary task group in a hospital working on policy and practice changes in response to confidentiality laws, undocumented immigrant admissions, indigent patients and the avian flu threat. The other is the HEART therapy group for teen girls with obesity. After completing each statement, compare your response with the modeled response, bearing in mind that the modeled response is only one of many possible acceptable responses.

Client Statements

1. **Task group member** [*in fifth meeting, having missed three*]: "Well, I think we should reconsider why we need to change the policy at all. After all, we've done it this way for years."
2. **Task group member** [*second meeting*]: "How are we going to make decisions—majority rule?"
3. **Task group member** [*third meeting*]: "You're just here for the paycheck."

Modeled Responses

1. "Gene, we talked about the reason we were convened in the first two meetings. I'm wondering why this is coming up at this point?"

2. [*to the group*] "What do you think are the pros and cons of different decision-making options?"
3. "It is true that I'm paid for this work, but I'm drawn here to help the course of groups like this one."

Notes

1. We also refer you to Hartford (1971), Henry (1992), Corey and Corey (2006), Tuckman and Jensen (1977), and Yalom (1995) as sources from which we have drawn information to complement the Garland, Jones, and Kolodny model.
2. Reid (1997) has reviewed procedures for evaluating outcomes in groups, including group testimonials, content analysis of audio- or videotapes, sociometric analysis, self-rating instruments, and other subjective measures. We refer you to Reid (1991) and to Corey (1990) for further discussion of these evaluative measures.
3. Although it is beyond the scope of this chapter to provide details, techniques abound in the literature to address the preceding issues and other self-defeating client attitudes, including those found in Meichenbaum (1977), Mahoney (1974), and Burns (1980). Both Toseland and Rivas (2009) and Rose (1989) offer specific ways of altering cognitions within a group context.

CHAPTER 17

Additive Empathy, Interpretation, and Confrontation

CHAPTER OVERVIEW

Chapter 17 builds on the skills introduced in Chapters 5 and 6 to assist clients in achieving a deeper understanding of their own behavior, the behavior of others, and their options in exploring change. Appropriate timing for and uses of confrontation are presented as a means of gaining greater self-knowledge and assisting clients in making informed decisions about their potential consequences. As in earlier chapters, examples from videos linked to this chapter are featured.

The Meaning and Significance of Client Self-Awareness

Self-awareness is a priceless ingredient generally acknowledged as essential to sound mental health. Humans have long known of the profound importance of self-awareness, as reflected by Socrates, the ancient Greek philosopher, in his often-quoted admonition, "Know thyself." Self-awareness is often sought by voluntary clients and is indispensable to the helping process they seek, particularly during the change-oriented phase. Individuals' efforts to solve problems and to change are effective only if they are properly directed, which in turn depends on accurate awareness of behaviors and circumstances that need to be changed. Indeed, many people experience incessant problems in daily living related to their lack of awareness of the forces that produce these problems.

As we employ the term, *self-awareness* refers largely to awareness of the various forces operating in the present. Social workers assist clients to expand their awareness of their needs or wants, motives, emotions, beliefs, and problematic behaviors, and of these items' impact on other people. We do *not* use self-awareness to refer to insight into the etiology of problems. As we noted in earlier chapters, people can and do change without achieving this type of insight. On occasion, brief excursions into the past may be productive and enlightening—for example, to determine which qualities attracted marital partners to each other, to identify factors that have contributed to sexual dysfunction, to assess the chronicity of problems, or to highlight previous successes. When making such brief excursions, however, it is important to relate the information elicited along the way to *present* work and *present* problems, emphasizing to clients that they can change the present. In other words, they can alter the current effects of history but not history itself.

Social workers have numerous tools at their disposal to assist clients to gain expanded self-awareness. Of these tools, additive empathy, interpretation, and confrontation are probably employed most extensively. This chapter defines these techniques, specifies indications for their use, presents guidelines for employing them effectively, and provides skill development exercises related to these tools.

Additive Empathy and Interpretation

There have been debates about whether empathy is a primarily a personal trait or a skill that can be learned (Fernandez-Olano, Montoya-Fernandez, & Salinas-Sanchez, 2008). Those who consider it to be a learnable trait often conceive it as requiring the practitioner to be in a special state of receptivity, learning to empty him- or herself of distractions and be open to the other person (Lu, Dane & Gellman, 2005; Block-Lerner, et al., 2007; Dimidjian & Linehan, 2003; Segal, Williams, & Teasdale, 2002). Other social work educators have argued that it requires specific training and experience for social workers to be empathic to the social conditions and experiences of low-income clients (Segal, 2007; Smith, 2006).

However conceived, empathy on the social worker's part is critical to the helping process. Earlier chapters

519

examined uses of empathy in the initial phase of the helping process. During the action-oriented phase, additive levels of empathy serve to expand clients' self-awareness, to cushion the impact of confrontations (discussed later in this chapter), and to explore and resolve relational reactions and other obstacles to change (which is discussed at length in Chapter 18). Of course, social workers also continue to use reciprocal levels of empathy during the goal attainment phase because the purposes for which empathy was employed in the initial phase persist throughout the helping process. The difference is that additive levels of empathy are employed sparingly in the initial phase but occupy a prominent position during the action-oriented phase.

Additive empathic responses go somewhat beyond what clients have expressed and therefore require some degree of inference by social workers. Thus, these responses are moderately interpretive—that is, they interpret forces operating to produce feelings, cognitions, reactions, and behavioral patterns. Indeed, after an exhaustive study of research involving psychoanalysis, Luborsky and Spence (1978) concluded that interpretation, as employed by psychoanalysts, is basically the same as empathic communication.

Insight through *interpretation*, it should be noted, is the "supreme agent" in the hierarchy of therapeutic principles that are basic to psychoanalysis and closely related therapies. Proponents of several other theories (most notably, client-centered, Gestalt, and certain existential theories) have avoided the use of interpretation. Still others (Claiborn, 1982; Levy, 1963) maintain that interpretation is essential to the counseling process, regardless of the social worker's theoretical orientation, and that many behaviors of social workers (whether intentional or not) perform interpretive functions.

Semantic and conceptual confusion have contributed to the divergence in views. Additional writings have sharpened concepts and reduced vagueness and confusion. Based on Levy's (1963) conceptualization, Claiborn (1982) posits that interpretation, whatever the social worker's theoretical orientation, "presents the client with a viewpoint discrepant from the client's own, the function of which is to prepare or induce the client to change in accordance with that viewpoint" (p. 442). Viewed in this light, interpretation assists clients to view their problems from a different perspective, thereby opening up new possibilities for remedial courses of action. This generic view, which emphasizes a *discrepant viewpoint*, is sufficiently broad to encompass many change-oriented techniques identified in different theories, including refraining (Watzlawick, Weakland, &

Fisch, 1974), relabeling (Barton & Alexander, 1981), positive connotation (Selvini-Palazzoli, Boscolo, Cecchin, & Prata, 1974), positive reinterpretation (Hammond et al., 1977), additive empathy, and traditional psychoanalytic interpretations. The content of interpretations concerning the same clinical situation thus can be expected to vary according to the theoretical allegiances of social workers. Research (summarized by Claiborn, 1982), however, indicates that "interpretations differing greatly in content seem to have a similar impact on clients" (p. 450).

Levy (1963) classifies interpretations into two categories: *semantic* and *propositional*. Semantic interpretations describe clients' experiences according to the social worker's conceptual vocabulary: "By 'frustrated,' I gather you mean you're feeling hurt and disillusioned." Semantic interpretations thus are closely related to additive empathic responses. Propositional interpretations involve the social worker's notions or explanations that assert causal relationships among factors involved in clients' problem situations: "When you try so hard to avoid displeasing others, you displease yourself and end up resenting others for taking advantage of you."

Social workers should avoid making interpretations or additive empathic responses (we are using the terms interchangeably) that are far removed from the awareness of clients. Research (Speisman, 1959) has indicated that moderate interpretations (those that reflect feelings that lie at the margin of the client's experiences) facilitate self-exploration and self-awareness, whereas deep interpretations engender opposition.[1]

Because the latter are remote from clients' experiences, they appear illogical and irrelevant to clients, who therefore tend to reject them despite the fact that such interpretations may be accurate. The following is an example of such an inept, deep interpretation:

Client: My boss is a real tyrant. He never gives anyone credit, except for Fran. She can do no wrong in his eyes. He just seems to have it in for me. Sometimes I'd like to punch his lights out.

Social worker: Your boss seems to activate the same feelings you had toward your father. You feel he favors Fran, who symbolizes your favored sister. It's your father who you feel was the real tyrant, and you're reliving your resentment toward him. Your boss is merely a symbol of him.

Understandably, the client would likely reject and perhaps resent this interpretation. Although the social worker may be accurate (the determination of which is purely speculative), the client is struggling with feelings toward his boss. To shift the focus to his feelings toward his father misses the mark entirely from the client's perspective.

The following interpretation, made in response to the same client message, would be less likely to create opposition because it is linked to recent experiences of the client:

Social worker: So you really resent your boss because he seems impossible to please and shows partiality toward Fran. [*Reciprocal empathy.*] Those feelings reminded me of similar ones you expressed about 2 weeks ago. You were talking about how, when your parents spent a week with you on their vacation, your father seemed to find fault with everything you did but raved about how well your sister was doing. You'd previously mentioned he'd always seemed to favor your sister and that nothing you did seemed to please him. I'm wondering if those feelings might be connected with the feelings you're experiencing at work.

In the preceding message, notice that the social worker carefully documented the rationale of the interpretation and offered it tentatively, a technique discussed later in the section titled "Guidelines for Employing Interpretation and Additive Empathy." Because we discussed, illustrated, and provided exercises related to additive empathy in Chapter 5, we will not deal with these topics in this chapter. Instead, we limit our discussion here to the uses of interpretation and additive empathy in expanding clients' self-awareness of (1) deeper feelings; (2) underlying meanings of feelings, thoughts, and behavior; (3) wants and goals; (4) hidden purposes of behavior; and (5) unrealized strengths and potentialities.

> Additive empathy or interpretation can provide a useful role in identifying and exploring patterns of couple behavior. In the video "Home for the Holidays," the practitioner, Kim, has heard discussions about different communications patterns in Jackie's and Anna's families of origin. She asks Jackie about whether the way her family handled her coming out as a lesbian was symbolic of how other such issues were dealt within her family. Rather than suggest that they are representative of other such issues, Kim asks a question. Similarly, later Kim asks whether the discussion about the wedding picture and Anna not being included in it is symbolic of challenges they have faced in making decisions or working out problems. Finally, Kim puts their difficulties in the context of becoming a new family: "Often when we are forming new families, new couples, we are torn between the family we come from and the new family we are creating; this plays out in logistical decisions about the holidays."

Deeper Feelings

Clients often have limited awareness of certain emotions, perceiving them only dimly, if at all. Moreover, emotional reactions often involve multiple emotions, but clients may experience only the dominant or surface feelings. Further, some clients experience only negative emotions, such as anger, and are out of touch with more tender feelings, such as hurt, disappointment, compassion, loneliness, fears, and caring. Additive empathic responses (semantic interpretations) may assist clients to become aware of the emotions that lie at the edge of their awareness, thereby enabling them to experience these feelings more sharply and fully, to become more aware of their humanness (including the full spectrum of emotions), and to integrate these emerging emotions into the totality of their experience.

Social workers frequently employ additive empathic responses directed at expanding clients' awareness of feelings for several purposes, which we identify and illustrate in the following examples.

1. To identify feelings that are only implied or hinted at in clients' verbal messages

   Client [*in sixth session*]: I wonder if you feel we're making any progress. [*Clients frequently ask questions that embody feelings.*]

   Social worker: It sounds as though you're not satisfied with your progress. I wonder if you're feeling discouraged about how it's been going.

2. To identify feelings that underlie surface emotions

   Client: I've just felt so bored in the evenings with so little to do. I play video games and surf the Internet, but that doesn't seem to help. Life's just a drag.

   Social worker: I'm getting the impression you're feeling empty and pretty depressed. I wonder if you're feeling lonely and wishing you had some friends to fill that emptiness?

3. To add intensity to feelings clients have minimized

Thirty-year-old mildly retarded, socially isolated woman: It was a little disappointing that Jana [*her childhood friend from another state*] couldn't come to visit. She lost her job and had to cancel her plane reservations.

Social worker: I can see how terribly disappointed you were. In fact, you seem really down even now. You'd looked forward to her visit and made plans. It has been a real blow to you.

4. To clarify the nature of feelings clients experience only vaguely

Gay male client: When Robert told me he didn't want to be with me any more, I just turned numb. I've been walking around in a daze ever since, telling myself, "This can't be happening."

Social worker: It has been a great shock to you. You were so unprepared. It hurts so much it's hard to admit it's really happening.

5. To identify feelings manifested only nonverbally

Client: My sister asked me to tend her kids while she's on vacation, and I will, of course. [*Frowns and sighs.*]

Social worker: But your sigh tells me you don't feel good about it. Right now the message I get from you is that it seems an unfair and heavy burden to you and that you resent it.

Underlying Meanings of Feelings, Thoughts, and Behavior

Used for this purpose, additive empathy or interpretation assists clients to conceptualize or make meaning of feelings, thoughts, and behavior. Social workers thus assist clients in understanding what motivates them to feel, think, and behave as they do; to grasp how their behavior bears on their problems and goals; and to discern themes and patterns in their feelings, thoughts, and behavior. As clients discern similarities, parallels, and themes in their behavior and experiences, their self-awareness gradually expands in much the same way as single pieces of a puzzle fit together, gradually forming discrete entities and eventually coalescing into a coherent whole. The previous interpretation made to the client who resented his boss for favoring a coworker is an example of this type of additive empathic response (it is also a propositional interpretation).

In a more concrete sense, then, social workers may employ this type of interpretation or additive empathy to assist clients to realize that they experience troublesome feelings in the presence of a certain type of person or in certain circumstances. For example, clients may feel depressed in the presence of critical people or feel extremely anxious in situations wherein they must perform (e.g., when expected to give a talk or take a test). Social workers may thus use additive empathy to identify negative perceptual sets and other dysfunctional cognitive patterns that can be modified by employing cognitive restructuring. Clients may attend exclusively to trivial indications of their imperfections and completely overlook abundant evidence of competent and successful performance.

Similarly, a social worker may assist a client to discern a pattern of anticipating negative outcomes of relatively minor events and dreading (and avoiding) the events because of his or her perception of those outcomes as absolute disasters. One client dreaded visiting a lifelong friend who had recently sustained a severe fall, leaving her partially paralyzed. When the social worker explored possible negative events that the client feared might occur if she were to visit the friend, she identified the following:

- *"What if I cry when I see her?"*
- *"What if I stare at her?"*
- *"What if I say the wrong thing?"*

Using an additive empathic response, the social worker replied, "And if you did one of those things, it would be a total disaster?" The client readily agreed. The social worker then employed cognitive restructuring to assist the client to view the situation in a more realistic perspective. The social worker discussed each feared reaction in turn, clarifying that anyone might react as the client feared reacting and that if she were to react in any of these ways it would be uncomfortable but certainly not a disaster. The social worker and client jointly concluded that the client had a certain amount of control over how she reacted rather than being totally at the mercy of circumstances. Following behavioral rehearsal, the client's fears of disaster gradually dwindled to manageable proportions.

Social workers may also employ this type of additive empathy to enhance clients' awareness of perceptual distortions that adversely affect their interpersonal relationships. For example, parents may reject children because they perceive characteristics in them that the parents abhor. Previous exploration, however, may have disclosed that parents identify the same qualities in themselves and project their self-hatred onto their children. By assisting clients to recognize how self-perceptions (which may also be distorted) warp their perceptions of their children, social workers enable such parents to make discriminations and to perceive and accept their children as unique individuals who are different from themselves.

Similar perceptual distortions may occur between marital partners. These problems may cause spouses to perceive and to respond inappropriately to each other as a result of unresolved and troublesome feelings that derive from earlier relationships with parents of the opposite sex.

> In the video associated with this chapter, "Adolescent mother and foster parent," the practitioner, Glenda, observes behavioral patterns that are conflicting between a teen parent, Twanna, and her foster parent, Janet. Twanna is coming home late from school, leaving her two-year-old child with the foster mother for extended periods. The foster mother is concerned that Twanna may not be around her child enough to bond with her. Meanwhile, the foster mother is at times pacifying the infant by giving her candy. When Twanna tries to stop this, her child has tantrums. Glenda hears the account of this interaction and suggests that when Twanna refuses to deal with the tantrums, going to her room and putting on her head phones, she may be thinking about Janet, "You made her this way… you deal with her."

Wants and Goals

Another important use of additive empathy is to assist clients to become aware of wants and goals that they imply in their messages but do not fully recognize. When beset by difficulties, people often tend to think in terms of problems and ways to obtain relief from them rather than in terms of growth and change—even though the latter two processes are often implied in the former. When they become more aware of the thrust toward growth implied in their messages, clients often welcome the prospect and may even wax enthusiastic about it. This type of additive empathy not only expands self-awareness, but may also enhance motivation.

As is apparent in the following excerpt, additive empathic messages that highlight implied wants and goals often results in the formulation of explicit goals that pave the way to change-oriented actions. Moreover, such messages play a critical role in arousing hope in dispirited clients who feel overwhelmed by their problems and have been unable to discern any positive desires for growth manifested in their struggles. This type of message plays a key role both in the first phase of the helping process and in the change-oriented phase.

Client: I'm so sick of always being imposed upon. All of my family just take me for granted. You know: "Good old Marcie, you can always depend on her." I've taken about all of this that I can take.

Social worker: Just thinking about it stirs you up. Marcie, it seems to me that what you're saying adds up to an urgent desire on your part to be your own person—to feel in charge of yourself rather than being at the mercy of others' requests or demands.

Client: I hadn't thought of it that way, but you're right. That's exactly what I want. If I could just be my own person.

Social worker: Maybe that's a goal you'd like to set for yourself. It seems to fit, and accomplishing it would liberate you from the oppressive feelings you've described.

Client: Yes, yes! I'd like very much to set that goal. Do you really think I could accomplish it?

Hidden Purposes of Behavior

Social workers sometimes employ interpretation to help clients become more fully aware of the basic motivations that underlie their concerns. Other people may misinterpret clients' motives, and clients themselves may have only a dim awareness of them because of the obscuring effect of their problematic behaviors.

Prominent among these motives are the following: to protect tenuous self-esteem (e.g., by avoiding situations that involve any risk of failing), to avoid anxiety-producing situations, and to compensate for feelings of impotency or inadequacy. The following are typical examples of surface behaviors and the hidden purposes served by those behaviors:

- *Underachieving students may exert little effort in school (1) because they can justify failing on the basis of not having really tried (rather than having to face their fears of being inadequate) or (2) because they are seeking to punish parents who withhold approval and love when they fall short of their expectations.*

- *Clients may present a facade of bravado to conceal from themselves and others underlying fears and feelings of inadequacy.*

- *Clients may set themselves up for physical or emotional pain to offset deep-seated feelings of guilt.*

- *Clients may engage in self-defeating behavior to validate myths that they are destined to be losers or to live out life scripts determined by circumstances beyond their control.*

- *Clients may avoid relating closely to others to protect against fears of being dominated or controlled.*

- *Clients may behave aggressively or abrasively to avoid risking rejection by keeping others at a distance.*

Interpretations must be based on substantial supporting information that clients have disclosed previously. Without supporting information, interpretations are little more than speculations that clients are unlikely to accept. Indeed, such speculations often emanate from social workers' projections and are typically inaccurate. Clients may regard such interpretations as offensive or may question social workers' competence when they receive such responses.

The following example illustrates appropriate use of interpretation to expand awareness of the motives underlying a client's behavior.

Case Example

The client, Mr. R, age 33, and his wife entered marital therapy largely at his wife's instigation. Mrs. R complained about a lack of closeness in the relationship and felt rejected because her husband seldom made affectional overtures. When she made overtures, he typically rebuffed her by pulling back. Mr. R had revealed in the exploratory interviews that his mother had been (and still was) extremely dominating and controlling. He felt little warmth toward his mother and saw her no more than was absolutely necessary.

The following excerpt from an individual session with Mr. R focuses on an event that occurred during the week when the couple went to a movie. Mrs. R had reached over to hold her husband's hand. He abruptly withdrew it, and Mrs. R later expressed her feelings of hurt and rejection. Their ensuing discussion was unproductive, and their communication became strained. Mr. R discussed the event that occurred in the theater:

Mr. R: I know Carol was hurt when I didn't hold her hand. I don't know why, but it really turned me off.

Social worker: So you're wondering why you turn off when she reaches for some affectional contact. I wonder what was happening inside of you at that moment. What were you thinking and feeling?

Mr. R: Gee, let me think. I guess I was anticipating she'd do it, and I just wanted to be left alone to enjoy the movie. I guess I resented her taking my hand. That doesn't make sense when I think about it. Why should I resent holding hands with the woman I love?

Social worker: Jim, I think you're asking an awfully good question—one that's a key to many of the difficulties in your marriage. Let me share an idea with you that may shed some light on why you respond as you do. You mentioned you felt resentful when Carol took your hand. Based on the feelings you just expressed, I'm wondering if perhaps you feel you're submitting to her if you respond positively when she takes the initiative and pull back to be sure you're not letting yourself be dominated by her [*the hidden purpose*]. Another reason for suggesting that is that as you were growing up you felt dominated by your mother and resented her for being that way. Even now you avoid seeing her any more than you have to. I'm wondering if, as a result of your relationship with her, you could have developed a supersensitivity to being controlled by a female so that you resent any behavior on Carol's part that even suggests her being in control. [*The latter part of the response provides the rationale for the interpretation.*]

Unrealized Strengths and Potentialities

Another vital purpose served by interpretation and additive empathy is to expand clients' awareness of their strengths and undeveloped potentialities. Clients' strengths are demonstrated in a variety of ways, and social workers need to sensitize themselves to these often subtle manifestations by consciously cultivating a positive perceptual set. This objective is vital, because clients are often preoccupied with their weaknesses. Moreover, becoming aware of strengths tends to arouse clients' hopes and to generate the courage they need to begin making changes.

Drawing clients' awareness to strengths tends to enhance self-esteem and to foster courage to undertake tasks that involve risking new behaviors. With conscious effort, social workers can become increasingly aware of their clients' strengths. For example, when a client faces a child welfare investigation because his or her children were left alone, part of the assessment must necessarily focus on the circumstances of danger that occurred and alternatives that were available to the client. This investigation often provokes defensive behavior from the client. Clients are more likely to respond positively to explorations for other solutions if their own strengths are recognized (De Jong & Miller, 1995; McQuaide & Ehrenreich, 1997). For example, the following response identifies both strengths and problems:

Social worker: You have explained that you did not intend to leave your children alone for any extended period. Your daughter was cooking for her little brother when the grease fire broke out. She knew how to call 911 and get the fire department. We would all want this situation to never have happened. Still, your daughter knew what to do in case of an emergency. She was able to prepare a meal. You have done many things to prepare your children to cope. We will need to plan together so that they are not left alone without adult supervision.

In this case, the supporting of strengths is paired with identification of continuing concerns and the need to plan together to eliminate dangers.

In the video "Serving the Squeaky Wheel" associated with this chapter, the practitioner, Ron Rooney, becomes aware of a pattern in many stories from Molly, the client, that concern grievances about being ill-served by other social workers and the health system. When she mentions not wanting to be the "greasy wheel" [squeaky wheel], Rooney suggests the possibility that Molly has, in fact, being acting as a squeaky wheel by complaining when she feels underserved, and that pattern of assertiveness is sometimes rewarded by the system and sometimes punished: "You seem to be courageous in fighting battles and you have learned some skills in assertiveness—and, as you say, that can be a two-edged or three-edged sword. Sometimes your assertiveness gets you what you want and sometimes your assertiveness causes some people to look at you as the squeaky wheel that has squeaked too much."

Guidelines for Employing Interpretation and Additive Empathy

Considerable finesse is required to employ interpretation and additive empathy effectively. The following guidelines will assist you in acquiring this skill.

1. *Use additive empathy sparingly until a sound working relationship has evolved.* Because these responses go somewhat beyond clients' current level of self-awareness, clients may misinterpret the motives of a social worker and respond defensively. Hence, when clients have brief contact with a social worker, such as in discharge planning, they are unlikely to develop the kind of relationship in which additive empathy is appropriate. When clients demonstrate that they are confident of a social worker's goodwill, they are able to tolerate and often to benefit from additive empathic and interpretative responses.

The exceptions to this guideline involve messages that identify (1) wants and goals and (2) strengths and potentialities, both of which are also appropriate in the initial phase of the helping process. Social workers must avoid identifying strengths excessively in the initial phase, because some clients will interpret such messages as insincere flattery.

2. *Employ these responses only when clients are engaged in self-exploration or have shown that they are ready to do so.* Clients or groups that are not ready to engage in self-exploration are likely to resist social workers' interpretive efforts and may perceive them as unwarranted attempts by social workers to impose their formulations upon them. Exceptions to this guideline are the same as those cited in the first guideline.

3. *Pitch these responses to the edge of clients' self-awareness, and avoid attempting to foster awareness that is remote from clients' current awareness or experiences.* Clients generally are receptive to responses that closely relate to their experiences but resist those that emanate from social workers' unfounded conjectures. It is poor practice to attempt to push clients into rapidly acquiring new insights, because many of these deep interpretations will prove to be inaccurate and produce negative effects, including reducing clients' confidence in social workers, conveying lack of understanding, or engendering resistance. Social workers should not employ interpretive responses until they have amassed sufficient information to be reasonably confident their responses are accurate. They should then take care to share the supportive information upon which the interpretation is based.

4. *Avoid making several additive empathic responses in succession.* Because interpretation responses require time to think through, digest, and assimilate, a series of such responses tends to bewilder clients.

5. *Phrase interpretive responses in tentative terms.* Because these responses involve a certain degree of inference, there is always the possibility that the social worker might be wrong. Tentative phrasing openly acknowledges this possibility and invites clients to agree or disagree. If social workers present interpretations in an authoritarian or dogmatic manner, however, clients may not feel free to offer candid feedback and may outwardly agree while covertly rejecting interpretations. Tentative phrases include "I wonder if … ," "Could it be that your feelings may be related to … ?", and "Perhaps you're feeling this way because … ." Using additive empathy to explore strengths is, of course, less threatening and can be done with less hesitance.

Note that in the video "Home for the Holidays," at several points, Kim, the family therapist suggests a tentative interpretation of what one or other of the couple might be feeling and then says, "I don't want to put words into your mouth," giving them an opportunity to correct her interpretation.

6. *To determine the accuracy of an interpretive response, carefully note clients' reactions after offering the interpretation.* When responses are on target, clients affirm their validity, continue self-exploration by bringing up additional relevant material, or respond emotionally in a manner that matches the moment (e.g., ventilate relevant feelings). When interpretations are inaccurate or are premature, clients tend to disconfirm them (verbally or nonverbally), change the subject, withdraw emotionally, argue or become defensive, or simply ignore the interpretation.

7. *If the client responds negatively to an interpretative response, acknowledge your probable error, respond empathically to the client's reaction, and continue your discussion of the topic under consideration.*

To assist you in expanding your skill in formulating interpretive and additive empathic responses, a number of exercises, together with modeled responses, appear at the end of this chapter.

Confrontation

Confrontation is similar to interpretation and additive empathy in that it is a tool to enhance clients' self-awareness and to promote change. Confrontation, however, involves facing clients with some aspect of their thoughts, feelings, or behavior that is contributing to or maintaining their difficulties. Social workers, perhaps more than members of some other helping professions, must struggle to maintain a dual focus on both the individual's rights and social justice. Some claim that the ability to juggle these sometimes conflicting demands is an essential strength of the profession (Regehr & Angle, 1997). Others argue that "there are some activities people can do that put them outside any entitlement to respect … some people called clients are not much respected" (Ryder & Tepley, 1993, p. 146). For example, individuals who act to harm or endanger others, such as the perpetrators of domestic violence or sexual abuse, challenge this dual commitment and social workers' ethical obligation (described in Chapter 4) to respect the inherent worth and dignity of all individuals regardless of the acts they may have committed.

In this context, when is confrontation appropriate? With whom? And under what conditions? Is confrontation a skill or a style of practice?

In some settings, confrontation has become a style of practice rather than a selective skill. That is, practitioners believe that some clients are so well defended with denial, rationalization, and refusal to accept responsibility that only repeated confrontations will succeed. For example, in work with batterers, some have claimed that "almost every word they [batterers] utter is either victim blaming or justification for their violence. So I have to start confronting all of that stuff right from the beginning and it gets very intense" (Pence & Paymar, 1993, p. 21). It was believed that only when the offender admitted responsibility for the behavior and accepted the label of offender could meaningful change occur. If the clients did not accept the label, and if they defended themselves, they were labeled as being in denial and resistant (Miller & Sovereign, 1989). Hence, confronting them in an authoritarian and aggressive style (Miller & Rollnick, 1991) was considered necessary to achieve an admission of guilt—that is, admission that they had a problem and were not in control of their behavior.

In short, clients were expected to give up their own views and to accept the views of those who had the power to confront them. It was assumed that disempowered persons—who had no motivation owned by them, and were incapable of making their own decisions and controlling their behavior—would then accept and cooperate with the formulation of the problem by the social workers and/or group (Kear-Colwell & Pollock, 1997). If they

TABLE-17-1 STAGES OF CHANGE MODEL

STAGE	CHARACTERISTIC BEHAVIOR	SOCIAL WORKER'S TASK
Precontemplation	Client does not believe that he or she has a problem; is considered unmotivated by others	Raise awareness of concerns held by others: "What does your partner think about the effect of your drinking on your home life?" Stimulate dissonance with risk-benefit analysis: "What are the benefits to you from making your living by selling drugs? What are the costs to you from living by selling drugs?"
Contemplation	Becomes aware of the existence of the problem but is not moved to action Appears ambivalent—shows awareness, then discounts it	Attempt to tip decisional balance by exploring reasons to change: "As you add it up, what do you think the benefits are in relation to the costs? If you get a legal job, then what?" Strengthen confidence in change as a possibility
Preparation	Recognizes problem; asks what can be done to change Appears motivated	Help client plan appropriate course of action
Action	Implements plan of action	Develop plan to implement action Plan details to make it possible (e.g., transportation, child care)
Maintenance	Sustains change through consistent application of strategies	Identify strategies to prevent lapses and relapse: "What have been the triggers to expose you to a dangerous situation?"
Relapse	Slips into problematic behavior and may return to precontemplation stage	Attempt to return to contemplation without being stuck or demoralized Reinforce achievement; treat with respect: "This is a difficult time. You have been at this point before and you overcame it. What do you think about whether you want to overcome it again?"

SOURCE: Adapted from Kear-Colwell & Pollock (1997); and Prochaska, DiClemente, and Norcross (1992).

reacted by showing disagreement and resistance, they were seen as persisting in denial, as lacking motivation, and often as demonstrating pathological personality patterns.

This view too often leads to an interactive cycle of confrontation and denial in which the client acts to protect his or her self-esteem by denying charges (Miller & Sovereign, 1989). Social workers and theorists in fields such as treatment of domestic abuse perpetrators, persons with addictions, and sexual offenders are now questioning whether this style is effective or ethical (Fearing, 1996; Kear-Colwell & Pollock, 1997; Miller & Sovereign, 1989; Murphy & Baxter, 1997). These helping professionals are questioning whether intense confrontation of defenses is beneficial or whether it may unwittingly reinforce the belief that relationships are based on coercive influences (Murphy & Baxter, 1997). They suggest that a supportive and collaborative working alliance is more likely to increase motivation in clients. Motivational interviewing is more likely to create dissonance and encourage offenders to own the

process. Even in work with addicted persons, new approaches acknowledge the importance of developing a positive, respectful approach toward the person who is the subject of the intervention (Fearing, 1996).

Instead of all-purpose confrontation delivered at any time, it may be more useful to acknowledge the stage of change the client is at regarding the problematic behavior when using this technique. Prochaska, DiClemente, and Norcross (1992) have proposed a six-stage process of change (see Table 17-1). Their model begins with precontemplation, in which the person has not considered the behavior to be a problem.

In the motivational interviewing approach, the social worker takes responsibility for pursuing a positive atmosphere for change based on accurate empathic understanding, mutual trust, acceptance, and understanding of the world from the offender's perspective (Kear-Colwell & Pollock, 1997). In this exploration, the focus is on the offending behavior and its effects and origins, not on the person of the offender (Kear-Colwell & Pollock, 1997). The effort seeks to be persuasive by creating an awareness that the person's problem behavior is dissonant with his or her personal goals. By engaging in a risk-benefit analysis, the social worker assists the client in deciding whether it makes sense to explore a change so as to better reach those goals. The social worker would then assist the client to make a decision.

Once a client has decided to act, then the form of influence can help him or her decide which action to pursue. For example, after he has decided to deal with a domestic violence problem, a male client can be helped to consider alternatives for how to go about it. When a decision has been made, efforts are aimed at planning useful action to reach the goal. When a change has occurred, efforts are aimed at exploring in detail the contingencies and triggers that have been associated with the behavior. Armed with such knowledge, alternatives can be planned and practiced to avoid a relapse into the offending behavior.

Confrontation is most likely to be heard when it comes from a source liked and respected by the client. Consequently, confrontations that occur early in contact are often not accurately heard or heeded. Nevertheless, social workers sometimes have responsibilities to confront clients with violations of the law and with dangers to themselves and others before a helping relationship has developed. Such confrontations should occur sparingly, given the likelihood that they will not be heeded so early in contact (Rooney, 2009).

In the middle phase of work, social workers employ confrontation to assist clients to achieve awareness of the forces blocking their progress toward growth and goal attainment and to enhance their motivation to implement efforts toward change. Confrontation is particularly relevant when clients manifest blind spots to discrepancies or inconsistencies in their thoughts, beliefs, emotions, and behavior that produce or perpetuate dysfunctional behavior. Of course, blind spots in self-awareness are universal because all humans suffer from the limitation of being unable to step out of their perceptual fields and look at themselves objectively.

Additive empathy and confrontation have much in common. Skillful confrontations incorporate consideration of clients' feelings that underlie obstacles to change. Because fears are often among these feelings, skill in relating with high levels of empathy is a prerequisite to using confrontation effectively. Indeed, effective confrontation is an extension of empathic communication because the focus on discrepancies and inconsistencies derives from a deep understanding of clients' feelings, experiences, and behavior.

It is important for social workers to possess a range of confrontation skills and not to confront clients primarily to vent their own frustration with clients' lack of progress. Social workers would more appropriately consider confrontation to exist along a continuum that ranges from fostering *self-confrontation* at one extreme to *assertive confrontation* at the other extreme (Rooney, 2009). That is, clients can often be engaged quickly in self-confrontation by asking them questions that cause them to reflect on the relationship between their behaviors and their own values.

Skillfully designed intake forms can serve a similar function, asking potential clients to reflect on concerns and their perceptions of the causes. Such confrontations are subtle and respectful, and they rarely engender strong client opposition. As clients gain expanded awareness of themselves and their problems through self-exploration, they tend to recognize and to confront discrepancies and inconsistencies themselves. Self-confrontation is generally preferable to social worker–initiated confrontation, because the former is less risky and because clients' resistance to integrating insights is not an obstacle when they initiate confrontations themselves.

Clients vary widely in the degree to which they engage in self-confrontation. Emotionally mature, introspective persons may engage in self-confrontations frequently. In contrast, individuals who are out of touch with their emotions, who lack awareness of their effects on others, and who blame others or circumstances for their difficulties are least likely to engage in self-confrontation.

Inductive questioning can be a form of confrontation that is more active on the social worker's part but is still conveyed in a respectful manner. The social worker asks questions that lead the client to consider potential discrepancies between thoughts, values, beliefs, and actions. Also, when the therapist asks a question that relates to facts rather than one that requires the client to label himself or herself, the question is more likely to be effective. For example, asking a client with a chemical dependency problem, "Are you powerless over alcohol?" would require the client to essentially label himself an alcoholic. On the other hand, "Do you ever have blackouts?", "Do you find it easier to bring up a problem with another person when you have had something to drink?", and "Do you ever find that once you begin drinking you can't easily stop?" are questions that, taken together, raise the possibility that drinking is a problem that might need attention (Citron, 1978).

When a danger is imminent, the social worker may not be able to rely on tactful self-confrontation facilitated by inductive questioning. Instead, he or she may have to engage in more assertive confrontation in which the connection between troubling thoughts, plans, values, and beliefs is stated in declarative form, connecting them explicitly for the client. Such assertive confrontation is a more high-risk technique because clients may interpret social workers' statements as criticisms, put-downs, or rejections. Paradoxically, the risk of these reactions is greatest among clients who must be confronted most often because they rarely engage in self-confrontation. These individuals tend to have weak self-concepts and are therefore prone to read criticism into messages when none is intended. Moreover, ill-timed and poorly executed confrontations may be perceived by clients as verbal assaults and may seriously damage helping relationships.

Using confrontation therefore requires keen timing and finesse. Social workers must make special efforts to convey their helpful intent and goodwill as they employ this technique. Otherwise, they may engender hostility or offend and alienate clients.

Effective assertive confrontations embody four elements: (1) expression of concern; (2) a description of the client's purported goal, belief, or commitment; (3) the behavior (or absence of behavior) that is inconsistent or discrepant with the goal, belief, or commitment; and (4) the probable negative outcomes of the discrepant behavior. The format of a confrontive response may be depicted as follows:

(want)
I am concerned because you (believe)
(are striving to)

_____
(describe desired outcome)

but your _____
(describe discrepant action, behavior, or inaction)

is likely to produce _____
(describe probable negative consequences)

This format is purely illustrative. You may organize these elements in varying ways, and we encourage you to be innovative and to develop your own style. For example, you may challenge clients to analyze the effects of behaviors that are incongruous with their purported goals or values, as illustrated in the following excerpt:

Social worker [*To male on parole*]: Al, I know the last thing you want is to have to return to prison. I want you to stay out, too, and I think you sense that. But I have to level with you. You're starting to hang out with the same bunch you got in trouble with before you went to prison. You're heading in the same direction you were before, and we both know where that leads.

In this confrontation, the social worker begins by referring to the client's purported goal (remaining out of prison) and expresses a like commitment to the goal. The social worker next introduces concern about the client's behavior (hanging out with the same bunch the client got in trouble with before) that is discrepant with that goal. The social worker concludes the confrontation by focusing on the possible negative consequence of the discrepant behavior (getting into trouble and returning to prison).

Notice these same elements in the following examples of confrontive responses:

- [To father in family session]: *Mr. D, I'd like you to stop for a moment and examine what you're doing. I know you want the children not to be afraid of you and to talk with you more openly. Right?* [Father agrees.] *Okay, let's think about what you just did with Steve. He began to tell you about what he did after the school assembly, and you cut him off and got on his case. Did you notice how he clammed up immediately?*

- [To mother in child welfare system]: *I have a concern I need to share with you. You've expressed your goal of regaining custody of Pete, and we agreed that attending the parents' group was part of the plan to accomplish that goal. This week is the second time in a row you've missed the meeting because you overslept. I'm very concerned that you may be defeating yourself in accomplishing your goal.*

Because employing assertive confrontation runs the risk of putting clients on the defensive or alienating them, expressing concern and helpful intent is a critical element because it reduces the possibility that clients will misconstrue the motive behind the confrontation. Tone of voice is also vital in highlighting helpful intent. If the social worker conveys the confrontation in a warm, concerned tone of voice, the client will be much less likely to feel attacked. If the social worker uses a critical tone of voice, any verbal reassurance that criticism was not intended is likely to fall on deaf ears. Keep in mind that people tend to attach more credence to nonverbal aspects of messages than to verbal aspects.

Guidelines for Employing Confrontation

To assist you in employing confrontation effectively, we offer the following guidelines.

1. *When a violation of the law or imminent danger to self or others is involved, a confrontation must occur no matter how early in the working relationship.* Such confrontations may impede the development of the relationship, but the risk of harm to self and others is more important than the immediate effect on the relationship.

2. *Whenever possible, avoid confrontation until an effective working relationship has been established.* This can occur when a client is contemplating action (or inaction) that impedes his or her own goals but is not an imminent danger to self or others. Employing empathic responsiveness in early contacts conveys understanding, fosters rapport, and enhances confidence in the social worker's perceptiveness and expertise. When a foundation of trust and confidence has been established, clients are more receptive to confrontations and, in some instances, even welcome them.

3. *Use confrontation sparingly.* Confrontation is a potent technique that generally should be employed only when clients' blind spots are not responsive to other, less risky intervention methods. Poorly timed and excessive confrontations can inflict psychological damage on clients (Lieberman, Yalom, & Miles, 1973).

Another reason to employ confrontation judiciously is that some clients may yield to forceful confrontation for counterproductive reasons. Seeking to please social workers (or to avoid displeasing them), they may temporarily modify their behavior. But changing merely to comply with the expectations of a social worker leads to passivity and dependence, both of which are anathema to actual growth. Some clients are already excessively passive, and pressuring them for compliance merely reinforces their passivity.

4. *Deliver confrontations in an atmosphere of warmth, caring, and concern.* If social workers employ confrontations in a cold, impersonal, or critical way, clients are likely to feel that they are being attacked. By contrast, if social workers preface confrontations with genuine empathic concern, clients are more likely to perceive the helpfulness intended in the confrontation.

5. *Whenever possible, encourage self-confrontation.* Recall from the previous discussion that self-confrontation has decided advantages over social worker–initiated confrontation. Learning by self-discovery fosters

independence and increases the likelihood that clients will act upon their newly gained self-awareness. Social workers can encourage self-confrontation by drawing clients' attention to issues, behaviors, or inconsistencies that they may have overlooked and by encouraging them to analyze the situation further.

For example, the social worker may directly intervene into dysfunctional interactions and challenge individuals, couples, families, or groups to identify what they are doing. Responses that encourage self-confrontation in such a context include the following:

- *"Let's stop and look at what you just did."*
- *"What did you just do?"*

Other inductive question responses that highlight inconsistencies and foster self-confrontation are as follows:

- *"I'm having trouble seeing how what you just said (or did) fits with …"*
- *"I can understand how you felt, but how did (describe behavior) make it better for you?"*
- *"What you're saying seems inconsistent with what you want to achieve. How do you see it?"*

Yet another technique is useful when clients overlook the dynamic significance of their own revealing expressions or when their manifest feelings fail to match their reported feelings. This technique involves asking them to repeat a message, to listen carefully to themselves, and to consider the meaning of the message. Examples of this technique follow:

- *"I want to be sure you realize the significance of what you just said. Repeat it, but this time listen carefully to yourself, and tell me what it means to you."*
- [To marital partner in conjoint interview]: *"Joan just told you something terribly important, and I'm not sure you really grasped it. Could you repeat it, Joan, and I want you to listen very carefully, Bob, and check with Joan as to whether you grasped what she said."*
- [To group member]: *"You just told the group you're feeling better about yourself, but it didn't come through that way. Please say it again, but get in touch with your feelings and listen to yourself."*

6. *Avoid using confrontation when clients are experiencing extreme emotional strain.* Confrontation tends to mobilize anxiety. When clients are under heavy strain, supportive techniques rather than confrontation

are indicated. Clients who are overwhelmed with anxiety or guilt generally are not receptive to confrontation and will not benefit from it. In fact, confrontation may be detrimental, adding to their already excessive tension.

Conversely, confrontation is appropriate for clients who experience minimal inner conflict or anxiety when such reactions would be appropriate in light of their problematic behavior as perceived by others. Self-satisfied and typically insensitive to the feelings and needs of others (whom they cause to be anxious), such clients—popularly referred to as having "character disorders"—often lack the anxiety needed to engender and maintain adequate motivation. Confrontation, when combined with the facilitative conditions, may mobilize the anxiety they need to examine their own behavior and to consider making constructive changes.

7. Follow confrontation with emphatic responsiveness. Because clients may take offense to even skillful confrontation, it is vital to be sensitive to their reactions. Clients often do not express their reactions verbally, so social workers need to be especially attuned to nonverbal cues that suggest hurt, anger, confusion, discomfort, embarrassment, or resentment. If clients manifest these or other unfavorable reactions, it is important to explore their reactions and to respond empathically to their feelings. Discussing such reactions provides opportunities (1) for clients to ventilate their feelings and (2) for social workers to clarify their helpful intent and to assist clients to work through negative feelings. If social workers fail to sense negative feelings or clients withhold expressions of them, the feelings may fester and adversely affect the helping relationship.

8. Expect that clients will respond to confrontation with a certain degree of anxiety. Indeed, confrontation is employed to produce a temporary sense of disequilibrium that is essential to break an impasse. The anxiety or disequilibrium serves a therapeutic purpose in impelling the client to make constructive changes that eliminate the discrepancy that prompted the social worker's confrontation. Empathic responsiveness following confrontation is not aimed at diluting this anxiety, but rather seeks to resolve untoward reactions that may derive from negative interpretations of the social worker's motives for making the confrontation.

9. Do not expect immediate change after confrontations. Although awareness paves the way to change, clients rarely succeed in making changes immediately following acquisition of insight. Even when clients fully accept confrontations, corresponding changes ordinarily occur by increments. Known as working through,

this change process involves repeatedly reviewing the same conflicts and the client's typical reactions to them, gradually broadening the perspective to encompass increasingly more situations to which the changes are applicable. Unfortunately, some naive social workers press for immediate change, sometimes inflicting psychological damage on their clients.

Indications for Assertive Confrontation

As noted previously, confrontation is appropriate in three circumstances: (1) when violations of the law or imminent threats to the welfare and safety of self or others are involved; (2) when discrepancies, inconsistencies, and dysfunctional behaviors (overt or covert) block progress or create difficulties; and (3) when efforts at self-confrontation and inductive questioning have been ineffective in fostering clients' awareness of these behaviors or attempts to make corresponding changes. Discrepancies may reside in cognitive/perceptual, emotional (affective), or behavioral functions or may involve interactions between these functions. A comprehensive analysis of types of discrepancies and inconsistencies has been presented elsewhere (Hammond et al., 1977, pp. 286–318); therefore, we merely highlight some of the most commonly encountered.

Cognitive/Perceptual Discrepancies

Many clients have behavioral or perceptual difficulties that are a product of inaccurate, erroneous, or incomplete information, and confrontation may assist them in modifying their problematic behaviors. For example, clients may lack accurate information about indicators of alcoholism, normal sexual functioning, or reasonable expectations of children according to stages of development.

Even more common are misconceptions about the self. The most common of these, in the authors' experience, involve self-demeaning perceptions. Even talented and attractive persons may view themselves as inferior, worthless, inadequate, unattractive, or stupid. Such perceptions are often deeply embedded and do not yield to change without extensive working through. Nevertheless, confronting clients with their strengths or raising their awareness of other areas of competence can prove helpful in challenging such self-deprecating views.

Other cognitive/perceptual discrepancies include interpersonal perceptual distortions, irrational fears, dichotomous or stereotypical thinking, denial of problems, placing responsibility for one's difficulties outside of oneself, failing to discern available alternative solutions to difficulties, and failing to consider consequences of actions.

Affective Discrepancies

Discrepancies in the emotional realm are inextricably linked to cognitive/perceptual processes, because emotions are shaped by the cognitive meanings that clients attribute to situations, events, and memories. For example, a client may experience intense anger that emanates from a conclusion that another person has intentionally insulted, slighted, or betrayed him or her. This conclusion is based on a meaning attribution that may involve a grossly distorted perception of the other person's intentions. In such instances, social workers can assist clients to explore their feelings, to provide relevant detailed factual information, to consider alternative meanings, and to realign their emotions with reality.

Affective discrepancies that social workers commonly encounter include denying or minimizing actual feelings, being out of touch with painful emotions, expressing feelings that are contrary to purported feelings (e.g., claiming to love a spouse or child but expressing only critical or otherwise negative feelings), and verbally expressing a feeling that contradicts feelings expressed nonverbally (e.g., "No, I'm not disappointed," said with a quivering voice and tears in the eyes). Gentle confrontations aimed at emotional discrepancies often pave the way to ventilation of troubling emotions, and many clients appreciate social workers' sensitivity in recognizing their suppressed or unexpressed emotions.

If a client appears unprepared to face painful emotions, the social worker should proceed cautiously. Indeed, it may be wise to defer further exploration of those hurtful emotions. Confronting the client vigorously may elicit overwhelming emotions and engender consequent resentment toward the social worker.

Behavioral Discrepancies

Clients may experience many behavioral concerns that create difficulties for themselves and for others. Even though these patterns may be conspicuous to others, clients may remain blind to their patterns or to the effects of their behaviors on others. Confrontation may be required to expand their awareness of these patterns and their pernicious effects.

Irresponsible behavior tends to spawn serious interpersonal difficulties for clients as well as problems with broader society. Neglect of children, weak efforts to secure and maintain employment, undependability in fulfilling assignments, failure to maintain property—these and similar derelictions of duty often result in severe financial, legal, and interpersonal entanglements that may culminate in loss of employment; estrangement from others; and loss of property, child custody, self-respect, and even personal freedom.

Irresponsible behavior often pervades the helping process as well, sometimes indicated by clients' tardiness to sessions, unwillingness to acknowledge problems, and failure to keep appointments or pay fees. Effective confrontation with such clients requires employing a firm approach couched in expressions of goodwill and concern about wanting to assist them to avoid the adverse consequences of not assuming responsibilities. Social workers do a disservice to their clients when they permit them to evade responsibility for their actions or inaction. Further, social workers must counter clients' tendency to blame others or circumstances for their difficulties by assisting them to recognize that *only they* can reduce the pressures that beset them.

Other common behavioral discrepancies involve repeated actions that are incongruous with purported goals or values. Adolescents may describe ambitious goals that require extensive training or education but make little effort in school, be truant frequently, and otherwise behave in ways that are entirely inconsistent with their stated goals. Spouses or parents may similarly espouse goals of improving their marital or family life but persistently behave in abrasive ways that further erode their relationships.

Confrontation often must be used to assist clients to desist from engaging in self-defeating behaviors. In some instances, therapeutic binds (a special form of confrontation discussed in Chapter 18) may be employed to supply needed leverage to motivate clients to relinquish destructive and unusually persistent patterns of behavior.

Three other common categories of discrepancies or dysfunctional behavior that warrant confrontation are manipulative behavior, dysfunctional communication, and resistance to change. In groups, certain members may attempt to dominate the group, bait group members, play one person against the other, undermine the leader, or engage in other destructive ploys. The price of permitting members to engage in such behaviors may be loss of certain group members, dilution of the group's effectiveness, or premature dissolution of the group. To avert such undesired consequences, the leader may elicit the reactions of other group members to this behavior and assist members to confront manipulators with their destructive tactics. Such confrontations should adhere to the guidelines delineated earlier, and the leader should encourage members to invite offending members to join with them in constructively seeking to accomplish the purposes for which the group was formed.

Because problematic communication frequently occurs in individual, conjoint, and group sessions, social workers encounter abundant opportunities to employ confrontation to good effect. Intervening during or immediately following dysfunctional communication is a powerful means of enabling clients to experience firsthand the negative effects of their dysfunctional behaviors (e.g., interrupting, attacking, claiming, or criticizing). By shifting the focus to the negative reactions of recipients of problematic messages, social workers enable clients to receive direct feedback about how their behavior offends, alienates, or engenders defensiveness in others, thereby producing effects contrary to their purported goals.

Summary

Chapter 17 discussed three vital tools in working through clients' opposition to change and to relating openly in the helping relationship: additive empathy, interpretation, and confrontation. If individual clients are left to struggle alone with negative feelings about the helping process or the social worker, their feelings may mount to the extent that they resolve them by discontinuing their sessions. If family members or groups are permitted to oppose change by engaging in distractive, irrelevant, or otherwise dysfunctional behaviors, they may likewise lose both confidence in the social worker (for valid reasons) and motivation to continue. For these reasons, social workers must accord the highest priority to being helpful to clients who encounter obstacles or who may be opposed to change.

Skill Development Exercises in Additive Empathy and Interpretation

To assist you to advance your skills in responding with interpretation and additive empathy, we provide the following exercises. Read each client message, determine the type of response required, and formulate a written response that you would employ if you were in an actual session with the client. Keep in mind the guidelines for employing interpretive and additive

empathic responses. Compare your responses with the modeled responses provided at the end of the exercises.

Client Statements

1. **White female client** [*to African American male social worker*]: You seem to be accepting of white people—at least you have been of me. But somehow I still feel uneasy with you. I guess it's just me. I haven't really known many black people very well.

2. **Married woman, age 28**: I feel I don't have a life of my own. My life is controlled by *his* work, *his* hours, and *his* demands. It's like I don't have an identity of my own.

3. **Prison inmate, age 31** [*1 week before the date of his scheduled parole, which was canceled the preceding week*]: Man, what the hell's going on with me? Here I've been on good behavior for three years and finally got a parole date. You'd think I'd be damned glad to get out of here. So I get all uptight and get in a brawl in the mess hall. I mean I really blew it, man. Who knows when they'll give me another date?

4. **Male, age 18**: What's the point in talking about going to Trade Tech? I didn't make it in high school, and I won't make it there either. You may as well give up on me—I'm just a dropout in life.

5. **Widow, age 54**: It was Mother's Day last Sunday, and neither of my kids did so much as send me a card. You'd think they could at least acknowledge I'm alive.

6. **Female secretary, age 21**: I don't have any trouble typing when I'm working alone. But if the boss or anyone else is looking over my shoulder, it's like I'm all thumbs. I just seem to tighten up.

7. **Female, age 26, in a committed relationship; she is 5 pounds overweight**: When I make a batch of cookies or a cake on the weekend, Terri [her partner] looks at me with that condemning expression, as though I'm not really trying to keep my weight down. I don't think it's fair just because she doesn't like sweets. I like sweets, but the only time I eat any is on the weekend, and I don't eat much then. I feel I deserve to eat dessert on the weekend at least.

8. **Disabled male recipient of public assistance (with a back condition caused by a recent industrial accident)**: This not being able to work is really getting to

me. I see my kids needing things I can't afford to get them, and I just feel—I don't know—kind of useless. There's got to be a way of making a living.

9. **Depressed male, age 53**: Yeah, I know I do all right in my work. But that doesn't amount to much. Anyone could do that. That's how I feel about everything I've ever done. Nothing's really amounted to anything.

10. **Mother, age 29, who is alleged to have neglected her children**: I don't know. I'm just so confused. I look at my kids sometimes, and I want to be a better mother. But after they've been fighting, or throwing tantrums, or whining and I lose my cool, I feel like I'd just like to go somewhere—anywhere—and never come back. The kids deserve a better mother.

Modeled Responses for Interpretation and Additive Empathy

1. [*To clarify feelings experienced only vaguely*]: I gather that even though you can't put your finger on why, you're still a little uncomfortable with me. You haven't related closely to that many African Americans, and you're still not altogether sure how much you can trust me.

2. [*Implied wants and goals*]: Sounds like you feel you're just an extension of your husband and that part of you is wanting to find yourself and be a person in your own right.

3. [*Hidden purpose of behavior, underlying feelings*]: So you're pretty confused about what's happened. Fighting in the mess hall when you did just doesn't make sense to you. You know, Carl, about your getting uptight—I guess I'm wondering if you were worried about getting out—worried about whether you could make it outside. I'm wondering if you might have fouled up last week to avoid taking that risk.

4. [*Underlying belief about self*]: Sounds like you feel defeated before you give yourself a chance. Like it's hopeless to even try. Jay, that concerns me because when you think that way about yourself, you *are* defeated—not because you lack ability but because you think of yourself as destined to fail. That belief itself is your real enemy.

5. [*Deeper feelings*]: You must have felt terribly hurt and resentful that they didn't so much as call you. In fact, you seem to be experiencing those feelings now. It just hurts so much.

6. [*Underlying thoughts and feelings*]: I wonder if, in light of your tightening up, you get to feeling scared, as though you're afraid you won't measure up to their expectations.

7. [*Unrealized strengths*]: I'm impressed with what you just said. It strikes me that you're exercising a lot of control by limiting dessert to weekends and using moderation then. In fact, your self-control seems greater than that of most people. You and Terri have a legitimate difference concerning sweets. But it's exactly that—a difference. Neither view is right or wrong, and you're entitled to your preference as much as she is entitled to hers.

8. [*Unrealized strength and implied want*]: Steve, I can hear the frustration you're feeling, and I want you to know it reflects some real strength on your part. You want to be self-supporting and be able to provide better for your family. Given that desire, we can explore opportunities for learning new skills that won't require physical strength.

9. [*Underlying pattern of thought*]: Kent, I get the feeling that it wouldn't matter what you did. You could set a world record, and you wouldn't feel it amounted to much. I'm wondering if your difficulty lies more in long-time feelings you've had about yourself, that you somehow just don't measure up. I'd be interested in hearing more about how you've viewed yourself.

10. [*Underlying feelings and implied wants*]: So your feelings tear you and pull you in different directions. You'd like to be a better mother, and you feel bad when you lose your cool. But sometimes you just feel so overwhelmed and inadequate in coping with the children. Part of you would like to learn to manage the children better, but another part would like to get away from your responsibilities.

Skill Development Exercises in Confrontation

The following exercises involve discrepancies and dysfunctional behavior in all three experiential domains—cognitive/perceptual, emotional, and behavioral. After reading the brief summary of the situation involved and the verbatim exchanges between the client(s) and social worker, identify the type of discrepancy involved and formulate your response (observing the guidelines presented earlier) as though you are the social worker in a real-life situation. Next, compare your response with the modeled one, keeping in mind that the model is only one of many possible appropriate responses. Carefully analyze how your response is similar to or differs from the modeled response and whether you adhered to the guidelines.

Situations and Dialogue

1. You have been working with Mr. Lyon for several weeks, following his referral by the court after being convicted for sexually molesting his teenage daughter. Mr. Lyon has been 15 minutes late for his last two appointments, and today he is 20 minutes late. During his sessions he has explored and worked on problems only superficially.

    Client: Sorry to be late today. Traffic was sure heavy. You know how that goes.

2. The clients are marital partners whom you have seen conjointly five times. One of their goals is to reduce marital conflict by avoiding getting into arguments that create mutual resentments.

    Mrs. J: This week has been just awful. I've tried to look nice and have his meals on time—like he said he wanted—and I've just felt so discouraged. He got on my back Tuesday and … [*Husband interrupts.*]

    Mr. J: [*angrily*]: Just a minute. You're only telling half the story. You left out what you did Monday. [*She interrupts.*]

    Mrs. J: Oh, forget it. What's the use? He doesn't care about me. He couldn't, the way he treats me. [*Mr. J shakes head in disgust.*]

3. The client is a slightly retarded young adult who was referred by a rehabilitation agency because of social and emotional problems. The client has manifested a strong interest in dating young women and has been vigorously pursuing a clerk (Sue) in a local supermarket. She has registered no interest in him and obviously has attempted to discourage him from further efforts. The following excerpt occurs in the seventh session.

    Client: I went through Sue's check stand this morning. I told her I'd like to take her to see a movie.

    Social worker: Oh, and what did she say?

    Client: She said she was too busy. I'll wait a couple of weeks and ask her again.

4. Tony, age 16, is a member of a therapy group in a youth correctional institution. In the preceding session, he appeared to gain a sense of power and satisfaction from provoking other members to react angrily and defensively, which disrupted the group process. Tony directs the following message to a group member early in the fourth session.

    Tony: I noticed you trying to get next to Meg at the dance Wednesday. You think you're pretty hot stuff, don't you?

5. The client is a mother, age 26, who keeps feelings inside until they mount out of control, at which time she discharges anger explosively.

    Client: I can't believe my neighbor. She sends her kids over to play with Sandra at lunchtime and disappears. It's obvious her kids haven't had lunch, and I end up feeding them, even though she's better off financially than I am.

    Social worker: What do you feel when she does that?

    Client: Oh, not much, I guess. But I think it's a rotten thing to do.

6. You have been working for several weeks with a family that includes the parents and four children ranging in age from 10 to 17. The mother is a domineering person who acts as spokesperson for the family, and the father is passive and soft-spoken. A teenage daughter, Tina, expresses herself in the following dialogue.

    Tina: We always seem to have a hassle when we visit our grandparents. Grandma's so bossy. I don't like going there.

    Mother: Tina, that's not true. You've always enjoyed going to her house. You and your grandmother have always been close.

7. Group members in their fifth session have been intently discussing difficulties of the members in social interaction. One of the members takes the group off on a tangent by describing humorous idiosyncrasies of a person she met while on vacation, and the other group members follow suit by sharing humorous anecdotes about "oddballs" they have encountered.

8. The client is an attractive, personable, and intelligent woman who has been married for 3 years to a self-centered, critical man. In the fourth session (an

individual interview), she tearfully makes the following statements:

Client: I've done everything he's asked of me. I've lost 10 pounds. I support him in his work. I golf with him. I even changed my religion to please him. And he's still not happy with me. There's just something wrong with me.

9. The clients are a married couple in their early thirties. The following excerpt occurs in the initial interview.

Wife: We just seem to fight over the smallest things. When he gets really mad, he loses his temper and knocks me around.

Husband: The real problem is that she puts her parents ahead of me. She's the one who needs help, not me. If she'd get straightened out, I wouldn't lose my temper. Tell her where her first responsibility is. I've tried, and she won't listen to me.

10. The clients are a family consisting of the parents and two children. Taylor, age 15, has been truant from school and smoking marijuana. Angie, age 16, is a model student and is obviously her parents' favorite. The family was referred by the school when Taylor was expelled for several days. The father, a highly successful businessman, entered family therapy with obvious reluctance, which has continued to this, the fourth session.

Mother: Things haven't been much different this week. Everyone's been busy, and we really haven't seen much of each other.

Father: I think we'd better plan to skip the next 3 weeks. Things have been going pretty well, and I have an audit in process at the office that's going to put me in a time bind.

Modeled Responses for Confrontation

1. [*Irresponsible behavior by the client*]: Ted, I'm concerned you're late today. This is the third time in a row you've been late, and it shortens the time available to us. But my concerns go beyond that. I know you don't like having to come here and that you'd like to be out from under the court's jurisdiction. But the way you're going about things won't accomplish that. I can't be helpful to you and can't write a favorable report to the court if you just go through the motions of coming here for help. Apparently it's uncomfortable for you to come. I'd be interested in hearing just what you're feeling about coming.

2. [*Discrepancy between purported goal and behavior, as well as dysfunctional communication*]: Let's stop and look at what you're doing right now. I'm concerned because each of you wants to feel closer to the other, but what you're both doing just makes each other defensive.

   [*To husband*]: Mr. J, she was sharing some important feelings with you, and you cut her off.

   [*To wife*]: And you did the same thing, Mrs. J, when he was talking.

   [*To both*]: I know you may not agree, but it's important to hear each other out and to try to understand. If you keep interrupting and trying to blame each other, as you've both been doing, you're going to stay at square one, and I don't want that to happen. Let's go back and start over, but this time put yourself in the shoes of the other and try to understand. Check out with the other if you really understood. Then you can express your own views.

3. [*Dysfunctional, self-defeating behavior*]: Pete, I know how much you think of Sue and how you'd like to date her. I'm concerned that you keep asking her out, though, because she never accepts and doesn't appear to want to go out with you. My concern is that you're setting yourself up for hurt and disappointment. I'd like to see you get a girlfriend, but your chances of getting a date are probably a lot better with persons other than Sue.

4. [*Abrasive, provocative behavior*]: Hold on a minute, guys. I'm feeling uncomfortable and concerned right now about what Tony just said. It comes across as a real put-down, and we agreed earlier that one of our rules was to support and help each other. Tony, would you like some feedback from other members about how you're coming across to the group?

5. [*Discrepancy between expressed and actual feeling*]: I agree. But I'm concerned about your saying you don't feel much. I should think you'd be ticked off and want to change the situation. Let's see if you can get in touch with your feelings. Picture yourself at home at noon and your neighbor's kids knock on

the door while you're fixing lunch. Can you picture it? What are you feeling in your body and thinking just now?

6. [*Dysfunctional communication, disconfirming Tina's feelings and experiences*]: What did you just do, Mrs. Black? Stop and think for a moment about how you responded to Tina's message. It may help you to understand why she doesn't share more with you. [*or*] Tina, could you tell your mother what you're feeling right now about what she just said? I'd like her to get some feedback that could help her communicate better with you.

7. [*Discrepancy between goals and behavior, getting off topic*]: I'm concerned about what the group's doing right now. What do you think is happening?

8. [*Misconception about the self, cognitive/perceptual discrepancy*]: Jan, I'm concerned about what you just said because you're putting yourself down and leaving no room to feel good about yourself. You're assuming that you own the problem and that you're deficient in some way. I'm not at all sure that's the problem. You're married to a man who seems impossible to please, and that is more likely the problem. As we agreed earlier, you have tasks of feeling good about yourself, standing up for yourself, and letting your husband's problem be his problem. As long as your feelings about yourself depend on his approval, you're going to feel down on yourself.

9. [*Manipulative behavior*]: I don't know the two of you well enough to presume to know what's causing your problems.

[*To husband*]: If you're expecting me to tell your wife to shape up, you'll be disappointed. My job is to help each of you to see your part in the difficulties and to make appropriate changes. If I did what you asked, I'd be doing both of you a gross disservice. Things don't get better that way.

10. [*Discrepancy between behavior and purported goals*]: What you do, of course, is up to you. I am concerned, however, because you all agreed you wanted to relate more closely as family members and give one another more support. To accomplish that means you have to work at it steadily, or things aren't likely to change much.

[*To father*]: My impression is that you're backing off. I know your business is important, but I guess you have to decide whether you're really committed to the goals you set for yourselves.

Notes

1. Claiborn (1982) presents numerous examples of both types of interpretation as well as a comprehensive discussion of this important topic. Other researchers (Beck & Strong, 1982; Claiborn, Crawford, & Hackman, 1983; Dowd & Boroto, 1982; Feldman, Strong, & Danser, 1982; Milne & Dowd, 1983) have also reported findings comparing the effects of different types of interpretations.

CHAPTER 18

Managing Barriers to Change

CHAPTER OVERVIEW

Chapter 18 focuses on potential barriers to change and ways of managing them so that they do not interrupt progress or cause unplanned termination by clients. Clients who have the best of intentions and who are highly motivated may nevertheless encounter obstacles that interfere with the helping process and goal attainment. These obstacles may occur within the individual (e.g., interpersonal or intrapersonal dynamics or a mix of both), or arise within the physical environment. Social workers' behaviors may either contribute to resolution of clients' barriers or unintentionally aggravate them. Guidelines for becoming aware of and responding to barriers to change are also discussed. Chapter 18 concludes with skill development exercises and modeled responses to clients' statements.

Barriers to Change

Barriers to change may be characterized as relational dynamics that occur in the social worker–client relationship. For instance, either the social worker or client may have a strong reaction to the other. Also, the social worker can become over- or under-involved with the client which can have an adverse impact on the relationship. In the best of circumstances, progress toward goal attainment is rarely smooth. Instead, the change process is one in which there are rapid spurts, plateaus, impasses, fears, relapses, and sometimes brief periods of regression. Think about the number of times that you have vowed to behave differently with a friend, spouse, or relative only to become involved in a situation that pushes your buttons, causing you to revert to old patterns of behaving. In the end, you might accomplish this goal that you have set for yourself, and the fact that you had a setback does not mean that you are unable or unwilling to change. The same is true for clients.

Even getting started can be a formidable challenge with involuntary clients, when compliance is required; the help that is offered has not been solicited, and may not be perceived as particularly useful. For example, social workers in their contact with parents suspected of abusing their children, or their encounters with individuals who have been charged with domestic violence, often face a range of client emotions, including hostility, anger, grief, and frustration. In these emotionally charged situations, another response from the involuntary individual might be to question your motive as well as the usefulness of the contact, with you, "What are you going to do?"

The degree and rate of change vary widely and are affected by many variables—most importantly, variations in the motivation and strengths of clients; the severity and duration of problems; the dynamics of the helping relationship; the environmental forces that support or work against change; and the responsiveness (or lack thereof) of institutions in providing resources when a need is indicated.

Barriers to change discussed in this chapter are:

- *Relational reactions and the interactions between clients and social workers.*
- *Dynamics that can emerge in cross-racial and cross-cultural relationships.*
- *Sexual attraction toward clients, and the ethical and legal implication of the related behavior.*

In the final section of the chapter, managing ambivalence or opposition to change as manifested by individuals, families, or groups is discussed. The discussion also highlights strategies that can be used to address these issues and provide client's with opportunities for growth.

Relational Reactions

Your relationship as a social worker with a client is the vehicle that animates the helping process, especially for voluntary clients. Relational reactions are those conscious and unconscious dynamics between people; for example, reactions of the social workers to the client, or those of the client in response to the social worker. Indeed, the quality of the helping relationship critically determines both the client's moment-to-moment receptiveness to the social worker's influence and intervention and the ultimate outcome of the helping process. Because of the profound importance of the helping relationship, it is crucial that you are skilled both in cultivating relationships and in keeping those relationships intact. Feelings that influence the relationship—for better or worse—constantly flow back and forth between the social worker and the client. To maintain positive helping relationships, you must be alert to threats to those relationships and manage them carefully.

Helping relationships that are characterized by reciprocal positive feelings between social workers and clients are conducive to personal growth and successful problem solving. Facilitative conditions, such as high levels of *warmth, acceptance, unconditional caring, empathy, genuineness*, and *sensitivity to differences* promote the development of positive relationships. Despite best efforts, however, some clients are unable to hear or respond positively for a number of reasons, including distrust, fear, or simply being overwhelmed. Social workers, too, may have difficulty responding positively to clients because of their own bias, or because clients' have certain personality traits, physical attributes, or types of problems. For example, consider the following exchange from a case consultation session:

Social worker, presenting a case: How can you feel empathy for every client? I have this one client, and when I go to her house, she is just sitting there like a big lump. She doesn't seem to understand that she may lose her children. She tells me that the man who abused her children is out of her life, but I don't believe her. She tells lies, she doesn't do anything to help herself, and she sits there in the midst of a cluttered filthy apartment watching television. I am just waiting to catch her in one of her lies. It is hard for me to feel anything for this client or to help her keep custody of her children.

Consultant: Wow, you really don't like this client and she knows it! Perhaps she feels, "Why bother to establish a relationship with you?"

Upon reflection, the social worker reluctantly agreed with the consultant's assessment of the dynamics in her interactions with the client. With the help of the consultant, she was able to focus on the work to be done in this case—specifically, ensuring the safety of the children.

As you think about this situation, you may want to review Chapter 6, which discussed the importance of developing and maintaining psychological contact with clients, and Chapter 8, which focused on exploring the nature of the problem. Also useful is content found in Chapter 12, which deals with motivational congruence and motivational interviewing, and Chapter 17 on the stages of change. Consider how the content in these chapters is relevant to the preceding situation.

What are the relational dynamics in the case? First, when we do not like clients, for whatever reasons, they are able to sense our feelings toward them and the psychological contract is unlikely to develop. Note, for example, how the social worker described the client as "sitting there like a big lump." What image of the client does her statement convey to you? Perhaps that she is overweight, passive, lazy, and uncaring about her children. Further, the bias of the social worker appeared to be slanted toward Weinberg's (2006) assertion that single mothers are often judged by accepted standards of motherhood behavior; in which case, this mother was sorely lacking. But there may be other explanations for the mother's behavior. For example, is the mother depressed? Because of the social worker's reaction, an exploration of pertinent factors may have been overlooked.

A social worker's perception of clients can also influence the manner in which clients are assessed and the decisions that are made. For example, Holland (2000) discusses findings from a study in which social workers' biases influenced their perceptions of a client's level of commitment. Clients who are perceived as cooperative and acknowledging their need for change are assessed in a positive manner. In contrast, if clients are behaving in an angry or passive way, like the mother in this case, they are perceived more negatively and are assessed as being less willing to change.

A second factor in this case was the social worker's preoccupation with whether the client was telling the truth. There are times when you may feel that you are working harder than a client, and therefore you can become sidetracked by their behavior, for example, truth telling. Obviously, truth telling is a reciprocal expectation in the helping relationship. Yet, is it really necessary to determine whether the mother was lying, unless her dishonesty threatened the welfare of her children?

With the help of the consultant, the social worker was able to refocus her work with this client on assessing issues relative to the safety of the children. The mother remained relatively passive; however, she did commit to a plan that supported the safety of her children. For example, her boyfriend who was suspected of abusing her children had been court-ordered to stay away from the home. When he was spotted in the alley behind her house, she promptly called the police. The decisive assessment question is whether this mother could, was willing to, and under what circumstances ensure that her children were safe? Did the social worker come to like the client? Perhaps not, but she was able to understand and therefore manage her reactions to the mother, beginning with examining her own behavior and bias.

Even when a positive relationship evolves, various events and moment-by-moment transactions may pose risks to initiating and sustaining a workable relationship. Social workers must be attentive to instances in their relationships with clients that indicate that something is "off-center." Failure to perceive that something has gone wrong and effectively manage the situation may result in a deadlock, in which problem solving becomes stalled. The next section elaborates on the threats to the relationship that result from the social worker's actions or behavior, those of the client, and from dynamic mixes of both.

Under- and Over-Involvement of Social Workers with Clients

Social workers desire to be attuned to clients and relational dynamics in the helping process. However, it is not unusual for contact to be less than facilitative in some circumstances. If clients experience negative emotional reactions during the contact with you, a temporary breach can occur in a helping relationship. If you fail to recognize and respond to those reactions, then they may expand into major obstacles. You may, in other instances become too caught up with a client and their situation to such an extent that your actions in the relationship are an inhibiting force. Raines (1996) has classified such reactions as *over-involvement or under-involvement*. Levels of over- or under-involvement can also be classified according to the social worker's general viewpoint or attitude toward the client, which can be positive or negative. Even though you may strive to maintain a balanced attitude, be appreciative of strengths, and be aware of obstacles, there are situations in which you may be inclined to emphasize one side of the story that is generally favorable or unfavorable to the client. Table 18-1 presents an adaptation of Raines's schema for classifying involvement (Raines, 1996).

1. *When the social worker is under-involved and has a negative attitude toward the client*, it can be reflected in lack of attention or empathy, tuning out, biased or judgmental views, or dismissing or not recalling pertinent information. All (or most) social workers (certainly including the authors of this book) have had less than

productive sessions with clients and even days in which their attentiveness was less than desirable. Table 18-1 highlights circumstances in which such under-involvement becomes associated with the social worker's services to a particular client. Such behaviors are signals that the cause of the behavior must be examined. Hence, part of professional behavior is the capacity for self-observation and correction when indicated. Noting one of these patterns and examining its cause in supervision or consultation with peers can assist you in developing plans for rectifying the behavior.

2. *Under-involvement when there is a positive social worker attitude* can occur when the social worker withholds assistance because of an overly optimistic assessment of the client's capacity and need for help. For example, a client making good progress was praised by the social worker. The client reported that she often wakes up feeling scared, angry, depressed and overwhelmed by her responsibilities. In response to the client's complaints, however, the social worker encouraged her to focus on her strengths (e.g., "Look what you have accomplished so far!"), promising the client that continued sessions will most likely resolve her concerns. Two relational issues are at risk in this scenario. First, the social worker's level of empathy can be rated as low and as such is a potential relational barrier. In addition, she did not pay attention to the concerns and feelings expressed by the client. Challenging the client to focus on her strengths hampered the social worker's ability to address what the client had said, a signal that she is under-involved. Finally, the promise of continued sessions lacks clarity about what is to be accomplished. Is the implication that by showing up overly optimistic, in particular that the client's feelings and fears will be resolved? Would it surprise you to learn that the client sporadically showed up for future appointments with the social worker and only then when she had a concrete need? Similarly, settling on assignments or tasks that the client feels incapable of completing can be a sign of positive under-involvement. In some cases, when the client fails, there is a tendency to question their commitment, rather than our own actions.

Under-involvement when there is a positive social worker attitude can also influence a social worker's decision making, as illustrated in the next case situation.

Social Worker, presenting a case: Police were called to the home due to a domestic violence incident. The husband was charged with interference of a 911 call because he had thrown the telephone into the pool while the wife was making the call. The

TABLE-18-1 SOCIAL WORKER'S UNDER- AND OVER-INVOLVEMENT WITH CLIENTS

	SOCIAL WORKER WITH UNFAVORABLE ATTITUDE TOWARD CLIENT	SOCIAL WORKER WITH FAVORABLE ATTITUDE TOWARD CLIENT
Under-involvement	• Finds it difficult to empathize with the client • Is inattentive to or "tunes out" the client • Has lapses of memory about important information previously revealed by the client • Is drowsy or preoccupied • Dreads sessions or comes late, cancels sessions inappropriately • Is off the mark with interpretations • Client perceives feedback as put-downs • Fails to acknowledge client growth • Never thinks about the client outside of sessions	• Withholds empathy inappropriately due to belief in client's strengths • Refrains from interpretation to promote insight • Reflects or reframes excessively without answering • Never considers self-disclosure • Gives advice or assignments that the client feels incapable of carrying out
Over-involvement	• Has an unreasonable dislike of the client • Is argumentative • Is provocative • Gives excessive advice • Employs inept or poorly timed confrontations • Disapproves of the client's planned course of action inappropriately • Appears to take sides against the client (or subgroup) or actually does so • Dominates discussions or frequently interrupts the client • Uses power with involuntary clients to interfere in lifestyle areas beyond the range of legal mandates • Competes intellectually • Has violent thoughts or dreams about the client	• Is overly emotional or sympathetic • Provides extra time inappropriately • Fantasizes brilliant interpretations • Is unusually sensitive to criticisms • Has sexual thoughts or dreams about the client • Seeks nonprofessional contact with the client

SOURCE: Adapted from Raines (1996).

court-ordered case plan identified improved communication between the couple and the resolution of their domestic violence issues.

In the initial session with the couple, they reported being involved in conflict-resolution sessions with their religious leader, and as a result they were now better able to communicate with each other. They also contended that "we don't have domestic violence issues." Their explanation, "The wife is pregnant, and they both attributed her hormonal changes mood swings to the incident that prompted the call." The social worker accepted their explanation, but stated that she did have one concern, that "Unless encouraged to do so, the wife rarely spoke."

Based on the session with the couple, the social worker's conclusion was that the case should be closed. The couple she noted "is involved in the community, both are professionals and happy the upcoming birth of their baby." Further, "they live in a spacious home, just off the golf course, in an outer-ring suburb."

As in negative under-involvement, positive decisions may happen with particular clients, at a particular time, and with clients who possess what is perceived to be positive attributes. Patterns of repeated positive under-involvement, however, call for examination and correction. Once again, reflection on these patterns with peers and supervisors can assist social workers in finding ways to adjust the involvement level. Hence, while generally focusing on client strengths and having a positive attitude toward clients is consistent with social work values, the possibility of positive under-involvement alerts us to ways that attention to strengths may be exaggerated and not completely helpful in all circumstances.

3. *Over-involvement with a negative social worker attitude* refers to negative attention such that clients feel punished or in combat with the social worker. Patterns of arguing, acting provocatively, using confrontation inappropriately, and power arbitrarily, and the like can signal negative over-involvement. Note that if the social worker is operating under a legal mandate to provide, for example, services to persons who have mistreated their children, then power and authority could be used appropriately and in an ethical manner. Facilitative conditions, for example, empathy, genuineness, and unconditional caring for the client are equally appropriate. In contrast, in cases of over-involvement with a negative social worker attitude, the use of power becomes personal and punishing rather than appropriate to the circumstances and safety of children. This behavior is contrary to social work values, but it does occur. This behavior is often observed in high-stress work settings in which social workers have close contact with clients who have been harmed and with individuals who have either harmed those clients or not acted fully to prevent the harm. Over-involvement with negative attitude may also be evident in court mandated case plans. It may also spill over into other relationships and can take the form of rigid rules of conduct in educational, residential, and corrections settings. Social workers in such settings and their supervisors should take special precautions to avoid stereotyping clients and ignoring client strengths and values. The following two case scenarios have similar dynamics. The first example demonstrates how *over-involvement* can cause negative interactions between you and other professionals when you are invested in a particular outcome for a client and perceive the actions of the other professional as being under-involved, negative, or unjust.

Social worker, presenting a case: Am I too mixed up in this case? Some of my colleagues believe that I am, and this is why I am presenting this case. First, there are many topics that I wish to discuss; for example, the county case manager's questioning of my professional boundaries, and the boundaries of our agency's (here the social worker distributes copies of a dictionary definition of boundaries), and the lack of due process in the county's decisions about the clients. The case manager raised concerns about boundaries after I submitted the first progress

report on the family. In my report, I indicated the family's diligence in addressing the concerns outlined in the county's case plan. He indicated that I had not done a comprehensive report as the report was too positive. Further, he said that I was more involved than necessary with the family. This particular case manager has done this with other families that receive a positive report from us as you all know.

The social worker continues her report. The real issue here about boundaries must be dealt with first. If he means providing the family with resources, listening to them, and advocating on their behalf then, so be it. Who am I to judge the family's practice of witchcraft, or the mother attending a witch's ball? I find these people different, but interesting, and hey, so are some of us! But I am concerned that my being an advocate for the family will have adverse consequences for them and for our agency. For example, what if the case manager reassigned the case or stopped making referrals to us, in which case my actions affect all of us. Help!

If you were a present at the team meeting in which this case was presented, how would you respond to the question of "Am I too involved in this case?" Would you conclude that asking the question was a credit to the social worker? Is it clear what help the social worker is seeking? Are you able to identify the relational dynamics between the two professionals that spilled-over into the work with the family?

Both of the cases illustrate the dynamics of over- and under-involvement. More importantly, the cases demonstrate how levels of involvement can obscure professional judgment, the results of which can have an adverse impact on client well-being.

The second illustration of *over-involvement* describes a social worker who appears to have little insight into her behavior that has implications for her clients and is counter to the goals of the agency. The scenarios also emphasize how over-involvement may arise as a result of a combination of positive and negative dynamics.

Case Example

Marta is a youth worker in a shelter for homeless youth. She is passionate about her work and believes that her relationship with her young clients will help them to become independent, productive adults. She sees herself as an example of a survivor. Her supervisor has approached her several times, because she believes that Marta sometimes crosses professional boundaries with her clients. Marta's primary goal is to prepare homeless youth to become independent. Actually, youth gaining independence is a program goal, so her behavior is consistent with the intended program outcome. Another goal of the program however, is to assist the youth to resolve conflicts with their parents whenever possible. Marta's work with youth is often in conflict with this goal.

Marta's own youth was marked by constant battles with her parents. At age 17, she left home, lived with friends for a period, and eventually became homeless. Her approach and her relationship with the youth on her caseload are generally as a "survivor of the streets," encouraging a dependency by urging her clients to rely on her for support. Whenever a youth expresses an interest in exploring reconnecting with his or her parents, Marta routinely rejects this idea as being unhealthy to the youth's progress and refuses to help make contact. The supervisor considers Marta's work with youth to be generally exemplary, with the exception of her negative attitude toward parents. Marta points to the fact that many on her caseload have in fact become independent; further, that they seek her out for ongoing support, which she finds frustrating at times.

4. *Over-involvement with a positive social worker attitude* entails excessive preoccupation with a particular client. The social worker tends to focus on a particular client in such a way that the client dominates the social worker's thoughts and dreams, and in some instances includes sexual fantasies. In the most extreme cases, that positive over-involvement attitude toward the client can lead to more serious consequences— for example, boundary violations such as sexual contact with clients. Because of the seriousness of boundary violations, we discuss this issue later in greater detail.

Burnout, Compassion Fatigue and Vicarious Trauma

Being under- or over-involved with clients may also be related to *burnout*. James (2008) attributes burnout to identifying too closely with clients and their problems, as well as to being dedicated and idealistic. Marta, in the previous case, for example, may be a candidate for burn-out as she appears to perceive herself as the primary vehicle for ensuring the success of the youth. Burnout occurs over a period of time in which initially

the individual is enthusiastic and involved but starts to move into stagnation, which leads to frustration and, eventually, apathy. These factors over a prolonged period can also result in a "crisis state of disequilibrium" and chronic indifference (James, 2008, p. 537).

The following describe different circumstances of burnout.

- *Negative under-involvement can occur when you feel frustrated because you are unable to solve certain problems, have a large caseload, and when the outcomes of your work are unknown or uncertain (Dane, 2000; James, 2008). In working with clients, you can become numb to demands that exceed your mental capacity. Thoughts such as "I have heard this story too many times," or "How can I change anything?" may occur to you, along with a feeling of helplessness.*

- *The strong need to be liked by a client or the urge to save a client, taking calls at home, feeling responsible for clients' mistakes or regressions, and panicking when carefully detailed plans fail to produce the expected results can also signal burnout. One social worker was challenged by her spouse when she began staying later and later at work in order to "get a handle on things." "Soon," he said, "you won't come home at all." At the administrative level, this level of burnout may take the form of micromanaging or feeling that nothing will get done or done correctly unless the individual is involved (James, 2008).*

- *When professionals have difficulty in bonding with and enlisting the cooperation of clients who are different (Fontes, 2005).*

- *In organizations in which the leadership is ineffective; there is a lack of rewards, recognition, or organizational support; decisions are perceived to be unfair or arbitrary; or an unsupportive environment in which the fit between organizational and individual beliefs are at odds (Leiter & Maslach, 2005).*

Many authors have recognized and studied compassion fatigue, vicarious or secondary or trauma, and the direct and indirect effects of stress on professionals (Bell, 2003; Cunningham, 2003; Dane, 2000; Figley, 2002). These authors are excellent resources, as is O'Hollaran and Linton (2000), for self-assessment and self-care strategies for professionals.

Compassion fatigue is different from burnout. Burnout is mainly associated with workload demands and stressors, the urgency and size of caseload, and the effects of clients' collective trauma. Compassion fatigue, in contrast, is a constant state of tension and pre-occupation with the individual and collective trauma of clients (Figley, 1995; 2002). Professionals are too deeply drawn into the trauma and emotions of their clients and their situations, and as a result they become mentally exhausted (Figley 2002; 1995). Compassion fatigue is also referred to as vicarious or secondary trauma, a situation in which knowledge of and exposure to others' trauma and wanting to help results in trauma for the professional. This form of trauma is most often evident in professionals who day after day listen to the traumatic narratives of clients in situations of family violence, child sexual abuse, and hospital oncology units. It may also be ignited by past experiences of the professional or provoked by the vulnerability of the client; for example, children who have been abused. Figley (2002; 1995) is an excellent resource for self-assessment with regard to compassion fatigue.

Research has shown that *Vicarious or Secondary Trauma has implications for the professional.* In a study of secondary trauma for family violence professionals, Bell (2003) found that constant "exposure to clients' stories negatively affects cognitions" of the professional (2003, p. 514). Similar results were reported by Dane (2000) in a study of child welfare workers and Cunningham's (2003) findings of group work with individuals with a history of trauma. Further, the response level of the professional was related to whether the client's situation was similar to his or her own experience, which can be the basis of positive or negative transference from the client or a countertransference reaction on the part of the professional.

The theoretical base of vicarious or secondary trauma includes psychoanalytic, developmental, and personality theories (Dane, 2000; James, 2008). General signs and symptoms associated with vicarious trauma as summarized by Dane (2000, p. 29) are

- *Decreased energy*
- *Lack of self-time*
- *Disconnecting from loved ones*
- *Social withdrawal*
- *Increased sensitivity to violence, threats, or fear*
- *Cynicism, generalized despair, and hopelessness*

Dane (2000) clarifies that the above are "endpoints" that over time result in the "erosion of beliefs about self and frame of reference."

Bell (2003), Dane (2000), and James (2008) emphasize the responsibility of the organization to recognize and support staff when there are indications of burn-out and vicarious trauma. Bell, (2003), for example, points out that the strengths perspective is applicable to staff as well as clients. She asserts that organizations can celebrate small successes, recognize the strengths and ways of coping of individual staff, and create a culture in which staff is supported. Dane (2000) proposes a model in which strategies for responding to staff needs include small group discussions and relaxation techniques.

Reactions of Clients: Assessing Potential Barriers and Intervening

The preceding discussion emphasized professional behavior, which influences the relationship with clients. There are other times when reactions occur as a result of the attitudes or misperceptions by clients. Whatever their source, sensing and addressing client's feelings and thoughts as they happen is also crucial to preventing them from escalating. Clients may not always initiate a discussion of their negative reactions. Their ability to do so may depend on their personality type, their age, cultural differences with regard to authority, their status (e.g., voluntary or involuntary), or their sense of power in your role or that of the organization, for example, a residential treatment or correctional facility. Keep in mind that in view of a real or perceived power differential between you and clients, sharing negative feelings and cognitions can be extremely difficult for some clients or have grave implications when they do so. You can reduce the threat that clients experience by being attentive and accepting, or by being an advocate even though you may believe that their interpretation is off the mark or entirely unrealistic. If you are insensitive to nonverbal cues, these feelings and cognitions will linger and remain unresolved.

To avert such a development, it is crucial to watch for indicators of negative reactions, including the following nonverbal cues: frowning, fidgeting, sighing, appearing startled, grimacing, changing the subject, becoming silent, clearing the throat, blushing, and tightening the muscles. When you observe these or other cues, it is important to shift the focus of the session to the client's here-and-now feelings and cognitions. You should do this tentatively, checking out whether your perception is accurate. If it is accurate, proceed by expressing genuine concern for the client's discomfort and conveying your desire to understand what the client is experiencing at the moment. Examples of responses that facilitate discussion of troubling feelings and thoughts follow:

- **To a youth**: *"I'm thinking, to use a phrase that I've heard from you, that what I said was a "flyover" [not paying attention] for you. What are thinking and feeling at this moment?"*

- **To a young minor**: *"Are you feeling sad right now? Would it help for you to draw a picture of how you feel, and we could look at it together?*

- **To an adult client**: *"You are quiet right now, looking away from me. I wonder if you have some feelings about my draft progress report to the court that I just shared with you?"*

Notice that in each of the above situations, the social worker was specific to the moment that the client reacted, but relied on the client to put forth his or her own thoughts or feelings.

By eliciting clients' feelings and thoughts, you also have the opportunity to correct any misunderstandings, clarify your intentions, remedy any blunders, and identify adverse beliefs or thought patterns. Indeed, some clients benefit from observing a model who can acknowledge mistakes and apologize without feeling humiliated. Moreover, they may gain self-confidence by realizing that social workers value them sufficiently to be concerned about their thoughts and feelings and to rectify errors of omission or commission. After productive discussions of here-and-now thoughts and feelings, most clients will regain their positive feelings and resume working on their problems.

On some occasions, a client may succeed in concealing negative thoughts and feelings, or you may overlook nonverbal cues. The feelings may escalate until it becomes obvious that the client is holding back, being overly formal, responding defensively, or engaging in other forms of reactance. Again, you should give priority to the relationship by shifting focus to what is bothering the client and responding to it. After you have worked through the negative reaction of the client, it is helpful to negotiate a "mini-contract" in which you and the client agree to discuss troublesome feelings and thoughts as they occur. The objective of this contract is to avert negative recurrences in the future. Learning to express negative feelings and thoughts can be a milestone for clients who may have habitually withheld their reactions to the detriment of themselves and others.

The following is an example of a message aimed at *negotiating an appropriate mini-contract*:

Social worker: Okay, we got passed the flyover, where you felt I was ignoring what you said. Thank you for telling me about how it feels for people to be telling you what you need to do. Because you told me how you felt, you helped me to understand and you gave me a chance to explain what I really meant last week. For us to work well together, it is important for both of us to put negative reactions on the table. What do you think about the two of us developing an agreement in which we agree to immediately alert each other to troubling thoughts and feelings that happen between us?

In developing the mini-contract, you are conveying to the youth client your willingness to be open to and respectful of his reactions.

Pathological or Inept Social Workers

Although all social workers occasionally commit errors, some social workers repeatedly make mistakes, causing irreparable damage to helping relationships. Repeated unchecked errors can even cause psychological damage to clients. Gottesfeld and Lieberman (1979) refer to such social workers as *pathological*, pointing out that "It is possible to have therapists who suffer from as many unresolved problems as do clients" (p. 388). Ineptness and unethical practices on the part of social workers can be observed in professionals who are abrasive, egotistical, controlling, judgmental, demeaning, patronizing, or rigid in their behavior. Being habitually late or unprepared for appointments and appearing to be detached or disinterested are further indicators of this behavior and are also disrespectful. In many cases, the same social worker would not tolerate similar behavior in a client.

The ineptness of social workers may also be attributed to anxiety, a lack of skill or experience, dealing with problems beyond their scope of practice, or an inability to build collaborative relationships with clients. According to Meyer (2001), agencies may also contribute to this problem by assigning the most difficult cases to professionals with the least amount of experience. These behaviors and attributes can create a range of additional difficulties for clients especially those whose contact is mandated. With voluntary clients, social workers who behave in this manner described tend to lose clients prematurely or to have clients who miss appointments.

The majority of voluntary clients who experience these behaviors or attributes and have the good sense to "vote with their feet" by terminating their contact with you. Mandated clients suffer greater consequences for deciding to terminate early. They are more likely to evade contact or attempt to be transferred to another social worker. Supervisors should be alert when there are several requests for transfer from the same social worker. Pathological social workers harm their clients, their agencies, and the profession as a whole.

Often, other social workers face a difficult situation in deciding which steps to take when they become aware of such situations. As Meyer (2001) observes, both agencies and professionals may ignore these dynamics, instead characterizing clients' behavior as resistant or oppositional. Of course, the privacy of the interaction between a client and a social worker may make it difficult to observe situations in which the behavior of a colleague is harmful to client well-being. However, individuals who act in a manner that is harmful or demeaning to clients are often quite open about what they do; for example, telling stories about clients in which their own status is heightened, giving clients demeaning names as descriptors, breaching confidentiality, and talking down to clients when other clients or staff are present. It is indeed a challenge to judge or question the behavior or competence of another professional social work colleague. At the same time, both you and your agency have a responsibility to protect clients.

The NASW Code of Ethics speaks directly to the "primacy of clients' rights" as well as to your obligation to peers and the employment organization. A caution by Gottesfeld and Lieberman (1979) is timeless in this regard. They assert that, to protect clients' rights, "agencies organized to help clients should not accept employee pathology that defeats the system's purpose" (p. 392). Actions to rectify such situations, however, must safeguard the rights of both social workers and clients. Reports should be based on facts, not judgments or bias and your motive should be clarified. Reviewing information with supervisors or a consultant provides an additional safeguard. You may also want to refer back to the guidelines on whistle-blowing in Chapter 14.

Ultimately, in some situations, a referral to the local NASW chapter and state licensing board or certification authority may become necessary. NASW chapters and regulatory boards have committees that investigate complaints of unethical and unprofessional conduct. Information about misconduct is shared between NASW chapters and state boards of social work. Infractions that constitute egregious harm are also reported to the Disciplinary Actions Reporting System (DARS), a national database to which the Association of Social Work Boards (ASWB) has access. "This system is a means by which social work regulatory boards can verify the historical disciplinary background of individuals seeking licensure or renewal" (*ASWB Member Policy Manual*).

Cross-Racial and Cross-Cultural Barriers

Clients and social worker may experience adverse reactions in cross-racial or cross-cultural relationships with social workers for a variety of reasons. Tensions in social relations that may be grounded in society may present as dynamics in the helping relationship. Involuntary status, in which racial or ethnic minorities or members of other oppressed groups are disproportionately represented, is also a significant factor. These factors may be macro-level, environmental issues, but they nevertheless influence micro-level practice and relationships.

In their most basic form, barriers to the social worker–client relationship may stem from either lack of knowledge of the client's culture or lack of experience in working with members of a given racial or minority group. Foster (1988), Hodge (2004), Hodge & Nadir (2008), and Sue (2006), suggest treatment goals, specifically those that aim to achieve separation from others and autonomy are bounded by assumptions of certain Western cultures. Conversely, persons from cultures in which interdependence and group belonging are valued may not aspire to goals of this nature. In cross-cultural, cross-racial situations, it is therefore important to understand clients from the viewpoint of their lifestyles and the standards for well-being established by their reference group.

Cross-racial and cross-cultural relationships are challenging on many levels. Social workers who are members of ethnic or racial minority groups perhaps can be more attuned to the values of majority-group clients. Conversely, as Proctor and Davis (1994) have noted, Caucasian social workers may have limited knowledge or exposure to the realities of other cultures. These differences are made greater by a diverse experiential and social distance (Clifford & Burke, 2005; Davis & Gelsomino, 1994; Green, Kiernan-Strong, & Baskind, 2005).

Social distance can also be influential in a relationship in which the social worker is a member of racial or ethnic minority groups. In U.S. society, social interactions and professional relationships remain configured around assumptions of sameness, including social class.

For the most part, however, a certain social distance separates social workers and their clients, irrespective of their racial or ethnic status. Clifford and Burke (2005) emphasized that the profession's ethical principle of having respect for differences is influenced by social distance. Specifically, respect for another individual becomes much more of a challenge when the individual is of a very different social standing.

Lacking familiarity and limited contact with clients who are different may cause social workers to fill in any information void with stereotypes, preconceived notions, and media images. There is also the resulting tendency to become overly positive or negative about a particular racial or ethnic group. On the positive side, social workers may over-identify with these clients, losing sight of their individuality as well as the subgroups within a racial or ethnic culture. On the negative side, perceptions or stereotypes may lead them to erroneously generalize clients' problems to the group in which they are members, thereby influencing the social worker's capacity to be empathetic to the individual's situation. Whaley (1998) asserts that racial and class bias is influenced by social and cognitive perceptions that fill in the blanks with general stereotypes; for example, black youth who are demonstrating the same traits as their white counterparts are four times more likely to be viewed as violent. In these and other situations, the professional's assessment may be directed toward interpreting behavior, in which the lens used in the process is skewed by misinformation or generalizations (Malgady & Zayas, 2001; Sue, 2006; Whaley, 1998).

Given the potential obstacles that may emerge in cross-racial and cross-cultural relationships, you might wonder if the solution is to match clients with social workers of the same racial or ethnic group. This solution is, of course, not practical, nor is there sufficient evidence that suggest that matching always works to the clients' advantage (James, 2008; Malgady & Zayas, 2001). In addition, some clients will react to and distrust *any* social worker—even those who share their background or heritage. This distrust often arises at a systems level—specifically, at the level of the organization that you represent—yet the dynamics emerge in your relationship with the client. In any of the situations previously described, it can be expected that dynamics in the client–social worker relationship will reflect a mutual strangeness. In some instances, social workers and agencies emphasize sameness rather than differences in an attempt to minimize potential barriers. Too often, differences of race and culture are ignored in a form of "color-blind" practice designed to avoid

conflict (Proctor & Davis, 1994; Davis & Gelsomino, 1994). Davis and Gelsomino also caution both majority and minority practitioners to be aware of their biases related to socioeconomic factors. In addition to the implications that these factors have for racial and ethnic minority groups, these authors suggest that they are equally relevant to the "social realities of low-income white clients." Social workers may perceive that these clients are responsible for their difficulties. Moreover, they may assess them at a higher level based on an assumption that these clients have failed to take advantage of their life opportunities.

Cultivating Positive Cross-cultural Relations

What can be done to minimize the dynamics of difference and its role as a relational barrier in the helping process? Empathy and empathic communication are basic skills that facilitate engagement and bridge the gaps that may be present in cross-racial and cross-cultural client-social worker relationships. Dyche and Zayas (2001) and Parson (1993) emphasize that knowledge of culture is insufficient to evoke empathy. Instead, they refer to *cultural empathy* as a more effective treatment tool. Cultural empathy is expressed by the social worker at the affective level, rather than solely at the cognitive level. Whereas the cognitive level references knowledge about different cultures, at the affective level social workers make an effort to see and hear the world through the client's eyes and experiences and to grasp meaning from the client's perspective. Parson (1993) further characterizes cultural empathy as *ethnotherapeutic*, meaning that it relies on the cross-cultural professional's capacity for introspection and self-disclosure when this information would support the helping process.

Relational empathy as described by Freedberg (2007) also facilitates helping as it demonstrates acceptance and understanding of the client's cultural and sociopolitical situation even though you may not be fully aware of each and every cultural or racial nuance. Relational empathy is grounded in relational culture theory, in which traditional boundaries may be crossed and in which the client–social worker relationship is based on a mutual sharing. Assessment skills in determining acculturation levels, including culturally derived behaviors or dysfunctions in the context of culture, are critical. How a problem is perceived and framed by the social worker can be either an inhibiting factor or a facilitative factor. Clients need to be able to trust that you understand their situation.

In a study that examined cross-cultural practices, Davis and Gelsomino (1994) found that social workers tended to ignore environmental factors and instead were more inclined to explore internal or personal difficulties as the source of client problems. Another facilitative measure is actively engaging the client in defining both the problem and the desired solution from his or her perspective. Lee (2003) for example, in applying the solution-focused approach in cross-cultural relationships, emphasizes utilizing the techniques of social constructivism—specifically, including the narrative and viewpoint of the client. Lee further suggests that empowerment-based practice, which focuses on client strengths, is essential in assisting clients to create solutions for themselves.

Minority clients, because they have had the normative experience of interacting with nonminority social workers, may have a combination of positive and negative feelings. Their negative feelings may be based on relational tensions in the larger society. You should also be aware that clients absorb and react to the negative media images and political messages that are used to describe them. For example, these hurtful messages may suggest that immigrants are taking jobs from Americans; teaching immigrant or refugee children diminishes education for others and contributes to higher costs for education; welfare recipients are averse to working; certain neighborhoods are dangerous and crime-ridden drug zones; minority children consistently have lower achievement scores on standardized tests; and minority groups do not hold the same values as the rest of society.

When clients have negative feelings, you can neutralize the situation by empathically confronting and responding to their feelings. As a preventive measure, in the initial contact you might inquire about whether the client has concerns on this front. In addition, you might ask how problems are handled in their culture and explore who else should be involved in the problem-solving effort. As one social worker in a mental health setting commented, "It is not unusual for 10 to 15 family members to accompany my client to sessions with me." Also, she noted, "I have to arrange transportation for the entire group." Her statement suggests an additional and crucial consideration in cross-racial and cross-cultural interactions—the need to be sufficiently flexible so as to accommodate cultural preferences and customs.

In addition to cultural and relational empathy and empathetic communications, "helper attractiveness" is an interpersonal factor to which diverse clients are reported to have responded to favorably (Harper & Lantz, 1996). Essentially, it means that the clients' perceive that the social worker has an interest in them and a genuine desire to help. Further, helper attractiveness implies that diverse clients experience respectful, warm, genuine, committed, and ethical behavior on the part of the social worker. The following are representative comments from focus group sessions, one with emancipated minority minors who had been wards of the state and the other, with staff who were considered to have established successful relationships with the minor clients.

Minors: Throughout your life in the system, you come in contact with a lot of indifferent professionals. They run in and tell you what to do, are disinterested in you as a person and your goals. They give you a case plan to follow and tell you to find a job. I want to go to college, but no, they tell you, go get a job. How is a minimum wage job going to sustain me and my baby in the long run? Having met with you because they are required to do, then they move on to the next case. In all fairness, they do have large caseloads, but you never really feel that they are interested in you or really see you as an individual. When I get a worker that listens to me, tries to understand me, and is willing to treat me like a real person, I do better. Sometimes, they act like a parent which is okay if they treat me right.

Staff: A large part of connecting with these kids is to remember that they are kids. They have been in the system so long, some, almost all of their lives. They don't want to sit in an office and have you talk at them. Sometimes, just riding around with them or going to get a hamburger is when you really are able to connect with them. They talk and you listen. Sometimes you point out the contractions in their words and behavior in a teasing way and they laugh. Even when they mess up, you have to respect them as individuals, do things with them. A lot of time, they say, "Miss X, I know that I let you down, and I felt bad, because you are real and you support me." A real turning point in even the most difficult cases often occurs when you support them unconditionally, are dependable, respond to them in a caring and empathetic way. Above all, you need to include them in the decisions about their future. Some of their negative reactions are developmental, others are because they are scared or testing you to make sure you aren't going to leave them, and still others because the court or the foster home failed to respect them or treat them as individuals.

Of course, no matter which facilitative measure you use and no matter how much goodwill, warmth, and empathy you convey, some clients will remain guarded or will test you for a period of time before finally engaging with you. The rationale for this behavior may be racial, cultural, or systems paranoia, all of which frequently overlap with involuntary client status.

Despite what may appear to be the challenging trials and tribulations inherent in cross-cultural and cross-racial relationships, it is quite possible to have productive helping relationships with clients who are different from yourself. Dean (2001), however, challenges the notion of cultural competence as an arrival point, stating that it is based on the "belief that knowledge brings control and effectiveness which is to be achieved above all else" (p. 624). Instead, she suggests, it is equally important for social workers to be aware of their lack of competence, and therefore to understand competence to be a process of evolving and changing. Williams (2006) proposes that organizations in which cultural competence is a goal need to "facilitate the availability of appropriate learning experiences, staff pathways for advocacy and time and space for culturally competent practice" (p. 214). Using a case to demonstrate levels of cultural competence, Williams, describes levels of cultural competence, in which the social worker's initial awareness of culture is an anthropological view of culture, specifically learning about culture. The highest level she maintains is embedded in critical theory in which social, political and economic arrangements are considered, and in which the outcomes sought are anti-oppression and social change.

Earlier, we noted some general indicators and conditions that can facilitate competence with diverse groups in an effort to lessen the impact of potential barriers in the helping relationship. In the spirit of Dean's (2001) evolving and changing competence as well as the levels proposed by Williams (2006) we add these measures to those previously discussed:

- *Being comfortable with differences*
- *Adopting a posture of discovery with individual clients, and assessing behavior in the context of their reality*
- *Taking steps to calm vulnerabilities, anxieties, and fears about making mistakes*
- *Focusing on cultural and racial strengths, including adaptive behaviors*
- *Understanding that rigid, reactive behavior on the part of clients may not be specific to you*

- *Continually evaluating your knowledge of differences, and increasing your level of cultural competence*
- *Understanding that clients' worldviews may be different from your own*
- *Being prepared to intervene at the micro, mezzo, or macro level, because racial and ethnic minority individuals' problems often involve all three levels*
- *Understanding macro-level influences in relationships as well as the extent to which macro-level conditions an marginalized status affect the lives of racial and cultural minority groups*

Finally, note that the literature suggests that racial and ethnic minority clients show a preference for time-limited, goal-directed, action-oriented intervention methods, in which they quickly experience change (Corwin, 2002; Al-Krenawi & Graham, 2000; Gelman, 2004).

Difficulties in Establishing Trust

Clients vary widely in their capacity to trust. Some clients have levels of interpersonal functioning that enable them to quickly engage in the helping process, after only a few moments of checking out the social worker. For others, including racial and ethnic minority clients, despite the goodwill, knowledge, and skills that you display, revealing their feelings, gaining their trust and dismantling their defenses may take a longer period of time. Involuntary clients who have not sought a helping relationship should not be expected to readily trust you. In fact, attempting to persuade such clients of your helpful intent is usually counterproductive. Many distrustful clients trust actions before words. That is, they see trust as a product of the relationship that emerges over time. Trust in this regard is a process and is reinforced by attributes and actions, such as your commitment, patience, respect, and completion of the tasks that you agreed to do.

With involuntary clients, pushing for self-disclosure before trust and a positive working relationship are established may alienate them or prolong the period in which you must prove yourself as being trustworthy. They can erect the barriers of social distance and their perceived or real powerlessness in their attitude and language; for example, referring to you formally, or to others as "them," or "the system" (G.D. Rooney, 2009). Because these clients do not enter helping relationships voluntarily, they may disclose their problems only superficially during early sessions. These clients often enter the helping relationship in the pre-contemplation stage of change. In essence, they may not readily own the problem as described by others or even agree that they have a problem. Time limits—in particular, when a mandate requires that certain actions or behavioral changed occur by a certain date—may further exacerbate the problem.

In seeking to establish trust and a viable working relationship, you may find it necessary to reach out to involuntary clients to engage them in the helping process. When they cancel or miss appointments, you can continue the contact by phoning them, making a home visit (if your agency permits), or writing a letter. You can review the work that needs to be accomplished, empathize with their situations, and reiterate your support for helping them resolve their difficulties with the court. Many involuntary clients urgently need and want help. In some instances, their failure to trust and engage or keep appointments may emanate from fear or a pattern of avoidance rather than from a lack of motivation. Your assisting clients to come to terms with their fear or avoidance behavior may be therapeutic, whereas allowing them to terminate by default can have grave consequences. The movies *Antoine Fisher* (with Denzel Washington as therapist) and *Good Will Hunting* (with Robin Williams as therapist) are excellent examples of reaching out to a client and building trust.

Transference Reactions

Unrealistic perceptions of and reactions directed toward the social worker or members of a group are known as *transference reactions* (Knight, 2006: Nichols, 2006). In such reactions, the client transfers to the social worker wishes, fears, and other feelings that are rooted in past experiences with others (usually parents, parental substitutes, and siblings). Trauma survivors can experience several stages of transference. Transference reactions not only affect the relationship between the client and social worker, they also impede progress. They can also create difficulties in other interpersonal relationships. For example, a male may transfer his positive or negative relationship expectations to all females based on his experience with his mother. Difficulties in his relationship with other females can occur if the dynamics with his mother were negative and punitive; he will similarly perceive other females in this manner.

Transference can also occur at the group or community level. In minority communities in which youth perceive that they are being unfairly harassed by police, for example, transference reactions can occur in interactions with other authority figures, including with the social worker. Also, when communities have experienced a high level of oppressive police tactics, members may be reluctant to assist police in solving crimes. Transference then is subject to racial and political overtones, and is often reinforced by the powerful messages of music about injustices and inequalities, which further shapes cognitions and worldviews.

Transference may also occur in treatment groups between clients and in work with couples where one or both partners are having a reaction to the other. Multiple transference reactions can emerge in groups. In group situations, a trauma survivor may assign motivations, thoughts, and feelings to other members, projecting the attributes of the individual who hurt them in hostile interactions (Knight, 2006). In other instances, reactions may be evoked by interactions with the social worker facilitator as an authority figure, or by interactions with individual members. An individual can be experienced as a mother by one member, as a father by another member, and as a sibling by still another member. Similarly, that individual can perceive friends, authority figures, and siblings in the group. In either case, transference reactions can stall the group's progress. Your role as group facilitator is to assess the impact of this dynamic on the group and intervene appropriately. You can then utilize group process and communication skills to refocus the attention of members on the group's purpose. You may also use this occasion as a teachable moment, emphasizing how distorted perceptions of group members are based on other interpersonal relationships, rather than members of the group.

The following case example illustrates a transference reaction on the part of one member of a couple and its effects of their relationship.

Case Example

Connie and Kim had been together for more than 20 years. They experienced what they believed to be the usual relationship tensions—disagreements about finances, household chores, and whose turn it was to walk the dog. Their families were supportive of their relationship, thus family relations are not a source of strain for the couple. They were generally able to work through their interpersonal conflicts with others, although neither reported being very good at resolving their own conflicts together. This lack of skill was most apparent when Kim would present solutions for issues over which they had disagreements. In their usual pattern, Connie would avoid dealing with unpleasant situations and brood. Kim would work out a solution on her own and then present it to Connie. Connie's explosive reaction would further escalate the situation, and each would retreat to a more comfortable place, that of avoidance.

They reached a crisis point when Connie became involved with another woman. At first she denied any involvement other than friendship, but eventually she admitted her attraction to this individual. The tension, stress, and strain on the couple's relationship escalated to the point that they agreed to seek professional help.

During a session with the social worker, Connie stated that she had no intention of dissolving their relationship, which she valued. She did, however, state that she was attracted to the other woman, because this person was affirming, praising her for her accomplishments, and generally thought her to be a worthwhile individual. She felt that Kim rarely behaved in this way toward her; in fact, she thought that Kim did not appreciate her at all.

After further probing by the social worker, Connie admitted that when Kim raised issues and presented solutions, it reminded her of her father, who was always telling her what to do, and how to do it. During her teenage years, he rarely found reasons to praise her, often finding fault with her decisions and just about anything that she did. Even now, although Connie is a successful professional, he rarely had anything good to say about her. Kim's behavior reminded Connie of her father, and her reactions to him spilled over into her relationship with Kim. When Kim presented solutions, in Connie's mind she was telling her what to do.

As observed in this case, transference reactions involve overgeneralized and distorted perceptions that create difficulties in interpersonal relationships and sometimes in systems relationships. On a system-to-individual or system-to-group level, transference can involve responses to authority in any form. Besides preventing a client from making progress in resolving problems, transference reactions in therapeutic relationships may also create opportunities for growth. The therapeutic relationship is, in effect, a social microcosm wherein clients' interpersonal behavior and conditioned patterns of perceiving and feeling are manifested. In this context, clients can recreate here-and-now interactions that are virtually identical to those that plague and defeat them in other relationships; for example,

Connie's projection of Kim's behavior based on her relationship with her father. The consequent challenge for the social worker is to assist clients to recognize their distorted perceptions and to develop perceptual sets that help them differentiate between individuals and situations, rather than relying on projections, mental images, beliefs, or attitudes.

The frequency with which transference reactions related to the social worker occur during the course of the helping process varies considerably. In time-limited, task-focused forms of intervention, the likelihood of transference reactions may be minimal because of a focus on current concerns. When treatment has a focus on the past, and involves in-depth analysis of intrapsychic processes, transference may assume a more prominent role in the helping process. Similarly, working with marital partners conjointly tends to discourage transference reactions involving social workers, whereas working with only one partner may foster transference by the client and over-identification on the social worker's part.

Identifying Transference Reactions

Whatever the agency setting and the intervention, you will occasionally encounter transference reactions. To manage transference reactions, you must first be aware of their manifestations. Here are examples of some behaviors symptomatic of transference:

- *Transference reactions involving interpersonal trauma are common. Examples are mistrust, fear, or anger (Knight, 2006).*
- *Fear, distrust, and hostile interactions or rage at the social worker, group members, or projections of significant others in response to their grief, frustration, and fears (James, 2008; Knight, 2006).*
- *Behaving provocative by arguing with or baiting the social worker or becoming silent and hostile, avoiding making progress (Nichols, 2006).*
- *Questioning the interest of the social worker; in particular, whether the social worker can understand their situation without having had a similar experience (James, 2008). Also, feeling that the social worker couldn't possibly have a genuine interest because helping clients is their job.*
- *Misinterpreting a message of the social worker or others as a result of feeling put down. Responding defensively, feeling rejected, or expecting criticism or punishment without realistic cause.*
- *Perceptions that their thoughts and feelings are extreme, and questioning whether others, even*

those with similar experience, can understand (Knight, 2006).

- *Trauma survivors seeing other's behaviors or reactions as signs of betrayal, abandonment, and rejection; assigning others the motivations, thoughts, and feelings of those who caused their trauma (Knight, 2006).*
- *Relating to the social worker in a clinging, dependent way or excessively seeking praise and reassurance.*
- *Attempting to please the social worker by giving excessive compliments and praise or by ingratiating behavior.*
- *Attempting to engage the social worker socially, offering personal favors, presenting gifts, or seeking special considerations, and in some cases, having dreams or fantasies about the social worker.*
- *Relating to the social worker or group members in a dependent manner, excessively seeking praise and reassurance.*
- *Difficulty in discussing problems because the social worker or a group member reminds them of someone else in appearance (Nichols, 2006).*

Clearly, although such reactions originate in the past, they become manifest in the here and now. This raises an interesting question: Are transference reactions best resolved by focusing on the past to enable clients to gain insight into their origins? We maintain that because reactions driven by past experiences are played out in the present, they can be resolved by examining clients' current inaccurate and distorted perceptions. Of course, when clients bring up experiences and circumstances from their past, brief historical excursions often facilitate productive emotional catharsis and lead to an understanding of the origins of their patterns of thinking, feeling, and behaving. Moreover, when clients have experienced traumatic stresses (e.g., physical or sexual abuse, sexual assault, war, injury, or other crisis events), probing and exploration of these experiences may be vital to gaining understanding of and recovery from the detrimental effects of those experiences (James, 2008; Knight, 2006; Wartel, 1991; Rosenthal, 1988).

Managing Transference Reactions

When clients manifest behaviors that are possible indications of transference reactions, after any necessary examination of the past, it is important to shift the focus to their here-and-now feelings, because such reactions generally cause clients to disengage from the relationship and from productive work, ultimately undermining the helping process. To assist you in managing transference reactions, we offer the following guidelines:

1. *Be open to the possibility that the client's reaction is not unrealistic* and may be a product of your behavior. If discussion and introspection indicate that the client's behavior is realistic, respond authentically by owning responsibility for your behavior.
2. *When clients appear to expect you to respond in antitherapeutic ways, as significant others have in the past, it is important to respond differently,* thereby disconfirming those expectations. Responses that contrast sharply with the client's expectations may produce temporary disequilibrium and force the client to differentiate the social worker from past figures. As a result, the client must thus deal with the social worker as a unique and real person, rather than perpetuating fictional expectations based on past experiences.
3. *Assist the client to determine the immediate source of distorted perceptions by exploring how and when the feelings emerged.* Carefully explore antecedents and meaning attributions associated with the feelings. Avoid attempting to correct distorted perceptions by immediately revealing your actual feelings. By first exploring how and when problematic feelings emerged, you can assist clients to expand their awareness of their patterns of overgeneralizing and making both faulty meaning attributions and unwarranted assumptions based on past experience. This awareness can enable them in the future to discriminate between feelings that emanate from conditioned perceptual sets and reality-based feelings and reactions.
4. *After clients have recognized the unrealistic nature of their feelings and manifested awareness of the distortions that produced these feelings, share your actual feelings.* This revelation can be a source of reassurance to clients who have felt offended, hurt, resentful, rejected, or the like.
5. *After you have examined problematic feelings, assist clients to determine whether they have experienced similar reactions in other relationships.* Through this exploration, clients may recognize patterns of distortions that create difficulties in other relationships.

The application of these guidelines is illustrated in the following excerpt taken from the eighth session with a 30-year-old female who had sought help because she was discouraged about her failure to find a marital partner.

Client: Wow, the weeks sure go by fast. [*Long pause.*] I don't have much to talk about today. [*Ambivalence.*]

Social worker [*sensing the client is struggling with something*]: I gather you didn't really feel ready for your appointment today. [*Empathic response.*] How did you feel about coming? [*Open-ended probing response.*]

Client: I didn't want to come, but I thought I should. Actually, it has been an eventful week. But I haven't felt I wanted to tell you about what has been happening. [*Indication of a possible transference reaction.*]

Social worker: Sounds like you've had some misgivings about confiding certain things in me. [*Paraphrasing response.*] Could you share with me some of your thoughts about confiding in me? [*Open-ended probing response/polite command.*]

Client: Okay. I've wanted to keep them to myself until I find out how things turn out. I've wanted to wait until it really develops into something. Then I would tell you. [*Testing.*]

Social worker: So you haven't wanted to risk it turning out bad and worrying about how I would feel if it did. [*Additive empathy, interpretation.*]

Client: I guess I've wanted to impress you. I had a date with the fellow we talked about last week. It was wonderful. He's just the opposite of the other creep I told you about. He either has a real line or he's a super guy. I couldn't believe how considerate he was. [*Seeking approval/praise.*]

Social worker: You can't be sure yet what he's really like, and you want to be sure he's for real before you tell me about him? [*Additive empathy/interpretation.*]

Client [*with an embarrassed smile*]: Yes! And if it really developed into something, then I could tell you.

Social worker: And that way you could be sure I'd be favorably impressed? [*Additive empathy/interpretation.*]

Client: Yes! I've felt I wanted you to know someone really good could be attracted to me.

Social worker: Hmm. Sounds like you've felt I've doubted you have much to offer a man and wanted to prove to me you do have something to offer. [*Additive empathy/interpretation.*]

Client: Yes, that's true. I have wanted you to think of me as a desirable person.

Social worker: I'd like to explore where those doubts or fears that I don't see you as a desirable person come from. I'm wondering how you've concluded I don't see you as having much to offer a man. Have I done or said something that conveyed that to you? [*Probing, addressing perceptions and feelings.*]

Client [*thinks for a moment*]: Well, no. Nothing that I can think of.

Social worker: Yet I gather those feelings have been very real to you. I wonder when you first became aware of those feelings.

Client [*after a pause*]: Well, I think it was when we began to talk about my feelings that guys are just interested in me for what they can get. I guess I wondered if you thought I was a real dud. I wanted you to know it wasn't so, that a desirable person could be attracted to me.

Social worker: You know when we were discussing your feelings toward your mother two or three weeks ago, you said essentially the same thing. [*Using summarization to make a connection between separate but related events.*]

Client: I'm not sure what you mean.

Social worker: You had said you felt your mother doubted you would ever marry because you were so cold you couldn't attract a man.

Client [*smiles pensively and nods affirmatively*]: You know I never wanted to elope. I always wanted to marry in my hometown and have a big wedding. When I had my ring on my finger, I would turn to mother and say, "See, you were wrong!"

Social worker: So you've felt you needed to prove to her that someone could love you. And that's also what you wanted to prove to me. [*Additive empathy reflection.*]

Client: Yes. [*Nods affirmatively.*]

Social worker: I'm interested you've thought maybe I, too, didn't see you as lovable. Could you share with me how you reached that conclusion? [*Social worker continues to explore the unrealistic nature of her perception and how it pervades other relationships. Focus on here and now.*]

By sensitively exploring the client's reluctance to attend the session, the social worker not only resolved an emerging obstacle to productive work, she also assisted the client to explore further her doubts about her attractiveness. Through this process, the social worker expanded the client's awareness of how these doubts distorted her perceptions of how others viewed her—in this instance, the social worker. Moreover, through the exploration, the social worker was able to identify a basic misconception that had influenced the client's relationships with others and to relate more comfortably with the social worker. Note also that the communication and facilitative skills used by the social worker brought the client to a place where she could examine her thoughts and feelings.

Countertransference Reactions

Social workers may also experience adverse relational reactions that can damage helping relationships if they are not recognized and managed effectively. Just as with clients, social workers' feelings may be realistic or unrealistic. The counterpart of transference, such reactions are known as *countertransference*. Like transference, this phenomenon involves feelings, wishes, and unconscious defensive patterns on the part of the social worker. They are derived from past relationships, interfere with objective perception, and block productive interaction with clients.

Countertransference in the traditional sense is grounded in psychoanalytic theory, in which the professional has conscious and unconscious emotional reactions to the client (McWilliams, 1999). The more contemporary view of countertransference is that the professional's reactions, real and unreal, to a client can occur irrespective of origin and can be based on their own past or present experiences or client characteristics (James, 2008; Knight, 2006; Nichols, 2006). Proposing a more transactional approach, specifically that of the person and the environment, Fauth (2006) examined transactional stress theory and countertransference. Findings showed that countertransference behavior was related to stressful interpersonal events and the professional's appraisal as to whether the situation was harmful, threatening, or taxed his or her coping resources.

Countertransference reactions are believed to contaminate helping relationships by producing distorted perceptions, blind spots, wishes, and antitherapeutic emotional reactions and behaviors (Kahn, 1997). Selected reactions that can result in counterproductive dynamics are:

- *The professional lacks the skills to integrate anger or conflict resolution into their coping repertoire or personality. For example, when confronted by a client who is angry, the tendency may be to become unduly uncomfortable and attempt to divert the expression of such feelings.*
- *Unresolved feelings about rejections by significant others and thus find it difficult to relate to clients who are cool and aloof.*
- *The failure of the social worker to resolve resentful feelings toward authority, resulting in, for example, over-identification with a rebellious adolescent.*
- *Controlling and over-identifying with clients who have similar problems and being blind to reciprocal behavior between clients; for example, taking sides when working with a couple in marital counseling.*
- *A social worker may have an excessive need to be loved and admired and may behave seductively or strive to impress clients by inappropriate disclosure of personal information. Of course, selective self-disclosure in the form of empathic responsiveness can be beneficial (Goldstein, 1997). Raines (1996) suggests that self-disclosure decisions may be considered within a range of over- and under-involvement; therefore, personal sharing should be rational and related to the current relationship.*

Knight (2006) and James (2008) assert that countertransference, including vicarious trauma, is a common reaction among professionals who are involved in crisis work and the intensity of work with trauma survivors. Salston and Figley (2004) also point to the consequences of trauma for professionals working with criminal victims. Countertransference, in high stress situations may also signal a stage of burnout. James and Gilliland (2001) note that crisis professionals may experience "reawakened" unresolved thoughts and feelings" as a result of working with clients who have had similar experiences (p. 419). Maintaining a professional distance may be difficult, especially when the countertransference reaction is related to the trauma experiences and "horror stories" of immigrants and refugees (Potocky-Tripodi, 2002). As a result, the tendency to become over-involved may emerge as professionals experience compassion fatigue or secondary trauma. Neither situation is productive in that either one can severely impair the ability to work effectively with clients. Your conscious assessment of these dynamics is critical to both you and the client. You may need to seek supervision and consultation and to consider whether taking time off will assist you to refocus and reenergize your professional work.

TABLE-18-2 TYPICAL PROFESSIONAL COUNTERTRANSFERENCE REACTIONS

- Being unduly concerned about or protective of a client, becoming his or her champion or rescuer
- Having persistent dreams or erotic fantasies about clients
- Dreading or anticipating sessions with clients
- Feeling uncomfortable when discussing certain problems with a client
- Hostility directed toward a client or inability to empathize with a client
- Blaming others exclusively for a client's difficulties
- Feeling bored, being drowsy, or tuning out a client
- Regularly being tardy or forgetting appointments with certain clients
- Consistently ending sessions early or extending them beyond the designated time
- Trying to impress or being unduly impressed by clients
- Being overly concerned about losing a client
- Arguing with or feeling defensive or hurt by a client's criticisms or actions
- Being overly solicitous and performing tasks that clients are capable of performing
- Probing into a client's sex life
- Liking or disliking certain types of clients (may also be reality based)
- Identifying with the role of an abuser in trauma situation or feeling responsible for their pain
- Attempts to manage feeling can include minimizing the stories of trauma clients, being disgusted with clients or acting in a voyeuristic manner

Before discussing how to manage countertransference reactions, it is first important to identify their typical manifestations (see Table 18-2). Portions of the indicators in the table are taken from Knight (2006) and Etherington (2000).

Note the similarity between the list in Table 18-2 and the reactions that were described in Table 18-1 for over- and under-involvement. Also note that these countertransference behaviors may evidence a lack of professional distance, unprofessional conduct, and burnout. Unrealistic feelings toward a client and reactions such as those in Tables 18-1 and 18-2 are indications that should prompt immediate appropriate corrective measures. Otherwise, they can contribute to the client's problem, and ultimately impair the helping relationship.

Ordinarily, the first step in resolving countertransference (and often all that is needed) is to engage in introspection. *Introspection* involves an analytical dialogue with oneself aimed at discovering sources of feelings, reactions, cognitions, and behavior. Examples of questions that facilitate introspection include the following:

- *"Why am I feeling uncomfortable with this client? What is going on inside me that I am not able to relate in a professional manner?"*

- *"How well do I manage my own anxiety, anger, or discomfort with this client's situations?"*
- *"Why do I dislike (or feel bored, impatient, or irritated) with this client? Are my feelings rational, or does this client remind me of someone else or my own experience?"*
- *"What is happening inside of me that I don't face certain problems with this client? Am I afraid of a negative reaction on the client's part?"*
- *"What purpose was served by arguing with this client? Was I feeling defensive or threatened?"*
- *"Why did I talk so much or give so much advice? Did I feel a need to give something to the client?"*
- *"What's happening with me that I'm fantasizing or dreaming about this client?"*
- *"Why am I constantly taking sides in my work with couples (parents or minors), thereby overlooking one side. Am I over-identifying with certain clients and, if so, why?"*
- *"Could my own experience, personality, or feelings block my objectivity?"*

Introspection and self-assessment, as well as the ability to maintain appropriate boundaries and distance, will assist you to achieve or regain a realistic perspective on your relationships with clients. Discussion of such topics should also be part of consultation with colleagues and supervisors, in which you expose and explore your feelings and obtain their perspective and advice. Just as clients are sometimes too close to their problems to view them objectively and thus benefit from seeing them from the vantage point of a social worker, so you can likewise benefit from the unbiased perspective of an uninvolved colleague, consultant, or supervisor. However, professionals who repeatedly experience countertransference reactions need professional help beyond mere introspection or the input of a colleague. Specifically, ongoing countertransference reactions limit their effectiveness and create relational barriers to effective work with clients.

Realistic Practitioner Reactions

Not all negative feelings toward certain clients represent countertransference reactions to clients or their situations or the transference reactions of clients toward the professional. Some clients are abrasive, arrogant, or obnoxious; have irritating mannerisms; or are exploitative of and cruel toward others. Even the most accepting social workers may have difficulty developing positive feelings toward such clients. Social workers, after all, are only human; thus they are not immune to disliking others or feeling irritated and impatient at times. Despite their behavior, clients are entitled to service. In fact, often these clients need help precisely because their behavior alienates others, leaving them isolated and confused about what created their difficulties.

When you look beyond the offensive behaviors of certain clients, you will often discover that beneath the facade of arrogance and toughness are desirable—even admirable—qualities and vulnerability. A social worker noted in an interview with one of the authors that "during contact with minors, in particular when race is a factor (the social worker is white), the minors often assume a negative posture with a big attitude." However, when you gain access to the private worlds of some clients, you may find that they have endured severe emotional deprivation, and perhaps physical or sexual abuse, or other traumatic experiences that have exceeded their coping ability and capacity to trust. For example, the same social worker stated that "In many cases, once you get past their behavior you find a fragile kid who has been exposed to a life that you can hardly imagine!" In her response to these individuals, in spite of their behavior, she continues her efforts to connect with them and to convey warmth, acceptance, and empathy. She also shared that there are days when she

is tired of their behavior, and "I tell them so. Oddly enough, most respond to me in a very caring way."

Abrasive clients need far more than acceptance, however: They need feedback about how certain aspects of their behavior offend you and others. You can also encourage these clients to risk new behaviors and give them opportunities to learn and practice those skills. Feedback can be extremely helpful if it is conveyed sensitively and imparted in the context of goodwill. In providing such feedback, you must be careful to avoid evaluative or blaming comments that tend to elicit defensiveness—for example, "You boast too much and dominate conversations" or "You are insensitive to other people's feelings and say hurtful things." Clients are far more likely to be receptive to messages that describe and document their behavior and that personalize your response. The following descriptive message embodies ownership of feelings: "When you sneered at me just now, I began to feel defensive and resentful. You've done that several times before, and I find myself backing away from you each time. I'm concerned because I suspect that this is how you interact with others." This message, of course, is highly authentic and would not be appropriate until a sound working relationship has been established.

Sexual Attraction toward Clients

Romantic and sexual feelings toward clients can be especially hazardous, although such feelings are by no means uncommon. One survey of 585 psychotherapists (psychologists) revealed that only 77 (13%) had never been attracted to any client (Pope, Keith-Spiegel, & Tabachnick, 1986). The majority (82%), however, had never seriously considered sexual involvement with a client; of the remaining 18%, 87% had considered becoming involved only once or twice. Of the 585 respondents, approximately 6% had actually engaged in sexual intimacies with clients.

In a more recent study, Strom-Gottfried (1999a) found that of the ethics complaints reported to NASW, 29% involved boundary violations. Of this total, almost three-fourths involved some form of sexual violation. As Strom-Gottfried notes, "Even a small incidence warrants the attention of the profession, particularly supervisors and educators, to assure that any measures available to reduce the incidence further are fully pursued" (1999a, p. 448). Social workers need to be informed about appropriate professional behaviors, exposed to good modeling, explore challenging situations, and use critical thinking skills in such examinations.

When the setting, location, or population exposes the social worker to particular risk (e.g., in rural areas; close religious, cultural, and ethnic communities; and substance abuse treatment settings), potential dilemmas and dual relationships must be explored. Raines (1996) suggests that in situations where sexual attraction is evident, but, self-disclosure decisions must be considered within a range of over- and under-involvement. Likewise, he suggests, personal sharing should be based on rational grounds and related to the current relationship.

As noted earlier, most social workers have at some point in their careers experienced sexual attraction toward a client. Managing such attraction appropriately is critical. Fortunately, data indicate that the majority of therapists handle their attractions successfully. Although 83% believed the attraction to be mutual, others assumed that the client was unaware of their attraction. When the latter was the case, they believed the attraction did not have any harmful effects on the helping process. By contrast, therapists who believed clients were aware of their attraction understood the detrimental impact on the helping process.

Although Strom-Gottfried (1999a) found that only 6% of those surveyed had engaged in sexual activities with clients, this percentage is quite alarming. Sexual involvement has grievous consequences for clients. They often experience confusion and intense guilt, and thereafter have great difficulty trusting professionals. Some social workers have justified engaging in sexual activities with clients on the basis of assisting them to feel loved or helping them to overcome sexual problems. Such explanations are often thinly disguised and feeble rationalizations for exploiting clients. Typically, such attractions or sexual activities involve clients who are attractive and relatively young. In other instances, justifications are based on the client's behavior toward the social worker. Irrespective of circumstance, this behavior is unacceptable. It is a grave disservice to the client and damaging to the public image of the profession and has legal implications for the social worker.

The consequences of sexual involvement are devastating for social workers as well. When such behaviors are discovered, offending social workers may be sanctioned, sued for unethical practice and have their license or certification revoked, essentially removing them from the profession. Ethical standards of conduct established by licensing boards and the NASW Code of Ethics are unequivocal in this regard. The NASW Code of Ethics states: "The social worker should under no circumstance engage in sexual activities or sexual contact with current clients, whether such contact is consensual or forced" (Section 1.09a).

Sexual attraction to a client is normal but must be managed, because acting on an attraction is always unethical in the client–social worker professional relationship. Effectively managing sexual attraction requires engaging in the corrective measures identified earlier for unrealistic feelings and reactions—namely, introspection and consulting with a supervisor. In this regard, it is noteworthy that in the Strom-Gottfried study previously cited, 57% of respondents had the good sense to seek consultation or supervision when they were attracted to a client. We cannot state too strongly that you must not allow feelings to go unchecked. Furthermore, you should take measures to prevent and avoid any problematic circumstances, by altering the manner in which you dress or behave so that it will not prompt either a client or you to become sexually attracted to or involved with each other. Social workers who frequently experience erotic fantasies about clients are particularly vulnerable, are considered impaired professionals, and should consider entering treatment.

Managing Opposition to Change

Social workers and other helping professionals have been inclined to label client behaviors that *oppose* the direction in which they wish them to go as *resistance*. Resistance has been defined as holding back, disengaging, or in some way subverting or sabotaging change efforts, whether knowingly or not, without open discussion and as any action or attitude that impedes the course of therapeutic work (Meyer, 2001; Nichols & Schwartz, 2004). Resistance as first conceptualized by Freud was described as a normal, healthy response. More recently, this concept has been used in a fashion that holds the client responsible for the opposition, which tends to cause further resistance (Meyer, 2001).

In understanding resistance as a normative self-protective function, think about a situation in which you were told that you needed to make certain changes, whether at work (complete your case notes on time), at home (be more helpful around the house), or a relationship (be more attentive).

- *What was your emotional response?*
- *What was your behavioral response?*

Now transfer your responses to clients, especially those who are meeting with you for the first time.

To see how resistance arises with involuntary clients, think about your response and emotional reaction when a telemarketer telephones your home at dinnertime and offers you a product for which you have little interest and no desire to have. In this situation, you have the option of disconnecting the call. In interactions with involuntary clients, they are often acting on these same feelings, but may feel that they do not have the option of disconnecting.

There are several factors involved in understanding the dynamic of resistance. Lum (2004) notes, for example, that resistance is prominent in interactions with persons of color. It may take the form of "minimal involvement, reserved or superficially pleasant." (pp. 152–153). The basis for resistance on the part of minority individuals, and indeed entire communities is rooted in a lack of trust or confidence in the professional. Establishing trust and reciprocity in relationships is a major thrust in overcoming the reluctance that people of color have about seeking help from agencies "that are controlled and dominated by whites" (Lum, 2004 p. 152).

Another factor in avoiding blaming clients for resistance is to recognize opposition to change as a universal phenomenon, as anyone who has attempted to break long-established habits knows all too well. The force of habits is relentless; moreover, making a change often means foregoing gratifications or coping head-on with frightening or aversive situations. In addition, making a change may entail risking new behavior in the face of unknown consequences. Even though the status quo may cause pain and distress, it is familiar, and the consequences of habitual behavior are predictable. Further, it is not uncommon for clients to have mixed feelings about change, both desiring it and being hesitant or ambivalent about implementing it. Opposing feelings generally coexist—that is, part of the client is motivated to change even as another part strives to maintain the familiar status quo.

Recognizing clients' ambivalent feelings about changing enables you to assist them to explore their feelings and to weigh the advantages and disadvantages of making changes. Indeed, as clients think through their feelings and reassess the implications of maintaining the status quo, the scales often tilt in favor of change. In the helping process, by accepting clients in spite of their opposition to change or the fact that they are in the *pre-contemplation stage* of change ("I am not sure that I have a problem"), you recognize their right to self-determination. It may be beneficial to ethical

persuasion to engage them in the change effort (See Chapter 17). Keep in mind that when clients feel free to make up their own minds, they are more likely to become engaged. This factor is crucial, because pressure often engenders an opposing force or reactance. Viewed in this light, recognizing and accepting oppositional feelings to change prevent such feelings from going underground, where they might subtly undermine the helping process. Recognizing, openly discussing, and accepting oppositional feelings thus can liberate a desire and willingness to change.

Reactance theory provides a more fruitful perspective for considering opposition to change. Rather than blaming clients for their oppositional behavior, this theory leads the social worker to objectively anticipate the range of responses to be expected when valued freedoms are threatened (Brehm, 1976). First, some clients may try to regain their freedom directly by attempting to take back what has been threatened (e.g., choice). Second, a frequent response is to restore freedom by implication or to "find the loophole" by offering up superficial compliance while violating the spirit of requirements (e.g., I will sit at my desk, but I won't so any work). Third, threatened behaviors and beliefs may be more valued than ever before. Finally, the person or source of the threat may be met with hostility or aggression (R.H Rooney, 1992, p. 130).

Reactance theory lends itself to proactive strategies designed to reduce this kind of opposition. For example, clients who perceive global pressure to change their lifestyle are likely to experience less reactance if those pressures are narrowed in scope and the change effort emphasizes behaviors that remain free. Second, reactance is likely to be reduced if the client perceives that he or she has at least some constrained choices (R. H. Rooney, 1992). Understanding the client's perspective on the situation and avoiding labeling can also act to reduce reactance (p. 135).

Preventing Opposition to Change

Opposition to change may emanate from sources other than ambivalence about changing. Clients may misunderstand the nature of service or of a specific intervention and may therefore be reluctant to cooperate fully. Should this occur, it is vital to explain fully the nature of the service or intervention (informed consent), exploring what is required and where there is room for choice. This discussion should also clarify the roles of the participants and permit voluntary clients to feel free to decide whether to proceed with the therapy. The best way of preventing opposition to change is to be thorough in formulating contracts, clarifying roles, developing specific goals, providing a rationale for specific interventions, inviting questions, eliciting and discussing misgivings, and fostering self-determination.

Other sources of opposition to change include apprehension or fear associated with engaging in behavior that is alien to one's usual functioning or cultural beliefs or having to face a situation that appears overwhelming. These feelings are generally so intense that clients are reluctant to complete essential actions. Their difficulties may then be compounded by embarrassment over failure to implement the actions, which may produce resistance to seeing the social worker or discussing the problematic situation further. This kind of opposition can also be prevented by anticipating and exploring the fears or values and beliefs and by preparing clients through modeling, behavioral rehearsal, and guided practice. These strategies are discussed at length in Chapter 13, along with other factors that may hinder the change process.

Transference Resistance

Some clients become so enmeshed in major transference reactions that their reactions create an obstacle to progress (Nichols, 2006). Some clients may idealize the social worker and attempt to use the helping relationship as a substitute for other relationships, for example. They may then become preoccupied with this dynamic, rather than focusing on goal attainment. Other clients may be disappointed and resentful because a social worker does not meet their unrealistic expectations. Perceiving the social worker as uncaring, withholding, and rejecting (as they likewise perceived their parents), these clients may struggle with angry feelings (negative transference) toward the social worker, which diverts them from working productively on their problems. Unless social workers recognize and assist such clients to resolve these feelings by discussing them, accepting them, and placing them in a realistic perspective, these clients may prematurely terminate the contact, convinced that their perceptions and feelings are accurate.

Manifestations of Opposition to Change

Opposition to change takes many forms, and the frequency with which clients manifest different forms varies according to the type of setting, the client's

personality, and the client's ethnicity and socioeconomic level. The following can be common manifestations of opposition:

- *Mental blocking (mind going blank)*
- *Lengthy periods of silence*
- *Inattention or mind wandering, changing the subject*
- *Rambling on at length or dwelling on unimportant details*
- *Restlessness or fidgeting*
- *Discussing superficialities or irrelevant matters*
- *Lying or deliberately misrepresenting facts*
- *Intellectualizing (avoiding feelings and problems by focusing on abstract ideas)*
- *Forgetting details of distressing events or of content of previous sessions*
- *Being tardy for or forgetting, changing, or canceling appointments*
- *Minimizing problems or claiming miraculous improvement*
- *Bringing up important content at the end of a session*
- *Not paying fees for service*
- *Not applying knowledge and skills gained in sessions in daily life*
- *Assuming a stance of helplessness*

Various verbal ploys to justify not engaging in the change process or taking the requisite corrective action may be expressed as follows:

- *"I couldn't do that; it just wouldn't be me."*
- *"I just can't!"*
- *"I've tried that, and it doesn't work."*
- *"I understand what you're saying, but …"*
- *"I'm not so different; isn't everyone … ?"*

Many of the preceding examples do not necessarily indicate opposition to change. Saying that one cannot complete a particular action needs careful exploration. In fact, if the client continues to work productively, then the phenomenon may not warrant special handling. If the client appears to have reached an impasse, however, one can safely conclude that opposition is involved and shift the focus to exploring the factors that underlie this opposition. Also, be aware the rambling or dwelling on unimportant information can also be clients' attempts to make some sense of their situation, to tell their story, or to air their grievances. It may also be an opportunity for catharsis, in which clients can vent their frustrations. Change should also take into consideration whether:

- *The client has the resources to change (e.g., developmental, social, cognitive)*
- *Environmental barriers (e.g., economic, political, cultural)*
- *The client–social worker relationship (relational barriers)*

Opposition can also emerge in family and group sessions. Individual members may engage in any of the preceding phenomena. In groups, members may form subgroups and ignore the total group process. Likewise, family members can organize in factions, which can be based on gender, age, or power. Resistance in groups and families can also manifest in scapegoating individual members. In families, one individual may be characterized as the source of the family's difficulties; in groups, a scapegoat may be faulted for poor group processes. In groups, oppositional behavior may take the form of a client or even several group members isolating themselves and not participating, attempting to force the leader to assume responsibility that belongs with the group, engaging in social banter, failing to stay on topic, and struggling for power rather than working cooperatively.

Bear in mind that the family or group member who appears to be opposing change may actually be presenting a concern that other members feel as well. As with individuals, when impasses occur, the social worker should shift the focus of group or family members to the dysfunctional processes so that energies are not diverted to counterproductive activities.[1]

Because opposition to change is a common phenomenon, it is not necessary to become alarmed about every possible occurrence. Moreover, focusing on trivial opposition may elicit adverse reactions from clients, who may feel that the social worker is attempting to scrutinize and analyze their most minute behavior. In fact, overreacting to manifestations of opposition may ultimately produce opposition. A rule of thumb is that if opposition is not strong enough to impede progress, then it is best ignored. Nevertheless, when an opposition blocks progress, it is imperative to grant the highest priority to its resolution.

Exploring and Managing Opposition

A first step in managing potential opposition to change involves bringing it into the light by focusing on the client's underlying here-and-now feelings. Sensitive and skillful handling is essential because personal feelings toward the social worker are commonly associated with such opposition, and clients find it difficult to risk sharing their feelings in this scenario. (Otherwise, they would have shared them already.) Empathy, warmth, and acceptance play a critical role in eliciting clients' feelings because these ingredients of the client–social worker relationship foster a non threatening interpersonal climate.

In exploring sources of opposition, the social worker should not focus on the manifestation per se but rather cite it as an indication that the client is experiencing troubling thoughts and feelings directed to the social worker or events in the helping process. An authentic response conveys the social worker's goodwill and concern that progress has bogged down; it also reaffirms the social worker's helpful intent and desire to work out whatever difficulties have arisen. Sometimes, the content discussed in an earlier session may yield cues as to the sources of difficulties. For example, the client may have previously discussed an extremely painful topic, disclosed personal feelings related to their shame or guilt, or bristled in response to being confronted with personal contributions to a problematic situation. In such instances, the social worker may open up these feelings for discussion: "You appear awfully quiet today, as though you're struggling. I know that our last session was upsetting to you. Could you share with me what you're feeling about it just now?"

Discussing sources of opposition often reveals fears about where exploring certain personal feelings might lead. Some clients mistakenly fear that they are losing their minds and that by revealing their thoughts and feeling the social worker will judge their mental competence. Other clients may fear that they will be condemned if they disclose negative feelings toward a child or discuss extramarital affairs. Still other clients may be concerned that they will be pressured to change their thoughts or be perceived as being ridiculous.

As you initiate exploration of the source of opposition, some clients may hesitate to reveal relevant feelings. One technique that often proves successful in cutting through such reluctance is to focus empathically on here-and-now fears about disclosing other troublesome feelings. Your sensitivity, empathy, and genuineness may well pave the way for the client to risk opening up more. The following empathic response is one example of this technique:

Social worker: I'm sensing that you're very uncomfortable about discussing your feelings. I may be wrong, but I get the impression you are afraid of how I will respond. I can't say for sure how I'd respond, but I want you to know I'd do my best to understand your feelings. It would be helpful if you would share with me what you're feeling at this moment?

When clients do risk sharing their feelings, it is often therapeutic to accredit their strength for their ability to take this risk and to express reassurance. Such positive responses further cultivate a climate that is conducive to reciprocal openness, obliterate the feared consequences, and reinforce the client for disclosing risky feelings. The following is an example of such a response:

Social worker: Thanks for expressing your anger. Clearly, you have felt this way for a long time. It took a lot of courage on your part. I accept your anger and now understand that it created a distance in our relationship. I feel bad that these feelings continued to build and I didn't notice or know about them. Your sharing your feelings with me gives both of us an opportunity to talk things out.

Positive Connotation

Positive connotation is another technique that is useful in reducing the threat level, thereby allowing clients to save face and protect their self-esteem that they risked in talking about their feelings. In positive connotation, constructive intentions are attributed to what would otherwise be regarded as a client's undesirable or negative behavior. In using this technique, the social worker recognizes that the meaning ascribed to behavior can be viewed both positively and negatively, depending on one's vantage point. When viewed as an obstacle to progress, opposition takes on a negative meaning. When viewed from the client's perspective, however, the same behavior may have positive intentions. The following examples clarify this point:

- *A client cancels an appointment and is withdrawn in the following session. Exploration reveals that she resented the social worker "pressuring her" to follow a certain course of action. The social worker empathizes with her feelings as evidence of self-direction.*
- *A client is preoccupied with thoughts or fantasies about the social worker, which causes him to be stalled in working on his problems. These feelings can also be interpreted as evidence that he is moving away from his self-imposed isolation and is permitting himself to risk feelings of closeness that can be transferred to social relationships.*
- *After an extended period of silence and an exploration of related feelings, a parent launches into a tirade over how the social worker takes sides with the minor. The response is considered as a legitimate effort by the parent to be to be understood.*

The goal of positive connotation is not to condone clients' opposition or to reinforce their distorted perceptions. Rather, the objectives are to minimize clients' needs to defend themselves, to safeguard their already precarious sense of self, and to act in a manner that is consistent with a strengths perspective. When using this technique, it is important to assist clients to recognize that their reactions are derived from distorted perceptions (if they are) and to encourage them to express their feelings directly.

Redefining Problems as Opportunities for Growth

The technique of *redefining problems as growth opportunities* is a close relative of positive connotation because it also involves relabeling or reframing. Both clients and social workers tend to view problems negatively. Moreover, clients often view remedial courses of action as "necessary evils," dwelling on the threat involved in risking new behaviors. Therefore, it is often helpful to reformulate problems and essential tasks as opportunities for growth and means to gain liberation from stifling and self-defeating behaviors. Relabeling or reframing emphasizes the positives—that is, the benefits of change rather than the discomfort, fear, and other costs of modifying one's behavior.

In using this technique, it is important to not convey an unrealistically positive attitude. The fears and threats are very real to clients who risk change, and being unduly optimistic may simply convey a lack of understanding on your part. Neither reframing nor relabeling minimizes clients' problems or ignores fears in risking new behaviors. Both do, however, enable clients to view their difficulties in a fuller perspective that embodies positive as well as negative factors. The following are examples of how problem situations might be relabeled as opportunities for growth:

Relabeling

- *A teenage foster child who has run away because the foster parents insisted he adhere to a night-time curfew refuses to return to the foster home because the foster parents "are unreasonable." The social worker describes returning as a challenge to deal with a problem head-on and to work it out rather than avoiding, which has been the youth pattern.*
- *An elderly female with a family history of breast cancer is reluctant to see a doctor because she fears she has cancer. The social worker empathizes with*

her fears but describes the checkup as an opportunity to rule out the frightening possibility or to receive treatment before the disease progresses, should she have cancer.

Reframing

- *A youth feels embarrassed about taking a battery of vocational tests and attending a vocational-technical school, rather than going to college. The social worker acknowledges his discomfort but emphasizes that taking the tests offers an opportunity to learn more about his aptitudes and to expand his choices in planning his future.*
- *A woman expresses apprehension about leaving her abusive spouse. The social worker empathizes with her fear, but points out that leaving her spouse will allow her to pursue opportunities she envisioned for herself and for her children.*

Confronting Patterns of Opposition

In some instances, clients fail to make progress toward their goals because of the persistence of pervasive particular patterns of behavior. For example, some clients may intellectualize extensively to avoid having to experience painful emotions such as loneliness or depression. Other clients may relate in a distant, aloof manner or in aggressive ways to protect against becoming close to others and risking rejection. Still others may consistently hold other people or circumstances responsible for their difficulties, failing to examine or acknowledge their part in creating the situation. Because such patterns of behavior often create impasses in therapy, social workers must be able to recognize and handle them. Confronting clients with discrepancies between expressed goals and behaviors that defeat accomplishment of those goals is often needed to break such impasses. Because Chapter 17 discussed confrontation at length, we will limit our discussion here to a special type of confrontation: therapeutic binds.

Therapeutic Binds

Occasionally, social workers may encounter clients who stubbornly cling to self-defeating behaviors despite awareness that these behaviors perpetuate their difficulties. In such instances, placing clients in a *therapeutic bind* may be the impetus needed to modify the problematic behaviors. In using a therapeutic bind, social workers confront clients with their self-defeating

behaviors in such a way that they must either modify their behaviors or own responsibility for choosing to perpetuate their difficulties despite their expressed intentions to the contrary (Nichols & Schwartz, 2004; Goldenberg & Goldenberg, 2004) The only way out of a therapeutic bind, unless one chooses to acknowledge no intention of changing, is to make constructive changes.

Following are some examples of situations in which therapeutic binds have been successfully used.

- *Despite efforts to resolve fears of being rejected in relationships with others, a client continued to decline social invitations and makes no effort to reach out to others. The social worker asked her about her apparent choice to continue her social isolation. "You can either risk being with others or continue as you are, but you said that you wanted your life to be different."*
- *A supervisor complained to an Employee Assistance Program (EAP) social worker about conflict with other members on his team. In exploring the situation, the supervisor admitted that he consistently made unilateral decisions despite repeated feedback and negative reactions from other team members. The social worker asked him, "Is it your decision that it is more important for you to be control, rather than to improve your working relationships with colleagues?'*
- *An adolescent persisted in being truant from school, violating family rules, and engaging in antisocial behaviors despite his assertion that he wanted to be independent. The social worker countered that he "seemed unprepared to use his freedom wisely." The social worker points out that by continuing to get in trouble, the juvenile court judge would further limit his choices until he demonstrated a capacity to set limits on his behavior.*
- *In marital counseling, a wife constantly brings up her husband's previous infidelity despite expressing a desire to strengthen their marriage. When this occurred, the husband's response was to withdraw and disengage from the relationship. Presenting the wife with the contradiction in her behavior, the social worker stated, "Despite your claim of wanting to preserve the marriage, by your behavior it appears to be more important for you to continue to talk about your husband's previous behavior."*

In using therapeutic binds, it is vital to observe the guidelines for confrontation, thereby avoiding "clobbering" or alienating the client. In this way, asking a question about the apparent contradiction or conclusion can be experienced as a more respectful form of confrontation leading to self-reflection. Be aware however, that a therapeutic bind is a potent but high-risk technique, and you should use it sparingly. In the best of circumstances, clients can experience an *aha* moment which allows them to move forward and out of a pattern of counterproductive behaviors. When the technique is used, care should be taken to modify its jarring effect with empathy, concern, and sensitive exploration of the dynamics behind the self-defeating patterns. Above all, the technique should be used to assist the client and not as a confrontational response to the social worker's own frustrations about the client's contradictory behavior or opposition.

Summary

This chapter described barriers to change with individuals, including relational reactions, over- and under-involvement, and racial and cultural barriers. Relational reactions can occur as a result of social workers' real or imagined perceptions of clients, or they may derive from perceptions that clients formulate about social workers. Other relational dynamics include transference and countertransference. Acting on sexual attraction toward clients is particularly damaging and exploitative and has severe consequences; instead, social workers should recognize these attractions and deal with them appropriately (i.e., ethically).

Relational reactions, including resistance, are normal manifestations of opposition to change. In view of this reality, this chapter discussed at length techniques for recognizing and managing these reactions and opposition to change. Your skillful handling of these dynamics is critical to ensuring that the helping relationship is productive and remains focused on the desired outcome. Be aware, however, that barriers to change can be the result of environmental factors beyond the control of the client; in such a case, you may need to assume the role of advocate.

Related Online Content

Visit the *Direct Social Work Practice* companion Web site at *www.cengage.com/social_work/hepworth* for additional learning tools such as glossary terms, chapter outlines, relevant Web links, and chapter practice quizzes.

Skill Development Exercises

1. Think about what your thoughts and reaction might be in the following situations. Then assess the nature of your reaction.

   - *You are an only child. Your client has four children and the house is a mess. The oldest child, age 14, complains that her mother rarely pays attention to her.*
   - *Both of your parents were heavy drinkers, and at times they were difficult. Your client becomes abusive to his wife and children when he has been drinking.*
   - *You grew up in a middle-class family. A majority of the clients that you work with are poor, and many live in homes where there is evidence of rodents.*
   - *A co-worker in the residential facility for minors where you work has posted pictures of former residents on his My Space page, indicating that the clients are his friends.*

2. Review the case examples in this chapter in which the social worker was over- or under-involved. As a colleague, what advice would you offer? What are the ethical and legal implications of the social worker's behavior in these cases?

3. After reading the section on cross-cultural barriers, what did you learn that could inform your practice with clients who are different?

4. Reflect on an occasion in which you had a strong reaction to a client. How would you handle the situation after reading this chapter?

5. Develop a checklist for yourself using the barriers to change discussed in this chapter. Use the checklist that you developed as a self-assessment tool in your work with clients.

Skill Development Exercises in Managing Relational Reactions and Opposition

The following exercises are intended to assist you in expanding your skills in responding appropriately to relational reactions and opposition to change. Study each client message and determine whether a relational reaction or opposition to change might be involved. Then write the response you would give if you were the social worker. Compare your response with the modeled response provided at the end of the exercises. Bear in mind that the modeled response is only one of many possible appropriate responses.

Client Statements

1. *Male client [has been discussing feelings of rejection and self-doubt after his partner broke up with him; suddenly he looks down, sighs, then looks up]*: Say, did I tell you I got promoted at work?
2. *Female client, age 23 [to male social worker, age 25]*: I've been feeling very close to you these past weeks. I was wondering if you could hold me in your arms for just a moment.
3. *Male client, age 27 [agitated]*: I've been coming to see you for 8 weeks, and things haven't changed a bit. I'm beginning to question whether you are able to help me.
4. *Delinquent on probation, age 16*: 1 think it's crazy to have to come here every week. You don't have to worry about me. I'm not getting into any trouble.
5. *Female in welfare-to-work program*: Sure, you say you want to help me. All you social workers are just alike. You don't understand the pressure I have to get a good job in the time I have left on welfare. If you really want to help, you would increase the time I have left.
6. *Client, age 27 [to male social worker]*: I've just never been able to trust men. My old man was alcoholic, and the only thing you could depend on with him was that he'd be drunk when you needed him most.
7. *Male client [to female mental health social worker]*: Sometimes I really felt I was cheated in life, you know, with parents who didn't give a damn what happened to me. I think about you—how warm and caring you are, and—I know it sounds crazy but I wish I'd had you for a mother. Sometimes I even daydream about it.
8. *Client [after an emotional prior session, the client yawns, looks out the window, and comments]*: Not much to talk about today. Nothing much has happened this week.
9. *Male client, age 24 [in fifth session]*: I have this thing where people never measure up to my expectations. I know I expect too much, and I always end up feeling let down.
10. *Middle-aged minority male [challenging]*: I suppose you see me in the usual stereotype, you people have for [minority] males. I want you to know that

I'm ambitious and want to do right by my family. I just need a job right now.

Modeled Responses

1. "Congratulations! No, you didn't tell me about your promotion, but before you do, I'd like to know more about what you were feeling just a moment ago when you were discussing your breakup with your partner. I was sensing that that you don't want to talk about this. Let's focus on how you feel about this situation."
2. "I'm flattered that you would want me to hold you and pleased you could share those feelings with me. I also feel close to you, too, but if I were to become romantically inclined toward you, I'd be letting you down and couldn't be helpful to you. I hope you can understand."
3. "I can see you're anxious to get things worked out, and that's a plus. [*Positive connotation.*] But you're pretty unhappy with your progress and seem to feel that I am not doing my job. I'd like to better understand your feelings. What do you feel I should be doing differently? [*Exploring feelings and expectations.*]"
4. "You sound pretty angry about having to report to me each week. I can't blame you for that. Still, the judge ordered it, and neither of us really has any choice. How do you suggest that we make the best of the situation?"
5. "I'm sorry you feel I'm not really interested in helping you. I gather you've had some bad experiences with other caseworkers, and I hope our relationship can be better. I sense your frustration at working under this time pressure and your anxiety about what will occur if you don't succeed in the time available. I will work with you to make the best use of the time to get a job you can feel good about. Sometimes as we come to the end of the time frame there are some possibilities for an extension, but that can't be guaranteed. I wonder if the best use of our time might be to do the best we can to get the kind of job you want in the time available."
6. "I can understand, then, that you might find it difficult to trust me—wondering if I'm really dependable."
7. [*Smiling.*] "Thank you for the compliment. I gather you've been experiencing my care for you and find yourself longing for the love and care you didn't receive as a child. I can sense your feelings keenly and appreciate your sharing them."

8. "Somehow that doesn't fit with what we talked about last week. You expressed some very deep feelings about yourself and your marriage. I'd like to hear what you've been feeling about what we discussed last time."

9. "I wonder if that's what you're feeling just now in our relationship—that I haven't measured up to your expectations in some way. Could you share with me what you've been feeling in that regard?"

10. "I appreciate your sharing those feelings with me. I gather you've wondered how I see you. I see you as an ambitious and responsible person, and I want you to know I appreciate those qualities in you."

Notes

1. In some instances, manifestations of group behaviors that may appear at first to be opposition will actually prove to be adjustment reactions of members to excessive changes (e.g., loss of members, canceled sessions, or a move to another meeting place), which tend to frustrate and discourage group members.

PART 4

The Termination Phase

The third and final phase of the helping process encompasses the final evaluation of progress and the termination of the helping relationship. Although it has received less attention in the literature than the beginning and middle phases of the helping process, the final phase is important. The way in which social workers bring the helping relationship to a close strongly influences whether clients will maintain their progress and continue to grow following termination. Further, many people who receive social work services have previously been subject to difficult endings—those which involved ambiguity, abandonment, anger, abruptness, or failure. Properly handled, termination may itself be an intervention to model the ways in which relationships are concluded in a constructive and meaningful manner. Social workers must understand how to sensitively and skillfully conclude their work with clients, even if the end of the helping process is unplanned.

This chapter introduces you to strategies for evaluating case progress in work with individuals, groups, and families. The bulk of the chapter addresses the varieties of planned and unplanned terminations. It addresses ethical considerations, the common worker and client reactions to termination, the strategies for maintaining client gains post-termination, and the use of rituals in effectively ending the helping relationship.

The Final Phase: Evaluation and Termination

CHAPTER OVERVIEW

Chapter 19 reviews methods for evaluating case progress, describes various factors that affect the termination process, identifies relevant tasks for both social workers and clients, and discusses skills essential to effectively managing termination. After reading it you will:

- Understand how evaluation builds on the assessment measures and goal-setting procedures employed earlier in the helping process

- Be able to distinguish between outcome, process, and satisfaction forms of evaluation

- Appreciate the dynamics associated with various forms of planned and unplanned endings

- Be able to assist clients in solidifying gains made in treatment

- Understand common termination reactions and how to address them

- Know how to use rituals to achieve closure

Evaluation

Evaluating outcomes of the helping process has assumed ever-increasing significance in direct practice; indeed, the majority of social workers engage in some form of practice evaluation. Chapter 12 introduced you to the ways that goals and objectives, client self-monitoring, and other measures are vital in creating clear directions for service and benchmarks against which progress can be measured. The conclusion of service is thus the final point at which goal attainment and other aspects of change can be assessed prior to termination. If you have systematically obtained baseline measures and tracked progress, clients will be prepared for evaluation at termination. You can further enhance

their cooperation by again reviewing the rationale and actively involving them in the process. For example, you can introduce this topic to the client by making any of the following statements:

- *"An important part of termination is to assess the results we have achieved and to identify what helped you most and least during our work together."*
- *"As an agency, we're committed to improving the quality of our services. Your honest feedback will help us to know how we're doing."*
- *"Our evaluation measures will help you and me see how your symptoms have changed since you were admitted."*
- *"One way we determine success on the case plan is to evaluate how your situation has changed since we began working together."*

Several different evaluation methods can be used to determine client progress throughout the helping process and at its conclusion—for example, standardized tests, direct observation, goal attainment scaling, and client self-reports though logs, journals, and surveys. The power of evaluation is strengthened when multiple sources of information are used. Whatever method is used, evaluations focus on three dimensions of service: (1) outcomes, (2) process, and (3) satisfaction.

Outcomes

Outcome evaluation involves assessing the results achieved against the goals that were formulated during the contracting phase of work. As described in Chapters 8 and 12, the methods utilized during the assessment and goal-setting phases will, in part, determine which outcomes you measure. For example, you may measure changes in the *frequency* of difficulties (e.g., getting to work on time, getting detention, binging, hoarding, experiencing negative cognitions, forgetting to take medications) or the frequency of target behaviors, such as exercise, use of "I" statements, safe sex practices, or family outings. You may also assess outcomes by looking at changes in the *severity* of problems (e.g., self-esteem scores on rapid assessment instruments, anxiety as measured by a self-anchored rating scale, sleep disturbance as measured by a client's journal, or distractibility as measured by observations from a child's classroom teacher and caregivers). These items, when compared with the baseline measures taken when the client first entered service, will help determine the extent of progress and the client's readiness for termination (Epstein & Brown, 2002). A third measure of outcomes involves the *achievement* of goals or tasks (e.g., applying for and getting a job, completing homework, improving parenting and disciplinary practices, retaining sobriety, developing a safety plan, completing assignments between task group sessions). A specific type of success measure is goal attainment scaling (GAS). In this process, the workers and client identify a handful of problem behaviors or targeted changes and the related goals. Then, together, the worker and client assign each a number corresponding to the likelihood of achievement or success. A −[minus]2 would be an unfavorable outcome or a task or goal the client is highly unlikely to meet. A rating of 0 would indicate an expected outcome and +2 would indicate the most favorable outcome or the task with the greatest likelihood of completion (Yegidis & Weinbach, 2002). Ratings of −1 or +1 would be used to indicate more moderate expectations. For example, if the client's goal in a weight-loss group is to keep a record of all food and exercise for a week, the scale might be as follows:

−2 = Keep inconsistent or incomplete records for the majority of days of the week.

−1 = Keep the log for 2 days, marking all food and exercise, along with related calories.

 0 = Keep the log for 4 days, marking all food and exercise, along with related calories.

+1 = Keep the log for 5 or 6 days, marking all food and exercise, along with related calories.

+2 = Keep the log for 7 days, marking all food and exercise, along with related calories.

The client's goal attainment, then, is weighed in light of the likelihood that he or she would achieve the goal, with better outcome associated with the ideal or "stretch" goals. Clearly GAS is best suited for clients who are motivated to complete tasks and are reliable in reporting the results. The consistent use of GAS will help the social worker and client track incremental steps toward service outcomes and can ultimately serve as one indicator of readiness for termination.

Manualized or evidence-based interventions typically contain measures as part of the work. Typically, these instruments would have been used as part of assessment and treatment or service planning to determine areas of difficulty and strength and to establish baseline scores against which progress can be measured. Numerous texts offer standardized scales and information on selecting and administering them in practice to target outcomes (Bloom, Fischer, & Orme 2006; Fischer and Corcoran 2006a, 2006b; Unrau, Gabor, & Grinnell, 2007). Some of these instruments lend themselves to repeated use, enabling workers and clients to track progress over time. Through such single-subject designs (also referred to as single-system research and single-case time series or $n=1$ designs) the client is compared to him or herself on baseline scores from earlier administrations. If the initial goals for work were vague or unmeasurable, or if no baseline measures were taken, social workers and clients can still evaluate the current status of the client's difficulties, symptoms or achievements, or goal attainment to develop an approximate sense of progress and readiness for termination; however, comparative analyses will be impossible.

In addition to comparative measures, you can use interviews or questionnaires to determine clients' views in order to evaluate their sense of progress against your own observations. The difficulty with these recollections and other forms of self-report are, of course, that they may be highly selective and may be affected by numerous factors, such as the client's desire to please (or punish) the social worker, the client's interest in concluding service, or the *hope* that problems are resolved and that further services are not necessary. Although it is unwise to challenge clients' perceptions, you can reduce biases by asking clients to provide actual examples of recent events ("critical incidents") that illustrate their attainment of goals, a decline in difficulties, or an increase in capacities. This discussion also provides an opportunity for you to reaffirm the client's accomplishments, which tend to heighten his or her confidence and satisfaction.

As noted above, clients' perceptions of their progress can be supplemented by other criteria or sources where feasible. For example, feedback from collateral contacts, such as family members, teachers, other helpers, or fellow clients (in families, groups, or residential settings), may provide perspectives on an individual's progress that can be contrasted with self-reports.

Process

Another aspect of evaluation involves identifying the aspects of the helping process that were useful or detrimental. Feedback about techniques and incidents that enhanced or blocked progress will help you to hone certain skills, eliminate others, and use techniques with greater discrimination. Such "formative evaluation" methods also help organizations to determine which elements of their programs were effective in bringing about the desired change or whether the techniques used were consistent with standardized agency protocols and delivered as efficiently as possible (Royse, Thyer, Padgett, & Logan, 2001). These evaluations capture the nuances of client–social worker interactions that contribute to treatment effectiveness. A technique that is useful with an assertive client, for example, may produce the opposite effect with a depressed client. Likewise, a family intervention may be most effective if it is structured in a particular way. A social worker may have attributed a positive outcome to a masterfully executed technique, only to find the client was helped far more by the practitioner's willingness to reach out and maintain hope when the client had almost given up (McCollum & Beer, 1995).

Clearly, client feedback can be used to assess beneficial aspects of the helping process, though self-reports about process are subject to the same biases as self-reports about outcomes described above. Evaluation instruments can also be used to more precisely measure the aspects of the helping process that were instrumental in achieving change.

With manualized or other evidence-based interventions, fidelity assessments can address how closely the process and skills used by the program or the individual social worker match the design of the intervention (Substance Abuse and Mental Health Services Administration [SAMHSA], 2003a). These can include qualitative case-study reviews in which supervisory meetings, observation of sessions, audit interviews with clinicians, or focus groups with colleagues are used to examine a particular worker's actions (O'Hare, 2005). Quantitative fidelity measures include statistics on the type, frequency, duration, and pattern of services; chart reviews and other administrative or quality assurance data; the level of congruence with the intervention model; and inventories that capture the degree to which the worker employs particular skills. One such instrument, the Practice Skills Inventory (PSI), documents the number of client contacts, and the frequency that particular skills were used (e.g., "Provided emotional support for my client," "Taught specific skills to deal with a certain

problem") (O'Hare, 2005, pp. 555–556), and examples of those skills for the case (e.g., "Acknowledged how painful it is to move from home into assisted living," "Role-played ways of meeting other residents").

Published measures are also available for social workers who wish to evaluate outcomes and processes in their work with groups and families. Toseland & Rivas (2009) describe six self-report measures that can capture feedback on the therapeutic elements of treatment groups. For example, Yalom's Curative Factors Scale (Stone, Lewis, & Beck, 1994) might identify the dimensions of treatment groups and their relative therapeutic effectiveness. You can also construct valid measures of practice effectiveness by combining measures (e.g., records about sessions, client self-reports, observations) to provide an approximate measure of the effectiveness of the intervention processes used.

With children and other clients who lack high written or verbal ability, the use of expressive techniques, such as collages or painting, may help to tap into evaluative content. For example, the client may be asked to draw or display something to illustrate "what I liked best/least about our work together" or "what helped me during my time here." Feedback from caregivers and other observers can be sought on a periodic basis, and their appraisals can be linked to the interventions being used at a given point in time.

Satisfaction

The outcomes achieved and the means used to achieve them are important measures of client progress. Another measure in the increasingly competitive and consumer-conscious practice environment seeks information about client satisfaction. You may gauge this level of satisfaction in your evaluative discussions with the client. Some settings facilitate gathering formal feedback by sending out written client feedback forms at the termination of service or at a specified follow-up period. Some payers, such as managed care companies, will also evaluate providers by directly seeking client input.

These instruments address satisfaction with the social worker's service by asking questions such as "Would you refer a friend or family member to us for services in the future?", "Were you and the clinician able to meet your goal?", and "Do you believe you needed additional services that were not provided?" (Corcoran & Vandiver, 1996, p. 57). Satisfaction surveys also evaluate structural or operational issues such as appropriateness of the waiting room, convenience of parking, time elapsed between the client's request for service and first appointment, the worker's promptness in making a home visit, and friendliness of reception staff (Ackley, 1997; Corcoran & Vandiver, 1996; Larsen, Attkisson, Hargreaves & Nguyen, 1979). Satisfaction measures may specifically evaluate particular elements of an agency's services or progress on particular initiatives. For example, they may inquire about the cultural competence of the staff, the openness of the facility to diverse populations, or the turnaround time in responding to client calls and requests.

The Kansas Consumer Satisfaction Survey utilizes a 26-item, Likert-type scale with ratings 1 to 5 (strongly agree to strongly disagree, or does not apply) in which clients respond to statements such as "If I have an emergency at night or on the weekend, I am able to get help from the program," "I can choose where I live," and "My opinions and ideas are included in my treatment plan" (SAMHSA, 2003a). A related instrument, the Quality of Life Self-Assessment, asks consumers to tell the agency "how things are going...these days" (SAMHSA, 2003b) by rating such issues as social life, level of independence, physical health, and access to transportation on a 4-point scale (poor–fair–good–excellent); it also measures mental health symptoms and the effects of alcohol and other drug use on a severe–moderate–minimal–none scale. The instrument also invites the client to indicate whether any of the items should be reflected on his or her service plan. Both the satisfaction and self-assessment surveys offer open-ended items to which clients can respond with other thoughts or questions. Clearly, the utility of these or any evaluation instrument depends on professionals' and agencies' willingness and ability to incorporate them into standard practices and procedures (Rzepnicki, 2004).

Termination

Termination refers to the process of formally ending the individual social worker–client relationship. It is a feature of practice with a variety of client systems, from individuals and families to task groups, coalitions, and communities, and it occurs regardless of the duration of the helping relationship.[1] Terminations can occur when goals are met, when clients make a transition to other services, when time-limited services are concluded, and when social workers or clients leave the helping relationship. Even if clients are likely to "come and go" from service over a period of time as their concerns and needs change, it is important to draw closure to each unique episode of care.

The notion of ending is often introduced at the beginning of service, when the social worker notes the likely duration of care, the number of sessions allotted, or the goals that will guide the helping process. In some time-limited treatment models, the fixed length of care is part of informed consent discussions at the outset. For example, the social worker might explain, "We believe that brief treatment is effective and helps both you and me make efficient use of our time together. So we'll begin today by getting an idea of the goals you want to work on, and the best way to use our time over the next 6 to 8 weeks to achieve those goals."

Whether in short- or long-term therapy models, successful termination involves preparing clients adequately for separation from the social worker and/or group and accomplishing other tasks that facilitate the transition from being a client to being "on one's own":[2]

1. Evaluating the service provided and the extent to which goals were accomplished[3]
2. Determining when to implement termination
3. Mutually resolving emotional reactions experienced during the process of ending
4. Planning to maintain gains achieved and to achieve continued growth.

The significance of these tasks and the extent to which they can be successfully accomplished are determined in large measure by the context in which the helping relationship takes place. The intensity of the termination process is affected by factors such as the type of contact (voluntary or involuntary), the size and characteristics of the client system, and the nature of the intervention used. Emotional reactions will vary depending on the nature and length of the helping relationship. That is, involuntary clients and those with more structured and time-limited services will be less likely to experience a sense of loss at termination than those who have engaged in longer and more voluntary relationships with the social worker. For example, termination of a time-limited educational group may be less intense and require less preparation of members than would the ending of an ongoing interpersonal support group or discharge from a residential treatment setting. Terminations from brief crisis intervention, case management, or discharge planning relationships may differ in intensity depending on the nature of the needs met and the length of service. Termination from family sessions may be less difficult than those from individual work, because most of the client system will continue to work and be together, albeit without the social worker's involvement.

Types of Termination

Terminations generally fall into one of two categories: unplanned and planned. *Unplanned terminations* occur

Ideas in Action

The "Squeaky Wheel" video illustrates the challenges for professionals who take over case responsibility after the unanticipated departure of a former worker. In the video, the unplanned termination of Nancy, the previous worker, created distress for Molly. Among her reactions were confusion, anger, and distrust targeted at the new worker and professionals in general. Ron, the current social worker, attempts to help Molly get some closure on that loss by asking "What would you say to Nancy?", which the client answers with a further elaboration of her mistrust of professionals. What other strategies can social workers use to get at the feelings created by unplanned, abrupt, or poorly managed endings?

when the clients withdraw prematurely from services or when social workers leave the helping relationship due to illness, job change, or other circumstances. *Planned terminations* occur when clients' goals are achieved, when transfer or referral is anticipated and necessary, or when service is concluded due to the time-limited nature of the setting (such as hospitals or schools) or the treatment modality used (such as brief treatment or fixed-length groups).

Unplanned Terminations

Unplanned terminations can be initiated by the actions of the client, the social worker, or both.

Client-initiated termination can be triggered by dropping out of treatment, by an adverse event that renders the client unavailable for service, or by the client behaving in such a way that services are withdrawn or he or she is ejected from the setting. Examples of adverse events include being arrested, running away, committing suicide, or otherwise dying unexpectedly. The category of "dropouts" from service is similarly broad, including clients who are seeking services involuntarily or are otherwise unmotivated, clients who are dissatisfied with the social worker but are unable to verbalize those concerns, clients who feel they have made satisfactory progress and thus "are done" whether the clinician thinks so or not, and clients who decide to quit for pragmatic reasons, such as a lack of funds or the inconvenience of the service setting. A mixed form of unplanned termination can be characterized as a "pushout," where the social worker and the client have failed to "click" and the client's discontinuation is prompted or reinforced by the practitioner's disinterest or lack of commitment (Hunsley, Aubrey, Vestervelt, & Vito, 1999).

A common theme of all these client-initiated endings is that they are unanticipated and thus allow no opportunity for discussion, processing, or closure, yet the residue of feelings and unfinished business remains. The tasks of termination (reflection on the work together, planning for the future, marking the end of treatment)

remain undone and both parties may experience feelings of abandonment, anger, rejection, failure, relief, and shame.

Similar issues can arise from certain forms of practitioner-initiated unplanned endings—for example, when the social worker dies, becomes incapacitated, or is dismissed. Other practitioner-initiated unplanned endings, such as those due to layoffs or job transfers, may elicit negative reactions from the client, but generally allow time for processing and closure. We will discuss managing those feelings and endings in a later section. Other unplanned endings require special measures so that the tasks of termination can be approximated to the extent possible.

Managing Unplanned Terminations. Some estimates suggest that 50% of the overall client population will drop out of service (Kazdin & Wassell, 1998; Sweet & Noones, 1989) and that this figure may be even higher for certain subgroups. Some settings may have their own protocols for dealing with "no shows," and a different mechanism may be needed for the client who fails to reappear after a first session (see Meyer, 2001) compared to one who ceases to appear for service midway through the course of treatment.

A common response to unplanned termination by the client is for the social worker to reach out to him or her by phone, email, or letter. The goal in doing so may be to acknowledge the decision to conclude services, to encourage the client to come in for a closing session, or to achieve the purposes of such a session through the communication itself. For example, one client who was arrested could not receive phone calls or return for services. Nevertheless, the social worker was able to write him a letter in which she reviewed the goals he had achieved and the issues with which he continued to struggle. She conveyed her regard for him and informed him of the availability of other services during his incarceration and following his release. A similar technique can be used when a social worker must leave abruptly, when a client quits service, or when a client leaves an institution against medical advice. Such endings are not ideal because they do not allow the client the opportunity to express his or her views or participate in evaluation, but they do help to mark the ending and "clear the air" regarding future services.

When a worker dies or otherwise becomes incapacitated, it is incumbent upon his or her colleagues to intervene for the care or transfer of the clients involved. They must also recognize that these clients' needs and reactions will be shaped by the abruptness and nature of the loss, their personal loss histories, and the particular issues for which they were seeking help (Philip & Stevens, 1992; Philip, 1994). Thus, grieving the lost relationship may become a primary task alongside continued work on their treatment goals identified earlier.

Likewise, when a client dies unexpectedly, whether through an accident or a traumatic act such as homicide or suicide, the loss has significant implications for the helping professionals left behind. For reasons of propriety and professional development, supervisory and collegial support should be the primary resource to the mourner, with coworkers offering empathy, permission to grieve, and encouragement to talk about and integrate the feelings that emerge (Chemtob, Hamada, Bauer, Torigoe, & Kinney, 1988; Krueger, Moore, Schmidt, & Wiens, 1979; Strom-Gottfried & Mowbray, 2006).

Formal processes for reviewing the case—referred to as "postvention" by Shneidman (1971)—can take the form of individual or group processing of the case (Pilsecker, 1987), a psychological autopsy (Kleepsies, Penk, & Forsyth, 1993; Chemtob et al., 1988) or critical incident stress debriefing (Farrington, 1995). Each of these mechanisms has a slightly different intent and focus, but each offers the opportunity for the social worker to acknowledge the loss, contemplate the experience with the client, have supportive review, and deepen understanding of what took place.

Unplanned terminations of a member from a group may occur for a number of reasons, both related and unrelated to the group itself, such as poor fit, discomfort with the group, transportation difficulties, or time conflicts (Toseland & Rivas, 2009). In any case, the unplanned departure presents challenges for achieving termination-related tasks. Because cohesion is central to the success of a group, the loss of a member can threaten that bond, make members question their own achievements or appropriateness for the group, and make them reluctant to continue building trusting relationships with the remaining group members. The social worker should try to encourage closure in some

form, both for the departing member and for the rest of the group. Even if it derails the group's preexisting agenda or timeline, this effort is time well spent because it supports the future health and success of the group process and the individual members.

Case Example

A cohort of 16 students had spent 18 months taking every class together. At the midpoint of the MSW program, however, one student decided to drop out to spend more time with family members who were aging and ailing. Moira was a respected and successful member of the class, and her decision took her instructors and faculty advisor by surprise. Nevertheless, they were persuaded by her confidence that her decision was the correct one for her at that particular point in time. Still, Moira felt sheepish about her decision. Although she e-mailed her classmates to let them know of her decision, she declined an instructor's suggestion that she come back for one more session to achieve closure for herself and the group. She did, however, give permission for the instructor to discuss her decision with the group and understood that they would be processing it in class the next time they met.

The day of the class, the instructor opened the conversation by noting Moira's empty seat and asking the class to share what they knew about her decision not to return. Because she had contacted many of them individually, it wasn't necessary for the instructor to share what she knew about Moira's decision. Next, the group discussed their reactions to Moira's departure, which included self-doubt ("If she can't do it all, how can we?"), anger and confusion ("She put so much into this—why quit now?"), sorrow ("She brought a lot of important things to this group"), hope ("Maybe this will just be a temporary choice"), and understanding ("I think she's doing what she needs to do for her family").

The instructor then asked, "What did Moira give to the group and how can we acknowledge that?" After discussing what they had learned from and valued in their time with Moira, class members wrote notes to her to share these impressions. The instructor collected the notes and, without reading them, included them with a letter to Moira in which she detailed her view on Moira's achievements, capacities, and options should she decide to return to the program in the future.

Following this, the class discussed the impact of acknowledging and processing her departure. They compared it to other losses that the class had experienced when classmates had earlier dropped out ("Here today, gone tomorrow") and the feelings evoked by the lack of closure on those losses, which included suspicion ("Were they forced out?"), apprehension ("Can I cut it? Am I next?"), guilt ("Was it something I said or did?"), and hurt ("Nobody really matters here"). The process of closure in Moira's case, even in her absence, achieved the goals of termination and sent a powerful message to the class—just as it does with other types of groups who experience such a loss.

Note that "closure," as used here and elsewhere in this chapter, does not mean that the matter is resolved, that the person and the loss are tucked away permanently and are not subject to further consideration. It does not mean, "Okay, I'm done. I can move on." Instead, closure simply means that the experience or episode has been reflected upon and the importance of the transition has been marked. It signifies an end in a way that helps free the participants to move on. Clinically, an ambiguous or mishandled termination may leave the social worker and client with a sense of unfinished business, and it may make it difficult for the client to invest easily or fully in future therapeutic relationships. Closure makes a difference.

Planned Terminations with Unsuccessful Outcomes

Sometimes termination occurs in a planned manner, but the endings are not marked by successful achievement of service goals. This may occur when

- *the social worker or the client is dissatisfied with the helping relationship,*
- *the client is hopelessly stalemated despite vigorous and persistent efforts to overcome his or her difficulties,*
- *the social worker is not competent to address the client's needs, or*
- *the client fails to comply with appropriate treatment requirements.*

Unlike unplanned terminations, these endings are not accompanied by abrupt disappearance from service and thus afford the social worker and client a chance to achieve the goals of closure. Groups also occasionally end with unsuccessful results, and members may be frustrated, disappointed, or angry with the leader or with other members (Smokowski, Rose, & Bacallao, 2001).

When the helping process ends unsuccessfully, termination should include discussion of (1) factors that prevented achieving more favorable results and (2) clients' feelings about seeking additional help in the future. This effort requires you to create as safe an atmosphere as possible so that both parties can honestly air concerns, with the intention of both achieving closure and keeping open possibilities for future service. It also requires the ability to hear and share feedback in a nondefensive manner. Sometimes, as a result of this termination conversation, you and a client may come to agreement on the conditions under which you would reconnect and develop a new contract for future services. At this final session, social workers should be prepared to offer referrals to other services if the issue for termination has been a poor fit with the individual practitioner or agency.

Planned Terminations with Successful Outcomes

As noted earlier, planned terminations can take many forms. The nature of the setting, intervention method, or funding source can all impose external pressures to terminate within a specific period of time. Other planned endings emerge from the helping relationship itself, as clients achieve their goals and move on to independence from the social worker. This step may not signal that the client has completed all of his or her desired goals or tasks (or that they are "done" in the social worker's eyes), but means only that the client has experienced "at least enough relief so that he no longer wants help *at that point*" (Reid, 1972, p. 199). Related to this development is what Cummings calls (1991) "brief intermittent therapy throughout the life cycle" (p. 35). That is, individuals who need social work services may come to use them as they do medical and other services—seeking them out in times of need to address acute problems rather than pursuing single episodes of extended treatment. In these termination situations, the social worker and client may therefore establish contingencies under which they will resume services in the future.

Termination Due to Temporal or Structural Limits

In organizations or agencies whose function involves providing service according to fixed time intervals, termination must be planned accordingly. In school settings, for example, services are generally discontinued at the conclusion of an academic year. In hospitals and other institutional settings, the duration of service is determined by the length of hospitalization, confinement, or insurance coverage.

Some service models, such as time-limited groups or fixed-length residential programs, are clearly designed to pace and conclude services within a specific time frame. For example, some treatment programs are organized such that clients progress from one program (and one set of workers) to another as their needs change. In residential programs or other settings with fixed lengths of stay, the course of treatment will involve a relatively predictable process whereby the client progresses through steps or phases leading to termination. Depending on the context of treatment, services may extend from several days to several months. Temporal factors are also central in termination for social work students, who leave a given practicum setting at the completion of an academic year.

Terminations that are prompted by program structure or preexisting time constraints involve certain factors peculiar to these circumstances. First, the ending of a school year or of a training period for students is a predetermined time for termination, which reduces the possibility that clients will interpret time limits as being arbitrarily imposed or perceive the social worker's leaving as desertion or abandonment. Knowing the termination date well in advance also provides ample time to resolve feelings about separation. Conversely, it also means that in school settings student clients may lose many supports all at one time.

Another factor common to terminations that are determined by temporal constraints or agency function rather than by individual factors is that the client's problems may not have been adequately resolved when termination occurs. The predetermined, untimely ending may lead to intense reactions from the client who is losing service and ending the helping relationship in what feels like midstream (Weiner, 1984). Social workers are therefore confronted with the dual tasks of working through feelings associated with untimely separation and referring clients for additional services when indicated.

Predetermined endings imposed by the close of a school year or a fixed length of service do not necessarily convey the same expectations of a positive outcome as do time limits that are determined by individual client progress. In other words, to say "I will see you until May because that is sufficient time to achieve your goals" conveys a far more positive expectation than "I will see you until May because that is all the time I will have available before leaving the placement."

Nevertheless, time-limited work does not necessarily lead to unsatisfactory outcomes. Clients can benefit from the focused nature of this work and may experience a fruitful relationship with the social worker even if termination results in referral for other services.

For example, one of the authors of this book worked with a client with serious, long-term mental health problems. During the time allotted for her field placement, she was able to help the client through a crisis and assist him to build his social supports so that future crises would not inevitably result in rehospitalization. In the termination process, they reviewed the accomplishments made during the year and the client met his new social worker, who would meet with him on a less intensive basis for support and maintenance of the gains made previously.

Other Determinants of Planned Termination

When terminations are not predetermined by agency setting, client circumstance, or form of service, how do the social worker and client know when to end? When services are highly goal directed, the termination point may be clear: it occurs when goals are reached and changes are sustained. When goals are amorphous or ongoing, however, determining a proper ending point can be more difficult. Theoretically, humans can grow indefinitely, and determining when clients have achieved optimal growth is no simple task. Ordinarily, it is appropriate to introduce the idea of termination when the client has reached the point of diminishing returns—that is, when the gains from sessions taper off to the point of being minor in significance. The client may indicate through words or actions that he or she is ready to discontinue services, or the social worker may initiate such discussion.

Two other variants on planned termination warrant discussion. "Simultaneous termination" occurs when the client and the social worker leave the service or agency at the same time. It offers the advantage of mutually shared, powerful experiences of ending, and it often focuses the time and attention devoted to termination tasks (Joyce, Duncan, Duncan, Kipnes, & Piper, 1996). Simultaneous termination also requires a good deal of self-awareness on the part of the social worker to ensure that his or her personal reactions to termination are not projected on the client. As with other endings involving the social worker's departure from the organization, the conditions and resources for future service should also be addressed.

The second type of planned termination occurs when the client dies, but the death is anticipated and planned for. Some settings, such as hospice care, nursing homes, or hospitals, expose social workers and other caregivers to death on a regular basis. The orientation and supervision offered in such settings must address this crucial aspect of practice, as particular skills are needed to assist clients in such circumstances and effectively manage social worker responses. For example, when the helping relationship is expected to end in conjunction with the patient's death, it may involve life review and reminiscences, plans to address end-of-life concerns, and attention to spiritual matters (Arnold, 2002).[4]

Understanding and Responding to Clients' Termination Reactions

Inherent in termination is separation from the social worker (and other clients, in the case of groups, inpatients, or residential settings). Separation typically involves mixed feelings for both the social worker and the client, which vary in intensity according to the degree of success achieved, the strength of the attachment, the type of termination, the cultural orientation of the client, and his or her previous experiences with separations from significant others (Bembry & Ericson, 1999; Dorfman, 1996). When clients successfully accomplish their goals, they experience a certain degree of pride and satisfaction as the helping process draws to a close. If they have grown in strength and self-esteem, they view the future optimistically as an opportunity for continued growth.

Most clients in individual, conjoint, family, and group therapy experience positive emotions in termination. The benefits from the gains achieved usually far outweigh the impact of the loss of the helping relationship. Clients may reflect on the experience by saying things like "I was such a wreck when I first came to see you—I'm surprised I didn't scare you away," "You helped me get my thinking straight, so I could see the options I had before me," or "Even if things didn't change that much with my son, it helped me a lot to be in the group and know I'm not alone."

As noted earlier, clients and social workers alike commonly experience a sense of loss during the termination process. Indeed, sadness is a common element of many of the endings that are a part of life itself (even positive ones), such as leaving parents to attend school, advancing from one grade to another, graduating, moving into a new community, or changing jobs. The loss in termination may be a deeply moving experience involving the "sweet sorrow" generally associated with parting from a person whom one has grown to value. Adept social workers help clients to give voice to these ambivalent feelings, acknowledging that transitions can be difficult but that successfully handling both good times and difficult ones is a necessary part of growth.

For the social worker, the nature of termination and the comfort with which it occurs appear to be linked to the overall health of the organization in which it takes place and the practitioner's level of job satisfaction (Resnick & Dziegielewski, 1996). In work sites where caseloads are high, where there is a rapid turnover in clients, or where staff support and effective supervision are lacking, sufficient attention may not be paid to the tasks and emotions that accompany clinical endings. Of course, like other elements of practice, the impact of termination on the social worker is also shaped by his or her overall "health," including the ability to maintain a proper balance between the practitioner's personal and professional lives.

Because termination can evoke feelings associated with past losses and endings, clients (and social workers) may respond to it in a variety of ways (and in any of these ways to varying degrees).

1. *Anger.* Clients may experience anger at termination, especially when termination occurs because the social worker leaves the agency. Because the termination is not goal related and occurs with little forewarning, reactions are sometimes similar to those that involve other types of sudden crises. The social worker may need to reach for the feelings evoked by his or her departure, as clients may have difficulty expressing negative emotions while they are simultaneously experiencing sadness or anxiety about the impending loss. It is important to encourage the verbal expression of emotions and respond empathically to them. It is vital, however, not to empathize to the extent of over-identification, thereby losing the capacity to assist the client with negative feelings and to engage in constructive planning.

   When the social worker's departure is caused by circumstances outside his or her control (layoffs or firing), it is important that the practitioner not fuel the client's anger to satisfy his or her own indignation or desire for vindication. Not only is this clinically unhelpful to the client, but it is at odds with the NASW Code of Ethics. The Code of Ethics cautions us not to "exploit clients in disputes with colleagues or engage clients in any inappropriate discussion of conflicts between social workers and their colleagues" (NASW, 1999, 2.04b).

2. *Denial.* Clients may contend that they were unaware of the impending termination or time limits on service and behave as if termination is not

imminent. They may deny having feelings about the termination or refuse to acknowledge that it affects them. Others may avoid endings by failing to appear for concluding sessions with the social worker (Dorfman, 1996). It is a mistake to interpret the client's "business as usual" demeanor as an indication that he or she is unaffected by the termination or is taking it in stride, because the unruffled exterior may represent "the calm before the storm."

A client's temporary denial of feelings represents an attempt to ward off the psychic pain associated with a distressing reality that must eventually be faced. To assist clients in getting in touch with their emotions, it is helpful to reintroduce the topic of termination and to express your desire to assist them in formulating plans to continue working toward their goals after your departure. As you bring up the topic of termination, be sensitive to nonverbal cues to clients' emotional reactions. We also recommend employing empathic communication that conveys understanding of and elicits the hurt, resentment, and rejection clients commonly experience when a valued person leaves. The following responses demonstrate this type of communication:

- *"I know that being discharged is scary and that makes you wish you didn't have to leave, but not talking about it won't keep it from happening. I want very much to use the time remaining to reflect on our work together so you are prepared to carry all that you've achieved here out into the world."*
- *"You've worked really hard here, and I know a lot of it wasn't easy for you. It's hard for me to believe you now when you shrug your shoulders and say it means nothing. I think it means a lot."*

3. *Avoidance.* Occasionally, clients may express their anger and hurt over a social worker's leaving by rejecting the social worker before the social worker can reject them. Some clients may silently protest by failing to appear for sessions as termination approaches. Others may ignore the social worker or profess that they no longer need him or her—in effect, employing the strategy that "the best defense is a good offense." When clients act in this fashion, it is critical to reach out to them. Otherwise, they may interpret the failure to do so as evidence that the social worker never really cared about them at all. In reaching out, a personal contact by telephone, email, letter, or home visit is essential, because it creates an opportunity for interaction in which the social worker can reaffirm his or her concern and

care and convey empathy and understanding of the client's emotional reaction.

4. *Reporting Recurrence of Old Problems or Generating New Ones.* Some clients tend to panic as treatment reaches an end and they experience a return of difficulties that have been under control for some time (Levinson, 1977). In an effort to continue the helping relationship, some may introduce new stresses and problems during the terminal sessions and even during the final scheduled session. Clients who normally communicate minimally may suddenly open up, and other clients may reveal confidential information they have previously withheld. Other clients may display more severe reactions by engaging in self-destructive or suicidal acts.

The severity of the client's revelation, regression, or return of symptoms will dictate how you respond. It is important to acknowledge the anxiety and apprehension that accompany termination. Some clients will benefit from a preemptive discussion of these issues as termination nears. The social worker might say, "Sometimes people worry that problems will reemerge once services end, but I'm confident about how far you've come. I trust that even if there are setbacks, they won't affect our ending." Some theoretical models suggest that the social worker engage the client in an explicit discussion about what it would take to return to the former level of functioning that necessitated treatment. The underlying idea here is that such a discussion creates significant discomfort and therefore, paradoxically, inoculates the client against future setbacks (Walsh, 2003).

At some occasions, it may make sense for you and the client to reconsider a planned ending. Limited "extensions by plan" (Epstein & Brown, 2002, p. 232) can be made to accomplish agreed-upon tasks if it appears that additional time would enable the client to achieve decisive progress. There may be legitimate reasons for recontracting for additional sessions—for example, identifying key problems only late in the helping process, returning to problems that were identified earlier but had to be set aside in favor of work on more pressing problems, or anticipating transitional events that bear on the client's problems (e.g., getting married, being discharged from an institution, regaining custody of a child). In these instances, continuing the working relationships may be warranted, if supported by the agency, especially if the client has achieved substantial progress on other problems during the initial contract period.

Determining whether the emergence of new issues (or the reemergence of old ones) is a ploy to avoid termination or a legitimate cause for developing a new contract can be tricky, but the decision should be based on your sense of the client's progress to date, the degree of dependency, and the significance of the issues being raised (Reid, 1972). Supervisory discussions can help workers look critically at these variables. If you believe that the problem is worthy of intervention but worry that continuing treatment may foster harmful dependence, you might consider referring the client to another clinician, or continuing work with the client yourself but in a less intensive format—through groups or through less frequent sessions, for example.

5. *Attempting to Prolong Contact.* Sometimes, rather than reveal new or renewed problems, clients may seek continued contact with the social worker more directly by suggesting a social or business relationship with the practitioner following termination. For example, the client may suggest meeting for coffee on occasion or exchanging cards or letters, or may propose joining a training program that will put him or her in regular contact with the social worker. This phenomenon is also evident when groups decide to continue meeting after the agency's involvement has concluded.

Unfortunately, the security brought by such plans is only fleeting and the negative effects of continued contact can be serious. Clearly, some requests for continued contact would be inappropriate, given the profession's ethical proscriptions against dual relationships. Other forms of contact, while not prohibited, may still be unwise in that they may undo the work done in the helping relationship and may undermine the client's confidence in his or her ability to function without the social worker. Further, continued informal involvement may constrain the client from becoming invested in other rewarding relationships (Bostic, Shadid, & Blotcky, 1996).

In the case of groups, it is not usually the social worker's role to discourage the group from continuing to meet, although he or she should be clear about his or her own stance and may share the wisdom of past experience. For example, at the conclusion of one bereavement group, the group members planned a cookout at one member's home. In response to the invitation to join them, the group leader simply said, "I'll be ending with you after our session next week, but I appreciate your offer to include me." In another group with a particularly

fragile and more easily disappointed membership, the social worker said, "I'm glad you feel close enough to one another to try to continue meeting after the group has formally ended. It's been my experience that sometimes it's hard to keep that going outside the group. If that happens to you, I hope you won't be discouraged or take it as a reflection on all you've accomplished in your time together."

This is not to say that planned follow-up phone calls, appointments, and "booster sessions" are always inappropriate. To the contrary, such plans are made within the goals of the helping process and have a clear therapeutic purpose, rather than being an attempt to evade the inevitability of ending.

6. *Finding Substitutes for the Social Worker.* Although finding one or more persons to replace the social worker may be a constructive way of developing social resources, it may also represent an attempt to locate a person on whom the client can become dependent, thereby compensating for the loss of the social worker. Group members may also seek to compensate for losses of group support by affiliating with other groups and never actually developing enduring social support systems. This problem is most likely to arise when the client has limited social supports. As such, the need for enhanced socialization should be visible during the helping process and may even be a goal for work. Indeed, plans for sustaining gains should include building networks and resources that can replace professionals as sources of assistance to the client.

Social Workers' Reactions to Termination

Clients are not the only ones who have reactions to termination. Social workers' responses may include guilt (at letting the client down or failing to sufficiently help the client), avoidance (delaying announcement of termination to avoid the feelings or reactions evoked), relief (at ending involvement with a difficult or challenging client), and prolonging service (because of financial or emotional fulfillment experienced by the clinician) (Dorfman, 1996; Joyce et al., 1996; Murphy & Dillon, 2008). In settings where premature terminations are the norm, workers may experience burnout and decreased sensitivity to clients after repeatedly working on cases where closure is not possible and treatment ends before interventions are carried out (Resnick & Dziegielewski, 1996). Self-understanding and good supervision are the essential elements by which even veteran social workers can recognize the reactions involved in terminations. These reactions negatively affect clients, so identifying and managing them is crucial.

Consolidating Gains and Planning Maintenance Strategies

In addition to managing the emotional and behavioral reactions to ending, another task of termination involves summarizing and stabilizing the changes achieved and developing a plan to sustain those changes. A similar aim of group work is to assist members to not only interact successfully within the group context but also transfer their newly developed interpersonal skills to the broad arena of social relationships.

Failure to maintain gains has been attributed to a variety of factors:

1. A natural tendency to revert to habitual response patterns (e.g., use of alcohol or drugs, aggressive or withdrawn behavior, poor communication patterns)
2. Personal and environmental stressors (e.g., family conflicts, pressures from landlords, personal rejection, loss of job, health problems, and deaths of loved ones)
3. Lack of opportunities in the environment for social and leisure activities
4. Absence of positive support systems (peer or family networks that have not changed in the same way the client has)
5. Inadequate social skills
6. Lack of reinforcement for functional behaviors
7. Inadequate preparation for environmental changes
8. Inability to resist peer pressures
9. Return to dysfunctional or destructive environments
10. Inadequately established new behaviors[5]

In planning maintenance strategies, you must anticipate such forces and prepare clients for coping with them. A monitoring phase may be useful for some clients. In this phase, the number and frequency of sessions decrease while support systems are called on to assist the client with new concerns. This technique, in effect, "weans" the client from the social worker's support, yet allows a transitional period in which the client can try out new skills and supports while gradually concluding the helping relationship.

When working with individuals and families, you may actively encourage clients to consider means for coping with setbacks. One model suggests asking what "would be required of each person to contribute to a resurgence of the problem" and organizing role-plays

in which the members engage in old behavioral patterns and describe afterward what thoughts and feelings they experienced in doing so (Walsh, 2003, p. 206). Similar forms of anticipation and practice may help inoculate clients against future relapses.

Social workers may encourage clients to return for additional help if problems appear to be mounting out of control. Although it is important to express confidence in clients' ability to cope independently with their problems, it is equally important to convey your continued interest in them and to invite them to return if they need to do so.

Follow-Up Sessions

Post-termination follow-up sessions are another important technique in ensuring successful termination and change maintenance. These sessions benefit both clients and social workers. Many clients continue to progress after termination, and follow-up sessions provide an opportunity to accredit such gains and encourage clients to continue their efforts.

These sessions also provide the social worker with an opportunity to provide brief additional assistance for residual difficulties. Social workers may assess the durability of changes in these sessions—that is, determine whether clients have maintained gains beyond the immediate influence of the helping relationship. Additional benefits of planned follow-up sessions are that they may soften the blow of termination and they allow opportunities for longitudinal evaluation of practice effectiveness.

By introducing the notion of the follow-up session as an integral part of the helping process, social workers can avoid the pitfalls of clients later viewing these sessions as an intrusion into their private lives or as an attempt to satisfy the social worker's curiosity. Wells (1994) recommends that in arranging for the follow-up session, social workers not set a specific date but rather explain that they will contact the client after a designated interval. This interval offers the client an opportunity to test out and further consolidate the learning and changes achieved during the formal helping period.

In the follow-up session, the social worker generally relates more informally than during the period of intervention. After observing the appropriate social courtesies, you should guide the discussion to the client's progress and obtain post-intervention measures when appropriate. The follow-up session also provides an excellent opportunity for further evaluation of your efforts during the period of intervention. In retrospect, what was most helpful? What was least helpful? Further efforts can be made to consolidate gains at this point as well. What was gained from treatment that the client can continue to use in coping with life? Finally, at this point you can contract for more formalized help if this step appears necessary. Follow-up sessions thus enable social workers to arrange for timely assistance that may arrest deterioration in functioning.

One caution related to follow-up sessions is warranted: They may not allow the client to make a "clean break" from services. Clients who had difficulty separating during termination may use follow-up sessions as an excuse to prolong contact with the social worker. This continued attachment is detrimental to the change process and inhibits the client from establishing appropriate attachments with social networks and with other helping professionals. Social workers should be alert to this possibility in proposing follow-up sessions and ensure that clients understand the specific purpose and focus of these sessions.

Ending Rituals

In many settings, termination may be concluded by a form of celebration or ritual that symbolically marks the goals achieved and the relationship's conclusion (Murphy & Dillon, 2003). For example, in residential programs and some treatment groups, termination may be acknowledged in "graduation" or "status elevation" ceremonies, during which other residents or members comment on the departing member's growth and offer good wishes for the future. Certificates, cards, or "memory books" (Elbow, 1987) are but a few of the symbolic gifts that terminating clients may receive from staff or fellow clients. In individual and family work, social workers may choose to mark termination with small gifts such as a book, a plant, a framed inspirational quote, a bookmark, or some other token that is representative of the working relationship or the achievements while in service. Groups may conclude by creating a lasting product that is symbolic of the group, such as a collage or mural; in the process of creating this item, participants can reflect on the meaning the group had for them as members (Northen & Kurland, 2001).

The decision to use rituals to mark termination should be based on an understanding of the client, the appropriateness of such actions for the agency or setting, and the meaning that the client may attribute to such actions. For example, giving a personal greeting card may be misinterpreted as a gesture of intimate friendship by some clients; for other clients, such as a

child leaving foster care for a permanent placement, it may be a source of comfort and continuity. A gift that is too lavish may cause discomfort if the client feels the need to reciprocate in some way. "Goodbye parties" may reinforce feelings of accomplishment and confidence, or they may obviate the feelings of sadness or ambivalence that must also be addressed as part of closure (Shulman, 1992). Graduation ceremonies may recreate past disappointments and lead to further setbacks if, for example, family members refuse to attend and acknowledge the changes the client has achieved (Jones, 1996).

Dorfman (1996) suggests asking the client how he or she would like to mark the final session and offering options if the client seems unsure what to suggest. Useful and meaningful ending rituals are numerous. For example, at the final session of the "Banana Splits" group for children of families undergoing divorce or separation, participants make and eat banana splits (McGonagle, 1986). A social worker may create a card depicting the "gift" or wish that he or she has for the client's continued success; participants in groups may write poems or rewrite lyrics to popular song melodies to mark the ending of a class or group (Walsh, 2003). Some clients may ask the social worker to create a "diploma" indicating what they have achieved and ask to have a photo taken together (Dorfman, 1996). Graduation ceremonies and other events to mark group terminations can facilitate the tasks of termination and model meaningful rituals in a way that clients might not have experienced previously (Jones, 1996). These endings can be linked symbolically to the goals for work and may help motivate other clients to strive toward the achievements being celebrated by fellow group or residence members.

Case Example

Horizons is a halfway house for youth whose behavioral problems have resulted in hospitalization or incarceration. The program is intended to help teenagers readjust to community life and establish social supports so that they can return to their homes or move successfully into independent living. Given this focus, the length of stay for any individual resident varies considerably. Some youth encounter difficulties or re-offend; they are then returned to jail or to inpatient settings or simply "drop out of sight." These endings can be difficult for staff as they deal with disappointment in the client's failure to "make it" this time around and perhaps question what they might have done to prevent this outcome. It is also disturbing for other clients as they worry about their own challenges and their ability to successfully move on to the next step.

When residents terminate prematurely from the program, they are asked to attend a community meeting, where they can process with the group their experiences in the program and the things they learned that can be of use in the future. Staff and other residents are also invited to share their observations and feelings, with the intention of giving supportive and constructive feedback from a caring community—one to which the resident might someday return. When clients quit the program and drop out of sight, such sessions are still held. In these sessions, the residents and staff who remain process their feelings about the departure and discern lessons they can take away from it.

When residents have met their goals and are ready to move on to a more permanent living situation, staff discuss the plan and timeline for departure and stay alert to the difficulties that can arise at termination. The staff members make a point of discussing, in groups and individual sessions, the fears that can arise in moving from some place "comfortable" to the unknown. Sometimes, alumni of the program will visit to talk about their experiences and offer advice and encouragement. At this time, goals are reviewed, progress is charted, and the client's views are sought on which aspects of the program facilitated change. Clients and staff work together to anticipate the challenges ahead and to put in place the strategies necessary to address them.

During a resident's final days, the Horizons staff and residents create a "graduation" ceremony, and each resident offers the one who is leaving symbolic gifts to take on "the journey." These gifts may consist of inspirational quotes, reminders of inside jokes or shared experiences, and more tangible items, such as towels or pots and pans to help get established in the new setting.

Family members, teachers, and workers from other agencies are encouraged to attend the graduation, and at the ceremony are asked to support the client in the next steps ahead. These ceremonies are often tearful and moving events, where the emphasis is on achievement and on hope for the future.

Summary

Social workers are well aware of the importance of engagement with clients and the skills and attitudes needed to build an effective working relationship. Unfortunately, when this relationship concludes, social workers may not be equally astute about "taking the relationship apart." Effective evaluation and termination leave both the practitioner and the client with a shared sense of the accomplishments achieved in their work together. This process affords the opportunity to model ending a relationship in a way that is not hurtful or damaging to the client. Effective termination equips the client with the skills and knowledge necessary to sustain gains or to seek further help as needed in the future.

Related Online Content

Visit the *Direct Social Work Practice* companion Web site at *www.cengage.com/social_work/hepworth* for additional learning tools such as glossary terms, chapter outlines, relevant Web links, and chapter practice quizzes.

Skills Development Exercises in Evaluation and Termination

In the companion video for this course involving Ali's last session with Angela and Irwin Corning, she engages the couple in reflection on the aspects of the helping process that were helpful and unhelpful to them. Based on your knowledge of evaluation and termination, address the following questions:

1. What goals were reached during the course of the Corning's work with Ali?
2. What goals were not achieved?
3. How could the worker evaluate the efficacy of the helping process, beyond asking for the clients' general feedback?
4. Based on the feedback Irwin and Angela provided, what further questions might Ali have asked to evaluate her intervention?
5. What risks do the Cornings face that might lead to a recurrence of problems?
6. What might Ali do in the final session to address those risks?
7. What feelings do Ali and her clients have about termination?

8. What steps might Ali take to strengthen her termination session with the Cornings?

Notes

1. For information on the concepts and steps of termination as they apply to macro practice, we suggest an article by Fauri, Harrigan, and Netting (1998).
2. For an excellent source on the considerations and strategies in termination across settings or using various theoretical orientations, see Walsh (2007).
3. See Meyer (2001) for a discussion of the dynamics of "no shows" and an effective clinical response.
4. For information on services in end-of-life care, see NASW's Standards of Social Work Practice in Palliative and End of Life Care (www.naswdc.org, 2004).
5. Feltenstein (2008); Koob & Le Moal (2008); Matto (2005); Baker, Piper, McCarthy, Majeskie, & Fiore (2004); Smyth (2005); Carroll (1996); Brownell, Marlatt, Lichenstein, and Wilson (1986); Daley (1987, 1991); Marlatt and Gordon (1985); and Catalano, Wells, Jenson, and Hawkins (1989) have authored articles and books that describe the neurobiology of relapse, identify various factors that contribute to relapse, discuss beliefs and myths associated with addictions, and delineate models for relapse education and treatment with addicted and impulse-disordered clients.

Bibliography

A

Abbott, A. A., & Wood, K. M. (2000). Assessment: Techniques and instruments for data collection. In A. Abbott (Ed.), *Alcohol, tobacco, and other drugs: Challenging myths, assessing theories, individualizing interventions* (pp. 159–186). Washington, DC: NASW Press.

Abramovitz, M. (2005). The largely untold story of welfare reform and the human services. *Social Work, 50*(2), 174–186.

Abramson, M. (1985). The autonomy–paternalism dilemma in social work. *Social Work, 27*, 422–427.

Abramson, J. S. (2002). Interdisciplinary team practice. In A. R. Roberts & G. J. Greene (Eds.), *Social workers' desk reference* (pp. 44–50). New York: Oxford University Press.

Ackley, D. C. (1997). *Breaking free of managed care.* Orlando, FL: Guilford Publications.

Adams, J. & Drake, R. (2006). Shared decision-making and evidence-based practice. *Community Mental Health Journal, 42*(1): 87–105.

Adams, K., Matto, H. & Le Croy, C. (in press). Limitations of evidence-based practice for social work education: Unpacking the complexity. *Journal of Social Work Education.*

Agbayani-Siewart, P. (2004) Assumptions of Asian-American similarity: The case of Filipino and Chinese American students. *Social Work, 49*(1), 39–51.

Aguilar, I. (1972). Initial contact with Mexican-American families. *Social Work, 20*, 379–382.

Aguilera, D., & Messick, J. (1982). *Crisis intervention: Theory and methodology* (4th ed.). St. Louis: Mosby.

Ahijevych, K., & Wewers, M. (1993). Factors associated with nicotine dependence among African American women cigarette smokers. *Research in Nursing and Health, 16*, 293–292.

Albert, V. (2000). Redefining welfare benefits: Consequences for adequacy and eligibility benefits. *Social Work, 45*(4), 300–310.

Alcabes, A. A., & Jones, J. A. (1985). Structural determinants of clienthood. *Social Work, 30*, 49–55.

Alexander, E. (1991). Sharing power among organizations: Coordination models to link theory and practice. In J. M. Bryson & R. C. Einsweiler (Eds.), *Shared power: What is it? How does it work? How can we make it work better?* (pp. 213–247). Lanham, MD: University Press of America.

Alexander, R., Jr. (2003). *Understanding legal concepts that influence social welfare policy and practice.* Pacific Grove, CA: Brooks/Cole, Thomson Learning.

Al-Krenawi, A. (1998). Reconciling western treatment and traditional healing: A social worker walks with the wind. *Reflections, 4*(3), 6–21.

Al-Krenawi, A., & Graham, J. (2000). Culturally sensitive social practice with Arab clients in mental health settings. *Health and Social Work, 25*, 9–22.

Allen, D, (2007). Black people have been let down by mental health services. *Nursing Standard. 22*(4), 28–31.

Allen-Meares, P. & Garvin, C. (Eds.). (2000). *The handbook of social work direct practice.* Thousand Oaks, CA: Sage.

Alley, G.R., & Brown, L.B. (2002). A diabetes problem-solving support group: Issues, process, and preliminary outcomes. *Social Work in Health Care, 36*, 1–9.

Alter, K., & Hage, J. (1992). *Organizations working together.* Newbury Park, CA: Sage Publications.

American Association of Retired Persons Foundation (October, 2007). State Fact Sheet for Grandparents and other relatives raising children.

American Association of Suicidology. (2004) *How do you recognize the warning signs of suicide?* Retrieved September 1, 2008, from http://www.suicidology.org/associations/1045/files/Mnemonic.pdf

American Psychiatric Association. (2000). *Diagnostic and statistical manual for mental disorders* (4th ed. text revision). Washington, DC: American Psychiatric Association.

Anderson, S., & Grant, J. (1984). Pregnant women and alcohol: Implications for social work. *Social Casework, 65*, 3–10.

Anderson, S. G., Halter, A. P., & Gryzlak, B. M. (2004). Difficulties after leaving TANF: Inner-city women talk about reasons for retuning to welfare. *Social Work, 49*(2), 185–194.

Anderson, D. A., & Worthen, D. (1997). Exploring a fourth dimension: Spirituality as a resource for the couple therapist. *Journal of Marital and Family Therapy, 23*(1), 3–12.

Anderson-Butcher, D., Khairallah, A. O., & Race-Bigelow, J. (2004). Mutual support groups for long-term recipients of TANF. *Social Work, 49*(1), 131–140.

Andrews, L. B. (2001). *Future perfect: Confronting decisions about genetics.* New York: Columbia University Press.

Andrews, A.B., & Ben-Arieh, A. (1999). Measuring and monitoring children's well-being across the world. *Social Work, 44*(2), 105–115.

Aponte, H. (1982). The person of the therapist: The cornerstone of therapy. *Family Therapy Networker, 21*(46), 19–21.

Applegate, J. S. (1992). The impact of subjective measures on nonbehavioral practice research: Outcome vs. process. *Families in Society, 73*(2), 100–108.

Arditti, J.A. (2008). Parental imprisonment and family visitation: A brief overview and recommendations for family friendly practice. Children of Incarcerated Parents, Conference Proceedings, Spring 2008, Center for Advanced Studies in Child Welfare, University of Minnesota.

Arnold, E. M. (2002). End-of-life counseling and care: Assessment, interventions and clinical issues. In A. R. Roberts & G. J. Greene (Eds.), *Social workers' desk reference* (pp. 452–457). New York: Oxford University Press.

Arnowitz, E., Brunswick, L., & Kaplan, B. (1983). Group therapy, with patients in the waiting room of an oncology clinic. *Social Work, 28*, 395–397.

Aronson, H., & Overall, B. (1966). Treatment expectations of patients in two social classes. *Social Work, 11*, 35–41.

Asai, M. O., & Kameoka, V. A. (2005). The influence of Sekentei on family caregiving and underutilization of social services among Japanese caregivers. *Social Work, 50*(2), 111–118.

Atchey, R. C. (1991). *Social forces and aging* (6th ed.). Springfield, IL: Charles G. Thomas.

Austin, C. D. (1990). Case management: Myths and realities. *Families in Society, 71*(7), 398–405.

Austin, K. M., Moline, M. E., & Williams, G. T. (1990). *Confronting malpractice: Legal and ethical dilemmas in psychotherapy.* Newbury Park, CA: Sage Publications.

Aversa, Jasmine (2008, June 15), "60,000 Joined the U.S. Jobless Rolls in June." Star Tribune, Minneapolis, Minnesota, A1, A9.

B

Baer, J. (1999). Family relationships, parenting behavior, and adolescent deviance in three ethnic groups. *Families in Society, 80*(3), 279–285.

Bailey, V. (2001). Cognitive-behavioral therapies for children and adolescents. *Advances in Psychiatric Treatment, 7*, 224–232.

Bailey-Dempsey, C., & Reid, W. J. (1996). Intervention design and development: A case study. *Research on Social Work Practice, 6*(2), 208–228.

Baker, T. B., Piper, M. E., McCarthy, D. E., Majeskie, M. R., & Fiore, M. C. (2004). Addiction motivation reformulated: An affective processing model of negative reinforcement. *Psychological Review, 11*(1), 33–51.

Bakker, L., Ward, T., Cryer, M., & Hudson, S. M. (1997). Out of the rut. A cognitive-behavioral treatment program for driving-while-disqualified offenders. *Behavioral Change, 14*, 29–38.

Balgopal, P., & Vassil, T. (1983). *Groups in social work: An ecological perspective.* New York: Macmillan.

Bandura, A. (1977). Self-efficacy: Toward a unifying theory of behavioral change. *Psychological Review, 84*, 191–215.

Bandura, A. (1986). *Social foundations of thought and action.* Englewood Cliffs, NJ: Prentice-Hall.

Bandura, A. (1988). Social cognitive theory. In R. Vasta (Ed.), *Annals of child development: Six theories of child development: Revised formulations and current issues* (pp. 1–60). Greenwich, CT: JAI Press.

Bandura, A. (1997). *Self-efficacy: The exercise of self control.* New York: Freeman

Bandura, A., & Locke, E. (2003). Negative self-efficacy and goal effects revisited. *Journal of Applied Psychology, 88*(1), 87–99.

Banerjee, M.M. (2002). Voicing realities and recommending reform in PRWORA. *Social Work, 47*(3), 315–328.

Barber, J. G. (1995). Working with resistant drug abusers. *Social Work, 40*(1), 17–23.

Bargal, D. (2004). Groups for reducing intergroup conflicts. In C. D. Garvin, L. M. Gutierrez, & M. J. Galinsky (Eds.), *Handbook of social work with groups* (pp. 292–306). New York: Guilford Press.

Barker, R. L. (1996). *The social work dictionary* (3rd ed.). Washington, DC: NASW Press.

Barker, R. L. (2003). *The social work dictionary* (5th ed.). Washington, DC: NASW Press.

Barnes, A. (2008). Race and hospital diagnoses of schizophrenia and mood disorders. *Social Work, 53*(1), 77–83.

Barsky, A. & Gould, J. (2002) *Clinicians in Court: A Guide to Subpoenas, Depositions, Testifying, and Everything Else You Need to Know.* New York: Guilford Press.

Barth, R., & Schinke, S. (1984). Enhancing the supports of teenage mothers. *Social Casework, 65,* 523–531.

Barth, R. P., Wildfire, J., & Green, R. L. (2006). Placement in to foster care and the interplay of urbanicity, child behavior problems and poverty. *American Journal of Orthopsychiatry, 76*(3) 358–366.

Bartlett, H. (1970). *The common base of social work practice.* New York: National Association of Social Workers.

Barton, C., & Alexander, J. (1981). Functional family therapy. In A. Gurman & D. Kniskern (Eds.), *Handbook of family therapy* (pp. 403–443). New York: Brunner/Mazel.

Barusch, A.S. (2002). Foundations of social policy, social justice, public programs, and the social work profession. Itasca, Ill: F.E. Peacock.

Beatrice, D. F. (1990). Inter-agency coordination: A practitioner's guide to a strategy for effective social policy. *Administration in Social Work, 14*(4), 45–60.

Beck, A. (1974). Phases in the development of structure in therapy and encounter groups. In D. Wexler & L. Rice (Eds.), *Innovations in client-centered therapy.* New York: Wiley.

Beck, A.T. (1975). *Cognitive therapy and emotional disorders.* New York: International Universities Press Inc.

Beck, A.T. (1976). *Cognitive therapy and the emotional disorders.* New York: International Universities Press

Beck, A.T. (1967) *Depression.* New York: Harper.

Beck, A., Kovacs, M., & Weissman, A. (1979). Assessment of suicidal intention. *Journal of Consulting and Clinical Psychology, 47,* 343–352.

Beck, A., Resnik, H., & Lettieri, D. (Eds.). (1974). *The prediction of suicide.* Bowie, MD: Charles Press.

Beck, A., Rush, A., Shaw, B., & Emery, G. (1979). *Cognitive therapy of depression.* New York: Guilford Press.

Beck, J. S. (1995). *Cognitive therapy: Basics and beyond.* New York: Guilford Press.

Becvar, D. S., & Becvar, R. J. (2000a). *Family therapy: A systemic integration* (4th ed.). Boston: Allyn & Bacon.

Becvar, D. S., & Becvar, R. J. (2000b). Family relationships, parenting behavior, and adolescent deviance in three ethnic groups. *Families in Society, 80*(3), 279–285.

Behroozi, C. S. (1992). A model for work with involuntary applicants in groups. *Social Work with Groups, 15*(2/3), 223–238.

Belkin, L. (1999, October 31). Parents blaming parents. *New York Times Sunday Magazine,* p. F61.

Bell, H. (2003). Strengths and secondary trauma in family violence work. *Social Work, 48*(4), 513–522.

Bell, J. L. (1995). Traumatic event debriefing: Service delivery designs and the role of social work. *Social Work, 40*(1), 36–43.

Bell, L. (2001). Patterns of interaction in multidisciplinary child protection teams in New Jersey. *Child Abuse and Neglect, 25*(1), 65–80.

Bembry, J. X., & Ericson, C. (1999). Therapeutic termination with the early adolescent who has experienced multiple losses. *Child and Adolescent Social Work Journal, 16*(3), 177–189.

Bennett, C. J., Legon, J., & Zilberfein, F. (1989). The significance of empathy in current hospital based practice. *Social Work in Health Care, 14*(2), 27–41.

Bepko, C., & Johnson, T. (2000). Gay and lesbian couples in therapy: Perspectives for the contemporary family therapist. *Journal of Marital and Family Therapy, 26*(3), 409–419.

Berg, I. K. (1994). *Family-based services: A solution-focused approach.* New York: Norton.

Berg, I. K., & Jaya, A. (1993). Different and same: Family therapy with Asian-American families. *Journal of Marital and Family Therapy, 19*(1), 31–38.

Berg. I. K., & Kelly, S. (2000). Building solutions in child protection. New York: W.W. Norton.

Bergeron, L. R., & Gray, B. (2003). Ethical dilemmas of reporting suspected elder abuse. *Social Work, 48,* 96–105.

Bergin & Garfield (2004). *Handbook of psychotherapy and behavioral change* (5th ed.). New York: Wiley

Berkman, B., Chauncey, S., Holmes, W., Daniels, A., Bonander, E., Sampson, S., & Robinson, M. (1999). Standardized screening of elderly patients' needs for social work assessment in primary care. *Health and Social Work, 24*(1), 9–16.

Berlin, S. B. (1996). Constructivism and the environment: A cognitive-integrative perspective for social work. *Families in Society, 77,* 326–335.

Berlin, S. B. (2001). *Clinical social work: A cognitive-integrative perspective.* New York: Oxford University Press.

Berlin, S. B., & Marsh, J. C. (1993). *Informing practice decisions.* New York: Macmillan.

Berman-Rossi, T., & Kelly, T. B. (2000, February). Teaching students to understand and utilize the changing paradigm of stage of group development theory. Paper presented at the 46th annual program meeting of the Council on Social Work Education, New York, NY.

Berman-Rossi, T., & Rossi, P. (1990). Confidentiality and informed consent in school social work, *Social Work in Education, 12*(3), 195–207.

Bernal, G., & Flores-Ortiz, Y. (1982). Latino families in therapy: Engagement and evaluation. *Journal of Marriage and Family Therapy, 8,* 357–365.

Bernhardt, B., & Rauch, J. (1993). Genetic family histories: An aid to social work assessment. *Families in Society, 74,* 195–205.

Bernstein, B. (1977). Privileged social work practice. *Social Casework, 66,* 387–393.

Bertcher, H., & Maple, F. (1985). Elements and issues in group composition. In P. Glasser, R. Sarri, & R. Vinter (Eds.), *Individual change through small groups* (pp. 180–202). New York: Free Press.

Bertolino, B., & O'Hanlon, B. (2002). *Collaborative, competency-based counseling and therapy.* Boston: Allyn and Bacon.

Beyer, J. A., & Balster, T. C. (2001). Assessment and classification in institutional corrections. In A. Walsh (Ed.), *Correctional assessment, casework, and counseling* (3rd ed., pp. 137–159). Lanham, MD: American Correctional Association.

Biesteck, F. (1957). *The casework relationship.* Chicago: Loyola University Press.

Bidgood, B., Holosko, M., & Taylor, L. (2003). A new working definition of social work practice: A turtle's view. *Research on Social Work Practice, 13*(3), 400–408.

Black, W. G. (1993). Military induced family separation: A stress reduction intervention. *Social Work, 38*(3), 273–280.

Block-Lerner, J., Adair, C., Plumb, J., Rhatigan, D. & Orsillo, S. (2007). The case for mindfulness-based approaches in the cultivation of empathy: Does non-judgmental present moment awareness increase capacity for perspective-taking and empathic concern? *Journal of marital and family therapy, 33*(4): 501–516.

Bloom, M., Fischer, J., & Orme, J. G. (2003). *Evaluating practice: Guidelines for the accountable professional.* Boston: Allyn & Bacon.

Bloom, M., Fischer, J. & Orme, J. (2006). *Evaluating practice: Guidelines for the accountable professional.* Boston: Allyn and Bacon.

Boehm, A., & Staples (2004). Empowerment: The point of view of consumers. *Families in Society: The Journal of Contemporary Human Services, 85*(2), 270–280.

Borys, D. S., & Pope, K. S. (1989). Dual relationships between therapist and client: A national study of psychologists, psychiatrists, and social workers. *Professional Psychology: Research and Practice, 20,* 283–293.

Bostic, J. Q., Shadid, L. G., & Blotcky, M. J. (1996). Our time is up: Forced terminations during psychotherapy. *American Journal of Psychotherapy, 50,* 347–359.

Bowen, M. (1960). A family concept of schizophrenia. In D.D. Jackson (Ed.). *The etiology of schizophrenia.* New York: Basic Books.

Bower, B. (1997). Therapy bonds and the bottle (establishment of therapeutic alliance linked to higher success rate in treatment of alcoholics). *Science News, 152,* 8.

Boyd-Franklin, N. (1989a). *Black families in therapy: A multisystems approach.* New York: Guilford Press.

Boyd-Franklin, N. (1989b). Major family approaches and their relevance to the treatment of black families. In N. Boyd-Franklin, *Black families in therapy: A multisystems approach* (pp. 121–132). New York: Guilford Press.

Boyd-Franklin, N., & Bry, B. H. (2000). *Reaching out in family therapy: Home-based school and community interventions.* New York: Guilford Press.

Bradshaw, W. (1996). Structured group work for individuals with schizophrenia: A coping skills approach. *Research on Social Work Practice, 6* (2), 139–154.

Brager, G., & Holloway, S. (1978). *Changing human service organizations: Politics and practice.* New York: Free Press.

Brager, G., & Holloway, S. (1983). A process model for changing organizations from within. In R. M. Kramer & H. Specht (Eds.), *Readings in community organization practice* (pp. 198–208.) Englewood Cliffs, NJ: Prentice-Hall.

Brandes, S. D. (1976). *American welfare capitalism, 1880–1940.* Chicago: University of Chicago Press.

Brehm, S. S. (1976). *The application of social psychology to clinical practice.* New York: Wiley.

Brehm, S. S., & Brehm, J. W. (1981). *Psychological reactance: A theory of freedom and control.* New York: Academic Press.

Brent, D. A., Johnson, B., Bartle, S., Bridge, J., Rather, C., Matta, J., et al. (1993). Personality disorder tendency to impulsive violence, and suicidal behavior in adolescents. *Journal of the American Academy of Child and Adolescent Psychiatry, 32*(1), 69–75.

Breton, M. (1985). Reaching and engaging people: Issues and practice principles. *Social Work with Groups, 8*(3), 7–21.

Breton, M. (2006). Path dependence and the place of social action in social work. *Social Work with Groups, 29*(4), 25–44.

Bridges, G. S., & Steen, S. (1998). Racial disparities in official assessments of juvenile offenders: Attributional stereotypes as mediating mechanisms. *American Sociological Review, 63,* 554–570.

Briggs, H. and Rzepnicki, T. (Eds.) (2004). *Using evidence in social work practice.* Chicago: Lyceum.

Brindis, C., Barth, R. P., & Loomis, A. B. (1987). Continuous counseling: Case management with teenage parents. *Social Casework, 68*(3), 164–172.

Brissett-Chapman, S. (1997). Child protection risk assessment and African American children: Cultural ramifications for families and communities. *Child Welfare, 76,* 45–63.

Bronfenbrenner, U. (1989). Ecological systems theory. In R. Vasta (Ed.), *Annals of child development: Six theories of child development: Revised formulations and current issues* (pp. 187–247). Greenwich, CT: JAI Press.

Brookins, G. K., Peterson, A. C., & Brooks, L. M. (1997). Youth and families in the inner city: Influencing positive outcomes. In H. J. Walberg, O. Reyes, & R. P. Weissberg (Eds.), *Children and youth: Interdisciplinary perspectives* (pp. 45–66). Thousand Oaks, CA: Sage Publications.

Brooks-Gunn, J., & Duncan, G. J. (1997). The effects of poverty on children: The future of children. *Children and Poverty, 7*(2), 55–71.

Brown, L. S. (1994). *Subjective dialogues: Theory in feminist therapy.* New York: Basic Books.

Brown, C. (2007, August 2). Liberians, anxious and grateful. *Star Tribune,* pp. B1, B7.

Brown, L., & Root, M. (1990). *Diversity and complexity in feminist theory.* New York: Haworth Press.

Brownell, K., Marlatt, G., Lichenstein, E., & Wilson, G. T. (1986). Understanding and preventing relapse. *American Psychologist, 41*(7), 765–782.

Brownlee, K. (1996). Ethics in community mental health care: The ethics of nonsexual relationships: A dilemma for the rural mental health professionals. *Community Mental Health Journal, 32*(5), 497–503.

Brueggemann, W. G. (2006). The practice of macro social work (3rd ed.). Thomson-Brooks/Cole.

Brunner, C., (1991). *Thinking collaboration: Ten questions and answers to help policy makers improve children's services.* Washington, DC: Education and Human Services Consortium.

Burford, G., & Pennell, J. (1996). Family group decision making: Generating indigenous structures for resolving family violence. *Protecting Children, 12*(3), 17–21.

Burford, G., & Pennell, J. (2004). From agency client to community-based consumer: The family group conference as a consumer-led group in child welfare. In C. D. Garvin, L. M. Gutierrez, & M. J. Galinsky (Eds.), *Handbook of social work with groups* (pp. 415–431). New York: Guilford Press.

Burnette, D. (1999). Custodial grandparents in Latino families: Patterns of service use and predictors of unmet needs. *Social Work, 44*(1), 22–34.

Burns, A., Lawlor, B. & Craig, S. (2004). *Assessment scales in old age psychiatry* (2nd ed.). London: Martin Dunitz.

Burns, D. (1980). *Feeling good.* New York: Avon Books.

Burns, D. (1995). The therapist's toolkit: Comprehensive assessment and treatment tools for the mental health professional. Philadelphia: D.D. Burns.

Buss, T. F., & Gillanders, W. R. (1997). Worry about health status among the elderly: Patient management and health policy implications. *Journal of Health and Social Policy, 8*(4), 53–66.

Butz, R. A. (1985). Reporting child abuse and confidentiality in counseling. *Social Casework, 66,* 83–90.

C

Cain, R. (1991a). Relational contexts and information management among gay men. *Families in Society, 72*(6), 344–352.

Cain, R. (1991b). Stigma management and gay identity development. *Social Work, 36*(1), 67–71.

Cameron, S., & turtle-song, i., (2002). Learning to write case notes using the SOAP format. *Journal of Counselling and Development, 80,* 286–292.

Campbell, J. A. (1988). Client acceptance of single-subject evaluation procedures. *Social Work Research Abstracts, 24,* 21–22.

Campbell, J. A. (1990). Ability of practitioners to estimate client acceptance of single-subject evaluation procedures. *Social Work, 35*(1), 9–14.

Canda, E. (1983). General implications of Shamanism for clinical social work. *International Social Work, 26,* 14–22.

Canda, E., & Phaobtong, T. (1992). Buddhism as a support system for Southeast Asian refugees. *Social Work, 37*(1), 61–67.

Canda, E. R. (1997). Spirituality. In R. L. Edwards (Ed.), *Encyclopedia of social work 1997 supplement* (19th ed., pp. 299–309). Washington, DC: NASW Press.

Capitman, J., MacAdam, M., & Yee, D. (1988). Hospital-based managed care. *Generations, 12*(5), 62–65.

Caplan, G. (1964). *Principles of preventive psychiatry.* New York: Basic Books.

Caplan, T. (1995). Safety and comfort, content and process: Facilitating open group work with men who batter. *Social Work with Groups, 18*(2/3), 33–51.

Caple, F. S., Salcido, R. M., & di Cecco, J. (1995). Engaging effectively with culturally diverse families and children. *Social Work in Education, 17*(3), 159–169.

Carkhuff, R. (1969). *Helping and human relations: Practice and research.* New York: Holt, Rinehart & Winston.

Carlozzi, A., Bull, K., Stein, L., Ray, K., & Barnes, L. (2002). Empathy theory and practice: A survey of psychologists and counselors. *Journal of Psychology, 36*(2), 161–171.

Carlton-LaNey, I. (1999). African American social work pioneers' response to need. *Social Work, 44*(4), 311–321.

Carniol, B. (1992). Structural social work: Maurice Moreau's challenge to social work practice. *Journal of Progressive Human Services, 3*(1), 1–19.

Carr, E. S. (2004). Accessing resources, transforming systems: Group work with poor and homeless people. In C. D. Garvin, L. M. Gutierrez, & M. J. Galinsky (Eds.), *Handbook of social work with groups* (pp. 360–383). New York: Guilford Press.

Carrell, S. (2000). Group therapy with adolescents. In *Group exercises for adolescents: A manual for therapists* (pp. 13–26). Thousand Oaks, CA: Sage Publications.

Carrillo, D. F., Gallant, J., & Thyer, B. (1995). Training MSW students in interviewing skills: An empirical assessment. *Arete, 18,* 12–19.

Carroll, K.M. (1996). Relapse prevention as a psychoosical treatment: A review of controlled clinical trials. *Experimental and Clinical Psychopharmacology, 4,* 46–54.

Carter, C.S. (2000). Church burning: Using a contemporary issue to teach community organization. *Journal of Social Work Education, 36*(1), 79–88.

Carter, B., & McGoldrick, M. (Eds.). (1988). *The changing life cycle: A framework for family therapy* (2nd ed.). New York: Gardner Press.

Carter, B., & McGoldrick, M. (Eds.). (1999a). *The expanded family life cycle: Individual, family, and social perspectives* (3rd ed.). Boston: Allyn & Bacon.

Carter, B., & McGoldrick, M. (1999b). Coaching at various stages of the life cycle. In B. Carter & M. McGoldrick (Eds.), *The expanded family life cycle: Individual, family, and social perspectives* (3rd ed., pp. 436–454). Boston: Allyn & Bacon.

Caspi, J., & Reid, W. J. (2002). *Educational supervision in social work. A task-centered model for field instruction and staff development.* New York: Columbia University Press.

Catalano, R., Wells, E. A., Jenson, J. M., & Hawkins, J. D. (1989). Aftercare services for drug-using institutionalized delinquents. *Social Service Review, 63*(4), 553–577.

Centers for Disease Control. (2005). *10 leading causes of death, United States.* Retrieved July 2, 2008, from http://webappa.cdc.gov/cgi-bin/broker.exe

Center for Economic and Social Justice. (n.d.). *Defining economic and social justice.* Retrieved August 23, 2008, from http://www.cesj.org/thirdway/economicjustice-defined.htm

Chan, C. L. W., Chan, Y., Lou, V. W. Q. (2002). Evaluating an empowerment group for divorced Chinese women in Hong Kong. *Research on Social Work Practice, 12*(4), 558–569.

Chandler, S. (1985). Mediation: Conjoint problem solving. *Social Work, 30,* 346–349.

Chapin, R., & Cox, E. O. (2001). Changing the paradigm: Strengths-based and empowerment–oriented social work practice with frail elderly. *Journal of Gerontological Social Work, 36,* (3/4), 165–169.

Charnley, H., & Langley, J. (2007). Developing cultural competence as a framework for anti-heterosexist social work practice: Reflections from the UK. *Journal of social work.* 7(3): 307–321.

Chau, K. L. (1990). A model for teaching cross-cultural practice in social work. *Journal of Social Work Education, 26*(2), 124–133.

Chau, K. L. (1993). Needs assessment for group work with people of color: A conceptual formulation. *Social Work with Groups, 15*(2/3), 53–66.

Chelune, G. J. (1979). Measuring openness in interpersonal communication. In G. Chelune & Associates (Eds.), *Self-disclosure.* San Francisco: Jossey-Bass.

Chemtob, C. M., Hamada, R. S., Bauer, G., Torigoe, R. Y., & Kinney, B. (1988). Patient suicide: Frequency and impact on psychologists. *Professional Psychology Research and Practice, 19*(4), 416–420.

Chen, S.W., & Davenport, D. (2005). Cognitive behavioral therapy with Chinese American clients: Cautions and modifications. *Psychotherapy Theory Research, Practice and Training, 42*(1), 101–110.

Chesler, M. (1994a). Strategies for multicultural organizational development. *Diversity Factors, 2*(2), 12–18.

Chesler, M. (1994b). Organizational development is not the same as multicultural organizational development. In E. Y. Cross, J. H. Katz, F. A. Miller, & E. H. Seashore (Eds.), *The promise of diversity* (pp. 240–351). Burr Ridge, IL: Irwin.

Child Welfare League of America. (1990). *Agency self-improvement checklist.* Washington, DC: Child Welfare League of America.

Chipungu, S. S., & Bent-Goodley, T. B. (2003). Race, poverty and child maltreatment. *APSAC Advisor, American Professional Society on the Abuse of Children, 15*(2).

Choi, G. (1997). Acculturative stress, social support, and depression in Korean American families. *Journal of Family Social Work, 2*(1), 81–79.

Christian, J. (2005). Riding the bus. *Journal of Contemporary Criminal Justice,* vol?, 31–48.

Cingolani, J. (1984). Social conflict perspective on work with involuntary clients. *Social Work, 29*, 442–446.

Citron, P. (1978). Group work with alcoholic poly-drug involved adolescents with deviant behavior syndrome. *Social Work with Groups, I*(1), 39–52.

Claiborn, C. (1982). Interpretation and change in counseling. *Journal of Counseling Psychology, 29*, 439–453.

Clifford, D., & Burke, B. (2005). Developing anti-oppression ethics in the new curriculum. *Social Work Education, 87*(2), 677–692.

Clinical social work association Clinical social work association http://www.associationsites.com/main-pub.cfm?usr=CSWA

Clinical Social Work Federation. (1997). Definition of clinical social work (revised). http://www.cswf.org/www/info/html

Cnaan, R. A., & Rothman, J. (1986). Conceptualizing community intervention: An empirical test of three models of community organization. *Administration in Social Work, 10*(3), 41–55.

Coady, N. & Lehmann, P. (Eds.). (2008). *Theoretical perspectives for direct social work practice: a generalist-eclectic approach* (2nd ed.). New York: Springer.

Coady, N. F., & Marziali, E. (1994). The association between global and specific measures of the therapeutic relationship. *Psychotherapy, 31*, 17–27.

Cobb, N. H. (2008). Cognitive-behavioral theory and treatment. In N. Coady & P. Lehmann (Eds.), *Theoretical perspectives for direct social work practice. A generalist-eclectic approach* (2nd ed., pp. 221–248). New York: Springer Publishing Company.

Cohen, J. A. (2003). Treating acute posttraumatic reactions in children and adolescents. *Biological Psychiatry, 53*, 827–833.

Cohen, E. D., & Cohen, G. S. (1999). *The virtuous therapist: Ethical practice of counseling and psychotherapy.* Belmont, CA: Brooks/Cole.

Collins, G. (2007, October 18). None dare call it child care. *The New York Times,* A27.

Collins, M. E., Stevens, J. W., & Lane, T. C. (2000). Teenage parents and welfare reform: Findings from a survey of teenagers affected by living requirements. *Social Work, 45*(4), 327–338.

Collins, P. M., Kayser, K., & Platt, S. (1994). Conjoint marital therapy: A social worker's approach to single-system evaluation. *Families in Society, 71*(8), 461–470.

Comer, E., Meier, A., & Galinsky, M.J. (2004). Development of innovative group work practice using the intervention research paradigm. *Social Work, 49*(2), 250–260.

Comfort, M. (2008). *Doing time together.* Place: University of Chicago Press.

Compton, B. R., & Galaway, B. (1994). *Social work processes* (6th ed.). Pacific Grove, CA: Brooks/Cole.

Compton, B., Galaway, B., & Cournoyer, B. (2005). *Social work processes.* (7th ed.) Pacific Grove, CA: Brooks/Cole.

Condrey, S. E., Facer, R. L., & Hamilton, J. P. (2005). Employees amidst welfare reform: TANF employees overall and organizational job satisfaction. *Journal of Human Behavior in the Social Environment, 12*(2/3), 221–242.

Congress, E. P. (1994). The use of culturegrams to assess and empower culturally diverse families. *Families in Society, 75*, 531–540.

Congress, E. P. (1999). Ethical dilemmas in interdisciplinary collaboration. In E. Congress (Ed.), *Social work values and ethics: Identifying and resolving professional dilemmas* (pp. 117–128). Chicago: Nelson Hall.

Congress, E. P. (2000). Crisis intervention with diverse families. In A.R. Roberts (Ed.). *Crisis intervention handbook: Assessment, treatment and research* (2nd ed., pp. 430–448), New York: Oxford University Press.

Congress, E. P. (2002). Using the culturegram with diverse families. In A. R. Roberts & G. J. Green (Eds.), *Social workers' desk reference* (pp. 57–61). New York: Oxford University Press.

Congress, E.P., & Lynn, M. (1994). Group work programs in public schools: Ethical dilemmas and cultural diversity. *Social Work in Education, 15*(2), 107–114.

Congress, E. P. & Lynn, M. (1997). Group work practice in the community: Navigating the slippery slope of ethical dilemmas. *Social Work with Groups, 20*(3), 61–74.

Connolly, C.M. (2006). A feminist perspective of resilience in lesbian couples. *Journal of Feminist Family Therapy, 18*(1/2), 137–162.

Constable, R., & Lee, D. B. (2004). Social work with families: Content and process. Chicago: Lyceum Books.

Cook, J.B., & Kaffenberger, C.J. (2003). Solution shop: A solution-focused counseling and study skills program for middle school. *Professional Counseling Journal, 7*(12), 116–124.

Corcoran, J. (1997), A solution-oriented approach to working with juvenile offenders, *Child and Adolescent Social Work Journal, 14*, 227–288.

Corcoran, J. (1998). Solution-focused practice with middle and high school at-risk youth. *Social Work in Education, 20*, 232–243.

Corcoran, J. (2000a). *Evidence based practice with families: A lifespan approach*. New York: Springer.

Corcoran, J. (2000b). Evidence based treatment of adolescents with externalizing disorders. In A. R. Roberts & G. J. Greene (Eds.), *Social workers' desk reference* (pp. 112–115). New York: Oxford University Press.

Corcoran, J. (2002). Evidence based treatment of adolescents with externalizing disorders. In A. R. Roberts and G. J. Greene (Eds.), *Social workers' desk reference* (pp. 793–796) New York: Oxford University Press.

Corcoran, J. (2008). *Solution-focused therapy*. In N. Coady & P. Lehmann (Eds.), *Theoretical perspectives for direct social work practice. A generalist-eclectic approach* (2nd ed., pp. 429–446). New York: Springer Publishing Company.

Corcoran, J., & Franklin, C. (1998). A solution-focused approach to physical abuse. *Journal of Family Psychotherapy, 9*(1), 69–73.

Corcoran, J., & Stephenson, M. (2000). The effectiveness of solution-focused therapy with child behavior problems: A preliminary report. *Families in Society: The Journal of Contemporary Human Services, 81*(5), 468–474.

Corcoran, K., & Fisher, J. (1999). *Measures for clinical practice* (3rd ed.). New York: Free Press.

Corcoran, K., & Gingerich, W. J. (1994). Practice evaluation in the context of managed care: Case recording methods for quality assurance reviews. *Research on Social Work Practice, 4*(3), 326–337.

Corcoran, K., & Vandiver, V. (1996). *Maneuvering the maze of managed care: Skills for mental health practitioners*. New York: Free Press.

Corcoran, K., & Winslade, W. J. (1994). Eavesdropping on the 50-minute hour: Managed mental health care and confidentiality. *Behavioral Sciences and the Law, 12*, 351–365.

Corey, G. (1990). *Theory and practice of group counseling*. Pacific Grove, CA: Brooks/Cole.

Corey, G., Corey, M. S., & Callanan, P. (2007). *Issues and ethics in the helping professions* (7th ed.). Pacific Grove, CA: Brooks/Cole.

Corey, G., Corey, M. S., Callahan, P. J., & Russell, J. M. (2004). *Group techniques* (3rd ed.). Pacific Grove, CA: Brooks/Cole.

Corey, M. S., & Corey, G. (2002). *Groups: Process and practice* (6th ed.). Pacific Grove, CA: Brooks/Cole.

Corey, M. S., & Corey, G. (1992). *Groups: Process and practice* (4th ed.). Pacific Grove, CA: Brooks/Cole.

Cormier, S., & Nurius, P. S. (2003). *Interviewing and change strategies for helpers: Fundamental skills and cognitive behavioral interventions*. Pacific Grove, CA: Brooks/Cole, Thomson Learning.

Cormier, S., Nurius, P. S., & Osborn, C. J. (2009). *Interviewing and change strategies for helpers: Fundamental skills in cognitive behavioral interventions* (6th ed.). Belmont, CA: Brooks Cole.

Cormier, W., & Cormier, L. (1979). *Interviewing strategies for helpers. A guide to assessment, treatment, and evaluation*. Pacific Grove, CA: Brooks/Cole.

Cornelius, L.J., Simpson, G.M., Ting, L., Wiggins, E., & Lipford, S. (2003). Reach out and I'll be there: Mental health crisis intervention and mobile outreach services to urban African Americans. *Health and Social Work, 28*(1), 74–78.

Corwin, M. (2002). *Brief treatment in clinical social work practice.* Pacific Grove, CA: Brooks/Cole.

Costello, E. J., Compton, S. N., Keeler, G., & Angold, A. (2003). Relationship between poverty and psychopathology: A natural experiment. *Journal of the American Medical Association, 290*(15), 2023–2029.

Council on Social Work Education (2008). Educational Policy and Accreditation Standards. Washington, DC: Council on Social Work Education.

Cournoyer, B. R. (1991). *Selected techniques for eclectic practice: Clinically speaking.* Indianapolis, IN: Author.

Cournoyer, B. (2004). *Evidence-based social work practice skills book.* New York: Allyn-Bacon.

Courtney, M. (1999). Challenges and opportunities posed by the reform era. Presented at the "Reconciling welfare reform with child welfare" conference. Center for Advanced Studies in Child Welfare, University of Minnesota, February 26.

Cowger, C. D. (1992). Assessment of client strengths. In D. Saleeby (Ed.), *The strengths perspective in social work practice* (pp. 139–147). New York: Longman.

Cowger, C. D. (1994). Assessing client strengths: Clinical assessment for client empowerment. *Social Work, 39*(3), 262–267.

Cowger, C. (1997). Assessing client improvement. In D. Saleebey (Ed.). *The strengths perspective* (2nd ed., pp. 52–73), White Plains, NY: Longman.

Cox, E. O. (1991). The critical role of social action in empowerment oriented groups. *Social Work with Groups, 14*(3/4), 77–90.

Crabtree, B. F., & Miller, W. L. (1992). *Doing qualitative research.* Newbury Park, CA: Sage Publications.

CRAFFT. (n.d.). Retrieved September 1, 2008, from http://www.projectcork.org/clinical_tools/pdf/CRAFFT.pdf

Crenshaw, A. B. (2003, October 14). "Middle-class families are richer, study shows." *The Dallas Morning News,* p. 3D.

Cross, T. L., Bazron, B. J., Dennis, K., & Issacs, M. R. (1989). *Toward a culturally competent system of care.* Washington, DC: Georgetown University Child Development Center.

Crosson-Tower, C. (2004). *Exploring child welfare: A practice perspective.* Boston: Allyn & Bacon.

Cull, J. G., & Gill, W. S. (1991). *Suicide Probability Scale (SPS).* Los Angeles: Western Psychological Services.

Cummings, N. A. (1991). Brief intermittent therapy throughout the life cycle. In C. S. Austad & W. H. Berman (Eds.), *Psychotherapy in managed health care: The optimal use of time and resources* (pp. 35–45). Washington, DC: American Psychological Association.

Cummins, H. J. (2007, July 24). Minimum wage increases today. *Star Tribune,* D1 & D2.

Cunningham, M. (2003). Impact of trauma social work clinicians: Empirical findings. *Social Work, 48*(4), 451–459.

Curry, R. (2007). Surviving professional stress. *Social Work Today* (November/December), 25–28.

Curtis, C. M., & Denby, R. W (2004). Impact of the Adoption and Safe Family Act on families of color: Workers share their thoughts. *Families in Society, 85*(1), 71–79.

D

Dahlen, E. R., & Deffenbacher, J. L. (2000). A partial component analysis of Beck's cognitive therapy for anger control. *Journal of Cognitive Psychotherapy, 14,* 77–95.

Daley, D. C. (1987). Relapse prevention with substance abusers: Clinical issues and myths. *Social Work, 32,* 138–142.

Daley, D. C. (1991). *Kicking addictive habits once and for all: A relapse prevention guide.* New York: Lexington.

Dane, B. (2000). Child welfare workers: An innovative approach for interacting with secondary trauma. *Journal of Social Work Education, 36*(1), 27–38.

Dane, B. O., & Simon, B. L. (1991). Resident guests: Social workers in host settings. *Social Work, 36*(3), 208–213.

Danish, J., D'Augelli, A., & Hauer, A. (1980). *Helping skills: A basic training program.* New York: Human Sciences Press.

Danzy, J., & Jackson, S. M. (1997). Family preservation and support services: A missed opportunity. *Child Welfare, 76*(1), 31.

Davidson, J. R., & Davidson, T. (1996). Confidentiality and managed care: Ethical and legal concerns. *Health and Social Work, 21*(3), 208–215.

Davis, B. (2005). Ms. Palmer on second street. *Social Work, 50*(1), 89–92.

Davis, L. E., & Gelsomino, J. (1994). An assessment of practitioner cross-racial treatment experiences. *Social Work, 39*(1), 116–123.

Davis, I. P., & Reid, W. J. (1988). Event analysis in clinical practice and process research. *Social Casework, 69*(5), 298–306.

Deal, K. H. (1999). Clinical social work students' use of self-disclosure: A case for formal training. *Arete, 23*(3), 33–45.

Deal, K. H., & Brintzenhofeszok-Szoc, K. M. (2004). A study of MSW students' interviewing skills over time. *Journal of Teaching in Social Work, 24*(1/2), 181–197.

Dean, R. G. (2001). The myth of cross-cultural competence. *Families in Society: The Journal of Contemporary Human Services, 82*(6), 623–630.

De Anda, D. (1984). Bicultural socialization: Factors affecting the minority experience. *Social Work, 29*, 172–181.

De Anda, D., & Becerra, R. (1984). Support networks for adolescent mothers. *Social Casework, 65*, 172–181.

De Angelis, D. (2000). Licensing really is about protection. *ASWB Association News, 10*(2), 11.

DeBord, K., Canu, R. F., & Kerpelman, J. (2000). Understanding a work-family fit for single parents moving from welfare to work. *Social Work, 45*(4) 313–324.

De Jong, P., & Berg, I. K. (1998). *Interviewing for solutions.* Pacific Grove, CA: Brooks/Cole.

De Jong, P. (2001). Solution-focused therapy. In A. R. Roberts & G. J. Greene (Eds.), *Social workers' desk reference* (pp. 112–115). New York: Oxford University Press.

De Jong, P., & Berg, I. K. (2001). Co-constructing cooperation with mandated clients. *Social Work, 46*(4), 361–374.

De Jong, P. & Berg, I. K. (2002). Lerner's workbook interviewing for solutions (2nd ed.). Pacific Grove, CA: Brooks/Cole, Thomson Learning.

De Jong, P., & Miller, S. D. (1995). How to interview for client strengths. *Social Work, 40*(6), 729–736.

Delgado, M. (1983). Activities and Hispanic groups: Issues and suggestions. *Social Work with Groups, 6*(1), 85–96.

DeLine, C. (2000). *The back door: An experiment or an alternative.* Alberta, Canada: The Back Door.

Denison, M. (2003). The PDR for mental health professionals. *Psychotherapy: Theory, Research, Practice, and Training, 40*(4), 317–318.

DePoy, E., & Gilson, S. F. (2003). *Evaluation practice. Thinking and action principles for social work practice.* Pacific Grove, CA: Brooks/Cole.

DePoy, E., Hartman, A., & Haslett, D. (1999). Critical Action Research: A model for social work knowing. *Social Work, 44*(6), 560–569.

Demer. S., Hemesath, C., & Russell, C. (1998). A feminist critique of solution-focused therapy. *The America Journal of Family Therapy, 26*, 239–250.

De Shazer, S. (1988). *Clues: Investigating solutions in brief therapy.* New York: Norton.

De Shazer, S., & Berg, I. K. (1993). Constructing solutions. *Family Therapy Networker, 12*, 42–43.

Devore, W., & Schlesinger, E. G. (1999). *Ethnic-sensitive social work practice* (5th ed.). Boston: Allyn & Bacon.

Dewayne, C. (1978). Humor in therapy. *Social Work, 23*(6), 508–510.

Di Clemente, C. C., & Prochaska, J. O. (1998). Toward a comprehensive transtheoretical model of change: stages of change and addictive behaviors. In W. R. Miller and N. Heather (Eds.), *Treating Addictive Behaviors* (2nd ed.) (pp. 3–24). New York: Plenum Press.

Dickson, D. T. (1998). *Confidentiality and privacy in social work.* New York: Free Press.

Dies, R. R. (1983). Clinical implications of research on leadership in short-term group psychotherapy. In R. R. Dies & R. McKenzie (Eds.), *Advances in group psychotherapy: Integrating research and practice* (American Group Psychotherapy Association Monograph Series) (pp. 27–28). New York: International Universities Press.

Dietz, C. (2000). Reshaping clinical practice for the new millennium. *Journal of Social Work Education, 36*(3), 503–520.

Dimidjian, S., & Linehan, M. M. (2003). Defining an agenda for future research on the clinical application of mindfulness practice. *Clinical Psychology: Science and Practice, 10*, 166–171.

Dobson, K. S., & Dozios, D. J. (2001). Historical and philosophical basis of cognitive behavioral therapies. In K.S. Dobson (Ed.). *Handbook of Cognitive therapies* (pp. 3–39). New York: Guildford Press.

Doherty, W. J. (1995). *Soul-searching: When psychotherapy must promote moral responsibility.* New York: Basic Books.

Dolan, S., Martin, R., & Rosenow, D. (2008). Self-efficacy for cocaine abstinence: pretreatment correlates and relationship to outcomes. *Addictive behaviors. 33*, 675–688.

Dolgoff, R., Loewenberg, F. M., & Harrington, D. (2005). *Ethical decisions for social work practice* (7th ed.). Itasca, IL: F.E. Peacock.

Dolgoff, R., Loewenberg, F. M., & Harrington, D. (2009). *Ethical decisions for social work practice* (7th ed.). Itasca, IL: F.E. Peacock.

Dore, M. M. (1993). The practice–teaching parallel in educating the micropractitioner. *Journal of Social Work Education, 29*(2), 181–190.

Dorfman, R. A. (1996). *Clinical social work: Definition, practice, and vision.* New York: Brunner/Mazel.

Dossick, J., & Shea, E. (1995). *Creative therapy III: 52 more exercises for groups.* Sarasota, FL: Professional Resource Press.

Doster, J., & Nesbitt, J. (1979). Psychotherapy and self-disclosure. In G. Chelunc & Associates (Eds.), *Self-disclosure* (pp. 177–224). San Francisco: Jossey-Bass.

Drisko, J. W. (2004). Common factors in psychotherapy outcome: Meta-analytic findings and their implications for practice and research. *Families in Society, Journal of Contemporary Social Sciences, 85*(1), 81–90.

Dubowitz, H., & DePanitilis, D. (2000). Handbook for child protection practice. Thousand Oaks, CA: Sage.

DuBray, W. (1985). American Indian values: Critical factors in casework. *Social Casework, 66,* 30–37.

Duehn, W., & Proctor, E. (1977). Initial clinical interactions and premature discontinuance in treatment. *American Journal of Orthopsychiatry, 47,* 284–290.

Duncan, B. L., & Miller, S. D. (2000). *The heroic client.* San Francisco: Jossey Bass.

Dunlap, E., Golub, A., & Johnson, B. D. (2006). The severely-distressed African American family in a crack-era: Empowerment is not enough. *Journal of Sociology and Social Welfare, 53*(1), 115–139.

Duvall, E. M. (1977). *Marriage and family development* (5th ed.). Philadelphia: Lippincott.

Dyche, L., & Zayas, L. H. (2001). Cross-cultural empathy and training the contemporary psychotherapist. *Clinical Social Work Journal, 29*(3), 245–258.

E

Eamon, M. K., & Zhang, S-J. (2006). Do social work students' assess and address economic barriers to clients implementing agreed task? *Journal of Social Work Education, 42*(3), 525–542.

Early, T. J., & GlenMaye, L. F. (2000). Valuing families: Social work practice with families from a strengths perspective. *Social Work, 45*(2), 118–130.

Educational Policy and Accreditation Standards (EPAS) (2008).

Eaton, T. T., Abeles, N., & Gutfreund, M. J. (1993). Negative indicators, therapeutic alliance, and therapy outcome. *Psychotherapy Research, 3*(2), 115–123.

Edwards, A. (1982). The consequences of error in selecting treatment for blacks. *Social Casework, 63,* 429–433.

Edwards, E. (1983). Native-American elders: Current issues and social policy implications. In R. McNeely &

J. Colen (Eds.), *Aging in minority groups.* Beverly Hills, CA: Sage Publications.

Edwards, E. (2007). *Saving Graces.* New York: Broadway.

Edwards, E. D., Edwards, M. E., Davies, G. M., & Eddy, F. (1987). Enhancing self-concept and identification of American Indian girls. *Social Work with Groups, 1*(3), 309–318.

Efran, J., & Schenker, M. (1993). A potpourri of solutions: How new and different is solution-focused therapy? *Family Therapy Networker, 17*(3), 71–74.

Ehrenreich, B. (2001). *Nickel and dimed. On (not) getting by in America.* New York: Metropolitan Books.

Ehrenreich, B. (2004, July 11). Let them eat cake. *The New York Times,* p. 3.

Elbow, M. (1987). The memory books: Facilitating termination with children. *Social Casework, 68,* 180–183.

Ell, K. (1995). Crisis intervention: Research needs. In E. L. Edwards (Ed.), *Encyclopedia of social work* (19th ed., pp. 660–667). Washington, DC: NASW Press.

Ellis, A. (1962). *Reason and emotion in psychotherapy.* New York: Lyle Stuart.

Ellis, A. (1978). Family therapy: A phenomenological and active-directive approach. *Journal of Marriage and Family Counseling, 4,* 43–50.

Ellis, A. (2001). *Overcoming destructive beliefs, feelings, and behaviors: New directions for rational emotive behavior therapy.* Amherst, NY: Prometheus.

Ellis, R. A., & Sowers, K. M. (2001). Juvenile justice practice. *A cross disciplinary approach to intervention.* Brooks/Cole- Thomson Learning.

Ellor, J. W., Netting, F. E., & Thibault, J. M. (1999). *Religious and spiritual aspects of human service practice.* Columbia, SC: University of South Carolina Press.

Enos, S. (2008). Incarcerated parents: Interrupted childhood. Children of Incarcerated Parents, Conference Proceedings, Spring 2008, Center for Advanced Studies in Child Welfare, University of Minnesota.

Ensign, J. (1998). Health issues of homeless youth. *Journal of Social Distress and the Homeless, 7*(3), 159–174.

Ephross, P. H., & Vassil, T. V. (1988). *Groups that work: Structure and process.* New York: Columbia University Press.

Epstein, H. (2003, October 12). Enough to make you sick. *The New York Times Magazine,* pp. 76–86.

Epstein, L. (1992). *Brief treatment and a new look at the task-centered approach* (3rd ed.). Boston: Allyn & Bacon.

Epstein, L., & Brown, L. B. (2002). *Brief treatment and a new look at the task-centered approach* (4th ed.). Boston: Allyn & Bacon.

Epstein, R. S., Simon, R. I., & Kay, G. G. (1992). Assessing boundary violations in psychotherapy: Survey results with the Exploitation Index. *Bulletin of the Menninger Foundation, 56*(2), 150–166.

Erford, B. T. (2003). Transforming the school counseling profession. Upper Saddle, NJ: Merrill Prentice Hall.

Erickson, S. H. (2001). Multiple relationships in rural counseling. *The Family Journal: Counseling and Therapy for Couples and Families, 9*(3), 302–304.

Etherington, K. (2000). Supervising counselors who work with survivors of childhood sexual abuse. *Counseling Psychology Quarterly, 13*, 377–389.

Evans, T. (2004). A multidimensional assessment of children with chronic physical conditions. *Health and Social Work. 29*(3), 245–248.

Ewalt, P. L., & Mokuau, N. (1996). Self-determination from a Pacific perspective. In P. L. Ewalt, E. M. Freeman, S. A. Kirk, & D. L. Poole (Eds.), *Multicultural issues in social work* (pp. 255–268). Washington, DC: NASW Press.

Ewing J. A. (1984). Detecting alcoholism: The CAGE questionnaire. *Journal of the American Medical Association. 252*(14). 1905–1907.

Ezell, M. (2001). *Advocacy in the human services.* Thousand Oaks, CA: Brooks/Cole, Thomson Learning.

F

Falicov, C. (1996). Mexican families. In M. McGoldrick, J. Giordano, & J. Pearce (Eds.), *Ethnicity and family therapy* (2nd ed.) (pp. 169–182). New York: Gullford Press.

Fallot, R. D., & Harris, M. (2002). The Trauma Recovery and Empowerment Model (TREM): Conceptual and practical issues in a group intervention for women. *Community Mental Health Journal, 38*, 475–485.

Farmer, R. L. (1999) Clinical HBSE concentration: A transactional model. *Journal of Social Work Education, 35*(2), 289–299.

Farrington, A. (1995). Suicide and psychological debriefing. *British Journal of Nursing, 4*(4), 209–211.

Fast, J. D. (2003). After Columbine: How people mourn sudden death. *Social Work, 48*(4), 484–491.

Fauri, D. P., Harrigan, M. P., & Netting, F. E. (1998). Termination: Extending the concept for Macro Social Work practice. *Journal of Sociology and Social Welfare 25*(4), 61–80.

Fauth, J. (2006). Counselors' stress appraisals as predictors of countertransference behavior with male clients. *Journal of Counseling and Development, 84*(4), 430–439.

Fearing, J. (1996). The changing face of intervention. *Behavioral Health Management, 16*, 35–37.

Feeny, S. L. (2004). The cognitive behavioral treatment of social phobia. *Clinical Case Studies, 3*(2), 124–146.

Feltenstein, M. W. (2008). The neurocircuitry of addiction: An overview. *British Journal of Pharmacology 154*(2), 261–274.

Ferguson, K. M. (2007). Implementing a social enterprise intervention with homeless, street-living youth in Los Angeles. *Social Work, 52*(2), 103–112.

Fernandez, M. (October 15, 2007). Study finds disparities in mortgages by race. *The New York Times*, A20.

Fernandez-Olano, C., Montoya-Fernandez, J. & Salinas-Sanchez, A. (2008). Impact of clinical interview training on the empathy level of medical students and medical residents. *Medical teacher, 30*(3): 322–324.

Figley, C. R. (Ed.). (1995). Compassion fatigue: Dealing with secondary traumatic stress disorder in those who treat the traumatized. New York: Bunner-Mazel.

Figley. C. R. (Ed.). (2002). *Treating compassion fatigue.* New York: Brunner-Rutledge.

Finn, J. L., & Jacobson, M. (2003a). Just practice: Steps toward a new social work paradigm. *Journal of Social Work Education, 39*(1), 57–78.

Finn, J. L., & Jacobson, M. (2003b). *Just practice: A social justice approach to social work.* Peosta, IA: Eddie Bowers.

Fingeld, D. (2000). Therapeutic groups online: The good, the bad, and the unknown. *Issues in Mental Health Nursing, 21*, 241–255.

Fischer, J. (1973). Is casework effective? A review. *Social Work, 18*, 5–20.

Fischer, J. (1978). *Effective casework practice: An eclectic approach.* New York: McGraw-Hill.

Fischer, J. & Corcoran, K. (2006). *Measures for Clinical Practice and Research: Couples, families, and Children: A sourcebook, Vol. 1 (4th ed)*. Oxford University Press.

Fischer, J. & Corcoran, K. (2007). *Measures for Clinical Practice and Research: Adults: A sourcebook, Vol. 2 (4th ed)*. Oxford University Press.

Flapan, D., & Fenchal, G. (1987). *The developing ego and the emerging self in group therapy.* Northvale, NJ: Aronson.

Flores, M. T., & Carey, G. (2000). *Family therapy with Hispanics: Toward appreciating diversity*. Boston: Allyn & Bacon.

Fong, R. (1997). Child welfare practice with Chinese families: Assessment issues for immigrants from the People's Republic China. *Journal of Family Social Work, 2*(1), 33–47.

Fong, L. G. W., & Gibbs, J. T. (1995). Facilitating service to multicultural communities in a dominant culture setting. An organizational perspective. *Administration in Social Work, 19*(2), 1–24.

Fontes, L. A. (2005). *Child abuse and culture. Working with diverse families*. New York: Guilford Press.

Fortune, A. E. (1985). Treatment groups. In A. E. Fortune (Ed.), *Task-centered practice with families and groups* (pp. 33–44). New York: Springer.

Fortune, A., Pearlingi, B., & Rochelle, C. D. (1992). Reactions to termination of individual treatment. *Social Work, 37*(2), 171–178.

Fowler, R. C., Rich, C. L., & Young, D. C. (1986). San Diego suicide study, II: Substance abuse in young cases. *Archives of General Psychiatry, 43*, 962–965.

Frager, S. (2000). *Managing managed care: Secrets from a former case manager*. New York: Wiley.

Frankenburg, W. K., Dodds, J., Archer, P., Shapiro, H., & Bresnick, B. (1992). The Denver II: A Major Revision and Restandardization of the Denver Developmental Screening Test. *Pediatrics, 89*, 91–97.

Franklin, C. (2002). Developing effective practice competencies in managed behavioral health care. In Roberts, A. R. & Greene, G. J. (Eds.) *Social workers desk reference*, (pp. 3–10). New York: Oxford.

Franklin, D. L. (1990). The cycles of social work practice: Social action vs. individual interest. *Journal of Progressive Human Services, 1*(2), 59–80.

Franklin, C., & Streeter, C. L. (2004). *Solution-focused alternatives for education: An outcome evaluation of Garza High School*. Retrieved December 11, 2008, from http://www.utexas.edu.libproxy.lib.unc.edu/courses/franklin/safed_report_final.doc

Freddolino, P., Moxley, D., and Hyduk, C. (2004). A differential model of advocacy in social work practice. *Families in Society, 85*(1), 119–128.

Fredriksen, K.I. (1999). Family caregiving responsibilities among lesbians and gay men. *Social Work, 44*(2), 142–155.

Fredriksen-Goldsen, K. I., & Scharlach, A. E. (2001). Families and work. *New Directions in the Twenty-First Century*. Oxford University Press.

Freed, A. (1988). Interviewing through an interpreter. *Social Work, 33*, 315–319.

Freedberg, S. (2007). Re-examining empathy: A relational-feminist point of view. *Social work 52*(3): 251–259.

Freeman, E. M., & Dyers, L. (1993). High risk children and adolescents: Families and community environments. *Families in Society, 74*(7), 422–431.

Freud, S. (1999). The social construction of normality. *Families in Society, 80*(4), 333–339.

Frey, G. A. (1990). Framework for promoting organizational change. *Families in Society, 7*(3), 142–147.

Frey, A. and Dupper, D., (2005). A broader conceptional approach to clinical practice for the 21st century. *Children and Schools, 29*(1), 33–44.

From, S. B. (2008) When mom is away: Supporting families or incarcerated mothers. Children of Incarcerated Parents, Conference Proceedings, Spring 2008, Center for Advanced Studies in Child Welfare, University of Minnesota.

Fullerton, C. D., & Ursano, R. J. (2005). *Psychological and psychopathological consequences of disasters*. In. J. J. Lopez-Ibor, G. Christodoulou, M. Maj, N. Sartorius & A. Okasha (Eds.), Disaster and mental health (pp. 25–49) New York: Wiley.

G

Gabbard, G. O. (1996). Lessons to be learned from the study of sexual boundary violations. *American Journal of Psychotherapy, 50*(3), 311–322.

Galinsky, M. J., & Schopler, J. H. (1989). Developmental patterns in open-ended groups. *Social Work with Groups, 12*(2), 99–114.

Galinsky, M. J., Terzian, M. A., & Fraser, M. W. (2006). The art of group work practice with manualized curricula. *Social Work with Groups, 29*, 11–26.

Galinsky, M. J., Turnbull, J. E., Meglin, D. E., & Wilner, M. E. (1993). Confronting the reality of collaborative practice research: Issues of practice, design, measurement, and team development. *Social Work, 38*(4), 440–449.

Gallo, J. J. (2005). Activities of Daily Living and Instrumental Activities of Daily Living Assessment. In J. J. Gallo, H. R. Bogner, T. Fulmer, & G. Paveza (Eds.), *Handbook of geriatric assessment* (4th ed., 193–234). Boston: Jones and Bartlett Publishers.

Gallo, J. J., & Bogner, H. R. (2005). The context of geriatric care. In J. J. Gallo, H. R. Bogner, T. Fulmer, & G. Paveza (Eds.), *Handbook of geriatric assessment* (4th ed., 3–14). Boston: Jones and Bartlett Publishers.

Gallo, J. J., Bogner, H. R., Fulmer, T., & Paveza, J. (Eds.). (2005). *Handbook of geriatric assessment* (4th ed.). Sudbury, MA: Jones and Bartlett Publishers.

Gallo, J. J., Fulmer, T., Paveza, G. J., & Reichel, W. (2000). Mental status assessment. In *Handbook of geriatric assessment* (3rd ed., pp. 29–99). Gaithersburg, MD: Aspen.

Gambrill, E. (1995). Behavioral social work: Past, present and future. *Research on Social Work Practice, 5*(4), 466–484.

Gambrill, E. (2004). Contributions of critical thinking and evidence-based practice to the fulfillment of the ethical obligation of professions. In H. Briggs, and T. Rzepnicki (Eds.), *Using evidence in social work practice.* (3–19). Chicago: Lyceum.

Gambrill, E. (2007). Views of evidence-based practice: Social workers' Code of Ethics and accreditation standards as guides for choice. *Journal of Social Work Education, 43,* 447–462.

Garcia Coll, C., Akerman, A. & Cichetti, D. (2000). Cultural influences on developmental processes and outcomes: Implicatons for the study of development and psychopathology. *Development and Psychopathology, 12,* 333–356.

Garcia Coll, C. T., Lamberty, G., Jenkins, R., McAdoo, H. P., Crnic, K., Wasik. B. H., & Vasquez Garcia, H. (1996). An integrative model for the study of developmental competencies in minority children. *Child Development, 67,* 1891–1914.

Gardner, F. (2000). Design Evaluation: Illuminating social work practice for better outcomes. *Social Work, 45*(2), 176–182.

Garland, J., Jones, H., & Kolodny, R. (1965). A model for stages in the development of social work groups. In S. Bernstein (Ed.), *Explorations in group work.* Boston: Milford House.

Gartrell, N. K. (1992). Boundaries in lesbian therapy relationships. *Women & Therapy, 12*(3), 29–50.

Gaudiano, B. A., & Herbert, J. D. (2006). Self-efficacy for social situations in adolescents with generalized social anxiety disorder. *Behavioral and Cognitive Psychotherapy, 35,* 209–223.

Gavin, D. R., Ross, H. E., & Skinner, H. A. (1989). Diagnostic validity of the Drug Abuse Screening Test in the assessment of DSM-III drug disorders. *British Journal of Addiction 84* (3): 301–307.

Garvin, C. (1981). *Contemporary group work.* Englewood Cliffs, NJ: Prentice-Hall.

Garvin, C. (1986). Family therapy and group work: "Kissing cousins or distant relatives" in social work practice. In M. Parnes (Ed.), *Innovations in social group work: feedback from practice to theory: proceedings of the annual group work symposium* (p. 1–16). NY: Haworth Press.

Garvin, C. (1987). *Contemporary group work* (2nd ed.). Englewood Cliffs, NJ: Prentice-Hall.

Garvin, C. D., & Galinsky, M. J. "Groups" *Encyclopedia of Social Work.* Terry Mizrahi. *Copyright © 2008 by National Association of Social Workers and Oxford University Press, Inc..* Encyclopedia of Social Work: (e-reference edition). Oxford University Press. University of North Carolina - Chapel Hill. 15 June 2008 http://www.oxford-naswsocialwork.com/entry?entry=t203.e167

Gelman, C. R. (2004). Empirically-based principles for culturally competent practice with Latinos. *Journal of Ethnic and Cultural Diversity in Social Work, 13*(1), 83–108.

Gelman, C. R., & Mirabito, D. M. (2005). Practicing what we teach: Using case studies from 911 to teach crisis intervention from a generalist perspective. *Journal of Social Work Education, 4,* 479–494.

Gelman, S. R., Pollack, D., & Weiner, A. (1999). Confidentiality of social work records in the computer age. *Social Work, 44*(3), 243–252.

Gendlin, E. (1974). Client-centered and experiential psychotherapy. In D. Wexler & L. Rice (Eds.), *Innovations in client-centered therapy.* New York: Wiley.

Gendolla, G. H. E. (2004). The intensity of motivation when the self is involved: An application of Brehm's Theory of Motivation to effort-related cardiovascular response. In R. Wright, J. Greenberg & S. S. Brehm (Eds.). Motivational analysis of social behavior (pp. 205–224). Lawrence Erlbaum Associates Publishers.

Gendron, C., Poitras, L., Dastoor, D. P., & Perodeau, G. (1996). Cognitive-behavioral group intervention for spousal caregivers: Findings and clinical observations. *Clinical Gerontologist, 17*(1), 3–19.

Genty, P. M. (2008). The inflexibility of the Adoption and Safe Family Act and the inintended impact upon the children of incarcerated parents and their families. Children of Incacerated Parents, Conference Proceedings, Spring 2008, Center for Advanced Studies in Child Welfare, University of Minnesota.

George, L., & Fillenbaum, G. (1990). OARS methodology: A decade of experience in geriatric assessment. *Journal of the American Geriatrics Society, 33,* 607–615.

Germain, C. (1979). Ecology and social work. In C. Germain (Ed.), *Social work practice: People and environments* (pp. 1–2). New York: Columbia University Press.

Germain, C. (1981). The ecological approach to people–environmental transactions. *Social Case-Work, 62,* 323–331.

Gerstel, N., Bogard, C. J., McConnell, J. J., & Schwartz, M. (1996). The therapeutic incarceration of homeless families. *Social Service Review, 70*(4), 542–572.

Getzel, G. S. (1991). Survival modes for people with AIDS in groups. *Social Work, 36*(1), 7–11.

Getzel, G. S. (1998). Group work practice with gay men and lesbians. In G. P. Mallon (Ed.), *Foundations of social work practice with lesbian and gay persons* (pp. 131–144). Binghamton, NY: Haworth Press.

Giacola, P. R., Mezzich, A. C., Clark, D. B., & Tarter, R. E. (1999). Cognitive distortions, aggressive behaviors and drug use in adolescent boys with and without prior family history. *Psychology of Addictive Behavior, 13*, 22–32.

Giannandrea, V., & Murphy, K. (1973). Similarity of self-disclosure and return for a second interview. *Journal of Counseling Psychology, 20*, 545–548.

Gibbs, J. (1995). *Tribes: A new way of learning and being together.* Sausalito, CA: Center Source Systems.

Gibson, P. A. (1999). African American grandmothers: New mothers again. *Affilia, 14*(3), 329–343.

Gilbar, O. (1992). Workers' sick fund (kupat holim) hotline therapeutic first intervention: A model developed in the Gulf War. *Social Work in Health Care, 17*(4), 45–57.

Gilbert, N. (1977). The search for professional identity. *Social Work, 22*, 401–406.

Gilbert, D. J. (2003). Multicultural assessment. In C. Jordan & C. Franklin (Eds.), *Clinical assessment for social workers: Quantitative and qualitative methods* (2nd ed., pp. 351–383). Chicago: Lyceum Books.

Gilgun, J. F. (1994). Hand to glove: The grounded theory approach and social work practice research. In L. Sherman & W. J. Reid (Eds.), *Qualitative research in social work* (pp. 115–125). New York: Columbia University Press.

Gilgun, J. F. (1999). CASPARS: New tools for assessing client risks and strengths. *Families in Society, 80*(5), 450–458.

Gilgun, J. F. (2001). CASPARS: New tools for assessing client risks and strengths. *Families and Society: The Journal of Contemporary Human Services, 82*, 450–459.

Gingerich, W. J., & Eisengart, S. (2000). Solution-focused brief treatment. A review of outcome research. *Family Process, 39*, 477–498.

Gingerich, W. J., & Wabeke, T. (2001). A solution-focused approach to mental health interventions in school settings. *Children in Schools, 23*(1), 33–47.

Gira, E., Kessler, M., & Poertner, J. (2001). *Evidence-based practice in child welfare.* Urbana-Champaign, ILL: University of Illinois at Urbana-Champaign.

Gitterman, A. (1996). Ecological perspectives: Response to Professor Jerry Wakefield. *Social Service Review, 70*(3), 472–476.

Giunta, C. T., & Streissguth, A. P. (1988). Patients with fetal alcohol syndrome and their caretakers. *Social Casework, 69*(7), 453–459.

Glancy, G., & Saini, M. (2005). An evidence-based review of psychological treatment of anger and aggression. *Brief Treatment and Crisis Intervention, 5*(2), 229–248.

Glisson, C. (1994). The effects of service coordination teams on outcomes for children in state custody. *Administration in Social Work, 18*(4), 1–25.

Global standards for social work education and training. (2004). International Association of Schools of Social Work and International Federation of Social Workers. Final document for discussion and adoption at the General Assemblies, Adelaide, Australia.

Golan, N. (1978). *Treatment in crisis situations.* New York: Free Press.

Golan, N. (1981). *Passing through transitions: A guide for the practitioners.* New York: Free Press.

Gold, M. (1986, November). (As quoted by Earl Ubell.) Is that child bad or depressed? *Parade Magazine, 2*, 10.

Gold, N. (1990). Motivation: The crucial but unexplored component of social work practice. *Social Work, 35*, 49–56.

Goldenberg, I., & Goldenberg, H. (1991). *Family therapy: An overview* (3rd ed.). Pacific Grove, CA: Brooks/Cole.

Goldenberg, I., & Goldenberg, H. (2000). *Family therapy: An overview* (5th ed.). Pacific Grove, CA: Brooks/Cole.

Goldenberg, I., & Goldenberg, H., (2004). *Family therapy: An overview* (6th ed.). Pacific Grove, CA: Brooks/Cole.

Goldfried, M. (1977). The use of relaxation and cognitive re-labeling as coping skills. In R. Stuart (Ed.), *Behavioral self-management* (pp. 82–116). New York: Brunner/Mazel.

Goldstein, E. G. (1997). To tell or not to tell: The disclosure of events in the therapist's life to the patient. *Clinical Social Work Journal, 25*(1), 41–58.

Goodman, H. (1997). Social group work in community corrections. *Social Work with Groups, 20*(1), 51–64.

Goodman, H., Getzel, G. S., & Ford, W. (1996). Group work with high-risk urban youths on probation. *Social Work, 41*(4), 375–381.

Goodwin, D. W., & Gabrielli, W. F. (1997). Alcohol: Clinical aspects. In J. H. Lowinson, P. Ruiz, R. B. Millman, & J. G. Langrod (Eds.), *Substance abuse: A comparative textbook* (3rd ed., pp. 142–148). Baltimore, MD: Williams & Wilkins.

Gordon, W. (1965). Toward a social work frame of reference. *Journal of Education for Social Work, 1*, 19–26.

Gordon, T. (1970). *Parent effectiveness training*. New York: P. H. Wyclen.

Gottesfeld, M., & Lieberman, F. (1979). The pathological therapist. *Social Casework, 60*, 387–393.

Goyer, A. (2006). *Intergenerational relationships: Grandparents raising grandchildren*. Policy and Research Report, American Association of Retired Persons.

Graham, P (1998). *Cognitive behavior therapy for children and families*. Cambridge: Cambridge University Press.

Graham, J. R., & Barter, K. (1999). Collaboration: A social work practice method. *Families in Society, 80*(1), 6–13.

Grame, C., Tortorici, J., Healey, B., Dillingham, J., & Wilklebaur, P. (1999). Addressing spiritual and religious issues of clients with a history of psychological trauma. *Bulletin of the Menninger Clinic, 63*(2), 223–239.

Green, J. W. (1999). *Cultural awareness in the human services: A multi-ethnic approach*. Boston: Allyn & Bacon.

Green, J. P., Duncan, R. E., Barnes, G. L., & Oberklaid, F. (2003). Putting informed into consent: A matter of plain language. *Journal of Pediatric Child Health, 39*, 700–703.

Green, R. G., Kiernan-Stern, M., & Baskind, F. R. (2005). White social worker's attitudes about people of color. *Journal of Ethnic and Cultural Diversity in Social Work, 14*(1/2), 47–68.

Greene, A. D. & Latting, J. K. (2004). Whistle-blowing as a form of advocacy: Guidelines for the practitioner and the organization. *Social Work, 49*(2), 219–230.

Greene, G. J., Lee, M. Y., & Hoffpauir, S. (2005). The language of empowerment and strengths in clinical social work: A constructivist perspective. *Families in Society, 86*(2), 267–277.

Greenberg, M. (2007). *Making poverty history*. Ending Poverty in America, Special Report of The American Prospect, The Annie E. Casey Foundation & The Northwest Area Foundation. A3–A4.

Greenberg, J., & Tyler, T. R. (1987). Why procedural justice in organizations. *Social Justice Research, 1*(2). 127–143.

Greenfield, P. M. (1994). Independence and interdependence as developmental scripts: Implications for theory, research and practice. In P. M. Greenfield & R. R. Cocking (Eds.), *Cross-cultural roots of minority child development* (pp. 1–24). Hillsdale, NJ: Lawrence Erlbaum Associates.

Gross, E. (1995). Deconstructing politically correct practice literature: The American Indian case. *Social Work, 40*(2), 206–213.

Grote, N. K., Zuckoff, A., Swartz, H., Bledsoe, S. E., & Geibel, S. (2007). Engaging women who are depressed and economically disadvantaged in mental health treatment. *Social Work, 53*(4), 295–308.

Guadalupe, K. L., & Lum, D. (2005). *Multidimensional contextual practice. Diversity and transcendence*. Thomson-Brooks/Cole.

Gulati, P., & Guest, G. (1990). The community-centered model: A garden variety approach or a radical transformation of community practice? *Social Work, 35*(1), 63–68.

Gumpert, J., & Saltman, J. E. (1998). Social group work practice in rural areas: The practitioners speak. *Social Work with Groups, 21*(3), 19–34.

Gutierrez, L. M. (1994). Beyond coping: an empowerment perspective on stressful life events. *Journal of Sociology and Social Welfare, 21*(3), 201–219.

Guiterrez, L., GlenMaye, L., & Delois, K. (1995). The organizational context of empowerment practice: Implications for social work in administration. *Social Work, 40*, 249–258.

Gutierrez, L. M., & Lewis, E. A. (1999). Strengthening communities through groups: A multicultural perspective. In H. Bertcher, L. F. Kurtz, & A. Lamont (Eds.), *Rebuilding communities: Challenges for group work* (pp. 5–16). New York: Haworth Press.

Gutierrez, L. M., & Ortega, R. (1991). Developing methods to empower Latinos: The importance of groups. *Social Work with Groups, 14*(2), 23–43.

Gutierrez, L. M., Parsons, R. J., & Cox, E. O. (1998). *Empowerment in social work practice: A sourcebook*. Pacific Grove, CA: Brooks/Cole.

Gurman, A. (1977). The patient's perception of the therapeutic relationship. In A. Gutman & A. Razin (Eds.), *Effective psychotherapy: A handbook of research*. New York: Pergamon Press.

H

Hackman, J. R., & Oldham, G. R. (1976). Motivation through the design of work: Test of a theory. *Organizational Behavior and Human Performance, 16*, 250–279.

Hackman, J. R., & Oldham, G. R. (1980). *Work design*. Reading, MA: Addison-Wesley.

Hackney, H., & Cormier, L. (1979). *Counseling strategies and objectives* (2nd ed.), Englewood Cliffs, NJ: Prentice-Hall.

Hage, D. (2004). *Reforming welfare by rewarding work.* Minneapolis: University of Minnesota Press.

Haight, W. L. (1998). Gathering the spirit at First Baptist Church: Spirituality as a protective factor in the lives of African American children. *Social Work, 43*(3), 213–221.

Hall, E.T. (1976). *Beyond culture.* New York: Anchor Press.

Halpern, R. (1990). Poverty and early childhood parenting: Toward a framework for intervention. *American Journal of Orthopsychiatry, 60*(1), 6–18.

Halpern, J., & Tramontin, M. (2007). Disaster. Mental health theory and practice. Thomson-Brooks/Cole.

Hammond, D., Hepworth, D., & Smith, V. (1977). *Improving therapeutic communication.* San Francisco: Jossey-Bass.

Hand, C. A. (2006). An Ojibwe perspective on the welfare of children: Lessons of the past and visions for the future. *Children Youth and Services Review, 28,* 20–46.

Handmaker, N. S., Miller, W. R., & Manicke, M. (1999). Findings of a pilot study of motivational interviewing with pregnant drinkers. *Journal of Studies on Alcohol, 60,* 285–287.

Hankin, B. L., Abramson, L. Y., Moffitt, T. E., Silva, P. A., McGee, R., & Angell, K. E. (1998). Development of depression from preadolescence to young adulthood: Emerging gender differences in a 10-year longitudinal study. *Journal of Abnormal Psychology, 107,* 128–140.

Hannah, G. (2006). Maintaining product-Process balance in community anti-poverty initiatives. *Social Work, 51*(2), 9–17.

Hardina, D. (2004). Guidelines for ethical practice in community organization. *Social Work, 49*(4), 595–604.

Hardy, K. (1993). War of the worlds. *The Family Therapy Networker,* 51–57.

Hare, J. (1994). Concerns and issues faced by families headed by a lesbian couple. *Families in Society, 75*(1), 27–35.

Harper, K. V., & Lantz, J. (1996). *Cross-cultural practice.* Chicago: Lyceum Books.

Harris, J. (1999). First steps in telecollaboration. *Learning and Leading with Technology, 27,* 54–57.

Harris, M., & Franklin, C. (2003). Effects of cognitive-behavioral, school-based group intervention with Mexican American pregnant and parenting adolescents. *Social Work Research, 27,* 74–84.

Hart-Hester, S. (2004). Elderly suicides: A need for prevention. *The Internet Journal of Mental Health. 2,* Retrieved July 2, 2008, from http://www.ispub.com/ostia/index.php?xmlFilePath=journals/ijmh/vol2n1/suicide.xml

Hartford, M. (1971). *Groups in social work.* New York: Columbia University Press.

Hartman, A. (1981). The family: A central focus for practice. *Social Work, 26,* 7–13.

Hartman, A. (1990). Many ways of knowing. *Social Work, 35,* 3–4.

Hartman, A. (1991). Social worker in situation. *Social Work, 36,* 195–196.

Hartman, A. (1993). The professional is political. *Social Work, 38*(4), 365, 366, 504.

Hartman, A. (1994). Diagrammatic assessment of family relationships. In B. R. Compton & B. Galaway (Eds.), *Social work processes* (5th ed., pp. 153–165). Pacific Grove, CA: Brooks/Cole.

Hartman, A., & Laird, J. (1983). *Family centered social work practice.* New York: Free Press.

Hasenfeld, Y., & Furman, W. M. (1994). Intervention research as an interorganizational exchange. In J. Rothman & E. Thomas (Eds.), *Intervention research: Design for human services* (pp. 297–313). New York: Haworth Press.

Hathaway, S. R. & McKinley, J. C. (1989). *MMPI–2 manual for administration and scoring.* Minneapolis: University of Minnesota Press.

Hawthorne, F. (2007, October, 23). Greater obstacles to retirement for women. *The New York Times,* Special Section, Retirement, p. H13.

Haynes, R., Corey, G., & Moulton, P. (2003). *Clinical supervision in the helping professions: A practical guide.* Pacific Grove, CA: Thomson, Brooks/Cole.

Haynes, K. S., & Mickelson, J. S. (2000). *Affecting change: Social workers in the political arena* (4th ed.). Boston: Allyn & Bacon.

Healey, M. (2007, September 27). Fact check: Children's health insurance. *Star Tribune,* p. A1.

Healy, L. M. (2007). Universalism and cultural relativism in social work ethics. *International Social Work, 50,* 11–26.

Hegar, R. (1999). The cultural roots of kinship care. In R. Hegar & M. Scannapieco (Eds.), *Kinship foster care, policy, practice, and research* (pp. 17–27). New York: Oxford University Press.

Henry, M. (1988). Revisiting open groups. *Group Work, 1,* 215–228.

Henry, S. (1992). *Group skills in four-dimensional approach* (2nd ed.). Pacific Grove, CA: Brooks/Cole.

Hernandez, M., & McGoldrick, M. (1999). Migration and the life cycle. In B. Carter & M. McGoldrick (Eds.), *The expanded family life cycle: Individual, family, and social perspectives* (3rd ed., pp. 169–184). Boston: Allyn & Bacon.

Hersen, M. and Thomas, J. (Eds). (2007). *Handbook of clinical interviewing with children.* Thousand Oaks, CA: Sage.

Hess, P. M., & Mullen, E. J. (1995). Bridging the gap. Collaborative considerations in practitioner–researcher knowledge-building partnerships. In P. M. Hess & E. J. Mullen (Eds.), *Practitioner–researcher partnerships* (pp. 1–30). Washington, DC: NASW Press.

Hill, B., Rotegard, L., & Bruininks, R. (1984). The quality of life of mentally retarded people in residential care. *Social Work, 29,* 275–281.

Hillier, A. (2007). Why social work needs mapping. *Journal of Social Work Education, 43*(2), 205–221.

Hines, P. H., Preto, N. G., McGoldrick, M., Almeida, R., & Weltman, S. (1999). Culture and the family life cycle. In B. Carter & M. McGoldrick (Eds.), *The expanded family life cycle. Individual, family and social perspectives* (3rd ed.). Needham Heights, Boston: Allyn & Bacon.

HIPAA medical privacy rule. (2003). Retrieved May 1, 2004, from http://www.socialworkers.org/hipaa/medical.asp.

Hirayama, K. K., Hirayama, H., & Cetingok, M. (1993). Mental health promotion for South East Asian refugees in the USA. *International Social Work, 36*(2), 119–129.

Ho, M. (1987). *Family therapy with ethnic minorities.* Newbury Park, CA: Sage.

Hodge, D. R. (2004). Working with Hindu clients in a spiritually sensitive manner. *Social Work, 49*(1), 27–38.

Hodge, D. R. (2005). Spiritual lifemaps: A client-centered pictorial instrument for spiritual assessment, planning and intervention. *Social Work, 50*(1), 77–87.

Hodge, D. R. (2007), Social justice and people of faith: A transnational perspective. *Social Work, 52*(2), 139–148.

Hodge, D. R., & Nadir, A. (2008). Moving toward culturally competent practice with Muslims: Modifying cognitive therapy with Islamic tenets. *Social Work* 53(1), 31–41.

Hoehn-Saric, R., Frank, J., Imber, S., Nash, E., Stone, A., & Battle, C. (1964). Systematic preparation of patients for psychotherapy—I. Effects on therapy behavior and outcome. *Journal of Psychiatric Research, 2,* 267–281. *Social Casework, 62,* 30–39.

Holbrook, T. L. (1995). Finding subjugated knowledge: Personal document research. *Social Work, 40*(6), 746–750.

Holland, S. (2000). The assessment relationship: Interaction between social workers and parents in child protection assessment. *British Journal of Social Work, 30,* 149–163.

Hollander, E. M. (2001). Cyber community in the valley of the shadow of death. *Journal of Loss and Trauma, 6,* 136–146.

Hollis, F. and Woods, M. (1981). *Casework: a psychosocial therapy* (3rd ed.). New York: Random House.

Holt, B. J. (2000). *The practice of generalist case management.* Needham Heights, MA: Allyn & Bacon

Homan, M. S. (1999). *Promoting community change: Making it happen in the real world* (2nd ed.). Brooks/Cole.

Homan, M. S. (2008). *Promoting community change. Making it happen in the real world* (4th ed.). Thomson Brooks/Cole.

Homeless Youth, National Coalition for the Homeless, NCH Fact Sheet # 13. Retrieved July 16, 2008, from http://www.nationalhomeless.org.

Hopfensperger, J. (2007, July 21). Divided by deportation, families ask why. *Star Tribune.* A1&A12.

Horesji, C., Heavy Runner, B., & Pablo, C. J. (1992). Reactions by Native American parents to child protection agencies: Cultural and community factors. *Child Welfare, 71*(4), 329–342.

Houston-Vega, M. K., Nuehring, E. M., & Daguio, E. R. (1997). *Prudent practice: A guide for managing malpractice risk.* Washington, DC: NASW Press.

Howard, M., Allen-Meares, P., & Ruffolo, M. (2007). Teaching Evidence-Based Practice: Strategic and Pedagogical Recommendations for Schools of Social Work; *Research on Social Work Practice*; *17,* 561–568.

Hoyt, M. F. (2000). *Some stories are better than others: Doing what works in brief therapy and managed care.* Philadelphia, PA.: Brunner/Mazel.

Hubble, M. A., Duncan, B. L., & Miller, S. D. (1999). Introduction. In M. A. Hubble, B. L. Duncan, & S. D. Miller (Eds.). *The heart and soul of change: What works in therapy.* Washington, DC: American Psychological Association.

Hudson, W. W. (1990). Computer-based clinical practice: Present status and future possibilities. In L. Videka-Sherman, & W. H. Reid (Eds.), *Advances in clinical social work research* (pp. 105–117). Silver Springs, MD: NASW Press.

Hudson, W. (1992). *The WALMYR assessment scales scoring manual.* Tempe, AZ: WALMYR.

Hudson, W. W. (1996). Computer assessment package. Tallahassee, FL: WALMYR.

Hudson, W., & McMurtry, S. L. (1997). Comprehensive assessment in social work practice: A multi-problem screening inventory. *Research of Social Work Practice, 7*(1), 79–88.

Huffine, C. (Summer, 2006). Bad conduct, defiance, and mental health. *Focal Point, 20*(2), 13–16.

Hulewat, P. (1996). Resettlement: A cultural and psychological crisis. *Social Work, 41*(2), 129–135.

Hull, G. Jr. (1982). Child welfare services to Native Americans. *Social Casework, 63,* 340–347.

Hunsley, J., Aubrey, T., Vestervelt, C. M., & Vito, D. (1999). Comparing therapist and client perspectives on reasons for psychotherapy termination. *Psychotherapy, 36*(4), 380–388.

Hurdle, D. E. (2002). Native Hawaiian traditional healing. *Social Work, 47*(2), 183–192.

Hurley, D. J. (1984). Resistance and work in adolescent groups. *Social Work with Groups, 1,* 71–81.

Hurvitz, N. (1975). Interactions hypothesis in marriage counseling. In A. Gutman & D. Rice (Eds.), *Couples in conflict* (pp. 225–240). New York: Jason Aronson.

Hutchison, E. (2003). Dimensions of Human Behavior Person and Environment (2nd ed.). Thousand Oaks, CA: Sage.

Hutson, R. Q. (2001). *Red flags: Research raises concerns about the impact of "welfare reform" on child maltreatment.* Washington, DC: Center for Law and Social Policy.

Hutxable, M. (January, 2004). Defining measurable behavioral goals and objectives. School Social Work Association of America, Northlake, Ill.

Hyde, C. (1996). A feminist's response to Rothman's "The interweaving of community intervention approaches." *Journal of Community Practice, 3*(3/4), 127–145.

I

Icard, L. D., Longres, J. F., & Spenser, M. (1999). Racial minority status and distress among children and adolescents. *Journal of Social Service Research, 25*(1/2), 19–40.

Indyk, D., Belville, R., Lachapelle, S. S., Gordon, G., & Dewart, T. (1993). A community-based approach to HIV case management: Systematizing the unmanageable. *Social Work, 38*(4), 380–387.

Ingersoll-Dayton, B., Schroepfer, T., & Pryce, J. (1999). The effectiveness of a solution-focused approach for problem behaviors among nursing home residents. *Journal of Gerontological Social Work, 32*(3), 49–64.

International Federation of Social Workers (2000). New definition of social work. Berne: International Federation of Social Workers.

Ivanoff, A. M., Blythe, B. J., & Tripodi, T. (1994). *Involuntary clients in social work practice: A research-based approach.* New York: Aldine de Gruyter.

J

Jackson, A. P. (1998). The role of social support in parenting for low-income, single, black mothers. *Social Service Review, 72*(3), 365–378.

Jackson, D. D., & Weakland, J. H. (1961). Conjoint family therapy: Some considerations on theory, technique, and results. *Psychiatry, 24,* 3–45.

Jacobs, E. E., Masson, R. L., & Harvill, R. L. (1998). *Group counseling strategies and skills.* Pacific Grove, CA: Brooks/Cole.

James, R. K. (2008). *Crisis intervention strategies* (6th ed.). Thomson-Brooks/Cole.

James, R. K., & Gilliland, B. E. (2001). *Crisis intervention strategies.* Pacific Grove, CA: Brooks/Cole, Thomson Learning.

James. R. K., & Gilliland, B. E. (2005). *Crisis intervention strategies* (5th ed.). Thomson- Brooks/Cole.

Jang, M., Lee, K., & Woo, K. (1998). Income, language, and citizenship status: Factors affecting the health care access and utilization of Chinese Americans. *Health and Social Work, 23*(2), 136–145.

Jansson, B. (2003). *Becoming an effective policy advocate* (4th ed.). Pacific Grove, CA: Thomson-Brooks/Cole.

Janzen, C., & Harris, O. (1997). *Family treatment in social work practice* (3rd ed.). Itasca, IL: F. E. Peacock.

Jarrett, R. L. (1995). Growing up poor: The family experience of socially mobile youth in low-income African American neighborhoods. *Journal of Adolescent Research, 10*(1), 111–135.

Jayaratne, S. (1994). Should systematic assessment, monitoring and evaluation tools be used as empowerment aids for clients? In W. W. Hudson & P. S. Nurius (Eds.), *Controversial issues in social work research* (pp. 88–92). Needham Heights, MA: Allyn and Bacon.

Jaycox, L. H., Zoellner, L., & Foa, E. B. (2002). Cognitive behavioral therapy for PTSD in rape survivor. *Journal of Clinical Psychology, 58*(8), 891–907.

Jenkins, A. (2007). *Inequality, race and remedy.* Ending Poverty in America, Special Report of The American Prospect, The Annie E. Casey Foundation & The Northwest Area Foundation. A8–A10.

Jennings, H. (1950). *Leadership and isolation.* New York: Longmans Green.

Jessop, D. (1998). 'Caribbean Norms vs. European Ethics', The Sunday Observer (Jamaica) (1 February): 13.

Jilek, W. (1982). *Indian healing: Shamanic ceremonialism in the Pacific Northwest today.* Laine, WA: Hancock House.

Jimenez, J. (2002). The history of grandmothers in the African American community. *Social Services Review, 76*(4), 524–551.

Johnson, H. C. (1989). Disruptive children: Biological factors in attention deficit disorder and antisocial disorders. *Social Work, 34*(2), 137–144.

Jones, D. M. (1996). Termination from drug treatment: Dangers and opportunities for clients of the graduation ceremony. *Social Work with Groups, 19*(3/4), 105–115.

Jordan, C., & Franklin, C. (1995). *Clinical assessment for social workers: Quantitative and qualitative methods.* Chicago: Lyceum Books.

Jordan, C., & Franklin, C. (2003). *Clinical assessment for social workers. Quantitative and qualitative methods* (2nd ed.). Chicago: Lyceum Books.

Jordan, C., & Hickerson, J. (2003). Children and adolescents. In C. Jordan & C. Franklin (Eds.), *Clinical assessment for social workers: Quantitative and qualitative methods* (pp. 179–213). Chicago: Lyceum Books.

Jordan, M. (2007, October 9). Exception to a meltdown. *The Wall Street Journal,* C1–C2.

Jose, P. E., Cafasso, L. L., & D'Anna, C. A. (1994). Ethnic group differences in children's coping strategies. *Sociological Studies of Children, 6,* 25–53.

Joseph, S., Williams, R., & Yule, W. (1993). Changes in outlook following disaster: Preliminary development of measures to assess positive and negative responses. *Journal of Traumatic Stress, 6,* 271–279.

Joshi, P. T., Capozzoli, J. A., & Coyle, J. T. (1990). The Johns Hopkins Depression Scale: Normative data and validation in child psychiatry patients. *Journal of the American Academy of Child and Adolescent Psychiatry, 29*(2), 283–288.

Joyce, A. S., Duncan, S. C., Duncan, A., Kipnes, D., & Piper, W. E. (1996). Limiting time-unlimited group therapy. *International Journal of Group Psychotherapy, 46*(6), 61–79.

Julia, M. C. (1996). *Multicultural Awareness in the health care professions.* Needham Heights, MA: Allyn & Bacon.

K

Kadushin, A. (1977). *Consultation in social work.* New York: Columbia University Press.

Kadushin, G., & Kulys, R. (1993). Discharge planning revisited: What do social workers actually do in discharge planning? *Social Work, 38*(6), 713–726.

Kagle, J. D. (1991). *Social work records* (2nd ed.). Chicago: Waveland Press.

Kagle, J. D. (1994). Should systematic assessment, monitoring and evaluation tools be used as empowerment aids for clients? Rejoiner to Dr. Jayaratne. In W. W. Hudson & P. S. Nurius (Eds.) *Controversial issues in social work research* (pp. 88–92). Needham Heights, MA: Allyn and Bacon.

Kagle, J. D. (2002). Record-keeping. In A. R. Roberts & G. J. Greene (Eds.), *Social workers' desk reference* (pp. 28–33). New York: Oxford University Press.

Kahn, M. (1997). Between therapist and client: The new relationship. New York: W.H. Freeman & Company.

Kane, N. (1995). Looking at the lite side. "I feed more cats, than I have T-cells." *Reflections, 1*(2), 26–36.

Kane, R. A., Penrod, J. D., Davidson, G., Moscovice, I., & Rich, E. (1991). What cost case management in long-term care? *Social Service Review, 65*(2), 281–303.

Kaplan, H. I., and Sadock, B. J., (Eds.). (2007). *Synopsis of Psychiatry* (10th ed.). Baltimore, MD: Williams and Wilkins.

Katz, S., Ford, A. B., Moskowitz, R. W., Jackson, B. A., & Jaffe, M. W. (1963). Studies of illness in the aged. The Index of ADL: A standardized measure of biological and psychosocial function. *Journal of the American Medical Association, 185,* 914–919.

Kauffman, J. M. (1997). *Characteristics of emotional and behavioral disorders of children and youth* (6th ed.). Upper Saddle River, NJ: Prentice-Hall.

Kazdin, A. E., & Wassell, G. (1998). Treatment completion and therapeutic change among children referred for outpatient therapy. *Professional Psychology: Research and Practice, 29*(4), 332–340.

Kear-Colwell, J., & Pollock, P. (1997). Motivation or confrontation: Which approach to the child sex offender? *Criminal Justice and Behavior, 24,* 20–33.

Keefe, T. (1978). The economic context of empathy. *Social Work, 23*(6), 460–465.

Kessler, M., Gira, E. & Poertner, J. (2005). Moving best practice to evidence based practice in child welfare. *Families in Society, 86*(2), 244–250.

Kettenbach, G. (2003). *Writing SOAP notes: With patient/client management formats* (3rd ed.). Philadephia: Davis.

Kettner, P. M., Daley, J. M., & Nichols, A. W. (1985). *Initiating change in organizations and communities.* Monterey, CA: Brooks/Cole.

Kilpatrick, A. C., & Holland, T. (1999). *Working with families: An integrative model by level of need* (2nd ed.). Boston: Allyn & Bacon.

Kilpatrick, A. C., & Holland, T. (2003). *Working with families: An integrative model by level of need* (3rd ed.). Boston: Allyn & Bacon.

Kilpartrick, A. C., & Holland, T. P. (2006). *Working with families. An integrative model by level of need* (4th ed.). Boston: Allyn & Bacon.

Kim, J. S. (2008). Examining the effectiveness of solution-focused brief therapy: A meta-analysis. *Research on Social Work Practice, 18*, 107–116.

Kirk, S. A., & Koeske, G. F. (1995). The fate of optimism: A longitudinal study of case managers' hopefulness and subsequent morale. *Research on Social Work Practice, 5*(1), 47–61.

Kirk, S. A., & Kutchins, H. (1992). *The selling of DSM: The rhetoric of science in psychiatry.* New York: Aldine De Gruyter.

Kleespies, P. M., Penk, W. E., & Forsyth, J. P. (1993). The stress of patient suicidal behavior during clinical training: Incidence, impact, and recovery. *Professional Psychology: Research and Practice, 24*(3), 293–303.

Klein, A. (1970). *Social work through group process.* Albany, NY: School of Social Welfare, State University of New York at Albany.

Knight, C. (2006). Groups for individuals with traumatic histories: Practice considerations for social workers. *Social Work, 51*(1), 20–30.

Knight, J. R., Sherritt, L., Shrier, L. A., Harris, S. K., & Chang, G. (2002). Validity of the CRAFFT substance abuse screening test among adolescent clinic patients. *Archives of Pediatrics and Adolescent Medicine, 156*, 607–614.

Knox, K. S., & Roberts, A. R. (2008). The crisis intervention model. In N. Coady & P. Lehmann (Eds.), *Theoretical perspectives for direct social work practice. A generalist-eclectic approach* (2nd ed., pp. 249–274). New York: Springer Publishing Company.

Kohn, L. P., Oden, T. M., Munoz, R. F., Robinson, A., & Leavitt, D. (2002). Adapted cognitive-behavioral group therapy for depressed low-income, African American women. *Community Mental Health Journal, 38*, 497–504.

Komar, A. A. (1994). Adolescent school crises: Structures, issues and techniques for postventions. *International Journal of Adolescence and Youth, 5*(1/2), 35–46.

Koob, J. J. (2003). Solution-focused family interventions. In A. C. Kilpatrick & T. P. Holland. *Working with families: An integrative model by level of need* (3rd ed., pp. 131–150). Boston: Allyn & Bacon.

Koob, G. F., & Le Moal, M. (2008) Addiction and the brain antireward system. *Annual Review of Psychology 59*(1), 29–53.

Kooden, H. (1994). The gay male therapist as an agent of socialization. *Journal of Gay and Lesbian Psychotherapy, 2*(2), 39–64.

Kopp, J. (1989). Self-observation: An empowerment strategy in assessment. *Social Casework, 70*(5), 276–284.

Kopp, J., & Butterfield, W. (1985). Changes in graduate students' use of interviewing skills from the classroom to the field. *Journal of Social Service Research, 9*(1), 65–89.

Korol, M. S., Green, B. L., & Grace, M. (1999). Developmental analysis of the psychosocial impact of disaster on children: A review. *Journal of the American Academy of Child and Adolescent Pyschiatry, 38*, 368–375.

Koss, M. P., & Shiang, J. (1994). Research on brief psychotherapy. In A. E. Bergin & S. L. Garfield (Eds.), *Handbook of psychotherapy and behavioral change* (3rd ed., pp. 664–700). New York: Wiley.

Kotlowitz, A. (1991). *There are no children here.* New York: Doubleday.

Kovacs, M. (1992). *Children's depression inventory manual.* Los Angeles: Western Psychological Services.

Krähenbühl S., & Blades, M. (2006). The effect of interviewing techniques on young children's responses to questions. *Child Care Health and Development 32*(3): 321–333.

Kreutzer. D. (2008, February 15). Wage mandates won't help the poor. *Star Tribune,* A17.

Kruger, L., Moore, D., Schmidt, P., & Wiens, R. (1979). Group work with abusive parents. *Social Work, 24,* 337–338.

Kuehlwein, K. T. (1992). Working with gay men. In A. Freeman & F. M. Dattillio (Eds.). Comprehensive casebook of cognitive therapy (pp. 249-252). New York: Plenum.

Kumabe, K., Nishada, C., & Hepworth, D. (1985). *Bridging ethnocultural diversity in social work and health.* Honolulu: University of Hawaii Press.

Kung, W. W. (2003). Chinese Americans' help seeking behavior for emotional distress. *Social Service Review, 77*(1), 110–134.

Kurland, R., & Salmon, R. (1998). Purpose: A misunderstood and misused keystone of group work practice. *Social Work with Groups, 21*(3), 5–17.

Kurtz, D. P., Kurtz, G. L., & Jarvis, S. V. (1991). Problems of maltreated runway youth. *Adolescence, 26,* 543–555.

Kurtz, D. P., Lindsey, E., Jarvis, S. & Nakerud, L. (2000). How runaway and homeless youth navigate troubled waters: The role of formal and informal helpers. *Child and Adolescence, 17*(2), 381–402.

Kutchins, H. (1991). The fiduciary relationship. The legal basis for social worker's responsibilities to clients. *Social Work, 36*, 106–103.

L

Laing, R. (1965). Mystification, confusion and conflict. In I. Boszormenyi-Nagy & J. Framo (Eds.), *Intensive family therapy: Theoretical and practical aspects.* New York: Harper & Row.

Laird, J. (1993). Family-centered practice: Cultural and constructionist reflections. *Journal of Teaching in Social Work, 8*(1/2), 77–109.

Lamb, M., & Brown, D. (2006). Conversational apprentices: Helping children become competent informants about their own experiences. *British Journal of Developmental Psychology, 24*, 215–234.

Lambert, M. J., Bergin, A. E., & Garfield, S. L. (2004). Introduction and historical overview. In M. J. Lambert (Ed.), *Handbook of psychotherapy and behavioral change* (5th ed., pp. 3–15). New York: Wiley.

Lambert, M. J., & Ogles, B. M. (2004). The efficacy and effectiveness of psychotherapy. In M. J. Lambert (Ed.), *Handbook of psychotherapy and behavioral change* (5th ed., pp. 139–193). New York: John Wiley.

Land, H. (1988). The impact of licensing on social work practice: Values, ethics and choices. *Journal of Independent Social Work, 2*(4), 87–96.

Lane, F. E. (1986). Utilizing physician empathy with violent patients. *American Journal of Psychotherapy, 40*, 448–456.

Lane, E. J., Daugherty, T. K., & Nyman, S. J. (1998). Feedback on ability in counseling, self-efficacy, and persistence on task. *Psychological Reports, 83*, 1113–1114.

Lang, N. (1972). A broad range model of practice in the social work group. *Social Service Review, 46*, 76–89.

Lantz, J. (1996). Cognitive theory in social work treatment. In F. Turner (Ed.), *Social work treatment: Interlocking theoretical approaches* (4th ed., pp. 94–115). New York: Free Press.

Larsen, D., Attkission, C., Hargreaves, W., & Nguyen, T. (1979). Assessment of client satisfaction: Development of a general scale. *Evaluation & Program Planning, 2*, 197–207.

Larsen, J. (1975). *A comparative study of traditional and competency-based methods of teaching interpersonal skills in social work education.* Unpublished doctoral dissertation, University of Utah, Salt Lake City.

Larsen, J. (1980). Accelerating group development and productivity: An effective leader approach. *Social Work with Groups, 3*, 25–39.

Larsen, J., & Hepworth, D. (1978). Skill development through competency-based education. *Journal of Education for Social Work, 14*, 73–81.

Larsen, J., & Mitchell, C. (1980). Task-centered, strength-oriented group work with delinquents. *Social Casework, 61*, 154–163.

Lavee, Y. (1997). The components of healthy marriages: Perceptions of Israeli social workers and their clients. *Journal of Family Social Work, 2*(1), 1–14.

Lazarus, A. A. (1994). How certain boundaries and ethics diminish therapeutic effectiveness. *Ethics and Behavior, 4*(3), 255–261.

Leadbeater, B. J., Kuperminc, G. P., Blatt, S. J., Hertzog, C. (1999). A multivariate model of gender differences in adolescents' internalizing and externalising problems. *Developmental Psychology, 35*, 1268–1282.

Leahy, R. H., & Holland, S. J. (2000). *Treatment plans and interventions for depression and anxiety disorders.* The Guildford Press.

LeCroy, C. W. (2002). Child therapy and social skills. In A. R. Roberts & G. J. Greene (Eds.), *Social workers' desk reference* (pp. 406–412). New York: Oxford University Press.

Lee, M. Y. (2003). A solution-focused approach to cross-cultural clinical social work practice: Utilizing cultural strengths. *Families in Society: The Journal of Contemporary Human Services, 84*(3), 385–395.

Lee, M. Y., Greene, G. J., & Rheinscheld, J. (1999). A model for short-term solution-focused group treatment of male domestic violence offenders. *Journal of Family Social Work, 3*(2), 39–57.

Lehman, A. F. (1996). Heterogeneity of person and place: Assessing co-occurring addictive and mental disorders. *American Journal of Orthopsychiatry, 66*(1), 32–41.

Leiter M. P., & Maslach, C. (2005). *Banishing burnout: Six involving feelings, attitudes, motives and strategies for improving your relationship expectations with work.* San Francisco: Jossey-Bass.

Leonhardt, L. (2007, September 12). Has the jump in wages met its end? *The New York Times,* C1 & C4.

Lesure-Lester, E. G. (2002). An application of cognitive behavioral principles in the reduction of aggression among abused African American adolescents. *Journal of Interpersonal Violence, 17*(4), 394–403.

Levi, D. (2007). *Group dynamics for teams (2nd ed.).* Thousand Oaks, CA: Sage Publications.

Levick, K. (1981). Privileged communication: Does it really exist? *Social Casework, 62,* 235–239.

Levine, C. O., & Dang, J. (1979). The group within the group: The dilemma of cotherapy. *International Journal of Group Psychotherapy, 29*(2), 175–184.

Levinson, H. (1977). Termination of psychotherapy: Some salient issues. *Social Casework, 58,* 480–489.

Levinson, D. J. (1996). *Seasons of women's life.* New York: Alfred A. Knopf.

Levy, C. (1973). The value base of social work. *Journal of Education for Social Work, 9,* 34–42.

Levy, L. (1963). *Psychological interpretation.* New York: Holt, Rinehart & Winston.

Lewis, E. (1991). Social change and citizen action: A philosophical exploration for modern social group work. *Social Work with Groups, 14*(3/4), 23–34.

Lewis, E. A., Skyles, A., & Crosbie-Burnett, M. (2000). Public policy and families of color in the new millennium. National Council on Family Relations Annual Program Meeting, Minneapolis, MN, November 12, 2000.

Lewis, J. A., Lewis, M. D., Packard, T., & Souflee, F. (2001). *Management of human service programs* (3rd ed.). Pacific Grove, CA: Wadsworth/Brooks/Cole.

Lewis, T., & Osborn, C. (2004). Solution-focused counseling and motivational interviewing. A consideration of confluence. *Journal of Counseling and Development, 82,* 38–48.

Liau, A. K., Barriga, A. Q., & Gibbs, J. C. (1998). Relations between self serving cognitive distortions and overt versus covert antisocial behaviors in adolescents. *Aggressive Behavior 24,* 335–346.

Lieberman, M., & Borman, L. (Eds.) (1979). *Self-help groups for coping with crisis.* San Francisco, CA: Jossey-Bass.

Lieberman, M., & Videka-Sherman, L. (1986). The impact of self-help groups on the mental health of widows and widowers. *American Journal of Orthopsychiatry, 56,* 435–449.

Lieberman, M., Yalom, I., & Miles, M. (1973). *Encounter groups: Firstfacts.* New York: Basic Books.

Ligon, J. (1997). Brief crisis stabilization of an African American woman. Integrating cultural and ecological approaches. *Journal of Multicultural Social Work, 6*(3/4), 111–123.

Lim, C., & Adelman, H. S. (1997). Establishing a school-based collaborative team to coordinate

resources: A case study. *Journal of Social Work in Education, 19*(4), 266–277.

Lindemann, E. (1944). Symptomatology and management of acute grief. *American Journal of Psychiatry, 101,* 141–148.

Lindemann, E. (1956). The meaning of crisis in individual and family. *Teachers College Record, 57,* 310.

Lindsey, M. A., Korr, W. S., Broitman, M., Bone, L., Green, A. & Leaf, P. J. (2006). Help-seeking behaviors and depression among African American adolescent boys. *Social Work, 51*(1), 49–58.

Linhorst, D. M. (2002). Federalism and social justice: Implications for social work. *Social Work, 47*(3), 201–208.

Linhorst, D. M., Hamilton, J., Young, E., & Eckert, A. (2002). Opportunities and barriers to empowering people with severe mental illness through participation in treatment planning. *Social Work, 47*(4), 425–434.

Linzer, N. (1999). *Resolving ethical dilemmas in social work practice.* Boston: Allyn & Bacon.

Lipchik, E. (1997). My story about solution-focused brief therapist/client relationships. *Journal of Systemic Therapies, 16,* 159–172.

Lipchik, E. (2002). *Beyond technique in solution-focused therapy: Working with emotions and the therapeutic relationship.* New York: Guilford Press.

Lister, L. (1987). Contemporary direct practice roles. *Social Work, 32,* 384–391.

Littell, J. & Girvin, H. (2004). Ready or not: Uses of the stages of change model in child welfare. *Child welfare. 83*(4), 341–366.

Lo, T. W. (2005). Task-centered group work: Reflections on practice. *International Social Work, 48,* 455–456.

Locke, D. (2001, February 22). With this ring. *Saint Paul Pioneer Press,* 17A.

Loewenburg, F., & Dolgoff, R. (1996), *Ethical decision for social work practice* (5th ed.) Itasca, Ill: F. E. Peacock.

Loewenberg, F. M., Dolgoff, R., & Harrington, D. (2005). *Ethical decisions for social work practice* (7th ed.). Itasca, IL: F.E. Peacock.

Logan, S. M. L., Freeman, E. M., & McRoy, R. G. (1990). *Social work practice with black families: A culturally specific perspective.* New York: Longman.

Long, K. A. (1986). Cultural considerations in the assessment and treatment of intrafamilial abuse. *American Journal of Orthopsychiatry, 56,* 131–136.

Long, D. L., Tice, C. J., & Morrison, J. D. (2006). *Macro social work practice. A strengths perspective.* Thomson-Brooks/Cole.

Longres, J. F. (1991). Toward a status model of ethnic sensitive practice. *Journal of Multi-cultural Social Work, I*(1), 41–56.

Longres, J. F. (1995). *Human behavior in the social environment*. Itasca, IL: F. E. Peacock.

Longres, J. F., & Torrecilha, R. S. (1992). Race and the diagnosis, placement and exit status of children and youth in a mental health and disability system. *Journal of Social Service Research, 15*(3/4), 43–63.

Loo, C. M., Ueda, S. S., & Morton, R. K. (2007). Group treatment for race-related stresses among Vietnam veterans. *Transcultural Psychiatry, 44*(1), 115–135.

Lowenstein, D. A., Amigo, E., Duara, R., Guterman, A., Kurwitz, D., Berkowitz, N., et al. (1989). A new scale for the assessment of functional status in Alzheimer's disease and related disorders. *Journal of Gerontology: Psychological Sciences, 44*, 114–121.

Lowinson, J. H., Ruiz, P., Millman, R. B., & Langrod, J. G. (Eds.). (2005). *Substance abuse: A comprehensive textbook* (4th ed.). Philadelphia, PA: Lippincott, Williams & Wilkins.

Lu, Y., Dane, B. & Gellman, A. (2005) An experiential model: teaching empathy and cultural sensitivity. *Journal of teaching social work. 25*(3/4), 89–103.

Luborsky, L., & Spence, D. (1978). Quantitative research on psychoanalytic therapy. In S. Garfield & A. Bergin (Eds.), *Handbook of psychotherapy and behavior change* (pp. 331–368). New York: Wiley.

Lukas, S. (1993). *Where to start and what to ask: An assessment handbook*. New York: Norton.

Lukton, R. (1982). Myths and realities of crisis intervention. *Social Casework, 63*, 275–285.

Lum, D. (1996). *Social work practice and people of color: A process-stage approach* (3rd ed.). Pacific Grove, CA: Brooks/Cole.

Lum, D. (2004). *Social work practice and people of color. A process-stage approach* (5th ed.). Pacific Grove, CA: Brooks/Cole.

Lum, D. (2007). *Culturally competent practice: A framework for understanding diverse groups and justice issues*. Pacific Grove, CA: Thomson-Brooks/Cole.

M

Macgowan, M. J. (1997). A measure of engagement for social group work: The group work engagement measure (GEM). *Journal of Social Service Research, 23*(2), 17–37.

Macgowan, M. J. (2004). Prevention and intervention in youth suicide. In P. Allen-Mears, & M. W. Fraser (Eds.), *Intervention with children and adolescents: An interdisciplinary perspective* (pp. 282–310). Boston: Pearson.

Mackelprang, R., & Hepworth, D. H. (1987). Ecological factors in rehabilitation of patients with severe spinal cord injuries. *Social Work in Health Care, 13*, 23–38.

Mackey, R. A., & O'Brian, B. A. (1998). Marital conflict management: Gender and ethnic differences. *Social Work, 43*(2), 128–141.

Madden, R. G., & Wayne, R. H. (2003) Social work and the law: A therapeutic jurisprudence perspective. *Social Work, 48*(3), 338–349.

Magen, R. (2004). Measurement issues. In C. D. Garvin, L. M. Gutierrez, & M. J. Galinsky (Eds.), *Handbook of social work with groups*. New York: Guilford Press.

Magen, R. H., & Glajchen, M. (1999). Cancer support groups: Client outcome and the context of group process. *Research on Social Work Practice, 9*(5), 541–554.

Maguire, L. (2002). *Clinical social work: Beyond generalist practice with individuals, groups and families*. Pacific Grove, CA: Thomson-Brooks-Cole.

Mahler, C. (1969). *Group counseling in the schools*. Boston: Houghton Mifflin.

Mahoney, M. J. (1974). *Cognition and behavior modification*. Cambridge, MA: Ballinger.

Mailick, M. D., & Vigilante, F. W. (1997). The family assessment wheel: A social constructionist perspective. *Families in Society, 80*(1), 361–369.

Malekoff, A. (2006). Strengths-based group work with children and adolescents. In C. D. Garvin, L. M. Gutierrez, & M. J. Galinsky (Eds.), *Handbook of social work with groups* (pp. 227–244). New York: Guilford Press.

Malgady, R. G. & Zayas, L. H. (2001). Cultural and linguistic considerations in psychodiagnosis with Hispanics: The need for an empirically informed process model. *Social Work, 46*, 39–49.

Mallory, K. (2004, May 8). Barbers cutting cancer out in Montgomery County. *The Washington Afro American, 112*, 39.

Mann, B., & Murphy, K. (1975). Timing of self disclosure, reciprocity of self-disclosure, and reactions to an initial interview. *Journal of Counseling Psychology, 22*, 304–308.

Marlatt, G. A., & Gordon, J. R. (1985). *Relapse prevention: Maintenance strategies in the treatment of addictive behaviors*. New York: Guilford Press.

Marlow, C. (1993). Coping with multiple roles: Family configuration and the need for workplace services. *Affilia, 8*(1), 40–55.

Marsh, J. C. (2002). Learning from clients. *Social Work, 47*(4), 341–342.

Marsh, J. (2003). Arguments for family strengths. *Social Work, 42*(2), 147–148.

Marsh, J. (2004). theory-driven versus theory-free research in empirical social work practice. pp. 20–35 in Briggs, H., & Rzepnicki, T. (eds). *Using evidence in social work practice.* Chicago: Lyceum.

Marsh, J. (2005). Social justice: social work's organizing value. *Social Work, 50,* 293–294.

Martin, L. L. (1993). *Total quality management in human service organizations.* Thousand Oaks, CA: Sage Publications.

Martin, P. Y., & O'Connor, G. G. (1989). *The social environment: Open systems applications.* Upper Saddle River, NJ: Longman.

Maschi, T. (2006). Unraveling the link between trauma and male delinquency: The cumulative versus differential risk perspective. *Social Work, 11*(1), 59–70.

Mason, J. L., Benjamin, M. P., & Lewis, S. A. (1996). The cultural competence model: Implications for child and family mental health services. In C. A. Heflinger & C. T. Nixon (Eds.), *Families and the mental health system for children and adolescents: Policy, services, and research* (pp. 165–190). Thousand Oaks, CA: Sage Publications.

Mattesich, P. W., & Monsey, B. R. (1992). *Collaboration: What makes it work.* Saint Paul, MN: Amherst Wilder Research Center.

Matto, H. C. (2005). A bio-behavioral model of addiction treatment: Applying dual representation theory to craving management and relapse prevention. *Substance Use & Misuse, 40*(4), 529–541.

Mau, W., & Jepsen, D. A. (1990). Help seeking perceptions behaviors: A comparison of Chinese and American graduate students. *Journal of Multicultural Counseling and Development, 18*(2), 95–104.

May, P., Hymbaugh, K., Aasc, J., & Samct, J. (1983). The epidemiology of fetal alcohol syndrome among American Indians of the Southwest. *Social Biology, 30,* 374–387.

Mayadas, N., Ramanathan, C., & Suarez, Z. (1998–1999). Mental health, social context, refugees and immigrants: A cultural interface. *Journal of Intergroup Relations, 25,* 3–14.

Mayer, J., & Timms, N. (1969). Clash in perspective between worker and client. *Social Casework, 50,* 32–40.

Mayo Clinic. (2007, January 12). Elder abuse: Signs to look for, action to take. Retrieved July 25, 2008, from http://www.mayoclinic.com/health/elder-abuse/HA00041

Mays, N. (2003, Fall). Investigating how culture impacts health. *Washington University in Saint Louis Magazine.*

McAdoo, J. L. (1993). Decision making and marital satisfaction in African American families. In H. P. McAdoo (Ed.), *Family ethnicity: Strength in diversity* (pp. 109–118). Thousand Oaks, CA: Sage Publications.

McChesney, K. Y. (1995). Urban homeless families. *Social Service Review, 69*(3), 428–460.

McCollum, E. E., & Beer, J. (1995). The view from the other chair. *Family Therapy Networker, 19*(2), 59–62.

McCollum, E. E, & Trepper, T. S. (2001). *Creating family solutions for substance abuse.* New York: Haworth Press.

McConaughy, S. H., & Auchenbach, T. M. (1994). *Manual for the semistructured clinical interview with children and adolescents.* Burlington, VT: University of Vermont, Department of Psychiatry.

McCubbin, H. (1988). *Resilient families in the military: Profiles of strengths and hardiness.* Madison, Wisconsin: University of Wisconsin.

McCubbin, H. I., & McCubbin, M. A. (1988). Typologies of resilient families. Emerging roles of social class and ethnicity. *Family Relations, 37,* 247–254.

McDonald, L. (2002). Evidence-based, family-strengthening strategies to reduce delinquency: FAST: Families and Schools Together. In A. R. Roberts & G. J. Greene (Eds.), *Social workers' desk reference* (pp. 717–722). New York: Oxford University Press.

McGoldrick. M. (Ed.) (1998). *Revisioning family therapy. Race, culture and gender in clinical practice.* New York: The Guilford Press.

McGoldrick, M., & Gerson, R. (1985). *Genograms in family assessment.* New York: Norton.

McGoldrick, M., Giordano, J., & Pearce, J. K. (Eds.) (1996). *Ethnicity and family therapy.* New York: Guilford Press.

McGonagle, E. (1986). *Banana splits: A peer support group for children of transitional families.* Ballston Spa, NY: Author.

McHale, J. P., & Cowan, P. A. (1996) (Eds.). Understanding how family-level dynamics affect children's development: Studies in two-parent families. Jossey-Bass Publishers.

McIntosh, J. L. (2003). Suicide survivors: The aftermath of suicide and suicidal behavior. In C. D. Bryant (Ed.), *The handbook of death and dying* (pp. 339–350). Thousand Oaks, CA: Sage Publications.

McKenry, P. C., & Price, S. J. (Eds.). (2000). *Families and change. Coping with stressful events and transitions* (2nd ed.). Thousand Oaks, CA: Sage Publications.

McKenzie, A. (2005), Narrative-oriented therapy with children who have experiencd sexual abuse. *Envision: The Manitoba Journal of Child Welfare, 4*(2), 1–29.

McLoyd, V. (1997). The impact of poverty and low socioeconomic status on the socioemotional functioning of African-American children and adolescents. In R. W. Taylor & M. C. Wang (Eds.), *Social and emotional adjustment and family relations in ethnic minority families* (pp. 2–34). Mahwah, NJ: Lawrence Erlbaum Associates.

McMillen, J. C. (1999) Better for it: How people benefit from adversity. *Social Work, 44*(5), 455–468.

McMillen, J. E., & Fischer, R. (1998). The perceived benefit scale: Measuring perceived positive life changes after negative events. *Social Work Research, 22*(3), 173–187.

McMillen, J., Morris, L., & Sherraden, M. (2004). Ending social work's grudge match: Problems versus strengths. *Families in Society, 85*, 317–325.

McMillen, J. C., Smith, E. M., & Fisher, R. (1997). Perceived benefit and mental health after three types of disaster. *Journal of Consulting and Clinical Psychology, 63*, 1037–1043.

McMillen, J. C., Zuravin, S., & Rideout, G. B. (1995). Perceptions of benefits from child sexual abuse. *Journal of Consulting and Clinical Psychology, 63*, 1037–1043.

McNeely, R., & Badami, M. (1984). Interracial communication in school social work. *Social Work, 29*, 22–25.

McPhatter, A. (1991). Assessment revisited: A comprehensive approach to understanding family dynamics. *Families in Society, 72*, 11–21.

McQuaide, S. (1999). Using psychodynamic, cognitive behavioral and solution-focused questioning to construct a new narrative. *Clinical Social Work, 27*(4), 339–353.

McQuaide, S., & Ehrenreich, J. H. (1997). Assessing client strengths. *Families in Society, 78*(2), 201–212.

McRoy, R. G. (2003, June 6). *Impact of systems on adoption in the African American community*. Keynote address presented at the meeting of the Institute on Domestic Violence in the African American Community, Minneapolis, MN.

McWilliams, N. (1999). Psychoanalytic formulation. Guilford Press.

Meenaghan, T. M. (1987). Macro practice: Current trends and issues. In *Encyclopedia of social work* (18th ed., pp. 82–89). Silver Spring, MD: National Association of Social Workers.

Meezan, W., & O'Keefe, M. (1998). Evaluating the effectiveness of multifamily group therapy in child abuse and neglect. *Research on Social Work Practice, 8*(3), 330–353.

Meichenbaum, D. (1977). *Cognitive-behavior modification*. New York: Plenum Press.

Meier, A. (1997). Inventing new models of social support groups: A feasibility study of an online stress management support group for social workers. *Social Work with Groups, 20*(4), 35–53.

Meier, A. (2002). An online stress management support group for social workers. *Journal of Technology in Human Services, 20*(1/2), 107–132.

Meier, A. (2006). Technology-mediated groups. In C. D. Garvin, L. M. Gutierrez, & M. J. Galinsky (Eds.), *Handbook of social work with groups* (pp. 13–31). New York: Guilford Press.

Metcalf, L. (1998). *Solution focused group therapy: Ideas for groups in private practice, schools, agencies, and treatment programs*. New York: Free Press.

Metcalf, L., Thomas, F., Duncan, B., Miller, S., & Hubble, M. (1996). What works in solution-focused brief therapy: A qualitative analysis of client and therapist's perceptions. In S. Miller, M. Hubble, & B. Duncan (Eds.), *Handbook of solution-focused brief therapy*. San Francisco: Jossey-Bass.

Meyer, C. (Ed.). (1983). *Clinical social work in the eco-systems perspective*. New York: Columbia University Press.

Meyer, C. (1990, April 1). *Can social work keep up with the changing family?* [Monograph]. The fifth annual Robert J. O'Leary Memorial Lecture. Columbus, OH: The Ohio State University College of Social Work, 1–24.

Meyer, W. (2001). Why they don't come back: A clinical perspective on the no-show client. *Clinical Social Work, 29*(4), 325–339.

Meyers, M. K. (1993). Organizational factors in the integration of services for children. *Social Service Review, 67*(4), 547–571.

Meystedt, D. M. (1984). Religion and the rural population: Implications for social work. *Social Casework, 65*(4), 219–226.

Milgram, D., & Rubin, J. S. (1992). Resisting resistance: Involuntary substance abuse group therapy. *Social Work with Groups, 15*(1), 95–110.

Miller, D. B. (1997). Parenting against the odds: African-American parents in the child welfare system—a group approach. *Social Work with Groups, 20*(1), 5–18.

Miller, J. A. (1994). A family's sense of power in their community: Theoretical and research issues. *Smith College Studies in Social Work, 64*(3), 221–241.

Miller, R., & Mason, S. E. (2001). Using group therapy to enhance treatment compliance in first episode schizophrenia. *Social Work with Groups, 24*(1), 37–52.

Miller, S. M., & Øyen, E. (1996). Remeasuring Poverty. *Poverty & Race, 5*(5), 1–4.

Miller, W. R., & Rollnick, S. (1991). *Motivational interviewing: Preparing people to change addictive behavior.* New York: Guilford Press.

Miller, W. R., & Rollnick, S. (2002). *Motivational interviewing: preparing people to change addictive behavior* (2nd ed.). New York: Guilford Press.

Miller, W. R., & Sovereign, R. G. (1989). The check-up: A model for early intervention in addictive behaviors. In T. Loberg, W. R. Miller, P. E. Nathan, & G. A. Marlatt (Eds.), *Addictive behaviors: Prevention and early intervention* (pp. 219–231). Amsterdam: Swets and Zeitlinger.

Millon, T., & Davis, R. (1997). The MCMI-III: Present and future directions. *Journal of Personality Assessment 68*(1) 68–95.

Minuchin, S. (1974). *Families and family therapy.* Cambridge, MA: Harvard University Press.

Mitchell, C. G. (1998). Perceptions of empathy and client satisfaction with managed behavioral health care. *Social Work, 43*(5), 404–411.

Mokuau, N., & Fong, R. (1994). Assessing the responsiveness of health services to ethnic minorities of color. *Social Work in Health Care, 28*(1), 23–34.

Moore, S. T. (1990). A social work practice model of case management: The case management grid. *Social Work, 35*(5), 444–448.

Morell, C. (2003). Empowerment theory and long-living women: A feminist and disability perspective. *Journal of Human Behavior in the Social Environment, 7*(3/4), 225–236.

Morgan, A. (2000). *What is narrative therapy?* Adelaide, South Australia: Dulwich Centre Publication.

Morgan, G. (1997). *Images of organizations.* Thousand Oaks, CA: Sage Publications.

Morrison, J. (1995). *The first interview: Revised for DSM-IV.* New York: Guilford Press.

Morrow, D. F. (1993). Social work with gay and lesbian adolescents. *Social Work, 38*(6), 655–660.

Morton, T. (1999). The increasing colorization of America's child welfare system. The overrepresentation of African American children. *Policy and Practice, 12*, 21–30.

Mosley, J. C., & Lex, A. (1990). Identification of potentially stressful life events experienced by a population of urban minority youth. *Journal of Multicultural Counseling and Development, 18*(3), 118–125.

Moyers, T., & Rollnick, S. (2002). A motivational interviewing perspective on resistance in psychotherapy. *Journal of Clinical Psychology, 58*(2), 185–193.

Munroe, E. (2004). Improving practice: Child protection as a systems problem. *Children Youth and Services Review, 27*, 375–391.

Munson, C. E. (2002). The techniques and process of supervisory practice. In A. R. Roberts & G. J. Greene (Eds.) *Social workers' desk reference* (pp. 38–44). New York: Oxford University Press.

Murdach, A. D. (1996). Beneficence re-examined: Protective intervention in mental health. *Social Work, 41*, 26–32.

Murphy, C. M., & Baxter, V. A. (1997). Motivating batterers to change in the treatment context. *Journal of Interpersonal Violence, 12*(4), 607–619.

Murphy, B. C., & Dillon, C. (1998). *Interviewing in action: Process and practice.* Pacific Grove, CA: Brooks/Cole.

Murphy, B. C., & Dillon, C. (2003). *Interviewing in action: Relationship, process, and change* (2nd ed.). Pacific Grove, CA: Brooks/Cole.

Murphy, B. C., & Dillon, C. (2008). *Interviewing in action in a multicultural world* (3rd ed.). Pacific Grove, CA: Brooks/Cole.

Murray, C. E., & Murray, T. L. (2004). Solution-focused premarital counseling: Helping couples build a vision for their marriage. *Journal of Marital and Family Therapy, 30*(3), 349–358.

Mwanza (1990). *Afrikan naturalism.* Columbus, OH: Pan Afrikan Publications.

Mydans, S. (2004, August, 1). Looking out for the many, saving the one. *The New York Times,* p. WR3.

N

Nader, K., & Mello, C. (2008). Interactive trauma/Grief-focused therapy with children. In N. Coady & P. Lehmann (Eds.), *Theoretical perspectives for direct social work practice. A generalist-eclectic approach* (2nd ed., pp. 493–519). New York: Springer Publishing Company.

Nadler, A. (1996). Help seeking behavior as a coping resource. In M. Rosen (Ed.), *Learning resourcefulness: On coping skills, self control and adaptive behavior* (pp. 127–162). New York: Springer Publishing.

Naleppa, M. J. (1999). Late adulthood. In E. D. Hutchison (Ed.). *Dimensions of human behavior: The changing life course.* Thousand Oaks, CA: Pine Forge Press.

Naleppa, M. J., & Reid, W. J. (2000). Integrating case management and brief-treatment strategies: A hospital-based geriatric program. *Social Work in Health Care, 31*(4), 1–23.

National Association of Social Workers (NASW). (1996). *Code of ethics.* Washington, DC: NASW Press.

National Association of Social Workers (NASW). (1999). *Code of ethics.* Washington, DC: NASW Press. http://www.naswdc.org/publs/code/code.asp

National Association of Social Workers (NASW). (2001). *NASW standard for cultural competence for social work practice.* Washington, DC: NASW Press.

National Association of Social Workers. (2006). *Immigration policy toolkit.* Washington, DC: NASW Press.

National Association of Scholars. (2007). *The scandal of social work education.* Retrieved August 24, 2008, from www.NAS.org

National Institute on Drug Abuse. (2008, January 2). *Commonly Abused Drugs.* Retreived June 30, 2008, from http://www.drugabuse.gov/DrugPages/DrugsofAbuse.html

Nelson, T. D., & Kelley, L. (2001). Solution-focused couples groups. *Journal of Systemic Therapies, 20,* 47–66.

Nelson-Zlupko, L., Kauffman, E., & Dore, M. M. (1995). Gender differences in drug addiction and treatment: Implications for social work intervention with substance abusing women. *Social Work, 40*(1), 45–54.

Netting, F. E., Kettner, P. M., & McMurtry, S. L. (2004). *Social work macro practice.* (3rd ed.) Boston: Allyn & Bacon.

Nevil, N., Beatty, M. L., & Moxley, D. P. (1997). *Socialization games for persons with disabilities: Structured group activities for social and interpersonal development.* Springfield, IL: C. C. Thomas.

Newman, K, & Chen, V. T (2007). *The missing class. Portraits of the near poor in America.* Boston: Beacon Press.

Nichols, M. P. (2006). *Family therapy. Concepts and methods* (7th ed.). Boston: Allyn & Bacon.

Nichols, M. P., & Schwartz, R. C. (1998). *Family therapy: Concepts and methods* (4th ed.). Boston: Allyn & Bacon.

Nichols, M. P., & Schwartz, R. C. (2004). *Family therapy: Concepts and methods.* (6th ed.) Boston: Allyn & Bacon.

Norcross, J. C. & Lambert, M. J. (2006). The therapy relationship. In J. C. Norcross, L. E. Beutler & R. F. Levant (Eds.). *Evidence-Based Practices in Mental Health: Debate and Dialogue on the Fundamental Questions* (pp. 208–217). Washington, D.C.: American Psychological Association.

Nord, M., & Luloff, A. E. (1995). Homeless children and their families in New Hampshire: A rural perspective. *Social Service Review, 69*(3), 461–478.

Norris, J. (1999). Mastering documentation, 2nd ed. Springhouse, PA: Springhouse.

Northen, H. (2006). Ethics and values in group work. In C. D. Garvin, L. M. Gutierrez, & M. J. Galinsky (Eds.), *Handbook of social work with groups* (pp. 76–89). New York: Guilford Press.

Northen, H., & Kurland, R. (2001). The use of activity. In *Social work with groups* (3rd ed., pp. 258–287). New York: Columbia University Press.

Norton, D. G. (1978). *The dual perspective: Inclusion of ethnic minority content in the social work curriculum.* New York: Council on Social Work Education.

Nosko, A., & Wallace, R. (1997). Female/male co-leadership in groups. *Social Work with Groups, 20*(2), 3–16.

Nugent, W. (1992). The effective impact of a clinical social worker's interviewing style: A series of single-case experiments. *Research on Social Work Practice, 2*(1), 6–27.

Nugent, W. R., & Halvorson, H. (1995). Testing the effects of active listening. *Research on Social Work Practice, 5*(2), 152–175.

Nugent, W. R., Umbriet, M. S., Wilnamaki, L., & Paddock, J. (2001). Participation in victim-offender mediation and reoffense: Successful replications? *Research on Social Work Practice, 11,* 5–23.

Nybell, L. M., & Gray, S. S. (2004). Race, place, space: Meaning of cultural competence in three child welfare agencies. *Social Work, 49*(1), 17–26.

O

Oettingen, G., Bulgarella, C., Henderson, M. & Collwitzer, P. M. (2004) The self-regulation or goal pursuit. In R. Wright, J. Greenberg & S. S. Brehm (Eds.). Motivational analysis of social behavior (pp. 225–244). Lawrence Erlbaum Associates Publishers.

Ogbu, J. U. (1994). *From cultural differences to differences in cultural frame of reference.* In P. M. Greenfield & R. R. Cocking (Eds.), *Cross-cultural roots of minority child development* (pp. 365–392). Hillsdale, NJ: Erlbaum.

Ogbu, J. U. (1997). Understanding the school performances of urban blacks: Some essential knowledge. In H. J. Walbery, O. Reyes, and P. R. Weissberg (Eds.). *Children and youth: Interdisciplinary perspectives.* Thousand Oaks, CA: Sage Publications.

O'Hanlon, W. (1996). Case commentary. *Family Therapy Networker*, January/February, 84–85.

O'Hare, T. (2005). *Evidence-based practices for social workers: An interdisciplinary approach.* Chicago: Lyceum Books, Inc.

O'Hollaran, T. M., & Linton, J. M. (2000). Stress on the job: Self-care resources for counselors. *Journal of Mental Health Counseling, 22*, 254–265.

Okun, B. F. (1996). *Understanding diverse families. What practitioners need to know.* New York: Guilford Press.

Okun, B. (2002). *Effective helping: Interviewing and counseling techniques.* Pacific Grove, CA: Brooks/Cole.

Okun, B. F., Fried, J., & Okun, M. L. (1999). *Understanding diversity. A learning-as-practice primer.* Pacific Grove, CA: Brooks/Cole Publishing Company.

Oliver, M. L., & Shapiro, T. W. (2007). *Creating an opportunity society.* Ending Poverty in America, Special Report of The American Prospect, The Annie E. Casey Foundation & The Northwest Area Foundation. A27–A28.

O'Melia, M., & Miley, K. K. (Eds.) (2002). *Pathways to power. Readings in contextual social work practice.* Boston: Allyn & Bacon.

Organista, K., Dwyer, E. V., & Azocar, F. (1993). Cognitive behavioral therapy with Latino clients. *The Behavior Therapist, 16*, 229–228.

Orme, J. (2002). Social work: Gender, care and justice. *British Journal of Social Work, 32*, 799–814.

Ortiz, L. P. A., & Langer, N. (2002). Assessment of spirituality and religion in later life: Acknowledging clients' needs and personal resources. *Journal of Gerontological Social Work, 32*, 5–20.

Ostroff, C., & Atwater, L. E. (2003). Does whom you work with matter? Effects of referent group gender and age composition on managers' compensation. *Journal of Applied Psychology, 88*(4), 725–740.

Othmer, E., & Othmer, S. C. (1989). *The clinical interview using DSM-III-R.* Washington, DC: American Psychiatric Press.

P

Pack-Brown, J. P., Whittington-Clark, L. E., & Parker, W. M. (1998). *Images of me: A guide to group work with African-American women.* Boston: Allyn & Bacon.

Padgett, D. K. (1999). *The qualitative research experience.* Brooks/Cole-Thomson.

Padgett, D. K. (Ed.). (2004). *The qualitative research experience.* Thomson-Brooks/Cole.

Padilla, Y., Shapiro, E., Fernandez-Castro, M., & Faulkner, M. (2008). Our nation's immigrants in peril: An urgent call to social workers. *Social Work, 53*(1), 5–8.

Palmer, N., & Kaufman, M. (2003). The ethics of informed consent: Implications for multicultural practice. *Journal of Ethnic and Cultural Diversity in Social Work, 12*(1), 1–26.

Palmer, B., & Pablo, S. (1978). Community development possibilities for effective Indian reservation child abuse and neglect efforts. In M. Lauderdale, R. Anderson, & S. Cramer (Eds.), *Child abuse and neglect. Issues on innovation and implementation* (pp. 98–116). Washington, DC: U.S. Department of Health, Education and Welfare.

Palmer, K. (2007, September 3). The new mommy track. *U.S. News & World Report*, pp. 40–44.

Panos, P. T., Panos, A., Cox, S., Roby, J. L. & Matheson, K. W. (2006). Ethical concerning the use of videoconferencing to supervise international social work field practicum students. *Journal of Social Work Education 38*(3), 421–438.

Parad, H. J. (1965). *Crisis intervention: Selected readings.* New York: Family Service Association of America.

Parad, H. J., & Parad, L. G. (Eds.). (1990). *Crisis intervention: Book 2.* Milwaukee, WI: Family Service America.

Parad, H. J., & Parad, L. G. (2006). *Crisis intervention book 2: The practitioner's source book for brief therapy* (2nd ed.). Tucson, AZ: Fenestra Books.

Parihar, B. (1994). *Task-centered management in human service organizations.* Springfield, Ill: Thomas.

Parlec, M. (1979). Conversational politics. *Psychology Today, 12*, 48–56.

Parloff, M., Waskow, I., & Wolfe, B. (1978). Research on therapist variables in relation to process and outcome. In S. Garfield & A. Bergin (Eds.),

Handbook of psychotherapy and behavior change (pp. 233–282). New York: Wiley.

Parsons, R. J. (2002). Guidelines for empowerment-based social work practice. In A. R. Roberts & G. J. Greene (Eds.), *Social workers' desk reference* (pp. 396–401). New York: Oxford University Press.

Parsons, R. J., Jorgenson, J. D., & Hernandez, S. H. (1988). Integrative practice approach: A framework for problem solving. *Social Work, 35*(5), 417–421.

Parsons, R. J., Jorgensen, J. D., & Hernandez, S. H. (1994). *The integration of social work practice.* Pacific Grove, CA: Brooks/Cole.

Patterson, D. A., & Lee, M. (1998). Intensive case management and rehospitalization: A survival analysis. *Research on Social Work Practice, 8*(2), 152–171.

Paveza, G. J., Prohaska, T., Hagopian, M., & Cohen, D., (1989). *Determination of need—Revision: Final report, Volume I.* Chicago: University of Illinois at Chicago.

Pavlov, I. P. (1927). *Conditioned reflexes.* Oxford, England: Oxford University Press.

Payne, M. (2005). *Modern social work theory* (3rd ed.). Chicago: Lyceum Books.

Paz, J. (2002). Culturally competent substance abuse treatment with Latinos. *Journal of Human Behavior in the Social Environment, 5*(3/4), 123–136.

Pazaratz, D. (2000). Task-centered child and youth care in residential treatment. Residential treatment for Children and Youth *17*(4), 1–16.

Pelton, L. H. (2003). Social justice and social work. *Journal of Social Work Education,* 433–439.

Pence, E., & Paymar, M. (1993). *Education groups for men who batter: The Duluth model.* New York: Springer.

Perlman, H. (1957) *Social casework: A problem-solving process.* Chicago: University of Chicago Press.

Peters, A. J. (1997). Themes in group work with lesbian and gay adolescents. *Social Work with Groups, 20*(2), 51–69.

Peterson, D. (2007, August 29). Income up: Fewer of us in poverty. *Star Tribune,* A1 & A10.

Petr, C. & Walter, U. (2005). Best practices inquiry: A multidimensional, value-critical framework. *Journal of Social Work Education, 41*(2), 251–267.

Philip, C. E. (1994). Letting go: Problems with termination when a therapist is seriously ill or dying. *Smith College Studies in Social Work, 64*(2), 169–179.

Philip, C. E., & Stevens, E. V. (1992). Countertransference issues for the consultant when a colleague is critically ill (or dying). *Clinical Social Work Journal, 20*(4), 411–419.

Pichot, T., & Dolan, Y. (2003). Solution-focused brief therapy: Its effective use in agency settings. New York: Haworth Press.

Pierce, W. J., & Elisme, E. (1997). Understanding and working with Haitian immigrant families. *Journal of Family Social Work, 2*(1), 49–65.

Piliavin, I., Wright, B. R. W., Mare, R. D., & Westerfelt, A. H. (1996). Exits from and returns to homelessness. *Social Service Review, 70*(1), 33–57.

Pilsecker, C. (1987). A patient dies—A social worker reviews his work. *Social Work in Health Care, 13*(2), 35–45.

Pincus, A., & Minahan, A. (1973). *Social work practice: Model and method.* Itasca, IL: F. E. Peacock.

Poindexter, C. C. (1997). In the aftermath: Serial crisis intervention for people with HIV. *Health and Social Work, 22*(2), 125–132.

Pokorny, A. D., Miller, B. A., Kaplan, H. B. (1972). The Brief MAST: A shortened version of the Michigan Alcoholism Screening Test. *American Journal of Psychiatry, 129*(3), 342–345.

Pollack, S. (2004). Anti-oppressive social work practice with women in prison: Discursive reconstructions and alternative practices. *British Journal of Social Work, 34*(5), 693–707.

Pollio, D. E. (1995). Use of humor in crisis intervention. *Families in Society, 76*(6), 376–384.

Pollio, D. (2006). The art of evidence based practice. *Research on Social Work Practice 16*(2), 224–232.

Polowy, C. I., & Gilbertson, J. (1997). *Social workers and subpoenas: Office of General Counsel Law Notes.* Washington, DC: NASW Press.

Pomeroy, E. C., Rubin, A., & Walker, R. J. (1995). Effectiveness of a psychoeducational and task-centered group intervention of family members of people with AIDS. *Social Work Research, 19,* 129–152.

Ponce, D. (1980). The Filipinos: The Philippine background. In J. McDermott, Jr., W. Tseng, & T. Maretski (Eds.), *People and cultures of Hawaii* (pp. 155–163). Honolulu: University of Hawaii Press.

Pope, K. S., Keith-Spiegel, P., & Tabachnick, B. G. (1986). Sexual attraction to clients. *American Psychologist, 41,* 147–158.

Potter-Efron, R., & Potter-Efron, P. (1992). *Anger, alcoholism and addiction: Treating anger in a chemical dependency setting.* New York: Norton.

Potocky-Tripodi, M. (2002). *Best practices for social work with refugees and immigrants.* New York: Columbia University Press.

Potocky-Tripodi, M. (2003). Refugee economic adaptation: Theory, evidence and implications for policy and practice. *Journal of Social Service Research, 30,* 63–91.

Poulin, J. (2000). *Collaborative social work. Strengths-based generalist practice.* Itasca, IL: F. E. Peacock.

Powell, M., Thomson, D. and Dietze, P. (1997). Memories of an event: interviewing separate occurrences. Implications for children. *Families in Society, 78*(6), 600–610.

Prochaska, J. O., & DiClemente, C. C. (1986). Towards a comprehensive model of change. In W. R. Miller & N. Heather (Eds.), *Treating addictive behaviors: Processes of change* (pp. 3–28). New York: Pergamon Press.

Prochaska, J., DiClemente, C. C., & Norcross, J. C. (1992). Transtheoretical therapy: Toward a more integrative model of change. *Psychotherapy: Theory, Research, and Practice, 19,* 276–288.

Proctor, E. (2007). Implementing Evidence-Based Practice in social work education: Principles, strategies, and partnerships. *Research on Social Work Practice; 17,* 583–591.

Proctor, E. K., & and Davis, L. E. (1994). The challenge of racial difference: Skills for clinical practice. *Social Work, 39*(3), 314–323.

Proehl, R.A. (2001). *Organizational change in human services.* Thousand Oaks, CA: Sage Publications.

Project Cork. (n.d.) *CAGE.* Retrieved September 8, 2008, from http://www.projectcork.org/clinical_tools/html/CAGE.html

Protecting the privacy of patients' health information. (2003). Retrieved May 1, 2004, from http://www.hhs.gov/news/facts/privacy.html

Puryear, D. (1979). *Helping people in crisis.* San Francisco: Jossey-Bass.

Q

Queralt, M. (1984). Understanding Cuban immigrants: A cultural perspective. *Social Work, 29,* 115–121.

R

Ragg, D., Okagbue-Reaves, J., & Piers, J. (2007, October 28). *Shaping student interactive habits: a critical function of practice education.* Presentation at Council of Social Work Education Annual Program Meeting #74a.

Raines, J. C. (1996). Self-disclosure in clinical social work. *Clinical Social Work Journal, 24*(4), 357–375.

Ramakrishman, K. R., Balgopal, P. R., & Pettys, G. L. (1994). Task-centered work with communities. In E. R. Tolson, W. J. Reid, & C. D. Garvin (Eds.). *Generalist Practice: A task-centered approach.* New York: Columbia University Press.

Ramos, B. M. & Garvin, C. (2003). Task-centered treatment with culturally diverse populations, In E. R. Tolson, W. J. Reid, & C. D. Garvin (Eds.), *Generalist practice: A Task-centered approach* (2nd ed., pp. 441–463). New York: Columbia University Press.

Ramos, B. M., & Tolson, E. R. (2008). The task-centered model. In N. Coady & P. Lehmann (Eds.), *Theoretical perspectives for direct social work practice. A generalist-eclectic approach* (2nd ed., pp. 275–295). New York: Springer Publishing Company.

Range, L. M., & Knott, E. C. (1997). Twenty suicide assessment instruments: Evaluation and recommendations. *Death Studies, 21,* 25–58.

Rank, M. R., & Hirschl, T. A. (1999). The likelihood of poverty across the American lifespan. *Social Work, 44,* 201–208.

Rank. M. R., & Hirschl, T. A. (2002). Welfare use as a life course event: Toward a new understanding of the U.S. safety net. *Social Work, 47,* 327–358.

Rapoport, L. (1967). Crisis-oriented short-term casework. *Social Service Review, 41*(1), 31–43.

Rapp, C. A. (1998). *The strengths model: Case management with people suffering from severe and persistent mental illness.* New York: Oxford University Press.

Eloise Rathbone-McCuan "Elder Abuse" *Encyclopedia of Social Work.* Terry Mizrahi and Larry E. Davis. *Copyright © 2008 by National Association of Social Workers and Oxford University Press, Inc..* Encyclopedia of Social Work: (e-reference edition). Oxford University Press. University of North Carolina - Chapel Hill. 25 July 2008 http://www.oxford-naswsocialwork.com/entry?entry=t203.e122

Ratliff, S. S. (1996). The multicultural challenge to health care. In M. C. Julia, *Multicultural awareness in the health care professions.* Needham Heights, MA: Allyn & Bacon.

Rauch, J. B. (1993). *Assessment: A sourcebook for social work practice.* Milwaukee, WI: Families International.

Ray, N. (2007). Lesbian gay, bisexual and transgender youth: An epidemic of homelessness. National Gay and Lesbian Policy Institute, July 30, 2007. Retrieved July 16, 2008, http://www.thetaskforce.org

Raymond, G. T., Teare, R. J., & Atherton, C. R. (1996). Is "field of practice" a relevant organizing principle for the MSW curriculum? *Journal of Social Work Education, 32*(1), 19–30.

Reamer, F. (1989). *Ethical dilemmas in social service* (2nd ed.). New York: Columbia University Press.

Reamer, F. G. (1994). *Social work malpractice and liability: Strategies for prevention.* New York: Columbia University Press.

Reamer, F. G. (1995). Malpractice claims against social workers: First facts. *Social Work, 40*(5), 595–601.

Reamer, F. G. (1998). *Ethical standards in social work: A critical review of the NASW code of ethics.* Washington, DC: NASW Press.

Reamer, F. G. (1999). *Social work values and ethics* (2nd ed.). New York: Columbia University Press.

Reamer, F. G. (2001). *Tangled relationships: Managing boundary issues in the human services.* New York: Columbia University Press.

Reamer. F. G., (2005). Ethical and legal standards in social work: Consistency and conflicts. *Families in Society, 86*(2), 163–169.

Reese, D. J., Ahern, R. E., Nair, S., O'Faire, J. D., & Warren, C. (1999). Hospice access and use by African Americans: Addressing cultural and institutional barriers through participatory action research, *Social Work, 44*(6), 549–559.

Regehr, C., & Angle, B. (1997). Coercive influences: Informed consent in court-mandated social work practice. *Social Work, 42*(3), 300–306.

Reinecke, M., Datillo, F. & Freeman, A. (2003). *Cognitive therapy with children* (2nd ed.). New York: Guilford Press.

Reisch, M. (2002). Social work and politics in the new century. *Social Work, 45*(4), 293–226.

Reid, K. E. (1991). *Social work practice with groups: A clinical perspective.* Pacific Grove, CA: Brooks/Cole.

Reid, K. E. (2002). Clinical social work with groups. In A. R. Roberts & G. J. Greene (Eds.), *Social workers' desk reference* (pp. 432–436). New York: Oxford University Press.

Reid, W. J. (1972). *Task-centered casework.* New York: Columbia University Press.

Reid, W. J. (1975). A test of the task-centered approach. *Social Work, 22,* 3–9.

Reid, W. J. (1977). Process and outcome in the treatment of family problems. In W. Reid & L. Epstein (Eds.), *Task centered practice. Self-help groups and human service agencies: How they work together.* Milwaukee: Family Service of America.

Reid, W. J. (1978). *The task-centered system.* New York: Columbia University Press.

Reid, W. J. (1985). *Family problem solving.* New York: Columbia University Press.

Reid, W. J. (1987). Task-centered research. In *Encyclopedia of social work* (vol. 2, pp. 757–764). Silver Spring, MD: NASW Press.

Reid, W. J. (1992). *Task strategies.* New York: Columbia University Press.

Reid, W. J. (1994). The empirical practice movement. *Social Service Review, 68*(2), 165–184.

Reid, W.J. (1996). Task-centered social work. In F. J. Turner (Ed.). *Social work treatment: Interlocking theoretical approaches* (4th ed., pp 617–640). New York: Free Press.

Reid, W. J. (1997a). Research on task-centered practice. *Social Work, 21*(3), 131–137.

Reid, W. J. (2000). *The task planner.* New York: Columbia University Press.

Reid, W.J., & Bailey-Dempsey, C. (1995). The effects of monetary incentives in school performance. *Families in Society, 76,* 331–340.

Reid, W.J., & Epstein, L. (Eds.). (1972). *Task-centered casework.* New York: Columbia University Press.

Reid, W. J., Epstein, L., Brown, L., Tolson, E. R., & Rooney, R.H. (1980). Task-centered school social work. *Social Work in Education, 2,* 7–24.

Reid, W. J., & Fortune, A. E. (2002). The task-centered model. In A. R. Roberts & G. J. Greene (Eds.), *Social workers' desk reference* (pp. 101–104). New York: Oxford University Press.

Reid, W., & Hanrahan, P. (1982). Recent evaluations of social work: Grounds for optimism. *Social Work, 27,* 328–340.

Reid, W., & Shyne, A. (1969). *Brief and extended casework.* New York: Columbia University Press.

Reilly, T. (2001). Collaboration in action: An uncertain process. *Administration in Social Work, 25*(1), 52–74.

Reisch M., & Sommerfeld, D. (2003a). Interorganizational relationships among nonprofits in the aftermath of welfare reform. *Social Work, 48*(3), 307–319.

Reisch, M., & Sommerfeld, D. (2003b). The "Other America" after welfare reform: A view from nonprofit sector. *Journal of Poverty 7*(1/2), 69–95.

Reitan, T. C. (1998). Theories of interorganizational relations in the human services. *Social Service Review, 72*(3), 285–309.

Renfrey, G. S. (1992). Cognitive-behavior therapy and the Native American client. *Behavior Therapy, 23,* 321–340.

Resnick, C., & Dziegielewski, S. F. (1996). The relationship between therapeutic termination and job satisfaction among medical social workers. *Social Work in Health Care, 23*(3), 17–33.

Reuben, D. B., & Siu, A. L. (1990). An objective measure of physical function of elderly outpatients: The Physical Performance Test. *Journal of the American Geriatrics Society, 38,* 1105–1112.

Reynolds, B. C. (1951). Must it hurt to be helped? In B. C. Reynolds, *Social work and social living:*

Explorations philosophy and practice. New York: Citadel Press.

Reynolds, T., & Jones, G. (1996). Trauma debriefings: A one-session group model. In B. L. Stempler, M. Glass, & C. M. Savinelli (Eds.), *Social group work today and tomorrow: Moving to advanced training and practice* (pp. 129–139). Binghamton, NY: Haworth Press.

Rheingold, A. A., Herbert, J. D., & Franklin, M. E. (2003). Cognitive bias in adolescents with social anxiety disorder. *Cognitive Therapy and Research, 27,* 639–655.

Ribner, D. S., & Knei-Paz, C. (2002). Client's view of a successful helping relationship. *Social Work, 47*(4), 379–387.

Rice, A. H. (1998). *Focusing on strengths: Focus group research on the impact of welfare reform.* A paper presented for the XX Symposium Association for the Advancement of Social Work with Groups, October 1998, Miami, FL.

Richey, C. A., & Roffman, R. A. (1999). One the sidelines of guidelines: Further thoughts on the fit between clinical guidelines and social work practice. *Research on Social Work Practice, 9,* 311–321.

Richman, L. S., Kohn-Woods, L., & Williams, D. R. (2007). Discrimination and racial identity for mental health service utilization. *Journal of Social and Clinical Psychology, 26*(4), 960–980.

Rittenhouse, J. (1997). Feminist principles in survivor's groups: Out-of-group contact. *The Journal for Specialists in Group Work, 22,* 111–119.

Rittner, B., & Dozier, C. D. (2000). Effects of court-ordered substance abuse treatment on child protective services cases. *Social Work 45*(2), 131–140.

Rivera, F. G., & Erlich, J. L. (1998). *Community organizing in a diverse society* (3rd ed.). Boston: Allyn & Bacon.

Roberts, A. R. (1990). *Crisis intervention handbook: Assessment, treatment, and research.* Belmont, CA: Wadsworth.

Roberts, A. R. (2000). *An overview of crisis theory and crisis intervention.* In A. R. Roberts (Ed.), *Crisis interviewing handbook: Assessment, treatment, and research.* Belmont, CA: Wadsworth.

Roberts, A. R., & Greene, G. J. (Eds.) (2002). *Social workers' desk reference* (pp. 112–115). New York: Oxford University Press.

Roberts, A. R. (2005). *Crisis intervention handbook: Assessment, treatment and research* (3rd ed.). New York: Oxford University Press.

Roberts, D. (2002). *Shattered bonds. The color of child welfare.* New York: Basic Books.

Roberts-DeGennaro, M. (1987). *Developing case.* New York: Columbia University Press.

Robinson, J. B. (1989). Clinical treatment of black families: Issues and strategies. *Social Work, 34,* 323–329.

Robinson, V. (1930). *A changing psychology in social work.* Chapel Hill: University of North Carolina Press.

Robinson, D. R. (2000). Challenges from the front line: A contemporary view. In A social justice framework for child welfare. The agenda for a 21st century. Conference Proceedings, University of Minnesota, June, 23, 2000.

Rodenborg, N. (2004, November). Services to African American children in poverty: Institutional discrimination in child welfare. *Journal of Poverty: Innovations on Social, Political and Economic Inequalities, 3*(3).

Rogers, C. (1957). The necessary and sufficient conditions of therapeutic personality change. *Journal of Consulting Psychology, 22,* 95–103.

Rodgers, A. Y., & Potocky, M. (1997). Evaluating culturally sensitive practice through single-system design: Methodological issues and strategies. *Research on Social Work Practice, 7*(3), 391–401.

Ronnau, J. P., & Marlow, C. R. (1995). Family preservation: Poverty and the value of diversity. *Families in Society, 74*(9), 538–544.

Rooney, G. D. (1997). Concerns of employed women: Issues for employee assistance programs. In A. Daly (Ed.), *Work force diversity: Issues and perspectives in the world of work* (pp. 314–330). Washington, DC: NASW Press.

Rooney, G. D. (2000). Examining the values and ethics reflected in policy decisions. In K. Strom-Gottfried (Ed.), *Social work practice: Cases, activities and exercises* (pp. 50–54). Thousand Oaks, CA: Pine Forge Press.

Rooney, G. D. (2009). Oppression and involuntary status. In R. H. Rooney (Ed.). *Strategies for work with involuntary clients* (2nd ed. In press). New York: Columbia University Press.

Rooney, G. D., Neathery, K., & Suzek, M. (1997). *Defining child neglect: A community perspective.* Minneapolis, MN: Minneapolis Human Services Network Research Report.

Rooney, R. H. (1981). A task-centered reunification model for foster care. In A.A. Maluccio & P. Sinanoglu (Eds.), *The challenge of partnership: Working with biological parents of children in foster care* (pp. 135–159). New York: Child Welfare League of America.

Rooney, R. H. (1992). *Strategies for work with involuntary clients.* New York: Columbia University Press.

Rooney, R. H. (2009). *Strategies for work with involuntary clients* (2nd ed.). New York: Columbia.

Rooney, R. H., & Bibus, A. A. (1996). Multiple lenses: Ethnically sensitive practice with involuntary clients who are having difficulties with drugs or alcohol. *Journal of Multicultural Social Work, 4*(2), 59–73.

Rooney, R. H., & Chovanec, M. (2004). Involuntary groups. In C. Garvin, L. Gutierrez, & M. Galinsky (Eds.), *Handbook of social work with groups.* New York: Guilford Press.

Rose, S. D. (1989). *Working with adults in groups: Integrating cognitive-behavioral and small group strategies.* San Francisco: Jossey-Bass.

Rose, S. M. (1992). *Case management and social work practice.* Menlo Park, CA: Longman Press.

Rose, S. D. (1998). *Group therapy with troubled youth: A cognitive behavioral interactive approach.* Thousand Oaks, CA: Sage Publications.

Rosen, A. (1972). The treatment relationship: A conceptualization. *Journal of Clinical Psychology, 38,* 329–337.

Rosenblatt, E. (1994). *Metaphor of family systems theory.* New York: Guilford Press.

Rosenthal, K. (1988). The inanimate self in adult victims of child abuse and neglect. *Social Casework, 69*(8), 505–510.

Rosenthal Gelman, C. (2004). Empirically-based principles for culturally competent practice with Latinos. *Journal of Ethnic and Cultural Diversity in Social Work, 13*(1), 83–108.

Ross, C. (1997). *Something to draw on: Activities and interventions using an art therapy approach.* London: Jessica Kingsley.

Roth, W. (1987). Disabilities: Physical. In *Encyclopedia of social work* (vol. *1,* pp. 434–438). Silver Spring, MD: NASW Press.

Rothman, J. (1991). A model of case management: Toward empirically based practice. *Social Work, 36*(6), 521–528.

Rothman, J. (1994). *Practice with highly vulnerable clients: Case management and community-based service.* Englewood Cliffs, NJ: Prentice-Hall.

Rothman, J. (1995). Approaches to community intervention. In F. M. Cox, J. L. Erlich, J. J. Rothman & J. Tropman (Eds.). *Strategies of community intervention.* Itasca, Ill: Peacock.

Rothman, J. (1999). Intent and consent. In J. Rothman (Ed.), *Reflections on community organizations: Enduring themes and critical issues* (pp. 3–26). Itasca, IL: F. E. Peacock.

Rothman, J., Erlich, J. L., & Tropman, J. (1995). *Strategies of community intervention* (5th ed.). Itasca, IL: F. E. Peacock.

Rothman,, J., Erlich, J. L., & Tropman, J. E. (1999). *Strategies of community interventions* (5th ed.). Itasca, IL: F.E, Peacock.

Rothman, J., Erlich, J. L., & Tropman, J. E. (2001). *Strategies of community interventions* (6th ed.). Itasca, IL: F. E. Peacock.

Rothman, J., Gant, L.M., & Hnat, S.A. (1985). Mexican-American family culture. *Social Service Review, 59,* 197–215.

Rothman, J., & Tropman, J. (1987). Models of community organization and development and macro practice perspectives. Their mixing and phasing. In F.M. Cox, J. L. Erlich, J. J. Rothman & J. Tropman (Eds.). *Strategies of community organizing* (pp. 3–26) Itasca, Ill: Peacock.

Rotunno, M., & McGoldrick, M. (1982). Italian families. In M. McGoldrick, J. Pearce, & J. Giordano (Eds.), *Ethnicity and family therapy* (pp. 340–363). New York: Guilford Press.

Rounds, K. A., Galinsky, M. J., & Stevens, L. S. (1991). Linking people with AIDS in rural communities: The telephone group. *Social Work, 36*(1), 13–18.

Rowan, A. B. (2001). Adolescent substance abuse and suicide. *Depression and Anxiety, 14,* 186–191.

Rowe, R., Maughan, B., Worthman, C. M., Costello, E. J., & Angold, A. (2004). Testosterone, antisocial behavior, and social dominance in boys: Pubertal development and biosocial interaction. *Biological Psychiatry, 55*(5), 546–552.

Royse, D., Thyer, B. A., Padgett, D. K., & Logan, T. K. (2001). *Program evaluation: An introduction* (3rd ed.). Belmont, CA: Brooks/Cole.

Rozzini, R., Frisoni, G. B., Bianchetti, A., Zanetti, O., & Trabucchi, M. (1993). Physical Performance Test and Activities of Daily Living scales in the assessment of health status in elderly people. *Journal of the American Geriatrics Society, 41,* 1109–1113.

Rubin, A. (2007). Improving the teaching of evidence-based practice: Introduction to the special issue. *Research on Social Work Practice, 17,* 541–547.

Rubin, A. & Babbie, E. (2005). *Research methods for Social Work,* (5th Ed.). Belmont, CA: Wadsworth/Thomson Learning.

Rudolph, K. D. & Clark, A. G. (2001). Conceptions of relationship in children with depression and aggressive symptoms. Social-cognitive distortions or reality. *Journal of Abnormal Child Psychology, 29*(1), 41–56.

Ryder, R., & Tepley, R. (1993). No more Mr. Nice Guy: Informed consent and benevolence in marital family therapy. *Family Relations, 42*, 145–147.

Rzepnicki, T. L. (1991). Enhancing the durability of intervention gains: A challenge for the 1990s. *Social Service Review, 65*(1), 92–111.

Rzepnicki, T. L. (2004). Informed consent and practice evaluation: Making the decision to participate meaningful. In H. E. Briggs, & T. L. Rzepnicki (Eds.), *Using evidence in social work practice: Behavioral perspectives* (pp. 273–290). Chicago, IL: Lyceum Books, Inc.

S

Safran, J. D., & Muran, J. C. (2000). Resolving therapeutic alliance ruptures: Diversity and integration. *In Session: Psychotherapy in Practice, 56*(2), 597–605.

Saleebey, D. (Ed.) (1992). *The strengths perspective in social work practice.* New York: Longman.

Saleeby, D. (1996). The Strength perspective in social work practice: Extensions and cautions. *Social Work, 41*(3), 296–305.

Saleebey, D. (Ed.) (1997). *The strengths perspective in social work practice* (2nd ed.). Needham Heights, MA: Allyn & Bacon.

Saleebey, D. (2002). The strengths perspective in social work practice (3rd ed.). New York: Allyn & Bacon.

Saleebey, D. (2004). The power of place: Another look at the environment. *Families in Society 85*(1), 7–16.

Salmon, R., & Graziano, R. (Eds.). (2004). *Group work and aging: Issues in practice research and education.* New York: Haworth Press.

Salston, M., & Figley, C. R. (2004). Secondary traumatic stress effects of working with survivors of criminal victimization. *Journal of Traumatic Stress, 16*(2), 167–174.

Salzar, M. S. (1997). Consumer empowerment in mental health organizations: Concepts, benefits and impediments. *Administration and Policy in Mental Health, 24*, 425–434.

Sandfort, J. (1999). The structural impediments to human services collaboration: Examining welfare reform at the front lines. *Social Service Review, 73*(3), 314–339.

Sands, R. G. (1989). The social worker joins the team: A look at the socialization process. *Social Work in Health Care, 14*(2), 1–14.

Sands, R. G., Stafford, J., & McClelland, M. (1990). "I beg to differ": Conflict in the interdisciplinary team. *Social Work in Health Care, 14*(3), 55–72.

Santos, D. (1995). Deafness. In *Encyclopedia of social work* (vol. *19*, pp. 685–703). Washington, DC: NASW Press.

Sarkisian, N., & Gerstel, N. (2004). Kinship support among blacks and whites: Race and family organization. *American Sociological Review, 69*, 812–836.

Sarri, R. (1987). Administration in social welfare. In *Encyclopedia of social work* (vol. *1*, pp. 27–40). Silver Spring, MD: NASW Press.

Satir, V. (1967). *Conjoint family therapy.* Palo Alto, CA: Science & Behavior Books.

Satir, V. M., (1972). *Peoplemaking.* Palo Alto, CA: Science and Behavior Books.

Saulnier, C. F. (1997). Alcohol problems and marginalization: Social group work with lesbians. *Social Work with Groups, 20*(3), 37–59.

Sauter, J., & Franklin, C. (1998). Assessing Post-Traumatic Stress Disorder in children: Diagnostic and measurement strategies. *Research on Social Work Practice, 8*, 251–270.

Savner, S. (2000, July/August). Welfare reform and racial/ethnic minorities: The questions to ask. *Poverty & Race, 9*(4), 3–5.

Schaffer, D. (1992). *NIHM diagnostic interview schedule for children, version 2.3.* New York: Columbia University, Division of Child and Adolescent Psychiatry.

Schein, E. H. (1985). *Organizational culture and leadership.* San Francisco: Jossey-Bass.

Scheyett, A. (2006). Danger and opportunity in teaching evidence-based practice in the social work curriculum. *Journal of Teaching in Social Work, 26*(1): 19–29.

Schiller, L. Y. (1997). Rethinking stages of development in women's groups: Implications for practice. *Social Work with Groups, 20*(3), 3–19.

Schneider, R. L., & Lester, L. (2001). *Social work advocacy. A new framework for action.* Brooks/Cole.

Schneider, R. L., & Netting, F. E. (1999). Influencing social policy in a time of devolution: Upholding social work's great tradition. *Social Work, 44*(4), 349–357.

Schopler, J., & Galinsky, M. (1974). Goals in social group work practice: Formulation, implementation and evaluation. In P. Glasser, R. Sarri, & R. Vinter (Eds.), *Individual change through small groups.* New York: Free Press.

Schopler, J. H., & Galinsky, M. J. (1981). Meeting practice needs: Conceptualizing the open-ended group. *Social Work with Groups, 7*(2), 3–21.

Schopler, J. H., Galinsky, M. J., & Abell, M. (1997). Creating community through telephone and computer groups: Theoretical and practice perspectives. *Social Work with Groups, 20*(4), 19–34.

Schopler, J. H., Galinsky, M. J., Davis, L. E., & Despard, M. (1996). The RAP model: Assessing a framework for leading multicultural groups. *Social Work with Groups, 19*(3/4), 21–39.

Schrier, C. (1980). Guidelines for record-keeping under privacy and open-access laws. *Social Work, 25,* 452–457.

Schwartz, G. (1989). Confidentiality revisited. *Social Work, 34*(3), 223–226.

Search Institute. (2002). National Survey of Parents. Minneapolis. Minnesota: Same.

Seay, H. A., Fee, V. E., Holloway, K. S., & Giesen, J. M. (2003). A multi component treatment package to increase anger control in teacher referred boys. *Child and Family Behavior Therapy, 25*(1), 1–18.

Secret, M., Jordan, A., & Ford, J. (1999). Empowerment evaluation as a social work strategy. *Social Work, 24*(2), 120–127.

Segal, U. A. (1991). Cultural variables in Asian Indian families. *Families in Society, 72,* 233–244.

Segal, E. A. (2007). Social empathy: A tool to address the contradictions of working but still poor. *Families in Society, 88* (3), 333–337.

Segal, Z. V., Williams, J. M., & Teasdale, J. D. (2002). *Mindfulness-based cognitive therapy for depression: a new approach to preventing relapse.* New York: Guilford.

Selekman, M. D. (2005). Pathways to change: Brief therapy with difficult children (2nd ed.). New York: Guilford Press.

Selvini-Palazzoli, M., Boscolo, L., Cecchin, G., & Prata, G. (1974). The treatment of children through brief therapy of their parents. *Family Process, 13,* 429–442.

Selzer, M. L. (1971). The Michigan Alcoholism Screening Test: The quest for a new diagnostic instrument. *American Journal of Psychiatry 27*(12), 1653–1658.

Senge, P. (1990). *The fifth discipline: The art and practice of learning organization.* New York: Doubleday Currency.

Senge, P. M. (1994). *The fifth discipline field book: Strategies and tolls for building a learning organization.* New York: Bantam, Doubleday, Dell.

Sengupta, S. (2001, July 8). How many poor children is too many? *The New York Times,* WK 3.

Serres, C. (2004, June 6). House of hurdles. *Minneapolis Star Tribune,* pp. A1, A21.

Shamai, M. (2003). Therapeutic effects of qualitative research: Reconstructing the experience of treatment as a by-product of qualitative evaluation. *Social Service Review, 77*(3), 454–467.

Shane, P. G. (2007). The effects of incarceration on children and families. National Association of Social Work, Child Welfare Section Connection, *1,* 1–5.

Shannon, T. R., Kleniewski, N., & Cross, W. M. (2002). Urban problems in sociological perspective. In *Nature of urban life* (4th ed., pp. 63–89). Long Grove, IL: Waveland Press.

Sharpe, L., & Tarrier, M. (1992). A cognitive-behavioral treatment approach for problem gambling. *Journal of Cognitive Psychotherapy, 5,* 119–127.

Shea, S. C. (1998). The chronological assessment of suicide events: a practical interviewing strategy for the elicitation of suicidal ideation. *Journal of Clinical Psychiatry, 59,* 58–72. Retrieved July 2, 2008, from http://www.suicideassessment.com/web/case/case-JCP.html

Sheafor, B., Horejsi, C. R., & Horejsi, G. A. (1994). *Techniques and guidelines for social work practice* (3rd ed.). Boston: Allyn & Bacon.

Sherraden, B., Slosar, B., & Sherraden, M. (2002). Innovation in social policy: Collaborative policy advocacy. *Social Work 47*(3), 209–211.

Sherwood, D. A. (1998). Spiritual assessment as a normal part of social work practice: Power to help and power to harm. *Social Work and Christianity, 25*(2), 80–90.

Shih, M., & Sanchez, D. (2005). Perspectives and research on the positive and negative implications of having multiple racial identities. *Psychology Bulletin, 131*(4), 569–591.

Shneidman, E. S. (1971). The management of the presuicidal, suicidal and postsuicidal patient. *Annals of Internal Medicine, 75,* 441–458.

Shoham, V., Rorhbaugh, M., & Patterson, J. (1995). Problem and solution-focused couples therapies: The MRI and Milwaukee modes. In N. S. Jacobson & A. S. Gurman (Eds.), *Clinical handbook for couple therapy.* New York: Guildford Press.

Shulman, L. (1984). *The skills of helping individuals and groups* (2nd ed.). Itasca, IL: F. E. Peacock.

Shulman, L. (1992). *The skills of helping individuals and groups* (3rd ed.). Itasca, IL: F. E. Peacock.

Shulman, L. (2009). *The Skills of Helping Individuals, Families, Groups, and Communities.* (6th ed.). Belmont, CA: Brooks/Cole.

Silberberg. S. (2001). Searching for family resilience. *Family Matters, 58,* 52–57.

Silvawe, G. W. (1995). The need for a new social work perspective in an African setting: The case of social casework in Zambia. *British Journal of Social Work 25,* 71–84.

Silove, D. (2000). A conceptual framework for mass trauma. Indications for adaptation, intervention and debriefing. In B. Raphael & J. P. Wilson (Eds.). *Psychology, debriefing, theory, practice and evidence* (pp. 337–350), New York: Cambridge University Press.

Simon, J. B., Murphy, J. J. & Smith, S. M. (2005). Understanding and fostering family resilience. *The Family Journal, 13*(4), 427–436.

Simonson, N. (1976). The impact of therapist disclosure on patient disclosure. *Journal of Transpersonal Psychology, 23,* 3–6.

Siporin, M. (1975). *Introduction to social work practice.* New York: Macmillan.

Siporin, M. (1980). Ecological systems theory in social work. *Journal of Sociology and Social Welfare, 7,* 507–532.

Skinner, B. F. (1974). *About behaviorism.* New York: Knopf.

Slater, S. (1995). *The lesbian lifecycle.* New York: Free Press.

Smagner, J. P., & Sullivan, M. H. (2005). Investigating the effectiveness of behavioral parenting with involuntary clients in child welfare settings. *Research of Social Work Practice, 15*(6), 431–439.

Smith, B. D., & Marsh, J. C. (2002). Client–service matching in substance abuse treatment for women with children. *Journal of Substance Abuse Treatment, 22,* 161–168.

Smith, C., & Carlson, B. E. (1997). Stress, coping and resilience in children and youth. *Social Service Review, 71*(2), 231–256.

Smith, C., & Nylund, D. (1997), Narrative therapies with children and adolescents. New York: Guilford Press.

Smith, N. (2006). empowering the "unfit" mother: increasing empathy, redefining the label. *Affilia. 21*(4), 448–457.

Smith, T. B. (2004). *Practicing multiculturalism: Affirming diversity in counseling and psychology.* Boston: Pearson.

Smokowski, P. R., Rose, S. D., & Bacallao, M. L. (2001). Damaging therapeutic groups: How vulnerable consumers become group casualties. *Small Group Research, 32*(2), 223–251.

Smyth, N.J. (2005) Drug Use, Self-Efficacy, and Coping Skills Among People with Concurrent Substance Abuse and Personality Disorders: Implications for Relapse Prevention. *Journal of Social Work Practice in the Addictions 5*(4), 63–79.

Social workers and psychotherapist–patient privilege: *Jaffee v. Redmond* revisited. (n.d.) Retrieved March 2, 2005, from http://www.socialworkers.org/ldf/legalrissue/200503

Solis, D., & Corchado, A. (2002, January 25). "Recession may hurt Hispanics the most." *The Dallas Morning News,* pp. 2D, 11D.

Solomon, P., & Draine, J. (1996). Service delivery differences between consumer and nonconsumer case managers in mental health. *Research on Social Work Practice, 6*(2), 193–207.

Sommers-Flanagan, R. (2007). Ethical considerations in crisis and humanitarian interventions. *Ethics and Behavior, 17*(2), 187–202.

Sosin, M., & Callum, S. (1983). Advocacy: A conceptualization for social work practice. *Social Work, 28,* 12–17.

Sotomayor, M. (1991). Introduction. In M. Sotomayor (Ed.), *Empowering Hispanic families: A critical issue for the 90s* (pp. xi–xxiii). Milwaukee, WI: Family Service America.

Sousa, L., Ribeiro, C., & Rodriques, S. (2006). Intervention with multiproblem poor clients: Toward a strengths-focused perspective. *Journal of Social Work Practice, 20*(2), 189–204.

Sowers-Hoag, K., & Thyer, B. (1985). Teaching social work practice: A review and analysis of empirical research. *Journal of Social Work Education, 21*(3), 5–15.

Specht, H., & Courtney, M. E. (1994). *Unfaithful angels: How social work abandoned its mission.* Toronto: Maxwell Macmillan Canada.

Speisman, J. (1959). Depth of interpretation and verbal resistance in psychotherapy. *Journal of Consulting Psychology, 23,* 93–99.

Spitalnick, J. S., & McNair, L. D. (2005). Journal of Sex and Marital Therapy, *31,* 43–56.

Spitzer, R., Williams, J., Kroenke, K., Linzer, M., DeGruy, F. III, Hahn, S., Brody, D., & Johnson, J. (1994). Utility of a new procedure for diagnosing mental disorders in primary care: The PRIME-MD 1000 study. *Journal of the American Medical Association, 272,* 1749–1756.

Spoth, R., Guyll, M., Chao, W., & Molgaard, V. (2003). Exploratory study of a preventive intervention with general population African American families. *Journal of Early Adolescence, 23*(4). 435–468.

Spriggs, W. E. (2007). *The changing face of poverty in America, Why are so many women, children, racial and cultural minorities still poor?* Ending Poverty in America, Special Report of The American Prospect, The Annie E. Casey Foundation & The Northwest Area Foundation. A5–A7.

Springer, D., & Franklin, C. (2003). Standardized assessment measures and computer-assisted assessment technologies. In C. Jordan & C. Franklin (Eds.), *Clinical assessment for social workers. Quantitative and qualitative methods* (2nd ed., pp. 97–137). Chicago: Lyceum Books.

Springer, D. W., Lynch, C., & Rubin, A (2000). Effects of Solution-focused mutual aid group for Hispanic children or incarcerated parents. *Child and Adolescent Social Work*, *17*(6), 431–442.

Srebnik, D. S., & Saltzberg, E. A. (1994). Feminist cognitive-behavioral therapy for negative body image. *Women and Therapy*, *15*(2), 117–133.

Staples, L. H. (1990). Powerful ideas about empowerment. *Administration in Social Work*, *14*(2), 29–42.

Steinmetz, G. (1992). Fetal alcohol syndrome. *National Geographic*, *181*(2), 36–39.

St Lawrence, J. S., Brasfield, T. L., Jefferson, K. W., O'Bannon, R. E., & Shirley, A. (1995). Cognitive-behavioral intervention to reduce the African adolescents' risk for HIV infection. *Journal of Counseling Psychology*, *63*(2), 221–237.

Stokes, J. P. (1983). Components of group cohesion: Intermember attraction, instrumental value, and risk taking. *Small Group Behavior*, *14*, 163–173.

Strean, H. (1997). Comment on James C. Raines' "Self disclosure in clinical social work" *Clinical Social Work Journal*, *25*(3), 365–366.

Steigerwald, F., & Stone, D. (1999). Cognitive restructuring and the 12-step program of Alcoholics Anonymous. *Journal of Substance Abuse*, *16*, 321–327.

Stoesen, L. (2004). End to Iraq prisoner abuse demanded. *NASW News*, *49*(7), 1.

Stone, M., Lewis, C., & Beck, A. (1994). The structure of Yalom's Curative Factors Scale. *International Journal of Group Psychotherapy*, *23*(2), 155–168.

Storm, C. (1991). The remaining thread: Matching change and stability signals. *Journal of Strategic and Systemic Therapies*, *10*, 114–117.

Strom-Gottfried, K. (1998a). Applying a conflict resolution framework in managed care. *Social Work*, *43*(5), 393–401.

Strom-Gottfried, K. J. (1998b). Informed consent meets managed care. *Health and Social Work*, *23*(1), 25–33.

Strom-Gottfried, K. J. (1999a). Professional boundaries: An analysis of violations by social workers. *Families in Society*, *80*, 439–448.

Strom-Gottfried, K. J. (1999b). *Social work practice: Cases, activities and exercises*. Thousand Oaks, CA: Pine Forge Press.

Strom-Gottfried, K. J. (2007) *Straight talk about professional ethics*. Chicago: Lyceum.

Strom-Gottfried, K. J. (2008). *The ethics of practice with minors: High stakes, hard choices*. Chicago: Lyceum.

Strom-Gottfried, K. J. (2009). The ethics of practice in home-based care. In S. Allen and E. Tracy (Eds.), *Delivering Home-based Services: A Social Work Perspective*. New York: Columbia University Press.

Strom-Gottfried, K., & Morrissey, M. (2000). The organizational diversity audit. In K. Strom-Gottfried (Ed.), *Social work practice: Cases, activities, and exercises* (pp. 168–172). Thousand Oaks, CA: Pine Forge Press.

Strom-Gottfried, K., & Mowbray, N. D. (2006). Who heals the helper? Facilitating the social worker's grief. *Families in Society: The Journal of Contemporary Social Services*, *87*(1), 9–15.

Saulnier, C. F. (2002). *Deciding who to see: Lesbians discuss their preferences in health and mental health care providers. Social Work*, *47*(4), 355–365.

Stuart, R. (1980). *Helping couples change*. New York: Guilford Press.

Stuart, P. H. (1999). Linking clients and policy: Social work's distinctive contribution. *Social Work*, *44*(4), 335–347.

Studt, E. (1968). Social work theory and implications for the practice methods. *Social Work Education Reporter*, *16*, 22–46.

Suarez, Z. E., & Siefert, H. (1998). Latinas and sexually transmitted diseases: Implications of recent research for prevention. *Social Work in Health Care*, *28*(1), 1–19.

Subramanian, K., Hernandez, S., & Martinez, A. (1995). Psychoeducational group work for low-income Latina mothers with HIV infection. *Social Work in Groups*, *18*(2/3), 53–64.

Substance Abuse and Mental Health Services Administration. (2003a). *Family Psychoeducation Fidelity Scale*. Retrieved June 19, 2008, from http://download.ncadi.samhsa.gov/ken/pdf/toolkits/family/12.FamPsy_Fidelity.pdf

Substance Abuse and Mental Health Services Administration. (2003b). *Assertive Community Treatment: Monitoring client outcomes*. Retrieved June 19, 2008, from http://download.ncadi.samhsa.gov/ken/pdf/toolkits/community/19.ACT_Client_Outcomes.pdf

Sukhodolsky, D. G., Kassinore, H., & Gorman, B. S. (2004). Cognitive behavioral therapy for anger in children and adolescents: A metaanalysis. *Aggression and Violent Behavior*, *9*, 247–269.

Sue, D. (1981). *Counseling the culturally different: Theory and practice*. New York: Wiley.

Sue, D. W. (2006). *Multicultural Social Work Practice*. Hoboken, NJ: John Wiley & Sons.

Sue, D. W., Capodilupo, C. M., Torino, G. C., Buccerri, J. M., Holder, A. M. B., Nadal, K. L., & Esquilin, M. (2007). Racial microagression in everyday life. *American Psychologist* (May-June), 271–285.

Sue, D. W., & Sue, S. (1990). *Counseling the culturally different: Theory and practice* (2nd ed.). New York: Wiley.

Sunley, R. (1997). Advocacy in the new world of managed care. *Families in Society*, *78*(1), 84–94.

Sweet, C., & Noones, J. (1989). Factors associated with premature termination from outpatient treatment. *Hospital and Community Psychiatry*, *40*(9), 947–951.

Swenson, C. (2002). Clinical social work practice: Political and social realities. In A. Roberts, & G. Greene (Eds.). *Social workers desk reference* (pp. 632–639). New York: Oxford.

Swenson, C. (1998). Clinical social work's contribution to a social justice perspective. *Social Work*, *43*(6), 527–537.

T

Taft, J. (1937). The relation of function to process in social casework. *Journal of Social Work Process*, *I*(1), 1–18.

Tate, T. (2001). Peer influencing positive cognitive relationship. *Reclaiming Children & Youth*, *9*(4), 215–218.

Teall, B. (2000). Using solution-oriented intervention in an ecological frame: A case illustration. *Social Work in Education*, *22*(1), 54–61.

Terr, L. C. (1995). Childhood trauma: An outline and overview. In G. S. Everly, Jr., & J. M. Lating (Eds.). *Psychotraumatology* (pp. 301–320). New York: Plenum.

Testa, M. (2002). Subsidized guardianship: Testing an idea whose time has finally come. *Social Work Research*, *26*(3), 145–158.

Teyber, E. (2006). Interpersonal processes in therapy: An integrative model (5th ed.). Pacific Grove, CA: Brooks/Cole.

Thibault, J., Ellor, J., & Netting, F. (1991). A conceptual framework for assessing the spiritual functioning and fulfillment of older adults in long-term care settings. *Journal of Religious Gerontology*, *7*(4), 29–46.

Thomas, H., & Caplan, T. (1997). Client, therapist and context: Addressing resistance in group work. *The Social Worker*, *65*(3), 27–36.

Thomas, H., & Caplan, T. (1999). Spinning the group process wheel: Effective facilitation techniques for motivating involuntary clients. *Social Work with Groups*, *21*(4), 3–21.

Thomlison, B. (2005). Using evidence-based knowledge in child welfare to improve policies and practices: current thinking and continuing challenges. *Research on Social Work Practice*, *15*(5), 321–322.

Thompson, C. (Ed.). (1989). *The instruments of psychiatric research*. New York: Willey.

Thyer, B. A. (2002). Principles of evidence-based practice and treatment development. In A. R. Roberts & G. J. Greene (Eds.), *Social workers' desk reference* (pp. 739–742). New York: Oxford University Press.

Thyer, B. A., & Wodarski, J. S. (1998). *Handbook of empirical social work practice*, volume *1*. New York: Wiley.

Tienda, M. (2007). *Don't blame immigrants for poverty wages*. Ending Poverty in America, Special Report of The American Prospect, The Annie E. Casey Foundation & The Northwest Area Foundation. A10–A11.

Tohn, S. L., & Oshlag, J. A. (1996). Solution-focused therapy with mandated clients: Cooperating with the uncooperative. In S. D. Miller, M. A. Hubble, & B. L. Duncan (Eds.), *Handbook of solution-focused brief therapy* (pp. 152–183). San Francisco: Jossey-Bass.

Tolan, P. H., & Gorman-Smith, D. (1997). Families and the development of urban children. In H. J. Walberg, O. Reyes, & R. P. Weissberg (Eds.), *Children and youth: Interdisciplinary perspectives* (pp. 67–91). Thousand Oaks, CA: Sage Publications.

Tolman, R. M., & Molidor, C. E. (1994). A decade of social group work research: Trends in methodology, theory and program development. *Research on Social Work Practice*, *4*(2), 142–159.

Tolson, E. R., Reid, W. J., & Garvin, C. D. (1994). *Generalist practice. A task-centered approach*. New York: Columbia University Press.

Toseland, R. W., Jones, L. V., & Gellis, Z. D. (2006). Group dynamics. In C. D. Garvin, L. M. Gutierrez, & M. J. Galinsky (Eds.), *Handbook of social work with groups* (pp. 13–31). New York: Guilford Press.

Toseland, R. W., & Rivas, R. F. (2009). *An Introduction to Group Work Practice* (6th ed.). Boston: Allyn and Bacon.

Tracy, E. M., & Whittaker, J. K. (1990). The social network map: Assessing social support in clinical practice. *Families in Society*, *71*(8), 461–470.

Trepper, T.S., Dolan, Y., McCollum, E.E., & Nelson, T. (2006), Steve De Shazer and the future of solution-focused therapy. *Journal of Marital and Family Therapy 32*(2), 133–139.

Tropman, J. E., & Morningstar, G. (1995). The effective meeting: How to achieve high-quality decisions. In J. E. Tropman, J. L. Erlich, & J. Rothman (Eds.), *Tactics and techniques of community intervention* (3rd ed., pp. 412–426). Itasca, IL: F. E. Peacock.

Trotter, C. (1999). *Working with Involuntary Clients.* London: Sage.

Trotter, C. (2006). *Working with Involuntary Clients: a guide to practice* (2nd ed.). London: Sage.

Truax, C., & Carkhuff, R. (1964). For better or for worse: The process of psychotherapeutic personality change. In *Recent advances in the study of behavior change* (pp. 118–163). Montreal: McGill University Press.

Truax, C., & Carkhuff, R. (1967). *Toward effective counseling and psychotherapy: Training and practice.* Chicago: Aldine-Atherton.

Truax, C., & Mitchell, K. (1971). Research on certain therapist interpersonal skills in relation to process and outcome. In A. Bergin & S. Garfield (Eds.), *Handbook of psychotherapy and behavior change* (pp. 299–344). New York: Wiley.

Tsui, P., & Schultz, G. L. (1985). Failure of rapport: Why psychotherapeutic engagement fails in the treatment of Asian clients. *American Journal of Orthopsychiatry, 55,* 561–569.

Tsui, P., & Schultz, G. L. (1988). Ethnic factors in group process: Cultural dynamics in multi-ethnic therapy groups. *American Journal of Orthopsychiatry, 58,* 136–142.

Tuckman, B. (1963). Developmental sequence in small groups. *Psychological Bulletin, 63,* 384–399.

Tuckman, B. W., & Jenson, M. A. (1977). Stages of small group development revisited. *Group and Organization Studies, 2,* 419–427.

U

U.S. Department of Health and Human Services. (2003). *Office for Civil Rights: HIPAA.* Retrieved August 4, 2003, from http://www.hhs.gov/ocr/hipaa/

Ussher, J. (1990). Cognitive behavioral couples therapy with gay men referred for counseling in an AIDS setting: A pilot study. *AIDS Care, 2,* 43–51.

V

Vakalah, H. F., & Khajak, K. (2000). Parent to parent and family to family: Innovative self-help and mutual support. In A. Sallee, H. Lawson, & K. Briar-Lawson (Eds.), *Innovative practices with children and families* (pp. 271–290). Dubuque, IA: Eddie Bowers.

Valencia, R. R. & Black, M. S. (2002). Mexican Americans don't value education! *Journal of Latinos and Education 1*(2), 81–103.

Van Hook, M. P., Berkman, B., & Dunkle, R. (1996). Assessment tools for general health care settings: PRIME-MD, OARS and SF-36. *Health and Social Work, 21*(3), 230–235.

Van Souest, D., & Garcia, B. (2003). *Diversity education for social justice.* Alexandria, VA: Council on Social Work Education.

Van Voorhis, R. M. (1998). Culturally relevant practice: A framework for teaching the psychosocial dynamics of oppression. *Journal of Social Work Education, 34*(1), 121–133.

Van Voorhis, R. M., & Hostetter, C. (2006). The impact of MSW education on the social worker empowerment and commitment to client empowerment through social justice advocacy. *Journal of Social Work Education, 47*(1), 105–121.

Van Wormer, K. (2002). Our social work imagination: How social work has not abandoned its mission. *Journal of Teaching in Social Work, 22*(3/4), 21–37.

Van Wormer, K., & Boes (1997). Humor in the emergency room: A social work perspective. *Health and Social Work, 22*(2), 87–92.

VandeCreek, L., Knapp, S., & Herzog, C. (1988). Privileged communication for social workers. *Social Casework, 69,* 28–34.

Varlas, L (2005). Bridging the widest gap: Raising the achievement of black boys. Education Update *47*(8). 1, 2, 8.

Vera, E. M., & Speight, S. L. (2003). Multicultural competencies, social justice and counseling psychology: Expanding our roles. *The Counseling Psychologist. 31,* 253–272.

Videka-Sherman, L. (1988). Meta-analysis of research on social work practice in mental health. *Social Work, 33*(4), 325–338.

Vodde, R., & Gallant, J. P. (2002). Bridging the gap between micro and macro practice: Larger scale change and a unified model of narrative-deconstructive practice. *Journal of Social Work Education, 38*(3), 439–458.

Voisin, D. R. (2007). The effects of family and community violence exposure among youth. Recommendations for practice and policy. *Journal of Social Work Education, 43*(1), 51–64.

Vosler, N. R. (1990). Assessing family access to basic resources: An essential component of social work practice. *Social Work, 35*(5), 434–441.

Voss, R. W., Douville, V., Little Soldier, A., & Twiss, G. (1999). Tribal and shamanic-based social work practice. A Lakota perspective. *Social Work, 44*(3), 228–241.

W

Wagner, C. C., & Conners, W. (2008, June). *Motivational interviewing: Resources for clinicians, researchers, and trainers*. Retrieved July 25, 2008, from http://www.motivationalinterview.org/

Waites, C., MacGowan, J. P., Pennell, J., Carlton-LaNey, I., & Weil, M. (2004). *Increasing the cultural responsiveness of family group conferencing*. Social Work, *49*(2), 291–300.

Wakefield, J. C. (1996a). Does social work need the ecosystems perspective? Part 1. Is the perspective clinically useful? *Social Service Review, 70*(1), 1–32.

Wakefield, J. C. (1996b). Does social work need the ecosystems perspective? Part 2. Does the perspective save social work from incoherence? *Social Service Review, 70*(2), 183–213.

Walen, S., DiGiuseppe, R., & Wessler, R. (1980). *A practitioner's guide to RET*. New York: Oxford University Press.

Walker, R., & Stanton, M. (2000). Multiculturalism in social work ethics. *Journal of Social Work Education, 36*(3), 449–462.

Walsh, F. (1996). The concept of family resilience: Crisis and challenge. *Family Process, 35*, 261–281.

Walsh, J. (2000). *Clinical case management with persons having mental illness: A relationship-based approach*. Pacific Grove, CA: Brooks/Cole.

Walsh, J. (2003). *Endings in clinical practice: Effective closure in diverse settings*. Chicago: Lyceum Books.

Walsh, J. (2006). *Theories for direct social work practice*. Belmont, CA: Thompson Brooks/Cole.

Walsh, J. (2007). *Endings in clinical practice: Effective closure in diverse settings* (2nd ed.). Chicago: Lyceum Books.

Walsh, J., & Bentley, K. J. (2002). Psychopharmacology basics. In A. R. Roberts & G. J. Greene (Eds.), *Social workers' desk reference* (pp. 646–651). New York: Oxford University Press.

Waltman, G. H. (1996). Amish health care beliefs and practices. In M. C. Julia, *Multicultural awareness in the health care professions*. Needham Heights, MA: Allyn & Bacon.

Wampold, B. (2001). *The great psychotherapy debate: Models, methods and findings*. Mahwah, NJ: Lawrence Erlbaum.

Warren, K., Franklin, C., & Streeter, C. L. (1998). New directions in systems theory: Chaos and complexity. *Social Work, 43*(4), 357–372.

Wartel, S. (1991). Clinical considerations for adults abused as children. *Families in Society, 72*(3), 157–163.

Washington, O., & Moxley, D. (2003). Promising group practices to empower low income minority women coping with chemical dependency. *American Journal of Orthopsychiatry, 73*(1), 109–116.

Watkins, A. M. & Kurtz, P. D. (2001). Using solution-focused intervention to address African American male overrepresentation in special education: A case study. *Children & Schools, 23*(4), 223–234.

Watzlawick, P., Weakland, J., & Fisch, R. (1974). *Change: Principles of problem formulation*. New York: Norton.

Weaver, H. N. (2004). The elements of cultural competence: Application with Native American clients. *Journal of Ethics & Cultural Diversity in Social Work, 13*(1), 19–35.

Webb, N. B. (1996). The biopsychosocial assessment of the child. In *Social work practice with children* (pp. 57–98). New York: Guilford Press.

Weick, A., & Saleebey, D. (1995). Supporting family strengths: Orienting policy and practice in the 21st century. *Families in Society, 76*, 141–149.

Weil, M. O. (1996). Community building: Building community practice. *Social Work, 41*(5), 481–499.

Weil, M. O. & Gamble, D. N. (1995). Community practice models. In R.L. Edwards (Ed.). *Encyclopedia of Social Work* (19th ed. pp. 577–593). Washington, DC: NASW Press.

Weinberg, M. (2006). Pregnant with possibility: The paradoxes of "help" as anti-oppression and discipline with a young single mother. *Families in Society, 67*(2), 161–169.

Weiner, M. F. (1984). *Techniques of group psychotherapy*. Washington, DC: American Psychiatric Press.

Weiner-Davis (1992). *Divorce-busting*. New York: Summit Books.

Weiss, C. H. (1998). *Evaluation: Methods for studying programs and policies* (2nd Edition). Upper Saddle River, NJ: Prentice Hall.

Wells, R. (1975). Training in facilitative skills. *Social Work, 20*, 242–243.

Wells, R. A. (1994). *Planned short-term treatment* (2nd ed.). New York: Free Press.

Wells, R. A., & Gianetti. V. J. (Eds.). (1990). *Handbook of the brief psychotherapies*. New York: Plenum Press.

Wenar, C. (1994). *Developmental psychopathology from infancy through adolescence* (3rd ed.). New York: McGraw-Hill.

West, L., Mercer, S. O., & Altheimer, E. (1993). Operation Desert Storm: The response of a social work outreach team. *Social Work in Health Care, 19*(2), 81–98.

Westermeyer, J. J. (1993). Cross-cultural psychiatric assessment. In A. C. Gaw (Ed.), *Culture, ethnicity and mental illness* (pp. 125–146). Washington, DC: American Psychiatric Press.

Weston, K. (1991). *Families we choose: Lesbians, gays, and kinship.* New York: Columbia University Press.

Wexler, D. (1992). Putting mental health into mental health law: Therapeutic jurisprudence. *Law and Human Behavior, 16*, 27–38.

Whaley, A. L. (1998). Racism in the provision of mental health services: A social cognitive analysis. *American Journal of Orthopsychiatry, 88*(1), 48–57.

Whitaker, C. (1958). Psychotherapy with couples. *American Journal of Psychotherapy, 12*, 18–23.

White, M., & Epston, D. (1990). *Narrative means to therapeutic ends.* New York: Norton.

White, M., & Morgan, A. (2006). *Narrative therapy with families and children.* Adelaide, South Australia: Dulwich Centre Publication.

Whiteman, M., Fanshel, D., & Grundy, J. (1987). Cognitive-behavioral interventions aimed at anger of parents at risk of child abuse. *Social Work, 32*(6), 469–474.

Whiting Blome, W. & Steib, S. (2004). Whatever the problem, the answer is "evidence-based practice" or is it? *Child welfare, 83*(6), 611–615.

Whittaker, J. K., & Tracy, E. M. (1989). *Social treatment: An introduction to interpersonal helping in social work practice.* New York: Aldine de Gruyter.

Will, G. F. (2007; October 14). Code of coercion. *The Washington Post*, pp. B07.

Williams, C. C. (2006). The epistemology of cultural. *Families in Society, 87*(1), 209–220.

Williams, A. (2007, August 1). Child abuse in military families. *Star Tribune*, pp. A1, A7.

Williams, L. F. (1990). The challenge of education to social work: The case for minority children. *Social Work, 35*(3), 236–242.

Williams, N., & Reeves, P. (2004). MSW students go to burn camp: Exploring social work values through service-learning. *Social Work Education, 23*, 383–398.

Wilson, W. J. (1997). *When work disappears: The world of the new urban poor.* New York: Random House

Withorn, A. (1998). No win ... facing the ethical perils of welfare reform. *Families in Society, 79*(3), 277–287.

Witkin, S. (1993). A human rights approach to social work research and evaluation. In J. Laird (Ed.), *Revisioning social work education: A social constructionist approach.* Binghamton, NY: Haworth Press.

Wodarski, J. S., & Thyer, B. A. (1998). *Handbook of empirical social work practice. Volume 2: Social problems and practice issues.* New York: Wiley.

Wolf, K. T. (1991). The diagnostic and statistical manual and the misdiagnosis of African-Americans: An historical perspective. *Social Work Perspectives, 10*(1), 33–38.

Wolfe, J. L. (1992). Working with gay women. In A. Freeman & F.M. Darrillio (Eds.). Comprehensive casebook of cognitive therapy (pp 249–255).

Wong, D. K. (2007). Crucial individuals in the help-seeking pathway of Chinese caregivers of relatives in early psychosis in Hong Kong. *Social Work 52*(2), 127–135.

Wood, S. A. (2007). The analysis of an innovative HIV-positive women's support group. *Social Work with Groups, 30*, 9–28.

Worden, J. W. (1991). *Grief counseling and grief therapy: A handbook for the mental health practitioner.* New York: Springer.

World Health Organization. (2008). *Suicide prevention (SUPRE)*. Retrieved July, 2, 2008, from http://www.who.int/mental_health/prevention/suicide/suicideprevent/en/index.html

Wright, O. L. Jr., & Anderson, J. P. (1998). Clinical social work practice with urban African American families. *Families in Society, 79*(2), 197–205.

Wright, R. A., Greenberg, J., & Brehm, S. S. (2004). Motivational analyses of social behavior. Lawrence Erlbaum Associates Publishers.

Wright, W. (1999). The use of purpose in on-going activity groups: A framework for maximizing the therapeutic impact. *Social Work with Groups, 22*(2/3), 33–57.

Wulczyn, F., & Lery, B. (2007). *Racial disparity in foster care admissions.* Chapin Hall Center for Children, University of Chicago, Chicago, Ill.

Wylie, M. S. (1990). Brief therapy on the couch. *Family Therapy Networker, 14*, 26–34, 66.

Y

Yaffe, J., Jenson, J. M., & Howard, M. O. (1995). Women and substance abuse: Implications for treatment. *Alcoholism-Treatment Quarterly, 13*(2), 1–15.

Yalom, I. D. (1995). *The theory and practice of group psychotherapy.* (4th ed.) New York: Basic Books.

Yalom, I. D., & Lieberman, M. (1971). A study of encounter group casualties. *Archives of General Psychiatry, 25,* 16–30.

Yamamoto, J., Silva, J. A., Justice, L. R., Chang, C. Y., & Leong, G. B. (1993). Cross-cultural psychotherapy. In A. C. Gaw (Ed.), *Culture, ethnicity and mental illness* (pp. 101–124). Washington, DC: American Psychiatric Press.

Yamashiro, G., & Matsuoka, J. (1997). *Help seeking among Asian and Pacific Americans: A multiperspective analysis.* Washington, DC: NASW Press.

Yegidis, B. L., & Weinbach, R. W. (2002). *Research methods for social workers.* Boston: Allyn and Bacon.

Yesavage, J. A., Brink, T. L., Rose, T. L., Lum, O., Huang, V., Adey, M., et al. (1983). Development and validation of a geriatric depression screening scale: A preliminary report. *Journal of Psychiatric Research, 17,* 37–49.

Yin, S. (2006). *Elderly white men afflicted by high suicide rates: U.S. medical system not set up to detect depression in the aging.* Retrieved July 2, 2008, from Population Reference Bureau Web site: http://www.prb.org/Articles/2006/ElderlyWhiteMenAfflictedbyHighSuicideRates.aspx

Yunus, M. (2007). *Creating a world without poverty. Social business and the future of capitalism.* NY: Public Affairs.

Z

Zastrow, C. (2003). *The practice of social work. Applications of generalist and advanced content* (7th ed.). Pacific Grove, CA: Thomson Brooks/Cole.

Zastrow, C., & Kirst-Ashman, K. (1990). *Understanding human behavior and the social environment* (2nd ed.). Chicago: Nelson-Hall.

Zechetmayr, M. (1997). Native Americans: A neglected health care crisis and a solution. *Journal of Health and Social Policy, 9*(2), 29–47.

Zeira, A., Astor, R. A., & Benbenishty, R. (2003). School violence in Israel: Findings of a national survey. *Social Work, 48*(4), 471–483.

Zimmerman, S. L. (1995). *Understanding family policy: Theories and applications* (2nd ed.). Thousand Oaks, CA: Sage Publications.

Zipple, M., & Spaniol, L. (1987). Current educational and supportive models of family intervention. In A. B. Hatfield & H. P. Lefley (Eds.), *Families of the mentally ill.* New York: Guilford Press.

Zuckerman, E. L. (2003). *The paper office, third edition: Forms, guidelines, and resources to make your practice work ethically, legally, and profitably* (3rd ed.). New York: Guilford Press.

Zung, W. (1965). A self-rating depression scale. *Archives of General Psychiatry, 12,* 63–70.

Author Index

Aase, J., 176
Abbott, A. A., 183
Abeles, N. 161
Abell, M., 274, 514
Abramovitz, M., 415, 416, 417, 429, 437, 444
Abramson, M., 63, 64, 515
Achenbach, 181
Adams, K., 12, 19, 42, 83
Adelman, H. S., 450
Agbayani-Siewart, P., 156
Aguilar, M., 44
Aguilera, D., 410
Ahern, R. E., 338, 419, 420
Ahijevych, K., 395
Akerman, A., 357
Albert, V., 232
Alcabes, A. A., 33
Alexander, E., 450, 451
Alexander, J., 520
Alexander, R., 418, 432
Al-Krenawi, A., 201, 306, 358, 550
Allen, D., 445
Allen-Meares, P., 20, 21
Alley, G. R., 363
Almeida, R., 258, 358
Alter, K., 450
Altheimer, E., 381
Anderson, S., 226
Anderson, S.G., 12, 416
Anderson, D. A., 463
Anderson, J. P., 457, 462
Anderson-Butcher, D., 275, 513
Andrews, L. B., 202, 338
Angle, B., 526
Angold, A., 201, 232, 418
Aponte, H., 469
Applegate, J. S., 337, 338
Archer, P., 196
Arditti, J.A., 448
Arnowitz, E., 221
Aronson, H., 83
Asai, M. O., 359
Astor, R. A., 382
Atchey, R. C., 238
Atherton, C. R., 24

Atwater, L. E., 234
Austin, K. M., 71, 450
Aversa, J., 412
Azocar, F., 395

Babbie, E., 339, 419
Bacallao, M. L., 294, 297, 497, 509
Badami, M., 44
Baer, J., 471
Bailey, V., 394
Bailey-Dempsey, C., 29, 363
Bakker, L., 394
Balgopal, P., 288, 363, 502
Balster, T. C., 172
Bandura, A., 39, 306, 316, 363, 372, 373, 390, 391, 395
Banerjee, M. M., 416, 429
Barber, J. G., 206
Bargal, D., 274
Barker, R. L., 273, 430
Barnes, A., 445
Barnes, G. L., 362
Barriga, A. Q., 384, 394
Barsky, A., 71
Barter, K., 451, 451
Barth, R. P., 221, 232
Bartlett, H., 23
Barton, C., 520
Barusch, 433
Baskind, F. R., 547
Baxter, V. A., 526
Bazron, B. J., 446
Beatrice, D. F., 450, 451
Beatty, M. L., 510
Becerra, R., 221
Beck, A., 180, 183, 226, 288, 390, 391, 455, 537
Becvar, D. S., 242, 269, 455, 475, 477, 483, 484
Becvar, R. J., 242, 269, 455, 475, 477, 483, 484
Behroozi, C. S., 282
Belkin, L., 380
Bell, J. L., 379, 380, 544, 545
Bell, L., 29
Belville, R., 221
Ben-Arieh, A., 338
Benbenishty, R., 382

Benjamin, M. P., 290
Bennett, C. J., 88
Bent-Goodley, T. B., 417, 444
Bentley, K. J., 226
Bepko, C., 471, 472
Berg, I. K., 38, 50, 249, 309, 311, 312, 403, 404, 405, 407, 408, 455, 456, 467, 468, 469, 483
Bergeron, L. R., 195
Bergin, A. E., 409
Berkman, B., 184, 220
Berlin, S. B., 18, 19, 263, 331, 333, 336, 356, 390, 391, 393, 395, 475
Berman-Rossi, T., 361, 362, 492, 494
Bernal, G., 249
Bernhardt, B., 225
Bernstein, B., 70, 71
Bertcher, H., 281
Bertolino, B., 181, 405
Beyer, J. A., 172
Bianchetti, A., 196
Bibus, A. A., 193, 250
Bidgood, B., 4
Biestek, F., 63, 67
Birmaher, A., 214
Black, M. S, 11, 233
Blades, M., 43
Blatt, S. J., 214
Bledsoe, S. E., 309
Block-Lerner, J., 519
Bloom, M., 175, 180, 184, 314, 319, 331, 332, 336, 351
Blythe, B. J., 45, 94
Boehm, A., 306
Boes, M., 160
Bogard, C. J., 421
Bone, L., 323, 382
Boroto, D. R., 537
Borman, L., 512
Borys, D. S., 67
Boscolo, L., 520
Bowen, M., 455
Bower, B., 564
Boyd-Franklin, N., 227, 236, 237, 249, 254, 379, 460, 462, 467, 468, 469, 487
Bradshaw, W., 274

Brager, G., 73, 438, 440
Brandes, S. D., 427
Brasfield, T. L., 395
Brehm, J. W., 158, 161, 317, 368, 559
Brehm, S. S., 158, 161, 368
Bresnick, B., 196
Breton, M., 288, 412, 415, 416
Bridges, G. S., 193
Briggs, H., 21
Brindis, C., 221
Brintzenhofe-Szok, K., 130
Brissette-Chapman, S., 220
Broitman, M., 323, 382
Bronfenbrenner, U., 395
Brooks, L. M., 425
Brooks-Gunn, J., 232, 417
Brookins, G. K., 425
Brown, C., 233
Brown, L. B. 39, 43, 44, 46, 149, 215, 363, 570, 578
Brown, L., 250
Brown, L. S., 395
Brownlee, K., 67
Bruce, M. L., 215
Brueggemann, W. G., 411, 412, 413, 415, 433
Bruininks, R., 221
Brunner, C., 451
Brunswick, L., 221
Bry, B. H., 227, 236, 237, 469
Bucceri, G. 360
Bulgarella, C., 303, 316
Burford, G., 43, 514
Burke, B., 306, 309, 547, 548
Burnette, D., 228
Burns, D., 183, 517
Burns, A., 184
Burroughs, J. C., 277
Buss, T. F., 201
Butterfield, W., 129
Butz, R. A., 69

Cafasso, L. L., 418
Cain, R., 189
Callanan, P., 69, 73, 74, 277, 513
Callum, S., 432
Cameron, S., 225
Campbell, J. A., 338
Canda, E. R., 201, 221, 425
Canu, R. F., 234
Capitman, J., 450
Caplan, G., 383
Caplan, T., 161, 274, 381, 410, 503
Caple, F. S., 241, 250, 251
Capodilupo, C. M., 360
Capozzoli, J. A., 215
Carey, G., 249, 462, 467, 468, 469, 470
Carillo, D. F., 129
Carkhuff, R., 95, 108
Carlson, B. E., 418
Carlton-LaNey, I., 307, 359, 428
Carniol, B., 3, 248
Carr, E. S., 274
Carrell, S., 277, 501, 502
Carter, B., 228, 243, 249, 254, 269, 270, 357, 433, 434, 468
Caspi, J., 318, 364, 368
Cecchin, G., 520
Cetingok, M., 230, 237, 250, 251, 424

Chan, C. L. W., 359
Chan, Y., 359
Chandler, S., 28
Chang, C. Y., 183, 201
Chao, W., 357
Chapin, R., 409, 409
Charnley, H., 35
Chau, K. L., 250, 290
Chelune, G. J., 107
Chen, S.W., 232, 395
Chesler, M., 446
Chipungu, S. S., 417, 444
Choi, G., 467
Chovanec, M., 105, 274
Christian, J., 448
Cicchetti, D., 357
Cingolani, J., 34, 89, 94, 121
Citron, P., 528
Claiborn, C., 520, 537
Clark, D. B., 394
Cleveland, 236, 236
Clifford, D., 306, 309, 547, 548
Cnaan, R. A., 433
Coady, N., 18, 20, 355
Coady, N. F., 161
Cobb, N. H., 390
Cohen, D., 410
Cohen, E. D., 62
Cohen, G. S., 62
Collins, G., 235
Collins, M. E., 232
Collins, P. M., 333, 475, 476
Comer, E., 453
Compton, B. R., 16, 17, 33, 232, 418, 443
Condrey, S. E., 437
Congress, E. P., 48, 202, 236, 248, 359, 362, 385, 450
Connolly, C. M., 359, 472
Constable, R., 227, 228, 230, 235
Cook, J. B, 404
Corchado, A., 234
Corcoran, J., 404, 405, 406, 407, 408
Corcoran, K., 30, 40, 42, 68, 184, 332, 351, 360, 394, 403
Corey, G., 59
Corey, G., 69, 73, 74, 277, 280, 282, 497, 501, 503, 504, 506, 510, 512, 513
Corey, M. S., 69, 73, 74, 277, 497, 501, 503, 504, 506, 510, 512, 513
Cormier, S., 181, 356, 393, 394, 395, 410
Cormier, L., 130, 139, 390, 402
Cormier, W., 139
Corwin, M., 303, 323, 344, 408, 469, 550
Costello, E. J., 201, 232, 418
Cournoyer, B., 19
Cournoyer, B. R., 356
Courtney, M. E., 23, 26, 415, 416, 428
Cowan, P. A., 358
Cowger, C. D., 7, 63, 178, 179, 251
Cox, E. O., 318, 409, 454, 454, 514
Coyle, J. T., 215
Crabtree, B. F., 338
Craig, S., 184
Crawford, J. B., 537
Crenshaw, A. B., 235
Crinic, K., 357
Crosbie-Burnett, M., 256
Cross, T. L., 446, 447

Cross, W. M., 436
Crosson-Tower, C., 228
Cryer, M., 394
Cull, J. G., 226
Cummings, N. A., 231
Cunningham, M., 544, 545
Curry, R., 380
Curtis, C. M., 417

Daguio, E. R., 65, 69, 71, 186, 346
Daley, J. M., 438, 440
Dane, B. O., 29, 519, 544, 545
Dang, J., 277
Danish, J., 107
D'Anna, C. A., 418
Danser, 537
Danzy, J., 425
Dastoor, D. P., 394
Dattilio, F. M., 409
D'Augelli, A, 107
Daugherty, T. K., 39
Davenport, D., 395
Davidson, G., 451
Davidson, J. R., 68
Davidson, T., 68
Davies, G. M., 510
Davis, I. P., 339
Davis, L. E., 44, 177, 274, 547, 548
Deal, K. H., 106, 130
Dean, R. G., 550
De Anda, D., 176, 193, 221
DeAngelis, D., 9
DeBord, K., 234
Deffenbacher, J. L., 394
De Jong, P., 38, 39, 50, 309, 311, 312, 403, 404, 405, 407, 408, 525
Delgado, M., 510
DeLine, C., 346
Delois, K., 414
Denby, R. W, 417
Denison, M., 202
Dennis, K., 446
DePoy, E., 332, 419, 420
Dermer, S. B., 404
de Shazer, S., 403, 405, 406, 455, 456, 466
Despard, M., 274
Devore, W., 344, 364, 379, 469
Dewart, T., 221
Dewayne, C., 161
di Cecco, J., 241, 250, 251
Dickson, D. T., 69, 70, 71
DiClemente, C. C., 35, 36, 217, 527
Dies, R. R., 504
Dietz, C., 149, 306, 309, 410
DiGuiseppe, R., 409
Dillon, C., 59
Dillon, D., 306
Dimidjian, S., 519
Dobson, K. S., 390
Dodds, J., 196
Doherty, W. J., 56
Dolan, S., 39
Dolan, Y., 356, 403, 404
Dolgoff, R., 318, 437
Dore, M. M., 27, 203, 280
Dossick, J., 298
Doster, J., 45
Douville, V., 359, 447

Dowd, E. T., 537
Dozier, C. D., 307
Dozios, D.J., 390
Draine, J., 450
Drake, R., 19
Drisko, J. W., 42, 83
Duberstein, 215
DuBray, W., 208
Duehn, W., 129
Duncan, 42, 83, 232, 362
Duncan, B., 406
Duncan, G. J., 417
Dunkle, R., 184
Dunlap, E., 307, 409
Dupper, D., 25
Duvall, E. M., 269
Dwyer, E.V., 395
Dyche, L., 548
Dyers, L., 418

Eamon, M.K., 371
Early, T. J., 251, 252, 409
Eaton, T. T., 161
Eckert, A., 409
Eddy, F., 510
Edwards, A., 44
Edwards, 515
Edwards, E., 176
Edwards, E. D., 510
Edwards, M. E., 510
Efran, J., 406
Ehrenreich, B., 234, 393, 429
Ehrenreich, J. H., 525
Eisengard, S., 404
Elisme, E., 462, 467, 468, 469
Ell, K., 385, 389, 390
Ellis, A., 180, 187, 209, 305, 324, 346, 455, 390
Ellor, J. W., 222
Emery, G., 183, 390
Enos, 448
Ensign, J., 201
Ephross, P. H., 297
Epstein, H., 418
Epstein, L., 39, 46, 121, 363, 408
Epstein, R. S., 67
Epston, D., 412, 413
Erford, B. T., 323
Erickson, S. H., 67
Erlich, J. L., 413, 433, 434, 435, 437
Esquilin, M., 360
Etherington, K., 556
Evans, T., 149
Ewalt, P. L., 250
Ezell, M., 431, 436, 437

Facer, R. L., 437
Fallot, R. D., 514
Farmer, R., 357, 409
Fast, J. D., 379, 381
Fauth, J., 555
Fearing, J., 527
Feeny, S. L., 394
Feldman, 537
Fenchal, G., 280
Ferguson, K. M., 412
Fernandez, 309
Fernandez-Olano, 519
Figley, C. R., 544, 545, 555

Fillenbaum, G., 184
Fingeld, D. L., 194, 274, 514
Finn, J. L., 3, 7, 227, 306, 415
Fisch, R., 520
Fischer, J., 18, 95, 175, 180, 184, 314, 319, 331, 332, 335, 336, 351
Fisher, R., 360, 383
Flapan, D., 280
Flett, 215
Flores, M. T., 249, 462, 467, 468, 469, 470
Flores-Ortiz, Y., 249
Fluhr, 301
Foa, E. B., 394
Fong, R., 201, 445, 462, 467, 470
Fontes, L. A., 271, 321, 324, 544
Ford, W., 276, 285, 454
Fortune, A. E., 42, 363, 456
Foster, 547
Fowler, R. C., 215
Frager, S., 178
Frankenberg, 196
Franklin, C., 18, 26, 180, 182, 184, 237, 252, 271, 306, 313, 332, 333, 338, 341, 351, 360, 394, 404, 406
Franklin, D. L., 428
Fraser, M. W., 286
Freddolino, P., 430, 432
Fredriksen, K. I., 308, 309
Fredriksen-Goldsen, K. I., 227, 228, 470
Freed, A., 47
Freeman, E. M., 344, 409, 418
Freud, S., 385, 403
Frey, G. A., 25, 73, 440, 441
Fried, J., 229, 240, 241, 249, 254, 255, 257, 258, 260
Frisoni, G. B., 196
From, S. B., 448
Fullerton, C.D., 361
Fuentes, 359
Furman, W. M., 451

Gabbard, G. O., 67
Gabrielli, W. F., 202
Galaway, B., 16, 17, 33, 443
Galinsky, M. J., 274, 277, 281, 286, 451, 492, 494, 514
Galisky, 285, 453
Gallant, J., 130, 402, 413
Gallo, J. J., 183, 196, 218
Gambrill, E., 19, 21, 58, 390
Gant, L. M., 359
Garcia, B., 357, 447
Garcia-Coll, 357
Garcia-Preto, N., 258
Gardner, F., 305, 307, 332
Garfield, S. L., 409
Garland, J., 492, 497, 504
Gartrell, N. K., 67
Garvin, 20, 285, 344
Garvin, C., 279, 280, 281, 364, 368, 500, 501, 502
Garvin, C. D., 363, 364, 379
Gavin, D. R., 183
Gelb, 277
Gelles, 295
Gellman, A., 519
Gelman, S. R., 68, 359, 379, 550
Gelsomimo, J., 547, 548

Gendlin, E., 103
Gendolla, G. H. E., 311
Gendron, C., 394
Genty, P. M., 448
George, L., 184
Germain, C., 15
Gershel, N., 421
Gerstel, N., 307, 409
Gerson, R., 236, 237
Getzel, G. S., 274, 276, 285, 513
Giacola, P. R., 394
Gianetti, V. J., 408, 410
Giannandrea, V., 45
Gibbs, J., 298, 394, 445
Gibson, P. A., 189, 228, 425
Giebel, 309
Giesen, J.M., 394
Gilbert, N., 8, 176, 177
Gilbertson, J., 71
Gilgun, J. F., 236, 237, 333, 338
Gill, W. S., 226
Gillanders, W. R., 201
Gilliland, B. E., 307, 358, 381, 385, 387, 388, 408, 555
Gilson, S. F., 332
Gingerich, W. J., 332, 404
Giordano, J., 177, 226, 251
Gira, E., 19
Gitterman, A., 18
Giunta, C. T., 225
Glancy, G., 394
Glajchen, M., 274, 302
GlenMaye, 251, 252, 409, 414
Glisson, C., 450
Golan, N., 383, 410
Gold, M., 35, 214
Goldenberg, H., 242, 455, 456, 467, 470, 563
Goldenberg, I., 242, 455, 456, 467, 470, 563
Goldfried, M., 395
Goldstein, E. G., 555
Gollwitzer, 303, 316
Golub, A., 307, 409
Gondolla, 306
Goodman, H., 274, 276, 285
Goodwin, D. W., 202
Gordon, G., 221
Gordon, W., 23
Gorman, B. S., 394
Gorman-Smith, D., 418
Gottesfeld, M., 546, 547
Gould, J., 71
Goyer, A., 228
Grace, M., 382
Graham, J., 306, 358, 394, 451, 550
Graham, J. R., 450, 451
Grame, C., 222
Grant, J., 225
Gray, 195, 445
Graziano, R., 274
Green, J. W., 230, 232, 237, 242, 249, 251, 323, 344, 358, 359, 362, 382, 424, 425, 547
Greenberg, M., 232, 306, 312, 317
Greene, G. J., 36, 404, 409, 410, 443
Greenfield, P. M., 424
Gross, E., 156, 208
Grote, N. K., 309
Gryzlak, B. M., 416
Guadalupe, K.L., 248, 306, 309, 359

Guadiano, 394
Guest, G., 433, 435
Gulati, P., 433, 435
Gumpert, J., 280, 282, 283, 514
Gurman, A., 107
Gutfreund, M. J., 161
Gutierrez, L. M., 409, 414, 415, 454, 454
Guyll, M., 357

Hackman, J. R., 439, 542
Hackney, H., 130
Hage, J., 450
Haight, W. L., 425
Hall, E.T., 307
Halpern, R., 381, 382, 383, 385, 445
Halter, A. P., 416
Halvorson, H., 155
Hamilton, J., 409, 437
Hammond, D., 95, 114, 520, 531
Hand, C. A., 263, 359
Handmaker, 564
Hanrahan, P., 46, 129
Hardina, D., 433, 437
Hardy, K. V., 177
Hare, J., 471, 488
Harper, K. V., 177, 549
Harrington, D., 318, 437
Harris, O., 264, 358, 469
Harris, S., 514
Hartford, M., 278, 288, 292, 296
Hartman, A., 7, 220, 228, 229, 230, 236, 237, 456
Harvill, R. L., 277
Harris, M., 183, 358, 404
Hartman, A., 419, 420
Hasenfeld, Y., 451
Haslett, D., 419, 420
Hathaway, S. R., 183
Hauer, A., 107
Hawthorne, F., 234
Haynes, K. S., 59, 428, 429, 430, 432
Hays, 395, 402
Healy, L. M., 61, 232
Heavy Runner, B., 250, 425
Hegar, R. L., 425
Heisel, 215
Hemesath, C., 404
Henderson, M., 303, 316
Henry, M., 281, 505, 509, 511, 513
Henry, S., 497, 499
Hepworth, D. H., 44, 95, 221
Herbert, J. D., 394
Hernandez, 357
Hernandez, M., 229, 506
Hernandez, S., 274, 278
Hernandez, S. H., 412, 413
Hersen, M., 149
Hertzog, C., 214
Herzog, C., 69
Hess, P. M., 451
Hester, 215
Hickerson, J., 182, 195
Hill, B., 221
Hillier, A, 419
Hines, P. H., 358
Hines, P. M., 258
Hirayama, H., 230, 237, 250, 251, 424
Hirayama, K. K., 230, 237, 250, 251, 424
Hirschl, T. A., 231, 417

Hnat, S. A., 359
Ho, M., 468
Hodge, D. R., 411, 547
Hodge, D. R., 307, 359, 360, 362, 395
Hoehn-Saric, R., 83
Hoffpauir, S., 409
Holbrook, T. L., 338
Holder, A. M. B., 360
Holland, T., 227, 228, 229, 237, 248, 249, 254, 257, 357, 391, 470, 540
Hollander, E. M., 514
Hollis, F., 18
Holloway, S., 73, 438, 441
Holosko, M., 4
Holoway, 394
Holt, B. J., 451
Homan, M. S., 419, 422, 432, 435
Hopfensperger, J., 233, 234
Horejsi, C. R., 14, 250, 425
Horejsi, G. A., 14
Hostetter, C., 415
Houston-Vega, M. K., 65, 69, 71, 186, 346
Hoyt, M. F., 379, 408
Howard, M. O., 20, 203
Hubble, M., 42, 83, 406
Hudson, W., 237
Hudson, S. M., 394
Hudson, W., 332, 336
Huffine, C, 322
Hull, G., 45, 221
Hurdle, D. E., 359
Hurley, D. J., 503
Hurvitz, N., 190
Hutchinson, 357
Hutson, R. Q., 416
Huxtable, 303, 323, 324
Hyde, C., 430, 434
Hyduk, C., 430, 432
Hymbaugh, K., 176

Icard, L. D., 418
Indyk, D., 221
Ingersoll-Dayton, B., 404
Issacs, M. R., 446
Ivanoff, A., 45, 94

Jackson, D.D., 455
Jackson, A. P., 425
Jackson, S. M., 425
Jacobs, E. E., 277
Jacobson, M., 3, 7, 227, 306, 415
James, R. K., 307, 344, 356, 358, 379, 380, 381, 382, 383, 384, 385, 386, 387, 388, 407, 408, 544, 545, 548, 552, 553, 555
Jang, M., 201
Janzen, C., 264, 358, 469
Jayaratne, S., 341
Jaycox, L. H., 394
Jefferson, K.W., 395
Jenkins, 231, 357
Jennings, H., 294
Jenson, J. M., 203
Jepson, D. A., 359
Jessop, 61

Jilek, W., 220
Jimenez, J., 228
Johnson, A. L., 201, 307, 409, 471, 472
Jones, 33, 295
Jones, B., 497, 504
Jones, G., 514
Jones, H., 492
Jordan, C., 180, 182, 195, 234, 237, 252, 271, 306, 313, 333, 338, 341, 351, 360, 406, 454
Jorgensen, J. D., 412, 413
Jose, P. E., 415
Joseph, S., 383
Joshi, P. T., 215
Julia, M. C., 201
Justice, L. R., 201

Kadushin, A., 29
Kaffenberger, C. J., 404
Kagle, J. D., 222, 225, 333, 341
Kahn, M., 555
Kales, 215
Kameoka, V. A., 359
Kane, R. A., 161, 451
Kaplan, B., 175, 183, 221
Kassinore, H., 394
Katz, S., 196
Kauffman, E., 203, 280
Kauffman, J. M., 214, 215
Kaufman, M., 360, 362
Kay, G. G., 67
Kayser, K., 333, 475, 476
Kear-Colwell, J., 526, 527
Keefe, T., 88
Keeler, G., 232, 418
Keith-Spiegel, P., 67, 557
Kelly, T. B., 403, 404, 492, 494
Kerpelman, J., 234
Kessler, M., 19, 20
Kettenback, 225
Kettner, P. M., 412, 413, 414, 438, 440
Khairallah, A. O., 275, 513
Khajak, K., 514
Kiernan-Strong, 547
Kilpatrick, A. C., 227, 228, 229, 236, 237, 248, 249, 254, 257, 357, 470
Kim, J. S., 20
Kirk, S. A., 175, 440
Kirst-Ashman, K., 14
Klein, A., 288
Kleniewski, N., 436
Knapp, S., 69
Knei-Paz, C., 303
Knight, 183, 380, 551, 552, 553, 555, 556
Knott, E. C., 183, 226
Knox, K.S., 379, 383, 384
Koeske, G. F., 440
Kohn, L.P., 395
Kohn-Woods, L., 445
Kolodny, R., 492, 497, 504
Komar, A. A., 379
Koob, J. J., 403, 405
Kooden, H., 83
Kopp, J., 130, 182
Korol, M. S., 382
Korr, W. S., 323, 382
Koss, M. P., 344
Kotlowitz, A., 418
Kovacs, M., 215, 226

Krähenbühl, S., 43
Kreutzer. D., 420
Kuehlwein, K.T., 395
Kulys, R., 29
Kumabe, K., 44, 220
Kung, W. W., 358
Kupermic, 214
Kurland, R., 274, 275, 276, 277, 282, 510
Kurtz, G. L., 404, 421
Kurtz, P. D., 421
Kutchins, H., 175, 320, 361

Lachapelle, S. S., 221
Langer, N., 222
Laing, K., 267
Laird, J., 230, 236, 237, 468
Lamb, M., 43, 44, 149
Lambert, M.J., 42, 83, 357
Land, H., 9
Lane, F. E., 39, 105, 232
Lang, N., 497
Langley, J., 35
Langrod, J. G., 205
Lantz, J., 177, 180, 209, 549
Larsen, J., 95, 108, 292, 364
Latting, J. K., 443
Lavee, Y., 467
Lawlor, B., 184
Lazarus, A. A., 66
Leadbetter, 214
Leaf, P. J., 323, 382
Leahy, R. H., 391
Leavitt, D., 395
LeCroy, C. W., 12, 42, 502
Lee, D. B., 227, 228, 230, 235
Lee, K., 201
Lee, M. Y., 306, 403, 404, 409, 410, 450, 549
Legon, J., 88
Leiter, M.P., 544
Lehman, A. F., 18, 20, 205, 355
Leong, G. B., 201
Leonhardt, L., 231
Lery, B., 417
Lester, L., 411, 430, 431
Lesure-Lester, E. G., 395
Lettieri, D., 226
Levi, D., 298
Levick, K., 71
Levine, C. O., 277
Levinson, H., 358
Levy, C., 8
Levy, L., 520
Lewis, E., 407, 419
Lewis, E. A., 256, 415, 514
Lewis, J. A., 332, 438, 440
Lewis, M. D., 332, 438
Lewis, S. A., 290
Lex, A., 418
Liau, A. K., 394
Lieberman, F., 546, 547
Lieberman, M., 107, 221, 512, 530
Ligon, J., 385
Lim, C., 450
Lindemann, E., 383
Lindsey, M. A., 323, 382
Linehan, M. M., 519
Linhorst, D. M., 409, 415, 416
Linton, J. M., 380, 544

Linzer, N., 63
Lipchik, E., 405, 406, 407, 410
Lipford, S., 385
Lister, L., 26
Little Soldier, A., 359, 447
Lo, T.W., 364
Locke, E., 39, 230
Loewenberg, F.M., 318, 437
Logan, T. K., 344
Long, D. D., 412, 414, 415
Long, K. A., 70
Longres, J. F., 44, 264, 418, 445
Loo, C. M., 395
Loomis, A. B., 221
Lou, V. W. Q., 359
Lowe, 439
Lowenstein, D. A., 196
Lowinson, J. H., 205
Lu, Y., 519
Luborsky, L., 520
Ludloff, A. E., 421
Lukas, S., 43, 103, 183, 186, 192, 195
Lukton, R., 382, 410
Lum, D., 44, 212, 248, 250, 306, 307, 309, 311, 341, 359, 379, 380, 381, 384, 385, 425, 454, 462, 559
Lynch, C., 404, 406
Lyness, 215

MacAdam, M., 450
Macgowan, M. J., 214, 286, 307, 359
Mackelprang, R., 221
Mackey, R. A., 467, 483
MacMillan, 409
Madden, R. G., 418
Magen, R., 274, 302, 513
Mahler, C., 512
Mailick, M. D., 236, 237, 248
Malgady, R. G., 424, 445, 548
Mallory, K., 426
Manicke, 564
Mann, L., 45
Maple, F., 281
Mare, R. D., 421
Marlow, C. R., 182, 470
Marsh, J. C., 18, 19, 263, 306, 311, 331, 333, 336, 409, 475
Martin, P. Y., 236, 252, 438, 440
Martinez, A., 274, 278, 506
Marziali, E., 161
Maschi, T., 382
Maslach, C., 544
Mason, J. L., 290
Mason, S. E., 514
Masson, R. L., 277
Matheson, K. W., 318
Matsuoka, J., 186
Mattesisch, P. W., 451, 452
Matto, H. C., 12, 42
Mau, W., 359
Maughan, B., 201
May, P., 176
Mayadas, N., 176, 193
Mayer, J., 83, 84, 102
Mays, N., 425
McAdoo, J. L., 241, 249, 250, 251, 254, 261, 357
McChesney, K. Y., 420, 421
McClelland, M., 29

McCollum, E. E., 356, 403, 404
McConaughy, S. H., 181
McConnell, J. J., 421
McCubbin, 235
McDonald, L., 511
McFarlane, W. R., 514
McGoldrick, M., 177, 202, 226, 227, 228, 229, 236, 237, 243, 249, 251, 254, 255, 258, 260, 269, 270, 357, 358, 468
McHale, J. P., 358
McIntosh, J. L., 214
McKenzie, A., 321, 324
McKinley, J. C., 183
McKenry, P. C., 229, 230, 269, 471
McLoyd, V., 418
McMillen, J. E., 33, 39, 252, 358, 383, 408, 409
McMurtry, S. L., 237, 412, 413, 414, 438
McNair, L. D., 241, 359
McNeely, R., 44
McPhatter, A., 249
McQuaide, S., 404, 525
McRoy, R. G., 344, 425
McWilliams, N., 555
Meenaghan, T. M., 14
Meezan, W., 514
Meglin, D. E., 451
Meier, A., 274, 275, 300, 301, 453, 514
Mello, C., 357, 382
Mercer, S. O., 381
Messick, J., 410
Meyer, C., 15, 228, 229, 269, 270
Meyer, W., 306, 311, 380, 546, 547, 558
Meyers, M. K., 452
Meystedt, D. M., 222
Mezzich, A. C., 394
Mickelson, J. S., 428, 429, 430, 432
Miles, M., 530
Miley, K. K., 434
Milgram, D., 280
Miller, 42, 83, 127, 183, 232, 303, 313, 316, 319, 325, 368, 407, 564
Miller, D. B., 274
Miller, J. A., 256
Miller, R., 514
Miller, S., 406
Miller, S. D., 404, 525
Miller, W. L., 338
Miller, W. R., 526, 527
Millman, R. B., 205
Millon, T., 183
Minahan, A., 15, 16
Minuchin, S., 238, 254, 255, 456, 486
Mirabito, D. M., 379
Mitchell, K., 107, 364
Mokuau, N., 201, 250
Molgaard, V., 357
Molidor, C. E., 513
Moline, M. E., 71
Monsey, B. R., 451, 452
Montoya-Fernandez, J., 519
Moore, S. T., 450
Morell, C., 409
Moreno, 294
Morgan, G., 321, 324, 338, 339, 340, 357, 438, 439
Morningstar, G., 515
Morris, L., 252, 408, 409

Morrison, J., 186, 192, 201, 208, 412, 414, 415
Morrissey, M., 446
Morrow, D. F., 249
Morton, T., 395, 417, 444
Moscovice, I., 451
Mosley, J. C., 418
Moulton, P., 59
Moxley, D., 39, 430, 432, 510
Moyers, T., 217
Mullen, E. J., 451
Munoz, R. F., 395
Munroe, E., 417
Munson, C. E., 30, 175
Muran, J. C., 161
Murdach, A. D., 6, 643
Murphy, K., 59, 235
Murphy, C. M., 527
Murphy, J. W., 45, 306
Murphy, K., 45
Murray, 403, 404
Mwanza, 220
Mydans, S., 412

Nadal, K. L., 360
Nader, K., 357, 382
Nadir, A., 362, 395, 547
Nadler, A., 359
Nair, S., 338, 419, 420
Nakerud, 421
Naleppa, M. J., 201, 451
Neathery, K., 262, 425
Neleppa, 363
Nelson, 356, 404
Nelson-Becker, 409
Nelson-Zlupko, L., 203, 280
Nesbitt, J., 45
Netting, F. E., 222, 412, 413, 414, 429, 438, 440
Nevil, N., 510
Newman, K., 232
Nichols, A. W., 338, 340
Nichols, M. P., 227, 245, 251, 264, 313, 342, 343,
        403, 455, 456, 460, 462, 487, 489, 551, 553,
        555, 558, 560, 563
Nishida, C., 44
Norcross, J. C., 42, 83, 527
Nord, M., 421
Norris, 225
Northen, H., 274, 276, 277, 282, 510
Norton, D. G., 249
Nosko, A., 277, 508
Novelli, 184
Nuehring, E. M., 65, 69, 71, 186, 346
Nugent, W., 28
Nugent, W. R., 88, 155
Nurius, P. S., 181, 356, 390, 393, 394, 395,
        402, 409
Nybell, L. M., 445
Nyland, 321
Nyman, S. J., 39

O'Bannon, R. E., 395
Oberklaid, F., 362
O'Brien, B. A., 467, 483
O'Connor, G. G., 236, 252, 438
Oden, T. M., 395
Oettingen, G., 303, 316
O'Faire, J. D., 338, 419, 420

Ogles, B. M., 83
Ogbu, J. U., 357, 424
O'Halloran, 380
O'Hanlon, W., 181, 405, 406
O'Hare, 179, 180, 181, 184
O'Hollaran, T. M., 544
Okagbue-Reaves, J., 155, 159, 165, 167
O'Keefe, M., 514
Okun, B., 228, 229, 240, 241, 249, 254, 255, 257,
        258, 260, 383, 384
Oldham, G. R., 439
Oliver, M. L., 231
O'Melia, M., 434
Organista, K., 395
Orme, J. G., 175, 180, 184, 307, 314, 319, 331,
        332, 335, 336, 351
Ortega, R., 415
Ortiz, L. P. A., 222
Osborn, 181, 407
Oshlag, J. A., 404, 407
Ostroff, C., 234
Othmer, E., 200
Othmer, S. C., 200
Otten, 380
Overall, B., 83
Oyen, 232

Pablo, C. J., 250, 425
Pablo, S., 45
Packard, T., 332, 419, 438
Pack-Brown, J. P., 273, 274, 276, 278, 290
Padgett, D. K., 339
Padilla, Y., 4
Palmer, B., 45, 234, 360, 362
Panos, 318
Parad, H. J., 379, 381, 383, 410
Parad, L., 379, 381, 410
Parihar, B., 363
Parker, W. M., 273, 274, 276, 278, 290
Parks, 184
Parlee, 119
Parloff, M., 107
Parson, E. R., 548
Parsons, R. J., 4, 7, 409, 412, 454, 454
Patterson, D. A., 450
Patterson, J., 405
Paulson, 277
Pavlov, I. P., 390
Paveza, G. J., 196
Paymar, M., 526
Payne, M., 12, 19
Paz, J., 306
Pazaratz, D., 363
Pearce, J., 177, 226, 251
Pearlingi, B., 42
Pearlman, 363
Pearson, 215
Pelton, L. H., 3
Pence, E., 526
Pennell, J., 43, 307, 359, 514
Penrod, J. D., 451
Perlman, H., 18, 315, 363, 409
Perodeau, G., 394
Peters, A. J., 274
Peterson, A. C., 425
Petr, C., 19
Petts, 363

Phaobtong, T., 425
Pichot, T., 404
Pierce, W. J., 462, 467, 468, 469
Piers, J., 155, 159, 165, 167
Piliavin, I., 421
Pincus, A., 15, 16
Platt, S., 333, 475, 476
Poertner, J., 19
Poindexter, C. C., 385
Poitras, L., 394
Pokorny, A. D., 183
Pollack, D., 68, 306, 307, 309, 359, 391, 394, 410
Pollio, D. E., 12, 160
Pollock, P., 526, 527
Polowy, C. I., 71
Pomeroy, E. C., 363, 364
Ponce, D., 220
Pope, K. S., 67, 557
Potocky, 446
Potocky-Tripodi, M., 307, 326, 333, 341, 343,
        359, 385, 395, 410, 424, 429, 462, 469, 555
Potter-Efron, P., 105
Potter-Efron, R., 105
Powell, M., 149
Prata, G., 520
Preto, N. G., 358
Price, S. J., 230, 269, 471
Proehl, R. A., 437
Prochaska, J., 36, 217, 527
Proctor, E. K., 19, 44, 129, 177, 547, 548
Poulin, J., 230, 331
Puryear, D., 410
Pryce, J., 404

Queralt, M., 226

Race-Bigelow, J., 275, 513
Ragg, D., 155, 159, 165, 167
Raines, J. C., 541, 542, 555, 558
Ramanathan, C., 176
Ramarkrishman, 363
Ramos, B. M., 356, 363, 364, 379
Range, L. M., 183, 226
Rank, M. R., 231, 417
Rapoport, L., 383
Rapp, C. A., 221
Rathbone-McCuan, E., 195
Ratliff, S. S., 222
Rauch, J. B., 218, 225
Ray, N., 412
Raymond, G. T., 24
Reamer, F. G., 58, 62, 64, 67, 69, 73, 74, 318, 320,
        342, 343, 361, 450
Reese D. J., 338, 419, 420
Reeves, P., 55
Regehr, C., 526
Reid, K. E., 273, 281, 282, 505, 513
Reid, W. J., 29, 30, 33, 39, 46, 129, 315, 318, 339,
        344, 356, 363, 364, 367, 368, 376, 379, 408,
        451, 455, 456
Reilly, T., 450, 451
Reinecke, M., 409
Reisch, M., 232, 437
Reitan, T. C., 451
Renfrey, G. S., 395
Resnik, H., 226
Ressler, 222

Reuben, D. B., 196
Reynolds, B., 424
Reynolds, T., 514
Rheingold, A. A., 394
Rheinscheld, J., 404
Ribeiro, C., 359
Ribner, D. S., 303
Rice, A. H., 430
Rich, C. L., 215
Rich, E., 451
Richey, C. A., 20
Richman, L. S., 445
Richmond, M., 227
Rittenhouse, J., 514
Rittner, B., 307
Rivas, R. S., 274, 275, 280, 285, 289, 295,
    297, 298, 496, 500, 501, 511, 512, 513,
    515, 516
Rivera, F. G., 434, 435
Roberts, 232, 384, 410
Roberts, A. R., 379, 381, 383, 432
Roberts, D., 417, 445
Roberts-DeGennaro, M., 450
Robinson, J. B., 39, 395, 417, 468
Roby, J. L., 318
Rochelle, C. D., 42
Rodenborg, N., 444
Rodenburg, 232
Rodgers, A. Y., 446
Rodriguez, 359
Roffman, R. A., 20
Rogers, C., 88
Rollnick, S., 127, 217, 303, 303, 313, 316, 319,
    325, 368, 407, 526
Ronnau, J. P., 182
Rooney, 105
Rooney, G. D., 4, 144, 248, 251, 262, 265, 309,
    311, 359, 410, 425, 442, 470, 550
Rooney, R. H., 44, 46, 48, 49, 83, 144, 162,
    177, 193, 207, 250, 274, 306, 311, 309,
    311, 312, 313, 316, 329, 361, 364, 377,
    379, 469, 528, 559
Root, M., 250
Rorhbaugh, M., 405
Rose, S. D., 280, 285, 294, 296, 297, 450, 497,
    502, 505, 509, 511, 513, 517
Rosen, A., 129
Rosenblatt, A., 463
Rosenthal, K., 553
Ross, C., 183, 280, 285, 511
Rossi, P., 361, 362
Rotegard, L., 221
Roth, W., 15
Rothman, J., 359, 413, 432, 434, 433, 450,
    451, 453
Rotunno, M., 258
Rounds, K. A., 274
Rowan, A. B., 215
Rowe, R., 201
Rozini, 196
Rubin, J. S., 19, 20, 280, 339, 363, 364, 404,
    406, 419
Rudolph, K. D., 394
Ruffolo, M., 20
Ruiz, P., 205
Rush, A., 183, 390
Russell, J. M., 277, 404, 513

Ryder, R., 526
Rzepnicki, T. L., 21, 42

Sadock, B. J., 175
Safran, J. D., 161
Salazar, 409
Salcido, R. M., 241, 250, 251
Saleeby, D., 7, 63, 178, 179, 229, 248, 409,
    415, 465
Salinas-Sanchez, A., 519
Salmon, R., 274, 275, 277
Salston, M., 555
Saltman, J. E., 280, 282, 283, 514
Saltzberg, E. A., 395
Samet, J., 176
Sanchez, D., 394
Sandfort, J., 451, 452
Sands, R. G., 29
Santos, D., 177
Sarkisian, N., 307, 409
Sarri, R., 14
Satir, V., 259, 266, 455
Saulnier, C. F., 274, 276, 307
Sauter, J., 184
Schaffer, D., 181
Scharlach, 227, 228, 470
Schein, E. H., 437
Schenker, M., 406
Scheyett, A., 19, 20, 21
Schiller, L. Y., 491, 506
Schinke, S., 221
Schlesinger, E. G., 344, 364, 379, 469
Schmidt, P., 380
Schneider, R. L., 411, 429, 431
Schopler, J. H., 274, 277, 281, 281, 492,
    494, 514
Schrier, C., 71
Schroepfer, T., 404
Schultz, G. L., 44, 102, 108, 130, 156, 289
Schwartz, G., 381
Schwartz, G., 71, 251, 264, 563
Schwartz, M., 421
Schwartz, R. C., 227, 245, 342, 343, 403, 455,
    456, 460, 462, 558
Seay, H. A., 394
Secret, M., 454
Segal, U. A., 231, 232, 468, 519
Selekman, M. D., 404
Selvini-Palazzoli, M., 520
Selzer, M. L., 183
Senge, P., 438
Sengupta, S., 232
Serres, C., 436
Shamai, M., 338, 339, 340
Shane, P. G., 358
Shannon, T. R., 437
Shapiro, 196, 231
Sharpe, L., 394
Shaw, B., 183, 390
Shea, S. C., 226
Shea, E., 298
Sheafor, B., 14
Sherraden, 252, 408, 409, 430, 437
Sherritt, L., 183
Sherwood, D. A., 221, 222
Shiang, J., 344
Shih, M.,, 394

Shirley, A., 395
Shoham, V., 405
Shrier, L. A., 183
Shulman, L., 502
Shyne, A., 363, 408
Siefert, H., 201
Silberberg. S., 229, 235
Silva, J. A., 201
Silvawe, G. W., 61
Silvo, 385
Simon, J. B., 235
Simon, B. A., 29
Simon, R. I., 67
Simonson, N., 45
Simpson, G. M., 385
Siporin, M., 8, 15
Siu, A. L., 196
Skinner, 183
Skyles, A., 256
Slater, S., 249
Slosar, B., 430, 437
Smagner, J. P., 356
Smith, C., 235, 311, 321, 519
Smith, B. D., 306
Smith, C., 418
Smith, E. M., 383
Smith, T. B., 176
Smith, V., 95
Smokowski, P. R., 294, 297, 497, 509
Solis, D., 234
Solomon, P., 450
Sommers-Flannagan, 361
Sosin, M., 432
Sotomayor, M., 220
Souflee, F., 332, 419, 438
Sousa, L., 359
Sovereign, R. G., 526, 527
Sowers, K. M., 305, 324, 346
Sowers-Hoag, K., 129
Spaniol, L., 221
Specht, H., 23, 26, 415, 428
Speight, S. L., 227, 306
Speisman, J., 520
Spence, D., 520
Spenser, M., 418
Spitalnick, J. S., 241, 359
Spitzer, R., 183
Spriggs, W. E., 232
Springer, D., 332, 404, 406
Srebnik, D. S., 395
Stafford, J., 29
Stanton, 445
Staples, L. H., 306, 409
Steen, S., 193
Steib, S., 19
Steigerworld, 394
Steinmetz, G., 225
Stephenson, M., 404, 406
Stevens, 232
Stevens, S. L., 274
St Lawrence, J. S., 395
Stoesen, L., 428
Stokes, J. P., 296
Stone, M., 394
Storm, C., 406
Strean, H., 113
Streeter, C. L., 18, 332, 404, 406

Streissguth, A. P., 225
Strom-Gottfried, K. J., 65, 67, 72, 74, 131, 135, 182, 220, 305, 318, 320, 342, 361, 362, 557, 558
Strong, 537
Stuart, P. H., 428, 479
Studt, E., 363
Suarez, Z. E., 176, 201
Subramian, K., 274, 278, 506
Sue, D. W., 228, 306, 307, 309, 311, 358, 359, 360, 385, 424, 425, 468, 547, 548
Sue, D., 220, 344
Sue, S., 344
Sukhodolsky, D. G., 394
Sullivan, M. H., 356
Sunley, R., 73
Suzek, M., 262, 425
Swartz, H., 309
Swenson, C., 25, 26

Tabachnick, B. G., 67, 557
Taft, J., 18, 39
Tarrier, M., 394
Tarter, R. E., 394
Tate, T., 394
Taylor, L., 4
Teal, 404
Teare, R. J., 24
Teasdale, J. D., 519
Tepley, R., 526
Terr, L. C., 382
Terzian, M. A., 286
Testa, M., 425
Teyber, E., 323
Thibault, J. M., 222
Thomas, J., 149, 453
Thomas, D. L., 274
Thomas, F., 406
Thomas, H., 503
Thomlinson, 19
Thompson, C., 184
Thomson, 149
Thyer, B. A., 40, 129, 180, 184
Tice, 412, 414, 415
Tienda, M., 234
Timms, N., 83, 84, 102
Ting, 385
Tohn, S. L., 404, 407
Tolan, P. H., 418
Tolman, R. M., 513
Tolson, E. R., 356, 363, 364, 368, 379
Torino, G. C., 360
Torrecilha, R. S., 445
Toseland, R. W., 274, 275, 280, 285, 289, 295, 297, 298, 364, 496, 500, 502, 511, 512, 513, 515, 516, 517
Trabucchi, M., 196
Tracy, E. M., 18, 221, 236, 237, 425
Tramontin, M., 381, 382, 383, 385
Trepper, T. S., 356, 403, 404, 405, 406
Tripodi, T., 45, 94
Tropman, J. E., 413, 433, 434, 515
Trotter, C., 3, 4, 24, 83, 160, 407
Truax, C., 95, 107, 108
Tsui, P., 44, 102, 108, 130, 156, 289
Tuckman, 492, 493, 494, 495

Turnbull, J. E., 451
Turtle-Song, i., 225
Twiss, G., 447
Tyler, T. R., 306, 312

Ueda, S. S., 395
Ursano, R. J., 361
Ussher, J., 395

Vakalah, H. F., 514
Valencia, R. R., 11
Valesquez, 357
VandeCreek, L., 69
Vandiver, V., 30, 40, 42
VanHook, M. P., 184
Van Soest, D., 447
Van Voorhis, R. M., 248, 359, 410, 415
Van Wormer, K., 3, 160
Varlas, L., 303
Vassil, T. V., 288, 297, 502
Vera, E. M., 227, 306
Videka-Sherman, L., 36, 48, 221
Vigilante, F. W., 236, 237, 248
Vodde, R., 402, 413
Voison, 382
Vosler, N. R., 235, 248, 333
Voss, R. W., 359, 447

Wabeke, T., 404
Waites, C., 307, 359
Wakefield, J. C., 18, 26
Walen, S., 409
Walker, 363, 364, 445
Wallace, R., 277, 508
Walsh, J., 12, 20, 180, 181, 226, 227, 235, 249, 391, 394, 410, 450
Walter, U., 19
Waltman, G. H., 202
Wampold, B., 83
Ward, T., 394
Warren, K., 18, 338, 419, 420
Wartel, S., 553
Washington, O., 39
Wasik. B. H., 357
Waskow, I., 107
Watkins, J., 404
Watzlawick, P., 520
Wayne, R. H., 418
Weakland, J., 455, 520
Weaver, H. N., 306, 447
Webb, N. B., 195
Weick, A., 465
Weil, M. O., 307, 359, 414, 415
Weinberg, M., 248, 306, 307, 309, 471, 540
Weiner, A., 68
Weiner-Davis, M., 473
Weiss, B., 339
Weissman, A, 226
Wells, R. A., 195
Wells, R., 95, 408, 410
Weltman, S., 258, 358
Wenar, C., 214
Wessler, R., 409
West, L., 381
Westerfelt, A. H., 421
Westermeyer, J. J., 200

Weston, K., 228
Wewers, M., 395
Wexler, D., 418
Whaley, A. L., 548
White, M., 321, 412, 413
Whiting Blome, W., 19
Whitaker, C., 455
Whittaker, J. K., 18, 221, 236, 237, 425
Whittington-Clark, L. E., 273, 274, 276, 278, 290
Wiggins, E., 385
Wildfire, J., 232
Williams, 55, 233, 308, 383, 519, 550
Williams, G. T., 71
Williams, L. F., 445
Williams, R., 380
Wilner, M. E., 451
Wilson, 232
Winslade, W. J., 68
Withorn, A., 232, 429
Witkin, S. L., 340
Wodarski, J., 180, 184
Wolf, K. T., 445
Wolfe, B., 107, 395
Wong, D. K., 307, 308
Woo, K., 201
Wood, S. A., 285, 286
Wood, K. M., 183
Woods, R. T., 18
Worden, J. W., 213
Worthen, D., 463
Worthman, C. M., 201
Wright, O. L. Jr., 306, 317
Wright, B. R. W., 421
Wright, O. L., 457, 462
Wright, W., 511
Wulczyn, F., 417
Wylie, M. S., 406

Yaffe, J., 203
Yalom, I. D., 107, 279, 285, 297, 493, 497, 501, 530
Yamamoto, J., 201
Yamashiro, G., 186
Yee, D., 450
Yesavage, J. A., 213
Yin, S., 215
Young, D. C., 215
Young, E., 409
Yule. W., 383
Yunus, M., 231

Zanetti, O., 196
Zastrow, C., 14, 419
Zayas, L. H., 424, 445, 548
Zechetmayr, M., 201
Zeira, A., 382
Zhang, S-J., 371
Zilberfein, F., 88
Zimmerman, S. L., 235, 256
Zipple, M., 221
Zivin, 215
Zoellner, L., 394
Zuckerman, E. L., 225
Zuckhoff, 309
Zung, W., 183

Subject Index

Abu Ghraib prison, 428
Abuse of children or elders, confidentiality and, 69–70
Accent responses, 130
Acceptance, 540
Action, 217, 527
Action system, 17
Activities of daily living (ADLs), 196, 219
  instrumental, 196
Adaptational theory, 384
Addictive and mental disorders, dual diagnosis of, 200, 205–206
Additive empathic responses. *See also* Interpretations
  accuracy of, 526
  avoid series of, 526
  examples of, 520–521
  interpretations as, 520
  negative response to, 526
  phrasing of, 526
Additive empathy
  confrontations distinguished from, 50–51, 526, 528
  deeper feelings, 521–522
  empathy distinguished from, 519–520
  guidelines for employing, 525–526
  hidden purposes of behavior, 523–524
  summarization employing, 151
  underlying meanings of feelings, thoughts, and behavior, 522–523
  unrealized strengths and potentialities, 524–525
  wants and goals, 523
Adjourning stage, 496
ADLs *See* Activities of daily living (ADLs)
Adolescents
  depression in, 214–215
  suicidal risk of, 214–215
Adoption and Safe Family Act (ASFA), 416, 417, 429, 448
Adult
  assessing, 194–196
  suicidal risk in older, 215
Advance directives, 64

Advising and giving of suggestions or solutions to clients prematurely, 159–160
Advocacy
  social action *See* Advocacy and social action
Advocacy and social action
  approach for, 432–433
  cause, 430
  competence and skills, 431–432
  defined, 430
  ethical principles for, 431–432
  goal of, 432
  indications for, 427–431
  on behalf of clients, 430
  models of, 430
  policies and legislation, 429–430
  process of, 430
  risks and limitations of, 432
  skills, 431–432
  steps in, 432
  strategic frame analysis, 433
  techniques of, 432–433
Advocate, 31, 430
Affective discrepancies, 532
Affective disorders
  bipolar disorder, 212
  major depressive disorder, 212–213
Affective words and phrases, 90–94
African American community, 417
Agency policies, communicating, 87
Agency program objectives, goals and, 305–306, 321
Agency system, 17
Agnosia, 210
Agreeable mandate strategy, 312
Agreement for professional services, 347–348
Agreements, 342
  purchase-of-service, 346
Alcoholism, 202–203
Alcohol use and abuse, assessing, 200, 202–203
All or nothing thinking, 391
All-purpose confrontations, 527
American Medical Association, 233
American Red Cross, 426

American Sign Language (ASL), 177
Analyzing social problems and conditions
  disparate impact and social justice, 416
  social justice questions, 416–417
  questions for, 415
  values and resource distribution, 415
  who is responsible, 417
  who is affected, 416
Anhedonia, 211, 212
Anticipated life transition, 384
Anticipatory guidance, 389
Aphasia, 210
Appearance, assessment of, 200–201
Applicants, 4, 16, 33
Approach/avoidance behavior, 492–493
Appropriateness of affect, 211–212
Apraxia, 210
Arbitrators, 28
Art therapy, 511
ASFA *See* Adoption and Safe Family Act (ASFA)
ASL *See* American Sign Language (ASL)
Assertive confrontation, 528
  affective discrepancies, 532
  behavioral discrepancies, 532–533
  cognitive/perceptual discrepancies, 531
  elements of, 529
  indications for, 531–533
  types of discrepancies, 531–533
Assertiveness, 41
Assessment(s), 4, 37–38
  background sheets, 181
  beginning, 185–186
  of behavioral functioning, 200, 215–217
  of biophysical functioning *See* Biophysical functioning
  case example, 178
  case management, 451
  checklist, 185
  of children, 194–196
  class factors, 193–194
  client concerns, 186–187
  client self-monitoring, 182
  cognitive flexibility, 208
  cognitive or thought disorders, 210

Assessment(s) (*continued*)
  cognitive/perceptual functioning *See* Cognitive/perceptual functioning
  coherence, 208
  collateral contacts, 181, 182, 183
  conducting, 172, 184–194
  consideration of other people or systems, 187
  coping efforts and skills, 192–193
  crisis intervention (CI), 379–380
  cultural factors, 193–194
  culturally competent, 175–177
  defined, 172
  depression *See* Depression
  developmental, 195
  developmental needs and wants, 187–188
  diagnosis and, 174–175
  direct observation of interactions, 181–182
  direct observation of nonverbal behavior, 180, 181
  drug use and abuse *See* Drug use and abuse
  duration of problem, 191
  of emotional functioning *See* Emotional functioning
  empathic responding to accurately assess client problems, 103
  emphasizing client strengths in, 177–179
  enactment, 182
  environmental systems *See* Environmental systems
  ethnic minority clients, 176
  external resources, 194
  family *See* Family assessment(s)
  of family power structure, 258–259
  focus of, 172–174
  formal, 172
  framework for, 178–179
  of group behaviors *See* Group member behaviors, assessment of
  of group processes *See* Group processes, assessment of
  health, 201–202
  influences on, 172–173
  information sources, 181–184
  instruments for, 183
  intellectual functioning, 206
  interview as information source in, 181
  intrapersonal systems, 199–200
  issues affecting client functioning, 191–192
  judgment, 207
  language differences, 177
  life transition stresses, 189
  meanings ascribed to problems, 189–190
  misconceptions, 209
  multidimensional, 36–38, 171–172
  older adults, 194–196
  personal experience in making, 181, 184
  physical environment, 218–219
  presenting problem, 186–187, 188–189
  problematic behaviors *See* Problematic behaviors
  problem identification, 186–187
  process, 172–174
  product of, 172–174
  questions to answer, 184–185
  reality testing, 207
  role of knowledge and theory in, 179–181
  self-awareness in making, 184
  self-concept, 209
  settings, 172
  of severity of problem, 189
  societal factors, 193–194
  solution-focused questions, 191–192
  of spirituality/religion, 221–222
  of strengths and problems, 172–173
  substance abuse *See* Drug use and abuse
  testing instruments, 183, 183
  tools, 180, 183
  typical wants involved in presenting problems, 188–189
  use of interpreters, 177
  values, 208–209
  written *See* Written assessments
Association of Retired Persons (AARP), 228
Association of Social Work Boards (ASWB), 547
ASWB *See* Association of Social Work Boards (ASWB)
Asymmetrical relationships, 483
Attributions, meaning, 190
Auditory hallucinations, 207
Authenticity, 106–107
  defined, 107
  as facilitative condition, 87–88
  relating assertively to clients, 118–122
  responding with *See* Responding authentically
  self-disclosure and *See* Self-disclosure
Autonomy, 439
Avolition, 210

Background sheets, 181
Barber's Cutting Cancer Out, 426
Bargaining, 312–313
Barriers to change, 539
  assessing potential barriers and intervening, 545–546
  countertransference reactions *See* Countertransference reactions
  cross-racial and cross-cultural, 547–550
  eliciting feelings and thoughts of clients, 546
  establishing trust, 548, 550–551
  interpersonal factors, 549
  pathological or inept social workers, 546–547
  positive connotation, 562
  redefining problems as opportunities for growth, 562
  relational reactions and potential *See* Relational reactions to helping process
  transference reactions *See* Transference reactions
Barriers to communication *See* Communication barriers
Baseline behaviors, retrospective estimates of, 335
Baseline measures, 334
  guidelines for obtaining, 336
Basis of conclusions drawn by clients, exploring, 138
Beck Depression Inventory, 183
Beck Scale for Suicidal Ideation, 183
Behavioral changes, 305
Behavioral discrepancies, 532–533
Behavioral functioning
  assessing, 200, 215–217
  dimensions of behavior, 216
Behavioral rehearsal, increasing self-efficacy through, 373–374
Behavioral tasks, 367
Behavioral treatment agreement, 350
Behaviors
  approach/avoidance, 492–493
  assessing physical attending, 169
  circular explanations of, 245–246
  counterproductive, 292
  dysfunctional behaviors, 287, 289
  enacted role, 264
  examples of nonverbal, 156–157
  family role behavior and life transition stresses, 265
  functional behaviors, 287, 288–289
  group member behaviors *See* Group member behaviors, assessment of
  hidden purposes of, 523–524
  interactional, 140–141
  interpretations of dynamics of behavior, 162–163
  linear explanation of, 245
  patterned behaviors *See* Patterned behaviors
  perceived role, 264
  prescribed role, 264
  problematic *See* Problematic behaviors
  problematic and functional group, 293
  social environment and human, 12
  thematic, 287
Beliefs, goal setting, 306–307
Big event, 380
Bilingualism, 177
Biophysical functioning
  physical characteristics and presentation, 200–202
  physical health, 201–202
Bipolar disorder, 212
Blaming, 391
Blaming clients, 161
Blaming the poor, 429
Boundaries, 17
  NASW Code of Ethics and, 66–67
  preservation of professional, 66–67
Boundaries and boundary maintenance, family, 252–256
  cultural and family variants, 254–255
  external family boundary maintenance, 253
  family subsystems and coalitions, 254
  flexibility in, 253
  internal family boundary maintenance, 253–254
  relationships in disengaged families, 256
Brainstorming, 367–368, 515
Brief Family Therapy Center, 403
Brief therapies, 363, 364
  solution-focused, 180
Brief treatment models, 363, 364
Brokers, 27–28, 422
BSW programs, 23
Burnout, 544
  circumstances of, 544

CAGE test, 183
Captive clients, 159
Cardinal values, 53–60

Case management
  assessment, 451
  characteristics of, 451
  functions, 450–452
  goals setting/case planning, 451
  linking clients, 451
  macro level, 450–451
  model, 452
  monitoring and reassessment, 451
  outcome evaluation/termination, 451
  planning interventions or identifying and
    indexing resources, 451
  steps of, 451
Case managers/coordinators
  functions of, 28
Case progress notes, 314–315, 332
Case records, confidentiality of, 68, 71–72
Casework, 23
CASPARS *See* Clinical Assessment Package for
    Assessing Risks and Strengths (CASPARS)
Catastrophizing, 392
CBT *See* Cognitive-behavioral therapy (CBT)
Challenges, 380
Change
  barriers to *See* Barriers to change
  opposition to *See* Opposition to change
Change maintenance strategies, planning, 42
Change-oriented approaches, 355
Change strategies, 440. *See also* Organizational
    change
Chaos theory, 384
Charity Organization Societies (COS), 227
Charity Organization Societies and the Settle-
    ment Houses, 227, 428
Checking out perceptions, 137–138
Child abuse, confidentiality and, 69–70
Child care cooperative, 425
Children
  assessing, 194–196
  cognitive restructuring, 394
  crisis, 381–383
  decision-making processes, 259
  depression in, 214–215
  positive feedback from parents to, 476
  poverty impact, 232–233
  rewards and incentives for, 369–370
  suicidal risk of, 214–215
  as undocumented individuals, 427
Children's Depression Scale, 215
Child Welfare League of America, 430, 446
CI *See* Crisis intervention (CI)
Circular causality, 245
Civil Rights Movement, 428
Clarify expectations, 461–462
Class factors in assessment, 193–194
Clichés, 166
Client advocate, 28–29
Client participation, 341
Client problems, empathic responding to ac-
    curately assess, 103
Client records, confidentiality of, 68, 71–72
Clients, 4, 33–34
  ability to trust, 548, 550–551
  arguing with, 161–162
  assessing problems of, 103
  assisting clients to personalize their state-
    ments, 138–139

biophysical functioning *See* Biophysical
    functioning
blaming, 161
captive, 159
confrontations with, 103–104
consoling, 159
contracting with, 341–342
coping efforts and skills, 193–193
counterattacking, 163
countertransference reactions *See*
    Countertransference reactions
criticizing, 158
dignity of, 443
eliciting details related to clients' experiences,
    140
emotional reactions to problems, 192
establishing relationships with, 102
ethnic minority, 176
excusing, 159
exploring basis of conclusions drawn by, 138
focusing *See* Focusing
instructing, 161–162
interrupting, 164
involuntary, 33–34
issues affecting client functioning, 191–192
judging, 161
"Leaning into" clients' anger, 120
lecturing, 161–162
legally mandated, 4
linking, 452
maintaining psychological contact with,
    129–130
making requests of, 118–119
managing anger and violence by, 104–105
misgivings/concerns of, 34–35
nonverbal communication barriers *See*
    Nonverbal communication barriers,
    eliminating obstacles presented by, 103
nonvoluntary, 4
participation in goal setting, 306
persuading, 162
realistic reactions toward offensive, 557
reassuring, 159
relating assertively to, 118–122
resistance to change by, 558–559
responding to nonverbal messages by, 103
rewards and incentives for, 369
roles of, 83–87
sexual attraction toward, 557–558
social worker's negative attitude toward, 541,
    543–544
social worker's positive attitude toward, 541,
    544
staying in touch with, 103
sympathizing with, 159
teaching reciprocal empathic responding to,
    105–106
threatening, 163
transference reactions *See* Transference
    reactions
verbal communication barriers *See*
    Verbal communication barriers,
    eliminating
voluntary, 4
warning, 163
Client self-monitoring, 182
Client system, 16

Clinical Assessment Package for Assessing Risks
    and Strengths (CASPARS), 236, 333
Clinical practice, 25, 26. *See also* Direct practice
Clinical Social Work Federation, 25
Clinical Social Work Practice: A Cognitive-
    Integrative Approach, 390
Closed-ended responses
  discriminant use of, 133–135
  examples of, 132
  exercises in identifying, 133
  information elicited by, 134
Closed-ended treatment groups, 281
Coalitions, family, 254
Code of Ethics, NASW, 5, 6, 7, 8, 9–10, 53, 61,
    411, 437
  confidentiality, 67–68
  informed consent, 65, 300
  key principles, 63–68
  primacy of clients' rights, 547
  professional boundaries, 66–67
  self-determination, 63–65
Cognitions
  functional and problematic, 292
  as obstacles to task completion, 372
Cognitive Behavioral
  integrative cognitive approach, 390
  cognitive distortions, 391
  cognitive restructuring, 390–391
  tenets of, 391
  theory of, 390
Cognitive behavioral approach to family
    systems, 455
Cognitive-behavioral therapy (CBT)
  cognitive restructuring as component of, 390
  defined, 390
  theoretical framework, 390
Cognitive dissonance, 209
Cognitive distortions, 391–393
Cognitive Distortions, categories of, 391
Cognitive flexibility, assessment of, 208
Cognitive functioning
  exploration of, 49
  goal to change, 305
Cognitive or thought disorders, assessment of,
    210
Cognitive patterns, assessment of individuals',
    290–291
  case example, 291
Cognitive patterns and myths, family, 263–264
Cognitive/perceptual discrepancies, 531
Cognitive/perceptual functioning
  assessing, 199, 206–209
  cognitive flexibility, 208
  cognitive or thought disorders, 210
  coherence, 208
  intellectual functioning, 206
  judgment, 207
  misconceptions, 209
  reality testing, 207
  self-concept, 209
  values, 208–209
Cognitive restructuring
  acceptance of self-statements, assumptions,
    and beliefs, 396–397
  application with diverse groups, 394–395
  assistance in clients rewarding themselves for
    successful coping efforts, 401–402

Cognitive restructuring (*continued*)
   assistance in identifying dysfunctional beliefs and patterns of thoughts, 397–399
   assistance in identifying situations that engender dysfunctional cognitions, 399–400
   assistance in substituting functional self-statements for self-defeating cognitions, 400–401
   assumptions of, 390,
   case example, 395
   clusters of misconceptions, 399
   cognitive-behavioral therapy (CBT) *See* Cognitive-behavioral therapy (CBT)
   culturally compatible adaptations, 395
   with diverse groups, 394–395
   empirical evidence for, 393
   explanation of
   goal of, 391
   limitations, strengths and cautions, 402
   with minority group clients, 402
   with minors, 394
   procedure of, 395–402
   self-monitoring, 399–400
   self-statements, 395–402
   social worker use of self, 396
   strengths, limitations, and cautions, 402–403
   steps in, 395–402
   tenets of, 391
   theoretical framework, 390
   uses of, 393–394
   utilization with minors, 394
Cognitive schema, 263
   Developmental stage, 269
   Negative, 474
   Culturally derived, 270
   Marginalized and oppressed people, 393
Cognitive sets, cultivating positive, 474–475
Cognitive tasks, 367
The Cognitive Therapy of Depression (Beck et al.), 390
Cognitive therapy (CT), tenets of, 391
Coherence, assessment of, 208
Cohesion
   assessment of group, 296–297
   importance of, 499–500
Collaboration, 450, 451
   case example, 452–453
   interorganizational *See* Service coordination and interorganizational collaboration
   phases of, 452
Collaborative practice, 229
Collateral contacts, information from, 182
Color blind practice, 548
Common Cause, 432
Communication
   drawing attention to repetitive, 465–466
   empathic, 88–89, 95–98
   helping process and, 35
   increasing effective, 507–508
   metacommunication, 477–478
   positive feedback *See* Positive feedback
   privileged communication and confidentiality, 70–71
   regulating communication in families, 456
Communication barriers
   eliminating nonverbal *See* Nonverbal communication barriers, eliminating

eliminating verbal *See* Verbal communication barriers, eliminating
   in families, 267–268
Communication patterns
   family *See* Communication styles, family
   gauging effectiveness of responses, 167–168
   impacts of counterproductive, 155
Communication styles, family
   barriers to communication, 267–268
   congruence and clarity of communications, 266–267
   mystification, 267
   receiver skills, 268
   sender skills, 268–269
   validating responses, 269
Communities United to Rebuild Neighborhoods (CURN), 434
Community organization, 433
   areas of focus, 433–434
   model, 435–436
   capacity building, 433–434
   community intervention strategies, 434–436
   contact with key informants, 435
   cultural guides, 435
   ethical decision making framework, 437
   ethical issues, 436–437
   levels of community contact, 435–436
   locality development, 433
   models and strategies, 433
   national programs and policies, 433–434
   natural helping networks, 435
   organizing and planning with diverse groups, 435–436
   planning with diverse groups, 435
   problem solving process, 434
   social action, 434
   social planning, 434
   steps and skills of, 434–436
   strategies of, 433–434
Community resources, mobilizing, 422–424
Community support systems and networks, 425–426
Compassion fatigue, 544–545
Compassionate conservatism, 429
Competence, social worker
   core duties, 10–14
   ethical requirement, 10
   evolving theory of, 15–18
Complainants, 406
Complementary interactions, modifying, 483
Complementary relationships, 483
Complementary roles, 264
Composition of treatment groups, 280–281
Computerized information systems, 332–333
Concreteness, seeking, 505–506
Concrete responses
   assisting clients to personalize their statements, 138–139
   blending open-ended, empathic and, 146–148
   challenges in seeking, 135–136
   checking out perceptions, 137–138
   clarification of meaning of vague or unfamiliar terms, 138
   eliciting details related to clients' experiences, 140

eliciting details related to interactional behavior, 140–141
   eliciting specific feelings, 139–140
   exercises in seeking, 142–143
   exploring basis of conclusions drawn by clients, 138–139
   exploring topics in depth using, 145–146
   focusing on here and now, 140
   specificity of expression by social workers, 141–142
   types of, 136–141
Confianza, 462
Confidentiality
   case records, 68, 71–72
   communicating about, 87
   danger to self or others, 69
   limits on, 68–72
   privileged communications, 70–71
   safeguarding, 67–68
   subpoenas, 70–71
   suspicion of child or elder abuse, 69–70
   waivers of, 69
Conflict
   assisting clients to disengage from, 482–483
   interrole, 265
Confrontations
   additive empathy distinguished from *See* Additive empathy
   all-purpose, 527
   anxiety in responses to, 531
   appropriateness of, 526
   of defenses, 527
   delivery of, 530
   extreme emotional strain and, 530–531
   follow with empathic responsiveness, 531
   guidelines for employing, 530–531
   hearing of, 528
   immediate change from, 531
   interpretation distinguished from, 526
   to manifest blind spots in thoughts, beliefs, emotions, and behavior, 528
   self-confrontation, 528
   spare use of, 530
   as style of practice, 526
   therapeutic binds, 563–564
   violations of law and, 530
   working relationship, 530
Confronting patterns of opposition, 563–564
Congruence and clarity of communications in families, 266–267
Consent, non-western perspective, 362
Consoling clients, 159
Consultant/consultee, 29–30
Consultations, confidentiality and, 68–69
Contact, duration, 381
Contacted persons, 16
Contemplation, 36, 217, 527
Content levels of family interactions, 242–246
Content relevance, 129
Contingency contract, 475
Contracting with clients, 341–342. *See also* Contracts
Contracts
   agreement for professional services, 347–348
   agreements, 342
   appointment times, 345
   behavioral, 340–341

behavioral treatment agreement, 350
contingency, 475
crisis situation, 342
developing, 343–346
duration of process, 344–345
financial arrangements, 346
formal, 342–343
forms of, 342
frequency of sessions, 343–344
goals to be accomplished, 343
housekeeping items, 345–346
informal, 342–343
interventions to be employed, 343
length and frequency of sessions, 343–344
monitoring progress, 345
negotiating, 38–39, 49–50
negotiating mini-contract, 546
participants' roles, 343
purpose of, 341–342
rationale for, 342
renegotiating, 345
roles of participants, 343
sample, 346
session length and frequency, 343–344
stipulating measurement and evaluation of
    progress, 345
stipulations for renegotiating, 345
techniques to be employed, 343
"the back door", 346
time-limited, 344
types of, 342
verbal, 342
written, 342
Convenience, 281
Cooperation, 450
Coordination, 450
Coping efforts and skills, client, 192–193, 374
Coping mechanism, 388
Coping questions, 405
Core conditions, 88
Council on Social Work Education (CSWE),
    411, 428
    core competencies, 10–14, 23
    curriculum policy statement, 23
    purposes of, 5–6
Counterattacking clients, 163
Counterproductive behaviors, 292
Counterproductive roles, 501–502
Countertransference reactions, 555–557
    introspection, 556
    steps in resolving, 556
    typical, 556
Covert behaviors, measuring, 335
Covert goals, 309
CRAFFT test, 183
Crisis
    assessment in, 379
    anticipated life transition, 384
    benefits, 383
    categories of, 384
    defined, 342
    definition and stages, 380
    dispositional, 384
    emotional reaction, 384
    events and situations, 380
    level of danger, 381
    maturational/developmental, 384

opportunity, 378–381
positive constructive thinking
    and action, 388
psychiatric emergency, 384
psychopathological, 384
reactions, 380
responses, 380
situational supports, 386–388
six categories of, 384
stages of, 380–381
traumatic stress, 384
traumatic stress reactions and
    developmental stage, 384
Type I, Type II, 382–383
types of, 384
Crisis intervention (CI)
    application with diverse groups, 384
    anticipatory guidance, 389
    assessment, 379–380
    case example, 386–387
    characteristics of, 379
    considerations for minors, 381–382
    crisis defined, 380
    define problem, 385–386
    delineating tasks, 383
    duration of contact, 381–383
    ensure client safety, 387
    equilibrium model, 379–380
    equilibrium model, tenets of, 379–380
    examine alternatives, 387–388
    expansion of, 389
    Interactive Trauma/Grief-Focus Therapy
        Model (IT/G-FT), 382
    key elements in equilibrium model, 379
    limitations of, 389–390
    make plans, 388
    obtaining commitment, 388–389
    planning, 388
    process and procedures of, 385–389
    promptness of response, 381
    provide support, 387
    psychosocial transitions as key
        element in, 380
    six-step model of, 385–389
    stages of crisis, 380–381
    strengths and limitation, 389
    strengths of, 389–390
    tenets of, 379–380
    theoretical framework, 383–384
    time limits, 379
    Triage Assessment System (TAS), 380
Crisis reaction, 380–381
Crisis situation contract, 342
Critical incidences, 339
Critical thinking, 10
Criticizing clients, 161–162
Cross-cultural contact, 177
Cross-racial and cross-cultural barriers to
    change, 547–550
CSWE See Council on Social Work Education
    (CSWE)
Cultivating positive cognitive sets,
    474–475
Cultural and ecological perspectives, family
    interventions
    communication style differences,
        467–468

differences in communication styles,
    467–468
engaging the family, 469–470
hierarchical considerations, 468
sensitivity to culture, 467
social worker authority, 468–469
use of ecological approach, 470
Cultural competence, 175–177, 446
    Self-Assessment Instrument, 446
Cultural Competence, organizations
    macro perspective, 445
    organizational competence, 445
    organizations, 446
    public policy, 447
    resources and tools, 446
    social worker's ethical responsibility, 444
    strategies to achieve, 446
Cultural dislocation, 194
Cultural differences, awareness, 10
Cultural empathy, 548
Cultural factors
    in assessment, 193–194, 254–255
    developing resources with diverse
        groups, 424
    in families, 228
    matching interventions to, 358–360
Culturalgram, 236
Culturally competent assessment, 175–177
Cultural self-awareness, 177
CURN See Communities United to Rebuild
    Neighborhoods (CURN)
Curriculum policy statement, CSWE, 23
Customers, 406

DAFS See Direct Assessment of Functioning
    Scale
Danger or threat to self or others,
    confidentiality and, 69
DARS See Disciplinary Actions Reporting
    System (DARS)
Data sources, 195–196
DAST See Drug Abuse Screening Test
DDST-II See Denver Developmental Screening
    Test for Children
Decision by consensus, 282
Decision-making processes
    family, 259–261
    groups, 294–295
Deeper feelings, 521–522
Deficiencies in judgment, 207
Deficiencies in social skills, 372
Delabeling strategy, 464
Delusions, 207
Dementia, 210
Denver Developmental Screening Test for
    Children (DDST-II), 196
Deployment, 233
Depression
    Beck Depression Inventory, 183
    children and, 214–215
    Children's Depression Scale, 215
    Geriatric Depression Scale, 213
    Johns Hopkins Depression Scale, 215
    major depressive disorder, 212–213
    older adults and, 215
Derailment, 208
Determination, 217

Determination of Need Assessment (DONA), 196

Developmental assessment, 195

Developmental needs and wants, assessment of, 187–188

Developmental phases, matching interventions to, 357

Diagnosis
  assessment and, 174–175
  defined, 174

Diagnostic and Statistical Manual (DSM-IV-TR), 174–175, 212, 382

Differentiation, 492, 495–496, 499

Dignity and worth
  privacy, 443
  promoting, 443
  staff behavior and attitudes, 443

Diligent working poor, 232

Dimensions of family assessment
  boundaries and boundary maintenance *See* Boundaries and boundary maintenance
  decision-making processes, 259–261
  family communication styles *See* Communication styles, family
  family context *See* Family context
  family goals, 261–262
  family life cycle, 269–270
  family myths and cognitive patterns, 263–264
  family roles, 264–265
  family strengths, 251–252
  format for employing, 247–248
  power structure *See* Power structure, family

Direct Assessment of Functioning Scale (DAFS), 219

Direct practice, 26
  defined, 25
  philosophy of, 26, 27

Direct practitioners, 25–26
  roles of, 25–26

Disciplinary Actions Reporting System (DARS), 547

Discounting positives, 392

Discovery, 359

Discrepant viewpoints, 520

Discrete general tasks, 315

Discrimination, 11

Disengaged families, 255

Disengaged family system, 255–256
  relationships in, 256

Disorientation, 207

Dispositional crisis, 384

Distorted attributions, 190

Distortions, 207

Disturbance in executive functioning, 210

Diversity, awareness, 10

Domain, 23

Dominating interaction, social worker, 164–165

DONA *See* Determination of Need Assessment

Drop-in model of groups, 281

Drop-out model *See* drop-in model

Drug Abuse Screening Test (DAST), 183

Drug use and abuse, 49
  alcohol, 202–203
  assessment of, 202
  illicit drugs, 202, 203–205

interviewing for potential of, 206
  medications, 202

DSM-IV-TR, 174–175

Dual diagnosis, 200, 205–206

Dual perspective, 249

Durable power of attorney, 64

Dwelling on past, 166

Dysfunctional family alignments, strategies to modify
  circumstances requiring, 486
  family sculpting, 487
  Genogram, 487
  goals, 486–487
  structural mapping, 486, 488

Dysfunctional family interactions, strategies to modify
  assisting clients to disengage from conflict, 482–483
  contracting for reciprocal changes, 483–485
  disengagement from conflict, 482–483
  metacommunication, 477–478
  modifying complementary interactions, 483
  modifying dysfunctional family rules, 478–480
  on-the-spot interventions, 480–482
  safeguarding mutual respect, 482

Dysfunctional family rules, 240–241
  modifying, 478–480

Dysfunctional patterns, 216

Dysfunctional processes, interrupting, 119–120

Dysfunctional role performance, 501–502

Dysphoria, 212

Earned Income Tax Credit (ETC), 231

Ecological approach with families, use of, 470
  examples of, 470–472

Ecological factors, assessment of, 37, 217–218

Ecological systems model, 15–18
  diagramming, 219, 220

Eco-map, 220, 237, 339, 340

Ecosystems theory, 384

Educational groups, 274

Educational Policy and Accreditation Standards (EPAS), 6, 411
  competencies, 10–14

Educator, social worker as, 26–27

Elder abuse, confidentiality and, 69–70

Embedded questions, 132–133

Emotional blunting, 211

Emotional constriction, 210

Emotional excesses, 210

Emotional functioning
  affective disorders, 212
  appropriateness of affect, 211–212
  assessing, 49, 199, 200, 209–215
  bipolar disorder, 212
  depression *See* Depression
  emotional control, 210–211
  emotional range, 211
  goal to change, 305
  suicidal risk, 213–214

Emotional reactions to problems, clients, 192

Emotional reasoning, 392

Emotions *See* Feelings

Empathic communication, 88–89
  levels of, 95–98

to mitigate cross-racial and cross-cultural barriers to change, 548

Empathic communication scale, 95–98

Empathic responding, 47, 95–99
  to accurately assess client problems, 103
  additive *See* Additive empathic responses
  blending open-ended, concrete and, 146–148
  employing, 102
  to establish relationship in initial sessions, 102
  exercises for discriminating levels of, 99–100
  exploring topics in depth using, 146
  to facilitate group discussions, 105
  family sessions, 461
  follow confrontation with, 531
  to handle obstacles presented by clients, 104
  levels of, 95–98
  to make confrontations more palatable, 103–104
  to manage anger and patterns of violence, 104–105
  reciprocal *See* Reciprocal empathic responding
  to respond to clients' nonverbal messages, 103
  to stay in touch with clients, 103
  teaching clients, 105–106
  uses of, 102–105

Empathy, 540
  additive *See* Additive empathy
  additive empathy distinguished from, 519–520
  conveyance of, 95–99
  cultural, 548
  as facilitative condition, 88
  reciprocal *See* Reciprocal empathic responding
  relational, 548

Empirical data, 19

Empowerment, 355, 448
  defined, 414
  macro practice in the context of, 414–415
  social work groups for, 514

Enabler, 422

Enacted role behavior, 264

Enactment, 182

Enhancing human well-being, 4–5

Enhancing social functioning, 5, 6

Enmeshment, in family systems, 249, 254–255

Environmental systems
  assessing, 200, 217–222
  basic environmental needs, 217–218
  in goal setting, 309
  goodness of fit, 217
  interaction with interpersonal and intrapersonal systems, 199
  physical environment, 218–219
  social support systems (SSSs) *See* Social support systems
  spirituality/religion, 221–222
  transactions, 217

EPAS *See* Educational Policy and Accreditation Standards (EPAS)

Equal Rights Amendment, 428

Equifinality, 18

ETC *See* Earned Income Tax Credit

Ethical Decision-Making Framework, 437

Ethical dilemmas, understanding and
    resolving, 73–76
    in groups, 299–301
Ethical Rule Screen, 437
Ethical tensions, 320
Ethics
    case example, 62–63
    Code of Ethics *See* Code of Ethics, NASW
    in community organizing, 436–437
    conflicts and, 73–76
    goal attainment strategies, 356
    in goal development, 306–307
    in groups, 299–301
    intersection of laws and, 62–63
    values and, 8–9
Ethnic minority clients, 176
Ethnotherapeutic, 548
Evaluation
    defined, 331
    function of, 331–332
    of groups, 513
    measurement and *See* Measurement and
        evaluation
    methods, 332
Evaluation in Clinical Practice, 360
Evidence-based practice, 19, 21
Exception questions, 405, 406
Exceptions, 406
Excusing clients, 159
Expectations, exploring client, 48
Expediters, 29
Exploration process, 47–48
    assessment of emotional functioning, 49
    cognitive functioning, 49
    focusing *See* Focusing
    focusing in depth, 48–49
    negotiating goals and contracts, 49–50
    outlines, 49, 144
    substance abuse, sexual abuse and violence, 49
    verbal following skills *See* Verbal following
        skills
Exploration skills, 36–37
External family boundary maintenance, 253
External resources for assessment, 194
Extreme distortions, 207

Facilitative conditions, 87–88
Facilitative responses, 165, 268
Facilitators, 29
Familismo, 228
FAE *See* Fetal alcohol effects (FAE)
Failure to complete tasks
    inadequate preparation, 377–378
    lack of commitment, 376–377
    lack of support, 377
    negative reactions to social worker, 377
    occurrence of a crisis, 376
    performance problems related to target
        problem, 378
    performance problems related to task,
        376–378
    vagueness of specified tasks, 377
Familiar, 359
Families
    assessing, 227, 236, 249
    collaborative practice with, 230
    cultural and family variants, 229, 254

level I, 228, 237
level 3, 237
gay and lesbian, 230
social work practice with, 227
resilience in, 235
Family
    case study, 464
    cultural and ecological perspectives in inter-
        ventions *See* Cultural and ecological
        perspectives, family interventions
    decision making, 259–261
    defined, 227–228, 455
    diversity, 250
    establishing rapport with, 460–461
    form, 249–250
    functions, 228–30
    grandparents, 247, 254, 256
    goals, 261–262
    homeostasis, 238–239
    influences on, 455
    initial contacts with *See* Initial contacts with
        families
    interactions with other social systems, 455
    interventions *See* Family interventions
        membership in, 227
    lifecycle, 357
    membership, 228
    military and, 233
    resilience, 235
    roles, 264
    rules *See* Rules, family
    separations, 233
    as social system, 455
    social work practice with, 227
    strengths, 251–252
    stressors, 230–235
    system, 252
    traditional, 227–228
    transitions, 233
Family assessment(s)
    assessing problems using systems frame-
        work, 246–247
    bounding patterns, 253, 255–256
    circular explanations of behavior,
        245–246
    Clinical Assessment Package for Assessing
        Risks and Strengths (CASPARS), 236
    content levels of interaction, 242–246
    decision-making, 260–261
    dimensions of *See* Dimensions of family
        assessment
    disengaged, 255–256
    dual perspective, 249
    factors in, 227–228
    of goals, 261–262
    instruments, 236–237
    interactions, 247
    power, 256–259
    power structure, 258–259
    process levels of interaction, 242–246
    rules, 239
    sequences of interaction, 243–245
    strength-based and risk, 237
    of strengths, 251–252
    strengths and risks, 237
    strengths based questions, 236
    systems concepts, 237–238

systems framework for *See* Systems frame-
    work for families
Family Assessment Wheel, 237
Family cognitive patterns and myths, 263–264
    case example, 263–264
Family, Communication styles of, 265
Family context
    diversity within groups, 250–251
    dual perspective, 249
    factors in assessing, 248–251
    family form, 249–250
    form, 249–250
    immigrant and refugee status, 251
Family form, 249–250
Family Functioning Style Scale (FSSS), 237
Family functions, 228–230
    case example, 229
Family goals, assessment of, 261–262
Family Homeostasis, 238
Family interactions
    case example, 243
    circular, 243–245
    circular explanation of behavior, 245
    circular motions of, 243
    communication styles of, 265, 268–269
    congruence and clarity, 266
    content and process levels of, 242–246
    linear explanation of, 245
    linear motions of, 243
    non verbal, 260
    sequences of, 243–245
    transactions, 243–246
    verbal, 266
Family interventions
    cultural and ecological perspectives *See*
        Cultural and ecological perspectives,
        family interventions
    dysfunctional interactions *See* Dysfunctional
        family interactions, strategies to modify
        feedback *See* Positive feedback
    focus on future, 472–473
    modifying dysfunctional family alignments
        See Dysfunctional family alignments,
        strategies to modify
    modifying misconceptions and distorted
        perceptions *See* Misconceptions and
        distorted perceptions, intervening with
        families
    positive feedback *See* Positive feedback
Family life cycle theory, 357
Family and Medical Leave Act, 234
Family myths and cognitive patterns
    case example, 263–264
    cognitive schema, 263
    social cognition, 263
Family life cycle, 269–270
Family relationships, factors influencing, 455
Family Resources Scale (FRS), 237
Family roles
    complementary, 264–265
    enacted, 264
    overload, 470–471
    interrole conflict, 265
    intrarole tension, 265
    perceived, 264
    prescribed, 264
    quid pro quo, 264–265

Family roles (*continued*)
  reciprocal, 264
  symmetrical, 264
  role transition, 264
Family rules
  assessing, 240
  cautions about, 240–241
  flexibility of, 241–242
  functional, 240
  labeling, 241
  mapping, 242
  morphostasis, 242
  morphogenesis, 242
  rigid, 240
  violation of, 241
Family sculpting, 487
Family Service of America, 430
Family sessions
  initial *See* Initial contacts with families
  manifestations of opposition to change in, 560–561
Family strengths, assessment of, 251–252
Family stressors
  extra-ordinary transitions, 235
  family transitions, 233–234
  impact on children, 232–233
  life cycle, 233
  life transitions, 233
  matching interventions to, 357–358
  public policy as source of, 230–231
  resilience of families, 235
  poverty, 231–232
  separations, 233
  transitions, 233–234
  types of, 230
  work and family balance as source of, 234–235
Family subsystems and coalitions, 254
Family systems
  approaches to intervening in, 455–456
  boundary maintenance, 252–253
  bounding patterns, 253–256
  coalitions, 254
  cognitive behaviorist approach to, 455
  concepts related to, 455
  disengaged, 255–255
  enmeshment, 254–255
  evolution of, 227–228
  included, 253
  influences on, 455–456
  intervening in, 455–456
  narrative, interpretative reality and social construction approaches to, 456
  open, 253
  regulating communication in, 455
  solution-focused therapy approach to, 455–456
  structural therapy approach to, 456
  subsystems and coalitions, 254
  task-centered, 456
Family, systems concepts
  application of, 238
Family therapy, 26
Family transitions, 233–234
Family values, 230
FAS *See* Fetal alcohol syndrome (FAS)
Fault-defend, 268

Feeling questions, 462
Feelings
  affective words and phrases, 90–94
  descriptive words for, 89–95
  developing perceptiveness to, 89–95
  surface and underlying, 94–95
Feeling stopper, 286
Fetal alcohol effects (FAE), 203
Fetal alcohol syndrome (FAS), 203
Field practicum, 14
Fishing expeditions, 166–167
Five-stage model for change, 217
Fixed beliefs about others, 190
Fixed principles, reference to, 190
Flexibility, 9
Flight of ideas, 208
Focal points of session, reviewing, 152
Focus, 432
Focusing
  blending open-ended, empathic and concrete responses, 146–148
  concrete responses, 140
  empathic responding, 146–148
  employing open-ended responses, 145
  exploring topics in depth, 144–146
  helping clients to focus or refocus, 149–150
  on here and now, 140
  maintaining focus, 119
  managing obstacles to, 148–150
  on the past, 166
  seeking concreteness, 145–146
  selecting topics for exploration, 143–144
  skills, 143–150
  summarizing responses to aid, 152
Focus on future in family interventions, 472–473
Food Stamp Program, 429
Formal assessment, 172
Forming stage, 492
Formula task, 406
Fostering safe social interaction, 165
Framework for assessment, 178–179
FrameWorks Institute, 415, 432–433
Frequency counts, 334
FRS *See* Family Resources Scale (FRS)
FSSS *See* Family Functioning Style Scale (FSSS)
Functional cognitions, 292
Functional family rules, 240–241
Functional group behavior, 293
Functional patterns, 216
Furthering responses, 47
  accent responses, 130
  minimal prompts, 130
Fusion, 249

GDS *See* Geriatric Depression Scale
GEM *See* Group work engagement measure (GEM)
Generalist practice, 13, 23–24
General tasks, goals and, 315–316
  partializing goals, 364–365
  partializing group goals, 365–366
Genogram, 202, 237, 254, 487
Genuineness, 88, 540. *See also* Authenticity
Geriatric Depression Scale (GDS), 213
George W. Bush Administration, 230, 234
Global goal, 315

Globalization, 392
Goal and task form, 333, 334
Goal attainment, 39–41, 50–51
  benefits, 328
  potential barriers, 328
  potential risks, 328
Goal Attainment Scaling, 30
Goal attainment strategies
  brief treatment models, 363, 364
  client involvement, 356–357
  empowerment, 355
  ethical practice, 360–361
  matching interventions to *See* Matching interventions
  models of practice, 363–364
  planning, 356–363
  task-centered system *See* Task-centered system
Goal development
  considerations in, 306
  ethical responsibility, 306–307
  factors influencing, 306–309
  minors, 321–322
  school-based group example, 322–325
Goal development (new)
  applying guidelines with minors, 321
  case example, 324
  client participation, 306
  considerations with minors, 323–326
  environmental conditions, 309
  factors that influence, 306–309
  family involvement, 307–308
  involuntary status, 309
  values and beliefs, 306–307
Goals
  agency program objectives and, 305–306, 321
  agreeable mandate strategy, 312
  assessment of family, 261–262
  bargaining, 313–314
  behavioral, 402, 404
  case example, 320
  case progress notes, 314, 315, 332
  changes sought by, 305
  consistent with agency function, 321
  contracts *See* Contracts defined in explicit and measurable terms, 313–315
  covert, 309
  defining, 306
  development of *See* Goal development family, 261–262
  discrete, 336
  explain purpose and function of, 326
  factors that influence the development of, 306–309
  feasibility of, 316–317, 328
  formulation of, 303
  general tasks and, 314–316
  guidelines for selecting and formulating, 310–311
  for involuntary clients *See* Involuntary clients
  function of, 303
  involvement of clients in establishing, 306
  linkage between target concern and, 303–304
  mandated *See* Mandated goals
  measurement, 331–341
  monitoring progress, 332–334
  motivational congruence, 311–312

mutual formulation of, 38–39
negative statements, 319
negotiating *See* Goals, negotiating ongoing, 371, 375
ongoing, 336, 3371, 375
overt, 309
partializing, 315, 364–365
positive statements, 319
prioritizing, 318
program objectives and, 305–306, 321
purpose and function of, 303, 325–326
purpose of, 303
reciprocal, 310
reservations about, 319
setting, 303, 305, 307, 451
shared, 310
and specific tasks, 315, 334
social worker skills, 318
statements of, 318–319
supervision or consultation of social worker, 318
types of, 309–310
ultimate (global), 315
use of additive empathy and interpretation to become aware of, 522
for voluntary clients, 310–311
Goals, feasible, feasibility
cookie cutter, 317
involuntary client and mandated case plan, 317
kitchen sink, 317
questions to facilitate (achieve), 316–317
Goals, jointly selecting
with involuntary clients, 329–330
Goals, negotiating, 38–39, 49–50
assisting clients to committing to specific goals, 328–331
benefits and risks discussion, 328
case example, 330–331
client readiness for, 325
explaining purpose and function of goals, 326
explicit definition of goals, 327
feasibility of, 328
involuntary clients, 325–326, 329
joint selection of appropriate goals, 326–327
process of, 325–331
ranking goals to clients' priorities, 330
readiness of involuntary clients, 325
Goals, reservations about
case example, 320
ethical and legal tensions, 320
referrals as a resource, 320
social worker values and goal tensions, 319
Goal setting
case example, 308–309
client participation, 306
environmental conditions, 309
example, 304
family involvement, 307–309
involuntary status, 309
social distance, 309
social proximity, 309
value inherent in, 307
values and beliefs, 306–307
Good faith, 484
Goodness of fit, 217

Graduate (MSW) programs, 23
Great society programs, 230
Group development, stages of, 491–492
common mistakes inhibiting, 504
creating therapeutic norms, 508–510
differentiation: developing group identity and internal frame of reference (stage 4), 492, 495–496, 499
encouraging balanced feedback, 506–507
enhancing awareness among task groups, 516
inclusion as leader intervention technique, 503
increasing effective communication, 507–508
intimacy: developing familial frame of reference (stage 3), 492, 494–495, 498–499, 510–511
leader interventions across, 503–513
leader's role in, 497
linking as leader intervention technique, 503
minimization of changes, 506
mistakes inhibiting, 504
monitoring treatment goals and tasks, 511
power and control: time of transition (stage 2), 492, 493–494, 498, 506–510
preaffiliation: approach and avoidance behavior (stage 1), 492–493, 498, 504–505
process as leader intervention technique, 503
seeking concreteness, 505–506
separation: breaking away (stage 5), 496, 499, 512–513, 513
termination *See* subhead: separation: breaking away (stage 5)
transition *See* subhead: power and control: time of transition (stage 2)
working phase, 510–511
Group diversity in assessment of family context, 250–251
Group interventions
cohesion, 499–500
facilitative, 491
group development stages *See* Group development, stages of
leadership structure, 502–503
normative structure, 500–501
role structure, 501–502
into structural elements of group, 497–503
subgroup structure, 502–503
Group leaders, 41, 287
alliance, 292–294
expediting distribution of power, 502–503
identifying cognitive patterns, 291–292
interventions across stages of group development *See* Group development, stages of
role in stages of group development, 491–492
structural aspects, 502
tasks of, 280
treatment groups, 277–278
Group member behaviors, assessment of
application of content and process concepts, 287
cognitive responses, 292
counterproductive behaviors, 292
developing profiles of individual behavior, 288–289

dysfunctional behaviors, 287, 289
examples of behavioral profiles of group members, 291–292
expressive roles, 287–288
formal roles, 287
functional behaviors, 287, 288–289
identifying growth of individuals, 289
identifying roles of group members, 287–288
impact of culture, 289–290
informal roles, 287
instrumental roles, 287
isolate role, 288
leadership roles, 287
maintenance roles, 287
patterned behaviors, 287–292
scapegoat role, 288
task-related roles, 287
thematic behaviors, 287
Group member cognitive patterns, assessment of, 291–292
Group processes, assessment of
alliances, 292–294
cognitive patterns, 291–292
cohesion, 296–297
decision making, 294–295
distribution of power, 294–295
group member behaviors *See* Group member behaviors, assessment of
group work engagement measure (GEM), 286
instruments for, 286
norms, 295–296
patterned behaviors, 287–292
subgroupings, 292–293
systems framework for, 286–287
values, 296
Groups
classification of, 273–275
concepts to practice in rural areas, 514
educational, 274
evaluation, 513
growth, 274
immigrant and refugee, 251, 427–428
involuntary clients and, 274
leaders *See* Group leaders
new developments in social work with, 513–515
online, 274
partializing group goals, 365–366
self-help, 275
single session meetings, 514
socialization, 274
social worker's goals in, 273
social work groups for empowerment, 514
support, 274
task *See* Task groups
technological tools aiding work with, 514–515
telephone, 274
therapy, 274
transference reactions, 551–552
treatment *See* Treatment groups
types of, 274
working group, 282
Group sessions
helping clients to focus or refocus in, 149–150
manifestations of opposition to change in, 560–561

Group sessions (*continued*)
summarizing responses *See* Summarizing responses
Group work, 273
Group work engagement measure (GEM), 286
Group work services, 26
Growth groups, 274
Guided practice, 374
Guidelines for treatment groups
attendance, 285
care of the room/cleanup, 285
decision making, 283–284
eating, drinking and smoking, 285
formulating, 282–283
group format, 283
help-giving/help-seeking roles, 284
individual contacts with social worker, 284–285
new members, 284
programming, 285–286
recordings of sessions, 285
touching, 286
visitors, 284
Gulf War, 233

Habitat, 15
Habitat for Humanity, 426
Hallucinations, 207
Health assessment, 201–202
Health care services
acceptability of, 201
affordability of, 201
availability of, 201
Health Insurance Portability and Accountability Act (HIPAA), 62
confidentiality standards, 68
Helper attractiveness, 549
Helping process
assessments, 37–38
barriers to goal accomplishment, 40
change maintenance strategies, 42
client misgivings/concerns, 34–35
communication, 35
enhancement of self-awareness, 41
enhancement of self-efficacy, 39
exploration skills, 36–37
facilitative conditions, 87–88
goal attainment, 39–41
implementation and goal attainment, 39–41
monitoring progress, 39–40
motivation techniques, 35–36
mutual formulation of goals, 38–39
overview, 33–52
Phase I, 34–39
Phase II, 39–41
Phase III, 41–42
rapport, 35–36
relational reactions, 40–41
role clarification in, 83–87
termination phase of, 41–42
use of self, 41
verbal following skills *See* Verbal following skills
Help-seeking behavior, 358–359
Heterogeneity versus homogeneity in treatment groups, 280

HIPAA *See* Health Insurance Portability and Accountability Act (HIPAA)
Homeless Against Homelessness (HAH), 420, 430
Homelessness, 420
Homeostasis, family, 238–239
family rules maintaining, 239–240
Homogeneity versus heterogeneity in treatment groups, 280
Host setting, 172
Human behavior, social environment and, 12
Human nature, assertion based on presumed laws of, 190
Human needs and resources, 5–6
Human problems *See* Intrapersonal systems
Human rights, 11
Humor inappropriately, using, 160–161

IFSW *See* International Federation of Social Workers (IFSW)
Illicit drugs, use and abuse of, 200, 202, 203–205
indications of commonly used drugs, 205
Image, 281
Immigrant and refugee status, 251
Immigrants and refugees
family transitions and, 233–234
status in assessment of family context, 251
support systems for, 427–428
Immigration and Customs Enforcement, 320
Immigration and Naturalization Service (INS), 320
Immigration laws, 233
Inability to disconfirm, 392
Inactive social workers, 166
Inappropriate affect, 211–212
Incentives
for adult clients, 369
for children, 369–370
Inclusion as leader intervention technique, 503
Individual casework or counseling, 26
Inductive questioning, 528
Influence, 430
Informal networks, 425–426
Information, eliciting essential, 48
Informative events, 339
Informed consent, 300–301
communicating about, 87
example of, 299–300
NASW Code of Ethics, 65
Integrative Cognitive Approach, 356
Initial contacts with families
begin helping members relate to each other positively, 466
clarification of choices about participation in helping process, 463
clarification of roles and nature of helping process, 463
confianza, 462
couples, 457
critical objectives of, 457–458
define problem as family problem, 464–465
delabeling strategy, 464
drawing attention to repetitive communications, 465–466
dynamics of minority status and culture, 462–467
eliciting family's perception of problems, 463

emphasize individual and family strengths, 465
ending session, 467
establish individual and family goals based on wants and needs, 466
establish personal relationships, 460–461
exploring reservations, 461–462
gauge interest in returning for future sessions, 466
guidelines, 457–458
identification of needs and wants of family members, 463–464
inquire about patterned behaviors and structure of family, 465–466
joining stage, 460
locations for, 458–459
managing initial contacts with couples and families, 456–459
managing initial contacts with parents, 459–460
negotiating a contract, 466
negotiating tasks to be accomplished during the week, 466–467
objectives of, 457–458, 460
orchestrating, 460–467
socializing technique, 460
social stage, 460
strengths-oriented statements, 465
summarizing session, 467
Initial interview
establishing rapport, 44–47
exploration process *See* Exploration process
with families *See* Initial contacts with families
open-ended responses, 135
selecting topics for exploration, 143–144
Inordinate apprehension, 211
Institutional environments
empowerment, 448
promoting dignity and worth, 443
prisons, 448
Institutionalized racism and discrimination *See* Racism and discrimination, institutionalized
Institutional programming, 448–449
Instrumental ADLs, 196
Intake forms, 528
Integrative Model by Level of Need, 237
Intellectual functioning, assessment of, 206
Interaction
direct observation of, 182
dominating, 164–165
fostering safe social, 165
reciprocal, 171
Interactional behavior, eliciting details related to, 140–141
Interactive Trauma/Grief-Focused Therapy (IT/G-FT), 382
Internal family boundary maintenance, 253–254
International Association of Schools of Social Worker, 428
International Federation of Social Workers (IFSW), 4, 428
International Statistical Classification of Disease and Related Health Problems, 174–175
Interorganizational collaboration *See* Service coordination and interorganizational collaboration

Interpersonal theory, 384
Interpretations. *See also* Additive empathic responses classifications of, 520
   confrontations distinguished from, 526–529
   deeper feelings, 521–522
   of dynamics of behavior, 162–163
   example of inept, 520
   guidelines for employing, 525–526
   hidden purposes of behavior, 523–524
   propositional, 520
   purpose of, 520
   semantic, 520
   as "supreme agent" in hierarchy of therapeutic principles, 520
   underlying meanings of feelings, thoughts, and behavior, 522–523
   unrealized strengths and potentialities, 524–525
   wants and goals, 523
Interpreters, use of, 46–47, 177
Interrole conflict, 265
Interrupting client, 164
Interventions, 343
   approach, 360
   cognitive restructuring *See* Cognitive restructuring
   crisis intervention (CI) *See* Crisis intervention (CI)
   deciding on and carrying out, 18–21
   family *See* Family interventions
   group *See* Group interventions
   guidelines influencing selection, 20–21
   macro-level, 412
   matching interventions to goal attainment strategies *See* Matching interventions
   on-the-spot *See* On-the-spot interventions
   planning, 452
   solution-focused treatment *See* Solution-focused treatment
Interviewing process, 42–51
   adults, 195–196
   children, 195–196
   conditions for productive interviews, 43
   ending, 50
   establishing rapport, 44–47
   exploration process *See* Exploration process
   focusing in depth, 48–49
   information obtained from, 181
   initial contacts with families *See* Initial contacts with families
   initial interview *See* Initial interview
   motivational interviewing, 526–527
   physical conditions, 43
   for potential of drug use and abuse, 206
   preliminary interview for treatment group, 278–279
   privacy, 43
   role induction interview, 83
   structure of interviews, 43–44
   treatment group preliminary interview, 278–279
   warm-up period, 44–45
Intimacy *See* Group development, stages of
Intrapersonal systems
   alcohol use and abuse, 200, 202–203
   assessment of, 199–200
   behavioral functioning, 215–217

biophysical functioning *See* Biophysical functioning
cognitive/perceptual functioning *See* Cognitive/perceptual functioning
drug use and abuse *See* Drug use and abuse
elements of, 199–200
emotional functioning *See* Emotional functioning
environmental systems *See* Environmental systems
interaction with interpersonal and environmental systems, 199
motivation, 217
Intrarole tensions, 265
Introspection, 556
Involuntary clients, 33–34
   establishing trust with, 550–551
   goals for, 311, 325–326, 329
   group work and, 274
   mandated case plans, 317–318
   minors, 323
   negotiating goals with, 325–326
Involuntary status, 309
IT/G-FT *See* Interactive Trauma/Grief-Focused Therapy

Jaffee v. Redmond, 70
Job feedback, 439
Johns Hopkins Depression Scale, 215
Johnson Administration, 231
Joining stage, 460
The Journal of Evidence-Based Social Work, 360
The Journal of Research on Social Work Practice, 360
Judging clients, 161
Judgment, assessment of, 207
Judgment focus, 392
Jumping to conclusions, 392

Kinship care, 425
Kitchen sink, 317
Knowledge base of social work practice, 8
Knowledge, role in assessments, 179–181

Language barriers
   establishing rapport, 44
   interpreters, 46–47
Laws, ethics and, 62–63
Leaders *See* Group leaders
Leadership structure, 502
Leading questions, 164
Leakage, nonverbal communication, 155
"Leaning into" clients' anger, 120
Learned helplessness, 217
Learning organization, 438
Legal
   tensions, 320
Legally mandated clients, 4
Lengthy messages, summarizing, 151–152
Liberian Immigration Act, 320
Liberian Refugee Immigration Act, 2007, 233
Life cycle, assessment of family, 269–270, 357
Life transaction patterns, 455
Life transition stresses, 189
   family role behavior and, 233, 265
Limits, setting, 120–122

Linear explanation of behavior, 245
Linking as leader intervention technique, 503
Locality development, 433
Logical analysis effects, 338–339
Looseness of association, 208
Loss, 380

Macro-level interventions, 412
   case example, 413
   opportunities for, 413
Macro-level practice, 13, 14, 24
Macro practice
   advocacy and social action *See* Advocacy and social action
   analyzing social problems and conditions, 415–418
   case study, 413
   community organization *See* community organization
   conceptual framework, 414
   defined, 412
   developing and supplementing resources *See* Resources empowerment, 414–415
   empowerment and strengths, 414–415
   evaluation, 453–454
   improving institutional environments *See* Organizations, improving social welfare
   improving organizations *See* Organizations, improving social welfare
   intervention strategies, 414–418
   linkage between micro practice and, 412–413
   professional titles associated with, 413
   Social work's commitment to, 407
   utilizing and enhancing support systems *See* Support systems, utilizing and enhancing
Maintenance, 217, 527
Major depressive disorder, 212–213
Maltreatment, 195–196
Managing opposition to change, 558–559, 561–562
Mandated goals, 311, 325, 329
   getting rid of, 313
   involuntary clients and, 317–318
Manifestations of opposition to change
   examples of, 560
   in family and group sessions, 560–561
Marital therapy, 26
Mary Richmond, 227
MAST *See* Michigan Alcohol Screening Test
Mastery, 374
Matching interventions
   to developmental phases, 356–357
   factors considered in, 356–357
   to problems, 356
   to racial and ethnocultural groups, 358–360
   to stressful transitions, 357–358
Maturational/developmental crisis, 384
MCMI. *See* Million Multiaxial Clinical Inventory-III
Meaning attributions, 190
Meaning of vague or unfamiliar terms, clarifying, 138
Measurement and evaluation
   challenges in, 331–332
   computerized information systems, 332–333
   contracts stipulation method for, 345
   evaluation defined, 331

Measurement and evaluation (*continued*)
  evaluation methods, 332
  function of evaluation, 332
  goal and task form, 333, 334
  goal attainment, 378
  limitations of standardized instruments
    for, 333
  macro practice, 453–454
  maximizing reliability and validity of mea-
    surements, 336
  measurement defined, 331
  methods of evaluation, 332
  qualitative measurements *See* Qualitative
    measurements
  quantitative measurements *See* Quantitative
    measurements
  record-keeping, 332
  resources for, 332–333
  standardized instruments for, 332–333
  strengths of standardized instruments for,
    333
  tools for, 333
Mediators, 28, 422
Medicaid, 231–232
Medications, assessing, 200, 202
Mental and addictive disorders, dual diagnosis
  of, 200, 205–206
Mental retardation, 210
Mental status exams, 210
Metacommunication, 477–478
Mezzo-level practice, 13, 14
Michigan Alcohol Screening Test
  (MAST), 183
Micro-level practice, 13, 14, 23
Micro practice
  case example, 412
  linkage between macro practice and,
    412–413
Mild distortions, 207
Military families, 233
Million Multiaxial Clinical Inventory-III
  (MCMI-III), 183
Mind reading, 392
Mini-contract, negotiating, 546
Minimal prompts, 130
Minimum wage, 231
Minnesota Multiphasic Personality Inventory
  (MMPI-II), 183
Minority group. *See also* Racial and ethno-
  cultural groups
  discovery procedure, 359
  microaggresion, 359–360
Minority group clients, cognitive restructuring
  with, 402
Minors *See* Children
  assent, 362
  applying goal development guidelines with,
    321–325
  cognitive restructuring, 394
  crisis, 381–383
  ethics of practice, 72
  informed consent, 362
  Intervention strategies with, 357
  involuntary and voluntary, 323
  rewards and incentives, 369
  self-determination and, 361–362
Miracle questions, 180, 405–406

Misconceptions
  assessment of, 209
  irrational fears and, 372
Misconceptions and distorted perceptions, in-
  tervening with families, 485–486,
  myths and unrealistic expectations, 485–486
  process, 486
Missing class, 232
MMPI *See* Minnesota Multiphasic Personality
  Inventory
Mobilizing community resources, 422–424
Modeling, increasing self-efficacy through,
  373–374
Models and Techniques of Practice, 363
Models of practice, 363–364
  task-centered system *See* Task-centered
    system
Moderate distortions, 207
Monitoring Progress, 39, 332, 337
Morphogenesis, 242
Morphostasis, 242
"Mother's night out" program, 425
Motivation
  aspects of, 217
  assessing, 200, 217
  direction of, 217
  enhance client's commitment to carry out
    task, 368–370
  for hiding behaviors, 523–524
  strength of, 217
  techniques, 35–36
Motivational congruence
  defined, 46
  goals for involuntary clients including, 311
Motivational interviewing, 526–527
MPSI *See* Multi-Problem Screening Inventory
  (MPSI)
MSW programs, 23
Multiaxial system, 175
Multidimensional assessments, 36–38
Multifinality, 18
Multi-Problem Screening Inventory (MPSI), 183
Multisystems, 237
Multisystems Approach, 237
Mutual formulation of goals, 38–39
Mystification of communications, 267
Myths and cognitive patterns, family, 263–264

NAMI *See* National Alliance for the Mentally Ill
  (NAMI)
Narrative, interpretative reality and social con-
  struction approaches to family systems,
  456
Narrative progress review, 345
NASW *See* National Association of Social
  Workers (NASW)
National Alliance for the Mentally Ill (NAMI),
  426
National Association of Social Workers
  (NASW)
  chapters and regulatory boards, 547
  Code of Ethics *See* Code of Ethics, NASW
  creation of, 23
  Pace Committee, 430
  social work mission statement, 4–5
  Standards for Cultural Competence in Social
    Work Practice, 411

National Association of Scholars, 10
National Doula Society, 426
National Welfare Rights Organization, 428
Natural helping networks, 435
Natural support systems, 194
Needs
  assessment, 419
  demand, 419
  mapping, 419
  normative, 419
Negative cognitive sets, 208
Negative filtering, 392
Negative goal statements, 319
Network therapy, 194
Niche, 15
Nickled and Dimed (Ehrenreich), 234
Nixon Administration, 231
Nominal group technique, 515
Nonlinear applications of systems theory, 18
Nonpossessive warmth, 88
Nonverbal communication barriers, eliminating
  assessing physical attending behaviors, 169
  cultural nuances to nonverbal cues, 156
  examples of nonverbal behaviors, 156–157
  leakage, 155
  physical attending, 155–156, 168
  taking inventory of nonverbal patterns of re-
    sponding, 157–158
Nonverbal communications
  direct observation of, 181
  eliminating barriers *See* Nonverbal commu-
    nication barriers, eliminating
  responding to clients' nonverbal, 103
Nonverbal cues, cultural nuances to, 156
Nonverbal minimal prompts, 130
Nonverbal patterns of responding, taking inventory of, 157–158
Nonvoluntary clients, 4
Non-western perspective, 362
Normative structure, 500–501
Norming stage, 494
Norms, 240
  assessment of group, 295–296
  examples of group, 296, 500–501, 508–510

OARS *See* Older Americans Resources and Services Questionnaire (OARS)
Objectives, 315
Oklahoma City bombing, 380
Older adult
  assessing, 194–196
  depression and suicidal risk with, 215
Older Americans Resources and Services Questionnaire (OARS), 184, 217
Ongoing general tasks, 315
Ongoing goals, 371, 375
Online groups, 274
On-the-spot interventions, 474, 480–482
  guidelines for making, 480–482
Open-ended responses
  blending empathic, concrete and, 146–148
  discriminant use of, 133–135
  examples of, 132–133
  exercises in identifying, 133
  exploring topics in depth using, 145
  information elicited by, 134–135
Open-ended treatment groups, 281

Opposition to change
  confronting patterns of opposition, 563–564
  exploring sources of, 561–562
  managing, 558–559, 561–562
  manifestations of, 560–561
  preventing, 559–560
  sources of, 559
  transference resistance, 560
Oppression, 11
Organizational analysts, 29
Organizational change, 437–438
  change strategies, 438
  effects of proposals, 440–441
  learning organization, 438
  organizational learning, 438
  risks, benefits and opposition, 440–441
  staff as agents of, 440
Organizational competence, 446
Organizational culture, 437
Organizational environments
  affect on clients, 440
  autonomy, 439
  characteristics of healthy, 439
  dynamics within, 439
  job feedback, 439
  skill variety, 439
  staff, 439–440
  task identity, 439
  task significance, 439
Organizational learning, 438–439
Organizational relationships
  collaboration, 451
  collaboration defined, 451
  coordination, 450
  cooperation, 450
  phases of collaboration, 451–452
Organizations, improving social welfare
  change strategies *See* Organizational change
  empowerment, 448
  examining policies and practices, 441–447
  institutionalized racism and discrimination
    See Racism and discrimination,
    institutionalized
  institutional programming, 448–449
  organizational change *See* Organizational
    change
  organizational culture defined, 437
  organizational environments *See* Organiza-
    tional environments
  policies and practices, 441–447
  privacy issues, 443–444
  promoting dignity and worth, 443–444
  resources and tools, 446–447
  safety concerns, 444
Organizations as support systems, 426–427
Outlines, interviewing, 49, 144
Overgeneralizations, 392
Overt behaviors, measuring, 334–335
Overt goals, 309
Over-the-counter medications, 202

Pace Committee, National Association of Social
  Workers, 430
Paraphrasing, 47
  examples, 131
  exercises in, 131–132
Parent-child conflict, 321

Parents
  managing initial contacts with, 459–460
  positive feedback to children, 476
Parents, Family, and Friends of Lesbians and
  Gays (PFLAG), 426
Parroting, 166
Partializing goals, 315, 364–365
Partializing group goals, 365–366
Participants. *See also* Clients
  roles of, 83–87, 343
Participatory Action Research, 419–420
Paternalism, 61, 63
Pathological or inept social workers, 546–547
Patterned behaviors
  assessment of groups', 291–292
  assessment of individuals', 287–290
  inquiries about patterned behaviors and
    structure of family, 465–466
Patterned cognitions, assessment of indivi-
    duals', 290–291
  case example, 291
Pause time, 467
Perceived role behavior, 264
Perceptions
  assessing, 214
  checking out, 137–138
Performing stage, 495
Personal experience in making assessment, use
  of, 181
Personalization of statements, assisting clients
  in, 138–139
Personalizing, 392
Personal responsibility, 230
Personal Responsibility and Work Opportunity
  Act of 2006 (PRWOR), 416, 429
Personal self-disclosing, 107, 108
Personal Work Opportunity and Reconciliation
  Act of 2006, 429
Personal values, conflicts between professional
  and, 53
Persuading clients, 162
Pew Partnership for Civic Change, 422
PFLAG *See* Parents, Family, and Friends of
  Lesbians and Gays (PFLAG)
Physical attending, 155–156
  assessing behaviors, 169
Physical characteristics and presentation,
  assessment of, 200–201
Physical environment, assessment of, 218–219
Physical examinations, 196
Planner, 30
Policies and legislative initiatives, 429–430
Policy and procedure developer, 30–31
Positive cognitive sets, cultivating, 474–475
Positive connotation, 562
Positive constructive thinking and action, 387
Positive feedback
  cultivating positive cognitive sets, 474–475
  educating clients about vital role of,
    473–474
  employing tasks to enhance cognitive sets,
    475
  enabling clients to give and receive, 475–477
  enabling family members to increase,
    475–477
  engaging clients in assessing how they give
    and receive, 473

  reviewing progress and accrediting incre-
    mental growth, 475
  sensitizing positive cognitive sets, 475
Positive feedback as form of authentic re-
    sponding, 116–118
Positive goal statements, 319
Post-intervention eco-map, 341
Post-traumatic stress disorder (PTSD), 380
Poverty, 417
  asset development, 231
  diligent and working poor, 232
  as family stressor, 231–232
  impact on children, 232–33
  missing class, 232
  reason for, 232
  Temporary Assistance for Needy Families
    (TANF) *See* Temporary Assistance for
    Needy Families (TANF)
Power of attorney, durable, 64
Power structure, family
  aspects of, 256
  assessment of, 258–259
  distribution and balance of power, 257–258
  elements of, 257
  multicultural perspectives, 258
Power structure, group, 294–295
Practice, evidence-based, 19
Practice models, 363–364
Preaffiliation *See* Group development, stages of
Precipitating events, 191
Precontemplation, 35, 217, 527
Prediction task, 406
Pregnancy, alcohol abuse and, 203
Pre-intervention eco-map, 340
Preliminary interview, treatment group,
  278–279
Preparation, 527
Prescribed role behavior, 264
Prescription medications, 202
Presenting problems
  importance of, 186–187
  typical wants involved in, 188–189
Preventing opposition to change, 559–560
Prevention, 5
Primary Care Evaluation of Mental Health Dis-
  orders (PRIME-MD), 183
PRIME-MD *See* Primary Care Evaluation of
  Mental Health Disorders (PRIME-MD)
Privileged communications
  confidentiality and, 70–71
Problematic and functional group
  behaviors, 293
Problematic behaviors
  frequency of, 191
  sites of, 190–191
  temporal context of, 190–191
Problematic cognitions, 292
Problematic group behavior, 293
Problem identification in assessment,
  186–187
Problem solving approaches
  as intervention strategies, 409
  compatible with values and ethics of social
    work, 360
  effectiveness of, 360
  empowerment, 409
  systematic generalist-eclectic practice, 355

Problem solving approaches (*continued*)
strengths in, 409
trends in, 409
Problems. *See also* Assessment(s)
assessment of strengths and, 172–173
causes of, 199
clients emotional reactions to, 192
duration of, 191
human *See* Human problems
interaction of multiple systems in, 199
matching interventions to, 356
meanings ascribed to, 189–190
multiple systems affecting, 199
presenting, 186–187, 188–189
severity of, 189
summarizing responses to highlight key
aspects of, 150–151
Process model, 19
Process as leader intervention technique, 503
Process levels of family interactions, 242–246
Professional boundaries, preservation of, 66–67
Professional values, conflicts between personal
and, 53
Program developer, 30
Program objectives, goals and, 305–306
Project Homeless Connect, 422–423
Propositional interpretations, 520
PRWOR *See* Personal Responsibility and Work
Opportunity Reconciliation Act of 2006
(PRWOR)
Pseudoscientific explanations, 190
Psychiatric emergency, 384
Psychoanalytic theory, 384
Psychological contact with clients, maintaining,
129–130
Psychological labeling, 190
Psychological scales, 336
Psychopathological crisis, 384
Psychotherapy, 25, 26
PTSD *See* Post-traumatic stress disorder
(PTSD)
Public policy, 447
Purchase-of-service agreement (POS), 346
"Putting Families First", 235

Qualitative measurements
advantages of, 338
assessment tools, 338
critical incidences, 339
criticisms of, 338
data collection process, 338
informative events, 339
logical analysis effects, 338–339
methods, 338–339
monitoring progress with, 339–340
Quantitative measurements
baseline measures, 333–334
covert behaviors, 335
frequency counts, 334
guidelines for obtaining baseline measures,
336
maximizing reliability and validity of measurements, 336
monitoring progress with, 337
overt behaviors, 334–335
psychological scales, 336
receptivity of clients to, 337–338

retrospective estimates of baseline behaviors,
335
self-administered scales, 336–337
self-anchored scale, 335–336
self-monitoring, 334–335
Questions
to answer in assessment, 184–185
coping, 405
embedded, 132–133
exception, 405, 406
feeling, 462
leading, 164
miracle, 405–406
scaling, 405
stacking, 163–164
Quid pro quo, 310
contract, 483

Racial and ethnocultural groups, matching interventions to, 358–360
Racism and discrimination, institutionalized,
444–445
cultural competence, 445
organizational competence, 445–446
public policy, 447
Rapport, establishing, 35–36, 44–47
with parents, 459
Rational-emotive therapy (RET), 390
Reactance theory, 158, 368, 559
Reactions
countertransference *See* Countertransference
reactions
realistic social worker, 557
transference *See* Transference reactions
Reactive effects, 334
Reality testing, assessment of, 207
Reason and Emotion in Psychotherapy (Ellis),
390
Reasons for Low Task Performance, 376,
378–379
Reassuring clients, 159
Receptivity, 268
Reciprocal changes, negotiating agreements for,
483–485
Reciprocal empathic responding, 97–98,
99–106
construction of, 100–101
leads for, 101–102
Reciprocal goals, 310
Reciprocal interaction, 171
Record-keeping
confidentiality and, 71–72
evaluations and, 332
Redefining problems as growth opportunities,
562
Referrals, 4, 16, 33, 194
making, 39
as resource, 320
Re-formed model of groups, 281
Reframing, 563
Refugees and immigrants
status in assessment of family context, 251
support systems for, 427–428
Regret orientation, 392
Relabeling, 562–563
Relapse, 527
Relating assertively to clients, 118–122

Relational dynamics, 539–541
Relational empathy, 548–549
Relational immediacy, 140
Relational reactions to helping process, 40–41,
539–558
assessing potential barriers and intervening,
545–546
barriers to change and, 539
characteristics of helping relationships, 540
eliciting feelings and thoughts of clients, 546
pathological or inept social workers, 546–547
social workers perception of helping relationship, 540
under- and over-involvement of social workers with clients, 541–544
Relationship rewards, 369–370
Relationships
asymmetrical, 483
complementary, 483
symmetrical, 483
Religion, assessment of, 221–222
Remediation, 5
Repetitive communications, drawing attention
to, 465–466
Replacement model of groups, 281
Request for Proposals (RFP), 305
Requests of clients, making, 118–119
Research, 11–12
Researcher/research consumer, 30
Resistance
avoiding blaming clients for, 559
defined, 558
factors in understanding dynamic of,
558–559
transference, 560
Resources
case example, 421–422
cautions and advice, 428
developing and supplementing, 418–424
developing resources with diverse groups, 424
four step process, 422
immigrant and refugee groups, 427
mobilizing community, 422–424
obtaining, 7
questions to guide, 419
referrals, 320
supplementing existing, 420–422
value and distribution of, 415–416
Respect, 88
Responding authentically
cues for, 112–116
guidelines for, 109–112
initiated by social workers, 114–116
paradigm for, 108–109
positive feedback as form of, 116–118
stimulated by client messages, 112–114
Restoration, 5
RET *See* Rational-emotive therapy (RET)
Retardation, mental, 210
Rewards and incentives
for adult clients, 369
for children, 369–370
Robert's Rules of Order, 515
Role changes, 189
Role clarification, 83–87
Role induction interview, 83
Role-play, increasing self-efficacy through, 373

Roles
  assessment of family, 264–265
  assessment of group, 501–502
  counterproductive, 501–502
  transition, 264
Romantic and sexual feelings toward clients,
    557–558
ROPES (Resources, options, possibilities, ex-
    ceptions and solutions), 237
Rules, family
  cautions about assessing, 240–241
  culturally based, 239
  flexibility of, 241–242
  functional and dysfunctional, 240–241
  maintaining homeostasis through, 239–240
  violations of, 241
Rural areas, group work concepts in, 514

Sarcasm or humor inappropriately, using,
    160–161
Saving a Generation, 425
Scaling
  motivation, 180
  problems, 180
  questions, 405
SCHIP *See* State Children's Insurance Program
Schizophrenia, 210
School-based group example, 322–325
Search Institute, 234
Secondary setting, 172
Secondary supervision
  conditions, 318
Section 8 Housing Choice program, 421
Self, use of, 41
Self-administered scales, 336–337
Self-anchored scale, 335–336
Self-awareness
  additive empathy *See* Additive empathy
  confrontation *See* Confrontations
  in creating assessments, 184
  cultural, 177
  defined, 519
  enhancement of, 41
  interpretation *See* Interpretations
  significance of, 519
Self-concept, assessment of, 209
Self-confrontation, 519, 520
  encouraging, 530
Self-determination, 9
  defined, 61
  fostering, 63–65
  as key principle of NASW Code of Ethics,
    63–65
  minors and, 361–362
  non-western perspective, 362
Self-disclosure
  defined, 106
  timing and intensity of, 108
  types of, 107–108
Self-efficacy, enhancement of, 39, 371
  increasing self-efficacy through behavioral
    rehearsal, modeling, and role-play,
    373–374
Self-help groups, 275
Self-involving statements, 107–108
Self-monitoring, 334–335, 399–400
Self-monitoring, client, 182

Self-statements, 396–402
Semantic interpretations, 520. *See also* Additive
    empathic responses
Senate Armed Services Committee, 428
Sensitivity to differences, 540
Separation, 492, 496, 499
  as family stressor, 233
September 11 terrorist attacks, 380, 412
Service agreements *See* Contracts
Service coordination and interorganizational
    collaboration, 449–453
  case example of collaboration, 452–453
  case management *See* Case management
  interdisciplinary teams, 450
  multidisciplinary teams, 450
  service fragmentation and duplication, 449
  types of, 450
  wraparound services, 451
Service fragmentation and duplication, 449
Setting limits, 120–122
Settings, assessment, 172
Sexual abuse, 49
Sexual attraction toward clients, 557–558
Shared goals, 310
Single session meetings with groups, 514
Situational context, assessment of, 37
Situational supports, 388
Skills, learning, 168, 170
Skill variety, 439
SOAP notes, 225
Social action, 430–431. *See also* Advocacy and
    social action
Social and economic justice, 6, 10
Social Cognition, 263
Social Diagnosis (Richmond), 227
Social empathy, 232
Social environment, 7
Social justice, 11
Social Learning Theory, 390
Social Work Day at the Capital, 430
Socialization groups, 274
Socializing technique, 460
Social Network Grid, 221
Social skills, deficiencies in, 372
Social stage, 460
Social Support Network Map, 236, 237, 253
Social support systems (SSSs), 220–221
  benefits from involvement with, 220
  eco-map, 220
  instruments for assessing, 221
  negative aspects of, 221
  positive aspects of, 221
Social work
  case example, 3–4, 24
  Code of Ethics *See* Code of Ethics, NASW
  core competencies, 10–14, 23
  core elements, 5
  mission of, 4–5
  purposes of, 5–6
  values *See* Values
Social workers
  authority of, 468–469
  case example, 3–4
  clinical, 25
  competence of, 15–18
  countertransference reactions *See* Counter-
    transference reactions

critical thinking, applying, 10
direct practitioners *See* Direct practitioners
diversity and cultural awareness, 10–11
eliciting feelings and thoughts of clients, 546
general tasks for, 366
generalist practitioner, 13
group goals, 273
groups served, 4
inactive, 165–166
interventions, 18–21
learning new skills, 168, 170
managing opposition to change *See* Opposi-
    tion to change
negative attitude toward client, 541, 543–544
negative reactions to, 377
obtaining resources, 7
pathological or inept, 546–547
positive attitude toward client, 541, 544
professional conduct, 10
realistic reactions toward offensive clients,
    557
relational reactions to helping process *See*
    Relational reactions to helping process
researcher/research consumer, 30
research and practice, 11–12
roles of, 26–31
sexual attraction toward clients, 557–558
skills in setting and reaching client goals, 318
specificity of expression by, 141–142
system linkage roles, 27–29
system maintenance and enhancement roles,
    29–30
transference reactions *See* Transference
    reactions
under- and over-involvement of, 541–544
values and goal tensions, 319–320
Social Work (journal), 23
Social work practice, 23
  advanced generalist, 24
  core competencies, 10–14
  evolving theory and competence, 15–18
  with families, 227–228
  generalist, 23–24
  integration of practice models, 15–18
  methods, 13–14
  models of, 15–18
  specialist, 24
Societal factors in assessment, 193–194
Sociograms, 294
Solution-focused approach, 38, 472, 514
Solution-focused assessment questions, 191–192
Solution-focused therapy approach to family
    systems, 455–456
Solution-focused treatment
  application with diverse groups, 404
  characteristics of, 403
  complainants, 406
  coping questions, 405
  customers, 406
  development of well-formed goals, 404
  empirical evidence and uses, 403–404
  exception questions, 405, 406
  formula task, 406
  interview questions, 404–405
  miracle questions, 405–406
  prediction task, 406
  procedures and techniques, 404–406

Solution-focused treatment (*continued*)
    scaling questions, 405
    strengths and limitations, 406–408
    tasks, 406
    tenets of, 403
    theoretical framework, 403
    uses of, 403–404
    utilization with minors, 404
    visitors, 406
Specific feelings, eliciting, 139–140
Specificity of responses *See* Concrete responses
Specific tasks, 315
    behavioral, 367
    cognitive, 367
    developing, 366–367
Spirituality, assessment of, 221–222
SSI *See* Supplemental Security Income (SSI)
SSSs *See* Social support systems (SSSs)
Stacking questions, 163–164
Staff
    as agents of change, 440
    behavior and attitudes, 443
    core job characteristics, 439
    issues affecting, 439
Stages of change model, 527
Standards for Cultural Competence in Social
        Work Practice, NASW, 411
"Starting where the client is", 103, 306, 321
State Children's Insurance Program (SCHIP),
        231
Stimulus-response congruence, 129
Storming stage, 493
Strategic frame analysis, 433
Strategies for developing with involuntary
        clients
    agreeable mandate, 312
    getting rid of the mandate, 313
    let's make a deal, 312
    motivational interviewing, 312, 313
    motivational congruence, 311
    questions for achieving, 312
    stages of change, 311
Strengths-oriented statements, 465
Stressful transitions, matching interventions to,
        357–358
Stressors, family *See* Family stressors
Structural mapping, 486, 488
Structural therapy approach to family systems,
        456
Subgroupings, 292–293
Subgroup structure, 502
Substance abuse, 49. *See also* Drug use and
        abuse
Subsystems and coalitions, family, 254
Successive approximation, 476
Suicidal risk
    Beck Scale for Suicidal Ideation, 183
    of children and adolescents, 214–215
    factors, 213–214
    of older adults, 215
Summarizing responses
    employing additive empathy, 151
    facets of, 150
    highlighting key aspects of problems, 150–151
    lengthy messages, 151–152
    to provide focus and continuity, 152
    reviewing focal points of session, 152

Supervisor of record, 318
Supervisors, 30
    confidentiality and, 68–69
Supplemental Security Income (SSI), 429
Support groups, 274
Support systems, utilizing and enhancing
    case example, 426, 427
    cautions and advice, 428
    community support systems and networks,
        424–428
    immigrant and refugee groups, 427–428
    importance of, 424–425
    organizations as support systems, 426–427
Surface and underlying feelings, 94–95
Symmetrical relationships, 483
Symmetrical roles, 264
Sympathizing with clients, 159
System development, 30
System linkage roles, 27–29
System maintenance and enhancement, 29–30
Systematic Generalist-Eclectic Practice, 355
Systems, intrapersonal *See* Intrapersonal
        systems
Systems framework for assessing
    case example, 236
    family functioning, 235
    micro, mezzo, macro, 236
    problems, 236, 238
Systems framework for assessment of group
        processes, 286–287
Systems framework for families
    application of, 238
    assessing problems using, 246–247
    assessment of family functioning, 235–237
    case example, 238
    homeostasis, 238–239
    morphogenesis, 242
    morphostasis, 242
    subsystems, 237
Systems models, 15–18
Systems theories, 18, 383
    limitations of, 18

TAF *See* Triage Assessment System (TAF)
TANF *See* Temporary Assistance for Needy
        Families (TANF)
Target concern, linkage between goals and,
        303–304
Target system, 16
Task-centered system
    adaptations of, 363–364
    advantages of, 363
    application to diverse groups, 364
    brainstorming task alternatives, 367–368
    central themes of, 363
    crisis intervention (CI) *See* Crisis interven-
        tion (CI)
    developing general tasks, 364–365
    empirical evidence, 363–364
    general tasks *See* General tasks, goals and
    maintaining focus and continuity, 375,
        378–379
    monitoring and evaluating progress,
        378–379
    partializing goals, 365–366
    procedures, 364
    Social worker tasks, 366

    specific tasks *See* Specific tasks
    Strengths and limitation, 378
    task alternatives, 367–368
    task-implementation sequence (TIS) *See*
        Task-implementation sequence (TIS)
    tenets of, 363
    theoretical framework, 363
    with minors, 367–368
Task groups
    beginning, 298
    composition of, 297, 515
    effective, 515
    enhancing awareness of stages of develop-
        ment, 516
    examples of, 273
    formation of, 297–298
    general, 366
    getting members involved, 515
    goal setting, 298
    membership, 297, 515
    planning for, 297–298
    problem identification in, 515
    roles, 298
    rules, 298
    treatment groups distinguished from, 274,
        515
    types of, 275
Task identity, 439
Task-implementation sequence (TIS)
    addressing barriers and obstacles, 372
    adherence to, 476
    analyze and resolve obstacles, 371–372
    assessing clients' readiness to begin tasks, 372
    conditions for tasks, 371
    enhance client's commitment to carry out
        task, 368–370
    enhancement of self-efficacy, 371
    guided practice, 374
    identification of potential barriers and obsta-
        cles, 371–372
    increasing self-efficacy through behavioral
        rehearsal, modeling, and role-play,
        373–374
    planning details of carrying out tasks,
        370–371
    rationale for implementing, 368
    rehearsing or practicing behaviors involved in
        tasks, 372–374
    rewards and incentives for adult clients, 369
    rewards and incentives for children, 369–370
    social worker's role in task planning, 370
    summarizing task plan, 375
Task plan, summarizing, 375
Task Planning
    address potential barriers and obstacles, 372
    analyze and resolve obstacles, 368, 371
    behavioral rehearsal, 373–374
    conditions for, 370
    coping efforts, 374
    details of, 370, 375
    emotional arousal, 373
    enhance client commitment, 373, 375
    guided practice, 373–374
    increasing self-efficacy, 373
    identify potential barriers and obstacles, 371
    mastery, 371–374
    modeling, 374

performance condition, 373
  role-play, 374
  social worker, role in, 370
  summarize plan, 375
  verbal persuasion, 373
  vicarious experience, 373
Tasks
  alternatives, 367–368
  behavioral, 367
  brainstorming alternatives, 367
  conditions for, 370
  cognitive, 367
  enhance client commitment, 328
  failure to complete *See* failure to complete
    tasks
  formula, 406
  general, 364–365
  inadequate preparation, 376–377
  lack of commitment, 376–377
  lack of support, 377
  maintaining focus and continuity, 375
  monitoring and evaluating progress,
    378–379
  occurrence of crisis, 376
  performance related to, 376
  plan details, 527
  prediction, 406
  specific, 366–367
  unspecified, 376
  vaguely specified, 377
Task significance, 439
Teachable moments, 474
Team member, 29
Telephone groups, 274
Temporary Assistance for Needy Families
    (TANF), 232, 275
Tenacity, 432
Termination
  phase of helping process, 41–42
Testing instruments for assessment(s), 181, 183
"the back door," sample contract, 346
Thematic behaviors, 287
Therapeutic binds, 563–564
Therapy groups, 274,
There Are No Children Here (Kotlowitz), 418
Thinking, 391
Threatening clients, 163
Threats, 380
Time-limited contracts, 344
TIS *See* Task-implementation sequence (TIS)
Traditional family, 227–228
Transactions, 217
  stressful, 357–358
Transference reactions
  case example, 551–552
  countertransference reactions *See* Counter-
    transference reactions
  defined, 551
  examples of, 552–553
  frequency of, 552
  with groups, 551–552
  guidelines for managing, 554
  identifying, 552–553
  managing, 553–555
  multiple, 551
  symptomatic behaviors of, 552–553
Transference resistance, 560

Transition in group development stages *See*
    Group development, stages of
Traumatic stress, 384
Treatment groups
  agency perspectives of purpose of, 276
  alliances, 292–294
  assessment of group processes *See* Group
    processes, assessment of
  client's perspectives of purpose of, 276–277
  closed, 281
  cohesion, 296–297
  co-leadership, 277–278
  composition of, 280–281
  counterproductive behaviors, 292
  diversity in, 281
  duration of meetings, 282
  educational groups, 274
  examples of, 273
  format, 283
  formation of, 275–286
  formulating guidelines for *See* Guidelines for
    treatment groups
  frequency of meetings, 282
  functional group behavior, 293
  goals of, 276, 278
  group goals, 278
  group processes *See* Group processes, as-
    sessment of
  growth groups, 274
  guidelines for *See* Guidelines for treatment
    groups
  homogeneity versus heterogeneity, 280
  individual goals, 278
  leaders *See* Group leaders
  leadership, 277–278
  location of, 281–282
  norms, 295–296
  open, 281
  overarching goals of, 276
  preliminary interview, 278–279
  problematic group behavior, 293
  purpose of, 275–277
  size, 281–282
  socialization groups, 274
  social worker's perspectives of purpose of,
    276
  subgroupings, 292–293
  support groups, 274
  task groups distinguished from, 274–275,
    515
  therapy groups, 274
  transference reactions, 551–552
  types of, 274
  values, 296
Triage Assessment System (TAF), 380
Trust, establishing, 548, 550–551
Tuning in, 474

UFW *See* United Farm Workers (UFW)
Ultimate goal, 315
Unchangeable factors, 190
Unconditional caring, 540
Under-and over-involvement of social workers
    with clients, 541–544
Undergraduate (BSW) programs, 23
Underlying feelings, 94–95
Undifferentiated ego mass, 249

Unfair comparisons, 393
Unfaithful Angels (Specht and Courtney), 428
United Farm Workers, 428
United Farm Workers (UFW), 428
United Way, 305
Universal Declaration of Human Rights, 411
Unrealized strengths and potentialities, 524–525
U.S. Department of Homeland Security, 233

Values, 6–10
  assessment of, 208–209
  assessment of group, 296
  cardinal, 53–60
  conflicts between professional and personal,
    53
  ethics and, 8–9
  goal setting, 306–307
Verbal communication barriers, eliminating
  advising and giving of suggestions or solu-
    tions prematurely, 159–160
  arguing with clients, 161–162
  assessing verbal barriers, 169
  clichés, 166
  common verbal barriers, 158–159, 163
  convincing clients about point of view, 161–162
  dominating interaction, 164–165
  dwelling on past, 166
  fishing expeditions, 166–167
  fostering safe social interaction, 165
  gauging effectiveness of responses, 167–168
  infrequent responses, 165–166
  instructing clients, 161–162
  interpretations, 162–163
  interrupting, 164
  judging, criticizing or placing blame, 161
  leading questions, 164
  lecturing clients, 161–162
  overusing phrases, 166
  parroting, 166
  persuading clients, 162
  reactance theory, 158
  reassuring, sympathizing, consoling or ex-
    cusing, 159
  stacking questions, 163–164
  threatening, warning or counterattacking, 163
  using sarcasm or humor inappropriately,
    160–161
Verbal contracts, 342
Verbal following skills
  analysis of, 152
  closed-ended responses *See* Closed-ended
    responses
  concrete responses *See* Concrete responses
  content relevance, 129
  focusing *See* Focusing
  functionality of, 130
  furthering responses, 130–132
  maintaining psychological contact with
    clients, 129–130
  open-ended responses *See* Open-ended
    responses
  paraphrasing responses, 130–132
  performance variables, 129–130
  stimulus-response congruence, 129
  summarizing responses *See* Summarizing
    responses
Verbal minimal prompts, 130

Vicarious trauma, 545
  signs and symptoms associated with, 545
Violence, 49
Visitors, 406
Visual hallucinations, 207
Voluntary clients, 4
  goals for, 310–311
  minors, 323

WAIS-III test *See* Wechsler Adult Intelligence
  Scale
Waivers of confidentiality, 69
WALMYR Assessment Scales, 183, 336
Wants and goals, 523

Warmth, 540
Warning clients, 163
War on poverty, 429
Welfare policy, 416, 429
Welfare reform, 416
Welfare to work, 234–235, 429, 563
Wechsler Adult Intelligence Scale
  (WAIS-III), 183
Wechsler Intelligence Scale for Children
  (WISC-III), 183
What ifs, 393
Will, George, 5, 10
WISC-III test *See* Wechsler Intelligence Scale
  for Children

Words and phrases, affective, 90–94
Work, and families, 234–235
Working group, 282, 500
Wraparound services, 451
Written assessments, 173, 222–225
  examples of, 223–225
  SOAP notes, 225
Written contracts, 342

YAVIS Client (young, articulate, verbal,
  intelligent and successful), 307

Zung Self-Rating Depression Scale, 183